WEAPONS

WEAPONS

an international encyclopedia from 5000 BC to 2000 AD

the Diagram Group

St. Martin's Press
New York

For information, write:
St. Martin's Press, Inc., 175 Fifth Ave.,
New York, N.Y. 10010
Manufactured in the United States of America

Library of Congress Cataloging-in-Publication Data

Weapons : an international encyclopedia from 5000 B.C. to 2000 A.D. / The Diagram Group.
p. cm.
Includes bibliographical references and index.
ISBN 0-312-03950-6 (pbk)
ISBN 0-312-03951-4 (hc)
1. Arms and armor—History—Dictionaries. I. Diagram Group.
U800.W39 1991
623.4'09—dc20
90-28498
CIP

10 9 8 7 6

The Diagram Group

Editor David Harding

Contributing editor Jefferson Cann

Editorial staff Hope Cohen, Norma Jack, Gail Lawther, Ruth Midgley

Art director Richard Hummerstone

Art editor Mark Evans

Artists Alan Cheung, Steven Clark, Brian Hewson, Susan Kinsey, Pavel Kostal, Kathleen McDougall, Janos Marffy, Graham Rosewarne

Art assistants Kerrigan Blackman, Steve Clifton, Richard Colville, Neil Connell, Roger Davis, Lee Griffiths, Alan Harris, Steve Hollingshead, Richard Prideaux, Kate Proud, Andrew Riley, Ray Stevens, Amanda Stiller, Mark Waite

Researchers Enid Moore, Linda Proud, Marita Westberg

Indexer Mary Ling

New edition staff

Editor Randal Gray

Consultants Will Fowler, Bill Gunston

Artists Darren Bennett, Peter Crossman, Brian Hewson, Lee Lawrence, Paul McCauley, Graham Rosewarne

The authors and publishers wish to extend their warmest thanks to the many museums, collections, research institutions and individuals without whose kind and generous assistance this book could not have been compiled. A list of acknowledgements is included on page 325.

Picture credits
Atlante ; R J Chinwalla, Lino Pellegrini p.93
Crown copyright photograph p.265
Deutsches Museum, Munich pp.234-235
Imperial War Museum, London pp.220-221 (bottom)
India Office Library and Records, London p.284
The Library of Congress, Washington DC pp.158-159
Clive Limpkin pp.74-75
McDonnell Douglas Helicopter Company p.279
Military Archive and Research Services pp.220-221 (top)
Novosti Press Agency p.264

INTRODUCTION

Weapons explains and illustrates the whole range of devices with which man has armed himself. It brings together, in one volume, a representative selection of all types of weapon from all ages and cultures.

The objects are arranged according to the simple criterion of function. Like is grouped with like, their basic functioning is explained, and a selection of examples—which may span many centuries and several continents—is illustrated. There is a general progression through the successive chapters from the simple to the complex, Chapter 1 beginning with clubs and Chapter 8 ending with maritime weapons. As the objects are not arranged historically, chronological tables are added for major topics such as small arms, to sketch in the dates of important developments. The visual indexes on pp. 296–317 also regroup all the "Western" weapons by historical periods, and the remainder by region.

The emphasis is kept on weapons in the strict sense of those used for combat between human beings. Similar objects made for the hunting of animals or for recreations such as target-shooting are generally excluded, even though their historical development may be inter-related.

Weapons has been carefully devised as a work of reference that not only contains a great fund of information, but also, through its indexes, provides several means of access to it. As well as placing specialist areas of interest in the context of the whole field of arms, it will serve as an unrivalled introduction to the subject for the general reader.

Since first publication in 1980 **Weapons** has established itself as the unrivalled one-volume international encylopedia of its subject. Not surprisingly, it is now hard and costly to obtain secondhand. This updated edition has a new 16-page chapter covering key developments in the decade since. They are also cross-referenced with the original coverage to which very few revisions have been necessary because the treatment is predominantly historical. Both index and bibliography have been fully updated to take account of new weapons systems and publications about them.

The illustration (opposite) is from Valturio's *Del 'Arte Militare* of 1483. It depicts soldiers armed with cannon, hand-cannon, crossbows, and a wide variety of pole-arms.

CONTENTS

Chapter 1

Chapter 2

Chapter 3

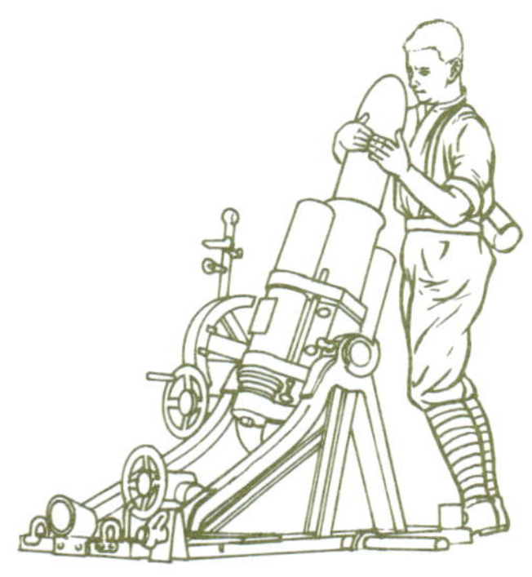

Chapter 4

Chapter 5

Chapter 6

Chapter 7

Chapter 8

Scale indicators

1 centimeter (thick bar)

10 centimeters (thin bar)

1 meter (pronged bar)

1.75 meters

The symbols shown here are used to indicate the size of objects that are illustrated in Chapters 1 to 7. They are not used where a perspective view of a particular object renders such a scale meaningless. Each appearance of a scale indicator is varied in proportion to the object it relates to.

Reference

Chapter 1

ARMING THE HAND

The weapons to be found in this chapter are all wielded in the hand, and not relinquished There is a great variety of such weapons and of ways that have been devised for using them, and it is not possible to place them all in a strict order that has any real significance. Nevertheless, we begin with clubs, surely one of the simplest purpose-made weapons, and end with bayonets, one of the last developments in hand-to-hand weaponry, and one of the few retained by modern conventional armies. Also included are fighting picks, war hammers, axes, daggers, swords, pole-arms (or staff weapons), and a selection of lesser-known hand weapons that fall outside the main categories.

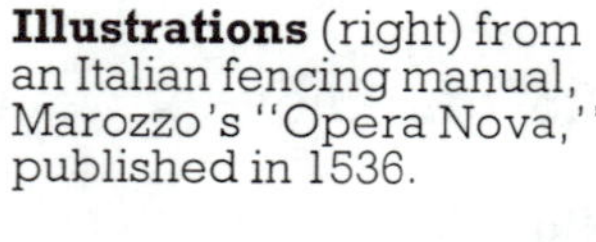

Illustrations (right) from an Italian fencing manual, Marozzo's "Opera Nova," published in 1536.

Clubs

The club can be regarded as the first purpose-made weapon. It has its origins in the unworked sticks and stones which would have come first to hand when primitive man needed a weapon, and it is a technological advance on both. The stone is made more effective by being mounted on a stick, and the stick by being made heavy at one end. Not all clubs are blunt. They have often been rendered more lethal by being given a sharp edge or sharp points, in which forms they anticipate the ax and the war-hammer. The all-metal mace for attacking armor, and the ceremonial club as a symbol of authority, represent clubs at their most sophisticated, beyond which there is no prospect of further development. Meanwhile the simple wooden truncheon continues to be used in law enforcement worldwide. (For thrown clubs see p. 78, in the chapter on hand-thrown missiles.)

Dynamics of the club (above) A heavy weight held in the hand (**a**), or a stick (**b**) can both be used to strike an enemy; but by mounting the weight on the stick (**c**), momentum, and hence the lethal force of the blow, are much increased.

Irish shillelagh (right), one of the simplest of all weapons, consists of a suitable piece of wood cut from a blackthorn tree.

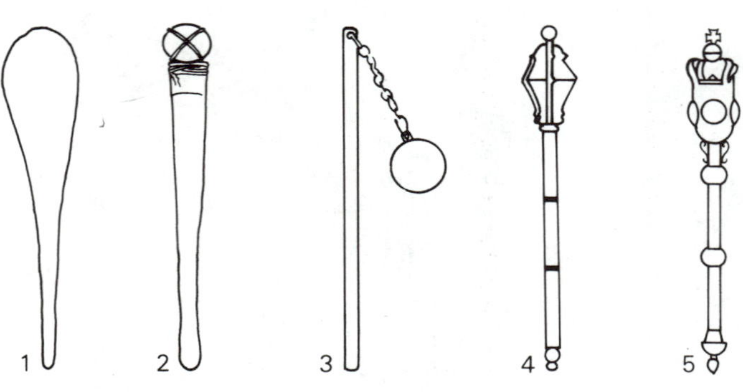
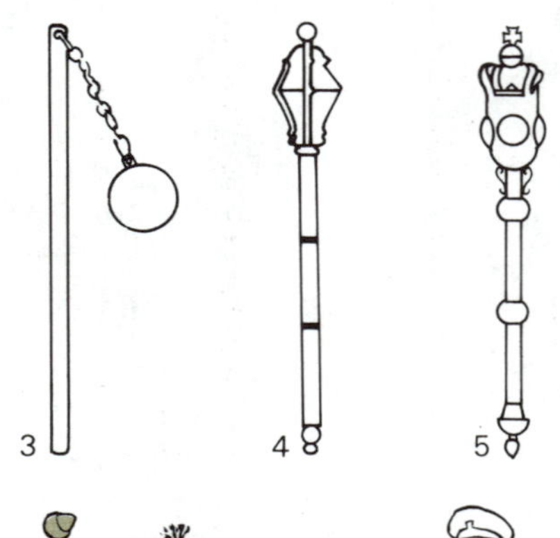

Types of club (left) Five types are differentiated here by the salient feature of their construction.
1 Simple Non-metal clubs made of only one material.
2 Composite Clubs using more than one material, non-articulated.
3 Articulated Clubs with a flexible head.
4 All-metal Known as maces.
5 Ceremonial Used as symbols of authority.

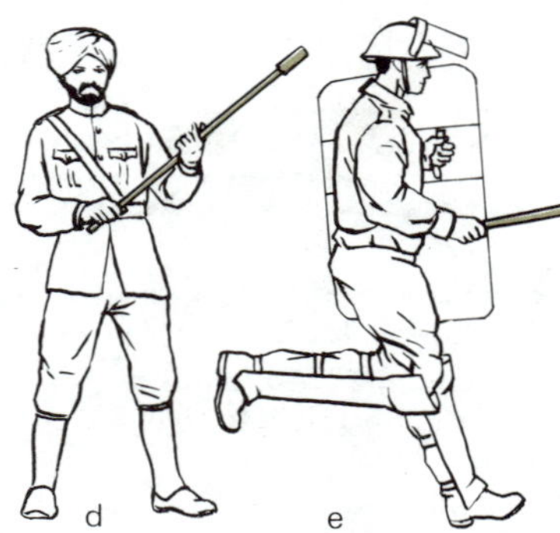

Clubs in use (left and above)
a Two figures possibly wielding clubs, from a South African rock painting of c.6000BC.
b In New Zealand and the Pacific, clubs were the main weapon before the coming of the Europeans. The finest simple clubs come from this area.
c In the West, the truncheon or night-stick is still carried by most police forces.
d The *lathi* is the weapon traditionally used for riot-control in the Indian subcontinent. It usually takes the form of a long bamboo pole weighted at the head with metal.
e Despite its great age and crudity, the club has a role in contemporary life, being much used in riot-control.

Simple clubs

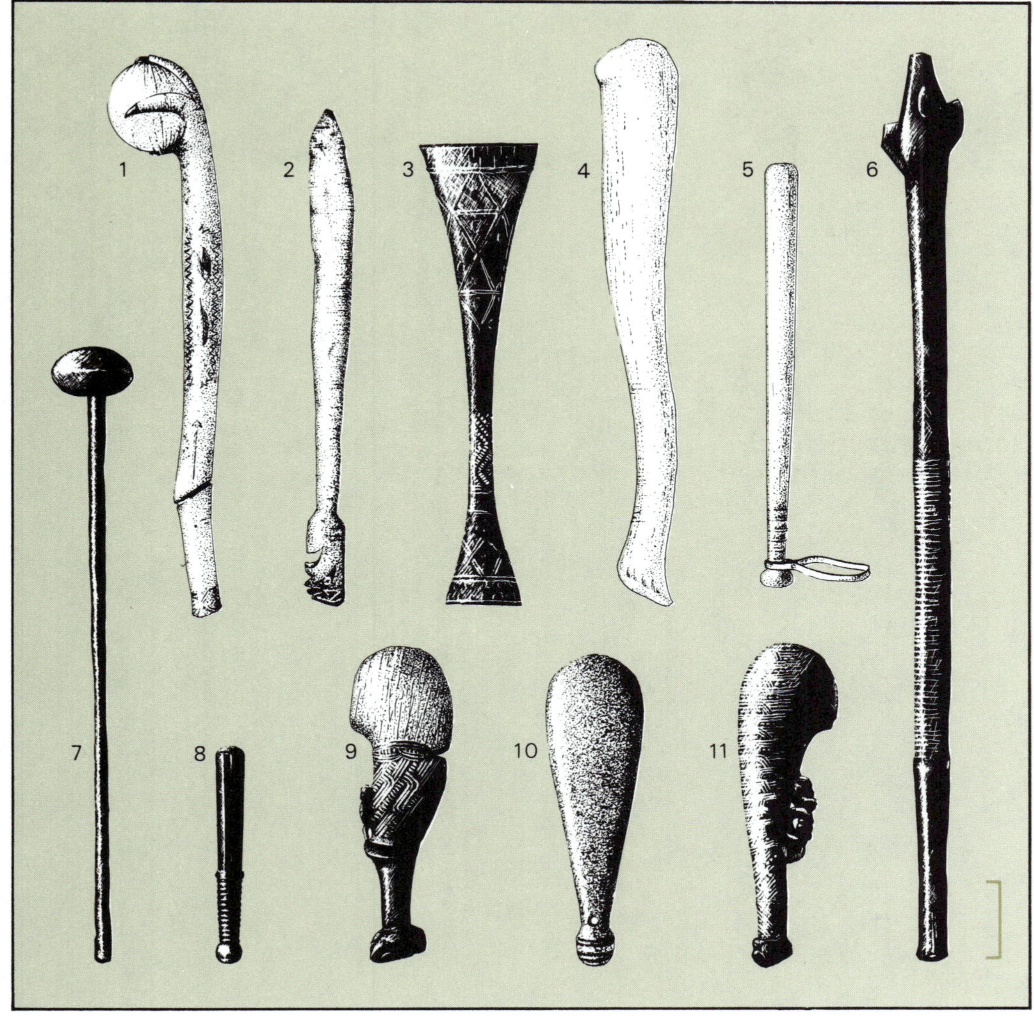

Simple clubs are those made all of one material, other than metal. Included are the simple stave, the riot batons of the present day, and also the carved wooden clubs of the Pacific that have developed into an art form. Wood and bone are the materials most commonly used. The varieties of shape are influenced by available materials, local tradition, or the search for a more effectively wounding form.

William the Conqueror is shown carrying a simple club in this detail from the Bayeux tapestry (left). William is depicted several times with a club in the tapestry, as also are Bishop Odo and some fleeing English foot soldiers.

Simple clubs (above)
1 Iroquois Indian bone club. Eastern USA.
2 Whalebone club from Unimak Island, Alaska.
3 Wooden club *macana*, bound with cane at the grip. Guyana.
4 Club consisting of a whale's penis bone. NW Coast Indians, USA.
5 British Army riot-control baton, c.1970. Hickory wood with leather wrist-strap.
6 Fijian wooden club, its grip bound with grass.
7 Zulu hardwood knobkerrie. South Africa.
8 New York City Police night-stick c.1960. Hard rubber.
9 Maori softwood club *patu*. New Zealand.
10 Maori club *mere*, of jade. Also known as *patu pounamou*. New Zealand.
11 Maori wooden club *wahaika*. This asymmetric type is of wood or bone.

Wooden club (above) from the Marquesas Islands, Central Pacific. Simple clubs of wood, bone or stone from New Zealand and the islands of the Pacific show the most imaginative designs and finest carving of all.

Composite clubs

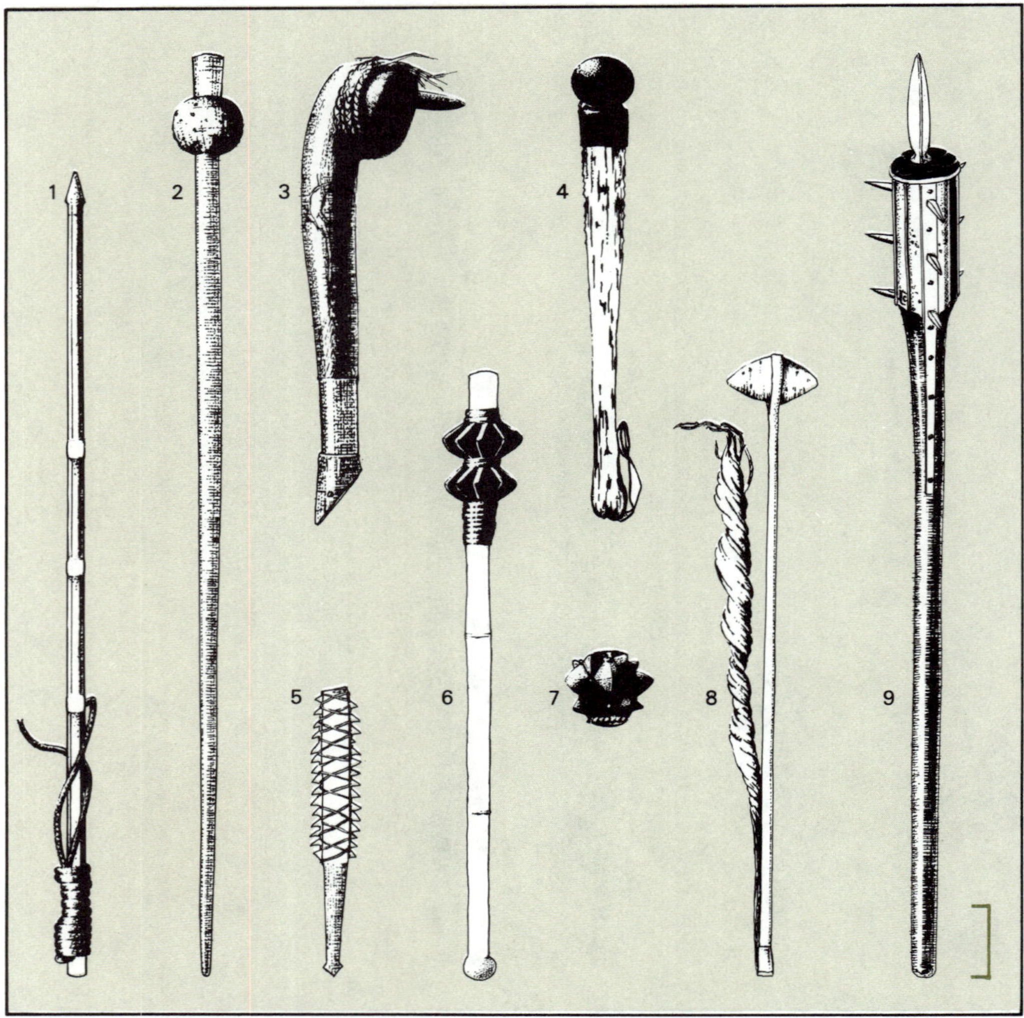

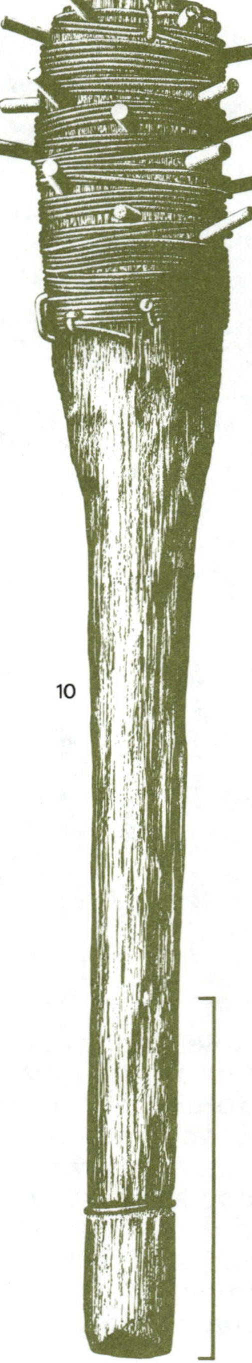

Composite clubs combine two or more materials in their construction as a means of increasing their efficiency. Most often a head of hard, weighty material is added to a wooden haft, the simplest form being a stone mounted on the end of a stick. Other examples are simple, wooden clubs to which a spike or metal sheathing is added in order to make blows more effective.

Plains Indian from North America is shown (left) carrying a stone-headed club and a lance, and wearing a bison headdress during a ritual dance. The stone-headed club — the original form of the tomahawk — was one of the main weapons of the Plains before the introduction of metals by the white man.

Composite clubs (above)
1 Japanese straight club *furibo*. Wood, bound and tipped with iron.
2 Club with pierced stone head fitted over a tapering wooden haft. Papua New Guinea.
3 Wooden club with a stone spike set in the head. Omaha.
4 North American Plains Indian club. A stone fixed to the haft with rawhide.
5 Light wooden club with sharks' teeth bound to the edges, a step toward the sword. Kiribati (Gilbert Islands.)
6 Club with bamboo haft and double steel flanges at the head. Northern India, 16th century.
7 Bronze mace-head from Sweden, 14th century.
8 North American Plains Indian club. Quartz head and rawhide-covered haft.
9 Spiked, iron-headed mace combining three gun barrels on a wooden haft. English, c.1510. (Tower of London.)
10 Club improvised by troops on the Western Front, 1914-18, for silent trench-raids. The spikes are nails with the heads clipped off; wire binding prevents them from splitting the wood. Nationality unknown. (The Castle Museum, York.)

Articulated clubs

Articulated clubs (left)
1 Swiss morning star mace, c.1530.
2 German morning star with short chain, 16th century.
3 German one-handed war-flail, wooden with iron mounts. Probably 17th century.
4 Indian flail with two balls and chains, 19th century.
5 Unusually short French morning star without spikes, 15th century.
6 Short German triple-headed iron flail, 15th century.
7 Modern German truncheon, commercially produced for riot-control by police. Telescopic, flexible haft consisting of two springs, and a casing which also forms the grip.
(Examples **1, 2, 5, 6** are from the Metropolitan Museum of Art, New York.)

Articulated clubs use flexibility in some form to multiply the force of a blow and to make it more difficult to parry. The simplest were war-flails, adaptations of the grain-threshing tool. More effective against armor were clubs of the "morning star" type, a spiked ball on a chain. The idea of an articulated club still survives in some modern flexible coshes.

The chigiriki (right) of Japan is a more aggressive variation of the parrying weapon *kusarigama*. It can be used to strike or entangle the opponent as well as to parry his blows.

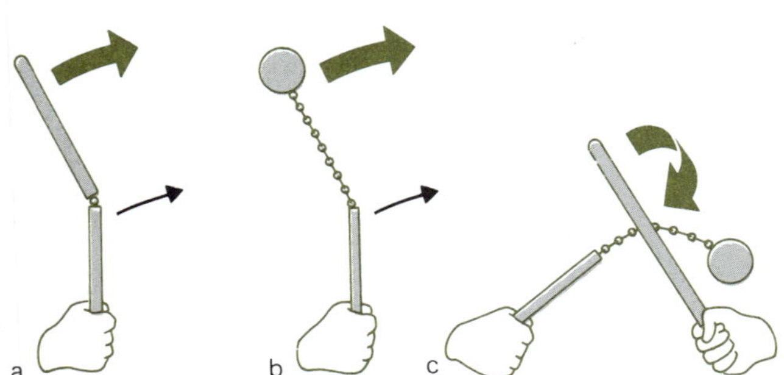

Principles (left) The joint of a war-flail (**a**) accelerates the swing of the free arm and so adds to the power of the blow. The mechanical principle of a ball and chain on a haft (**b**) is the same as for a flail, but the flexibility of the chain makes it even harder to parry (**c**).

All-metal maces

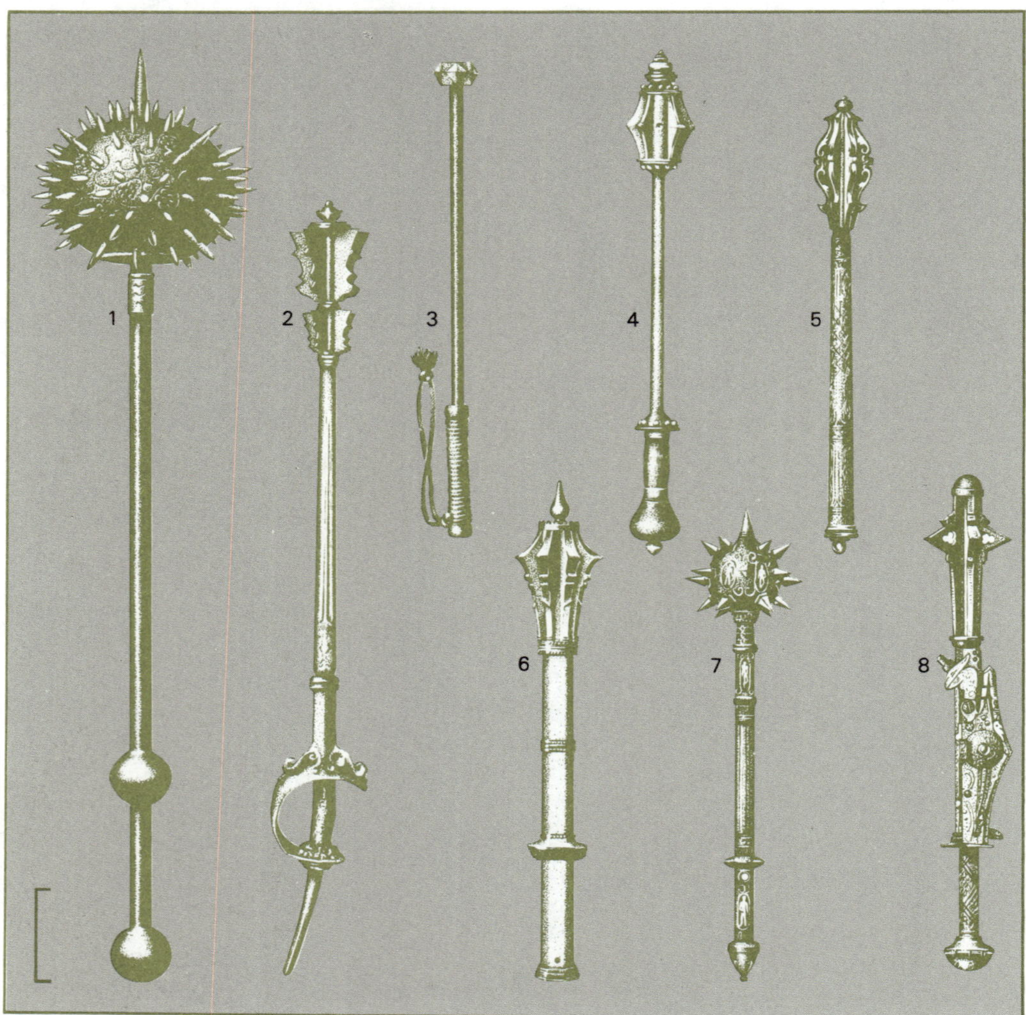

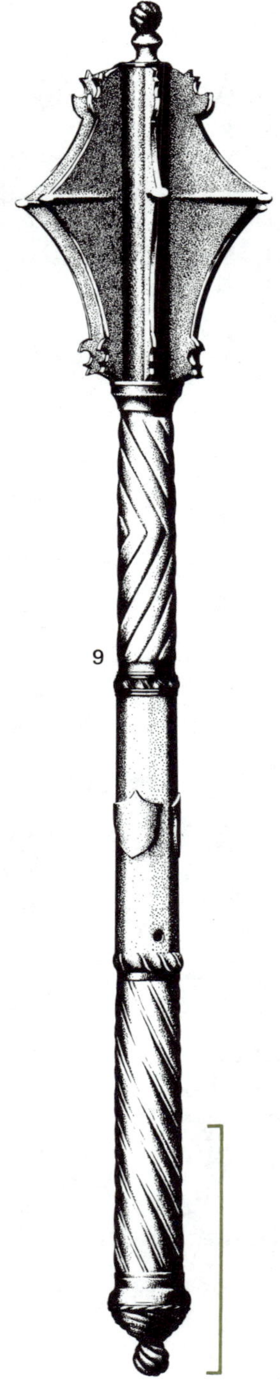

Maces made all of iron or steel are found wherever body armor has been used. Their weight and hardness, especially when focused into a spike or a narrow flange, made them more effective against an armored enemy than any type of sword. Although usually directed against the head, a mace blow on a limb could break a bone even if the armor was not pierced.

All-metal maces (above)
1 Indian mace, 18th century. Hollow, steel head, chased and set with many spikes.
2 Indian steel mace from Madras, 18th century. Sword-like hilt of *khanda* form (see p. 38).
3 Chinese iron mace, 18th century. With wrist-loop and rattan-bound grip.
4 German gilded iron mace, early 16th century. (Livrustkammaren, Stockholm.)
5 Italian flanged mace from Milan, c.1580. Gold inlay and damascene. (Wallace Collection, London.)
6 German iron mace, c.1530, from the Habsburg arsenal. (Kunsthistorisches Museum, Vienna.)
7 Italian morning star mace from Milan, c.1560. Iron, decorated with gold on russet (chemically rusted) surface. (Wallace Collection, London.)
8 Combined steel mace and wheellock pistol. Probably German, late 16th century. (Tower of London.)
9 European flanged steel mace, 16th century. The hole pierced in the shaft is for a wrist-thong, since if an armored horseman dropped his weapon he could not easily retrieve it. (Metropolitan Museum of Art, New York.)

Hungarians of the early 16th century are armed with heavy metal maces in the illustration (left).

Ceremonial maces

Perhaps because the club is such a fundamental weapon — a sign of brute force — ceremonial clubs have long been carried as symbols of power. This ancient development had a parallel in Europe after the Renaissance, when the iron mace, so effective against plate armor, gave rise to the metal ceremonial mace of civic officialdom, again a symbol of authority.

Maces in Ancient Egypt
King Nar-mer of Upper Egypt is depicted using a mace to smite a prisoner (right), from a stone palette of c.2900BC.
The stone mace-head of the "Scorpion King" (far right) is also Egyptian, dating from c.3200BC.

Symbols of authority
(right) derived from clubs.
a Civic mace-bearer of Colchester, England.
b British army drum major with parade mace.
c Court jester, with his traditional mock-scepter of a bladder on a stick.
d Coin of John Sigismund, Elector of Brandenburg, 1608-19. He is shown holding a scepter, symbol of his power.

Maces and scepters (right)
1 Civic mace of the town of Stamford, Lincolnshire. Silver gilt, made c.1660. (Stamford Town Hall, England.)
2 Scepter from the Crown Jewels of the English monarchs. (Tower of London.)
3 Stone scepter from ancient Colombia. (Museo del Oro, Bogota.)
4 Wooden scepter set with pearl shell, Solomon Islands.

Picks and war-hammers

The pick is a piercing weapon, with a dagger-like blade set at right-angles to a haft, so allowing it to be swung with great effect. A related weapon, the war-hammer, was used in Europe, Persia and India when plate armor and chain mail were common. This took the form of a small hammer-head, used to stun a helmeted opponent, and was invariably combined with a pick.

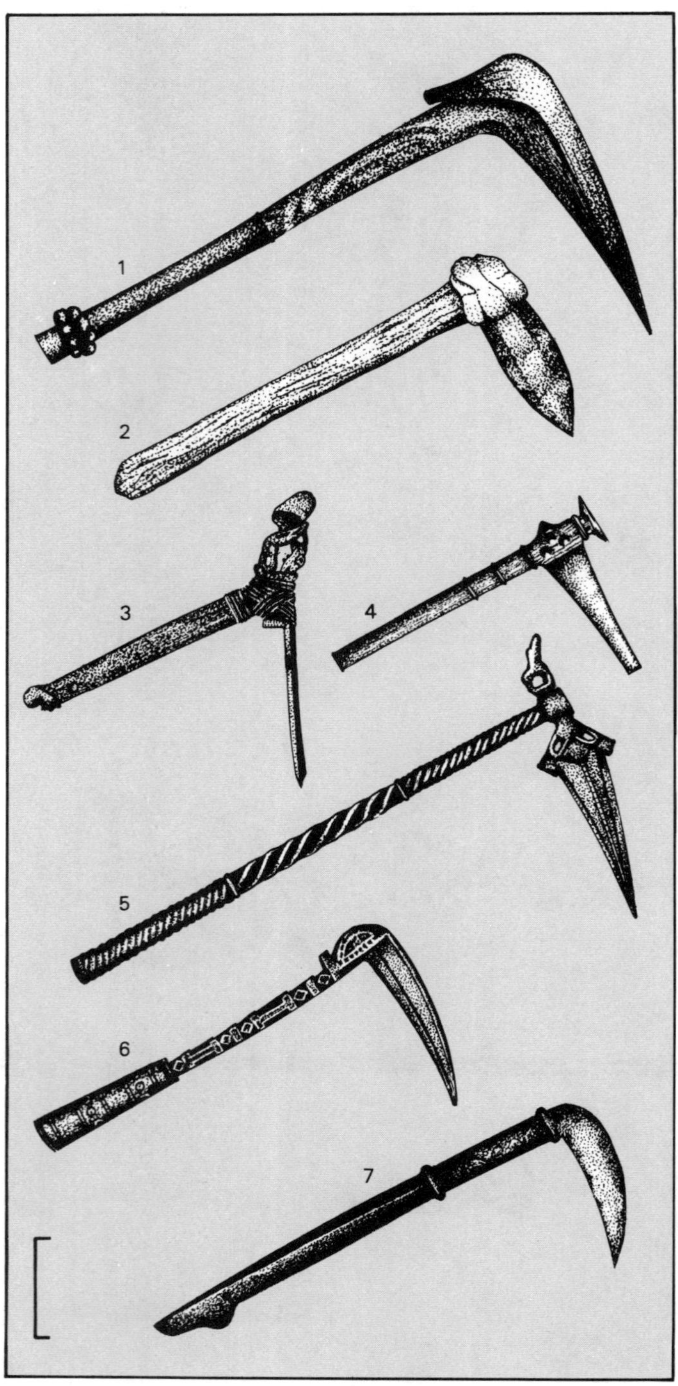

Picks (left)
1 Wooden pick or pointed club from New Caledonia.
2 Australian Aboriginal fighting pick. A stone blade set on a wooden haft by means of gum.
3 *Toki*, a Maori war-adz from New Zealand. Jade blade bound to a carved wooden haft.
4 Bronze Age pick, known to archeologists as a halberd, found at Skane, Sweden. An ordinary dagger-blade was often attached to a bronze haft in this way, though some examples may have been purely ceremonial.
5 *Zaghnal*, an Indian fighting pick. All-steel, with silver-plated haft.
6 All-steel fighting pick from the Afghanistan-Pakistan border. Decorated with brass and silver.
7 *Kama yari*, a Japanese fighting pick. When used as a parrying weapon with chain and ball attached, it is known as *kusarigama*.

Fighting pick (right) from India, sometimes called a crowbill by collectors. The finest examples of this type of weapon are from India and Persia, where they were used against the chain-mail armor popular in those areas.

War-hammer in use (right) from a detail of "The Rout of San Romano," by Uccello (National Gallery, London). Also called the horseman's hammer, the blunt head of this weapon could stun an opponent or fracture bones even without penetrating the armor. The pick at the other side of the haft was probably the most efficient weapon for piercing plate or mail armor.

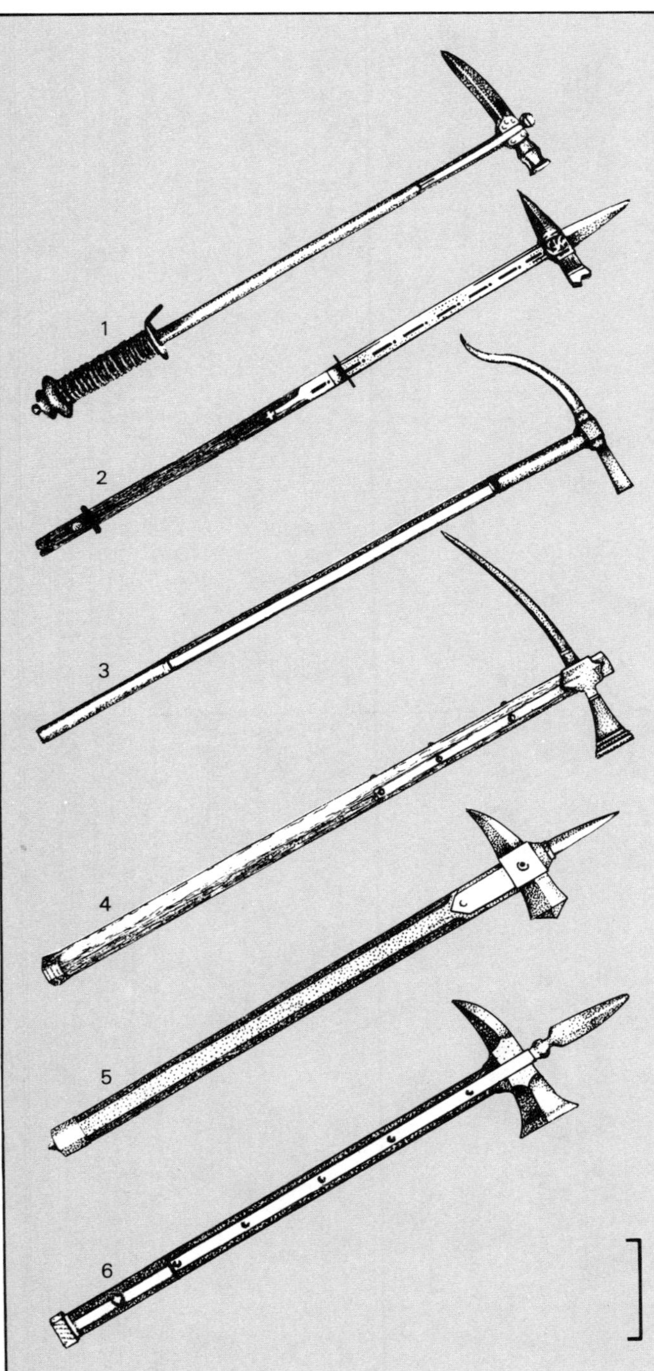

War-hammers (left)
1 Typical plain horseman's hammer. Wrought iron haft, bound with copper wire at the grip.
2 Wooden haft clad with iron on the upper half. Bavarian, c.1450-1500.
3 All-steel, damascened in gold, with a velvet covering to the grip. Indian or Persian.
4 Square hammer-head and octagonal pick, on a wooden haft. Possibly Italian, 16th century.
5 Diamond-shaped pick and slightly pointed hammer-face, on an oak haft. Possibly French, c.1450.
6 Wooden haft protected by long securing straps or langets. Italian, c.1490.

South German war-hammer (right) decorated with hunting scenes in gold and silver overlay. Made in the second half of the 16th century. (Victoria and Albert Museum, London.)

Axes 1

An ax is a familiar object, quickly recognized by anyone. Yet it is often difficult — especially with ancient specimens — to say with confidence whether a particular example was made for war or for cutting wood. Doubtless many served both purposes, and here we have included some which, although perhaps domestic tools, represent a stage in the development of both kinds. While the stone ax is thought to be the true ancestor of both wood- and war-axes, in some parts of the world there are also sharp-edged wooden or bone clubs that are ax-like in form. These have an adequately lethal edge for fighting, but would be no use for cutting timber. They are included here with true axes. (For axes commonly used as thrown weapons see p. 80, in the chapter on hand-thrown missiles.)

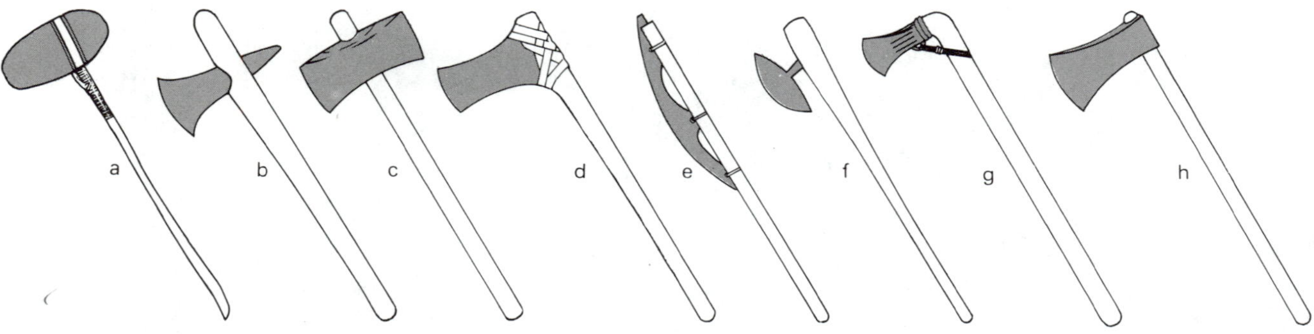

Means of attachment (above) Illustrated are some of the different methods used for attaching the ax-head to the haft.
a Haft of supple wood wrapped around a groove in a stone ax-head (North American Indian).
b Stone or bronze ax-head wedged through a hole in a wooden haft.
c Wooden haft fixed in a hole drilled through a stone ax-head.
d Copper or bronze head with a splayed back, lashed to a wooden haft (ancient Egyptian).
e Copper or bronze narrow blade slotted into a grooved wooden haft and bound through holes in the blade (ancient Egyptian).
f Narrow tang on an iron head thrust into a wooden haft (African).
g Curved wooden haft thrust into a hollow socketed bronze head, and bound in place through a loop cast on the underside of the head (European Bronze Age).
h Wooden haft fixed through a transverse hole in a cast iron head (Iron Age design in use ever since).

Ax-heads (right) of the Stone, Bronze and Iron Ages.
1 Hand-ax of the Middle Pleistocene period, from Oldoway, Tanzania. A stone tool that was simply held in the hand.
2 Polished stone ax-head of the Neolithic period, c.2500BC. Found in Yorkshire, England.
3 Perforated stone battle-ax head of the early Bronze Age, found in London.
4 Polished stone battle-ax head of an important European culture known as the Battle-ax People. Dates from c.2000BC.
5 Bronze battle-ax head from Ancient Egypt, bearing the name of Pharoah Sanusert I.
6 Broad scalloped ax-blade of the 12th dynasty, Ancient Egypt.
7 Coptic broad ax-blade of copper, from Egypt.
8 Bronze Age ax-head from Denmark.
9 Socketed bronze ax-head, also known as a palstave. Late Bronze Age, from Yorkshire, England.
10 Bronze ax-head from Luristan (Iran), an area famous for fine casting in this metal.
11 Cast bronze ax-head with a crouching lion on the socket, from Luristan, c.2400-1200BC.
12 Middle Bronze Age battle-ax head with cast and engraved decoration. From Hungary.
13 Ceremonial bronze ax-head from Sweden. Dates from c.800-700BC.
14 Battle-ax head from Syria, c.1300BC. Iron blade set in a socket of bronze with gold inlay, in the form of a pig.

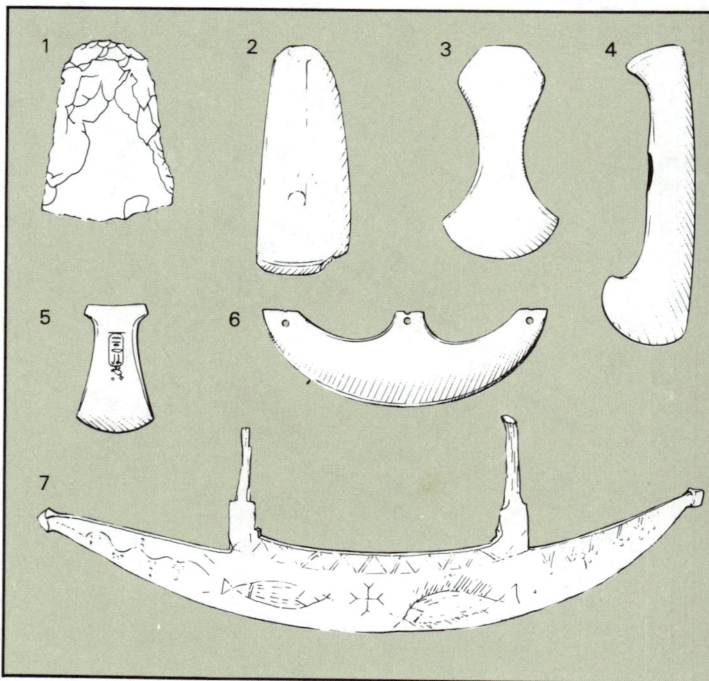

Ceremonial war-ax (right) from Ancient Egypt (Cairo Museum). The blade is of bronze and gold, bound to a wooden haft. The decoration depicts King Ahmose smiting an enemy, a common theme on Egyptian weapons (compare with the mace-head on p.19).

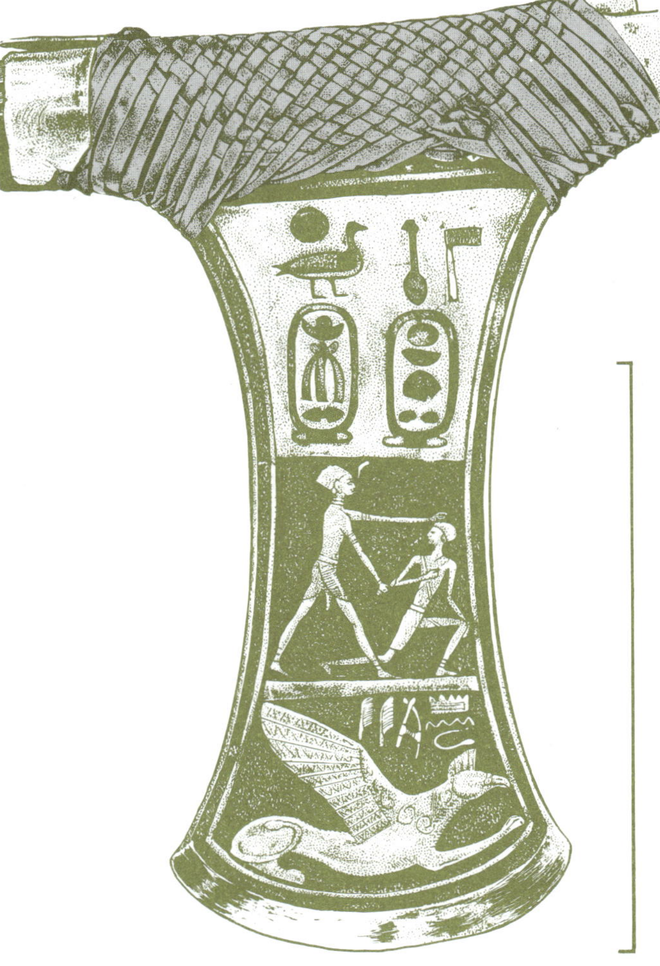

Shaping a flint ax (above) by the flaking method. Flint was an excellent material for an ax as it offered a naturally sharp, hard edge. In the late Stone Age, the ax-head was often polished, achieving great beauty of form.

Casting an ax-head (above) in the Bronze Age. Initially, open molds were used to cast simple shapes. The cutting edge was then hardened by a hammering process and sharpened. In time, the techniques of casting the complex shape of a socketed ax were also mastered.

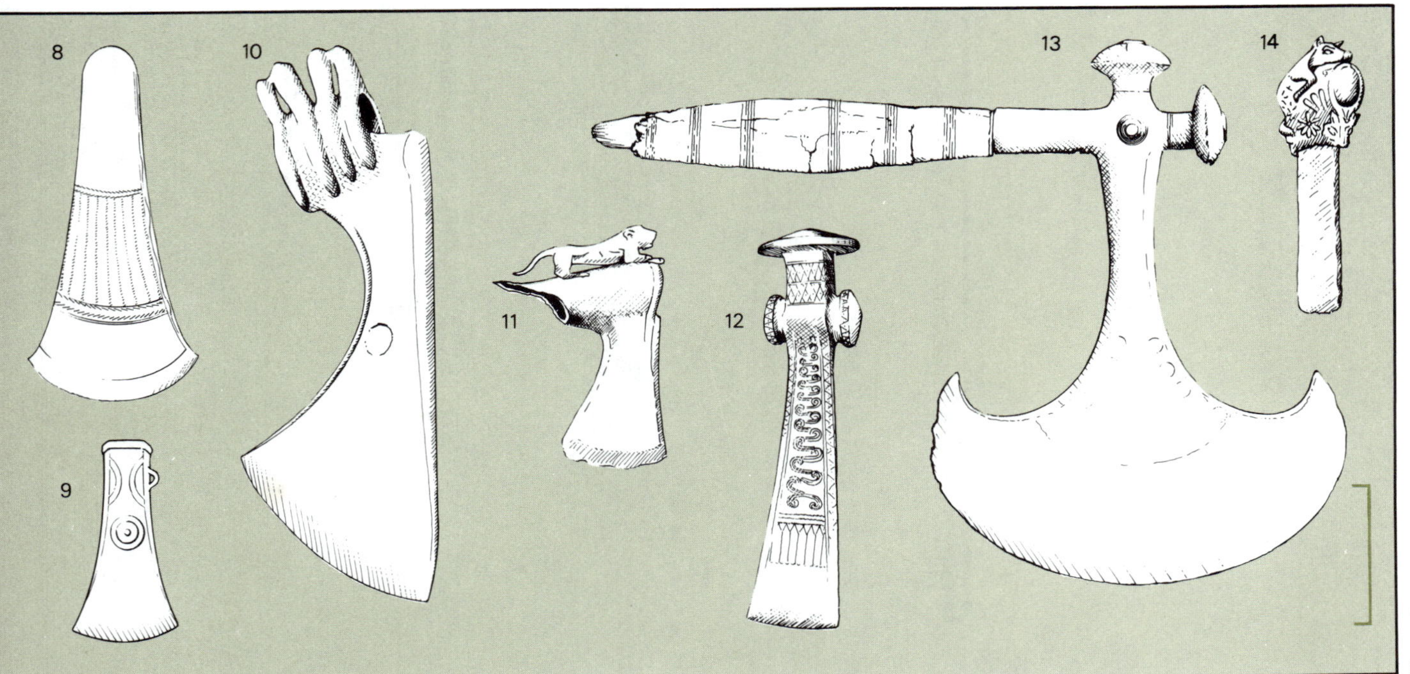

Axes 2

Viking ax (below) of iron, with geometric patterns and a stylized dragon inlaid in silver. Dates from the 10th century. Found in Jutland, Denmark. (Nationalmuseet, Copenhagen.)

Fighting axes (below)
1 North American tomahawk, combining a tobacco pipe. Made by Europeans as a trade item. Early 19th century.
2 American rifleman's belt-ax from the Revolutionary War period.
3 Battle-ax, probably German, 15th or early 16th century. The haft is a reconstruction.
4 Double-headed European battle-ax, early 16th century.
5 Norwegian farmer's ceremonial ax, dated 1610.
6 German mine-owner's ceremonial ax, late 17th century.
7 *Shoka*, war-ax of the Basuto people, from the Lake Tanganyika area.
8 Indian all-steel ax, probably dates from the 18th century.
9 Double-headed all-steel Indian or Persian ceremonial or war-ax.

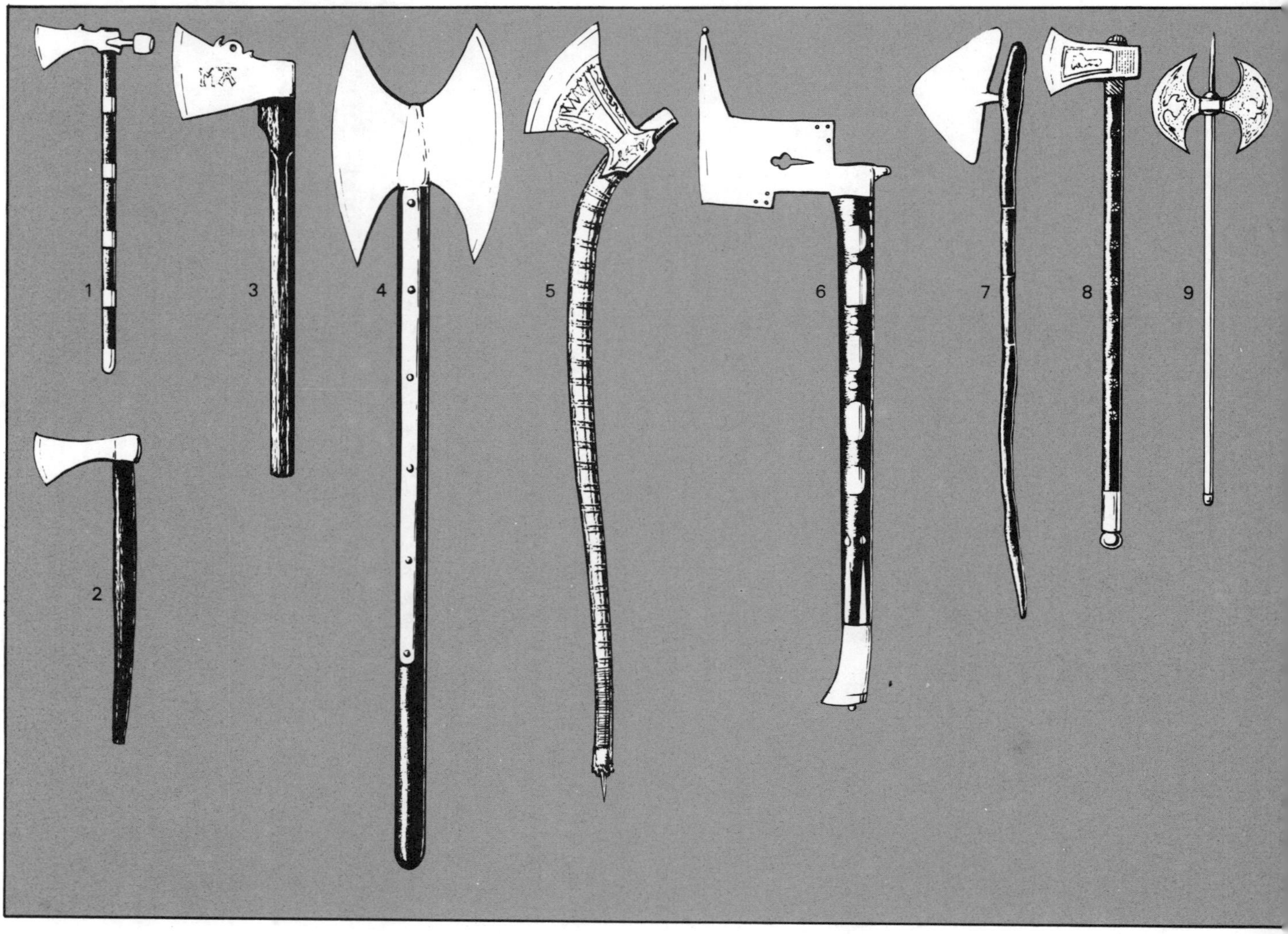

10 Knife-like Indian ax, known to Western collectors as a *bhuj*.
11 Indian fighting ax, one of many varieties from the Chota Nagpur region.
12 Indian fighting ax from the Chota Nagpur region.
13 War-ax of the Naga people of Assam, called a *dao*. This name is applied to a variety of ax- and sword-like weapons, from Nepal to Burma.
14 *Tungi*, ax of the Khond people of Southern India.
15 Ax of the Igorot people of Luzon in the Philippines. Known to be a domestic tool as well as a weapon.
16 *Biliong*, a fighting ax from Sarawak, Borneo. The head is fixed to the shaft by a sharp tang, and secured with binding.

Indo-Persian fighting ax (right) All-steel with Persian inscription on the crescent-shaped blade.

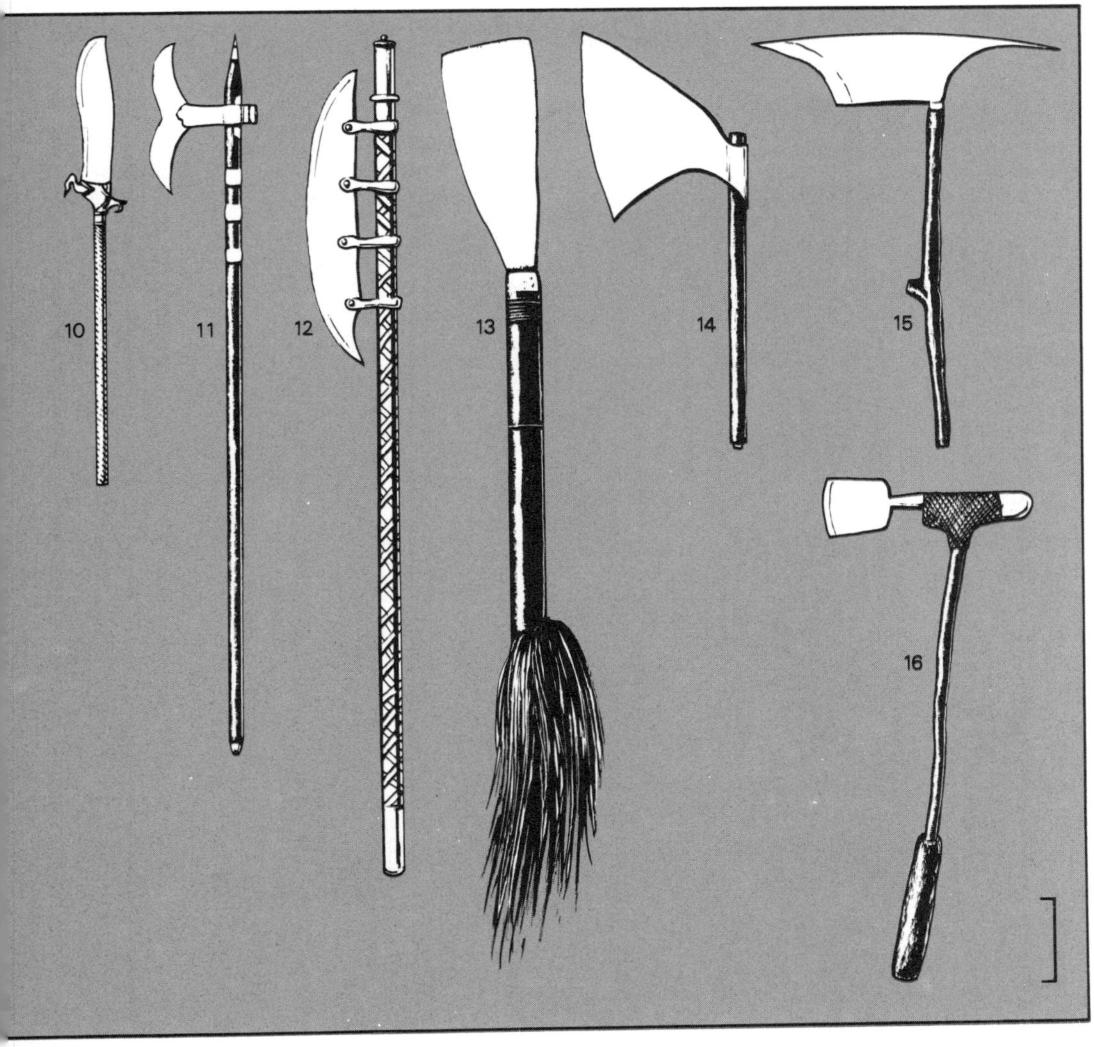

10 11 12 13 14 15 16

Daggers

One of the basic ways to kill or wound is to stab. The dagger is the simplest stabbing weapon. It is short-bladed, held in one hand, and while used primarily for thrusting, many will also cut in the manner of a domestic knife. As one of man's basic weapons it is found in all parts of the world and has been in use since the Stone Age.

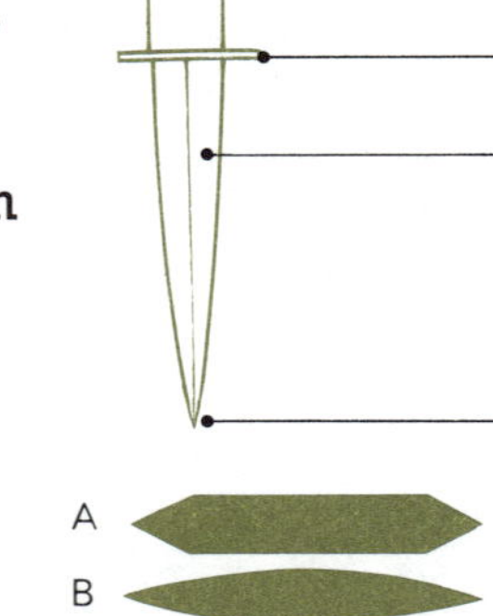

Characteristics (left) The basic characteristics of a dagger are sharpness and stiffness. All have a hilt or grip (**a**) and a blade (**c**) with a sharp point (**d**). Some have a form of guard (**b**) to protect the hand. In trying to fulfill the requirements, examples vary as to material, blade outline and cross-section, and less crucially, hilt style and attachment.

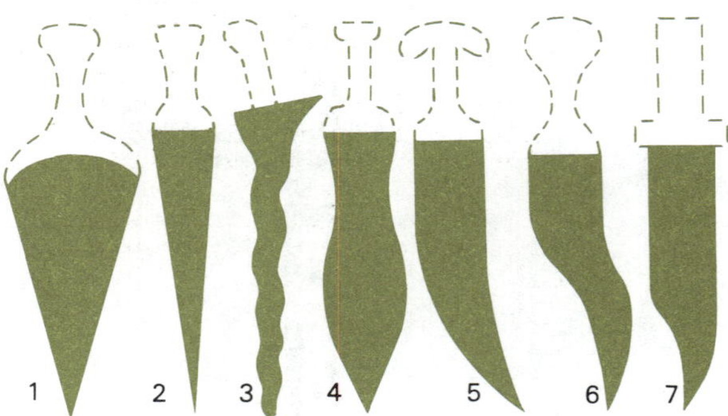

Blade outline (above) For the purpose of stabbing, the blade is usually tapered and often two-edged. However, the variety of blades is almost limitless. Certain shapes have become traditional in certain areas. Others are dictated by the material. The diagrams show some of the main types.

1 Broad taper, often to compensate for soft metal.
2 Narrow taper, an ideal blade shape.
3 Asymmetric Malay *kris*; blade is not always wavy.
4 Leaf-shape, heavy and severely wounding.
5 Curved *jambiya* shape from the Arab world.
6 Double curve, popular in India and Persia.
7 Bowie shape, clipped back to form a double-edged tip.

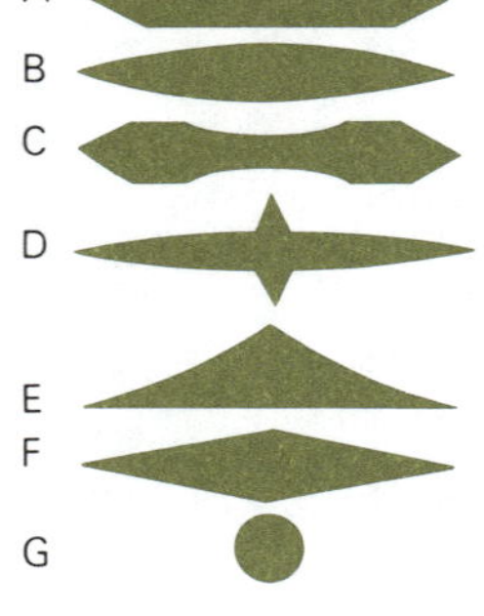

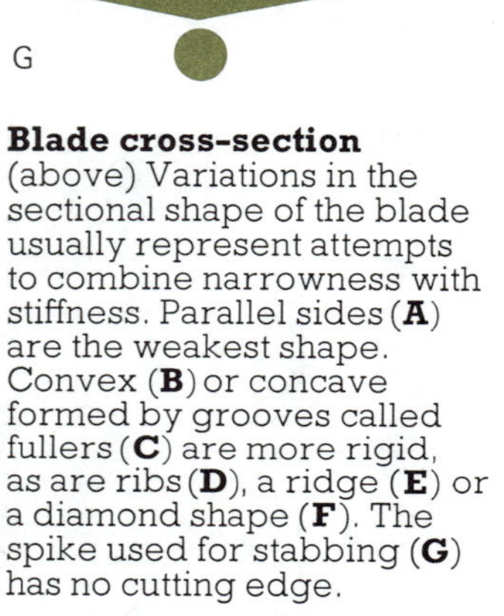

Blade cross-section (above) Variations in the sectional shape of the blade usually represent attempts to combine narrowness with stiffness. Parallel sides (**A**) are the weakest shape. Convex (**B**) or concave formed by grooves called fullers (**C**) are more rigid, as are ribs (**D**), a ridge (**E**) or a diamond shape (**F**). The spike used for stabbing (**G**) has no cutting edge.

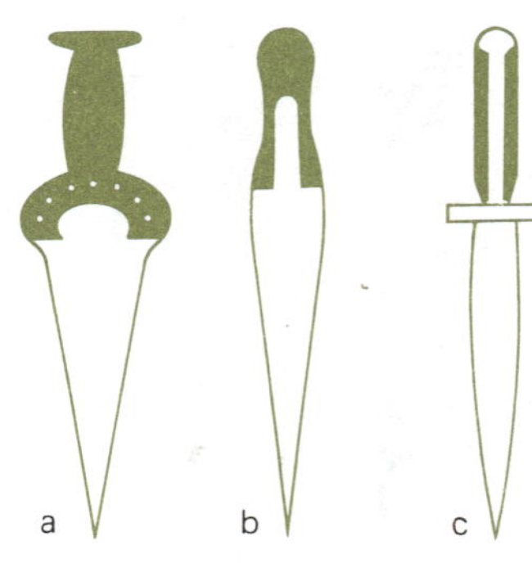

Hilt (left) Secure fixing of the hilt is vital in a metal dagger. The earliest ones have hilts riveted to the blade to save scarce bronze (**a**). Stronger is the short tang (continuation of the blade) thrust into the hilt (**b**). Strongest is the full-length tang (**c**) with the grip of another material. Varieties of grip shape and material are endless.

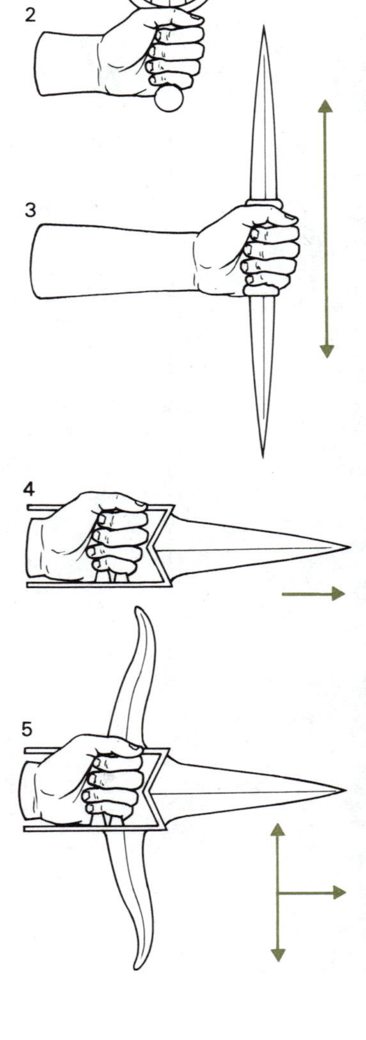

Holding and direction of thrust (right) The usual grip is with the blade away from the thumb (**1**), as a downward stab is the most powerful. Most daggers can also be held point upward (**2**), and some combine both possibilities (**3**). Others, notably the Indian *katar*, are punched forward (**4**). *Katars* that work in all three directions have also been made (**5**).

Use (left) The dagger's chief uses are for self-defense and in clandestine attack. It is quick to handle, easy to conceal, and has often been acceptable for ornamental wear. In prolonged fights it is often used in brawling clinches, where a long blade could not be drawn back far enough to make a stab. Other uses have been in religious ceremony and ritual sacrifice.

Non-metal daggers

Non-metal daggers make less satisfactory weapons than daggers made of metal. Minerals, although sharp, tend to be brittle; other common materials — bone, horn and wood — offer an acceptable point but will not keep a sharp edge. For these reasons, metal is usually the preferred material for daggers whenever it is available. Daggers for ritual use are sometimes an exception to this rule.

Flint dagger (left) A late example, dating from c.1600BC. Probably imitating the shape of early bronze daggers, it achieves a beauty of its own. Found in Sweden. (Statens Historiska Museum, Stockholm.)

Non-metal daggers (below)
1 Flint dagger of the earliest form, the grip scarcely distinct from the blade. Could also be fixed to a shaft as a spear point. Scandinavia, c.1800BC.
2 Flint dagger with a distinct grip. Intermediate in development to the other two flint daggers shown on this page. From Denmark.
3 North American Indian dirk of elk antler. A simple point without a cutting edge. California, 19th century.
4 Aztec sacrificial dagger with a blade of chalcedony. Used to cut out the heart of human victims. Given by Montezuma to Cortes for the King of Spain, c.1500. (British Museum, London.)
5 Australian Aboriginal dagger with quartzite blade and gum and wood handle. A Stone Age weapon made in the 20th century AD.
6 Ancient Chinese dagger of green jade. Probably for ritual or purely ornamental use.
7 Bone dagger with hilt in the shape of a reindeer. A spike without a cutting edge. From the Dordogne, France. Paleolithic period.
8 *Bich'wa*, a Dravidian dagger from Central India with characteristic voided hilt. This example is made of horn.
9 Jivaro Indian double-ended dagger of wood. Combines the two common directions of thrust. From Ecuador.
10 North American Indian wooden dagger. NW coast area.
11 Eskimo bone dagger, its grip bound with animal sinew.

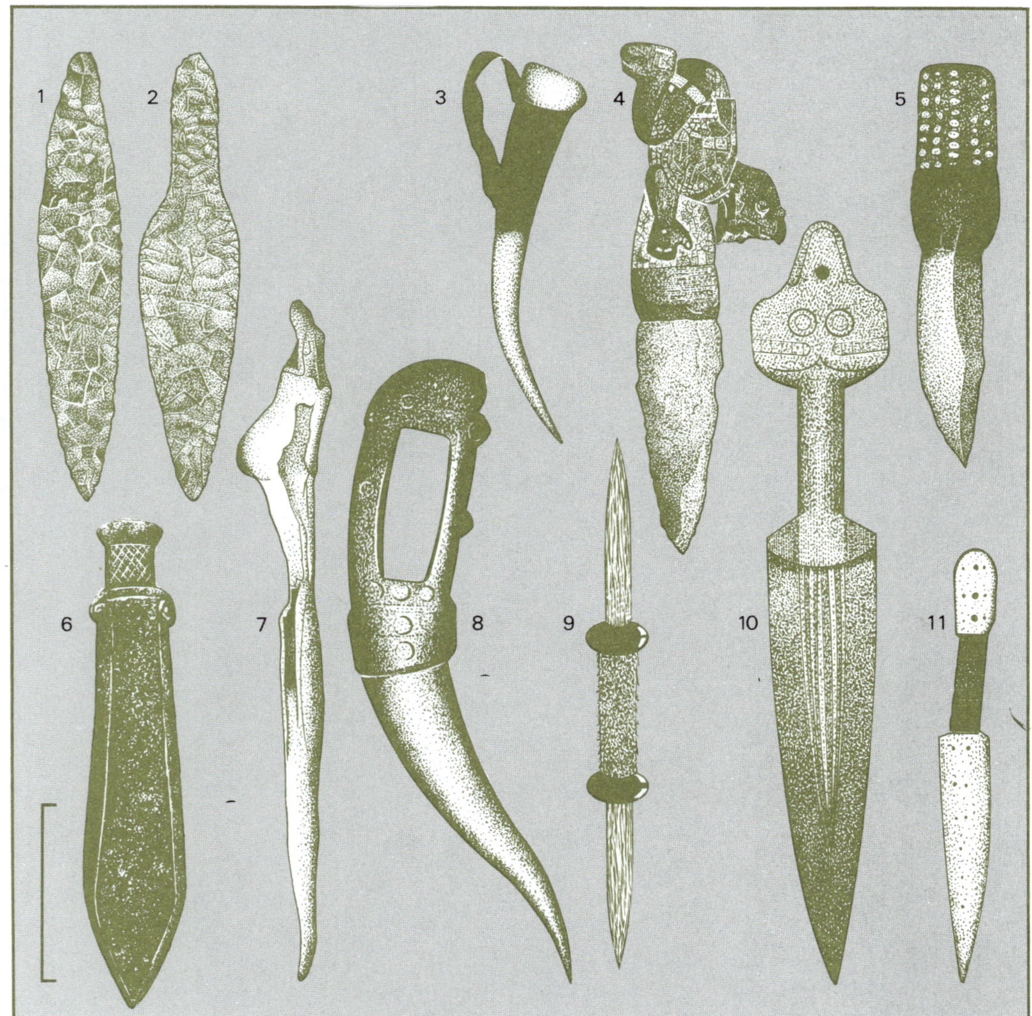

World daggers 1

A wide variety of hilt and metal blade shapes is found in daggers from all parts of the world. In general, types vary in accordance with their function (ranging from efficiency in fighting to ceremonial use), how they are worn, and the development of technology in each society. Daggers vary in length from around 6in (15cm) to around 20in (50cm), and at the longer end of the scale begin to merge with the short-sword.

A Swanetian man (left) from the Caucasus, wearing his *kindjal* dagger at his waist.

Straight-bladed daggers

1 North American Indian knife. Beaver-tail blade of steel obtained through trading. 19th century.

2 *Skean dhu*, Scottish dagger worn in the stocking top. Usually has a semiprecious stone set on the pommel.

3 *Pesh kabz*, a dagger popular in Persia and Northern India. The blade of T-shaped section was well suited to penetrating chain mail.

4 Arm knife, worn on the upper left arm in the Sudan. Wooden hilt. Not all have the cross-guard.

5 Chinese bronze dagger of the Chou dynasty, c.600-500BC. One-piece construction with a hollow, pierced hilt.

6 *Kard*, a single-edged Persian knife with watered steel blade inlaid with gold. 17th century.

7 *Fusetto*, a multipurpose stiletto for artillerymen. Used to measure the bore and shot, clear the vent and pierce the powder-bag. The blade is usually of an isosceles triangle section. Italy, 17-18th centuries.

8 *Telek*, a dagger used by the Tuareg people of North Africa. Worn along the inside of the left forearm, hilt forward, it is drawn with the right hand.

9 *Kindjal*, a long dagger from the Caucasus. Blade usually straight as shown, but occasionally slightly curved toward the point.

10 *Kwaiken*, a Japanese woman's dagger. This example has a double-edged blade, but some are single-edged. Said to have been used for ceremonially committing suicide by cutting the veins of the neck.

1 2 3 4 5 6 7 8 9 10 11 12

11 *Tanto*, a Japanese dagger with a small guard and a single edge. The types known as *hamidashi* and *aikuchi* are similar but have a vestigial guard or none at all.
12 *Piha-kaetta*, a dagger from Sri Lanka. Reminiscent of the Bowie shape, double-edged at the tip, and heavy as if for chopping. Often engraved and inlaid with silver and brass.
13 Punching dagger known as a scissors *katar*, from India. At rest, it looks like a common *katar* (see large illustration, right). When the bars are squeezed together the two side blades spread out to be used to parry or trap the enemy's blade.
14 *Katar* with three fixed blades and a hand-guard. A rare variation, combining all three possible directions of thrust with a dagger.
15 *Katar* with bifid blade. A variation of the common single-bladed type. The advantage is mainly psychological, but it could be used to trap the blade of an opponent.
16 Push dagger from the USA. A type that had a short vogue in the mid-19th century. Clearly related to the *katar* in principle, the blade protrudes between the fingers when gripped.

Katar (right), a punching dagger from India. Gripped by the two close-set bars, with the long tangs along either side of the wrist and forearm, it allows a most powerful blow. The point is sometimes reinforced so that it will pierce chain mail.

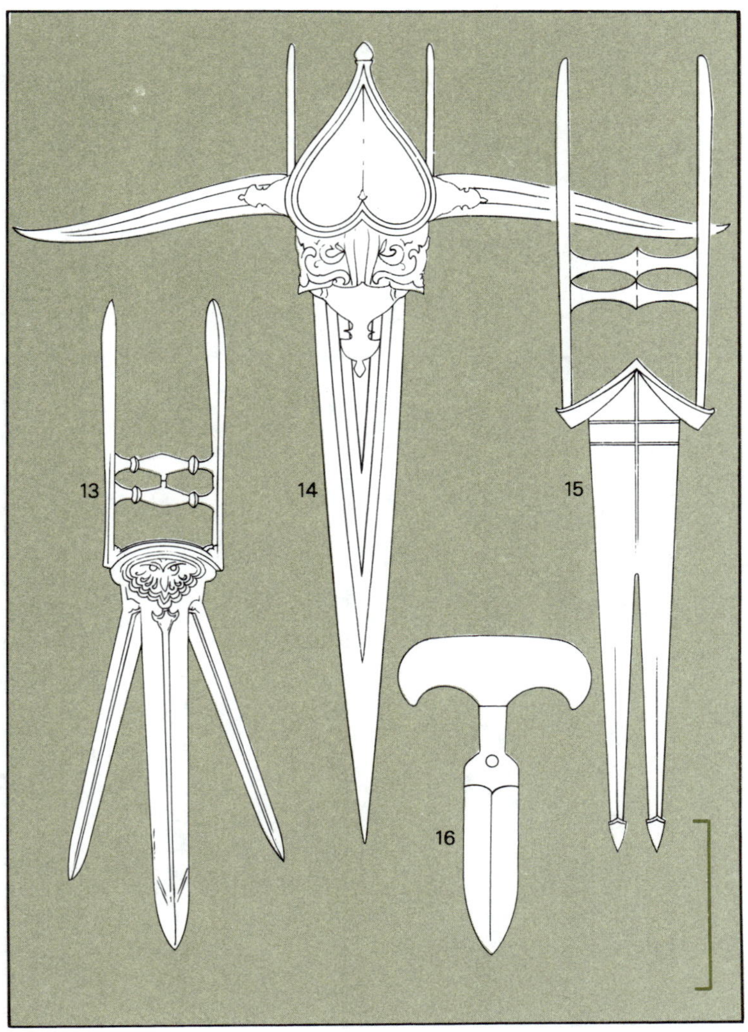

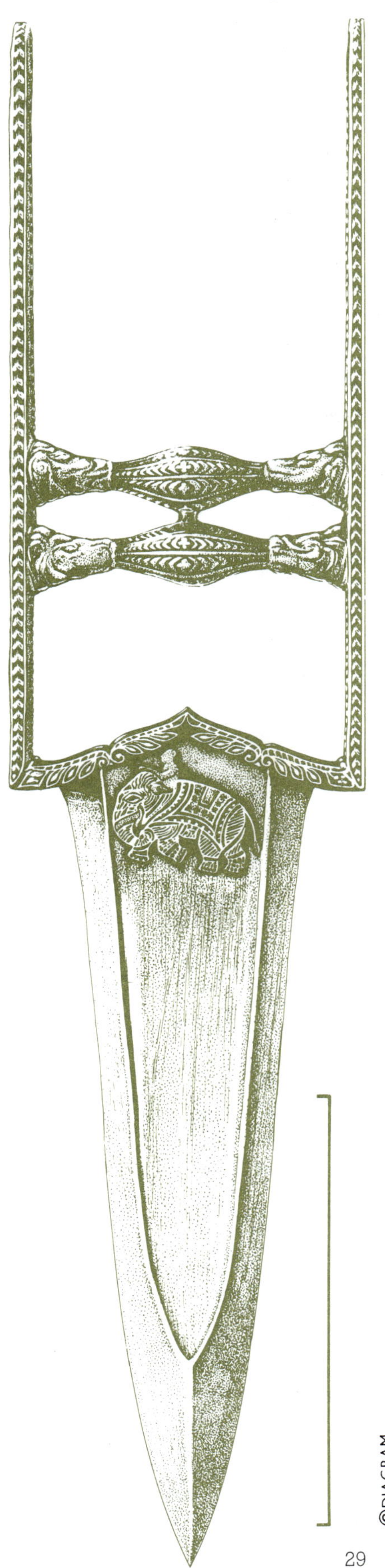

World daggers 2

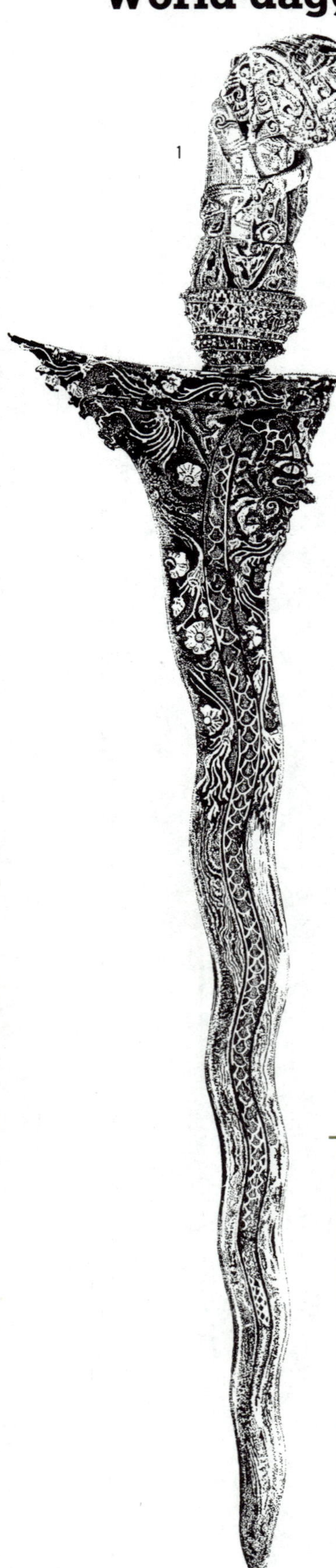

Daggers with curved blades

1 *Kris*, Malay weapon characterized by the curve to an asymmetrical spur at the base of the blade. The remainder of the blade may be either wavy or straight. The fine example (left) has an ivory handle and intricate gold inlay on the laminated steel blade.

2 *Khanjar*, a dagger from India and Persia. The type is distinguished more by the pistol-like grip of jade or ivory than by the blade, which can curve forward or back, or can recurve like that of the *khanjarli* (3).

3 *Khanjarli*, an Indian dagger with a double-curved, double-edged blade and characteristic pommel. Not all examples have the guard.

4 Dagger of jambiya form, from India. Has a steel blade and a gilt metal hilt.

5 *Jambiya*, an Arab dagger found in many variations. All have a curved, two-edged blade, usually with a reinforcing rib down the center. This example is from Muscat.

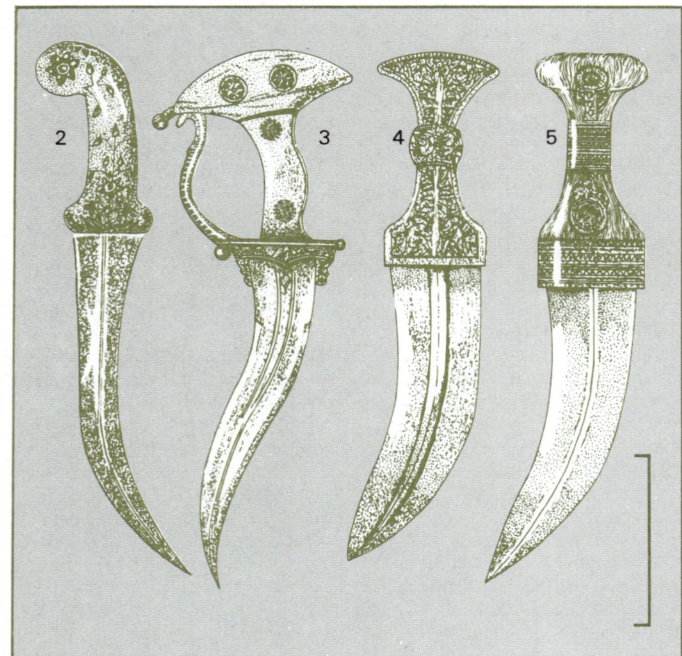

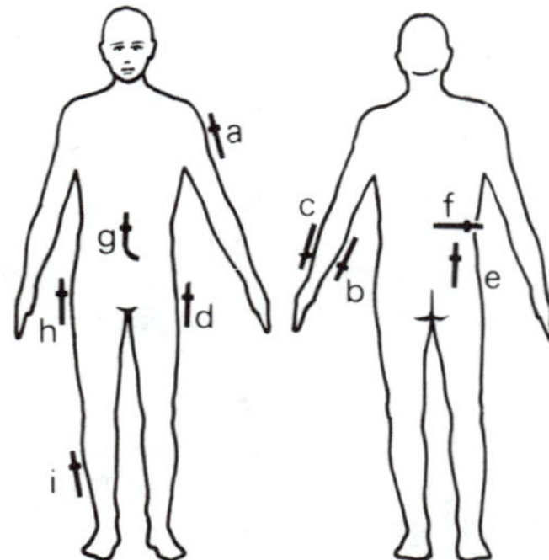

Wearing (left) Daggers are worn in different places for concealment, convenience of carrying, speed of draw.

a Upper arm (Sudan)
b Inner forearm (Sahara)
c Outer forearm (British Commandos)
d Left hip
e Right buttock, vertical
f Small of back, horizontal
g Center front (Arabs)
h Right hip
i Stocking or boot-top

Scabbards (right) Shown are examples of common types.

1 All leather, for US Marine fighting knife, with a strap to retain the knife.

2 Gilt and pierced copper over wood — this method can be used with other metals. Switzerland, 16th century.

3 All metal, for Nazi German dress dagger. Hung from the belt by two slings attached to the rings.

4 Leather-covered wood. Construction common to many countries. This one is for a Nepalese dagger.

5 Leather with metal mounts. A very common type. This is for a Scottish *skean dhu*.

6 All wood. Shown here in its simplest form, for a World War 1 trench dagger.

7 Thin metal over wood, for an Arab *jambiya*. Light and hard-wearing.

European daggers 1

The history of the European dagger relies less on logical development than on a succession of fashions. The advantages of a full-length tang or one-piece construction were established in the Bronze Age. Thereafter conventional styles were periodically modified by specific uses, such as formal dueling or penetrating the joints in armor. We illustrate examples of each of the main types.

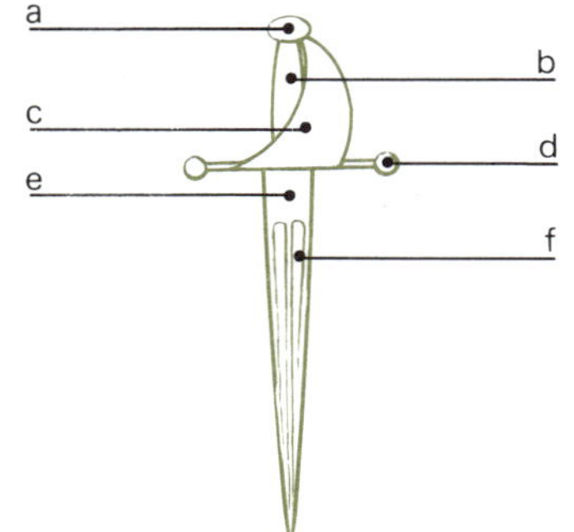

Parts of a dagger (left) In the Western world, the principal parts of a dagger are as follows.
a Pommel
b Grip(s)
c Knuckle-guard
d Quillons
e Ricasso
f Fullers (grooves)
(Not all these features are always present.)

Ancient and medieval daggers (left and below)
1 Bronze dagger with separate hilt riveted to the blade. Typical early construction. Sweden, c.1350-1200BC. (Statens Historiska Museum, Stockholm.)
2 Bronze dagger of the short, broad type commonly found in Bronze Age burial places in England. Yorkshire, c.2000-1600BC.
3 Iron Age dagger of the Hallstatt culture. Central Europe, c.500BC. Iron was first used in c.3000BC but was strengthened by the discovery of a steeling process in c.1500BC.
4 *Pugio*, a Roman military dagger of c.100AD. An even shorter version of the *gladius* short-sword.
5 *Scramasax*, an iron dagger of the Franks and Saxons. Dates from c.AD 550.
6 Rondel dagger. A modern name for a medieval type characterized by a diskoid pommel and guard. Blades are usually very narrow, and of various sectional shapes. From c.1320-1550.
7 *Baselard*. The medieval name for a type with a cross-piece at the guard and pommel. Most have tapered, double-edged blades. From c.1300-1500.

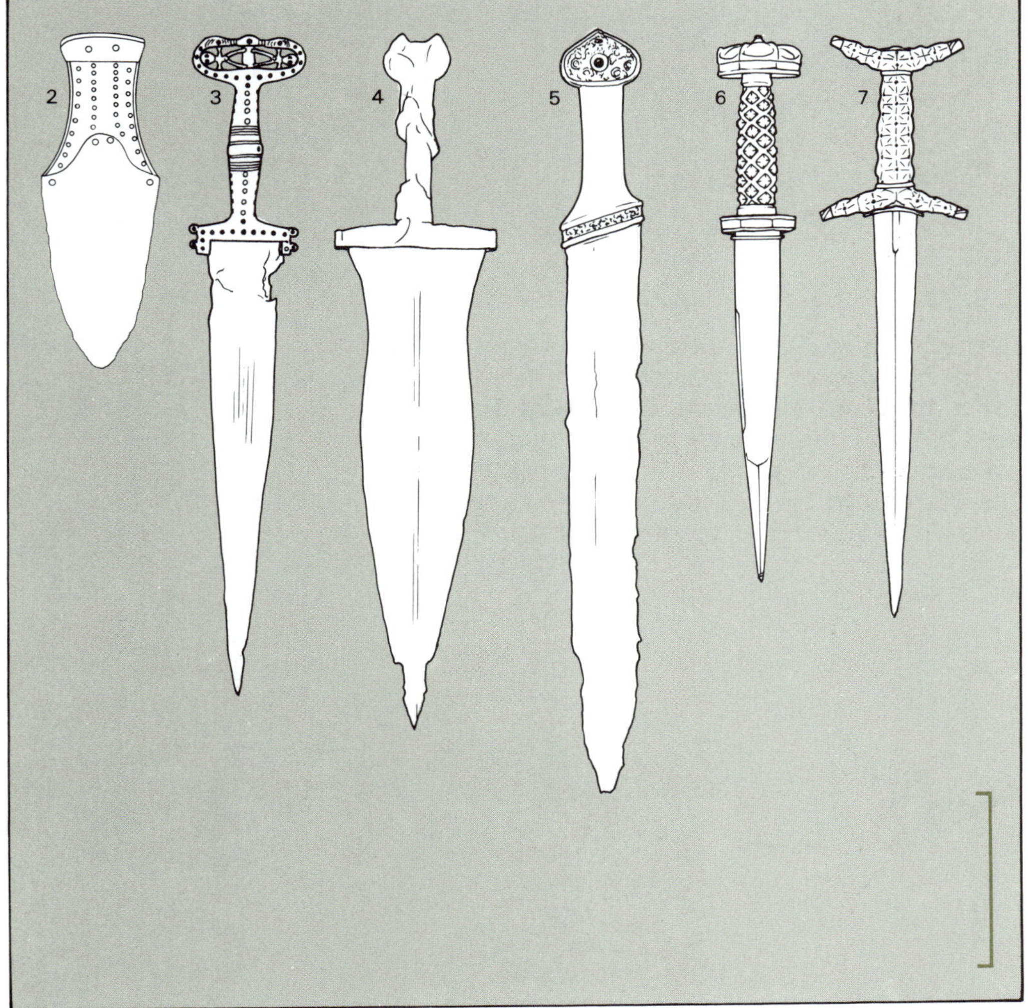

European daggers 2

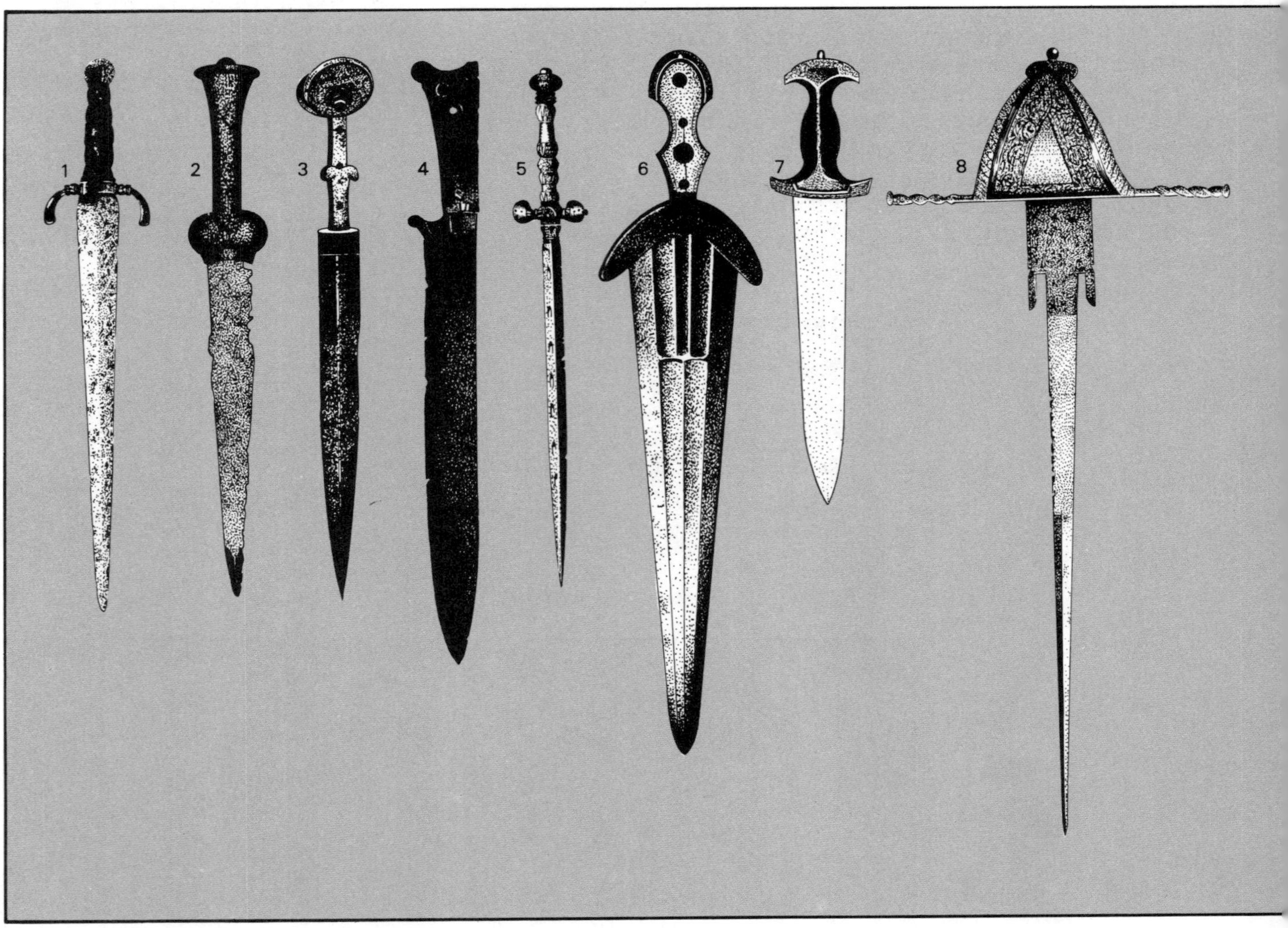

In the Middle Ages, a dagger was commonly worn by men of all classes for self-defense, for eating and also as an ornament. In Spain and Italy its use was formalized as a left-hand adjunct to the rapier, mainly for parrying. In the 16th century, the dagger began to give way to the sword as an item of wear.

Swordbreaker (below) A development of the left-hand dagger which, instead of simply parrying the opponent's blade, would trap and even break it. Characteristic toothed blade. Probably Italian, c.1600. (Wallace Collection, London.)

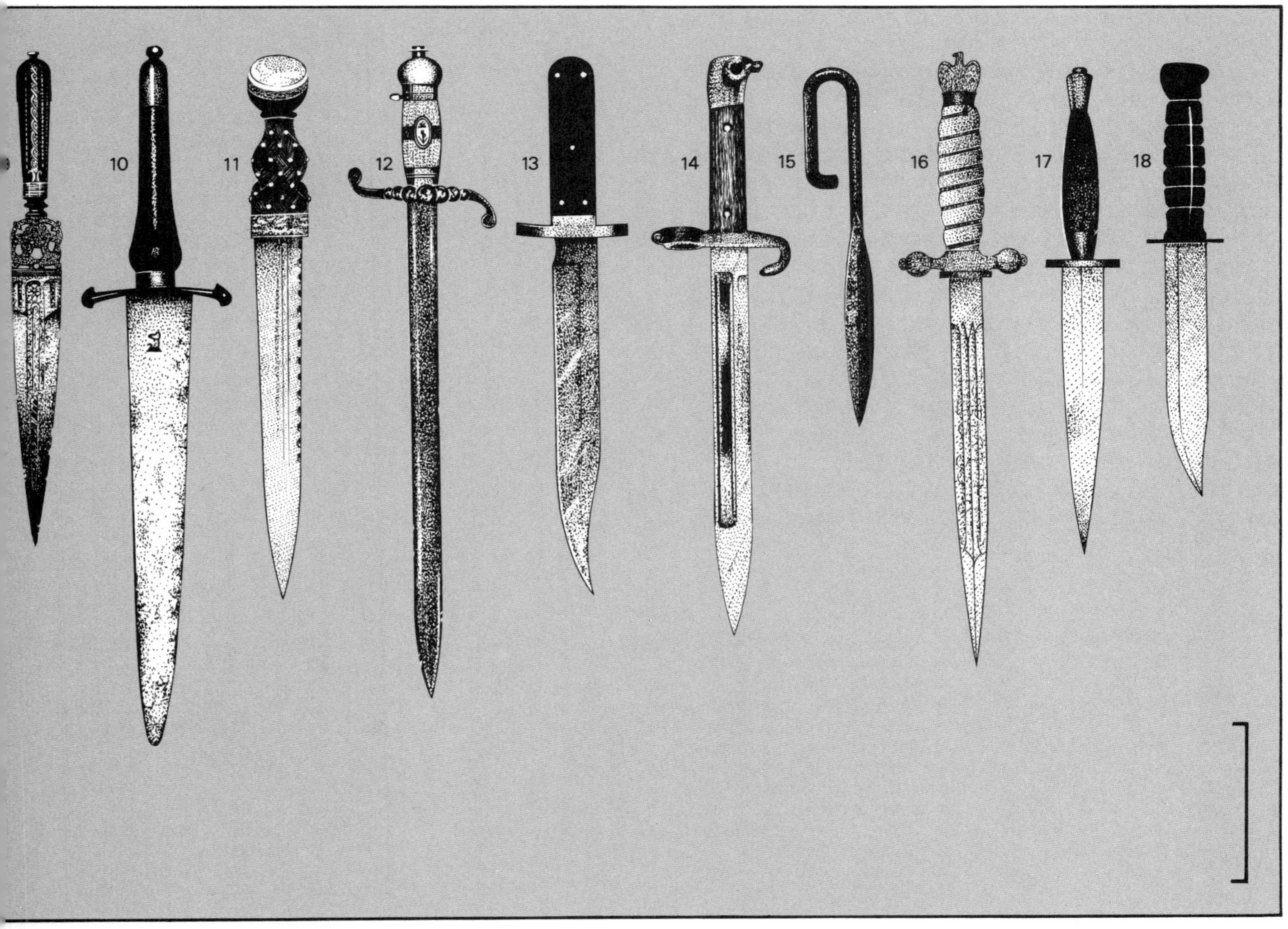

Late medieval and modern daggers (above)
1 Quillon dagger. A type with several sub-varieties. All have two projections at the guard. From c.1250-1500, and later as a left-hand weapon.
2 Kidney or ballock dagger. So-called because of the shape at the guard. Popular c.1300-1600. Shown is a late 14th century example.
3 Eared dagger, a type characterized by two disks at the pommel. Usually ornate and costly. From c.1400-1550. This example is Italian, 15th century.
4 Peasant knife or *Hauswehr*. A multipurpose knife of the peasant class, usually single-edged. Swiss, 16th century.
5 *Stiletto*, a purely stabbing weapon with no cutting edge. Common in Italy in the 17th and 18th centuries. Blade may be of square or triangular section. Early 17th century example.
6 *Cinquedea*, meaning "five fingers," the approximate width of the blade at the base. A heavy civilian arm, worn at the back. Italian example, c.1500.
7 Holbein dagger. A modern name for a style popular in Switzerland, and copied by the Nazis as a dress-dagger in the 1930s. The example is Swiss, mid-16th century.
8 *Main gauche* or left-hand dagger. Here in its fully developed form with pierced triangular knuckle-guard. Used with a rapier for dueling. Spanish, c.1650.
9 Mediterranean dagger. A type almost like a table knife, without a guard. Italian, late 18th century.
10 Plug bayonet. In the late 17th century, daggers were made to be stuck in the muzzle of a musket to create a pike. Tapered round hilt. German, c.1700.
11 Scottish dirk. Still very much a functional weapon in the 18th century; by the late 19th century (as shown here) it was a ceremonial ornament.
12 Naval dirk. In the 18th century, naval officers in many countries began to wear dress dirks as an ornament and sign of rank. British, 1790-1810.
13 Bowie knife. This example of c.1860 is the true Bowie shape — double-edged at the point. Most kinds of 19th century US fighting and hunting knives now go under this name.
14 Knife-bayonet. In the late 19th century bayonets once more resembled a dagger, and most still take this form. Austrian, 1888.
15 Trench dagger. World War 1 emergency-issue, combining a simple knuckle-duster guard.
16 Dress dagger. The Nazis used daggers as an item of uniform, special to each branch of the services. This one is naval, 1938.
17 Sykes-Fairbairn commando dagger. Worn on the left forearm. A simple, effective blade shape first used in Ancient Egypt. British, 1939-45.
18 US Marine fighting knife. A typical post-WW2 multipurpose weapon and survival-knife.

Swords

The concept of a sword is very simple; it is a long blade with a grip at one end. But it is a weapon that offers many possible varieties in form as well as great versatility in use. It is more adaptable and more subtle than the ax, one of its close antecedents, being easily adapted to thrusting and parrying as well as cutting. Longer than a dagger and not easily concealed, it has been regarded as an honorable weapon in many cultures. More than any other type of weapon, the sword has achieved special status — as an art form, a valued heirloom, and a symbol of war, justice, military skill and honor.
We survey the main varieties of sword worldwide, including its antecedents and also its development into a purely ceremonial object. Special attention is paid to swords from Europe, India and Japan.

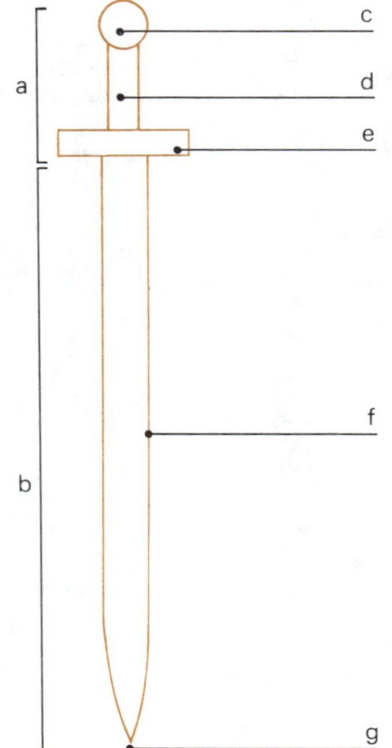

Basic parts of a sword (left)
a Hilt
b Blade
c Pommel
d Grip
e Guard
f Edge
g Point
(The specialized names for the parts of Japanese and some European swords are shown on pp. 41 and 50 respectively.)

Combat (left) A sketch by Hokusai shows the essential feature of sword combat — the confrontation of two men at just over arm's reach. The inherent equality of such combat probably accounts for the honorable status of the sword worldwide. Its versatility, for parrying, cutting and thrusting, has often led to the formalization of its use in "schools" or theories of fencing.

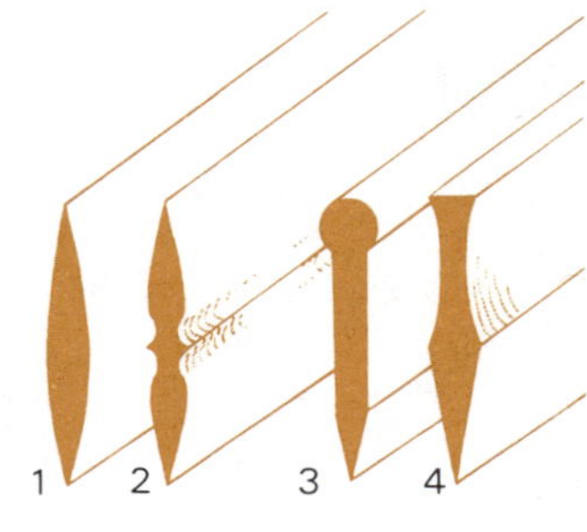

Blade cross-sections (left) There is great variety of sectional shape in sword-blades. Choice has usually been determined simply by fashion; but the origin of such fashions has often been an attempt to make a blade which is sufficiently rigid but as light as possible. Shown are two double-edged (**1**, **2**) and two single-edged (**3**, **4**) solutions to this problem.

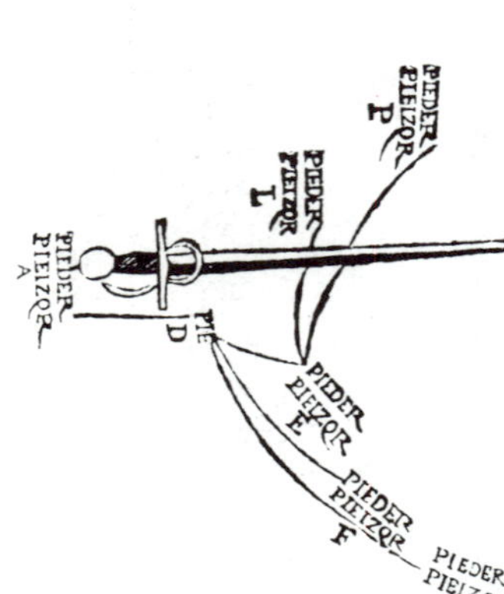

Cut versus thrust (above) This illustration from a 17th century Spanish fencing manual outlines a debate which is as old as the sword itself, expressed in terms of East versus West. In general, Eastern swords have tended to be made for cutting, while European swordsmen have been more ready to use the point for thrusting.

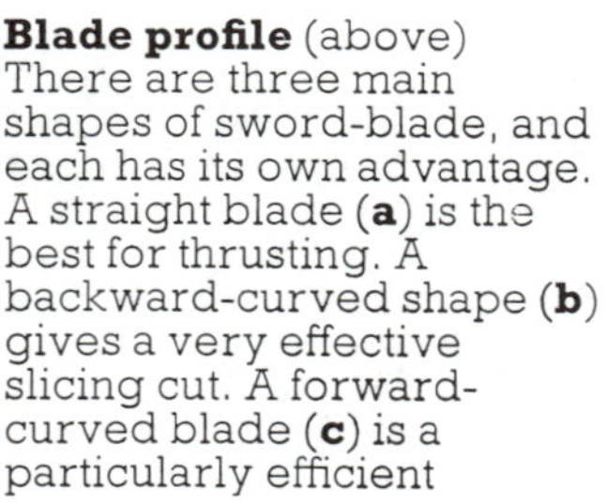

Blade profile (above) There are three main shapes of sword-blade, and each has its own advantage. A straight blade (**a**) is the best for thrusting. A backward-curved shape (**b**) gives a very effective slicing cut. A forward-curved blade (**c**) is a particularly efficient chopper, especially when, as is often the case, it is broad and heavy toward the tip. Whereas civilian preference has usually been determined by the current vogue, armies have often tried to design the ideal blade — one that is equally effective for both cutting and thrusting.

Status of the sword (above) The sword is a uniquely prestigious weapon, and has often accrued special significance. Several examples are illustrated here.

a In Japan the sword was at the heart of the cult of the Samurai warrior.

b In medieval Europe the simple cross-shaped sword was a symbol of Christianity associated especially with Crusaders, and later with the cult of chivalry.

c In many armies the sword is retained for ceremonial use, especially for officers, and has thus become a sign of rank.

d The sword is also used as a symbol of just retribution under the law.

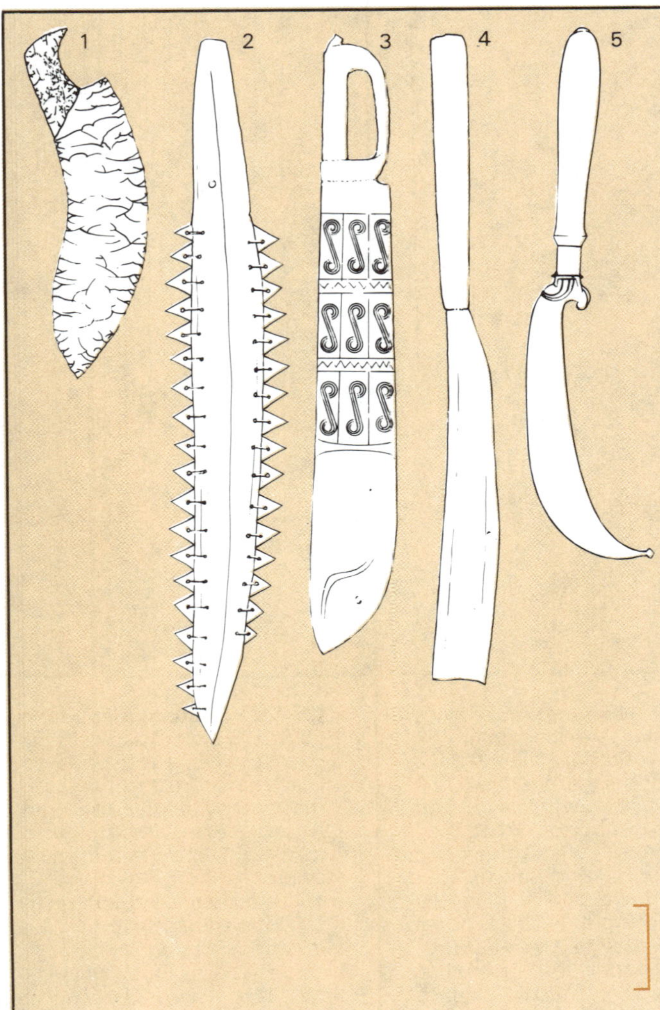

Proto-swords (left) Sword-like weapons have been produced by cultures lacking the metals needed to make a true sword. Sword-like "choppers" or axes also exist.

1 Flint knife from Ancient Egypt. This is about as long a blade as can be made in stone, and is too brittle for practical use.

2 Wooden club edged with sharks' teeth, from Kiribati (Gilbert Islands).

3 Wooden sword from New Guinea, made in imitation of the cutlass of a visiting Western sailor.

4 *Dao* from Assam. Although usually classed as axes, specimens as long as this are almost swords.

5 "Chopper" from Malabar, India, a simple form of sword.

Aborigine (below) of Australia, about to strike with a long wooden sword-like weapon.

Bronze sword (above) from Ancient Babylon. It was the discovery of bronze that allowed the development of the true sword. The inscription on the blade, in cuneiform script, reads "Son of Enlil-Nirari, King of Assyria." (Metropolitan Museum of Art, New York.)

African and Middle Eastern swords

Here we illustrate swords from Africa, the Middle East, Turkey, southern Russia and Iran. Although a common weapon in most of these areas, swords from Black Africa are scarcer, and are particularly hard to date. The majority of those in museums and on the collectors' market in the West were brought back by travelers in the 19th and early 20th centuries.

Dervish warrior (left), one of the fanatical followers of the Mahdi, who fought the British in the Sudan campaigns of the late 19th century. The legend has grown that their straight, cross-shaped swords were relics of the Crusades.

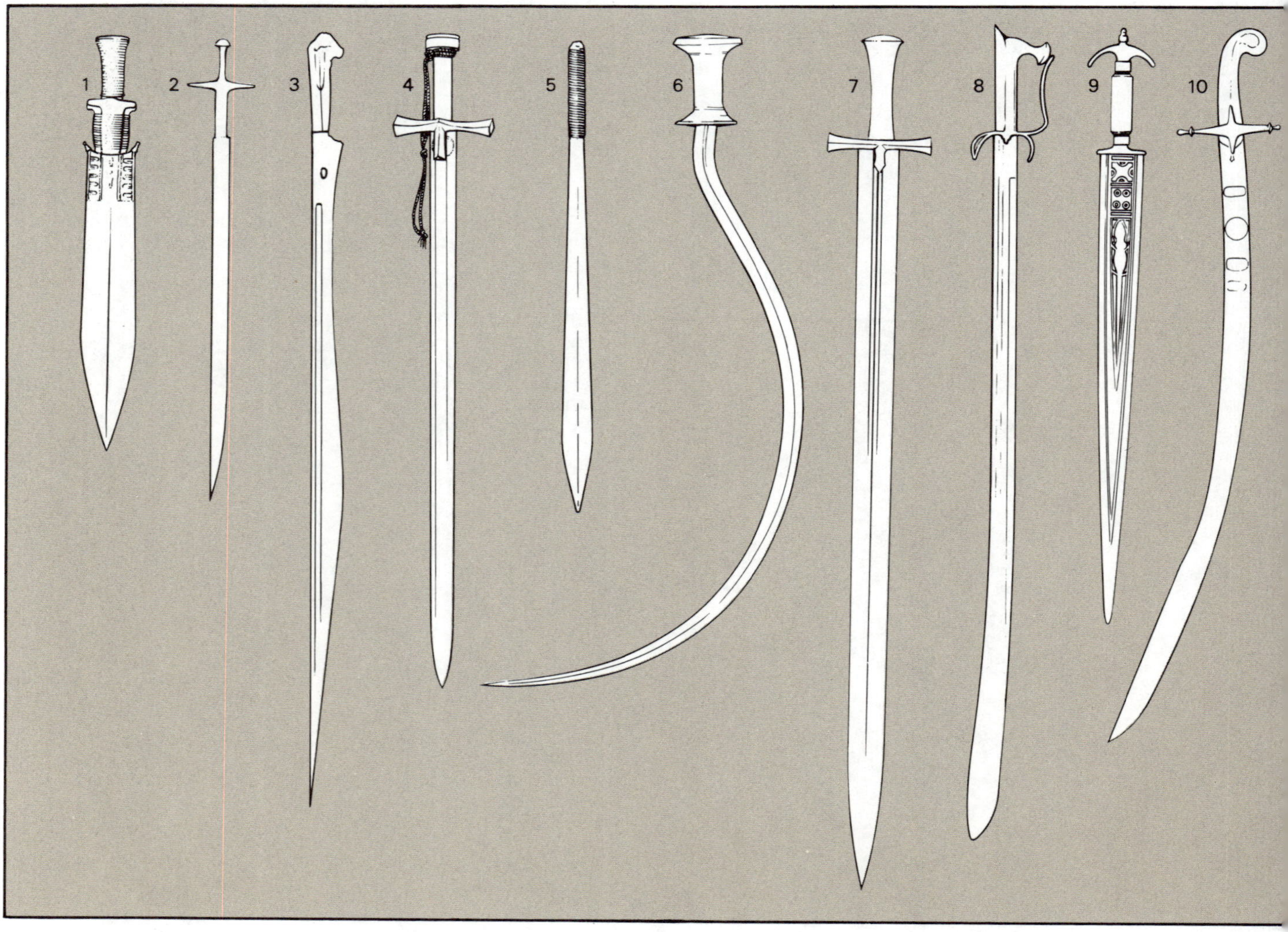

African swords
1 Two-edged sword from Gabon, West Africa. Thin steel blade, the grip bound with copper and brass wire.
2 *Takouba*, sword of the Tuaregs of the Sahara. Compare with the Tuareg dagger *telek* (p. 28).
3 *Flyssa*, sword of the Kabyles people of Morocco. Single-edged blade, engraved and inlaid with brass.
4 *Kaskara*, two-edged straight sword of the Baghirmi people of the Sahara. Similar in style to Sudanese swords.
5 Two-edged sword of the Masai people, East Africa. Blade of flat diamond-shaped section, no guard.
6 *Shotel*, two-edged, double-curved sword from Ethiopia. The curved tip is used to reach behind an opponent's shield.
7 Sudanese sword with characteristically straight, two-edged blade and cross-shaped guard.
8 Arab sword with a blade probably of European make, 18th century. Silver gilt hilt and mounts.
9 Arab sword from Dongola, with a tapered, two-edged steel blade, having geometric patterns and a crocodile cut into it. Ebony and ivory hilt.

Middle Eastern swords
10 *Kilij*, Turkish saber. This example has a 15th century blade and 18th century mounts. Typically, the blade broadens near the tip, with a straight sharp edge on the back.
11 *Yataghan* of typical form. Turkish sword with forward-curved, single-edged blade. Bone grips with large pommel, no guard.

Iron sword (right), a rare relic of the Sarmatians, a nomadic people from the steppes who were scattered throughout Europe between c.300BC and c.600AD. Examination by modern techniques such as X-rays are now revealing the original fine quality of many early iron swords, invariably found in poor condition.

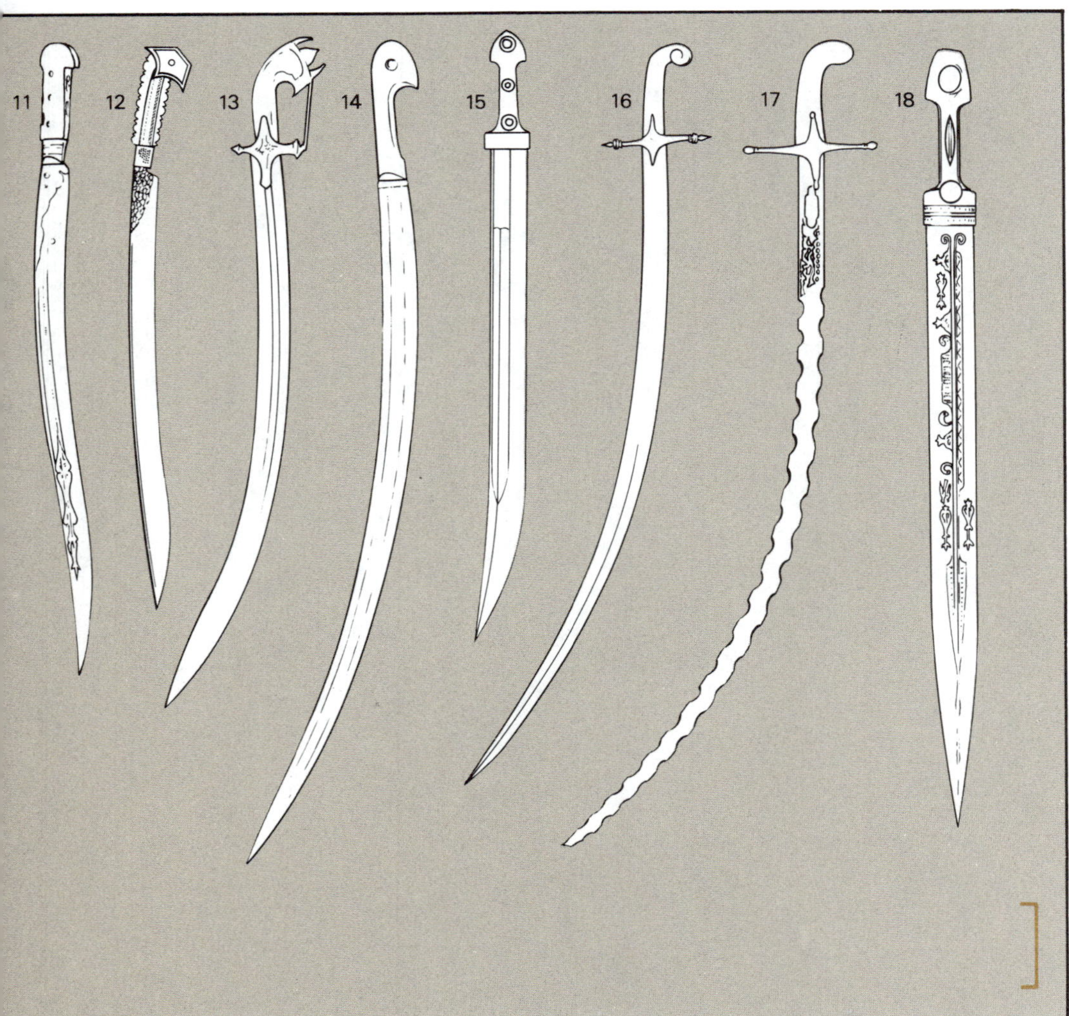

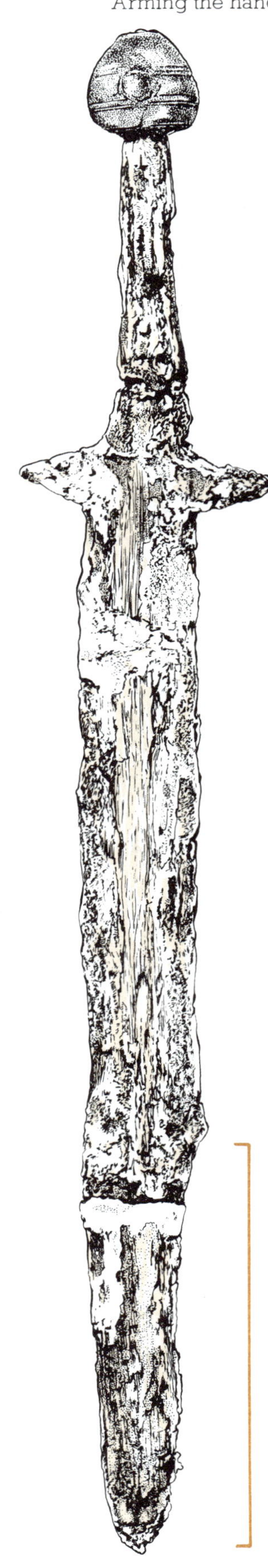

12 *Yataghan* with solid silver hilt and blade set with coral stones. Turkish.
13 *Saif*, a curved Arab sword with distinctive pommel. Found wherever there have been Arab communities.
14 *Shashqa*, a sword from the Caucasus, originally Circassian, but later in widespread use with Russian cavalry. Persian blade dated 1819.

15 *Kindjal*, a weapon from the Caucasus, found in short-sword size as here, and in dagger size (see p. 28).
16 *Shamshir* of typical form. The classic Persian saber, with curved blade and distinctive hilt. Also found in India.
17 *Shamshir* with flamboyant blade and gold inlaid steel hilt. Persian.

18 *Quaddara*, a name given sometimes to a large *kindjal* (see 15). Horn hilt, the blade etched and inlaid with gold.

Swords of the Indian subcontinent

The swords on these two pages are from the Indian subcontinent and adjacent areas. It is a region rich in varieties of sword, and has produced some of the best steel blades and richest decoration in the world. It is often difficult to ascribe a name, date and exact provenance to these swords, as much basic research is still to be done. Dates, where given, apply only to the example illustrated.

Rajput warrior (left) holding a *tulwar* and carrying a shield on his shoulder. Most of the martial races of Northern India used some variety of *tulwar*.

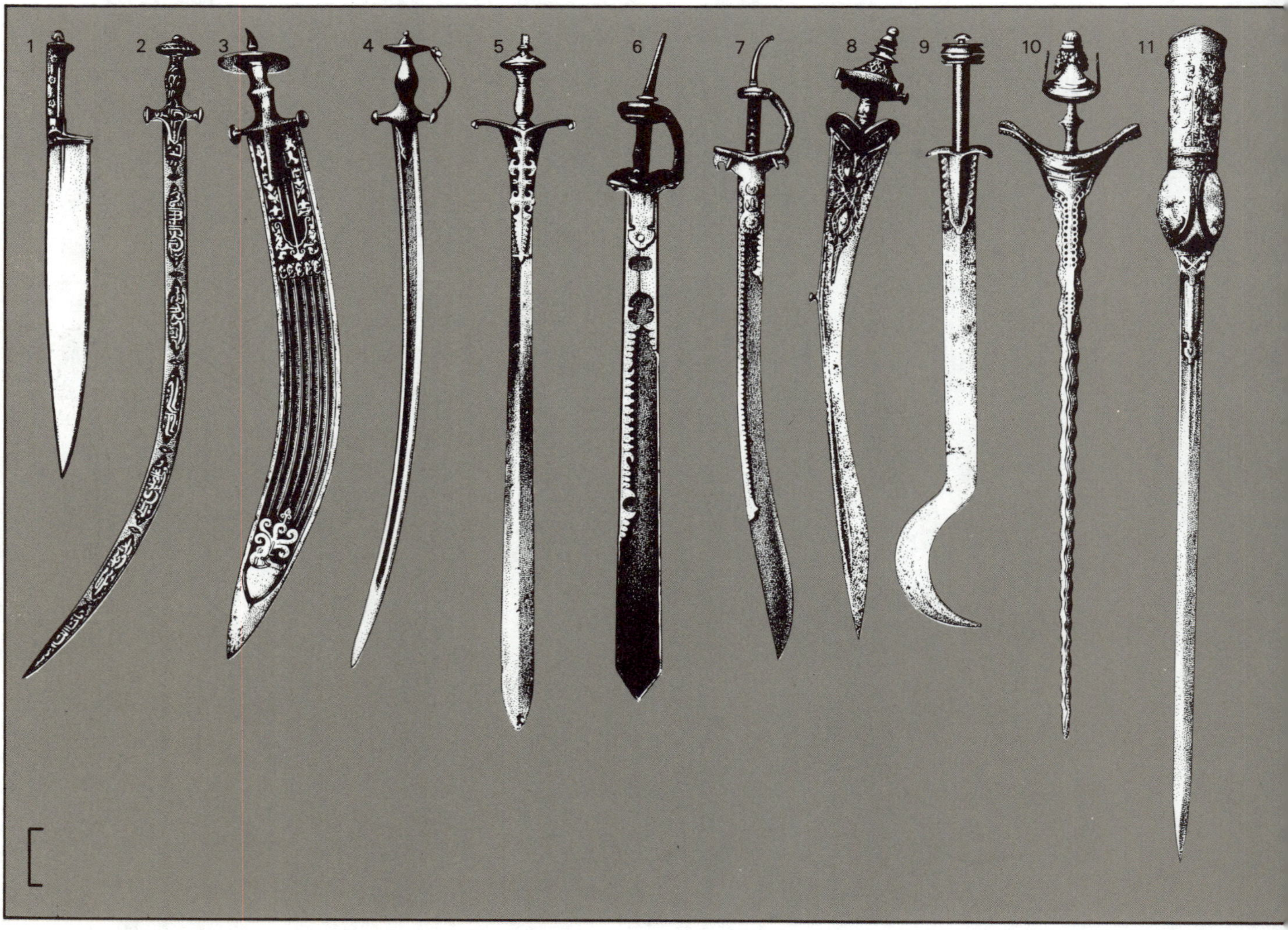

Indian subcontinent swords (above)
1 *Choora*, or Khyber knife. The heavy, single-edged sword of the Afghans and Pathans, from the border of Afghanistan and Pakistan.
2 *Tulwar* (or *talwar*), Indian sword characterized by a curved blade and a distinctive hilt with disk-shaped pommel. This one is Muslim, from Northern India, 17th century.
3 *Tulwar* with broad blade, for executions. Northern India, 18th or 19th century.
4 *Tulwar* with Punjabi style steel hilt incorporating a knuckle-guard. From Indore, late 18th century.
5 *Khanda* with gilt steel hilt of the "Old Indian" style. Straight two-edged blade. From Nepal, 18th century.
6 *Khanda* of more typical form than the previous one. Hilt of "Hindu basket" style with a spur to allow a two-handed grip. Note the blade's reinforcing trim. Maratha, 18th century.
7 *Sosun pattah*. Hilt of Hindu basket style. Forward-curved reinforced blade with a single edge. Central India, 18th century.
8 South Indian sword with steel hilt, square wooden pommel and forward-curved blade. Madras, 16th century.
9 Sword from a temple of the Nayar people, with a brass hilt and two-edged steel blade. From Tanjore, Southern India, 18th century.
10 South Indian sword with steel hilt and flamboyant two-edged blade. From Madras, 18th century.
11 *Pata*, Indian gauntlet sword with steel guard for the hand and wrist, chased and gilded. From Oudh

Gurkha (left) wearing his *kukri*, a short sword and general-purpose implement. Until the 19th century, the *kora* (see 16, below) was also much used by these Nepalese soldiers, but is less well-known than the *kukri*, which is still carried by Gurkha troops in the British, Indian and Nepalese armies. Contrary to popular belief in the West, the *kukri* is not thrown.

Detail of a tulwar (below) made in a style associated with the city of Lahore in the Punjab. The hilt is of steel, chiseled in relief and gilded. Subtle variations in the proportions of the hilt are often the expert's only guide to the origins of a particular *tulwar*. This one was probably made in the early 19th century. (Victoria and Albert Museum, London.)

(now Uttar Pradesh), 18th century.
12 *Adya katti* of typical form. Short, heavy blade with forward-angled cutting edge. Silver hilt. From Coorg, SW India.
13 *Zafar takieh*, Indian sword of a type traditionally held by a ruler giving an audience. The pommel is shaped to form a hand-rest.
14 *Firangi*, a word meaning foreign, applied in India to a European blade having an Indian hilt. This one is a Mahratta sword using a 17th century German blade.
15 Two-handed, two-edged sword with hollow iron grip. From Central India, 17th century.
16 *Kora* of typical form. Sharpened along the tip and the inside edge of the curve. Nepal, 18th century.
17 *Kukri* of a long, narrow form popular in the 19th century. Nepal, c.1850.
18 *Kukri* with chiseled iron hilt and gracefully curved blade. Nepal, probably 19th century.
19 *Kukri*, Indian Army issue, WW2. Made by a contractor in Northern India, 1943.
20 *Ram dao*, a sword used in Nepal and Northern India for the sacrifice of animals. A variety of extravagant shapes is known.

Far Eastern swords

Naga (left) wearing a *dao* in a scabbard slung from the right shoulder. In the areas near the Assam-Burma border where the Nagas live, the *dao* is carried as a general-purpose implement as well as a weapon.

Dyak head-hunter (left) from Borneo, wearing his sword at his waist.

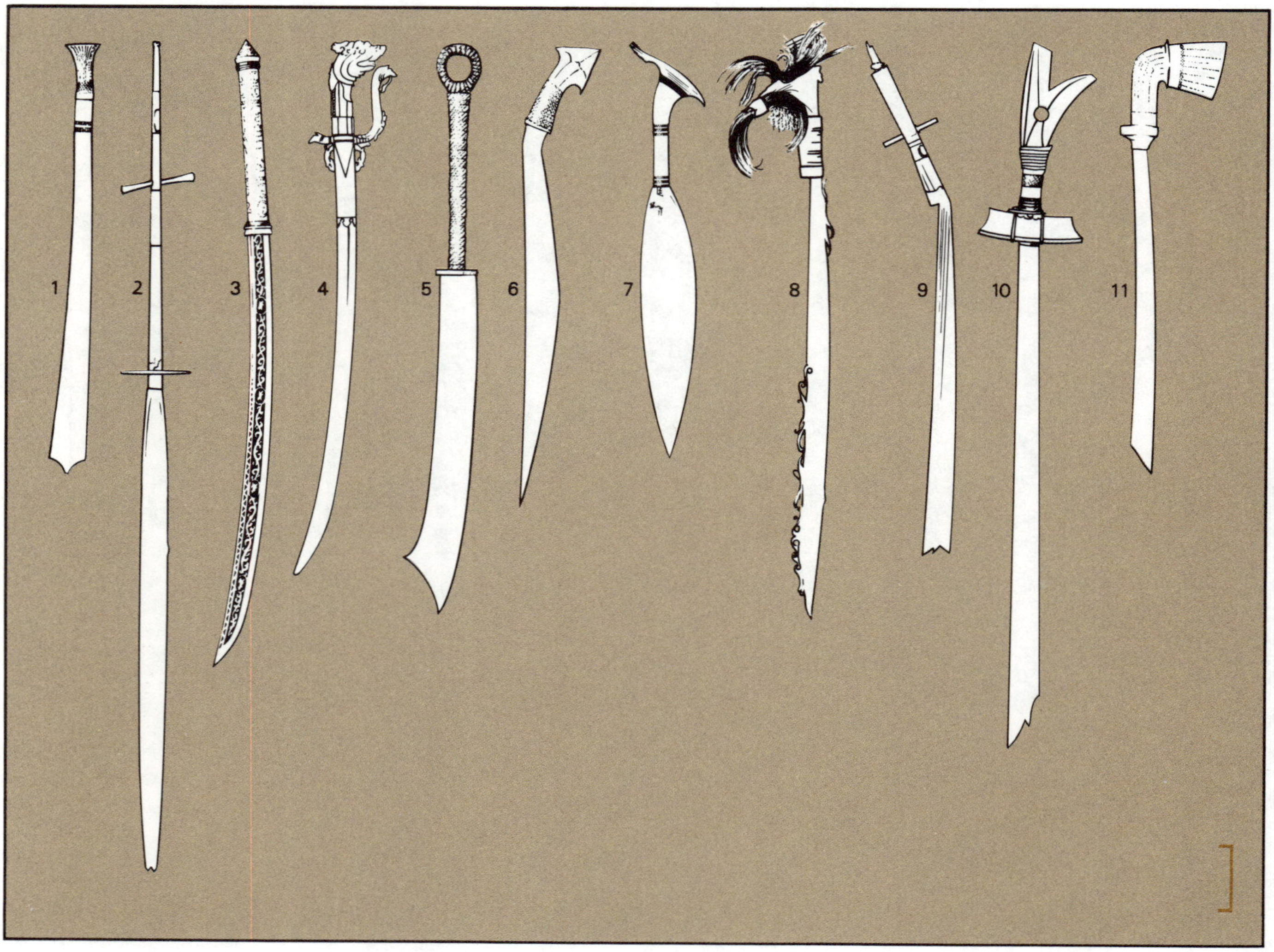

Far Eastern swords (above)
1 *Dao*, sword of the Kachin people of Assam. This is one of the commoner of the many shapes found in the region.
2 *Dao* or *noklang*, two-hand sword of the Khasi people of Assam. Iron grip with brass mounts.
3 *Dha*, sword with a single-edged blade, from Burma. Cylindrical grip covered with a white metal, the blade inlaid with copper and silver.
4 *Kastane*, sword from Sri Lanka with carved wooden grip and pommel, and steel knuckle-guard. Decorated with silver inlay and brass.
5 Chinese iron sword, single-edged. The hilt is simply the tang of the blade bound with cord.
6 *Talibon*, short sword of the Christian community in the Philippines. The grip is wooden with cane binding.
7 *Barong*, short sword or knife of the Moro people of the Philippines and Sabah.
8 *Mandau* or *parang ihlang* (the Malay name). Sword of the Dyak head-hunters of Borneo.
9 *Parang pandit*, sword of the Sea Dyaks of SE Asia, with a single-edged, forward-angled blade.
10 *Campilan*, single-edged sword of the Moros and Sea Dyaks. Carved wooden hilt.
11 *Klewang*, sword from the Celebes archipelago. Single-edged blade and distinctive carved wooden hilt.

Japanese swords 1

The Japanese sword is famous for its style and quality. It is a rich, specialized field of study, about which much information has been preserved. We describe the main types and terminology, and illustrate examples of those kinds most often seen on the collectors' market.

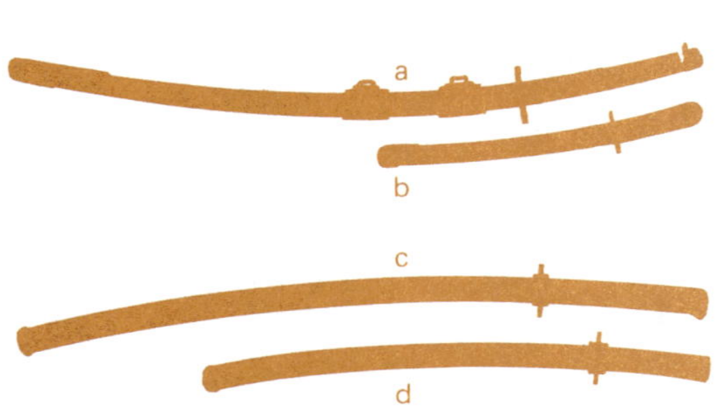

Daisho (above) Meaning "large-small," this name is applied to pairs of swords carried by the Samurai. There were two forms.
a, b A *tachi* and a shorter *tanto* were worn with court dress or armor, hanging from the girdle by a cord.
c, d A *katana* and a shorter *wakizashi* were tucked through the girdle of civilian dress, with their cutting edges upward.

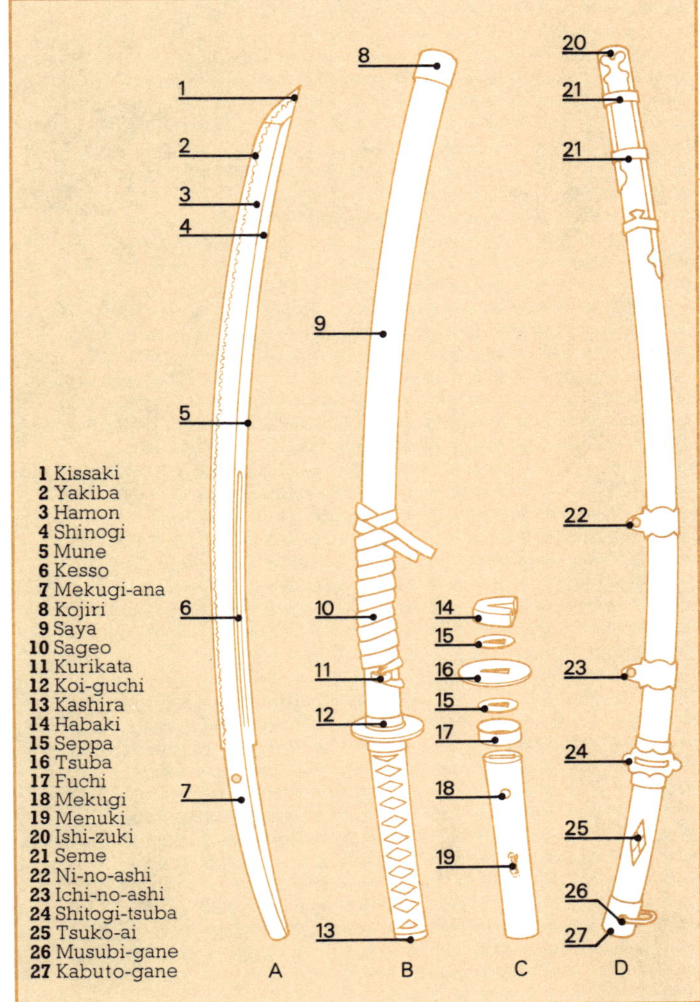

Parts (right) Shown are the parts of a blade (**A**), and of the fittings of a *katana* (**B**, **C**) and a *tachi* (**D**).
Western collectors commonly use the Japanese terms, as given here. The main difference between the two types is in the fittings, the blades differing only in the side on which the maker's mark appears (outward side when correctly worn).

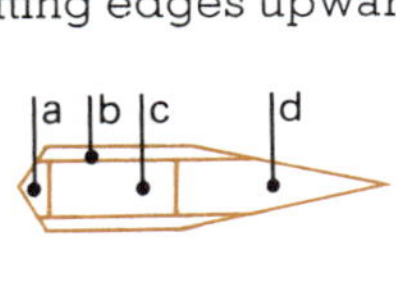

Parts of a blade (left)
a Back **b** Skin
c Core **d** Edge

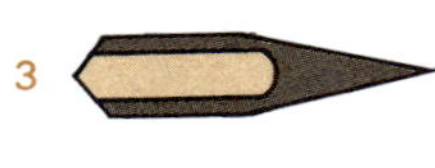

Blade cross-sections (left) Blades were formed from strips of iron and steel, arranged to give a sharp, hard edge and a resilient back. Four types of cross-section are shown here.
1 *Maru-kitae*, all hard.
2 *Wariha tetsu kitae*, only the edge hard.
3 *Kobuse san mai kitae*, soft core and back.
4 *Shihozume kitae*, soft core with medium-hard skin and back.

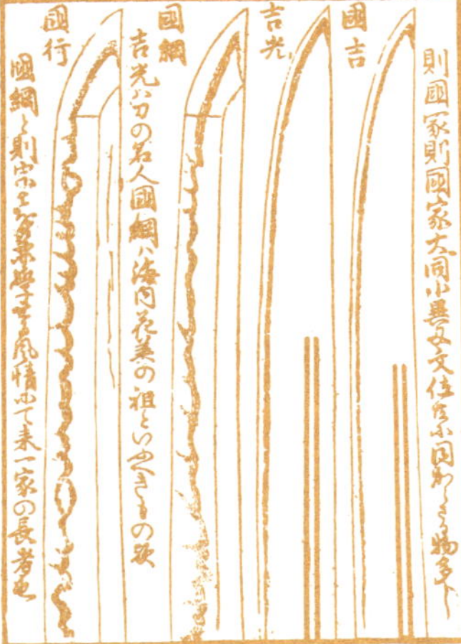

Blade patterns (left) The pattern at the border of the hard metal of the cutting edge can identify the swordsmith who forged it, as shown in this page from "Honcho Tanya Biko."

Ken (below) The form of sword, of Chinese origin, that was used in Japan in the 8th century AD, before the familiar *daisho* were developed. This is an 18th century votive example. (Rijksmuseum voor Volkenkunde, Leiden.)

Japanese swords 2

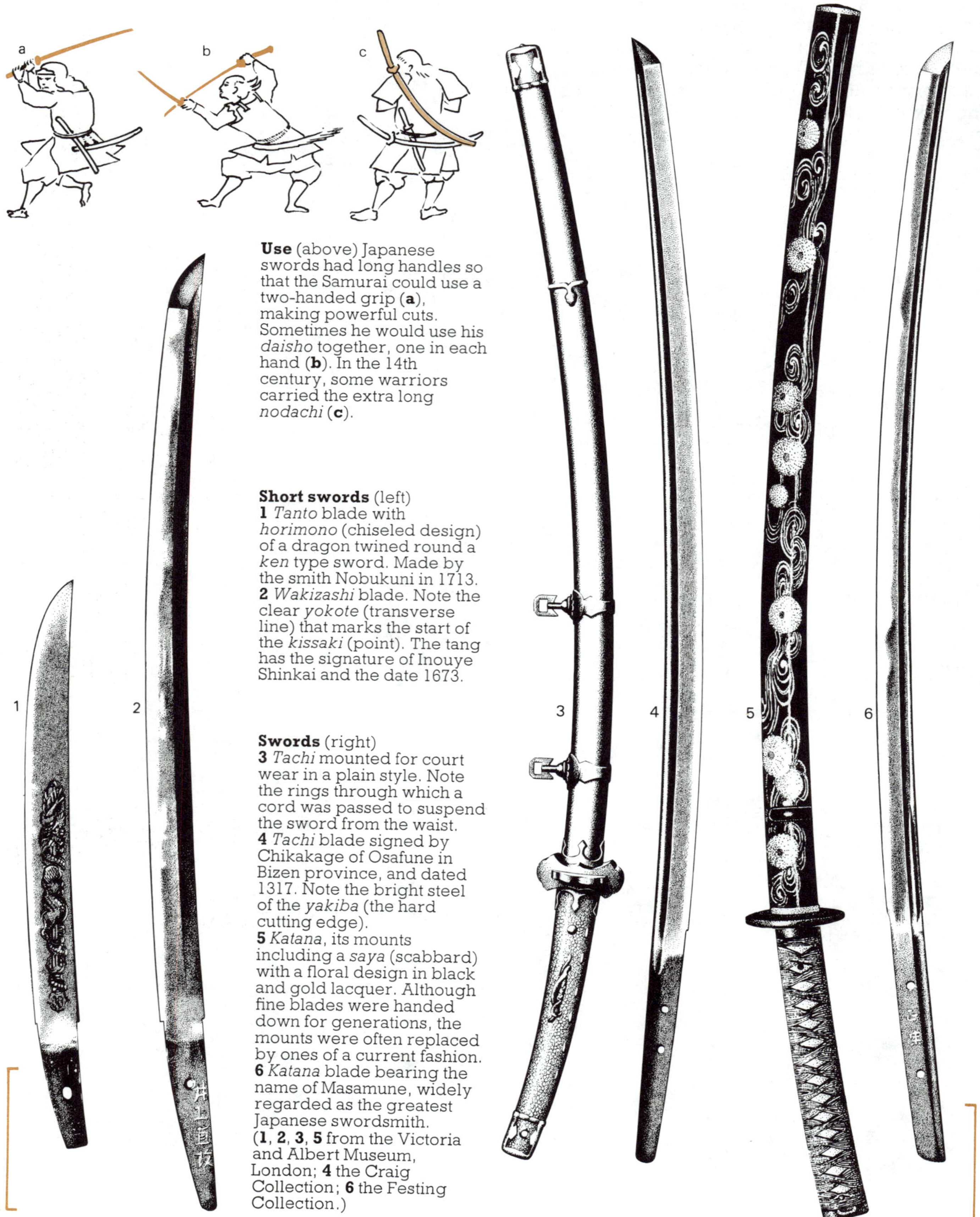

Use (above) Japanese swords had long handles so that the Samurai could use a two-handed grip (**a**), making powerful cuts. Sometimes he would use his *daisho* together, one in each hand (**b**). In the 14th century, some warriors carried the extra long *nodachi* (**c**).

Short swords (left)
1 *Tanto* blade with *horimono* (chiseled design) of a dragon twined round a *ken* type sword. Made by the smith Nobukuni in 1713.
2 *Wakizashi* blade. Note the clear *yokote* (transverse line) that marks the start of the *kissaki* (point). The tang has the signature of Inouye Shinkai and the date 1673.

Swords (right)
3 *Tachi* mounted for court wear in a plain style. Note the rings through which a cord was passed to suspend the sword from the waist.
4 *Tachi* blade signed by Chikakage of Osafune in Bizen province, and dated 1317. Note the bright steel of the *yakiba* (the hard cutting edge).
5 *Katana*, its mounts including a *saya* (scabbard) with a floral design in black and gold lacquer. Although fine blades were handed down for generations, the mounts were often replaced by ones of a current fashion.
6 *Katana* blade bearing the name of Masamune, widely regarded as the greatest Japanese swordsmith.
(**1**, **2**, **3**, **5** from the Victoria and Albert Museum, London; **4** the Craig Collection; **6** the Festing Collection.)

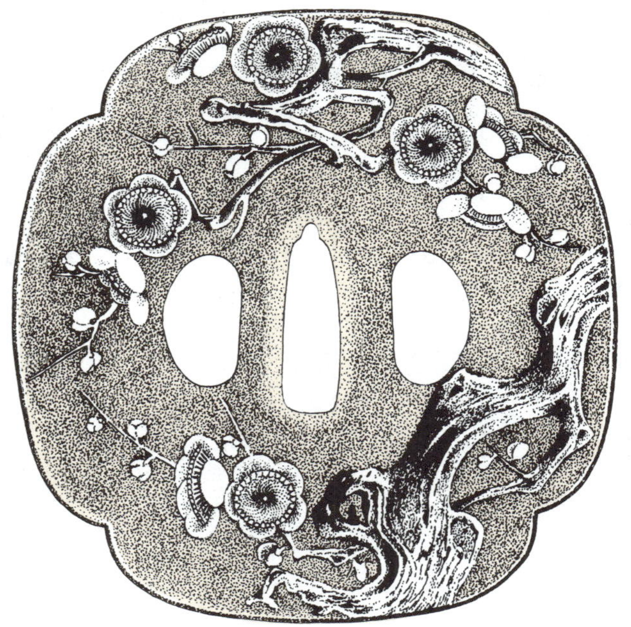

Guard (left) Called the *tsuba*, the guard is of interest in its own right, occurring in a variety of styles. Usually flat, it has a central hole for the tang and one or two holes beside this to take other fittings. The example illustrated is of bronze with a silver design in high relief (Ashmolean Museum, Oxford).

Other fittings (right) A small knife *kozuka* (**a**) and the hairpin *kogai* (**b**) were carried at either side of the scabbard, with their handles passing through the holes in the *tsuba*. The hilt or *tsuka* (**c**) was of wood covered with rayfish skin (*same*). Over this was wound silk braid, so as to leave visible a pair of ornamental plates, called *menuki*, and lozenge-shaped areas of *same*.

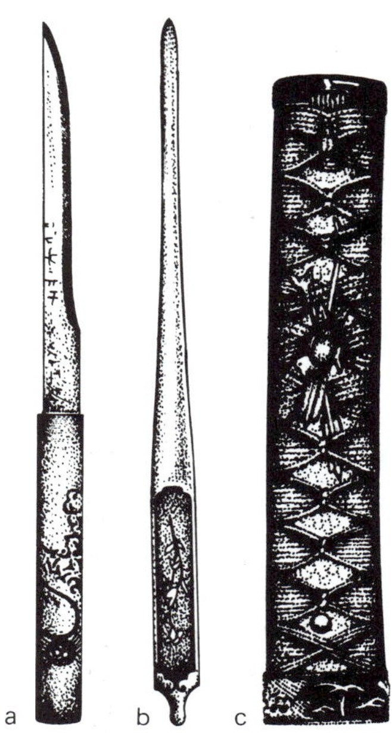

Tsuba examples (left) are often found on their own and are collected as a minor art form. Outlines and pierced decoration are extremely varied, as shown here. In addition, examples are to be found decorated with most of the techniques of metalwork known in Japan, including inlay with other metals and relief carving.

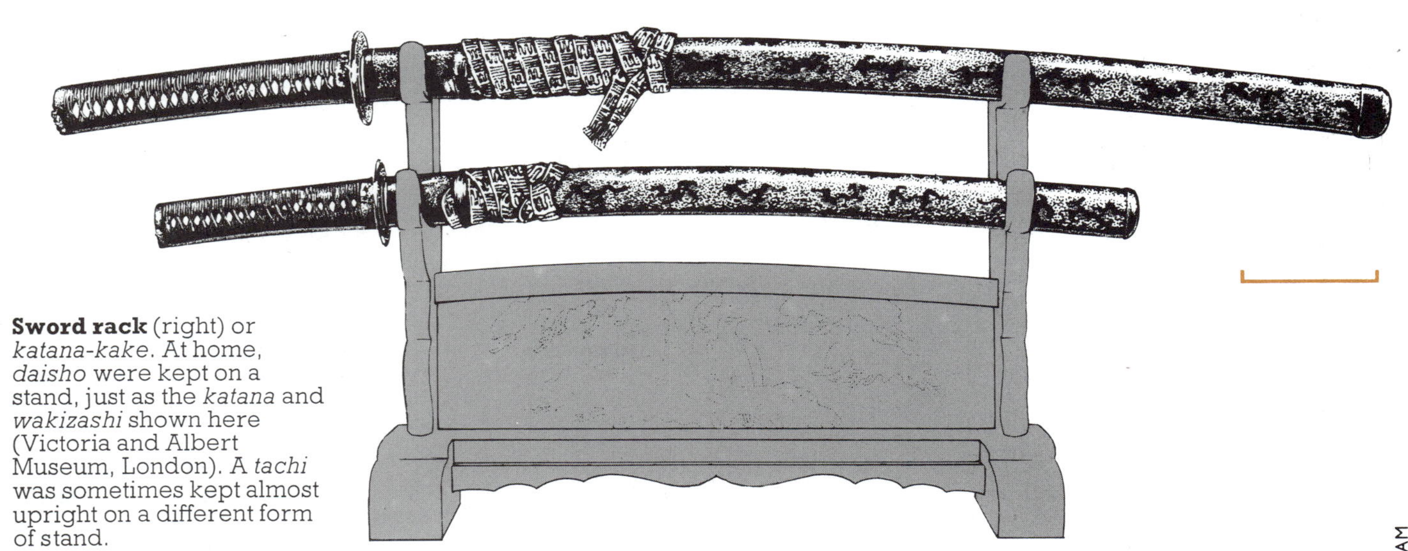

Sword rack (right) or *katana-kake*. At home, *daisho* were kept on a stand, just as the *katana* and *wakizashi* shown here (Victoria and Albert Museum, London). A *tachi* was sometimes kept almost upright on a different form of stand.

European bronze and early iron swords

The history of the European sword, as is the case with the dagger, is not so much a process of functional improvement as a series of changes in fashion. Better steels came, of course, to replace bronze and iron, and military swords were sometimes redesigned to match new theories of fighting; but no innovation was great enough to render all other swords obsolete. We present European swords in a loosely chronological order, beginning with Bronze Age, Iron Age and then medieval swords. From the Renaissance period onward, we pay special attention to two-handed swords, and deal separately with rapiers and smallswords, two distinctive new forms. In the 18th and 19th centuries, regulation military swords are the center of attention, ending with the ceremonial swords of this century.

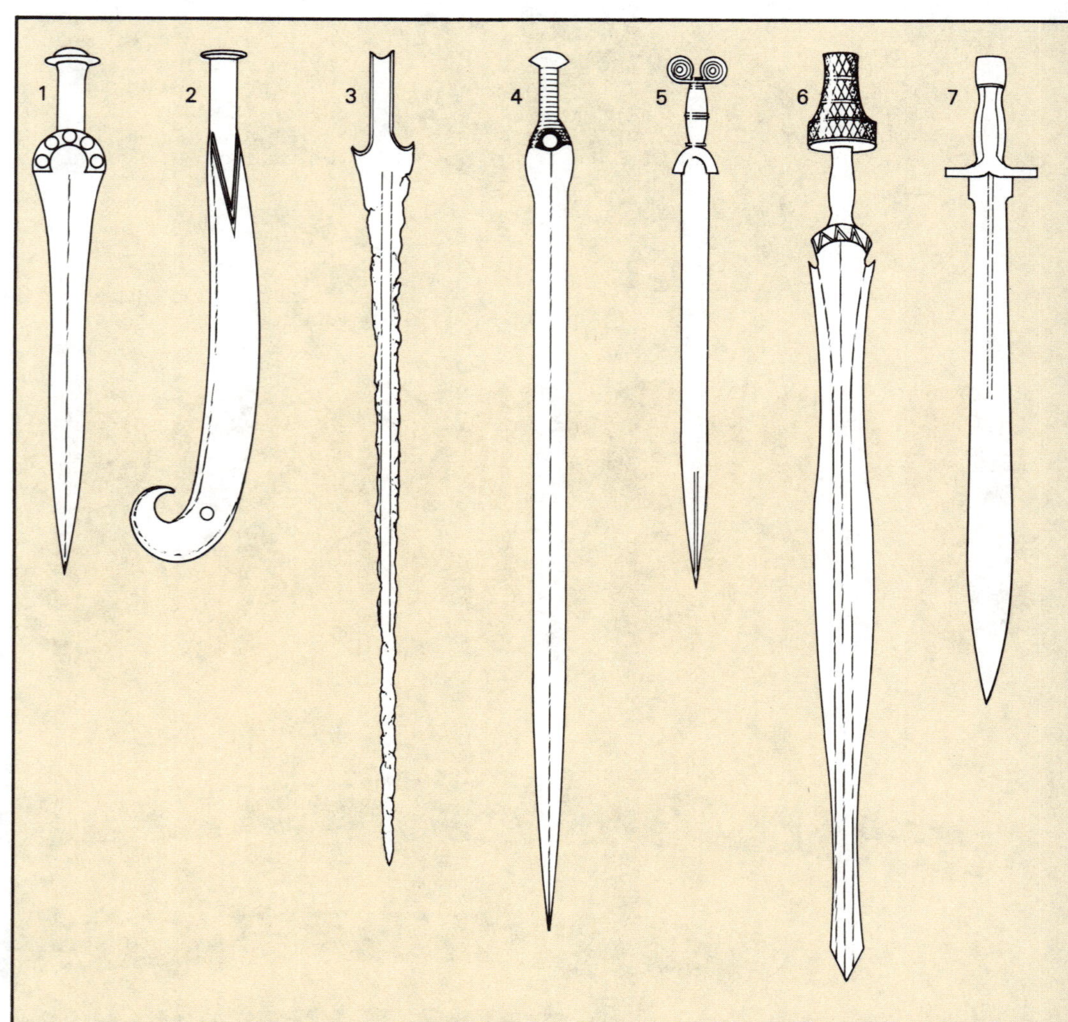

Nordic short-sword (left) of c.1350-1200BC. Made of one piece of bronze, but in the earlier style that had the hilt riveted to the blade. Decorated with typical incised geometric designs. (Statens Historiska Museum, Stockholm.)

Bronze and early iron swords (above)
1 Central European short-sword of the early Bronze Age, the hilt riveted to the blade.
2 Curved, single-edged short-sword from Sweden, c.1600-1350BC. Made of one piece of bronze.
3 Greek bronze sword of the Homeric Age, c.1300BC. Found at Mycenae.
4 Long bronze sword, made in one piece, c.1200-1000BC. Found on a Baltic island.
5 Central European sword of the late Bronze Age, c.850-650BC. Of the "antennae-sword" type.
6 Iron sword of the Hallstatt culture, Austria, c.650-500BC. The hilt is of ivory and amber.
7 Iron sword of the type used by Greek hoplites or infantry, c.6th century BC.

Greek warrior (left) of the classical period, wielding his short-sword. From a ceramic vase.

Roman legionary (right) wearing his *gladius* short-sword high on his right hip. From a replica armor. (National Museum of Wales, Legionary Museum of Caerleon.)

8 Iron single-edged sword from Spain, c.5th-6th centuries BC. This type was also used in classical Greece.
9 Iron sword-blade of the La Tène "B" culture, c.6th century BC, in Switzerland.
10 Iron sword with a bronze hilt, from Aquila, Italy, c.3rd century BC.
11 Gaulish iron sword with an anthropomorphic bronze hilt. From Aube, France, c.2nd century BC.
12 Iron sword with hilt of bronze and enamel. From Cumbria, England, c.1st century AD.
13 Roman iron *gladius*, the short-sword carried by the legionaries. Of early 1st century AD date.
14 Roman iron *gladius* of a later type with parallel edges and a shorter point. From Pompeii, late 1st century AD.

Roman gladius (right) with a steel blade, still in its scabbard. Made to be given as a reward for military achievement, this example has a scabbard of tinned bronze, decorated with brass fittings. The hilt is missing. Thought to mark a battle of 71AD. Found at Mainz, West Germany. (British Museum, London.)

European Dark Age and Medieval swords

The sword was an important weapon throughout the Dark Ages, particularly in Northern Europe. Many Nordic swords show rich decoration in the hilt, and X-rays have revealed high-quality pattern-welding in their now corroded steel blades. In contrast, the medieval sword, despite its prestige as a knightly weapon, is often of a plain cross-shape with an iron blade, only the pommel giving scope for fancy.

Swords for cutting Early medieval swords were made with broad blades for cutting, as seen in this detail from the Bayeux Tapestry (right). From the 13th century onward, more tapered blades, suited to thrusting, became common. This is thought to have been due to the increased use of plate-armor, which was best penetrated by a thrust at the joints.

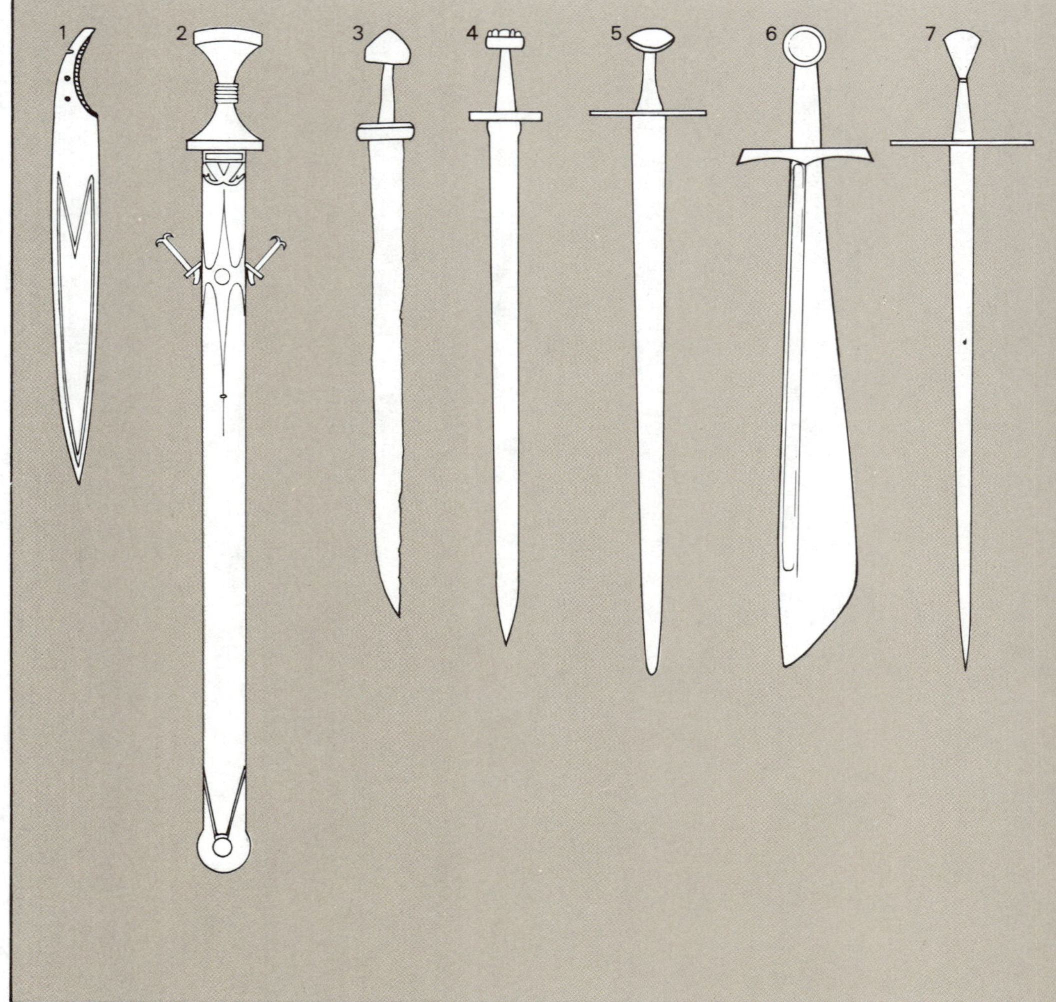

Viking sword (left) of the 10th century, with the original fine quality of such weapons still evident. The hilt is clad in silver foil, with an impressed "woven" pattern picked out in copper and niello. The two-edged steel blade has a broad, shallow fuller. This sword was found in a lake at Uppland, Sweden. (Statens Historiska Museum, Stockholm.)

Dark Age and medieval swords (above)
1 Broad, single-edged iron short-sword of c.100-300AD, found in a Danish bog.
2 Two-edged iron sword with bronze hilt and scabbard-mounts, c.400-450AD, from Denmark.
3 Viking single-edged iron sword, Norway, c.800AD.
4 Scandinavian two-edged iron sword 9th or 10th centuries AD.
5 German two-edged sword of c.1150-1200, with a "brazil-nut" pommel.
6 English falchion of c.1260-70, preserved in Durham Cathedral. Falchions were short and heavy, with a curved edge. The back of the blade may be straight, curved or clipped near the point.
7 Two-edged sword with triangular pommel, of c.1380. Nationality unknown.

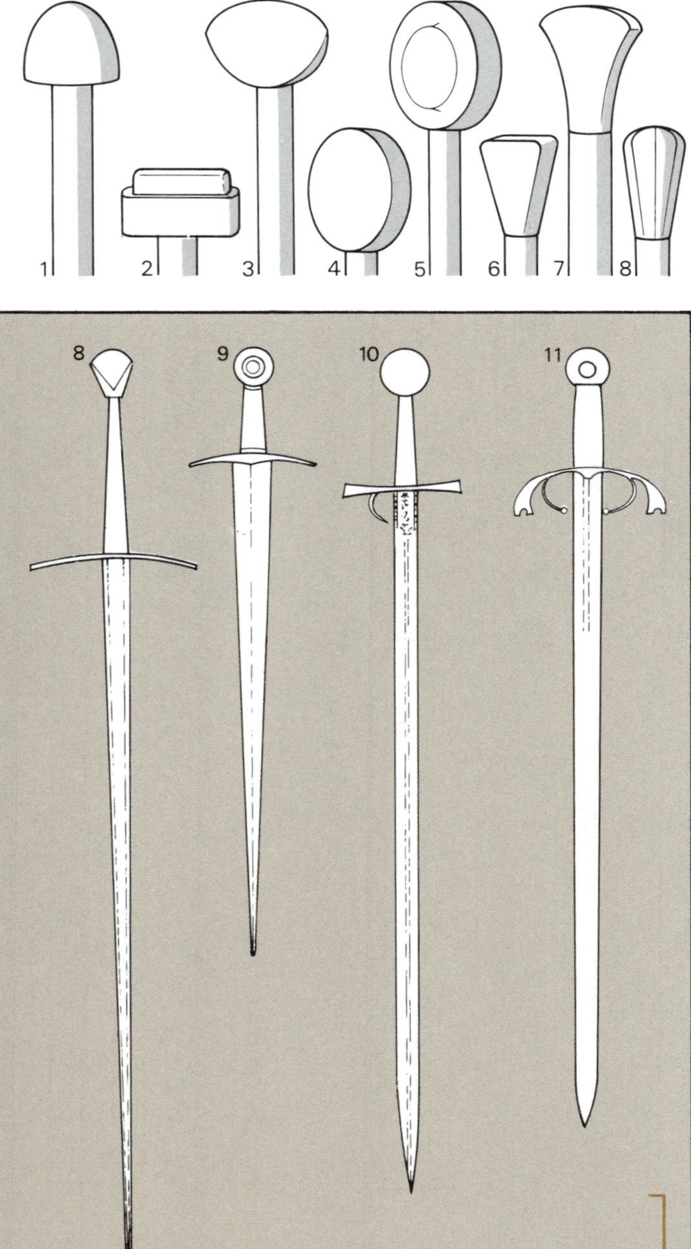

Pommel-shapes (left)
Heavy pommels were fitted to medieval swords to improve their balance. Here are some common types and their modern names.

1 Mushroom
2 Tea-cosy
3 Brazil-nut
4 Disk
5 Wheel
6 Triangular
7 Fish-tailed
8 Plummet-shaped

8 Bastard-sword of c.1380. These swords had a hilt long enough to be gripped, on occasion, by both hands, and are thus also called hand-and-a-half swords.
9 French sword of the late 14th century, with a tapered blade for thrusting.
10 Italian sword of the late 14th century with a simple finger-guard. The forefinger was sometimes hooked over the quillon to improve the user's grip.
11 Spanish sword with two finger-guards, or "arms of the hilt." Of late 15th century date.

Memorial brass (above) of an English knight who died in 1442. He is shown with a thrusting-sword, with a plummet-shaped pommel, slung typically low on his left hip. The familiar cross-shaped medieval sword has long been regarded as a symbol of the Christian knight. (From the brass of Sir Simon de Felbrigg, Felbrigg Church, Norfolk.)

Hand-and-a-half sword (right) of c.1440, found in the River Thames near London. (Museum of London.)
Compare the size of the one-handed sword (far right), preserved at Westminster Abbey, London. It is believed to have belonged to Henry V of England, and dates from c.1410-20.

Renaissance and 17th century swords

The 16th and 17th centuries saw a number of changes in swords. Initially, two-handed swords gained in popularity, for war and later for ceremonial use. At the same time, the one-handed sword was undergoing more change than it had for several centuries. The hilt became ever more elaborate, to protect the hand as the use of armor declined. The rapier also appeared; it is covered separately on p.50.

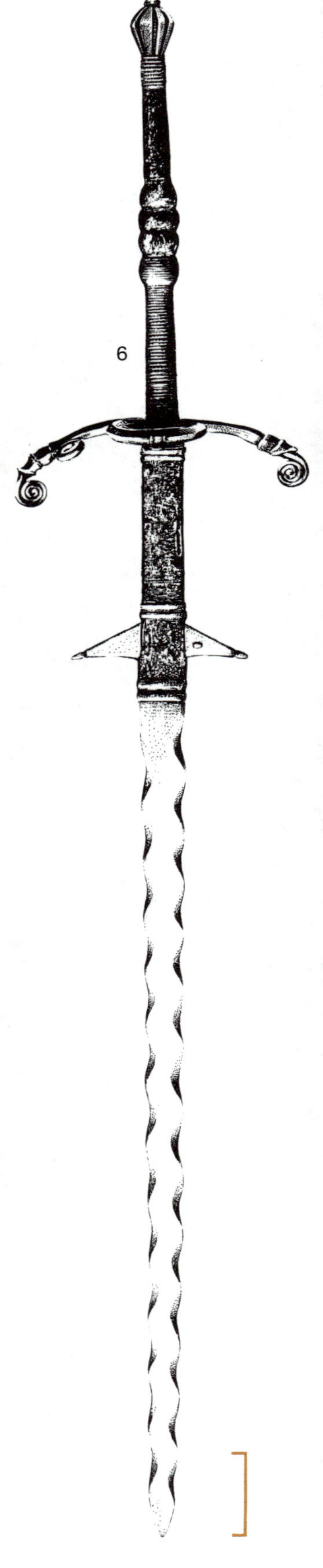

Two-hand and hand-and-a-half swords (above)
1 South German hand-and-a-half sword of the early 16th century, with spiral pommel and drooping quillons.
2 German two-hand sword of the early 16th century, with a blade of flat diamond section.
3 German two-hand *estoc* or thrusting-sword, of the first half of the 16th century. The blade is of diamond section with no cutting edge.
4 Scottish two-hand sword of the mid-16th century. This is the true claymore or *claidheamh mòr.*
5 German hand-and-a-half sword of c.1540-80. The blade is single-edged except for the one-third nearest the point.
6 German two-hand processional or "bearing" sword of the late 16th century. The ricasso or blunt base of the blade is covered in leather, to be gripped by the hand, and is guarded by two spurs. The flamboyant blade is sometimes called the "flamberge" type. (Castle Museum, York.)

Famous blade-marks
(right) All were later copied, especially by makers at Solingen in Germany.
1 Running wolf, originally used by blade-makers at Passau in Germany.
2 The name of Andrea dei Ferari (1530-c.1583), an Italian swordsmith. This example is a later fake.
3 Mark of the Sahagun family of Toledo in Spain, from c.1570.

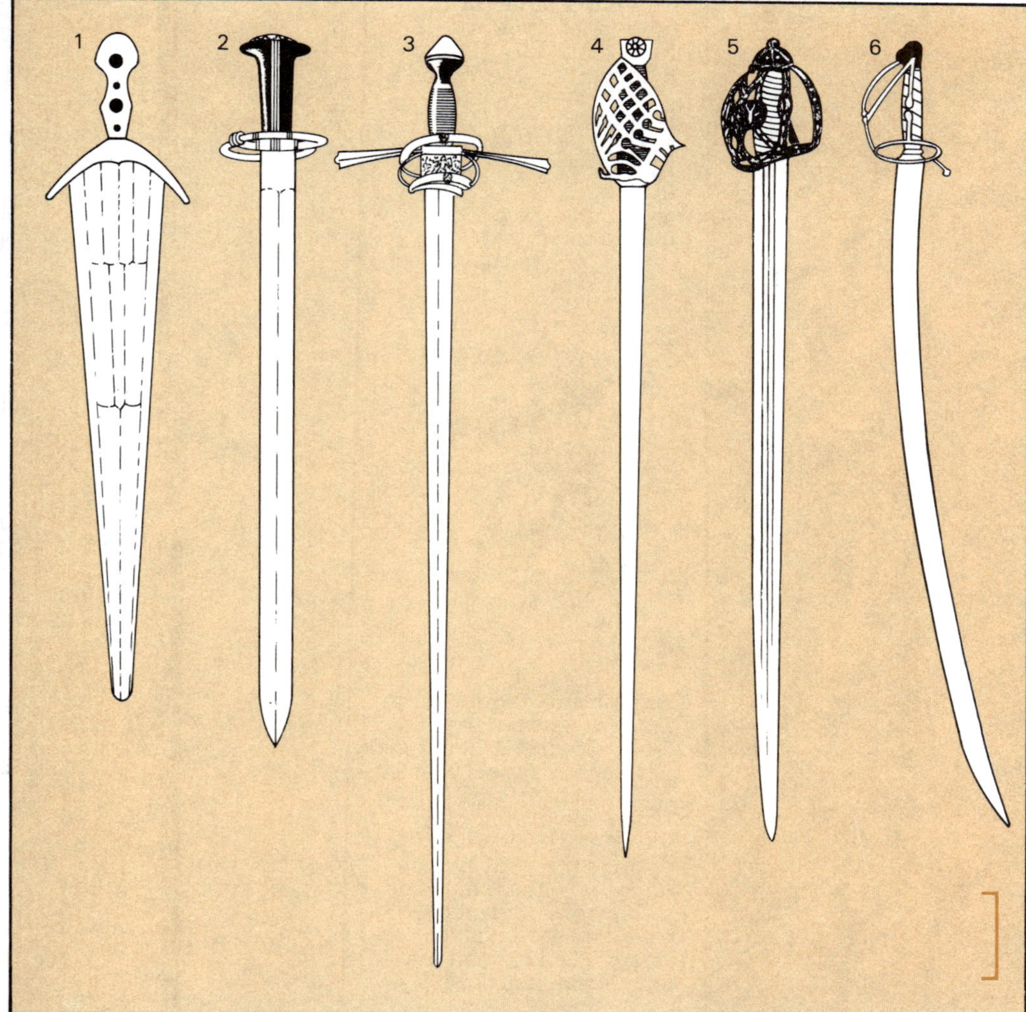

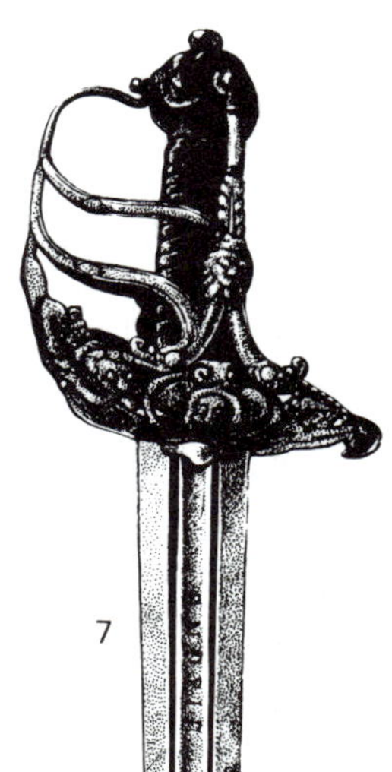

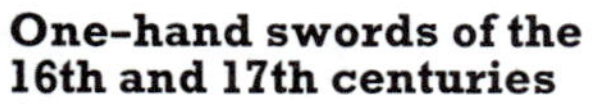

One-hand swords of the 16th and 17th centuries
(above)
1 *Cinquedea*, an Italian weapon of c.1500. It is also found in a shorter form as a dagger.
2 Two-edged sword popular among German *Landsknecht* mercenaries in the early 16th century. The type, with its horizontal S-shaped quillons, is known in German as a *Katzbalger*.
3 Sword of King Gustav Vasa of Sweden, made in Germany, c.1550. (Livrustkammaren, Stockholm.)
4 *Schiavona*, a two-edged sword with a basket-hilt, of c.1600, a style that originated in Venice.
5 Scottish two-edged, basket-hilted broadsword of c.1610.
6 Swiss saber of the mid-17th century, with a characteristic open guard.
7 English basket-hilted broadsword of c.1640, of the type known as a "mortuary" sword. The name refers to the faces that are chiseled on the iron hand-guard, once supposed to commemorate King Charles I, executed in 1649. (Castle Museum, York.)

Rapiers and smallswords

The rapier, a long-bladed thrusting-sword, appeared in Europe in about 1530, at once an item of dress and a weapon for which elaborate systems of fencing were devised. The varieties of hilt design were almost infinite. From c.1630, the rapier began to be replaced by the smallsword, a lighter weapon, highly fashionable until c.1780. Later developments of it still survive in ceremonial dress.

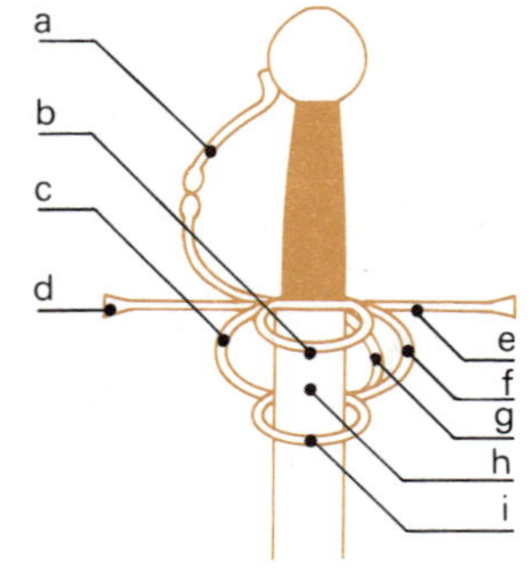

The parts of the hilt (above) of a swept-hilt rapier.
a Knuckle-bow or knuckle-guard
b, i Side-rings
c, f Arms of the hilt or *pas d'âne*
d, e Quillons
g Counterguard
h Ricasso

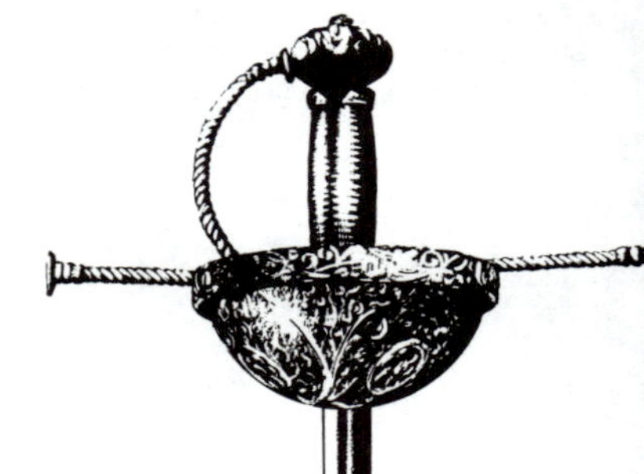

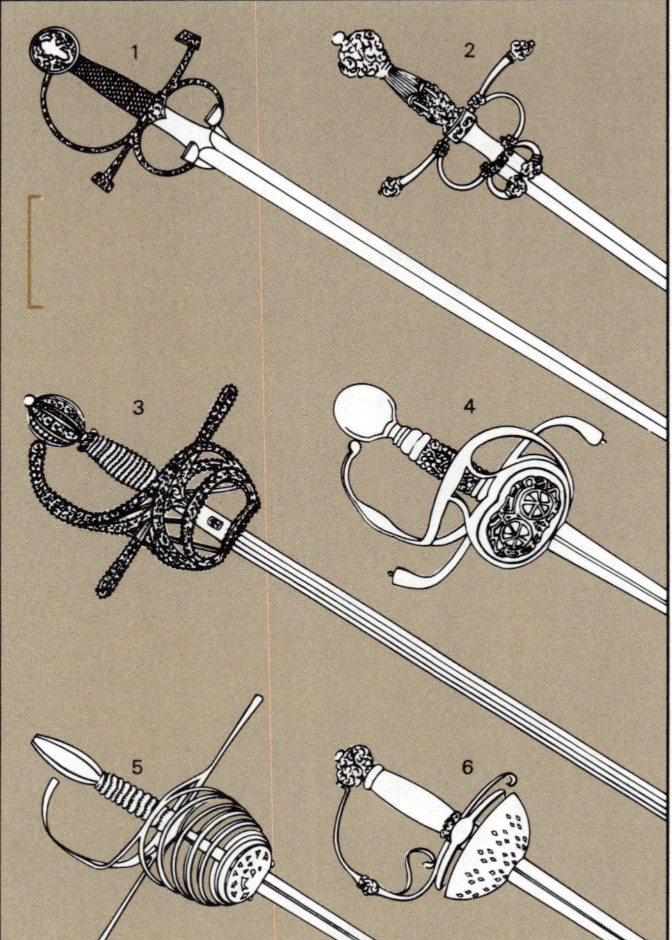

Rapier hilts (above)
1 Spanish, c.1530, with gold damascene decoration. Said to have belonged to Pizarro, the Conquistador. (Real Armería, Madrid.)
2 Italian, c.1570. With chiseled and gilt work, and no knuckle-bow.
3 French, c.1580. Of the swept-hilt type, with pierced silver decoration.
4 Probably German, c.1620. Of the "Pappenheimer" type. Carried by Gustav II Adolf of Sweden at the Battle of Lützen in 1632. (Livrustkammaren, Stockholm.)
5 Probably Spanish, c.1620. Steel, with an unusual number of side-rings.
6 English, c.1640-50. Iron, of the cup-hilt type, with pierced decoration.

Rapier and dagger play (above) A common way of fencing in the 16th and early 17th centuries was with a rapier in the right hand and a *main gauche* dagger in the left for parrying an opponent's thrusts. Such daggers (one is shown on p. 32) were often made in a matching set with the rapier. (Drawing after a fencing manual of 1628.)

Spanish cup-hilt rapier (right) of c.1650. The chiseled and pierced work on the hilt is typical of this classic style of rapier. The two-edged blade has a short fuller near the hilt, and is then of flattened diamond section. (Museo Lázaro Galdiano, Madrid.)

The smallsword was a fashionable item of dress for gentlemen from c.1630 to c.1780, and during this time was still used for fencing and dueling. It survived its fall from high fashion through being retained in the formal court dress (right) of European kingdoms well into the 20th century.

The shell-guards (above) of the classic smallsword hilt were developed from the side-rings of the rapier. As well as protecting the hand when parrying, they provided an area for the hilt-maker to show off his skill in decorative metalwork. Common mediums were solid silver, russet-and-gold, and, later, polished steel.

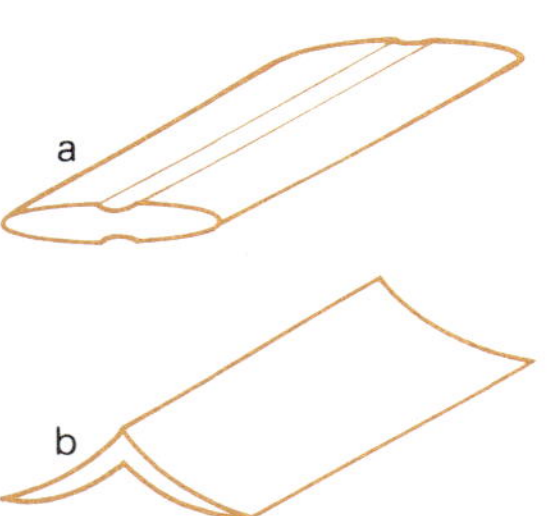

Blade sections (above) The early smallswords and pillow-swords usually had a fullered, two-edged blade (**a**). However, the majority of smallswords had blades of hollow triangular section (**b**). This shape allowed a very light blade that was still stiff enough for thrusting.

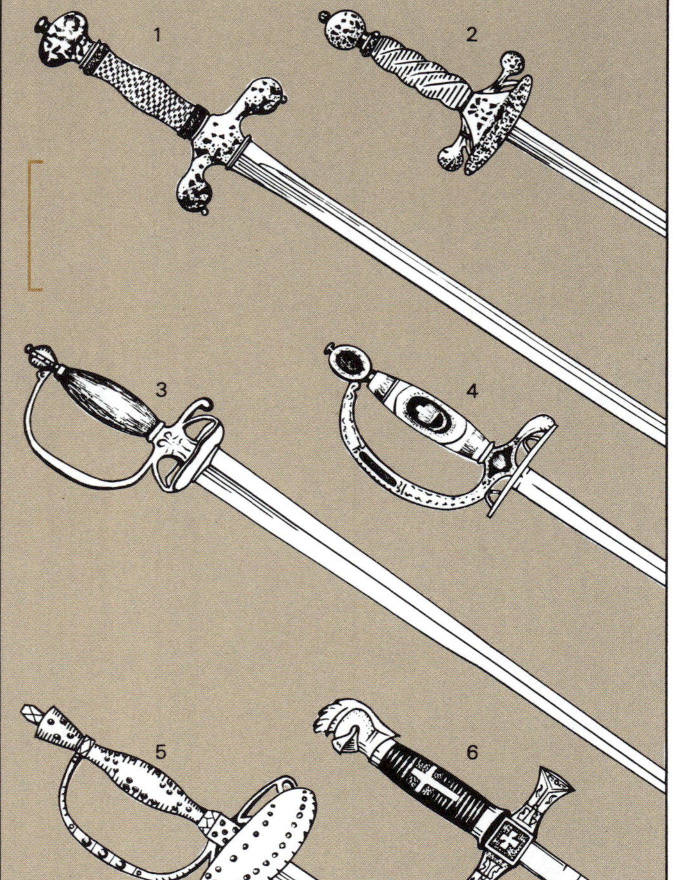

Smallswords (above)
1 So-called "pillow sword," the hilt made in Denmark c.1650; the blade made at Solingen, Germany.
2 Italian smallsword, made at Brescia, c.1680. Of a variety without a knuckle-bow.
3 English smallsword with a solid silver hilt, c.1750. Note the blade, which is of the "Colichemarde" type.
4 Smallsword presented as a reward to a British officer at the siege of Seringapatam in 1799. Gilt and enameled hilt.
5 English courtsword, c.1900. The cut-steel hilt is typical of late courtswords.
6 Society sword from the USA, of early 20th century date. The hilt is gilded, and decorated with gothic and masonic motifs.

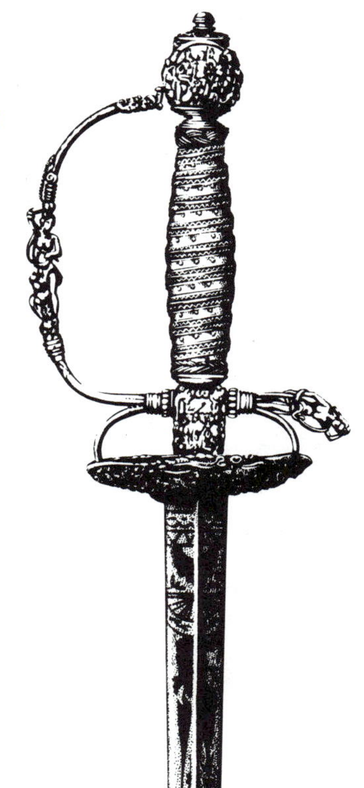

Fine quality smallsword (right) of typical form. The hilt is French, c.1660-80, with pierced and chiseled relief-work on a background of matt gold, depicting Neptune, mermaids and sea-monsters. The blade, of later date, has foliate and geometric designs "blued" onto its surface. (Wallace Collection, London.)

Regulation military swords 1

In the 18th century, the form of military swords began to be regulated by the authorities for the sake of uniform appearance, ease of supply and the maintenance of quality.
Although kept by other branches of the services as a secondary weapon, the sword was principally a cavalry arm. It survives to the present day chiefly as an item of ceremonial dress for officers.

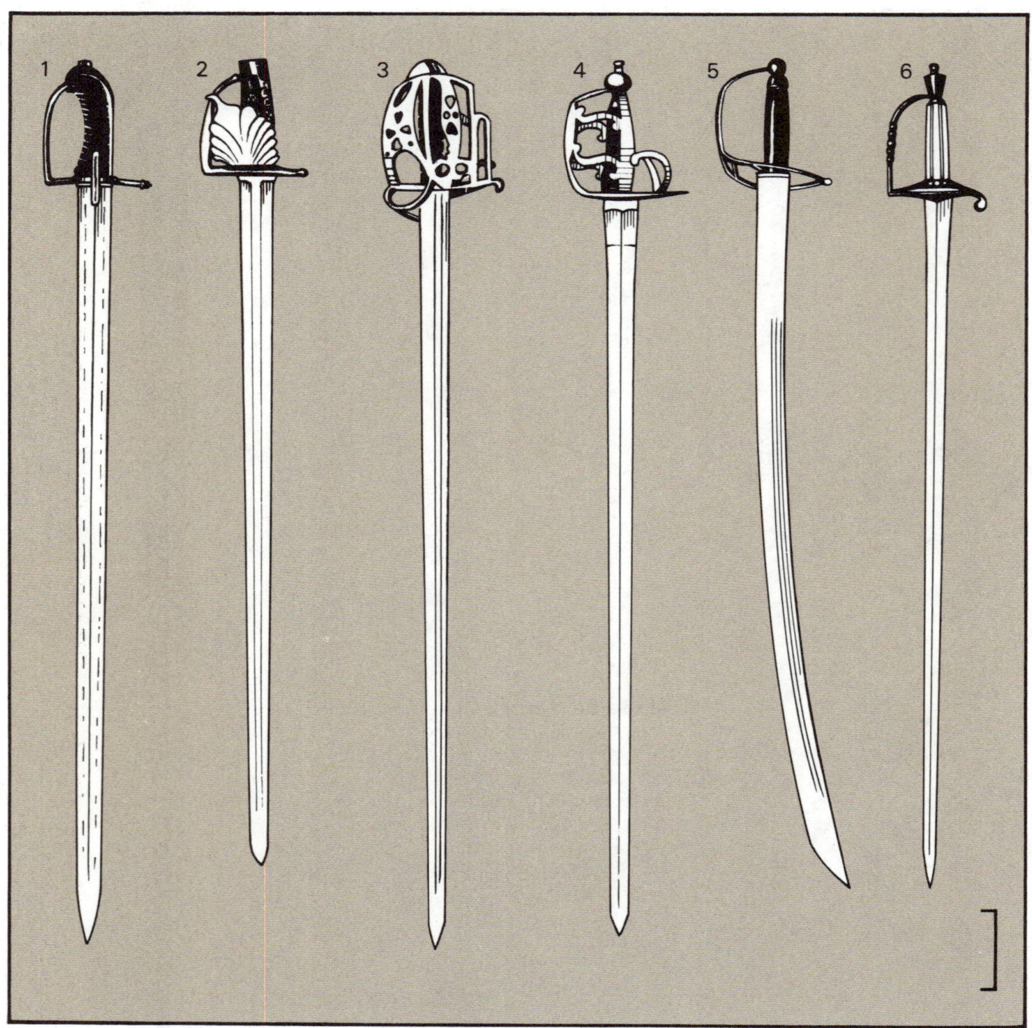

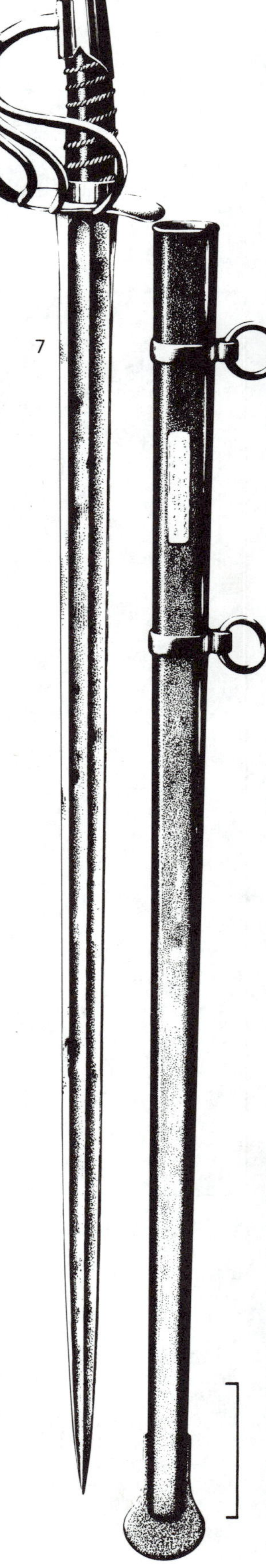

Regulation military swords (above)
1 Austrian sword of 1716 for heavy cavalry. The hilt is a simple brass knuckle-guard with a "langet," the vertical projection where the blade joins the hilt.
2 Danish cavalry sword of 1734, with a straight, two-edged blade. The steel hilt has a knuckle-bow and shell-like guard.
3 British cavalry sword with the hilt in the Scottish full-basket style. This blade is single-edged, but many were double-edged.
4 Swedish sword of 1775 for heavy cavalry, with a brass full-basket hilt.
5 American saber, c.1775, with a brass knuckle-guard of a style popular with both sides in the War of Independence.
6 British 1786 Pattern infantry officer's sword, an example of the type known as a "spadroon."
7 French saber for heavy cavalry, model of Year XIII on the Republican calendar (1805-06). This type was used by Napoleon's *Cuirassier* regiments. Its steel scabbard is also shown. (The Castle Museum, York.)

Cavalryman (right) charging with the point of his sword leveled. This method for shock action could be used with straight or slightly curved blades. Very curved blades were meant for cutting or slashing once level with an opponent. The sword was regarded as an important cavalry weapon until World War 1.

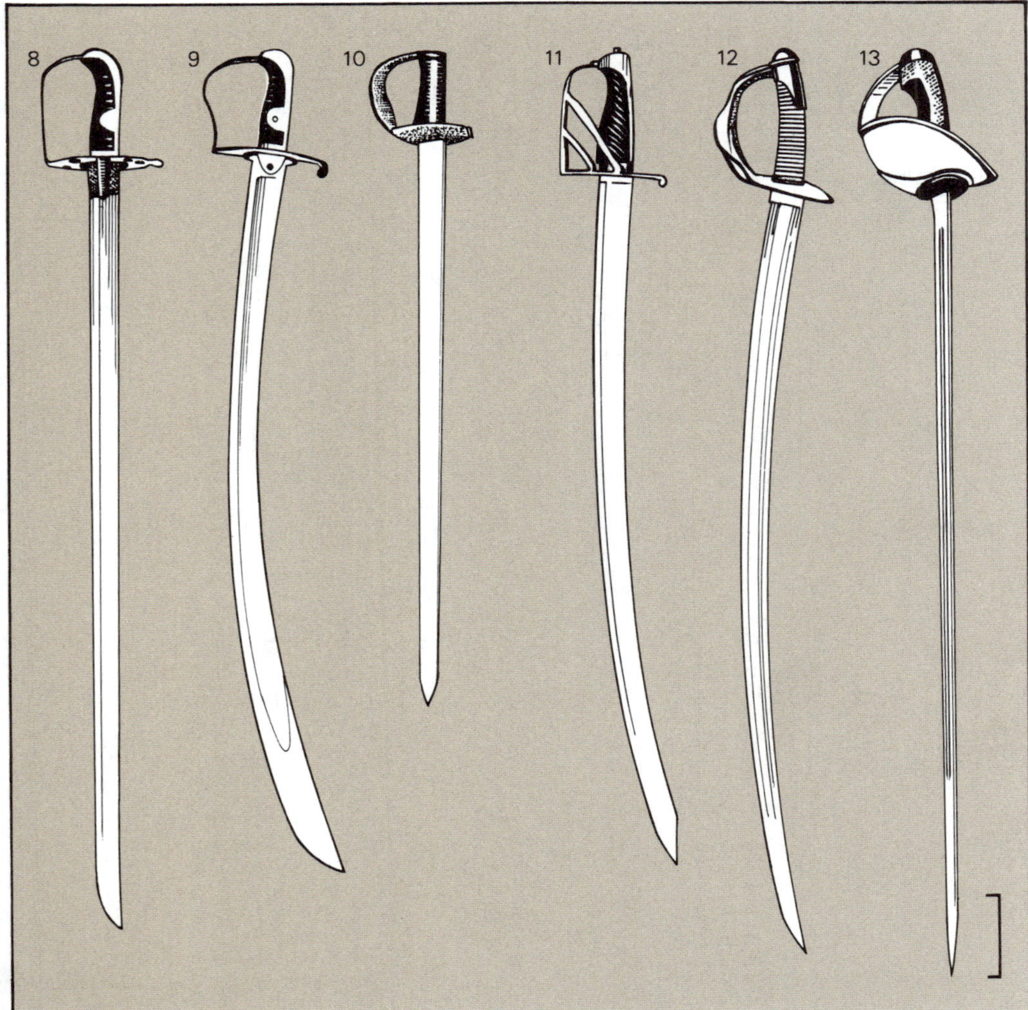

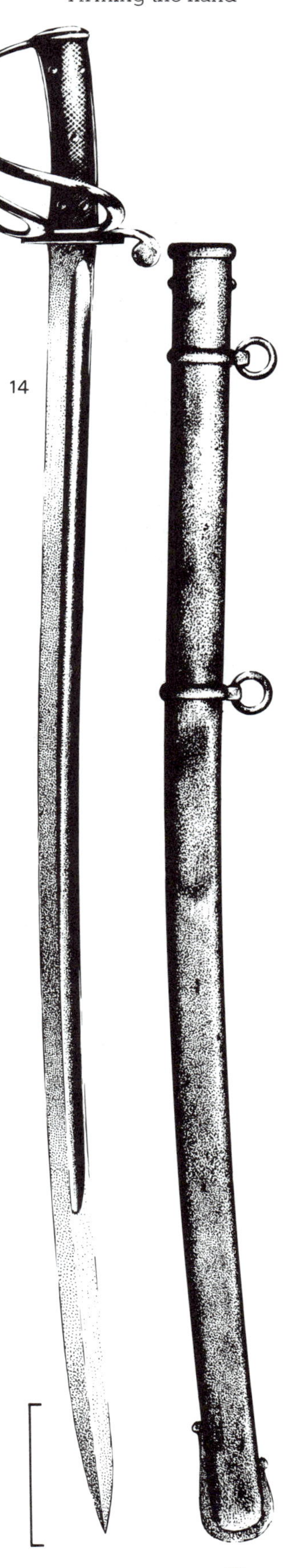

8 British 1796 Pattern sword for heavy cavalry. Designed purely for cutting, it has a hatchet point.
9 British 1796 Pattern saber for light cavalry. A slashing sword of which many were made during the Napoleonic wars.
10 British naval cutlass of 1804. Of typically plain appearance, with grips of cast iron and a sheet iron guard.

11 Prussian saber for light cavalry, of c.1806. The hilt is of stirrup shape, but with two bars added.
12 US Model 1840 dragoon saber, with a triple-bar brass hilt. This model was still in use in the Civil War of 1861-65.
13 British 1908 Pattern cavalry sword. A carefully designed thrusting-sword, still in service in WW1.

14 British 1853 Pattern sword for heavy and light cavalry. The blade was a compromise design, meant for cutting and thrusting. This pattern was used by at least two of the regiments in the Charge of the Light Brigade in the Crimean War, in 1854. (Private Collection.)

Regulation military swords 2

French infantryman (right) wearing his short sword slung from a shoulder-belt. Such swords, known as hangers or sidearms, were commonly used as secondary weapons, in addition to the musket and bayonet, by 18th century infantry. In many armies, troops such as artillery, engineers and bandsmen carried such sidearms throughout the 19th century.

Types of point (right)
a Hatchet point, found on swords designed solely for cutting.
b False edge, where the back of a single-edged blade is sharpened at the tip to form a sharp point for thrusting.
c Spear point, symmetrical, with a ridge down the center. Found on two-edged and false-edged blades.

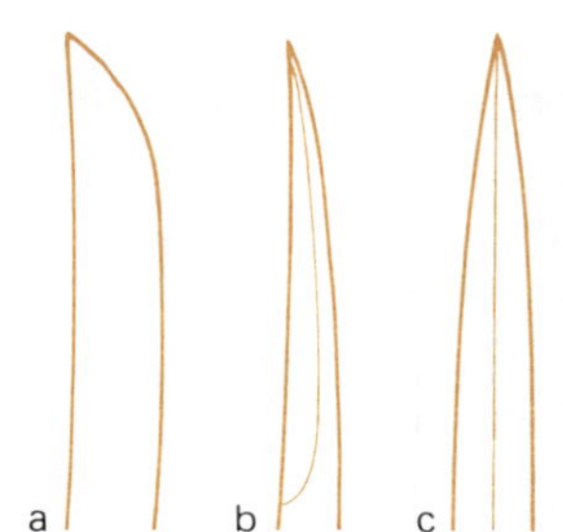

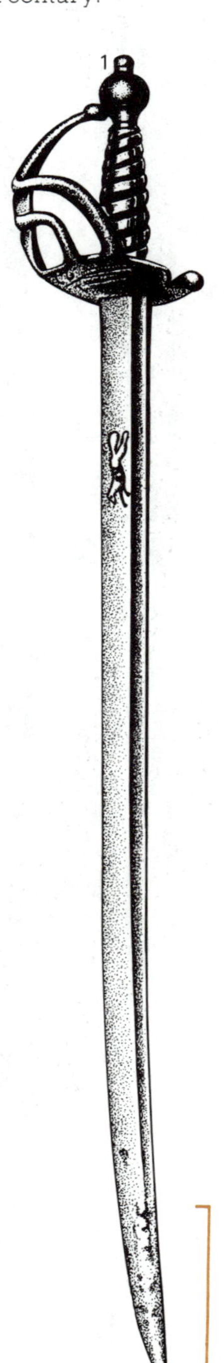

Hangers and sidearms (left and above)
All have brass hilts.
1 British infantry hanger, Pattern 1751. The single-edged fullered blade bears the mark of Samuel Harvey, the maker. (Castle Museum, York.)
2 Prussian infantry hanger of c.1740 with a flat, single-edged blade and a heart-shaped guard.
3 French infantry hanger, Modèle 1816, known as a *briquet*. The blade has a false edge at the tip.
4 Russian pioneers' sidearm of 1827. The blade is of falchion type, with a saw back for cutting wood.
5 French neo-classical sidearm of 1831. Based on the Roman *gladius*, it was nicknamed *coupe-choux*, meaning "cabbage-cutter."
6 Spanish machete, Modelo 1843, for artillery and engineers. The back of the broad, single-edged blade is clipped to a point.
7 British pioneers' sidearm, Pattern 1856. The blade is saw-backed and spear-pointed.

Types of hilt (right)
These common styles have generally accepted names:
A Full-basket hilt
B Half-basket hilt
C Stirrup hilt
D Mameluke hilt

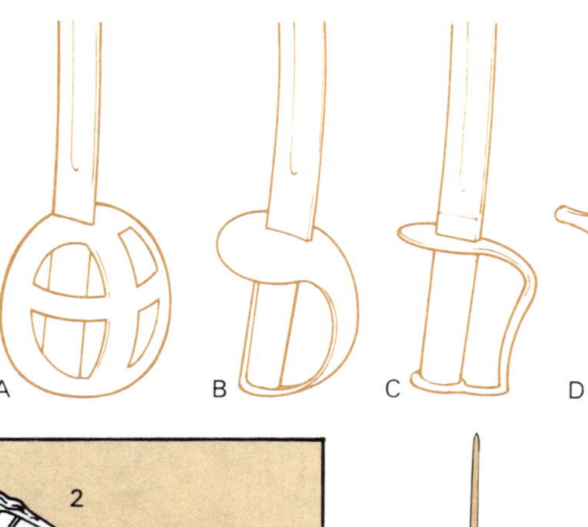

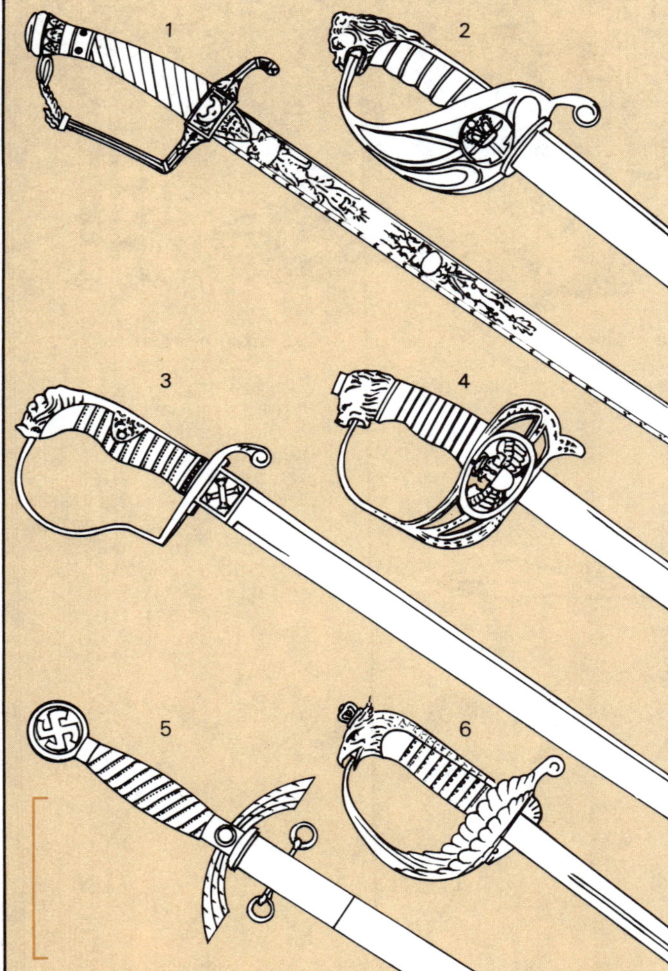

Officer (above) saluting by bringing the junction of hilt and blade to his lips. This custom is said to have originated from an act of Christian piety: kissing the cross-like guard of a medieval sword.

Ceremonial sword-hilts (above)
1 French Napoleonic general's sword with gilt brass hilt, and blued and gilt blade decoration.
2 British Royal Navy officer's sword, Pattern 1827, which is still in use, with modifications.
3 Imperial German Army mounted artillery officer's sword, c.1900. Gilt brass hilt.
4 Serbian Army officer's sword, c.1910. Nickel-plated three-bar hilt bearing the Serbian eagle.
5 Nazi German Luftwaffe officer's sword, c.1940. The mounts are nickel-plated and the grips and scabbard of blue leather.
6 Italian air force officer's sword, c.1940, with eagle-head pommel and the guard chiseled as feathers.

Ceremonial sword and scabbard (right) presented in 1809 to Lt Col James Stirling by the NCOs and privates of the 42nd Highlanders (now the Black Watch). Being regarded as a symbol of the soldier's profession, fine swords have for centuries been presented as rewards for military achievement. (Scottish United Services Museum, Edinburgh Castle.)

Pole-arms 1

It is easy to see that the addition of a long haft to weapons for cutting, thrusting or clubbing might give the user the advantage of reach over an enemy with a short weapon. It can also give a foot soldier the means to attack a horseman, or to keep him at a distance. These elementary advantages have produced a vast array of pole-arms (or staff weapons), from most areas and periods of history. Such objects have often come to be made in elaborate form for ceremonial display. Here we examine the different ways in which pole-arms have been used, and illustrate the variety of heads or blades that is to be found. Special attention is paid to those carried by European foot soldiers in the Middle Ages and Renaissance, and also to cavalry lances.

Basic parts of a pole-arm (below)
a Butt
b Shaft or haft
c Langets, cheeks or straps (one at each side)
d Socket
e Blade
(The socket and blade together form the head).

Infantry combat (above) in a woodcut by Hans Burgkmair (1473-1532). Pikes are most in evidence, but halberds, bills, partisans and a glaive can also be seen. Infantry pole-arms were variously made for clubbing, cutting, thrusting, hooking, parrying or picking (as with a pick-ax).

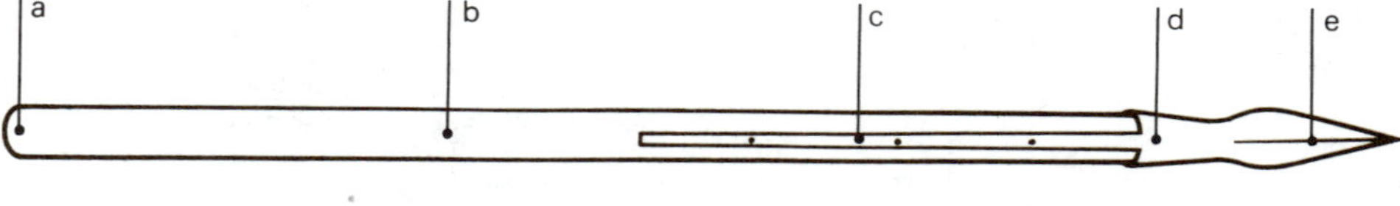

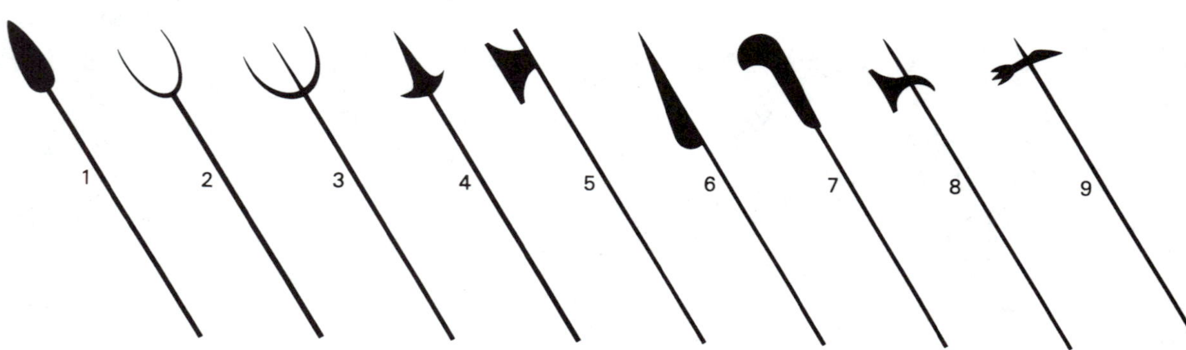

Size (left) Pikes were the longest of pole-arms, those used to defend squads of musketeers in the 17th century (**a**) being about 16ft (4.8m) long. The *sarissa* used in the Macedonian phalanx formation c.350BC was of similar length. We have excluded from this section any weapons much less than the height of a man (**b**).

Shapes of pole-arm heads (above) These are the essential shapes of the main types recognized in Europe. Most can be found in a number of elaborate variations. The same names are sometimes applied to weapons of similar shape from elsewhere in the world.
1 Thrusting-spear.
2 Military fork.
3 Trident.
4 Partisan — a broad spear point with wing-like projections at the base.
5 Pole-ax.
6 Glaive — a long knife-like blade with one cutting edge.
7 Bill — based on a tool for cutting hedges. The sharp edge is on the inside of the curve.
8 Halberd — combines an ax blade, a point and a beak.
9 Hammer for fighting on foot.

Infantry pole-arms in use (right) Pole-arms served many functions for the foot soldier in battle.
Pikes (**1**) were used, particularly in the 17th century, to form a hedge of points against cavalry attack, so protecting the musketeers while reloading.
From about the 7th century BC, Greek hoplites (**2**) used thrusting-spears and the phalanx formation to create an unbreakable wedge of armed men, abandoning the throwing-spear of Homeric times.
Renaissance Europe produced some of the finest pole-arms, decorated for processional display (**3**).
Even after this, spontoons and halberds lingered on as "leading staves" or signs of military rank. Shown is a British sergeant, c.1815 (**4**).
The quarterstaff (**5**) was the simplest of pole-arms, a plain length of wood, used in medieval Europe more for fencing or in brawls than in war.
The halberd (**6**) was one of the most versatile pole-arms of the 15th and 16th centuries. It could be used to hook an enemy to the ground, even if he was on horseback, as well as for chopping and thrusting.

The lance (right) was the horseman's pole-arm. It functioned by the momentum of the horse and rider, being held steady in the hand as they charged. Although most often associated with formal jousting in medieval (**7**) and renaissance Europe, it had been known in the ancient world. A light form of lance continued to be used in Poland and Hungary (**8**), and it enjoyed a new vogue in Western Europe when Napoleon adopted it for his Grande Armée. The fashion he set lasted into the First World War. The lance was also adopted by the Plains Indians of North America (**9**) after the coming of the horse.

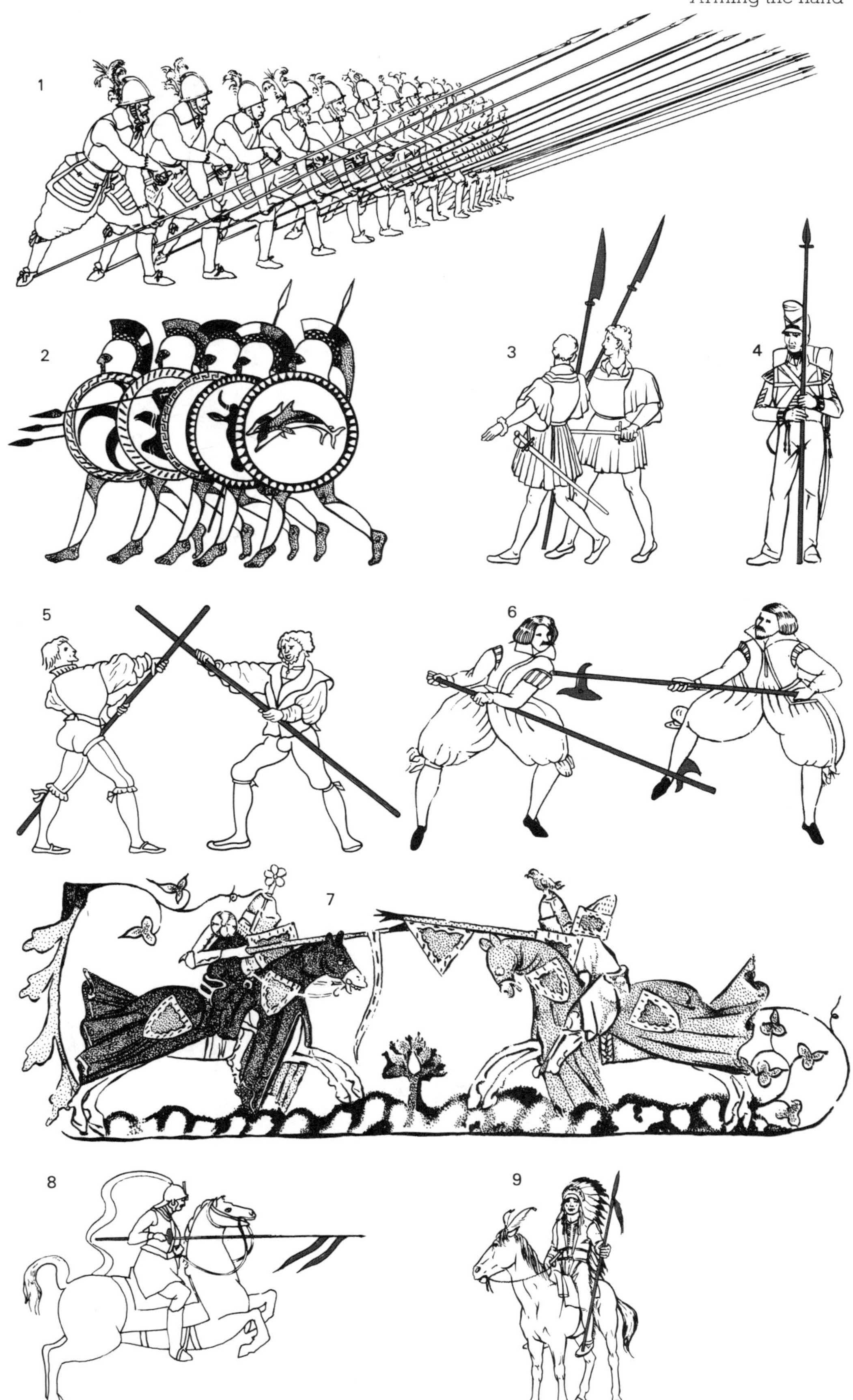

Pole-arms 2

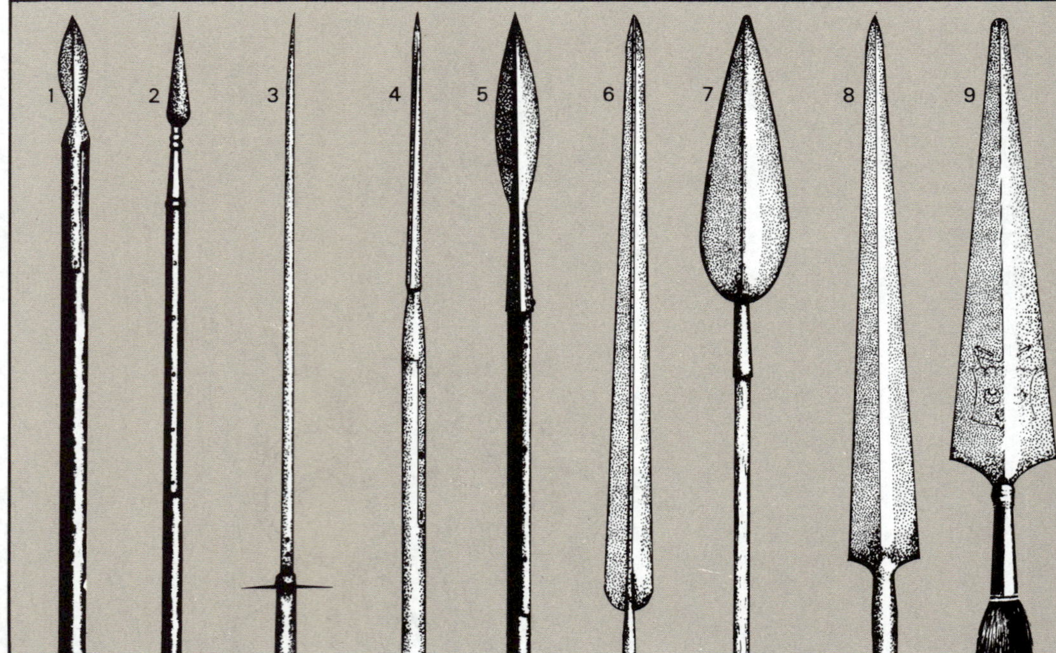

Spears and related weapons
1 Pike with leaf-shaped point. Swiss, 15th century.
2 Pike. European, c.1700.
3 *Ahlspiess* or awl-pike. Four-sided point. Swiss or German, 15th century.
4 Naval boarding pike. Spanish, 19th century.
5 Boar spear. German, 16th century.
6 Spear of the Masai of East Africa. 20th century.
7 Spear with bamboo shaft. Dervish, from Sudan, c.1880.
8 *Langdebeve* or ox-tongue partisan. Probably Swiss, c.1450-1550.
9 *Langdebeve* or ox-tongue partisan, bearing the arms of Duivenoord. Dutch, 1510.
10 *Langdebeve* or ox-tongue partisan. Probably Swiss, c.1450-1550.
11 Partisan. European, probably 16th century.
12 Partisan or spontoon of Dutch make. Carried at the battle of Lützen by a Swedish officer, 1632.
13 Partisan. Swedish, with the arms of King Gustav II Adolf, 1626.
14 Partisan of the Palace Guard of King Christian V of Denmark, c.1670.
15 Partisan from Piedmont, NW Italy. 18th century.
16 *Patisthanaya*, a partisan from Sri Lanka.

17 18 19 20 21 22

Processional boar spear (above) of a retainer of the Holy Roman Emperor Ferdinand I. It is dated 1558, by which time spears of this type were used more for hunting or display than in war. (Kunsthistorisches Museum, Vienna.)

17 Partisan bearing the arms of Poland and Lithuania, c.1700.
18 Spontoon of an English sergeant, c.1800.
19 Winged spear, similar to a partisan, sometimes called a "Bohemian ear-spoon," c.1500.
20 *Corsesca*. Italian, c.1550.
21 *Runka*. German, c.1475.
22 *Corsesca*. Italian, c.1550.
(**20–22** The names *rawcon, ranseur, corsèque, chauve souris* and *spetum* have also been applied to this form.)
23 *Magari yari*, a Japanese trident or winged spear.
24 Trident with gold inlay. Persian.
25 Trident from Korea, the side points emerging from dragons' mouths.
26 Feather staff or brandistock. The blades retract into the shaft when not required. Venetian, 1565.
27 Linstock, Swiss, 1590. Used to hold a slow-match for igniting artillery, and to defend the cannon.
28 Linstock. Northern European, late 17th century.

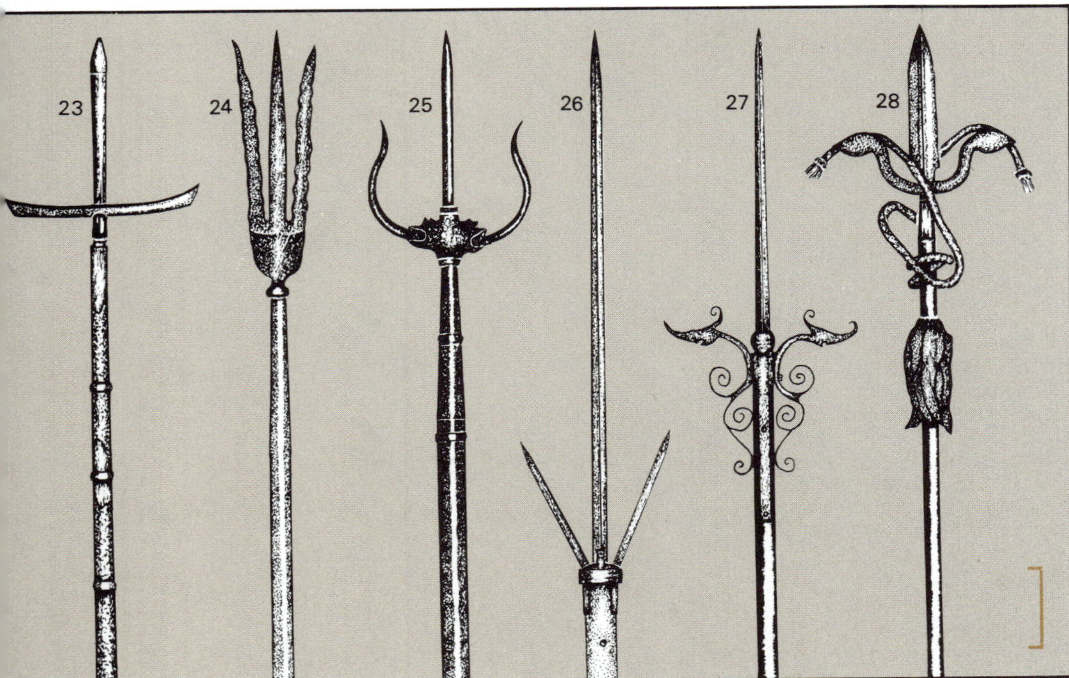

Processional partisan (above) of an officer of the guard of Louis XIV of France. Pierced, chiseled, etched and gilt decoration, including the figures of Hercules and Apollo. c.1670-80. (Wallace Collection, London.)

Pole-arms 3

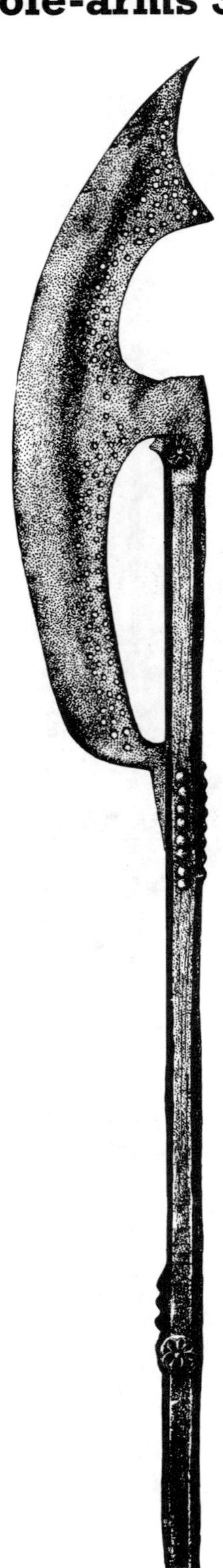

Axes and halberds (right)
1 *Bardiche*, a Russian form of pole-ax with a long cutting edge. Early 18th century.
2 Lochaber ax, the name given to a variety of related pole-arms from Scotland, c.1600.
3 Lochaber ax, with a hook said to have been used in scaling walls, c.1600.
4 Lochaber ax, of a form with all the features of a halberd. The name Jedburg ax has in modern times been applied to this form of Scottish pole-arm.
5 Halberd. Swiss, c.1475. Of a form that is sometimes called a Swiss *vouge*. It was in Switzerland that the name and form of the halberd originated.
6 Halberd. Swiss, c.1400. This early shape of halberd is sometimes called the Sempach type, but the term is not old.
7 Halberd of fully developed form. Swiss, early 16th century.
8 Halberd of the guard of the Elector of Saxony, c.1600. The cutting edge is of an unusual double-curved shape, and the top spike is especially broad.

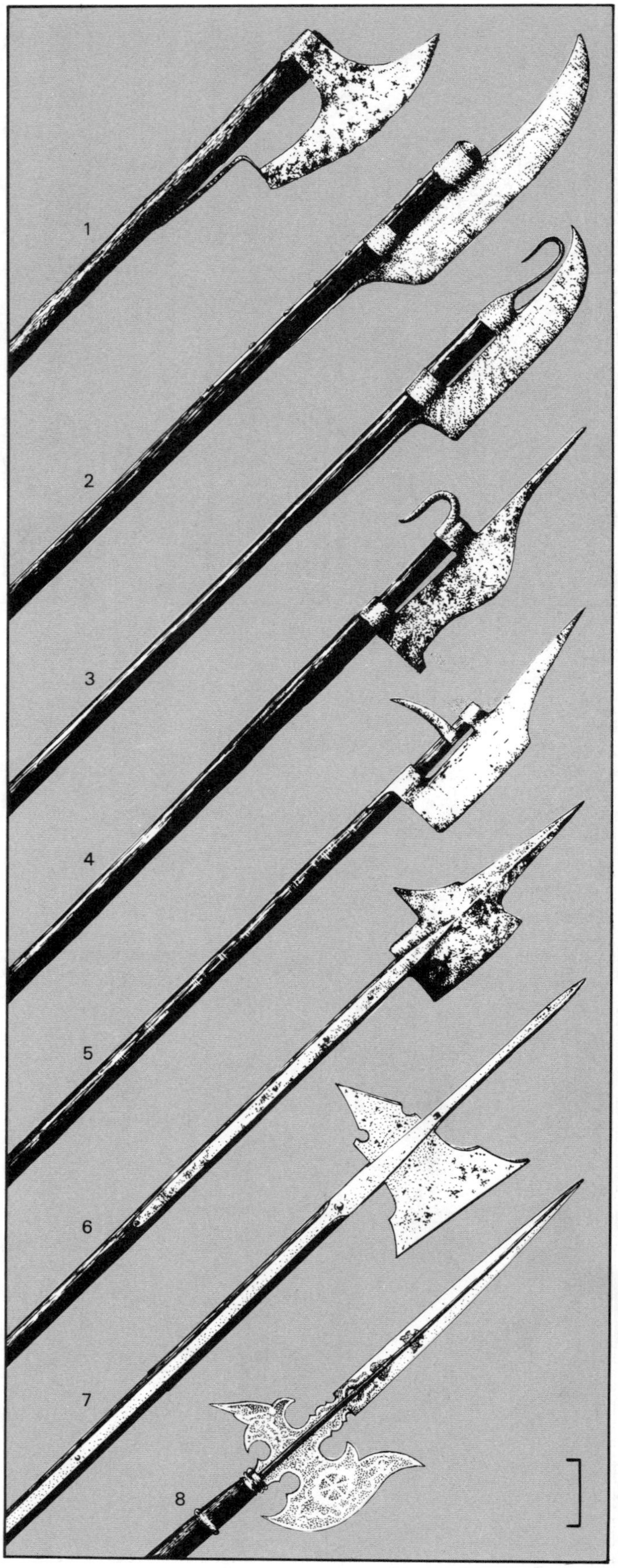

Bardiche (left) The characteristic Russian form of pole-ax used from the 16th to the 18th century. Typically, the cutting edge is long and convex, and the blade attached to the shaft at two points. This one is of the late 16th century. (Livrustkammaren, Stockholm.)

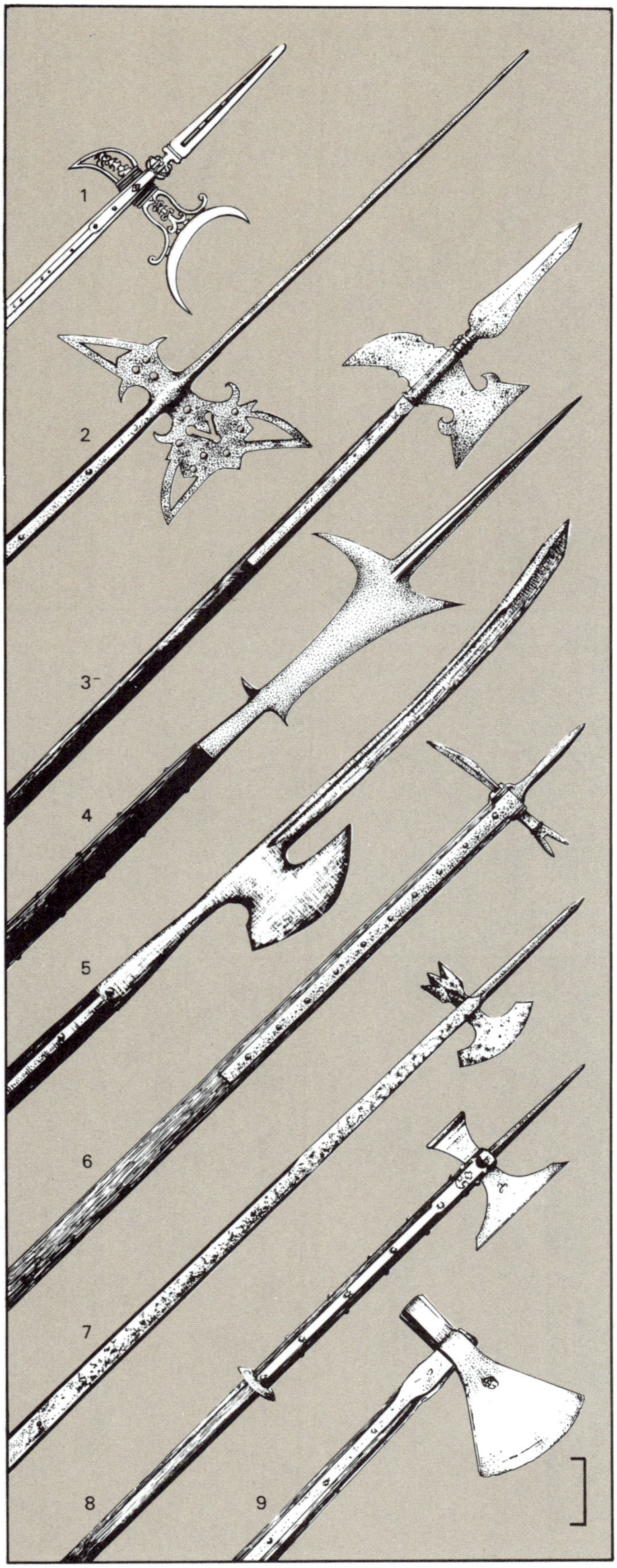

Processional halberd (below) for a retainer of Holy Roman Emperor Ferdinand I. Dated 1563. Decoration etched by Hans Polhaimer the Younger. (Kunsthistorisches Museum, Vienna.)

Axes and halberds (left)
1 Halberd. Spanish, of the 16th century. The crescent-shaped cutting edge is common on Spanish halberds.
2 Halberd, made in Arboga, Sweden, in the second half of the 16th century. The blade and beak are pierced and the spike is particularly long.
3 Sergeant's halberd. English, late 18th century. The blade is marked "3rd Regt. Guards." Halberds were carried as "leading staves" or signs of rank in the British army until 1792, when they began to be replaced by spontoons.
4 Halberd or bill. Italian, c.1510. This weapon has features of both these types.
5 Saber halberd. Swiss or German, c.1650. An unusual variant.
6 Foot soldier's hammer, a variety of pole-ax sometimes called a *bec de corbin* or a Lucerne hammer. European, c.1550.
7 Pole-ax. Probably French, c.1400-50. Combines a hammer with an ax-blade.
8 Pole-ax. Probably French, c.1470. Intended for use in fighting on foot in the lists. Note the disk-shaped hand-guard.
9 Pole-ax with hammer-head. Probably Swiss, 16th century.

Pole-arms 4

Glaives, bills and other infantry pole-arms
1 Agricultural scythe adapted as a pole-arm. English, Monmouth Rebellion 1685.
2 *Naginata*, a Japanese pole-arm with a sword-like blade.
3 Glaive or *couteau de breche*, etched with the monogram of Emperor Rudolf II. Augsburg c.1577.
4 Glaive or *fauchard*. French, 15th century.
5 Glaive. Venetian, c.1500.
6 Glaive. Italian, c.1500.
7 Processional glaive of the guard of the Doge's Palace, Venice. Mid-17th century.
8 Bill, a common soldier's weapon developed from the agricultural bill-hook. English, c.1500.
9 Bill. Probably Swiss, 15th century.
10 Bill, of a complex form common in Italy, c.1515.
11 *Guisarme*. English, c.1450.
12 Military fork. German or Swiss, early 16th century.
13 Military fork. French, c.1675.
14 Pole-arm from Java. The center prong is in the form of a diver.
15 Half moon. Spanish, c.1600.
16 Man-catcher, used by guards or watchmen to trap fugitives by the neck or by a limb. German, c.1600.
17 *Sode garami* or sleeve tangler. Japanese pole-arm said to be used to catch, unhorse or disarm an enemy wearing a loose-sleeved garment common in Japan.
18 Man-catcher or catchpole, similar in concept to 16, with sprung arms to trap a man's limb. English, c.1530.

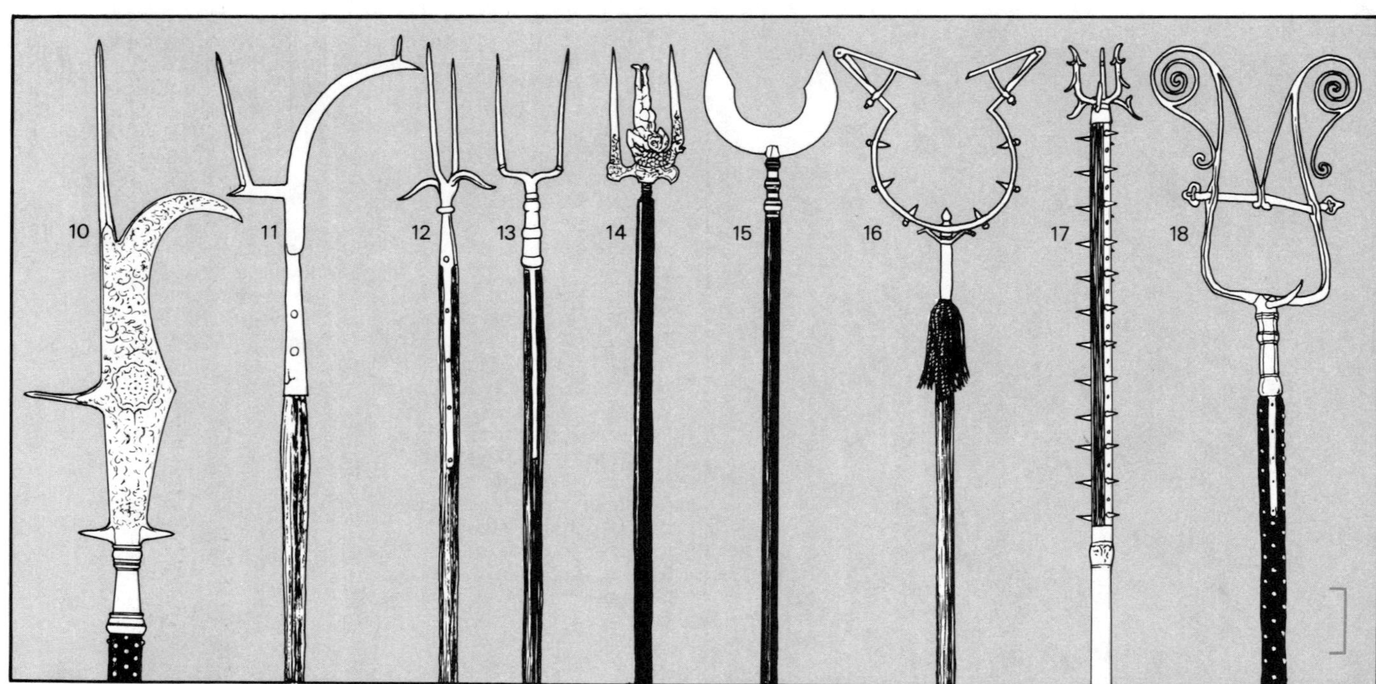

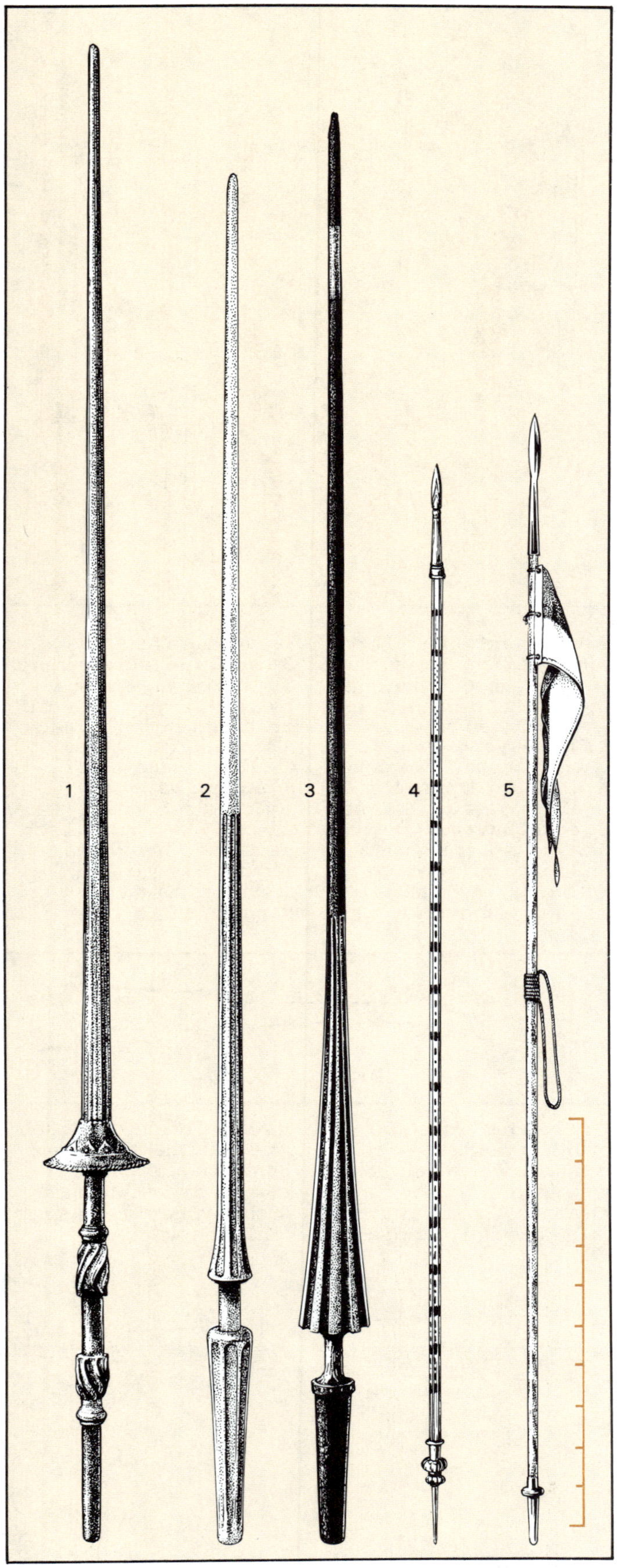

Lancer (above) of the Indian Army, 1916. Lances were still carried by the cavalry of many armies during the First World War, as they waited to exploit the hoped-for breakthrough.

Engraved point (below) of a Spanish cavalry lance, model 1842. The steel blade is of rhomboid section, set on a cylindrical socket and with two short langets to protect the top of the wooden shaft. Overall length of the lance is 8ft 2in (2.5m). (Museo de Artilleria, Madrid.)

Lances (left)
1 Jousting lance fitted with an iron handguard. Associated with a late 15th century German suit of armor.
2 A wooden jousting lance of a common, fluted design. The narrow "waisted" section is intended to be gripped by the hand. Associated with an early 16th century German suit of armor.
3 Hollow wooden jousting lance believed to have belonged to Henry VIII of England. This form of lance was designed to shatter if it struck an opponent fairly and squarely. (Tower of London.)
4 Hollow steel lance of the Mahratta people of western and central India. 18th century.
5 British pattern 1885 cavalry lance. Ash shaft, steel point and leather wrist-strap. The colors of the small pennon were red and white.

Bayonets

A bayonet is a blade that can be attached to the muzzle of a gun. In its original and most important role, it converts an infantryman's musket or rifle into a pike.

In the 17th century, ranks of pikemen were employed to protect musketeers against cavalry while they were reloading. The invention of the bayonet allowed a musketeer to defend himself, as he now in effect had a pole-arm, the foot soldier's traditional weapon.

Infantry were drilled in the use of their long bayonets against cavalry and other infantry until well into this century. Since WW1 there has been a change of emphasis, with most armies adopting short bayonets possessing a useful secondary function as a general-purpose knife.

Attachment (above) The form of a bayonet is dictated by the method of attachment to the gun. The main types are described here.
1 Plug bayonet Simply a dagger or short sword with a round grip tapered to fit tightly into the gun muzzle.
2 Socket bayonet A tubular sleeve fits over the muzzle, and has a slot to engage with a stud on the barrel. The socket forms a rudimentary hilt.
3 Sword and knife bayonet The hilt is adapted usually by a slot that fits onto a bar or stud on the barrel. Often also reinforced with a ring to fit around the muzzle.
4 Integral bayonet Attached permanently to the gun, often folding back under the barrel when not required. May have a spring for instant deployment.

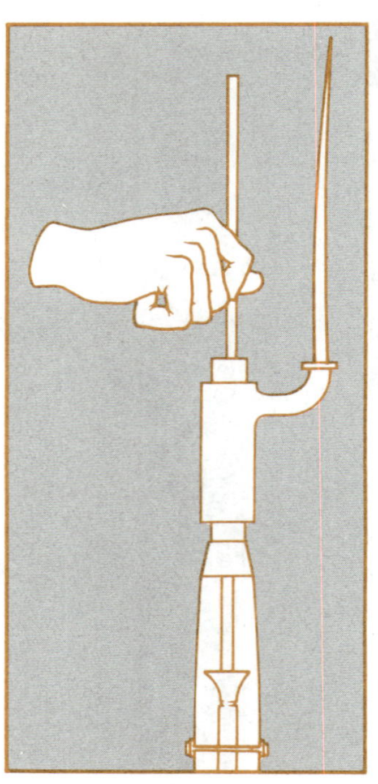

The fixed position (left) of military bayonets was long determined by the process of muzzle-loading. The blade could not be set above the bore, as it would interfere with aiming, nor below as that was where the ramrod fitted when not in use. The blade was thus offset far enough to the side to allow the fingers to grip the ramrod during loading. The socket bayonet with its characteristic "elbow" was the simplest shape that met all the requirements.
With the coming of breech-loading these constraints disappeared, and the blade could be set below the bore and closer to its axis.

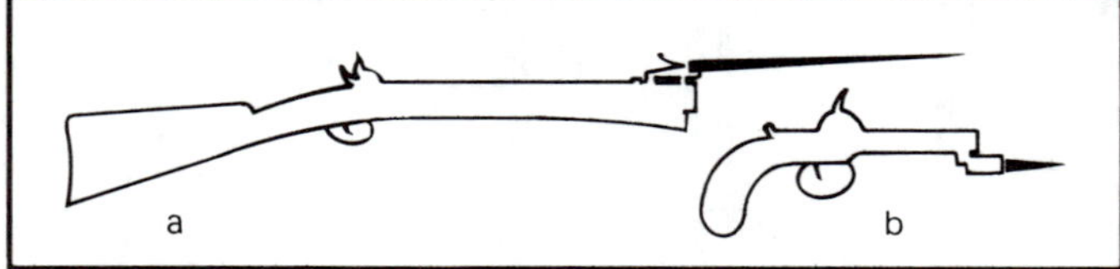

Civilian firearms (above) of the 18th and 19th centuries were often fitted with integral, folding bayonets. The blunderbuss (**a**) and pocket pistol (**b**) are the types of gun most often fitted with these bayonets. Being intended for emergency self-defense, such bayonets have a spring for fast deployment.

The earliest bayonet
The first known reference to "bayonettes" was made in France in 1647. They were of the plug type, the blade and hilt each about 1ft (30cm) long, and are thought to have looked like the bayonet shown in the 19th century illustration (above).

Use of bayonets (above)
a Primary use The greatest danger to musketeers was from cavalry, who could attack quickly before it was possible to reload. Partly because of this threat, the combined length of musket and bayonet was kept at about 6ft (2m) — long enough to reach a mounted opponent.

b Bayonets in defense In the bayonet's heyday in Europe, in the 18th and 19th centuries, a common tactic was to form two ranks of infantrymen, one kneeling in front of the other, so confronting the enemy with a hedge of bayonets, those of one rank protecting the second as they reloaded.

c Bayonets in attack The bayonet could also be used for shock attack, when the infantry charged. There is evidence that actual clashes were rare; one side or the other usually lost its nerve and fled. To use even this moral effect of the threat of the bayonet, troops needed to have better discipline than their enemies.

d The "pike mentality," which placed such emphasis on the bayonet, survived well into the 20th century. Even now the latest rifles and submachine guns are fitted with bayonets. But bayonet practice is used more as an exercise to develop aggression than as training for likely combat use. Secondary use as a general-purpose knife is now its chief justification.

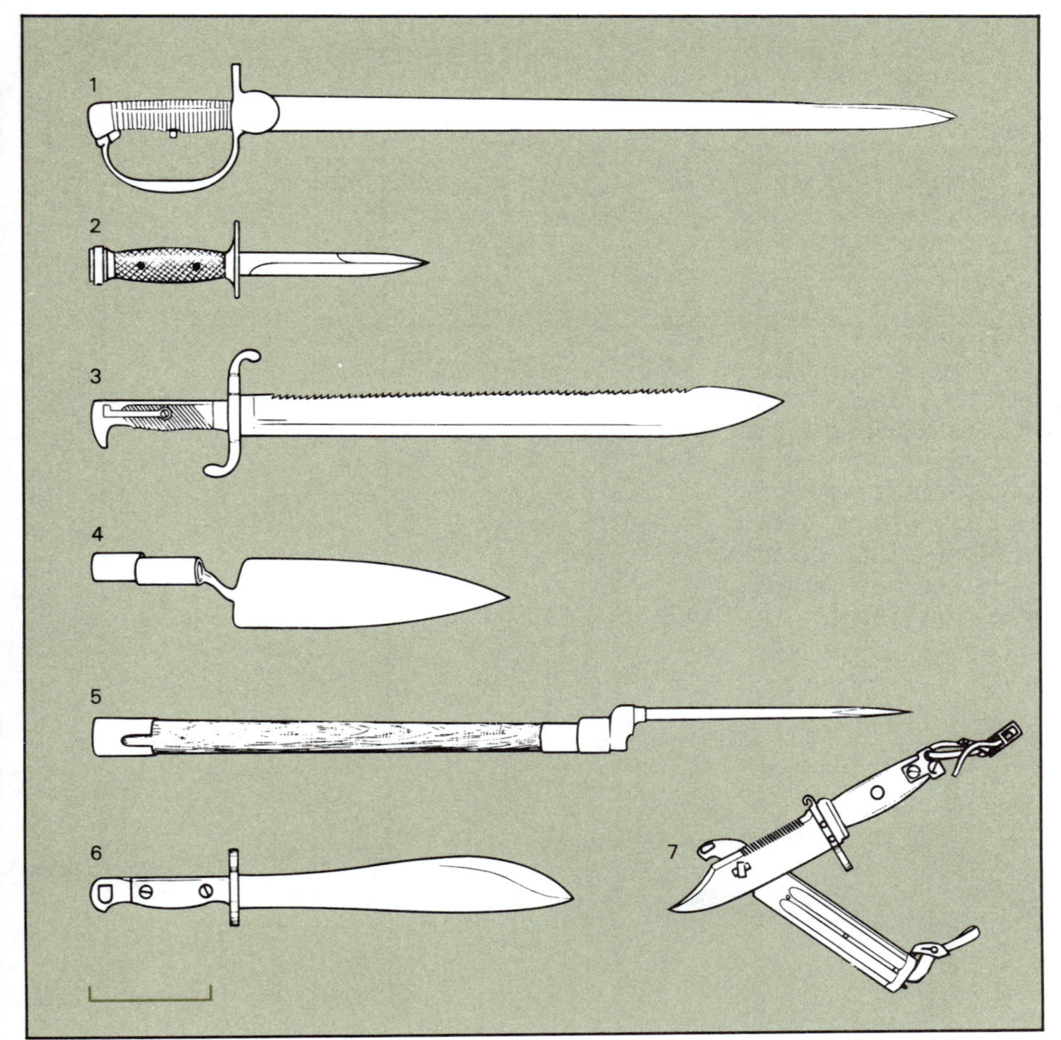

Types of secondary use
1 Sword bayonet This example is the second type made for the British Baker rifle, in 1801. Brass hilt.
2 Knife or dagger bayonet Originally, and now once again, the commonest secondary role. This is the US M7 for the M16 rifle, 1962.
3 Saw bayonet Usually issued to engineer, pioneer or artillery units, who needed an effective wood-saw to clear obstacles or prepare gun-positions. Prussian M1871.
4 Trowel bayonet An uncommon type meant to double as an entrenching tool. This is the US M1873 for the Springfield rifle.
5 Mine-probe British No4 spike bayonet attached to an entrenching-tool handle. This allowed troops to use this short bayonet to probe the ground for mines without needing to stoop.
6 Machete bayonet Australian experimental attempt to combine the jungle machete with the bayonet. For the SMLE No1 rifle, 1943.
7 Wire-cutter bayonet When linked to its special scabbard, this Soviet knife bayonet for the AK47 rifle forms a pair of wire-cutting shears.

Plug bayonets

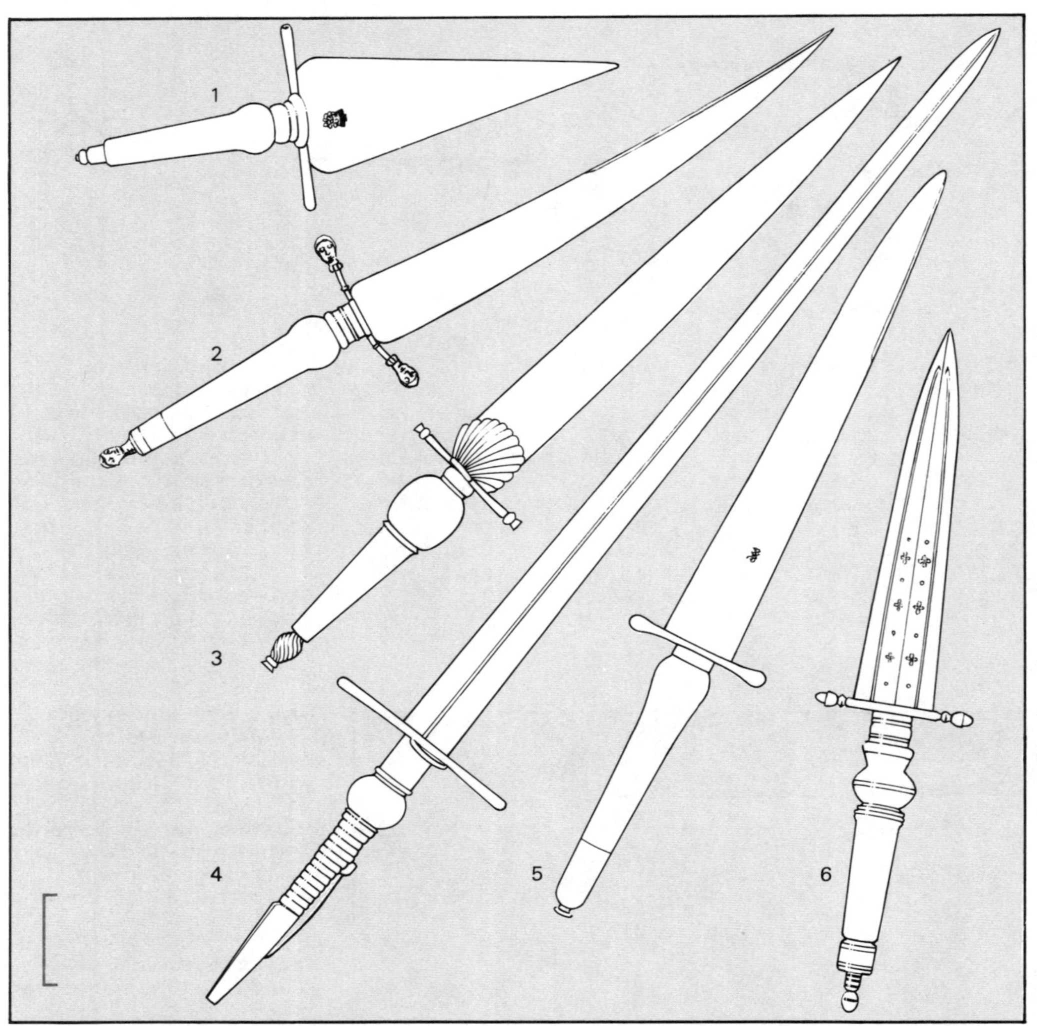

Plug bayonets (left)
1 Plug bayonet with broad, tapered blade. English, c.1680.
2 Plug bayonet with slight curve to the blade, double-edged near the tip. The helmeted heads on the pommel and quillons are quite common on late 17th century bayonets.
3 Plug bayonet with shell-guard, c.1670. Blade marked "Carolus Rex Dei Gratia."
4 Swedish M1692. Long enough to be used as a sword. The hilt fitted into two rings beside the barrel, and was held there by the spring, the only addition to an otherwise conventional plug bayonet. An important stage in development.
5 Plug bayonet of the plainest type, issued to common soldiers in the late 17th century.
6 Sporting plug bayonet as used in Spain until the mid-19th century. Could be used as a last resort defense against wild boar and as a general hunting and skinning knife.

The plug bayonet is the earliest and simplest form of bayonet, being merely a dagger with a tapered handle that can be stuck in the gun muzzle. The disadvantages were that it could easily work loose or jam in position, and of course it prevented the musket being loaded or fired. The type nevertheless survived into the 19th century among hunters, particularly in Spain, as a defense against wild boar.

English plug bayonet (below) of the late 17th century. Flamboyant iron blade, ivory grip and brass fittings.

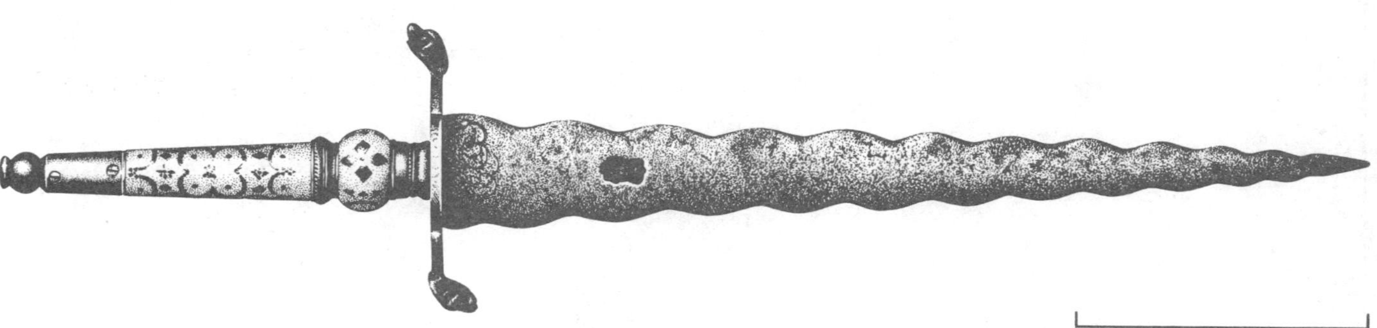

Integral bayonets

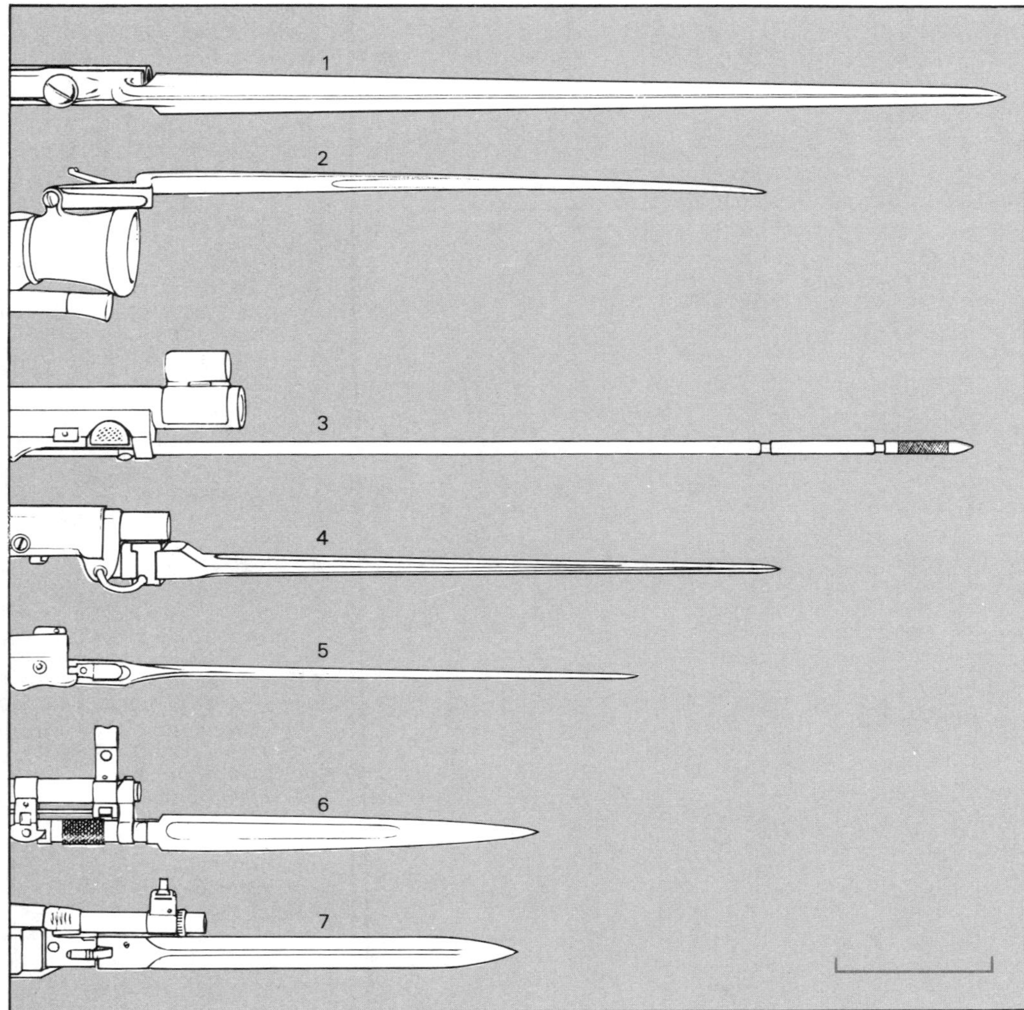

Integral bayonets (left)
1 Swiveling bayonet for the Dutch M1826/30 musketoon. Has the elbow and blade of the common triangular socket bayonet.
2 Civilian blunderbuss spring bayonet. A household defense weapon. The blade was held back above the barrel by a catch. When released, the leaf-spring flicked the blade into place.
3 Telescopic "ramrod" bayonet for US Springfield rifle M1884. Slid back into the stock in place of the ramrod, no longer needed for a breech-loading rifle. Shown partly extended. Full blade length 35.5in (101.6cm)
4 Japanese Type 44 folding bayonet, 1911, for Arisaka carbine. Held in position by a hook on the muzzle and a spring clip.
5 Italian folding bayonet for the Mannlicher-Carcano M1891 carbine. One of a variety of blade shapes and catches used on this short rifle.
6 Chinese Type 53 folding knife bayonet, fitted to the Chinese version of the Soviet SKS short rifle.
7 Czechoslovakian folding knife bayonet for the M1952 self-loading rifle. Folds back against the side of the barrel when not in use.

Integral, or retractable, bayonets are permanently attached to the gun and can be slid or folded back along the barrel when not needed. They were often fitted to pistols and blunderbusses of the 18th and 19th centuries, for use in personal and household defense. They are also found on 20th century military rifles in some countries, notably the USSR, Italy and China.

Type 56/1 (below) Chinese rifle with integral triangular bayonet shown partially unfolded. The rifle is a copy of the Soviet AK47, and the bayonet fixing is derived from that of the Soviet SKS rifle. The blade, 8.7in (22.1cm), is of Chinese design.

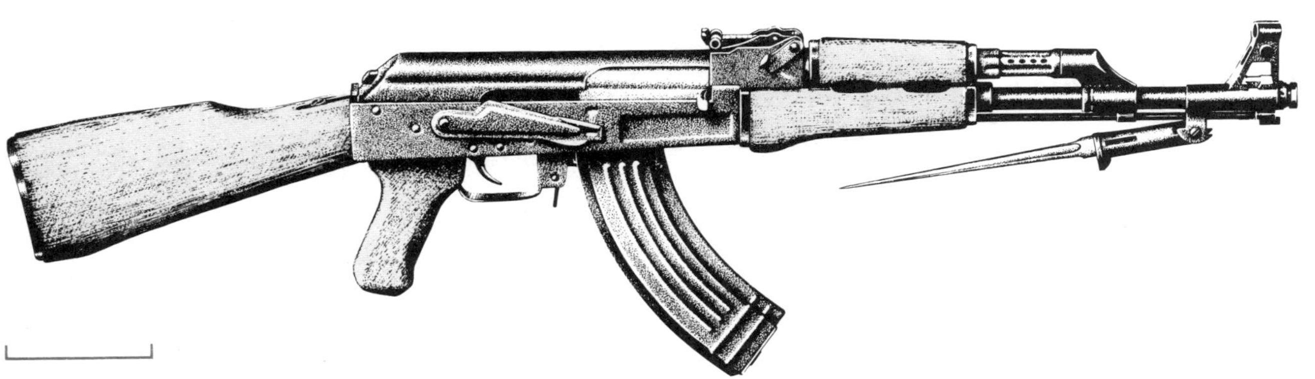

Socket bayonets

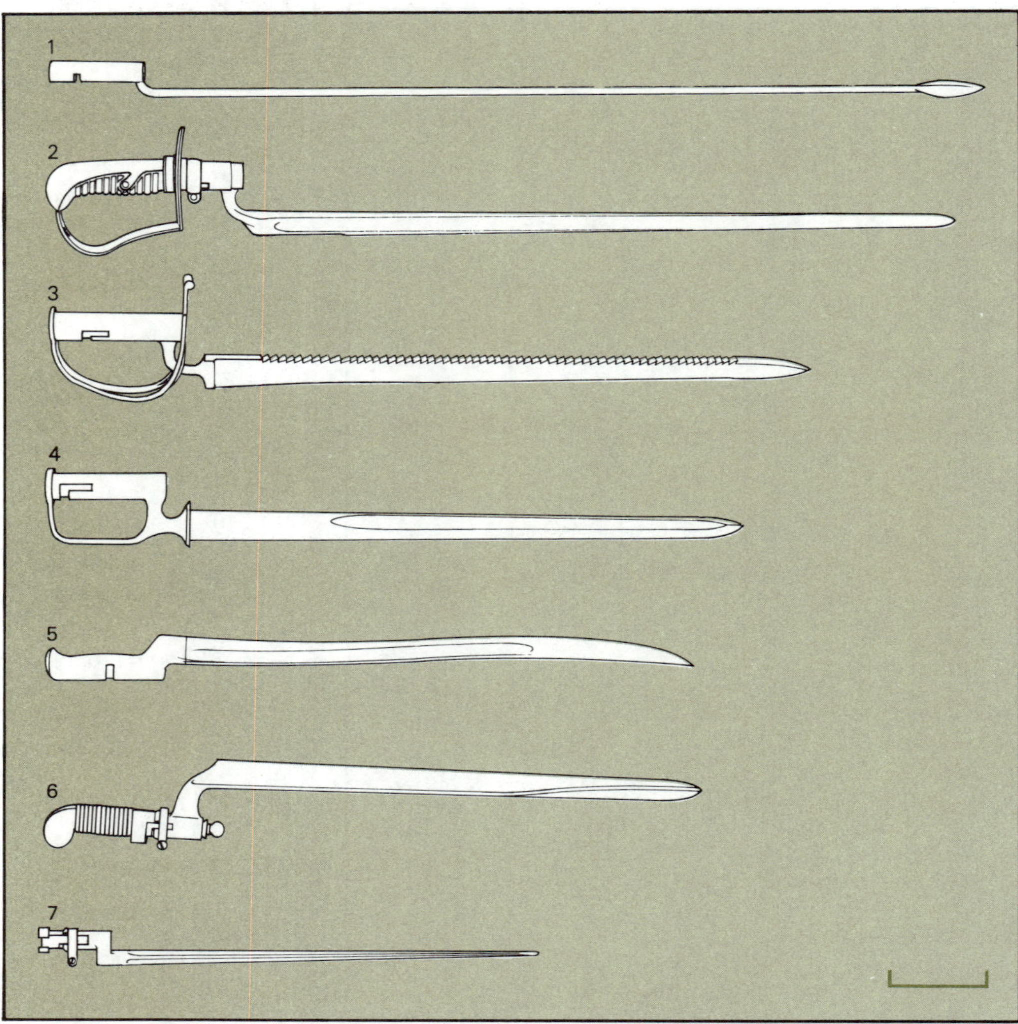

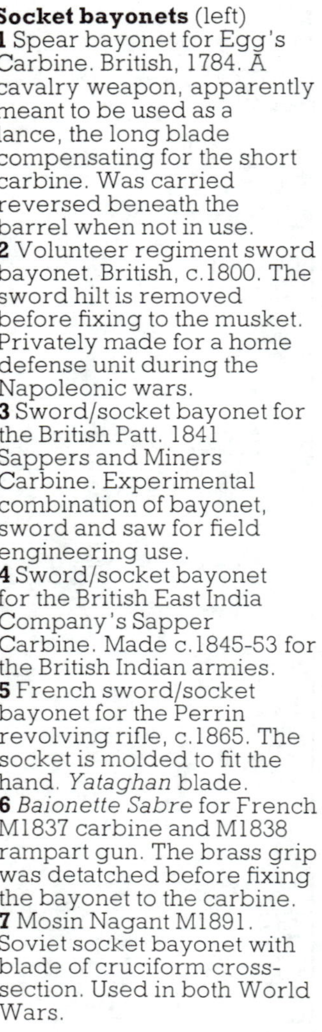

Socket bayonets (left)
1 Spear bayonet for Egg's Carbine. British, 1784. A cavalry weapon, apparently meant to be used as a lance, the long blade compensating for the short carbine. Was carried reversed beneath the barrel when not in use.
2 Volunteer regiment sword bayonet. British, c.1800. The sword hilt is removed before fixing to the musket. Privately made for a home defense unit during the Napoleonic wars.
3 Sword/socket bayonet for the British Patt. 1841 Sappers and Miners Carbine. Experimental combination of bayonet, sword and saw for field engineering use.
4 Sword/socket bayonet for the British East India Company's Sapper Carbine. Made c.1845-53 for the British Indian armies.
5 French sword/socket bayonet for the Perrin revolving rifle, c.1865. The socket is molded to fit the hand. *Yataghan* blade.
6 *Baionette Sabre* for French M1837 carbine and M1838 rampart gun. The brass grip was detatched before fixing the bayonet to the carbine.
7 Mosin Nagant M1891. Soviet socket bayonet with blade of cruciform cross-section. Used in both World Wars.

The socket bayonet was an improvement over the plug type because, when fixed, it permitted the musket to be loaded and fired. The socket is a metal tube fitting over the barrel, with a slot for the foresight, and later a locking catch. The blade is usually offset to the right of the barrel, allowing both the ramrod to be drawn from beneath and the hand to grip it while ramming down the charge.

Parts of the socket bayonet
a Socket
b Locking slot
c Elbow
d Shoulder
e Blade

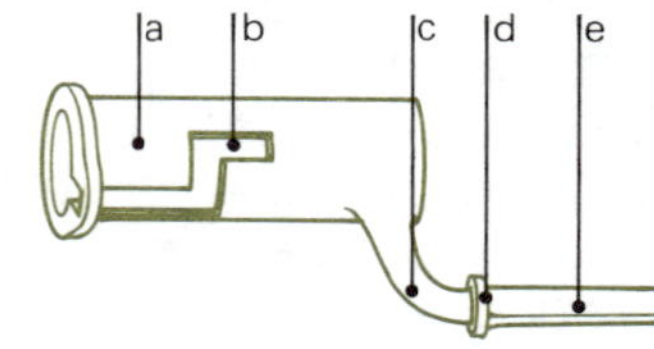

Socket bayonet (below) and scabbard, for the Brown Bess musket. The standard British infantry bayonet from c.1720 to c.1840. The scabbard is of stiff leather with brass mounts.

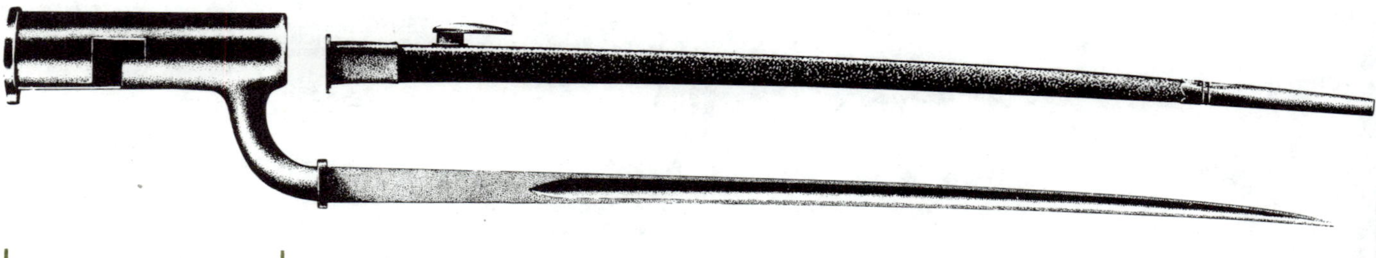

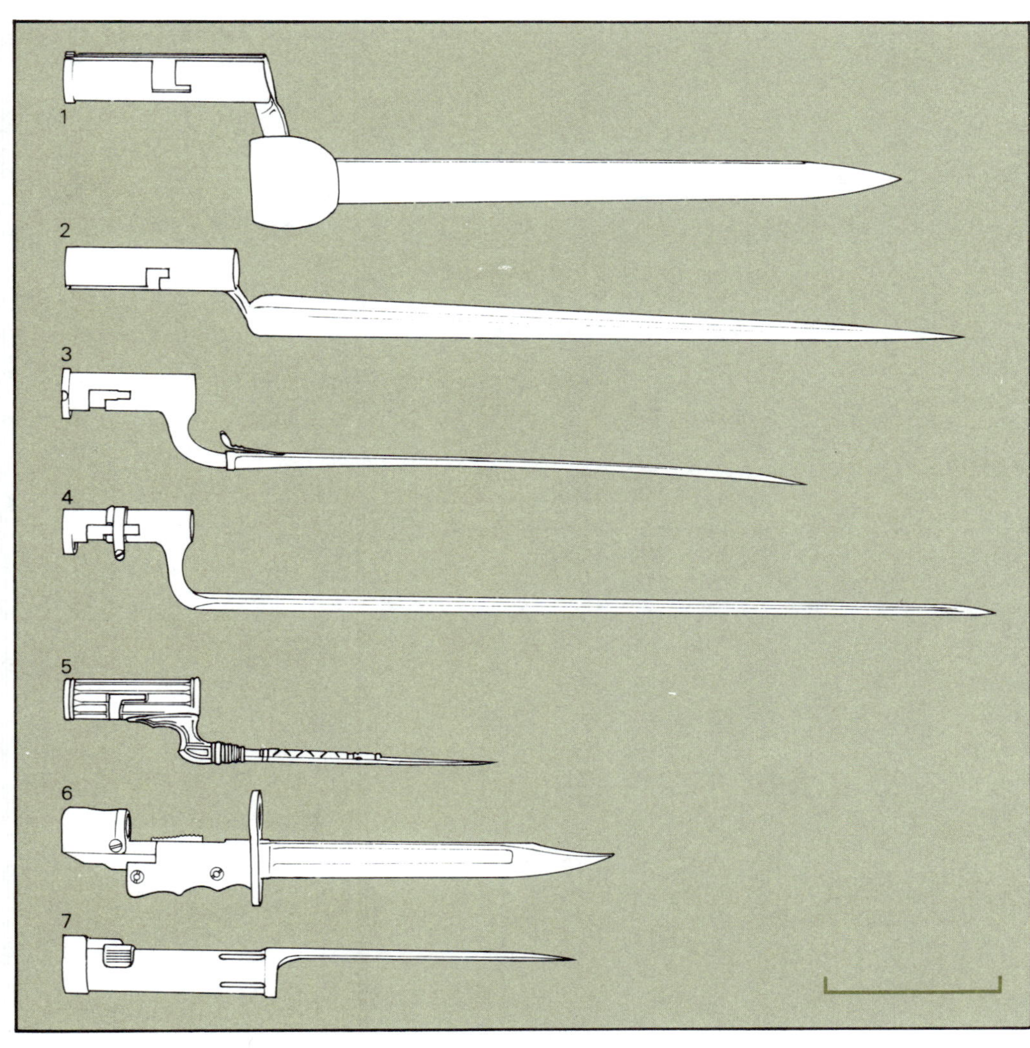

Socket bayonets (left)
1 Split socket bayonet. Probably English, c.1700. Flat blade and crude shell-guard at the elbow. The split socket could be pinched or prised open to fit any barrel.
2 Socket bayonet with flat two-edged blade, a type used in England in the early 18th century.
3 Constabulary bayonet. British 1840. The spring catch on the blade prevented the weapon from being snatched from its scabbard by a prisoner or a crowd.
4 US M1872 socket bayonet for the Springfield breech-loading rifle of that year. Triangular blade section.
5 Sporting socket bayonet. Spanish, mid-19th century. All brass. Flat blade, serrated on one edge. More ornate than military bayonets.
6 British No7 bayonet, 1946. For the No4 rifle and Mk5 Sten submachine gun. The socket swivels through a half turn to form the pommel when used as a dagger — a unique arrangement.
7 Modern socket bayonet for the Belgian FN automatic rifle, currently used by the Netherlands, the Republic of Ireland and South Africa.

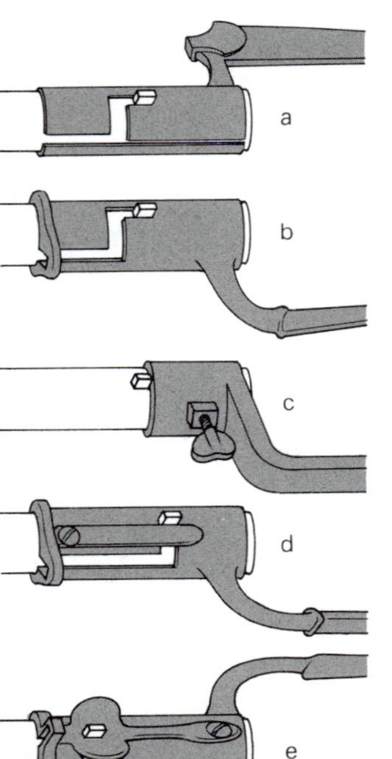

Socket varieties
a Split An early type that could be made to fit any of the irregular-sized barrels in use c.1720.
b Common Used with the British Brown Bess musket from c.1720 to c.1840, and with its equivalent in other armies.
c Wing bolt Swedish, 1696. Simple and effective, but not much copied elsewhere.
d East India Company spring In limited use with the British Indian armies in the early 19th century.
e Kyhl's spring catch A Danish invention of 1794, used by them for over 50 years. To unfasten, the spring is pulled up by the wing-like lugs and the bayonet pulled straight off.

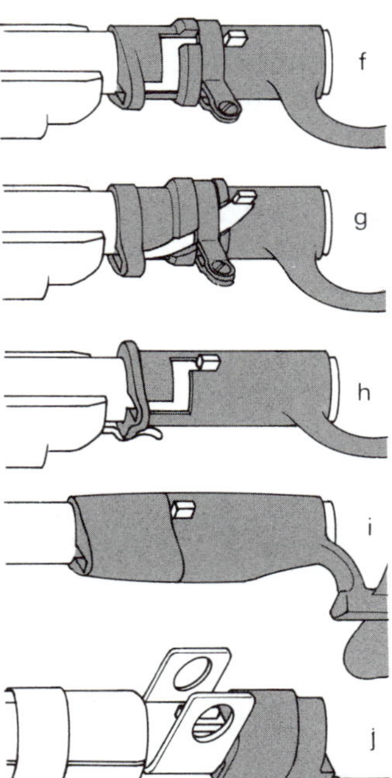

f French ring On fixing, the arch in the ring coincides with the zig-zag slot. The ring is then rotated to close the slot behind the sight.
g Austrian slot with ring The same principle as the French ring, but with an oblique slot.
h Hanoverian catch A hook-like spring-catch, fixed to the musket, grips the thick collar of the socket.
i US M1873 Trowel bayonet socket. After being slipped over the muzzle, the rear half of the socket rotates to close the slot and grip the back of the foresight.
j No4 spike bayonet British WW2 revival of the socket idea, using two lugs on the sides of the muzzle and a sliding section inside the socket (not visible).

Sword and knife bayonets

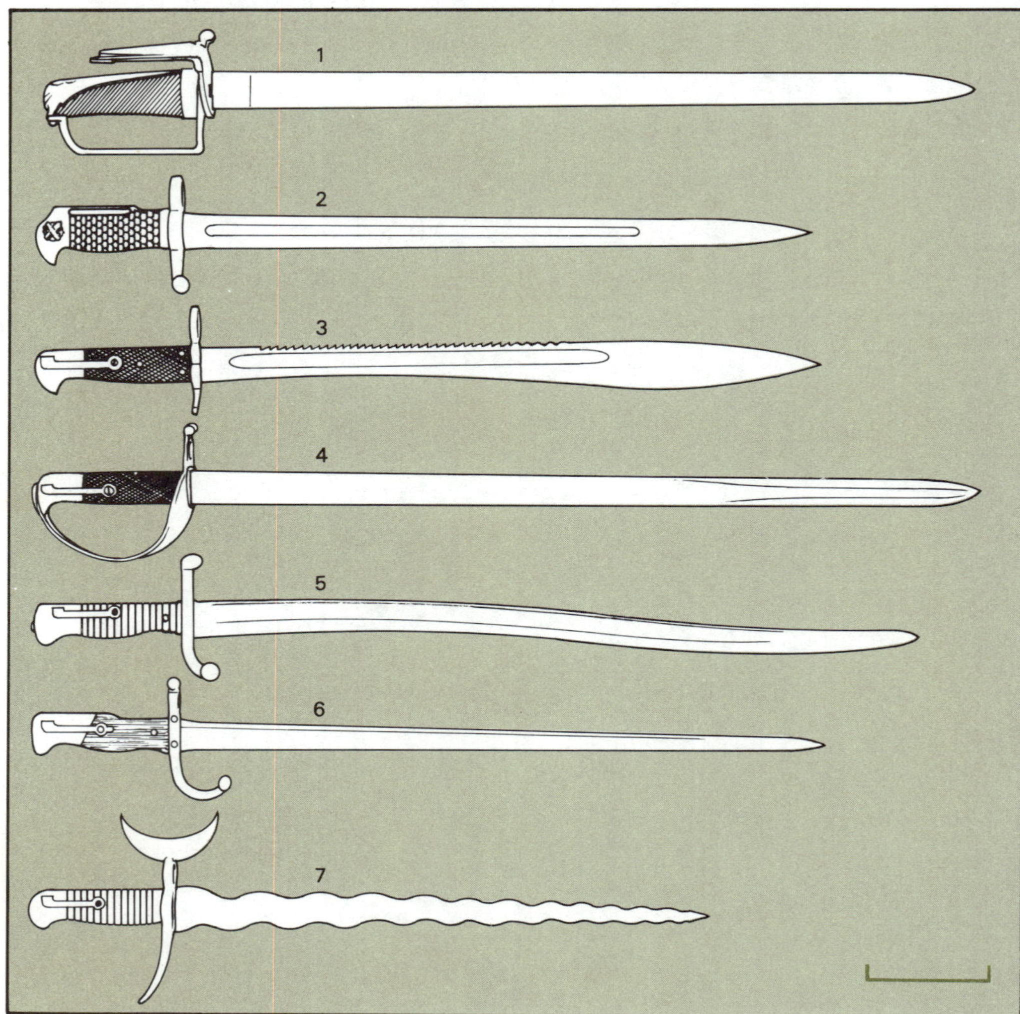

Sword bayonets (left)
1 Danish P1788/1801 hanger bayonet. 18th century foot soldiers carried a short sword called a hanger, here adapted as a bayonet. Bar fixing, but reversed, the bar being on the bayonet, not the gun muzzle.
2 US Navy sword bayonet, first type, for M1870 rifle. Brass hilt with fish-scale pattern on the grips, a feature of some US and Spanish bayonets.
3 Elcho bayonet, second type. British, 1871, for the Martini-Henry rifle. Blade modeled on the Gurkha *kukri*, an efficient chopping knife, with a saw added. Steel hilt, black composition grips. Limited issue only.
4 P1859 Naval cutlass bayonet, British, for the Enfield Short Naval rifle. An obvious combination for the navy, but clumsy as a bayonet. Steel hilt, black composition grips.
5 M1866 French bayonet for the Chassepot rifle. Retains the *yataghan* blade shape, widely used on earlier muzzle-loading rifles as it left space for the hand to grip the ramrod during loading. Brass hilt.
6 M1874 Epée bayonet for the French Gras rifle. Light and effective in the primary role, and made in huge numbers. Brass pommel, wood grips.
7 Halberd bayonet. Spanish, for M1857 carbine. Flamboyant blade with crescent ax-blade and spike of halberd form added to the cross-guard.

Sword and knife bayonets have fully formed hilts but are adapted to fit a gun muzzle, usually by means of a ring formed as part of the cross-guard, and a slot in the pommel to fit over a stud on the barrel. In general, those which are effective as swords are clumsy as bayonets. Most modern bayonets are of the knife type, and intended as general-purpose implements when not fixed on the rifle.

German M84/98 (below)
Made 1914-45, and still used in a few countries. Fitted the Mauser rifles of the Imperial and Nazi German armies. Shown with its steel scabbard and the leather "frog" by which it was attached to the soldier's waistbelt.

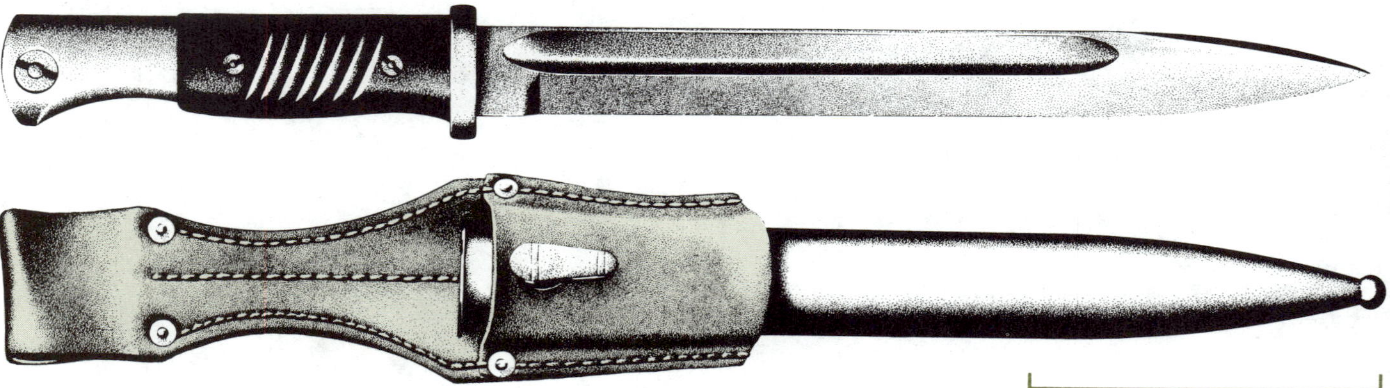

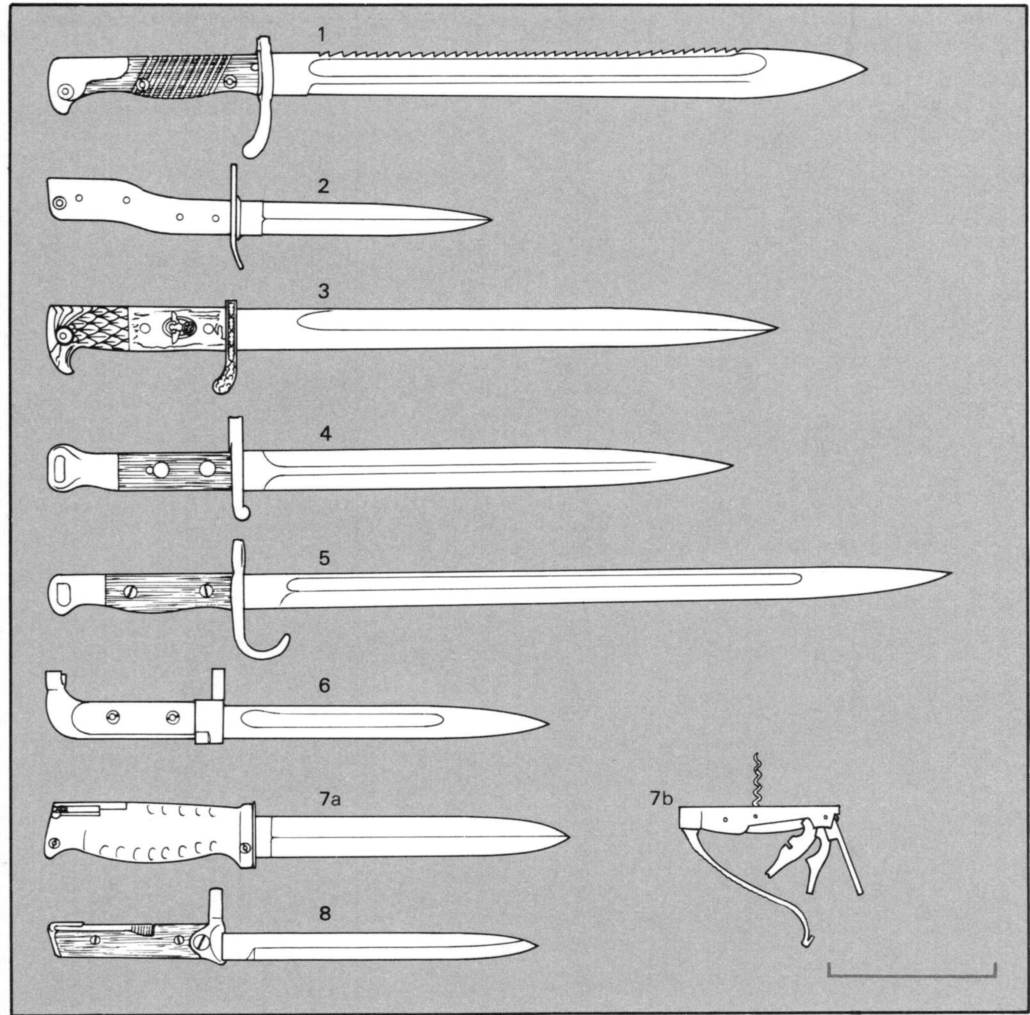

Sword and knife bayonets
(left)

1 German M1898/05, often called the "butcher's knife" blade-shape. Pioneer model with saw back. Used in WW1 on the Gew98 Mauser.

2 Trench-knife bayonet for the German Mauser rifle, WW1. A semi-official pattern which troops were allowed to buy. All steel.

3 Nazi German police dress bayonet, c.1940. Some were never intended to be fitted to a rifle, having no fixing slot or catch. Worn at the belt for show. Staghorn grips with metal badge.

4 British Patt. 1888 Mk2 for the Lee-Metford rifle. The first modern knife bayonet to be adopted by Britain. Double-edged blade.

5 British 1907 Pattern for the Short Magazine Lee-Enfield rifle. Note the hook-like "fighting quillon" meant to be used to trap an opponent's blade, omitted after 1913.

6 Soviet knife bayonet for the AK47 assault rifle in current use. Plastic grips.

7a Commercial knife bayonet for the Armalite AR10 rifle. The penknife-like combination tool (**7b**) fits in the hilt when folded.

8 Finnish M1960 knife bayonet for the AK60 assault rifle. Hinged to fold like a penknife when not on the rifle.

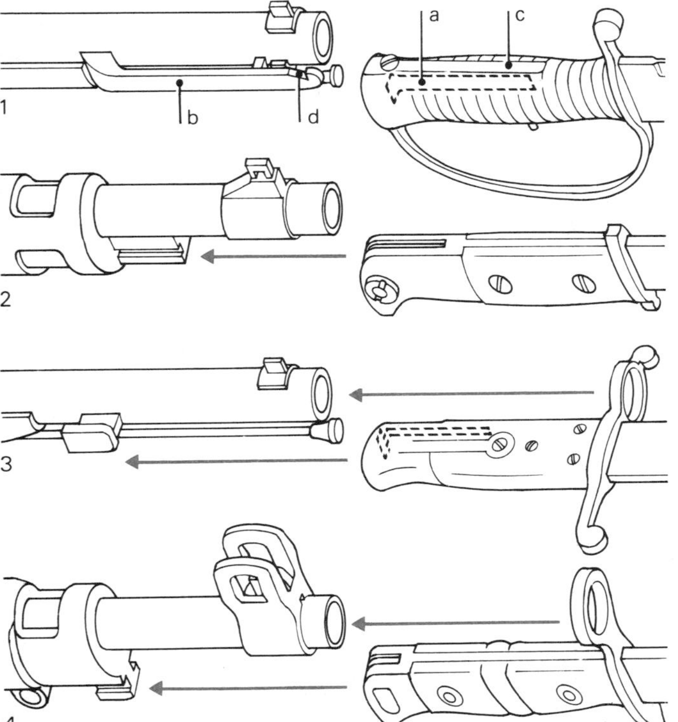

Attachment methods (left)
The two main methods are: by a bar alone (**1**, **2**) or a bar and ring (**3**, **4**). Shown are representative examples.

1 Baker rifle. British, 1800. The brass hilt has a slot (**a**) to fit over the bar (**b**), and a spring-catch (**c**) to grip the notch (**d**). The bayonet is at the side of the muzzle with the blade in the vertical plane.

2 Mauser. German, 1888 onward. A modern version of the bar fitting. The spring-catch is in the pommel of the hilt.

3 Enfield Short Rifle. British, 1850s onward. As with 1, the ramrod needed for muzzle-loading dictated that the bayonet be fixed at the side.

4 Enfield P14 and M17. British and US, 1914. The bayonet can be beneath the barrel as the rifle is a breech-loader.

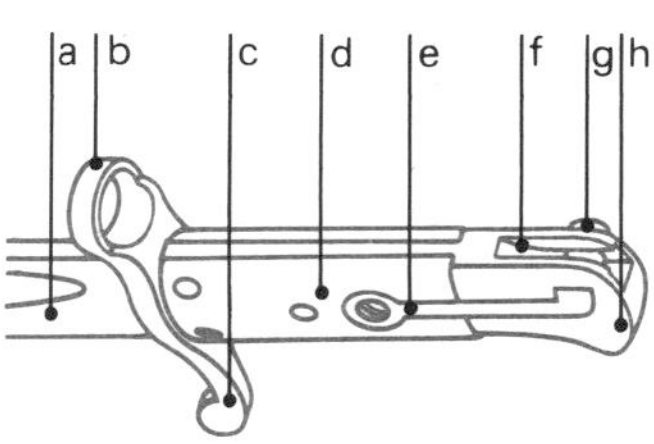

Parts of a hilted bayonet
(above)

a Blade
b Muzzle ring
c Quillon
d Grips
e Catch spring
f Fixing slot
g Catch or press-stud
h Pommel

Parts (**b**) and (**c**) form the cross-guard.

Miscellaneous hand weapons

Here we describe a number of weapons outside the mainstream of military arms. They range from devices for reinforcing the punch of a man's fist, to those meant primarily for parrying an opponent's blow. Many of those shown combine more than one offensive device, for use as the need and opportunity may occur.

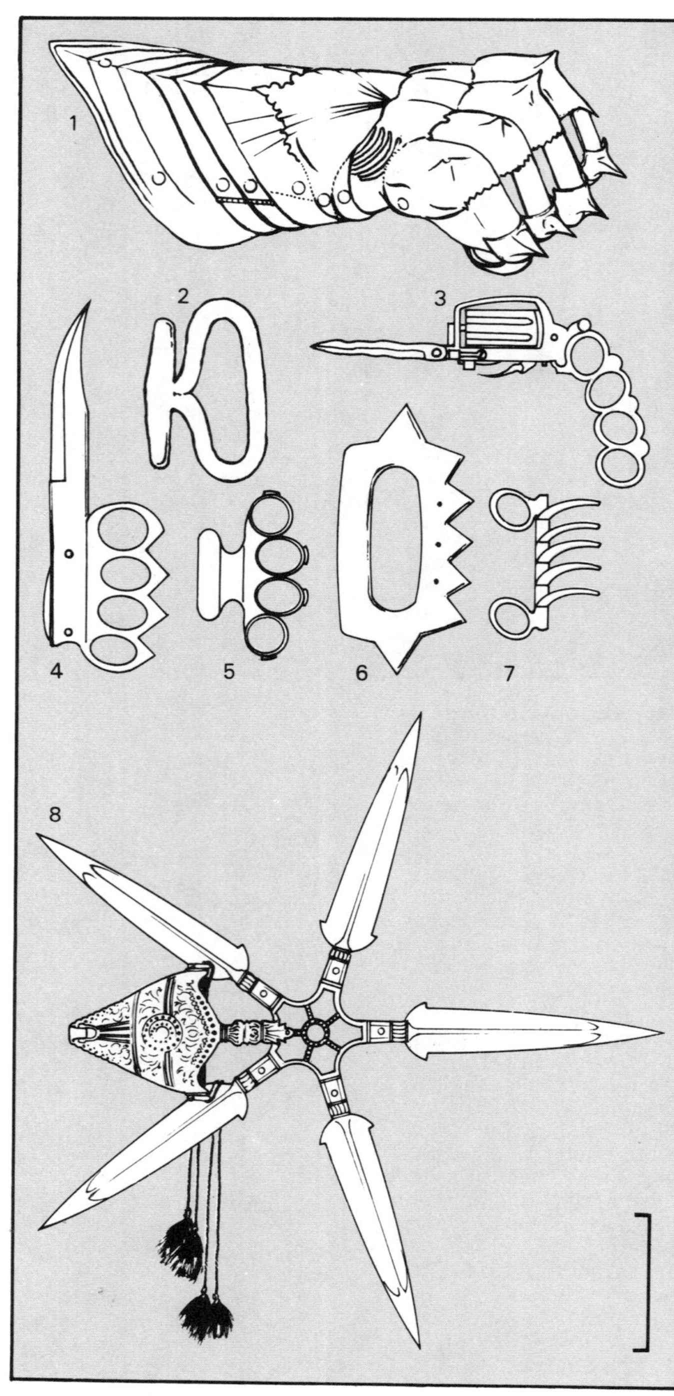

Reinforcing the fist
The idea of adding to the fist to make a blow more effective goes back at least to the Roman sport of boxing, as shown by the statue (above).

Fist weapons (left)
1 Gauntlet from a late medieval suit of armor, with spiked knuckles.
2 Lead "knuckle-duster" found on a battlefield of the American Civil War.
3 "Apache pistol," the commercial name for a 19th century weapon combining a dagger, metal knuckles and a small revolver.
4 Knuckle-duster-dagger. Made for use in trench raids during WW1. The blade is sharpened on the back edge to facilitate cutting a sentry's throat after approaching him from behind.
5 Modern French commercially made metal knuckle-duster.
6 *Hora*, knuckle-duster of horn, from India.
7 *Bagh nakh*, meaning "tiger's claws," a weapon from India, originally meant to cause wounds that would simulate an attack by a wild animal.
8 Indian weapon with five blades. A variation of the *katar* thrusting dagger (see p. 29).

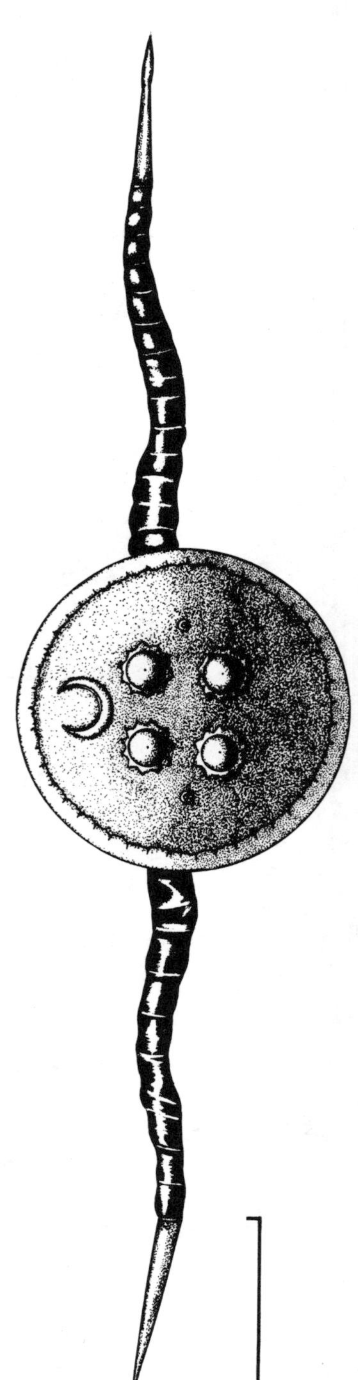

Madu (right) An Indian parrying weapon consisting of a pair of antelope horns with a shield to protect the hand. It was often used in the left hand as an adjunct to a sword in the right. The points could be used to wound if the opportunity arose.

Kusarigama (right) A Japanese parrying weapon consisting of a pick (see p. 20) with a ball and chain attached. It was used (far right) to block sword cuts and to strike back as the chance occurred.

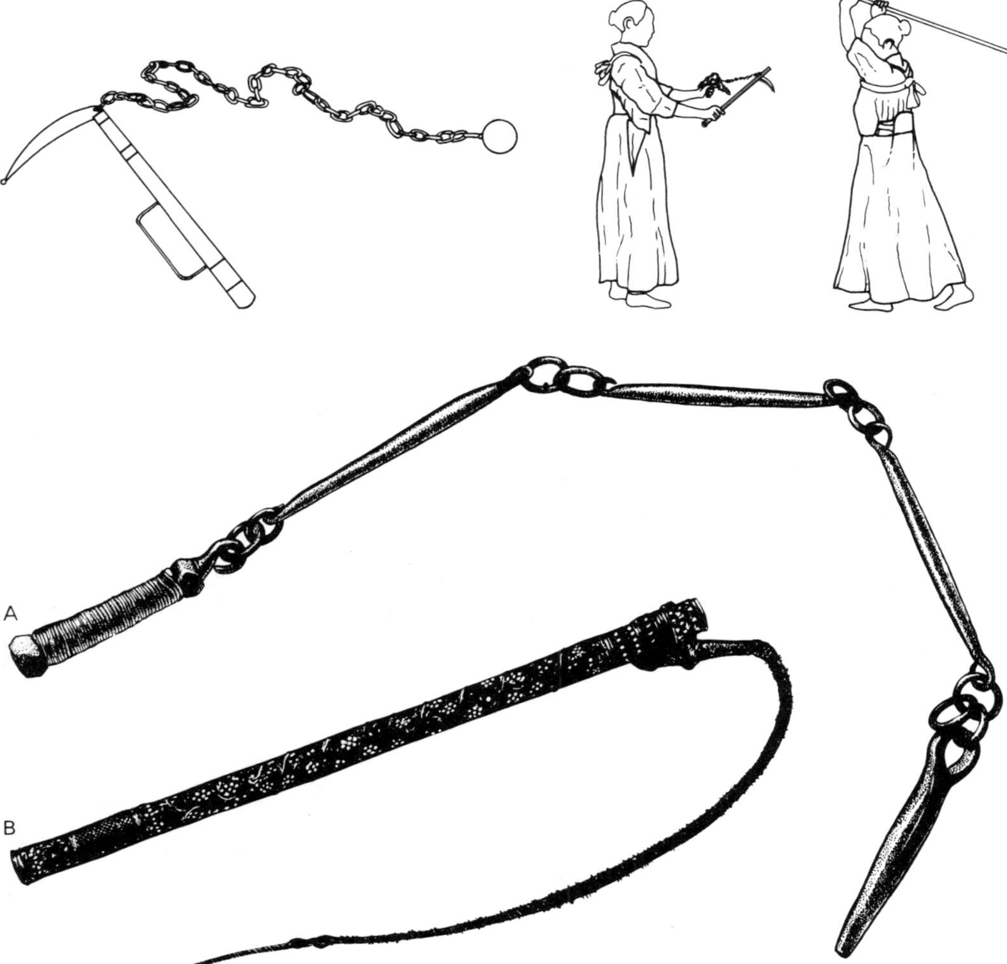

Parrying weapons (left)
1 Round iron shaft, pointed at each end, with a crescent-shaped blade at the middle. Chinese.
2 *Jittei*, simply a steel rod with a hilt. Japanese.
3 *Hachiwara*, meaning "helmet breaker," said also to have been used in the left hand to block sword cuts and break the opponent's blade. Japanese. (Cf the sword-breaker on p. 32.)

Whips (above)
A *Kau sin ke*, a Chinese chain-like weapon of iron, which could give a lethal blow.
B Turkish whip of hide, with a silver-gilt handle. Although not effective for military use, such objects have often been used as impromptu weapons.

Improvised weapons (right) A list of all the objects known to have been used as weapons on occasion would be almost endless. One that is characteristic of recent decades is the bike-chain, notorious for use in gang-fights. (Compare with the *kau sin ke*, above.)

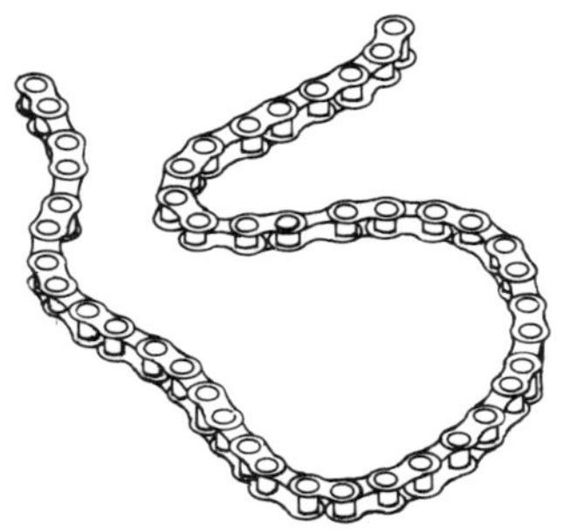

Chapter 2

HAND-THROWN MISSILES

Missiles thrown by hand are a simple and obvious means of aggression. They all derive originally from the stick or stone, and are developments parallel to the simpler of the hand-held weapons. In some cases, such as spears, the two are practically indistinguishable.

Yet, although they are simple in concept, most of these weapons require great skill, as well as strength, to be used effectively. Where this skill has been acquired by long practice, as can still be seen among the Australian Aborigines armed with the boomerang, a hand-thrown missile can give the user a great tactical advantage.

The power and effective range of hand-thrown weapons can be extended considerably by a number of simple devices that assist the thrower's arm. These devices, such as slings and spear-throwers, are included in this chapter rather than the next because the energy for propulsion is not stored in them as it is in a bow or in gunpowder. They are not true missile-throwers as the power still derives directly from the user's arm, and is merely enhanced by the device.

Photograph (right) of a stone-throwing incident in Londonderry, Northern Ireland, in 1972. The simplest missile weapon of all is still in use.

Devices to assist throwing

Here we survey ways that have been used to enhance the power of the thrower's own arm. In some cases the device is an integral part of the missile or simply an aspect of its shape; in others the device is separate from the missile and can be reused. The more important and widely used of these devices are covered in greater depth later in this chapter.

Exploiting gravity (left)
The simplest means of adding to the power of a thrown missile is to have the advantage in height over the enemy, as in this detail after a medieval illustration of a siege. Stones are being hurled from the walls onto attackers who are climbing scaling ladders.

Integral devices (right)
1 A rigid handle can extend the thrower's arm and act as a lever to increase the momentum of the heavy head (e.g. throwing-club).
2 A flexible handle, such as a cord, allows a weight to be swung at speed before release (e.g. *bolas*).
3 A thin cross-sectional shape allows a missile to skim through the air with minimum drag (e.g. quoit or *chakram*, *shuriken*).
4 An aerodynamic cross-sectional shape can help sustain the missile in flight (e.g. *boomerang*).
5 A loop of cord fixed to a spear can give added leverage to the hand at the moment of release (e.g. Roman *amentum*).

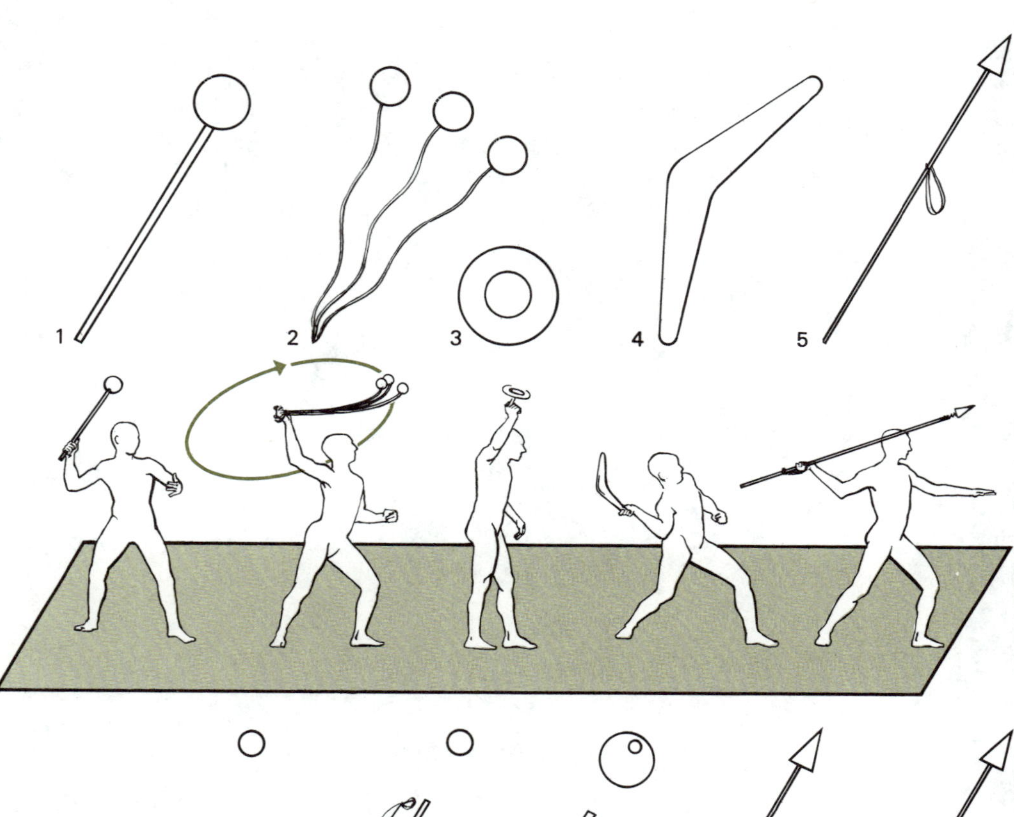

Separate devices (right)
A A sling allows a stone to be swung at high speed, then released (see opposite page).
B A staff-sling combines the leverage of a rigid handle with the release mechanism of a sling (e.g. medieval *fustibal*).
C A launching stick can be used as a lever to fling a perforated stone. If the stick has a forked end, a thin, flat stone can be thrown (e.g. as used by the Peruvians against the Spanish Conquistadores).
D A spear-thrower is a lever adapted to increase the momentum given to a throwing-spear (e.g. the Australian *woomera*).
E A separate, knotted cord, looped in a "half hitch" round a spear-shaft can be used to give added leverage at the moment of release.

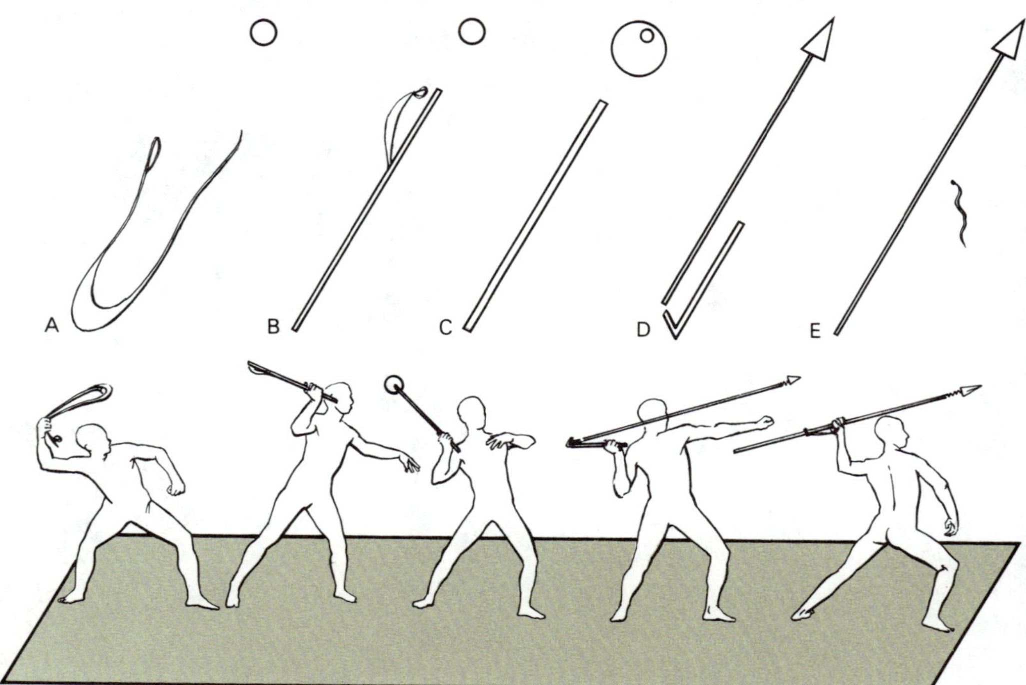

Slings

The sling is the simplest and probably the best means of increasing the distance over which a stone can be thrown. It is known to have been used in Europe and the Middle East from the Stone Age until the end of the Middle Ages at least. Examples are known from most parts of the globe. We show a small selection of slings from around the world, and some ancient sling-bullets.

Assyrian slingers (right) depicted in a bas-relief from Nineveh.

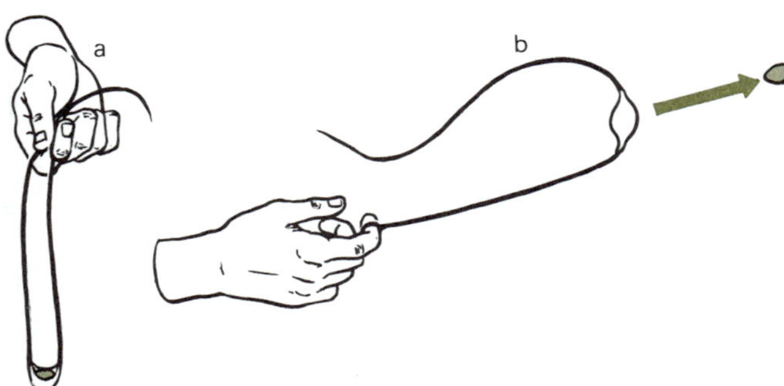

Using a sling (left) One end of the sling is looped over a finger, and the other end simply gripped by the thumb (**a**). A bullet is put in the pouch. The sling is swung vigorously around the user's head, and at the correct moment the loose end is released, spilling out the bullet, which is sent on its way by centrifugal force (**b**).

Slings (left)
1 Cord sling from Ancient Egypt, with one end missing. It was probably used by a mercenary or an invader, as the Egyptians are believed not to have used slings.
2 Leather sling from Eritrea, East Africa. Late 19th century AD.
3 Sling of two-colored cord, from Mongolia.
4 Braided sling from Hawaii, 18th century.

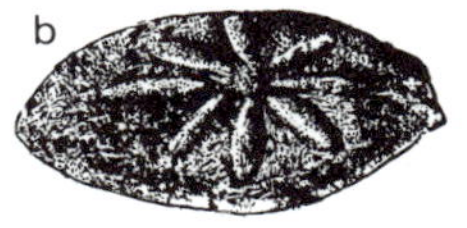

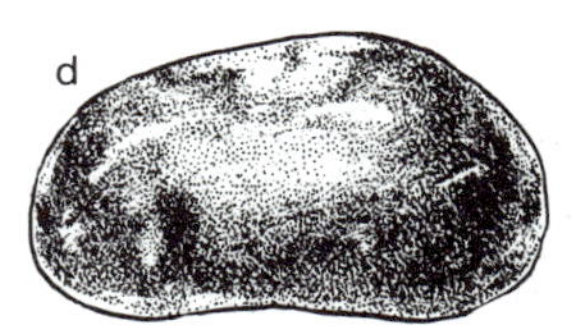

Sling bullets (right) all shown at actual size.
a Lead bullet with the emblem of an anchor, from Memphis, Egypt. Probably a relic of a siege by the Syrians in 171BC.
b As for (**a**) but with the emblem of a star.
c Ancient Greek lead sling bullet bearing the words, "Take that!" (British Museum, London.)
d Sling-stone from Maiden Castle, Dorset, England. One of the many thousands of beach pebbles stored in pits by the Celtic defenders at the time of the Roman storming of the fort in 44AD.

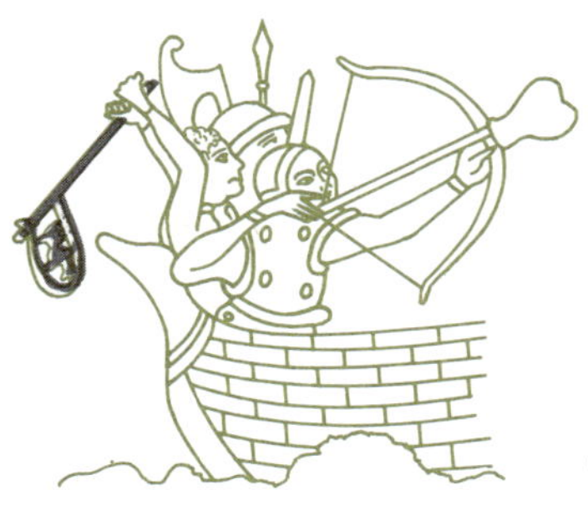

The staff-sling (right) or *fustibal* was used in medieval Europe to fling stones. It used the same method of release as the ordinary sling, but had a rigid handle. (After a manuscript illustration.)

Throwing-clubs

Most clubs are capable of being thrown. Here we illustrate some which are known to have been made with this use in mind. The addition of a handle increases the momentum of the head, but even so, there is a poor return for the trouble of manufacture, as compared with an unworked rock. The main advantage of a throwing-club would seem to be its amalgamation of striking and throwing properties.

Wooden throwing-club (right) of the Aborigines of the DeGrey River area of NW Australia. The serrations carved in relief around the head are designed to make a blow more effective. When it is thrown, the pointed tip is intended to strike the victim. (Museum of Mankind, London.)

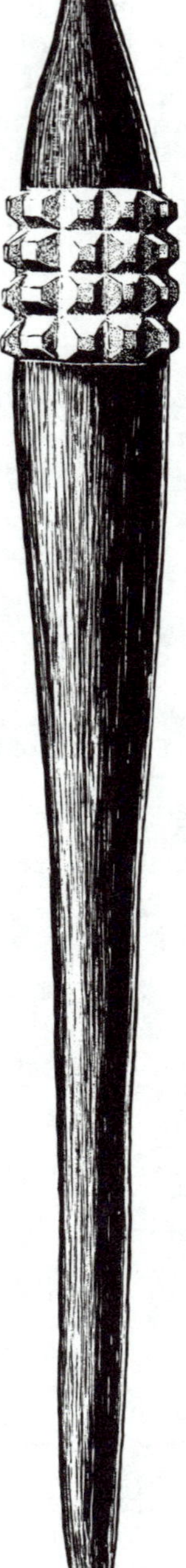

Throwing-sticks have seen wider use in the hunting of birds and small game than have throwing-clubs in war. The Ancient Egyptian nobleman (above) is depicted in pursuit of birds with a light throwing-stick. (After a wall-painting in a tomb.)

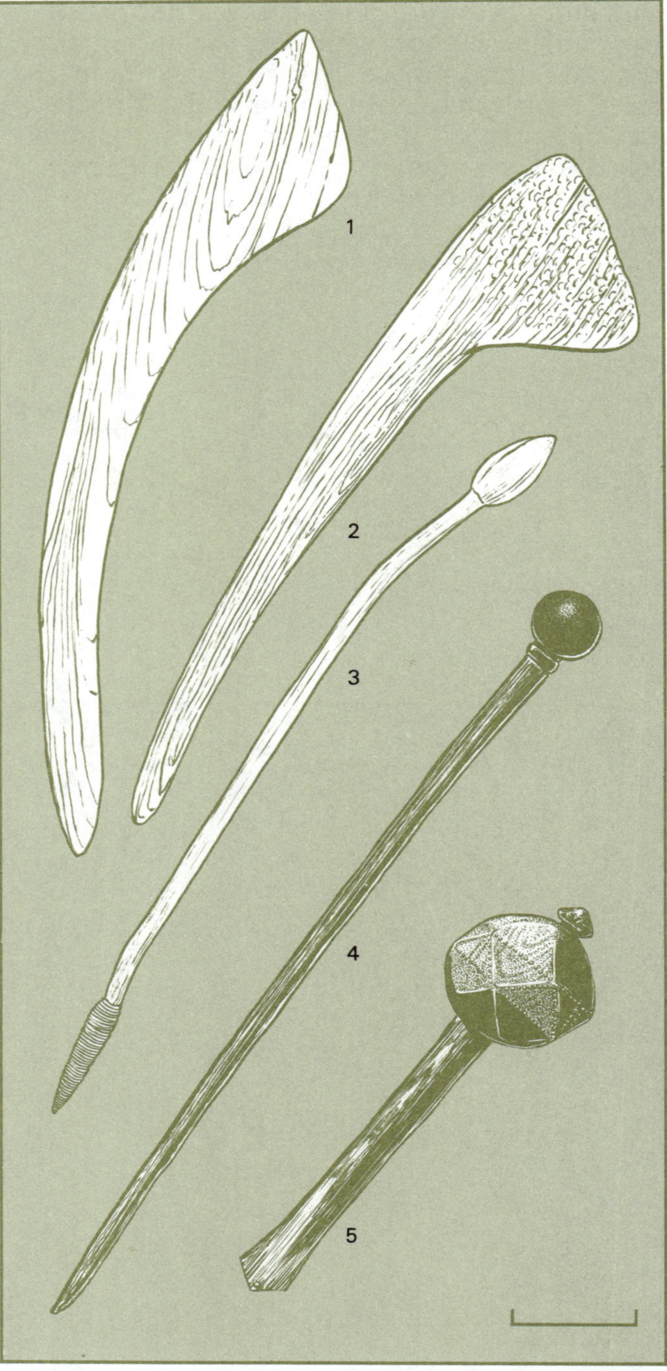

Throwing-clubs (above) All are made of wood.
1 Australian Aboriginal throwing-club from Victoria.
2 Australian Aboriginal throwing-club from Melville Island, off NW Territory, Australia.
3 Australian Aboriginal throwing-stick with binding at the grip ; from Victoria.
4 Zulu hardwood knobkerrie or *iWisa*, sometimes used as a thrown weapon.
5 Hardwood throwing-club from Fiji.

Boomerangs

The boomerang is a highly developed form of throwing-stick that makes use of an aerodynamic shape to extend its flight. The name is that used by Australian Aborigines in an area of New South Wales. It is now also applied to similar hunting weapons from other areas in Australia and elsewhere. The boomerangs shown here are of the non-returning type used in war and for hunting large animals.

Fighting boomerang (below) from the Brisbane area on the Eastern coast of Australia. It is made of dark wood with deeply incised wavy lines, and less deep diagonal shading. (Museum of Mankind, London.)

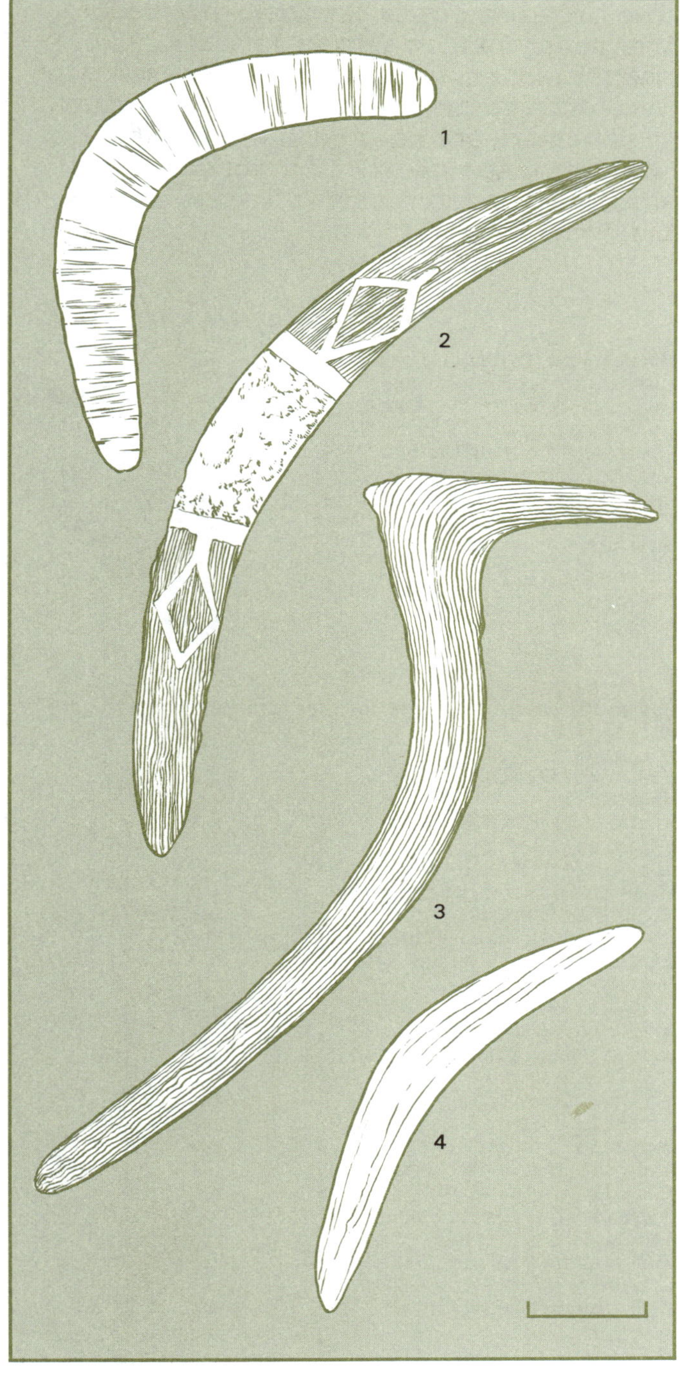

Aborigine (above) of Australia, about to throw a "beaked" war boomerang. All fighting boomerangs are designed to fly straight, although turning end-over-end. They wound by stunning, or by cutting with a sharpened edge. They do not return to the thrower even if the target is missed.

War boomerangs (above) All are of Australian Aboriginal origin.
1 Sharply curved boomerang with plain wood finish, from Victoria.
2 Red-painted boomerang with a design in white ; from Queensland.
3 "Beaked" boomerang, uncolored, but with longitudinal shallow fluting.
4 Small boomerang with plain wood finish, from the Swan River area of Western Australia.

Edged throwing-weapons

The broad category of edged throwing-weapons includes a great variety of shapes, some of which are recognizable to Western eyes as axes or knives, but many of which are unlike any other sort of weapon. The richest variety of edged throwing-weapons comes from West and Central Africa.

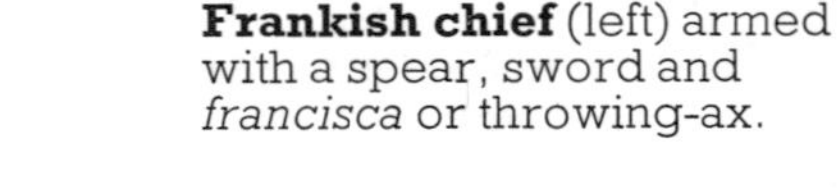

Frankish chief (left) armed with a spear, sword and *francisca* or throwing-ax.

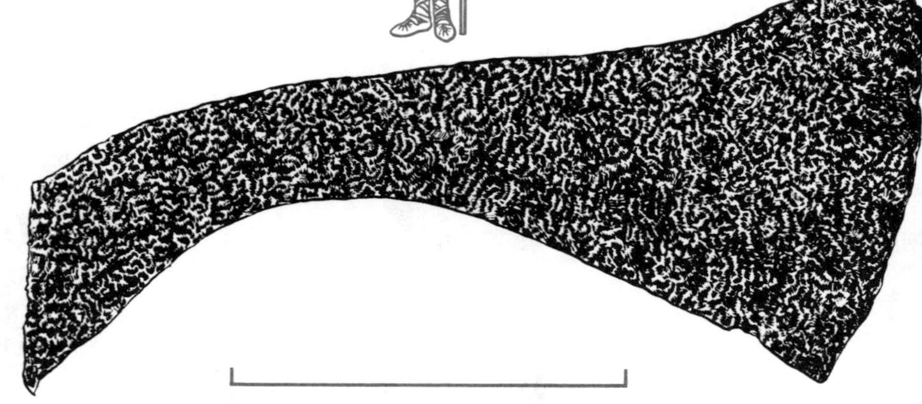

Francisca (right), the iron throwing-ax of the Franks, who inhabited parts of what is now France and West Germany in about the 5th and 6th centuries AD. This example was found in Kent, England. (British Museum, London.)

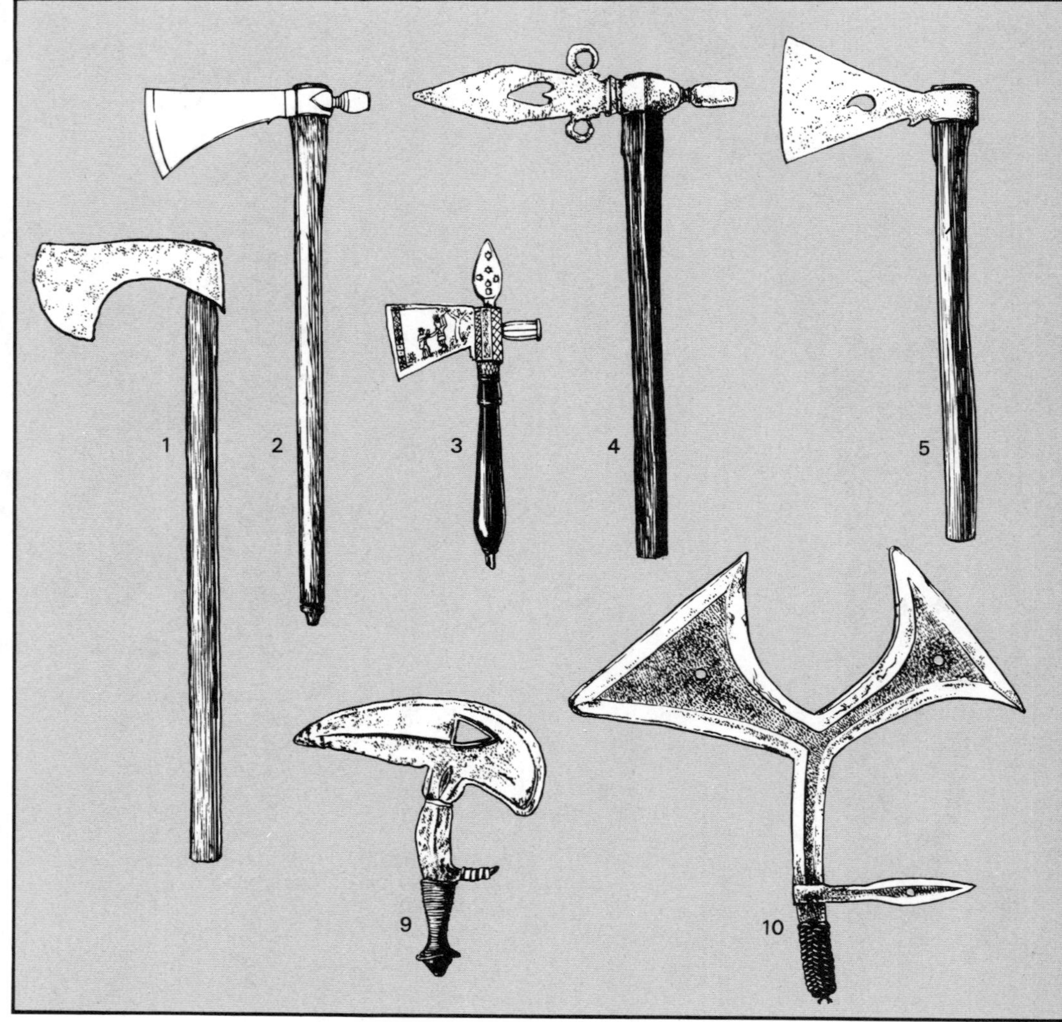

Edged throwing-weapons (right)
1 *Francisca* of the 5th or 6th century AD found on the Isle of Wight, off the South coast of England. (British Museum, London.)
2 Iron-bladed pipe-tomahawk made in Britain for the North American trade in the 19th century, combining an ax and a tobacco pipe.
3 Tomahawk of European make with Indian decoration, 18th or early 19th century.
4 "Spontoon" type pipe-tomahawk, so-called because of its similarity to the pole-arm of that name.
5 Iron trade tomahawk recovered from the Sisseton Sioux; 19th century.
6 Throwing-knife from the Darfur region of the Sudan.
7 Throwing-knife from NE Nigeria.
8 Throwing-knife from the region of the Congo river.
9 "Bird's head" throwing-knife of the Kota and Fang people of Gabon.
10 Throwing-knife from The Central African Empire.
11 *Chakram* or war-quoit of the Sikhs of the Punjab region of NW India.
12 Another, smaller, *chakram*, of the 19th century.

Throwing-knife (right) of the Bwaka people of central Africa, made of steel, engraved, and bound with leather at the grip. Many-pointed throwing-knives of extravagant shape are found widely in Africa. In flight they turn about the center of gravity and can cut or pierce at almost any attitude of impact.

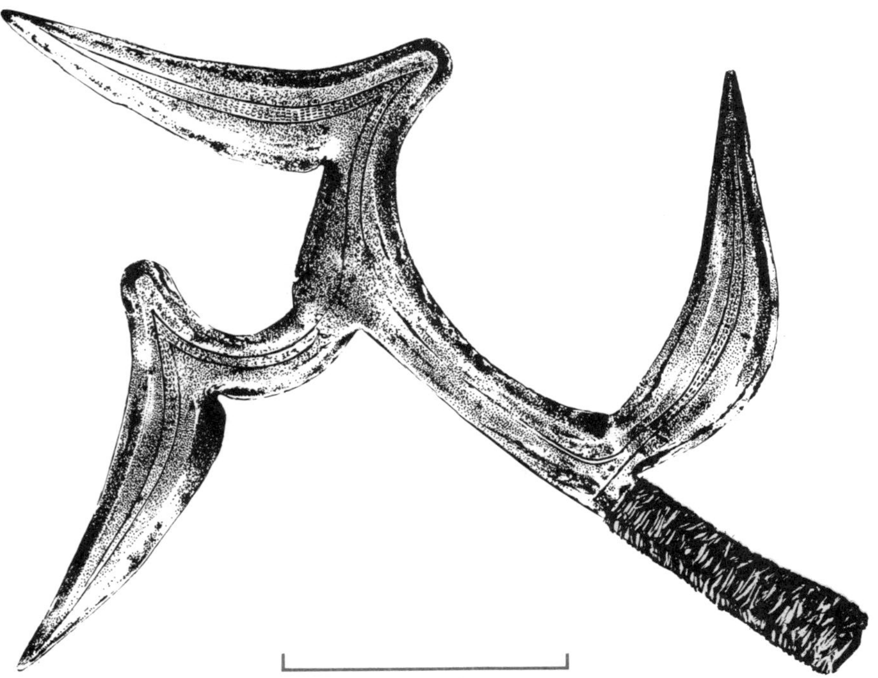

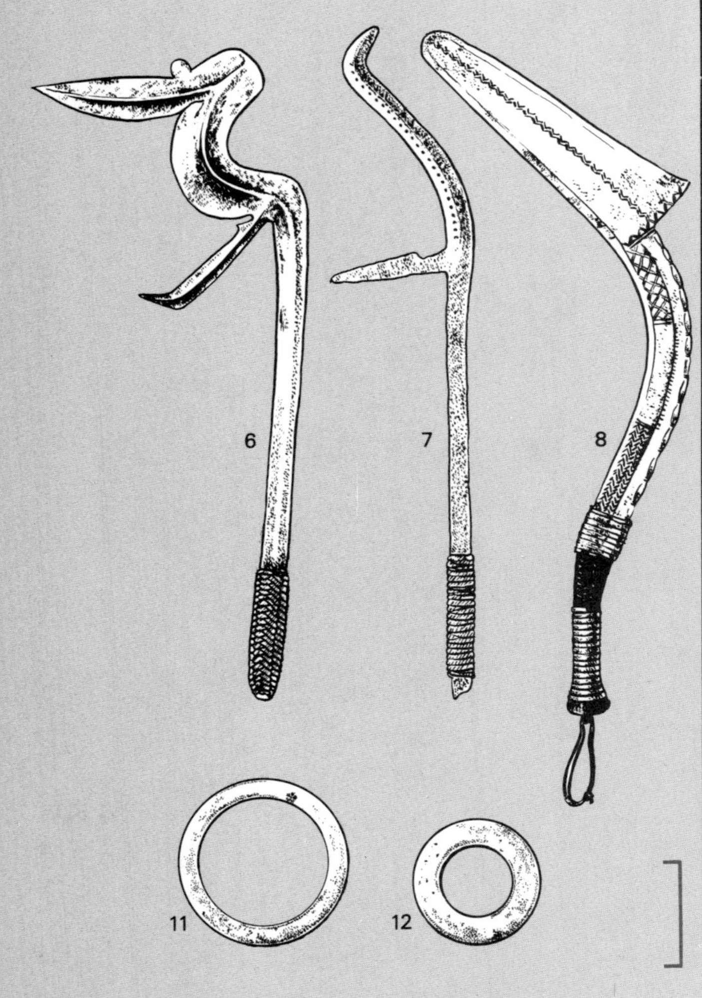

Chakram (above) or war-quoit, a thin, razor-sharp steel ring, once the characteristic weapon of the Sikhs. This example has inlaid gold decoration and dates from the 19th century. (Wallace Collection, London.)
The *chakram* is said to have been thrown as shown (left), by being whirled around the index finger before release.

Throwing-spears

Under this heading we survey the variety of long, pointed throwing weapons, of which the most important is the universally familiar spear. Their form and functioning is simple ; the long shaft ensures that the sharp tip is delivered point first, and its additional weight serves to increase the kinetic energy behind the blow. Spears that are not necessarily thrown will be found in Chapter 1.

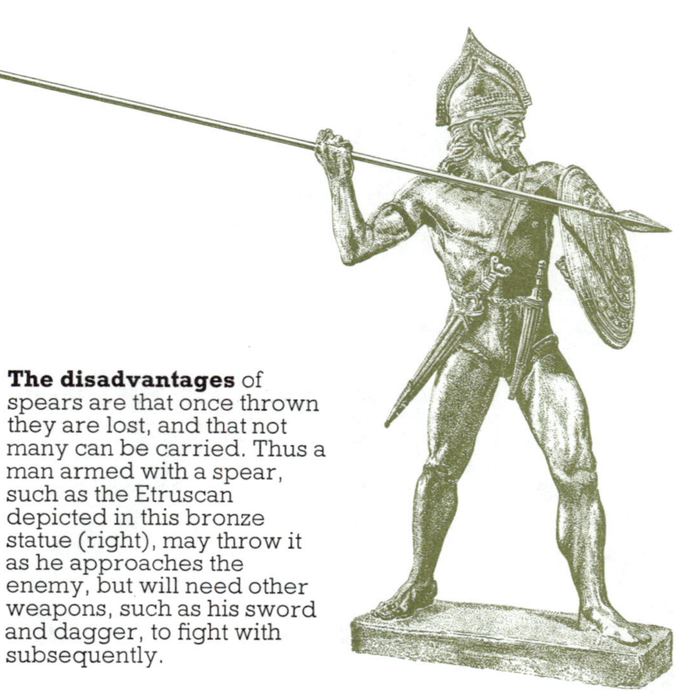

The disadvantages of spears are that once thrown they are lost, and that not many can be carried. Thus a man armed with a spear, such as the Etruscan depicted in this bronze statue (right), may throw it as he approaches the enemy, but will need other weapons, such as his sword and dagger, to fight with subsequently.

The size range (above) of throwing-spears is great. Most are in excess of the height of the user (**a**). However, there also exist shorter varieties (**b**), sometimes called javelins or darts, from about one foot (0.3m) in length

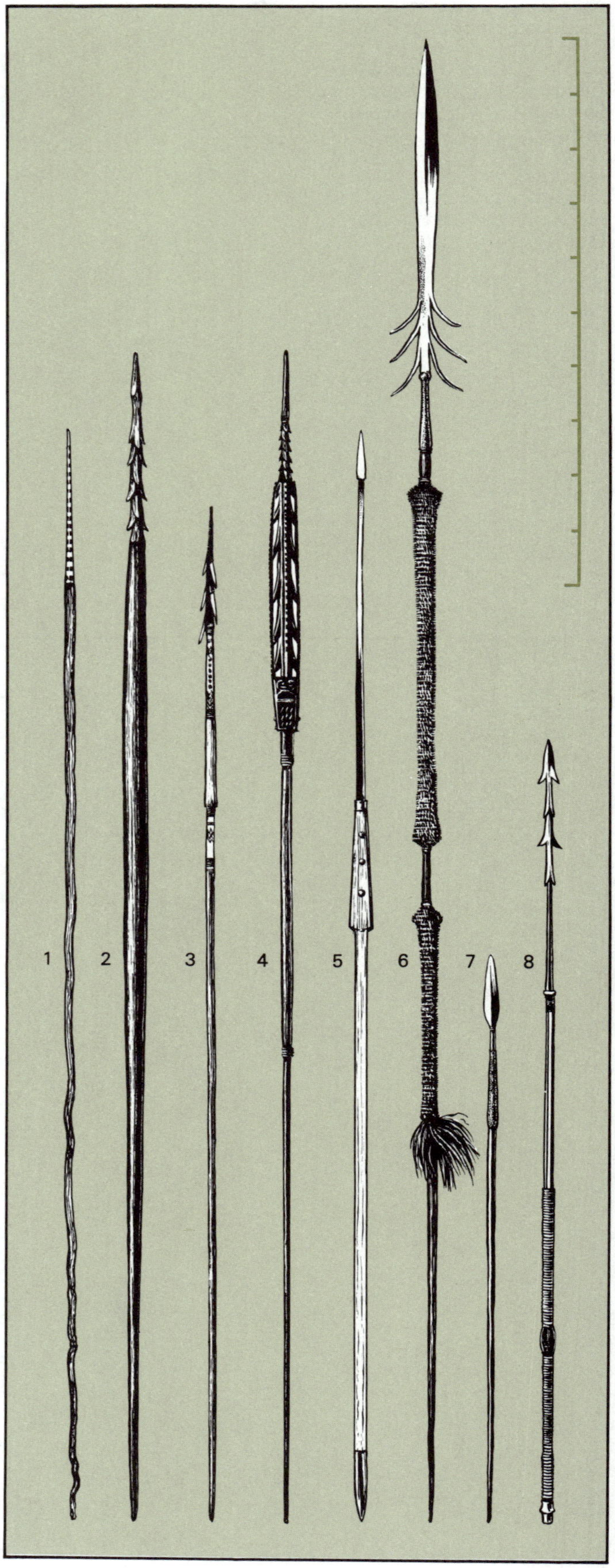

Throwing-spears (right)
1 Simple, one-piece wooden spear from Western Australia.
2 Highly-finished one-piece Hawaiian wooden spear, a relic of the fight in which Captain Cook was killed in 1779. (Museum of Mankind, London.)
3 Spear with barbs of bone, from the Solomon Islands.
4 Spear with carved and pierced wooden point, from the Solomon Islands.
5 Reconstruction of a Roman heavy javelin or *pilum*, with a long, iron point. 1st century AD.
6 Iron-bladed spear of the Naga people of Assam, the shaft decorated with colored hair.
7 Iron-bladed Zulu throwing-spear, from South Africa. Late 19th century.
8 Barbed, iron-bladed spear of the Mobati people of Zaire.

1 2 3 4 5 6 7 8

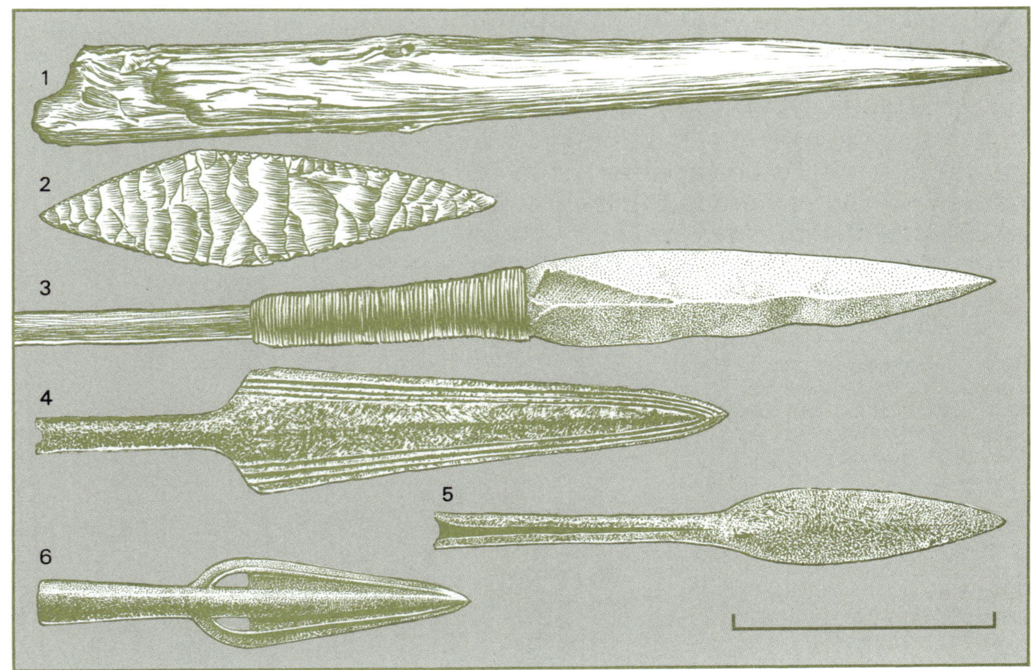

Spear points (right) A selection of different materials and attachment methods.
1 Broken-off point of a wooden spear of the Early Paleolithic Age, from Essex, England.
2 Flint spear point of the Late Stone Age, from France.
3 Stone point glued and lashed to a wooden shaft. Australian Aboriginal.
4 Bronze spearhead with tang for insertion into split top of shaft.
5 Hammered copper socketed spearhead from ancient Egypt.
6 Cast bronze socketed spearhead with loops for lashing to the shaft. Late Bronze Age Europe.

Short, spear-like weapons (right)
a All-wooden javelin from Hawaii.
b Turkish *jarid*, an all-steel short javelin.
c Japanese *nageyari*, a short throwing-spear.
d Japanese *uchi-ne*, a fighting dart with feather flights.

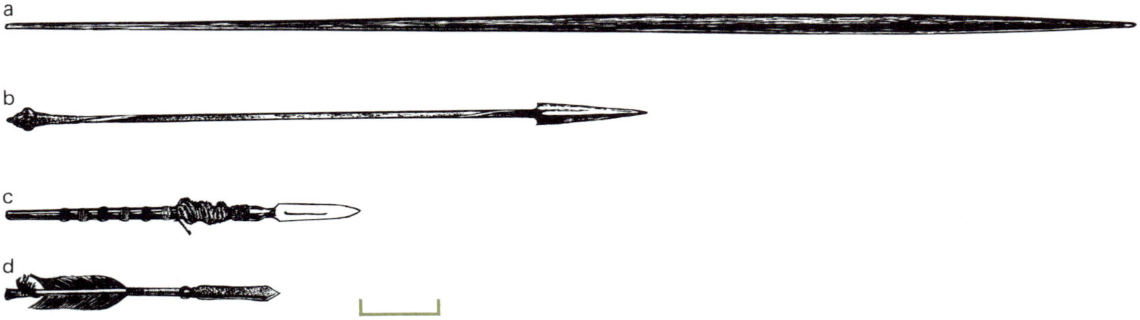

Spear-throwers (right) These devices have been used to assist spear-throwing at various periods in the Americas, Asia, the Pacific Islands, Australia and prehistoric Europe.
1 Australian Aboriginal spear-thrower or *woomera*, of wood.
2 Bone spear-thrower carved with a blackcock, from prehistoric France.

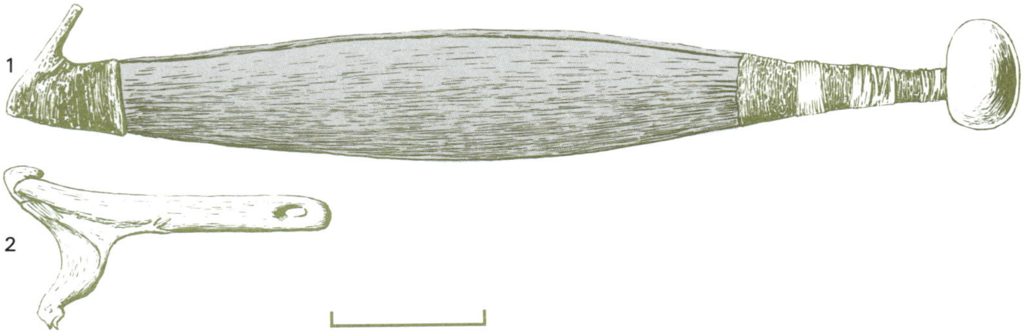

Using a spear-thrower (right)
a One end of the device is gripped in the throwing hand, and the spear laid on top with its butt-end against the small hook.
b On bringing the arm forward in the act of throwing, the device acts as a lever to give added momentum to the spear.

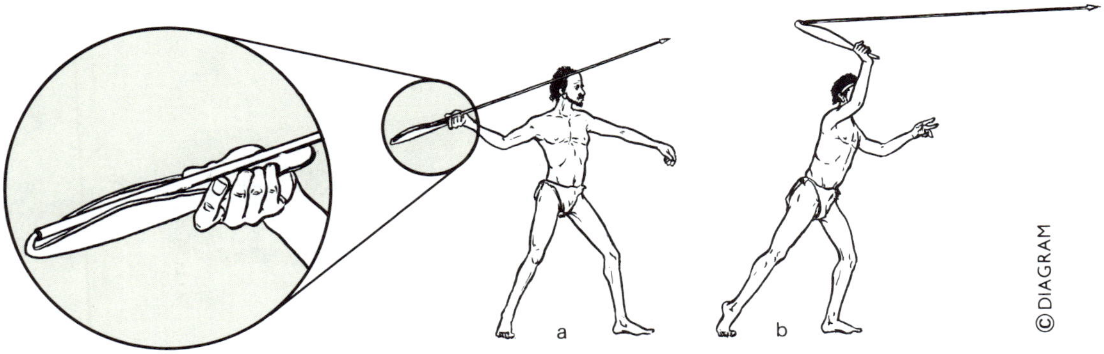

Hand grenades 1

The hand grenade is the most important form in which hand-thrown missiles survive in military use. It was known in the 16th century, and was in general use from the late 17th to the early 19th century. It was revived in the Russo-Japanese War of 1904, and came into its own in the trench warfare of 1914-18. We discuss anti-personnel grenades first, followed by the more specialized types.

Grenadier (left) of the 18th century, performing one of the motions in the grenade-throwing drill. He is blowing on the lighted end of a slow-match, to increase the spark, before using it to ignite a rope fuze protruding from the grenade. Simple, time-fuzed iron grenades were used, especially in siege warfare, throughout the 18th century.

Types of grenade (right) The main categories of hand-grenade now in use are the following.
1 Anti-personnel which may wound by fragmentation, blast, or both.
2 Specialized grenades, such as incendiary, smoke and anti-riot gas.
3 Anti-tank which may work by blast, or by the shaped charge effect (see p.91).

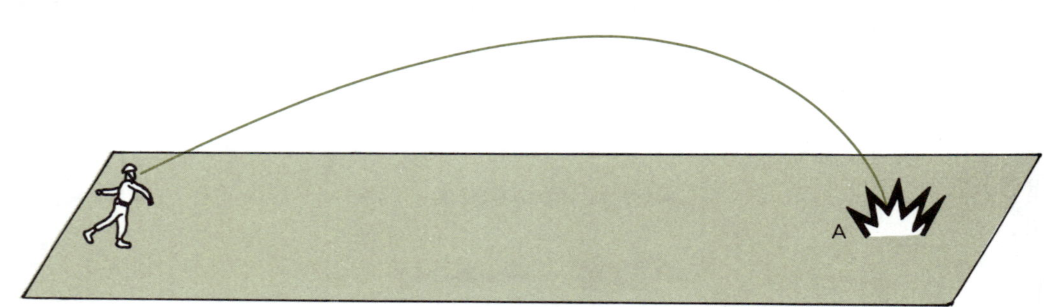

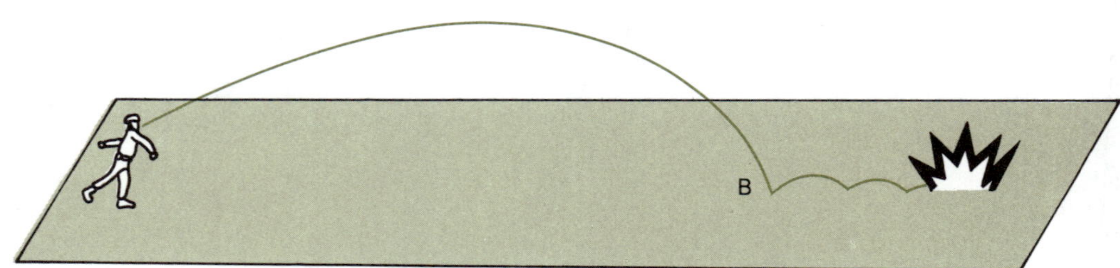

Fuzes (right) Whatever the effect of a grenade when it explodes, it may be fitted with either an impact fuze or a time fuze.
A Impact fuzes or percussion fuzes are designed to detonate a grenade as it strikes the ground. The advantages are that the grenade cannot be avoided or thrown back by an opponent before it explodes, and it will not roll back toward the user if thrown uphill.
B Time fuzes are designed to detonate a grenade after a pre-set delay, regardless of when it may hit the ground. They are more common than impact fuzes as they are generally safer to use. The fuze may be initiated in one of several ways. A four or five second delay is now usually considered best.

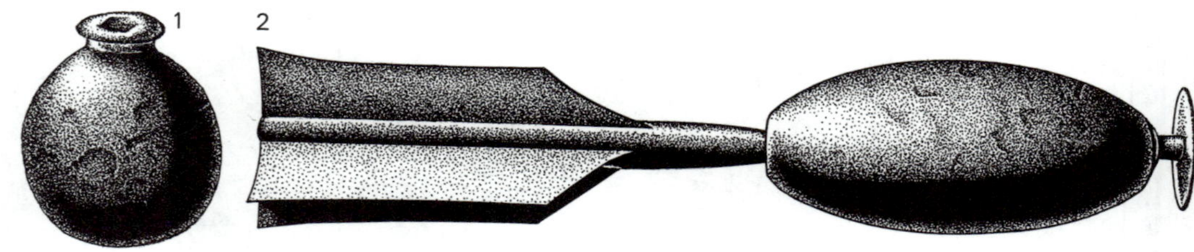

Early hand grenades (right)
1 Iron grenade found at Fort Ticonderoga, typical of the time-fuzed grenades used in the 18th century. (Washington's Headquarters, Newburgh, New York.)
2 Ketchum's grenade, a fin-stabilized percussion-fuzed type, used quite extensively in siege warfare during the American Civil War.

French "racket" grenade (right) improvised by troops on the Western Front in early 1915. It consists of some high explosive and a length of fuze tied to a wooden handle. Lengths of heavy gauge wire have been added to increase the fragmentation effect. In WW1, front-line troops soon recognized the usefulness of grenades in trench warfare.

Improvised hand grenades (right)
1 Blast grenade of 1914-15 consisting of a stick of high explosive (HE) with a length of fuze, to be lit with a match.
2 British "jam tin" grenade of early 1915, filled with "gun cotton" explosive and metal scraps to create a fragmentation effect.
3 British blast grenade of 1914-15 with a fuze lit by a friction igniter.
4 French "nail bomb" of 1914-15, with large nails bound round a stick of explosive.
5 German "racket" grenade of early 1915, with an old tobacco tin filled with HE and wired to a wooden handle.
6 "Nail bomb" as used by rioters in Northern Ireland in the early 1970s.

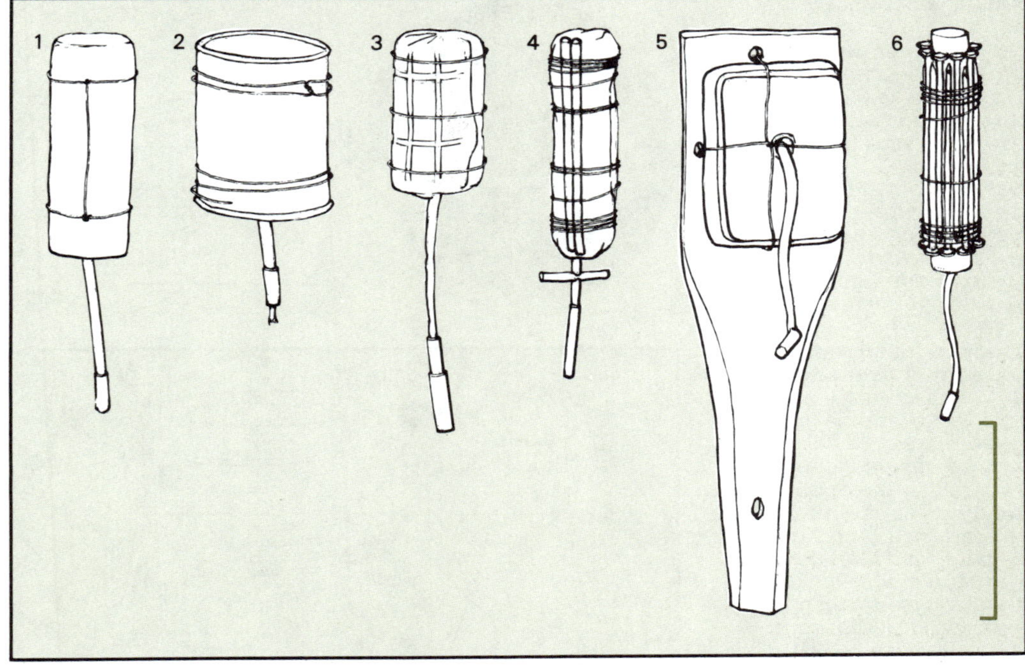

Tactical advantages (right) Hand grenades are much used for fighting in confined spaces such as trenches (**a**), when attacking bunkers (**b**) or in street-fighting (**c**). A grenade can often be thrown in without the thrower being exposed to rifle-fire. On detonation, the confined space is instantly filled with blast and lethal fragments.

Types of anti-personnel grenade (right) Blast or "offensive" grenades (**A**) have a limited danger-zone, and can thus be used safely by troops attacking in the open. However, the splinters from fragmentation or "defensive" grenades (**B**) can kill or wound at ranges beyond the maximum throwing distance. Thus the thrower needs protective cover.

Hand grenades 2

Percussion or impact fuzes (right) are of three main kinds. A direct action fuze (**A**) has a plunger which hits the ground first and is forced back against a detonator. A graze fuze (**B**) has an internal weight which is thrown forward on to the detonator when the grenade hits the ground. Both these types must land point first, unlike an "all-ways" fuze (**C**).

Hanes' Excelsior (right), an all-ways percussion grenade, was patented during the American Civil War, but was too dangerous to see wide use. It is shown ready for use (**1**) and open for priming (**2**). The theory was that, on hitting the ground, at least one cap would be crushed between the outer case and a nipple and explode, igniting the powder in the inner sphere.

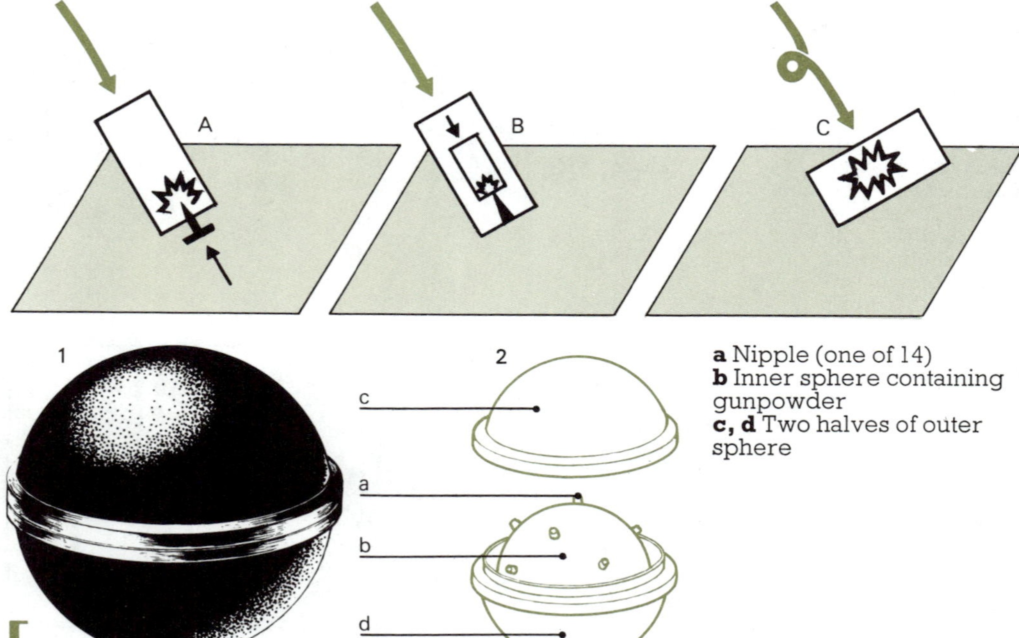

a Nipple (one of 14)
b Inner sphere containing gunpowder
c, d Two halves of outer sphere

Impact-fuzed anti-personnel grenades (right)
1 French grenade of 1915 fitted with a graze fuze. The pear-like shape helped ensure impact base-first, assisted by the opened safety lever and a small drogue on a cord.
2 Italian SRC Modello 35 grenade of WW2. This had an all-ways impact fuze.
3 British No1 Mk2 hand grenade of 1908-1915. This was similar to the No2 grenade (see opposite page) except that it had a direct-action fuze. The No1 Mk1 was similar but had a longer handle.
4 Czechoslovakian RG4, a modern offensive grenade with an all-ways impact fuze.
5 US M68 impact fragmentation hand grenade. This has the latest of impact fuzes. An electrical impact mechanism is armed 1-2sec after throwing. If this fails, a pyrotechnic time-delay takes over and detonates after 3-7sec.

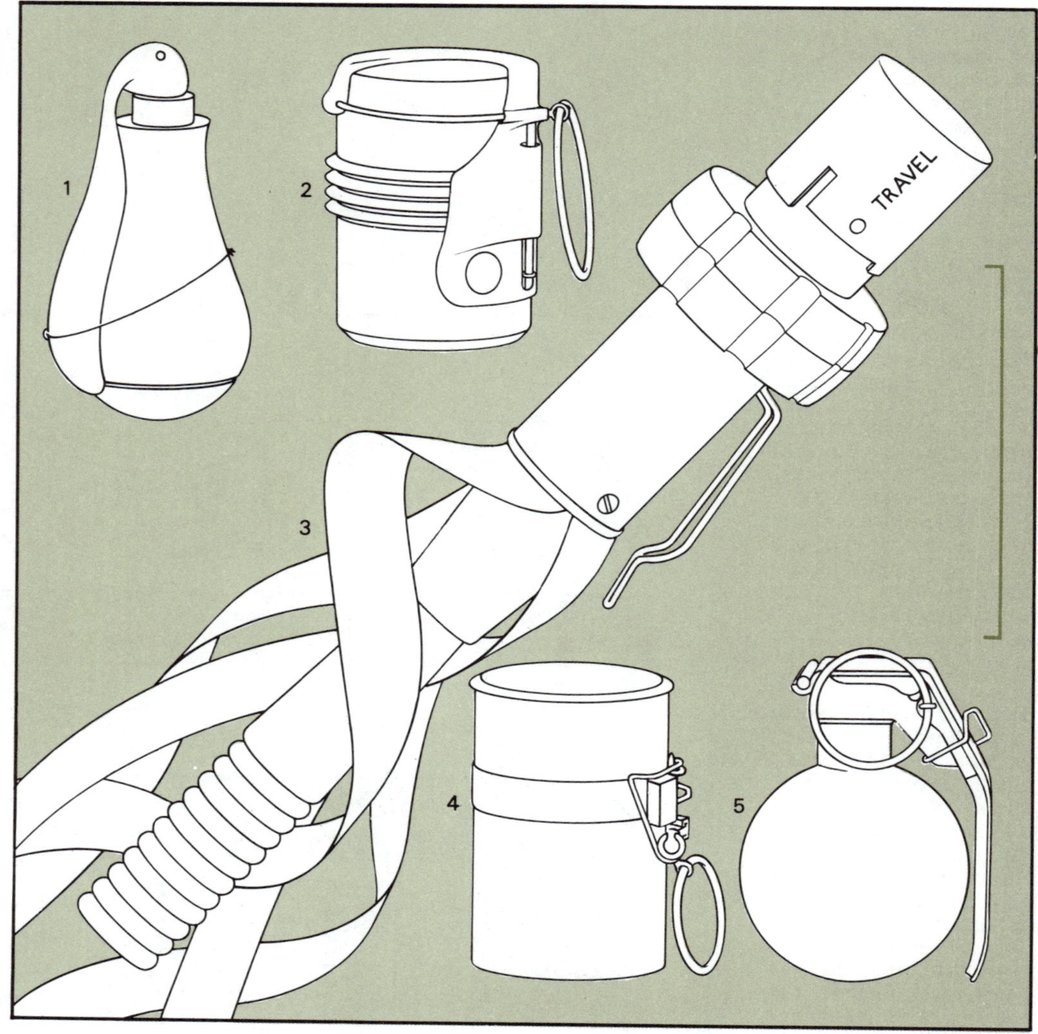

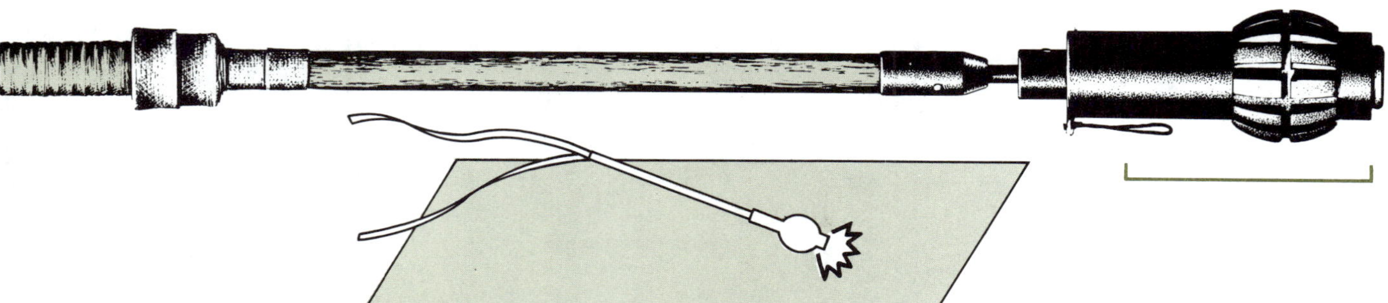

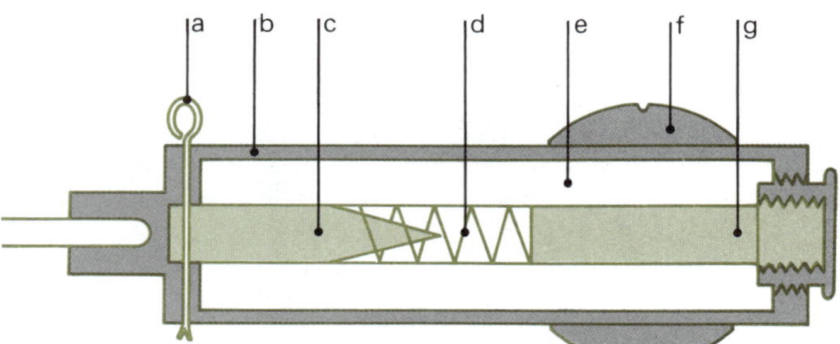

British No2 or Hale's percussion grenade (above and right) of 1914. The forward position of the heavy iron fragmenting sleeve, and the cloth streamers that unwound in flight, made sure the grenade hit the ground point first (above right), so setting off the graze fuze. Later models had shorter handles for use in trenches.

a Safety pin and ring
b Sheet brass body
c Inertial striker
d Creep spring
e Explosive filling
f Iron fragmenting sleeve
g Detonator

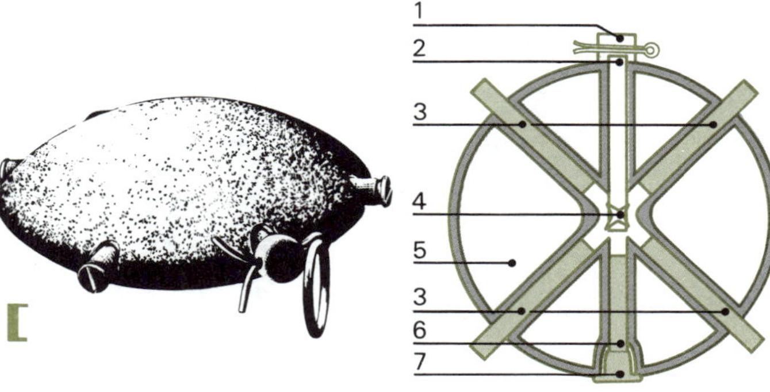

German discus grenade (right) of WW1, an early all-ways percussion type. To use, the safety pin and cap were removed and the grenade thrown like a discus. In flight, the safety pellet fell out, so exposing the points of the central star. On hitting the ground edge-on, the rearmost striker pellet was thrown against the star and exploded the grenade.

1 Safety cap held by pin
2 Safety pellet
3 Four striker pellets
4 Star with four points
5 HE filling
6 Detonator
7 Screwed plug

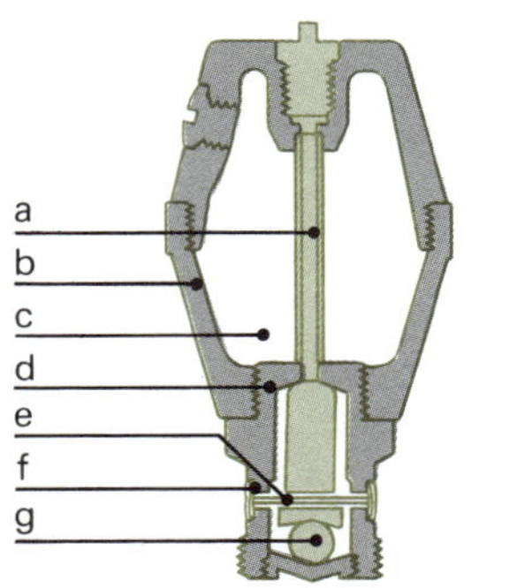

British No69 grenade (right) of WW2. This was an offensive type with an all-ways percussion fuze, and made of black "bakelite" plastic. To use, the safety cap was unscrewed to reveal a weighted tape wound around the fuze. The tape fell away in flight, pulling out a pin and so arming the fuze. This held a heavy ball which set it off however the grenade fell.

a Detonator
b Light plastic body
c HE filling
d Fuze body
e Pin
f Tape with lead weight
g Metal ball

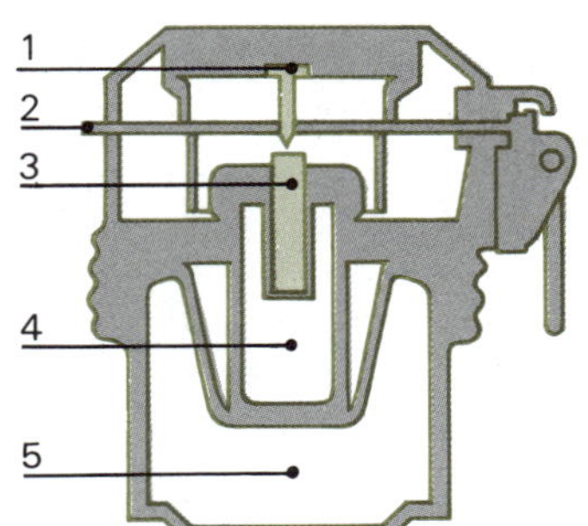

Czechoslovakian RG34 (right), a modern grenade with an all-ways impact fuze. To use, the safety ring is pulled, stripping off a metal tape around the body of the grenade. This action also withdraws a safety pin, allowing the striker to move to a central point over the primer, ready for ignition on impact with the ground.

1 Striker
2 Safety pin
3 Primer
4 Gaine or amplifying charge
5 Main HE filling

Hand grenades 3

Time-fuzed anti-personnel hand grenades (right)
1 German *Eiergranate* 39 or "egg grenade" of WW2. The button on top was the toggle for a pull-cord attached to a friction igniter.
2 French *Grenade á main offensive, OF* of WW2. A conventional finger-lever design (see the No36 or Mills Bomb, below).
3 US Mk2 or "pineapple" fragmentation grenade of WW2. This was the US Army's defensive grenade, an improvement on the British Mills Bomb.
4 Soviet M1914/30 grenade with a unique striker mechanism, worked by the long grip-lever protruding from the handle.
5 Communist Chinese fragmentation stick-grenade, used also by the Viet Cong in the Vietnam War. It functions like the German stick-grenade (see opposite page).
6 Soviet RG-42, a defensive grenade of WW2, thought to be still in use with Warsaw Pact reserve units.
7 British L2A1, the current anti-personnel grenade of the British Army. A pre-notched wire coil provides the fragments.
8 Dutch V40 "mini-grenade," the smallest hand grenade in current manufacture.

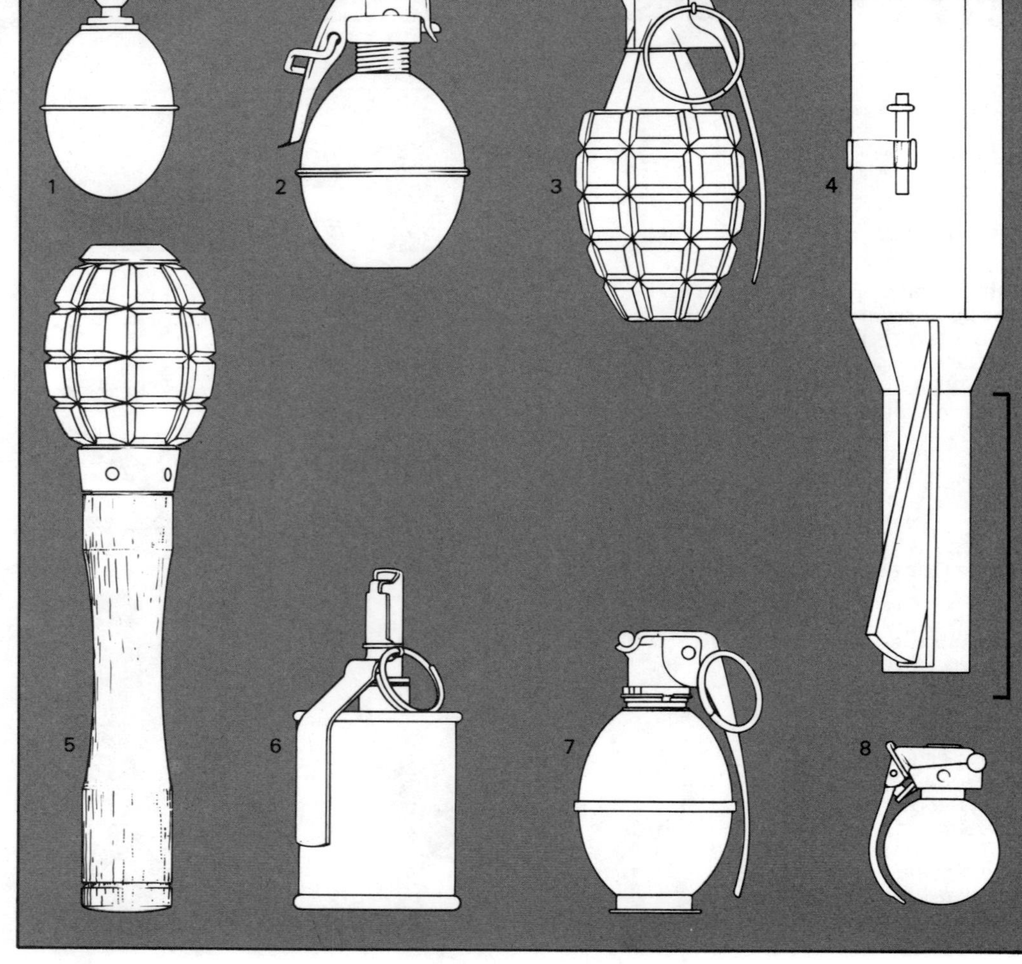

The British No36 grenade (below) was introduced in 1915 and known in WW1 as the Mills Bomb. It was a time-fuzed fragmentation grenade with a cast iron body and brass or zinc alloy fittings.

a Filler plug
b HE filling
c Striker and spring
d Cap
e Base plug
f Safety pin on ring
g Lever
h Detonator
i Time fuze

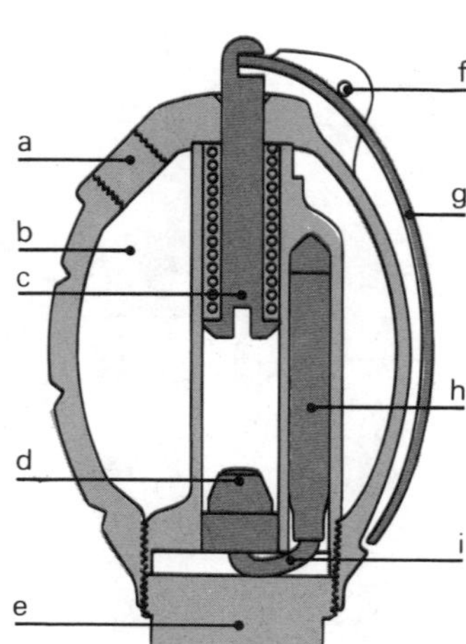

Functioning (right) of the No36 Grenade. The time fuze starts to burn only as the grenade leaves the thrower's hand. This system, using a finger lever, has been widely copied.
1 Immediately before throwing, the user grips the grenade so that the lever is pressed against the side, and pulls out the safety pin.
2 He throws the grenade, and as it leaves his hand the lever flies off as the striker spring forces the striker down on to the cap, so lighting the four-second time-fuze.

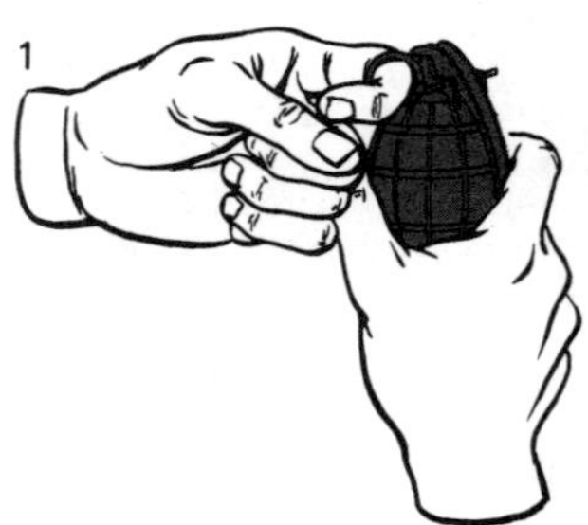

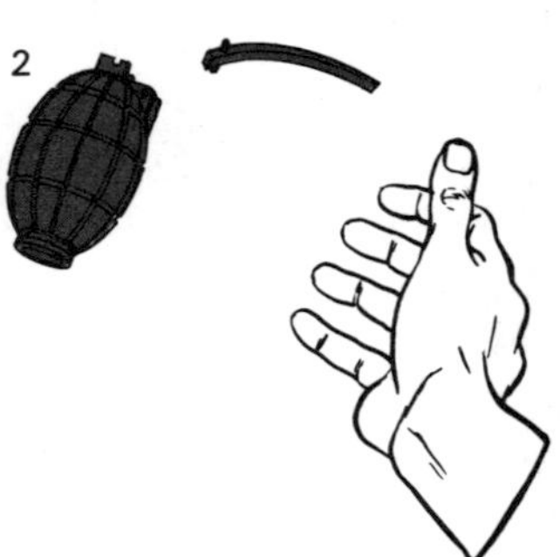

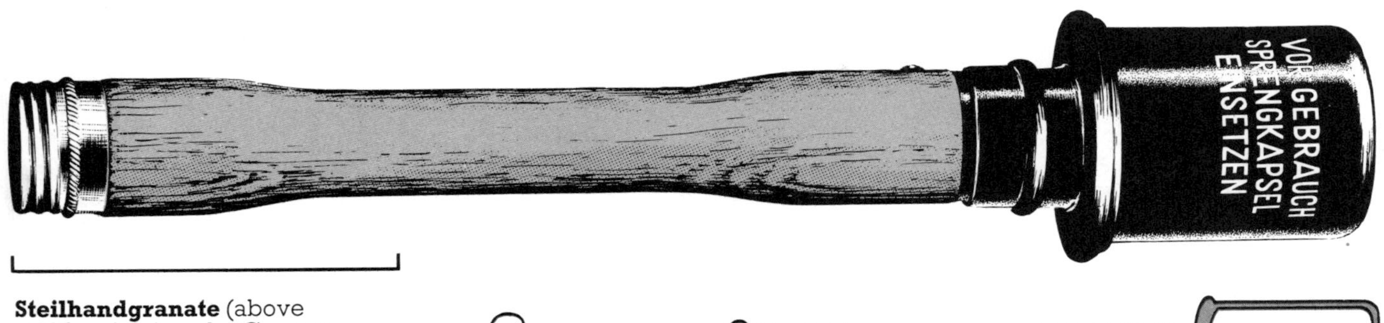

Steilhandgranate (above and far right) or the German stick-grenade was basically the same in both World Wars. It was a time-fuzed blast or offensive grenade. The fuze was ignited before throwing by removing the closing cap and pulling a cord (right) revealed inside the handle. There was a delay of four to five seconds before the explosion.

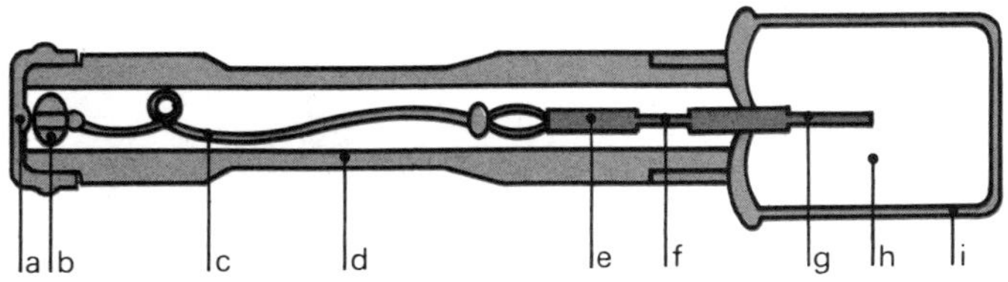

a Closing cap
b Porcelain toggle
c Cord
d Wooden handle
e Friction igniter
f Time-fuze
g Detonator
h HE filling
i Sheet metal casing

French "bracelet" grenade (far right) of 1915. This was a unique arrangement for igniting the time-fuze at the last possible moment. A leather leash connected to the primer was slipped over the wrist of the throwing hand and tightened (right). On throwing, the leash pulled out a friction wire, so lighting the time-fuze.

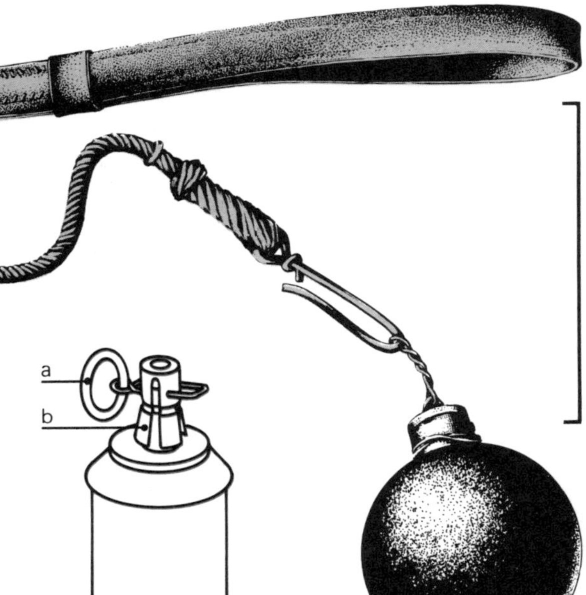

Japanese Type 97 grenade (center right) of WW2. Immediately before use, the ring (**a**) was pulled and a metal safety cap (**b**) fell away from the impact igniter which protruded from the end of the grenade. To start the time-fuze, this igniter was smashed down on any hard surface (right). The grenade was immediately thrown, and exploded 4-5sec later.

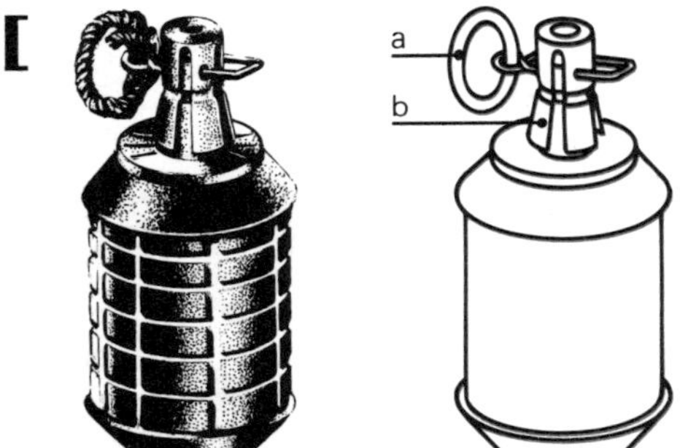

The DM 51 (right), a modern West German grenade. It functions in the same general way as the No36 grenade (see opposite), but has refinements typical of recent designs. It can be used as an offensive type (**1**), or a defensive type if the fragmentation sleeve (**2**) is slipped on. This is of hollow plastic, filled with about 3800 steel balls (**3**).

1 2 3

Hand grenades 4

Smoke and gas grenades (right) are both found in two forms. Some generate a steady pall of agent (**a**), which may be smoke for screening movement, or gas for suppressing riots. Others burst, giving an instantaneous effect. The commonest of these is the white phosphorus grenade (**b**) which combines smoke, incendiary and anti-personnel effects.

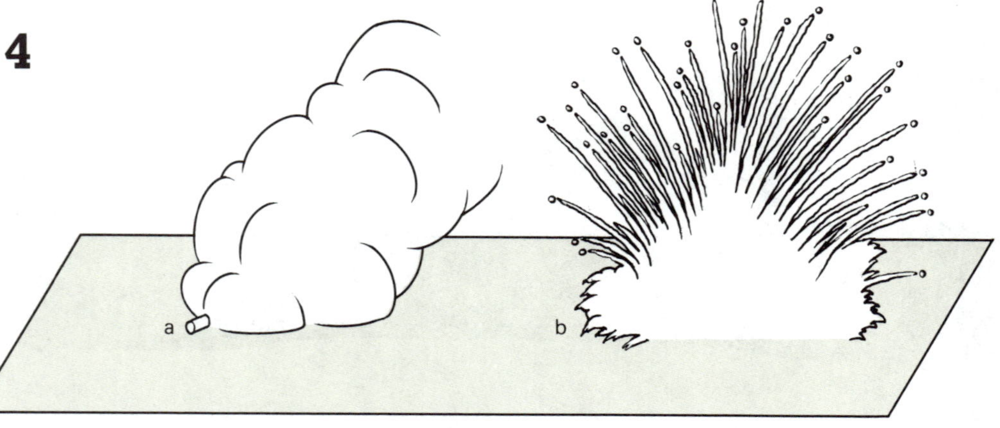

US M54 CS hand grenade (right and below), of the slow emission type. Ignition is by release of the finger lever (**a**) on throwing, and there follows an 8-12sec delay. As the fuel mixture and CS pellets (**b**) begin to burn, pressure-sensitive tape covering the emission holes (**c**) is ruptured, and lachrymatory gas is emitted for 15-35sec.

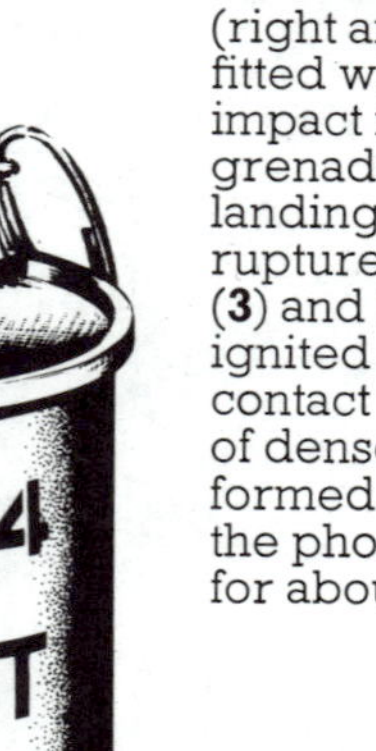

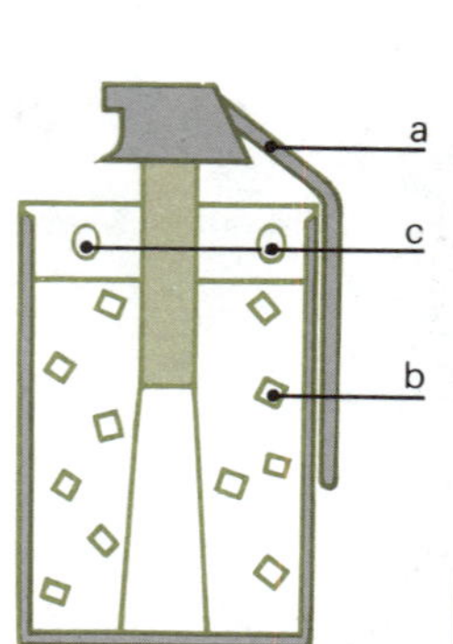

British No77 WP grenade (right and below) of WW2, fitted with the same all-ways impact fuze (**1**) as the No69 grenade (see p. 87). On landing, the detonator (**2**) ruptured the tin plate case (**3**) and the phosphorus (**4**) ignited spontaneously on contact with the air. A cloud of dense white smoke was formed instantaneously and the phosphorus burned for about a minute.

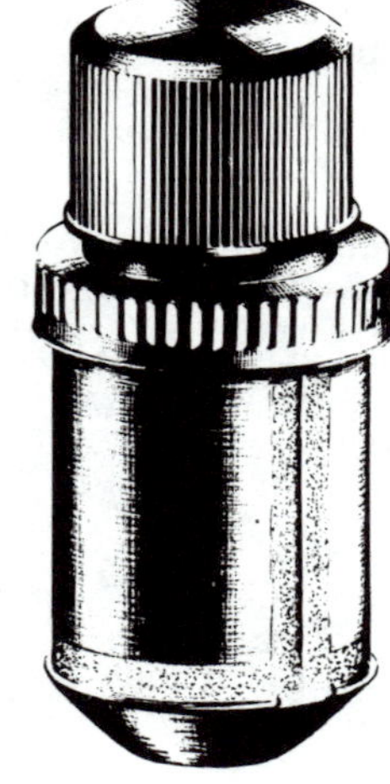

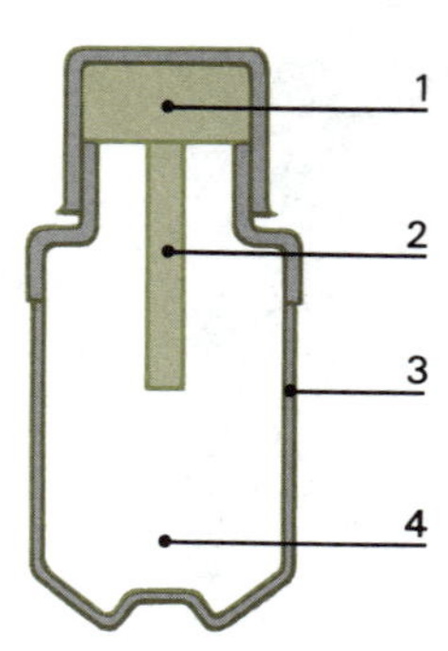

Smoke, gas and incendiary hand grenades (right)
a British No80 WP (white phosphorus) bursting smoke/incendiary grenade. In current use but now obsolescent. Time-fuzed.
b British L1 A2 CS gas grenade, as used against rioters in Northern Ireland in the early 1970s. Slow emission, time-fuzed.
c US TH3 AN-M14 incendiary grenade of the 1960s. Used for destroying equipment such as vehicles, it burned with intense heat for 30-45sec. Time-fuzed.
d DM19, a current West German bursting smoke/incendiary grenade, using a phosphorus filler. It has a pull-cord arming device, but detonation occurs when the body breaks, on impact with the ground.

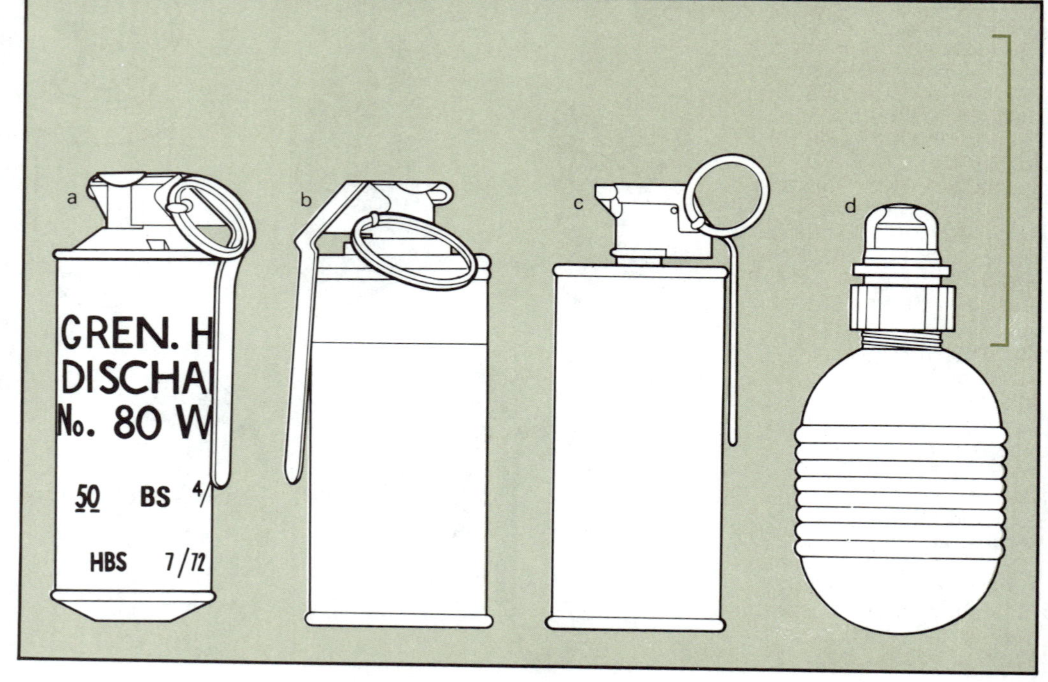

Anti-tank grenades (right) Early types relied on blast and were best directed against the tracks and sprocket wheels (**a**) of the tank. The use of the "shaped charge" effect in WW2 allowed main armor (**b**) to be penetrated. A charge with a conical cavity (**i**) focuses the heat of its explosion and sears a hole through several inches of armor plate (**ii**).

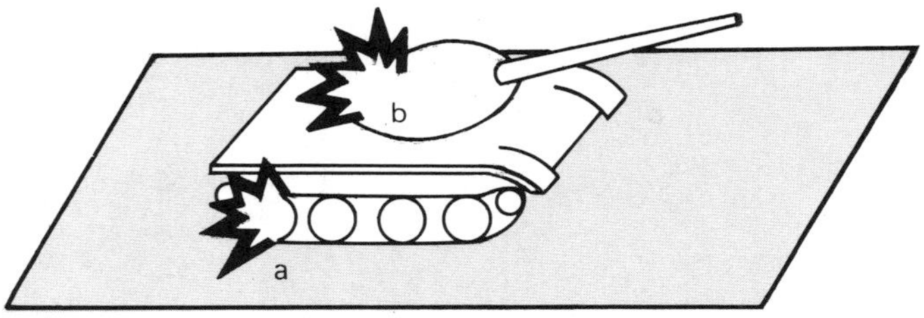

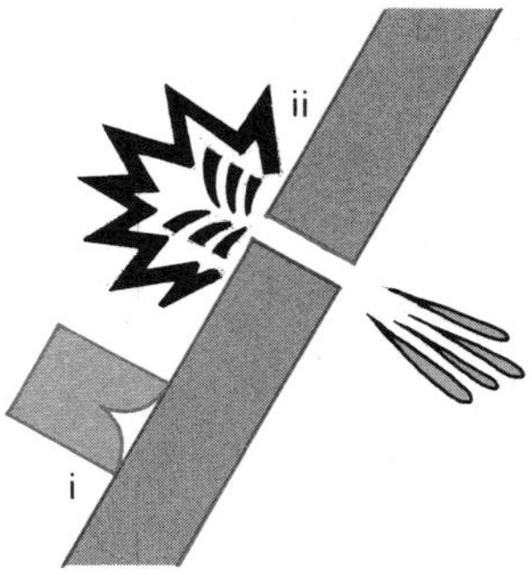

British No74 (ST) (right) or "sticky bomb" of early WW2. This was issued as shown at (**1**), and the two hemispherical covers had to be removed (**2**) before use, to reveal a spherical charge covered in strong adhesive. The handle was grasped, a safety pin pulled out and the grenade thrown. Five seconds later, while adhering to the tank, it exploded.

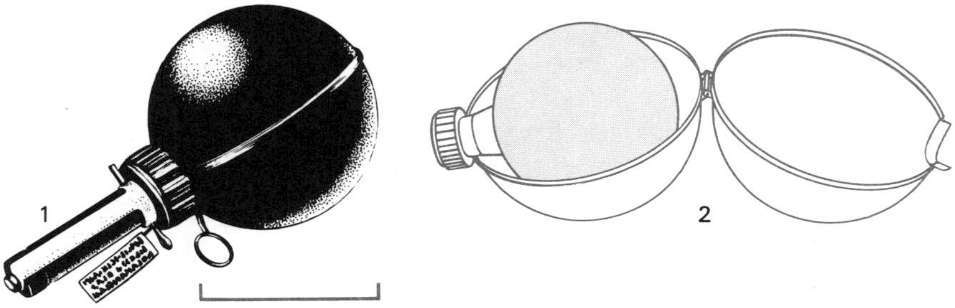

Japanese Type 3 anti-tank grenade (right) of WW2. This was a simple, shaped charge fitted with a graze fuze at the apex and a tail of hemp to make it fly and strike the tank at the correct attitude (far right).

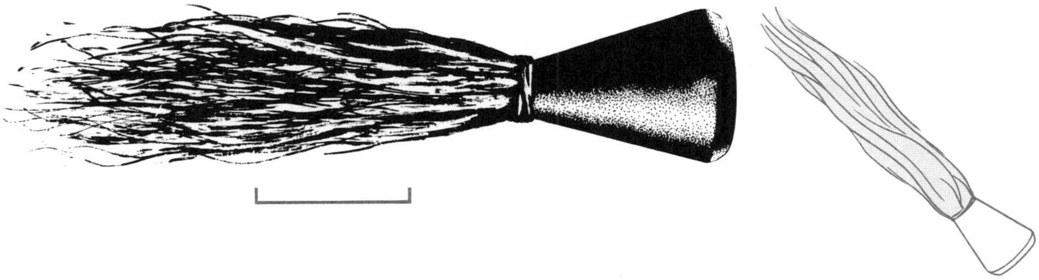

Panzerwurfmine (L) (right), a German weapon of WW2. This was a shaped-charge stick-grenade, fitted with an impact fuze and four canvas fins. Until throwing, these were kept folded by a cap on the end of the handle. On leaving the hand the cap slipped back and the fins sprang out, ensuring that the grenade flew head first (far right).

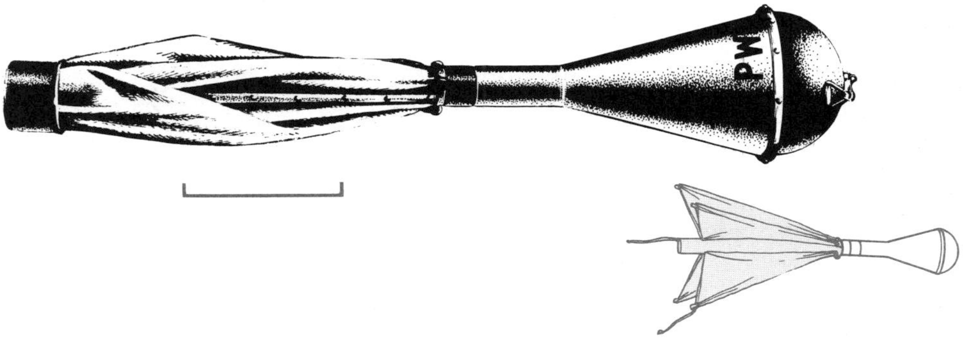

Soviet RPG-43 (right), another shaped-charge grenade, first used in WW2, and still used by Egypt in the 1973 war with Israel. On throwing, the conical tin drogue was forced back by a spring and dragged out two cloth strips as stabilizers (far right). A safety pin dropped out in flight, arming the graze fuze ready for impact.

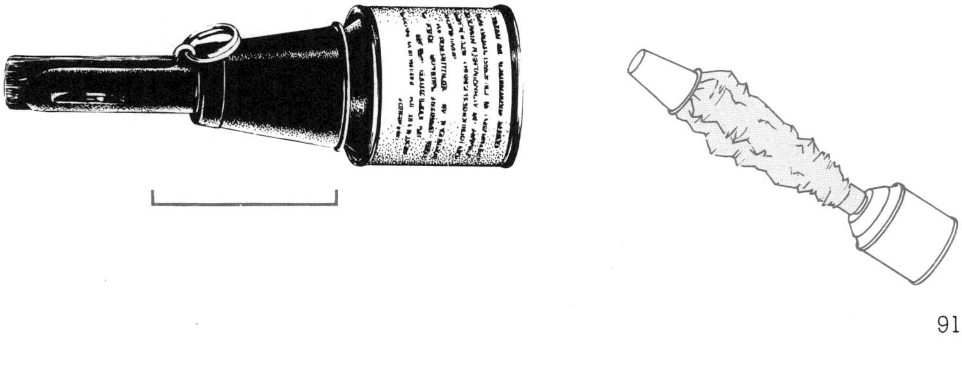

Chapter 3

HAND-HELD MISSILE-THROWERS

In this chapter we cover all weapons that propel a missile and that are fired from the hands or the shoulder without a support. They are personal weapons, wielded by one individual.

We begin with bows and crossbows. In these, although the energy used to throw the missile is still supplied by the firer, it is now stored in the spring of the bow, which was not the case with the simpler sling or spear-thrower.

Then follow the weapons which use gas or air-pressure to propel the missile. This category includes the simple blowpipe and the more complex airgun, although the latter is rarely seen in an effectively lethal form.

Next comes the most important category of hand-held missile-throwers : small arms. These are firearms, using explosive force to propel the missile. We have subdivided them according to the simplest functional distinctions, in a way that generally coincides with the historical development of firearms.

The chapter ends with some hand-held missile-throwers technically outside the category of small arms. These are mainly large-caliber weapons, now often used to destroy tanks. They are in a sense miniature artillery, and thus anticipate the mounted missile-throwers of Chapter 4.

Illustrations (near right) from a British Army small arms training manual of 1931. The two Ainu men in the photograph (far right) are armed with one of the oldest and one of the newest of hand-held missile-throwers : a bow and a semi-automatic shotgun.

Bows

A bow is a spring that stores and releases energy. By means of the bowstring, the slow strength of the archer, as he bends the bow, is rapidly transmitted to the arrow, propelling it farther and faster than it could be thrown by hand. This simple device, in its various forms, had the advantage in range and accuracy over all other hand-held missile throwers until long after the emergence of firearms.
We first examine bows that are drawn and released by hand (i.e. not crossbows), dividing them into types according to construction. There are several possible further subdivisions, but variations exist in the terminology used by reputable authorities.

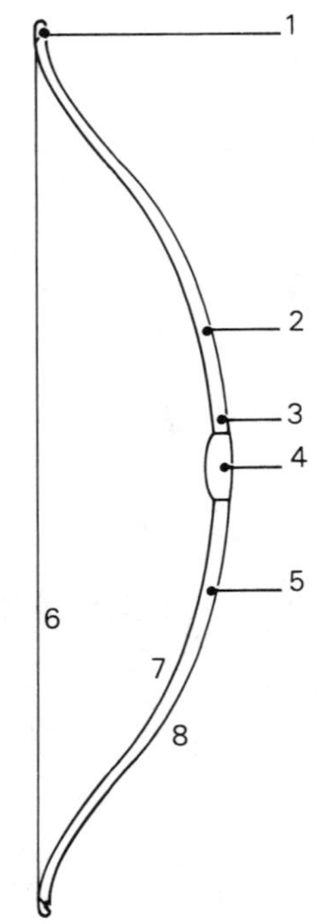

Basic parts of a bow (left)
1 Nock – a groove for the attachment of the bowstring at each end of the bow. It is sometimes on a separate piece of horn, fitted over the tip of the bow.
2 Upper limb
3 Arrow pass
4 Handle or grip
5 Lower limb
6 Bowstring
7 Belly – the side of the bow toward the archer.
8 Back – the side of the bow toward the target.

Bow profiles (right) Bows have many possible profile shapes, some of which are illustrated here.
a Curved
b Recurved
c Double-curved
d Asymmetric
e B-shaped
f Four-curved
g Triangular
h Joined angular

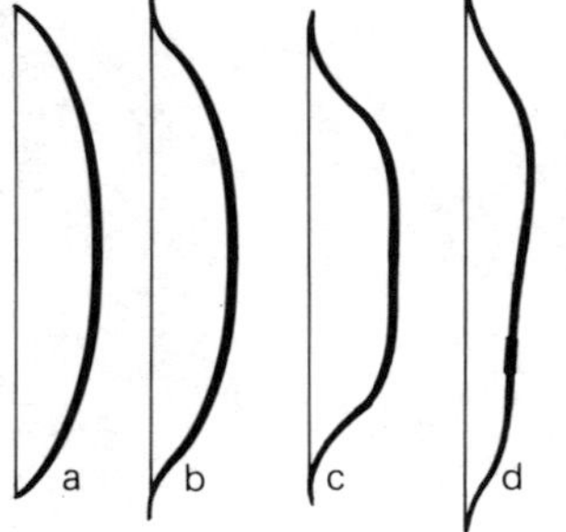

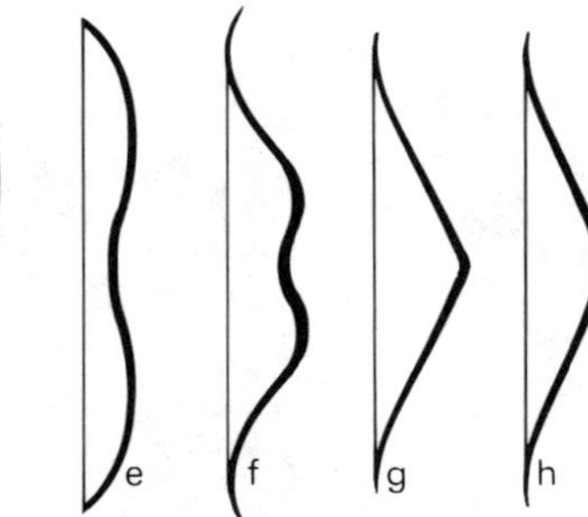

Comparative sizes (below) The 16th century drawing of a Mongol archer shows how short a composite bow can be. Drawn alongside for comparison is a Veddah from Sri Lanka, who wields a simple bow in excess of his own height.

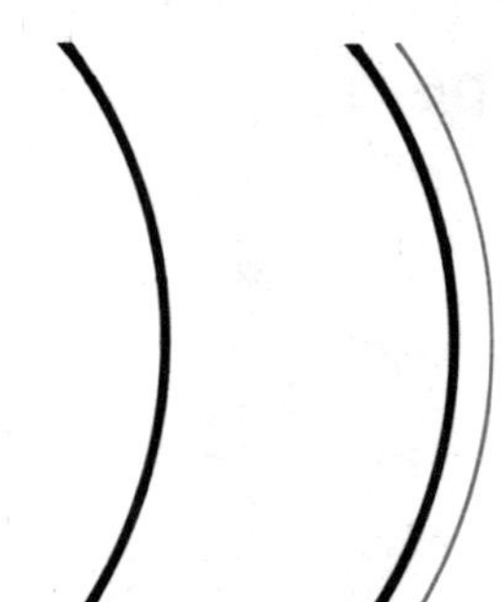

Types of bow construction (above)
1 Simple bows or self bows are those made from a single material, usually wood.
2 Backed bows A bow may be "backed" with a layer of resilient material—perhaps another kind of wood, or more often a layer of sinew—to strengthen the bow-stave.
3 Laminated bows These are made up from three or more layers of similar material — usually wood.
4 Composite bows These are made from three basic layers of dissimilar materials – most commonly wood, horn and sinew.
Note: The term "compound bows" is sometimes used. It includes both the laminated and composite types.

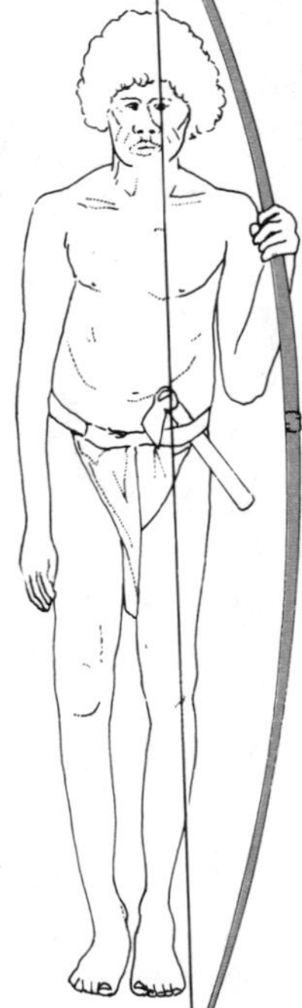

Stringing As shown in the illustration (right) longer bows are strung while standing; the archer places one tip on the ground and uses his body weight to help bend the bow. The detail from a Greek dish (below) shows a Scythian archer stringing his shorter composite bow while sitting, using the strength of his legs to bend the powerful bow.

Common methods of drawing (right)
a Primary draw, which can only be used with comparatively weak bows.
b Draw used in North America and SE Asia, using two fingers to hold the string below the arrow. Called the tertiary draw.
c Draw used in Europe from the Middle Ages onward, and in Africa and Asia, with two or three fingers gripping the string.
d Use of a thumb-ring, found in most parts of Asia from Turkey to China and Korea. The detail shows an archer's jade thumb-ring from India.

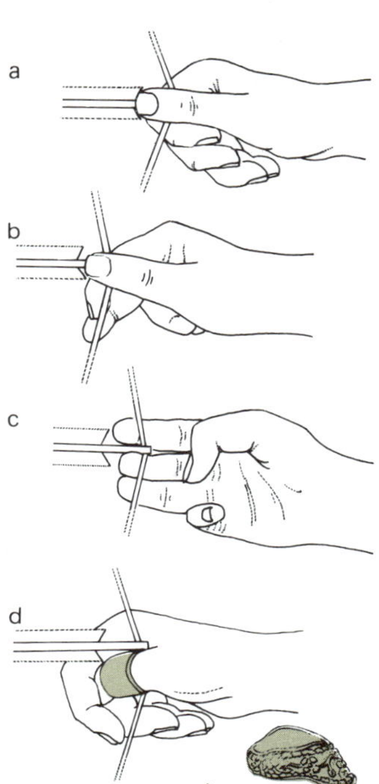

Bowstrings (right) Flax, hemp, ramie, silk, cotton and sinew are the materials most used. Shown are three unusual variants.
1 Detail of a Chinese bowstring consisting of stiff sections of tightly bound thread, jointed for flexibility.
2 Turkish bowstring, silk with sinew end loops.
3 Two strips of wood, for a Chinese pellet bow.

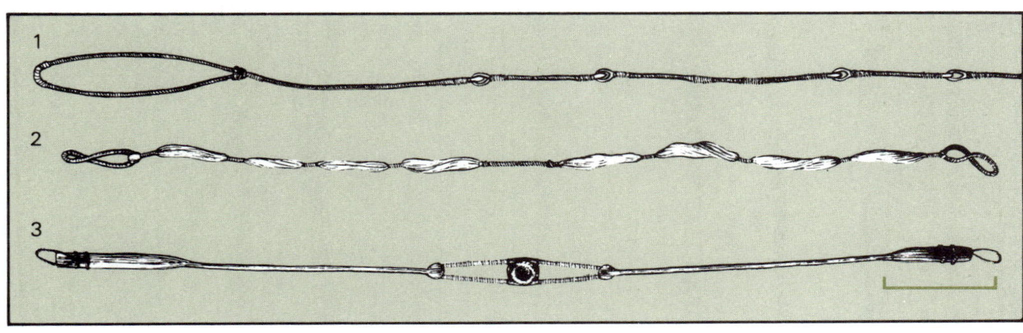

Accessories (right)
Common accessories for an archer are: a bowcase to carry and protect the bow when not in use; a quiver to carry the arrows; and a bracer, a pad worn on the inside of the left forearm to protect it from the released string.
a Japanese arrow-case of leather with gilt mounts.
b North American Indian combined bowcase and quiver of deerskin.
c Dutch bracer of ivory, 16th century.
d Bracer of bark, from an island off Queensland, Australia.

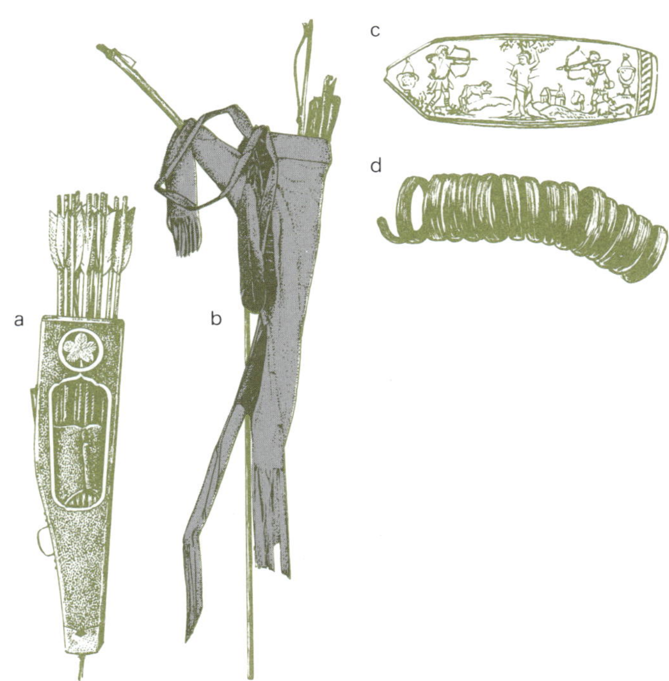

Tartar horseman (left) with a quiver of arrows and his bow in a bowcase slung over his shoulder.

Simple bows

Simple or self bows are those composed of a stave of only one material, usually wood. The earliest bows were of this type. At its best, as in the medieval Welsh and English longbow, its simplicity and rate of shooting outweighed, militarily, the advantages in power and accuracy of crossbows, at least in the open field.

Prehistoric use of bows
Cave paintings provide the oldest known illustrations of bows in use, c.10,000-c.5000BC. Although hunting scenes predominate, bows are also shown being used in combat (right, in a painting from Castellon, Spain). The detail (below) shows an archer about to draw his bow, gripping spare flighted arrows in the hand that holds the bow.

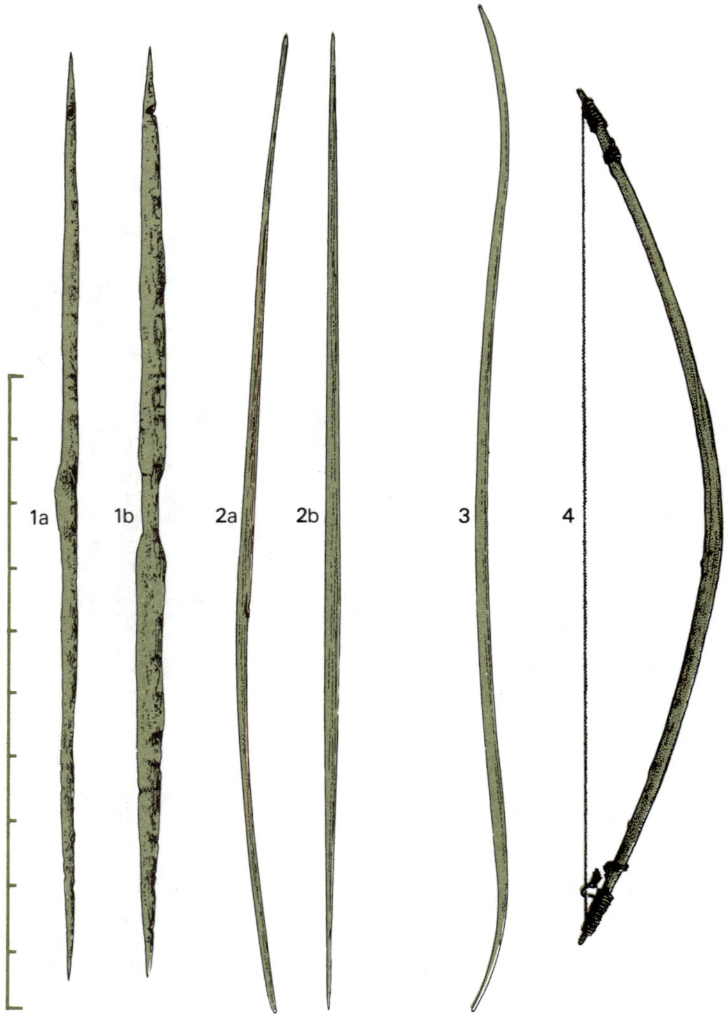

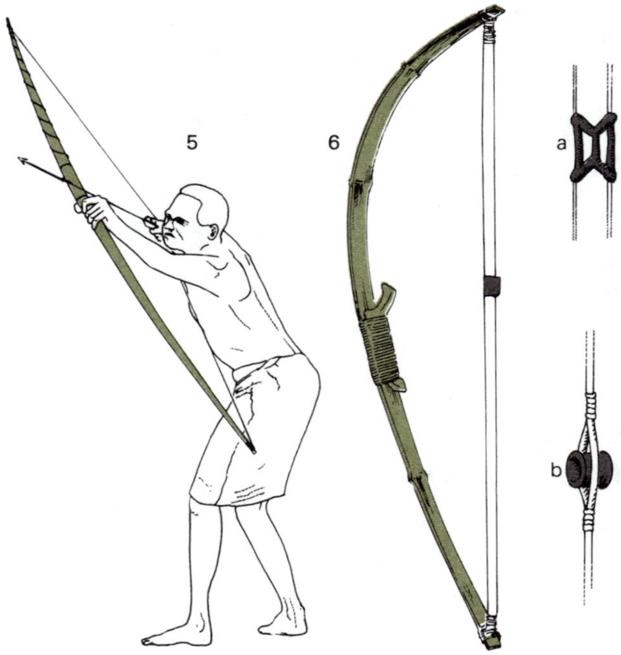

Ancient bows (above)
Although made of perishable wood, ancient bows have been found in a remarkable state of preservation.
1 Flat bow, thought to be of the late Mesolithic period (c.6000BC), found preserved in a bog at Holmegaard, Denmark. Side (**a**) and back (**b**) views of the unstrung bow are illustrated here.
2 Oak bow, found in peat at Viborg in Denmark. Dates from the late Stone Age, c.2000-c.1500BC. Shown here unstrung, from the side (**a**) and the back (**b**).
3 Egyptian bow of the New Kingdom, c.1400BC. Made of acacia wood. Double convex shape when unstrung, shown here from the side.

Recent bows (above) from Africa and Asia, primarily used for hunting.
4 Bow of the nomadic Hadza people of Tanzania.
5 Bow from Kenya, here shown in use. One of the most powerful simple bows, it has a draw-weight of up to 130lb (58.9kg). This compares with an average draw-weight of 80lb (36.2kg) for a medieval longbow.
6 Burmese pellet bow, made from bamboo. Of asymmetric shape, it has a separate grip-piece bound onto the stave below the center. To shoot pellets, some kind of pocket is needed on the string. Details are shown of two kinds, for double (**a**) and single (**b**) strings. Pellet bows cannot compete with arrows for lethality, and so have seldom been used in combat.

English archer (above) from a manuscript illustration of the Battle of Shrewsbury, 1403. Despite their military importance, bowmen at the height of the English longbow's success, in the 14th and 15th centuries, were among the lowliest soldiers, few of them wearing armor.

Henry VIII of England (above) at archery practice. Henry attempted to preserve the traditional skills of the longbow in England by law, decreeing that men of military age must keep bows and practice after morning service on Sundays. Despite his efforts and the weapon's cheapness and efficiency, it gave way to firearms as the main source of firepower.

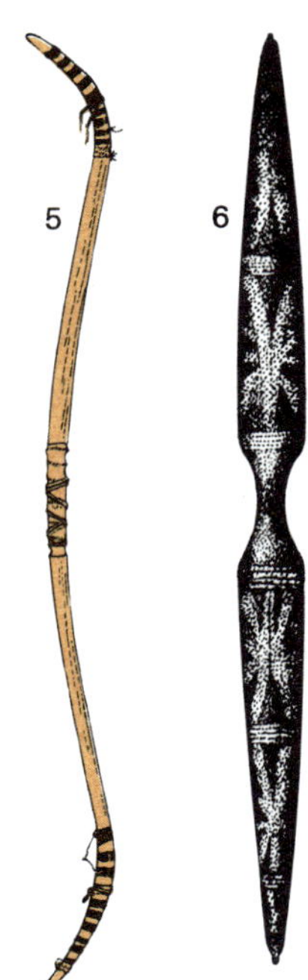

The longbow (above) This name is applied to the classic Welsh and English simple bows, in military use in the 14th to 16th centuries. Yew was the wood preferred, with elm as a substitute. The bow was about the height of the archer, and the arrow half that.

1 Longbow said to have been used at the Battle of Flodden, 1513.

2 Longbow recovered from the wreck of the *Mary Rose*, which sank in 1545.

3 A strung longbow is here shown in profile. The detail of the bow's cross-section (**a**) demonstrates how bows were cut so that there was sapwood at the flat back of the bow and denser heart wood at the curved belly. Detail (**b**) shows the horn nock for attaching the bowstring.

North American bows (above) Simple wooden bows were found across the continent. In the east, where suitable wood was plentiful, they were used to the exclusion of complex bows.

4 Indian from Florida, holding a long simple bow. Drawn from a watercolor by John White, who accompanied Ralegh's first colonizing expedition in the 1580s.

5 Sioux Indian bow of recurved shape. Painted, and partially bound with cloth strips. From South Dakota.

6 Modok Indian bow of flattened shape, narrowed at the center for the grip. Decorated with geometric patterns. From Oklahoma.

Laminated and backed bows

**Laminated bows differ from simple bows in being made up from three or more layers of the same basic material.
Simple bows are sometimes strengthened by the addition of "backing," usually in the form of animal sinew, applied to the back of the stave. If simply bound in place it is called "free" backing. If glued in place it is "close" backing.**

Plains Indian (left) from the American West, shown holding a backed bow and a lance.

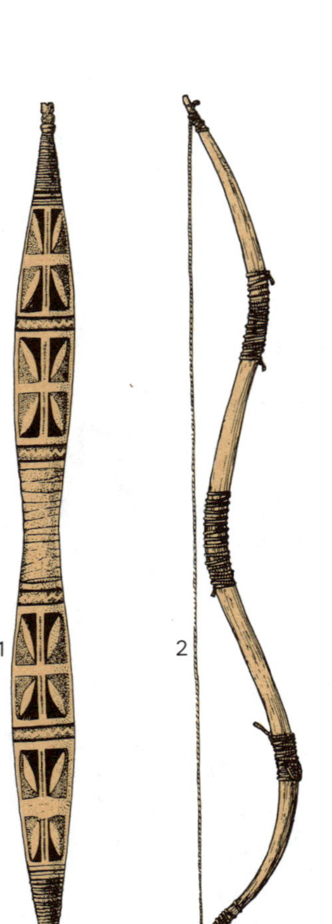

Asymmetric Japanese bows (above) The Samurai warrior (**a**), drawn from an armor in the Victoria and Albert Museum, London, is holding a bow of *shige-to-yumi* type — a laminated wood bow, bound with rattan and lacquered. This was regarded as a nobleman's weapon, and despite its length was often used from horseback. Note how far down the bow the grip is positioned. Both the laminated *shige-to-yumi* and the simple bow *maru-ki* are found in this shape and size. Illustration (**b**) shows the shape and proportions of a Japanese asymmetric bow when drawn. Note how far back the bow is drawn; the arrows were correspondingly long, heavy and destructive.

North American backed bows (above)
1 Flat bow from NW California, known as the Yurok-Hupa type. Of yew wood, with sinew glued to the back, painted over with geometric designs. Shown from the back, unstrung.
2 Indian bow from the American West, shown in side view. Composed of several pieces of horn, the joints and grip bound with animal sinew.
3 Eskimo bow of wood with "free" sinew backing, shown in back (**a**) and side (**b**) views.
4 Eskimo compound bow made from three pieces of reindeer horn, with sinew backing.

Composite bows

Composite bows are made up from three basic layers of dissimilar materials, combined so as to enhance the elastic efficiency of each. The traditional composite bow, seen at its best in Turkey, was made from horn and sinew applied to a core of wood. Modern composite bows for target shooting use materials such as glass-reinforced plastic and carbon fiber, but they do not concern us here.

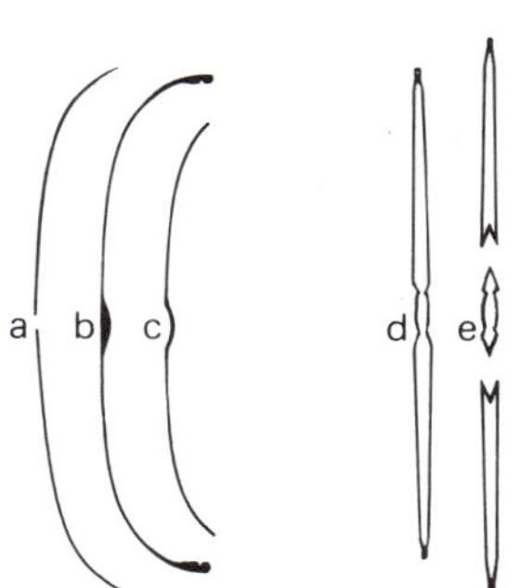

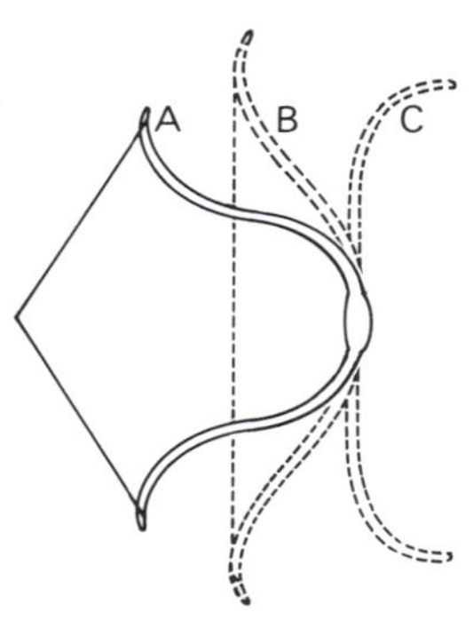

The Turkish bow is widely regarded as perhaps the most efficient type devised until this century.
The diagrams (left) show the shape of a Turkish bow when drawn (**A**), strung (**B**) and unstrung (**C**). The shape is designed to make best use of the naturally elastic components.

Components of the Turkish bow (above) Two strips of horn (**a**) were glued to a wooden core (**b**), which was further reinforced on the back by a strip of sinew (**c**). The wooden core was itself made up from three pieces, as shown (**d**, **e**). The back of the bow was covered either with bark or skin, and then painted.

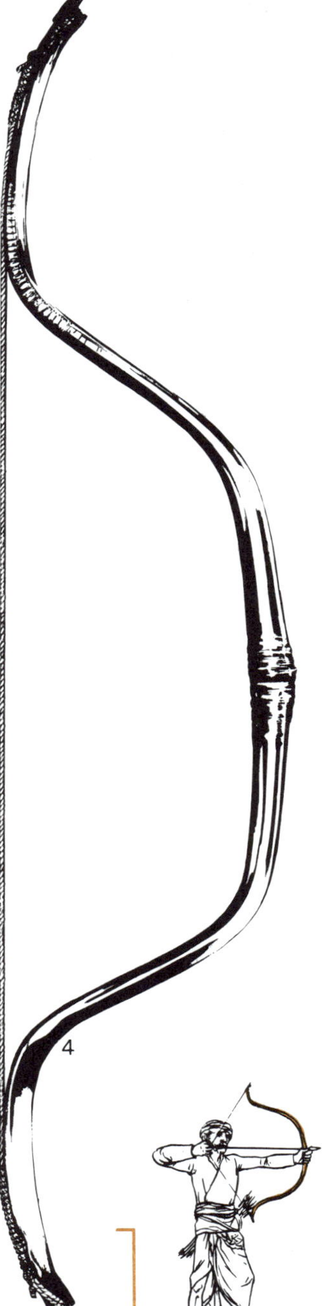

1

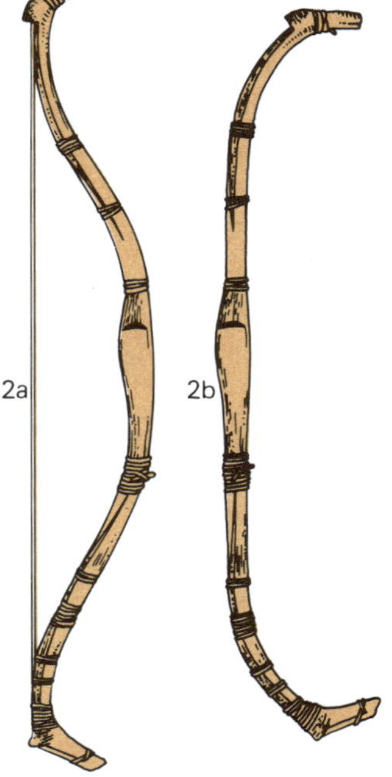

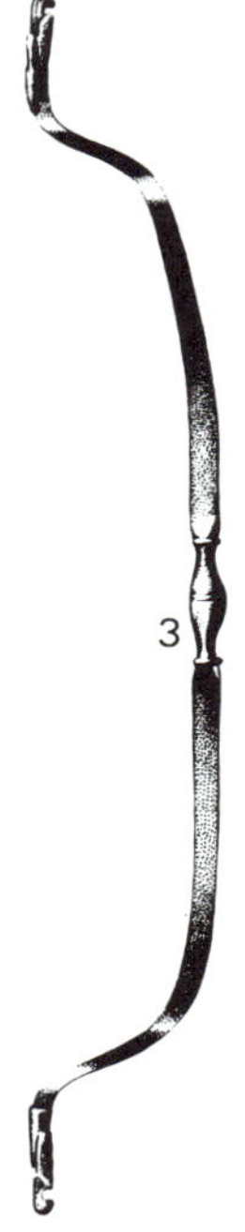

1 Turkish bow of the 19th century, painted crimson, with gold decoration near each tip. Silk bowstring with sinew ends. Tests show such weapons to have had a greater range than any other bow. The expert Sir Ralph Payne-Gallwey accepted figures of over 660yd (600m) with special flight arrows, and about 440yd (400m) with war arrows.

2 Bashkir bow Composite bow from the Bashkir region of the USSR, another variety of the Asian tradition in bowmaking. It consists largely of wood, with horn spliced into the belly side toward the tips, and with sinew reinforcement on the back. It is shown here from the side, strung (**a**) and unstrung (**b**).

Indian bows (above)
3 Steel bow from Northern India. Even before the coming of Europeans, India was able to produce fine steel in limited quantities. It was sometimes used for making bows, usually in the shape of the Indian composite bow. The example illustrated is probably a hunting weapon of the 19th century.

4 Composite bow from Northern India, consisting of a wood core with horn on the belly side and sinew on the back, and lacquered overall. Such bows were used in India even after the coming of firearms. Also shown in use.

Arrows

The arrow is a highly efficient projectile. It out-ranges the spear and the hand-thrown dart, and being small and light, many can be carried. Although simple in concept, great care is needed in manufacture. It must match the bow in length and weight, be perfectly straight and well fletched, have the correct degree of flexibility in the shaft, and have a point of suitable design to defeat the intended target.

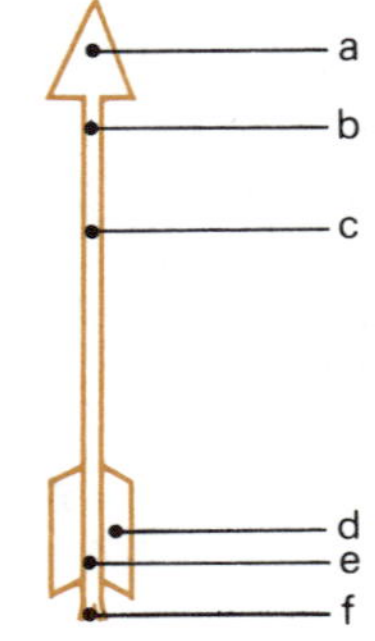

Parts (left) Shown are the parts of a typical arrow.
a Head
b Foot
c Shaft or stele
d Flights or feathers
e Shaftment
f Nock
Not all arrows have a separate head — some are merely sharpened at the tip. Some do not have feathers, but their range is severely limited.

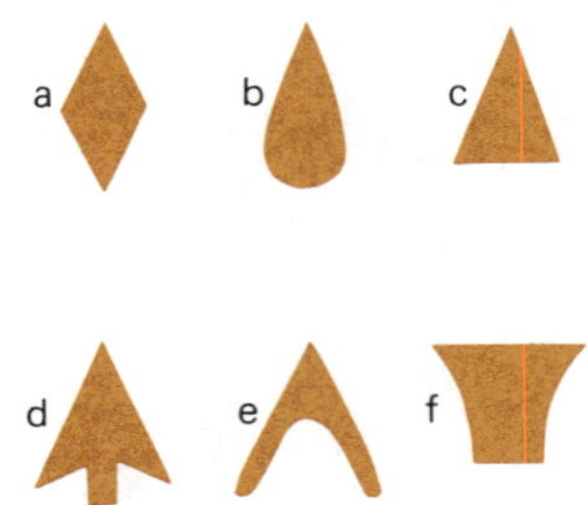

Shapes of arrowheads (left) These common profiles were developed in the Stone Age. Most of them were adapted and continued to be used on the coming of metals.
a Lozenge
b Leaf
c Triangular
d Barbed
e Swallowtail
f Chisel

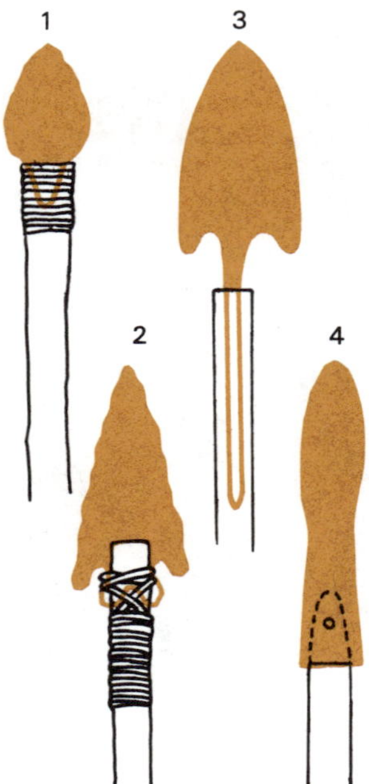

Attachment (left) Shown are some common methods of attaching head to shaft.
1 The simplest leaf-shaped stone tips were pushed into the split end of the shaft and gripped by binding tightly.
2 The barbs of more sophisticated stone tips could be used to improve the binding.
3 The long slender tang of a Japanese steel tip was pushed into the hollow core of a reed, a convenient shaft material also used elsewhere.
4 Where solid wood shafts were used, as in medieval Europe, iron tips were forged with a hollow socket, into which the tip of the shaft could be glued and sometimes pinned.

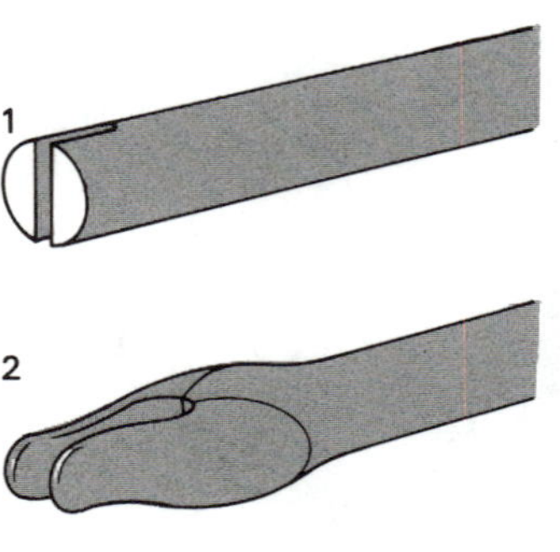

The nock or notch (left) The function of the nock is to keep the arrow in place on the bowstring until the transfer of energy (release) is complete. It may be a simple groove cut on the butt end of the arrow (**1**). Or, as on arrows found in Turkey (**2**), it may be a separately applied horn clip, designed to hold an arrow in place on the bowstring.

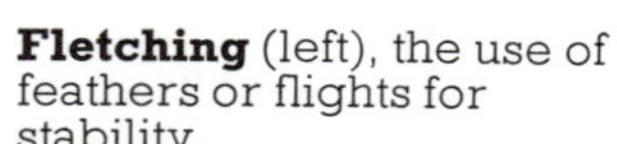

Fletching (left), the use of feathers or flights for stability.
a Some arrows, such as those of the Bushmen of Southern Africa, have no feathers.
b, **c**, **d** The feathers (or flights if of another material) are arranged symmetrically in twos, threes or fours, near the butt-end of the shaft. Sometimes one feather is colored and for regularity is always placed in the same plane when the arrow is fitted to the bowstring.
e In Turkey, feathers were sometimes fitted spirally on practice arrows.
f Attachment of feathers is often by binding with thread over the split quill at each end of the feather. Glue may also be used, as may additional thread spaced at intervals.

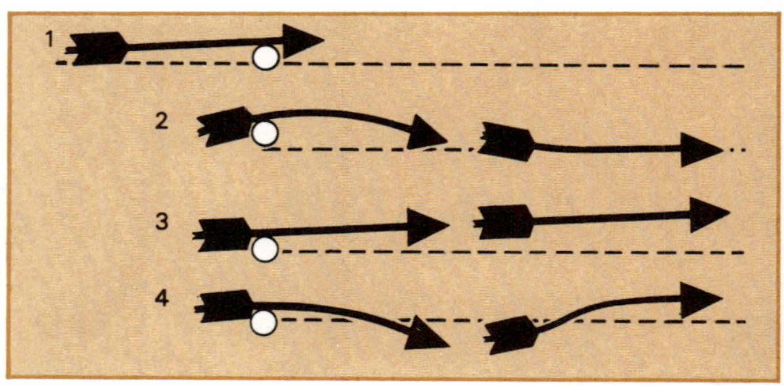

The archer's paradox (above) Because of this phenomenon, it is important that an arrow shaft is of the correct "spine" or flexibility.
1 Before release, the arrow is at a slightly divergent angle from the line of flight.
2 On release, the inertia of the head and butt causes the shaft to bend. If it is of the correct spine, it will resume the correct line of flight.
3 But if the shaft is too stiff, the arrow will fly off to the side.
4 If the shaft is not stiff enough, it will continue to bend, impairing flight.

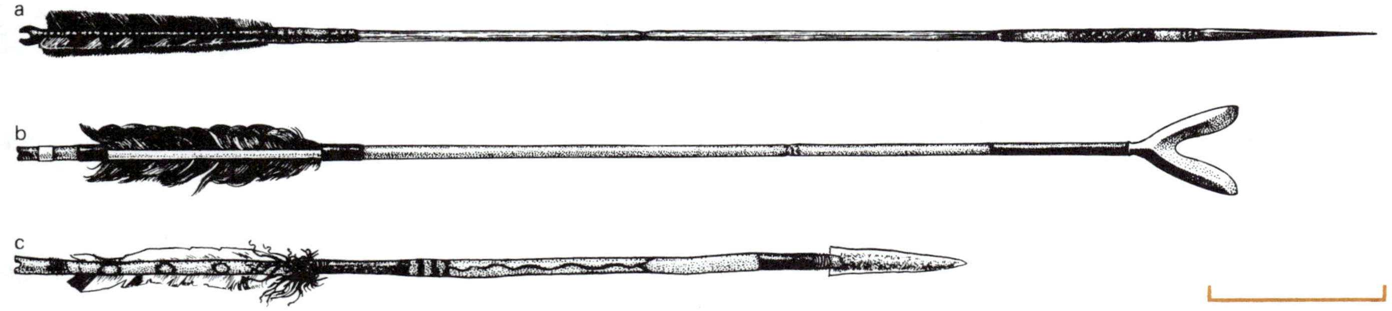

Arrows (above)
a Arrow from Northern India with painted designs, four flights, and a long, hexagonal steel tip for piercing mail armor.
b Japanese arrow with reed shaft and forked steel tip.
c Sioux Indian "medicine" arrow, painted with geometric designs, and having ritual significance.

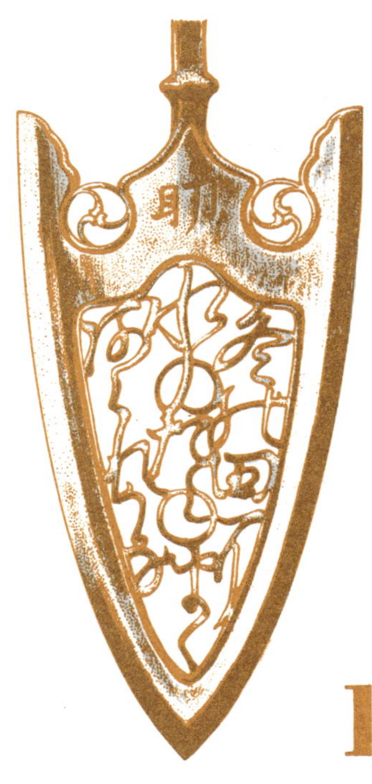

Arrowheads (above)
Shown here is a selection of arrowheads. They are grouped according to material, and illustrate the diversity of shapes. Details of origin are given in the list.

Flint arrowheads
1 England
2 Egypt
3, 4 France
5, 6 Northern Ireland
7 England
8, 9 Denmark
10 Sweden (flint microliths on a bone shaft)
11 Eskimo

Other non-metal arrowheads
12 Eskimo (bone)
13 NW American coast (ivory)
14–17 N America (obsidian)
18–21 N America (stone)
22 N America (petrified wood)

Metal arrowheads
23 Assyria (bronze)
24 Scythia (bronze)
25 Luristan (bronze)
26 Mesopotamia (bronze)
27–33 Medieval Europe (iron)
34–37 Japan (steel)
38 Kashmir (steel)

Japanese arrowhead
(above) of steel. The design, cut out with a saw, is a poem on falling hail. It was made as a gift or votive offering, and was not intended for shooting.

Crossbows 1

A crossbow is a bow attached to a stock, so that it can be kept in the loaded state without effort from the user. The stock also allows bending and release to be mechanically assisted. The result is an accurate and powerful projectile weapon, which can be used by a man lacking the skill and strength demanded by conventional bows. Crossbows vary as to the intended method of spanning (bending), the material of the bow-spring itself, the release mechanism, the projectile to be fired, and the use intended. As regards the last, the crossbow was obsolete as a weapon of war by 1550; thereafter its use was confined to hunting and target shooting.

Names of parts
The crossbow or arbalest
a Butt
b Stock or tiller
c Trigger
d Nut
e Groove
f Bowstring
g Bridle or bow iron
h Bow
i Stirrup

The bolt or quarrel
j Butt
k Feathers or flights
l Shaft
m Head

Using a crossbow (right)
The process differs significantly from that of "conventional" archery.
1 Spanning At its simplest, as shown, this involves drawing the string back by hand until it is held by the nut (see detail). Improved mechanical aids (see p.104) allowed more powerful bows to be made and used in the course of time.

1

2 Fitting the bolt This entailed holding the weapon roughly horizontal, and laying the bolt in the groove with its butt close to the nut (see detail). A leaf-spring was sometimes fitted to hold the bolt in place at any attitude.

2

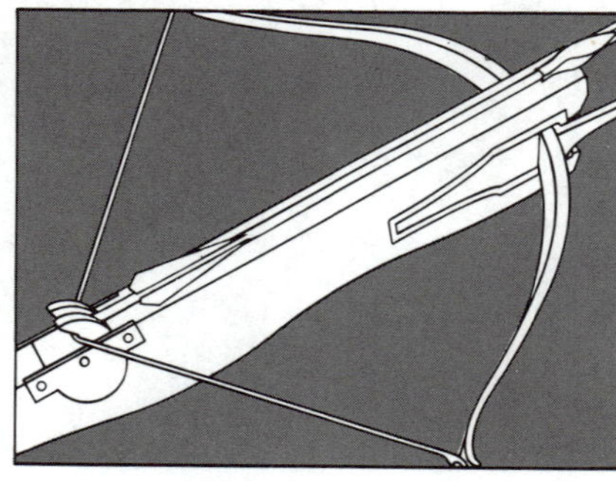

3 Aiming and release
Crossbows can be aimed much as a rifle, at or near the shoulder, and the trigger pressed with minimum disturbance to the aim. The detail shows one of the simplest release mechanisms, as found on military bows. On later target bows, great ingenuity was shown in trying to perfect this mechanism.

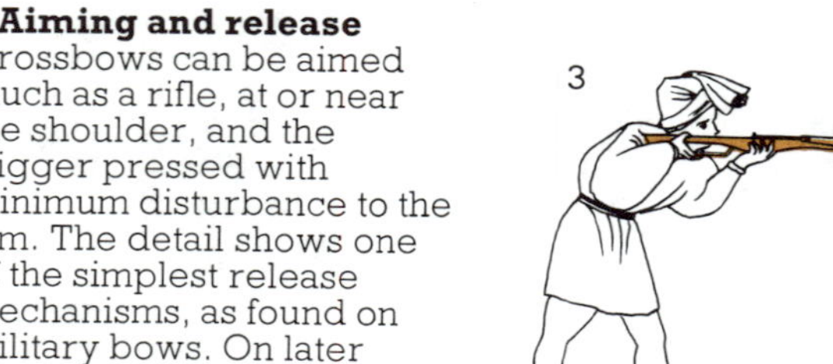

3

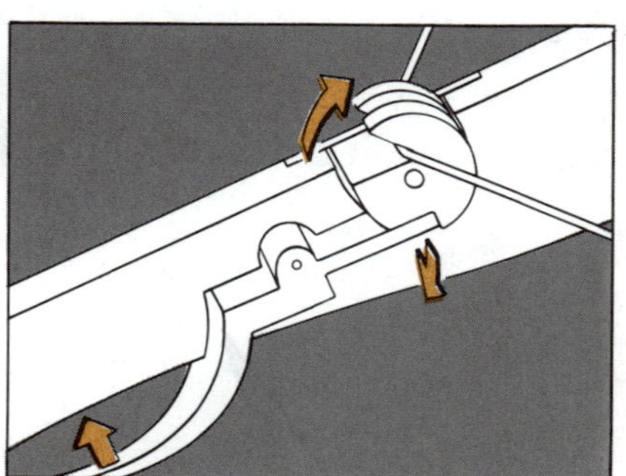

Chronology
500BC Sun Tzu in "The Art of War" mentions powerful arrow-shooting crossbows.
206BC-220AD (Han dynasty) Crossbows in regular use in China.
0-100AD Chinese repeating crossbow thought to have emerged.
1100 Crossbow in common use in Europe, especially with mercenaries.
1139 Use against Christians prohibited by Pope Innocent II, but used nevertheless.
1199 Richard I of England, an advocate of the crossbow, killed by one at the siege of Chaluz.
Late 13th century Replaced in England by the longbow, but still dominant in continental Europe.
Early 14th century The steel bow first fitted to crossbows.
14th and 15th centuries French and Belgian towns protected by civic companies of crossbowmen.
1521 and 1524 Cortes and Pizarro take crossbowmen to the New World.
1555-57 Swedes use crossbows against Russia
16th century Hand-held firearms replace the crossbow for war.
16th century onward Use in Europe confined to hunting and target shooting.
1894-95 Chinese use repeating crossbows in the Sino-Japanese War.
1914-18 A few instances of use in trench warfare.

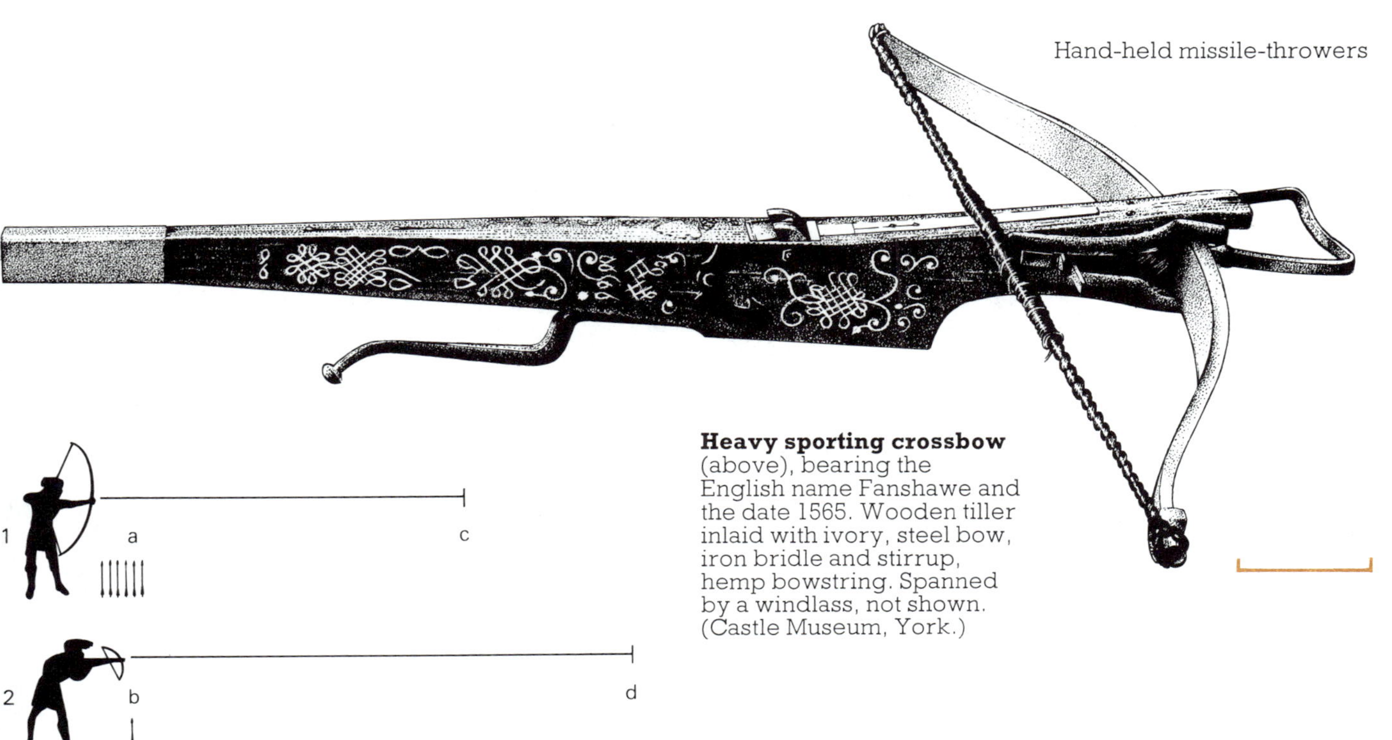

Heavy sporting crossbow (above), bearing the English name Fanshawe and the date 1565. Wooden tiller inlaid with ivory, steel bow, iron bridle and stirrup, hemp bowstring. Spanned by a windlass, not shown. (Castle Museum, York.)

Comparative potential (above) Compared are the English longbow (**1**) and the crossbow (**2**) — rivals in European warfare in the 14th and 15th centuries.

Rate of shooting
a Longbow, about six aimed arrows per minute (or twelve with less accuracy)
b Crossbow with windlass, about one bolt per minute (or four using a belt and claw)

Extreme range
c Longbow about 280yd (255m)
d Crossbow about 380yd (360m)
(The effective tactical ranges were of course less.)

Power Both were capable of piercing plate armor at tactical ranges with a correctly tempered arrowhead.
(Data after Sir Ralph Payne-Gallwey.)

Accuracy of aim (left) Inherently accurate, a crossbow could also be aimed precisely, using the top of the bolt much as the sights of a rifle.

Types of crossbow (left) Silhouettes of the two main types are shown here.
A Bolt-shooting crossbow for war or hunting large game.
B Stone- or bullet-shooting crossbow, with double bowstring, for hunting birds or small ground game.

Military bolts (below) These surviving examples are typical of the military bolts or quarrels of the late Middle Ages. The tips are iron, the shafts wooden and the flights of wood (**1**) and parchment (**2**).
(**1** is in the Castle Museum, Grandson, Switzerland; **2** in the Tower of London.)

Crossbows 2

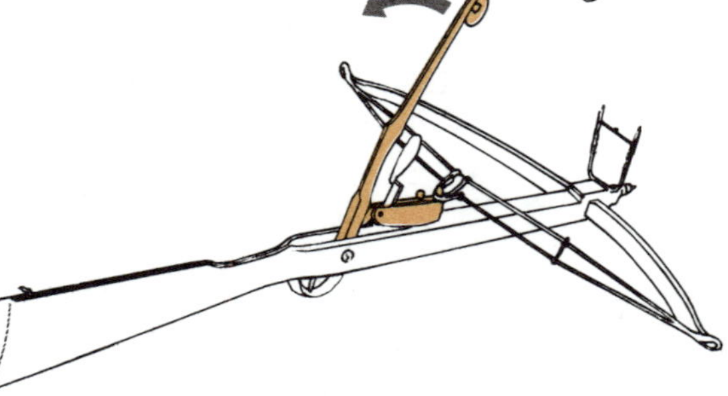

Devices for spanning (left)
a Stirrup and hands Went out of use as military bows became more powerful.
b Belt and claw The bowman bent down and attached the claw to the bowstring. As he straightened his back the bow was bent.
c Cord and pulley An improvement on (**b**), permitting more powerful bows.
d Goatsfoot lever The curved limbs slid over pivots on either side of the tiller as the opposite end of the lever was pulled back.
e Push lever Hooked onto a small stirrup at the front of the bow. Gave the user's arm a mechanical advantage as he pulled back the upper limb of the lever.
f Windlass Used with the most powerful crossbows. Used effectively in war despite being slow and cumbersome, but not popular for hunting.
g Cranequin A neat device using a rack and pinion system. Invented c.1450 and more popular with hunters than soldiers, as the gearing made it slow to wind.
h Built-in lever Much used on later stone-bows, and especially English sporting bullet-bows c.1800.

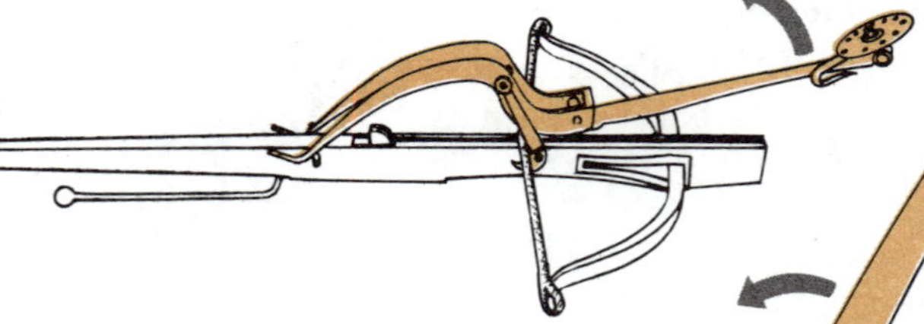

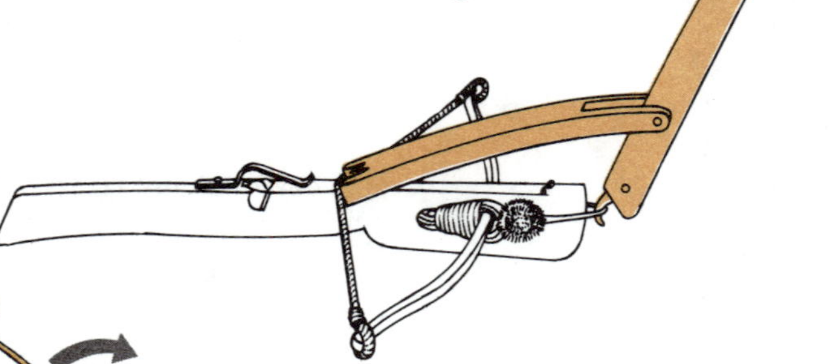

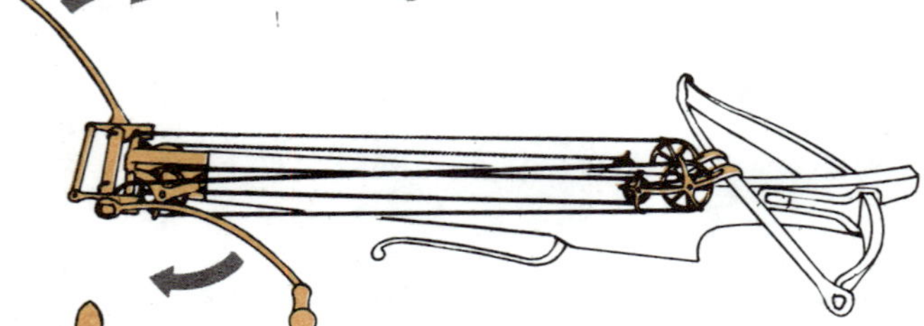

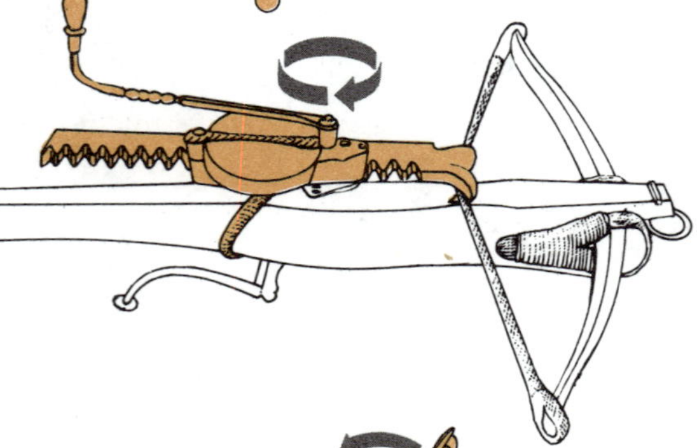

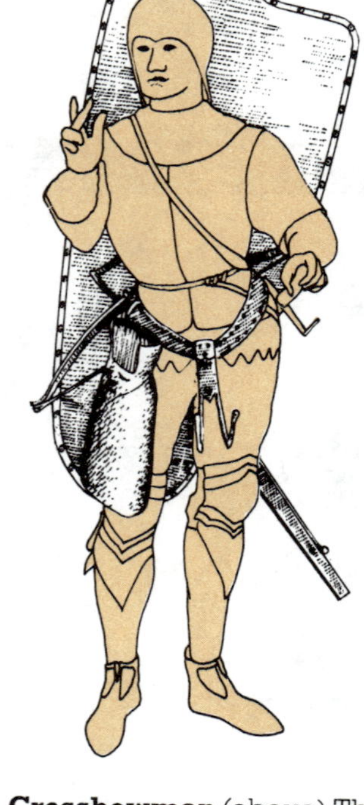

Crossbowman (above) The drawing after Viollet le Duc shows a crossbowman with his equipment. The bow is slung behind him at waist level, where he also carries a quiver full of bolts, a light sword, and a spanning device (in this case a belt and claw). The *pavise* or long shield carried on his back was made necessary by the slow process of loading.

Pavise (left) or shield for a crossbowman. The shield was placed on the ground to provide shelter during loading. A second man, called a paviser, was often employed to move and support the shield, allowing the bowman to concentrate on his work. Illustrated is a Swiss example from the second quarter of the 15th century. (Schweizerisches Landesmuseum, Zürich.)

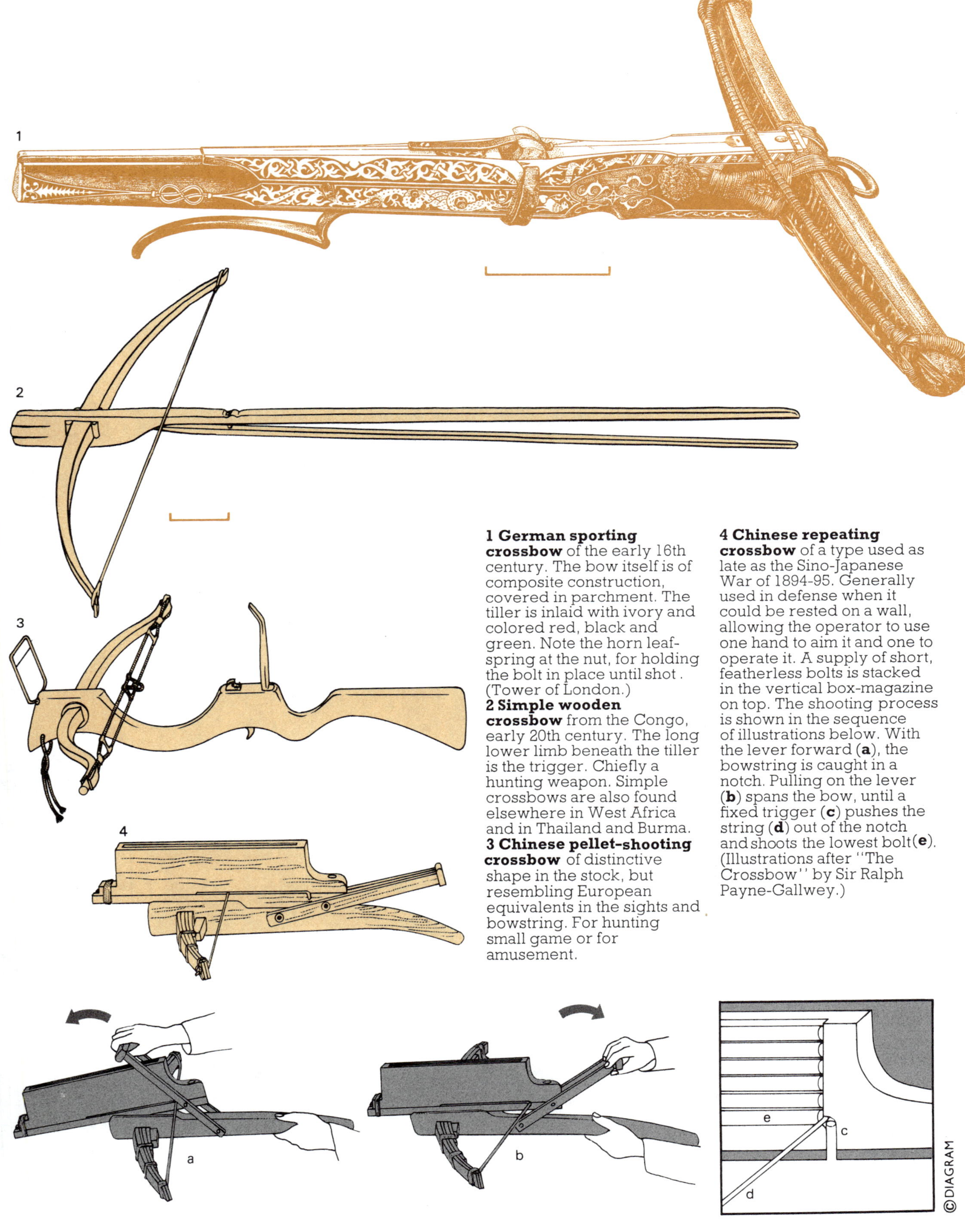

1 German sporting crossbow of the early 16th century. The bow itself is of composite construction, covered in parchment. The tiller is inlaid with ivory and colored red, black and green. Note the horn leaf-spring at the nut, for holding the bolt in place until shot . (Tower of London.)
2 Simple wooden crossbow from the Congo, early 20th century. The long lower limb beneath the tiller is the trigger. Chiefly a hunting weapon. Simple crossbows are also found elsewhere in West Africa and in Thailand and Burma.
3 Chinese pellet-shooting crossbow of distinctive shape in the stock, but resembling European equivalents in the sights and bowstring. For hunting small game or for amusement.
4 Chinese repeating crossbow of a type used as late as the Sino-Japanese War of 1894-95. Generally used in defense when it could be rested on a wall, allowing the operator to use one hand to aim it and one to operate it. A supply of short, featherless bolts is stacked in the vertical box-magazine on top. The shooting process is shown in the sequence of illustrations below. With the lever forward (**a**), the bowstring is caught in a notch. Pulling on the lever (**b**) spans the bow, until a fixed trigger (**c**) pushes the string (**d**) out of the notch and shoots the lowest bolt(**e**). (Illustrations after "The Crossbow" by Sir Ralph Payne-Gallwey.)

Blowguns

Blowguns, or blowpipes, are wooden tubes out of which light darts are propelled by the user's breath. They are known to have been used for hunting or recreation in many parts of the world, but are most common in Malaysia and South America; in these areas blowguns are used by the aboriginal inhabitants for war as well as hunting. The tube can be constructed in many different ways.

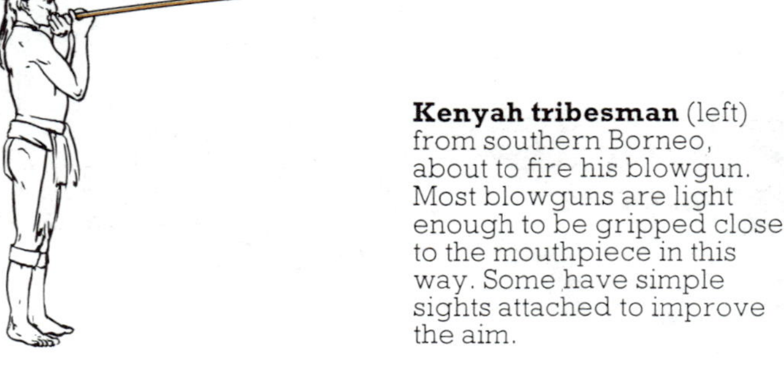

Kenyah tribesman (left) from southern Borneo, about to fire his blowgun. Most blowguns are light enough to be gripped close to the mouthpiece in this way. Some have simple sights attached to improve the aim.

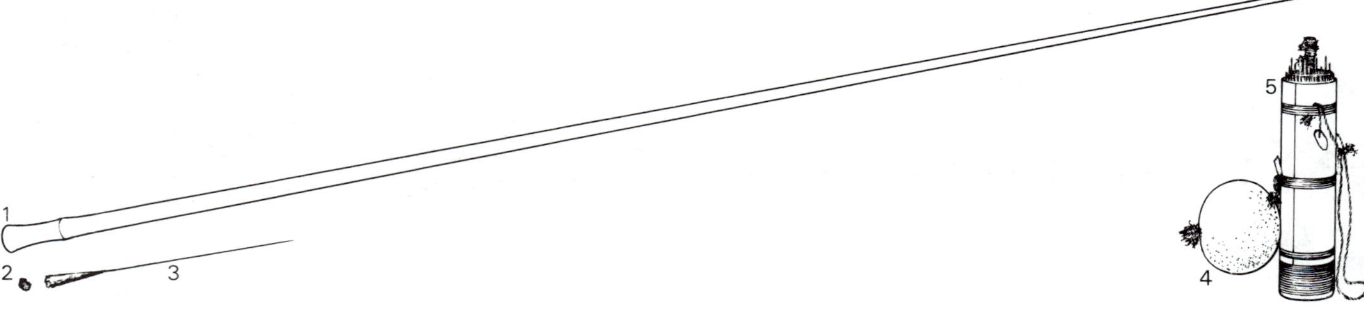

Blowgun and accessories (above) from South America.
1 Blowgun, the tube of reed bound with pliable wood fiber.
2 Tuft of cotton for use as wadding.
3 Dart, made from the spine of a leaf, set in a soft plug to fit the bore.
4 Gourd, to hold cotton for wadding.
5 Quiver for darts.

Cross-section (right) through the "breech" end of a typical blowgun with a dart in place for firing.
a Mouthpiece
b Tube or barrel
c Wadding
d Butt of dart
e Blade of dart
The commonest materials for wadding and the butt of the dart are cotton in South America and pith in Malaysia.

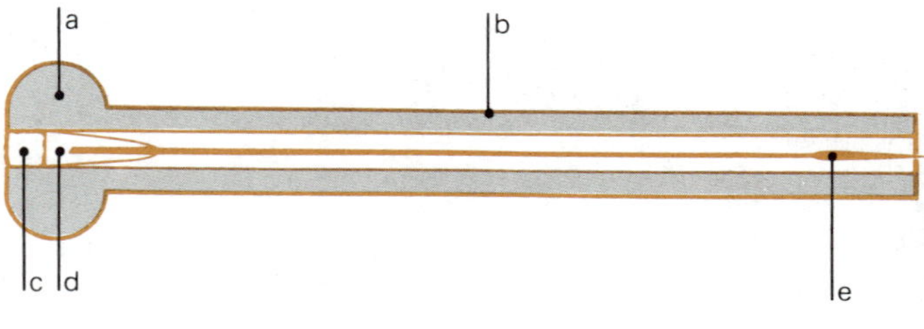

A

B

Blowguns (above) from Malaysia and Indonesia.
A Made with a narrow inner tube of bamboo inside a stronger, decorated tube, by the Sakai people of the Malay Peninsula.

B Made from a solid piece of wood, bored out, and fitted with a spear point, by the Dyaks of Borneo.

The mouthpiece (below) and "breech" end of a Sakai blowgun from the Malay Peninsula, shown at actual size.

Airguns

Airguns are the direct descendants of blowguns, having the addition of a mechanical device to provide the necessary air pressure. The pressure may be generated by a spring when the trigger is pulled, but airguns of this type are generally suited only to target shooting or the hunting of small game. The weapons shown here are of a more lethal kind, using a reservoir of pre-compressed air.

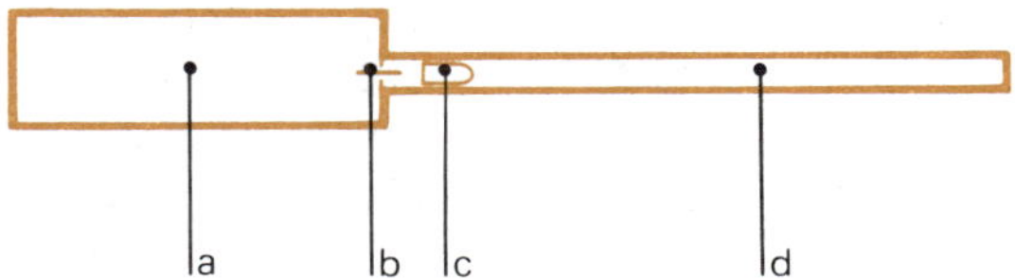

The principle (above) of a reservoir type airgun. The reservoir or pressure-vessel (**a**) contains enough compressed air for several shots. A valve (**b**) is opened briefly on pulling the trigger, allowing a blast of air to escape and propel a bullet (**c**) down the barrel (**d**).

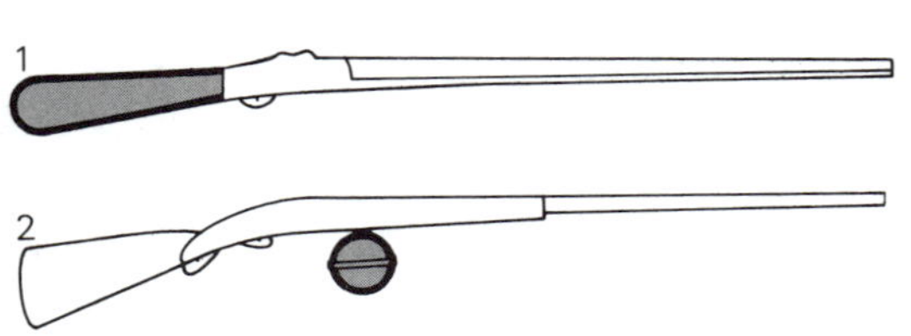

The storage of air (left) In the 18th and 19th centuries, the reservoir often formed the butt of the gun (**1**) or took the form of an external sphere (**2**). To fill the reservoir it was removed from the gun and attached to a pump, often of the hand-and-foot kind shown in use at (**3**) and (**4**).

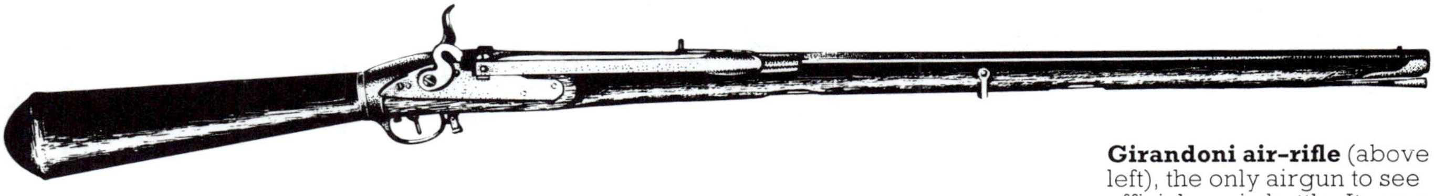

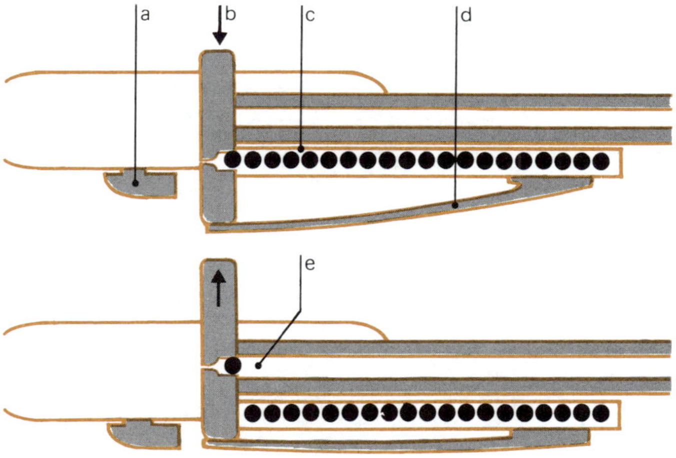

Girandoni air-rifle (above left), the only airgun to see official use in battle. It was a 20-shot repeater of 13mm (.51in) caliber, in limited use with Austrian sharpshooters from 1793 to 1801. The sectional top views (left) show the main working parts. The "hammer" (**a**) was pulled back to cock the valve release mechanism. The breechblock (**b**) was pushed across to pick up a lead ball from the magazine (**c**), and returned by its spring (**d**), so aligning the ball with the barrel (**e**). When the trigger was pulled, a blast of air from the butt-reservoir sent the ball to an effective range of about 130yd (120m).

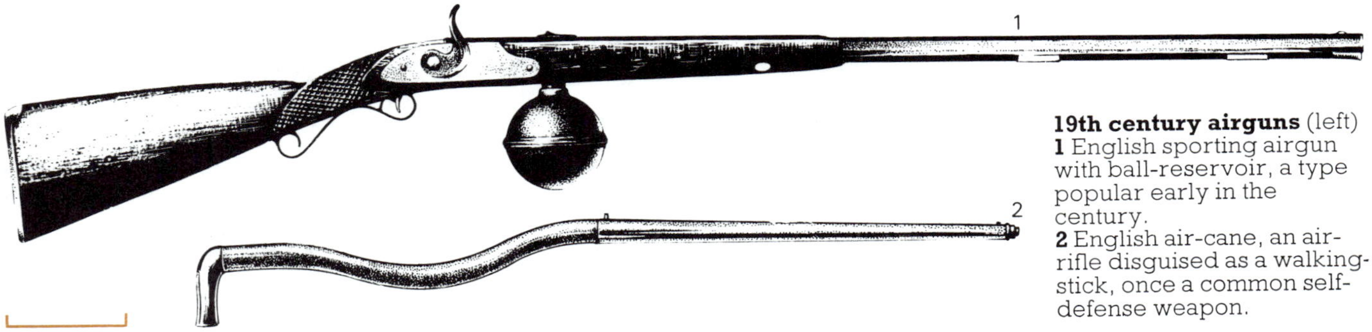

19th century airguns (left)
1 English sporting airgun with ball-reservoir, a type popular early in the century.
2 English air-cane, an air-rifle disguised as a walking-stick, once a common self-defense weapon.

Small arms

Under the heading of small arms, we explain and illustrate those hand-held missile-throwers that use an explosion to propel a missile from a tube. This definition includes some large-caliber weapons, fired from the shoulder, which are sometimes not counted as small arms, and it excludes most machine guns, as, except for submachine guns, they are commonly mounted on some form of support. Any such related weapons that cannot be picked up and fired by one man will be found in Chapter 4.

We have attempted to make the vast field of small arms intelligible by categorizing according to the simplest functional distinctions. Thus muzzle-loaders are presented before breech-loaders, and each of these categories is subdivided logically, by identifying the weapons' most essential feature. This system of classification corresponds in general with the historical development of military small arms.

We have added a brief explanation of the theory of small arms fire, to help explain the practicalities of exploiting these weapons in combat. There is also a section on the complex subject of small arms ammunition, and this is added to later alongside the relevant weapons. Firearms were for many years inferior to bows in range, accuracy, rate of fire and expense, but they succeeded probably because they could be used with effect by weaker and less skilful men than were needed to wield a bow. For the first time, the power for the shot was not supplied, even indirectly, by the firer's muscles. This was the "magic" of gunpowder.

Propulsion (right) However else they may differ, the small arms we show all use the same means of throwing a missile. An explosion is caused in a tube which is closed at one end. Expanding gases force the projectile out of the tube at high speed (**a**). This is true of firearms of any age (**b, c**).

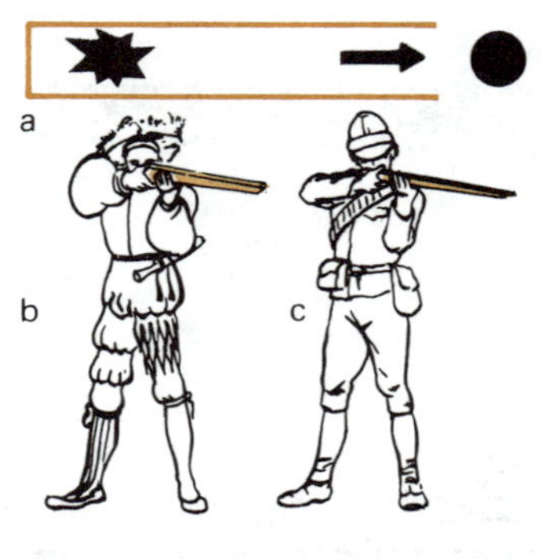

Loading (right) The most fundamental division of small arms is according to the way they are loaded.
1 Muzzle-loading small arms are loaded at the front of the barrel, the powder and ball being forced down the barrel with a rod. This simple method was predominant until the mid-19th century.
2 Breech-loading small arms are loaded at the rear of the barrel. This method has important advantages, but for technical reasons was not in common use until the mid-19th century.

Functioning (right) Small arms can also be classified by the way they function, a matter that involves the frequency with which they can be fired.
a Single-shot small arms need to be reloaded by hand before every shot.
b Multi-barreled small arms can fire a shot from each barrel before needing to be reloaded by hand.
c Repeaters have some form of magazine, an integral store of ammunition. Before each shot, the user need only work some form of lever, by hand, to feed the next cartridge into the breech. Revolvers are technically a subdivision of this category.
d Semi-automatic small arms are similar to repeaters, but use some of the energy of the exploding charge to work the mechanism. The weapon fires one shot at each pull of the trigger, and the next round is immediately fed into the breech. This type is also called self-loading or auto-loading.
e Fully-automatic small arms are similar to semi-automatics, but can fire in bursts of several shots at each pull of the trigger.

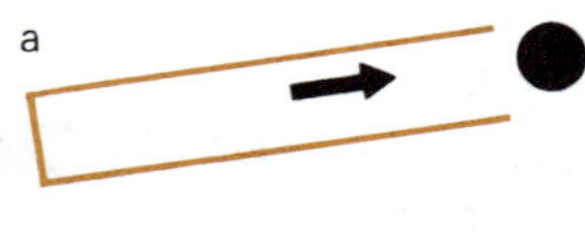

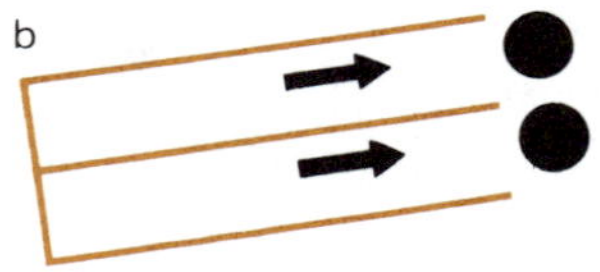

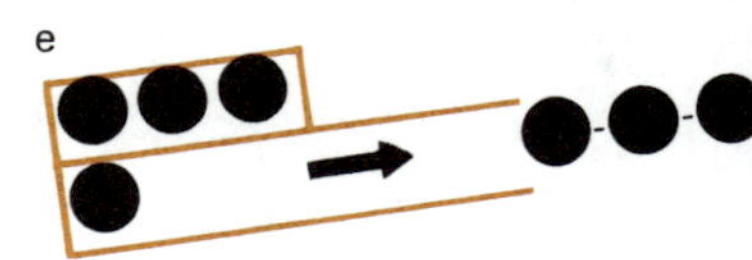

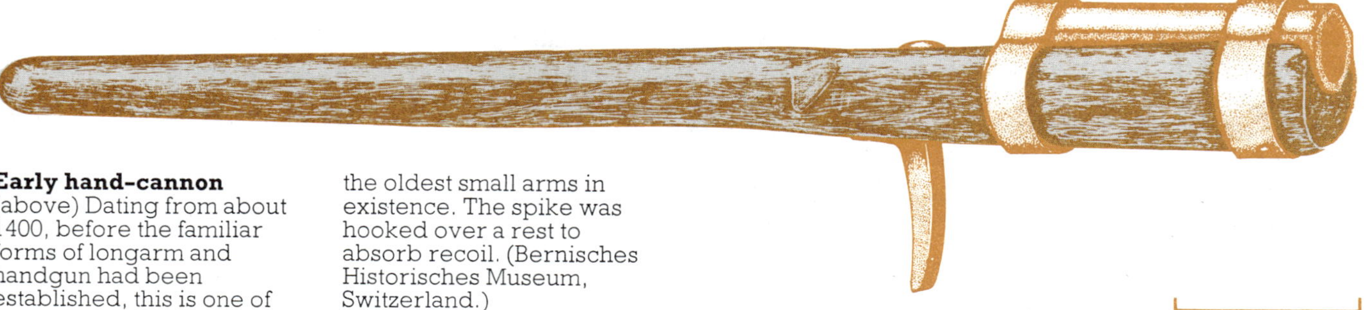

Early hand-cannon (above) Dating from about 1400, before the familiar forms of longarm and handgun had been established, this is one of the oldest small arms in existence. The spike was hooked over a rest to absorb recoil. (Bernisches Historisches Museum, Switzerland.)

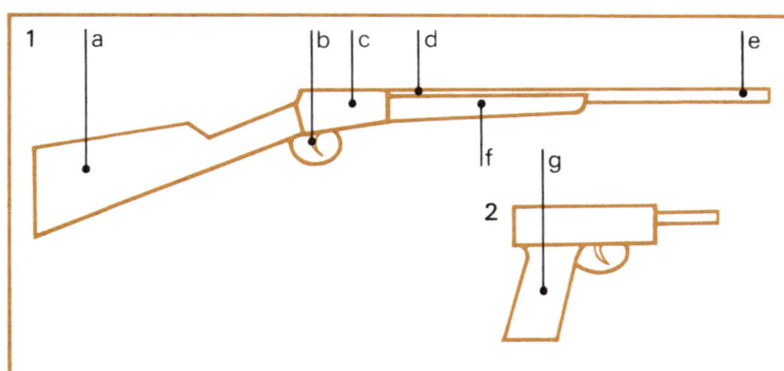

The basic parts (above), with their functions, of a longarm (**1**) and a handgun or pistol (**2**).
The longarm is held in both hands with the butt or stock (**a**) against the firer's shoulder. The trigger (**b**) allows him to activate the lock or action (**c**) with minimum disturbance to his aim and grip. The lock sets off the charge in the breech end (**d**) of the barrel, and the projectile emerges from the muzzle end (**e**). The wooden fore-end (**f**) protects the supporting hand from a hot barrel. The butt or grip (**g**) of a pistol permits it to be aimed and fired in one hand. In all cases, the bore is the inside of the barrel, with the chamber where the explosion occurs at its breech end.

A
a
B
b

Types of bore (above) There are two kinds.
A Smoothbore barrels have a plain inner surface and are best suited to firing a round ball or a quantity of buckshot, both of which are unstabilized in flight. There is often a gap (**a**), called "windage," between the bullet and bore. This reduces the power and accuracy of the shot.

B Rifled barrels have spiral grooves cut into the surface of the bore, leaving raised "lands" (**b**). These bite into the bullet and spin it as it is fired, so stabilizing its flight. The bullet's tight fit in the bore and its gyroscopic stability in flight make rifled firearms much more accurate than smoothbores.

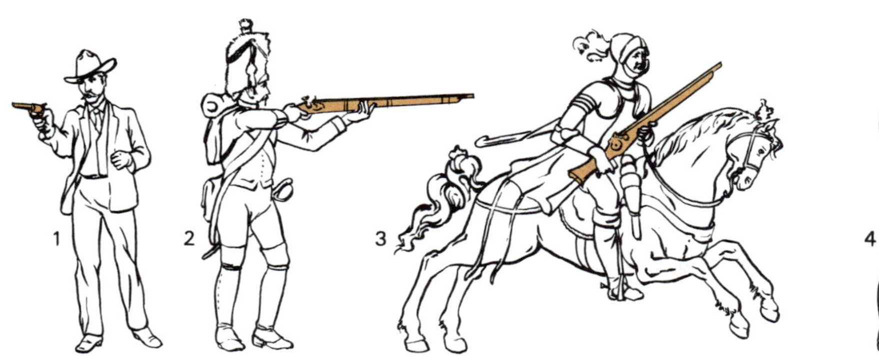

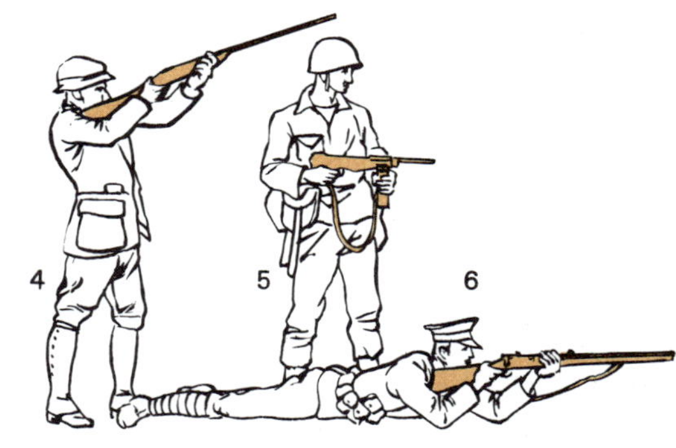

Types by use (above) Many of the terms applied to small arms are defined more easily by their use than their appearance. In some cases, a term has been current for many years, during which time the actual form of the weapon referred to has changed greatly. Here we explain six common terms.

1 Handgun or pistol Can be used in one hand. Even if a handgun has a rifled barrel, it is not called a rifle.

2 Musket, a smoothbore military longarm, usually muzzle-loading, once used by infantry.

3 Carbine, a short-barreled longarm, used originally by cavalry because of its convenience on horseback.

4 Shotgun, a smoothbore longarm for firing buckshot, more often used for hunting than for fighting.

5 Submachine gun, a handy fully-automatic weapon, the only type of machine gun light enough always to be fired without a support.

6 Rifle, a longarm with a rifled barrel, as distinct, originally, from a musket, and now from a submachine gun.

Theory of small arms fire

Ballistics, the science of projectiles, is divided into three parts: interior ballistics concerns what happens inside the gun-barrel; exterior ballistics covers the bullet's flight; terminal ballistics is concerned with its impact. Here we explain the essentials of exterior ballistics as they affect the tactical use of small arms.

Illustration (left) from a British Army training manual of World War 1. It shows the correct position when firing standing. In the early 20th century, when the rifle was at the height of its military importance, such manuals taught soldiers the theory of small arms fire in an academic fashion. They were expected to fire at distances of over a mile.

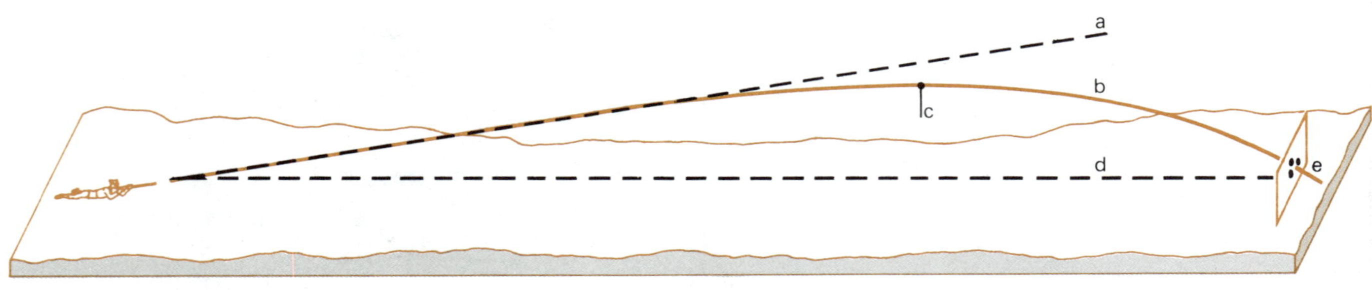

The bullet's flight (above) On firing, the rifle recoils in reaction to the forward motion of the bullet, and the muzzle usually tends to jump. Independently of this, when firing at longer ranges, the muzzle must be raised so that the initial "line of departure" (**a**) of the bullet takes account of the effect of gravity on its flight. Owing to gravity, the bullet soon begins to drop, so that in fact its path or "trajectory" (**b**) is a curve. The trajectory rises to the "culminating point" (**c**) and falls more steeply as the range increases, owing to air-resistance. If the firer has allowed for range correctly, by setting his sights, the trajectory will coincide with the "line of sight" (**d**) at the target. The line of sight is imaginary and straight, from the firer's eye, across the sights and out to the target.
The greater the "muzzle velocity," or speed of the bullet, the flatter the trajectory and the easier it becomes to allow for range. Except at point blank range, no rifle will put all its shots through the same hole. A series of shots forms a "group" (**e**) at the target. It is by the size of this group that the accuracy of rifle and ammunition together is assessed.

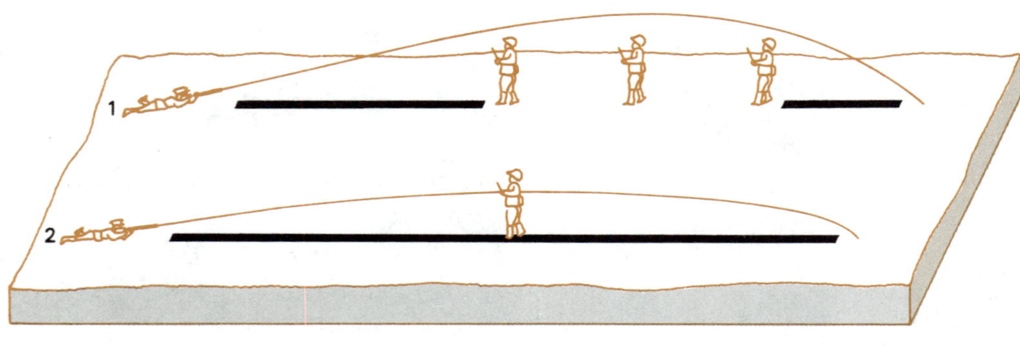

Danger space (left) The danger space is the distance over which the bullet remains within a man's height of the ground. If the bullet's velocity is low (**1**), the trajectory curves steeply, and there may well be an area in which the bullet will pass harmlessly over a man's head. With a flatter trajectory (**2**), this non-effective zone can be eliminated.

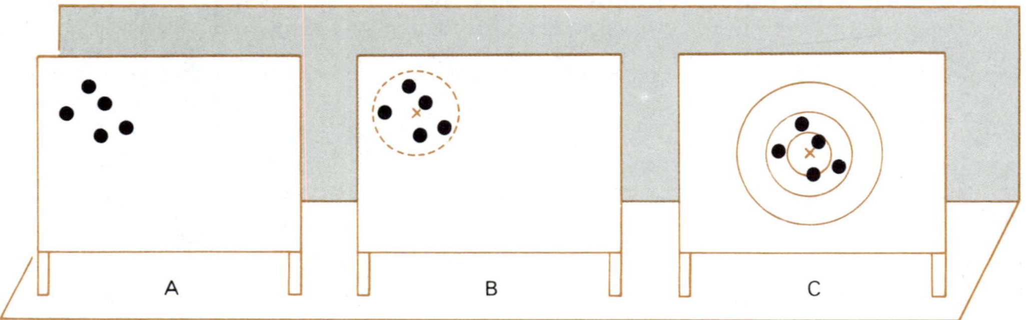

Zeroing (left) If a rifle is picked at random and fired, the group of shots may be anywhere on or off the target (**A**). The center of the group is assessed and called the Mean Point of Impact (MPI) (**B**). The firer must adjust the rifle-sights to cause the MPI to coincide with the point of aim (the center of the target) (**C**). This process is called zeroing.

Small arms chronology

Chronology (right) Here we set the main events in the history of firearms against important wars. While it is true that a war can give a temporary impetus to improvements in weaponry, there are several other factors contributing to progress in firearms design.
The greatest impetus of all came, of course, from the industrial revolution in the 19th century. General improvements in technology allowed hitherto impractical ideas to be used. The first and most vital product of 19th century inventiveness in the sphere of firearms was Dr Alexander Forsyth's development of percussion ignition. First used to set off the charge in muzzle-loaders — the first major improvement since the 17th century — it later opened the way for the self-contained cartridge. This highlights another factor in firearms development, namely the needs and ingenuity of sportsmen. Forsyth's initial concern had been to facilitate duck-shooting in wet weather. And again, the first successful self-contained cartridge was Lefaucheux's pinfire, designed for use in a sporting shotgun. However, since the late 19th century, sporting firearms have followed a different and slower course of development from the fighting weapons. It can be argued that, from the first adoption of percussion ignition by the European and American armies in the 1840s, a form of arms race can be traced. This steady process, of one innovation leapfrogging another, in peacetime as well as war, is probably the most important factor of all in firearms development.

Century	Wars	Firearms
1300		**1326** First illustration of a cannon
	1338 Outbreak of Hundred Years War	
		1364 Documentary evidence of hand-held firearms at Perugia
		c.1375 Firearms becoming common in Europe
1400		**1411** Earliest illustration of a simple matchlock
	1453 End of Hundred Years War	
	1453 Fall of Constantinople	
		c.1470 Shoulder-stocks developed
		c.1470 Snapping matchlock developed
	1494 Italian Wars begin	
1500		**c.1500** Leonardo da Vinci illustrates wheellock mechanism
	1503 Battle of Cerignola	**1503** At Cerignola hand-held firearms make first big impact
		1518 Wheellocks banned within Holy Roman Empire
		c.1540 The pistol emerges
		1543 Portuguese introduce matchlock firearms to Japan
		1547 Earliest documentary evidence of snaphance lock
	1559 Italian Wars end	**c.1550-** Rifling in limited use
	1568–1648 Revolt of the Netherlands	**c.1570** Heavy "Spanish" musket fired from a rest becomes popular
	1588 Spanish Armada	
1600	**1618–48** Thirty Years War	**c.1610** True flintlock emerges
	1642–48 English Civil War	**c.1640** Turn-off pistols emerge
		1641 Peter Kalthoff granted a monopoly on magazine guns in the Netherlands
		c.1650- Flintlocks widely used
	1689–97 War of the League of Augsburg	
1700	**1700–21** Great Northern War	**c.1700** Matchlock ignition obsolete in Europe
	1701–14 War of the Spanish Succession	
	1740–48 War of the Austrian Succession	
	1756–63 Seven Years War	**1770s** Special dueling pistols emerge
	1775–83 American War of Independence	**1775–83** Wide use of rifles in American Revolution
	1792 French Revolutionary Wars begin	
	1796–1815 Napoleonic Wars	
1800		**1807** Dr Forsyth patents percussion ignition
		1812 Pauly patents the first cartridge breech-loader
		1835 Lefaucheux patents the pinfire cartridge
		1835 Colt patents his first revolver design
		1840 Prussians adopt the needle-gun
		c.1840 European and American armies adopt percussion ignition
	1848 Year of Revolutions	**1849** Minié bullet designed
	1854–56 Crimean War	**1850s–60s** Minié rifles replace smoothbore muskets
	1861–65 American Civil War	**1886** French adopt first military smallbore smokeless-powder cartridge
	1870–71 Franco-Prussian War	**1887–88** Nobel patents important smokeless propellants
	1899–1902 Anglo-Boer War	**1888** Britain adopts the Lee-Metford bolt-action repeater
1900	**1904–05** Russo-Japanese War	
	1914–18 World War 1	**1914–18** Most combatants use bolt-action repeaters
		1918 First SMGs developed
	1936–39 Spanish Civil War	
	1939–45 World War 2	**1939–45** Self-loading rifles emerge
		1947 Kalishnikov designs the AK47 assault rifle
	1950–53 Korean War	
	1961–75 Vietnam War	**1961** US Army adopts the Armalite rifle
	1979 Chinese-Vietnamese Conflict	
	1980–88 Iran-Iraq War	**1980s** Caseless ammunition

Small arms ammunition

Small arms ammunition always consists of three main elements: priming, propellant and projectile. These were once carried separately, but are now sealed in a convenient metallic cartridge-case. The many thousands of specific varieties are now the subject of collectors' interest. Here we show at actual size the characteristic forms of military ammunition.

Parts (left) of a modern cartridge.
a Bullet
b Case
c Rim
d Bullet jacket
e Bullet core
f Propellant
g Primer
h Headstamp

Propellants (right) From the 13th to the late 19th century, the only gunpowder available was the traditional "black" powder, made in varying sizes of grain (**a, b**) and from varying proportions of charcoal, sulphur and saltpeter. In the 1880s, the first "smokeless" propellants were developed by Vieille in France, Nobel in Sweden and Abel and Dewar in Britain. Most are based on nitrocellulose and nitroglycerine. Cordite (**c**) is formed as pale brown strands. Nitrocellulose is usually gray, shaped as flakes (**d**), sticks (**e**) or spheres (**f**), the surface area calculated to adjust the speed of burning. These powders make less smoke and fouling, and are less dangerous in bulk than black powder.

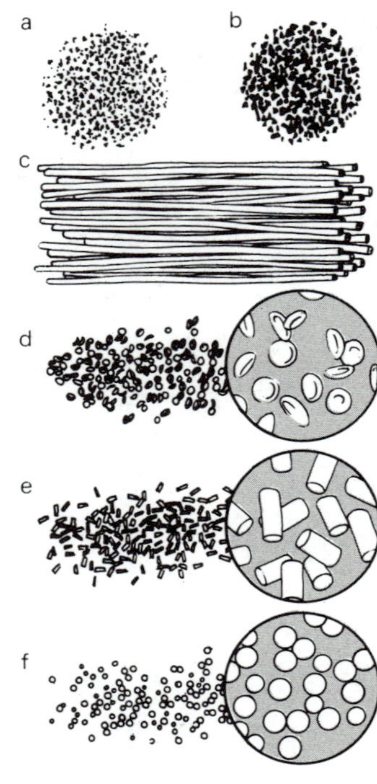

Projectiles (right) The universal projectile for smoothbore small arms was a lead ball (**1**), a shape suited to unstabilized flight. A rifled barrel, however, stabilizes the bullet gyroscopically, ensuring that an elongated shape (**2**) will fly point first. Such a shape allows a heavier bullet to be fired from a rifle of small caliber. Since the late 19th century, bullets have usually been covered with a jacket of harder metal which grips the rifling even at high velocity (**3,** shown after firing). In this century, rifle bullets have mostly been of the pointed "spitzer" shape (**4**), often with a streamlined "boat-tail" base (**5**). The trend now is to small caliber bullets fired at high velocity.

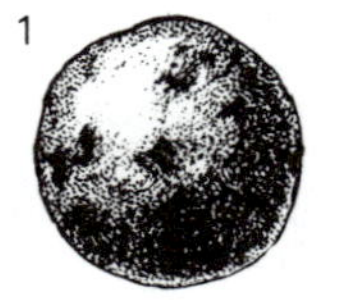

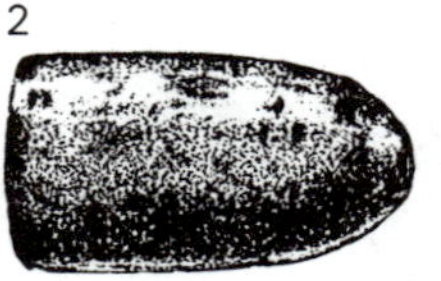

Priming materials (right) These were originally separate from the other components.
1 Gun flint. It sparked for about 20 shots before being replaced.
2 Copper percussion caps, containing detonating compound, and fired once only. At left is a military "top hat" cap, and at right a "common" cap.

Cartridge primers (right) Shown are three main types.
a The pinfire, with an integral pin which is struck by a hammer on the gun and sets off a cap inside the case.
b The rimfire, in which detonating compound inside the rim is crushed by the gun's firing pin.
c The centerfire, in which the gun's firing pin hits a cap located in the base of the cartridge.

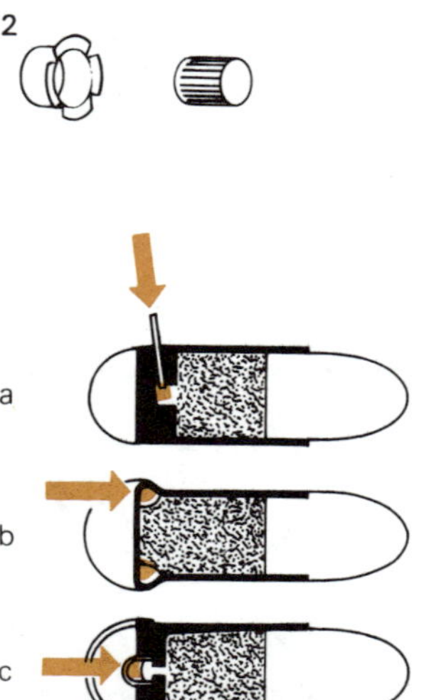

Cartridges (right) The materials needed to fire a muzzle-loader could be carried in bulk in flasks and pouches. But for military use, simple paper cartridges (**A**) were made up, containing a bullet and enough powder for one shot. The paper wrapper was torn open on loading. In the mid-19th century, many firearms were designed to use a combustible paper or linen cartrige (**B**), which was loaded as a unit but was still ignited by an external percussion cap.
The invention of the metallic cartridge (**C**) greatly eased the problems of breech-loading and rapid fire. Its brass case holds the propellant, bullet, its own means of ignition, and seals the breech on firing. It is waterproof and safe to handle.

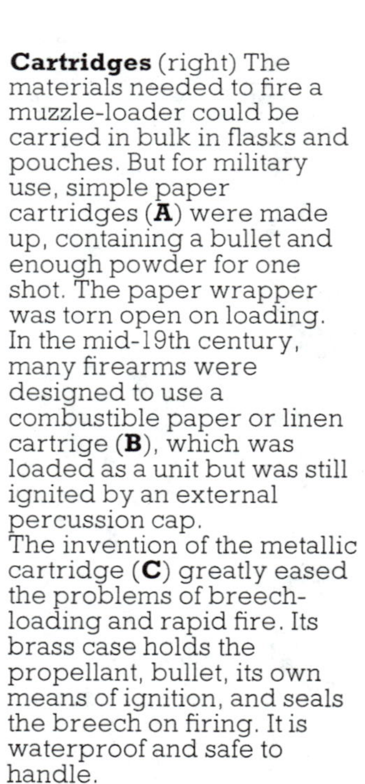

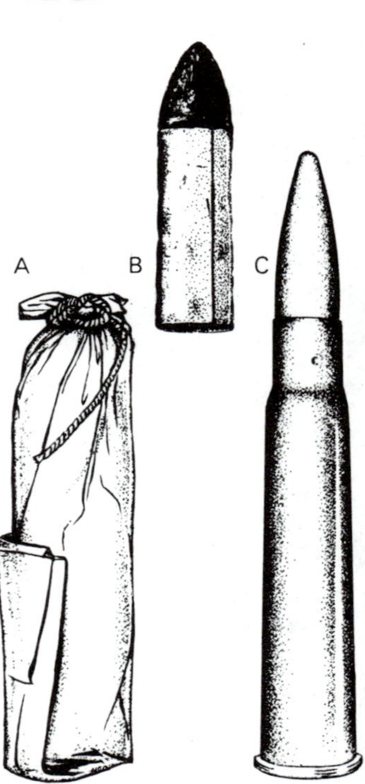

Bore size (right) can be described in two ways. The more usual way now is to give the measurement of the internal diameter of the bore (**1**). An older method is to give the gauge or bore number, for example 12-bore. This indicates that 12 perfect lead balls exactly fitting the bore would weigh one pound (**2**). Thus a 16-bore is smaller in caliber than a 12-bore.

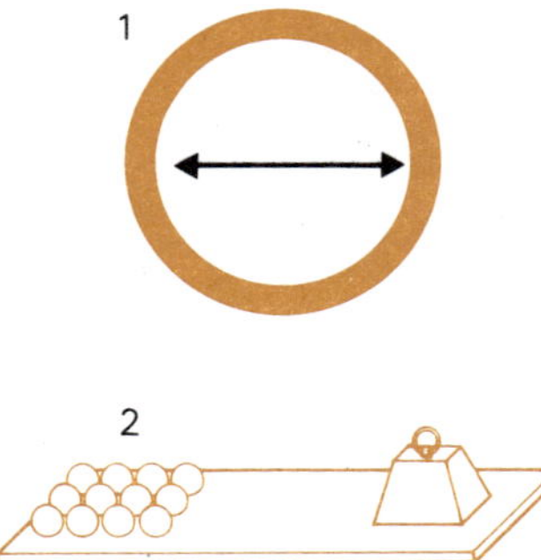

Extremes of caliber (right) The smallest calibers in common use are about .17in (4.3mm), shown (**a**). The largest guns fired from the shoulder rarely exceed 4-bore (**b**). In modern firearms usage, a caliber of 20mm (**c**) is often taken as the upper limit of the small arms category. Beyond that a weapon is classed as artillery.

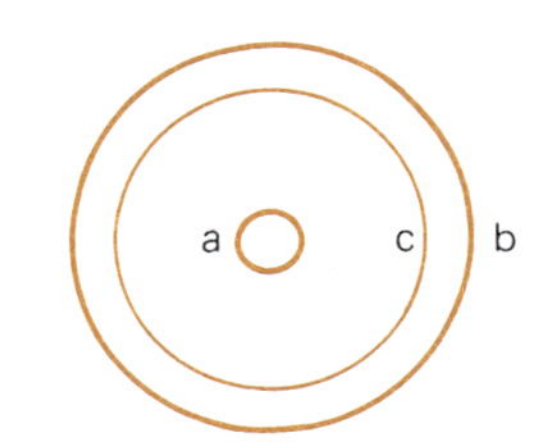

The caliber of modern firearms and ammunition is a complex subject. It may be expressed in metric or imperial units, according to the country of origin. However, the clearest means of notation is the metric system, which gives two figures. For example, the cartridge shown (right) is the German 7.92mm x57. The first figure is the nominal diameter of the bore (**A**). The second is the length of the case (**B**) in millimeters. This is usually sufficient to distinguish between types of ammunition with the same bullet diameter but different case shapes. The addition of the letter R, as in the Russian 7.62mm x54R, indicates that the case has a rimmed base (**C**), as opposed to the more usual so-called rimless type (**D**).

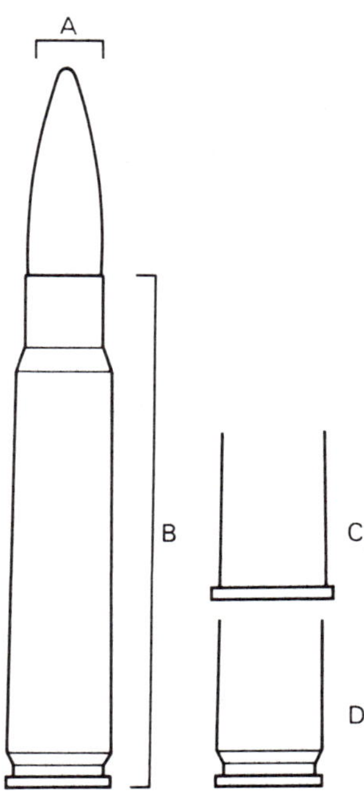

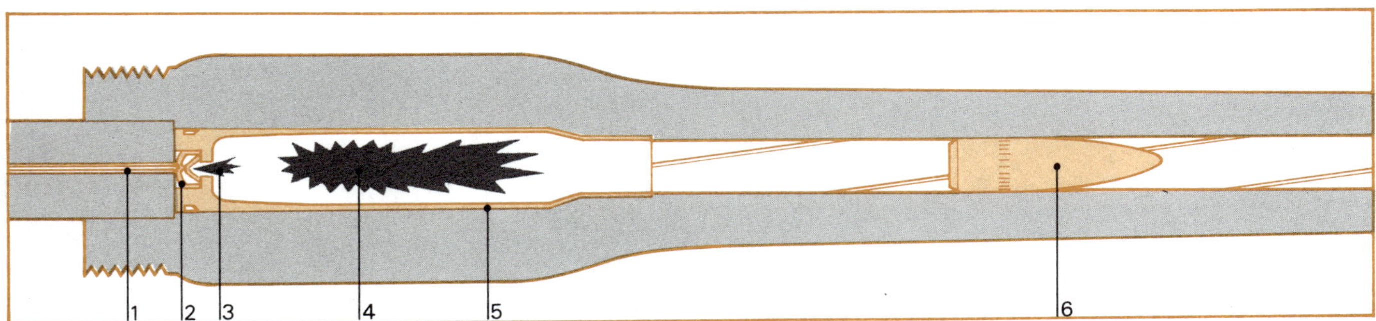

Internal phenomena (above) of the firing of a 20th century rifle cartridge. The example used is the US .30in Model 1906. The firing pin (**1**) dents the cap (**2**) in the cartridge base, crushing a detonating compound against a brass anvil. The resulting flash (**3**) ignites the main charge (**4**) which burns rapidly, the temperature reaching 2700°C. After 0.0005 seconds from ignition, the propellant has produced 14,000 times its own volume in gas. The pressure in the chamber reaches about 51,000 lbf/in² (3585.6 kgf/cm²). The sides of the brass cartridge case (**5**) are forced so tightly against the walls of the chamber that no gas can leak to the rear. The pressure forces the bullet (**6**) up the bore.

External phenomena (below) The table gives basic statistics on the same bullet's performance after it leaves the barrel. Note that it can penetrate less sand at short than at medium range. Penetration through timber and metal decreases as the velocity of the bullet decreases. (Information from the handbook for US Rifle, Model of 1917.)

	At the muzzle	**At 500yd (457.2m)**	**At 1000yd (914.4m)**
Speed of bullet	2700fps (822.9m/s)	1668fps (508.4m/s)	1068fps (325.5m/s)
Time of flight	Nil	0.709sec	1.864sec
Penetration through:			
dry sand	6.3in (16cm)	13in (33.02cm)	10.8in (27.43cm)
seasoned oak	34in (86.36cm)	14in (35.46cm)	Not known
mild steel plate	0.528in (1.34cm)	0.01in (0.0254cm)	Nil

Muzzle-loading small arms

Muzzle-loading firearms were generally preferred to breech-loaders until the mid-19th century, thanks to their advantages of simplicity and cheapness. This long period of popularity resulted in countless variations and minor improvements on the simple basic design of lock, stock and barrel. The many civilian and military muzzle-loaders that survive are now eagerly collected.

A sportsman (left) of the 18th century, ramming down the charge in his muzzle-loading shotgun, known then as a fowling piece.

Ignition systems (below) Here we show the six main types of ignition mechanisms (locks) used on small arms in the muzzle-loading era. Their purpose is to make fire, when required, at a narrow vent leading to the powder charge in the barrel. The examples shown are all of the simplest form, assembled on a metal lock-plate.

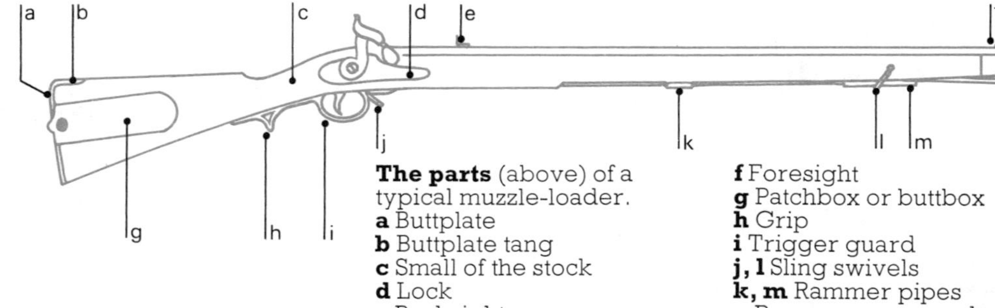

The parts (above) of a typical muzzle-loader.
a Buttplate
b Buttplate tang
c Small of the stock
d Lock
e Backsight
f Foresight
g Patchbox or buttbox
h Grip
i Trigger guard
j, l Sling swivels
k, m Rammer pipes
n Rammer or ramrod

Matchlock
Used in Europe until about 1700, it was used in India and Japan until the mid-19th century. On the trigger being pressed, the glowing tip of the match is plunged into the priming powder in the pan. Many varieties exist. In most, the pan and its cover are part of the barrel not of the lock, and must be opened by hand.

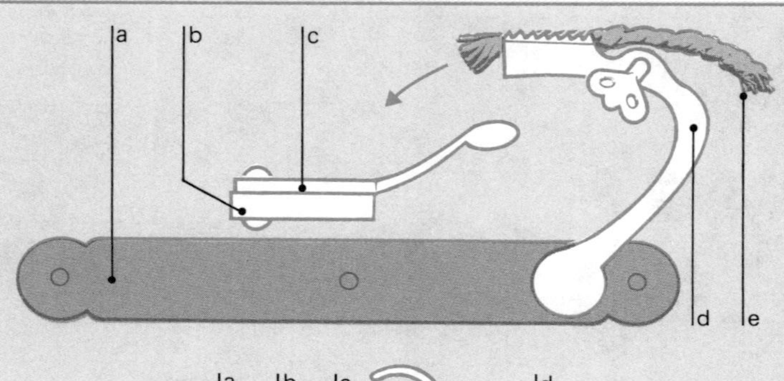

a Lockplate
b Pan
c Pan-cover
d Serpentine
e Match

Wheellock
Efficient, but internally complex and thus expensive, this type never wholly replaced the matchlock for military use. On pressing the trigger, the pan-cover slides forward and the pyrites is pressed against the wheel as it turns. The resulting sparks ignite the priming in the pan.

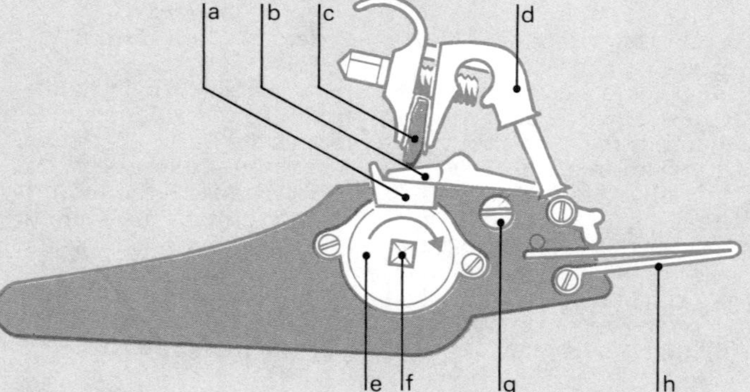

a Pan
b Pan-cover
c Iron pyrites
d Cock or dog-head
e Wheel
f Wheel-arbor or spindle
g Pan-cover release
h Cock-spring

Snaphance
An important innovation, using flint and steel for the first time. On pulling the trigger, the pan-cover is opened mechanically. At the same time, the cock swings forward to scrape the flint down the face of the steel, so pushing it away. The resulting sparks fall into the powder in the pan below.

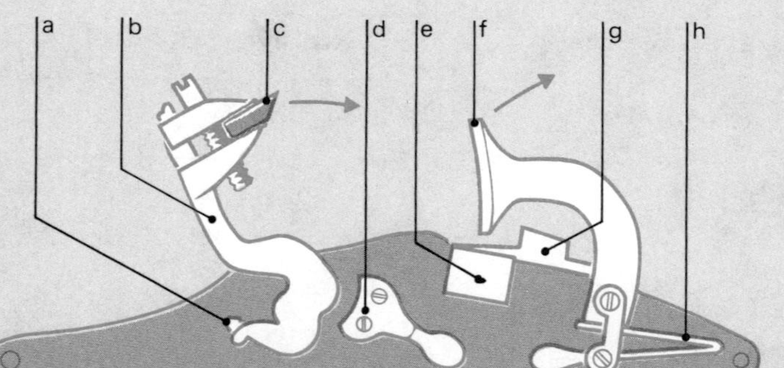

a Sear
b Cock
c Flint
d Buffer
e Pan
f Steel
g Pan-cover
h Steel-spring

Loading drill (right) for a flintlock musket. Armies used a strict drill in order to reduce errors in the heat of battle. The main actions were:
1 Biting the cartridge.
2 Priming the pan.
3 Pouring powder and ball into the muzzle.
4 Ramming down the charge.
5 Setting the lock to "full cock."
6 Aiming and firing.

Accessories (right) for use with muzzle-loaders.
a 17th century musketeer's powder flask.
b Rifleman's powder flask c.1810.
c Sportsman's powder flask c.1840.
d Military "combination tool," incorporating several implements.
e, f Bullet molds.

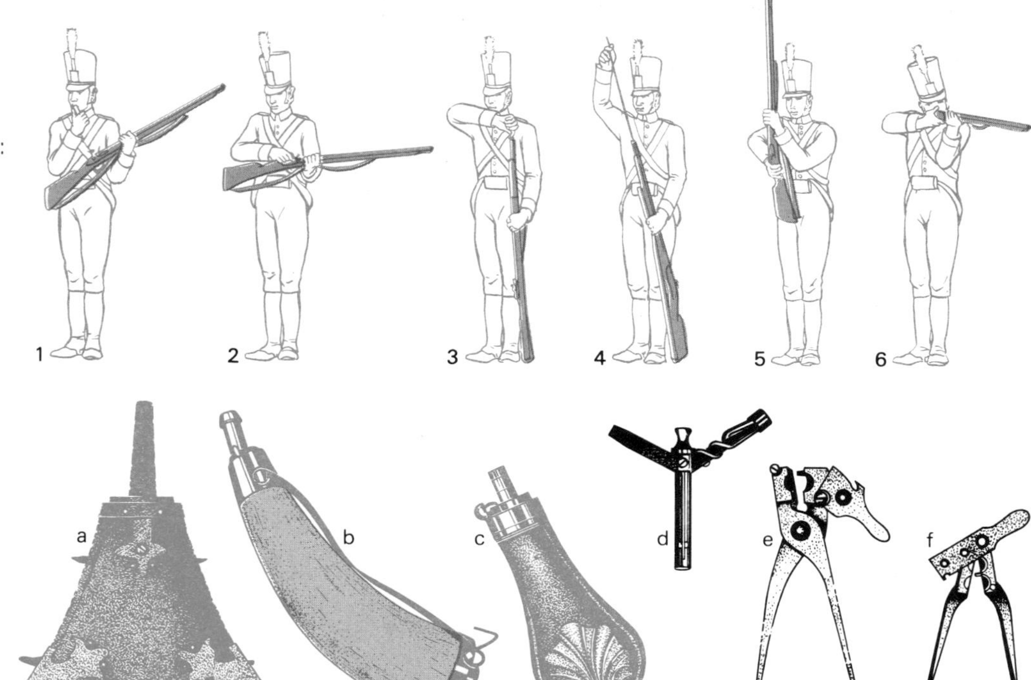

Flintlock
A refinement of the snaphance, with the steel and pan-cover made in one piece. On pressing the trigger, the cock scrapes the flint down the length of the steel, simultaneously uncovering the pan and exposing the priming to a shower of sparks. Simple and effective, this system replaced the matchlock and wheellock in Europe.

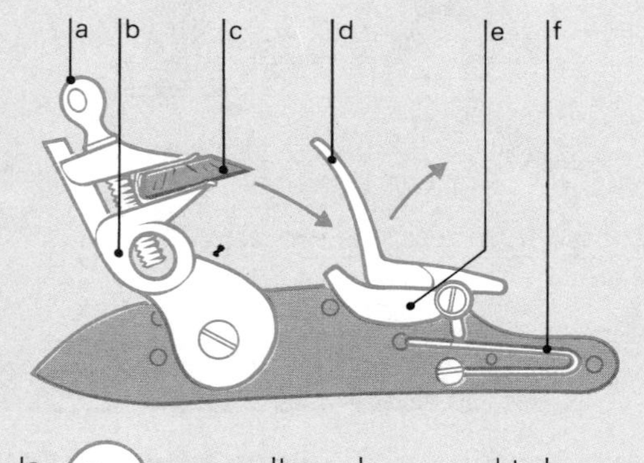

a Top-jaw screw
b Cock
c Flint
d Steel
e Pan
f Steel-spring

Miquelet
A close relation of the flintlock, long preferred in some Mediterranean areas. It differs in style, and in having an external mainspring. On pressing the trigger, the sear retracts from the toe of the cock, which is tipped forward by the spring pressing up at the heel. (In one variation the spring presses down on the toe.)

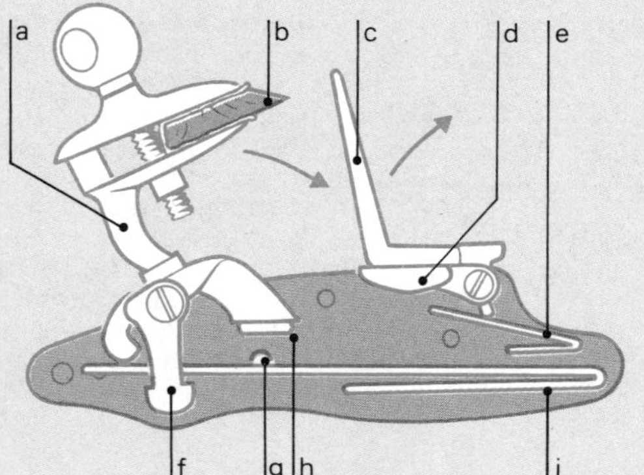

a Cock
b Flint
c Battery or steel
d Pan
e Battery-spring
f Cock-bridle
g Half-cock sear
h Full-cock sear
i Mainspring

Percussion
This is the commonest of the many ways found to use detonating compounds for ignition in the 19th century. On pressing the trigger, the hammer strikes the copper cap, crushing the compound against the end of the nipple. The resulting flash travels down the hollow nipple to the main powder charge in the barrel.

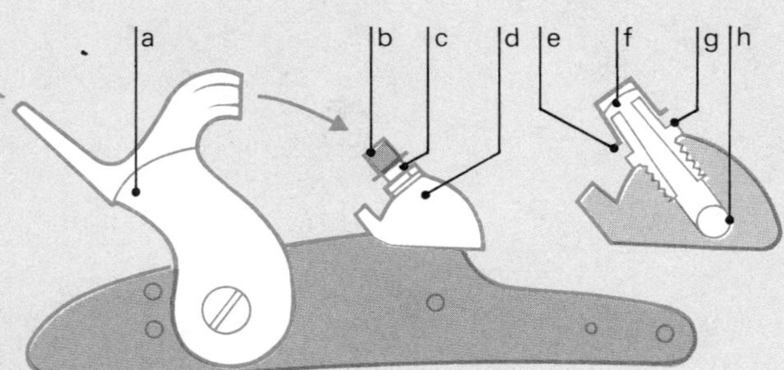

a Hammer
b Percussion cap
c Nipple
d Nipple lump or bolster

Section through nipple and lump:
e Percussion cap
f Detonating compound
g Nipple
h Vent to barrel

Single-shot muzzle-loading longarms 1

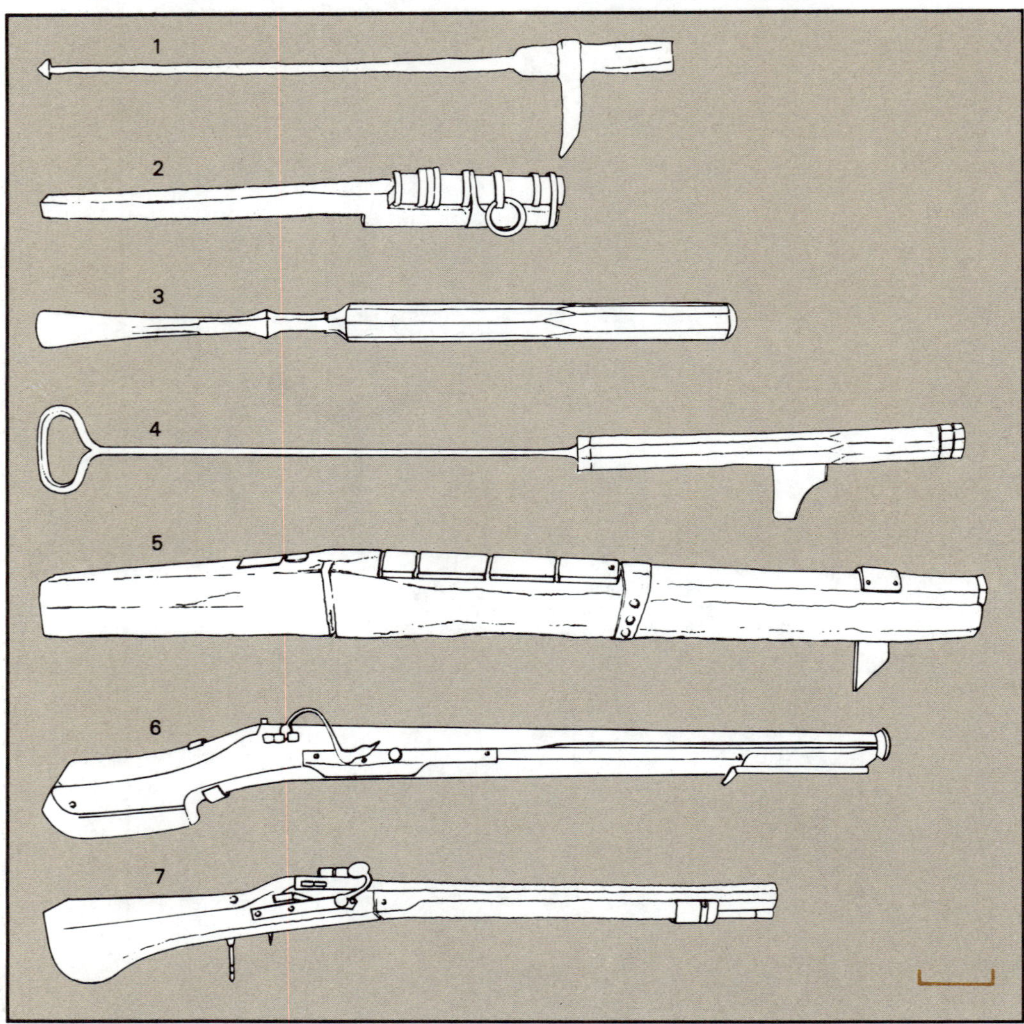

Hand-cannon and arquebuses (left)
1 All-iron hand-cannon with hook, c. 1400. Found in South Schleswig. (Tøjhusmuseet, Copenhagen.)
2 Hand-cannon with a wrought-iron barrel, found in the river Tiber at Rome. The wooden stock has been restored. From c. 1400-50. (Bernisches Historisches Museum, Switzerland.)
3 Hand-cannon with a socket for a wooden haft (now missing), c.1450. (Museum of Art and History, Geneva.)
4 All-iron hand-cannon with hook, from the second half of the 15th century. (Bernisches Historisches Museum, Switzerland.)
5 Large hackbut or arquebus, c.1470. (Museum of Art and History, Geneva.)
6 Arquebus with a matchlock mechanism. Swiss, c.1500. (Basle Historical Museum, Switzerland.)
7 Matchlock arquebus with a tubular backsight, from southern Germany. Dated 1537. (Bayerisches Nationalmuseum, Munich.)

Here we show single-shot muzzle-loading longarms, the basic firearm for over four centuries. Some are rifled, but smoothbores predominate in military use until c.1850. By that time, the type had been refined from the crude hand-cannon to the accurate and powerful Minié rifles of the Crimean and American Civil Wars.

Using a longarm (below)
a The illustration shows the firing of a large arquebus without a lock. It is hooked over a portable rest to absorb the recoil, yet one man still needs both hands to aim with, while another man puts a taper to the vent.
b In this illustration from the same source (watercolors by Nicolaus Glockenthon, c.1505), a gunstock, as we still know it, allows the firer to hold and aim with two hands, and to absorb the recoil with his shoulder, while a simple lock sets off the charge. Other designs of butt were placed against the cheek or chest.
c For about 100 years from c. 1567, heavy muskets in the Spanish style were fired, throughout Europe, from a simple forked rest.

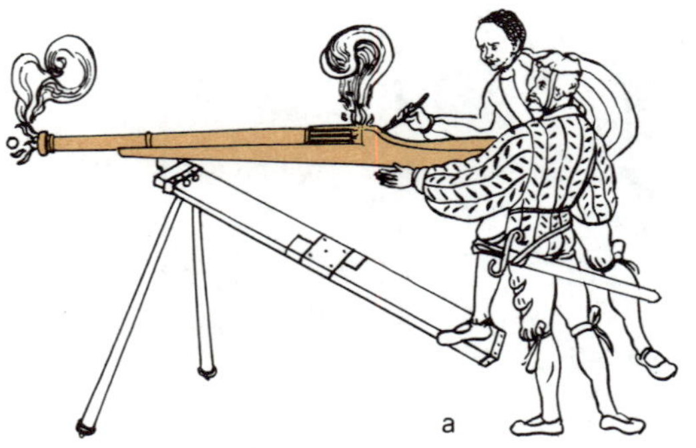

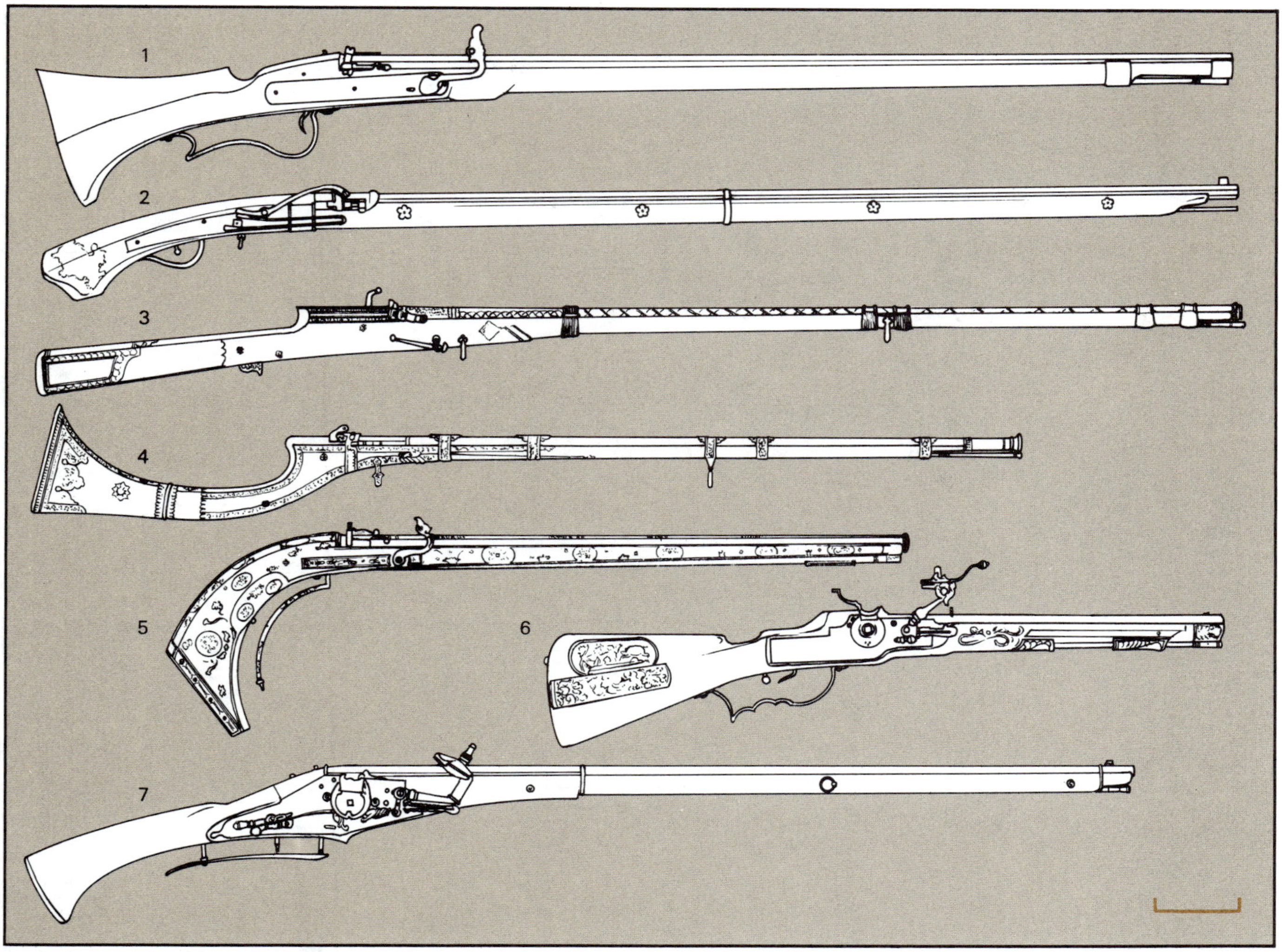

Matchlocks and wheellocks (above)
1 Matchlock caliver, a type of gun that was lighter than the musket of the time. This one is Austrian, c.1600.
2 Matchlock from Japan. The type was introduced by Portuguese traders in the 1540s, and was used, virtually unchanged, until the 1860s.
3 *Bandukh torador*, Indian matchlock musket. This form of ignition was in use in areas of India until this century.
4 *Jezail*. Matchlock musket with the Sind shape of butt, from what is now Pakistan. Also found with percussion or flint locks.
5 *Petronel*. Light French weapon with a butt designed to be held against the chest. This example, with bone inlay on the stock, is from c.1575.
6 Wheellock carbine with a rifled barrel. The stock inlaid with staghorn and bone. Probably German, 1675.
7 Military wheellock musket of plain style. Unusual, in that this mechanism was generally too expensive for issue to the rank-and-file. Italian, c.1600.

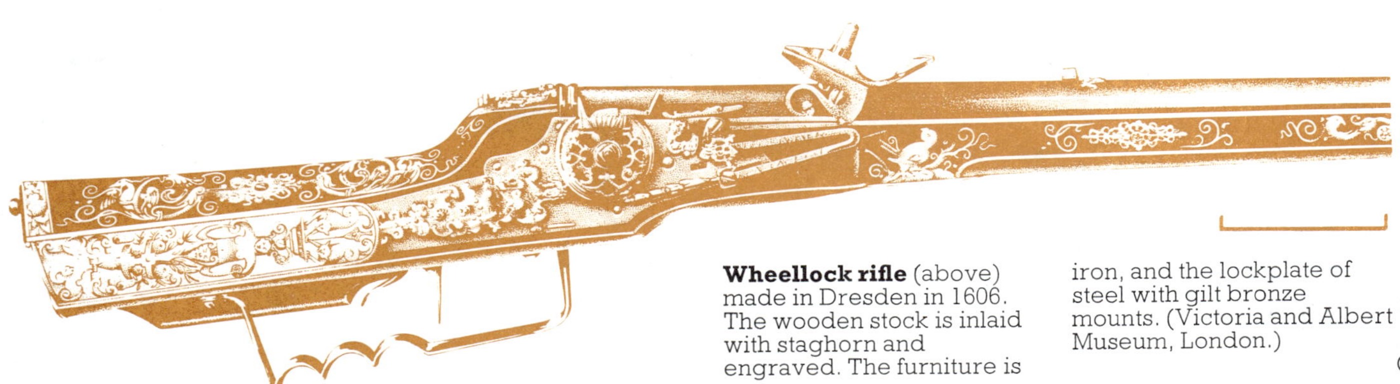

Wheellock rifle (above) made in Dresden in 1606. The wooden stock is inlaid with staghorn and engraved. The furniture is iron, and the lockplate of steel with gilt bronze mounts. (Victoria and Albert Museum, London.)

Single-shot muzzle-loading longarms 2

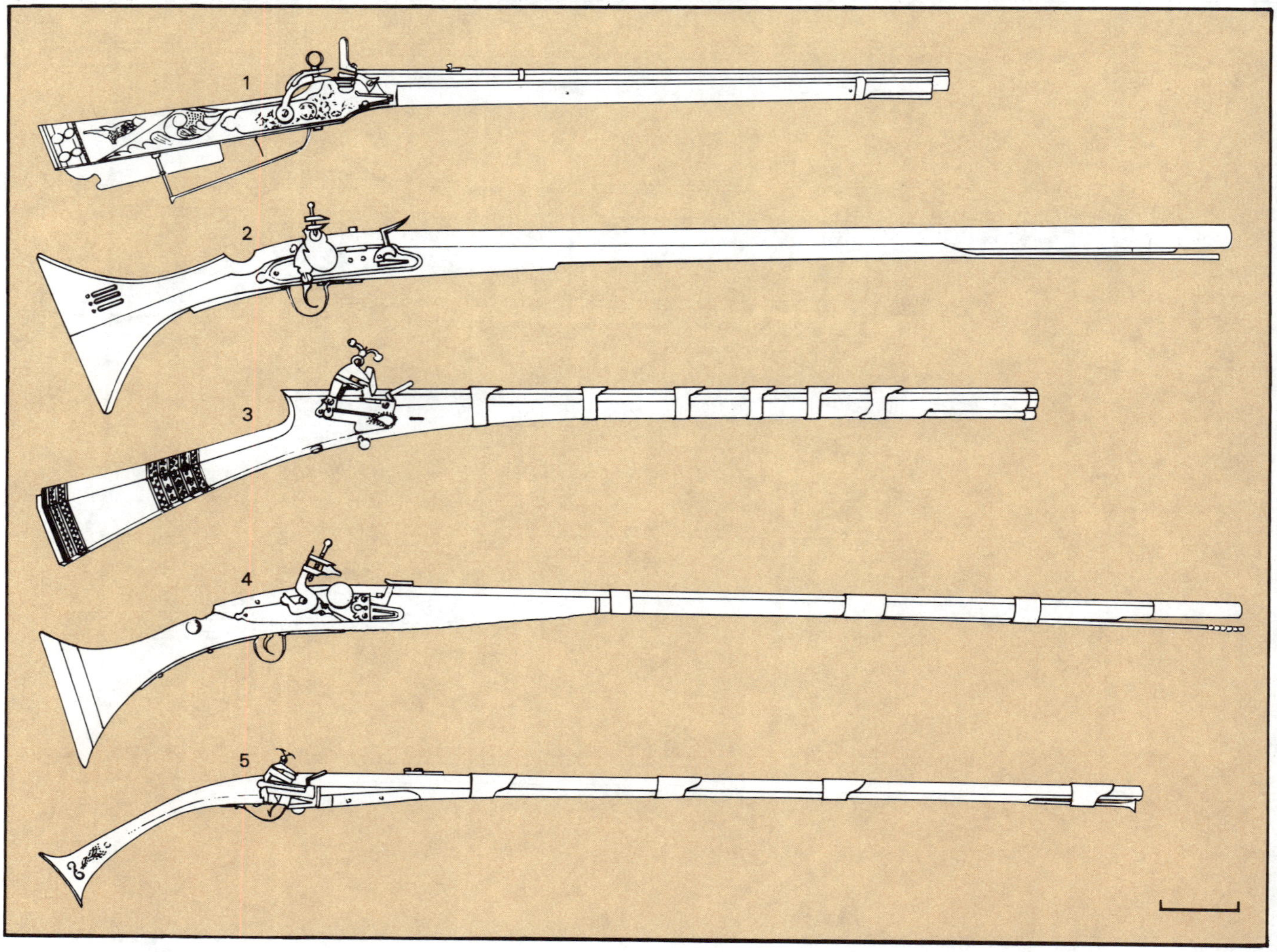

Some regional varieties (above) of smoothbore longarms.
1 Rifle with a Baltic type lock, a close relation of the flintlock, popular in Scandinavia in the 17th and 18th centuries. This one is probably Swedish, c.1650.
2 Dog-lock musket made in the American colonies, c.1640. The "dog" is the hook-like catch behind the cock of what is otherwise a flintlock. It is found on many 17th century English guns.
3 Turkish miquelet rifle of the 19th century. Turkish longarms in this characteristic style are often of high quality and richly decorated.
4 Algerian gun with a snaphance lock in the Dutch style, a form adopted widely in North Africa. 18th or 19th century.
5 Miquelet longarm from the Balkans, with a characteristic, slender butt. 19th century.

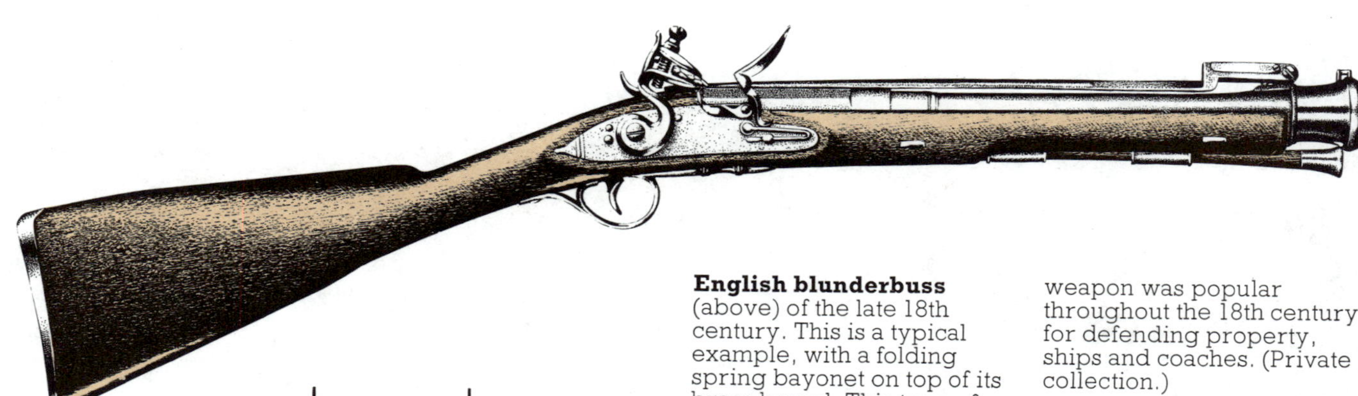

English blunderbuss (above) of the late 18th century. This is a typical example, with a folding spring bayonet on top of its brass barrel. This type of weapon was popular throughout the 18th century for defending property, ships and coaches. (Private collection.)

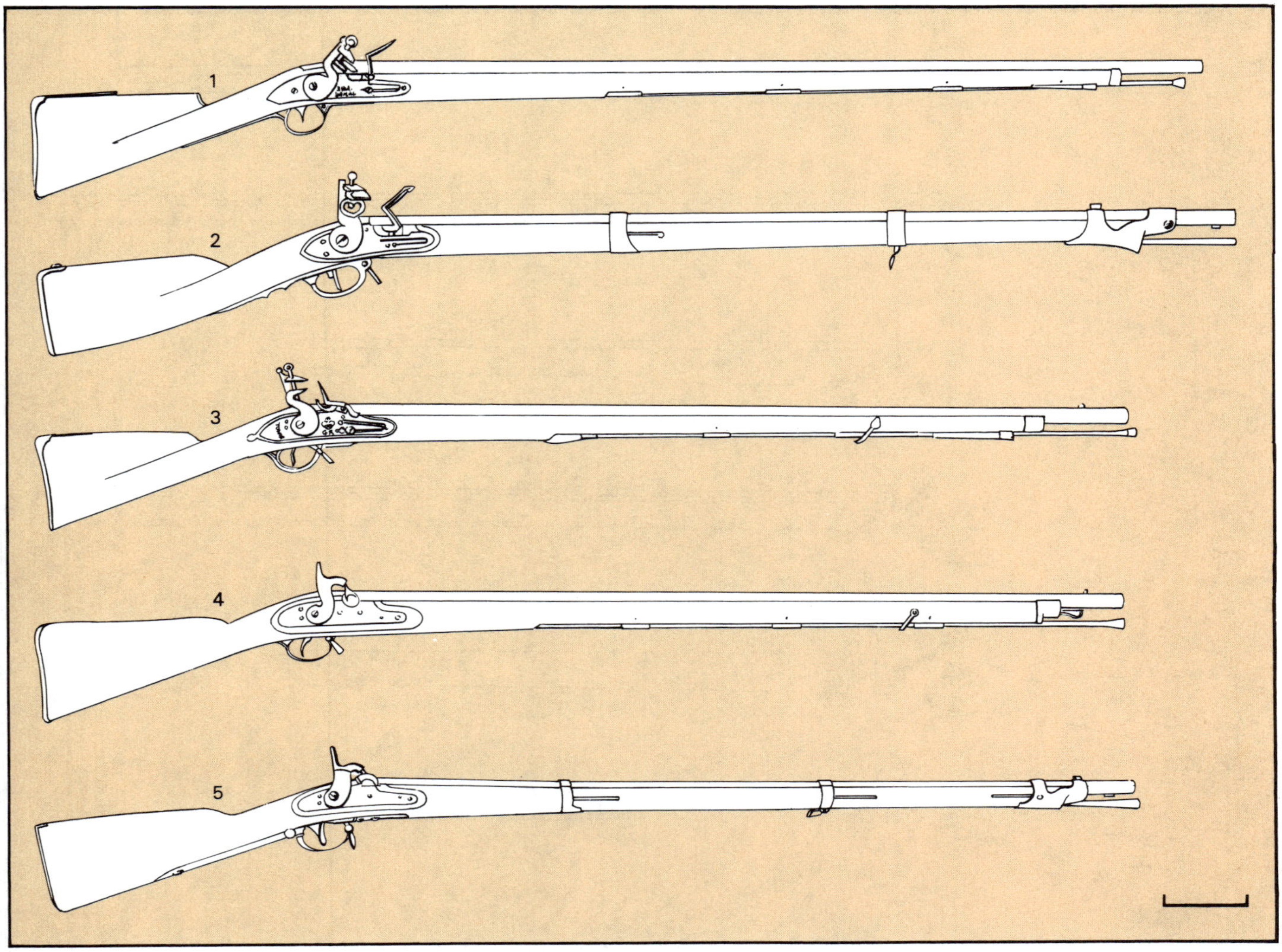

Volley firing (above) By modern standards, the smoothbore muzzle-loading muskets of the 17th, 18th and early 19th centuries were inaccurate and slow to load. A trained soldier could fire a shot about every 20 seconds, but could not expect to hit an individual enemy above about 80 yards (about 80 meters). But the infantry tactics of the time allowed for these defects. Ranks of men fired disciplined volleys, one sub-unit firing while others were loading. Thus an effective hail of bullets could be delivered at brief intervals to keep attackers at bay. Alternatively, a whole unit could fire together to overwhelm the enemy before attacking with the bayonet.

Smoothbore muskets (above)
1 American flintlock in the English style. Made for one of the "Committees of Safety" set up by the colonists in the War of Independence, 1776. Caliber .70in.
2 French Model 1777 musket. The main French infantry weapon, with modifications, of the Revolutionary and Napoleonic periods. Note the bands that hold the barrel to the fore-end, a characteristic of many continental European arms of the time. Caliber 17.5mm.
3 British "Brown Bess." Variations of this weapon served as the main British infantry arm from c.1720 until the 1840s. The model shown is the Short Land Pattern musket, distinguished by its 42in (106.7cm) barrel. It was adopted by the infantry in 1768, and was gradually replaced by the cheaper India Pattern musket from 1793. Caliber .75in.
4 British Pattern 1839 percussion musket. This was a transitional type, made up mostly from parts originally intended for flintlocks. Most armies changed to percussion ignition in about 1840. Caliber .75in.
5 US Model 1842, the US Army's last smoothbore percussion musket. Many were later rifled, and used in the Civil War (1861-65). Caliber .69in.

Single-shot muzzle-loading longarms 3

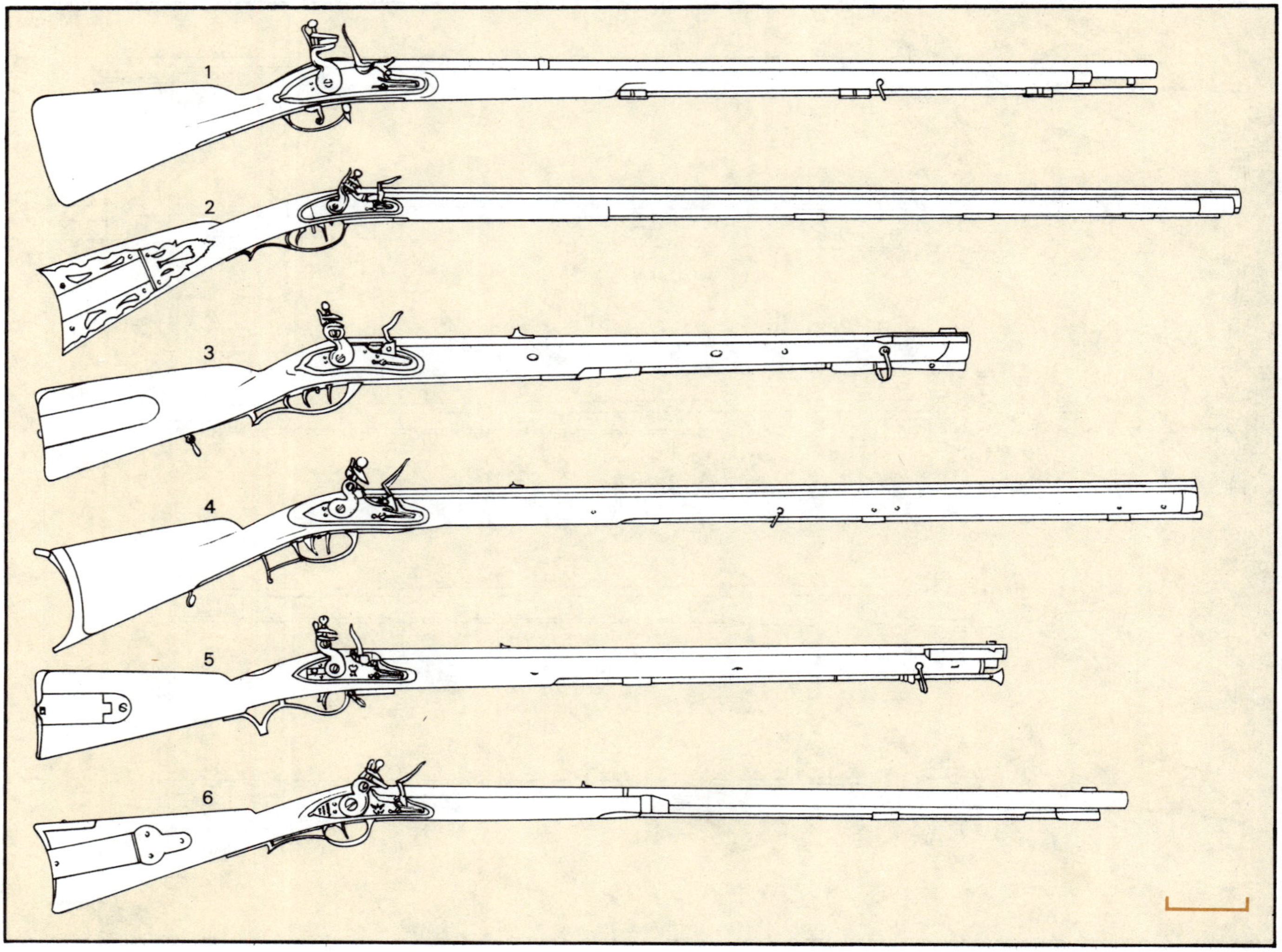

Flintlock rifles (above)
1 Danish Model 1763 rifled musket. There was very little external difference between this and the ordinary smoothbore musket of the time. Caliber 27mm.
2 Pennsylvania rifle, commonly but less correctly called a Kentucky rifle. The long barrel and elegant curved butt are typical of the classic American rifle of the 18th and 19th centuries. Caliber .44in.
3 Prussian Jäger rifle, Model 1810. Such rifles from the German states were successful and much copied in the late 18th century. Caliber 14.7mm.
4 Swiss Jäger rifle c.1800. Note the two triggers, one of which is a "set" trigger for accurate shooting, needing only a light touch to fire a shot. Caliber .72in.
5 British Baker rifle, in use c. 1800-40. This was the first rifle used in quantity by the British Army. The variation shown is c.1806-15. Caliber .625in.
6 US Model 1803 Harpers Ferry rifle. The first US Army rifle to be produced in a government arsenal. Caliber .54in.

The butt and lock (below) of a Pennsylvania long rifle. The curve of the butt and the decorative brasswork around the patch-box are characteristic of these rifles. Note the subtle vertical grain in the wood of the stock, which is of "tiger-stripe" maple. The small size of the lock is also typical of these stylish weapons.

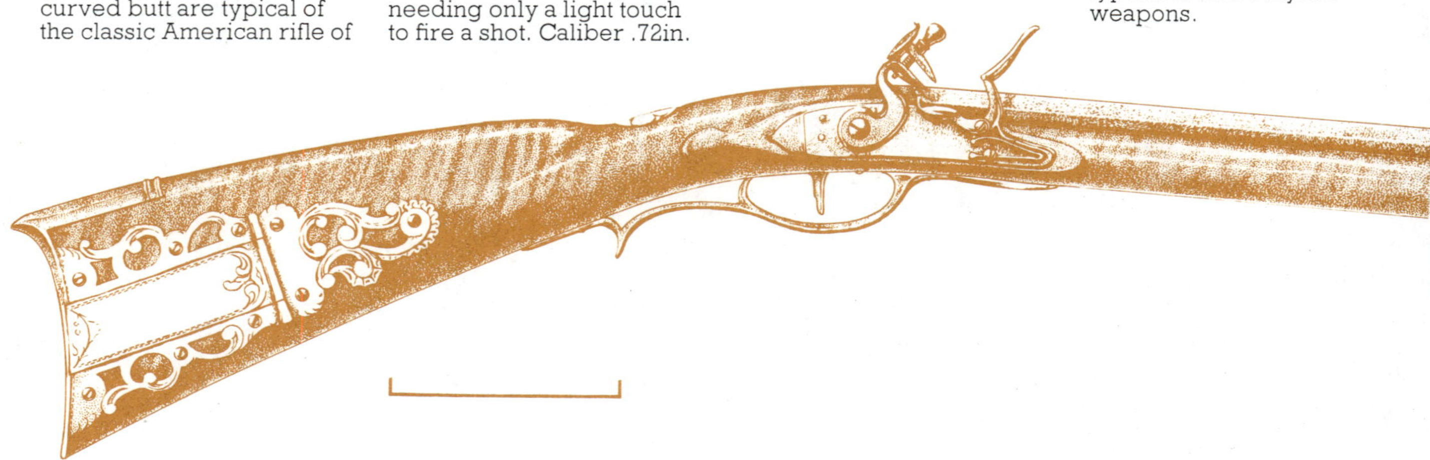

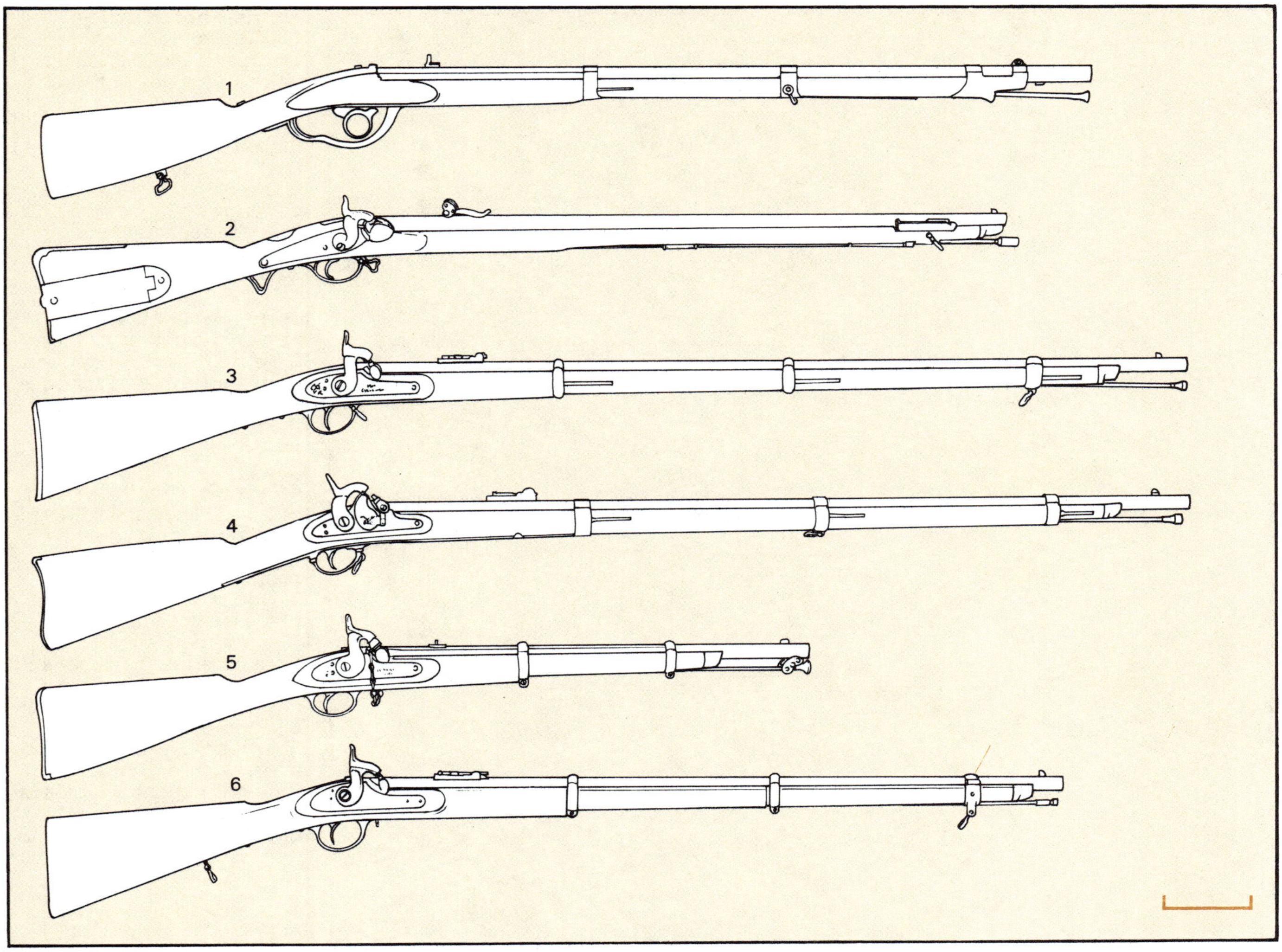

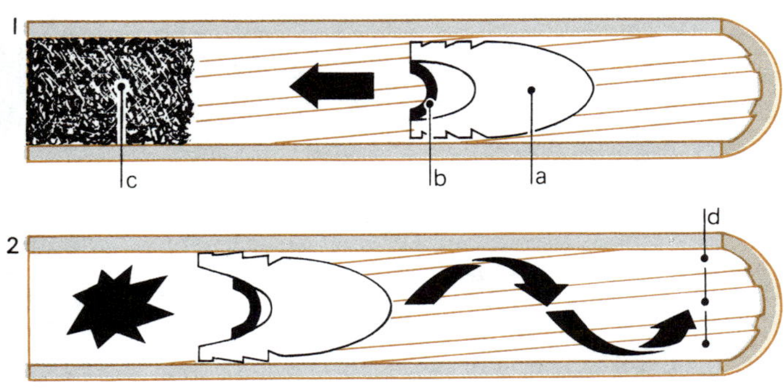

The Minié principle (above) was a French invention. It revolutionized military small arms in the 1850s by putting accurate rifles into the hands of all infantrymen.
1 A bullet (**a**), small enough to be pushed easily down a barrel dirty from much firing, has an iron cup (**b**) fitted into a hollow in its base.
2 When the powder (**c**) explodes, the cup is thrust into the hollow, forcing the skirt of the bullet into the rifling grooves (**d**). Thus the ease and speed of loading of the old smoothbore musket was combined with the accuracy of a rifle. Many older arms were altered to the new system. It was later found that a wooden plug in the bullet, or none at all, achieved the same effect.

Percussion rifles (above)
1 Danish underhammer rifled musket made in 1841. Several countries tried similar inverted locks. The main advantage was safety for the eye from the exploding cap. Caliber .69in.
2 Russian Model 1851 rifle. Fired a conical bullet with flanges to fit the bore's two wide grooves. The British Brunswick rifle was similar, but fired a ball cast with a belt around it to fit the grooves. Caliber .702in.
3 British Pattern1853 Enfield rifled musket. An influential Minié type rifle, used and copied widely. This is the second variation, as used in the Crimea and the Indian Mutiny. Caliber .577in.
4 US Model 1855 rifled musket. Fitted with Maynard's patent tape primer. This fed a roll of detonating caps over the nipple automatically as the hammer was cocked, and avoided fumbling for loose caps. Caliber .58in.
5 Carbine made at the Confederate States Arsenal at Tallassee, Alabama, in the American Civil War (1861-65). Derived from the Pattern 1853 Enfield. Caliber .58in.
6 British Whitworth military short rifle, 1863. Had a bore of hexagonal section, with a bullet shaped to fit it closely. One of the most accurate muzzle-loaders, but more successful as a target rifle than as a weapon. Caliber .451in.

Single-shot muzzle-loading pistols 1

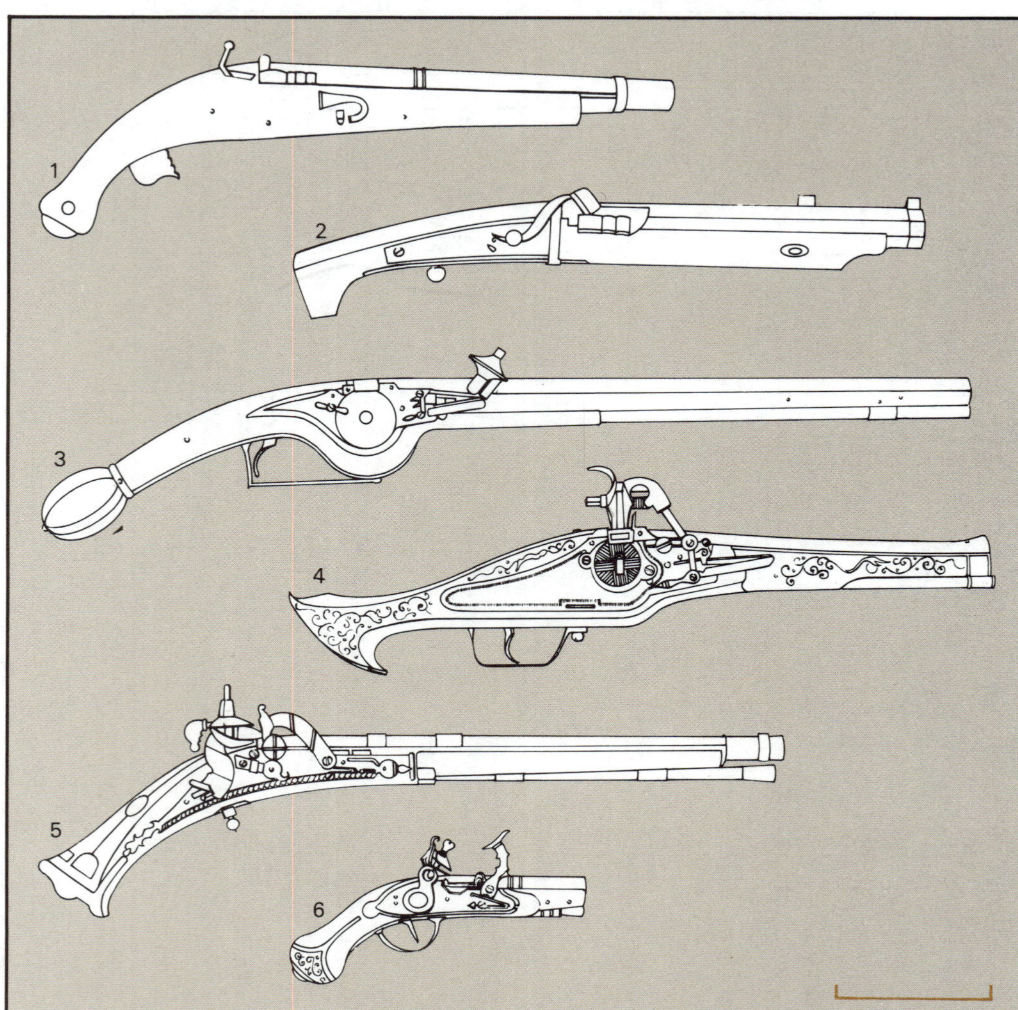

Single-shot muzzle-loading pistols (left)
1 Indian matchlock pistol with the trigger in the shape of a lotus flower. In the Indian form of matchlock, the serpentine rises clear of the pan as soon as the trigger is released. 18th century.
2 Japanese matchlock pistol with an octagonal iron barrel. Fitted with a snap-action lock which must be cocked by hand before firing. 19th century.
3 Dutch military wheellock holster pistol. This shape is characteristic of northern European cavalry pistols of the early and mid-17th century.
4 German wheellock "dag" or pistol. The shallow angle between barrel and butt is typical of early European pistols. Late 16th century.
5 Scottish snaphance pistol of the early 17th century. The snaphance lock was popular enough in Scotland for a recognizable national style to emerge.
6 Italian snaphance pistol, from the Tuscany region. A late example of this type of ignition; note how it differs from a true flintlock, in having a separate steel and pan-cover.

The pistol or handgun is a subdivision of small arms that did not appear until the early 16th century, in Europe. At that time the wheellock made a one-handed gun more practicable. Because of the pistol's limited accuracy, range and power, it has always been less important militarily than longarms. Yet its greater convenience has made it popular with civilians, chiefly as a defensive weapon.

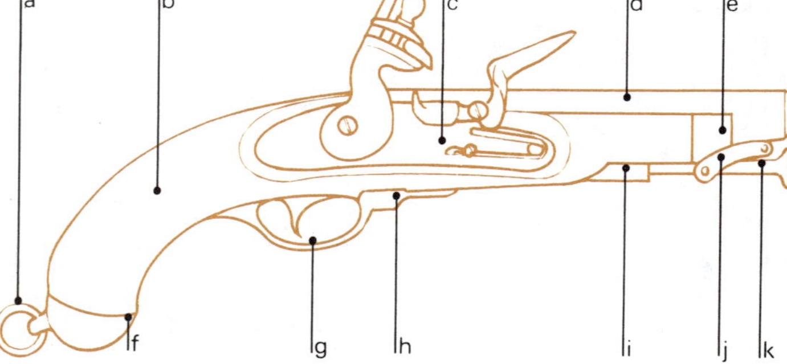

The parts (above) of a muzzle-loading pistol. All the features shown are common, especially on cavalry pistols, but are not necessarily present in every case.
a Lanyard ring
b Butt or grip
c Lock
d Barrel
e Fore-end-cap or nose-cap
f Butt-cap
g Trigger-guard
h Trigger-guard finial
i Rammer pipe
j Rammer swivel
k Rammer

Horseman's weapon (right) Being a one-handed weapon, the pistol was well suited to use on horseback, the other hand being left free to hold the reins. From the 16th century to the third quarter of the 19th, it was the custom in most Western armies for a cavalryman to carry a pair of pistols in holsters attached to his saddle. (After a woodcut of 1601.)

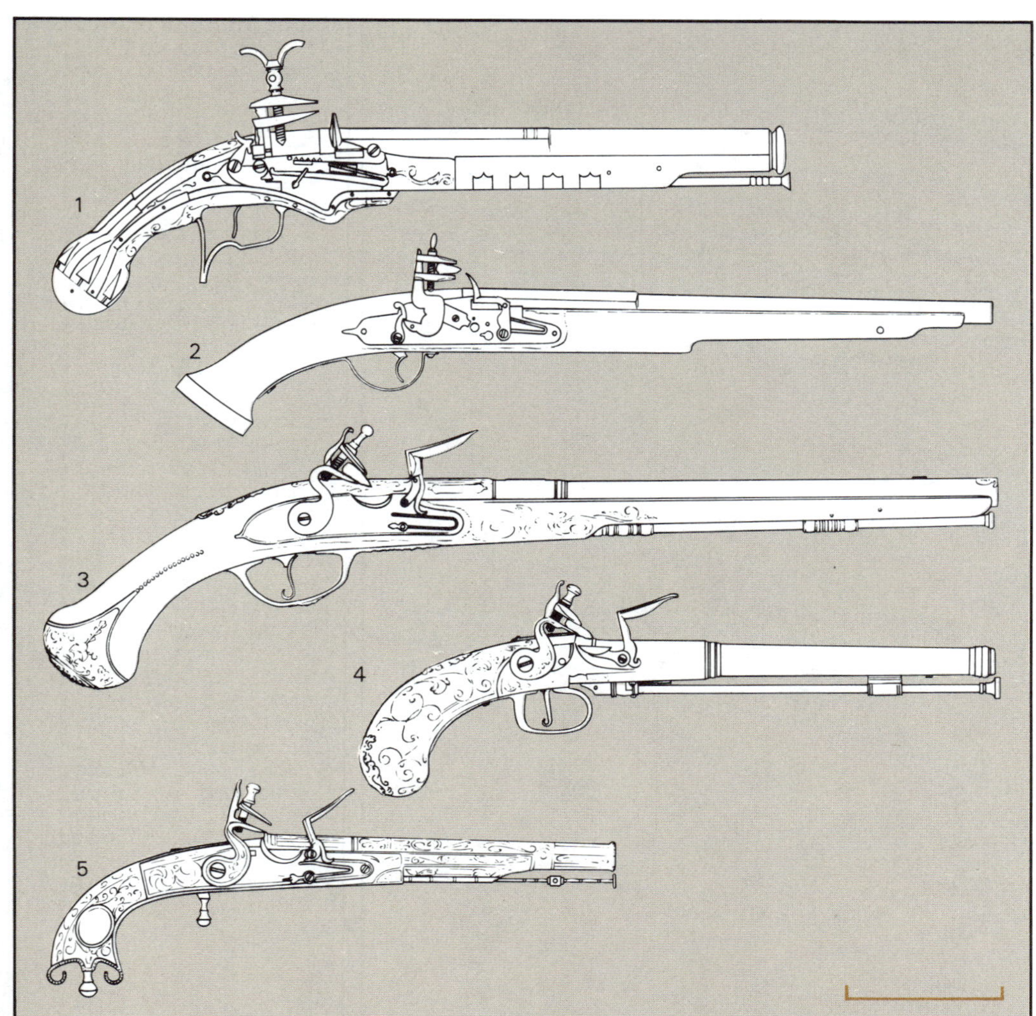

Single-shot muzzle-loading pistols (left)
1 Miquelet pistol from Ripoll, a town in the Pyrenees that once produced firearms in its own distinctive style. The lock is a variation in which the mainspring presses down on the toe of the cock. Dates from c.1600-50.
2 Holster pistol with an "English dog-lock," an early variety of flintlock, c.1640. The dog was a safety catch behind the cock.
3 French flintlock holster pistol of the 1680s. This style, with its elegant lock and long-eared butt-cap, remained popular in France and England for about a century.
4 Belgian all-metal rifled pistol with a flintlock mechanism made as part of the frame. Made at Liège, c.1725.
5 Scottish all-metal flintlock pistol by J. Murdoch of Doune, a celebrated maker of pistols in this style. The ball on the butt unscrews to reveal a pricker, used to clear fouling from the vent. Dates from c.1770.

Wheellock pistol (left) from South Germany, made in the late 16th century. A cavalryman would have carried a pair of such pistols in holsters at the front of his saddle. The wooden stock is inlaid with bone and mother-of-pearl. The lock is fitted with a safety catch. The iron barrel is of .60in (15.24mm) caliber. (Castle Museum, York.)

Single-shot muzzle-loading pistols 2

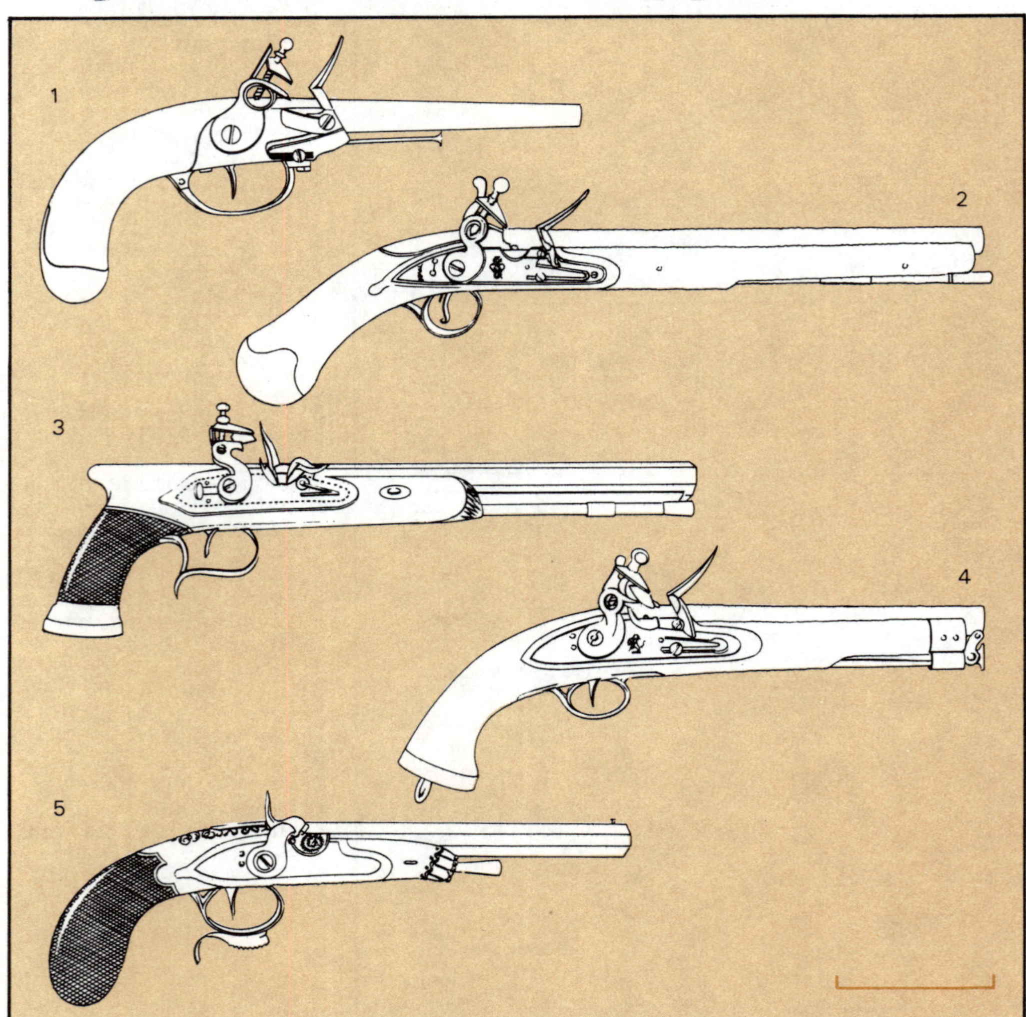

Later flintlock pistols (left)
1 French Model 1777 cavalry pistol, an unusual design. The lockplate is integral with the frame, the spring for the steel is reversed, and the rammer is set deep in the stock. Caliber 17.1mm.
2 British sea-service pistol. Pistols and muskets were kept on board warships for use in close-quarter fighting and by landing parties. Dated 1800. Caliber .56in.
3 One of a pair of "saw-handled" dueling pistols made by T. Mortimer and Son of London, c.1820. A late, refined flintlock with a rain-proof pan and a roller-bearing on the steel-spring. Caliber .52in.
4 East India Company cavalry pistol. Made in London c.1820-40 for the Native cavalry in British India. The rammer is attached to the muzzle by a swivel, and held in place by an external spring. Caliber .65in.
5 One of a pair of Russian pistols. Fine quality, with octagonal rifled barrel. Made c.1820 as a flintlock, and converted to percussion ignition c.1840. Caliber .50in.

Dueling pistols (left) in a fitted case, with a set of typical accessories. Special pairs of pistols for dueling were made, chiefly in England and France, from the 1770s. English dueling pistols were usually plain but of high quality, with octagonal smoothbore barrels.

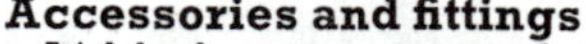

Accessories and fittings
a Lidded compartment for lead balls, flints or rags.
b Rod for loading and cleaning, incorporating a mallet.
c Tin for linen patches.
d Powder flask.
e Brush for cleaning the pan.
f Pewter oil bottle.
g Bullet mold.
h Turnscrew.
i Spring cramp.
j Punch for making patches.
k Second lidded compartment.

Dueler (below) waiting to fire his pistol.

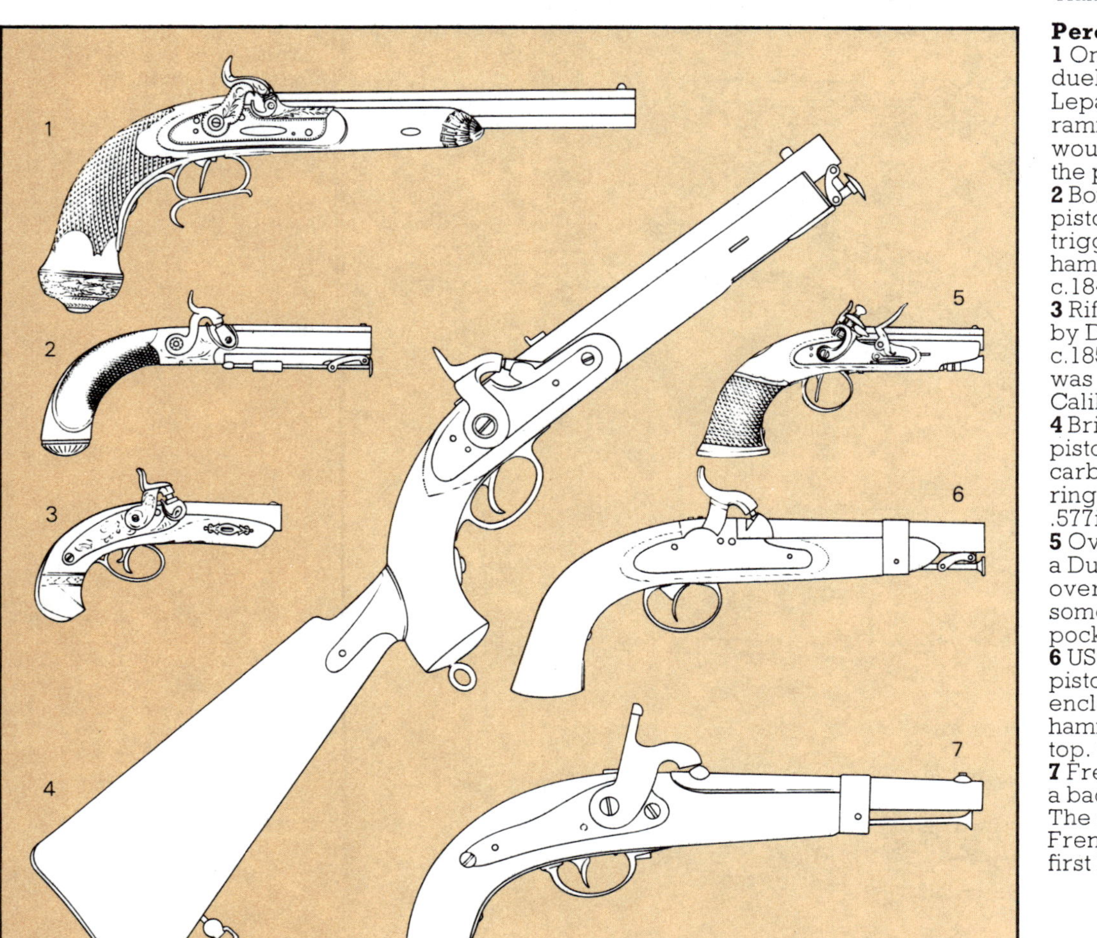

Percussion pistols (left)
1 One of a pair of rifled dueling pistols made by Lepage of Paris, c.1825. No rammer is fitted, as this would have been kept in the pistols' fitted case.
2 Boxlock side-hammer belt pistol. The concealed trigger appears when the hammer is cocked. English, c.1840.
3 Rifled pocket pistol made by Deringer of Philadelphia, c.1850. This maker's name was often pirated by others. Caliber .45in.
4 British Pattern 1856 rifled pistol. With a detachable carbine stock and a lanyard ring on the butt. Caliber .577in.
5 Overcoat pistol by Rigby, a Dublin gunsmith. An overcoat pistol was somewhat larger than a pocket pistol.
6 US Navy Model 1843 pistol. Note the distinctive enclosed lock, with the hammer emerging at the top. Caliber .54in.
7 French cavalry pistol with a back-action lock, c.1845. The style is typical of French military pistols of the first half of the 19th century.

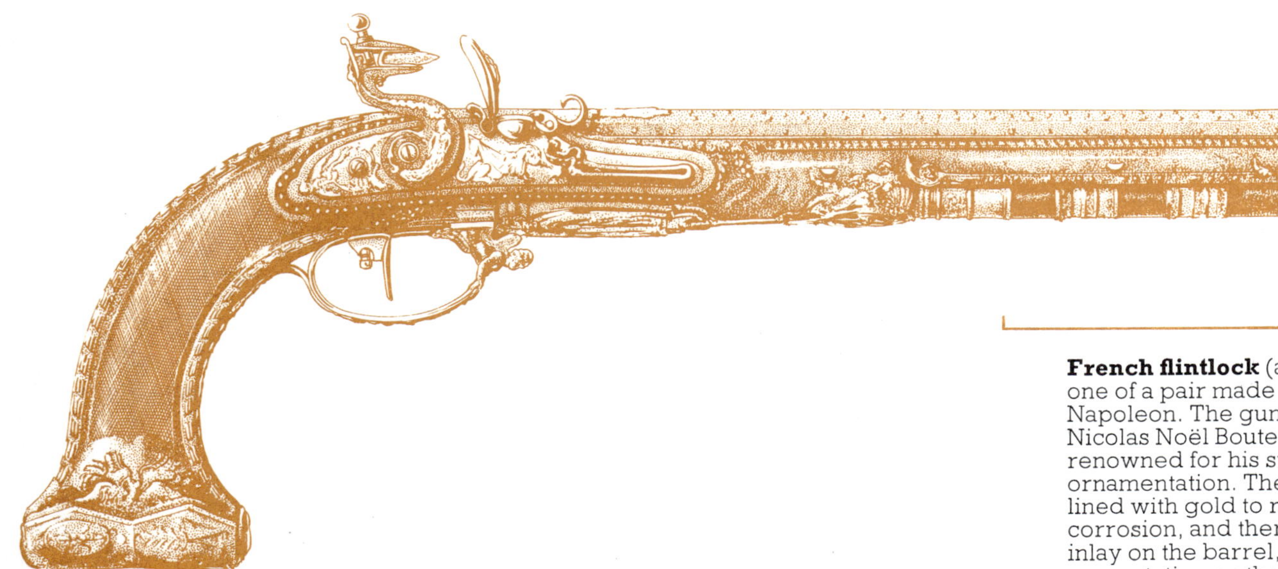

French flintlock (above), one of a pair made for Napoleon. The gunsmith, Nicolas Noël Boutet, was renowned for his superb ornamentation. The pan is lined with gold to resist corrosion, and there is gold inlay on the barrel, and gold encrustation on the lock. (Musée de l'Armée, Paris.)

Multi-shot muzzle-loaders

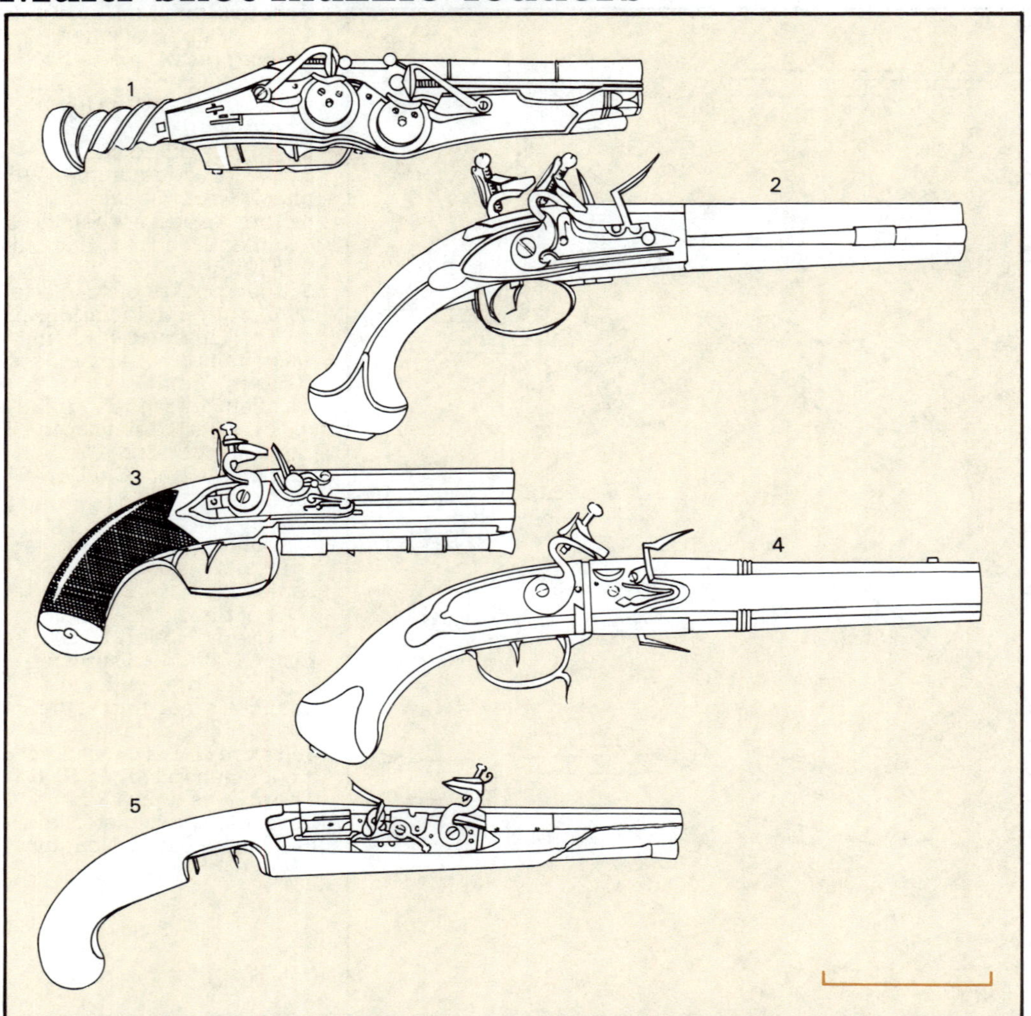

Multi-shot muzzle-loading pistols (left)
1 Wheellock over-and-under pistol, with two mechanisms on one lockplate. Made in Munich, c.1600.
2 Flintlock over-and-under pistol with a lock at each side. The locks have external mainsprings. English, c.1750.
3 Flintlock over-and-under officer's pistol, with a lock on each side. Made by Durs Egg of London, c.1790.
4 Flintlock "turnover" pistol, with two hand-rotated barrels. There is only one cock, but each barrel has its own pan and steel. European, c.1700.
5 Flintlock pistol for firing several superimposed loads from one barrel. The lock slides rearward to the next touch-hole as the second "trigger" is pulled. English, c.1785.

Many attempts were made to improve the rate of fire of muzzle-loaders. Some tried to superimpose many shots in one barrel. More commonly, several barrels were built into one weapon. Yet once the available shots had been fired, reloading was as slow as ever. Nevertheless, the initial advantage over an opponent using a single-shot weapon could be valuable, and many of these firearms were made.

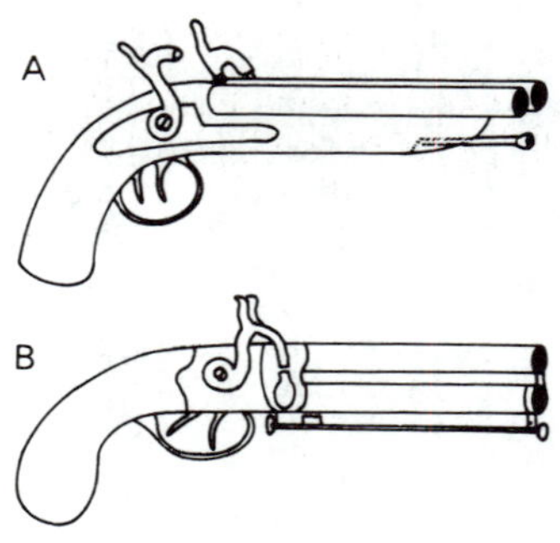

One lock per barrel (left) was the commonest system for multi-barreled guns. Most of these had two barrels, placed side-by-side (**A**), or over-and-under (**B**). Their advantage was that, should one lock missfire, the other was instantly available. The disadvantages were heaviness and an awkward shape.

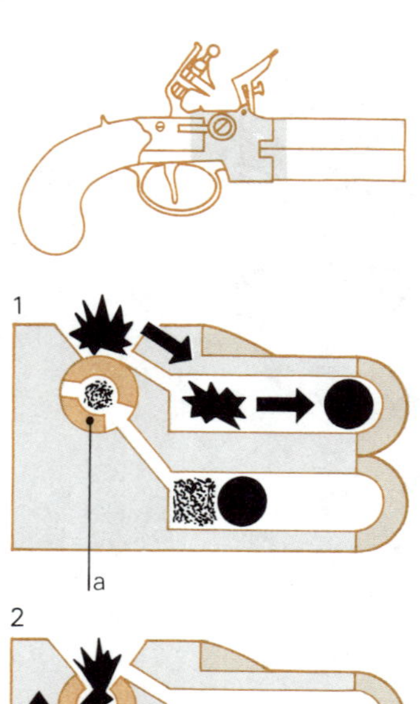

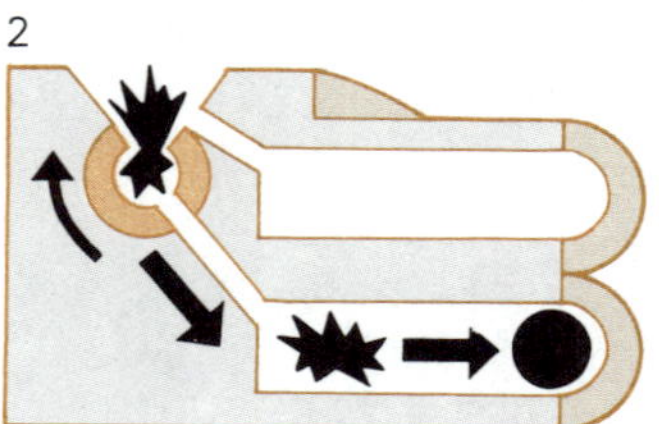

Tap-action pistol (left)
This was a system that allowed one lock to fire each barrel in turn. The pistol was fired once as at (**1**), when the flashpan was connected only to the top barrel. The tap (**a**) was then turned and the pistol re-cocked. On pulling the trigger again, the flash in the pan was connected to the lower barrel as at (**2**). It follows that if the pistol was first fired with the tap in this position, both barrels would go off simultaneously, but this was not the intention of the design.
There were a number of variations on this idea, with sliding pan-covers and more barrels, but the one shown was the most common. All were civilian self-defense weapons.

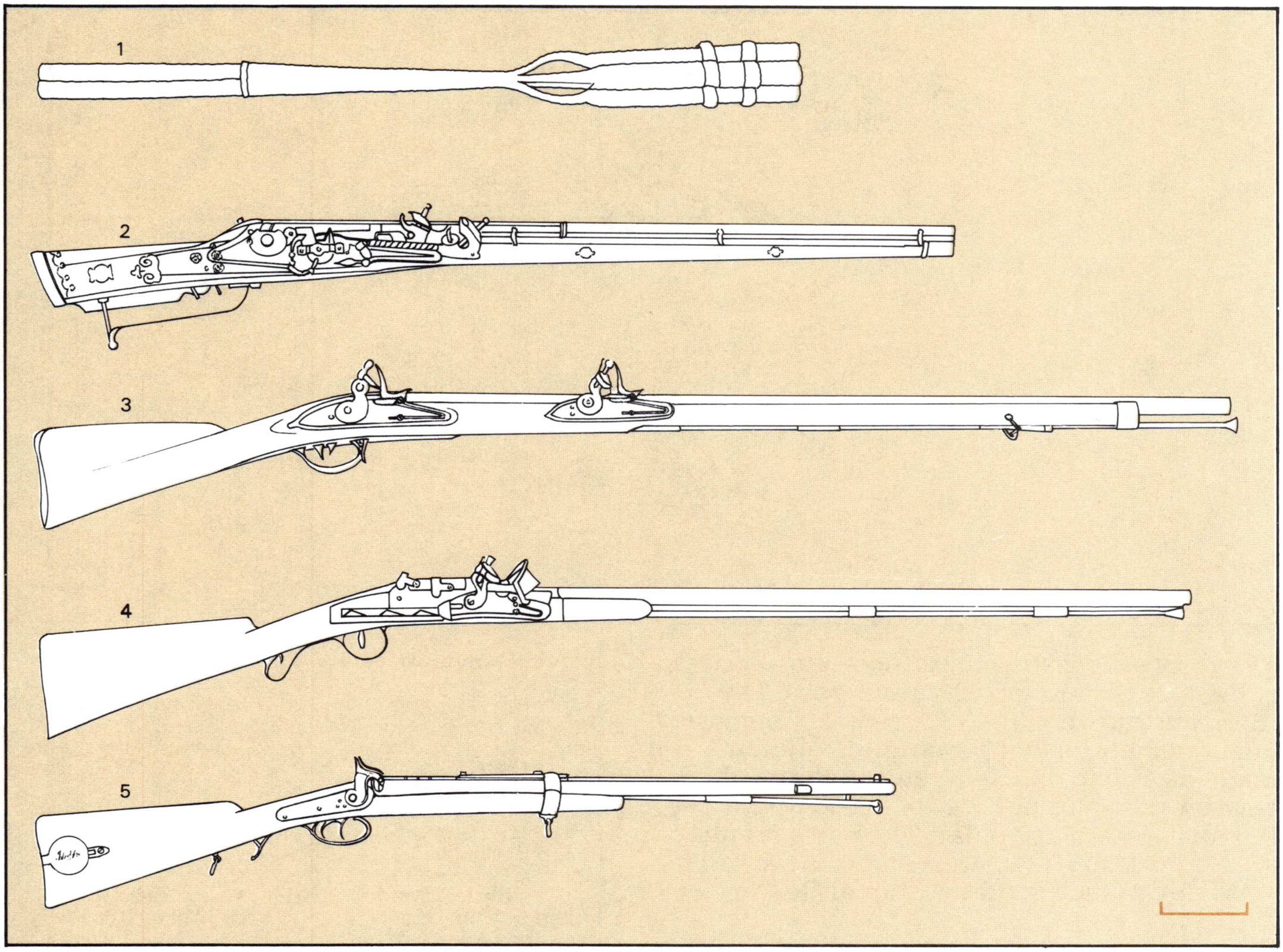

Multi-shot, muzzle-loading longarms (above)
1 Four-barreled hand-cannon of iron, on a wooden stock. European, mid-15th century.
2 Double-barreled wheellock rifle, with two locks mounted on one lockplate. Saxon, dated 1588.
3 Experimental English flintlock musket, 1815. The front lock ignited a fusilade of 11 superimposed, interconnecting charges. One charge was kept in reserve to be fired by the rear lock, which also allowed the weapon to be used as a normal single-shot musket.
4 Flintlock superimposed-load gun by H.W. Mortimer of London, c.1800. Each load was ignited via a separate touch-hole as the lock moved to the rear.
5 Jacob rifle. A double-barreled percussion rifle with four-groove rifling. It fired pointed bullets or miniature explosive shells, and was sighted up to 2000yd (1828m). British Indian Army, 1858.

Volley gun (below) invented by James Wilson in 1779, and made for the Royal Navy by Henry Nock of London in 1780. All seven barrels fired together. This is the earlier of two variations. (Castle Museum, York.)

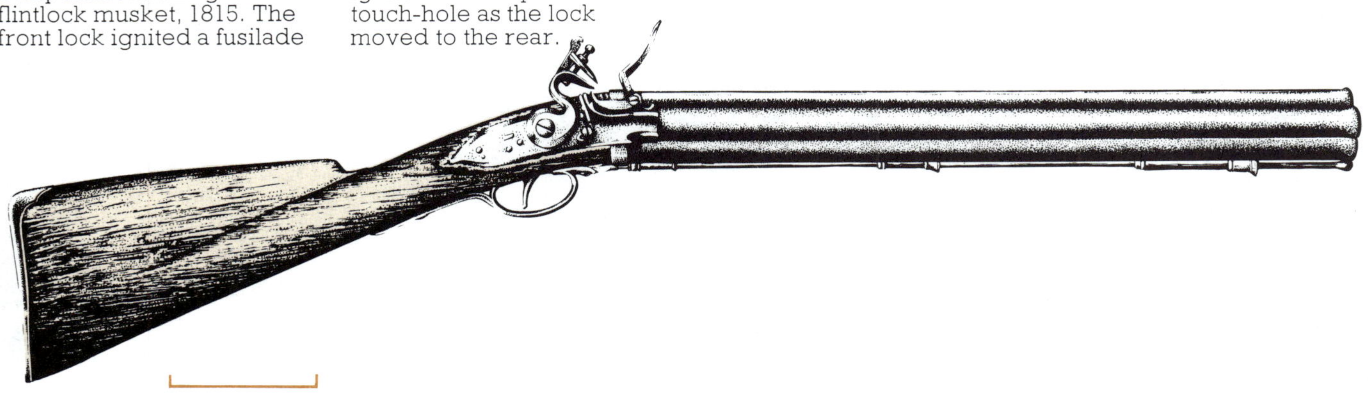

Front-loading revolvers

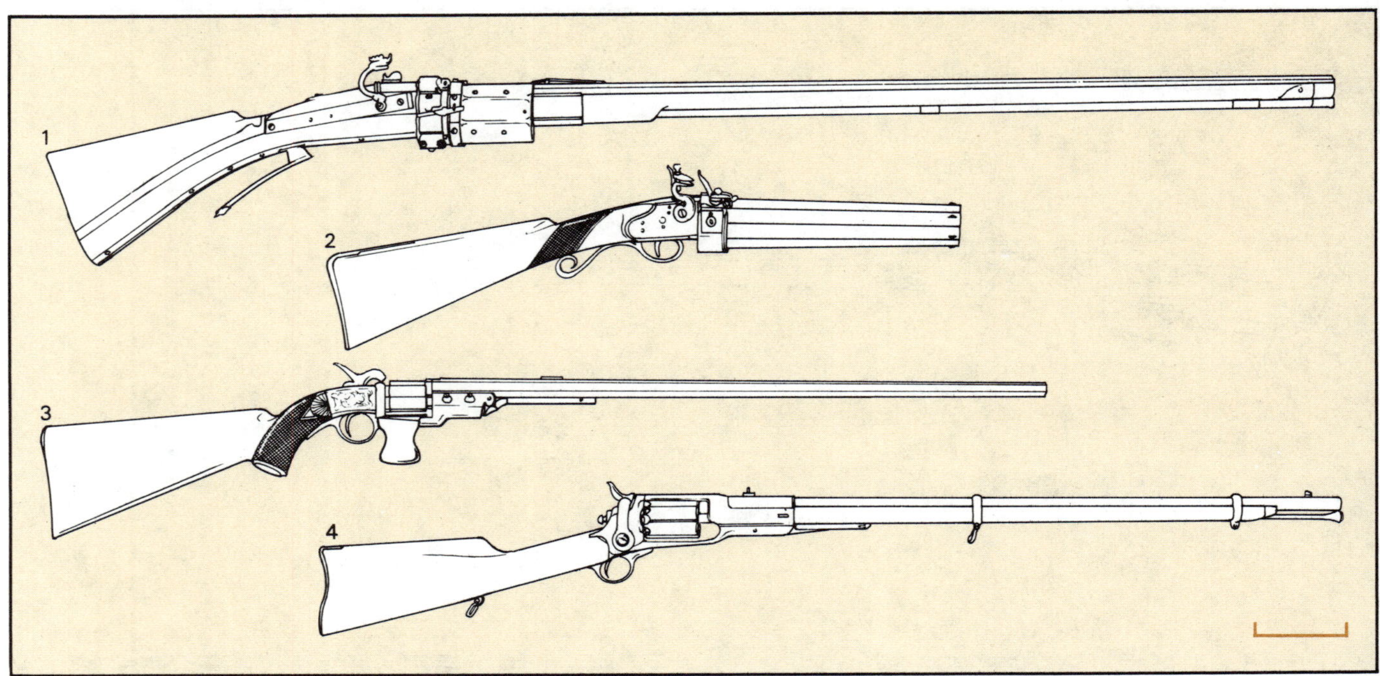

The most successful muzzle-loading repeaters by far were the revolvers. The idea was known in the 17th century, but it was not until the 19th that percussion ignition made its application far simpler. Pepperbox revolvers, with a number of full-length barrels, became popular. The more familiar type, with a short cylinder and one barrel, was later popularized by Samuel Colt.

Revolving longarms (above)
1 Revolving matchlock once in the collection of Louis XIII of France (reigned 1610-43). (Musée de l'Armée, Paris.)
2 Flintlock revolving carbine by Artemus Wheeler of Concord, Massachusetts. A seven-shot, hand-turned design patented in 1818. Of "pepperbox" type, with full-length barrels, and of .50in caliber.
3 Revolving rifle by Lang of London, c.1850. Note the grip below the cylinder, placed to avoid injury to the hand if several chambers fired at once — a danger with all these types.
4 Colt Model 1855, five-shot percussion revolving musket. Made in several lengths, Colt's revolving rifles were the most successful of the type. Caliber .56in.

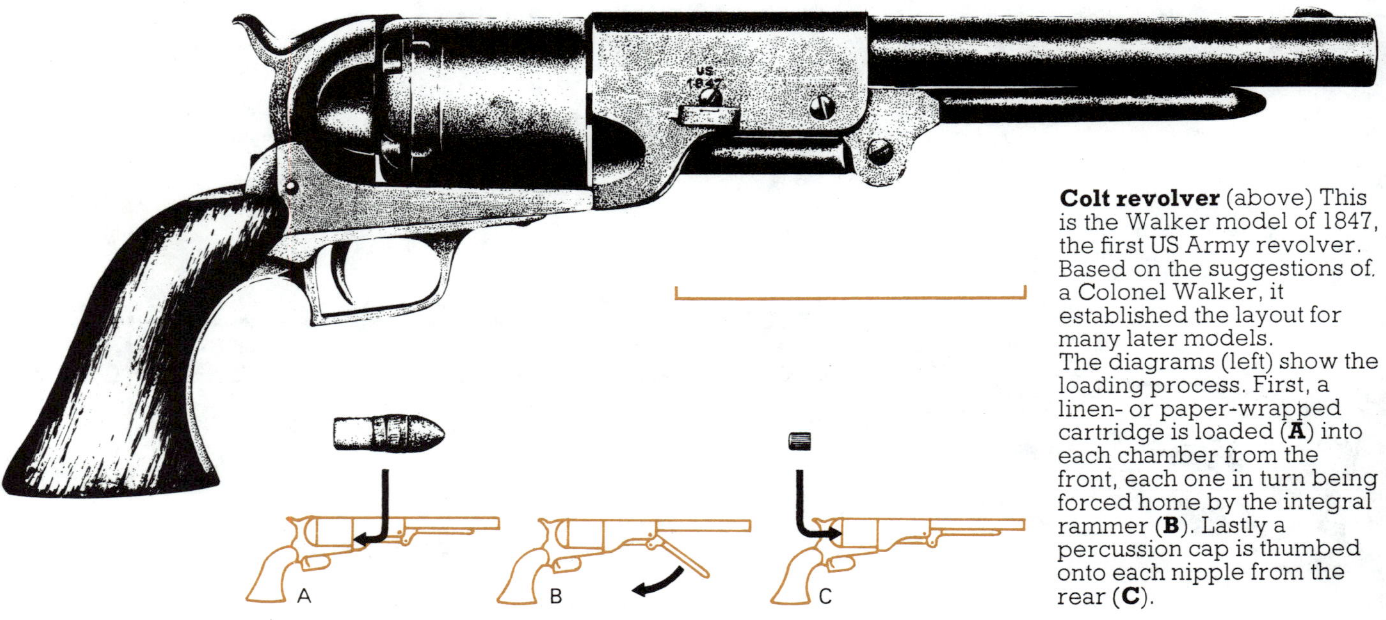

Colt revolver (above) This is the Walker model of 1847, the first US Army revolver. Based on the suggestions of a Colonel Walker, it established the layout for many later models.
The diagrams (left) show the loading process. First, a linen- or paper-wrapped cartridge is loaded (**A**) into each chamber from the front, each one in turn being forced home by the integral rammer (**B**). Lastly a percussion cap is thumbed onto each nipple from the rear (**C**).

Single-action revolvers (right) are those requiring the firer to cock the hammer — usually with his thumb (**a**) — before each shot. This system allows an accurate aim to be taken before the trigger is squeezed (**b**).

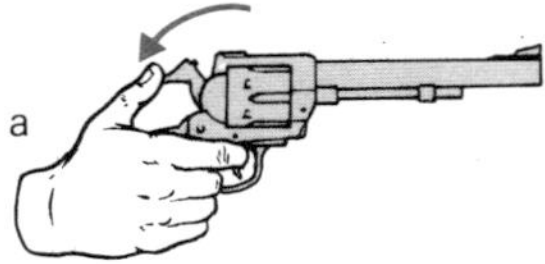

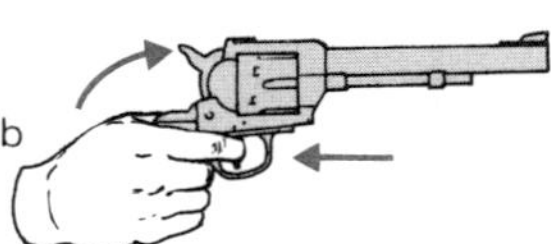

Double-action or self-cocking revolvers (right) are those fired simply by pulling the trigger. The first stage of the pull cocks the hammer (**a**), and further pressure fires the shot (**b**). This system is faster but less accurate than the single-action type.

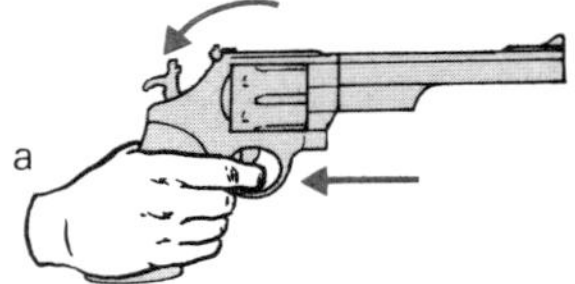

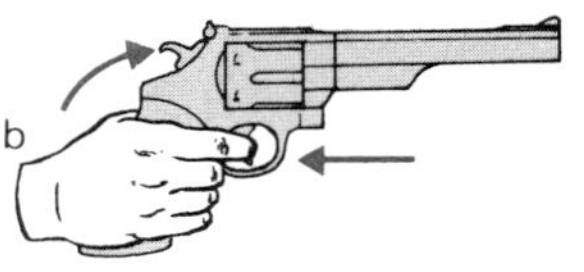

Revolving pistols (left) All are single-action, mechanically rotated types unless stated otherwise.
1 English six-shot snaphance revolver, c.1680. An early example of the cylinder type, rotated by hand. Caliber .5in.
2 Collier's five-shot flintlock revolver. Fitted with a self-priming steel. Developed from the Wheeler patent (see opposite). Caliber .44in.
3 Allen's patent double-action pepperbox revolver. This example is six-shot and of .36in caliber. Allen's pepperboxes were widely used in the 1840s, before being displaced by the Colt.
4 English "transitional" percussion revolver, c.1850. An adaptation of a double-action pepperbox design to the cylinder type. Caliber .36in.
5 Double-action pepperbox revolver, typical of the English type of the 1840s. Six-shot. Caliber .34in.
6 French LeMat "grapeshot" percussion revolver. So-called because of the shotgun barrel which forms the axis of the cylinder. Nine-shot, .42in caliber cylinder. 20-gauge central barrel (15.5mm).
7 Adams' patent double-action percussion revolver. An English rival of Colt's revolvers, found in many variations. This one is five-shot, .442in caliber.
8 Colt Paterson five-shot percussion revolver. This was the first of Colt's many successful revolver designs, patented in 1836. So-called because it was made at Paterson, New Jersey. Caliber .36in.

Breech-loading small arms

Although the idea of breech-loading is almost as old as the gun, it did not supersede muzzle-loading until metallic cartridges were devised and could be mass-produced cheaply. Once this occurred the way was opened for the development of efficient repeaters and automatic arms. Breech-loaders have higher rates of fire and are generally more accurate, and thus military tactics had to change.

Using a breech-loader (left), after a drawing by Frederic Remington. The firer has opened the breech and is taking a cartridge from his pouch. Breech-loaders were far easier to load from behind cover, or lying down, or on horseback than the old muzzle-loaders.

Breech-loading gun (below) which belonged to King Henry VIII of England. Such early examples were imperfect and not widely used. (Tower of London.)

Turn-off pistol (right), a simple form of breech-loader in use c.1640 to c.1850. To load, the barrel was unscrewed, and loose powder and a ball inserted into the other half as indicated by our arrow. The barrel was then screwed back on. Note that this system was then primed externally, just like a flint or percussion muzzle-loader.

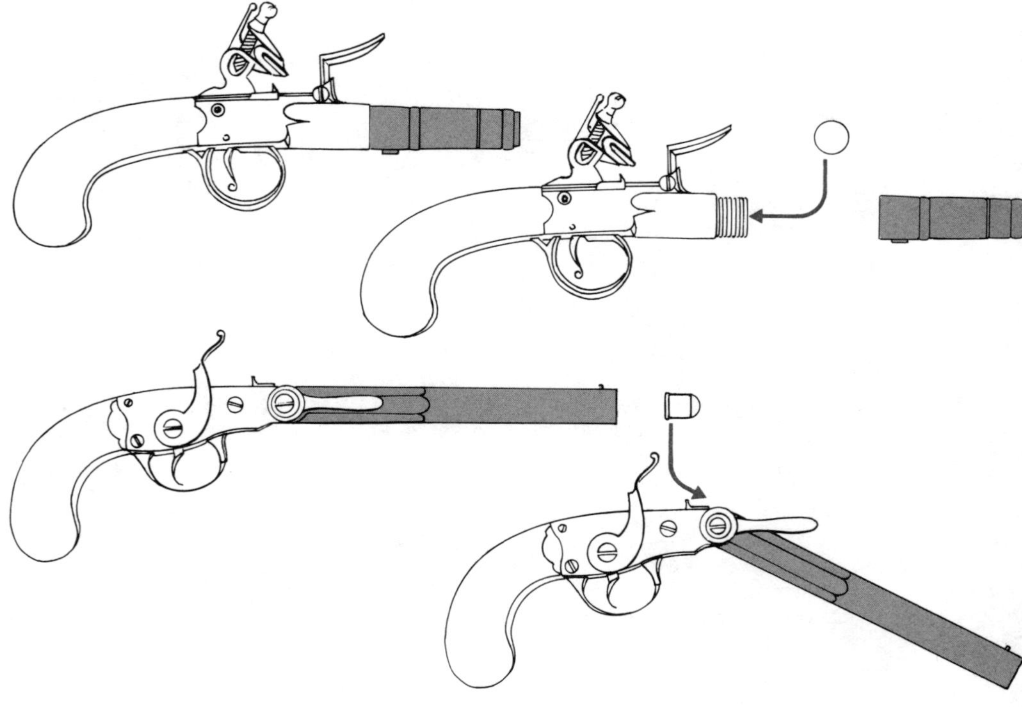

Pauly pistol (right) Pauly, a Swiss-born inventor, solved most of the problems of breech-loading in his Paris patent of 1812. He devised a self-contained cartridge and several forms of gun from which to fire it. The barrel swivels down and the cartridge is inserted as arrowed. The hammer-like lever serves to cock an internal striker.

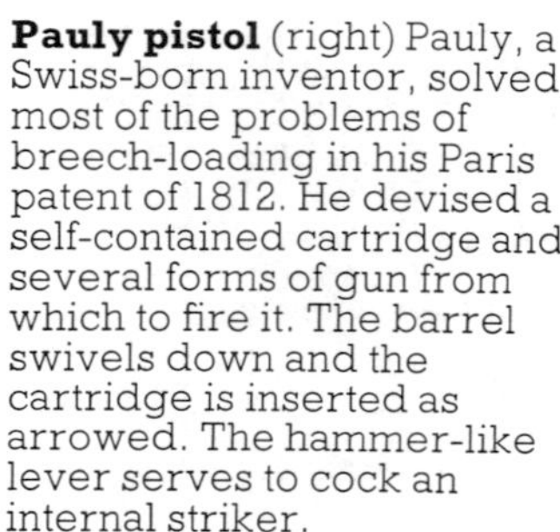

Pauly's cartridge (right) was one of the most important innovations in the history of small arms. For the first time, powder, ball and priming were combined in one unit, easily loaded via the breech. The example shown is a version with a separate brass base, and the remainder covered in thin paper. (Tøjhusmuseet, Copenhagen.)

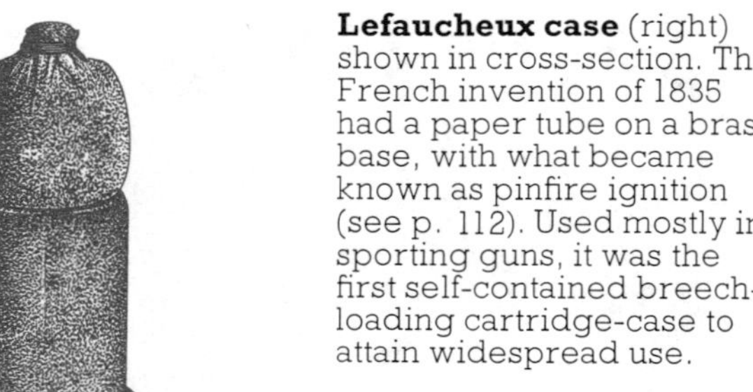

Lefaucheux case (right) shown in cross-section. This French invention of 1835 had a paper tube on a brass base, with what became known as pinfire ignition (see p. 112). Used mostly in sporting guns, it was the first self-contained breech-loading cartridge-case to attain widespread use.

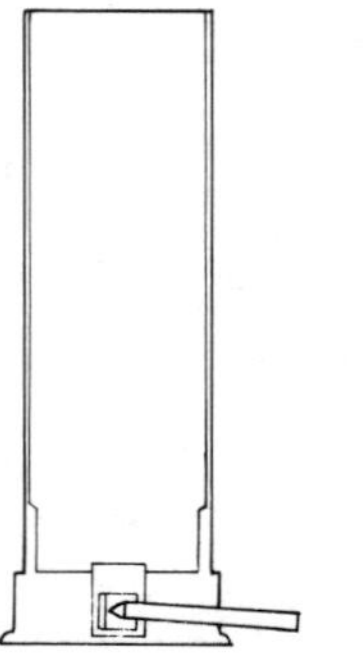

Boxer cartridge (right) for the British Snider rifle of 1867. This was one of the first metal-cased designs in widespread military use. It had sides (**a**) of coiled brass sheet on an iron base (**c**). The centerfire primer (**b**) was also of Colonel Boxer's own design, and is still in common use today.

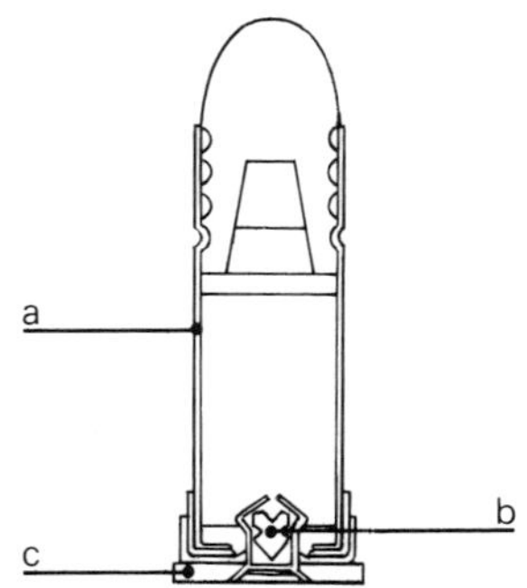

Sealing the breech (right) A major advantage of metal-cased cartridges is that the case seals the breech automatically on firing. This is achieved by the pressure from the exploding charge forcing the sides of the case so tightly against the walls of the breech that no gas can leak back. The correct technical term for sealing the breech is obturation.

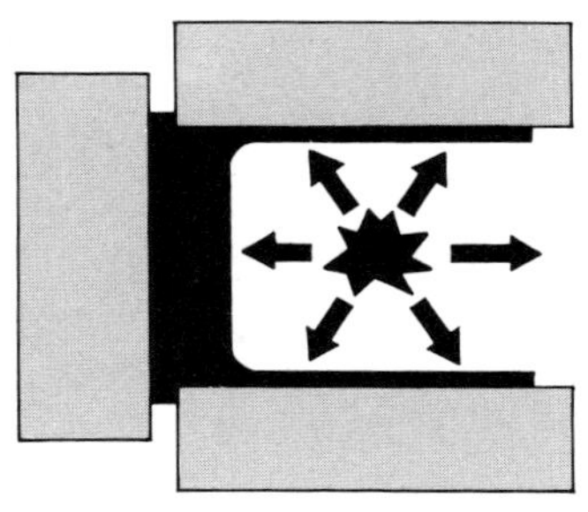

Single-shot rifles (right) are loaded by hand before each shot. In the Martini action shown, pushing down the lever lowers the front of the breech-block and cocks the firing pin inside it. A cartridge is pushed by hand into the chamber as arrowed. The lever is raised to close the breech before the trigger is pulled.

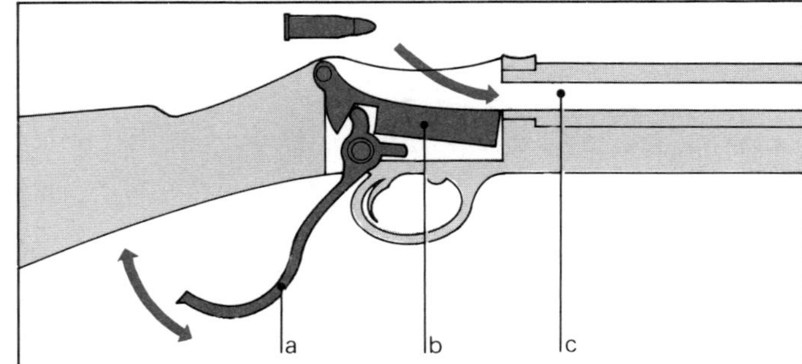

a Lever
b Breech-block
c Breech or chamber

Repeaters (right) have a number of cartridges stored in some form of magazine. These are fed into the chamber by a hand-powered mechanism. In the Winchester action shown, working the lever up and down between shots slides the breech-block back and forth to chamber the next cartridge and re-cock the hammer.

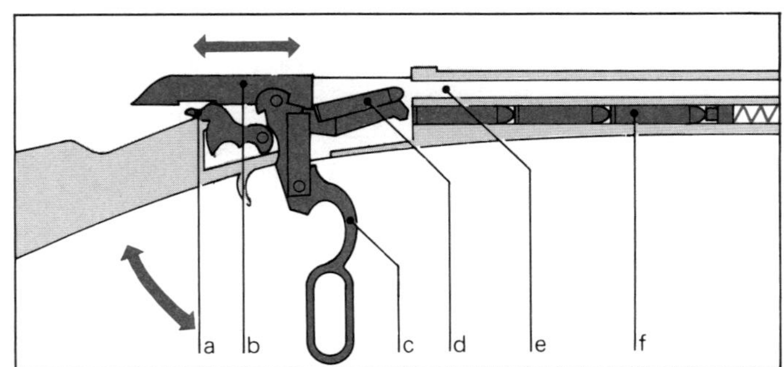

a Hammer
b Breech-block
c Lever
d Next cartridge
e Breech or chamber
f Tubular magazine

Automatic firearms (right) can fire a burst of shots at each pull of the trigger. In the Thompson submachine gun shown, the explosion of each cartridge blows back the breech-block against a spring. As it comes forward again it picks up another round from the magazine and fires it. It will continue to do this until the trigger is released or the ammunition runs out.

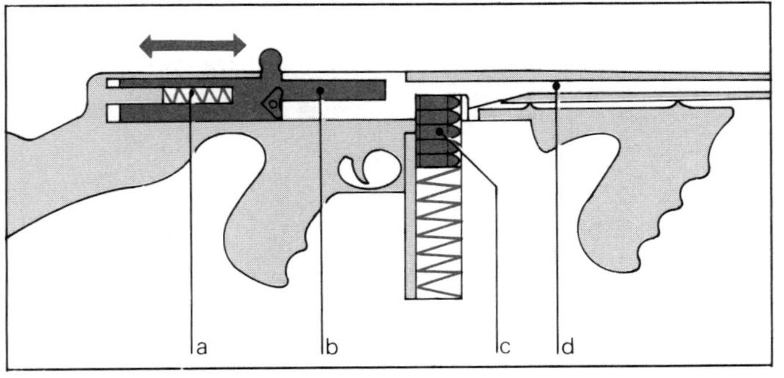

a Return spring
b Breech-block
c Cartridges in magazine
d Breech or chamber

Self-loading (right) or semi-automatic firearms fire one shot at each pull of the trigger without further action by the firer. In the Russian SKS action shown, gas is bled off from the barrel to drive back a piston. This opens the breech and re-cocks the hammer. A spring then returns the breech-block, so feeding the next round.

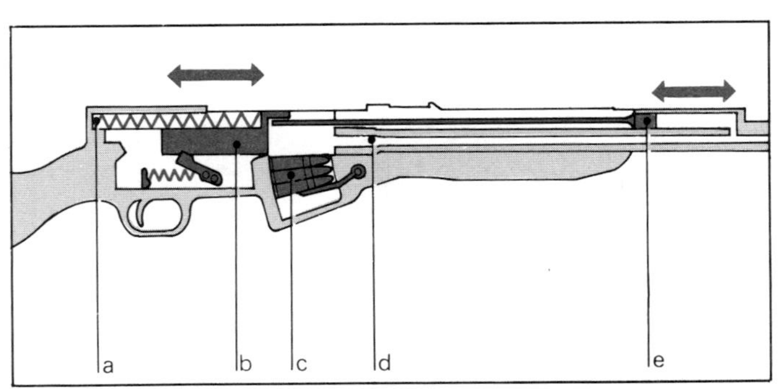

a Return spring
b Breech-block
c Cartridges in magazine
d Breech or chamber
e Gas piston

Single-shot breech-loaders

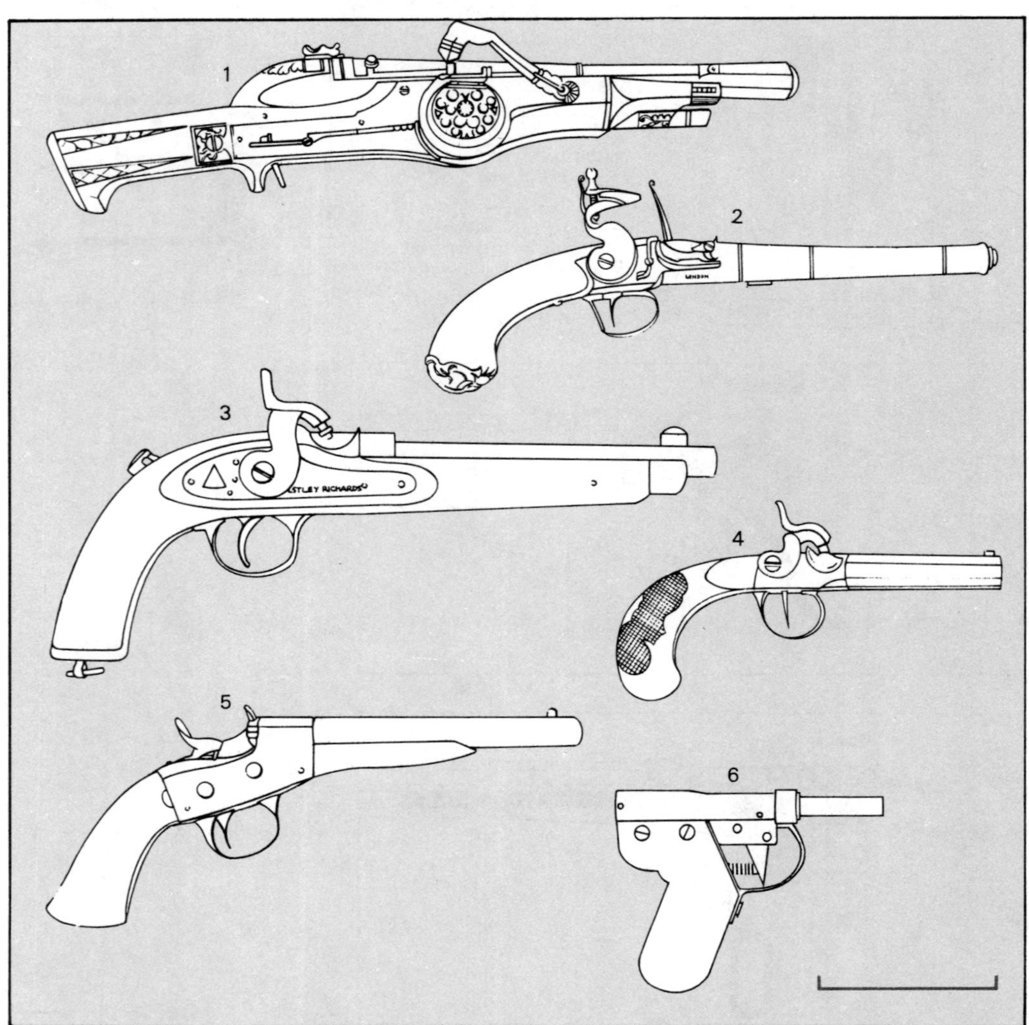

Single-shot breech-loading pistols (left)
1 Breech-loading wheellock pistol. It has a breech-block hinged at the side, and used a detachable steel chamber, like a crude cartridge. South German, c.1540.
2 Flintlock turn-off pistol, sometimes called a "Queen Anne cannon-barreled" pistol. For an explanation of the turn-off system see p. 130. English, c.1730.
3 Capping-breechloader pistol by the English maker Westley Richards. Known as the "monkey-tail" action, from the long, curved opening lever. An externally primed design, using a combustible cartridge. Made in 1867. Caliber .451in.
4 Percussion turn-off pocket pistol with octagonal barrel. Boxlock mechanism with side hammer. Belgian, c.1850.
5 Remington Model 1867 pistol for the US Navy. Fitted with the rolling-block breech mechanism, more often seen on rifles. Caliber .50in centerfire.
6 Home-made single-shot pistol from Northern Ireland, c.1972. Caliber .22in rimfire.

The heyday of the single-shot breech-loader as a military weapon was in the second half of the 19th century. Many of these designs were simple, accurate and reliable, and are still used for hunting and for target shooting. But militarily, the convenience of the metallic cartridge soon permitted efficient repeating firearms with high rates of fire, and the single-shot designs became obsolete.

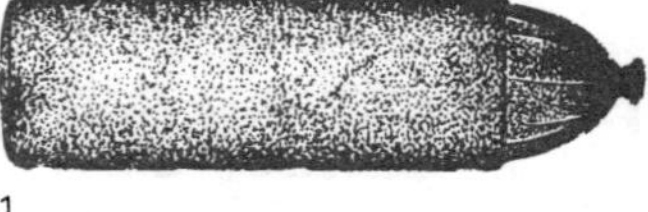

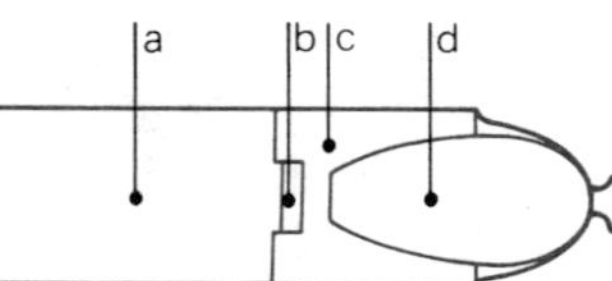

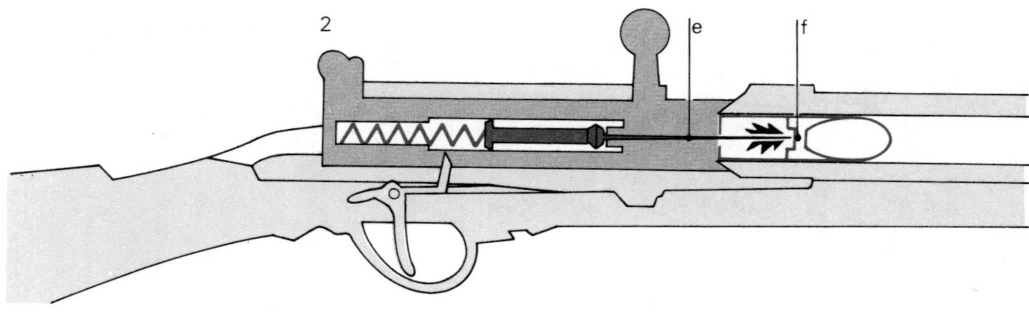

Dreyse cartridge and mechanism (left) This system, adopted by the Prussian Army in 1848, was an important innovation, having a bolt action and a self-contained cartridge.
1 The cartridge had a paper case, which burned away on firing. Internally, it consisted of a powder charge (**a**), a primer (**b**) at the base of a sabot or wad (**c**), and a bullet (**d**).
2 The mechanism was a single-shot bolt-action, loaded and closed by hand. On pulling the trigger, the needle (**e**) was impelled forward by its spring. It had to pierce the paper case and the whole length of the powder charge before hitting the primer (**f**) and igniting the charge. Despite some problems with fouling and escaping gas, the system was successful, and ahead of its time.

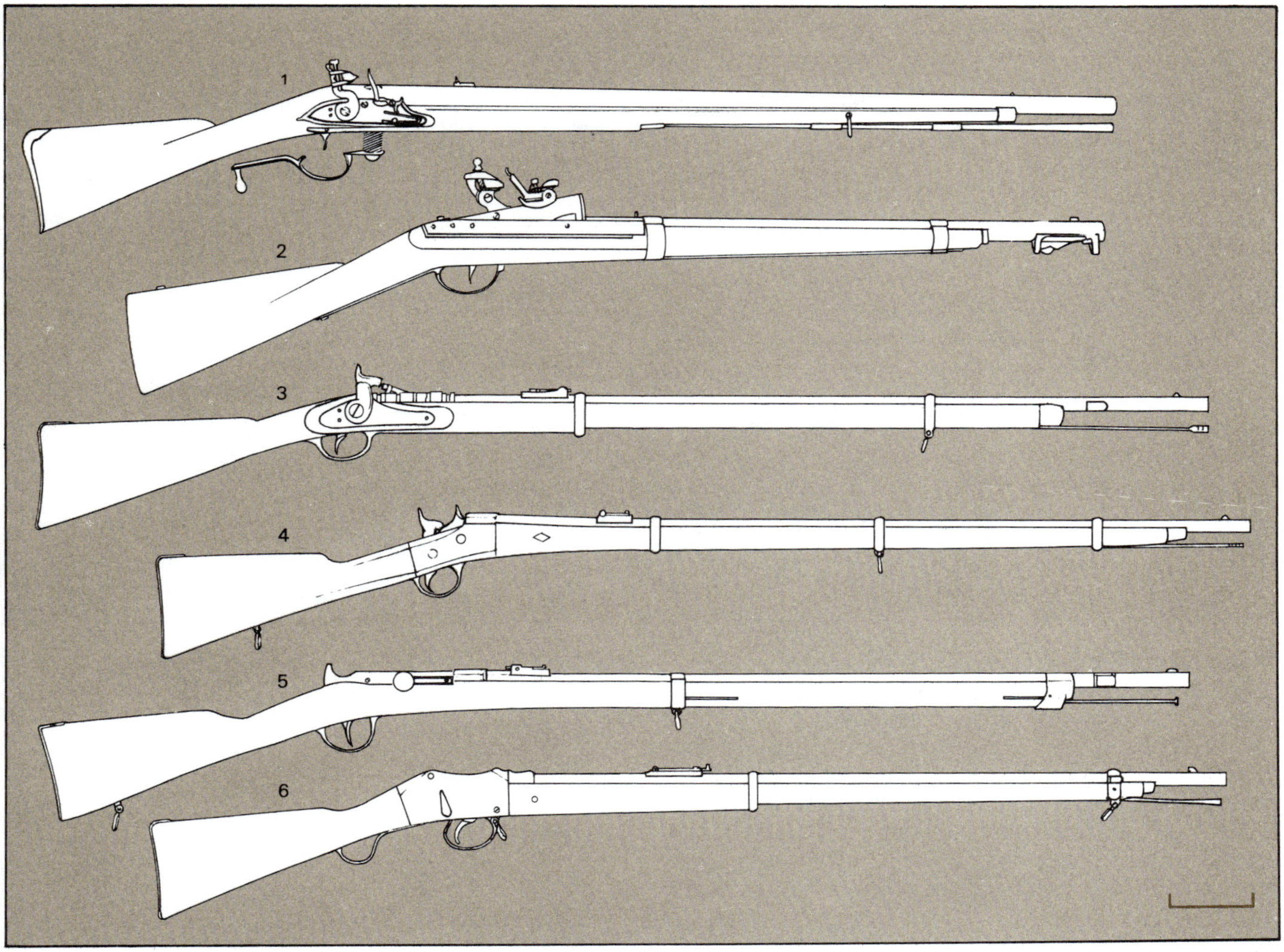

Single-shot breech-loading longarms (above)
1 Ferguson rifle. British improvement of the French La Chaumette system, using a screw-down breech-plug (shown open). In limited use in the American War of Independence in 1776.
2 Hall carbine. One of a series of US flint and percussion arms with a tip-up breech (shown partly opened). Issued from 1819.
3 Snider. British Army conversion of an Enfield muzzle-loader, using Boxer's cartridge. In service from 1867 in various barrel-lengths. Caliber .577in.
4 Remington Rolling-block. A simple and reliable American design, made in many versions and used in many countries. This is the Spanish Model 1871. Caliber 11mm.
5 Chassepot Modèle 1866. French bolt-action needle-rifle, used in the Franco-Prussian War of 1870. Fired a combustible paper cartridge. Caliber 11mm.
6 Martini-Henry. British service rifle using Von Martini's mechanism and Henry's rifling. Adopted in 1871. The cartridge was a reduced-caliber version of the Snider's; hence its odd designation .577/.450in.

Springfield Model 1873 (below) The carbine used by 7th US Cavalry at the Battle of the Little Bighorn in 1876. Caliber .45"-70 metallic cartridge.
Sharps Model 1855 carbine (bottom) American made, also used by the British. It was a "capping breech-loader," having external percussion priming and a combustible linen cartridge case. Caliber .577in.

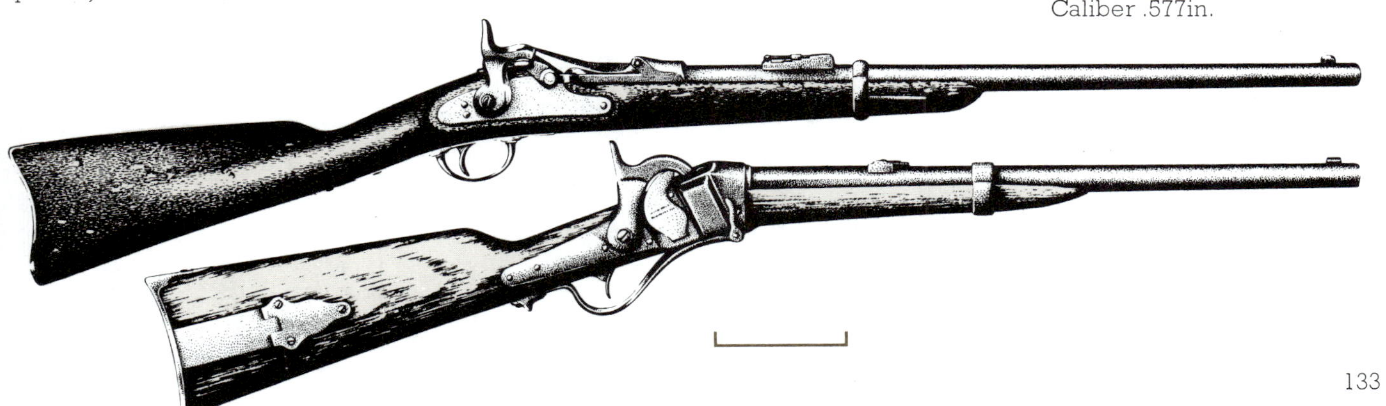

Multi-barreled breech-loaders

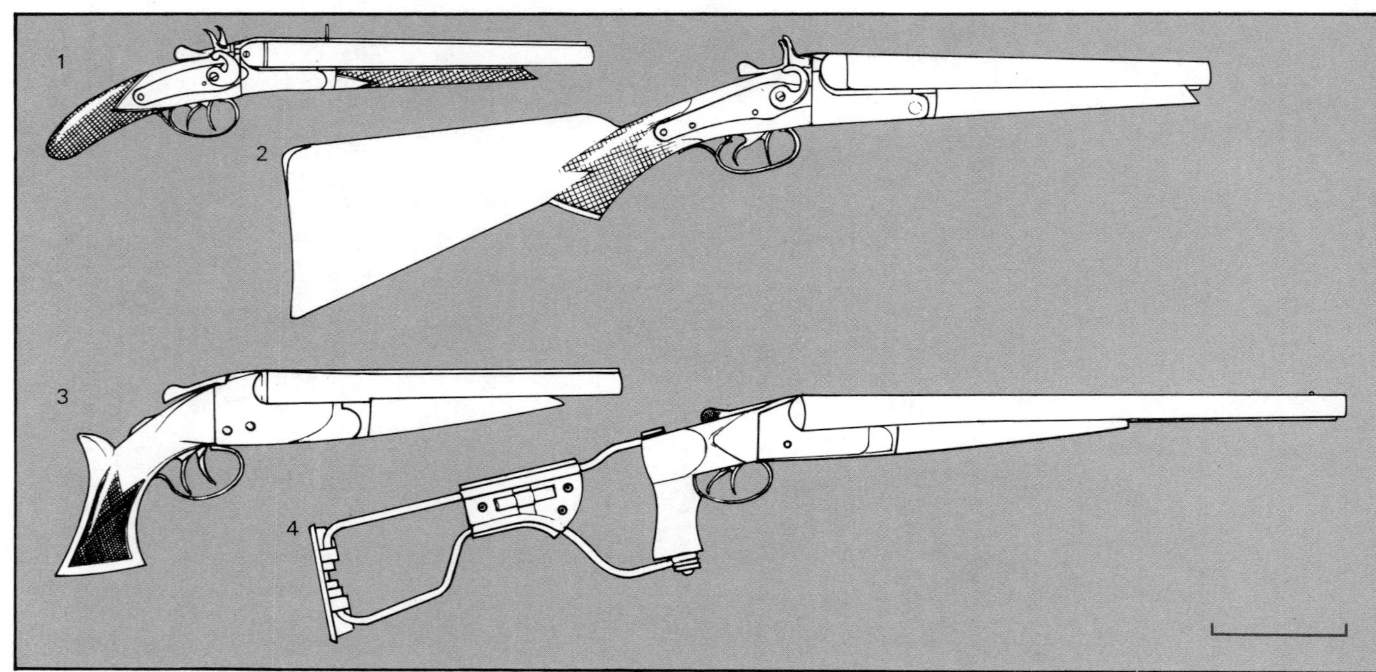

The old concept of the multi-barreled gun was easily adapted to breech-loading with self-contained cartridges. However, competition from repeaters limited the use of the idea mainly to cheaply made pistols for the civilian market. The great majority of multi-barreled breech-loading longarms are sporting guns rather than true weapons for use against human adversaries, and are not included here.

Double-barreled combat shotguns (above) All are of the break-open type.
1 Sawn-off Belgian hammer-shotgun used by "Doc" Holliday at the OK Corral fight in 1881. Barrels and stock have been cut down. 10-gauge.
2 Stage-coach guard's hammer-shotgun. Used in Arizona in the late 19th century. Shortened barrels. 12-gauge.
3 Ithaca Model A Auto and Burglar gun. A pistol for personal defense, based on a familiar boxlock "hammerless" shotgun design. A US commercial venture of the 1920s. 20-gauge.
4 Viet Cong adaptation of a boxlock "hammerless" shotgun. It has been fitted with a folding stock from a US M1 Carbine. Adapted c.1968. 12-gauge.

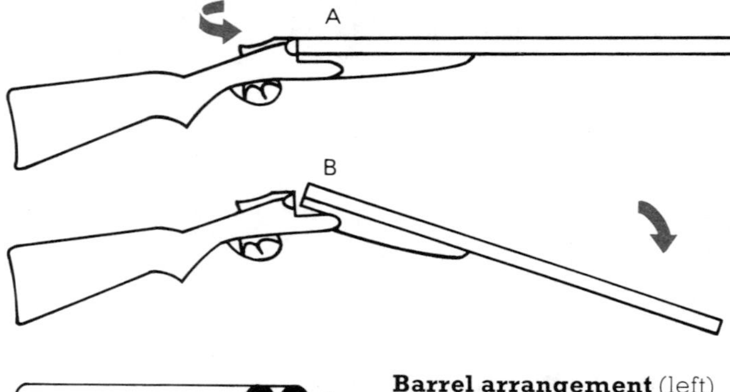

Break-open (left) Most double-barreled shotguns and many multi-barreled pistols are made on this simple system. A catch of some sort (there are many varieties) is released (**A**) and the gun hinges open at the breech (**B**), allowing the cartridges to be loaded.

a
b
c
d

Barrel arrangement (left) The two most common types are those used in double-barreled firearms and known as side-by-side (**a**) and over-and-under (**b**). A wide variety of arrangements can be found in the higher multiples (**c, d**), but these have no well-established names.

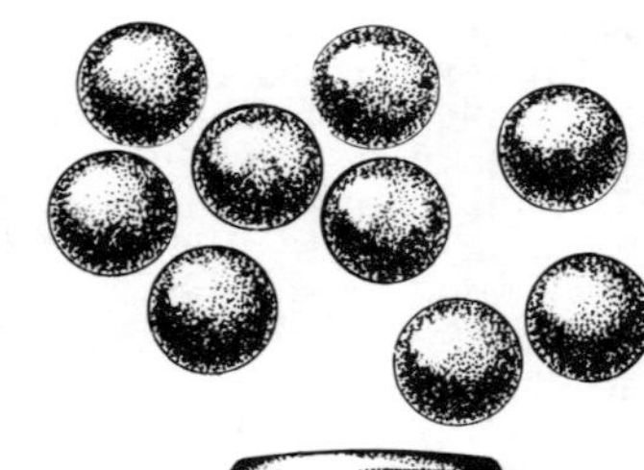

British 12-bore cartridge (right) as issued to the Home Guard in 1940, for use in private shotguns against the expected German invasion. It contains nine lead buckshot of SG size (.33in or 8.3mm), also shown separately (above right).

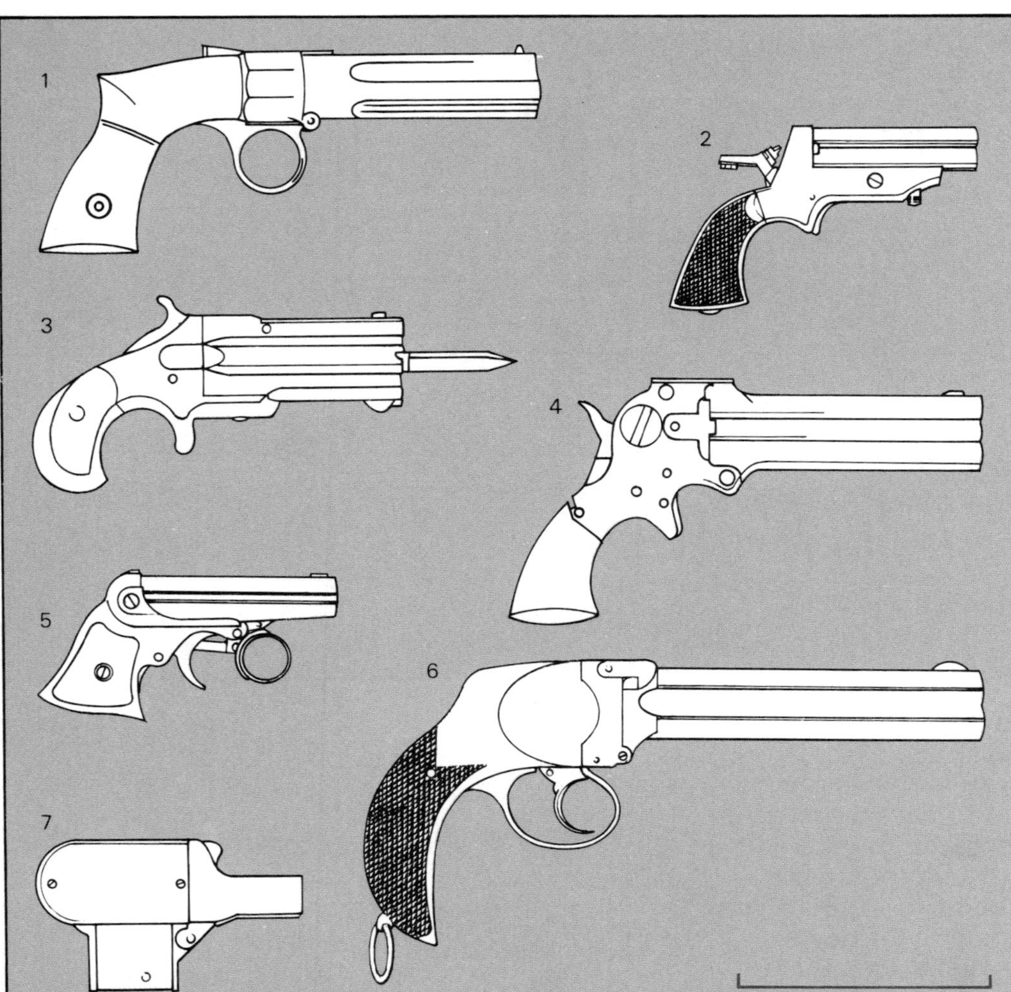

Multi-barreled breech-loading pistols (left) All are of US manufacture unless otherwise stated.

1 Robbins and Lawrence pepperbox An 1849 patent modified to breech-loading. The barrels remain still and the internal striker revolves to fire each in turn. Break-open. Five-shot. Caliber .31in.

2 Sharps "derringer" Patented in 1859. The hammer-nose is revolved to fire each barrel in turn. The barrels swing to the right to load. Four-shot. Caliber .30in rimfire.

3 Frank Wesson dagger-pistol Patented in 1868. The over-and-under barrels were rotated by hand. Two-shot. Caliber .41in rimfire.

4 Marston pistol model 1864. A break-open design. A stud had to be turned by hand to fire each barrel in turn. Three-shot. Caliber .32in rimfire

5 Remington-Elliot "derringer" Patented in 1860. The ring "trigger" is pulled between shots to rotate the internal striker. Four-shot. Caliber .32in rimfire.

6 Lancaster's pistol British, c.1882. A break-open design, also made as a shotgun. Four-shot. Caliber .476in Enfield.

7 Shattuck palm pistol Held with the barrels protruding between the fingers. Self-cocking. Patented 1906. Four-shot, smoothbored. Caliber .22in rimfire.

Remington derringer (left) A double-barreled, over-and-under design, in which the barrels hinge upward to load. First manufactured in the 1860s, copies of this model are still made. Caliber .41in rimfire. (Shown at actual size.)

Breech-loading repeaters 1

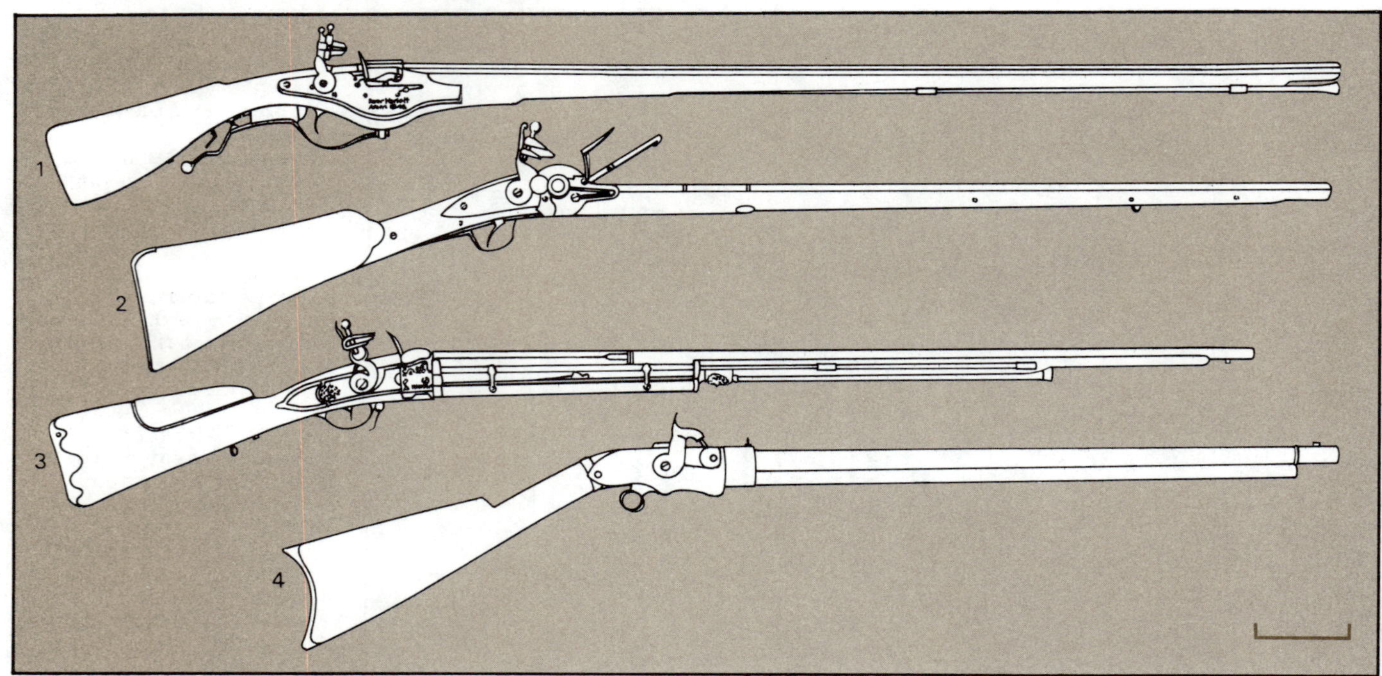

The large-scale use of repeating firearms had to await two developments in the 19th century. Problems of design were eased by the development of the metal-cased cartridge in the 1860s. Problems of fouling in the breech and bore were also overcome by new, smokeless propellants in the 1880s. The new rifles were so successful that many designs introduced in the 1890s are still in use.

Early repeaters (above)
1 Flintlock repeating rifle made in Denmark by Peter Kalthoff in 1646. It has a sliding breech-block worked by turning the trigger-guard. Wheellock versions also exist.
2 Flintlock repeating rifle on the Lorenzoni system. Italian, late 17th century. There are separate tubes in the butt to hold loose powder and balls.
3 Flintlock repeater by the Frenchman Chalembron, made in India c.1780-85. Powder and balls for 20 shots are held in the tubes below the barrel.
4 Jenning's repeating rifle, made in the USA c.1849. A forerunner of the Winchester repeaters, but using external pill-lock ignition, a variety of percussion.

Repeating actions (right)
There are three main types of operation, named according to the device that forms their chief visual characteristic. Within each general type there are many variations of precise design.
A Lever action
B Bolt action
C Slide or pump action

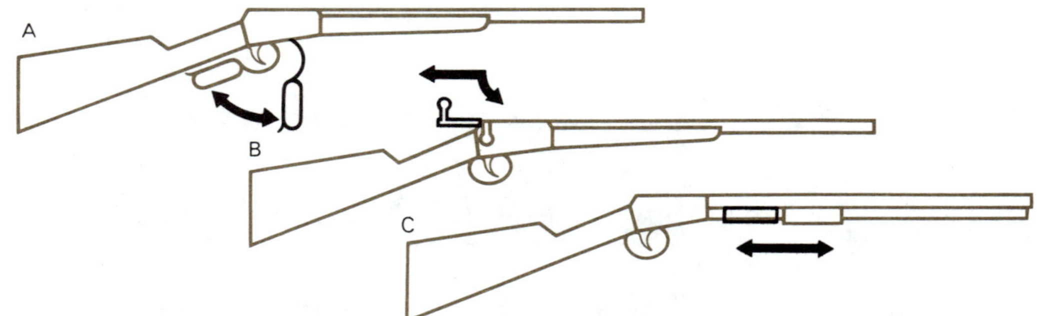

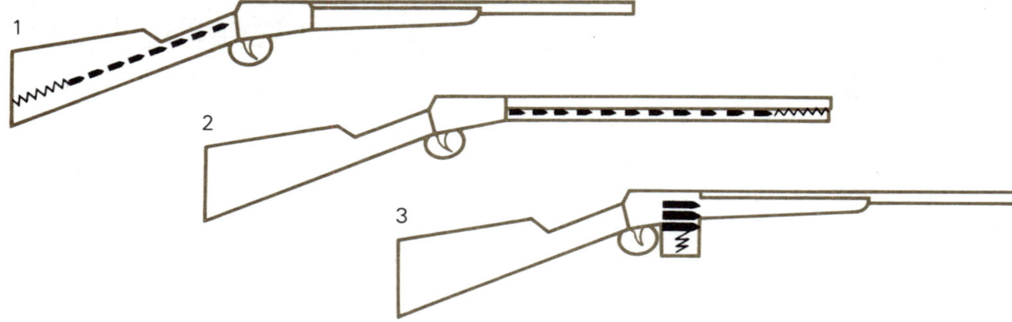

Magazines (left) are stores where ammunition is kept ready to be fed into the breech. Shown are the most common types and locations. In each case, a spring pushes the cartridges toward the breech.
1 Tubular magazine in the butt
2 Tubular magazine below the barrel
3 Box magazine below the breech mechanism

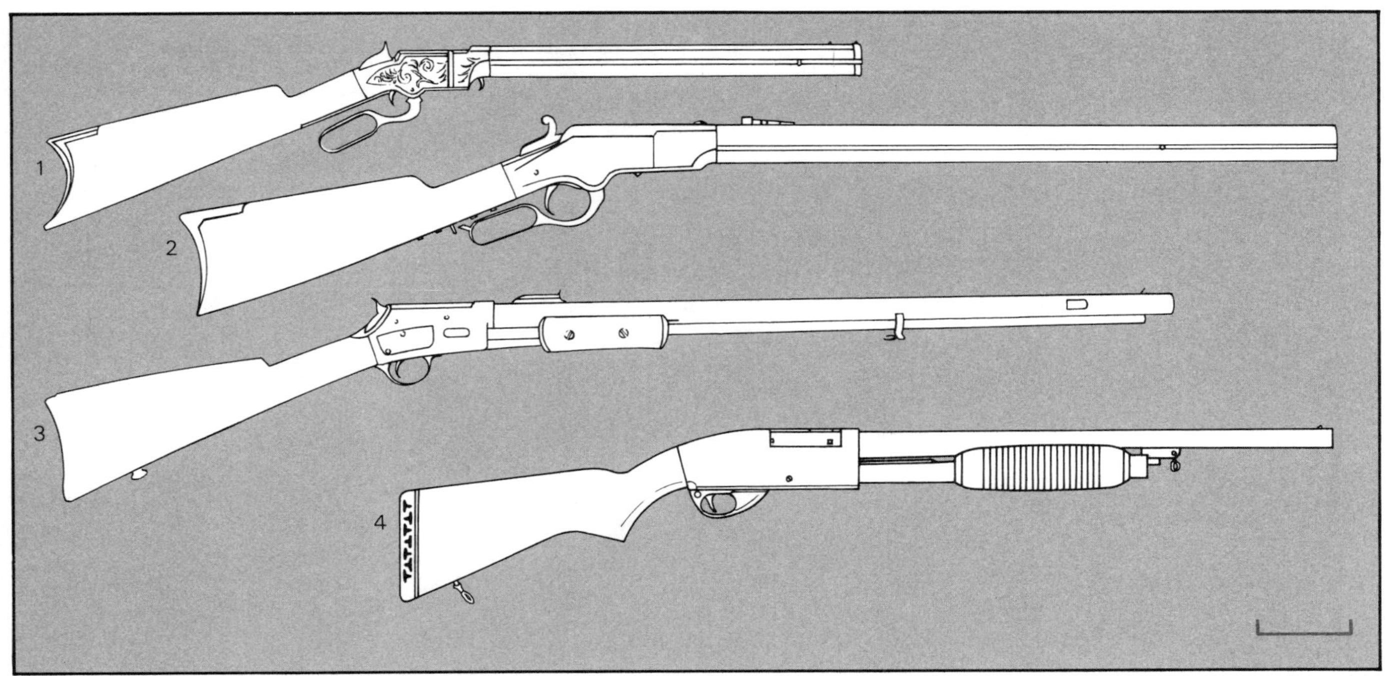

Repeaters (above) All are examples with tubular magazines below the barrel.
1 Volcanic lever-action carbine, USA, c.1855. Volcanic arms used a lead bullet with powder and priming in its hollow base. Caliber .38in.
2 Henry lever-action rifle, USA 1860. The immediate predecessor of the Winchester rifles. Caliber .44in rimfire.
3 Colt Lightning slide-action repeater, c.1885. This is the military version, exported to South America. The slide-action has been used widely for hunting-rifles. Caliber .44″-40.
4 Savage Model 77E slide-action (or pump-action) combat shotgun, used by the US Marines in Vietnam. Five-shot, 12-gauge.

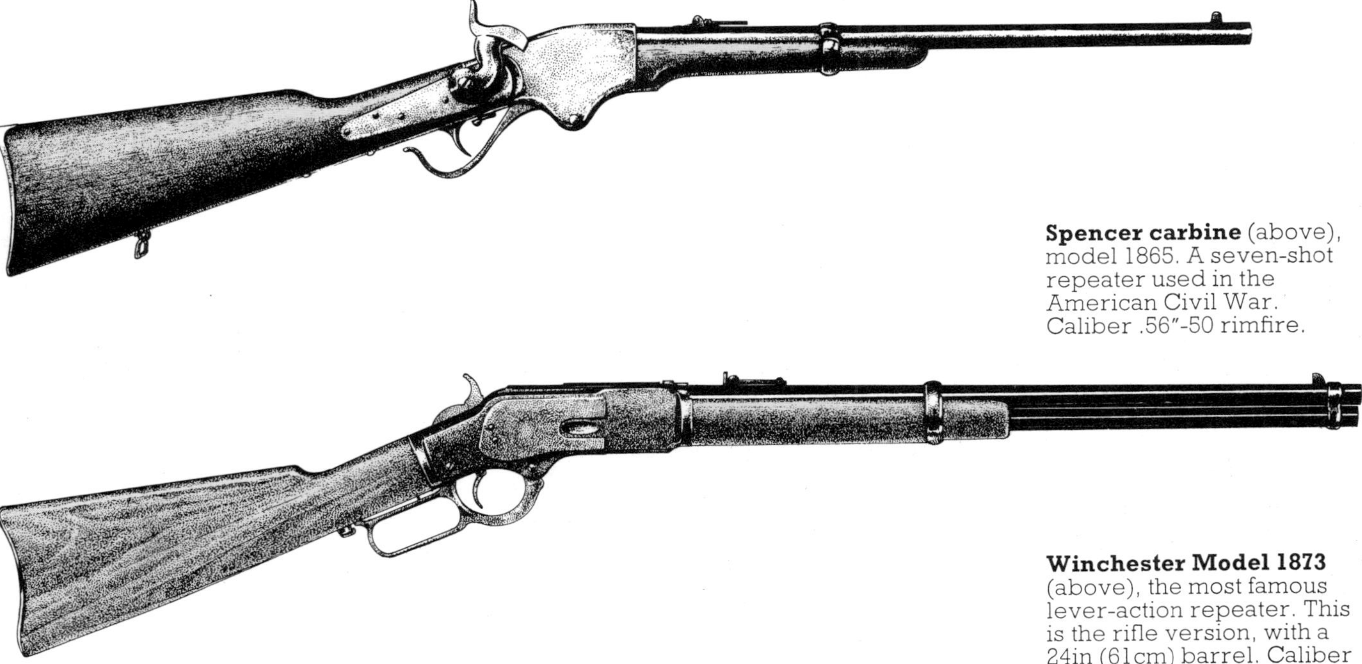

Spencer carbine (above), model 1865. A seven-shot repeater used in the American Civil War. Caliber .56″-50 rimfire.

Winchester Model 1873 (above), the most famous lever-action repeater. This is the rifle version, with a 24in (61cm) barrel. Caliber .44″-40 centerfire.

Breech-loading repeaters 2

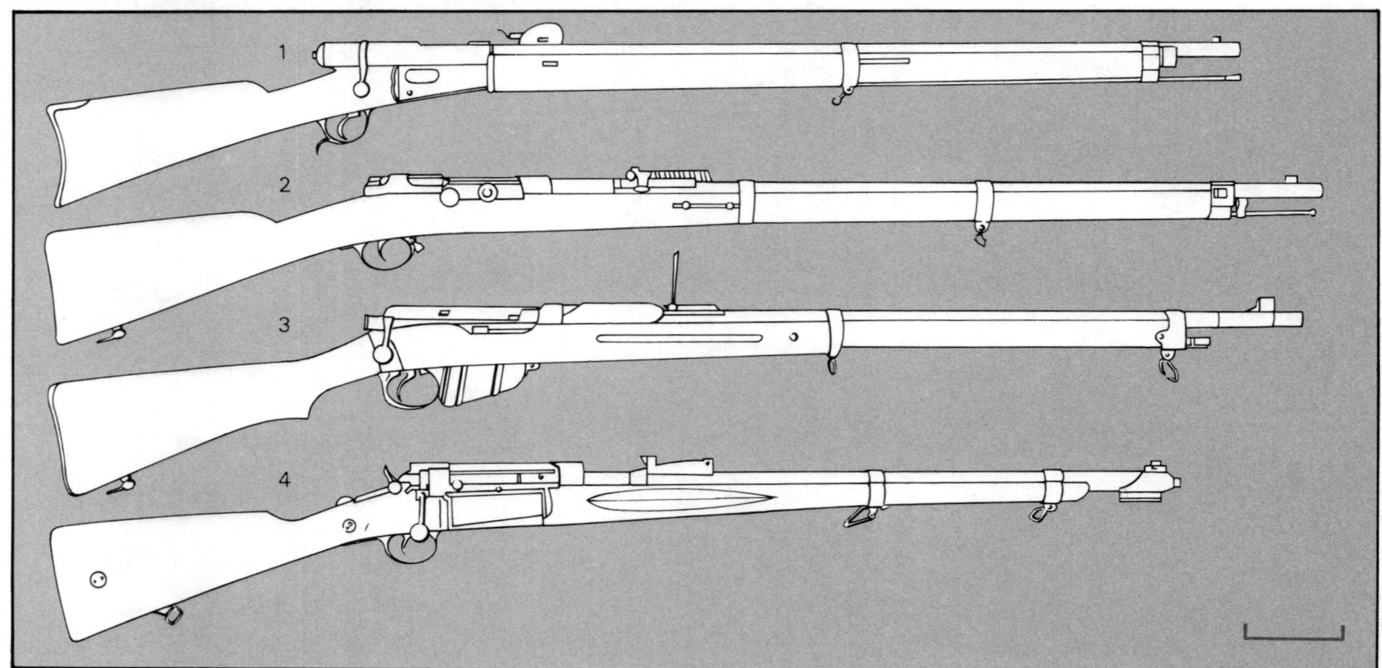

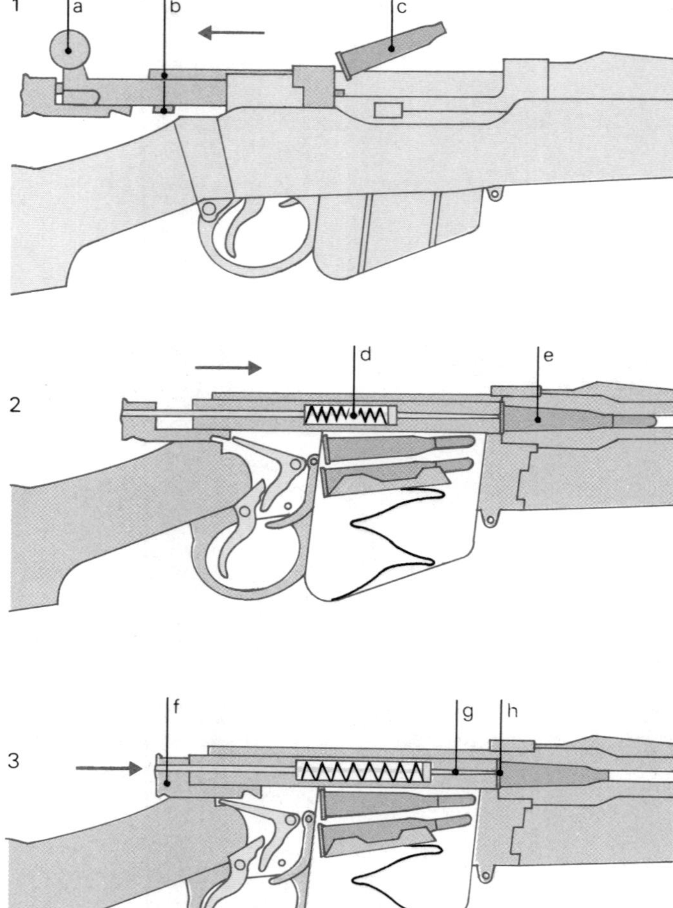

The functioning (left) of a bolt-action mechanism. The example shown is the Lee system, as used on the British Lee-Metford and Lee-Enfield service rifles from 1888 onward.
1 The bolt is unlocked as the handle (**a**) is raised. Note the locking lugs (**b**) toward the rear of the bolt. As the bolt is pulled back, the empty case from the last shot is extracted from the breech and then ejected (**c**).
2 On pushing the bolt forward again, the firing-pin spring (**d**) inside the bolt is compressed. At the same time, the bolt-face pushes the top cartridge from the magazine forward into the chamber (**e**). When the handle is finally turned down, the bolt is locked.
3 When the trigger is pressed, the cocking-piece (**f**) and the firing-pin (**g**) which is attached to it, fly forward and strike the primer on the base of the cartridge (**h**).
The Lee was one of the best bolt-action designs. Its main rival, the Mauser action, differs chiefly in having the locking lugs at the front of the bolt, and in cocking as the handle is raised on opening.

Early bolt-action repeaters (above)
1 Vetterli Model 1881 Swiss, a variant of the Model 1869. The 13-shot tubular magazine below the barrel is filled via a loading gate on the right side of the action. Caliber 10.4mm.
2 Mauser Model 71/84 German, the first of many Mauser bolt-action repeaters, converted from the single-shot Model 1871 in 1884. An eight-shot tubular magazine is fitted below the barrel. Caliber 11mm.
3 Lee-Metford The British Army's first repeater, using Lee's bolt action and box magazine, and Metford's rifling. Introduced in 1888. Eight-shot. Caliber .303in.
4 Krag-Jørgensen This is the Danish Model 1889 carbine version. Other variations were used by the USA, and by Norway where the design originated. All have a characteristic five-shot box magazine on the right side of the action. Caliber 8mm x58R.

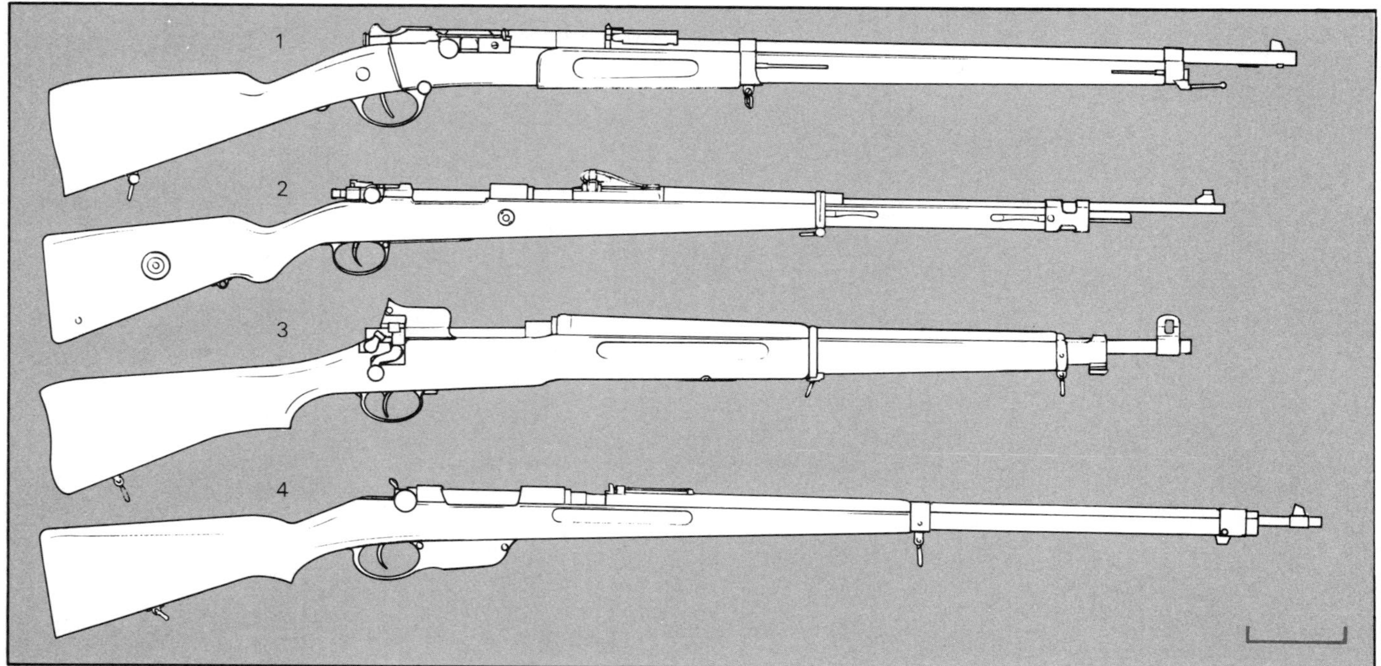

Rifles of World War 1 (above) Most armies were equipped with bolt-action repeaters.
1 Lebel Mle 1886/93 French. This design set the trend for the world's armies. It was the first smallbore military rifle using smokeless powder. Eight-shot tubular magazine below the barrel. Caliber 8mm x50R Lebel.
2 Mauser Gewehr 98 German. Widely copied and much modified, this was one of the most successful bolt-action designs. Five-shot box magazine. Caliber 7.92mm x57 Mauser.
3 P14 British experimental rifle, hastily adapted for the old .303in cartridge. In limited use only. Also used by the USA in .30in-'06 caliber as the M17 Enfield. Five-shot box magazine.
4 Mannlicher Model 1895 Used by Bulgaria and the Austro-Hungarian Empire. Five-shot magazine. Caliber 8mm x50R.

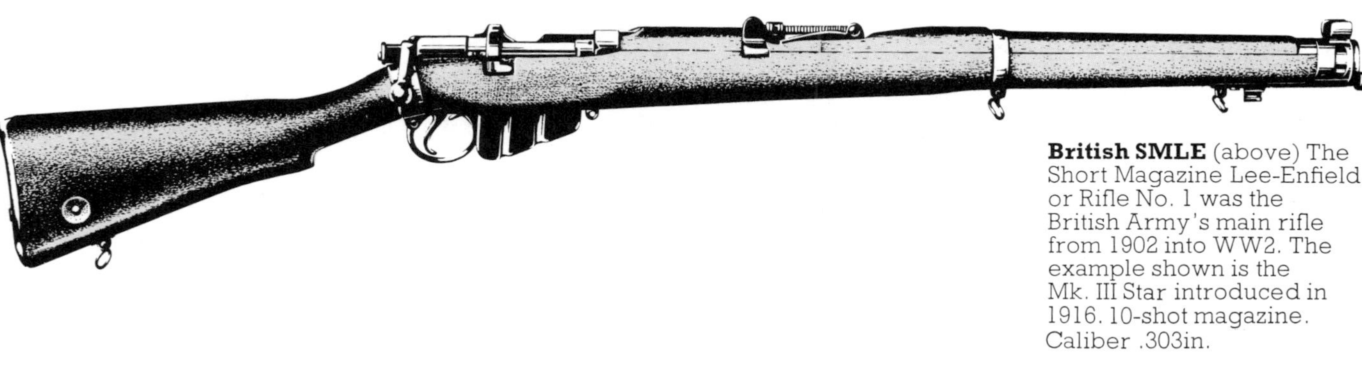

British SMLE (above) The Short Magazine Lee-Enfield, or Rifle No. 1 was the British Army's main rifle from 1902 into WW2. The example shown is the Mk. III Star introduced in 1916. 10-shot magazine. Caliber .303in.

US Model 1903 (above) or Springfield rifle. This was the US Army's principal arm, with modifications, until the beginning of WW2. Five-shot magazine. Caliber .30in-'06.

Breech-loading repeaters 3

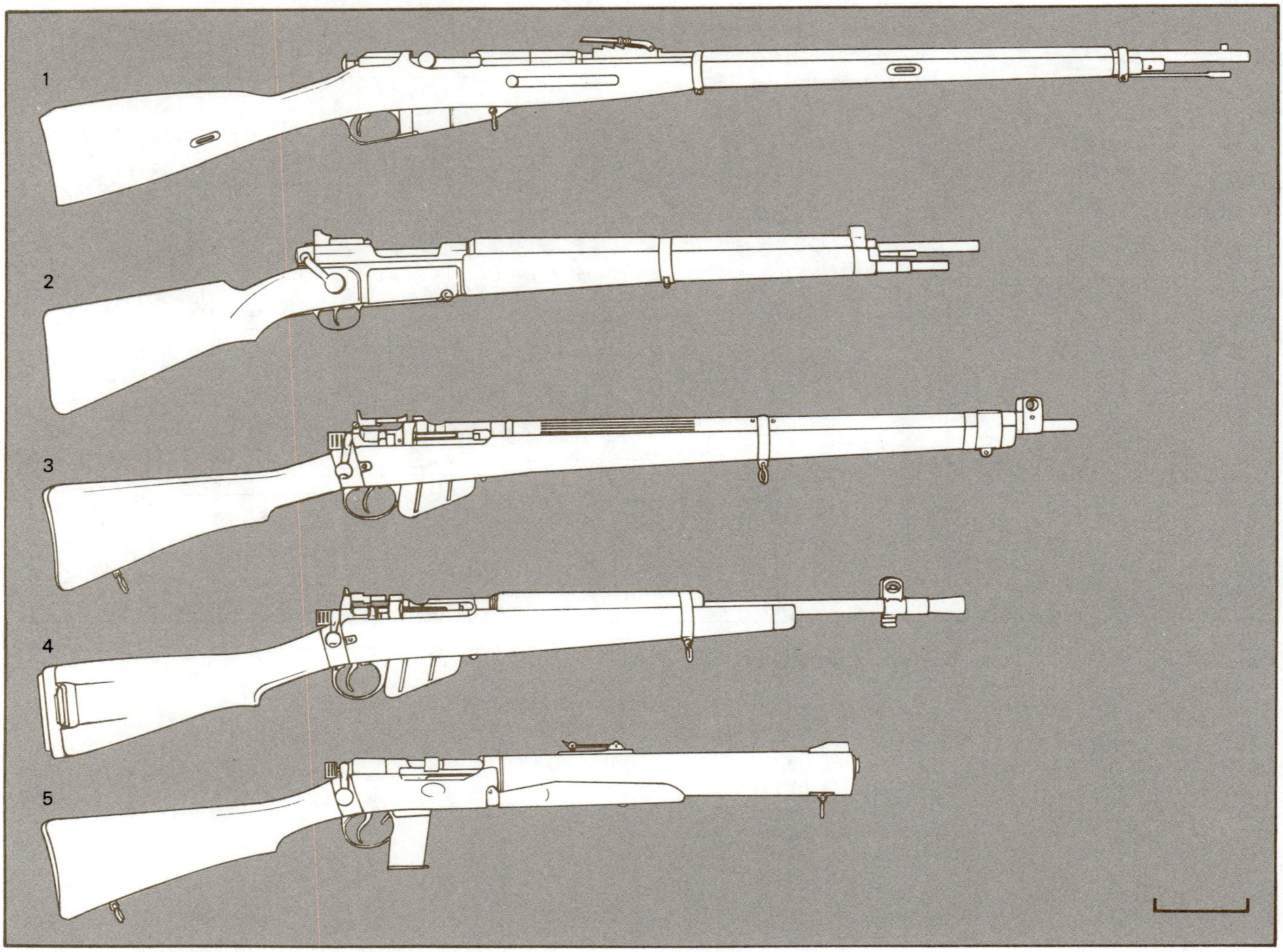

Charger or clip loading (right) To speed up the filling of box magazines, ammunition for most bolt-action rifles was supplied in steel clips. Shown are two common types for rimmed (**a**) and rimless (**b**) cartridges. The clip, usually containing five rounds, was placed over the open breech (**c**) and the rounds pushed down into the magazine in one motion with the thumb (**d**). The empty clip was then discarded. If the magazine held 10 rounds, this process was repeated before closing the bolt. In some designs the clip entered the magazine with the rounds.

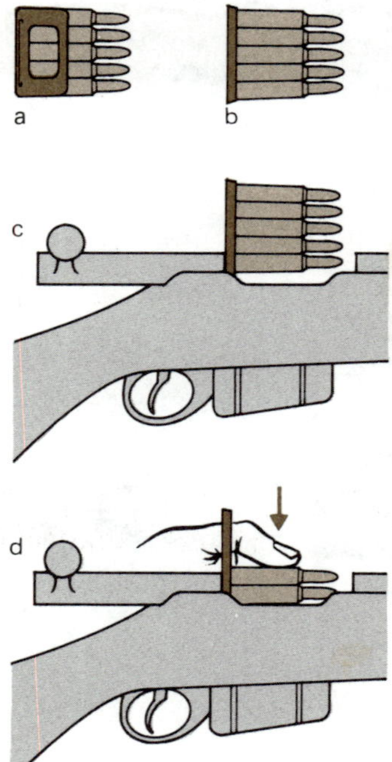

Allied bolt-action rifles of World War 2 (above)

1 Mosin-Nagant Soviet. This is the Model 1891/30, revised for mass-production in 1930. Five-shot box magazine. Caliber 7.62mm x54R.

2 MAS M1e 1936 French. One of the last bolt-action repeaters to be adopted by a major power. Five-shot box magazine. Caliber 7.5mm x54 M1929.

3 No4 MkI British. This was the SMLE (see p.139) revised for mass-production and with a new aperture sight. 10-shot box magazine. Caliber .303in.

4 No5 MkI British. Also called the Jungle Carbine. It was a lighter version of the No4 rifle, for use in tropical jungle. 10-shot magazine. Caliber .303in.

5 De Lisle carbine British. A silenced weapon made for clandestine use. It was based on the SMLE rifle, but used the same cartridge as the Thompson submachine gun. Caliber .45in ACP.

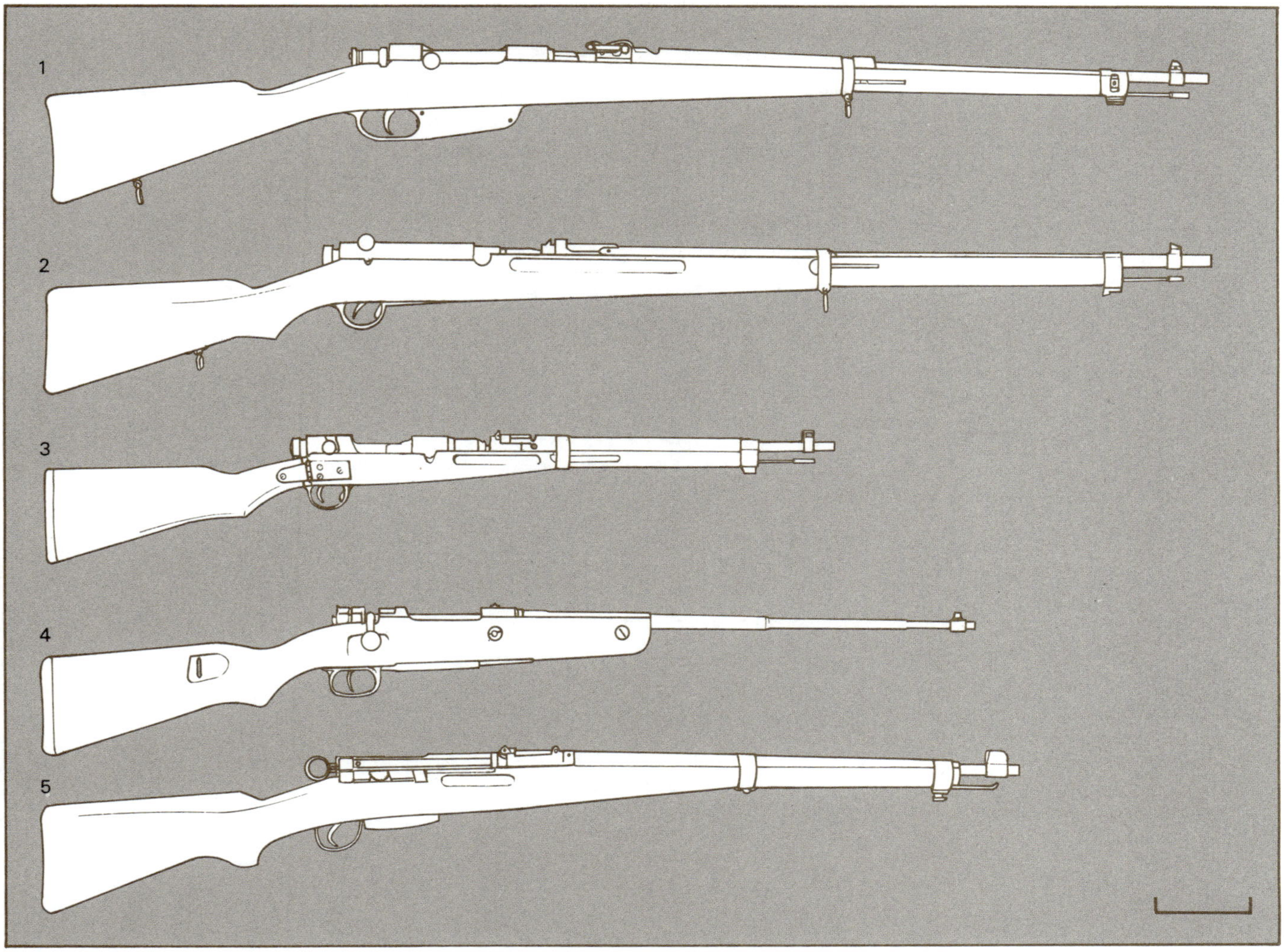

Axis bolt-action rifles of World War 2 (above)
1 Carcano Model 91/24 Italian. The externally identical M38 was also used, but in 7.35mm x51 caliber. Six-shot magazine. Caliber 6.5mm x52.
2 Arisaka Type 38 rifle Japanese. "Type 38" refers to the 38th year of the Meiji calendar (1905), when this type was introduced. Five-shot magazine. Caliber 6.5mm x50.
3 Arisaka Type 38 Carbine Japanese. Shown is the paratroop version with a folding stock. Note the hinge behind the trigger-guard. Caliber 6.5mm x50.
4 VG2 German. This was one of several makeshift weapons issued to local defense units late in the war. Five-shot magazine. Caliber 7.92mm x57 Mauser.

Rifle of a neutral country
5 Schmidt-Rubin Model 1931 Carbine Swiss. This was a "straight-pull" bolt-action design, which did not require a separate turning motion to unlock it. It was made in many variations from 1889 until the 1950s. Six-shot magazine. Caliber 7.5mm x54 M11.

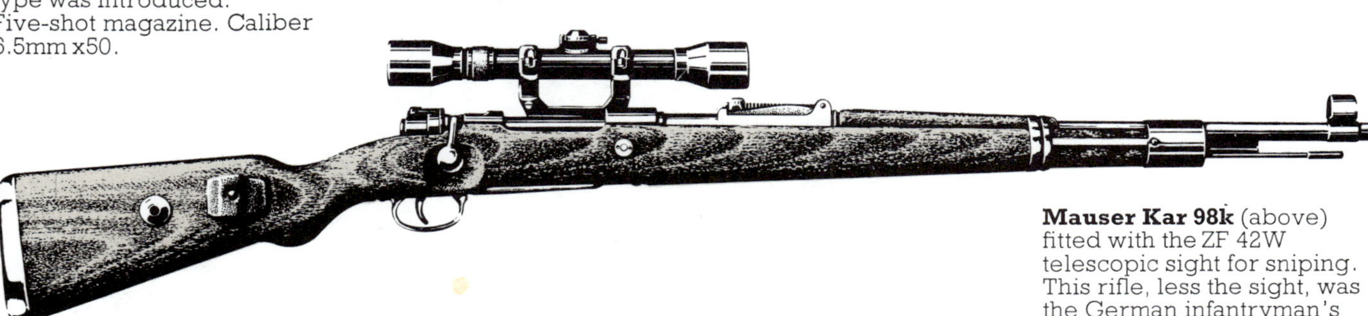

Mauser Kar 98k (above) fitted with the ZF 42W telescopic sight for sniping. This rifle, less the sight, was the German infantryman's main weapon in WW2. Five-shot magazine. Caliber 7.92mm x57 Mauser.

Breech-loading revolvers 1

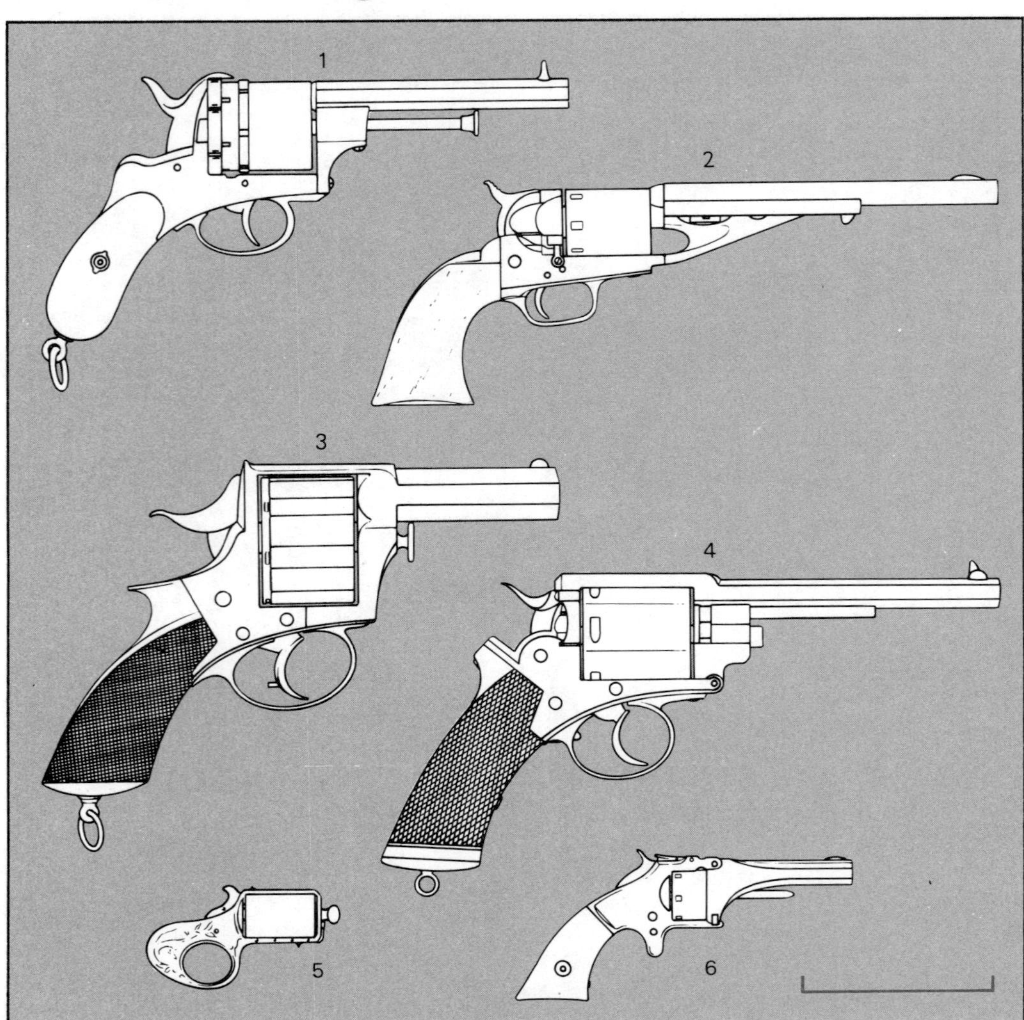

Early breech-loading revolvers (left)
1 Lefaucheux pinfire revolver. French, patented in 1845 and made in many variations. This one is six-shot, with side-gate loading. Caliber 12mm.
2 Colt Model 1861 Navy revolver, converted to breech-loading on the side-gate system in the 1870s. Six-shot. Caliber .38in centerfire.
3 British "man-stopper" revolver based on a Tranter design. The cylinder was removed for reloading. Date c.1870-80. Six-shot. Caliber .577in centerfire.
4 Adams revolver of 1872. British, side-gate loading. Note the solid frame around the cylinder. Five-shot. Caliber .45in Adams.
5 Reid's "Knuckle-duster" revolver, a US patent of 1865. Seven-shot cylinder, which was removed for loading. Caliber .22in rimfire.
6 Smith and Wesson Model No1. The first Smith and Wesson revolver, dating from 1857. A break-open design, but hinged at the top. Seven-shot. Caliber .22in rimfire.

Most of the major design developments in breech-loading revolvers occurred in the second half of the 19th century. In this century, the process has mainly been one of refinement in safety features and in the alloys and steels used. The great reliability of revolvers has prevented their replacement by semi-automatic pistols, especially for police use.

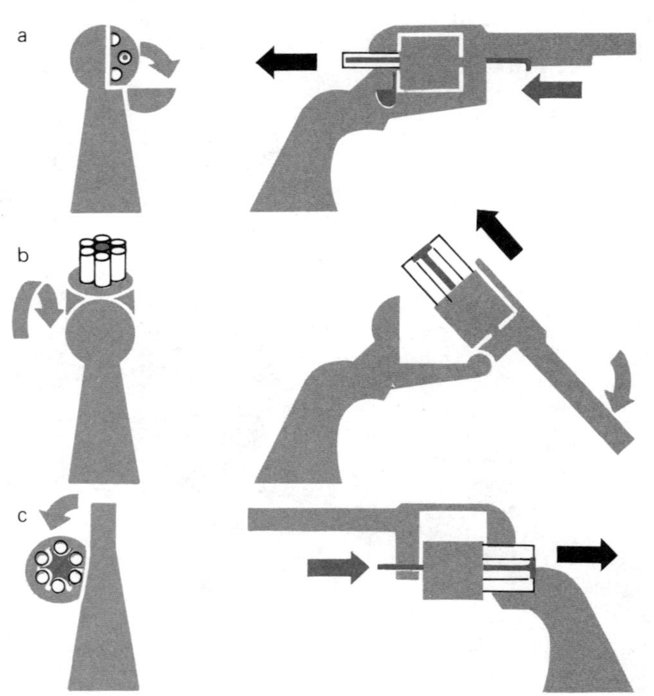

Opening and ejection (right) The most basic respect in which breech-loading revolvers vary is in the way they are opened and the spent cases ejected. Many designs have been produced and used successfully. We illustrate the three most widely used. All first appeared in the 19th century, but are still in production.

a Side-gate Each case is pushed out to the rear singly by the hand-operated rod alongside the barrel.
b Break-open All the cases are pushed out at once by a star-shaped extractor which rises as the revolver is opened.
c Swing-out cylinder This also has a star-shaped extractor, but it is worked by hand after opening.

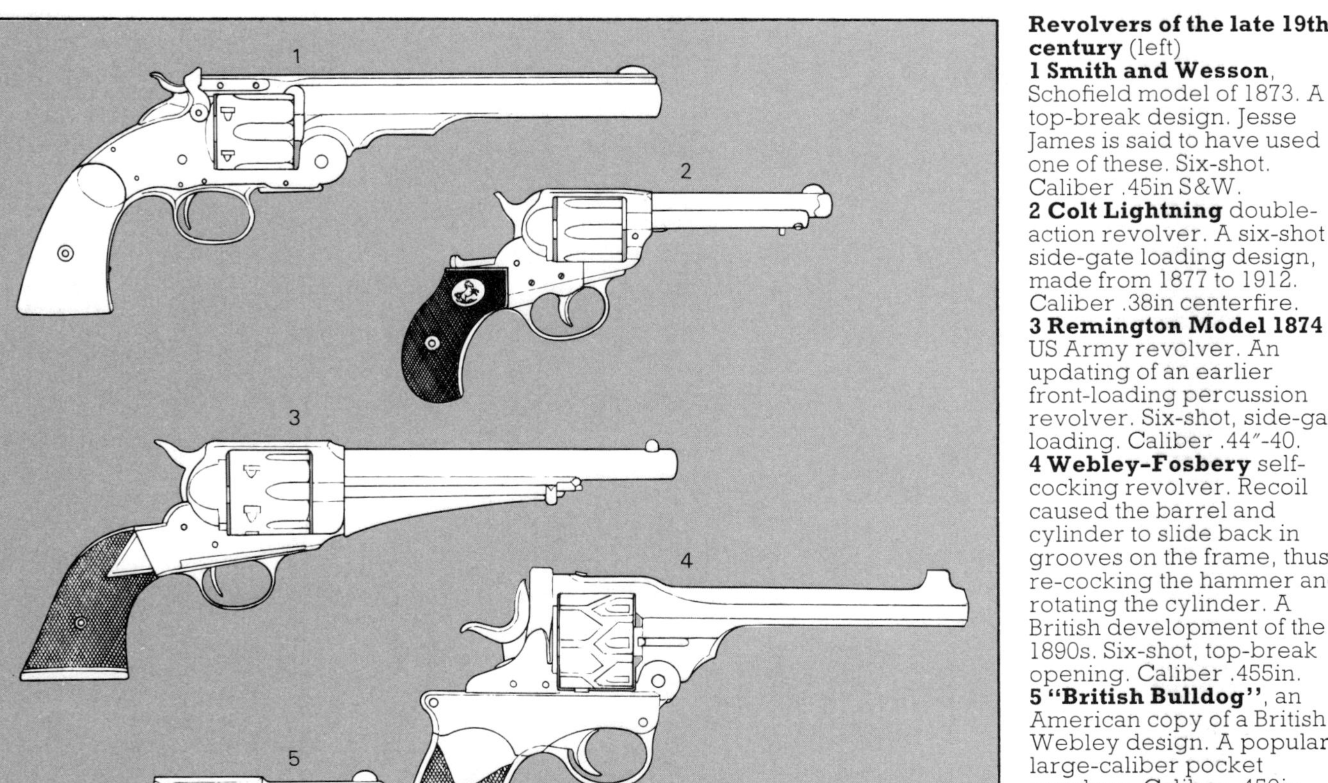

Revolvers of the late 19th century (left)
1 Smith and Wesson, Schofield model of 1873. A top-break design. Jesse James is said to have used one of these. Six-shot. Caliber .45in S&W.
2 Colt Lightning double-action revolver. A six-shot side-gate loading design, made from 1877 to 1912. Caliber .38in centerfire.
3 Remington Model 1874 US Army revolver. An updating of an earlier front-loading percussion revolver. Six-shot, side-gate loading. Caliber .44″-40.
4 Webley-Fosbery self-cocking revolver. Recoil caused the barrel and cylinder to slide back in grooves on the frame, thus re-cocking the hammer and rotating the cylinder. A British development of the 1890s. Six-shot, top-break opening. Caliber .455in.
5 "British Bulldog", an American copy of a British Webley design. A popular large-caliber pocket revolver. Caliber .450in.

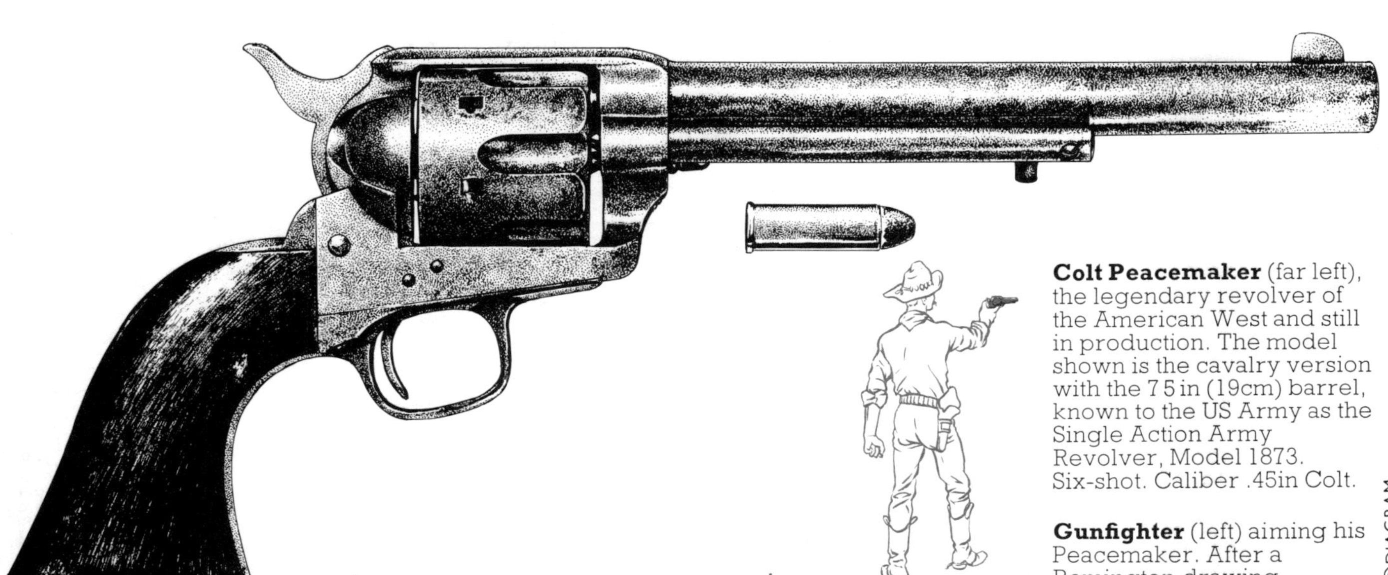

Colt Peacemaker (far left), the legendary revolver of the American West and still in production. The model shown is the cavalry version with the 7.5in (19cm) barrel, known to the US Army as the Single Action Army Revolver, Model 1873. Six-shot. Caliber .45in Colt.

Gunfighter (left) aiming his Peacemaker. After a Remington drawing.

Breech-loading revolvers 2

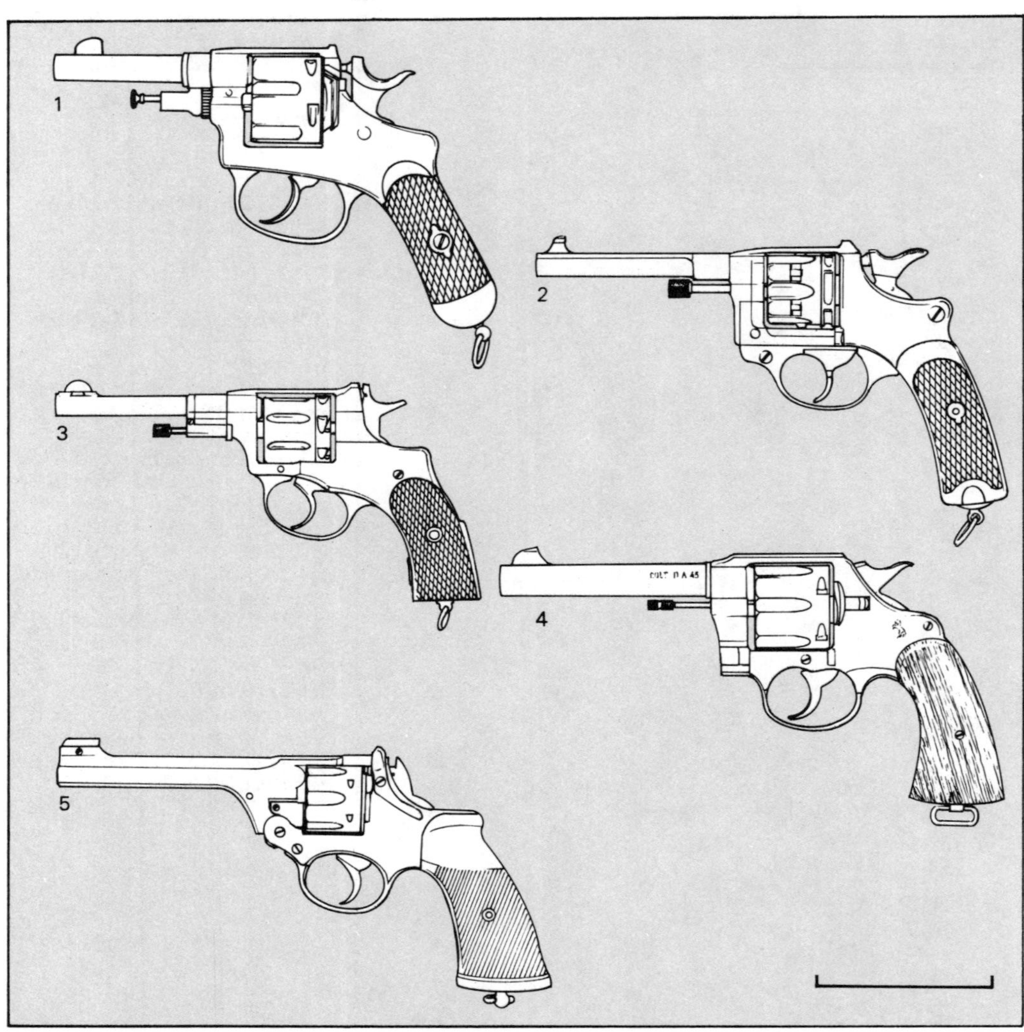

Military revolvers of the World Wars (left)
1 Modello 89B Italian. Made in several variations from 1889 until the 1920s. Six-shot, side-gate loading. Caliber 10.35mm.
2 Modèle 1892 French. Used in both World Wars. Double-action. Six-shot, swing-out cylinder. Caliber 8mm Lebel revolver.
3 Nagant Model 1895G Russian. Used by the Tsarist armies and by the Soviets in both World Wars. Seven-shot, side-gate opening. Caliber 7.62mm Nagant.
4 Colt New Service M1917 Used by both the USA and Britain, in slightly different calibers. Six-shot, swing-out cylinder. Calibers : .45in ACP (US service) ; .455in (British service).
5 Enfield No2 Mk1 Star British. A smaller caliber updating of the earlier Webley (see illustration below). This version was double-action only. Six-shot, top-break opening. Caliber .380in.

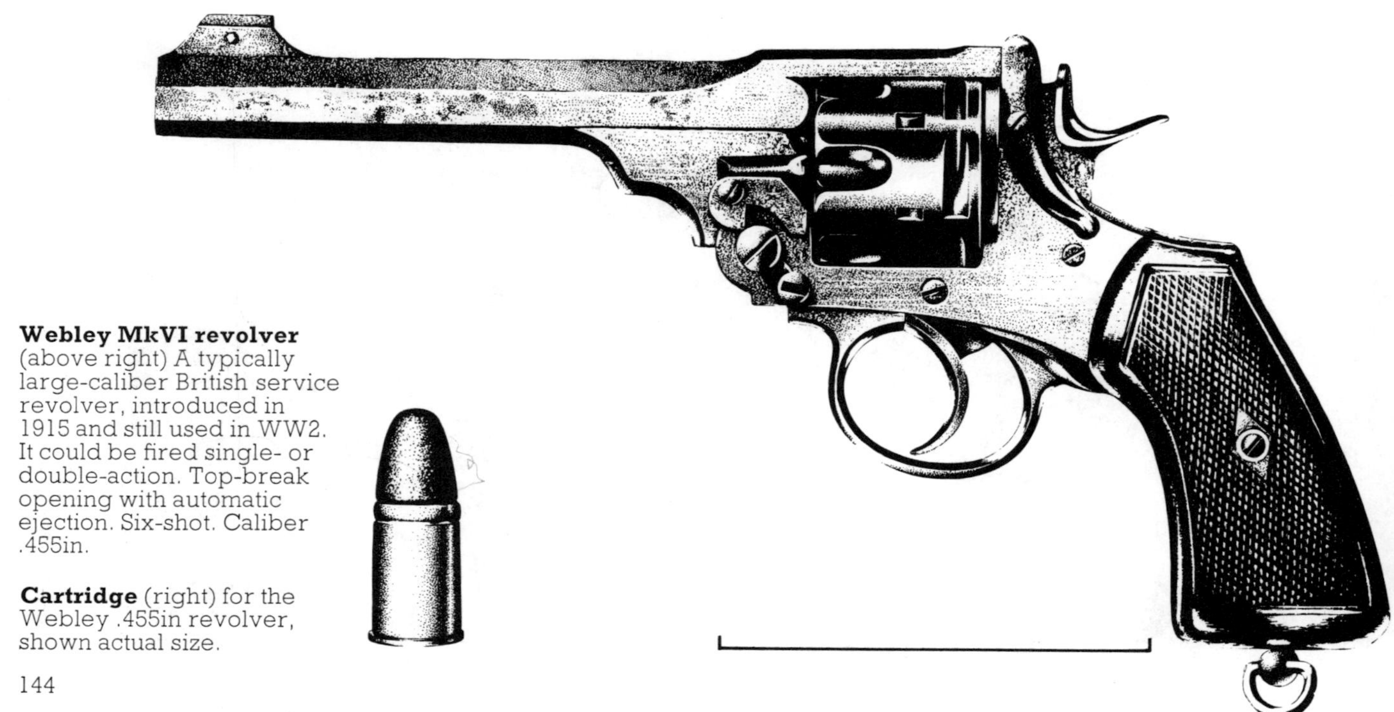

Webley MkVI revolver (above right) A typically large-caliber British service revolver, introduced in 1915 and still used in WW2. It could be fired single- or double-action. Top-break opening with automatic ejection. Six-shot. Caliber .455in.

Cartridge (right) for the Webley .455in revolver, shown actual size.

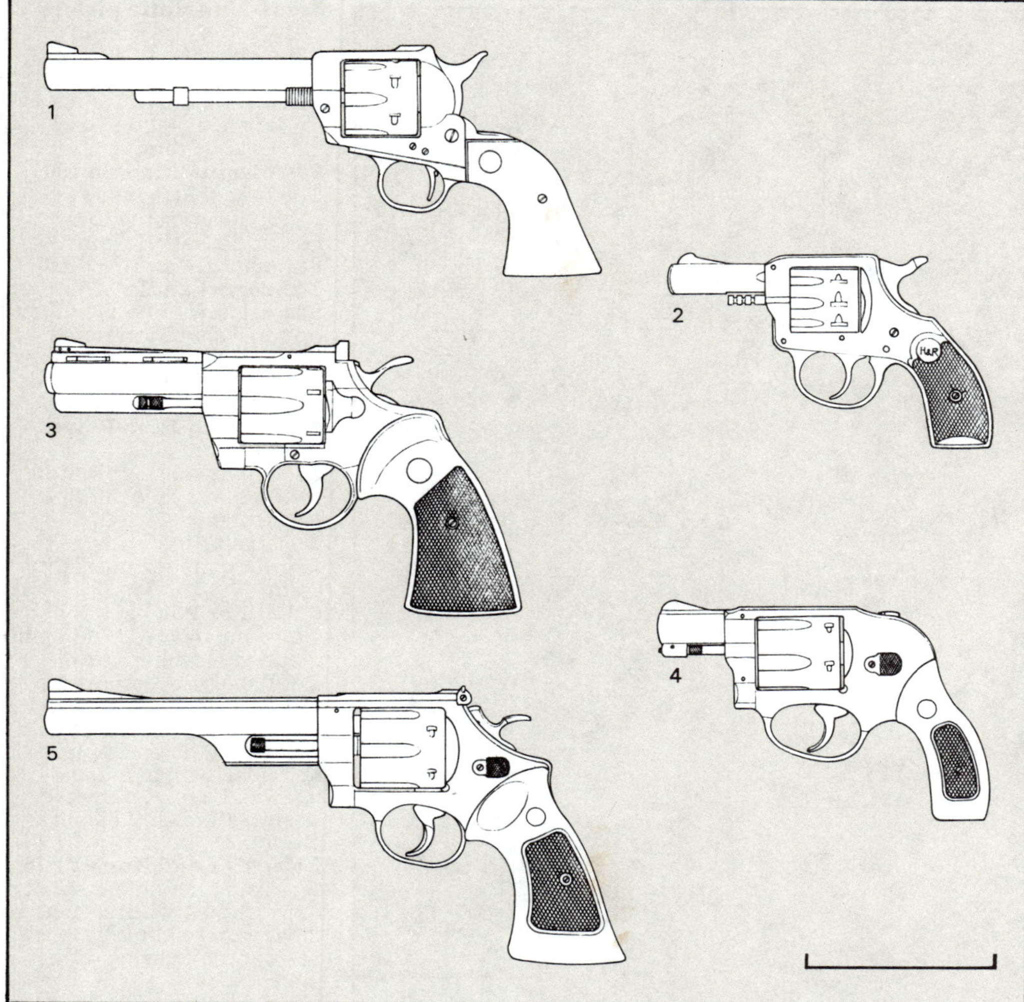

Modern commercial revolvers (left) All are of US manufacture and all except (**1**) are double-action.

1 Ruger Blackhawk New Model. Single-action. Made chiefly for hunting and target use. Six-shot, side-gate loading. Made in calibers .38in Special and .357in Magnum.

2 Harrington and Richardson Model 900 A typical low-cost revolver for personal protection. Nine-shot cylinder removes for loading. Caliber .22in rimfire.

3 Colt Python A powerful police and combat revolver, available in stainless steel. Six-shot, swing-out cylinder. Caliber .357in Magnum.

4 Smith and Wesson Bodyguard Airweight Model Weight 14½oz (0.411kg), compared with 47oz (1.33kg) for (5) below. Enclosed hammer. Alloy frame. Caliber .38in Special.

5 Smith and Wesson .44in Magnum Model 29. The most powerful pistol in the world. The muzzle-energy of the .44in Magnum is about 30% greater than its nearest commercial rival. Six-shot, swing-out cylinder. Also made in .41in Magnum caliber.

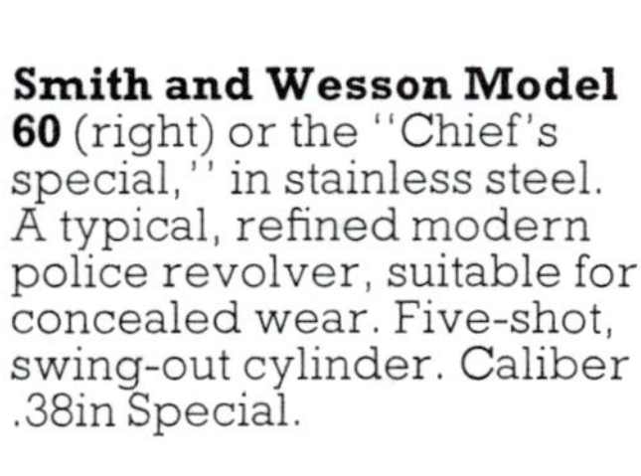

Smith and Wesson Model 60 (right) or the "Chief's special," in stainless steel. A typical, refined modern police revolver, suitable for concealed wear. Five-shot, swing-out cylinder. Caliber .38in Special.

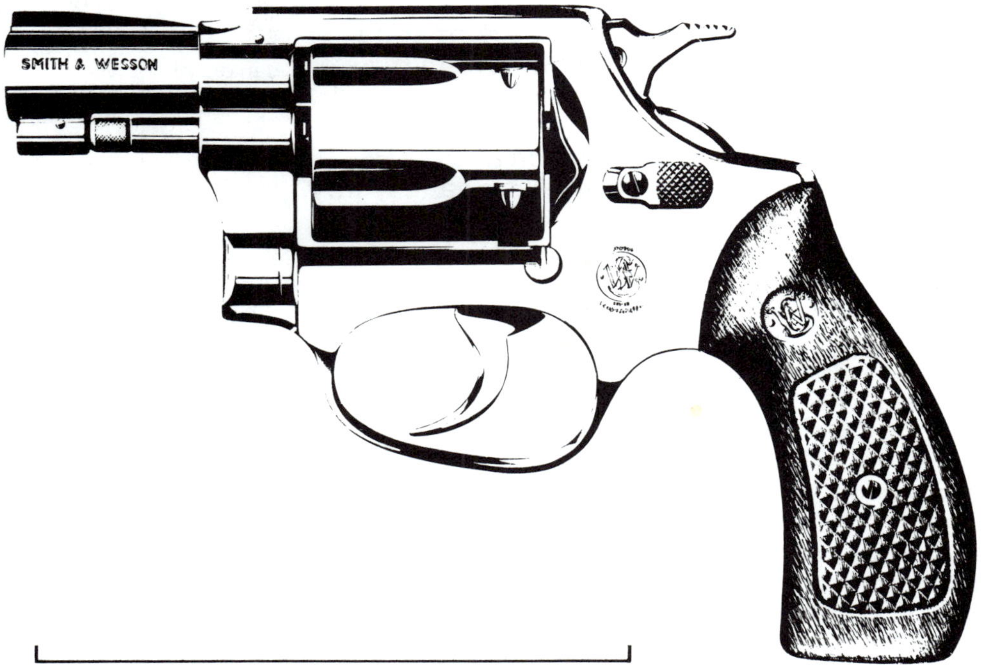

Semi-automatic pistols

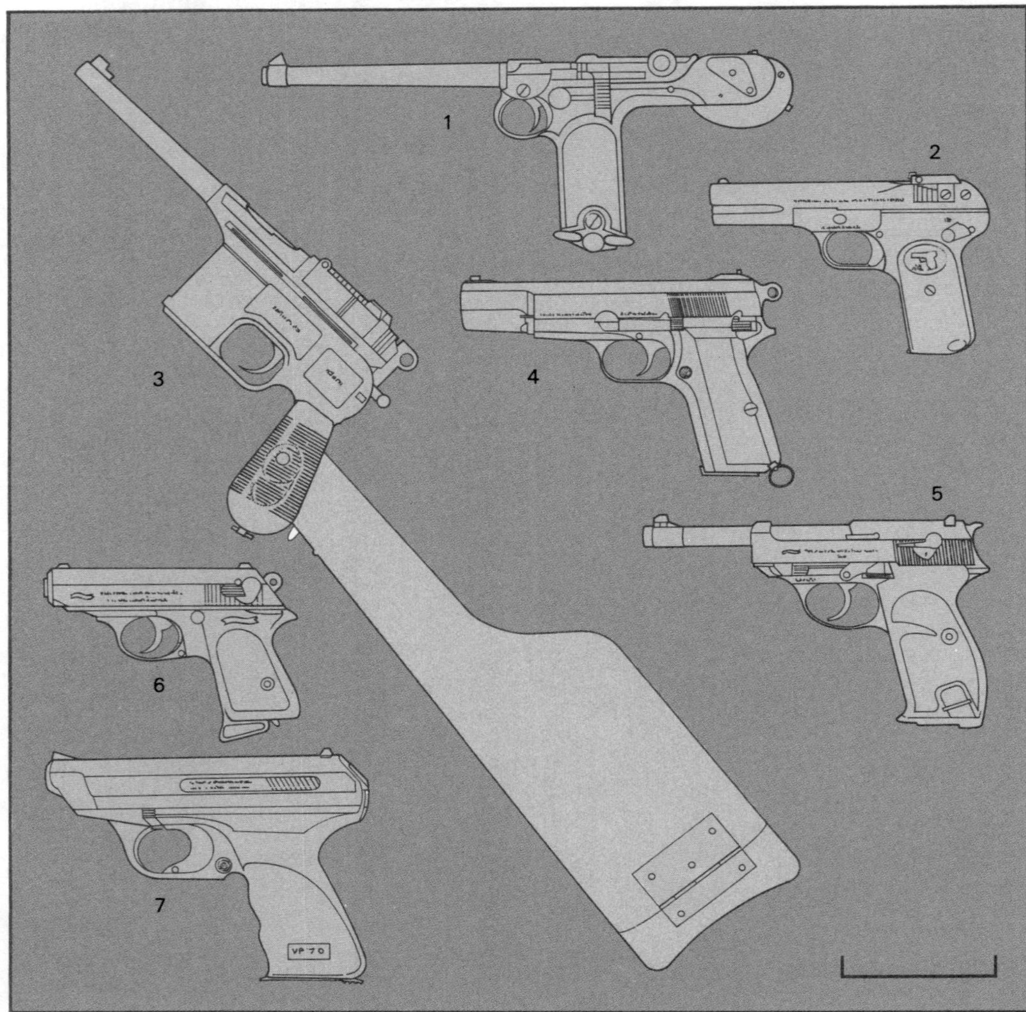

Semi-automatic pistols (left)
1 Borchardt pistol of 1893. One of the first successful pistols of the type, and a forerunner of the Luger. Caliber 7.63mm.
2 Browning Modèle 1900 The first of Browning's pistol designs, made by Fabrique Nationale in Belgium. Caliber 7.65mm.
3 "Broomhandle" Mauser pistol, shown fitted with the optional shoulder-stock. Produced in many versions from 1896. This is the Model 1916, in 9mm caliber.
4 Browning High Power pistol, or the GP35. Originally made in Belgium in 1935. Shown is the No2 Mk1 version made in Canada for the British Army. 13-round magazine. Caliber 9mm.
5 Walther P38 Used by Germany in WW2, and still made in modified form. Double-action hammer. Caliber 9mm.
6 Walther PPK The initials stand for Polizei Pistole Kriminal, which indicates its intended use. A blowback design. Caliber 7.65mm and others.
7 Heckler and Koch VP70 A recent innovation, able to fire three-shot bursts when fitted with a shoulder stock. 18-round magazine. Caliber 9mm.

These pistols, often called "automatics," are more correctly called autoloaders or semi-automatic pistols, as they do not fire in bursts. Before use, a full magazine must be inserted and the mechanism "cocked" by hand to feed a cartridge into the breech and to compress the striker-spring. Thereafter, they fire a shot each time the trigger is pressed. Most designs date from before WW1.

Position of the magazine (right) Several early designs of semi-auto pistol had the magazine placed in front of the trigger-guard (**a**), as on a rifle. Far more common and compact are pistols with the magazine placed inside the grip (**b**). As well as being neater, this solution improves the balance of the weapon.

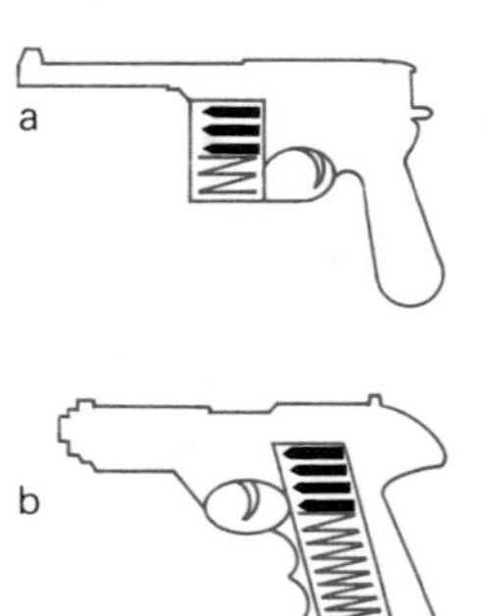

Blowback system (right) This is the simplest of the semi-auto systems, but it can only be used with weaker types of ammunition. The essential point is that barrel and breech are not locked together on firing (**A**). The mass of the slide (or breech-block) and the strength of the return-spring delay opening (**B**) until the bullet has left the barrel and bore pressure is low. In addition, the cartridge has a case with parallel sides. The detail (**C**) shows how this continues to seal the breech during opening until the whole length of the case is clear of the barrel.
As with all semi-auto designs, the return-spring pushes the slide forward again, feeding the next cartridge into the breech.

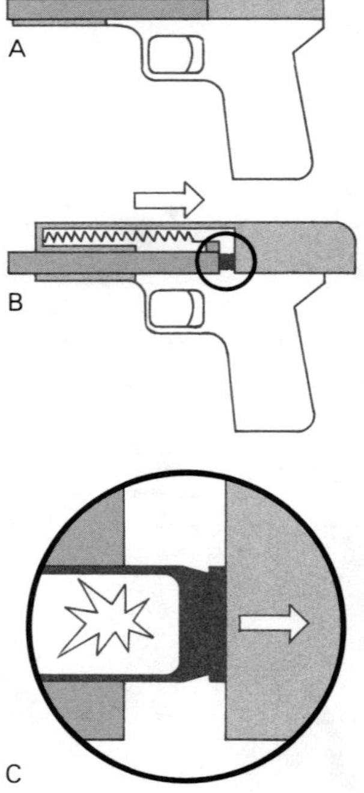

Locked breech systems (below) In order to use more powerful ammunition than is possible with blowback designs, many semi-auto pistols have barrel and breech-block locked together at the moment of firing. Here we examine how two famous designs of pistol unlock and open by using recoil.

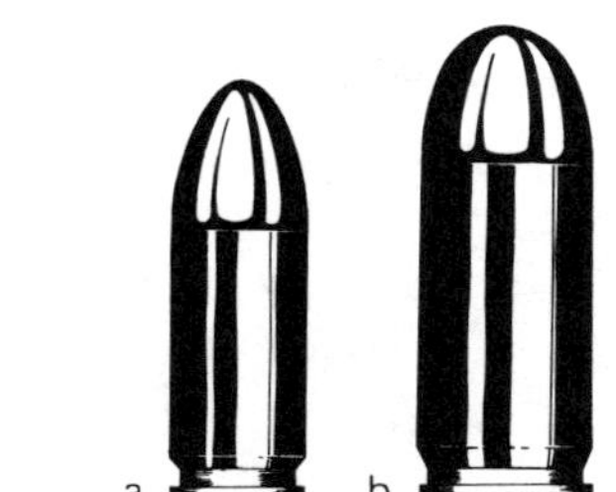

Cartridges (left) of the two calibers most widely used in semi-auto pistols. Shown actual size.
a 9mm Parabellum. This caliber is particularly popular in Europe.
b .45in ACP. The letters stand for Automatic Colt Pistol, which indicates its origins. Favored in the USA for its great power.

Luger P'08 (right) This well-known German pistol (**1**) uses a "toggle" action. A series of joints, like the joints of a finger, lock the breech-block to the barrel as long as the center joint is below the other two (**a**). On firing, barrel and breech-block are thrust back by recoil, sliding in grooves on the frame of the pistol. After a short distance the toggle is knocked upward (**b**) by sloping projections on the frame. This unlocks the breech-block, which continues to the rear to eject the spent case. The barrel moves no further back.
Many variations of Luger exist, differing chiefly in the length of barrel. Eight-shot magazine. Caliber 7.65mm Parabellum or 9mm Parabellum.

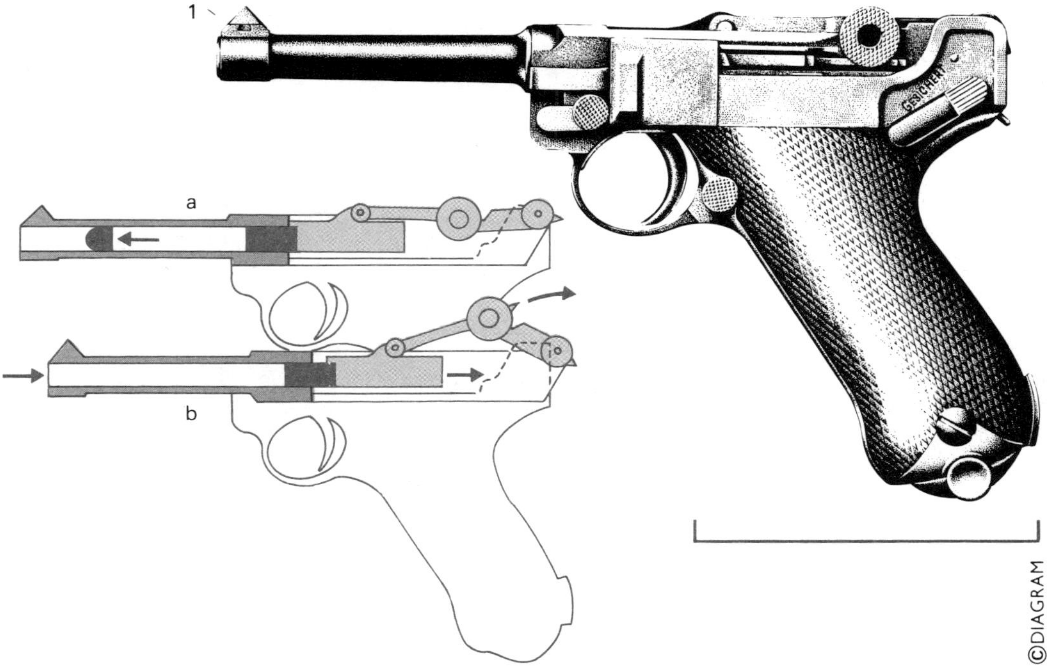

Colt 1911 A1 (right) The most popular of US semi-autos, this design (**2**) uses a variety of "short recoil" system. Before firing (**a**), the barrel is locked, by ribs on its upper surface, to the slide. A short flexible link attaches the barrel to the lower body of the pistol. On firing, barrel and slide recoil together until the link swings the barrel down (**b**), freeing it from the locking recesses on the slide. The slide then continues to the rear to eject the spent case and complete the operating cycle.
The 1911 A1 was produced in 1923 as a result of improvements to the original 1911 design. The 1911 A1 is still in production and in use in many parts of the world. Caliber .45in ACP.

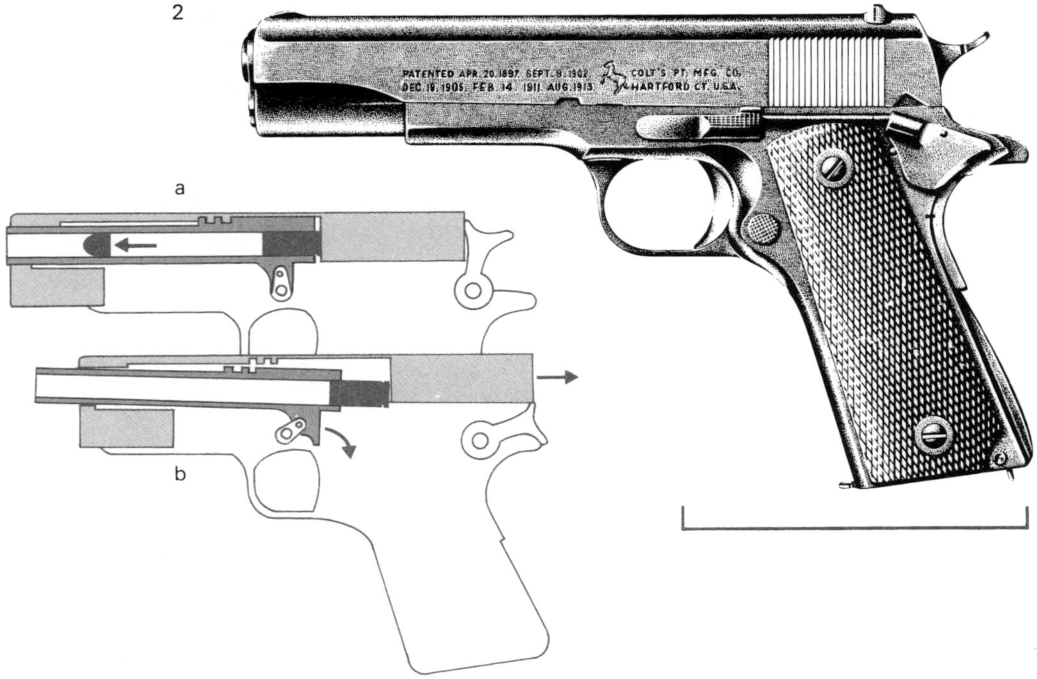

Submachine guns

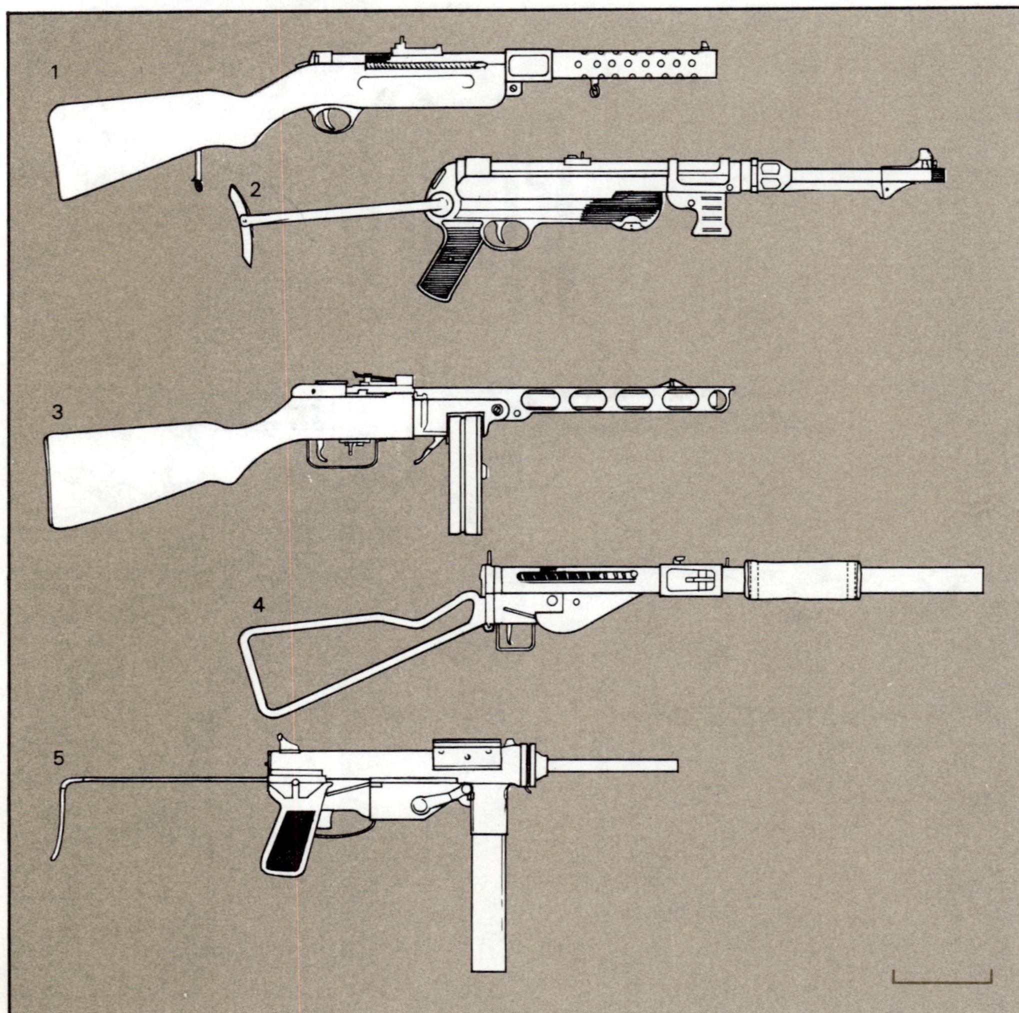

Submachine guns of the World Wars (left)
1 Bergmann MP 18/1 One of the first SMGs, used by the German army in 1918. Its "snail" magazine (not shown) was fitted on the left. Automatic only.
Rate of fire 400rpm.
Caliber 9mm.
2 MP40 German. Often called the Schmeisser. A simpler version of the similar MP38, the first SMG with a folding stock.
Automatic only.
Rate of fire 500rpm.
Caliber 9mm.
3 PPSh41 Soviet. Crude but effective. One of the main Soviet infantry weapons of WW2. Drum-shaped magazine.
Selective fire.
Rate of fire 900rpm.
Caliber 7.62mm x25 Tokarev.
4 Sten Mk2 One of the series of cheap British SMGs of WW2. The version shown has a long silencer over the barrel.
Selective fire.
Rate of fire 450rpm (550rpm without silencer).
Caliber 9mm.
5 US M3 Often called the "grease-gun" because of its resemblance to the mechanic's implement.
Telescopic stock.
Automatic only.
Rate of fire 450rpm.
Caliber .45in ACP.

Submachine guns (SMGs) are portable, fully-automatic firearms, used for close combat. The concept was a product of trench warfare, although most designs were too late to be used in WW1. Most use pistol-caliber ammunition, and recoil is light enough for them to be fired from the hip as well as from the shoulder. (For heavier types of machine gun and their functioning, see Chapter 4, p. 211.)

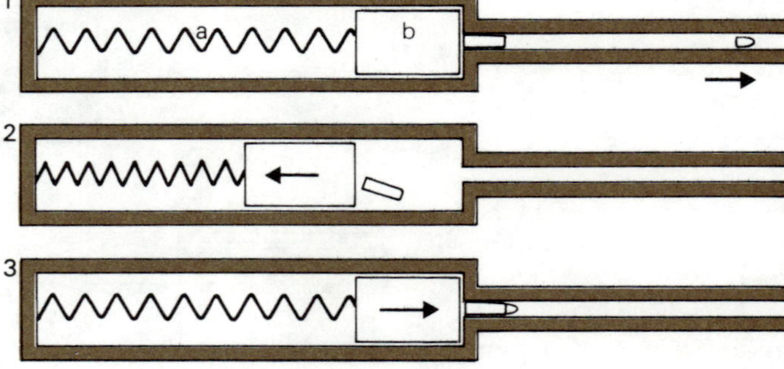

Collapsible stocks (right)
One of the SMG's main advantages is its handiness. This is often further enhanced by fitting a metal skeleton-stock, which can be collapsed when carried, for example, in a vehicle cab. Most such stocks either fold under the action (**A**) or telescope alongside it (**B**).

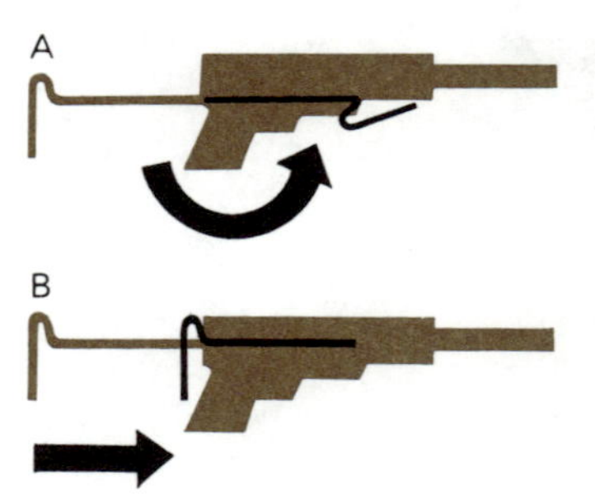

Blowback system (above)
Most SMGs use this simple operating principle.
1 At the moment of firing, the breech is kept closed merely by the strength of the spring (**a**) and by the weight and inertia of the breech-block (**b**).
2 Thus the opening of the breech and extraction of the empty case is delayed until the pressure in the bore is down to a safe level. As the block moves back, the empty case is ejected.
3 The spring then pushes the block forward again, to feed the next round into the breech and fire it. The ammunition is usually supplied from a box- or drum-like magazine. (For other systems used with more powerful ammunition, see p. 211 under "Machine Guns.")

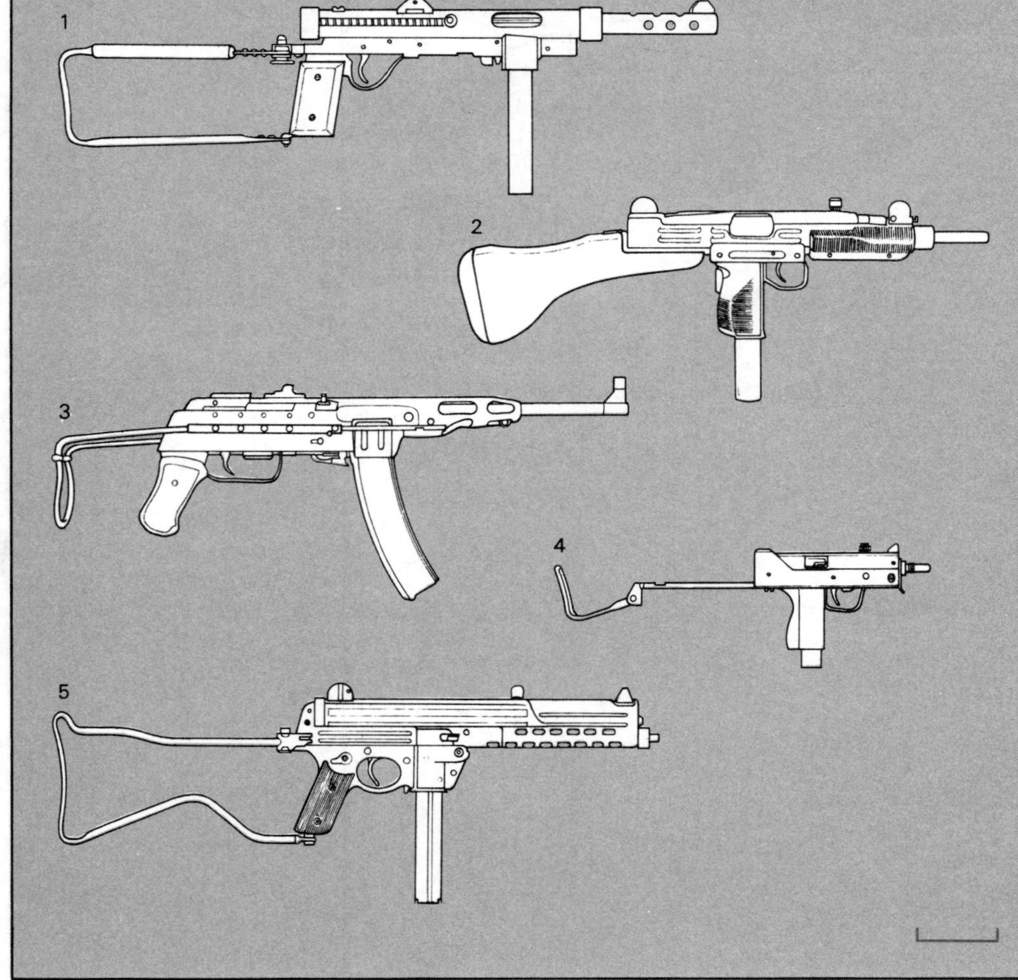

Some SMGs in current use (left)

1 "Port Said" An Egyptian copy of the Swedish Model 45B. The stock folds sideways. Automatic only. Rate of fire 600rpm. Caliber 9mm x19.

2 Uzi Israeli designed and produced. A compact design, with the magazine inserted through the grip. A version with a folding metal stock is also made. Selective fire. Rate of fire 600rpm. Caliber 9mm x19.

3 K-50M North Vietnamese. An adaptation of the Soviet PPSh 41, with a telescopic stock. Automatic only. Rate of fire 700rpm. Caliber 7.62mm x25 Tokarev.

4 Ingram Model 11 US commercial product, bought by several countries, often for undercover use. The stock slides in and folds. Selective fire. Rate of fire 1200rpm. Caliber .380in ACP.

5 Walther MPL West German commercial venture, bought by the police and border guards in that country. The stock folds sideways. Selective fire. Rate of fire 550rpm. Caliber 9mm x19.

Thompson Model 1928 SMG (above), the original "tommy-gun," which became famous through its use by gangsters (left) during Prohibition in the USA. It was later modified several times, and saw much use in WW2. The M1928 could use a 20-round (as here) or 30-round box magazine, or 50- and 100-round drum magazines. Caliber .45in ACP.

Rates of fire Note that figures for rates of fire indicate the cyclic rate of fire; that is to say the theoretical rate, ignoring the need to change magazines and re-cock the mechanism.

Self-loading and assault rifles 1

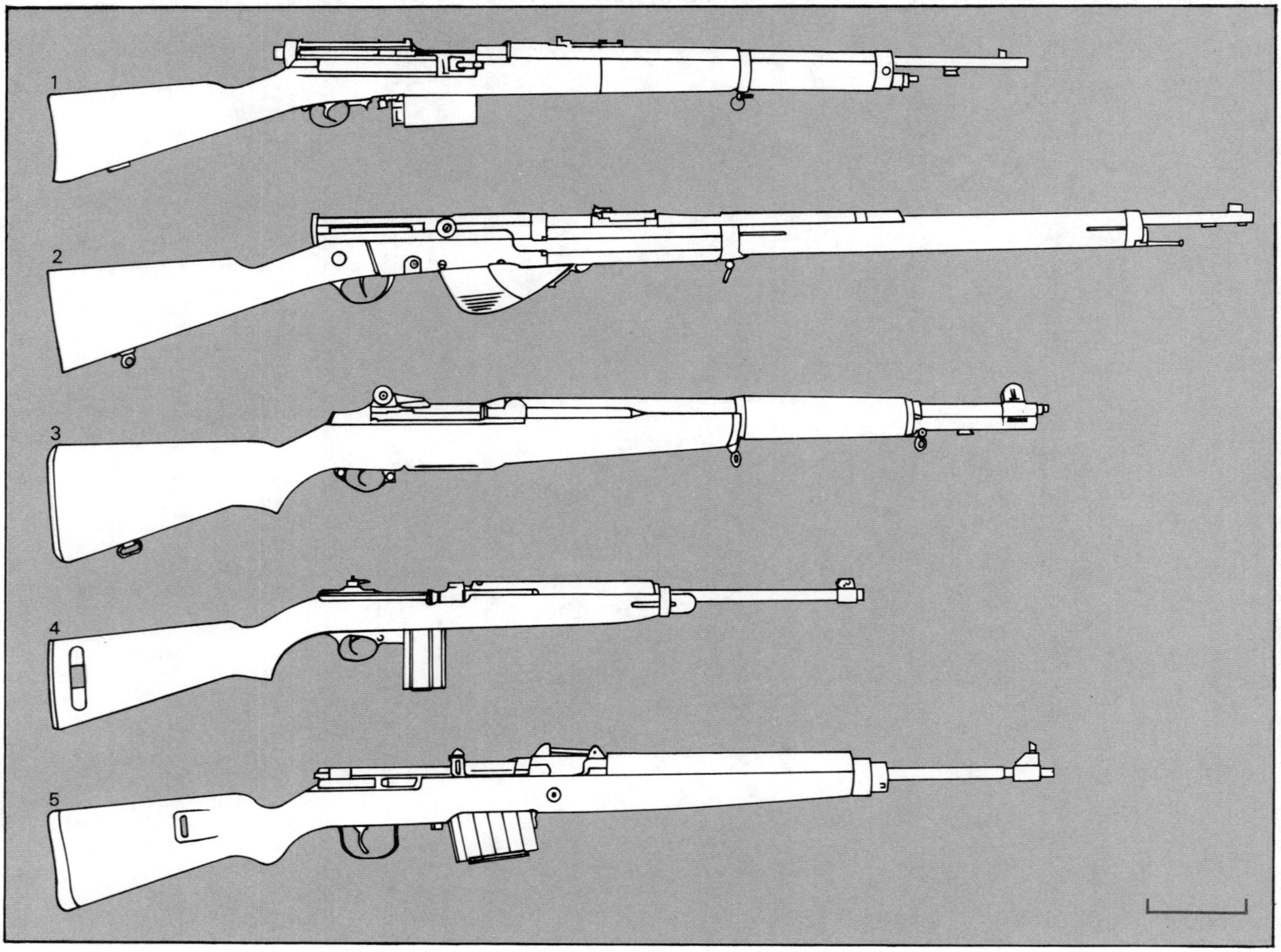

All these rifles use some of the power of the exploding cartridge to re-cock the striker and to feed the next round into the breech. Those that fire only one shot at each pull of the trigger are usually called self-loading rifles. Others, now usually called assault rifles, can also fire in bursts at the flick of a switch. As they fire less powerful ammunition, they can also be used as SMGs.

Early self-loading rifles (above)
1 Mondragon Modelo 1908 Designed and used by Mexico, but made in Switzerland.
Gas-operated.
Eight-round magazine.
Caliber 7mm x57 Mauser.
2 RSC Modèle 1917 French gas-operated weapon, in limited use in WW1.
Five-round magazine.
Caliber 8mm x50R Lebel.
3 US M1 Rifle, often called the Garand after its designer. The first SLR to be a general issue in any army, it was used throughout WW2 and in the Korean War.
Gas-operated.
Eight-round magazine.
Caliber .30in-'06.
4 US M1 Carbine used alongside the Garand when a lighter weapon was required. The M2 version could also fire in bursts.
Gas-operated, using a short-stroke piston.
15-round (shown) or 30-round magazine.
Caliber .30in M1 Carbine.
5 Gewehr 43 German design in limited use in WW2.
Gas-operated.
10-round magazine.
Caliber 7.92mm x57.

Gas-operation (right) Most semi-automatic and assault rifles use some variety of gas-operated mechanism. Breech-block and barrel are locked together on firing (**a**). Gas is bled off from behind the bullet to drive back a piston (**b**). This unlocks and opens the breech (**c**), extracting the empty case. The return spring will then repeat the cycle.

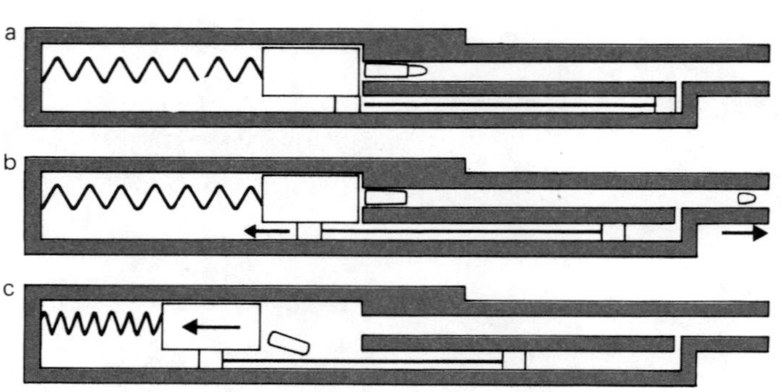

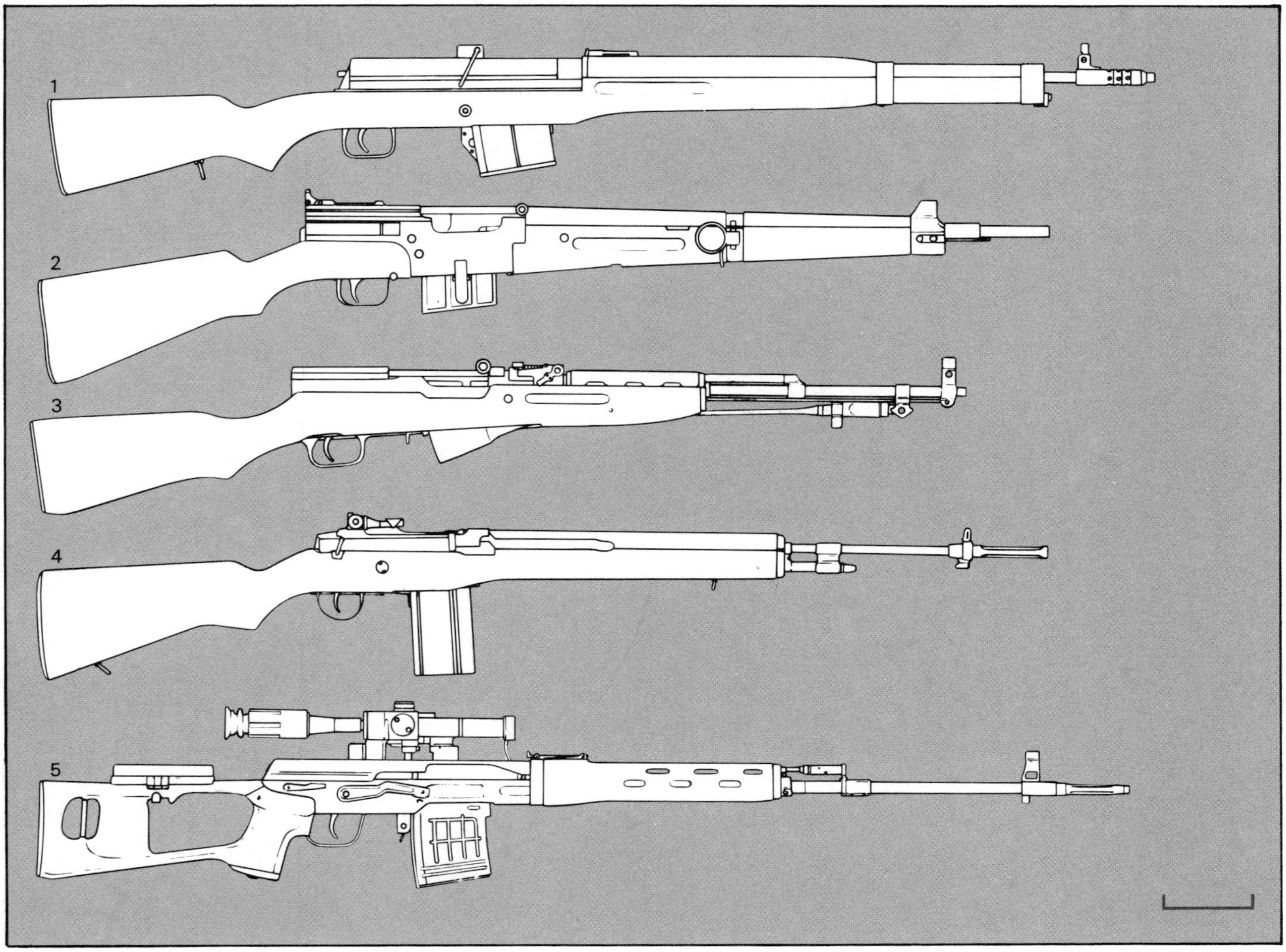

Post 1945 self-loading rifles (above)
1 Hakim An Egyptian copy of the Swedish Ljungmann rifle.
Gas-operated.
10-round magazine.
Caliber 7.92mm x57.
2 MAS 49 French design, gas-operated, but having no piston. Used by the French army since 1949.
10-round magazine.
Caliber 7.5mm x54 M1929.
3 Type 56 carbine. Chinese copy of the Soviet SKS. Still in use with militia units in China.
Gas-operated.
10-round magazine.
Caliber 7.62mm x39 M43.
4 US M14 Rifle based on the M1 Garand. Now partially replaced by the M16.
Gas-operated.
20-round magazine.
Caliber .308in (7.62mm x51 NATO).
5 SVD sniper rifle. Soviet weapon, known in the West as the Dragunov. It is fitted with a telescopic sight, and uses an obsolete cartridge for the sake of its accuracy.
Gas-operated.
10-round magazine.
Caliber 7.62mm x54R.

L1 A1 Rifle (below) This is the British version of the Belgian FN FAL, one of the most widely used of modern designs. The rifle shown has the latest black plastic stock.
Semi-automatic only.
Gas-operated.
20-round magazine.
Caliber 7.62mm x51NATO

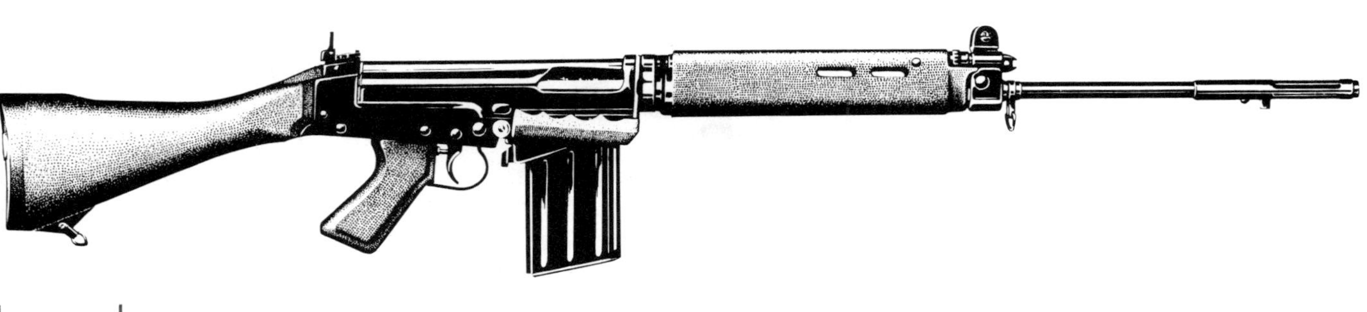

Self-loading and assault rifles 2

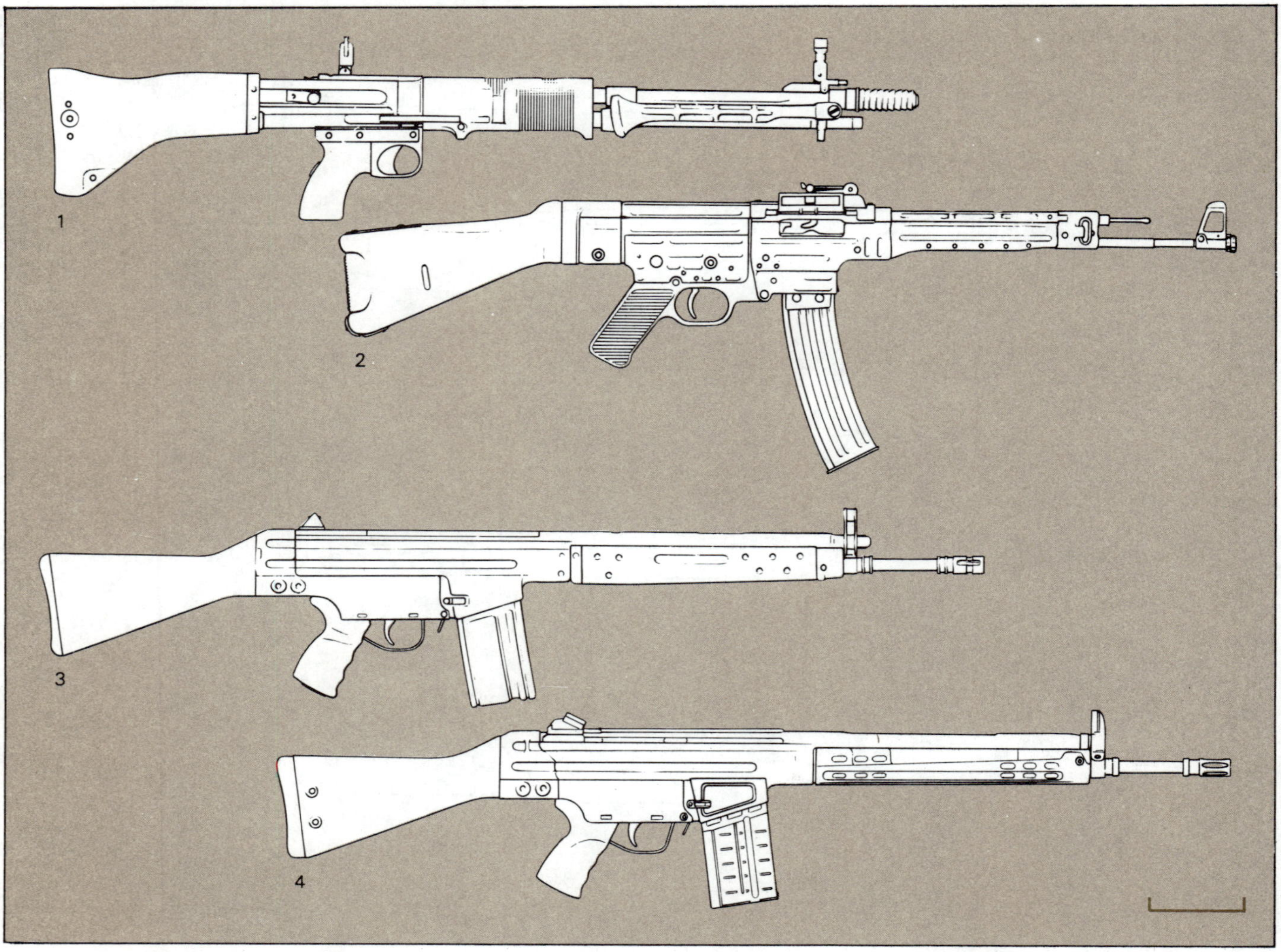

Stock alignment (right) The conventional, downward-angled stock (**a**) is not suited to fully-automatic fire. Recoil, acting in line with the barrel's axis, tends to make the muzzle rise when firing bursts, causing inaccuracy. This is avoided by the modern straight-line stock (**b**), which places the firer's shoulder directly in line with the barrel.

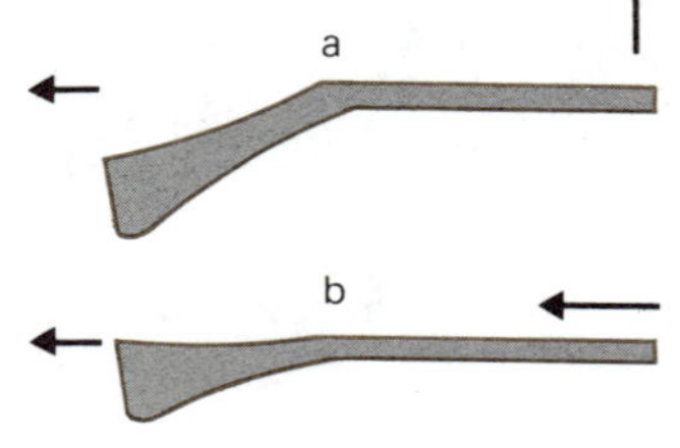

Cartridges (right) of the Warsaw Pact and NATO. The AK47 rifle and its derivatives, used by most Eastern bloc troops, fire the 7.62mmx39 intermediate powered round (**1**). NATO has standardized the more powerful but older-fashioned 7.62mm x51 (**2**). Note that although of the same nominal caliber, these cartridges are not interchangeable.

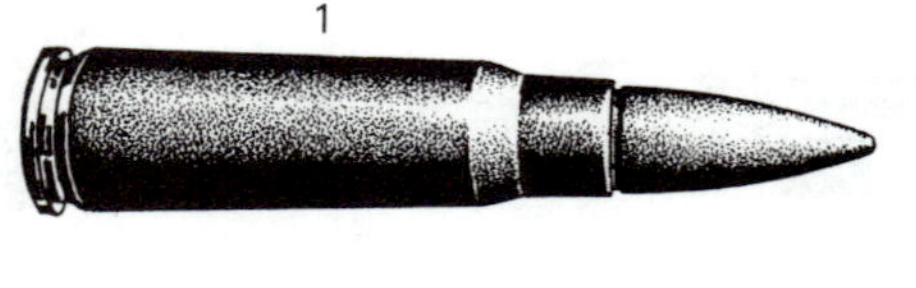

Assault rifles (above) All can fire at full- or semi-automatic.
1 FG42 German paratroop weapon of WW2. It was one of the first rifles to have a straight stock to reduce "climb" when firing at full-automatic.
Gas-operated.
Rate of fire 750rpm.
20-round magazine on the left side.
Caliber 7.92mm x57 Mauser.
2 MP44 Later called the Sturmgewehr 44 (StG44). This weapon established the name and form of the modern assault rifle. On limited issue in WW2.
Gas-operated.
Rate of fire 500rpm.
30-round magazine.
Caliber 7.92mm x32 Kurz.
3 CETME Model C Spanish rifle, made in several variations. Shown is the current light version.
Delayed blowback operation.
Rate of fire 550-650rpm.
20-round magazine.
Caliber 7.62mm x51 NATO and variants.
4 Gewehr 3 A3 this is the current West German army rifle, derived from the Spanish CETME. It has also been bought by other armies.
Delayed blowback operation.
Rate of fire 550rpm.
20-round magazine.
Caliber 7.62mm x51 NATO.

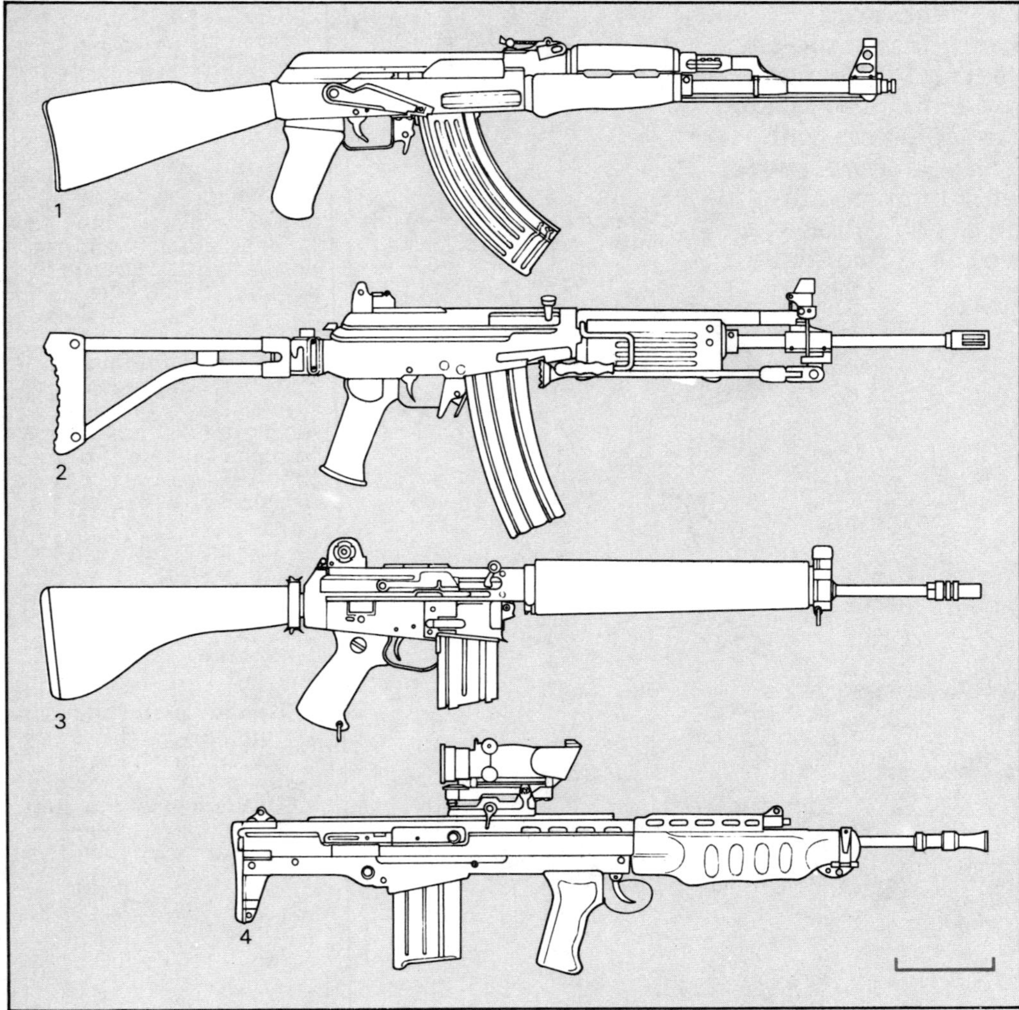

Assault rifles (left) All can fire at full- or semi-automatic.
1 AK47 Soviet assault rifle, also used in several variations by many other armies and guerrilla organizations. Shown is the basic version with fixed wooden stock.
Gas-operated.
Rate of fire 600rpm.
30-round magazine.
Caliber 7.62mm x39.
2 Galil ARM Israeli rifle developed since the Arab-Israeli War of 1967. Shown with the optional folding stock.
Gas-operated.
Rate of fire 650rpm.
35-round magazine.
Caliber 5.56mm x45.
3 AR18 The latest US commercial version of the Armalite rifle.
Gas-operated.
Rate of fire 800rpm.
20-round magazine.
Caliber .223in (5.56mm x45).
4 IW (Individual weapon.) Proposed British Army rifle, using the so-called "bull-pup" layout. This places the grip and trigger unit in front of the breech, so allowing a long barrel in a short overall length. Optical sight fitted as standard.
Gas-operated.
Rate of fire 700-850rpm.
20-round magazine.
Caliber 4.85mm. Became SA80 rifle, in service 1986.

US M16 A1 Rifle (left) The chief rifle currently used by US Forces. The main body of the rifle is made of aluminum alloy, and the stock is plastic.
Gas-operated.
Rate of fire 700-950rpm.
20- or (as shown) 30-round magazine.
Caliber .223in (5.56mm x45).

Soviet AKM (below left) The current army rifle of the USSR, an improved version of the AK47.
Gas-operated.
Rate of fire 600rpm.
30-round magazine.
Caliber 7.62mm x39.

Grenade guns and rifle grenades

Here we cover a variety of hand-held devices for projecting grenades. Some are grenade guns — true firearms. Others are grenades made to be fired from the muzzle of a rifle, with or without an adaptor. Both ideas are old, and have seen renewed use since World War 1, especially in an anti-tank role. We show a selection of examples and explain some different means of projection.

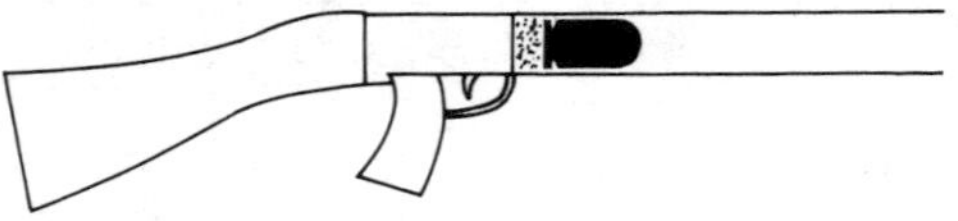

Grenade guns (above) are simply large-caliber small arms, firing a grenade instead of a bullet. Many can also fire anti-riot projectiles and signal flares. They may be muzzle-loaders, but most now load at the breech.

Methods of holding (left) Because of the recoil from firing a heavy projectile, most grenade guns are fired from the shoulder (**a**). Some have been made as pistols (**b**), similar to flare pistols.

1 Grenade pistol fitted with a combined matchlock/ wheellock mechanism. German, late 16th century.
2 Flintlock grenade gun with a bronze barrel. European, early 18th century.

3 US M79 grenade launcher, a rifled, breech-loading weapon. It fires a fixed cartridge (**3a**), and breaks open to load. Used in Vietnam with high-explosive and buckshot loads. Maximum range of grenade approximately 350yd (350m). Caliber 40mm.

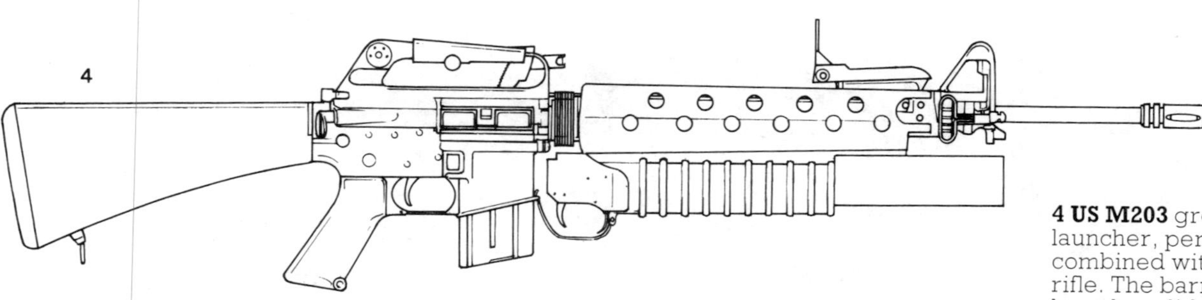

4 US M203 grenade launcher, permanently combined with an M16 A1 rifle. The barrel of the launcher slides forward to load. Caliber 40mm.

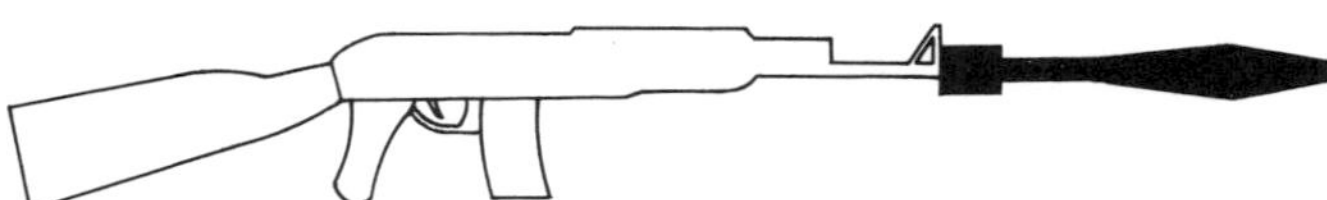

Rifle grenades (above) are fired from the muzzle of a longarm. A propellant cartridge is loaded into the rifle separately.

Firing positions (right) for absorbing the recoil.
a Rifle-butt on ground.
b Rifle-butt clasped under the armpit.

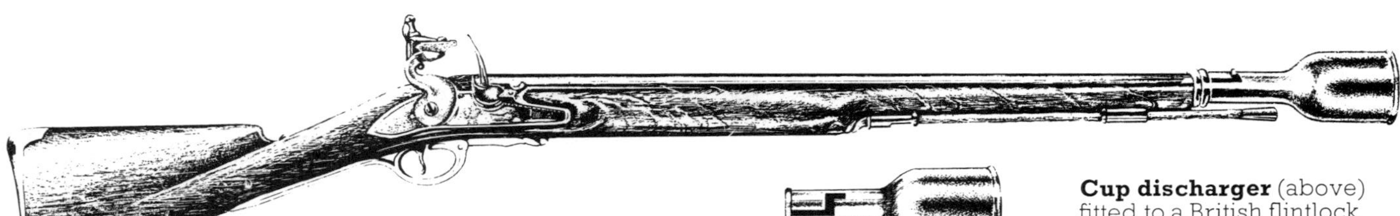

Cup discharger (above) fitted to a British flintlock carbine of 1747. It was used to fire cast-iron hand-grenades. The cup is also shown detatched (left). (Tower of London.)

Projection of grenades (right)
1 Cup discharger A wide-mouthed extension is fitted to the rifle muzzle and a grenade inserted. A blank cartridge is fired in the rifle barrel, and its gases propel the grenade on its way. This method is the most suitable for projecting normal hand-grenades. Variations exist which use a bulleted cartridge for propulsion, the bullet by-passing the grenade or passing via a tube through its center. The cup may be rifled or smooth.
2 Rod grenade The grenade is fitted with a steel rod, which is inserted into the rifle barrel. Projection is by blank cartridge only.
3 Spigot grenade The purpose-made grenade has a fin-stablized tube behind it. This is slipped over the rifle muzzle. Propulsion is usually by blank cartridge. However, versions do exist which use bulleted ammunition, the bullet being absorbed by a special trap in the top of the tube. The fins improve accuracy and make the grenade fly point-first. This is especially useful for anti-tank grenades.

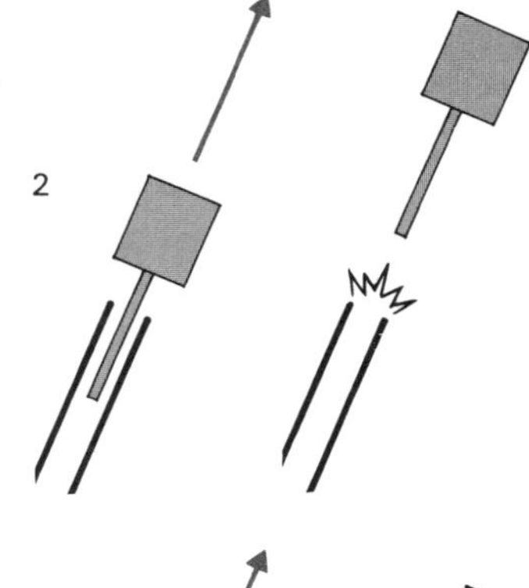

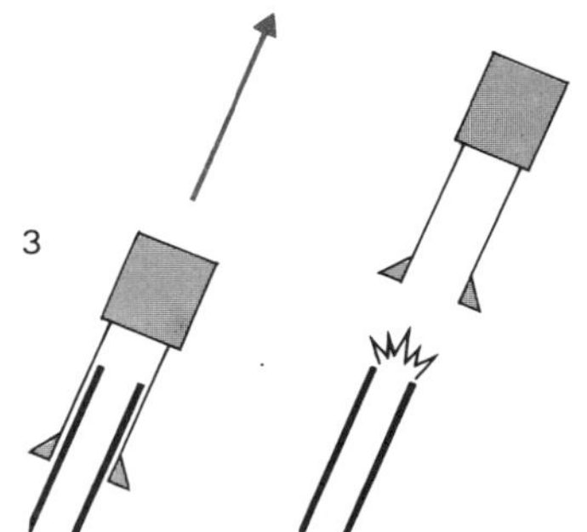

Examples (right) of rifle-grenades, representing each of the four main uses of this weapon.
a Anti-personnel Shown is the British No36 or Mills Grenade, of WW1 and WW2. It was a normal hand grenade, adapted for cup-discharge by fitting a base-plate. Like most anti-personnel grenades, it acted by blast and fragmentation.
b Anti-tank Shown is the French STRIM Light Anti-tank Rifle Grenade. Like most anti-tank grenades, it is spigot-launched and fin-stabilized, as its hollow-charge warhead (see p.156) must strike the target point first. In current use.
c Smoke Although meant primarily to obscure the enemy's vision, many types contain white phosphorus which has secondary anti-personnel and incendiary effects. Shown is the US M19 A1 WP grenade, which is spigot-launched.
d Anti-riot gas Rifle-grenades are a convenient way of delivering irritant gas or smoke. Shown is the Belgian LAC M2, which is spigot-launched but unstabilized in flight, as the tube is internal. Non-lethal rubber "grenades" are also made for anti-riot use.

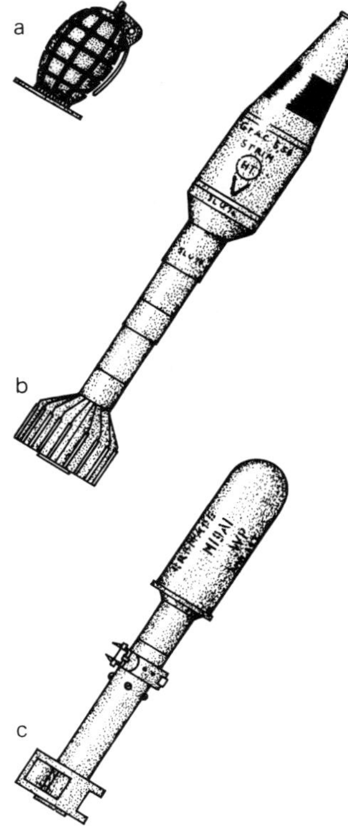

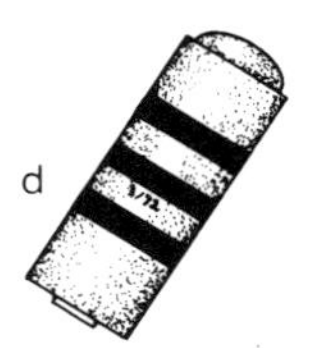

Hand-held recoilless guns

The recoilless gun is an ingenious product of World War 2. It allows a projectile the size of an artillery shell to be fired from a man's shoulder. It is in common use as a man-portable anti-tank weapon. Although effective in this role, its great back-blast is a disadvantage, as it can easily reveal the firer's position, and can kill anyone left close behind the gun at the moment of firing.

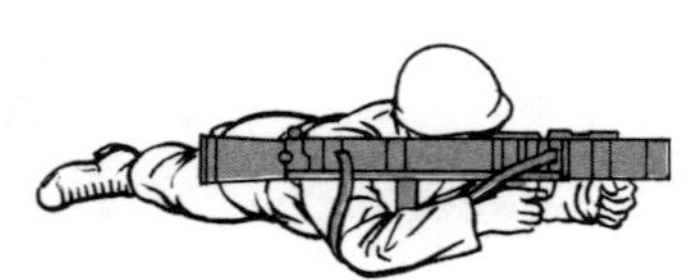

Firing from the shoulder (above) with these weapons is made possible by the lack of recoil and the lightness of the barrel, which only has to contain comparatively low stresses. The kneeling position is often used when aiming at a moving tank. In the lying position, the legs must be kept to one side to aviod injury from the backblast.

The principle (right) of the recoilless gun is based on Newton's third law, which states that, "To every action there is an equal and opposite reaction." The forward motion of the projectile is balanced by the rearward motion of a counterweight (**A**), or more often of a mass of high velocity gas (**B**), which takes the form of a violent backblast.

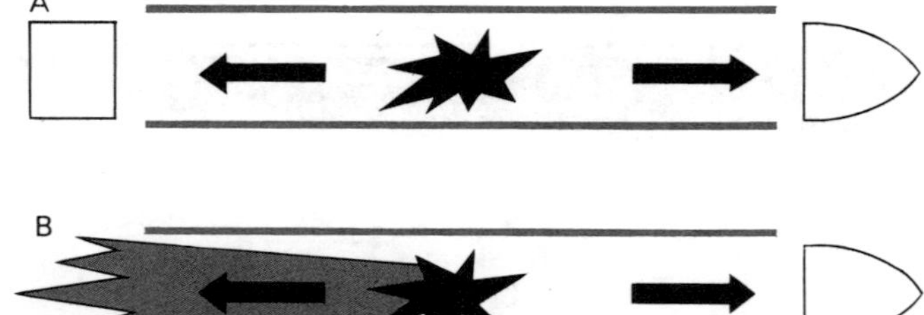

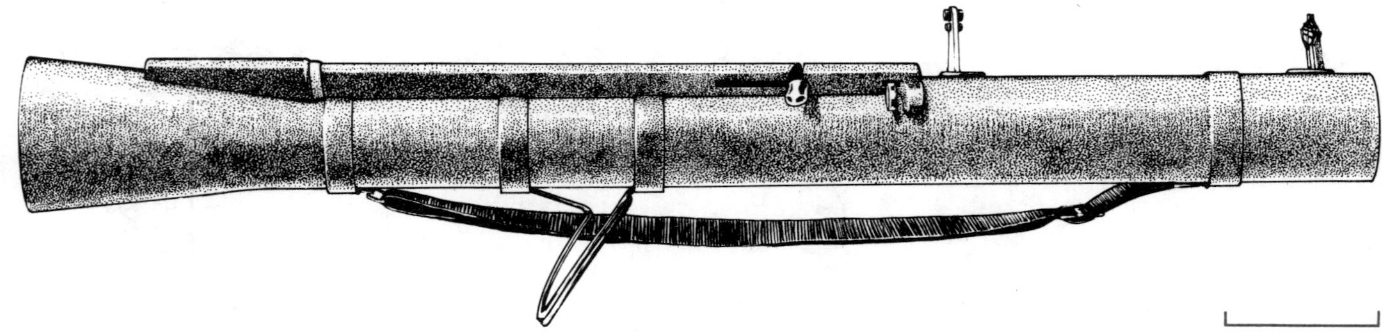

Miniman (above) A Swedish recoilless and disposable anti-tank gun, now in use. Its shell is stabilized by small fins which develop on leaving the barrel. Its maximum range is 250m (273yd) against stationary targets and 150m (163yd) against moving targets. The barrel is made of plastic and fiberglass. Weight 2.9kg (6.39lb).

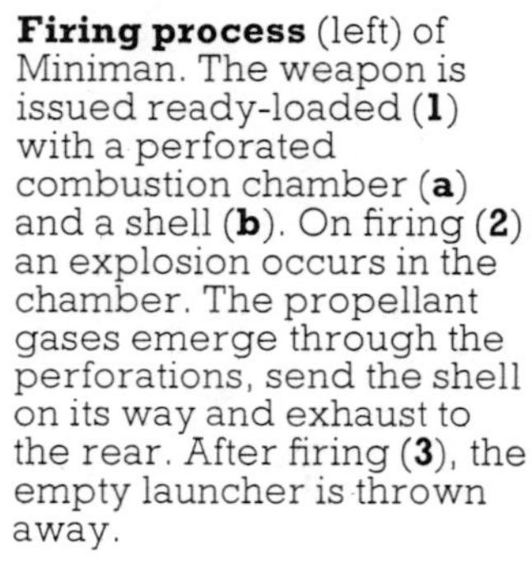

Firing process (left) of Miniman. The weapon is issued ready-loaded (**1**) with a perforated combustion chamber (**a**) and a shell (**b**). On firing (**2**) an explosion occurs in the chamber. The propellant gases emerge through the perforations, send the shell on its way and exhaust to the rear. After firing (**3**), the empty launcher is thrown away.

Shaped-charge shells (right) are used with Miniman and most other recoilless guns in the anti-tank role. A hollow cone of explosive (**A**) is detonated at its apex when the distance tube (**B**) hits the target (**C**). The force of the explosion focusses into a jet of hot gas at high velocity, which melts a narrow hole through the armor plate. Hot gases and molten metal are injected into the tank's interior, killing the crew or exploding their ammunition. This system has the great advantage that it will pierce as much armor at long ranges as at short. Miniman can penetrate 30cm (11.8in) of armor. The name HEAT (High Energy/Explosive Anti Tank) is given to this form of shell.

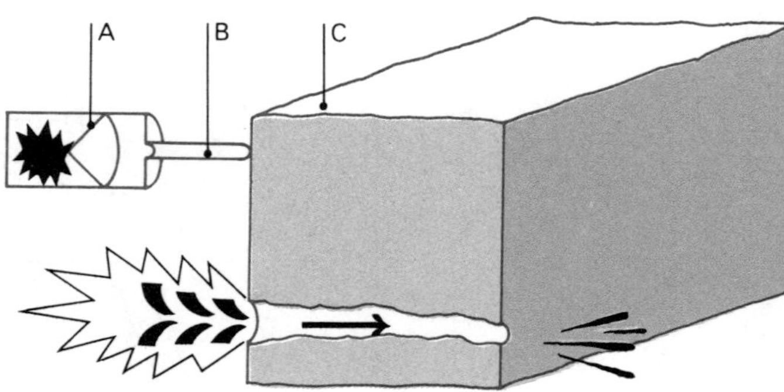

84mm RCL Carl-Gustaf (right), a Swedish design of recoilless gun, now used by several armies. It is made of high-grade steel, rifled, and its HEAT shell can destroy a tank at up to 500m (546yd). It can also fire high explosive, smoke and illuminating rounds. It is served by a two-man crew, and can be fired unsupported, or from a flexible bipod.

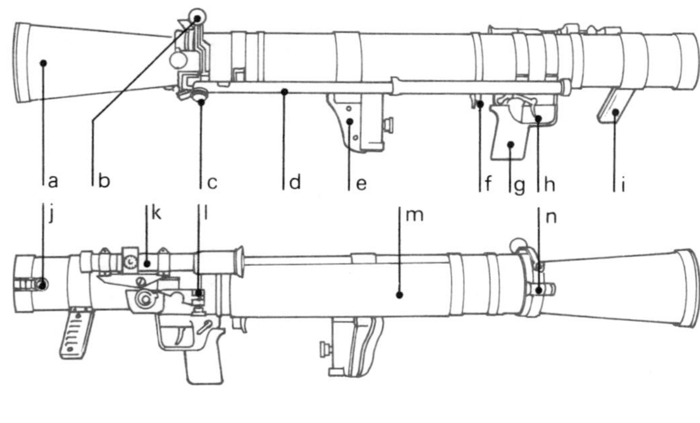

a Venturi
b Venturi fastening-strap
c Firing-pin unit
d Firing-rod tube
e Shoulder pad
f Cocking lever
g Pistol grip
h Trigger
i Front grip
j Iron foresight
k Telescopic sight
l Iron backsight
m Face pad
n Venturi axis-pin

The functioning (right) of the Carl-Gustaf RCL.
1 The basis of the system is a rifled steel tube with a venturi at the rear.
2 To load, the venturi rotates to one side on a pin and a fixed cartridge is inserted.
3 Ignition is by a percussion cap on the side of the cartridge case, struck by an external firing pin mechanism.
4 The explosion of the propellant charge pushes the shell up the tube and the frangible base of the cartridge is blown out by the rearward blast.
5 The venturi is opened and the now baseless empty cartridge-case removed. The weapon is normally aimed and fired by one man, and loaded and unloaded by another.

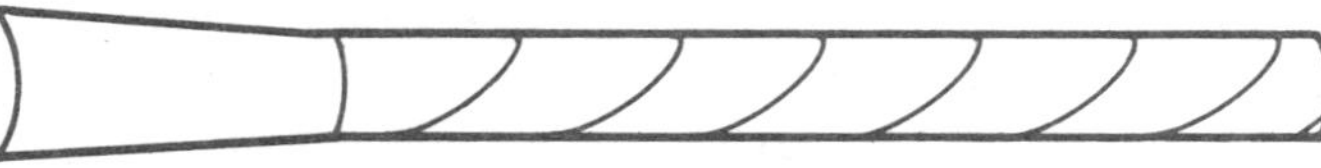

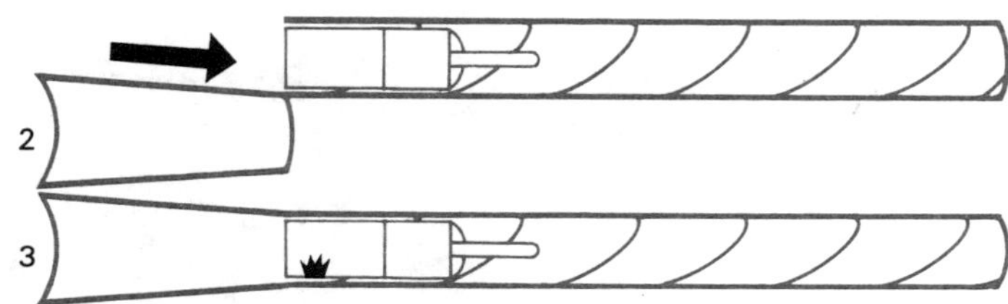

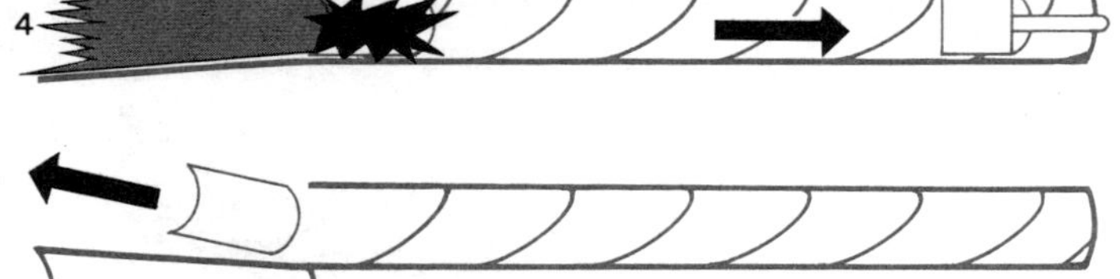

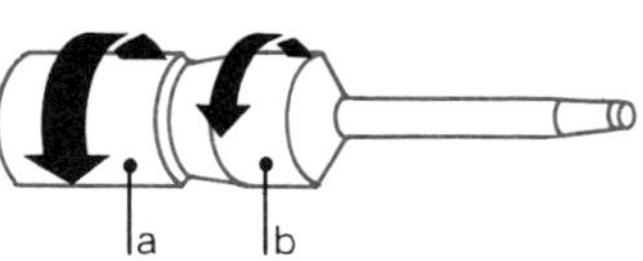

Stabilization (above) The Carl-Gustaf's shell is spin-stabilized by the rifling in the barrel. But as spin tends to reduce the penetrating effect of the shaped charge, a sleeve (**a**) is fitted which rotates on bearings, independently of the explosive filling (**b**). The spinning sleeve imparts sufficient gyroscopic stability without downgrading penetration.

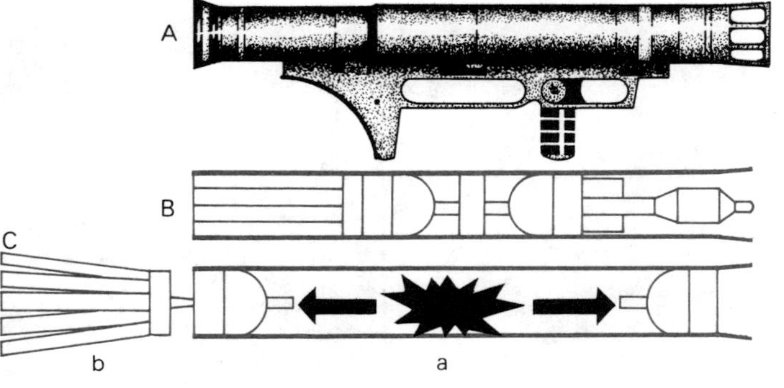

Armbrust (left) is a West German disposable anti-tank weapon which uses the recoilless principle in a new way. It is issued as a pre-loaded unit (**A**), shown also in section (**B**). On firing (**C**), the propellant (**a**) explodes between two pistons. These are driven to each end of the tube and stopped there. One ejects a counterweight (**b**), the other the shell (**c**).

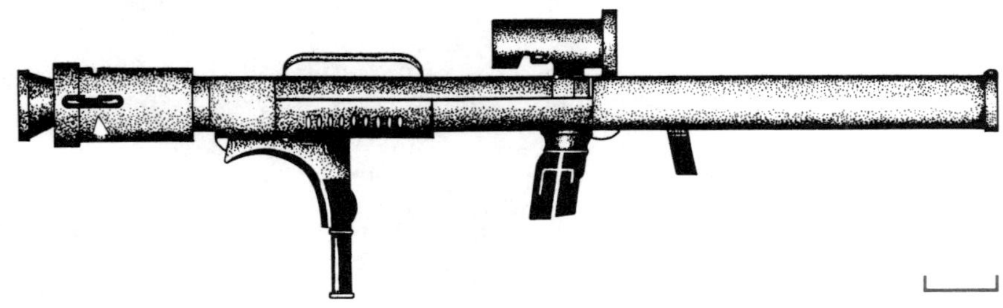

ACL-APX (left) is a French example of a quite common combination of systems. Its projectile is fired from the tube on the recoilless gun principle, but a rocket motor then ignites and propels the warhead to the target. The shaped-charge warhead is of 80mm (3.14in) caliber and reaches its maximum effective range of 580m (660yd) in 1.25sec.

Chapter 4

MOUNTED MISSILE-THROWERS

The difference between the missile-throwing weapons covered in this chapter and those in Chapter 3 is principally one of weight and size, and thus of portability. These devices hurl larger, more destructive missiles, and are therefore heavier in themselves and must be fired from some form of mounting. They are too unwieldy or too complex to be taken into battle by one man as his personal weapon or to be used by a civilian for self-defense. They are team weapons ; even the simplest of them, the ancient siege engines, required a special degree of organization and co-operation between men to make, deploy and fire them. They are thus exclusively military weapons.

After illustrating the mechanical engines, there is a discussion of the use of explosive propellants. Artillery using such propellants is then divided into its two main sub-varieties for detailed coverage. Muzzle-loading artillery is followed by breech-loading, an arrangement that corresponds in general with historical developments. The chapter ends with machine guns that are fired from mountings – the majority, that is, with the exception of the entirely hand-held submachine guns or machine pistols that are to be found in Chapter 3.

Photograph (right) taken during the American Civil War of 1861-65. It shows a Union battery of 100-pounder rifled guns at Fort Brady on the James River, Virginia.

Mechanical artillery

Before gunpowder was known and used as a propellant, three mechanical devices for storing and releasing energy were developed to throw heavier missiles to greater distances than a man on his own is capable of. These were a simple spring, a twisted skein of cord or hair, and a counterweighted lever. Although the Romans used small, mobile devices as field artillery, such engines were best suited to the frequent, long, static sieges of ancient and medieval warfare, when they could be built as big and powerful as current technology allowed. Surviving illustrations are often inaccurate or fanciful, and are supported by very few archeological remains of engines, but their missiles are more commonly found. What is known of the practicalities of mechanical artillery we owe to studies and experiments made since 1860.

Roman ballista (above) This detail from Trajan's Column in Rome shows two legionaries using a ballista during the Dacian Wars (101-107AD).

Name	Power source	Basis of data	Missile	Range
a Spring engine	Spring	Experimental model: Ash spring 3 × 4 × 60in (7.6 × 10.1 × 152cm)	3oz (85g)	160yd (146m)
b Catapult	Torsion skein	Experimental model: Arm 84in (213cm) Skein 8in (20.3cm) diameter	10lb (4.5kg)	350yd (320m)
		Estimate for largest example	*50lb (22.6kg)	*400yd (365m)
c Ballista	Two torsion skeins	Experimental model: Arms 24in (61cm) Skeins 3in (7.6cm) diameter	2.5lb (1.1kg)	300yd (274m)
		Estimate for largest example	*10lb (4.5kg)	*400-450yd (365-420m)
d Trebuchet	Counterweight	Estimate: Arm 50ft (15.2m) Weights 20,000lb (9,070kg)	*300lb (136kg)	*300yd (274m)

Comparative power (above) The table gives the power of various types of mechanical artillery. The data is derived from the experiments of Sir Ralph Payne-Gallwey, c.1900.
a This type is basically a simple spring set in a vertical plane (see p.161).
b Catapult powered by twisted fibers.
c Bow-like engine, powered by two sets of twisted fibers.
d A lever with a heavy counterweight at the bottom and a sling at the top.
(The data marked with an asterisk (*) is an estimate for the largest practicable weapon of that type. The remaining data on performance was actually achieved in experiments.)

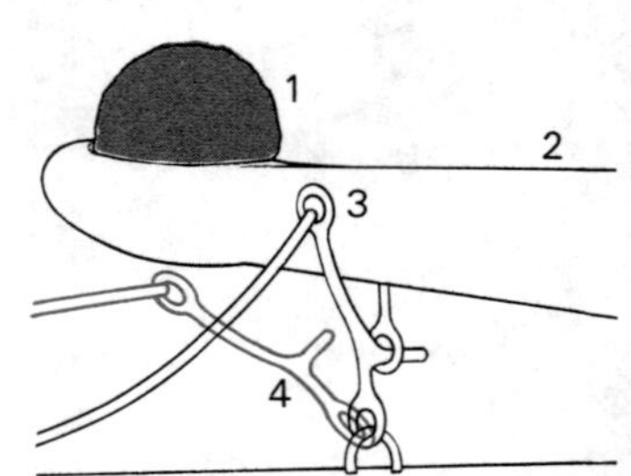

Release catch (right) All mechanical artillery needed a safe but easily released catch. The type shown, fitted to the arm of a catapult, could be adapted to suit various types of engine, and seems to have been widely used.
1 Projectile
2 Throwing-arm
3 Catch before release
4 Catch after release

Spring-powered engines

Spring-powered artillery used a single simple leaf-spring or a double one (a bow) to project a spear or a stone. Huge crossbows on a stand, with a mechanical aid to bend them, may have been the first of all siege engines. The spring was usually of wood, or a composite of horn and sinew as used in light crossbows. None of these devices seems to have been as efficient as those using torsion or a counterweight.

Mounted crossbow (left) Illustrated is a conjectural model of an ancient Greek mounted crossbow, bent by means of a windlass and ratchet. Many engines were devised by Archimedes to defend Syracuse when besieged by the Romans in 211BC. This was one of the most lavish uses of mechanical artillery of which accounts survive.

Spring engine (above) A medieval European device using a laminated wooden spring to project a spear. The frame allows adjustment of elevation and direction. (Illustration from Viollet le Duc's "*Dictionnaire Raisonné de l'Architecture Française*," 1868.)

Spring engine (right) shown about to throw two stones. One is placed directly on the wooden arm, and the other in a sling. From a drawing by Leonardo da Vinci in "Il Codice Atlantico". Probably a theoretical design rather than a drawing from an existing object.

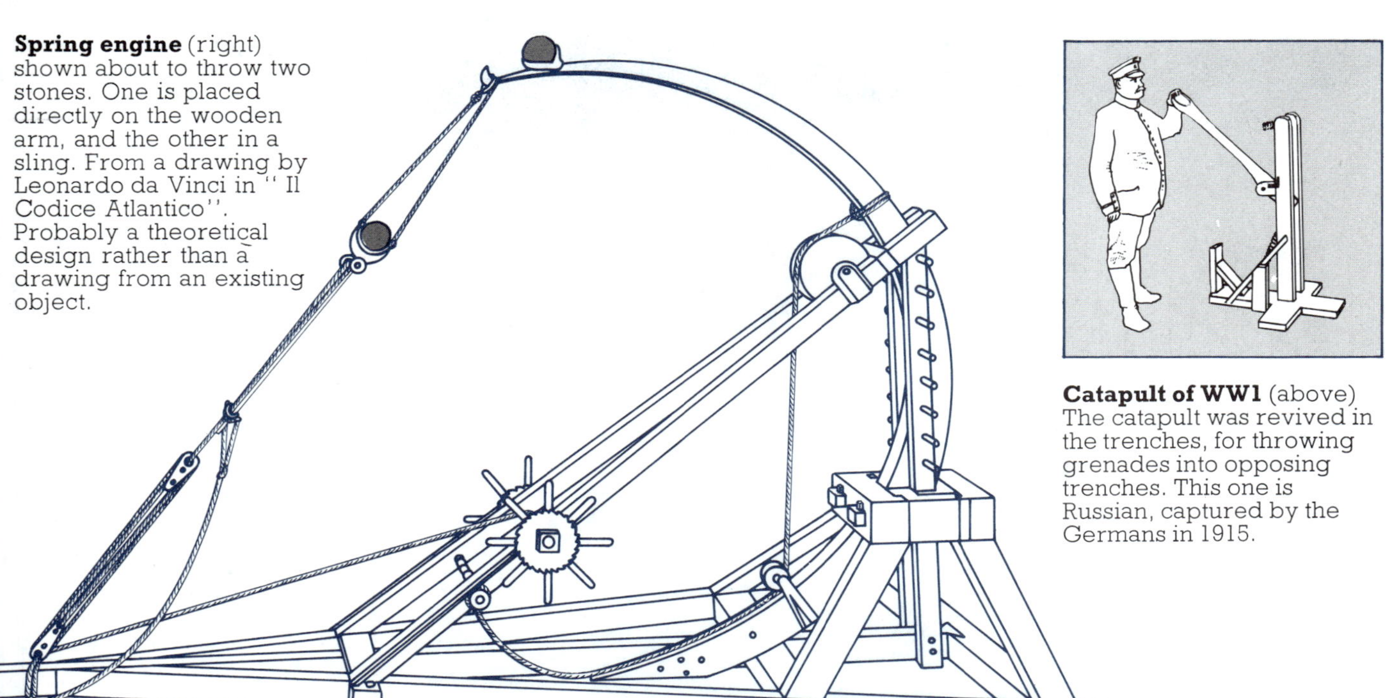

Catapult of WW1 (above) The catapult was revived in the trenches, for throwing grenades into opposing trenches. This one is Russian, captured by the Germans in 1915.

Torsion-powered engines

Torsion-powered artillery used the elasticity of a twisted skein of hair or cord to fling a missile. The system was much used by the ancient Greeks and Romans to power siege engines and field artillery. Projectiles of up to about 60lb (27.2kg) could be thrown by the largest catapults at higher velocities than from any other mechanical system, and accuracy was good. The frame had to be heavily built to withstand the stresses.

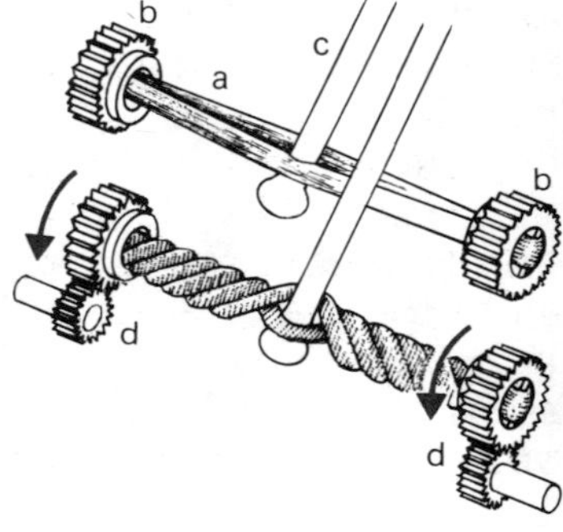

A skein (above) is formed as follows. A long strand of cord or hair (**a**) is wound many times round two axles (**b**), and the base of the arm (**c**) is placed in the center. The ends of the skein are then twisted by winches and ratchets (**d**).

1

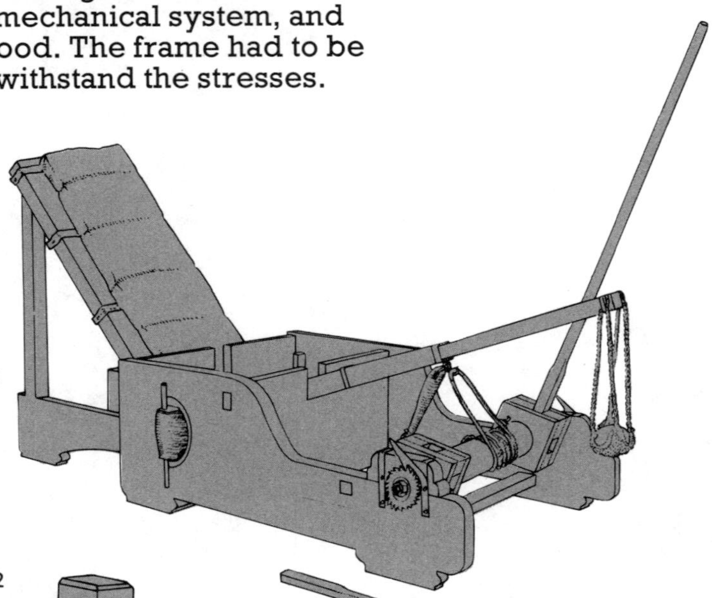

2

3

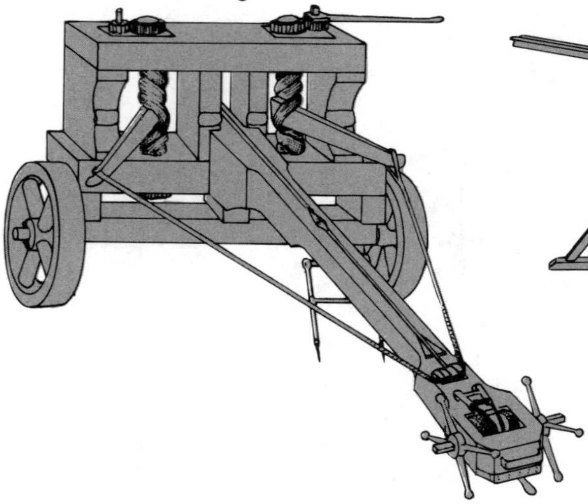

4

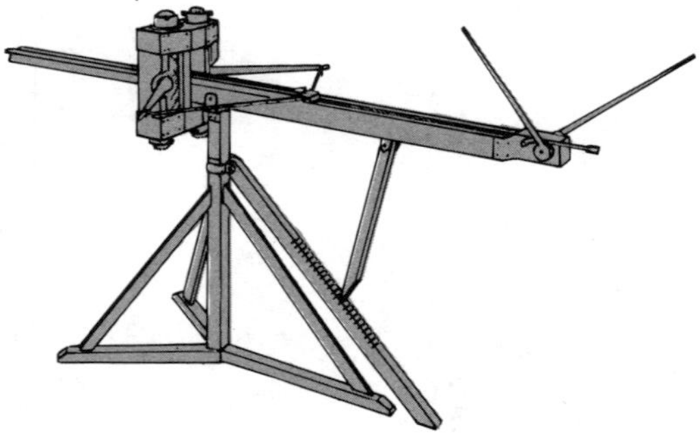

1 Roman onager A replica of the siege and field engine, thought to have been developed in the 3rd century AD. The name is that of a wild ass, a reflection of the violent kick as the arm reaches the end of its travel against the padding at the front. (Corinium Museum, Cirencester, England.)

2 Catapult The classic torsion-powered engine of medieval, Roman and even earlier times. It is one of the most efficient of all siege engines. Shown here is a reconstruction made and tested by Sir Ralph Payne-Gallwey, c.1900.

3 Ballista A device made by the Romans in various sizes for field and siege use. It could fire stones or javelins accurately on a low trajectory, but was complex in construction. (After a reconstruction by Sir Ralph Payne-Gallwey.)

4 Light field ballista Shown is a reconstruction of a Roman ballista, based on contemporary sources.

Counterweight-powered engines

Counterweight-powered engines could throw heavier missiles than any other mechanical artillery, although range and velocity were inferior to those of the biggest torsion-powered catapults. The massive counterweight and throwing arm called for a huge frame and consequently such machines were suited only to siege-work, by both sides. Surprisingly, this simple system was not in widespread use until after 1250.

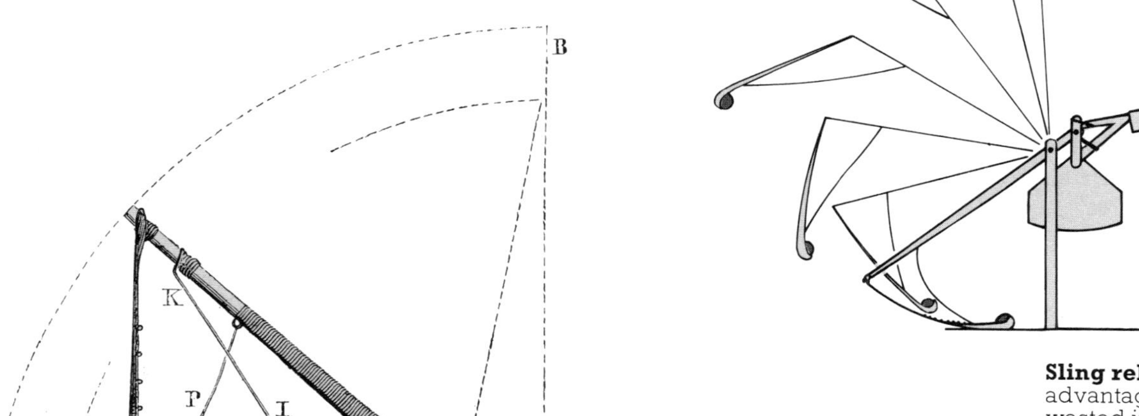

Sling release (above) The advantage of a sling was wasted if it did not release the stone at the correct moment. In the system used on the trebuchet shown here, the stone remains in the pouch until the stay-rope (**a**) becomes taught. The sling then kinks at (**b**) and the stone spills out.

Trebuchet (above) Engraving from Viollet le Duc showing a practicable design for a sophisticated medieval trebuchet. Note the system of windlasses, ropes and a pulley needed to raise such a huge counterweight — a box filled with earth and stones. Even with these aids many men would need to crowd around the windlasses in order to set the mechanism.

Sling release (right) An alternative system is shown in the sequential drawing and the detail above it. The angle of the horn (**a**), and the position of the stop (**b**) in relation to the shackle (**c**) are critical in releasing the stone at the optimum moment. (All illustrations on this page are from Viollet le Duc.)

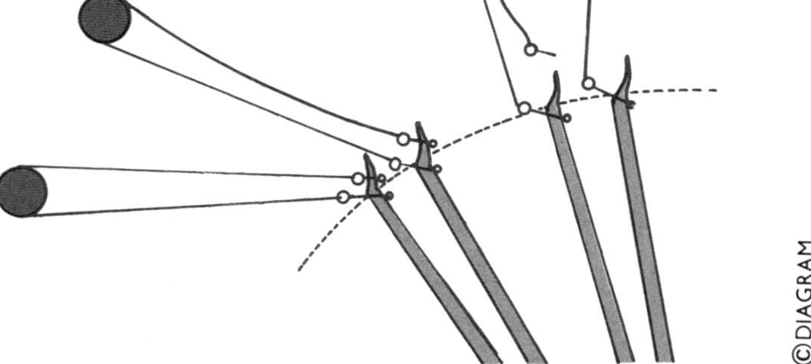

Explosion-powered artillery

The harnessing of explosive force to throw a projectile was one of the vital steps in the escalation of weapons technology. Although gunpowder had been known in China since the 11th century, it was in Europe in about 1300 that it began to be exploited as a propellant. The first handguns and cannon appeared together shortly after that date. Since then the cannon has very rarely been absent from any battlefield, a monster of a weapon, destroying or disheartening the enemy in large numbers. Its development has been a process of maximizing rate of fire, range and the lethality of the projectile on the one hand, and of minimizing the inherent problems of smoke, flash, fouling (soot), recoil and overheating on the other. This process and that of meeting new specialized needs is still going on.

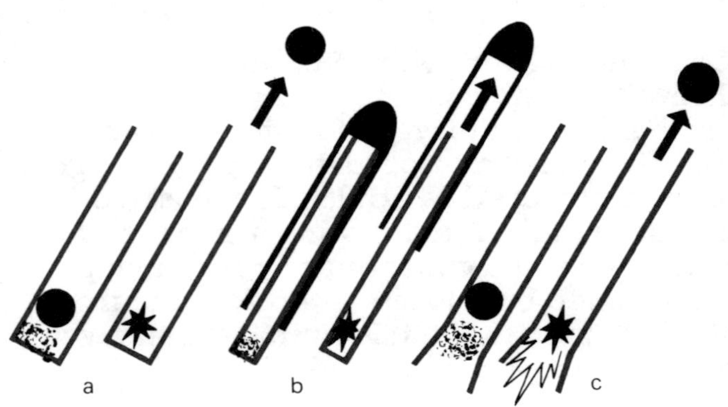

Explosive force (above) can be harnessed in several ways. All use the sudden change of solids into a large volume of high pressure gas to propel the missile.
a The usual way is to put the projectile in front of the propellant, in a tube closed at one end — the gun.
b Less common is the spigot principle, where the projectile is itself tubular, fitting over the barrel.
c Another method now in use is the recoilless gun. In this case the barrel is open at the rear. On firing, the forward motion of the projectile is counteracted by the rearward thrust of gases, and the barrel remains motionless.

The smoke, flash and noise of a fired cannon (left) were startling, and were as potent against the enemy as the shot itself. Today, the terrifying arrival of exploding shells can demoralize even if they do not kill; the gun that fired them may be miles away, with its flash and smoke minimized to avoid detection. (Pastiche in 16th century style.)

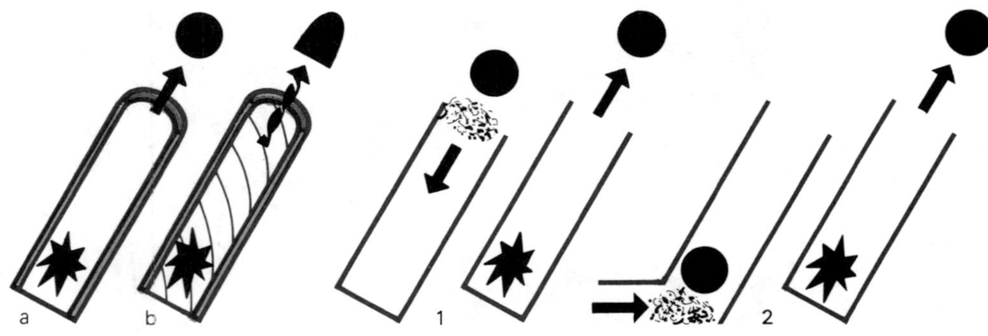

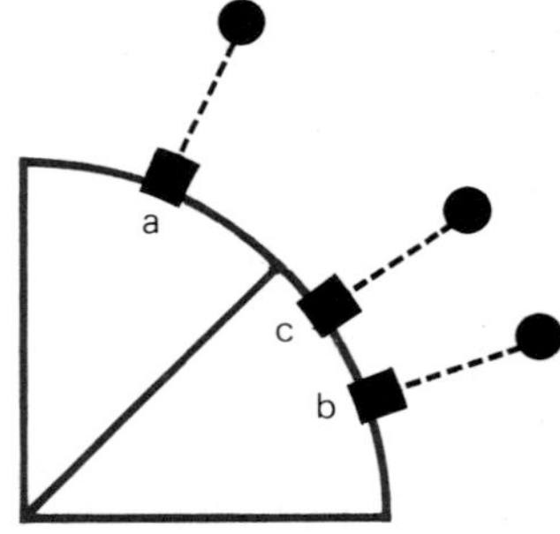

A gun barrel (above) can be either smoothbored (**a**) or rifled (**b**). The latter is the more accurate and powerful and was known before 1600, but technology did not allow its widespread use until after 1850. The spiral grooves spin the projectile, giving it gyroscopic stability. Thus an elongated projectile can be made to fly point first.

Muzzle- versus breech-loading (above)
1 Loading from the front or muzzle was long preferred because such a simple barrel was cheaper and easier to make. But there were disadvantages. Loading was slow, and in a ship or fort the cannon had to be hauled back inside to get at the muzzle. Also the shot had to be a loose fit to be pushed down the sooty bore, resulting in lost power and poor accuracy.
2 Breech-loading, where technology and finance permit, has the advantages of speed in loading, a tight fit between shot and bore (especially suited to rifled barrels), and convenience in ships and forts. Such guns need not be pulled back to reload, and even in the field the crew can stay behind a protective shield.

Types, by trajectory (above) Combustion-powered artillery has long been classified according to the path of its trajectory.
a The mortar lobs its shell in a high parabola.
b The gun has a direct, fast trajectory.
c The howitzer makes a useful compromise, firing a large shell by less powder and from a lighter barrel than that of the gun.

The history of combustion-powered artillery (right) is shown alongside the major wars since gunpowder became known in Europe. The most important developments were the supersession of wrought iron strip-and-hoop construction by cast barrels of bronze, iron or brass, and some later, simultaneous developments dating from the mid-19th century. These were the coming of reinforced and then steel barrels, loading via the breech, and rifling, all part of the current technological progress.
Roles The main uses of artillery were soon established and remained until this century; there were field, siege, fortress and naval guns. In this century the most important additions are the tank, anti-tank and anti-aircraft roles.

Propellants The gunpowder described by Friar Roger Bacon in c.1242 consisted of 1 part sulphur, 6 parts saltpeter and 2 parts charcoal. Although the proportions were altered, this black powder was not replaced as a propellant until nitrocellulose-based powders were developed between 1846 and 1887. In this latter year, Alfred Nobel of Sweden patented a propellant from which most modern types are derived. Black powder gave off dense clouds of white smoke, obscuring the gunners' vision and revealing the gun's position to the enemy. The new powders are called generally "smokeless" propellants, as they give off only a little thin gray smoke on firing. They also have another great advantage in that their rate of burning can be controlled, during design, to give the shell a smoothly accelerating push up the barrel.
High explosives It took longer for black powder to be replaced as an explosive shell-filling. Early "high explosives" such as dynamite were too sensitive to the shock of firing to be used in this way. This problem was overcome first with "lyddite" (picric acid).

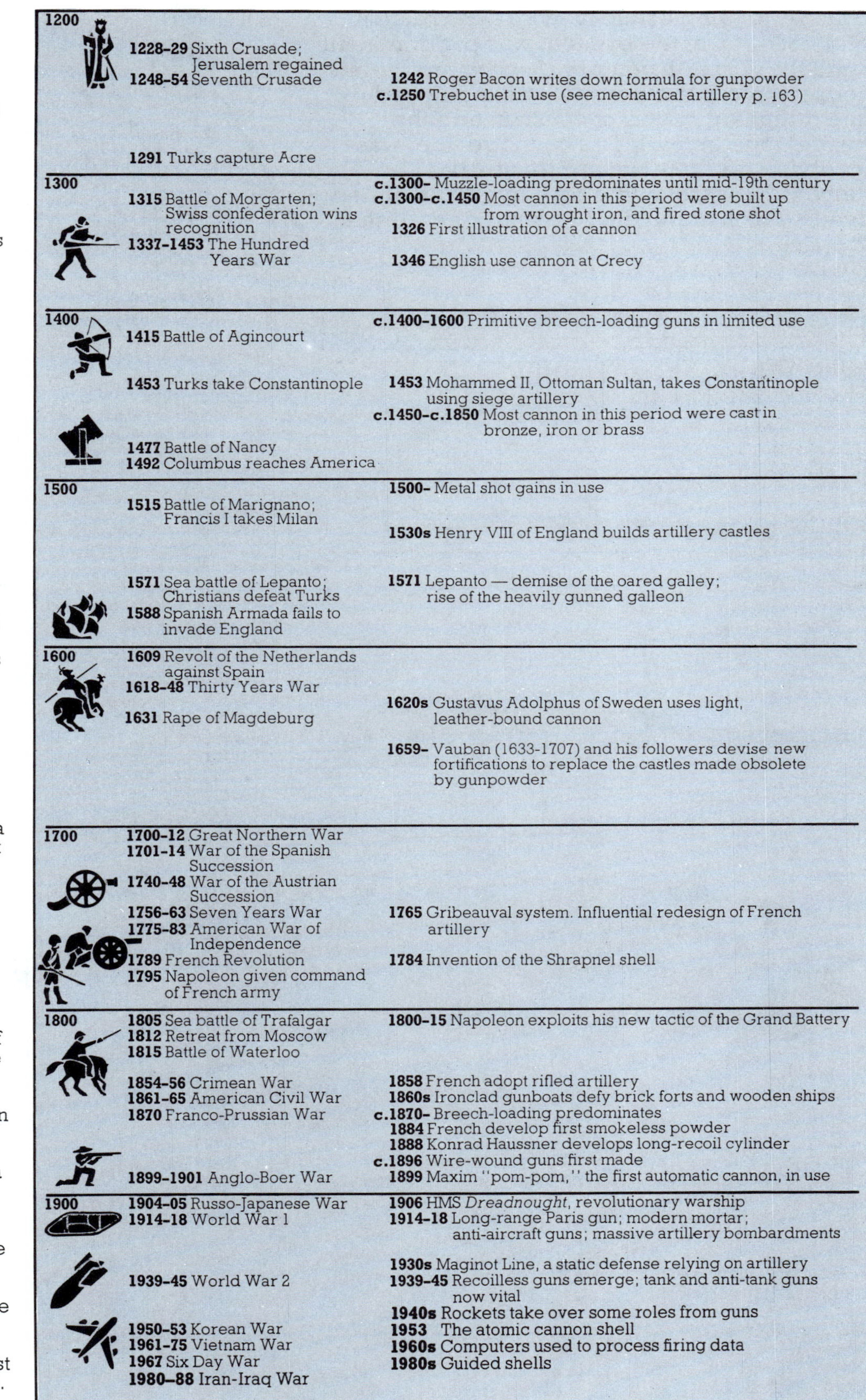

Century	Wars and events	Artillery developments
1200	**1228–29** Sixth Crusade; Jerusalem regained **1248–54** Seventh Crusade **1291** Turks capture Acre	**1242** Roger Bacon writes down formula for gunpowder **c.1250** Trebuchet in use (see mechanical artillery p. 163)
1300	**1315** Battle of Morgarten; Swiss confederation wins recognition **1337–1453** The Hundred Years War	**c.1300–** Muzzle-loading predominates until mid-19th century **c.1300–c.1450** Most cannon in this period were built up from wrought iron, and fired stone shot **1326** First illustration of a cannon **1346** English use cannon at Crecy
1400	**1415** Battle of Agincourt **1453** Turks take Constantinople **1477** Battle of Nancy **1492** Columbus reaches America	**c.1400–1600** Primitive breech-loading guns in limited use **1453** Mohammed II, Ottoman Sultan, takes Constantinople using siege artillery **c.1450–c.1850** Most cannon in this period were cast in bronze, iron or brass
1500	**1515** Battle of Marignano; Francis I takes Milan **1571** Sea battle of Lepanto; Christians defeat Turks **1588** Spanish Armada fails to invade England	**1500–** Metal shot gains in use **1530s** Henry VIII of England builds artillery castles **1571** Lepanto — demise of the oared galley; rise of the heavily gunned galleon
1600	**1609** Revolt of the Netherlands against Spain **1618–48** Thirty Years War **1631** Rape of Magdeburg	**1620s** Gustavus Adolphus of Sweden uses light, leather-bound cannon **1659–** Vauban (1633-1707) and his followers devise new fortifications to replace the castles made obsolete by gunpowder
1700	**1700–12** Great Northern War **1701–14** War of the Spanish Succession **1740–48** War of the Austrian Succession **1756–63** Seven Years War **1775–83** American War of Independence **1789** French Revolution **1795** Napoleon given command of French army	**1765** Gribeauval system. Influential redesign of French artillery **1784** Invention of the Shrapnel shell
1800	**1805** Sea battle of Trafalgar **1812** Retreat from Moscow **1815** Battle of Waterloo **1854–56** Crimean War **1861–65** American Civil War **1870** Franco-Prussian War **1899–1901** Anglo-Boer War	**1800–15** Napoleon exploits his new tactic of the Grand Battery **1858** French adopt rifled artillery **1860s** Ironclad gunboats defy brick forts and wooden ships **c.1870–** Breech-loading predominates **1884** French develop first smokeless powder **1888** Konrad Haussner develops long-recoil cylinder **c.1896** Wire-wound guns first made **1899** Maxim "pom-pom," the first automatic cannon, in use
1900	**1904–05** Russo-Japanese War **1914–18** World War 1 **1939–45** World War 2 **1950–53** Korean War **1961–75** Vietnam War **1967** Six Day War **1980–88** Iran-Iraq War	**1906** HMS *Dreadnought*, revolutionary warship **1914–18** Long-range Paris gun; modern mortar; anti-aircraft guns; massive artillery bombardments **1930s** Maginot Line, a static defense relying on artillery **1939–45** Recoilless guns emerge; tank and anti-tank guns now vital **1940s** Rockets take over some roles from guns **1953** The atomic cannon shell **1960s** Computers used to process firing data **1980s** Guided shells

Muzzle-loading artillery

Muzzle-loading artillery, with a barrel that did not open at the breech, was predominant until the late 19th century. Such weapons fall loosely into three periods, distinguished by the dominant means of constructing the barrel (see below). The carriage, too, was evolving; as the means whereby the unwieldy barrel could be moved and aimed, it tells much about the role intended for the gun.

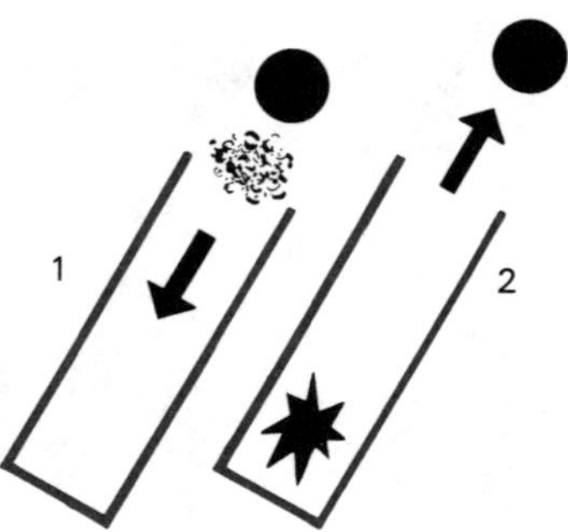

Muzzle-loading (left) The basic process is as follows.
1 A charge of powder is pushed to the bottom of the barrel, followed sometimes by a wad, and then the projectile.
2 A light is applied to a narrow vent leading to the powder, which explodes, propelling the shot out of the barrel.
(For details of the loading drill, see opposite page.)

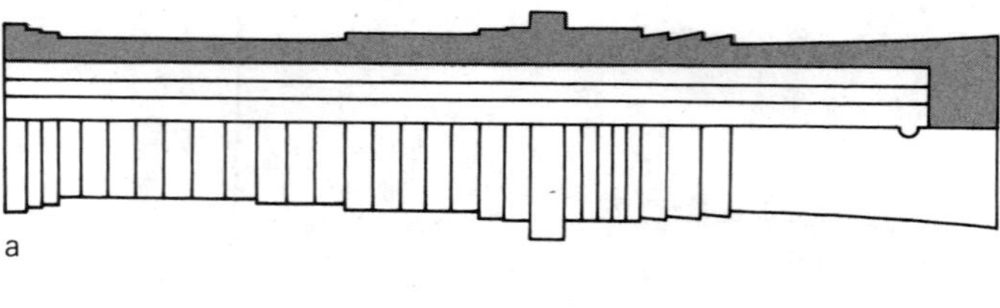

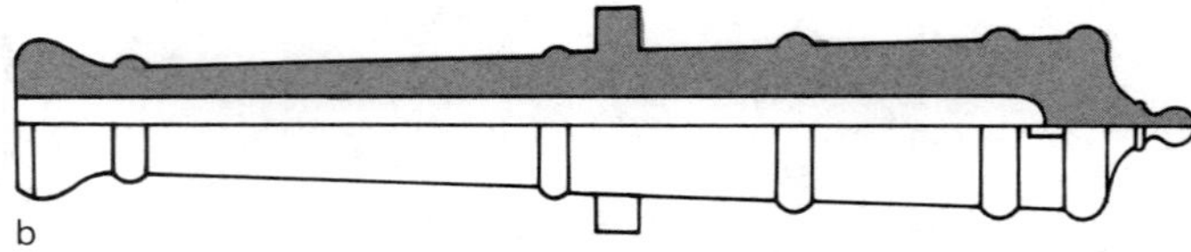

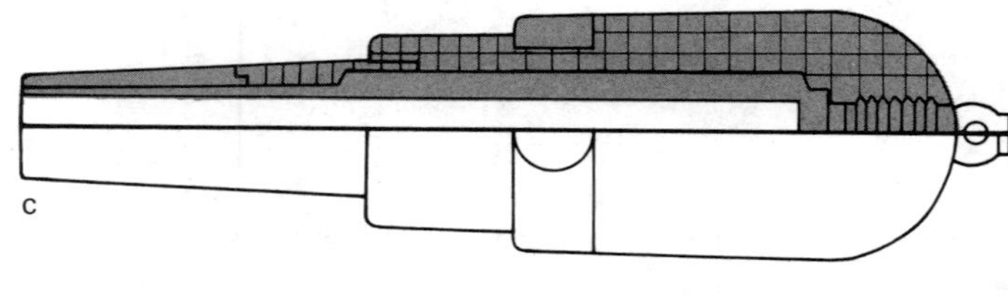

Barrel construction (left) Types in the three periods.
a At first, most cannon-barrels were built in wrought iron. Strips running lengthwise were bound together with hoops to resist the radial stresses of the explosion.
b From the late 15th century, barrels began to be cast in bronze, using the techniques of bell-founding. Such guns were generally safer to use, and of better appearance. Cast iron and brass came to be used also, and were favored until c.1860.
c Reinforced. From about 1860, artillery in the bigger calibers was usually strengthened at the breech because new demands led to greater bore pressure. Wrought iron came back into use in the form of thick collars coiled or shrunk over the basic barrel-tube.

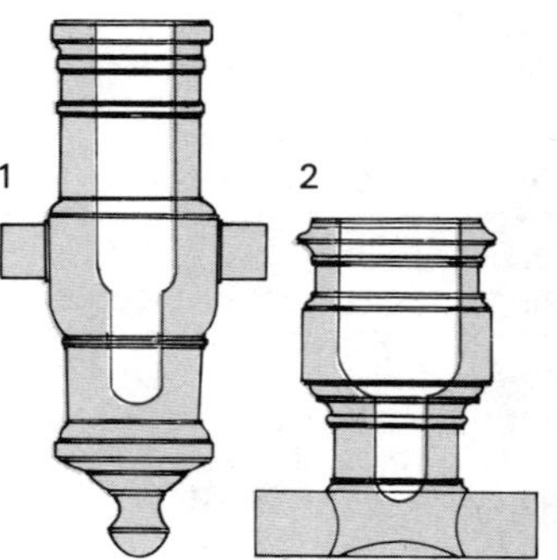

Mortar and howitzer (above) For most of the muzzle-loading period, these high-angle weapons took the general form shown here. The howitzer (**1**) had a narrow powder chamber, and pivots (trunnions) at the point of balance. The mortar (**2**) had trunnions at the base. Pérrier and bombard were names for early types similar to later howitzers.

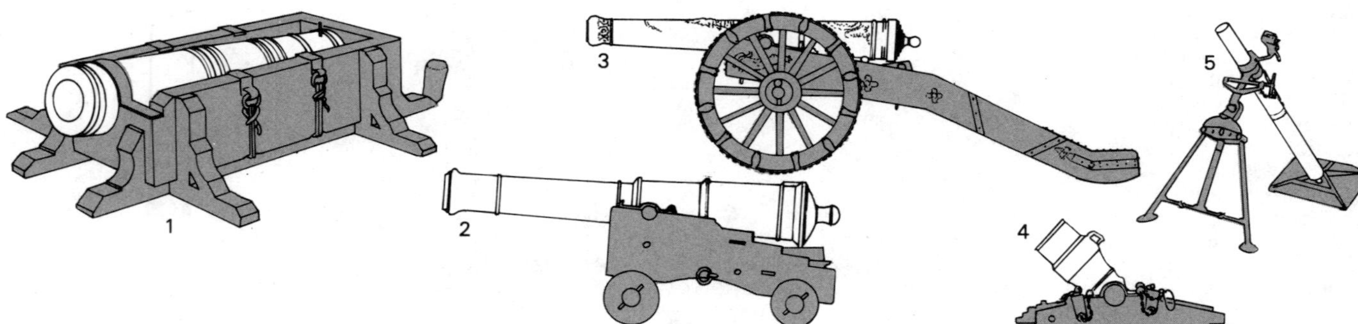

Carriages (above)
1 Early static mount In medieval manuscripts, cannon are often depicted in simple wooden troughs, as above. This reflects the chief use of cannon at the time, in static sieges of towns and castles. As the purpose was usually to batter down the walls in one place, the cannon was not often realigned.

2 Naval carriages typically had small wheels, as the only movement needed was in hauling the gun back to load, forward to fire, and in aiming — all on a flat deck. Fortress carriages were similar in shape, but often made in iron. The "steps" were used as a fulcrum when levering up the breech to reduce the angle of elevation.

3 The field carriage had to give the best possible cross-country and road mobility. This usually meant large wheels, and a compromise between strength and lightness in the frame. For movement it was usually hooked behind an ammunition limber (cart), and drawn by a team of six or more oxen, mules or horses.

4 Mortar beds were static and inflexible. The whole weapon was moved in aiming. For transportation, the mortar had to be hauled up onto a wagon.
5 The modern mortar, the last surviving muzzle-loading weapon, can usually be broken down into man-portable loads. The bipod can be adjusted and the charge varied to alter the aim of the piece.

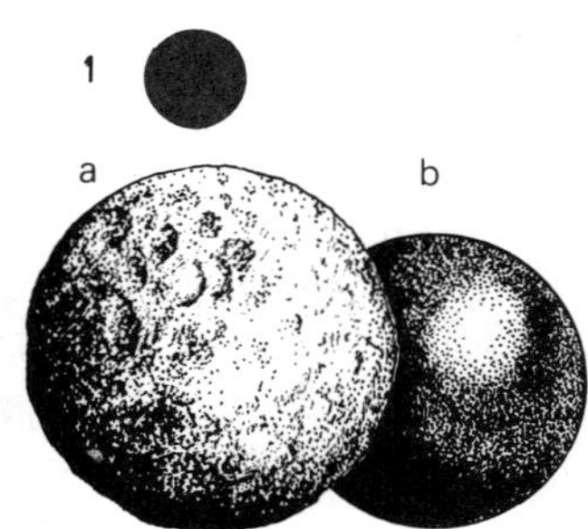

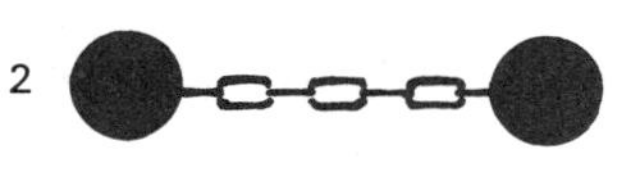

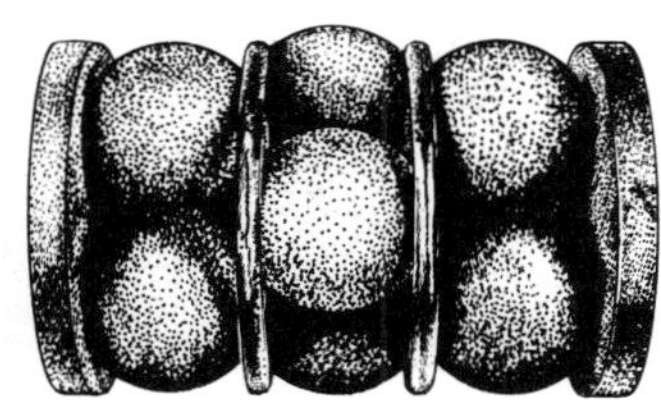

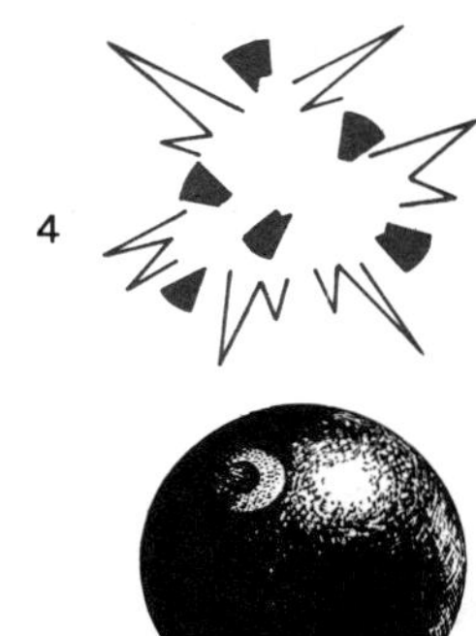

Types of projectile (above)
1 Solid Stone shot (**a**) was used initially, but by 1500 it was being replaced by cast iron roundshot (**b**), ideal for battering walls. In the field, it smashed through ranks of men, remaining lethal to great distances as it skimmed the ground. At sea, it pierced the enemy's hull, wrecked cannon, and cut down vital masts.

2 Expanding These were all naval projectiles, designed to be compact when loaded and fired, but then tumbling and spreading in flight. Thus the chance of cutting vital rigging on the enemy's ship was much increased. The chain-shot shown was a common variety of the expanding type of projectile. (See also p.173.)

3 Spreading This type of shot effectively turned a cannon into a huge shotgun for use against personnel. For ease of loading, a number of lead or iron balls was sealed in a tin (canister or case shot), or grouped together as shown (grapeshot). The container was broken up by the shock of firing, and the shot spread out to cover a wide area.

4 Explosive Common shell, a hollow iron sphere filled with gunpowder and fitted with a fuze to set it off, was fired against buildings, and men in the open at longer ranges. The latter role was later met by shrapnel, a variety of shell filled also with small shot. A time fuze set the bursting charge off over the heads of opposing troops.

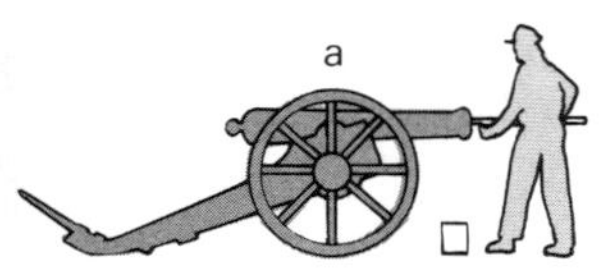

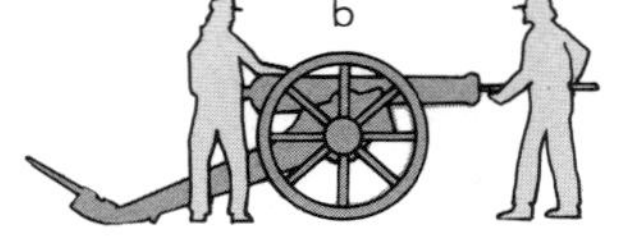

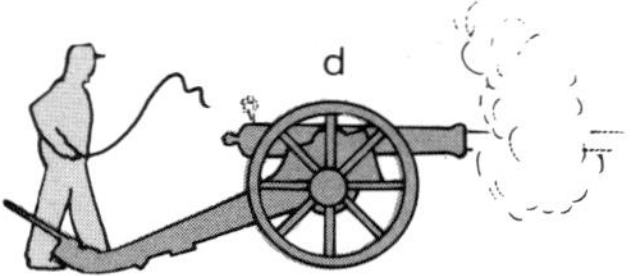

Gun drill (above) A strict drill was vital to ensure that the loading process was done correctly in the heat of battle. We show the steps common to most armies' drill sequences.
a The bore is sponged out to dampen sparks from the last shot and to soften the soot.
b One man puts his thumb over the touch-hole for safety as the powder and shot are rammed down (separately in the early years, fixed together by the end of the muzzle-loading period).
c The gun is aimed, on orders from the gunner as he sights along the barrel, and then primed (prepared for ignition).
d The gun is fired, the effect of the shot observed, and the process repeated.

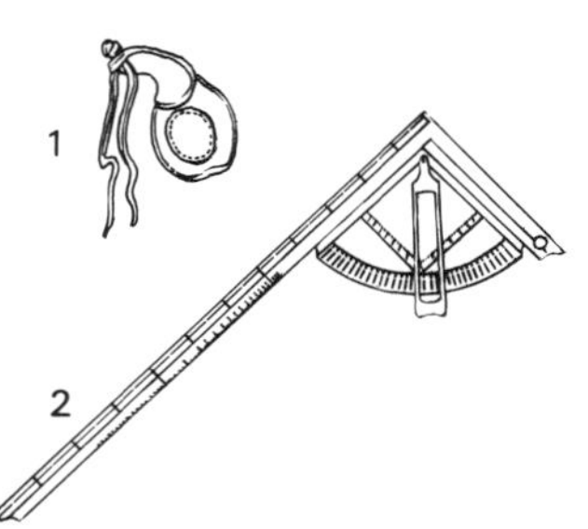

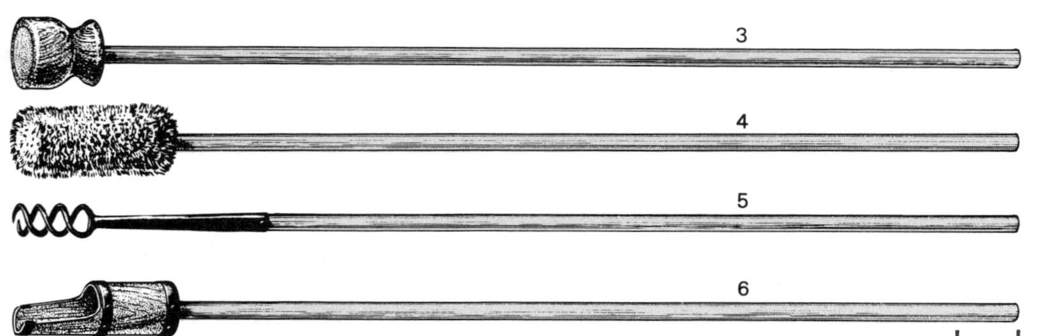

Accessories (left)
1 Thumbstall, used to protect the thumb from the hot barrel while covering the vent as powder and shot are rammed down the bore.
2 Quadrant, used to measure the angle of elevation of the barrel.
3 Rammer, for pushing the powder-bag and shot down the bore.
4 Sponge, for swabbing out the bore between shots.
5 Worm, used to clear obstructions, such as damp charges, from the bore, and to hold rags when cleaning it.
6 Powder-scoop, used to measure and load loose gunpowder if a bagged charge was not being used.

Wrought-iron muzzle-loaders

Wrought iron was commonly used to construct the earliest cannon. The barrel was built up from strips and hoops rather like a beer-barrel. By this means, guns were made in calibers as big as any that came later. Such guns, being still the subject of awe and superstition, were often given names. (For a breech-loading cannon made on this system, see p. 178).

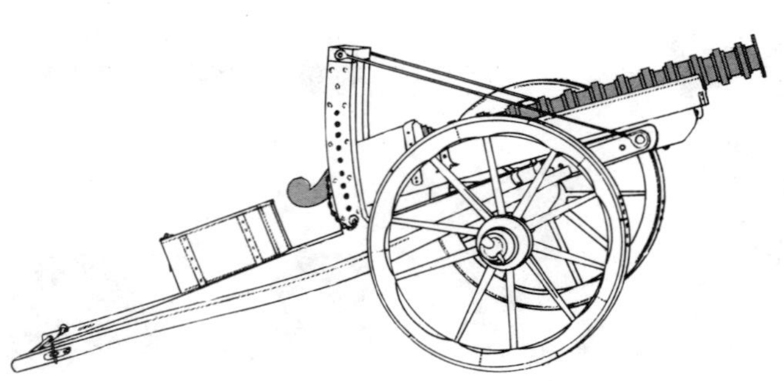

Culverin (above) This example, of 3in (7.62cm) caliber, was probably made in Burgundy in the 1460s. The word culverin was applied variously to calibers from 1.5in to 6in (3.8cm to 15.2cm) according to local usage. (Musée de la Neuveville, Bern, Switzerland.)

"Mons Meg" (left), a cannon of 19.5in (49.5cm) caliber, made in Flanders before 1489 and kept since then in Edinburgh Castle. It fired a stone ball of 550 lb (249.5kg) to 2800yd (2560m), or a heavier iron ball half as far. The barrel burst on firing a salute in 1680. Although used as a muzzle-loader, the narrower breech section could be unscrewed.

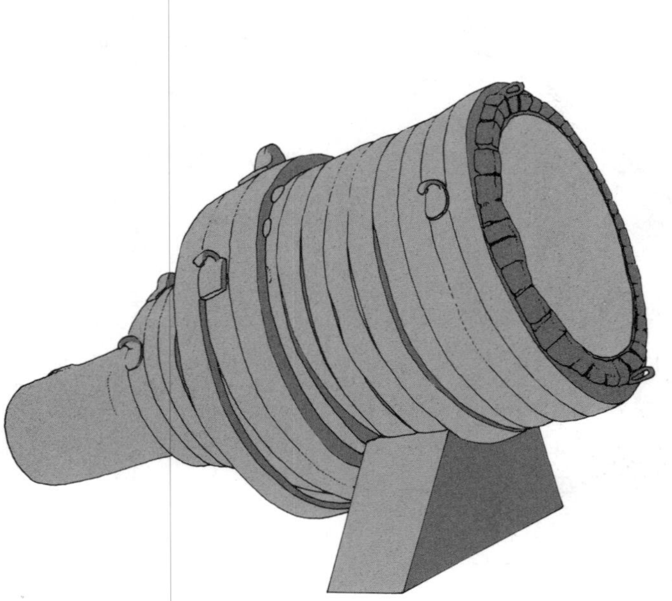

"Pumhardt" (left), a huge pérrier of 35in (88.9cm) caliber, dating from the early 15th century. Note the powder chamber at the breech end, narrow in proportion to the bore, resembling later howitzers (Heeresgeschlichtliches Museum, Vienna.)

Elevating gear (above) An engraving from Viollet le Duc shows a design of elevating gear for heavy barrels. The barrel pivots about the axle, under maximum leverage from the split trail at the rear. Compare with the system used for the lighter culverin at the top of this page.

Cast muzzle-loaders

Cast bronze was used increasingly to make cannon after about 1450, by adapting the techniques of bell-founding. Cast with designs in relief which were then finished with a hammer and chisel, some of these guns are, artistically, the finest ever produced. Bronze resists corrosion better than iron, an advantage in use which has also preserved many examples through centuries on the seabed.

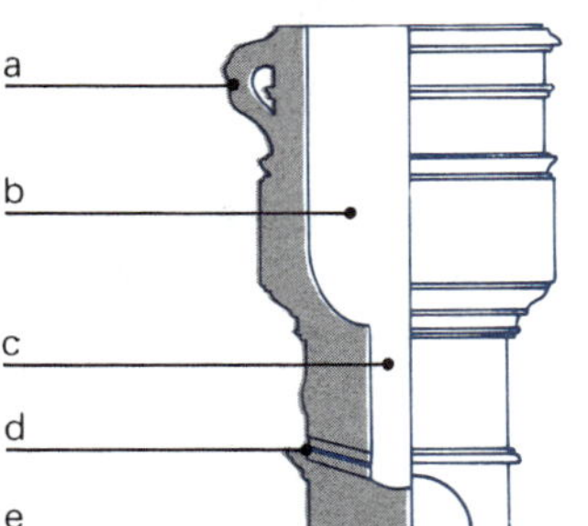

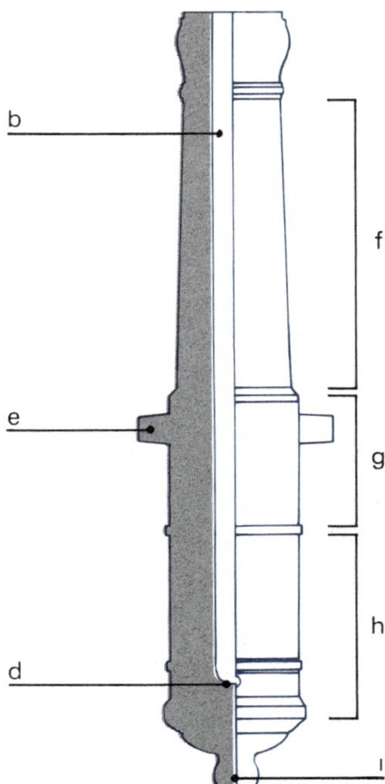

Parts of the barrel, of a mortar (above) and a gun (right).
a Dolphin or handle
b Bore
c Powder chamber
d Vent
e Trunnions
f Chase
g 2nd reinforce
h 1st reinforce
i Cascabel or button

1

2

3

1 Bronze mortar cast in the form of a crouching tiger. Made in South India in the late 18th century, probably for Tippoo Sultan — "The Tiger of Mysore" — or for his father Hyder Ali. Tippoo was defeated and killed by the British at Seringapatam in 1799. Caliber 9.5 in (24cm) (Tower of London).

2 Bombard of the late 15th century. Cast for the Order of St John, Rhodes. Caliber 23in (58.4cm). The barrel only is shown, as the carriage has not survived. (Musée de l'Armée, Paris.)

3 Bronze falconet, one of the lightest field pieces, firing a ball of up to 3 lb (1.3kg). (Prince Liechtenstein's Collection, Vaduz.)

4 Cannon Reproduced here is a design for a cannon cast in Venice in 1708. It bears the heraldic device of St Mark, and an inscription recording that it was cast in the presence of King Frederick IV of Denmark and Norway.

4

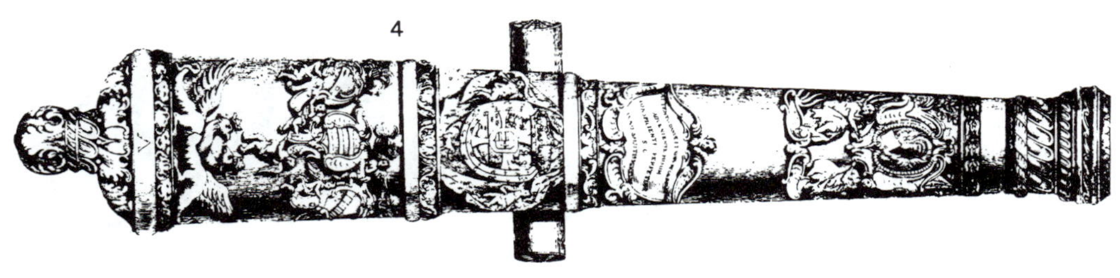

Smoothbore field artillery

The barrels of most artillery used in the 300 years up to c.1860 were made by casting in bronze, brass or iron. Any improvements were mostly confined to the carriage, or to lightening the barrel. The weapons shown on these two pages were for use on land as field artillery.

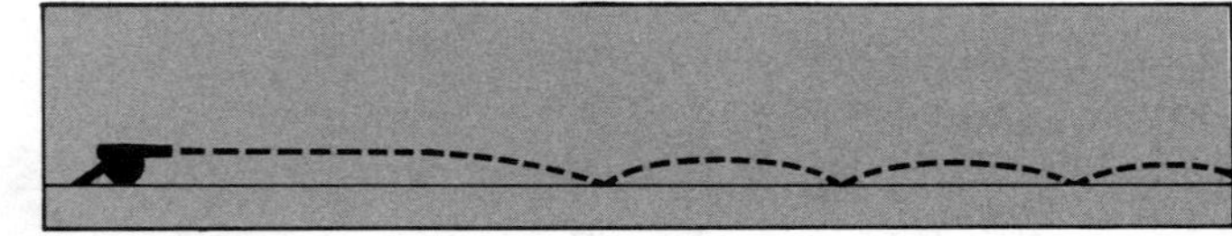

Roundshot was the solid iron sphere that formed the main ammunition supply on campaign. Also used for battering through walls, in the field it was fired almost parallel to the ground (above) to smash through many ranks of men or to break opposing cannon. Even after bouncing several times and moving slowly enough to be seen, it was heavy enough to maim.

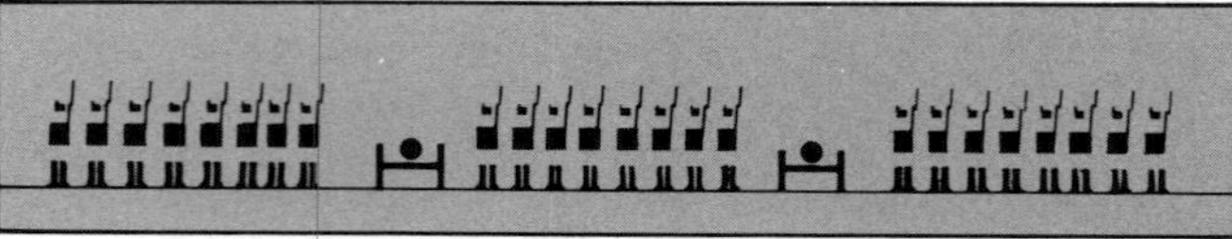

Regimental guns (above) In 18th century Europe, it was common practice to put the guns in the front rank, interspersed with the foot soldiers, to meet the enemy's expected main advance in the center of the line. To advance against such a combination of weapons required remarkable discipline.

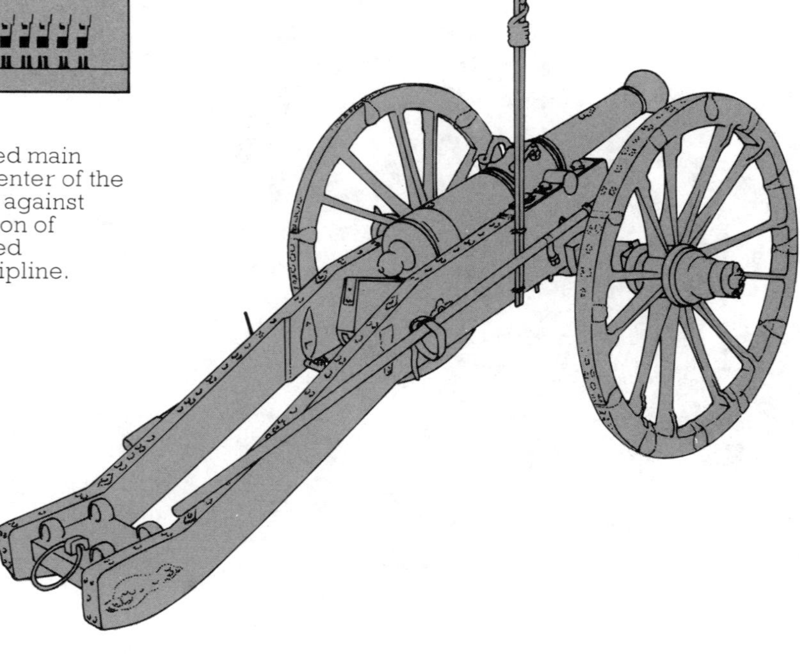

Light regimental gun (right) Swiss, 1757. In European armies of the time, a few such mobile guns were often used by each infantry regiment to supplement the firepower of its muskets. The box-like trail of the carriage is typical of the time. Caliber of 2.7in (6.8cm), firing a ball of 2 lb (0.9kg). (Bernisches Historisches Museum.)

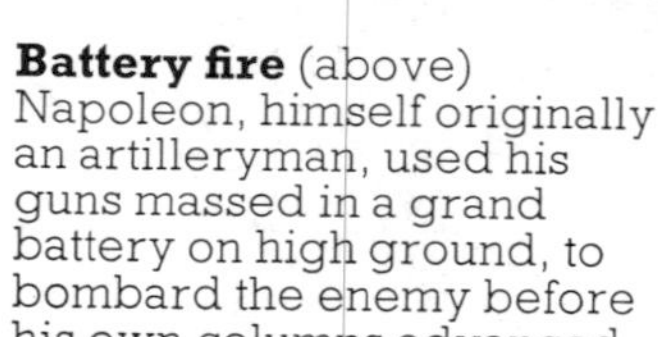

Battery fire (above) Napoleon, himself originally an artilleryman, used his guns massed in a grand battery on high ground, to bombard the enemy before his own columns advanced.

French 18-pounder field gun (right) of Napoleon's Grande Armée, captured by the British at Waterloo in 1815. The battle opened with a cannonade from batteries of such guns, firing at the British over the heads of the French troops. The barrel is cast brass of 5.2in (13.2cm) caliber. (Royal Military Academy, Sandhurst.)

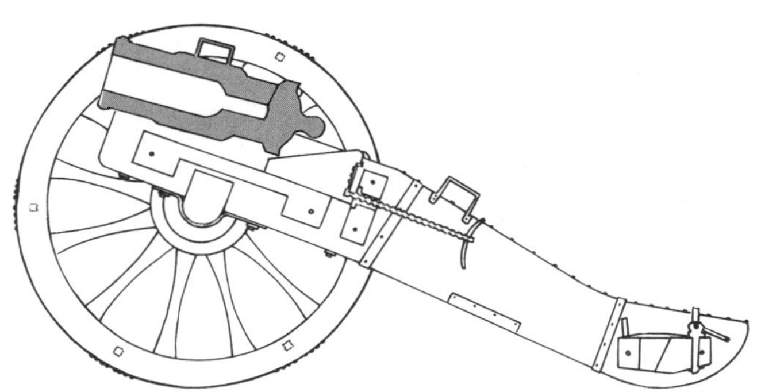

Section (left) through a French 24-pounder (16.5cm) caliber field howitzer, c.1765. An example from the Gribeauval system, a full redesign of French artillery. Note the screw-adjusted elevating wedge, and the narrow powder chamber which is characteristic of howitzers.

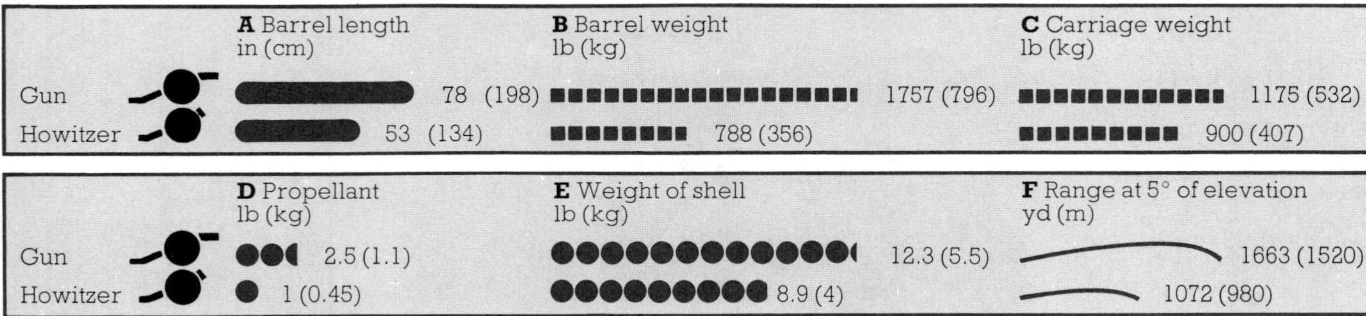

	A Barrel length in (cm)	B Barrel weight lb (kg)	C Carriage weight lb (kg)
Gun	78 (198)	1757 (796)	1175 (532)
Howitzer	53 (134)	788 (356)	900 (407)

	D Propellant lb (kg)	E Weight of shell lb (kg)	F Range at 5° of elevation yd (m)
Gun	2.5 (1.1)	12.3 (5.5)	1663 (1520)
Howitzer	1 (0.45)	8.9 (4)	1072 (980)

Gun and howitzer compared (above). The table presents data for a gun and howitzer of the same caliber — nominal 12-pounder, 4.62in (11.73cm) — both of them US Model of 1841-44.
The main advantage of a howitzer is its lightness (**B**, **C**) compared with a gun of the same caliber. The range is less (**F**) and the flight slower, but at a good saving in propellant (**D**). This small charge means there is less shock to the shell on firing, so its walls are thinner but it holds more powder and is thus more effective though lighter (**E**).

US 12-pounder field gun (below) of 1857, known as the "Napoleon." One of the last and best smoothbore muzzle-loading cast guns, much used in the American Civil War (1861-65). Originally a French design, named after Napoleon III. Maximum effective range 2000yd (1828m).

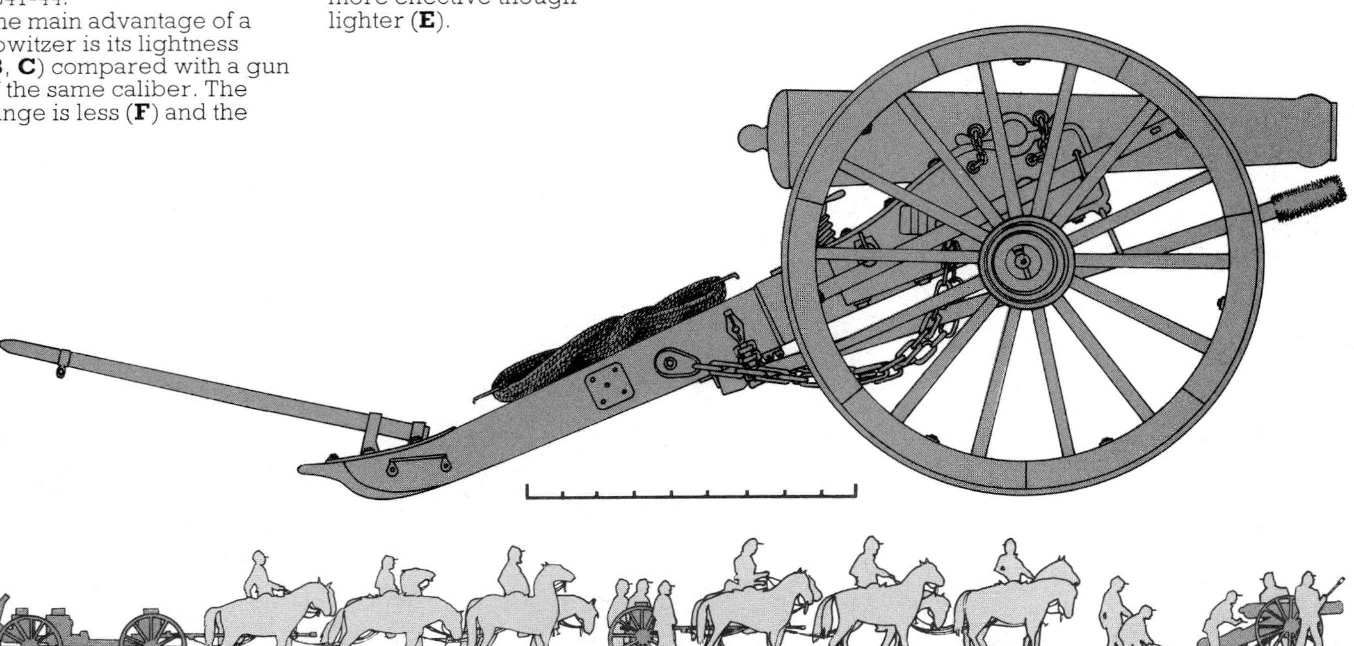

Men and horses (above) needed to serve one 12-pounder field gun at the time of the American Civil War. Ideally there were 8 gunners, 6 drivers and 12 horses, but crews were trained to work with fewer in case of casualties. On the move, the crew rode on the limber and caisson, or walked. (In battle, the limbers and horses would be farther to the rear.)

Smoothbore garrison artillery

The main difference between field artillery and that intended for use in defending fortresses was one of weight. The gun barrels could be of larger caliber as they and their ammunition were left in static garrisons. The interest for us lies mainly in the special carriages, designed to maximize the field of fire.

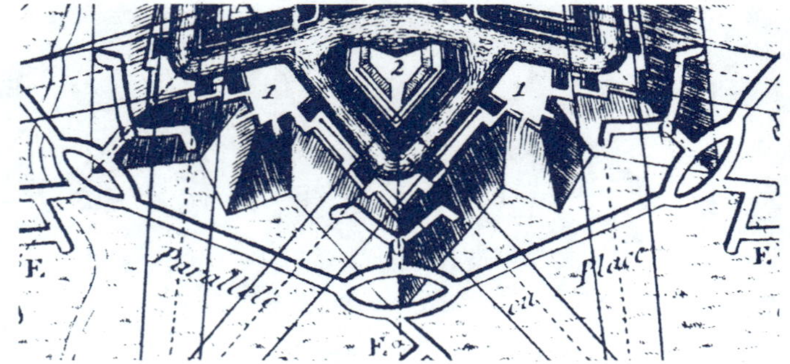

Fortifications (above)
From the 16th century onward, fortifications had to take account both of small arms and cannon. Shown here are distinctive angular plans devised by Vauban, a Frenchman. Shot was deflected by slopes or absorbed by earth more effectively than by vertical stone or brick walls. In Europe, whole cities were defended by such systems.

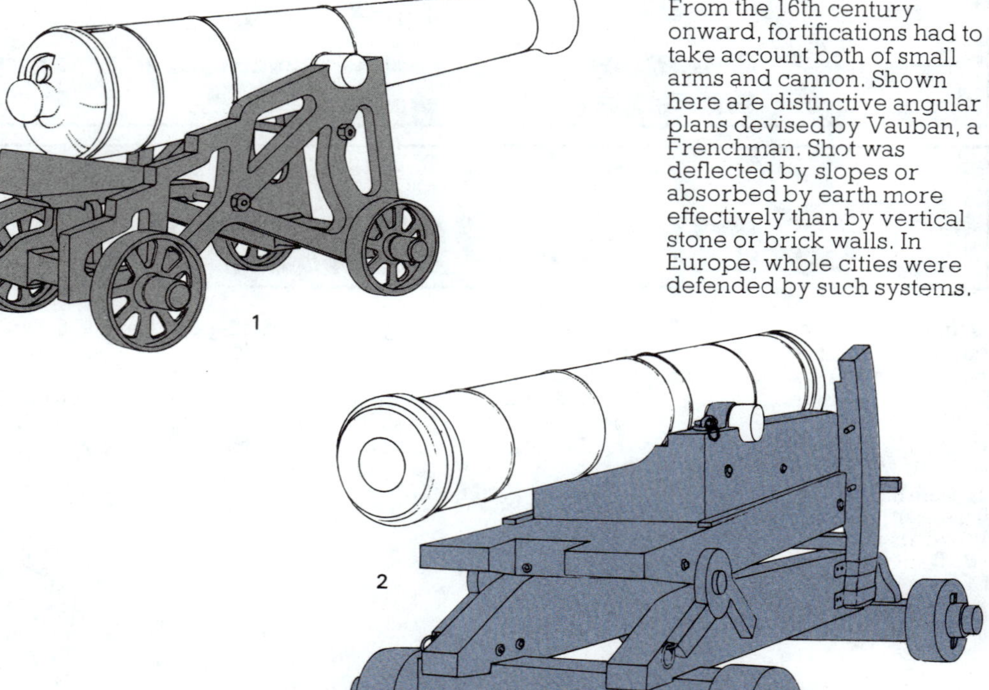

1 Iron garrison carriage
More durable than wood and less vulnerable in action, iron was often used to mount fortress guns, where weight was not a problem. The barrels of such guns were often of naval origin. Shown is a 24-pounder of the early 19th century. (Edinburgh Castle.)

2 Depression carriage
enabling a cannon to fire down on attackers from forts, which were often sited on high ground. This British example was called a Gibraltar carriage, after its development for the defense of the Rock in the siege of 1779-83. A special wad was used to stop the shot rolling out of the bore.

3 Rodman Columbiad of 15in (38.1cm) caliber, c.1863, on a center-pintle barbette carriage of iron. In Rodman guns, the inside of the bore was cooled by water-flow during casting. This put the surrounding metal in compression and increased its strength. The mount gave all-round traverse and absorbed recoil by friction. Weight of barrel 22.3 tons (22.6t).

Smoothbore naval guns

For 300 years, from c.1550 to c.1860, warships took the form of floating gun batteries. Each gun had a very limited traverse within the broadside, but had to be run back for loading each shot. These requirements, and thus the design of guns, changed little in this period. Improvements were limited chiefly to ammunition and the means of ignition.

The hull (below) of HMS *Victory*, Nelson's flagship at Trafalgar, shows the simple tiers of gundecks that typified the warship for 300 years.

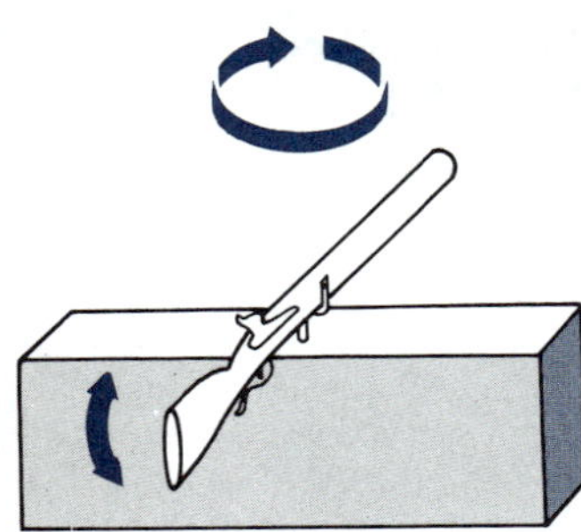

Swivel guns were mounted on small boats, and on the side-rail of ships-of-the-line to repel boarding parties. The stirrup mounting gave a good field of fire (left), and allowed the gun to be turned round for loading.
a (right) Malayan *lantaka*, of cast brass, also used on stockades on land.
b US brass percussion gun of 1858.

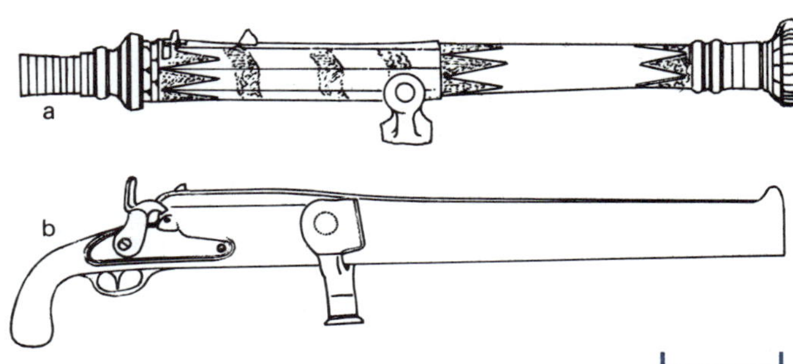

Specialized naval missiles (below) Three types are illustrated below, closed as on loading and open as in flight.
a Extending bar shot.
b, c Types of chain shot.

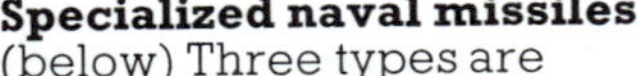

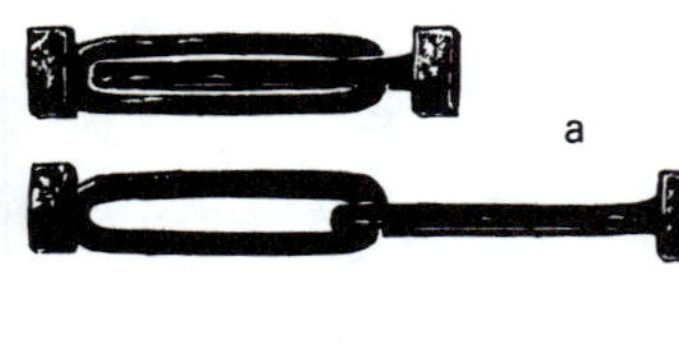

The main armament (right) of warships remained the same in principle from the 17th to the mid-19th century. Thus the difference between a gun from the Swedish ship *Vasa* of 1628 (**1**), and one from HMS *Victory* in 1805 (**2**), was chiefly one of style. The only functional improvement was the use of flintlock ignition. The thick breeching rope controlled recoil, and the thin ropes and pulleys were for hauling the gun forward once it had been loaded. The carronade (**3**) was a short, large-bore design, first made at Carron in Scotland, 1779. It was economic in weight, space and crew, and very destructive at short range.
Movement (below) The diagram shows the limited movement required of a naval gun.

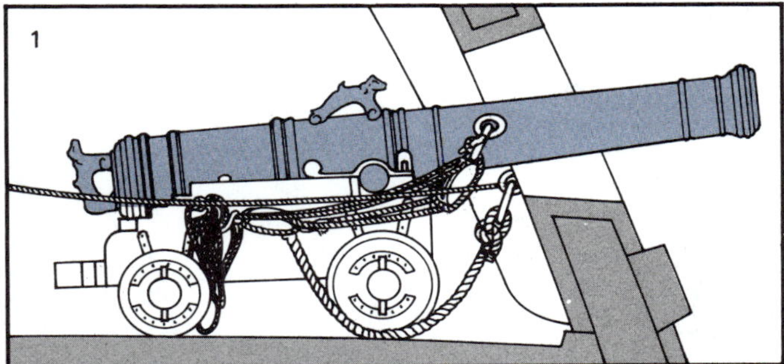

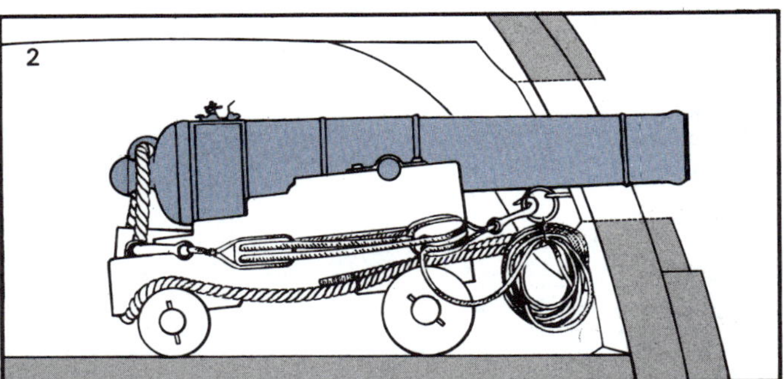

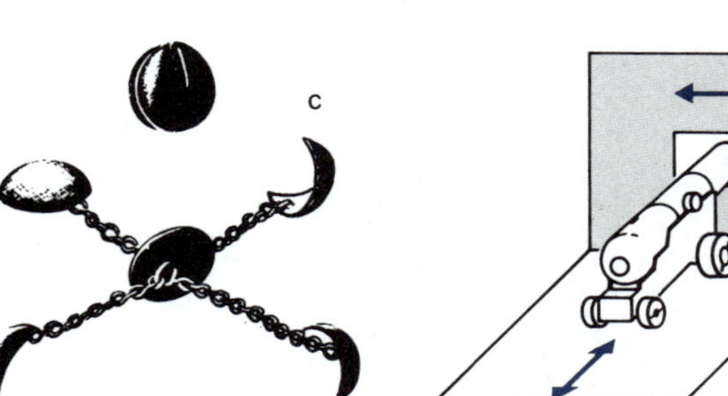

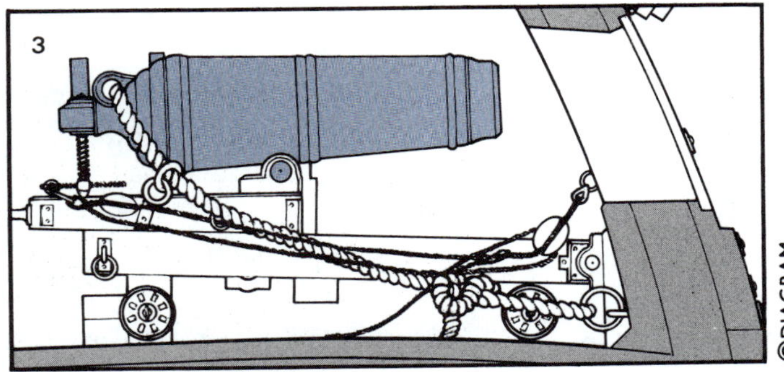

Late smoothbore artillery

By the 1860s cast smoothbore artillery, essentially unchanged for over 300 years, was being made obsolete by new developments — chiefly the rifled barrel and the ironclad warship. Here we examine the refinements used at the end of the smoothbore era, mostly improvements made possible by general advances in technology.

US siege mortar (above) of 13in (33cm) caliber, which weighed 7.6 tons (7.7t). It was given unheard-of mobility by mounting it on a railroad truck at the siege of Petersburg, Virginia in 1865. The shell was lifted by two men with tongs, who stood on the carriage's integral steps while placing it in the bore.

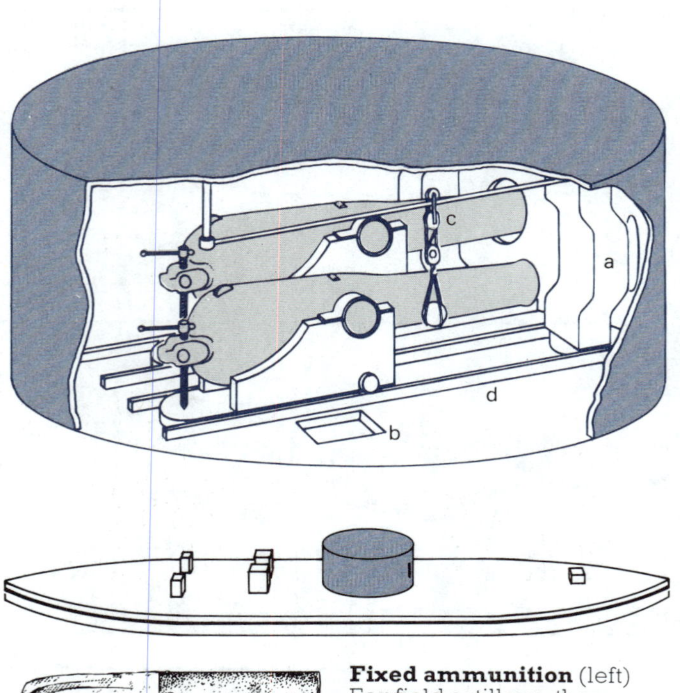

USS Monitor (left), a typical early ironclad warship of the 1860s, is shown here in half plan, with an enlarged section above showing the design of the gun turret. Two 11in (28cm) smoothbore guns were carried in the central, rotating turret. During loading, the gunport was blocked by turning a crank-shaped bar (**a**). Ammunition was passed up through a hatch (**b**) and taken to the muzzle on a system of rails and pulleys (**c**). The guns recoiled on friction rails (**d**) when fired. In these cramped conditions, muzzle-loading was difficult, and each gun could only be fired once in 2½ minutes. Nevertheless, such vessels made all wooden broadside-firing ships obsolete.

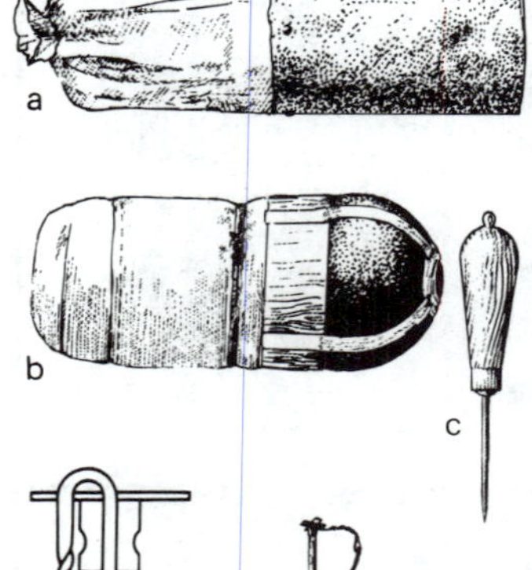

Fixed ammunition (left) For field artillery, the powder charge was usually attached to the projectile in a cloth bag for speed in loading. Shown are a canister round (**a**) and a round of common shell (**b**), both for a 12-pounder (about 11cm) gun of c.1860. On firing, the bag was burned and the tinned straps burst.

d
e

Priming and ignition (left) Once the cartridge had been rammed down, the bag was pierced through the vent with a pricker (**c**). A friction primer (**d**) was put in the vent and a lanyard (**e**) hooked to it. On tugging the lanyard, a coarse wire in the primer ignited a match-like composition, sending a flash into the powder charge below.

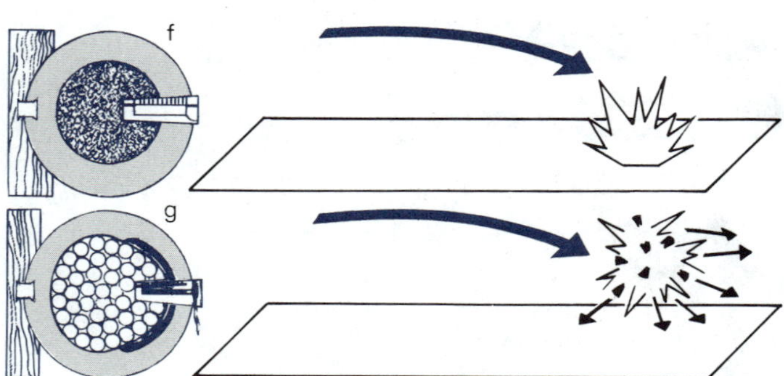

Explosive projectiles (above) By the 1860s, two quite advanced types were in use. Both are shown with a wooden base attached. This helped seal the bore, and kept the fuze facing forward. Both fuzes were lit by the flash of firing. Common shell (**f**) exploded after impact, so had thick walls and a comparatively small bursting charge of powder inside it. Boxer's diaphragm shrapnel shell (**g**) was an improvement of earlier types. A thin metal sheet separated the bursting powder from the balls, so avoiding premature ignition due to friction. The walls of the shell were thinner, as it was designed to explode in the air and shower the target with shot and fragments.

Reinforced and rifled muzzle-loaders

In the 1860s the principle of rifling was applied to artillery, following similar developments in small arms design. At the same time, new methods of reinforcing the barrel against the pressure of ever-increasing charges were introduced. These consisted mostly of surrounding the breech with wrought iron collars. Soon whole barrels were made in this way.

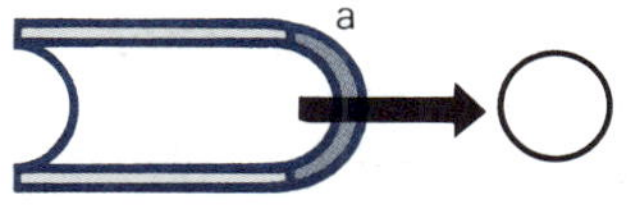

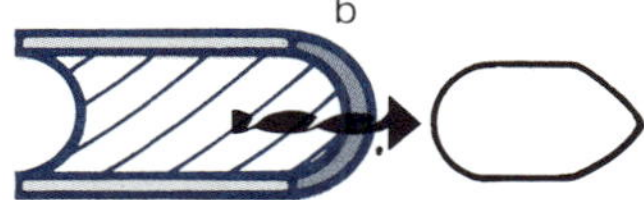

Rifled barrels (left) Fired from the old smoothbore barrels (**a**), projectiles had to be spherical, as they were unstabilized and tumbled in flight. The spin imparted by a rifled barrel (**b**) gave a shell gyroscopic stability, so it could be cylindrical and still fly point first. Longer, heavier shells could thus be fired from a given caliber of gun.

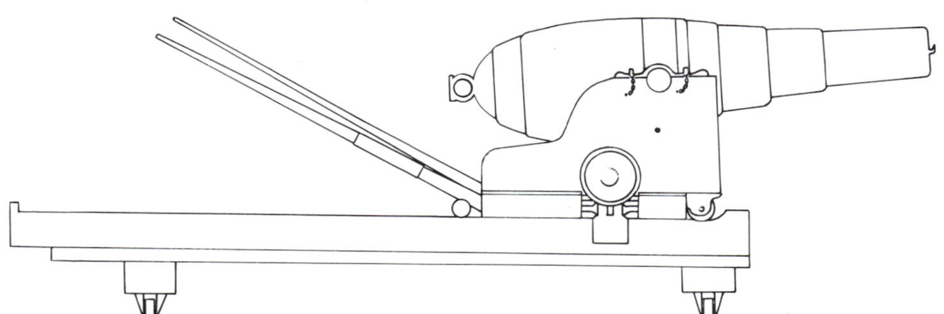

Armstrong 150-pounder (left), rifled muzzle-loading fortress gun, c.1863. Note the concentric sleeves used to form the barrel.

Sectional strength (below) of a reinforced barrel. The inner tube is under compression from the reinforcing outer sleeve, efficiently countering the radial stresses of firing. Cast metal lacked this oriented strength.

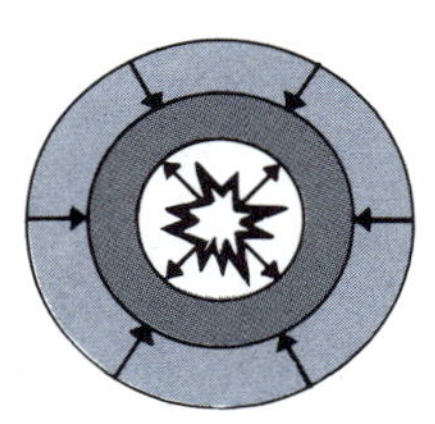

US 10-pounder (left), Parrot rifled field gun. Smaller in bore than the old 6-pounder smoothbore, but rifling increased the weight of shell by 55% and range by 26%, outclassing even the 12-pounder Napoleon. Parrot guns used a cast barrel with one wrought iron collar. Although cheap, they had a reputation for bursting in use.

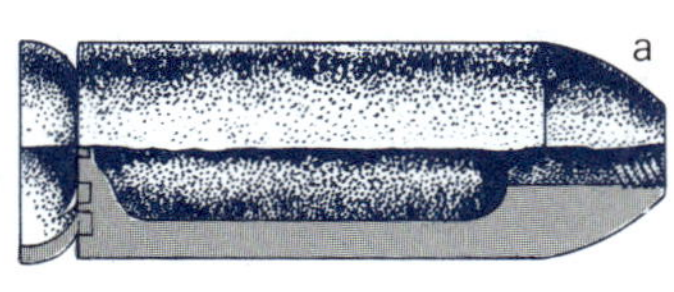

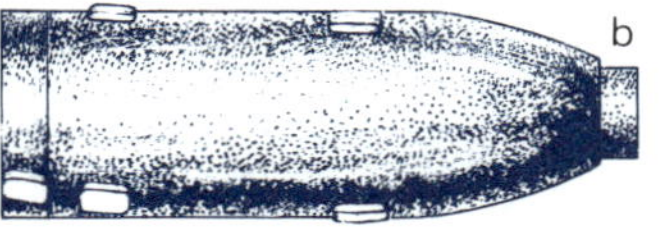

Shells for rifled guns (left) To grip the rifling grooves, various devices were tried on shells. Parrot shells (**a**) had a soft metal cup on the base, which was forced out into the grooves by the propellant gases on firing. Studded shells (**b**) had projections added to match the grooves in the bore.

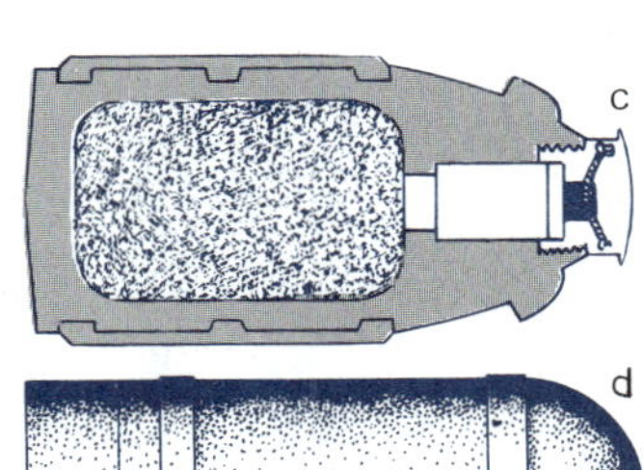

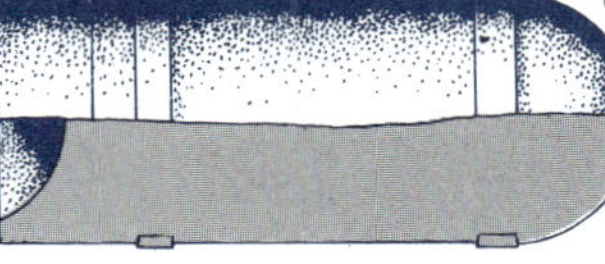

Stabilized projectiles (left) fired from rifled guns had two big advantages. Firstly, percussion fuzes could be fitted to the nose (**c**) and be relied on to detonate the shell on impact. Secondly, elongated solid shot (**d**) was heavier in proportion to its cross-section, and thus could pierce a greater thickness of armor-plate or masonry.

Modern mortars

The modern mortar is the only important survival of muzzle-loading artillery in the 20th century. Characteristically it is a portable, smoothbore weapon firing a fin-stabilized bomb at a high angle. It forms the infantry's own miniature artillery. Although its antecedents go back as far as the mortars of the 14th century, in its present form it dates only from the trenches of 1915.

Loading (right) Mortars are loaded by sliding a bomb tail-first down the barrel from the muzzle. The only exceptions are those that are too long for a man to reach the muzzle with a heavy bomb, and which must therefore have a simple breech mechanism.

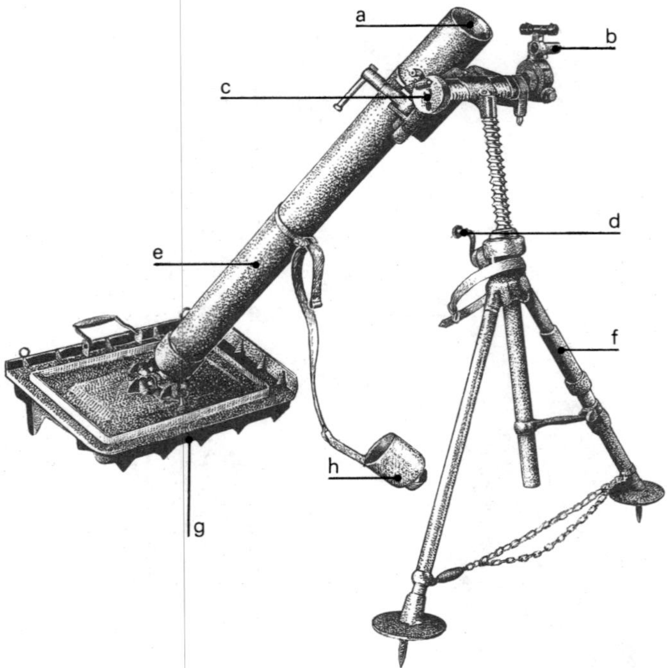

Typical medium mortar (left), the Swiss 81mm Model 1933. This basic format, called the Stokes-Brandt design, has been used by many armies. Its three main elements are the barrel, the bipod by which it is aimed, and the baseplate to stop it sinking into the ground on firing.

The parts (left) of a typical modern mortar (Stokes-Brandt layout) are indicated on the illustration.
a Muzzle
b Sights
c Traversing handle
d Elevating handle
e Barrel
f Bipod legs
g Baseplate
h Muzzle cap

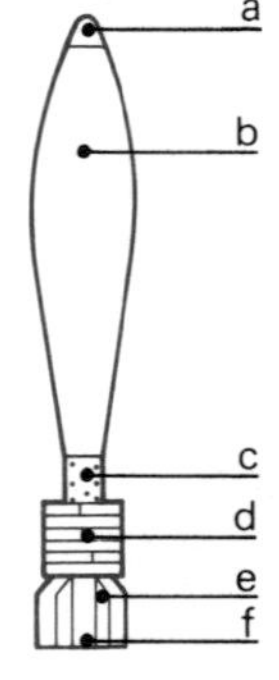

Parts of a fin-stabilized mortar bomb (above)
a Fuze, to activate the contents of the bomb.
b Body, containing the active agent.
c Primary charge of propellant in stem of fins.
d Augmenting charges, removed for short-range fire.
e Fins, to make the bomb fly point first.
f Percussion cap, to ignite the propellant.

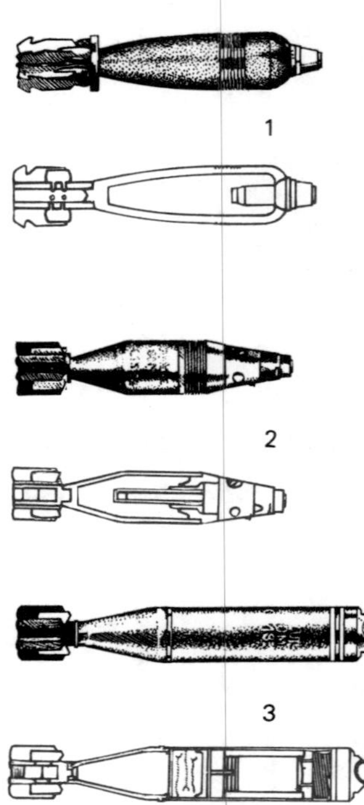

Mortar bombs (left)
Three common types are illustrated by specific examples:
1 High explosive can act in one of three ways according to the fuze: instantaneous impact; delayed action (which penetrates before exploding); or air-burst. Shown is a French 60mm Mk61.
2 Smoke is used to prevent enemy observation. This is the US 60mm M302 which uses white phosphorus to make a sudden dense white cloud. There are also slow emission types which give off a steady pall of smoke for several minutes. Most have a secondary incendiary effect.
3 Illuminating The fuze is set to open the bomb high over the enemy. A brilliant flare on a small parachute lights up the ground as it floats down. (US 60mm M83A3.)

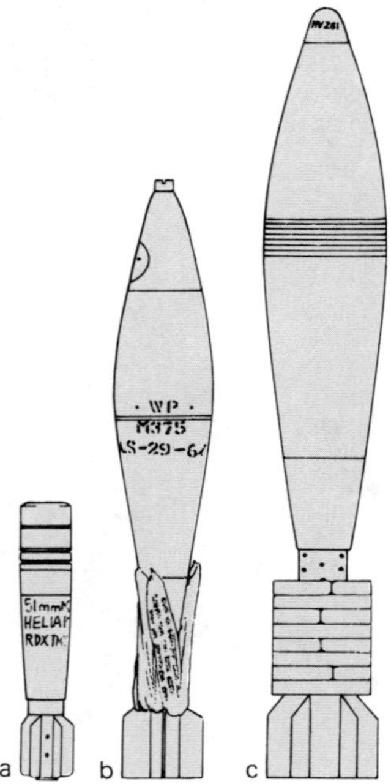

Size of bombs (left)
Typical light, medium and heavy mortar bombs are illustrated here.
a British 51mm
b US 81mm
c Swiss 120mm
(The Warsaw Pact countries also have 160mm and 240mm mortars, but these are breech-loading weapons.)

Minenwerfer (below) WW1 German rifled 25cm model being loaded carefully to match the pre-engraved copper driving band to the rifling grooves in the bore. Such weapons could not be safely drop-fired, so had a separate firing mechanism, activated after the loader had stepped clear of the muzzle.

Disposable mortar (right), the Belgian PRB 424. Issued as a bundle of four tubes, the kit consists of a barrel (**a**), baseplate (**b**), and three tubes containing seven bombs. The bombs (**c**) are multipurpose, and can also be used as grenades, or fired from the multi-spigot launcher (see below). Total weight 25 lb (11.5kg).

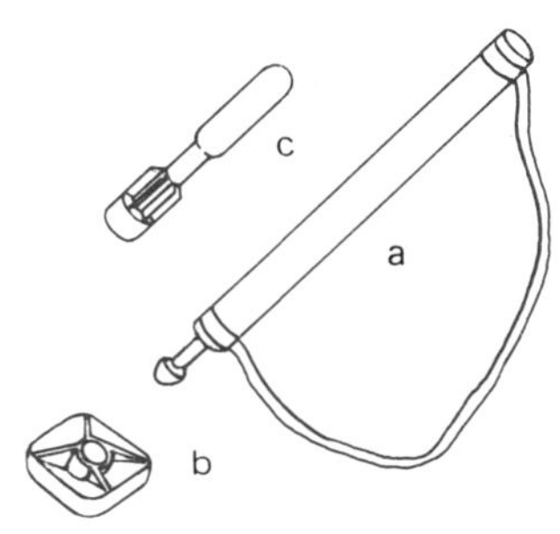

PRB 424 in use (right) The correct elevation for a given range is set by placing the foot at the appropriate mark on the sling. Then, when the sling is tightened by gripping the barrel as shown, the angle of elevation will be correct.

Bombs (right) for rifled mortars are fitted with pre-engraved driving bands, i.e. with a serrated metal collar which exactly fits the shape of the bore. The German WW1 *Minenwerfer* gas bomb (**1**) closely resembles a conventional shell. The modern French 120mm bomb (**2**) is closer to the design of a finned bomb.

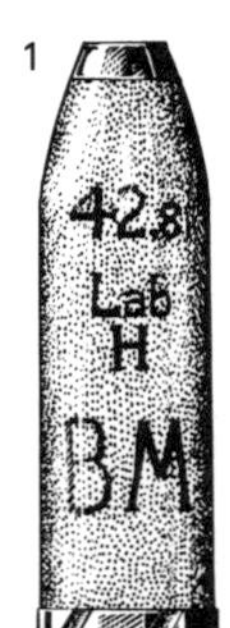

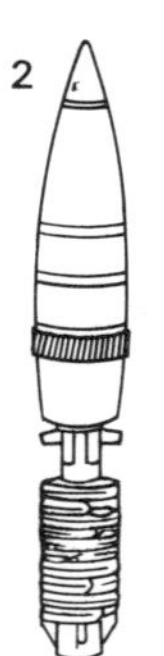

Multi-spigot launcher (right), the Belgian PRB 426. A combination of spigot and jet-shot propulsion used for firing grenades. The angle and rate of fire are adjustable. Range about 440yd (400m). An area of $1\frac{1}{4}$ acres (2 hectares) can be covered with lethal fragments, a useful facility in a planned defensive position.

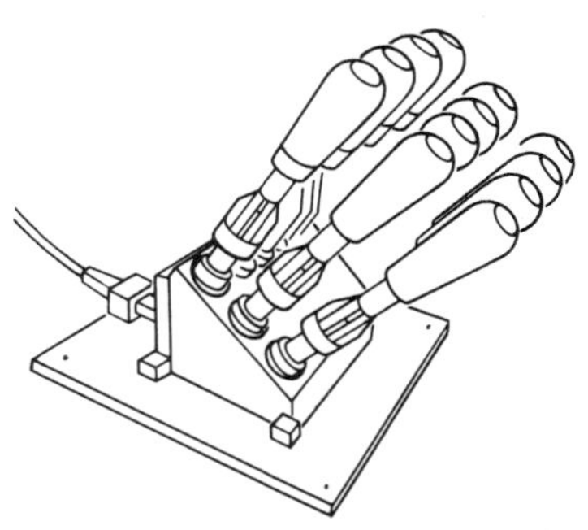

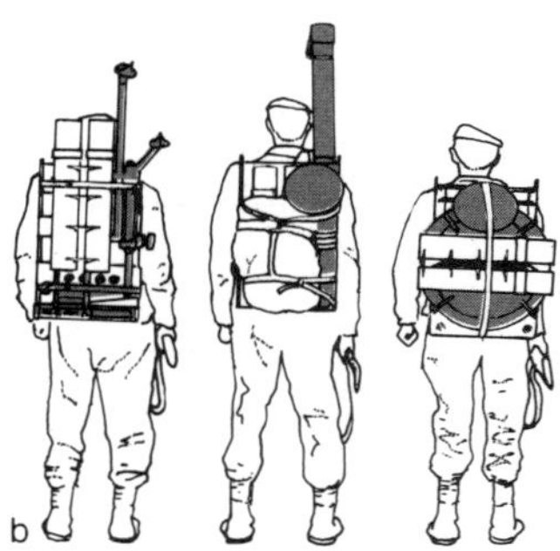

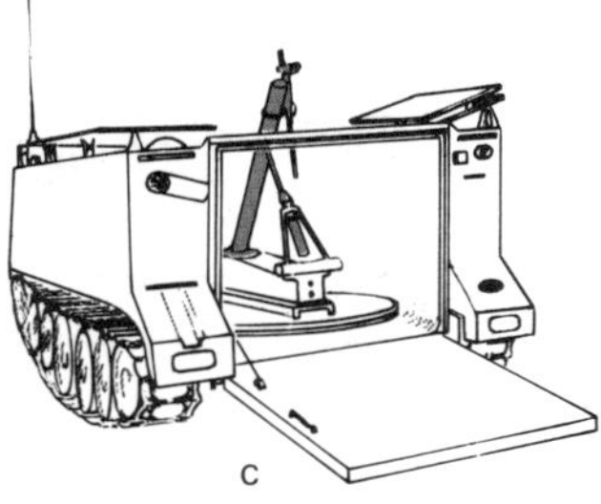

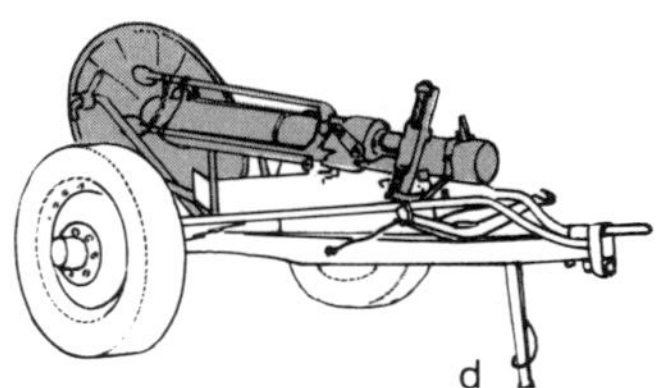

Portability (above) is a characteristic of modern mortars, but it is a relative term.

a A light mortar and several bombs can be carried and fired by one man, even from the prone position.

b Medium mortars (of about 81mm caliber) can mostly be stripped down into three man-portable loads. Here each man is carrying two bombs as well as a main component of the mortar.

c Medium and heavy types are now also mounted on armored personnel carriers, ready to fire out of a hatch on top as soon as the vehicle stops. This system has the great advantages of easing the carriage of ammunition, and of protecting the crew without their needing to dig in.

d Some heavy mortars are towed on wheeled carriages. This system is particularly popular with Warsaw Pact countries.

Breech-loading artillery

In the mid 19th century, general advances in technology permitted breech loading—an old concept with many theoretical advantages—to replace muzzle loading in the design of artillery. We explain the form taken by these technical changes, and their implications for ammunition. In subsequent pages breech-loading guns are surveyed, and classified according to their role, first on land then at sea.

Loading via the breech (left) has several main advantages. The shell can be a tight fit in a rifled bore, thus adding to power and accuracy. Loading is generally faster, and also easier in turret and casemate mountings.

15th century breech-loader (right) The idea of breech-loading is about as old as that of muzzle-loading. The field carriage of this piece is a reconstruction, but the barrel and breech mechanism were made in c. 1460-70. It has a slightly tapered bore of about 2in (5cm) caliber. (Bernisches Historisches Museum, Switzerland.)

Sealing the breech (right) In the late 19th century, two efficient ways were found of preventing the dangerous escape of propellant gases at the breech. These were:
A The "Quick Firing" (QF) system, using a brass cartridge case as the seal. The case is forced so tightly against the inside of the barrel that no gas can leak back.
B The De Bange system, without a cartridge case. The explosion of the propellant forces the mushroom piece back. The soft obturator ring is trapped against the breech block and squeezed out hard against the barrel walls, so forming a seal. The ammunition for each of these types is necessarily different. It is shown on p. 180.

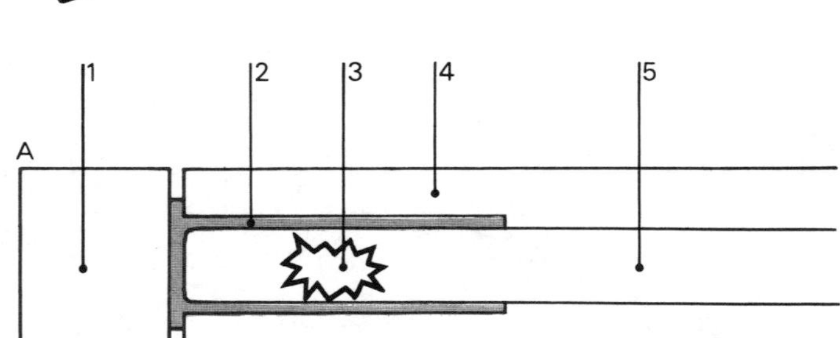

1 Breech block
2 Brass cartridge case
3 Explosion of propellant
4 Barrel walls
5 Bore

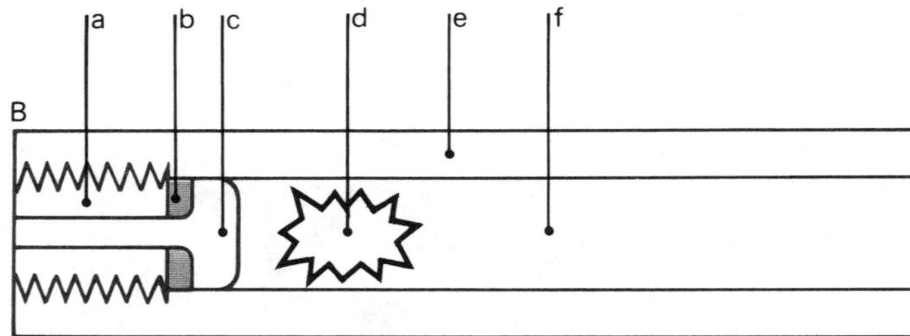

a Breech block
b Obturator ring
c Mushroom piece
d Explosion of propellant
e Barrel walls
f Bore

Sliding breech blocks (right) Many simple and effective mechanisms for opening and closing the breech have been based on a sliding block, moved aside or down to permit loading (**a**), and back again to close the breech (**b**). Variants of this type are generally used in conjunction with the QF system of sealing the breech.

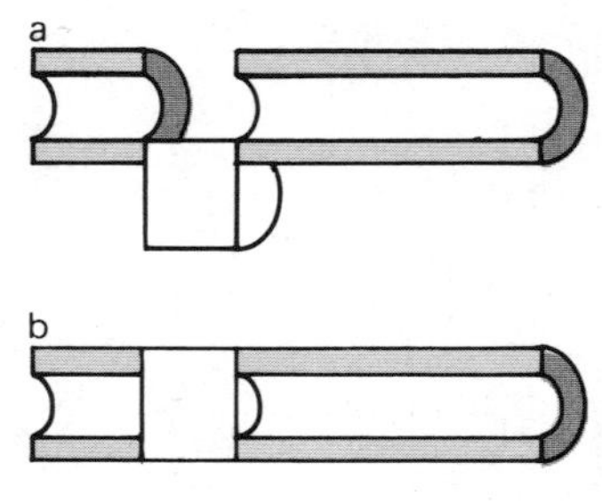

Interrupted screw breech (right) Another common breech mechanism uses a screw thread, but with sections cut away lengthwise (**1**). Thus a turn through a few degrees will lock (**2**) or unlock the breech, and permit rapid reloading. There are several minor variants of this type, most of which are usually combined with the De Bange obturator system.

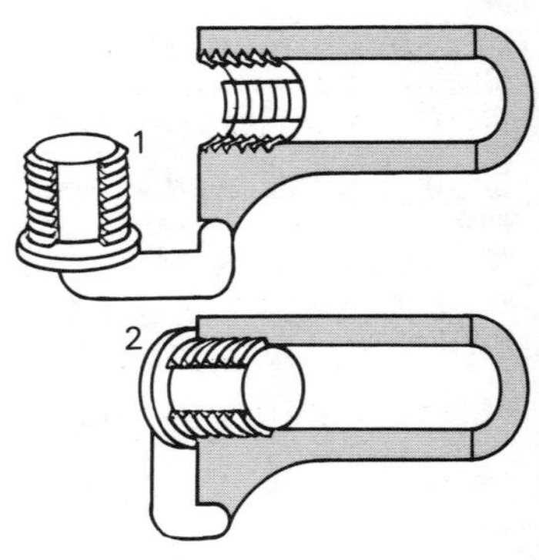

12-pounder Armstrong gun (right), adopted for British field batteries in 1859, and one of the first practical breech-loaders of the modern era. The elongated iron shell was coated with lead to "take" the rifling in the bore, and was very accurate. Some of these guns were used in the American Civil War of 1861-1865.
The caliber of the 12-pounder version was 3in (76.2mm). The propellant was loaded separately after the projectile, which could be one of three kinds: shrapnel, case shot or explosive shell, which weighed 11.56 lb (5.24kg).

Artillery fire (below) Here we explain three important aspects of the application of artillery fire to a target, as carried out since about 1900. These principles apply as much to naval gunfire as to land.

Direct and indirect fire (above) Until about the end of the 19th century, it was the custom to aim and fire artillery pieces "over open sights" (**a**), directly at the target. Since then it has been much more common to keep the guns well to the rear (**b**) and to place an observer (**c**) forward to direct the fire onto the target.

The ranging process (above) Lateral corrections are simple, but it is difficult to tell how far "short" or "over" a miss has fallen. Thus the "bracketing" system is used. Shell (**1**) falls short, so a bold correction is made, and (**2**) is over. Then alternate subtractions and additions are made (**3**), halving the correction each time, until shell (**4**) is on target.

The beaten zone (above) At tactical ranges, no gun can hit the same spot with every shell. This fact has to be allowed for when applying fire to a target. The imaginary rectangle containing all shots (**A**) is longer than it is broad. It has been found that 50% of shots fall within an inner area a quarter as long. This is called the 50% zone (**B**).

Factors affecting accuracy Among the factors that must be considered when "laying" or aiming an artillery piece are: meteorological conditions such as wind speed and air pressure; "drift," a gyroscopic phenomenon caused by the projectile's spin-stabilization; and, at long ranges, even the direction of the earth's rotation.

Ammunition for breech-loading artillery

The subject of artillery ammunition is complex, and it is important to understand the many forms that it takes: it is after all the projectile that inflicts the damage, the gun being merely the machine that delivers it. In addition to the basic information on these two pages, more details of specific types, such as anti-tank projectiles, are given later on the appropriate pages.

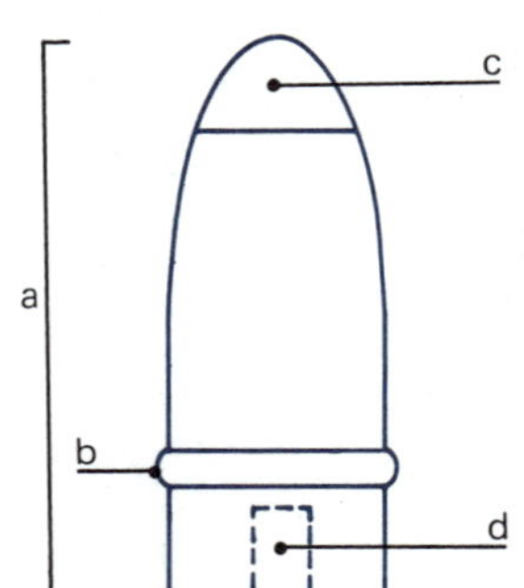

Characteristic features (left) of a breech-loading projectile. Projectiles for breech-loaders are of elongated shape (**a**). A "driving band" (**b**) of soft copper is set into the projectile to be gripped by the rifling lands and grooves in the barrel. A fuze is fitted either at the nose (**c**) or base (**d**) of an explosive shell to ignite its contents.

Caliber (right) The caliber of a gun or howitzer is the diameter of the bore (**1**) excluding the depth of the rifling grooves. The length of a barrel (**2**) is sometimes expressed as the number of calibers to which it is equal (**3**). For example a howitzer described as "4.5in (11.43cm) of 13.33 calibers" has a barrel 60in (152.4cm) long.

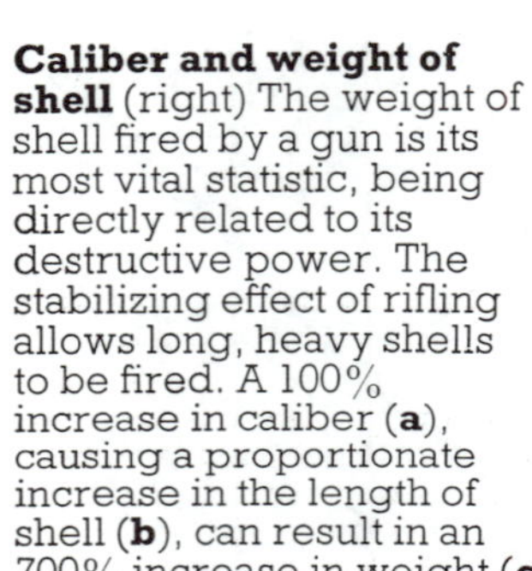

Caliber and weight of shell (right) The weight of shell fired by a gun is its most vital statistic, being directly related to its destructive power. The stabilizing effect of rifling allows long, heavy shells to be fired. A 100% increase in caliber (**a**), causing a proportionate increase in the length of shell (**b**), can result in an 700% increase in weight (**c**).

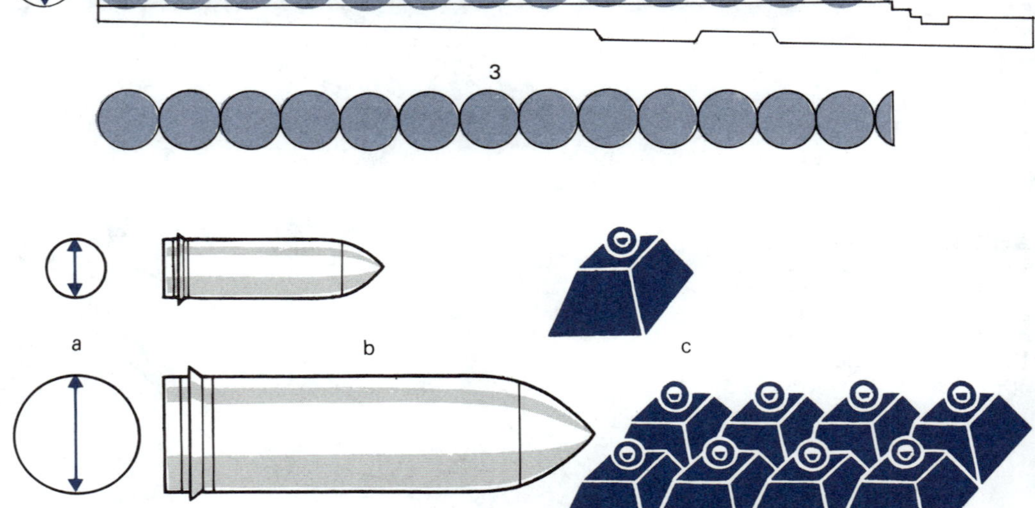

Types of ammunition (right) There are three main types for artillery, classified by how they are loaded into the gun.
A Fixed Loaded as one unit, the shell being fixed to the cartridge case, which also contains a primer. (French 75mm M1897 shown.)
B Semi-fixed Primer and charge are in a metal case, but the shell is loaded separately first. (German 10.5cm howitzer of WW2 shown.)
C Separate loading This type is used mostly with the De Bange breech. The projectile, charge (in a cloth bag) and primer or "vent tube" are each loaded separately. (British 6in Naval gun of WW1 shown.)
Types (**B**) and (**C**) have the advantage that the charge can be varied to adjust the trajectory and range.

Anti-personnel shells (right)

1 Shrapnel This was the main anti-personnel shell until early in WW1. It was set off by a time fuze, to fire a hail of spherical bullets over a wide area of ground as it descended. An impact element was sometimes added to the fuze to achieve some effect should the time element fail.

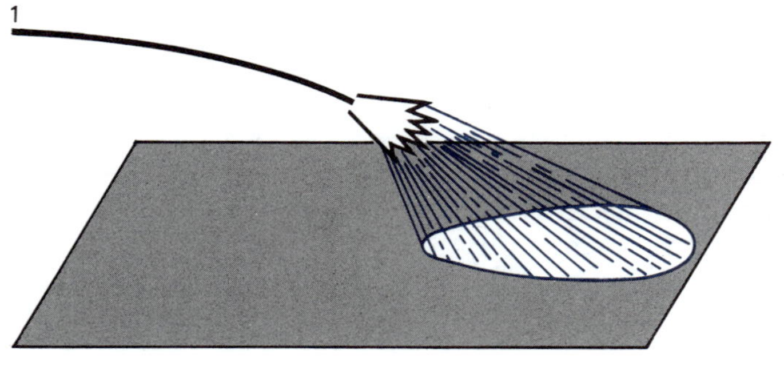

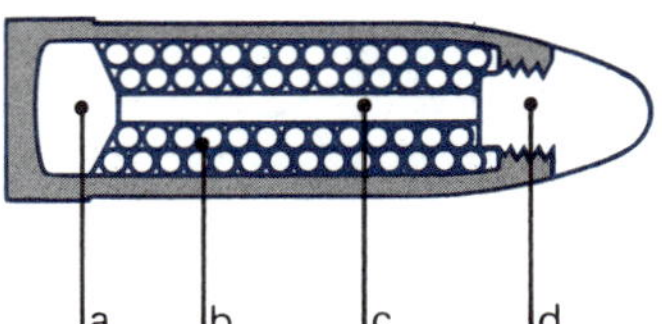

Typical shrapnel shell (above)
a Bursting charge
b Bullets
c Flash tube from fuze
d Fuze

2 High explosive (HE) This type uses blast and fragmentation to attack troops in the open or in trenches. It may be set off by an instantaneous (**A**), or delayed impact fuze, but an "airburst" effect (**B**), using a time or a proximity fuze, is often more effective.

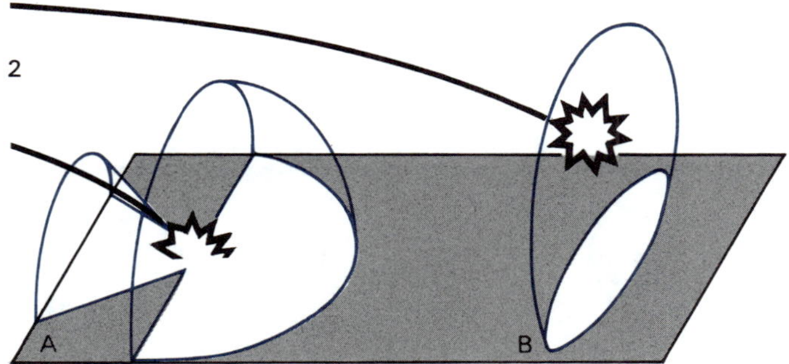

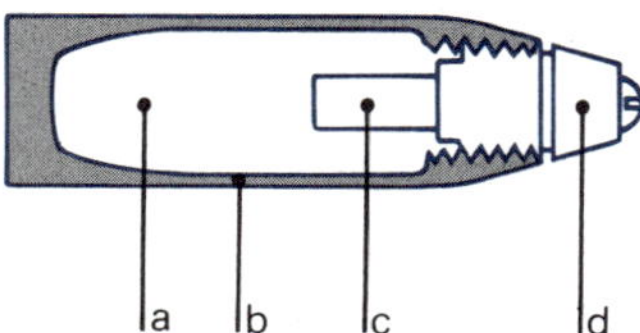

Typical HE shell (above)
a High explosive filling
b Fragmenting walls
c Amplifying charge
d Fuze

3 Chemical shell In WW1, lethal and harrassing gases were often delivered by artillery shell. The filling was usually in liquid form, scattered by a weak bursting charge on impact. Nerve gases may be used on future battlefields. White phosphorus, which has smoke and incendiary effects, is delivered in a similar manner.

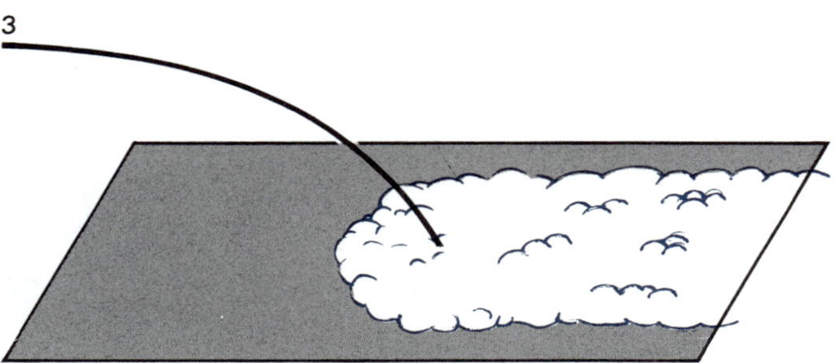

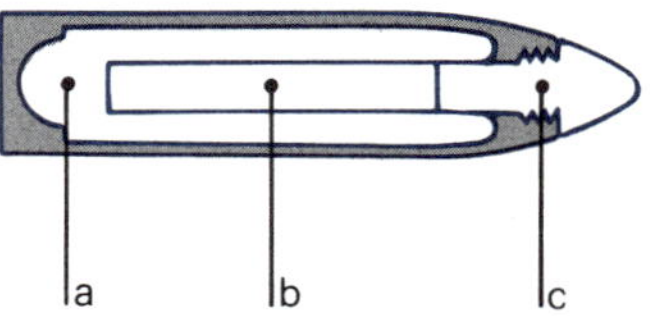

Typical gas or white phosphorus shell (above)
a Chemical agent
b Bursting charge
c Fuze

Fillings, fuzes and effects
Projectiles have been devised to defeat a wide variety of targets. They vary as to the filling contained in them and the fuze used to set them off. The table (right) sets out the combinations of filling and fuze most often used to attack some common targets.
Time fuzes may work by combustion or clockwork. Proximity fuzes transmit and receive radio waves to measure the distance from the target and then set off the shell at the optimum moment. Some impact fuzes are designed to go off after a slight delay, when the whole shell has penetrated the target.
For more detailed information on ammunition, see subsequent pages.

Role	Type of projectile/filler	Type of fuze
Anti-personnel	Shrapnel	Time Time and impact
	Explosive/fragmentation	Time Proximity Instantaneous impact
	Gas	Impact
	White phosphorus	Impact
Anti-structure	Explosive/fragmentation	Instantaneous impact Delayed impact
Anti-armor (Warship or tank target)	Solid shot	None
	Armor-piercing shell	Delayed impact base fuze
	HEAT (Hollow charge)	Impact
	HESH (Squash head)	Impact base fuze
Anti-aircraft	Explosive/fragmentation	Time Proximity Impact
	Shrapnel	Time

Breech-loading field artillery 1

Field artillery in the general sense consists of the mobile guns and howitzers that are designed to accompany an army on campaign. It is sometimes subdivided into light, medium and heavy categories, although these classes cannot be strictly defined. On the next six pages we illustrate the forms that field artillery has commonly taken during the breech-loading era.

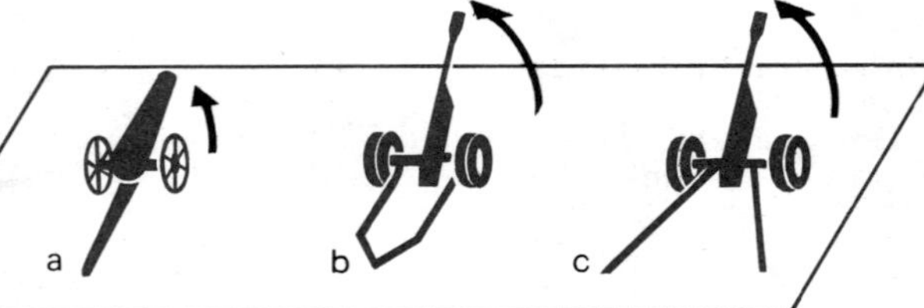

Types of trail (above) The old solid trail or pole trail (**a**) had the disadvantage that it limited elevation and thus range by obstructing the lowering of the breech. This problem was overcome with the box trail (**b**) and the split trail (**c**) that characterize field guns and howitzers of post-WW1 design.

Transportation (right) In the era of animal transport, the term "field artillery" often had a specific sense. Gun and limber were towed by horses, mules or oxen, and most of the crew walked (**1**). Distinct from this was horse artillery (**2**), where the crew rode, so that they could keep up with the cavalry. Horse-drawn artillery survived into WW2 in many armies.
In the motor transport era, the two main forms of field artillery are towed (**3**) and self-propelled (**4**). Towed guns are still useful in air-portable formations, while self-propelled guns are necessary to match the cross-country mobility and degree of protection of an armored formation.

15-pounder BL Mk2 (right), the breech loading field gun used by British field batteries in the Anglo-Boer War of 1899-1902. The carriage still resembles those of the muzzle-loading era, but the trail is made of steel. A recoil spade is fitted below the axle, attached to a spring on the trail. On firing, the spade dug into the ground and the spring absorbed the recoil.

Caliber 3in (76.2mm)
Range 6000yd (5500m)
Type of ammo : separate ; shrapnel.
Weight of shell 14 lb (6.34kg)

a Elevating screw
b Seat for gunner when traveling
c Barrel
d Spring case
e Steel rope
f Recoil spade

b
c
a
d
e
f

The problem of recoil (below) In the muzzle-loading era, field guns had been allowed to recoil freely. On firing, the gun usually ran back several feet and had to be pushed forward by hand and re-aimed. To exploit the advantages of breech-loading for rapid fire, a way had to be found to control this violent movement.

The French M1897 75mm Field Gun (right), the famous "Seventy-five," was the first design to control recoil successfully.
A The parts The barrel (**a**) was attached to a recoil device (**b**) which acted as a buffer and a recuperator. This device was fixed to the carriage (**d**), itself anchored to the ground by a spade-trail (**e**). A steel shield (**c**) could now be fitted to protect the crew.
B The effect of the buffer The buffer was a hydraulic brake, which absorbed recoil by forcing oil through a narrow valve. At the same time, air was being compressed in a cylinder.
C The effect of the recuperator The elasticity of the compressed air was used to push the barrel forward to its original position.

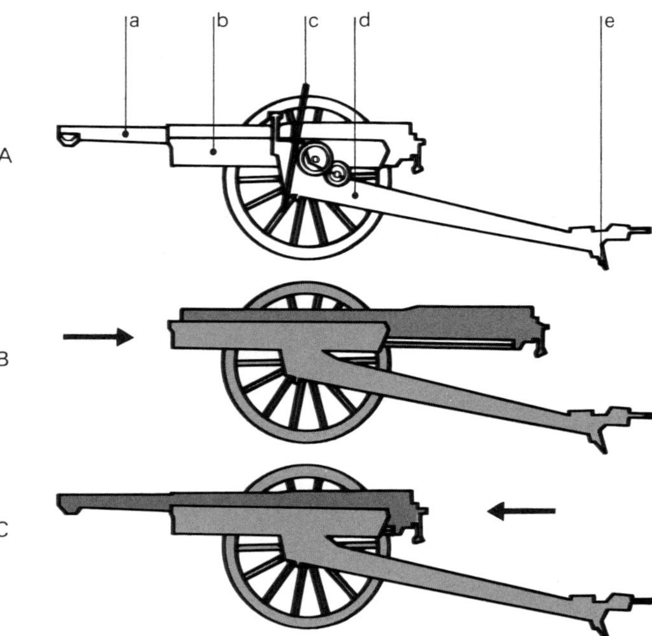

Quick-firing gun of WW1 (below) The British 13-pdr QF Horse Artillery gun displays the features of a modern field piece at the outbreak of the war. A buffer/recuperator is fitted to control the thrust of the barrel as it recoils to the rear, and then push it forward again. Any remaining tendency to recoil is checked by the spade digging into the ground. With the recoil thus controlled, two of the crew can remain on the seats fitted to the trail. There is also a steel shield to protect them from enemy fire. A gearing system is fitted that allows the barrel to be traversed a few degrees without moving the whole gun. There is a telescopic sight for direct fire at targets within the gun-layer's view. For indirect fire, controlled by a forward observer, there is a clinometer to measure elevation and a dial sight for lateral alignment. The gun was pulled behind an ammunition limber by a team of six horses, as can still be seen in London where the 13-pdr is still used for firing ceremonial salutes.

Data of 13-pdr QF gun
Caliber 3in (76.2mm)
Range 5900yd (5400m)
Type of ammo : fixed ; shrapnel, star.
Weight of shell 12.5 lb (5.66kg)

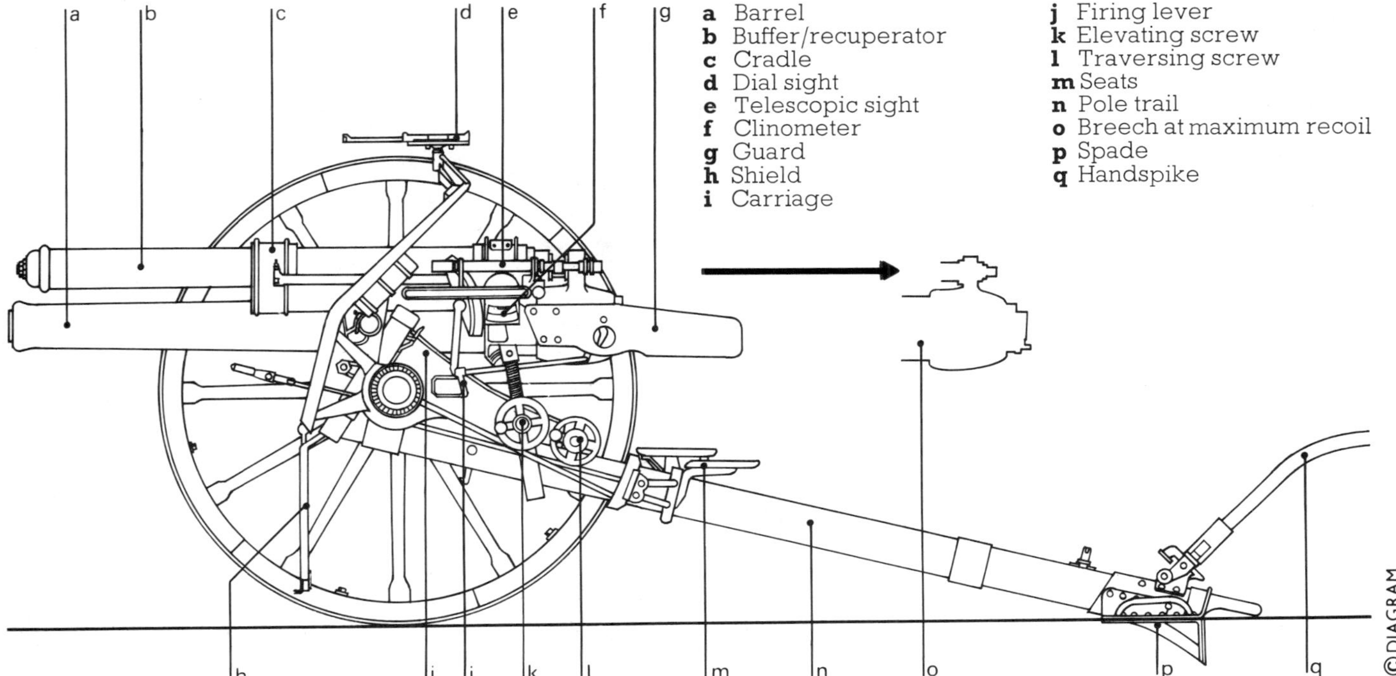

a Barrel
b Buffer/recuperator
c Cradle
d Dial sight
e Telescopic sight
f Clinometer
g Guard
h Shield
i Carriage
j Firing lever
k Elevating screw
l Traversing screw
m Seats
n Pole trail
o Breech at maximum recoil
p Spade
q Handspike

Breech-loading field artillery 2

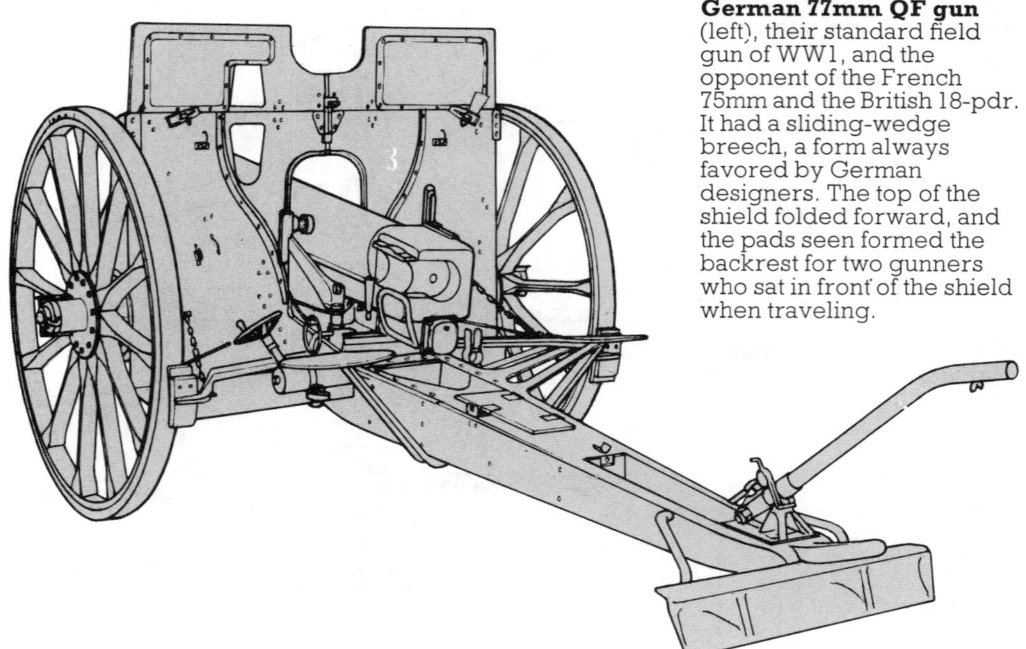

German 77mm QF gun (left), their standard field gun of WW1, and the opponent of the French 75mm and the British 18-pdr. It had a sliding-wedge breech, a form always favored by German designers. The top of the shield folded forward, and the pads seen formed the backrest for two gunners who sat in front of the shield when traveling.

Caliber 3.03in (77mm)
Range 9200yd (8400m)
Type of ammo : semi-fixed ; shrapnel, HE.
Weight of shrapnel shell 15 lb (6.8kg)

British 6in 26cwt howitzer (right), so called to distinguish it from an older model weighing 30 hundredweight, without its carriage. As the main British medium howitzer, this type fired 22.4 million rounds on the Western Front between 1915 and 1918.

Caliber 6in (152.4mm)
Range 9500yd (8700m)
Type of ammo : separate ; shrapnel, HE, gas.
Weight of shell 100 lb (45.3kg)

Self-propelled guns saw some action in WW1. Among them was the French St Chamond tracked mount (right). The forward tractor carried a generator to power the electric motors of both units. In WW2, field, anti-tank and anti-aircraft guns were all at times deployed on self-propelled mounts.

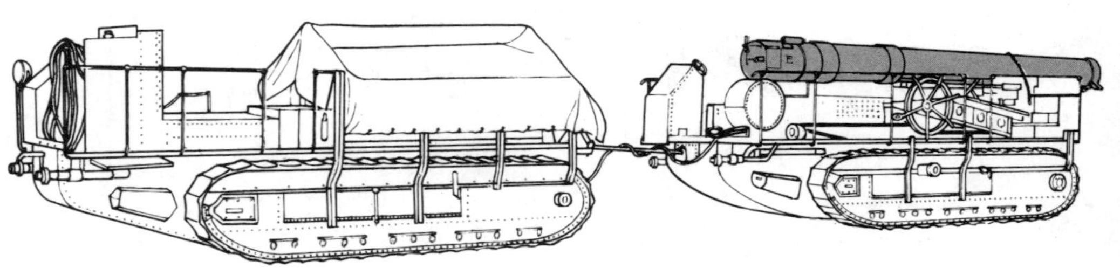

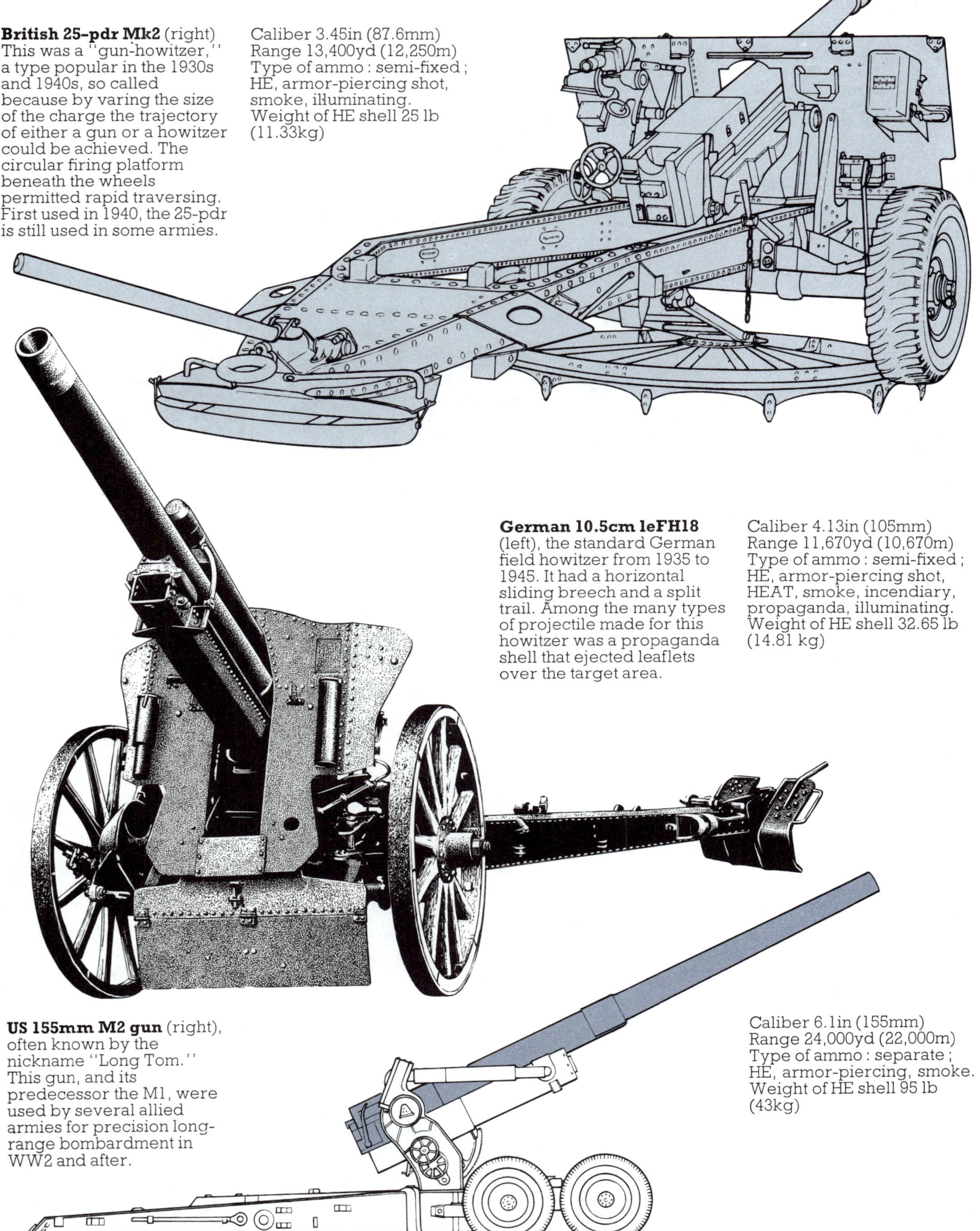

British 25-pdr Mk2 (right) This was a "gun-howitzer," a type popular in the 1930s and 1940s, so called because by varing the size of the charge the trajectory of either a gun or a howitzer could be achieved. The circular firing platform beneath the wheels permitted rapid traversing. First used in 1940, the 25-pdr is still used in some armies.

Caliber 3.45in (87.6mm)
Range 13,400yd (12,250m)
Type of ammo : semi-fixed ; HE, armor-piercing shot, smoke, illuminating.
Weight of HE shell 25 lb (11.33kg)

German 10.5cm leFH18 (left), the standard German field howitzer from 1935 to 1945. It had a horizontal sliding breech and a split trail. Among the many types of projectile made for this howitzer was a propaganda shell that ejected leaflets over the target area.

Caliber 4.13in (105mm)
Range 11,670yd (10,670m)
Type of ammo : semi-fixed ; HE, armor-piercing shot, HEAT, smoke, incendiary, propaganda, illuminating.
Weight of HE shell 32.65 lb (14.81 kg)

US 155mm M2 gun (right), often known by the nickname "Long Tom." This gun, and its predecessor the M1, were used by several allied armies for precision long-range bombardment in WW2 and after.

Caliber 6.1in (155mm)
Range 24,000yd (22,000m)
Type of ammo : separate ; HE, armor-piercing, smoke.
Weight of HE shell 95 lb (43kg)

Breech-loading field artillery 3

French 155mm MkF3 (right), the self-propelled medium howitzer that is deployed in support of the French army's mechanized divisions. Ammunition and most of the eight-man crew are carried on a second vehicle. Note the two angled spades at the rear of the vehicle, shown also in the diagram (below). These transmit some of the recoil forces to the ground, so allowing a comparatively light chassis.

Caliber 6.1in (155mm)
Range 21,900yd (20,000m)
Type of ammo: separate loading; HE, smoke, illuminating.
Max speed 37mph (60kmh)
Weight of shell 94 lb (43kg) approximately

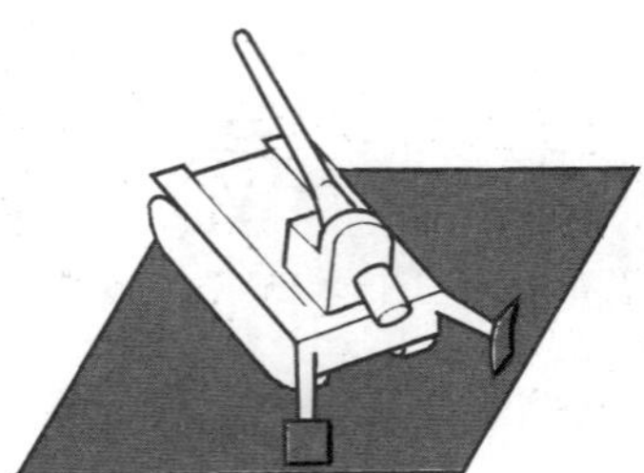

The US 8in Howitzer (right) is found in two forms: the M110 self-propelled version (**1**) and the M115 towed variant (**2**). The barrel, ammunition and performance are identical in each case. Nuclear shells are available for attacking tactical targets on the battlefield. Both versions are in service with NATO and several other countries as well as the USA. The reuse of major components in different forms is common military practice. It simplifies manufacture and supply, whilst in this instance providing a lighter, air-portable weapon as well as one suited to use in a mechanized or armored formation.

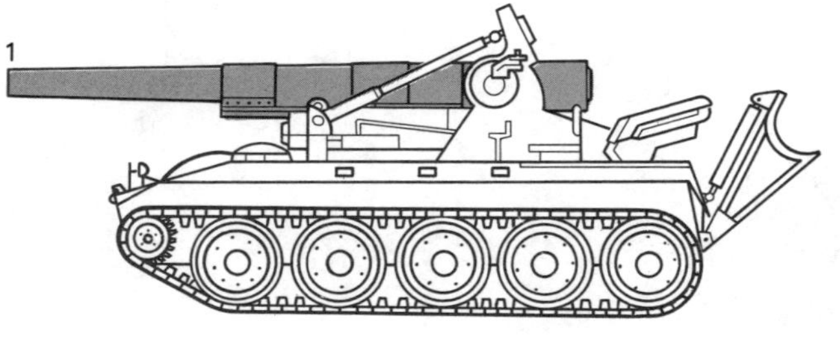

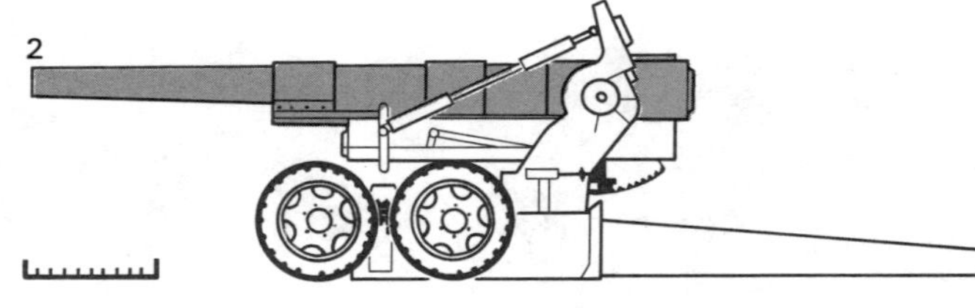

M110
Weight 58,000 lb (26,308kg)
Max speed approx 34mph (54kmh)

M115
Weight traveling 32,000 lb (14,515kg)

Common data
Caliber 8in (203mm)
Range 18,370yd (16,800m)
Type of ammo: separate loading; HE, HE spotting, rocket-assisted HE, nuclear.
Weight of HE shell 200 lb (91kg)

Soviet 76.2mm M1942 (ZiS-3) (right), a successful light field gun first produced in 1942 and still in use with at least 20 Eastern Bloc and non-aligned states. As with many Soviet field guns, the barrel is long in order to improve the muzzle velocity and thus boost the gun's anti-tank capabilities.

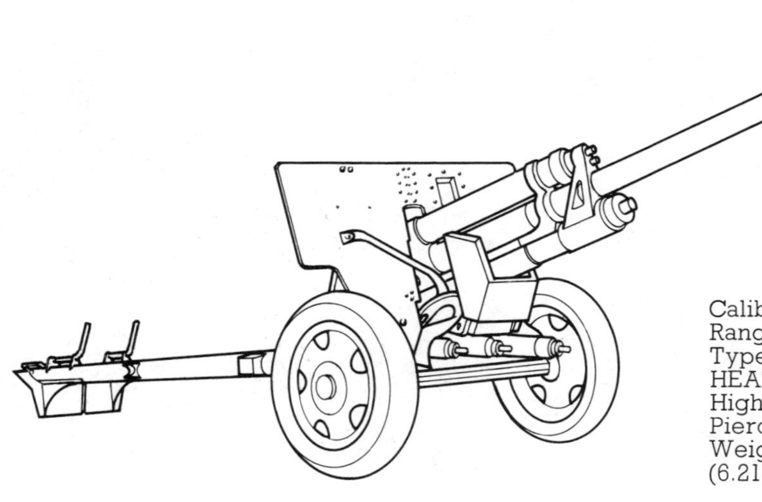

Caliber 3in (76.2mm)
Range 14,500yd (13,290m)
Type of ammo: fixed; HE, HEAT, armor-piercing HE, High Velocity Armor-Piercing Tracer (HVAPT).
Weight of HE shell 13.7 lb (6.21kg)

US 155mm M109 (right), a self-propelled medium howitzer now in use also with several NATO countries including Britain. The enclosed turret of aluminum armor plate helps protect the crew against chemical and light conventional weapons as well as some nuclear weapon effects. The howitzer is capable of both low and high angle fire as the ground requires.
Caliber 6.1in (155mm)
Range 15,970 yd (14,600m)
Type of ammo : separate loading ; HE, chemical, canister, nuclear (US only).
Weight of HE shell 95 lb (43kg)
Max speed 34mph (55kmh)

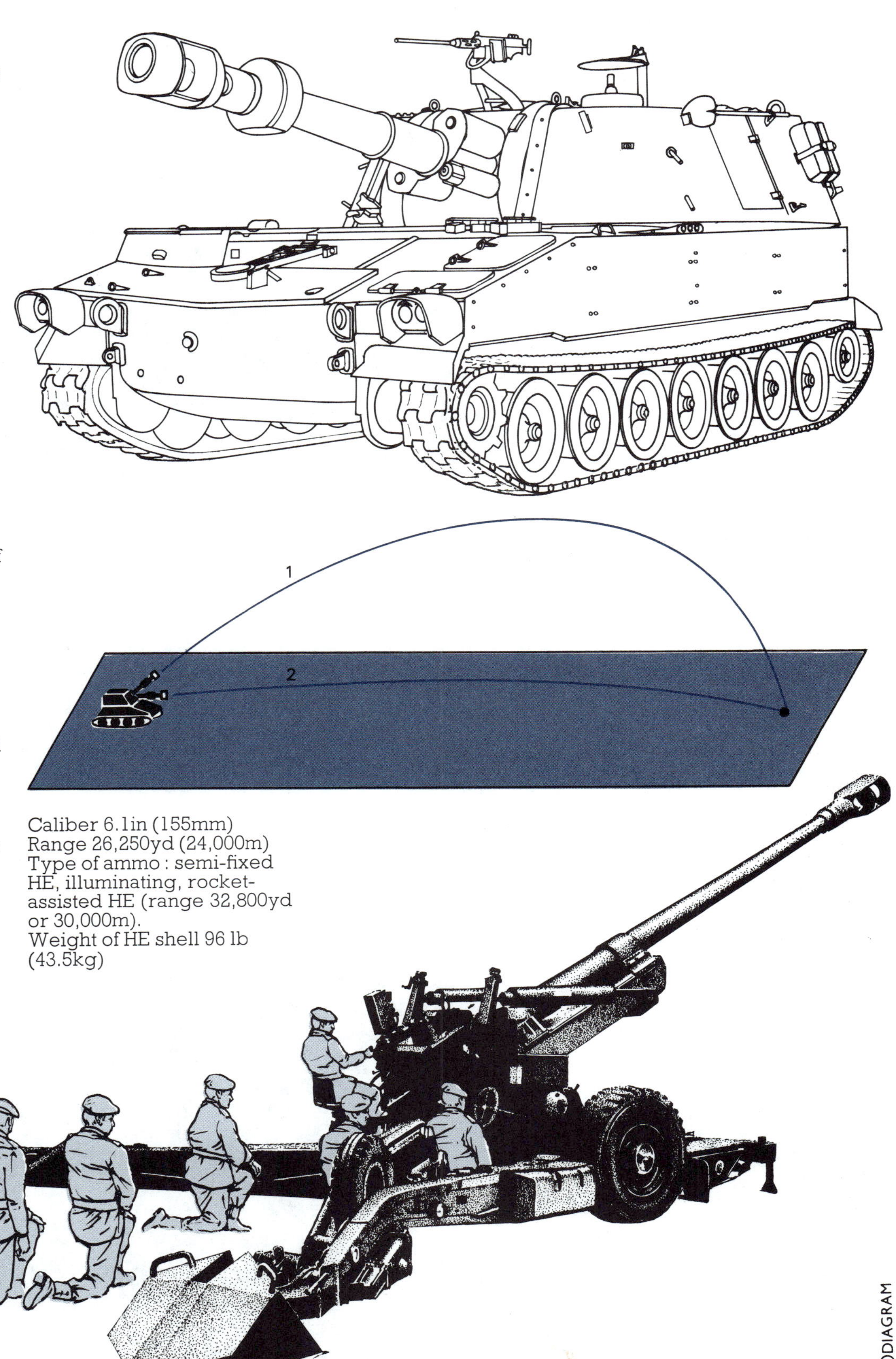

High- and low-angle fire (right) By varying the size of the charge, a modern separate-loading howitzer such as the M109 (see above) can cause two shells to hit the target at the same instant. First a small charge is used to fire a shell on a high, slow trajectory (**1**). Then a heavier charge is used to fire the second shell on a fast, flat trajectory (**2**).

Field Howitzer 70 (right) The FH70, a combined West German, Italian and British project, is one of the most advanced medium field pieces in use. It has excellent performance figures, and is fitted with an auxiliary motor to assist in maneuvering the weapon into position.

Caliber 6.1in (155mm)
Range 26,250yd (24,000m)
Type of ammo : semi-fixed HE, illuminating, rocket-assisted HE (range 32,800yd or 30,000m).
Weight of HE shell 96 lb (43.5kg)

Siege and railroad artillery

The deployment of the biggest artillery pieces, movable either by rail or piecemeal by road, was practicable only in the static conditions of siege warfare. The heyday of these weapons was in WW1, in the early attacks against fortresses and later in support of the trench systems. Although some survived into WW2, their role of heavy and long range bombardment was taken over by bomber aircraft.

German 42cm (16.5in) Siege Howitzer (right), a version of the original "Big Berthas" that destroyed the concrete and steel forts defending Belgium in 1914. Its shell weighed 205 lb (930kg).

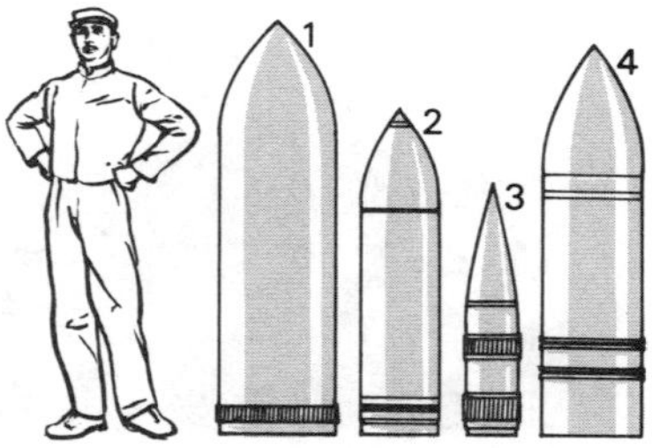

Size of shell (left) The shells for the four weapons shown on these two pages are drawn in scale with each other and with the figure of a man.
1 42cm "Big Bertha"
2 12in M4 Siege Howitzer
3 21cm "Paris Gun"
4 40cm Modèle 1916

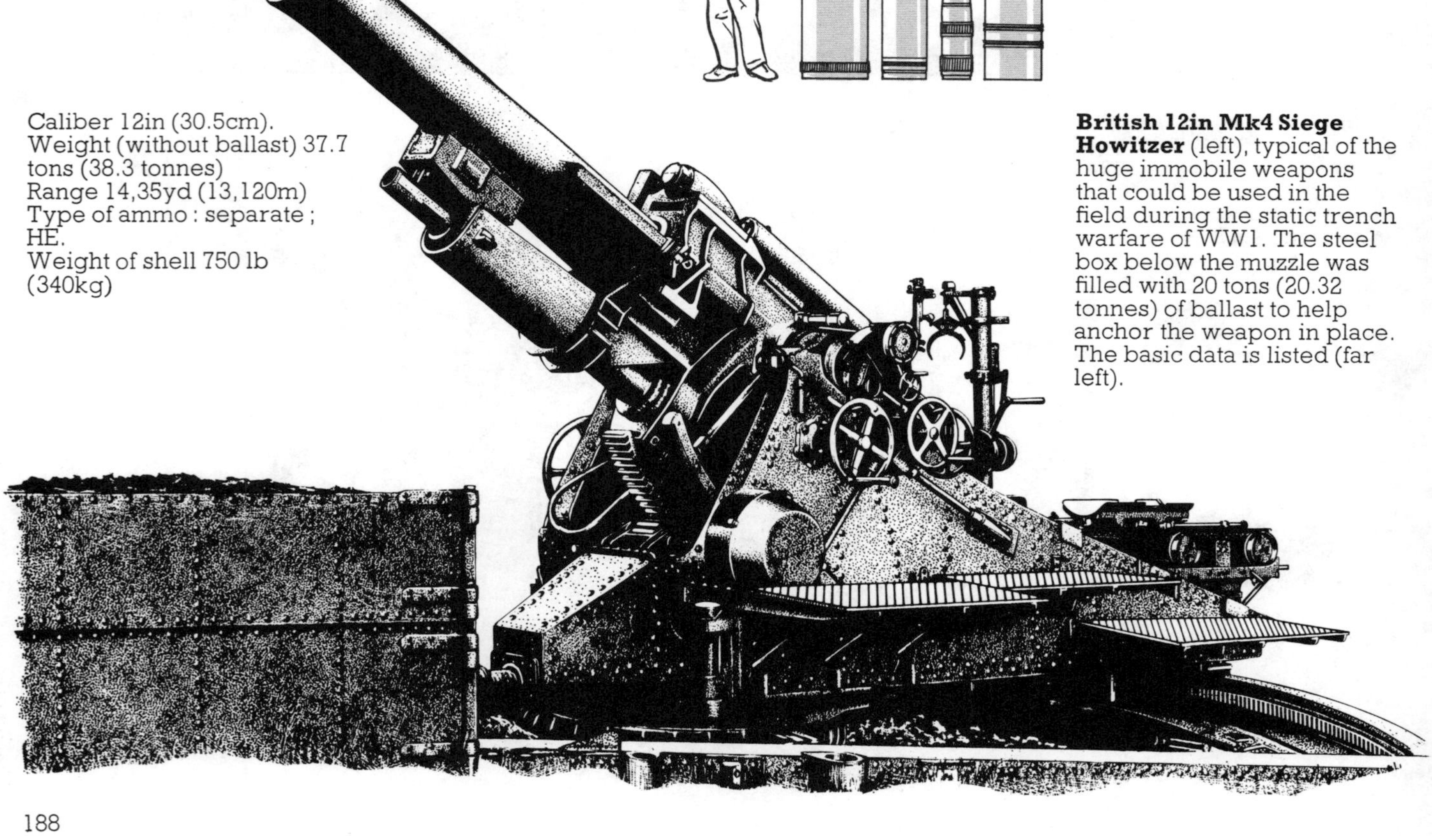

Caliber 12in (30.5cm).
Weight (without ballast) 37.7 tons (38.3 tonnes)
Range 14,35yd (13,120m)
Type of ammo : separate ; HE.
Weight of shell 750 lb (340kg)

British 12in Mk4 Siege Howitzer (left), typical of the huge immobile weapons that could be used in the field during the static trench warfare of WW1. The steel box below the muzzle was filled with 20 tons (20.32 tonnes) of ballast to help anchor the weapon in place. The basic data is listed (far left).

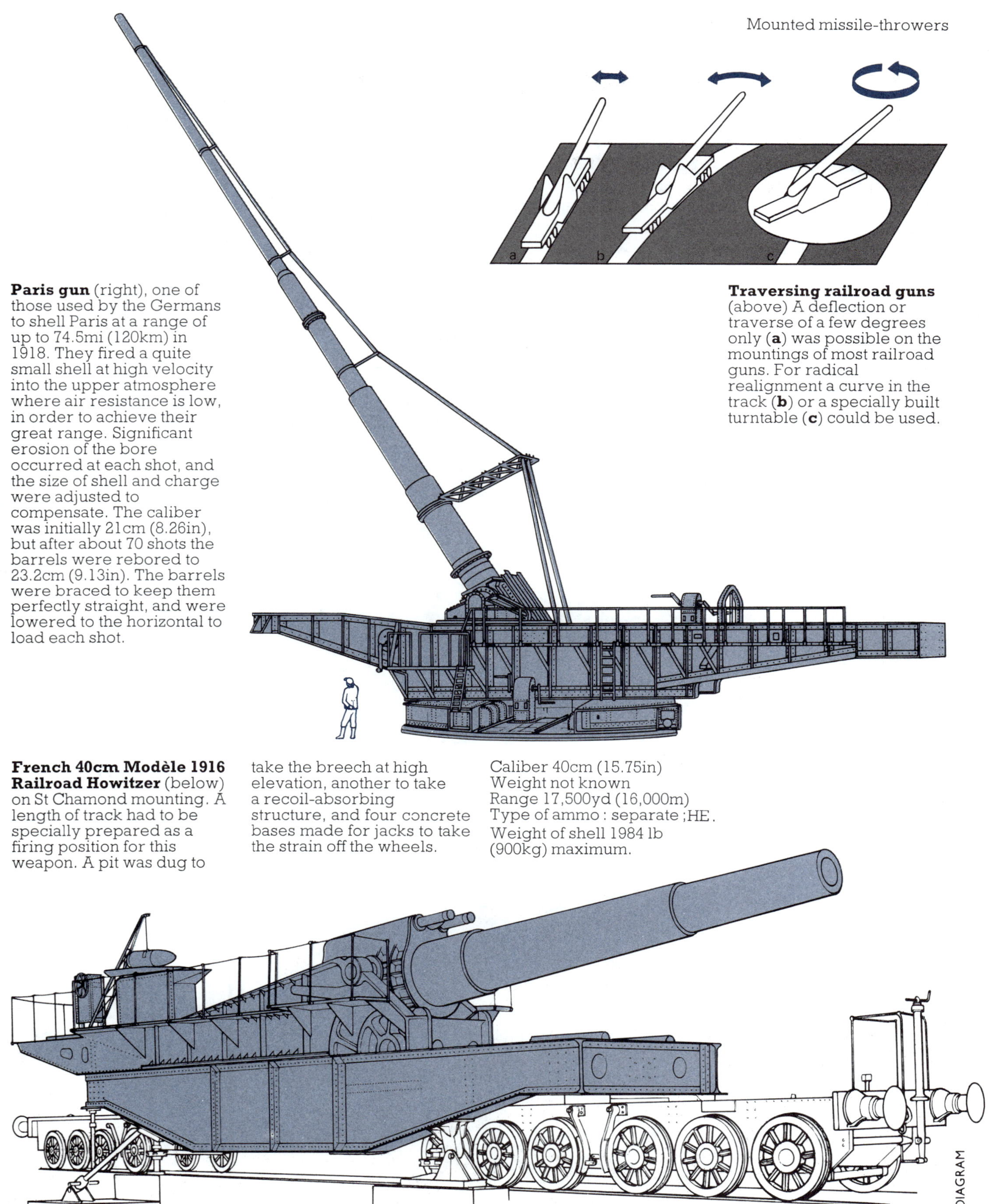

Traversing railroad guns (above) A deflection or traverse of a few degrees only (**a**) was possible on the mountings of most railroad guns. For radical realignment a curve in the track (**b**) or a specially built turntable (**c**) could be used.

Paris gun (right), one of those used by the Germans to shell Paris at a range of up to 74.5mi (120km) in 1918. They fired a quite small shell at high velocity into the upper atmosphere where air resistance is low, in order to achieve their great range. Significant erosion of the bore occurred at each shot, and the size of shell and charge were adjusted to compensate. The caliber was initially 21cm (8.26in), but after about 70 shots the barrels were rebored to 23.2cm (9.13in). The barrels were braced to keep them perfectly straight, and were lowered to the horizontal to load each shot.

French 40cm Modèle 1916 Railroad Howitzer (below) on St Chamond mounting. A length of track had to be specially prepared as a firing position for this weapon. A pit was dug to take the breech at high elevation, another to take a recoil-absorbing structure, and four concrete bases made for jacks to take the strain off the wheels.

Caliber 40cm (15.75in)
Weight not known
Range 17,500yd (16,000m)
Type of ammo : separate ;HE.
Weight of shell 1984 lb (900kg) maximum.

Pack artillery

Since the early 19th century, armies operating in mountainous country have deployed light guns or howitzers that can be broken down into several loads for transport by mule. Some armies have used similar weapons for the close support of infantry in any terrain. A new role for these light pieces emerged in WW2, for airborne delivery in support of parachute and glider troops.

Pack mule (left) carrying the barrel of a mountain howitzer. In steep terrain, the good power-to-weight ratio and the high-angle fire of a howitzer make it preferable to the true gun. The mule has still not been completely ousted by helicopter or parachute delivery.

British 10-pounder Mountain Gun (right) Issued to the mountain batteries of the British-Indian Army between 1901 and c. 1915. It could be carried by five mules, the barrel being separated into two lengths. This form of jointed barrel gave rise to the nickname, "screw-gun." No recoil system was fitted.

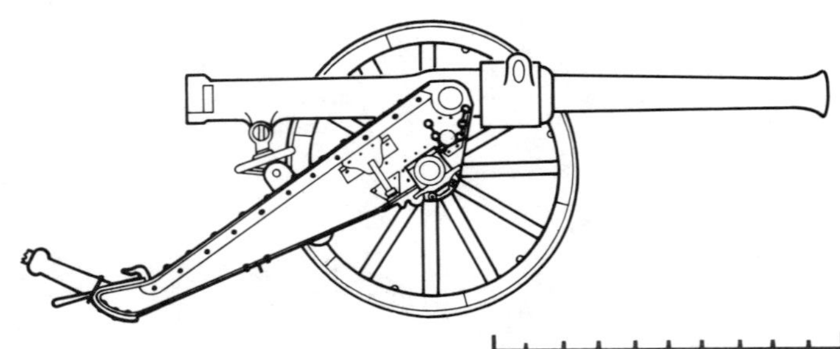

Caliber 2.75in (70mm)
Range 6000yd (5500m)
Type of ammo : separate loading ; shrapnel.
Weight of shell 10 lb (4.5kg)

Japanese 70mm Type 92 Infantry Gun (right), used to great effect in WW2, when it was often man-packed through the jungle. It was fitted with sheet steel wheels and a shield. The height of one or both wheels could be adjusted to suit the ground. Still used in China and Vietnam.

Caliber 2.75in (70mm)
Range 3000yd (2745m)
Type of ammo : semi-fixed ; HE, smoke, shrapnel, armor-piercing.
Weight of HE shell 8.36 lb (3.8kg)

US 75mm M1A1 Pack Howitzer (right), shown on the M8 carriage. Originally designed for carriage in six mule loads, it was more often delivered by parachute or glider in WW2. After the War, its designation was changed to M116. Used by the British 1st Airborne Division at Arnhem in 1944.

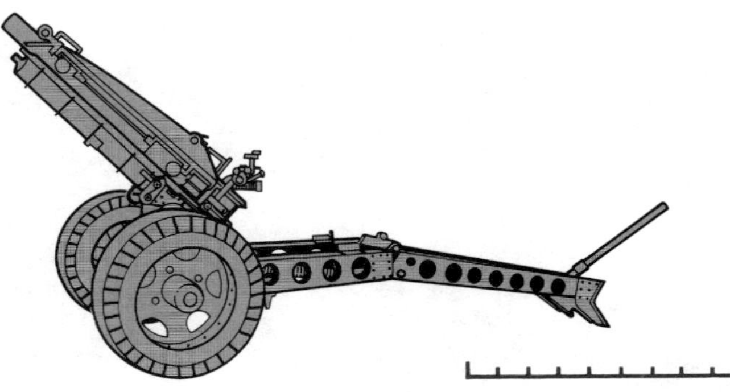

Caliber 2.95in (75mm)
Range 9760yd (8925m)
Type of ammo : fixed (HEAT) and semi-fixed (HE).
Weight of HE shell (M41A1) 13.76 lb (6.24kg)

Italian 105/14 Model 56 105mm Pack Howitzer (right) Introduced in 1957, this versatile weapon was later adopted by at least 17 other countries, including Britain. It is suited to transport by aircraft, helicopter, parachute, light towing vehicle, or in 11 mule loads. It can even be man-packed for short distances.

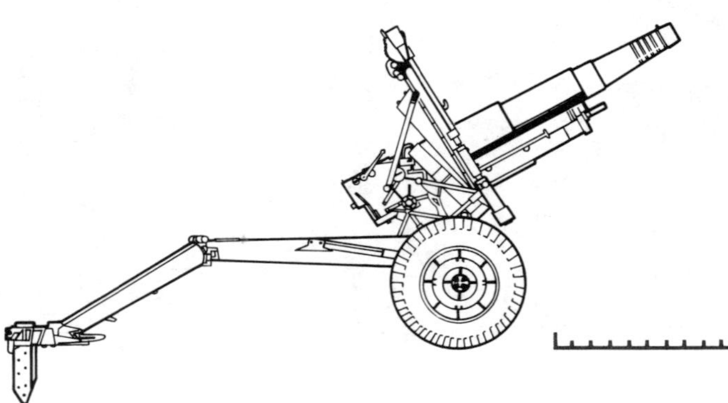

Caliber 4.13in (105mm)
Range 11,564yd (10,575m)
Type of ammo : semi- fixed (HE, smoke illuminating) ; fixed (HEAT).
Weight of HE shell 42 lb (19.06kg)

Coastal and fortress artillery

Artillery of all sizes, but especially the largest, had always been a vital element in any fixed defense system. The coming of breech-loading made it easier to protect the crew now that they did not need access to the gun muzzle, so turret, cupola and casemate mountings proliferated. New technology allowed bigger and more complex guns, but by the end of WW2 rockets and aircraft had made them all obsolete.

Types of emplacement (below) Illustrated in diagrammatic form are the four main types used for permanent fortifications.
1 Casemate The gun fires through an embrasure in the wall of the fort, at which point also its carriage is pivoted.
2 Barbette The centrally pivoted gun fires over a parapet curved to match its arc of traverse.
3 Disappearing mount The gun is mounted in a pit, where it is loaded. It is raised only briefly to fire. Once a common type of coastal emplacement.
4 Cupola The gun protrudes from a steel dome that is usually set in concrete, its rim flush with the ground. Used in the Maginot line.

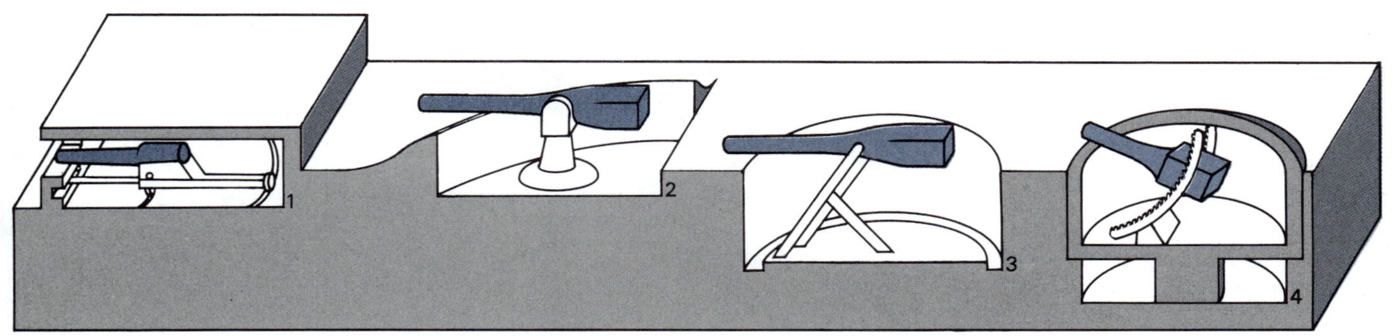

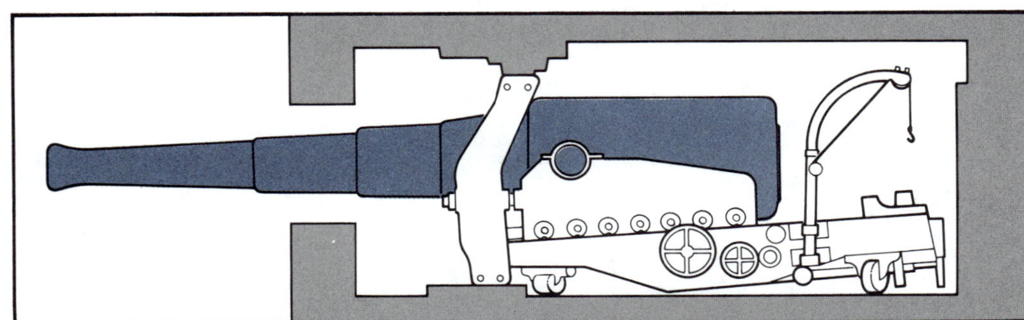

British 12in Coast Defense Gun (left) as mounted in an armored casemate c. 1881. To control recoil, hydraulic buffers were linked to the angled struts at the front of the carriage, to spread the strain between roof and floor. Used in the defenses of Portsmouth.
Range 8000yd (7315m).
Weight of shell 714 lb (323kg)

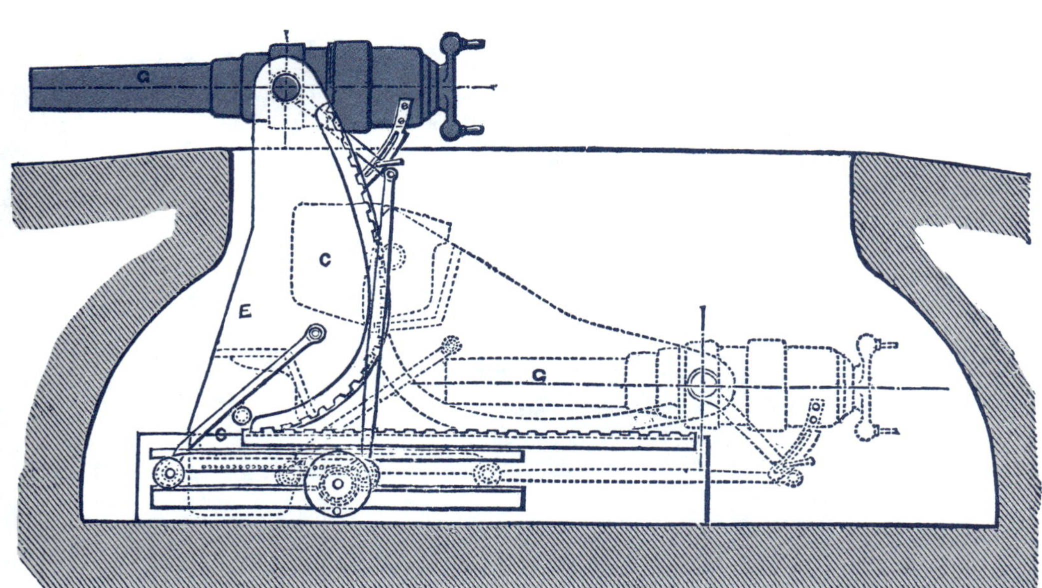

Disappearing mount (left), one of the first of its kind, designed by Captain Moncrieff of Edinburgh. When fired, the recoil forced the gun down into the pit on its curved ratchet cradle. At the same time a counterweight was lifted, so storing the energy needed to raise the gun for the next shot. Thus the crew was well protected and the gun exposed for the minimum time. Later types of disappearing carriage were used in coastal batteries until the demise of such defense systems after WW2. The illustration shows an early Armstrong breech-loader fitted on the mount. (From Cooke's "Naval Ordnance and Gunnery," 1875.)

Automatic cannon

Automatic cannon are in a sense scaled-up machine guns, capable of firing projectiles of a caliber and complexity that put them in the artillery category. Here we explain their essential features and list the roles in which they are used. More examples and information will be found under the headings of tank guns, anti-aircraft guns and naval guns.

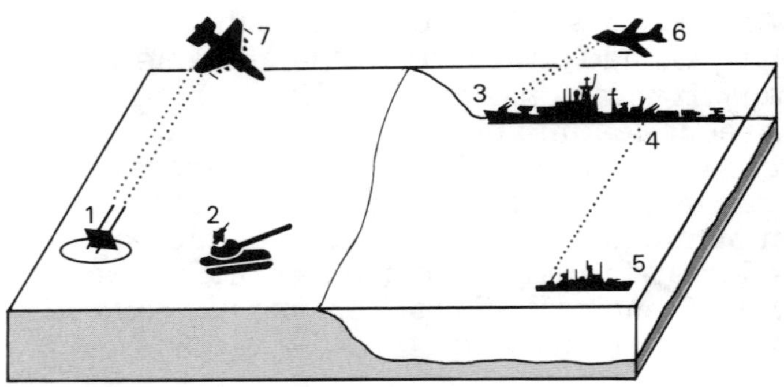

Uses for automatic cannon (above) These weapons fill a gap between machine guns of small arm calibers—too weak for some roles—and true artillery, which is often too cumbersome and slow firing for certain tasks. The variety of projectiles and the high volume of fire that they can deliver make automatic cannon useful in a number of roles:

Land
1 Anti-aircraft
2 On armored vehicles

Sea
3 Anti-aircraft
4 Anti-torpedo boat
5 On small fast boats

Air
6 On fighter aircraft
7 On ground-attack aircraft

Maxim 1-pounder "Pom-pom" (right) This was in effect an oversized version of Maxim's famous machine gun of the 1880s. The model shown is British, of WW1 date, on a high-angle field carriage. An earlier version had been used by both sides in the Anglo-Boer War (1899-1902). The Maxim was a truly automatic gun, deriving the energy for its mechanism from the explosion of the cartridge. Simpler, hand-cranked cannon had been used to defend warships against small torpedo boats since the 1870s.

Caliber 1.457in (37mm)
Range (on mount shown) 4500yd (4110m)
Weight of shell 1 lb (0.45kg)

The mechanism (below) of the Swiss KAA 20mm cannon, illustrating the similarity of a typical automatic cannon to a machine gun. The ammunition is belt-fed. Although a gas piston is used to unlock the breech, the breech-block is then forced to the rear by residual pressure in the bore. The mechanism is thus classed as a "blowback" design (see p. 211).

1 Bore
2 Gas port
3 Gas piston
4 Firing pin
5 Breech-block or bolt
6 Bolt tail
7 Travel of bolt to rear
8 Bolt buffer
a Cartridge in chamber
b Next cartridge to be fed
c Empty case ejected

Swiss KAA 20mm automatic cannon (right), one of the famous Oerlikon designs in current use. The Swiss firms of Hispano-Suiza and Oerlikon have always been leaders in this field.

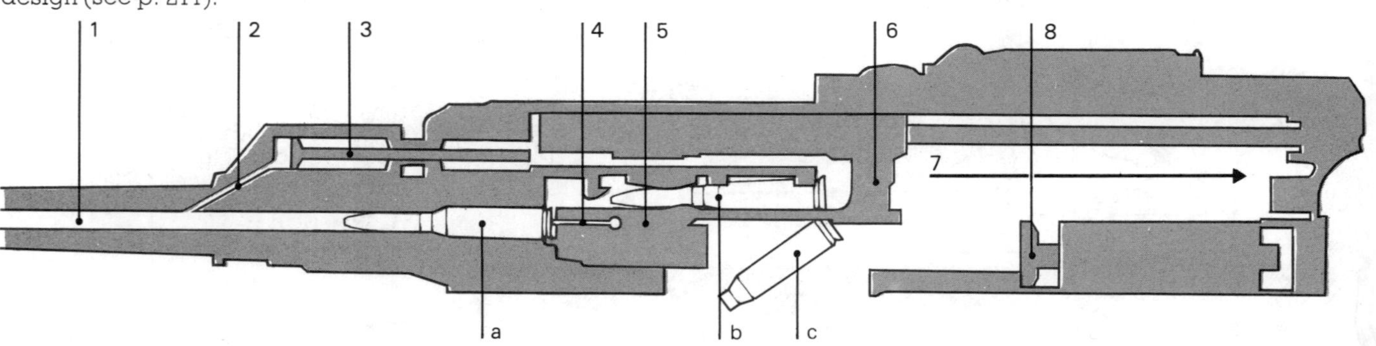

Aircraft armed with cannon (right) A selection of mountings is illustrated here by specific examples.
1 Firing through airscrew axis of German WW2 Bf109G Messerschmitt fighter.
2 Four wing-mounted cannon on British WW2 Mk9 Spitfire fighter.
3 In underwing "pod" of modern US Navy A-7 fighter.
4 In "chin" mount on US Huey Cobra helicopter.

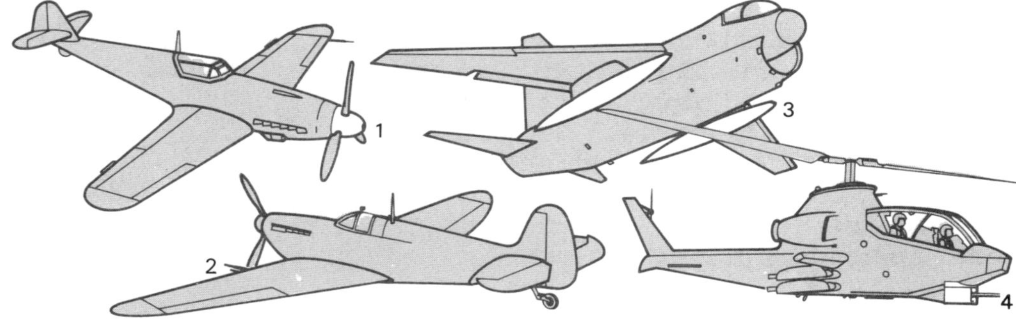

Aden 30mm cannon (right), a British development of a German design, in use as an aircraft gun since the 1950s. It is a belt-fed, five-chambered revolver, operated by recoil and a gas piston.
Weight 192 lb (87kg)
Cyclic rate of fire 1200-1400 rounds/min

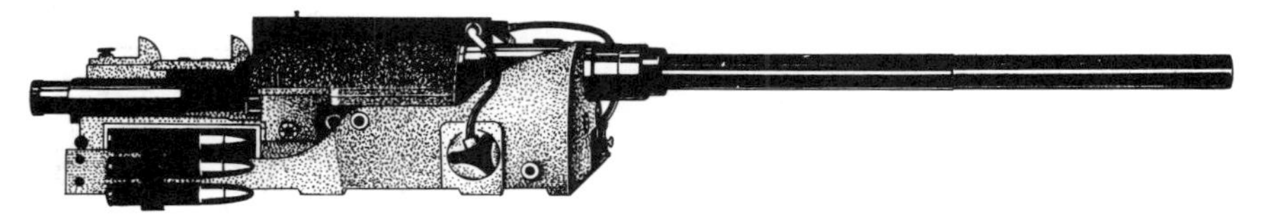

US M61 A1 (right) This is an electrically powered 20mm cannon that can be fitted in helicopters or fixed-wing aircraft. It is based on the Gatling gun principle (see p. 207) and has six revolving barrels. Their combined rate of fire is 6000 rounds per minute, or about 100 per second. There is a version adapted for air-defense use on the ground, the M168.

US 20mm cartridge (below) of the M50 series for aircraft cannon, in use since the 1950s. This is only one of many varieties of 20mm ammunition from around the world, few of which are interchangeable. 20mm is considered the minimum caliber in the category of automatic cannon. This type has an electric primer.

Cross section (right) through a US M56 A1 high explosive incendiary shell, one of two operational types loaded in the M50 series cartridge shown (below). The other is an armor-piercing incendiary projectile.
1 Copper driving band
2 Steel body
3 High explosive
4 Incendiary agent
5 M505 fuze (not sectioned)

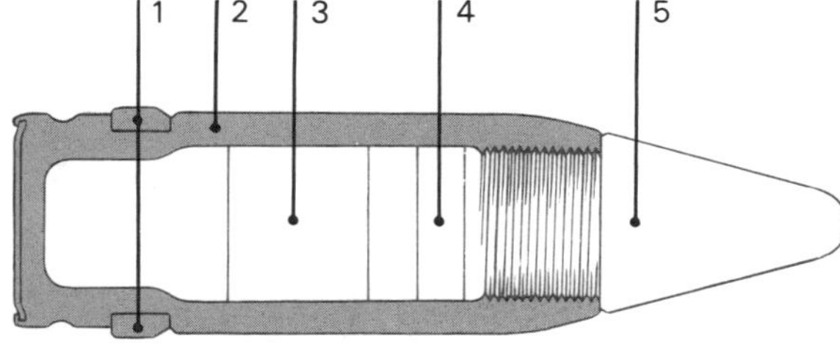

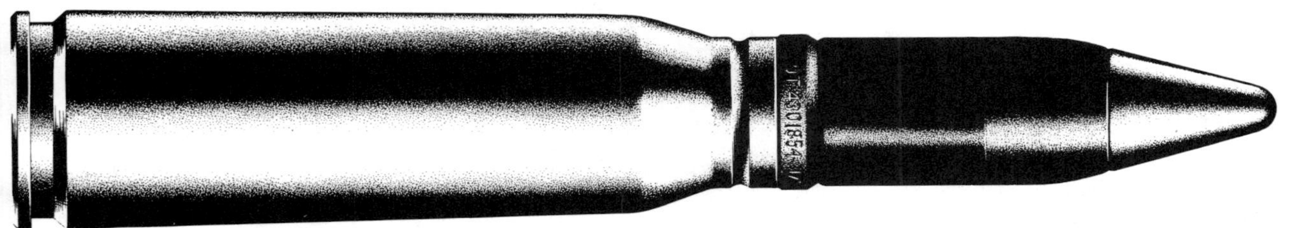

Anti-aircraft guns

The introduction of military aircraft in WW1 created a need for specialized Anti-Aircraft (AA) guns on mounts that allowed high-angle fire and an all-round traverse. By WW2 there were two general types of AA gun: heavy, single-shot guns for attacking high-flying planes, and light, fast-firing guns for low-level defense. The former have now largely been replaced by guided missiles.

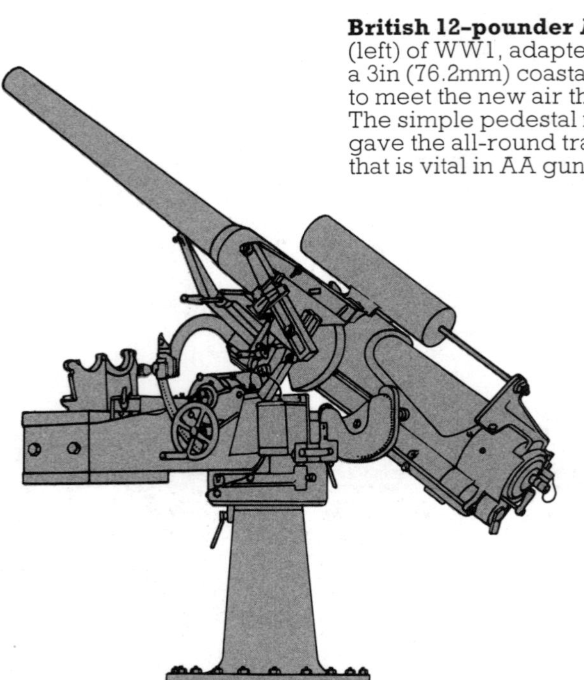

British 12-pounder AA gun (left) of WW1, adapted from a 3in (76.2mm) coastal gun to meet the new air threat. The simple pedestal mount gave the all-round traverse that is vital in AA guns.

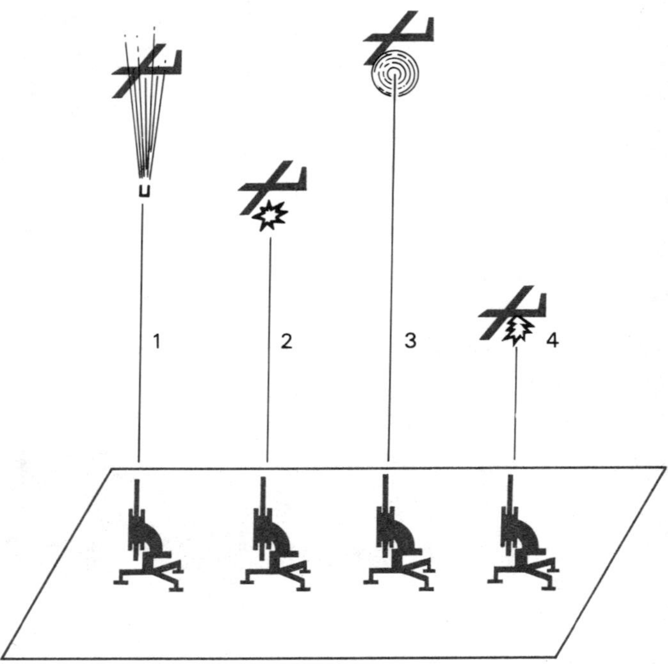

AA shells and fuzes (above)
1 Shrapnel shell fitted with a time fuze was used sometimes in WW1 to spray the path of the plane with a hail of bullets.
2 High explosive (HE) shell, with a time fuze set to explode on reaching the height of the plane, was the main heavy AA projectile of both World Wars.
3 Proximity fuzes, first developed in WW2, make HE shells more effective. They detect the presence of a plane within lethal range by using radio waves, and then detonate the shell.
4 Impact fuzed HE shells are commonly fired from the smaller, fast-firing AA guns used against low-flying aircraft.
AA shells are usually made to self-destruct if they miss the target, to lessen the danger to those below.

Swedish Bofors guns (left), mostly of 40mm (1.57in) caliber, have been used by most of the world's armies since the 1930s for low-level air defense. The example shown is the post-war L70, with improved ammunition and powered, radar-directed aiming. It is shown on a mobile mounting, but static, self-propelled and naval mounts have also been used.

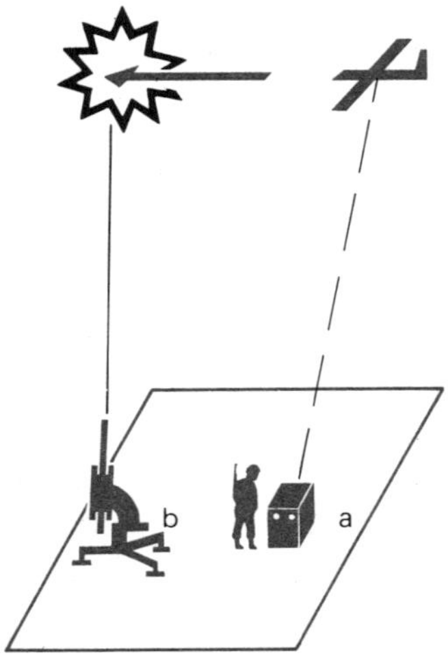

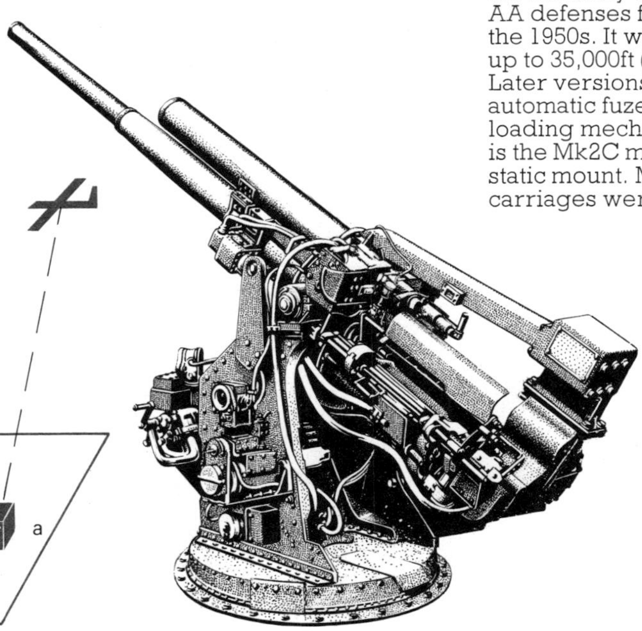

3.7in (94mm) AA gun (left), the mainstay of British heavy AA defenses from 1937 into the 1950s. It was effective at up to 35,000ft (10,700m). Later versions had automatic fuze-setting and loading mechanisms. Shown is the Mk2C model on a static mount. Mobile carriages were also made.

Predictors (above) In the 1930s, mechanical "predictors" (**a**) were devised that converted observations of the target's path automatically into data for elevation, direction and fuze-setting at the gun (**b**). Several guns could be linked to one predictor. The gunners simply obeyed these instructions and, in theory, shell and plane met at the predicted point.

88mm FLAK36 (right) The Flugabwehrkanone of 1936 was an early version of the famous German 88mm (3.46in) gun, the basis of several AA and anti-tank weapons of WW2. It was effective at up to about 26,250ft (8000m). It is shown on the mobile mount, ready for action with the wheels removed.

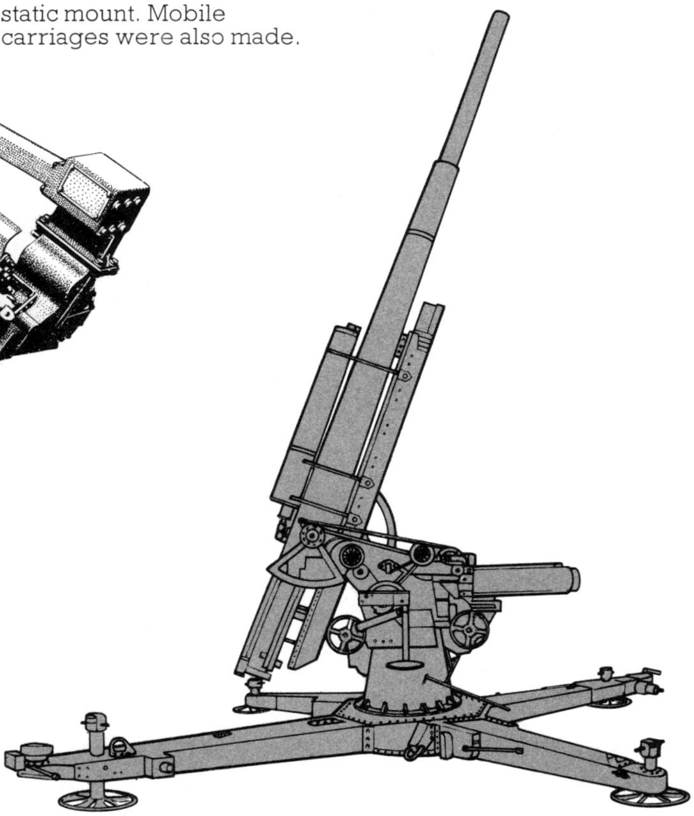

French AMX DCA 30 (left), a 30mm AA gun, typical of the sophistication of modern light AA guns. It has two 30mm (1.18in) automatic cannon and a radar fire-control system in a revolving turret, mounted on an AMX 13 type tracked chassis. Such mountings are necessary to allow the guns to match the mobility and protection of other elements in a modern armored division.

Although guided missiles have all but replaced heavy AA guns, smaller caliber fast-firing guns can still be effective against low-level air attack. Such guns are still used on static, towed and self-propelled mounts in many armies.

Tank guns

A major development in artillery in this century has been its adaptation for use in Armored Fighting Vehicles (AFVs). Self-propelled guns and howitzers, some of which are armored, have been dealt with under the heading of field artillery, of which they are now a major sub-variety. Here we deal specifically with the main armament of tanks and armored cars, which are used well forward on the battlefield in their own, specialized, aggressive roles. However, a full discussion of the tank as a vehicle and a complete weapon system is beyond the scope of this book. We concentrate on the gun itself—the types of gun and the ways used to mount them in tanks—and on the aids now used to assist accuracy. Armor-piercing ammunition will be found on p. 199, and tank machine guns on p. 218.

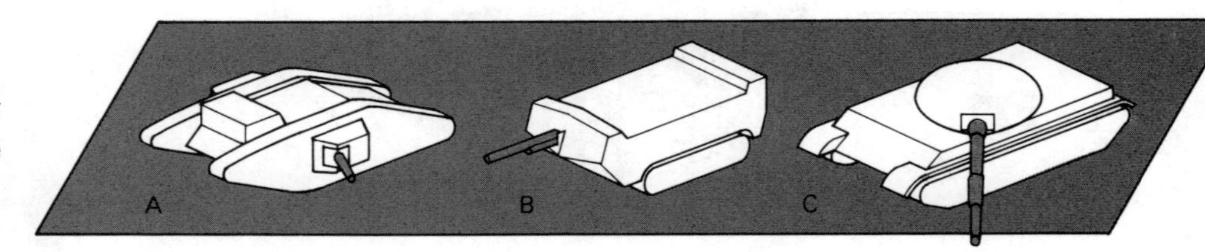

Gun mountings (right) British tanks of WW1 — the first to see action — had two guns, mounted in box-like "sponsons," one on each side of the hull (**A**). Some tanks have been fitted with one forward-firing gun mounted directly on the hull (**B**). The commonest arrangement is to mount the gun in a revolving turret, so permitting all-round traverse (**C**).

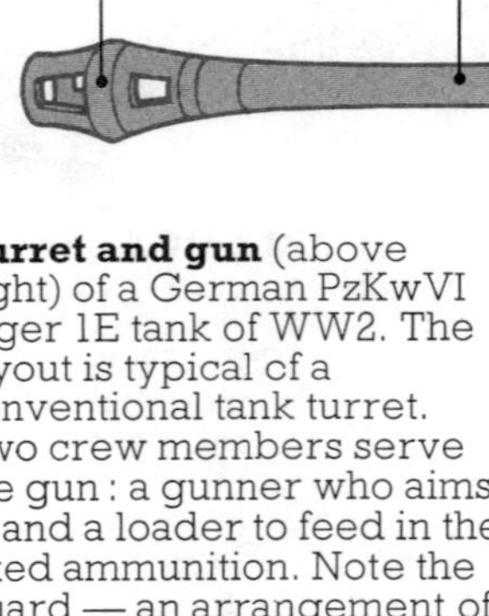

Turret and gun (above right) of a German PzKwVI Tiger 1E tank of WW2. The layout is typical of a conventional tank turret. Two crew members serve the gun: a gunner who aims it, and a loader to feed in the fixed ammunition. Note the guard — an arrangement of rails to keep the crew safely out of the path of the recoiling breech.

a Muzzle-brake
b Barrel
c Mantlet
d Recoil cylinders
e Sliding breech-block
f Loader's seat
g Elevating wheel
h Fine traverse wheel
i Sight
j Gunner's seat
k Turret drive gear
l Guard
m Bin for empty cases
n Tank commander's seat

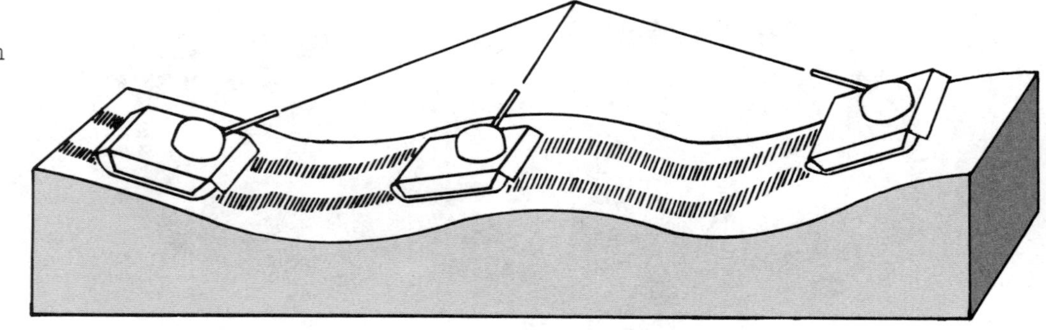

Stabilization of the gun (right) Soon after WW2, tanks began to be fitted with stabilizing systems, usually worked by hydraulics. The stabilizer keeps the tank gun pointing at the selected target, in both horizontal and vertical planes, however uneven the ground beneath the tank.

Ranging machine guns (right) A heavy-caliber machine gun is often fitted parallel to the main gun. Its ammunition follows the same trajectory as that of the main gun and can be seen in flight and on impact. After aiming, a burst is fired (**1**); if this hits, the main gun is instantly fired (**2**) and a hit is guaranteed. Lasers can now be used in the same way.

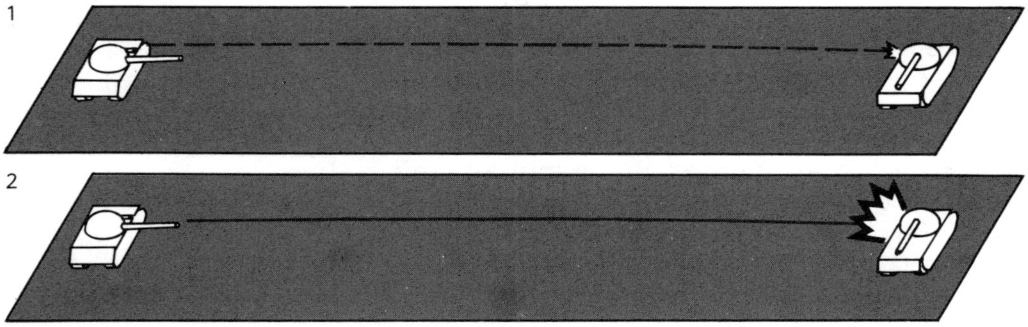

Stridvagn 103A (right) or the Swedish S-Tank caused a stir among tank designers in the 1970s. In order to fit a self-loading breech mechanism (too bulky for a revolving turret), its 105mm gun is mounted directly on the tank hull (**a**). The suspension system allows the whole tank to be tilted for elevation (**b**) or turned to aim left and right (**c**).

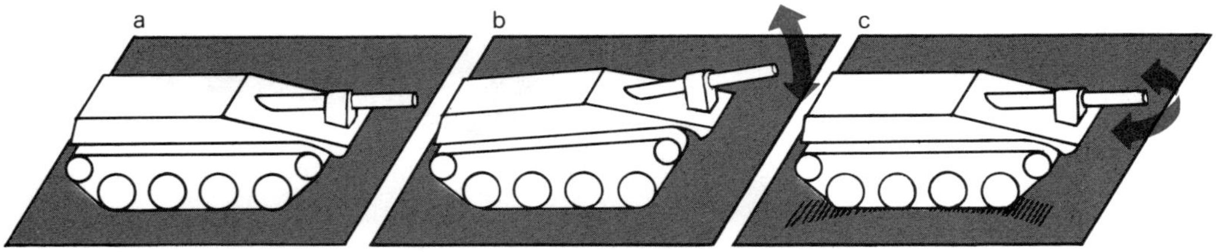

Rifled versus smoothbore guns (right) Most tanks have used rifled guns (**A**). However, in recent years many Soviet tanks have been fitted with smoothbore guns (**B**) firing fin-stabilized projectiles. This is thought to be in order to exploit the maximum effectiveness of the HEAT type of shell (see p. 199), which is hindered if spun by rifling.

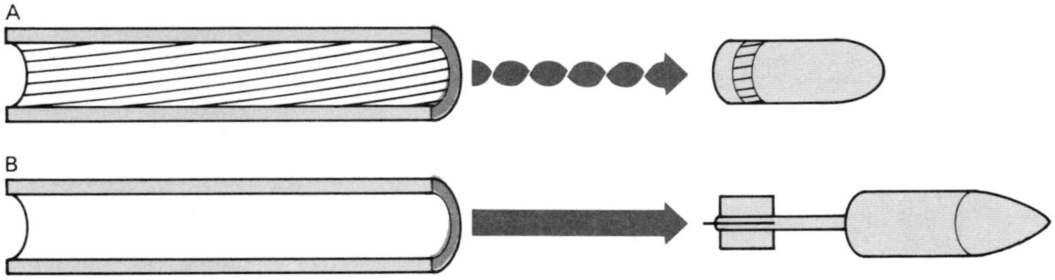

Rarden 30mm cannon (right) This is a British automatic cannon for light AFVs, and entered service in 1974. It illustrates one modern solution to the priorities of AFV gun design. The emphasis is on accuracy, with a slow rate of fire of 90 rounds/min. It is designed to penetrate the armor of Armored Personnel Carriers (APCs) and the side armor of main battle tanks. The gun is loaded from the rear with clips of three rounds of ammunition. The diagram (lower right) shows a sectional top view of the turret in which the Rarden is mounted. Note how little the crew's fighting compartment (**A**) is intruded on by the gun's compact breech (**B**). The turret can be mounted on a choice of light tanks, armored cars and APCs.

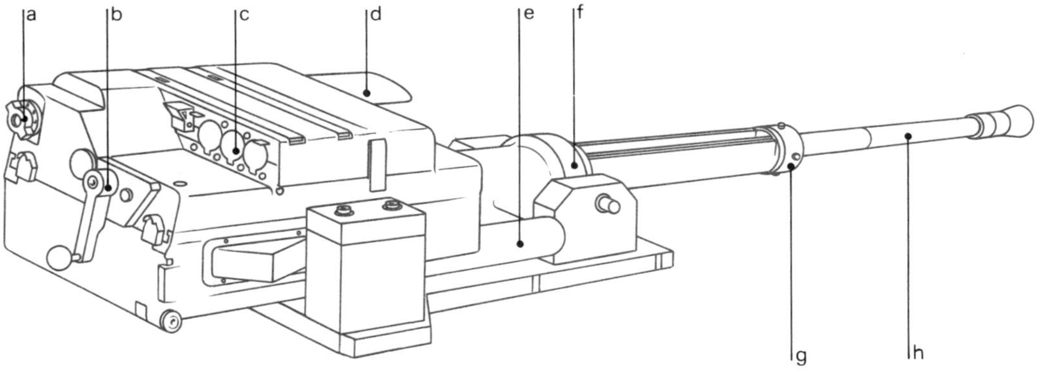

Parts of the Rarden cannon (above)
a Firing button
b Loading handle
c Loading apertures
d Ejection tube
e Recuperator
f Front barrel bearing
g Barrel vibration damping pads
h Barrel

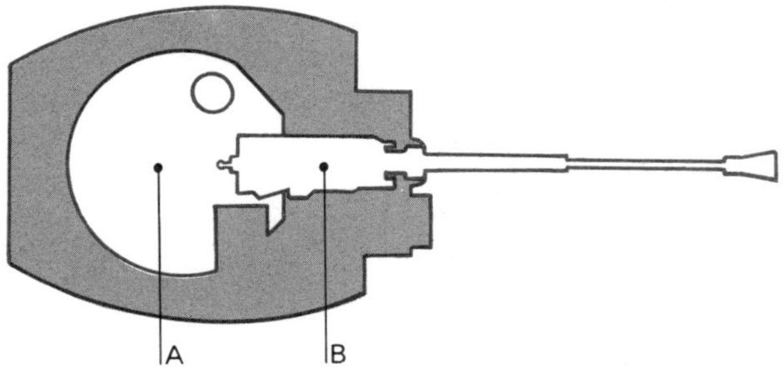

Anti-tank guns

The first specialized anti-tank weapons were outsize high-velocity rifles. In WW2 these were soon found inadequate, and a process of escalation ensued, with the thickness of tank armor and the power of anti-tank guns leapfrogging each other. Some anti-aircraft and field guns were also used in this role. Since WW2, recoilless guns (see p. 200) and rockets (p. 254) have all but replaced the conventional anti-tank gun.

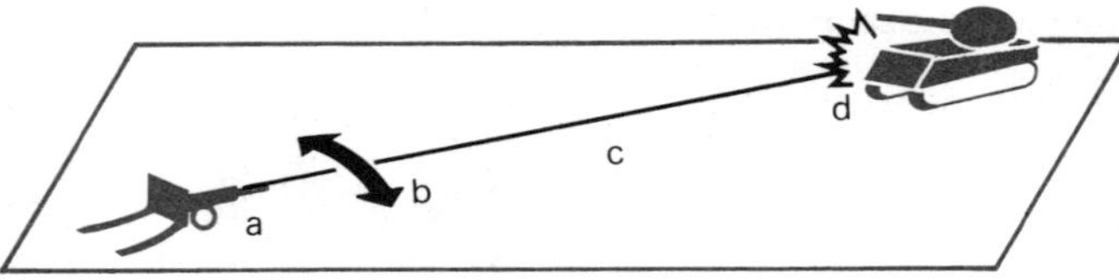

Characteristics (above) that are desirable in an anti-tank gun: a low shape (**a**) to aid concealment; a good traverse (**b**) to follow a moving target; a fast, flat trajectory (**c**) to aid a first shot kill before the tank can fire; and the power in the projectile to destroy any type of opposing tank (**d**).

Tankgewehr 1918 (right) The first weapon made specifically to attack tanks was this German rifle of WW1. It was simply a scaled-up, single-shot Mauser bolt-action rifle on a bipod. It was well able to pierce the armor of WW1 tanks. More sophisticated anti-tank rifles were still on issue in most armies in 1939.

Abbreviations
A/Tk Anti-tank
AP Armor piercing
APT Armor piercing tracer
MV Muzzle velocity

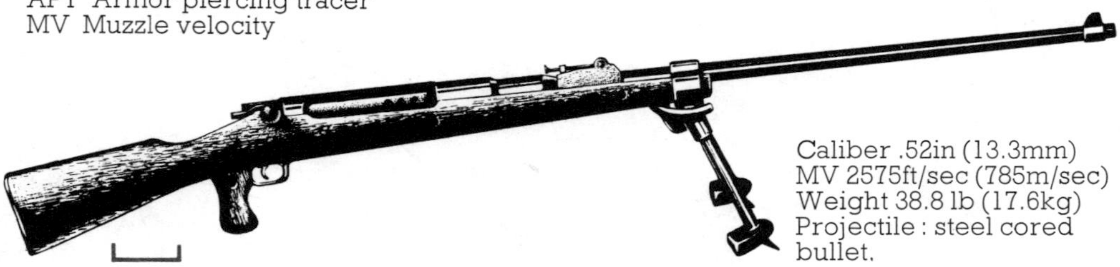

Caliber .52in (13.3mm)
MV 2575ft/sec (785m/sec)
Weight 38.8 lb (17.6kg)
Projectile: steel cored bullet.

37mm PAK36 (right) The Panzerabwehrkanone of 1936 was the German anti-tank gun at the outbreak of WW2. Most armies had comparable guns to supplement their anti-tank rifles, but both were soon outmoded by thicker tank armor. A new projectile was later made to extend the PAK36's service life. It was a large fin-stabilized bomb, fired from the gun muzzle.

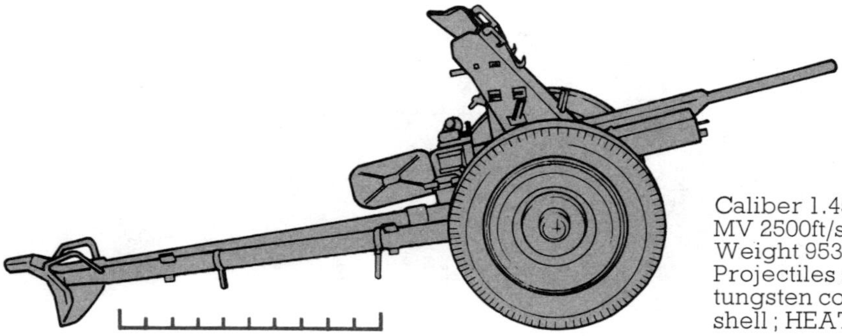

Caliber 1.45in (37mm)
MV 2500ft/sec (762m/sec)
Weight 953 lb (432kg)
Projectiles: APT shell; tungsten cored APT; HE shell; HEAT bomb.

British 6-pounder (right), the anti-tank gun adopted in 1941 to replace earlier, underpowered weapons. It was itself superseded by a 17-pounder gun in 1942, but was not withdrawn at once. It is still in use with the armies of at least 12 Third World countries.

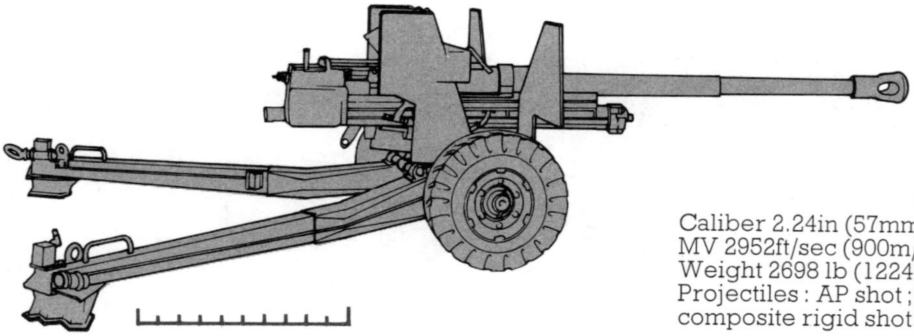

Caliber 2.24in (57mm)
MV 2952ft/sec (900m/sec)
Weight 2698 lb (1224kg)
Projectiles: AP shot; APDS; composite rigid shot.

Soviet M1944 100mm anti-tank gun (right), showing how big a conventional anti-tank gun must be to defeat modern tanks. Still used in some armies, but not that of the USSR.

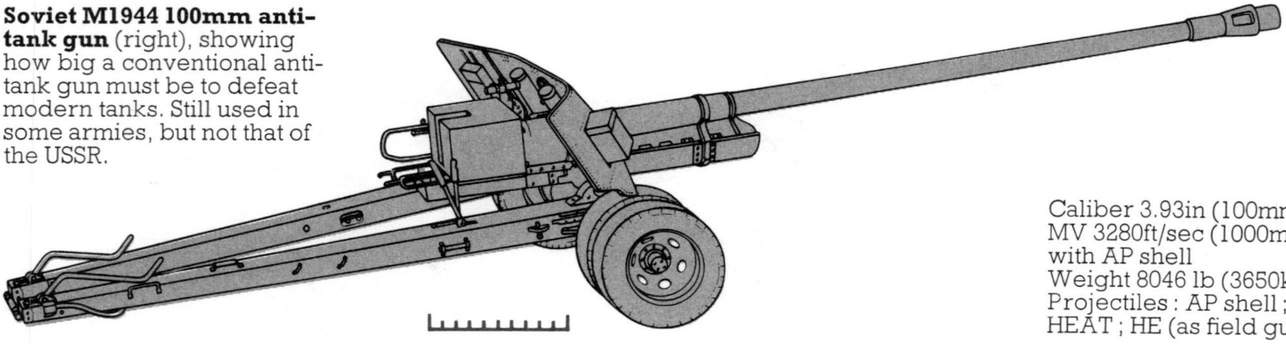

Caliber 3.93in (100mm)
MV 3280ft/sec (1000m/sec) with AP shell
Weight 8046 lb (3650kg)
Projectiles: AP shell; HEAT; HE (as field gun).

German 88mm PAK43 (right) This was developed from the famous 88mm FLAK37 anti-aircraft gun. It was towed into place on four wheels. These were then removed, and four outriggers swung out to form a stable, cruciform firing platform, as shown here. Like almost all anti-tank guns, it used fixed ammunition, but with the addition of a semi-automatic breech that ejected the cartridge case after firing.

Caliber 3.46in (88mm)
MV 3280ft/sec (1000m/sec) with APT shell
Weight 8159 lb (3700kg) in action as shown
Projectiles: APT shell; tungsten-cored composite rigid shot; HEAT; HE (as a field gun).

28mm sPzB41 (right), a German WW2 gun using the Gerlich principle. The tapered bore concentrates an increasing pressure on a decreasing base area of the shot, so multiplying the shot's velocity and energy. The version shown was for airborne troops, having a light carriage.

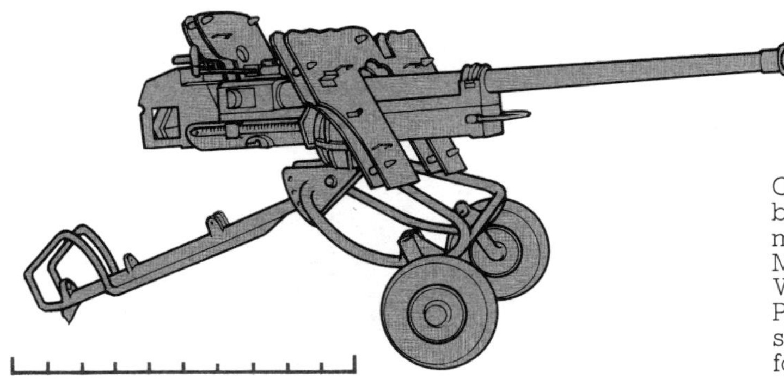

Caliber 1.1in (28mm) at the breech; .79in (20mm) at the muzzle
MV 4593ft/sec (1400m/sec)
Weight 505 lb (229kg)
Projectiles: tungsten cored skirted shot; HE shell (not for A/Tk use).

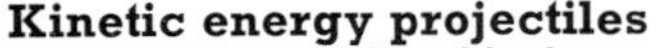

Kinetic energy projectiles (right) All use a hard bolt of steel or tungsten fired at high velocity to punch a hole through the armor plate.
a AP shot Inert, of full caliber diameter. It may have a soft metal cap to support the point during penetration.
b AP shell As for (**a**) but containing HE and a fuze in the base, to explode after penetration.
c Composite rigid shot This has a hard core inside a soft, hollow casing of full caliber diameter.
d Gerlich or arrowhead shot The "skirts" are squeezed down by the tapered bore of the gun.
e APDS or Armor-Piercing Discarding Sabot. As for (**c**) but the casing (sabot) falls away on leaving the barrel, and the core flies on at high velocity.

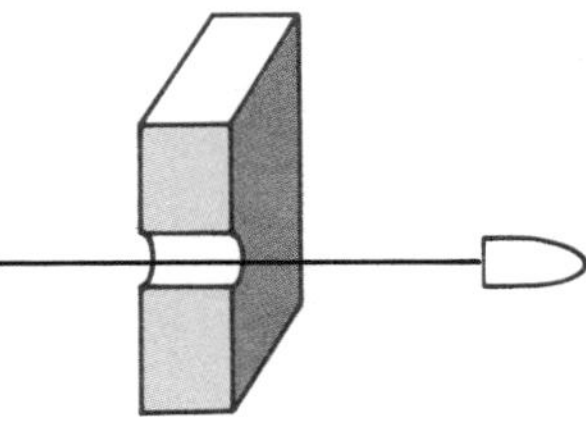

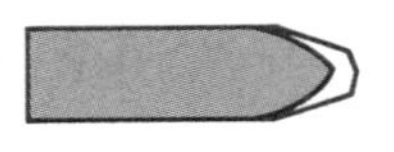

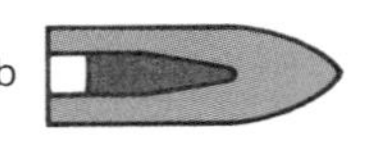

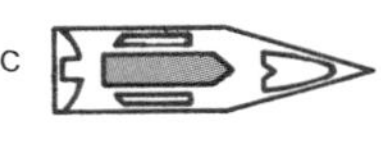

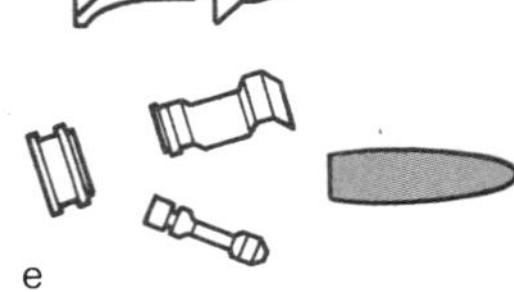

Chemical energy projectiles (right)These use high explosives to defeat armor plate, and are equally effective at any range.
1 HEAT or High Explosive Anti-Tank. This exploits the shaped or hollow charge effect, also known as the Monroe effect. A conical hollow, lined with metal, is formed at the front of the HE filling. If exploded at a short distance from the armor, the force is concentrated on a small spot, searing through the armor and injecting blast and hot metal into the tank.
2 HESH or High Explosive Squash Head. The shell has a thin casing and a base fuze. On impact, the HE spreads against the armor. On detonation, shock waves break fragments of steel off at high velocity inside the tank. Also called High Explosive Plastic (HEP).

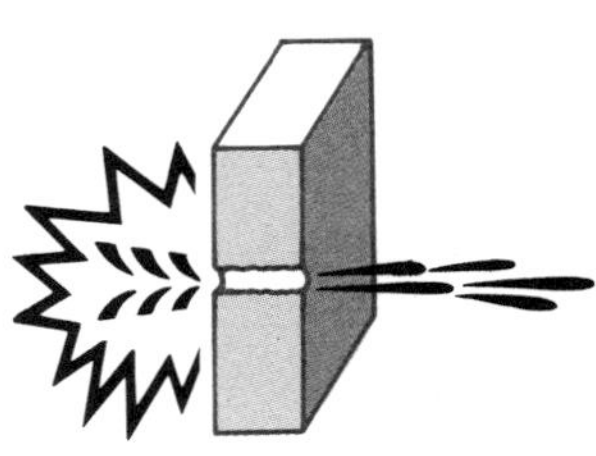

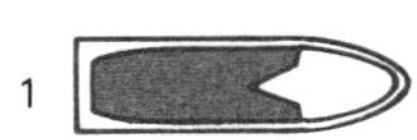

Recoilless guns

The development of recoilless guns, first put to use in WW2, provided armies with light, highly mobile artillery pieces that can nevertheless fire a heavy shell. These weapons have mostly been put to use by the infantry, either as light-support field guns, or more often as anti-tank guns. The difference between these guns and those hand-held weapons shown on pp. 156-157 is one of size and portability only.

The principle (above) of the recoilless gun is based on the balancing of thrust at each end of an open-ended barrel. The forward impetus given to the shell creates an equal reaction that is transformed into a rearward blast of gases. The barrel does not move and does not require the recoil-absorbing mechanism and heavy construction of conventional artillery.

Backblast is the main disadvantage of recoilless guns. It makes the siting of the gun difficult as there must be a large clear area behind in which the blast can dissipate. It can reveal the gun's position, damage the crew's hearing, and even kill anyone in its path. The wartime danger zone behind WOMBAT (see opposite page) is shown (right).

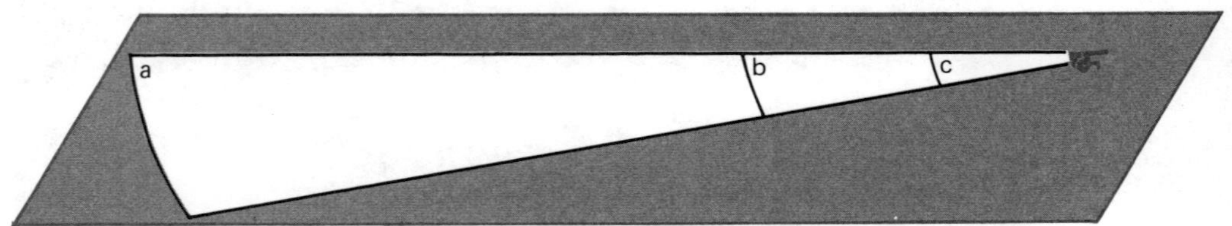

a Dangerous to troops in the open up to 100yd (91m).

b Troops within 15-35yd (14-32m) must be dug in.

c No troops may be within 15yd (14m) of the gun.

10.5cm LG40 (right) The German Leicht Geschütz of 1940 was a recoilless gun that could be dismantled for delivery by parachute. The shell was loaded first, followed by a charge in a case with a frangible plastic base that shattered and blew out rearwards on firing. A smaller 7.5cm (2.95in) version was used in the invasion of Crete in 1941.

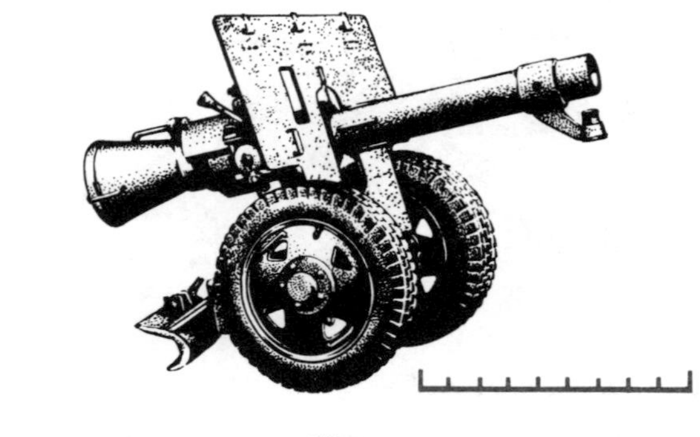

Caliber 4.13in (105mm)
Weight 855 lb (388kg)
Range 8695yd (7950m)
Type of projectile : HE.

The US M20 recoilless rifle (right), introduced in 1945, was used to fire HE and smoke rounds in a field gun role, and HEAT shells against tanks. When split into two loads of barrel and tripod it was man-portable. The tripod used was the same as for the Browning M1917 machine gun.
The breech, shown in cross-section in the diagram (below right), is of the "Kromuskit" type. The cartridge case is perforated, and supported only at the base and neck. A proportion of combustion gases forces the shell down the bore, and the remainder emerges through the perforations and escapes to the rear as backblast, through vents equal in area to the bore. The central part of the breech piece is removable for loading.

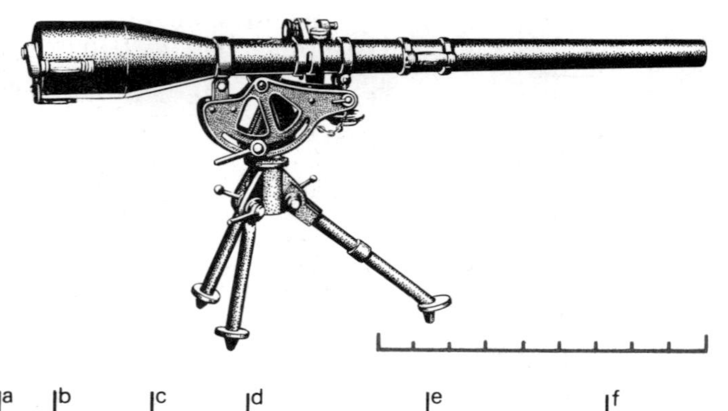

Caliber 2.95in (75mm)
Weight 158 lb (71.6kg)
Range 7000yd (6400m)

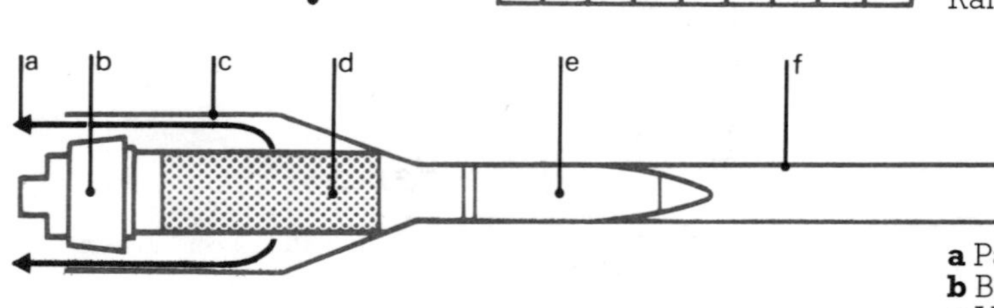

a Path of backblast
b Breech piece
c Venturi
d Perforated cartridge case
e Shell
f Barrel
g Complete round of ammunition

US M40 recoilless rifle (right), similar to the M20 (see preceding page) in having a Kromuskit type breech, but of the larger 106mm caliber. It has a .50in spotting rifle mounted on top of the barrel. A post-WW2 development, it is still used by many armies, but in US service it has been replaced by guided missiles.

British L6 WOMBAT (right) The Weapon Of Magnesium, Battalion Anti-Tank is a heavy caliber but physically lightweight recoilless anti-tank gun. It is fitted with an M8 .50in (12.7mm) spotting rifle. The gun works on the frangible base system, as shown in the cross-section (below right). The venturi swings to one side to load the cartridge, which has a brass case with a plastic base disk. As the pressure from the explosion of the propellant builds up, the base disk disintegrates and the backblast escapes straight back through the venturi. The WOMBAT'S weight is kept down by the use of alloys and a light carriage not intended for towing—the weapon is carried on a jeep. It is now being replaced by a guided missile system.

Swedish PV-1110 (right), a recoilless rifle that uses the same frangible base system as the WOMBAT. It too is fitted with a semi-automatic spotting rifle above the main barrel. The circular platform on the carriage serves as an elbow rest for the crew member who aims and fires the gun.

The use of spotting rifles (right) The user aims at the tank and fires the spotting rifle until a good hit is obtained. The special bullet can be seen burning in flight, and gives off a flash and puff of smoke on impact (**1**). The main gun is immediately fired. As the trajectories and alignment of both systems are matched, a hit with the main shell is practically assured (**2**).

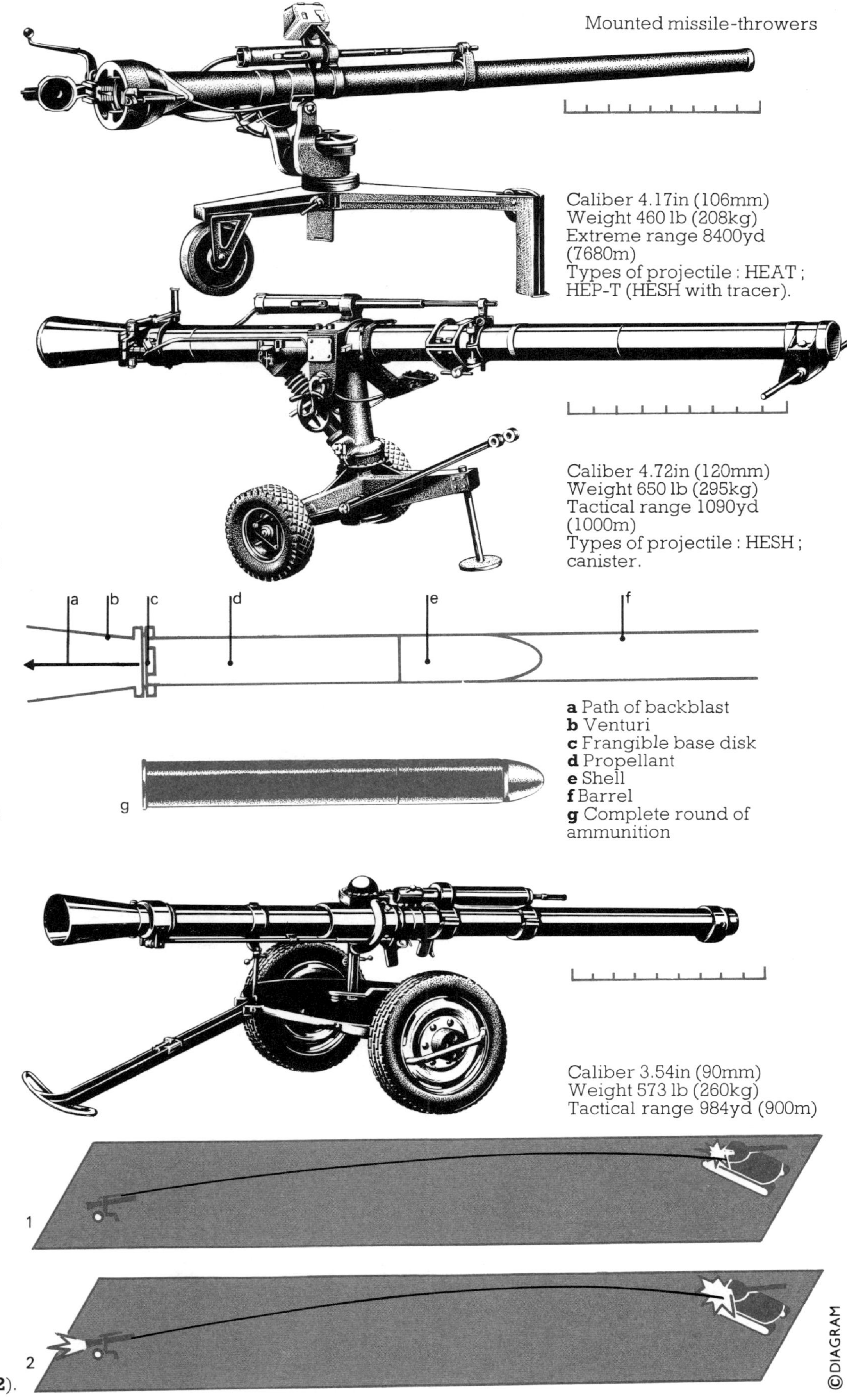

Breech-loading naval guns 1

Naval armament since the mid-19th century is a complex subject. In the second half of the century, the same general advances in technology that produced the breech-loading gun also produced the iron steamship. Here we are not concerned with the ships themselves or with the detailed developments in naval gunnery during the years of change. We concentrate mainly on the guns as they were in the early 20th century—the heyday of the big-gun battleship, before air-power made such a combination of vessel and armament obsolete.

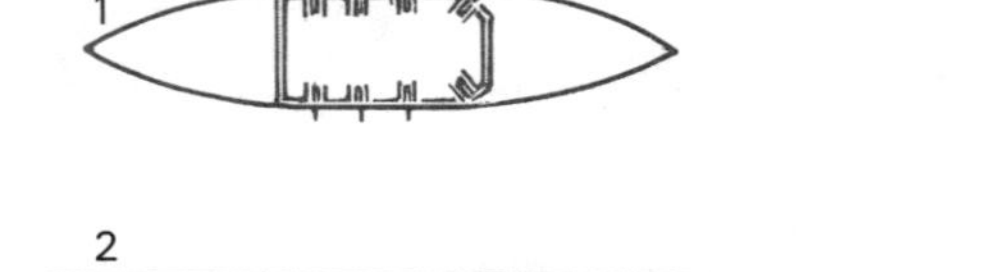

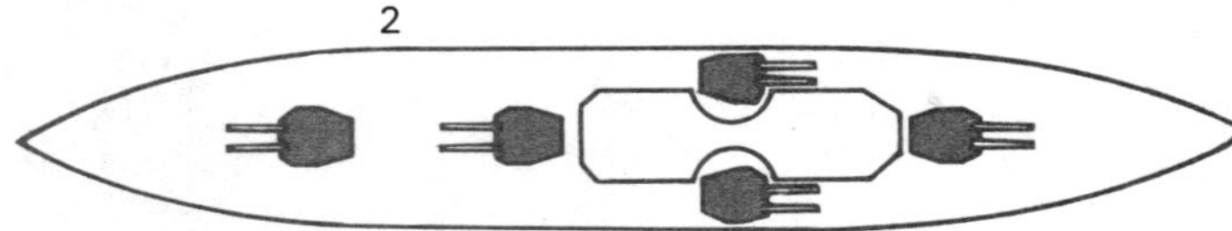

The mounting of guns on warships (above) underwent great changes in the late 19th century. The trend was toward fewer but bigger guns, as shown in the plan view of the Austrian battleship, "Don Juan de Austria" (**1**), launched in 1875. (Compare this with the older HMS Victory, shown on p. 173.) The guns are still mounted in casemates, with limited fields of fire. Countless permutations of gun mount and distribution about the ship were tried, before the British HMS Dreadnought (**2**) set the new pattern for all navies in 1906. Her ten 12in guns were mounted in five armored turrets, allowing a broadside of eight guns. She had 24 12-pounder guns as secondary armament.

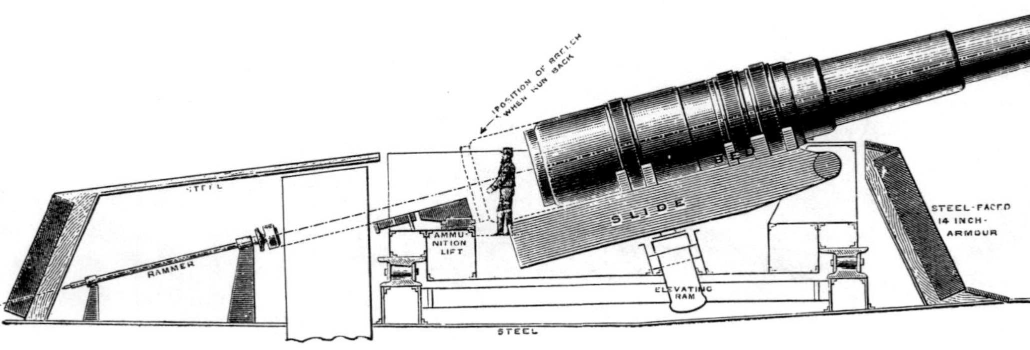

111 ton gun (left) of 16.25in (412mm) caliber, as mounted on HMS Benbow in the 1880s. Note that it is mounted in an open-topped barbette—a step toward the enclosed rotating turret. (From "The Naval Annual" of 1887.)

Armor-piercing shells (right) In the late 19th and early 20th centuries much research was done into the protection of ships by armor —and into its penetration by shells. The ideal naval shell had a point (**a**) hard enough to overcome the armor, but not so brittle as to shatter or to separate from its softer body (**b**). It had to contain enough explosive (**c**) to inflict significant damage, and needed a reliable fuze (**d**) to set off the shell-filling after penetration. It was also desirable to have a shell that could penetrate at an oblique angle (below right) and not glance off the smooth, hard armor plate. (See also p. 206.)

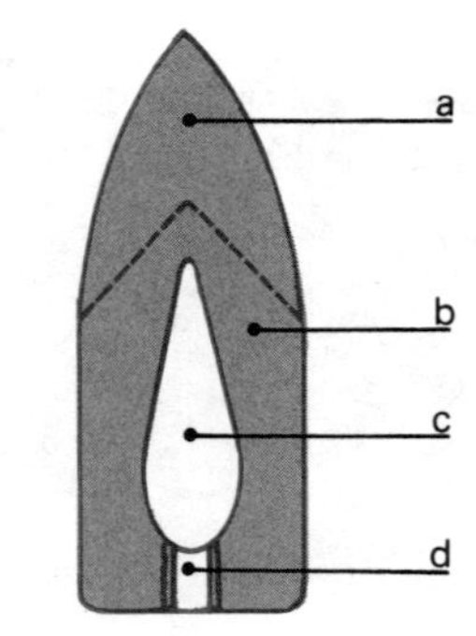

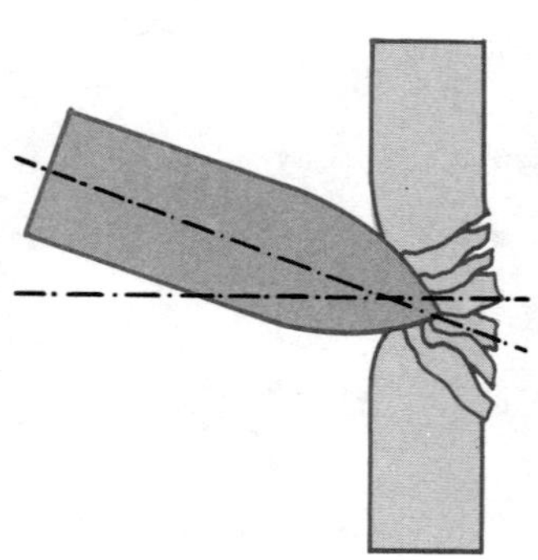

Electric ignition (right) First used in this way in the 1870s, electricity became the usual means for igniting the propellant in naval guns. The diagram (above right) shows in cross-section an electric firing-pistol of the 1890s. The cable (**A**) leads to the primer in the cartridge, and (**B**) to an electric battery. When the gun was loaded a "sounder"(**C**) announced whether the circuit was correct. On pulling the trigger (**D**), the current was passed to the primer. The cross-section (below right) shows an electric primer. Its bronze body (**1**) was screwed into the base of a brass cartridge case. To fire, the current passed down the spindle (**2**) and across a thin wire or "bridge" (**3**) which fuzed, igniting the powder (**4**).

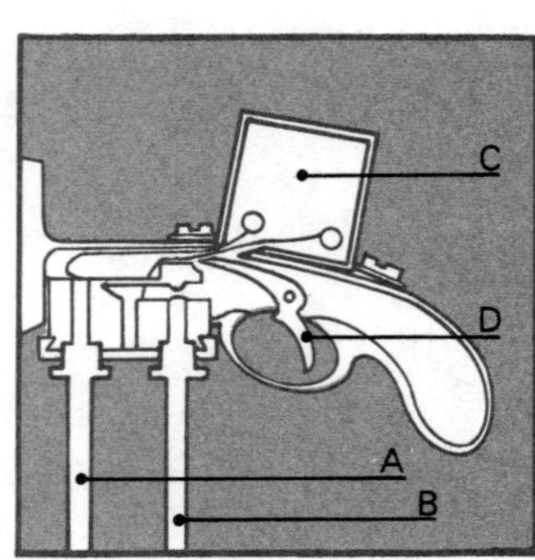

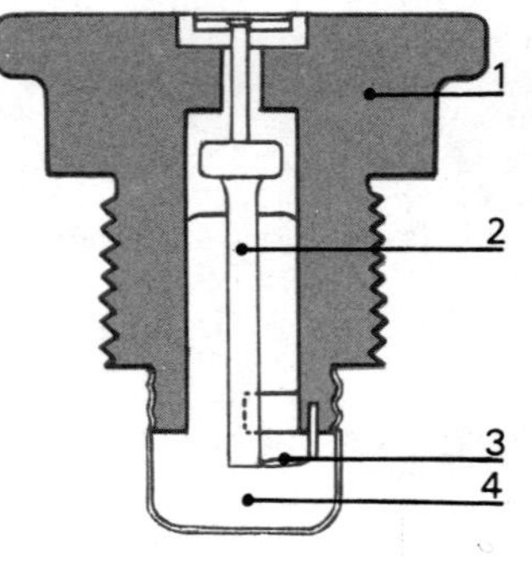

The armament (right) of a "Dreadnought" battleship was of several kinds. In addition to the main guns mounted in turrets (**A**), there was a secondary armament of smaller guns, usually in "between decks" mountings (**B**) or on pedestal mountings either on top of the main turrets (**C**) or on the open decks (**D**).

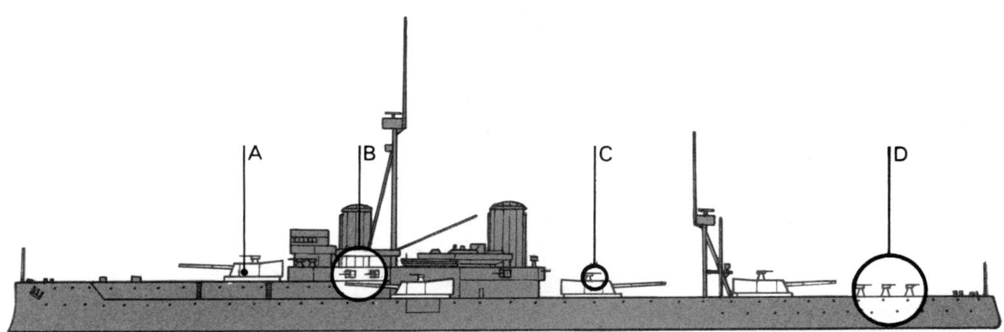

Pedestal-mounted Quick-Firing (QF) gun (right) of the 1890s. It was aimed and fired by one man with his shoulder pressed against the padded rest at the rear, while others loaded for him. 25 shots per minute could be fired. Fixed cartridges with percussion primers were used. The shoulder piece was attached to the carriage, not the gun, so that no recoil was felt by the firer.
Such light, simple, quick-firing guns were needed to counter the threat that arose in the 1880s from small, fast torpedo boats. These could sink even a battleship, and the latter's main armament was too unwieldy to be of use against such attackers.

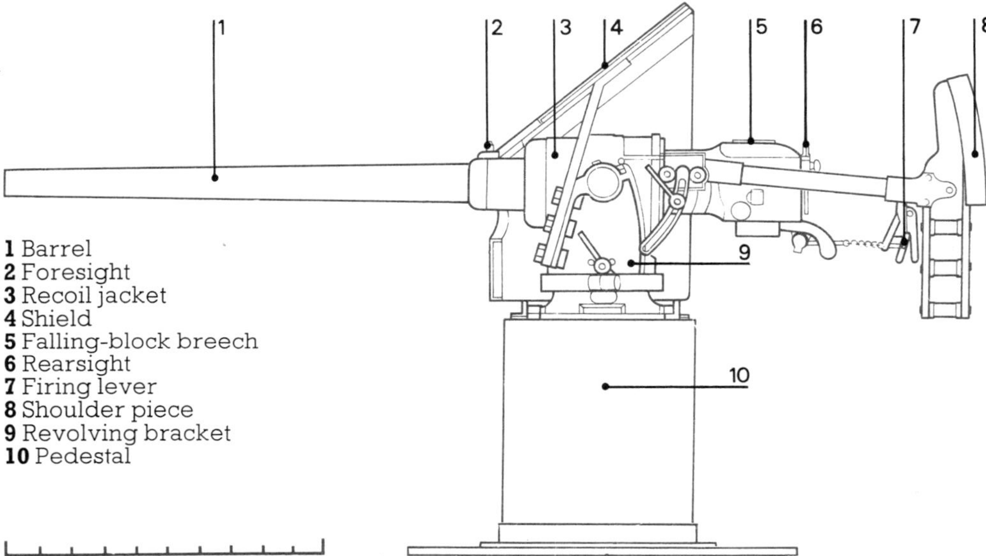

1 Barrel
2 Foresight
3 Recoil jacket
4 Shield
5 Falling-block breech
6 Rearsight
7 Firing lever
8 Shoulder piece
9 Revolving bracket
10 Pedestal

6in QF gun (right) on a Between Decks (BD) mount. Although different in external appearance, being more enclosed, the design shown was basically another pedestal mount. The 6in (152mm) gun shown was British, introduced in 1890, and could fire seven 100 lb (45.3kg) shells per minute. The ammunition was semi-fixed; that is, the shell was loaded first, followed by the charge of cordite in a brass case. Priming was electrical, but percussion primers could be fitted quickly if the supply of electricity failed. Guns in BD mounts were a feature to be seen on many battleships of WW1, but by WW2 most had been replaced by High Angle (HA) guns, that could also be used against aircraft.

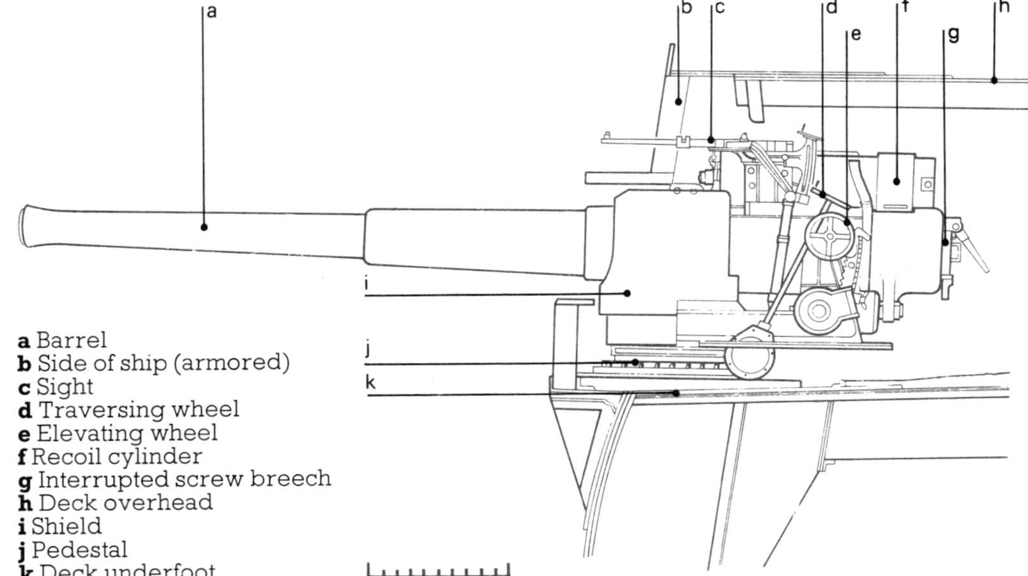

a Barrel
b Side of ship (armored)
c Sight
d Traversing wheel
e Elevating wheel
f Recoil cylinder
g Interrupted screw breech
h Deck overhead
i Shield
j Pedestal
k Deck underfoot

Breech-loading naval guns 2

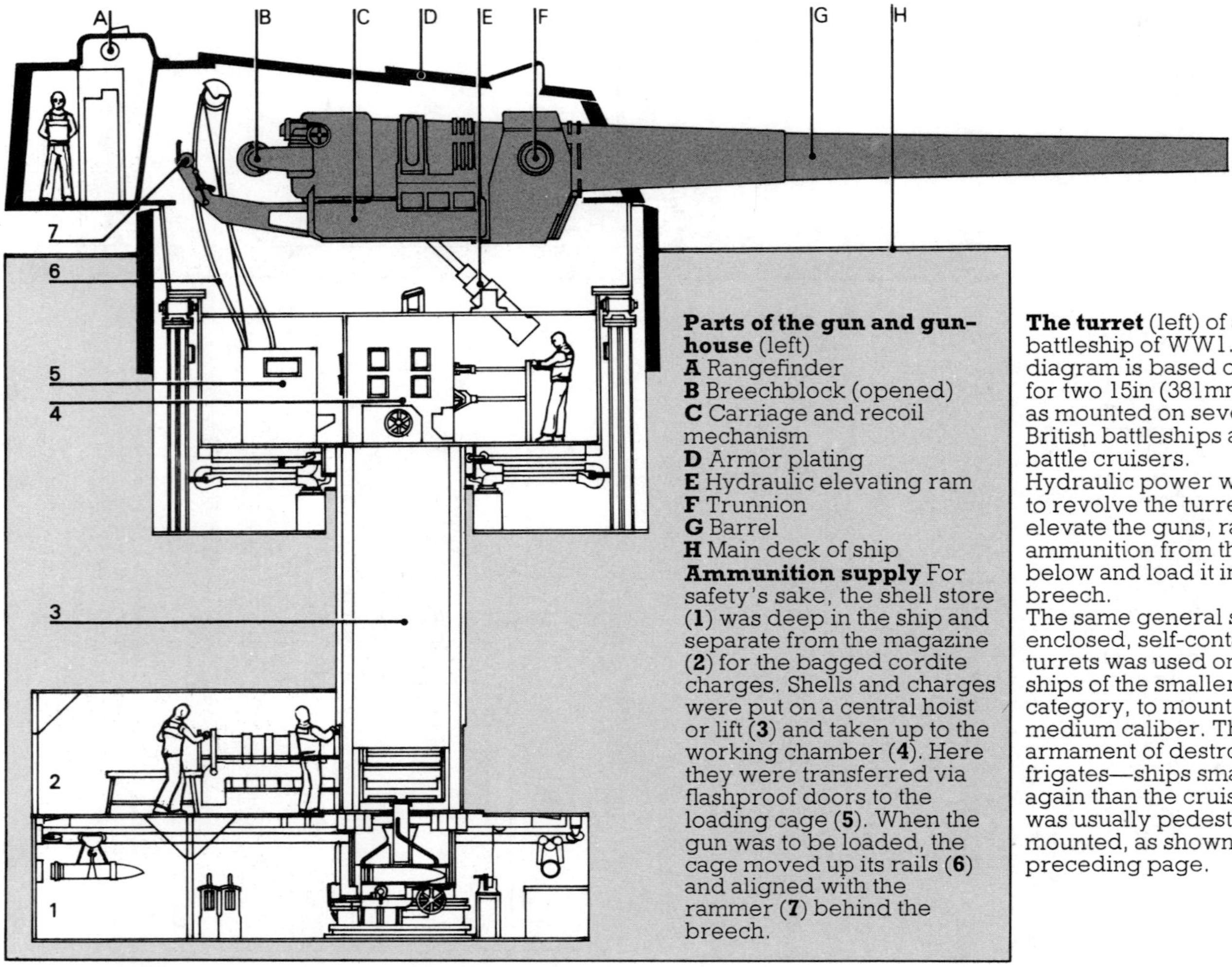

Parts of the gun and gun-house (left)
A Rangefinder
B Breechblock (opened)
C Carriage and recoil mechanism
D Armor plating
E Hydraulic elevating ram
F Trunnion
G Barrel
H Main deck of ship

Ammunition supply For safety's sake, the shell store (**1**) was deep in the ship and separate from the magazine (**2**) for the bagged cordite charges. Shells and charges were put on a central hoist or lift (**3**) and taken up to the working chamber (**4**). Here they were transferred via flashproof doors to the loading cage (**5**). When the gun was to be loaded, the cage moved up its rails (**6**) and aligned with the rammer (**7**) behind the breech.

The turret (left) of a typical battleship of WW1. The diagram is based on a turret for two 15in (381mm) guns, as mounted on several British battleships and battle cruisers.
Hydraulic power was used to revolve the turret, elevate the guns, raise the ammunition from the stores below and load it into the breech.
The same general system of enclosed, self-contained turrets was used on many ships of the smaller, cruiser category, to mount guns of medium caliber. The armament of destroyers and frigates—ships smaller again than the cruisers—was usually pedestal-mounted, as shown on the preceding page.

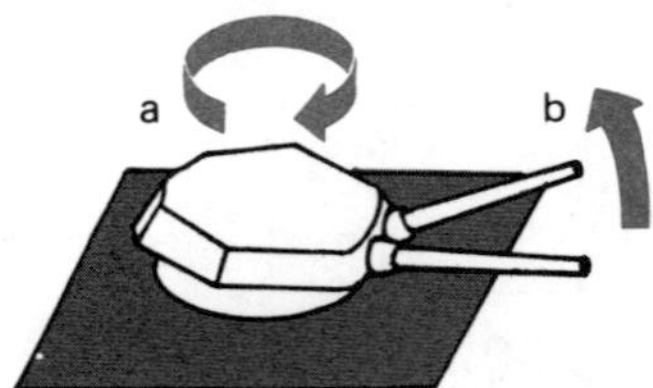

Turrets (left) provided the ideal solution for mounting big naval guns. The crew were well protected and the guns had a wide field of fire. Changes in direction were made by revolving the whole turret (**a**), and changes in elevation by altering the angle of the guns within the turret (**b**). Up to four guns were mounted in one turret.

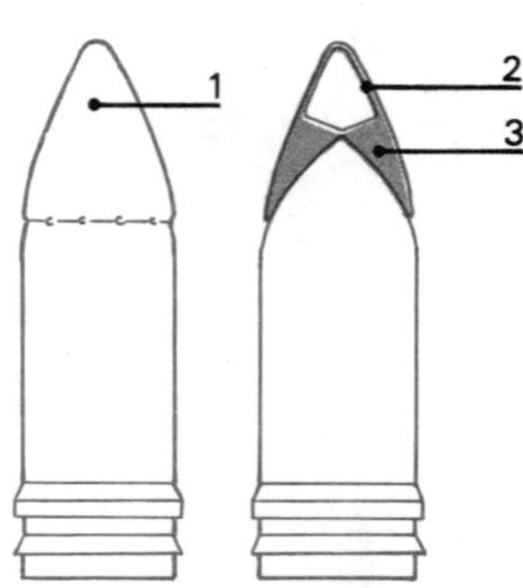

Capped shell (left) It was found that the ability of a shell to pierce armor plate was improved by adding a soft steel cap (**1**) over the point. The example shown is Hadfield's improved cap, as used by the British. It had a strealined "ballistic" cap (**2**) over a blunt "penetrating" cap (**3**), so shaped to aid penetration at oblique angles.

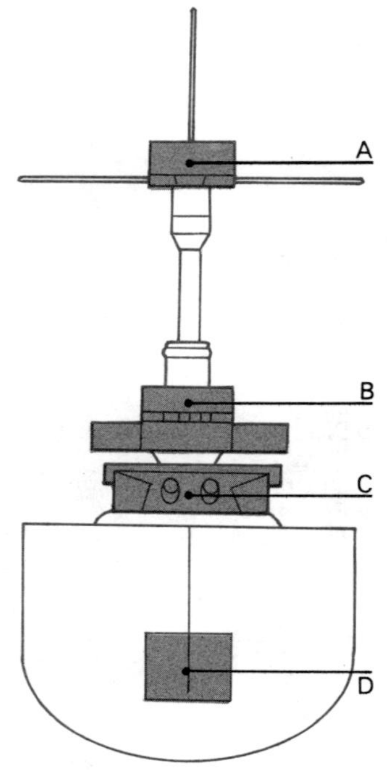

Fire control (left) The main armament of a battleship, dispersed in a number of turrets, was all controlled centrally. In general, there would be a team of observers, range takers and fire controllers high up in the ship's superstructure (**A**) above the smoke and spray. The whole system came under the command of the Captain on the bridge (**B**). There were also separate range-finders on each turret (**C**). Data from all sources on the movements of the ship and its target was processed at the fire control table—a kind of simple computer—below decks (**D**).
When all factors affecting aiming had been taken into account and the guns laid accordingly, they could be fired together by an electric circuit.

Anti-aircraft guns (right) or High Angle (HA) guns were of vital importance by WW2. Some took the form of dual-purpose guns of medium caliber in turrets (**a**), which could also engage surface targets. Automatic cannon (**b**) were easily installed, and came to be used in multiple mountings (**c**).

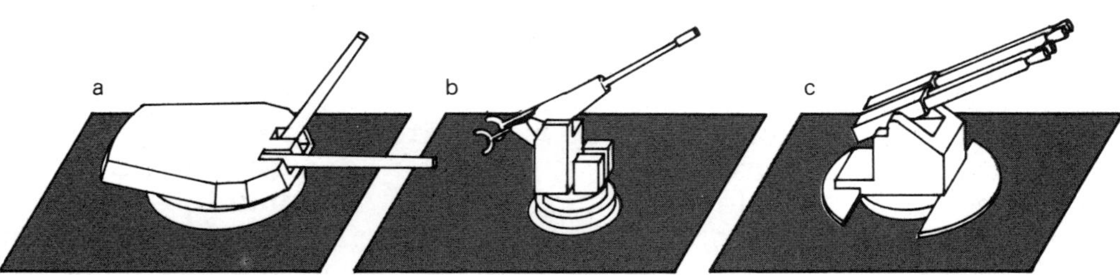

US 40mm Bofors gun (right) on a quadruple mounting for naval use. Since their first appearance in 1932, the various models of Swedish Bofors 40mm (1.57in) anti-aircraft gun have been used as widely by the world's navies as by the land forces (see p. 194). Multiple mountings, with several guns fitted together as here , have often been used on board ship where weight is less of a disadvantage than on mobile land-based weapons. Their purpose is to put more shells into the air around the target aircraft and thus increase the chance of a hit. The modern versions of the Bofors gun can be directed by radar, but retain a manual aiming system as a backup.

US 5in Mk45 (near right), a modern dual-purpose naval gun for engaging both surface and airborne targets. It is fully automated, so that the turret is unmanned during firing. The diagram (far right) shows the general arrangement of the system. The gun itself (**1**) is mounted on the open deck, the mechanism protected by a close-fitting shield of narrow frontal section. It is controlled remotely from the consoles (**2**) below decks. The fixed ammunition is supplied to the gun through a central hoist (**3**) from the magazine still deeper inside the ship (**4**). Modern automatic naval guns of medium caliber, such as this, can fire a weight of shells in a given time that compares favorably with the huge guns of earlier in the century.

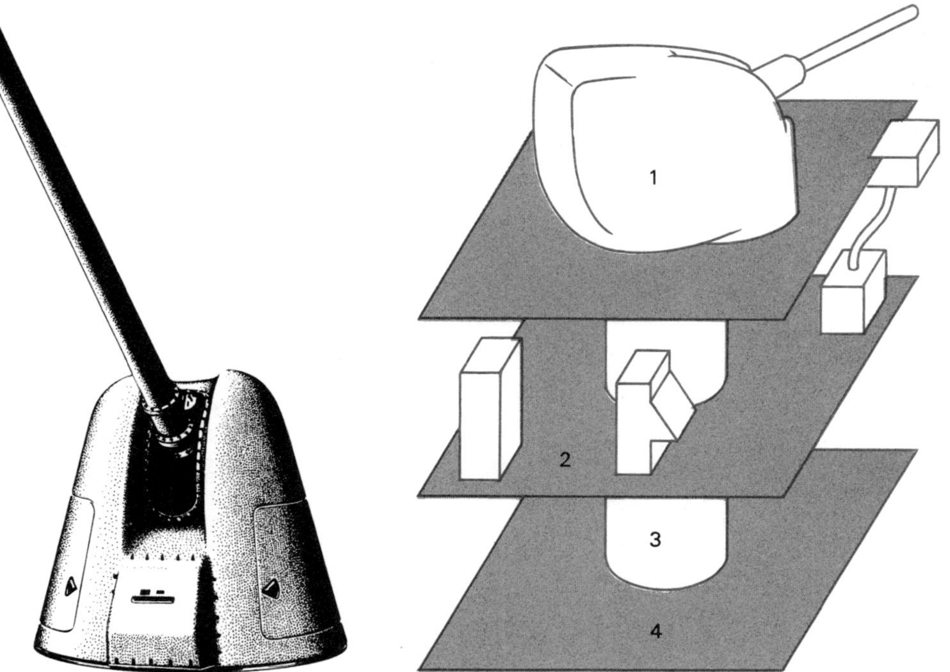

Machine guns

In the broadest sense any rapid-firing small arm is a machine gun, but the term is now applied only to modern fully automatic weapons. These guns are the product of the desire to increase the destructive power of one man and his gun so that he can defeat many men. One solution is to equip him to fire many more shots in a given time.

Ever since the first single-shot muzzle-loading firearms appeared in Europe in the late Middle Ages, people have tried to devise a weapon that will fire many times in quick succession. For certain reasons this desire was not realized until the late 19th century.

The main obstacle was the limitation of muzzle-loading. Contraptions were made to produce a volley or ripple of fire, but the rate could not be maintained because of the time inevitably taken to reload.

Advancing technology eased the problems in the mid-19th century by the invention of the metallic cartridge, which was robust enough to be machine-fed, contained its own means of ignition, and sealed the breech automatically against the escape of hot propellant gases. Efficient manually operated designs were in use in the 1860s, but it was not until 1884 that Hiram Maxim produced the first fully automatic machine gun. His revolutionary innovation was to harness some of the energy of the exploding charge to power the operating cycle. Armies now had to find the best way of using the machine gun tactically.

(Repeating rifles and pistols are closely related to the machine gun in principle, development and use. They are treated in the chapter on hand-held missile throwers, see p. 131.)

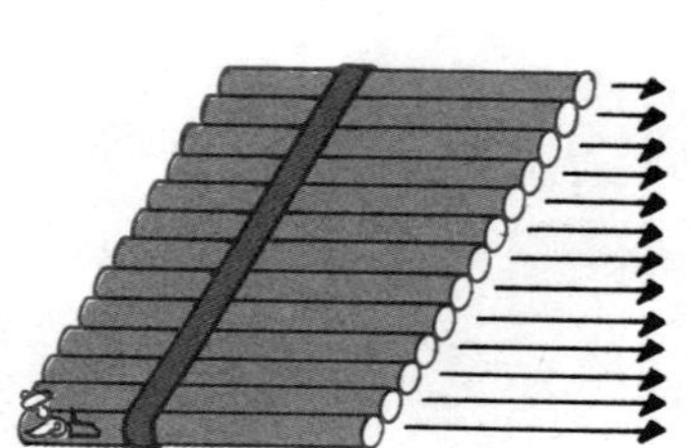

Muzzle-loading did not lend itself to rapid fire. One possibility, many loads superimposed in one barrel, proved dangerous and uncontrollable. Another solution, many barrels mounted on a carriage (left) produced a volley, but the rate of fire could not be kept up as they took so long to reload. It remained more practicable to have ranks of men firing volleys.

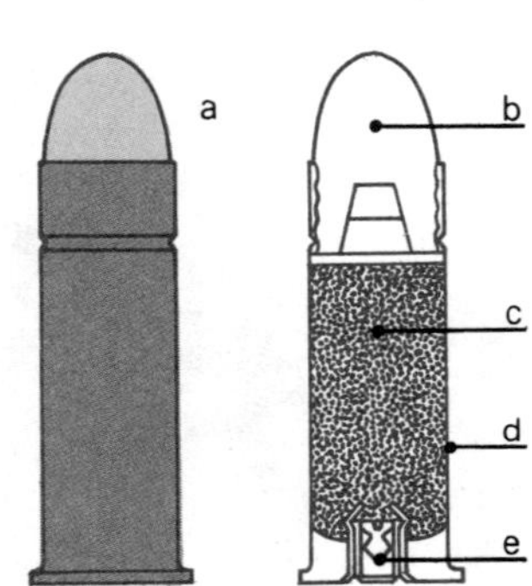

Cartridge breakthrough (left) Rapid loading via the breech was made possible by the metallic cartridge (**a**), which had its own ignition, could be mechanically fed, and sealed the breech on firing. Also, new smokeless propellant powders meant the firer was not blinded by smoke. Cartridge parts: bullet (**b**), propellant (**c**), brass case (**d**), percussion cap (**e**).

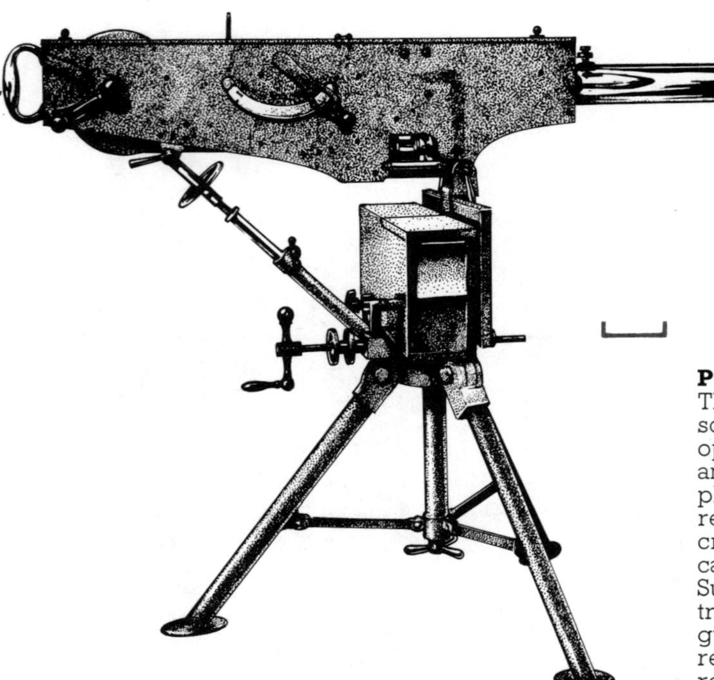

Prototype Maxim gun (left) This needed no external source of power to work the operating cycle. Once the ammunition belt was in place, a handle near the rear of the body had to be cranked twice to place a cartridge in the breech. Subsequently, when the trigger was pressed, the gun would start to fire and reload by means of the recoil from the explosion, and would continue to do so until the trigger was released or the ammunition ran out. Improved versions were adopted by Britain, Germany and the US Navy in the 1890s.
Recoil operated; belt fed; water cooled
Caliber .450in
Weight of gun 60 lb
Rate up to 600 round/min
(Imperial War Museum, London)

Early machine guns

Early machine guns (right)
1 Organ gun or volley gun, c.1670. Similar to a design by Leonardo da Vinci. Guns on this principle were still used in the American Civil War (1861-65). (Prince Liechtenstein's Collection, Vaduz.)
2 Puckle's gun, 1718. In essence a large revolver on a stand, it once fired 63 shots in 7 minutes. (Tower of London.)

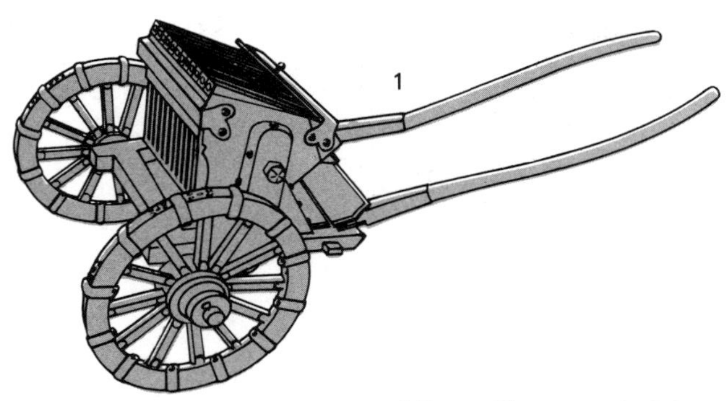

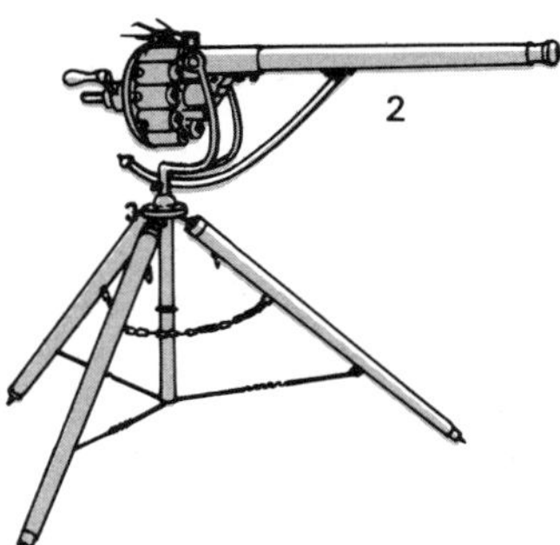

Manually operated types (right) Initially, even after the advent of the metallic cartridge, inventors were obsessed with multi-barreled, man-powered designs. These mostly used a lever (**a**) or a crank (**b**). The rate of fire depended mainly on how fast the firer worked the handle, but some mechanisms were inherently faster than others.

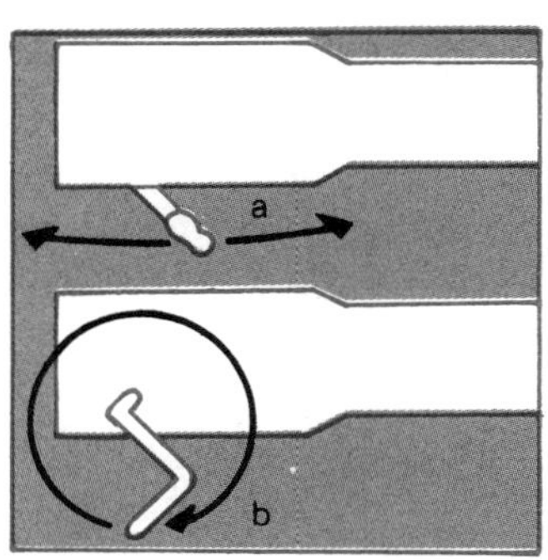

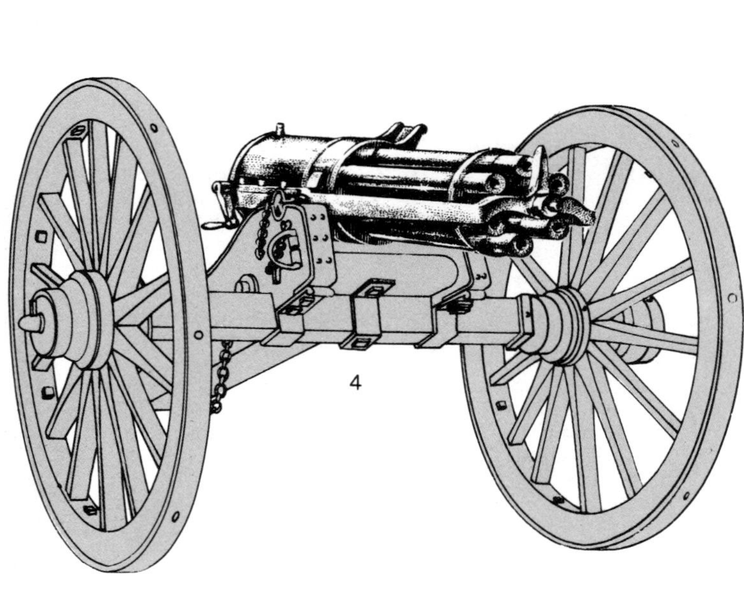

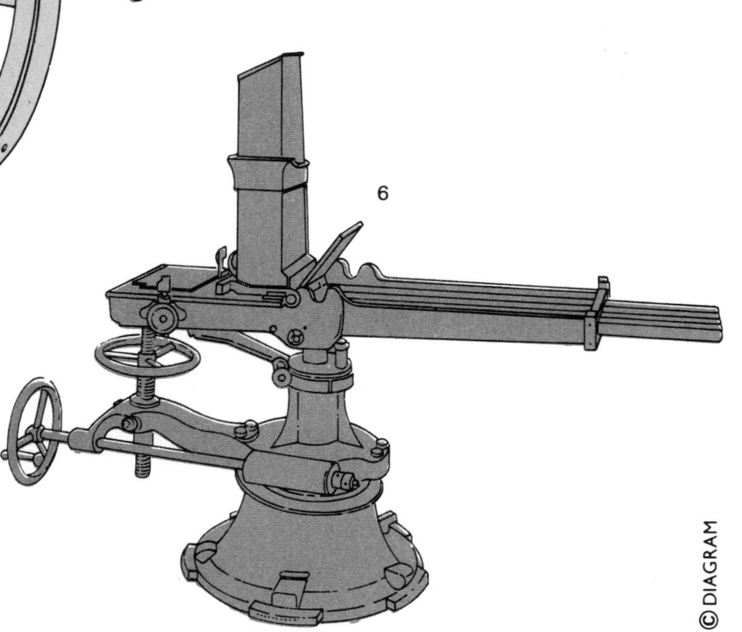

Manually operated guns
3 Agar "coffee mill," c.1860. An advanced design, but using steel tubes as cartridge cases. Used in the American Civil War. Rate 100-120 rounds/min.
4 Gatling, 1862. The most successful hand-cranked machine gun. Made in several calibers with 6 to 10 barrels. Rate up to 1200 rounds/min in later models.
5 Montigny Mitrailleuse, 1870. French. 37 barrels in one tube, fired in volleys or quick succession. A metal plate held 37 cartridges for loading.
6 Nordenfelt, 1873. Swedish design, made in several calibers and with from 2 to 12 barrels. Shown is a naval deck-mounted version. Rate of fire about 100 rounds/min per barrel.

Machine gun ammunition

Whenever possible, armies prefer to make their machine guns in the same caliber as their rifles. This has generally been practicable with light and medium types, but heavy machine guns necessarily use bigger, more powerful cartridges, Also, specialized uses, such as in aircraft, demand special varieties of projectile within a given caliber. Here we compare and explain the varieties, and their use.

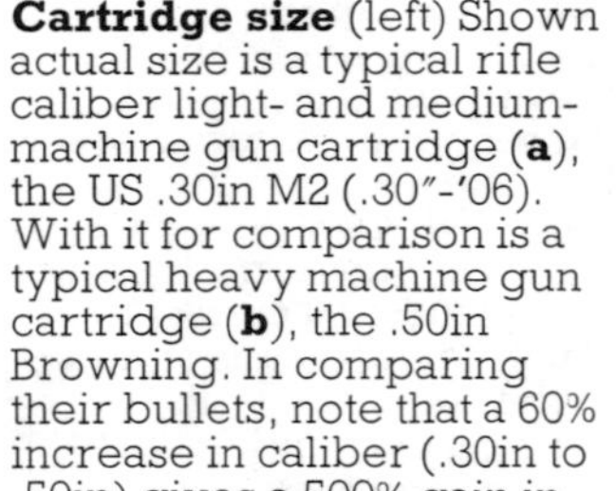

Cartridge size (left) Shown actual size is a typical rifle caliber light- and medium-machine gun cartridge (**a**), the US .30in M2 (.30″-'06). With it for comparison is a typical heavy machine gun cartridge (**b**), the .50in Browning. In comparing their bullets, note that a 60% increase in caliber (.30in to .50in), gives a 500% gain in weight (150 grains to 710).

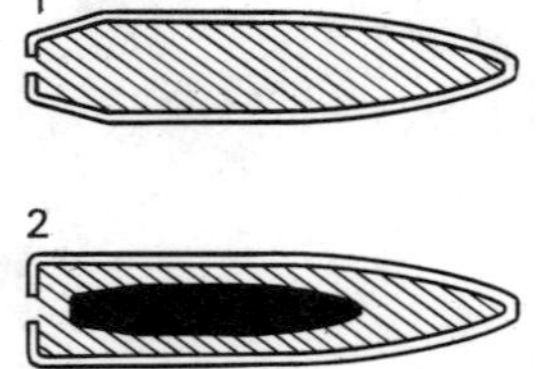

Cartridge types (left)
1 Ball The common inert bullet designed to kill or wound men. Typically, the outer jacket is a cupronickel alloy, and the core a lead alloy.
2 Armor-piercing Mainly for aircraft, to do more damage than ball types. A hardened steel core is covered with layers of softer metal to be gripped by the rifling grooves.

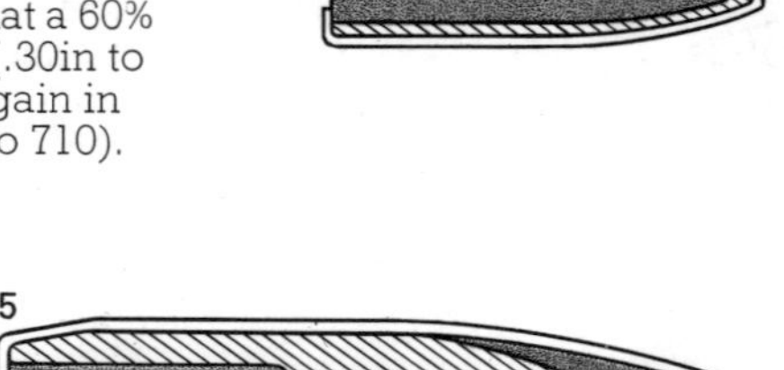

3 Tracer A firework-like composition inside is lit on firing, and burns as it flies, showing the gunner where his stream of fire is going. Used on land and in the air. Lead in the tip.
4 Incendiary Designed to penetrate and burn, setting fire to vehicles and aircraft. Contains a chemical that ignites on impact.

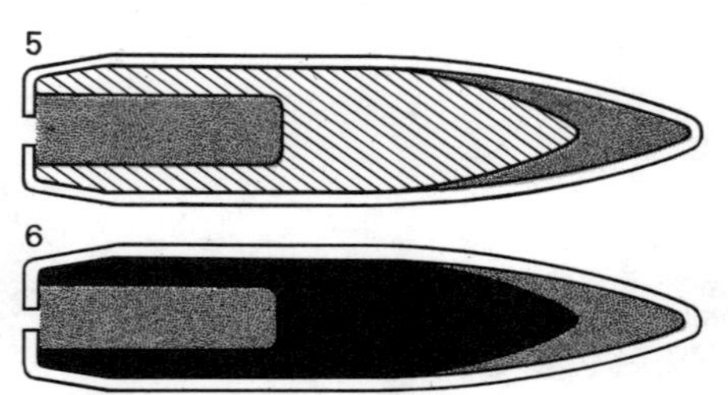

5 Spotter or observation The nose is filled with a chemical to give a flash and puff of smoke on hitting a hard object. Used to check the aim of a tank's main gun before firing.
6 Combinations Types shown above may be combined in one bullet, especially in the larger calibers. Shown is a .50in armor-piercing incendiary tracer (APIT).

Theory of machine gun fire (below) Machine guns on the ground exploit three characteristics of small-arms fire.
The dangerous space (A) is the distance within which the bullets remain within a man's height of the ground. This is used to clear or deny a strip of ground to the enemy.
The cone of fire produces a dispersal of shots (**B**) around the line of fire and so increases the chance of a hit on a point target at short and medium range.
The beaten zone (C) is the pattern of shots on the ground as they descend steeply at long range. It is wider but shorter as the range increases, and is applied to likely areas of enemy activity, often beyond the gunner's vision. (The distances given on the diagram below are approximate, but are typical of the most widely used rifle-caliber machine guns of both World Wars. Since 1945, these ranges have been shortening due to new tactical theories.)

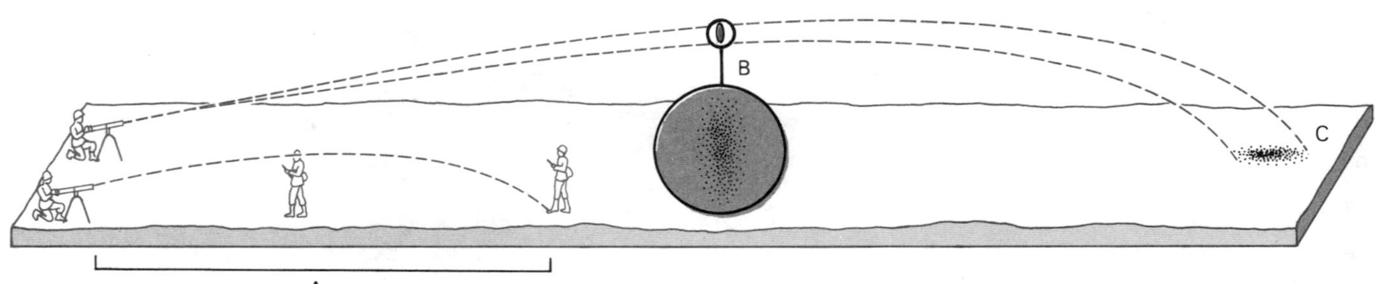

Machine gun chronology

Although the importance of machine guns was apparent in the Anglo-Boer War of 1899-1902 and the Russo-Japanese War of 1904-05, only Germany fully appreciated the lessons and equipped its army with sufficient Maxim guns by 1914.

Largely as a result of the effectiveness of machine guns and barbed wire in defense, World War 1 remained a stalemate for many months. By the end of the war, however, new applications of the machine gun were helping to find ways of overcoming the great new defensive combination. Tanks were well adapted to carry and exploit the machine gun, and the fleeting targets of both aircraft and anti-aircraft combat called for weapons with high rates of fire. In the infantry there was found to be a need for a light machine gun, especially in the tactics that began to replace the mass attacks of the earlier battles. Small groups advancing in rushes, "covering" each other with small-arms fire, were used successfully by the Germans in their attacks of March 1918, and copied by other armies.

In the 1930s and 1940s weapons were perfected to apply the lessons of 1918. The general- purpose machine gun (GPMG) emerged — a light machine gun capable of being put on a tripod to give sustained fire support.

In World War 2, the importance of the infantry machine gun was restricted by the influence of mortars, strike aircraft and tanks (these last two, of course, themselves carrying machine guns), but it was nevertheless an important weapon.

Since World War 2, the roles of machine guns have been blurred by the emergence of assault rifles (see p.150) and "weapon kits" such as the Stoner system, whereby one basic weapon,with additional or replacement parts, can fulfill all the infantry's needs.

The multi-barreled Gatling principle has been revived in the Minigun, using electric power to produce an aircraft or anti-aircraft machine gun with a very high rate of fire — up to 10,000 rounds per minute.

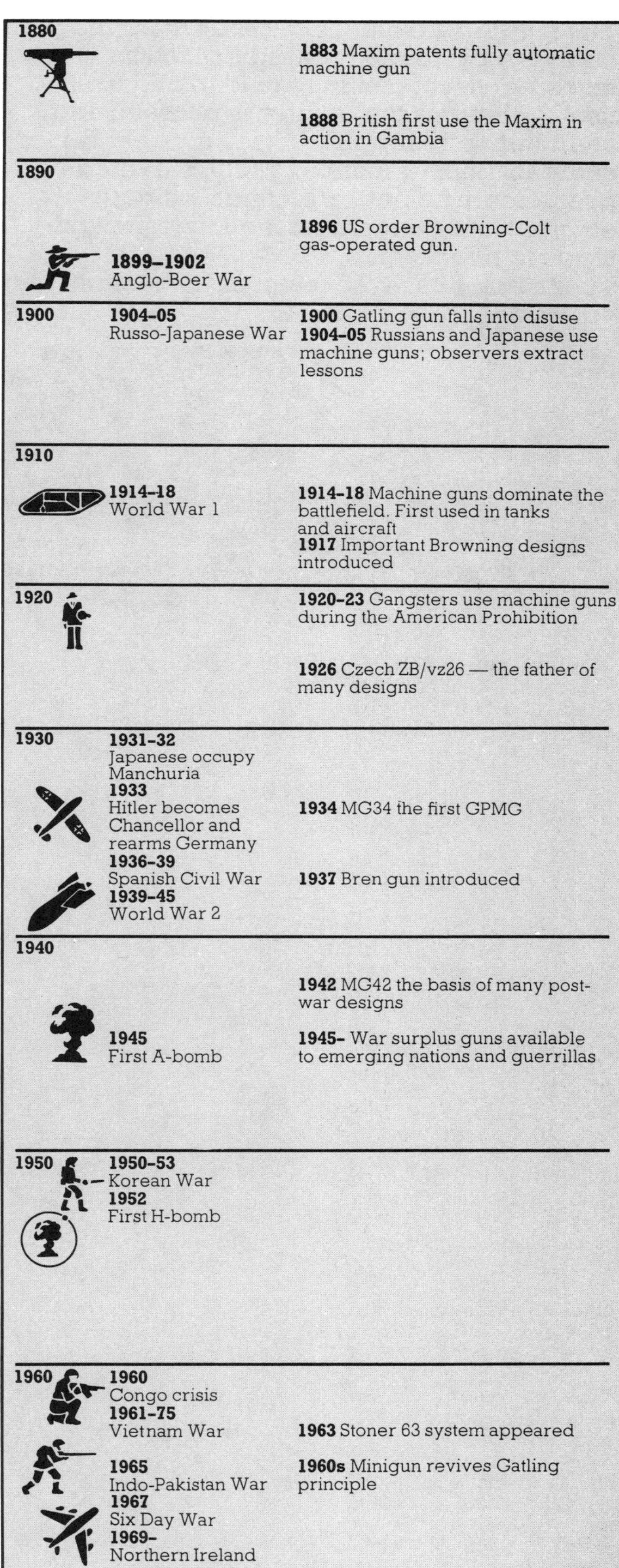

Decade	Events	Machine gun developments
1880		**1883** Maxim patents fully automatic machine gun **1888** British first use the Maxim in action in Gambia
1890	**1899–1902** Anglo-Boer War	**1896** US order Browning-Colt gas-operated gun.
1900	**1904–05** Russo-Japanese War	**1900** Gatling gun falls into disuse **1904–05** Russians and Japanese use machine guns; observers extract lessons
1910	**1914–18** World War 1	**1914–18** Machine guns dominate the battlefield. First used in tanks and aircraft **1917** Important Browning designs introduced
1920		**1920–23** Gangsters use machine guns during the American Prohibition **1926** Czech ZB/vz26 — the father of many designs
1930	**1931–32** Japanese occupy Manchuria **1933** Hitler becomes Chancellor and rearms Germany **1936–39** Spanish Civil War **1939–45** World War 2	**1934** MG34 the first GPMG **1937** Bren gun introduced
1940	**1945** First A-bomb	**1942** MG42 the basis of many post-war designs **1945–** War surplus guns available to emerging nations and guerrillas
1950	**1950–53** Korean War **1952** First H-bomb	
1960	**1960** Congo crisis **1961–75** Vietnam War **1965** Indo-Pakistan War **1967** Six Day War **1969–** Northern Ireland emergency	**1963** Stoner 63 system appeared **1960s** Minigun revives Gatling principle

Machine gun systems

The single-barreled, automatic machine gun takes the principle of rapid fire to its extreme: it will continue to load and fire itself as long as the trigger is pressed and ammunition is supplied. It is lighter and more compact than its manual, multi-barreled predecessors, but it demands a highly efficient and convenient feed system, and tends to overheat.
There are thus three features of machine gun design that interest us as solutions to the technological challenge:
Operating principle — how does the gun load and fire?
Feed — how is the ammunition supplied?
Cooling system — how is the barrel kept from overheating?
Design is, of course, also influenced by the evolution of new tactical roles on the battlefield.

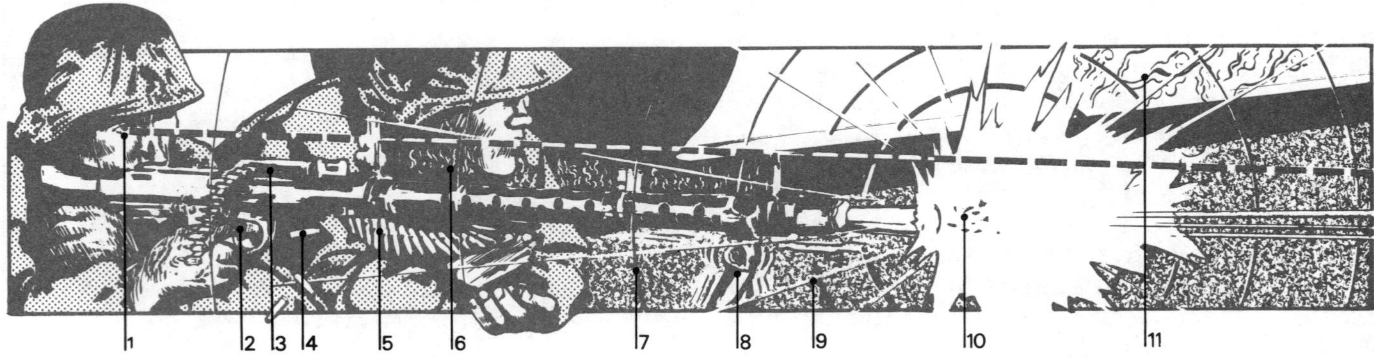

Machine gun in action (above) The illustration demonstrates the powerful phenomena of a machine gun firing.

1 Gun aimed at target.
2 Trigger pressed.
3 Empty belt emerging.
4 Empty cartridge cases ejected.
5 Ammunition fed in.
6 Haze from hot barrel.
7 Noise — painful to the firer, can deafen him.
8 Vibration. Accuracy depends on its control by the mounting and the firer.
9 Blast felt if near muzzle.
10 Flash visible in poor light.
11 Smoke. Faint gray, soon disperses.

Feed systems (right)
a Hopper — relies on gravity.
b Magazine — box or drum with cartridges under pressure from a spring.
c Strip — stiff metal clip holding a number of cartridges.
d Belt — continuous, often made of canvas.
e Belt — made up of metal links, disintegrating as rounds are withdrawn.

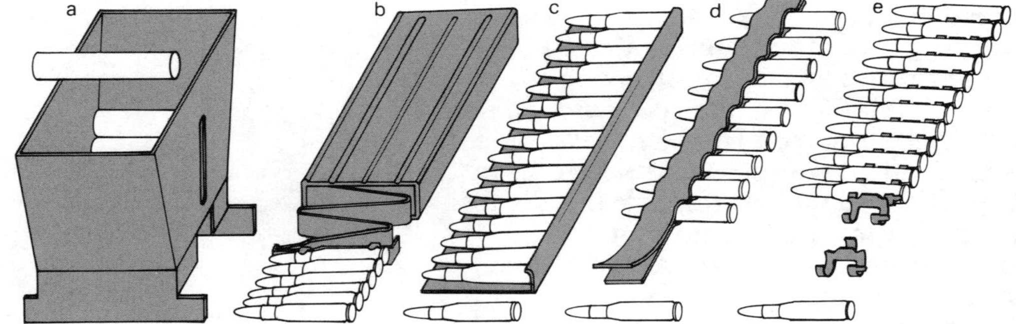

Cooling systems (right)
1 Water-cooled: a jacket of water around the barrel helps disperse the heat. When the water boils, the steam may be condensed in a can and re-used.
2 Air-cooled: may use radiating fins (**a**), or the heat-absorbing mass of a heavy barrel (**b**), often aided by a spare quick-change barrel (**c**).

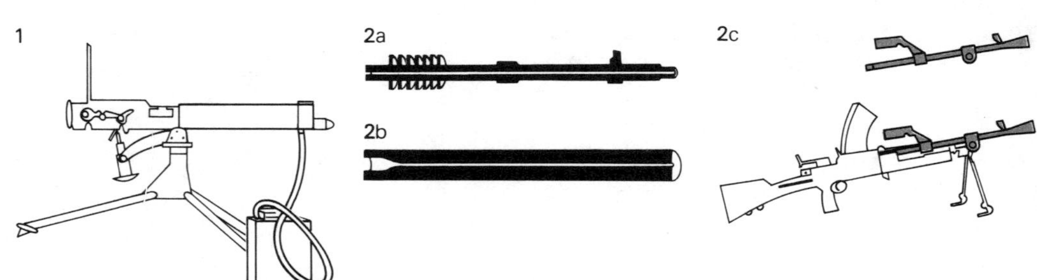

Operating principles (right)
A Recoil Before firing (**1**) the breechblock (**a**) and barrel (**b**) are locked together and held forward each by its own spring (**c**, **d**). On firing (**2**) they are driven back together by the rearward thrust in reaction to the forward motion of the bullet (**e**) and then unlocked, the pressure in the barrel now being down to atmospheric. The breech block continues to the rear and the empty case (**f**) is ejected (**3**). This principle was the first to be invented of the three main ways of using the energy of the exploding propellant charge to power the operating cycle.

B Blowback In this system, shown before firing (**1**), the breechblock (**a**) is not actually locked to the barrel (**b**). On firing (**2**), the strength of the spring (**c**), the inertia of the breechblock and sometimes a simple retarding device (delayed or retarded blowback system) delay the extraction of the empty case (**d**) until the barrel pressure is down to a safe level (**3**). Nevertheless it is gas pressure which powers the operating cycle, not recoil.

C Gas In this system the breechblock (**a**) is locked to the barrel (**b**) as shown at (**1**). Gas at high pressure from the explosion of the cartridge is bled off into a cylinder (**c**) where it drives back a piston (**d**) to unlock (**2**) and then push back the breechblock, extracting and ejecting the empty case (**3**).

Open breech Any of the three systems — recoil, blowback or gas — can be designed to operate "from an open breech," whereby until the trigger is pressed the feeding of the cartridge is delayed. Thus it cannot be ignited prematurely by remaining in a hot barrel during a pause in heavy use.

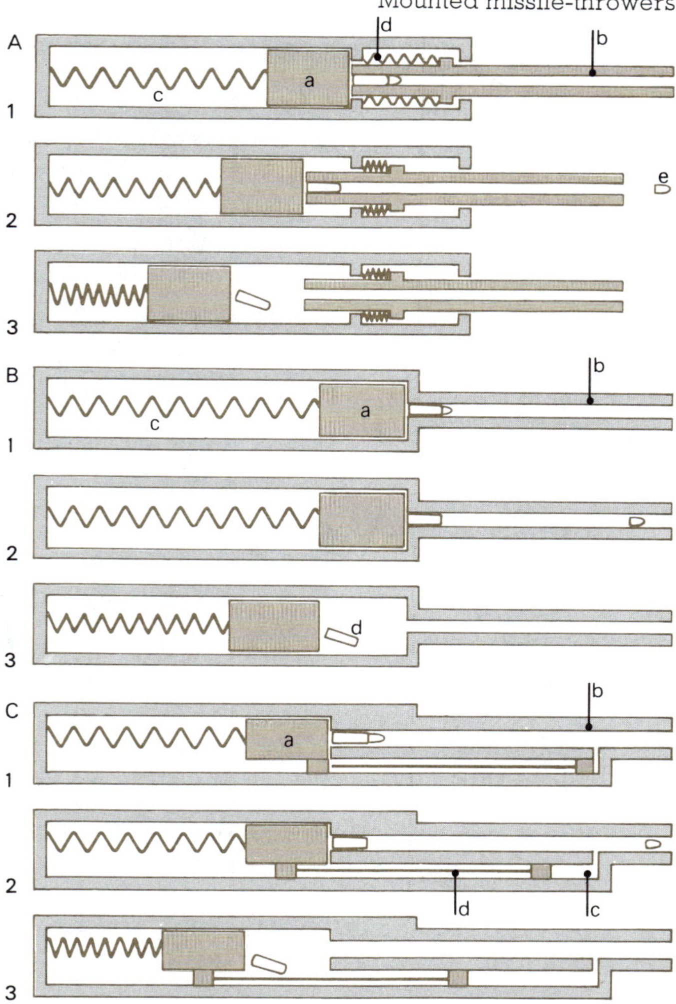

Roles and types Infantry machine guns are classified by their intended role, which is closely linked to their portability. We shall use the British terms of classification, which are comparative (light, medium, heavy), simply as access to an understanding of the tactical possibilities. The US equivalents are given below. (For submachine guns, see p. 148.)

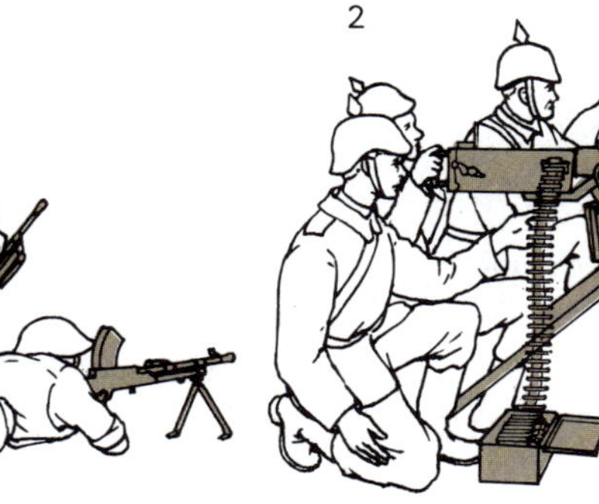

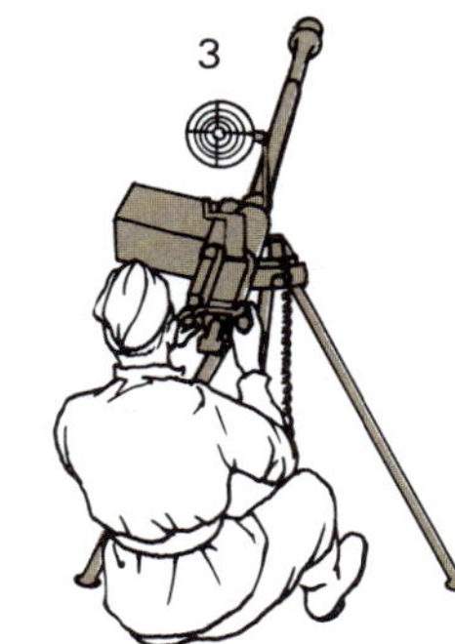

British terms and uses

1 Light machine gun (LMG) Intended to be fired from a bipod on the ground, the firer lying behind it, and easily carried by him. "No2" carries ammo, spare barrel.

2 Medium machine gun (MMG) Fired from a carriage or tripod, served by several men. Used to give sustained fire support, often over the heads of own troops.

3 Heavy machine gun (HMG) The difference between this and an MMG is more one of caliber than of role. About .50in (12.5mm). Greater power useful for AA defense.

US terms and uses

1 "Squad automatic" Used in the same role of close support of riflemen as the LMG. The first adopted, the BAR (see p. 212), could be fired standing.

2 All US Army guns of this type have been Browning designs, so no general term has emerged. Often used farther forward than in European armies.

3 "Fifty" Named from the .50in caliber of the Browning M2 series. More often used as a ground support weapon than in Europe.

Light machine guns

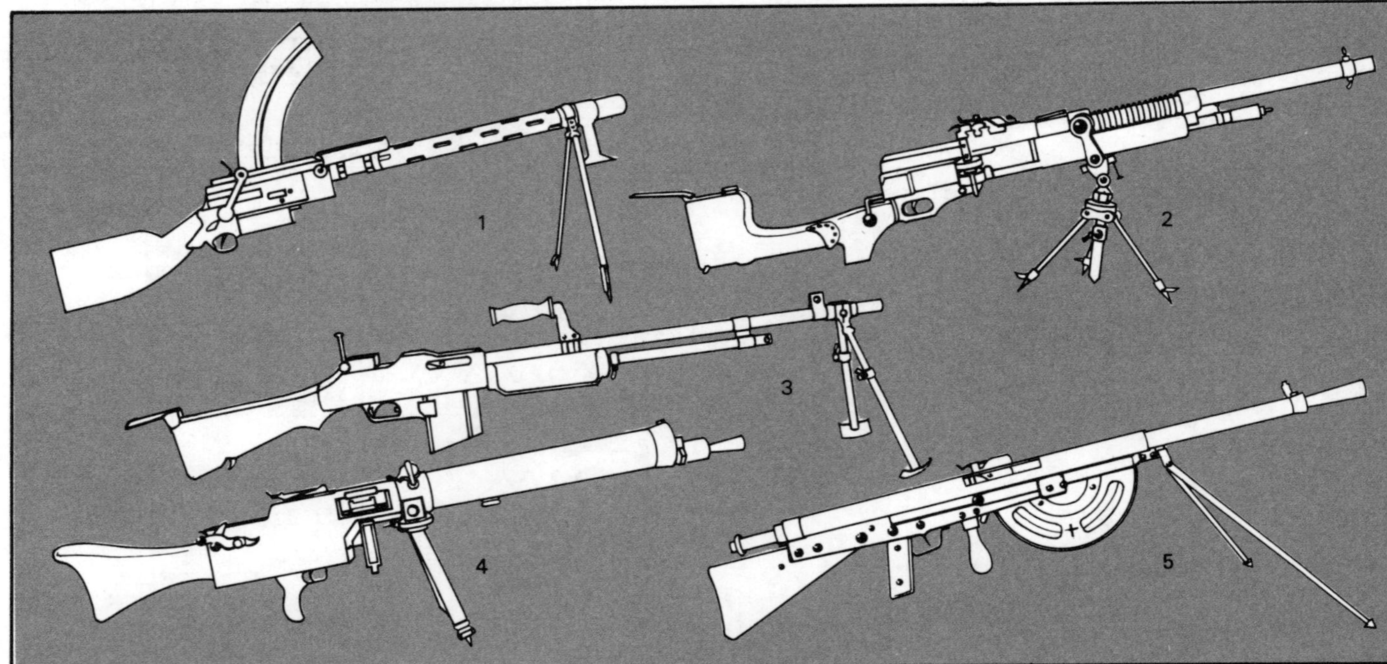

These machine guns are light enough to be carried by one man, who would be expected to keep pace with the riflemen and give them instant fire support. They are not expected to sustain their rates of fire for long without overheating. Most use magazines as being better suited to mobility than belts. General-purpose machine guns in the light role now meet this need for instant concentrated firepower.

Data key
a Caliber
b Weight unloaded
c Rate of fire
d Operating principle
e Method of feed
f Cooling system

Lewis gun (below) Designed by an American but used mainly by the British from 1915-39. The aluminum barrel casing was designed to use muzzle blast to draw air over internal cooling vanes.
a .303in British
b 26 lb (11.8kg)
c 550rpm
d Gas
e Drum magazine
f Air

1 Madsen Danish design produced for many countries in many different models. Shown is M1903/24.
a 8mm and many others
b 20 lb (9.07kg)
c 450rpm
d Recoil
e Curved magazine
f Air

2 Hotchkiss Mkl 1916. British version of a French design, also used by USA and Greece. In limited use in WW2.
a .303in and others
b 27 lb (11.7kg)
c 500rpm
d Gas
e Strip (Mkl also belt)
f Air

3 BAR M1918 A2 (Browning Automatic Rifle) US "squad automatic" of WW2. Could be shoulder-held but basically an LMG.
a .30"-'06
b 19.4 lb (8.82kg)
c 500rpm
d Gas
e Magazine
f Air

4 Maxim '08/15 German adaptation of the M1908 MMG. Heavy, but used successfully.
a 7.92mm
b 39 lb (17.7kg)
c 450rpm
d Recoil
e Belt
f Water

5 Chauchat French, 1914. An unsuccessful design by a committee, but used by France and the USA in WW1.
a 8mm Lebel
b 20 lb (9.07kg)
c 250rpm
d Recoil
e Magazine
f Air

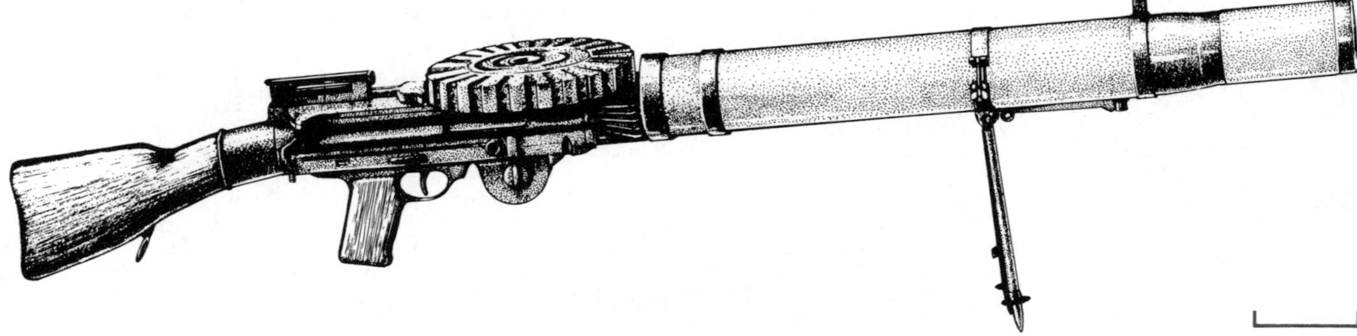

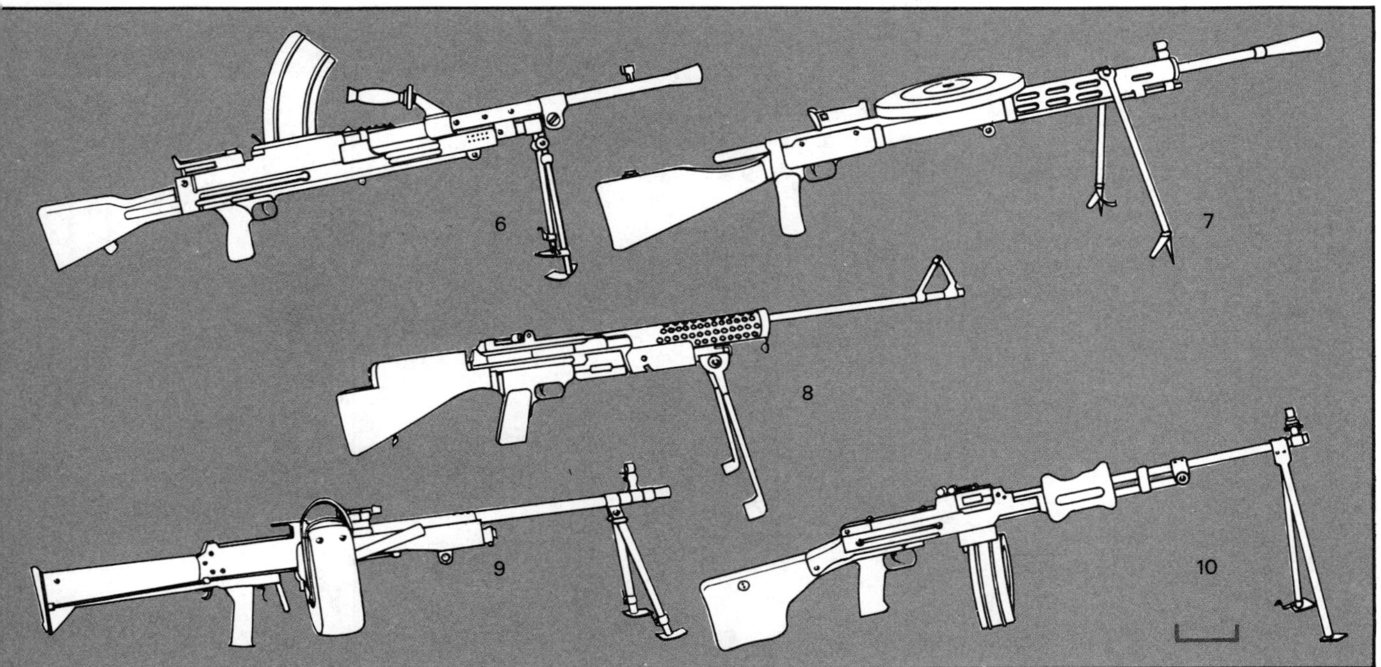

6 Bren MkI 1937. British adaptation of Czech ZB/vz26. One of the most successful LMGs, later marks still in use.
a .303in (and others later)
b 22 lb 5oz (10.15kg)
c 500rpm
d Gas
e Magazine
f Air plus spare barrel

7 Degtyarev DPM 1945. Soviet modification of their DP of 1928. Still in use in Far East and Africa.
a 7.62mm × 54 rimmed.
b 26 lb 13oz (12.2kg)
c 520-580rpm
d Gas
e Drum magazine **f** Air

8 Johnson M41 An advanced American design, but only ever used by US Rangers, Special Services and the Dutch East Indies (Indonesia).
a .30″-'06
b 14 lb 5oz (6.48kg)
c 300-900rpm adjustable
d Recoil
e Magazine
f Air

9 Finnish KK62 Designed, produced and used by Finland post-WW2.
a 7.62mm × 39
b 18.3 lb (8.3kg)
c 1000-1100rpm
d Gas
e Belt
f Air

10 Type 56 Chinese copy of Soviet Degtyarev RPD, also used by Egypt, N Korea, Vietnam, Pakistan.
a 7.62mm M43
b 15 lb 7oz (7kg)
c 700rpm
d Gas
e Belt
f Air

ZB/vz26 (below) Czechoslovak, 1926. Very successful in its own right, also the parent of the Bren.
a 7.92mm and others
b 21lb 5oz (9.6kg)
c 500rpm
d Gas
e Magazine
f Air

Rates of fire Note that figures for rates of fire indicate the cyclic rate of fire; that is to say the theoretical rate, ignoring the need to change magazines and re-cock the mechanism.

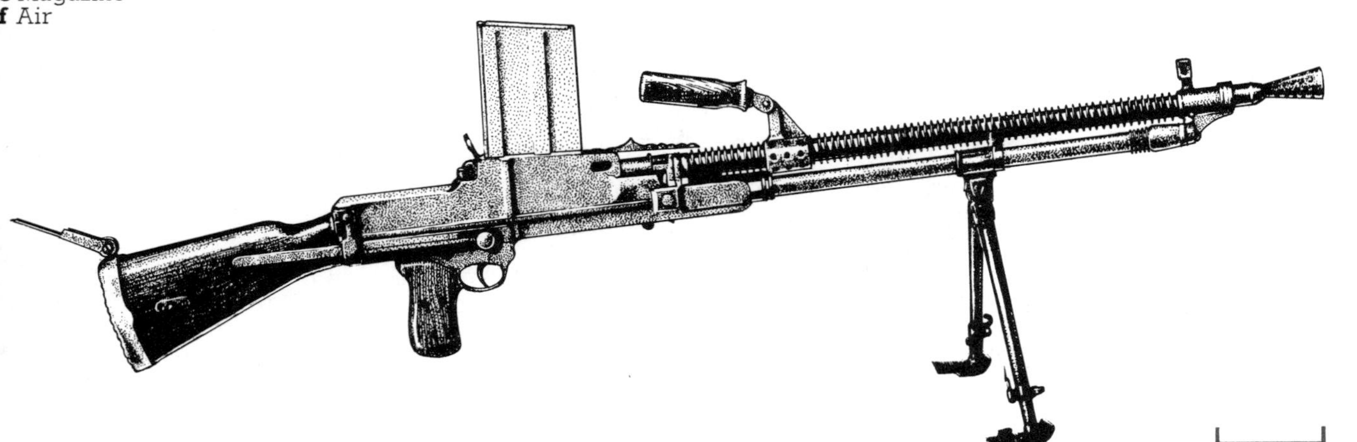

Medium and heavy machine guns

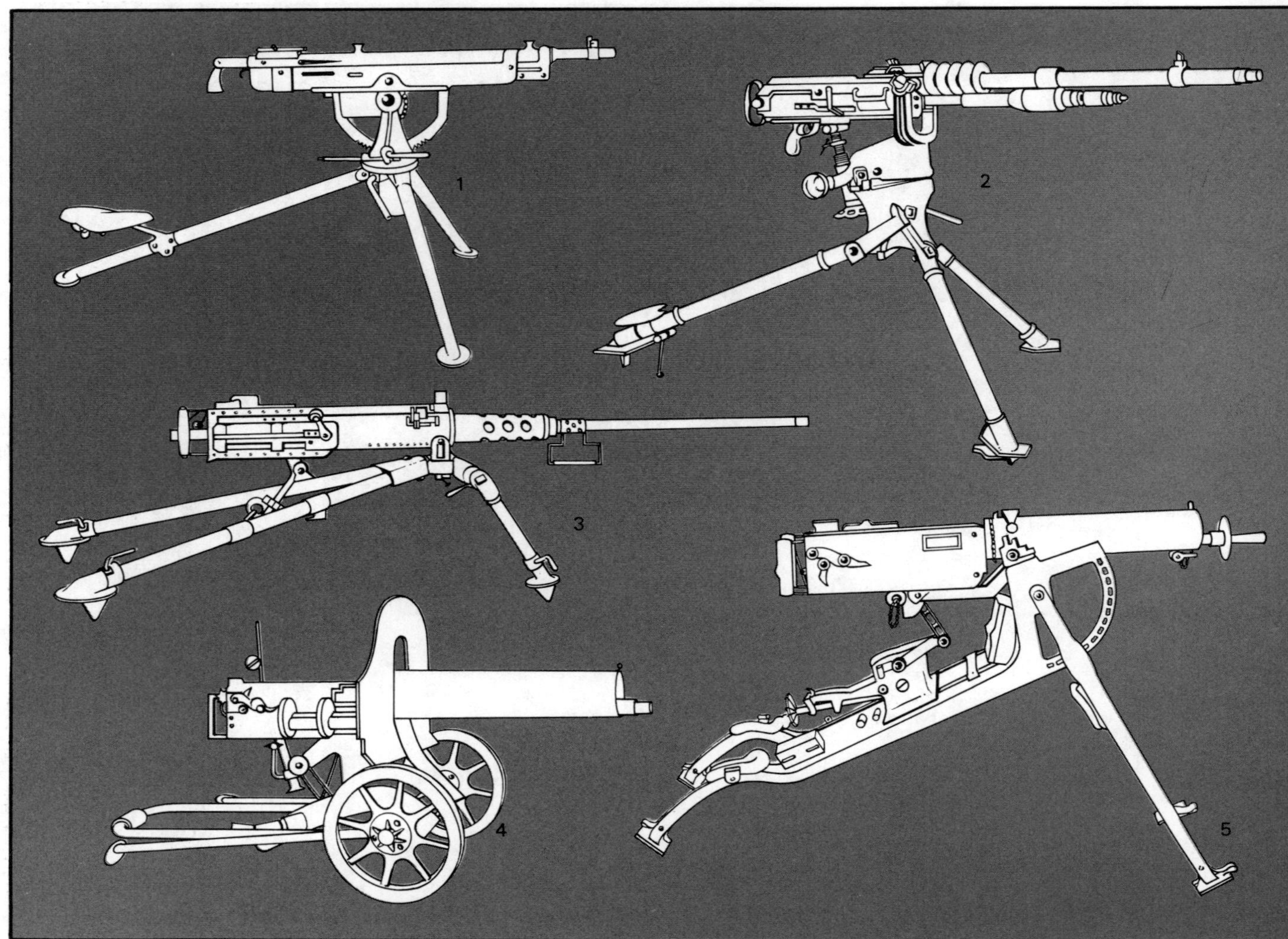

These are the machine guns of popular imagination, used to mow down advancing hordes of enemy, an image based on the appalling slaughter of 1916. The best of these types, the Vickers, Maxim '08 and Browning M1917, could fire 10,000 rounds per hour if the supply of ammunition, new barrels and and water was maintained. The coming of mortars, tanks and aircraft diminished the need for such sustained performance.

Data key
a Caliber
b Weight complete
c Rate of fire (rounds per minute)
d Operating principle
e Method of feed
f Cooling system

1 Browning-Colt Model 1914. American. Nicknamed the "potato digger" from the swinging lever below.
a .30"-'06 and others
b 101lb (45.8kg)
c 400-500rpm
d Gas **e** Belt **f** Air

2 Hotchkiss Model 1914. French. Used in both World Wars by several countries.
a 8mm Lebel Mle 1886
b 88 lb (40kg) **c** 600rpm
d Gas **e** Strip **f** Air

3 Browning M2 American. A heavy machine gun developed in 1918 and still in use in many countries.
a .50in
b 109 lb (49.4kg)
c 600rpm
d Recoil **e** Belt
f Air (in this version)

4 Maxim PM1910 Russian. Used in both World Wars; still in use in SE Asia.
a 7.62mm Russian
b 152 lb 8oz (69.2kg)
c Up to 600rpm
d Recoil **e** Belt **f** Water

5 Maxim '08 German, 1908. Fully exploited from 1914. Caused many of the 60,000 British casualties on July 1, 1916 on the Somme.
a 7.92mm
b 70 lb 8oz (32kg)
c 450rpm with booster
d Recoil **e** Belt **f** Water

6 Schwarzlose Model 07/12. Austrian. One of the few successful blowback medium guns. Used by several other countries in both World Wars.
a 8mm Mod 93 Austrian
b 44 lb (19.9kg) gun only
c 400rpm **d** Blowback
e Belt **f** Water

7 Fiat-Revelli Model 1914. Italian. Updated in 1935 and used to end of WW2.
a 6.5mm M95
b 37 lb 8oz (17kg) gun only
c 500rpm
d Delayed blowback
e Unique clip system; later belt
f Water; later air

8 Degtyarev DShK 1938 Soviet HMG, also much used as an anti-aircraft gun. Still in service.
a 12.7mm
b 78lb 8oz (35.5kg)
c 550rpm
d Gas **e** Belt **f** Air

9 Type 92 Japanese, 1938. The Japanese based all designs on the Hotchkiss.
a 7.7mm rimless and semi-rimless.

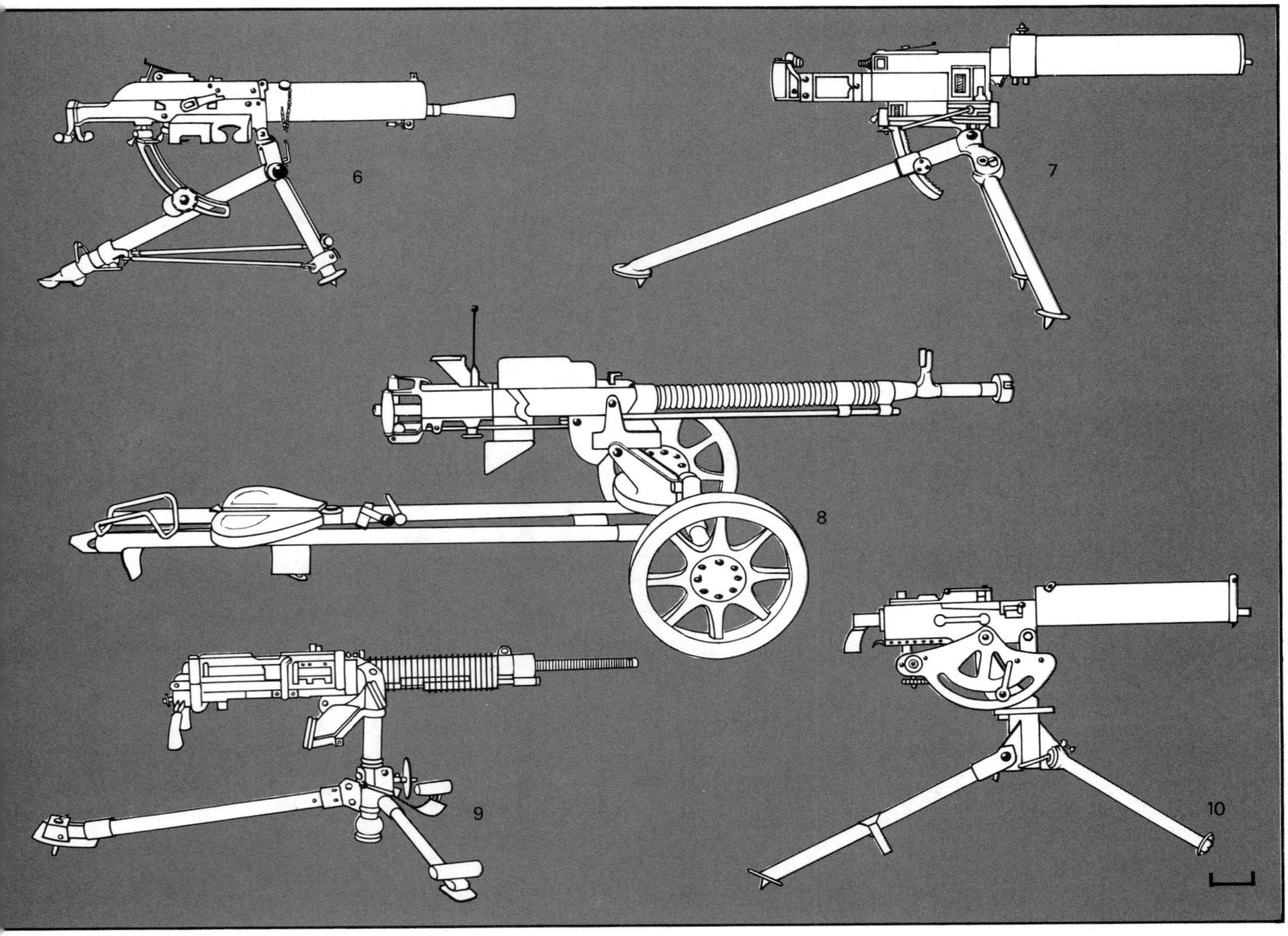

b 122lb (55.4kg)
c 450-500rpm **d** Gas
e Strip with oil device
f Air

10 Browning M1917
American. Successful basis of a family of designs, many of which are still in use.
a .30"-'06
b 41lb (18.6kg)
c 450-600rpm
d Recoil **e** Belt **f** Water

11 Vickers Mk 1 British. Used 1912-65. Late WW2 version shown with its accessories, typical also of other water-cooled types. A hose leads steam to the condenser can for re-use. Dial sight at top rear permitted firing by compass bearing at up to 4500yd (4100m) with Mk8z ammunition. Complicated, but famous for its reliability.
a .303in British
b 88 lb 8oz (40.2kg)
c 450-500rpm
d Recoil **e** Belt **f** Water

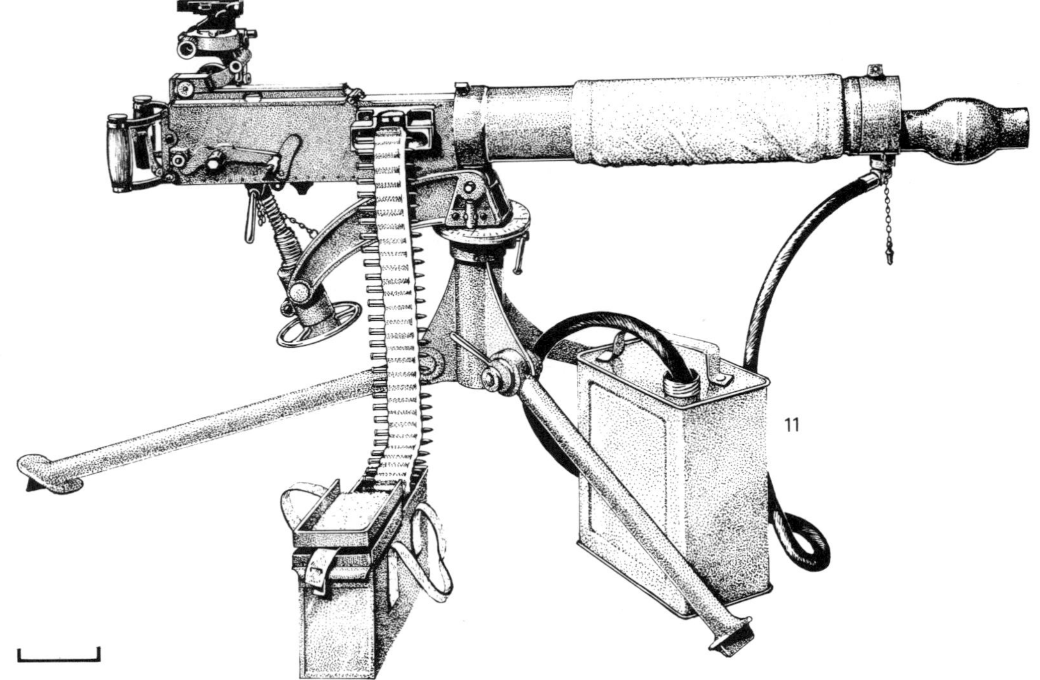

General purpose machine guns

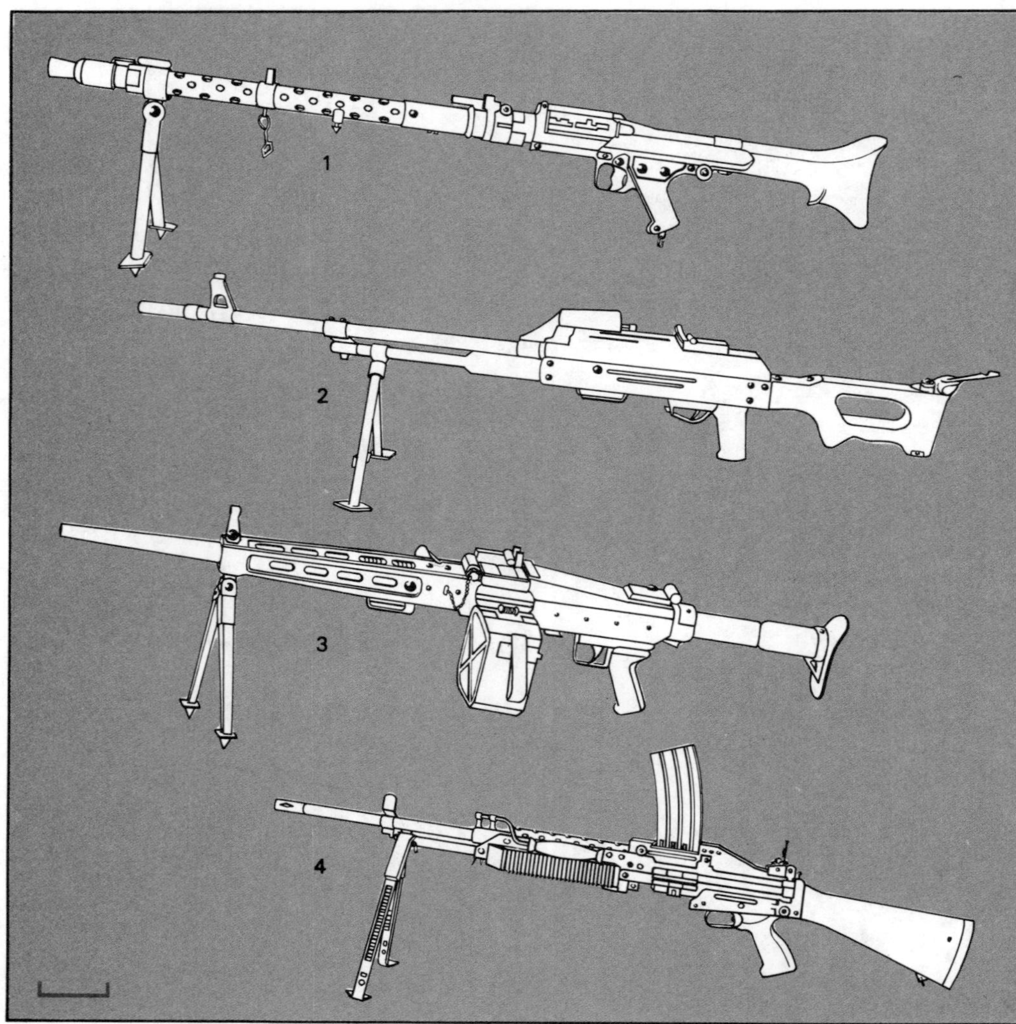

1 MG34 German, 1934. The first gun successfully to combine the roles of the LMG and MMG. Used all through WW2.
a 7.92mm × 57
b 26 lb 11oz (12.1kg)
c 800-900rpm
d Recoil **e** Belt **f** Air

2 Kalashnikov PK Soviet, c.1964, in current service. In the sustained fire role it is called the PKS. Uses an old-fashioned cartridge for the sake of long range.
a 7.62mm × 54 rimmed
b 19 lb 12oz (8.9kg)
c 650rpm
d Gas **e** Belt **f** Air

3 SIG MG710-3 Swiss, 1961. Exported to some South American countries. The spare barrel can be fitted very quickly.
a 7.62mm NATO
b 20 lb 4oz (9.25kg)
c 600rpm
d Delayed blowback
e Belt **f** Air

4 Stoner 63A American, 1963. Shown in the magazine-fed LMG role. The exchange of three parts adapts it to belt feed. First designed in 7.62mm NATO caliber, the series now uses 5.56mm × 45 (.223 in).
a 5.56mm × 45
b 11 lb 11oz (5.3kg)
c 700rpm
d Gas
e Belt or magazine
f Air

In most modern armies, GPMGs fill two needs. In the light role on a bipod, they are used as LMGs, and in the sustained fire role, on a tripod mount, they can be used as MMGs. They are all air-cooled, which means they cannot maintain as high a rate of fire as the old water-cooled MMGs, but the availability of mortars to supplement infantry firepower at longer ranges makes this limitation acceptable.

Data key
a Caliber
b Weight of gun in light role (with bipod)
c Rate of fire
d Operating principle
e Method of feed
f Cooling system
g Weight of tripod (where shown)

The Stoner system In 1963 an American, Eugene Stoner, designed a weapons kit, a range of parts to adapt one basic weapon to six roles. Although it has not sold well, it is thought the idea will shape future MG design. Shown are the parts that form the magazine- and belt-fed LMGs of the 63A series; common parts (**a**); magazine-feed parts (**b**): and belt-feed parts (**c**).

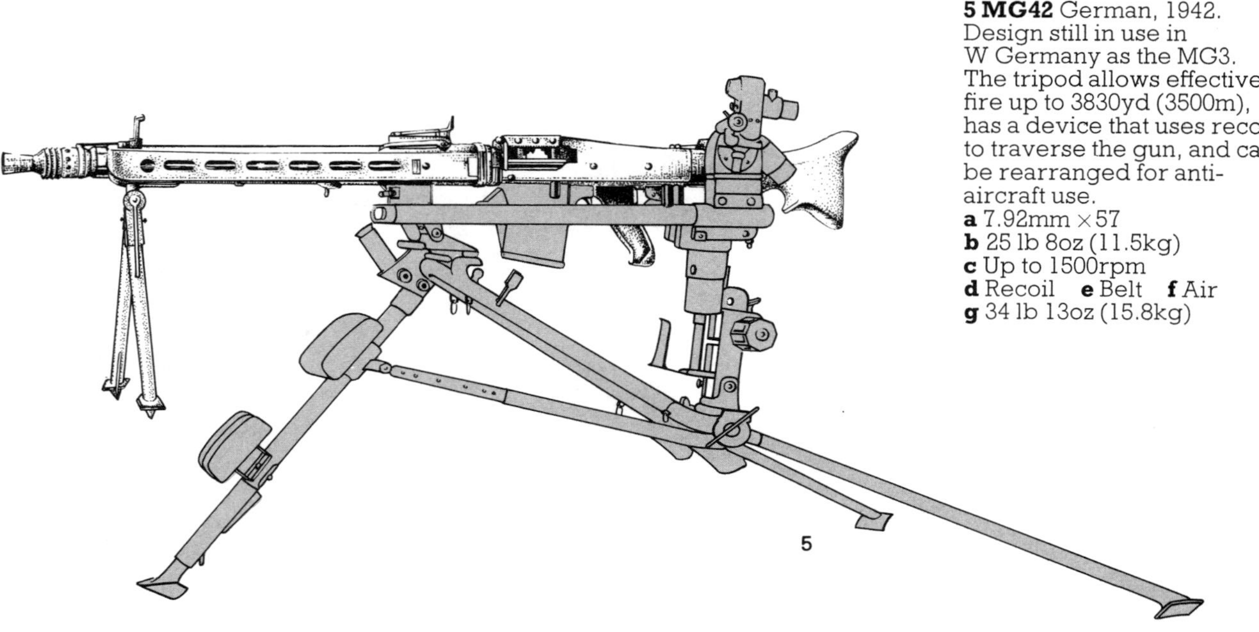

5 MG42 German, 1942. Design still in use in W Germany as the MG3. The tripod allows effective fire up to 3830yd (3500m), has a device that uses recoil to traverse the gun, and can be rearranged for anti-aircraft use.
a 7.92mm × 57
b 25 lb 8oz (11.5kg)
c Up to 1500rpm
d Recoil **e** Belt **f** Air
g 34 lb 13oz (15.8kg)

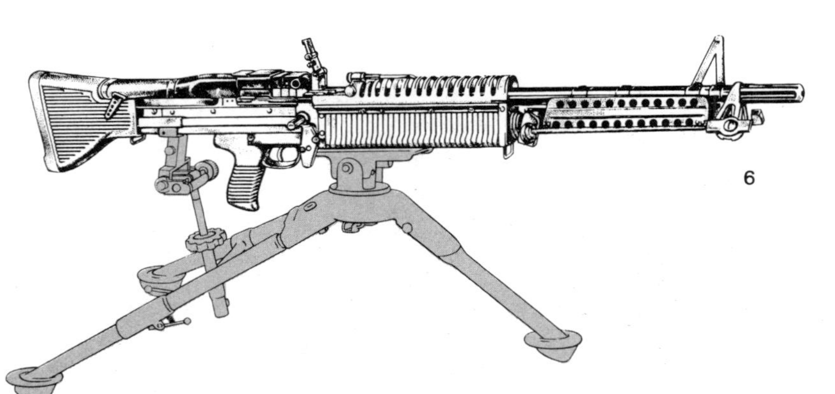

6 US M60 Current US Army issue GPMG, developed in the 1950s. Design owes much to the German MG42 and FG42. Metal stampings, plastic and rubber are used in place of wood and steel where possible.
a 7.62mm NATO
b 23 lb (10.4kg)
c 600rpm
d Gas **e** Belt **f** Air
g 15 lb (6.8kg)

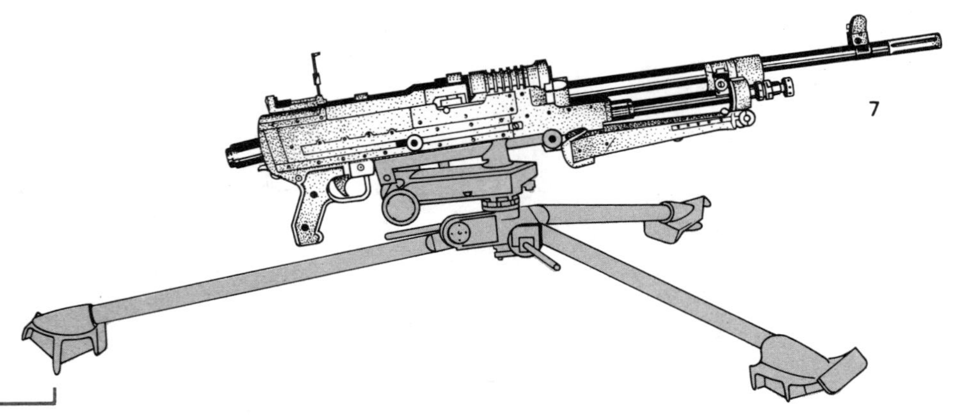

7 L7 A1 British GPMG. This is the Belgian FN MAG as made under license in the UK. Developed by FN in the early 1950s, and now used by at least 20 countries. In this role, the wood butt is replaced by the small buffer shown.
a 7.62mm NATO
b 22 lb 4oz (10.1kg)
c 750-1000rpm
d Gas **e** Belt **f** Air
g 29 lb 15oz (13.6kg)

Vehicle-mounted machine guns

Machine guns lend themselves to use on mechanized vehicles. Weight of gun and ammunition is no longer a problem, and one crew member can control great firepower. On the ground, armored fighting vehicles use MGs against personnel and aircraft. At sea they are used chiefly against air attack. In aerial warfare, their high rate of fire is exploited to hit fleeting targets.

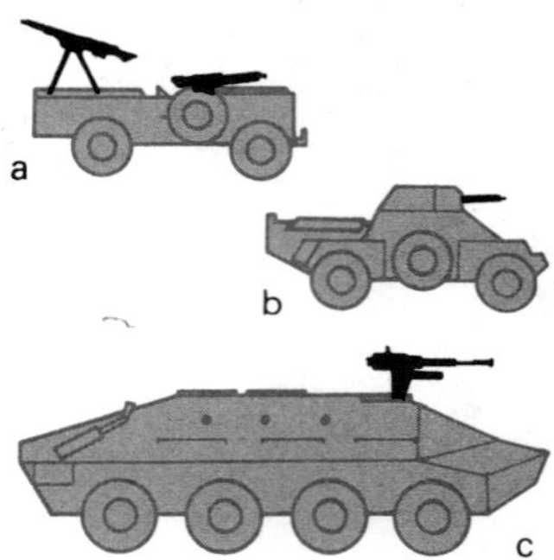

Vehicle mounts (left) For reconnaissance and small raids, MGs are mounted on "jeeps" (**a**) or armored cars (**b**). Mounts on the latter, as on armored personnel carriers (**c**), may be open or enclosed in a small turret.

Naval mountings (right) tend to be multiple, as weight is no problem. This is a quadruple Vickers Mk3 .5in mounting on a World War 2 frigate.

Tank mountings (below) Early tanks could mount up to four MGs in side sponsons (**a**), and a fifth in the hull (**b**). Typically WW2 and modern tanks have MGs on the hull (**c**) and the commander's hatch (**d**). Two co-axial MGs (**e**) are often fitted, one firing spotting rounds (see p. 208) to check the aim of the main gun next to it, the other to be used normally.

Tank machine guns (below)

1 Vickers .5in MkV 1933. Typical of British inter-war heavy tank MGs. The water cooling system was connected to that of the vehicle engine.
a .5in Vickers
b 58 lb (26.3kg)
c 700rpm
d Recoil **e** Belt **f** Water

2 BESA MkIII British version of the Czech Zb53 of 1937. Used in tanks throughout WW2. Also used by the Germans after taking the BRNO factory.
a 7.92mm × 57
b 54 lb (24.5kg)
c 450rpm (variable to 75rpm in Mks I and II)
d Gas **e** Belt **f** Air

3 L37 A1 British, in current use. Another variation of the Belgian FN MAG, used on the commander's hatch.
a 7.62mm NATO
b 24 lb (10.9kg)
c 750-1000rpm
d Gas **e** Belt **f** Air

4 US MG73 Currently used in M60 tank. Typically compact design for co-axial use, where space inside the turret is limited and fumes must exhaust to the outside. Fed from either side.
a 7.62mm NATO
b 29 lb 5oz (13.3kg)
c 450-500rpm
d Recoil **e** Belt **f** Air

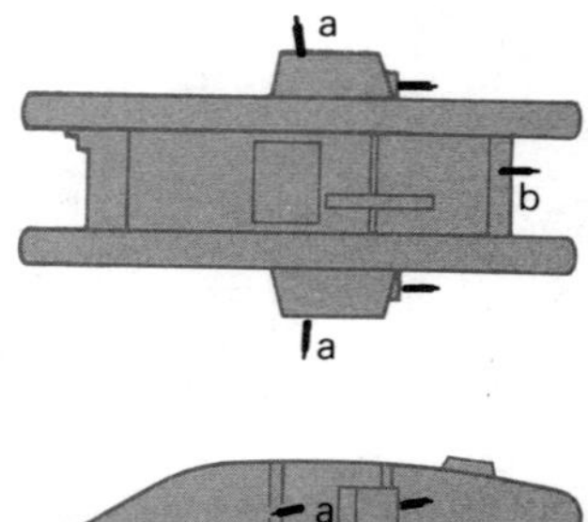

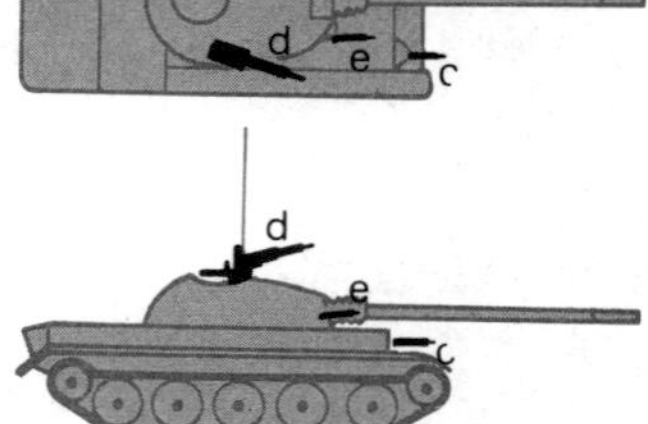

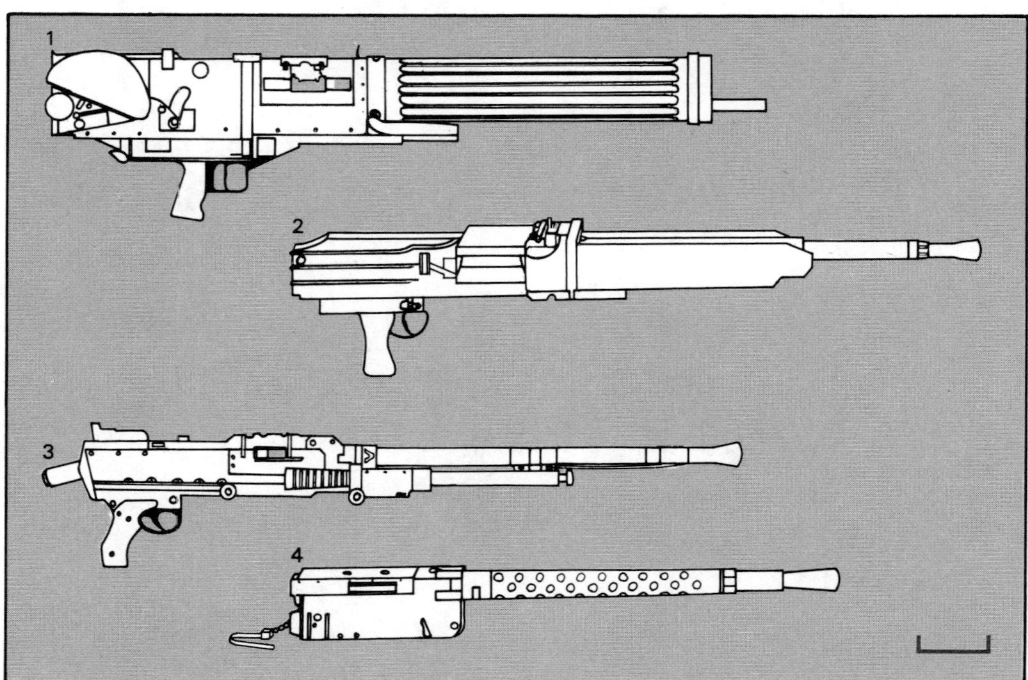

Positions of aircraft MGs (right)
1 WW1 biplanes could have an MG firing over the propellor from the top wing, rearward from the observer's cockpit, or, after the invention of synchronizing gear, forward between the spinning blades.
2 WW2 fighters mounted MGs in the wings, on the nose sides, or in the engine, firing through the center of the propellor boss.
3 WW2 bombers had defensive MGs in windows or movable turrets in many locations.
4 Though rockets are superseding MGs in this role, modern jet aircraft may still mount two heavy MGs in pods under the wings or fuselage.
5 Helicopters are used to attack ground targets with fixed forward-firing MGs or flexible side-mounts.

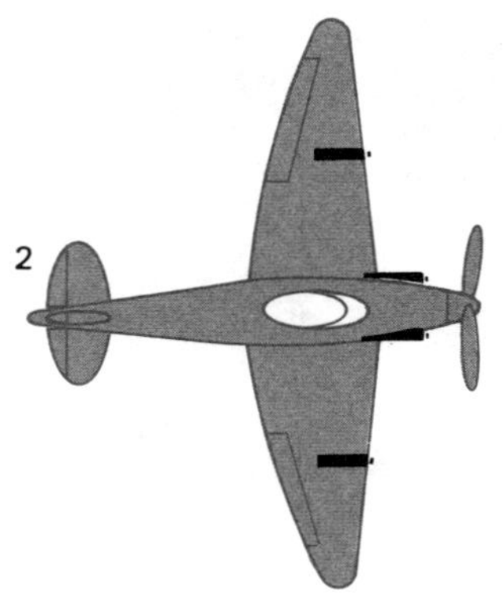

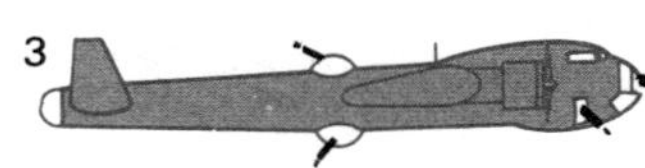

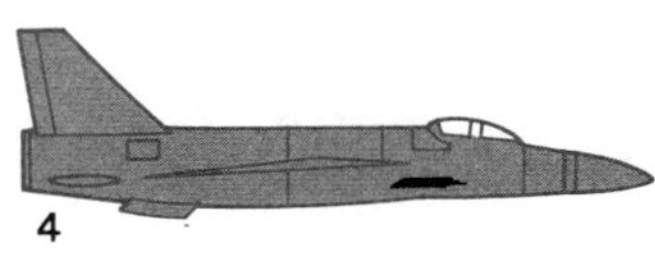

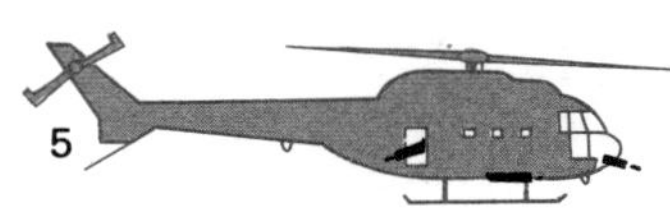

Data key
a Caliber
b Weight of gun
c Rate of fire
d Operating principle
e Method of feed
f Cooling system

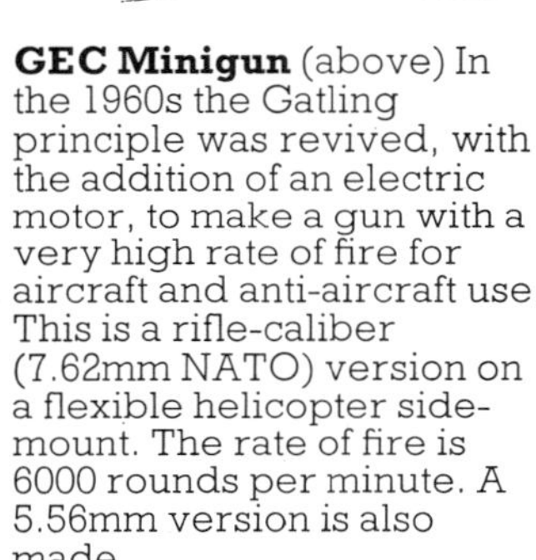

GEC Minigun (above) In the 1960s the Gatling principle was revived, with the addition of an electric motor, to make a gun with a very high rate of fire for aircraft and anti-aircraft use. This is a rifle-caliber (7.62mm NATO) version on a flexible helicopter side-mount. The rate of fire is 6000 rounds per minute. A 5.56mm version is also made.

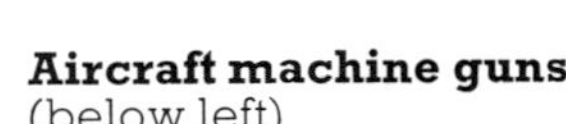

Aircraft machine guns (below left)
1 Parabellum Model 14 German WW1 aircraft gun, using a lightened Maxim recoil system.
a 7.92mm × 57
b 21 lb 9oz (9.8kg)
c 650-750rpm
d Recoil **e** Belt **f** Air
2 Lewis Mk2 Aircraft MG, 1915. Together with the Mk2 Vickers, this was the main British and American WW1 aircraft machine gun.
a .303in and .30″-'06
b 23 lb (10.4kg)
c 550rpm
d Gas **e** Drum magazine
f Air
3 Browning M2 .50in Perhaps the most used aircraft MG of WW2, in both turret and wing mountings. This caliber was very effective against the aircraft of the time.
a .50in
b 65 lb 2oz (29.5kg)
c 800rpm
d Recoil **e** Belt **f** Air
4 Browning Mk2 .303in The British version mounted in Spitfire and Hurricane fighters in the Battle of Britain, and also in bomber turrets.
a .303in
b 26 lb 8oz (12kg)
c 500rpm
d Recoil **e** Belt **f** Air

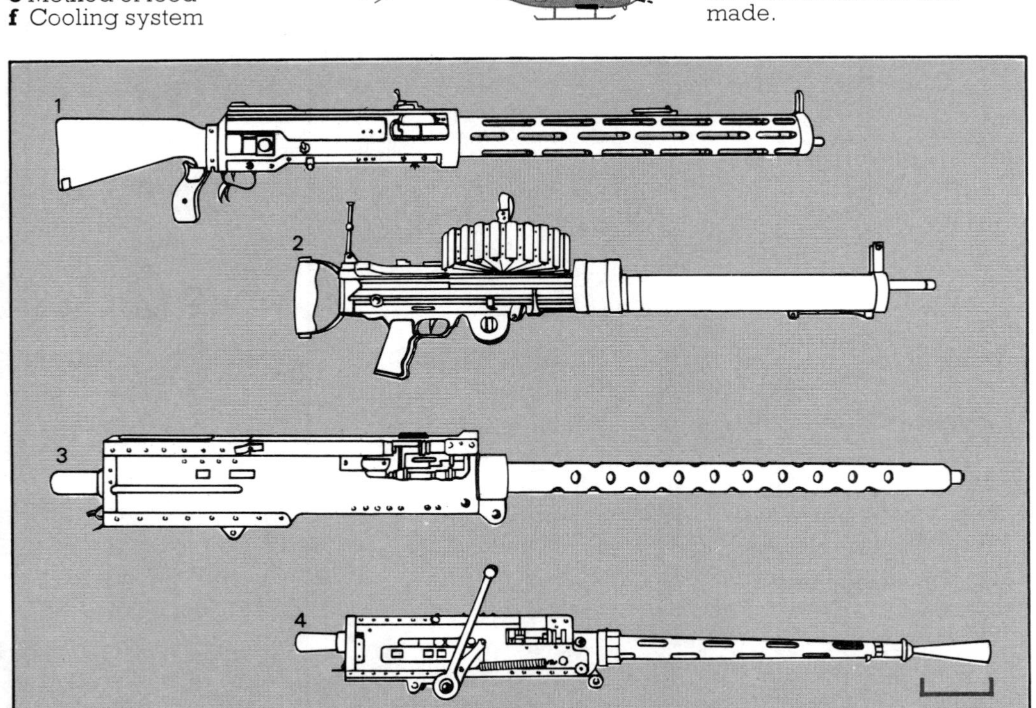

Chapter 5

POSITIONED WEAPONS

Under the heading of positioned weapons, we survey devices that can kill or wound by means of their location. They are all traps of a sort, placed in the enemy's likely path. A few of them are missile-throwers of a kind, but they are neither hand-held nor mounted in the manner of ordinary firearms or artillery. The category of positioned weapons ranges from immobile obstacles that are capable of wounding an incautious enemy, through many kinds of mechanical and explosive trap, to the mines of conventional sea and land warfare. It includes the "bombs" of the urban guerilla.
Many of these weapons have been condemned at times as "infernal machines," and were for a long time disregarded by conventional armies. This attitude would seem to be explained by the impersonal way in which they are used, being put in place and left, without the user requiring the courage to face his enemy.

Photograph (above right) taken from a reconnaissance aircraft over a beach in Normandy, in about May 1944. It shows the preparation, by the Germans, of obstacles designed to wreck landing-craft in the event of a seaborne invasion. Some of the angled stakes have been tipped with high explosive mines. Note the working-party running for cover.

Four frames (below right) from a film of the explosion of a tunneled mine on the Western Front in World War 1. In preparation for their great attack on the Somme on July 1, 1916, the British had placed 18 tons (18.28 tonnes) of high explosive under the German position known as Hawthorn Redoubt. It was detonated at 7.20 AM, ten minutes before H-hour.

Obstacles

The weapons described on these two pages are obstacles intended to deter an enemy by their obvious, unconcealed ability to inflict injury. We are not concerned with the history of fortification, or with hidden obstacles and traps (these will be found on subsequent pages). These obstacles must be "covered" by the defenders' missile weapons, otherwise they are easily neutralized by the attackers.

Injurious obstacles (below) Obstacles that carry the threat of injury have often been used to supplement fortifications such as walls (**a**) and ditches (**b, c**). The devices that we examine here may be as permanent and immobile (**d**) as the main fortifications; or they may be movable, scattered about as and where required (**e**).

Key
a Wall with rampart
b Dry ditch or moat
c Water-filled ditch
d Ditch with spikes
e Scattered obstacles

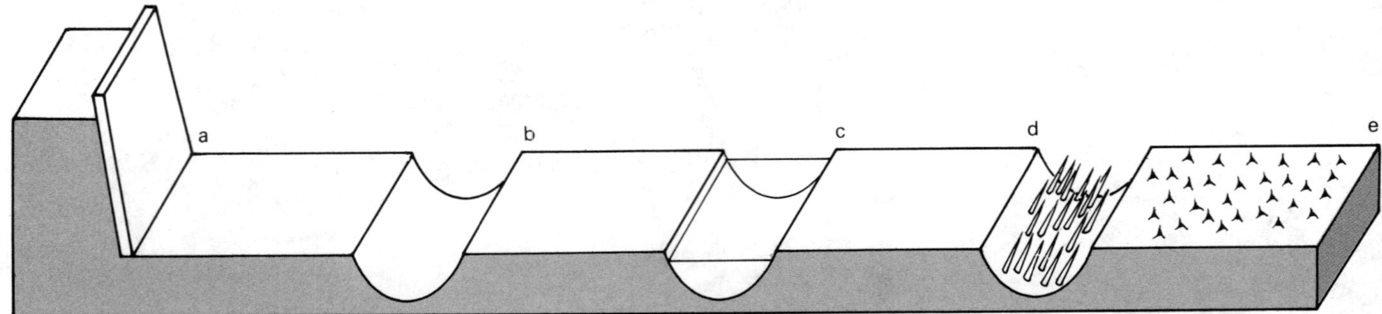

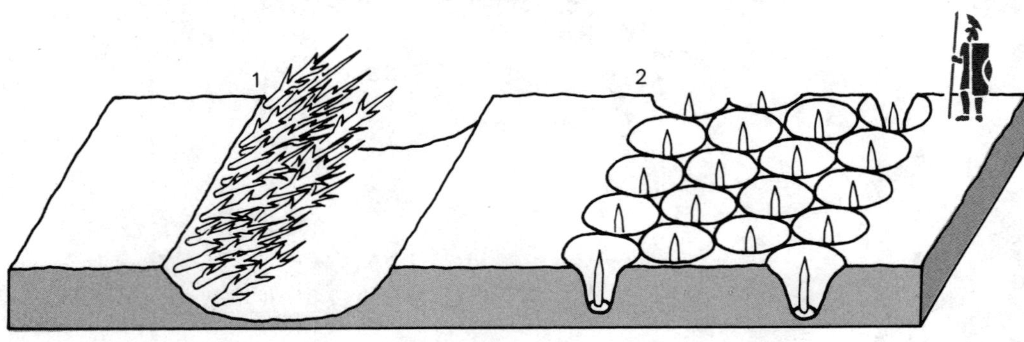

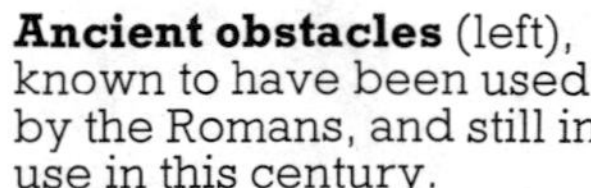

Ancient obstacles (left), known to have been used by the Romans, and still in use in this century.
1 Abatis Trees and bushes, their branches sharpened and laid toward the enemy, were set in the ground, often in combination with a ditch.
2 Trous de loup These were interlocking pits, each containing a sharp spike.

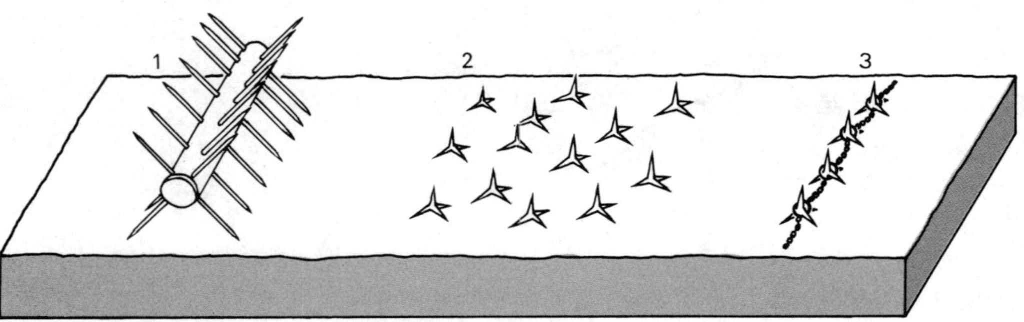

Movable obstacles (left) The main use of these is to block roads.
1 Cheval-de-frise, a log set with spikes.
2 Caltrops or crows' feet. These could be scattered on roads during a retreat to injure the enemy's horses.
3 Caltrop chain. Can be quickly pulled across a road to stop wheeled vehicles at check-points.

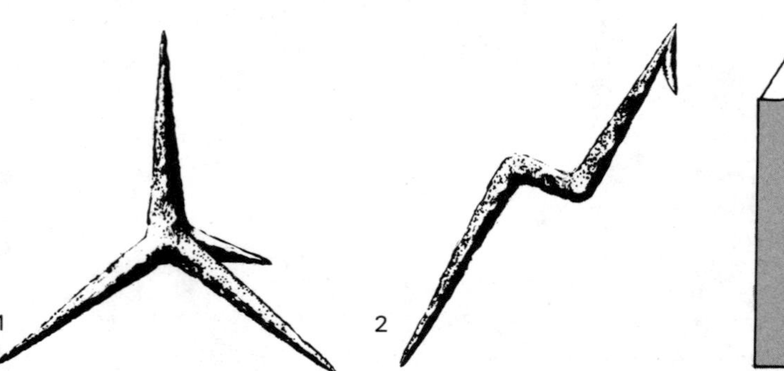

Roman obstacles (left)
1 Roman caltrop of iron.
2 Iron spike found at the site of the siege of Alesia (52BC), in what is now France. The siege was an incident in Julius Caesar's conquest of Gaul. The spike would originally have been set in the end of a short stake hammered into the ground, as shown in the diagram (near left).

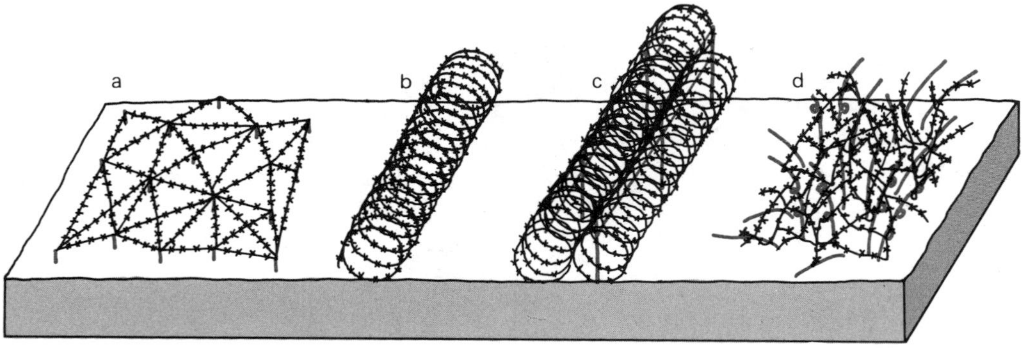

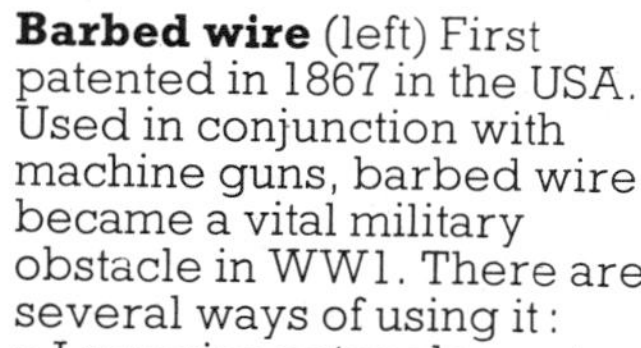

Barbed wire (left) First patented in 1867 in the USA. Used in conjunction with machine guns, barbed wire became a vital military obstacle in WW1. There are several ways of using it:
a Low wire entanglement, strung between pickets at ankle height.
b Coiled or "dannert" wire.
c Fences of several coils.
d Wire thicket, haphazard to hinder clearance.

Two types of wire (left)
1 Length of wire from a WW1 battlefield in Belgium, made in the usual way with sharpened wire barbs twisted round a central strand.
2 German WW1 wartime economy "razor wire." This was a sharp-edged zig-zag tape cut from sheet steel.

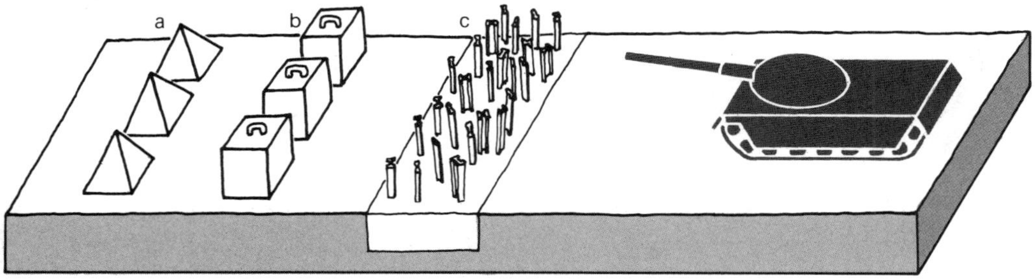

Anti-tank obstacles (left) Massive obstacles are needed to block the movement of tanks. Most are pointed, being designed to break the tracks of a tank should it try to cross. Obviously, they also bar the way for wheeled vehicles.
a Concrete "dragons' teeth"
b Concrete blocks
c Steel girders or railroad tracks set in concrete

Beach obstacles (left) These are a feature of 20th century warfare, erected on vulnerable shorelines as a defense against amphibious landings. They consist mainly of large timber or steel posts, placed below high-water mark to pierce the hulls of enemy landing-craft. They were sometimes tipped with explosives. (See also photo pp.220–221.)

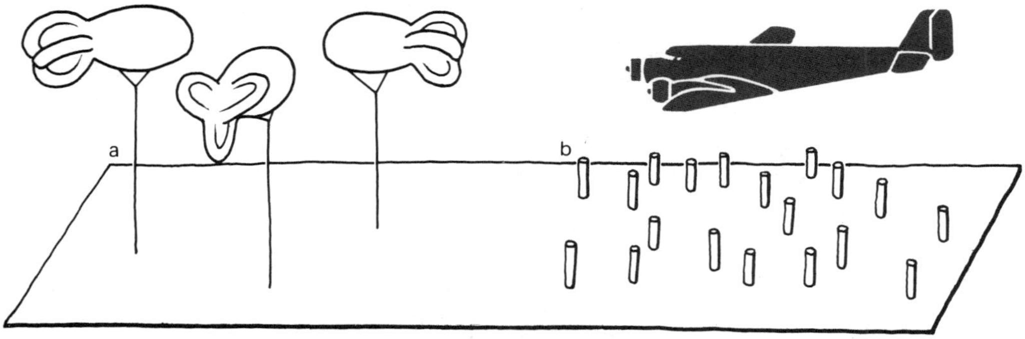

Anti-aircraft obstacles (left)
a In both World Wars, barrage balloons were used to help defend cities against bomber aircraft. The cables below the balloons were especially dangerous to raiders at night.
b In WW2, open spaces were sometimes sown with posts to prevent the landing of troop-carrying gliders.

Simple and mechanical traps

The devices shown under this heading are concealed with the intention of killing or wounding the enemy. Thus they are more aggressive in intention than obstacles, which are usually displayed with a view to deterring his approach.
These traps are most effective and most easily improvised in jungles, and that is where they are most often encountered. Most are also used for hunting animals.

Assyrian bas-relief (left) of Eannatum, King of Lagash, with his enemies caught in a net. Although in this case the net may be only a symbol of captivity, nets are one of the oldest forms of trap. (Louvre, Paris.)

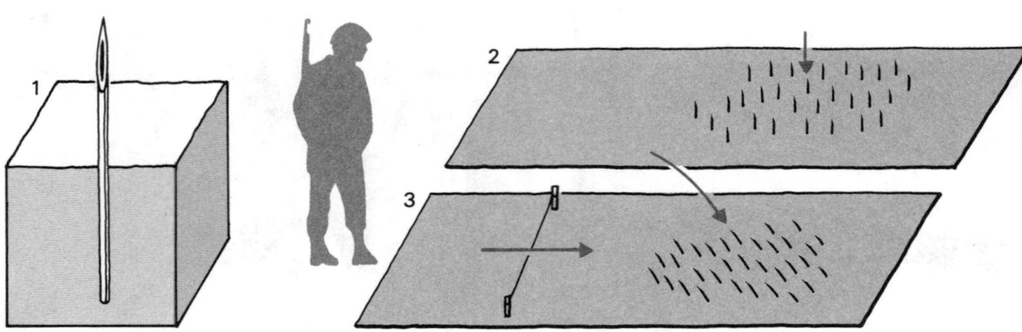

Panjis (right), or punjis, are spikes made usually from bamboo, which is hard and naturally sharp when cut (**1**). They may simply be placed on jungle paths (**2**) to pierce the sole of a boot, or be combined with a trip-wire (**3**) so that the victim falls onto the spikes.
Panjis are often smeared with dung to cause an infected wound.

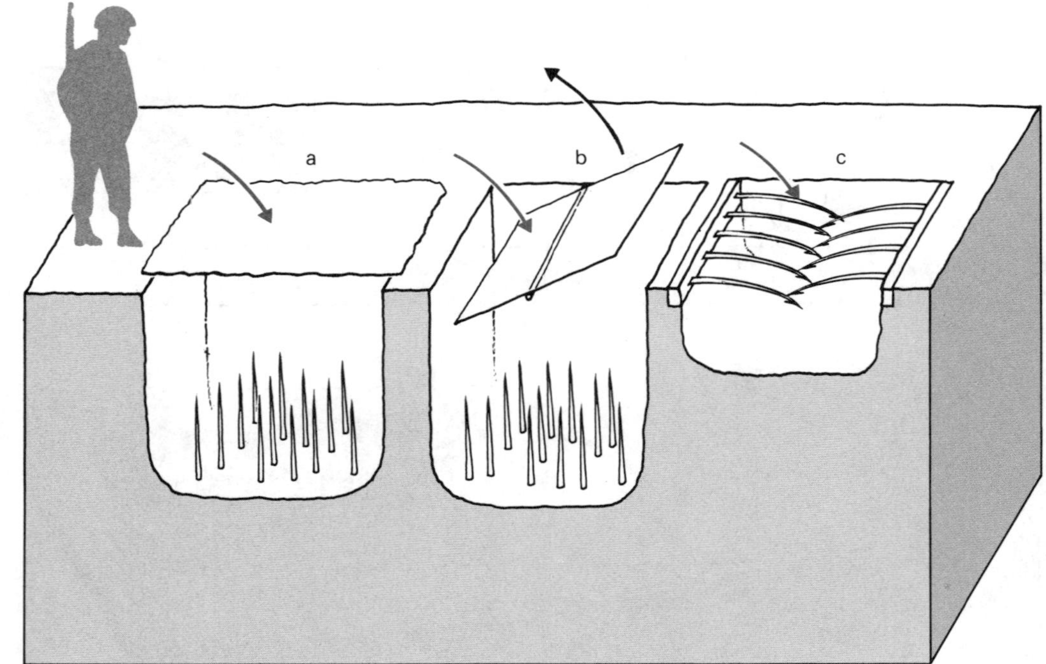

Pits (right) are often combined with spikes to increase the wounding effect of both. We show three types encountered during the Vietnam War of 1961–75.
a Panji pit covered with leaves.
b Panji pit covered with a platform balanced on a pole.
c "Venus' flytrap," a pit with flexible metal spikes across the top. The spikes are set in a wooden frame (see bottom of page) and support the camouflage. The victim's leg is trapped, and any attempt to pull it out will only worsen the injury.

Spiked frame (right) from a Vietcong pit trap, as shown at (**c**) above. The frame is wooden and the barbed spikes are steel.

Descending traps (right)
1 A spiked log is hidden in a tree above a trail, held there by a catch linked to a tripwire. When the tripwire is disturbed, the log swings down along the path to strike the victim.
2 A variation on the spiked log trap uses a weighted flat board with spikes on the under surface, falling vertically.

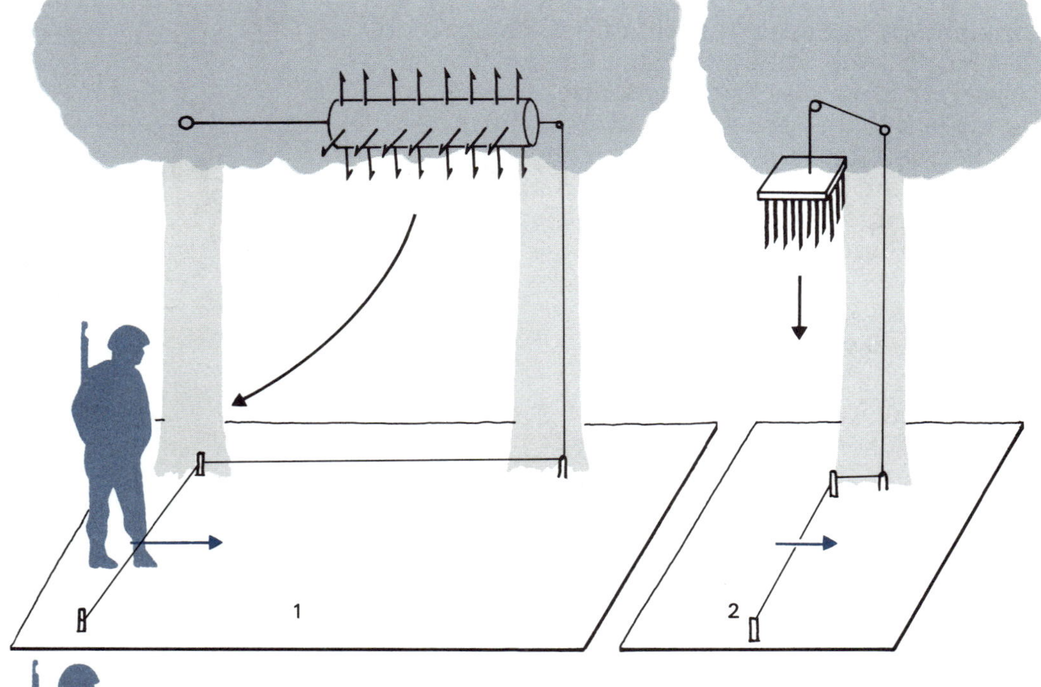

Two mechanical traps (right)
A The victim treads on the small board which pivots down into the pit and simultaneously levers up the spiked board, striking the victim in the chest or face.
B An arrow, powered by strong elastic, is concealed in a pit beside the trail, and is released by a tripwire.

Man-traps (right) were often set by 19th century landowners to catch or deter trespassers and poachers. Most consisted of two hinged jaws that closed about the victim's leg when he stepped on a central tilting plate (**1, 2**). The jaws were forced together by a loop on a flat spring (**3**). The example (below) is from Yorkshire. (Castle Museum, York.)

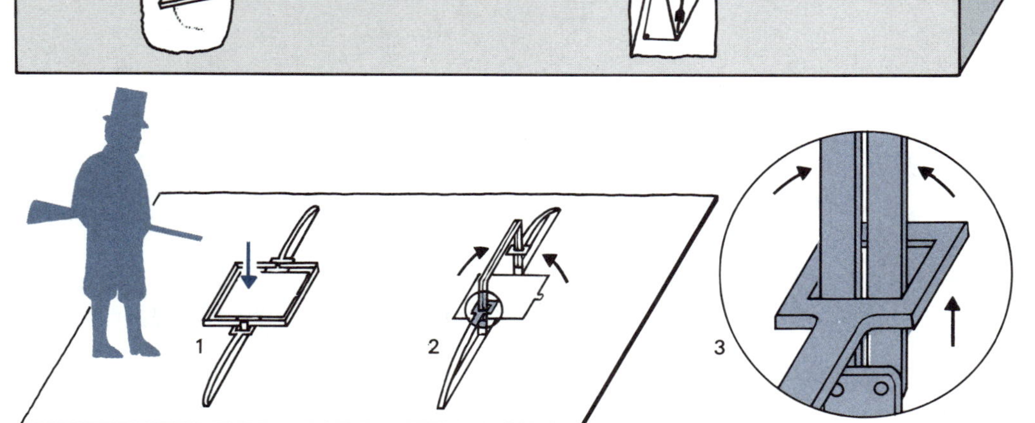

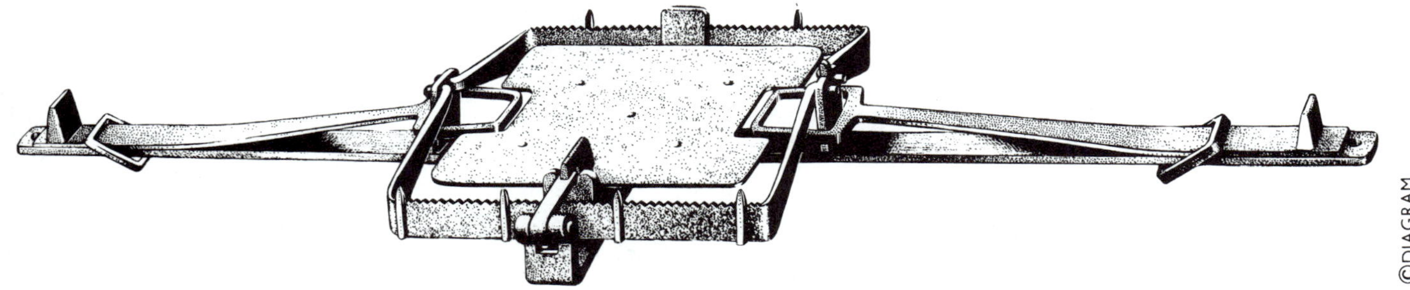

Explosive positioned weapons

The use of explosives, whether to propel a missile or to create a blast effect, has greatly extended the effectiveness of traps. These weapons, usually known as boobytraps, or simply bombs, are now in almost daily use with guerillas and terrorist groups. We distinguish between three main kinds: self-acting devices; command detonated devices; and time bombs.

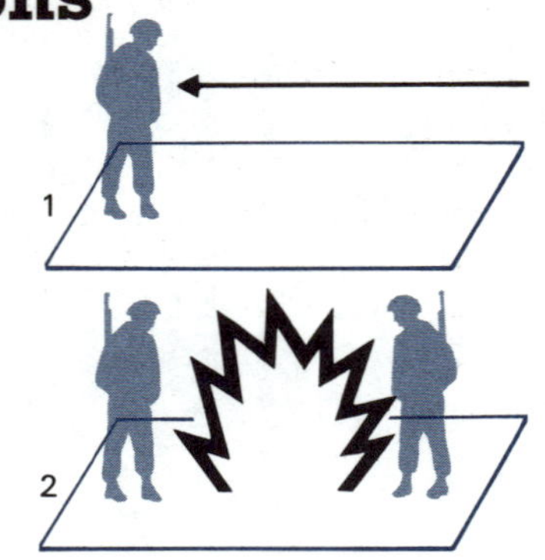

Weapon effects (left)
Whatever type of trigger mechanism may be fitted, the explosive device used in a boobytrap may be one of two kinds.
1 Firearms are sometimes adapted as boobytraps.
2 Most boobytraps, however, use blast and/or fragmentation effects, as being more likely to catch one or more victims.

Self-acting devices (right) are triggered off by the victim. Among the trigger mechanisms that have been used are those that are set off by:
a Disturbing a tripwire
b Applying pressure
c Releasing pressure
d Causing vibration
e Shedding light
Such trigger mechanisms may be used to set off a variety of charges.

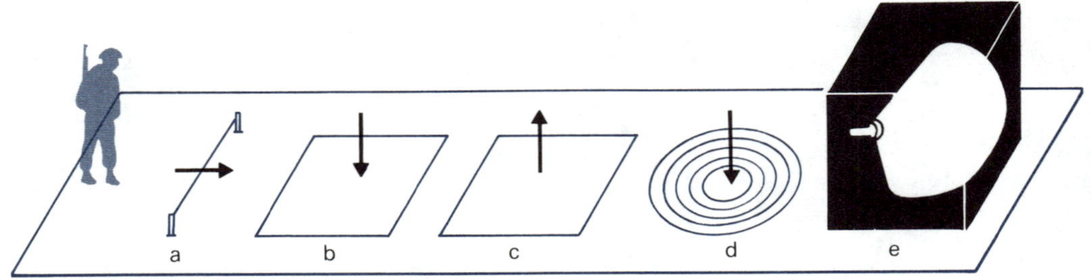

Command detonated (right) or controlled traps are set off from a safe distance by an observer. The link with the bomb may be made by pulling a cord (**1**) or more usually now by electric cable (**2**) or a radio beam (**3**). Such devices have often been used in recent years by terrorist groups, to ambush their opponents.

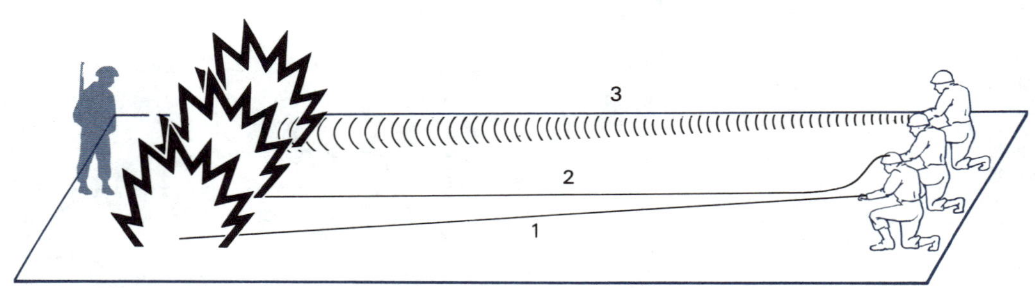

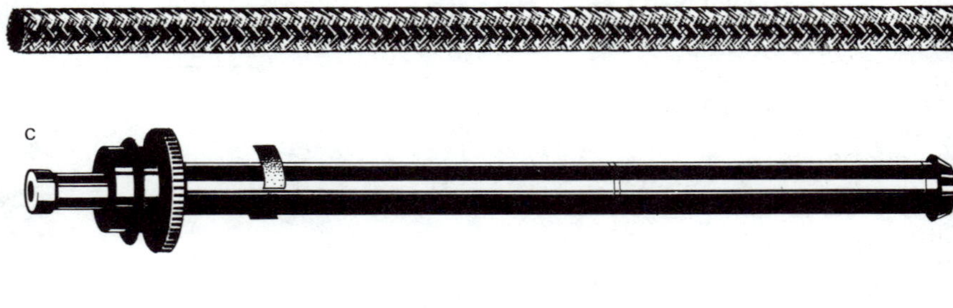

Time bombs (above)
There are three categories of timing device commonly used to achieve delayed detonation of time-bombs:
a Clockwork
b Combustible fuze
c Chemical "clocks," which often work by the slow action of acid making or breaking an electrical connection.

a Clockwork delay device developed for the US and British secret services for use in sabotage in WW2. The model shown had a delay of up to 24hrs, and there were also 12hr and eight-day models. At the pre-selected time, a spring-loaded firing-pin was released to strike a percussion primer and so set off the bomb. One use was on naval limpet mines.

b Bickford fuze was the first successful combustible delay cord, invented by an Englishman in 1831. It had a core of compressed fine gunpowder bound with jute or flax thread and waterproofed with asphalt or gutta-percha. It burned at the rate of about one yard in 70sec. Modernized plastic-covered versions are still in use.

c "Time pencil" developed by Britain and the US in WW2 for initiating explosive devices. After being screwed in place, the thin metal case of the tube is crushed. This releases a corrosive liquid, which then eats away a wire restraining a sprung firing-pin. It was the main initiator supplied to resistance movements.

Positioned missile-throwers

Firearms, or other missile-throwing weapons, when fixed in position and set up as boobytraps, have an obvious application in the defense of ground. They are especially useful if manpower is scarce. "Robot" guns are known to be in place on the eastern side of the "iron curtain" that divides East from West Germany. Directional mines are also in common military use for defense and ambush.

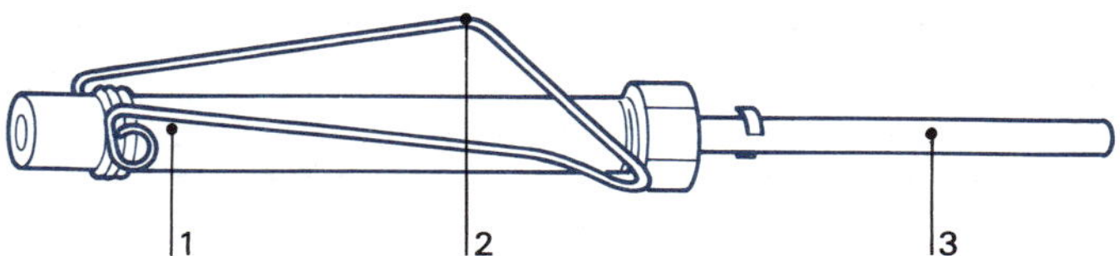

"Bushmaster" (above), the codename for a WW2 US device for deceiving the enemy in the jungle by simulating sniper fire. It was a crude firearm of .45in (11.5mm) caliber, consisting of a barrel (**1**) attached to a tree by a clip (**2**) and set off by a "time pencil" delay unit (**3**).

Spring gun (right), used in England c. 1800 to deter trespassers. The gun would be concealed beside a likely approach, perhaps on a path through a wood containing valuable "game" birds. Two tripwires could be attached to the ring at the end of the trigger-rod. If either wire was disturbed, the gun would swivel in that direction and fire. Such lethal devices were made illegal in the 1830s. Since then many designs for non-lethal alarm guns, firing blank charges to scare away intruders, have been patented.

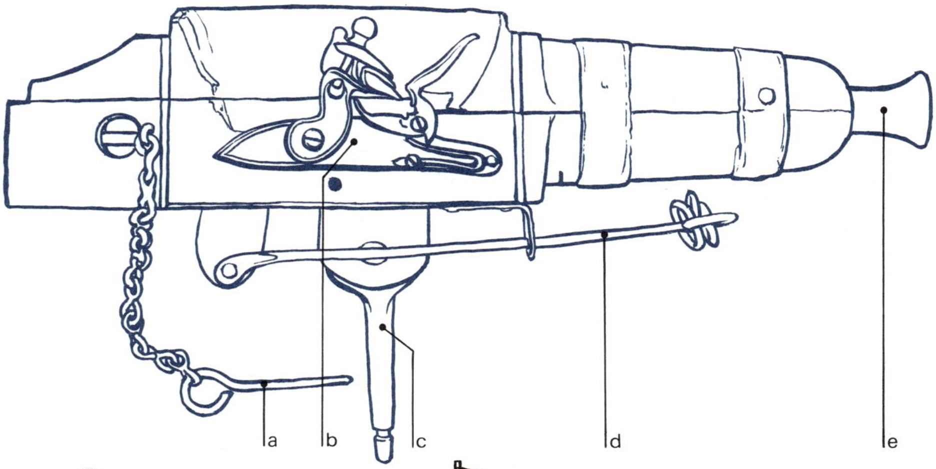

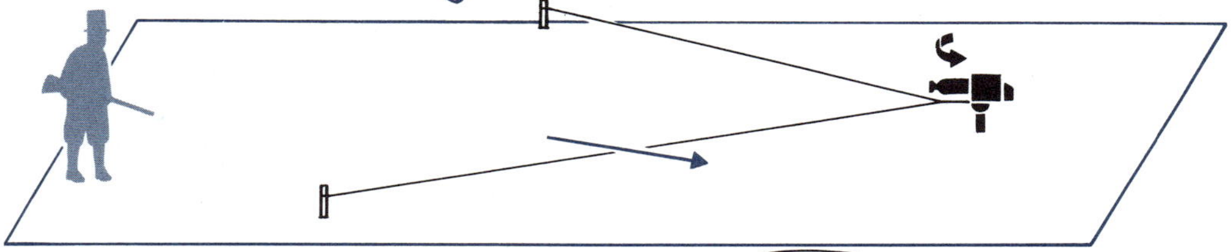

a Peg and chain to limit the arc of fire
b Flintlock mechanism
c Swivel pin
d Trigger-rod and ring
e Barrel

Fougasses (right) were used in fixed defensive systems from the 16th century to the early 20th.
A In the bottom of a sloping pit, explosives were placed, covered by boards and a filling of rocks or brick rubble.
B During an enemy attack, the explosives could be set off, showering a large area with heavy missiles.

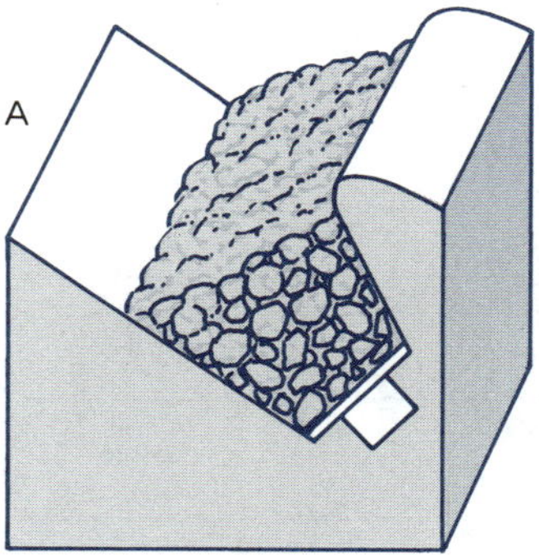

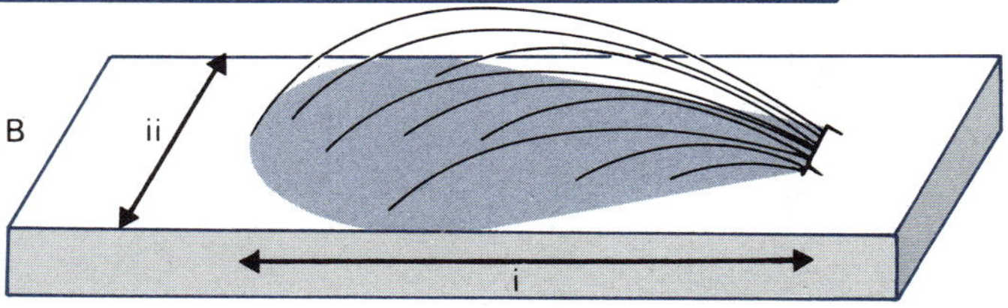

Beaten zone with a charge of 80lb (36kg) of powder and 5 tons (5.08 tonnes) of rocks.

Length (i) 450ft (137m)
Greatest breadth (ii) 350ft (106m)

Claymore mine (right), a "directional mine" that scatters a hail of steel balls out to 270yd (250m) over a 60° arc. It consists of a plastic case holding a curved slab of explosive, faced with hundreds of ball-bearings set in plastic. It can be laid as a self-acting boobytrap, or be "command detonated." In service with the British, US and other armies.

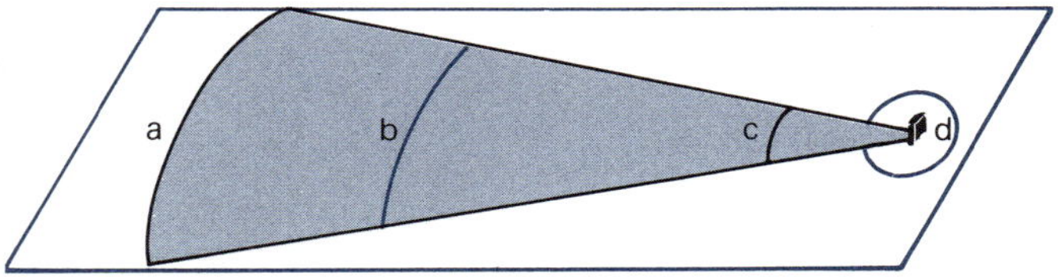

a Extreme range 270yd (250m)
b Arc of fire 60°
c Effective range 55yd (50m)
d Slight danger in other directions

Explosives in bulk

Despite their cumbersome and often dangerous form, explosives have been used in bulk as weapons in many ways, from the undermining of late medieval fortifications to the parcel bombs of 20th century urban terrorists. Before illustrating some of these uses, we explain the main types of chemical (as distinct from mechanical and nuclear) explosive, and the ways in which they explode.

Guy Fawkes (left) shown checking the barrels of gunpowder that he and other conspirators had placed under the Houses of Parliament in London in 1604. This famous plot to assassinate King James I and the whole of Parliament was discovered hours before the explosion was due.

Low and high explosives (right) There are several ways of classifying chemical explosives. The main division is between low or deflagrating and high or detonating types. Low explosives (**a**) explode simply by burning very rapidly, and have a comparatively gentle, heaving effect. In high explosives (**b**), a shock wave can be set up which, by compressing the explosive and thus raising its temperature, causes self-ignition at very high speed. The resulting detonating wave travels, in TNT for example, at about 15,600mph (7000m/sec). Thus high explosives have a shattering rather than a heaving effect, and are not so suitable for use as propellants.

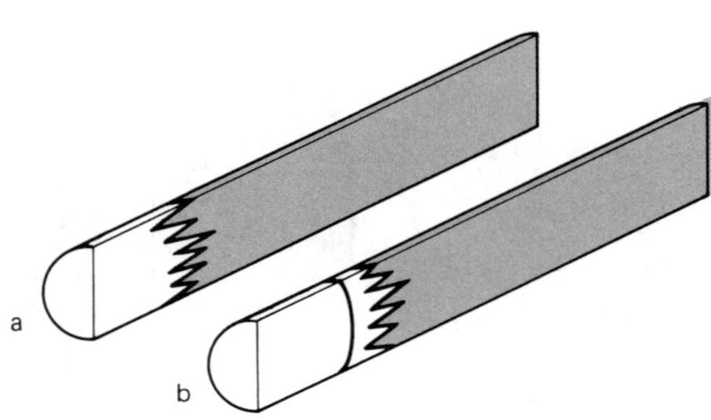

Name	Main constituents or chemical name	Low explosive	High explosive	Primer	Detonator	Detonating fuze	Slow fuze	Propellant	Shell-filling	Insensitive	Sensitive	Highly sensitive	Remarks
Black powder (Gunpowder)	Carbon, sulfur, potassium nitrate	●					●	●	●	●			Versatile and still in specialized use
Nitroglycerin	Glycerol, nitric acid, sulfuric acid		●									●	Too sensitive alone, but used in making other explosives
Nitrocellulose	Nitric acid, cellulose		●					●			●		Used mostly in propellants
Picric acid (Lyddite, melinite, trinitrophenol)	Phenol, sulfuric acid, nitric acid		●						●	●			Main Allied shell-filling in WW1
Ammonium picrate	Picric acid, ammonium		●						●	●			Filling for anti-tank shells
Trinitrotoluene (TNT)	Toluene, nitric acid		●						●	●			The main high explosive of WW2
Amatol	TNT, ammonium nitrate		●						●	●			Shell and bomb filling in WW1 and 2
RDX (Cyclonite, Hexogen)	Cyclotrimethylene trinitramine		●		●	●			●		●		WW2 and still in wide use, often mixed with TNT
PETN	Pentaerythitol tetranitrate		●		●	●			●		●		Often mixed with TNT
Torpex	TNT, RDX, aluminum		●								●		Filling for torpedoes and bombs in WW2
Mercuric fulminate	Mercury, alcohol, nitric acid		●	●	●						●		Ignited by spark, flame, friction or shock
Lead azide	Lead, nitrogen		●	●	●						●		Substitute for mercuric fulminate

Military explosives (left) The table gives some basic facts about important military explosives. Since the 1860s, many high explosives have been developed that satisfy the military requirements of chemical stability in storage, cheapness, and insensitivity to shock. Some famous names such as dynamite and gelignite have been excluded from this list as they have been used more in civil engineering than in war. More information on the use of explosives as propellants in missile-throwing weapons can be found on pp.112, 164 and 227. Plastic explosives (PE) are formed by adding waxes, oil or other plasticizers to a suitable high explosive to give it the useful quality of being able to be molded by hand.

Ignition Many high explosives are difficult to ignite—a useful safety feature. It may be necessary to use a series of three explosives : an impact-sensitive one as a primer, to make a flash to set off a detonating compound, which in turn sets up a shock wave to ignite the insensitive but powerful main charge.

Mines in the older sense of explosives placed by tunneling under enemy defenses (right) were used in siege warfare from the late Middle Ages onward.
1 In WW1, the procedure was that a "sap" was dug forward, and from the end of this a tunnel was made to a point under the enemy trench. Explosives were stacked in a side chamber, a fuze laid, and the tunnel "tamped" or sealed. Troops were held ready to rush over and occupy the crater.
2 The explosion had two effects: it ruptured the surrounding earth, and made a crater in the ground above. Mines were classified by their proportions, a "common mine" having a "two-lined" crater with a diameter of twice its depth. (See also photos, pp.220–221.)

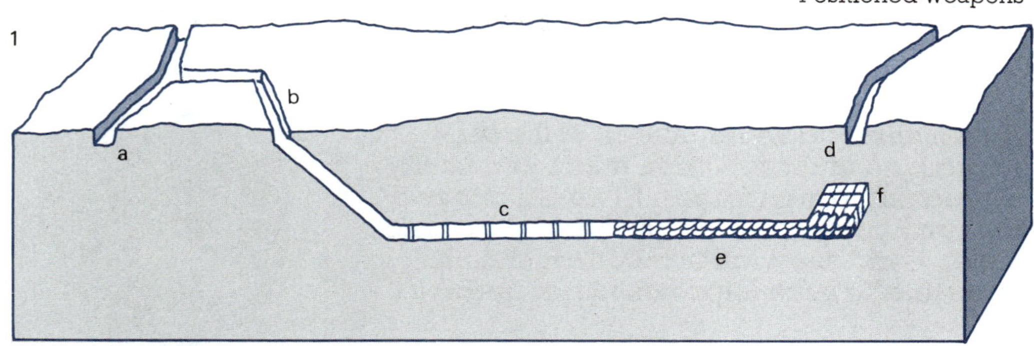

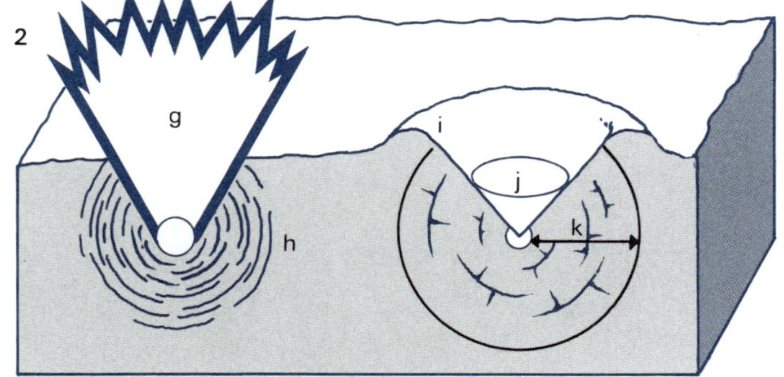

Key
a Own front line trench
b Sap
c Tunnel gallery
d Enemy front line trench
e Tamping
f Explosives
g Main force of explosion
h Shock waves
i, j Debris
k Radius of rupture

Demolitions and sabotage
Explosives are used by both regular and irregular forces to attack structures and people.
1 Communications (right) are a favorite target. Railroads (**i**) and roads (**ii**) can be cut, and the blast may be timed to catch passing traffic. Bridges (**iii**) are often chosen for attack, being especially vulnerable and important.

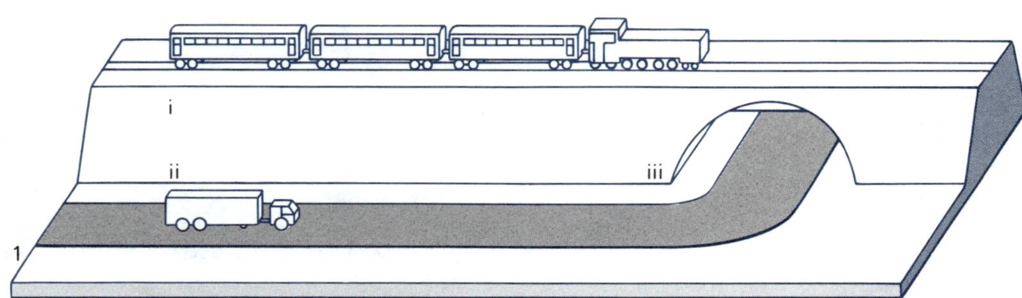

2 Indiscriminate attacks on personnel (right) Explosive boobytraps or time bombs may be left behind by retreating armies or placed by guerillas or political activists. Favorite targets are public or military buildings (**A**) or transport (**B**), shopping areas (**C**), or any essential services. The bomb is usually hidden inside an everyday object.

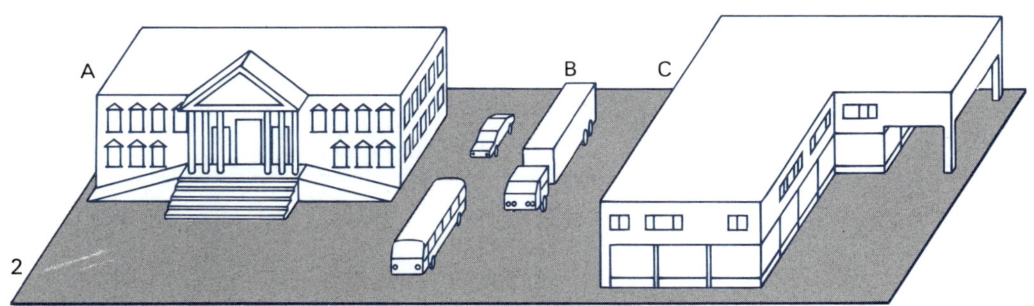

3 Attacks on individuals (right) Explosive devices in many forms have been used to assassinate specific individuals. In the July 1944 plot against Hitler, explosives in a briefcase (**a**) were placed near him. Other devices are explosives in parcels (**b**) or letters (**c**) addressed to the victim, or in his or her automobile, often set to explode on starting (**d**).

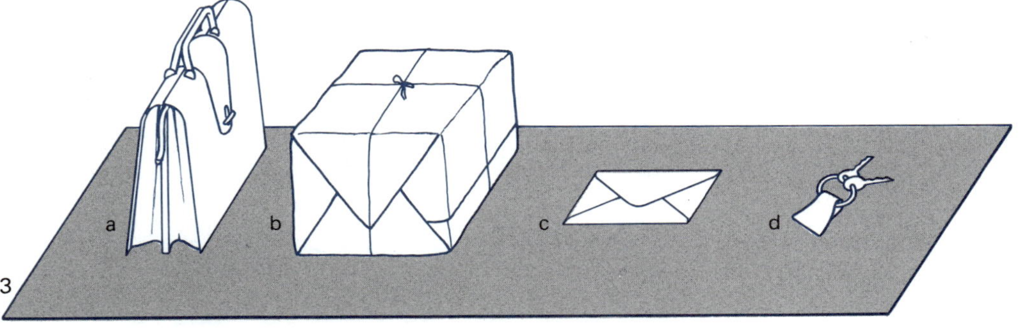

Land mines

Land mines are the same in principle as some of the explosive boobytraps shown on the preceding two pages. The selection of mines shown here, however, are all of the self-acting kind and have been made in quantity for regular armed forces. They fall into two general types—anti-tank and anti-personnel mines—and are used in more systematic ways than are the improvised boobytraps.

Land mine (left) of the American Civil War (1861–65). Land mines, then often called "land torpedoes," are known to have been used occasionally in that war despite prevailing disapproval of such "infernal devices." The one shown was improvised from a 24-pounder artillery shell, fitted with a sensitive percussion fuze.

Minelaying (right)
A Land mines are still often laid by hand—the original method.
B Some armies now use plows to sow strips of anti-tank mines. The plow is usually towed behind an armored personnel carrier.
C Mines can now also be sown from aircraft. This method can be used behind enemy lines.

A

B

C

Tellermine 35 (right), a typical anti-tank mine, used by the Germans in WW2. It was made of steel and contained 12lb (5.4kg) of TNT. It was buried a few inches below the surface, and would detonate only if a tank or other heavy vehicle passed over it—the pressure required to set it off being over 250lb (113kg). Note the secondary igniter well, designed to be fitted with an anti-lifting device that detonated the mine if the enemy attempted to dig it up. Being made of steel, its presence in the ground could be sensed by an electro-magnetic detector.

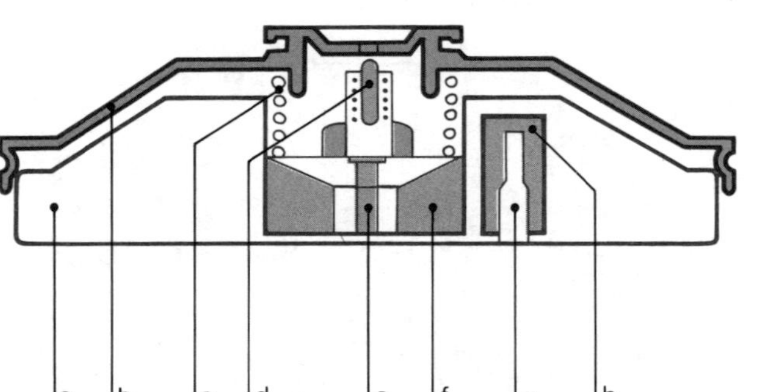

a Main charge of TNT
b Pressure-plate
c Pressure-plate spring
d Striker and spring
e Detonator
f Main booster
g Bottom fuze well
h Booster

L9 A1 Barmine (right) This modern British anti-tank mine is designed to be laid by plow (see above). The diagram (far right) shows how the short pressure-plate (**a**) ensures there is enough explosive (**b**) under the tank's track (**c**) to cut it on detonation. The barmine is all plastic, to make it more difficult to detect. It weighs 24.25lb (11kg).

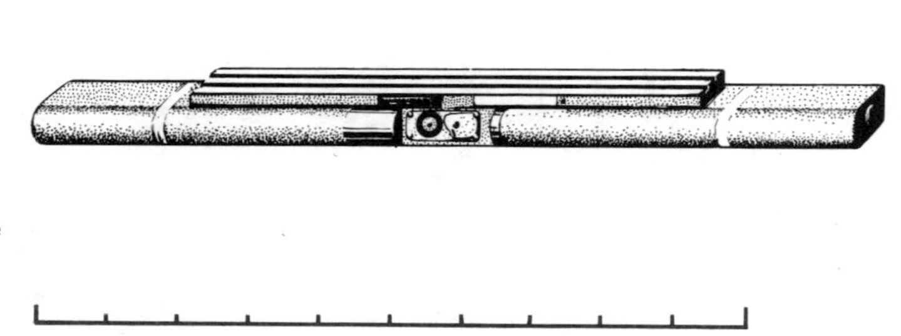

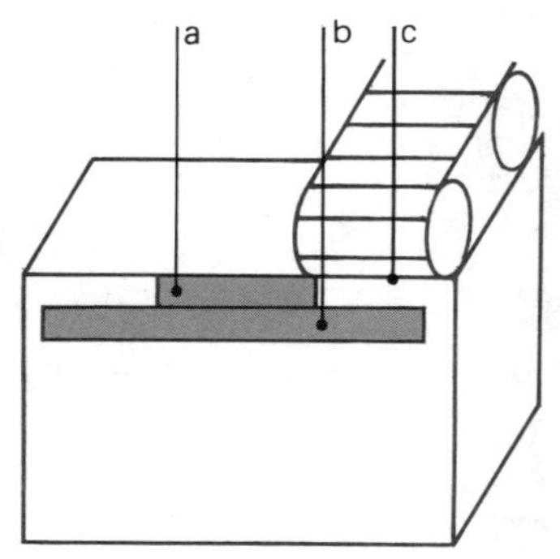

US M14 (right), a small anti-personnel mine of the 1950s that kills or wounds by blast. The casing is of plastic. Before burial, a safety clip is removed and the pressure-plate turned until the arrow points to "A." The pressure from a man's foot will then set off the mine.

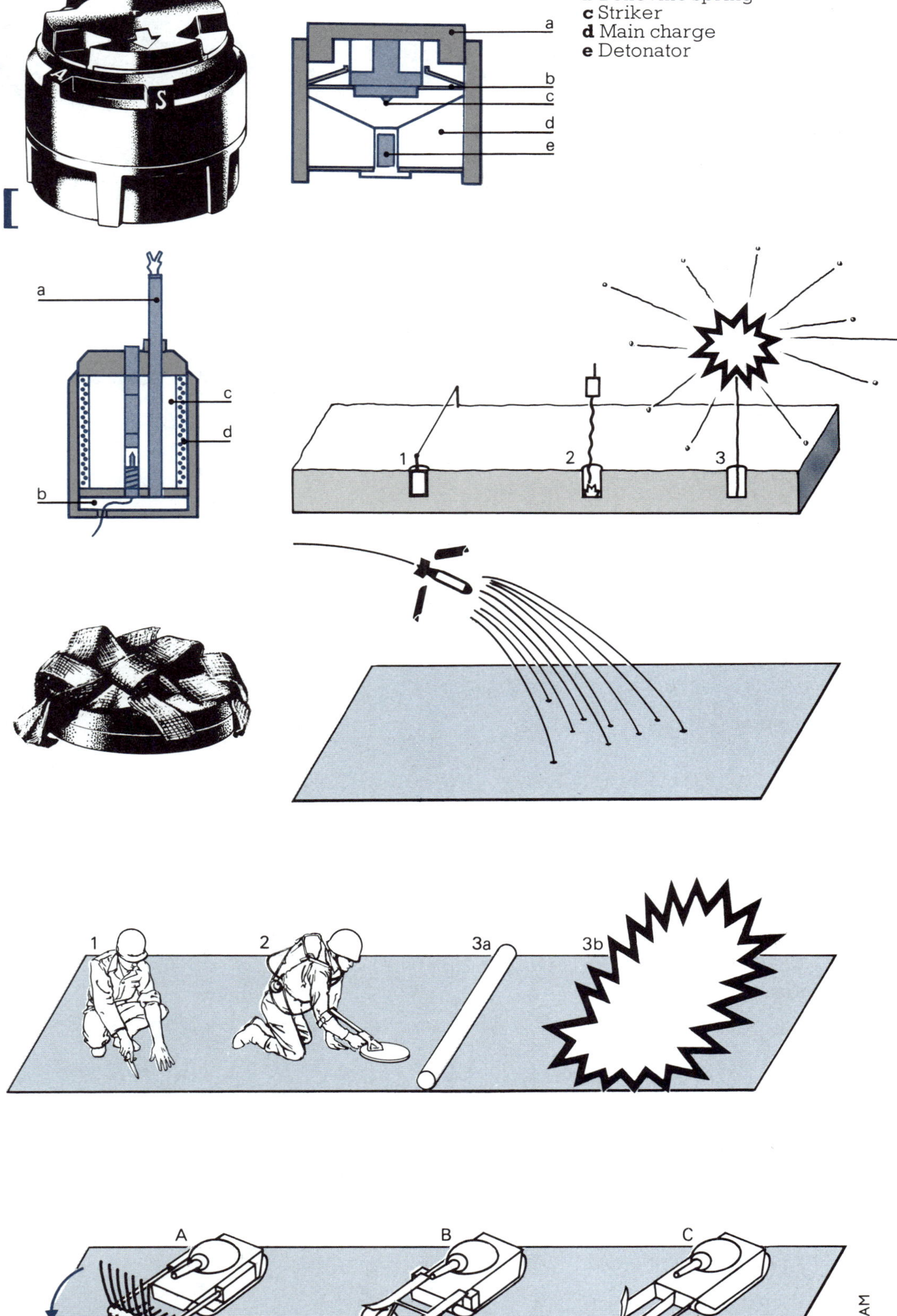

Sprengmine 44 (right), a German anti-personnel mine of WW2, much copied since.
1 A tripwire was attached to the protruding igniter (**a**).
2 If the wire was touched, a propellant charge (**b**) fired the mine in the air.
3 On reaching waist height, an anchor wire set off the main charge (**c**), firing steel balls (**d**) over a wide area.

Scattered mines (right) Mines are now available that can be scattered from the air by means of a "cluster bomb" (far right) or from projectors mounted on vehicles. They are small, and usually covered in camouflage cloth to hide them as they lie on the surface. They arm themselves automatically after release.

Mine clearance (right) The simplest method of locating mines is by probing gently with a bayonet (**1**). Mines made of ferrous metal can be located with a detector (**2**) by using magnetism. Another, faster method uses a rocket to lay an explosive-filled hose across the minefield (**3a**). This is then detonated (**3b**) to set off all mines in its path.

Mine-clearing tanks (right) have also been used to open a safe path quickly across a minefield. Some use a flail of heavy chains (**A**) or rollers (**B**) to set the mines off. However, such tanks can be defeated by fitting the mines with fuzes that detonate only when pressed twice. For this reason, plows are sometimes preferred that push the mines aside (**C**).

Naval mines

Under this heading we show a range of explosive devices for attacking ships and submarines. Most are self-acting devices which, laid in great numbers, constitute a strategic weapon that is a vital part of any blockade. Mines of this type can be set off by physical contact or by acoustic, magnetic, and pressure-sensitive devices. Other mines are tactical weapons, placed by hand on a specific ship.

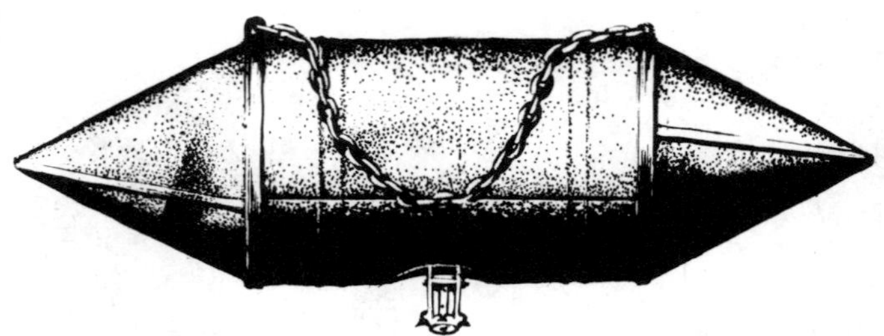

Confederate mine (above) of the American Civil War (1861–65). In this war the South, especially, devised many naval mines, then known as "torpedoes," to supplement its defenses.

Types of mine (right) Naval mines may be divided into four broad types. Drifting mines (**A**) are of limited use, being an uncontrolled hazard to all shipping. More common are moored mines (**B**), laid in planned minefields. Other mines lie on the seabed (**C**), or are attached covertly to the hull of a specific target ship (**D**).

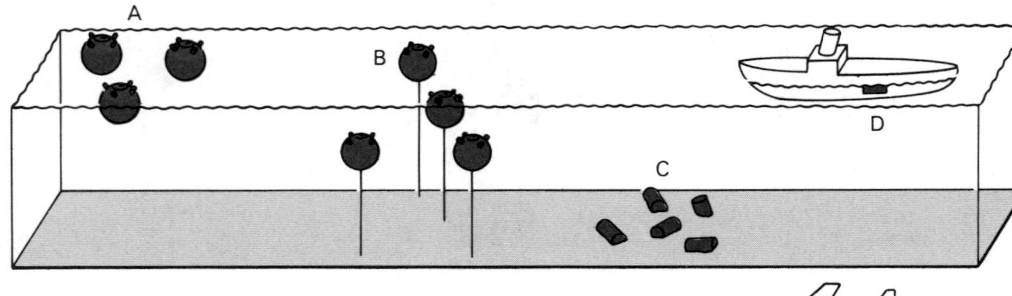

Minelaying (right) Mines are most commonly laid by surface ships—usually purpose-built "minelayers" (**1**). Submarines can lay mines covertly close to enemy ports (**2**). Aircraft are also useful for mining waters that are unsuitable for other methods (**3**).

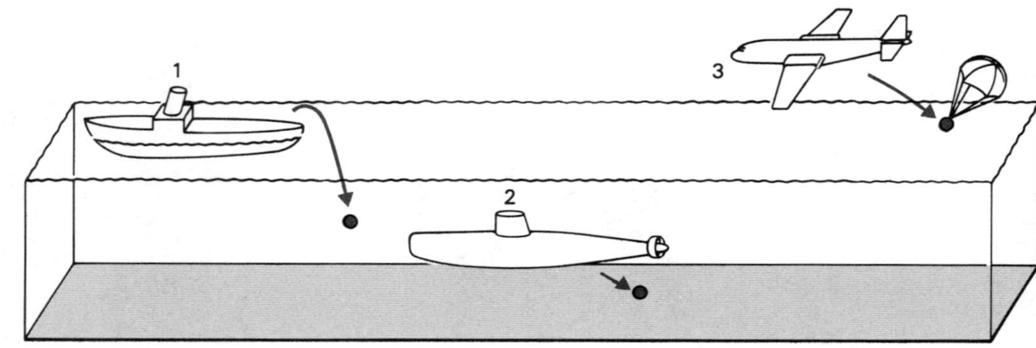

Elia mine (right), of the moored type, used by the British in WW1. The mine is shown in cross-section, still attached to its sinker mechanism—the form in which it was pushed over the stern of the minelayer. The diagram (far right) shows what happened next.
1 The air in the mine itself kept it afloat while the sinker descended, reeling out a cable as it went down.
2 When the depth regulator hanging below the sinker struck the seabed, the cable drum was locked automatically.
3 The mine was then pulled below the surface to the required depth.
The mine would detonate if the firing lever (now protruding horizontally) was struck by a ship or submarine.

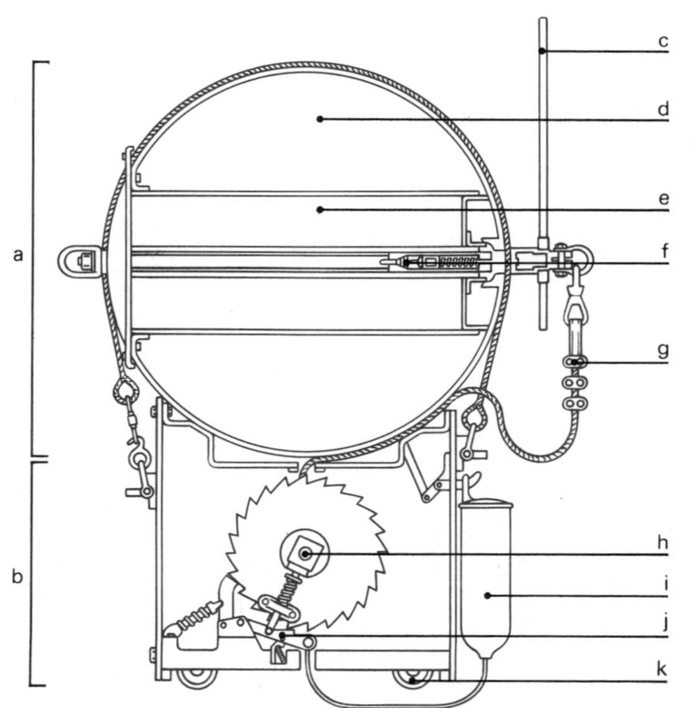

a Mine
b Sinker assembly
c Firing lever
d Buoyancy chamber (air)
e High explosive
f Striker and detonator
g Mooring cable
h Cable drum and ratchet
i Depth regulator
j Pawl to lock cable drum
k Wheels for launching

1 2 3

Mine with Herz horns (right), typical of both World Wars. The Herz horn was a German invention for triggering contact mines. Each horn consisted of a metal tube covering a phial of bichromate solution. When the horn was crushed, the solution completed a simple electric cell, the current from which ignited the detonator.

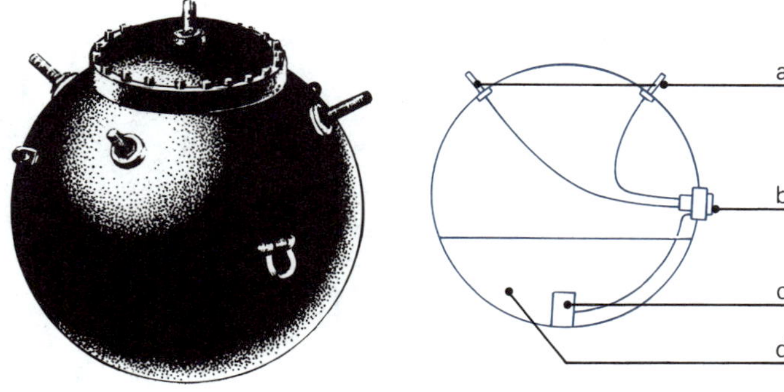

a Herz horns
b Safety switch (closed when the mine is laid)
c Detonator
d High explosive

British aerial magnetic mine (right) of WW2. When dropped by the aircraft, the casing at the rear fell away and the parachute opened. On entering the water, the parachute was released and the mine sank to the seabed. The hydrostatic device "armed" the mine, which would be set off by the magnetic field of a passing ship.

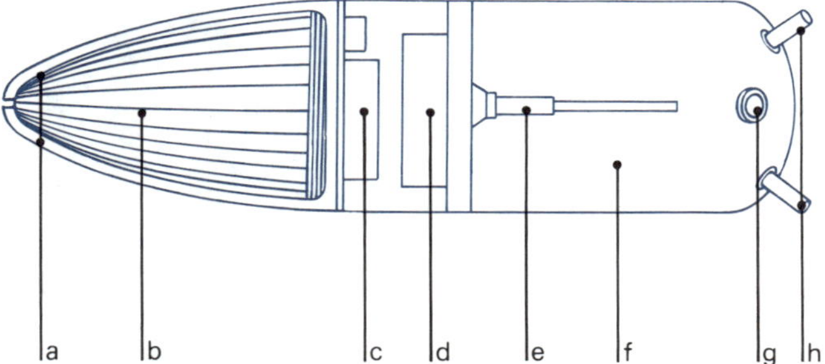

a Two halves of casing
b Parachute
c Magnetic switch
d Battery
e Detonator
f High explosive
g Hydrostatic device
h Feet to steady mine on seabed

US MK12 Mod0 mine (right), designed to be laid via the torpedo tube of a submarine. It happens also to be a magnetic mine. Iron hulled ships can be protected against magnetic mines by "degaussing." This involves winding a cable around the hull and passing an electric current through, to neutralize the ship's magnetic field.

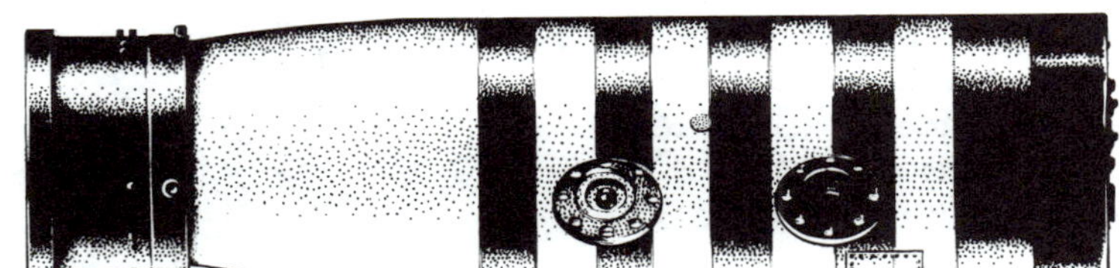

Limpet mine (right) The US model shown weighed less than 10lb (4.5kg), had a plastic casing, a charge of Torpex HE, and was fixed to the target ship's hull by six magnets. Other designs used explosive nails for attachment. Limpet mines were applied to the hulls of enemy ships below the waterline by divers, or by agents in small boats.

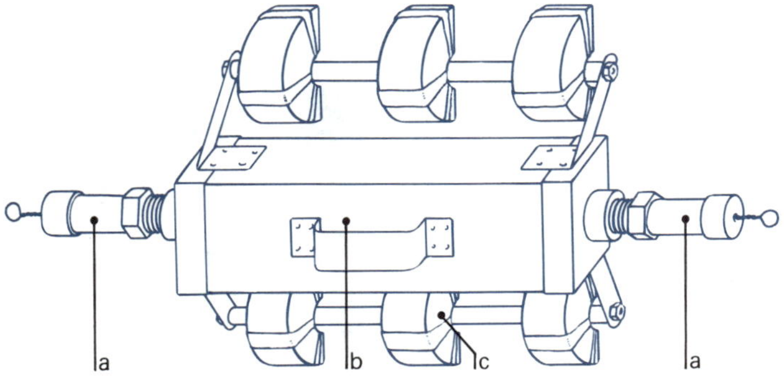

a Delay fuzes (two)
b Main charge
c Magnet (one of six)

"Human torpedo" (right), of the general type used by the Italians in WW2 and then copied by the British. It was an electrically powered, two-man underwater vessel for penetrating enemy harbors. The warhead was detached next to the target ship, to detonate when the divers had escaped. It was taken close to the target area by a parent submarine.

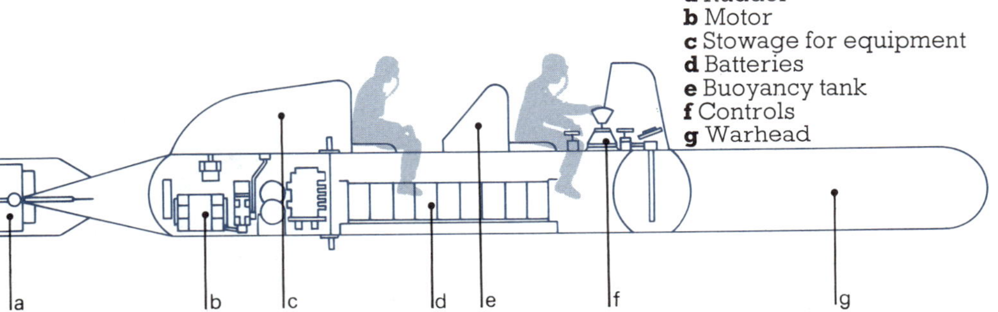

a Rudder
b Motor
c Stowage for equipment
d Batteries
e Buoyancy tank
f Controls
g Warhead

Chapter 6

BOMBS AND SELF-PROPELLED MISSILES

In this chapter we explain and illustrate bombs—in the strict sense of munitions dropped from aircraft—and self-propelled missiles of all kinds, from naval torpedoes to nuclear missiles.
The heyday of the aerial bomb was in WW2, when it was used both in strategic attacks on cities and in tactical roles on the battlefield. In the same war there rose to prominence the rocket and other self-propelled missiles (these terms should not be confused—see p.241). Since 1945 these new weapons have found even more applications than the bomb, at every level of conflict. Certain of the destructive agents that all these weapons are used to deliver—namely incendiary and other chemical agents, and nuclear explosives—are covered in more detail in Chapter 7.
Abbreviations used in this chapter:
ICBM: Intercontinental Ballistic Missile
IRBM: Intermediate Range Ballistic Missile
MRBM: Medium Range Ballistic Missile
ALCM: Air Launched Cruise Missile
SLCM: Submarine Launched Cruise Missile
SLBM: Submarine Launched Ballistic Missile
MIRV: Multiple Independently-targeted Re-entry Vehicle
MARV: Multiple Alternative-targeted Re-entry Vehicle

Photograph (right) of three German V2 rockets being prepared for launch in the latter stages of WW2. The V2 was the first true rocket to be used in a strategic role.

Aerial bombs 1

Aerial bombs—or simply "bombs"—are unpowered missiles dropped from aircraft. They are generally of streamlined shape, and fitted with stabilizing fins, fuzes, and an arming device to set the fuzes. The first specific aerial bomb was the German APR of 1912. Serious development began in WW1, with such bombs as the German PuW of 1915, which had a streamlined steel case and a centrifugal arming device. By the end of WW1, bombs of 2200lb (1000kg) were being used. WW2 saw a proliferation of bomb designs, from many weights of general purpose (GP) bomb, and many types and weights of incendiary, to specially designed bombs for specific missions, as well as napalm and nuclear bombs. Modern developments include "low-drag" shaping, retarding devices, and guided or "smart" bombs.

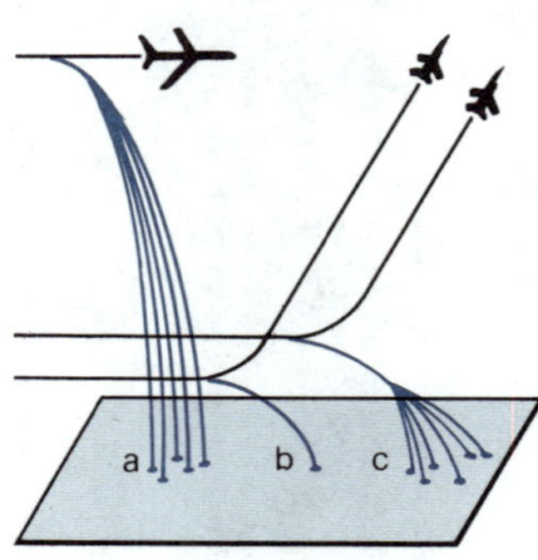

Methods of attack (left) In area and pattern bombing (**a**), as used in WW2, the aircraft drops its load from a high altitude over a relatively large area. Low level attack and precision bombing (**b**) are now favored. These modern methods can be made more effective against group targets by the use of "cluster" bombs containing many small bomblets (**c**).

	Types of bomb
	**Explosive** General purpose Fragmentation Demolition (blast) Anti-armor Fuel Air Explosive
	**Chemical** Gas Smoke Incendiary
	**Pyrotechnic** Photoflash Target indication
	**Nuclear** Fissionable Fusionable
	**Biological** Inert pathogenic organisms
	Guided Radio Laser Electro-optical (TV)

Types of bomb The table (left) classifies bombs according to their broad use (bold type) and filler or sub-variety (light type). Demolition bombs rely on blast to destroy structures, fragmentation bombs are used against personnel, and general-purpose bombs combine both effects. Next to high explosive bombs, incendiaries are the most widely used and the most deadly. Incendiary, fragmentation, Fuel Air Explosives (FAEs) and anti-armor bombs are now often dropped in clusters of small bomblets. The development of rocket-assisted and guided bombs began in WW2, and a radio-controlled version of the Grand Slam—the VB-13 Tarzon—was used in the Korean conflict.

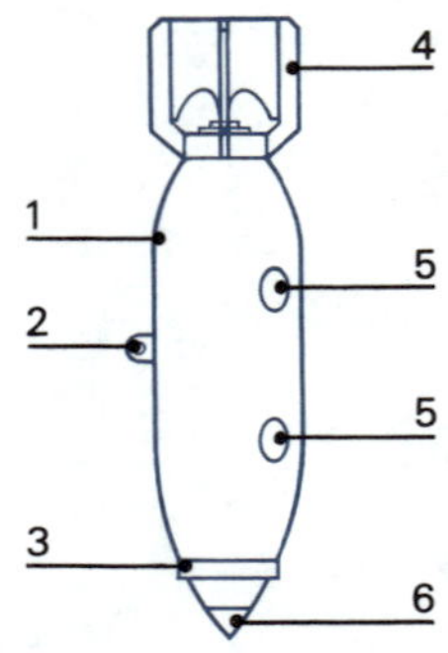

Parts of a typical bomb (left)
1 Casing
2 Suspension lug
3 Anti-ricochet device
4 Tail fins
5 Side pockets for fuzes
6 Position for a nose fuze
There may be a separate arming device in the tail, or it may be combined with a nose fuze.

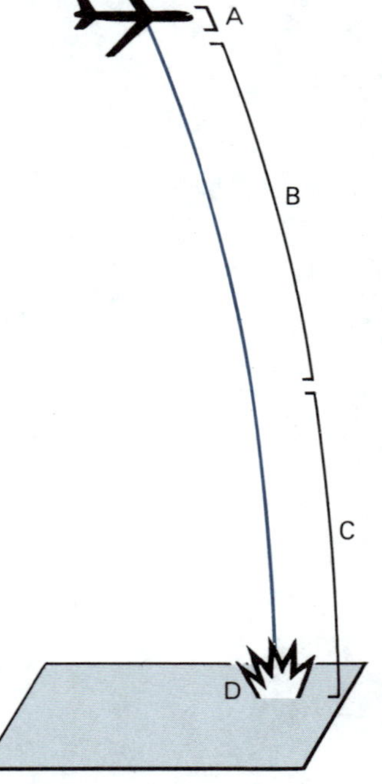

Dropping a bomb (left) There are several distinct phases in the dropping of a simple, impact-fuzed bomb as used in the great air-raids of WW2.
A Release. The bomb may have been carried attached beneath the aircraft or in an internal "bomb-bay." Soon after release the tail-fins cause the bomb to fall point-first.
B Arming. For the safety of the bombing aircraft the bombs do not become fully "live" until they have fallen some way. The arming device is often a small propeller, turned as the air rushes past.
C For the remainder of its descent, the bomb and its fuze are liable to explode on impact.
D Impact. The fuze reacts to impact, and detonates the bomb either instantly or after a pre-set delay.

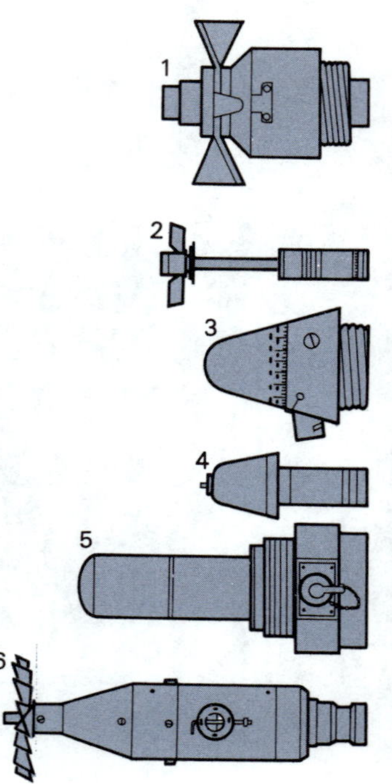

Fuzes (left) are devices that set off a bomb's main charge. They are classified according to their position on the bomb and their operating principle. The type of fuze fitted depends on the nature of the expected target, the method of attack, and the type of bomb-filling used. Proximity fuzes can sense, usually by radio waves, the approach of the target or ground. Hydrostatic fuzes are activated by water-pressure. Multi-position or "all-ways" fuzes, used mostly on unstabilized incendiaries, act on impact from any angle.
US bomb fuzes (left)
1 Impact nose fuze (1945)
2 Impact tail fuze (1940)
3 Mechanical time nose fuze (1960)
4 Proximity fuze (1965)
5 All-ways fuze (1970)
6 Hydrostatic fuze (1965)

Aerial bombs (right)
First World War
1 British Cooper bomb
2 British 112lb bomb
3 British 230lb bomb
4 French "Giant" bomb
5 US MkIII 50lb High Capacity Drop bomb
Between the World Wars
6 British 20lb HE bomb
7 US M31 300lb GP bomb
8 US Mk5 30lb fragmentation bomb
Second World War
a US M41 20lb fragmentation bomb
b Cluster of four M41 bombs
c US M34 2000lb GP bomb
d British 4lb incendiary bomb (US AN-M50 A1)
e British 250lb MC (Middle Capacity) bomb
f British 12,000lb HC (High Capacity) bomb
g British 30lb incendiary bomb
h British 12,000lb bomb "Tall Boy"
i British 22,000lb bomb "Grand Slam"
j German SB 1000kg high capacity bomb
k German PC 1000 RS (rocket-assisted armor-piercing) bomb
l German brand C50A incendiary bomb
Post WW2 and contemporary
1 US Mk20 Mod2 476lb "Rockeye II" anti-tank cluster bomb
2 US M118 3000lb GP bomb
3 US B1 755 anti-armor weapon cluster bomb
4 US Mk81 250lb GP bomb (with retarder open)
5 US Mk83 "Destructor" 1000lb bomb (with retarder open)
6 US Mk79 Mod1 1000lb fire bomb
7 US M117 750lb GP bomb
8 US Mk77 Mod0 750lb fire bomb

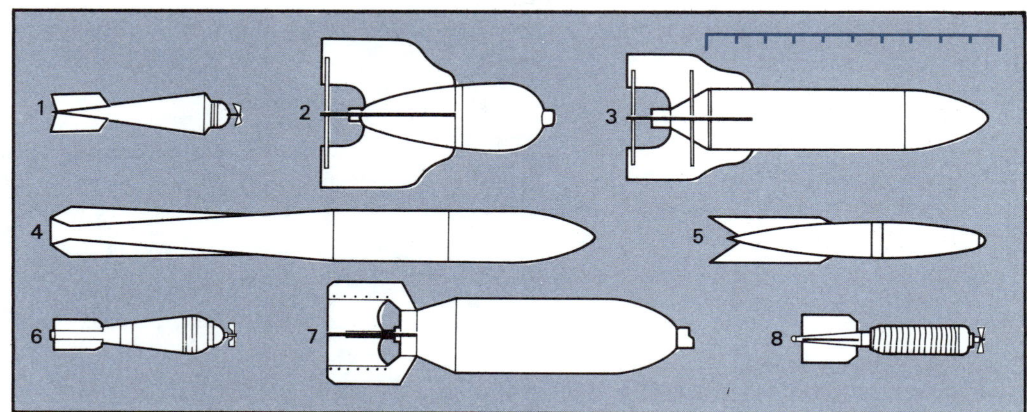

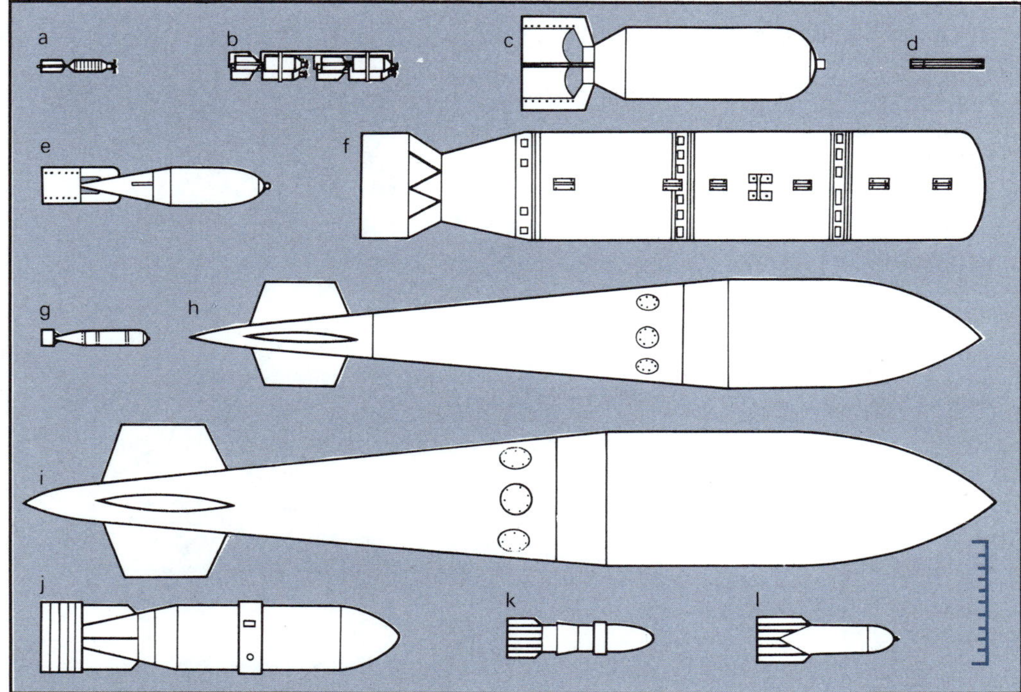

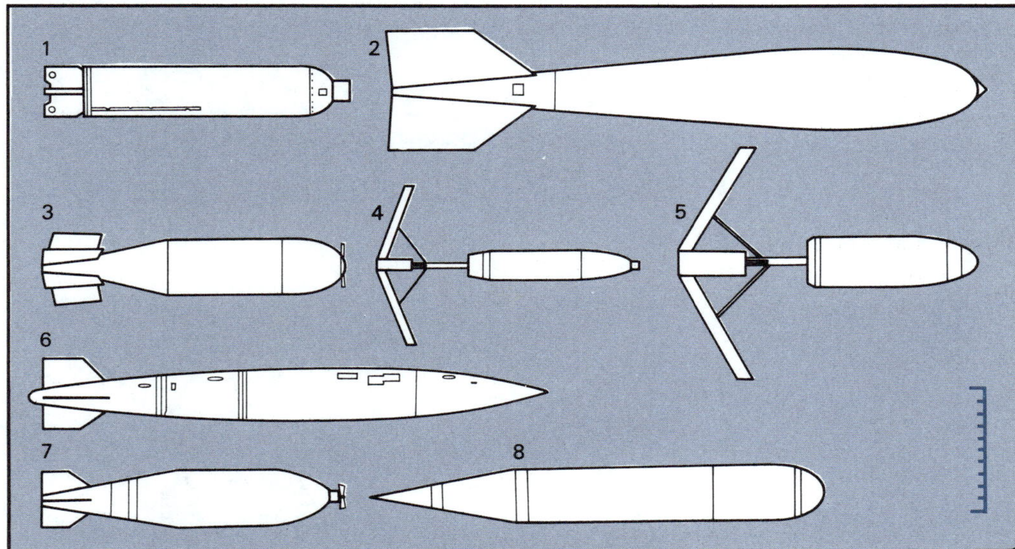

Note: The nominal weight of a bomb is often used as its name or official designation. The accurate weight is usually slightly different. For these reasons, the figures and units given above are those used by the country of origin, and have not been converted to metric or imperial units of measure.

Aerial bombs 2

Modern bombing (right) The effectiveness of modern air defense systems has made the older methods of high and medium level bombing infeasible. Strike aircraft are now designed for low-level approach and attack—the only way to maintain a degree of safety and the element of surprise. Typical mission profiles are : Hi-Lo-Hi (**1**), Lo-Lo-Hi (**2**) and Lo-Lo-Lo (**3**).

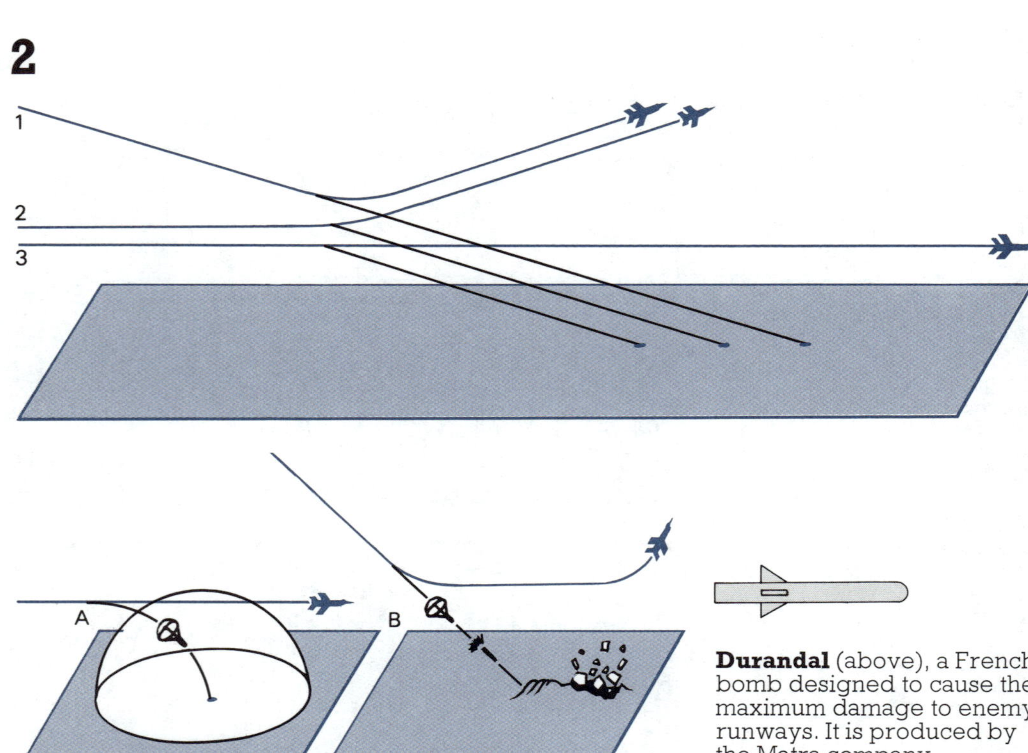

Retarding parachutes or airbrakes (right) can be fitted to some conventional bombs to allow an aircraft on a low-level attack to reach a safe distance (**A**) before the bomb explodes. **The Matra Durandal** (**B**) is a penetration bomb. It is first retarded to adjust the angle of descent, then rocket-boosted to maximize penetration.

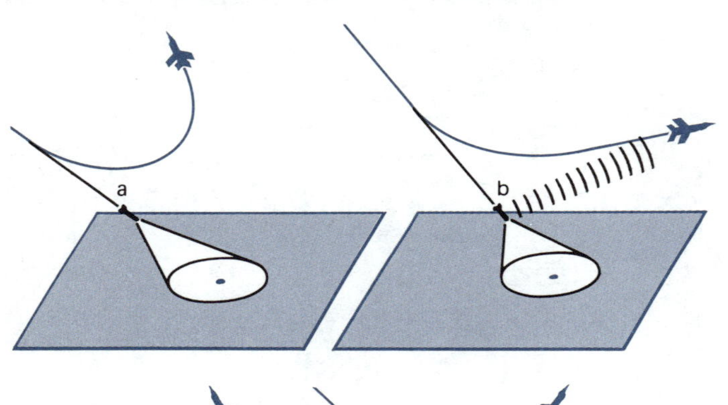

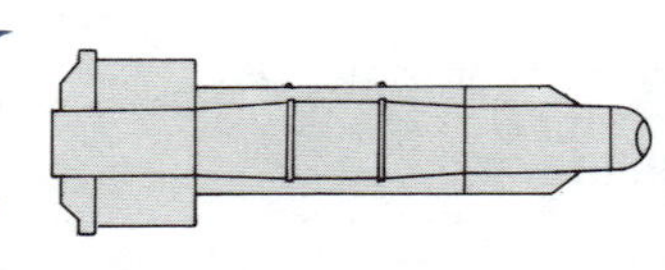

Durandal (above), a French bomb designed to cause the maximum damage to enemy runways. It is produced by the Matra company.

Electro-optically guided bombs (right) or HOBOS (homing bomb systems) are fitted with TV guidance units at the front and control surfaces (fins) at the rear. They are either locked onto the target by the aircrew and then home in on the target themselves (**a**), or are continually guided by transmitting pictures to the crew (**b**). Accuracy is to within a few feet.

US HOBO (above), an example of a T.V-guided bomb, used in the Vietnam war from 1969.

"Paveway" laser guided bombs (right) are conventional bombs with a laser detector and guidance and control unit at the front and a wing unit at the tail. The target is illuminated by laser either from the ground (**A**), from another aircraft (**B**) or from the bombing aircraft. The bomb's sensors pick up the reflected beam and follow it to the target.

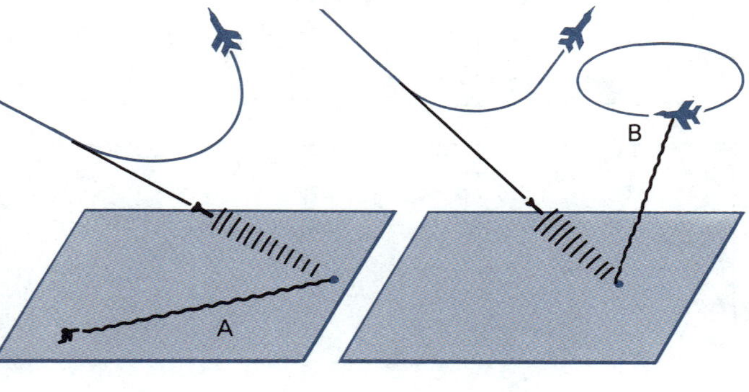

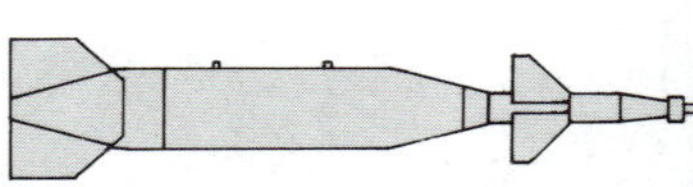

Paveway (above), a US laser-guided bomb used in the Vietnam war in pin-point attacks on strategic targets.

Fuel Air Explosives (FAEs) (right) use volatile hydrocarbons to create a new weapon effect. The US CBU-55 FAE has three bomblets (**a**) each containing 71.8lb (32.6kg) of ethylene oxide. This has five times the blastwave effect of TNT. It forms a cloud (**b**) of about 50ft (15m) across and 8ft (2.5m) high before detonation (**c**). FAEs are used to clear minefields.

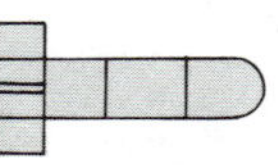

Bomblet (above) from the US CBU-55 Fuel Air Explosive bomb system. The use of explosive vapor is a new development in weaponry.

Depth charges

Depth charges were first used in 1916 when the British introduced the "D" type MkIII, to combat the U-Boat. As submarines became able to dive deeper, heavier charges shaped to sink faster were developed. Simple depth charges, dropped overboard, have now been superseded by mortars, rocket delivery systems, or by deep-running acoustic torpedoes (see also p.261).

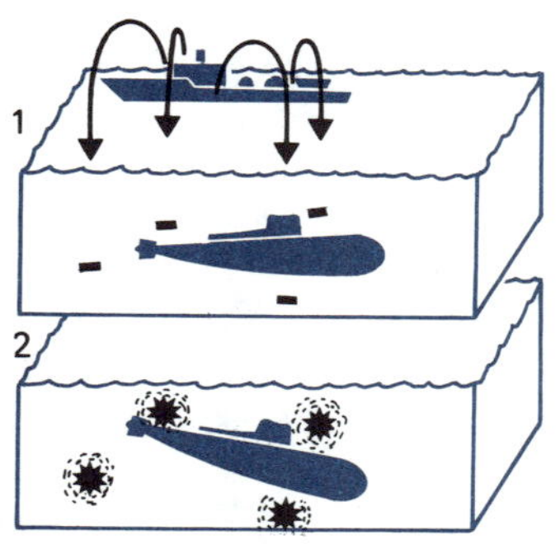

Dropping-patterns (left) The lethal blast radius of a depth charge was quite small—25ft (7.6m) for 300 lb (136kg) of TNT. But the damaging shock waves reached much further. Thus the attacking ship would try to drop a pattern of depth charges around the sub (**1**) Pressure waves from the explosives would combine to cause damage (**2**) and force the sub to surface.

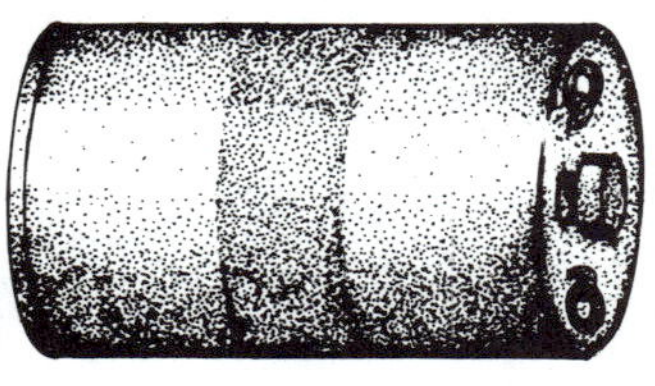

The British MkVII depth charge (left) is typical of those used in WW2. It weighed 410 lb (185kg) with a charge of 396 lb (179kg). The US Mk7 was heavier, with 600 lb (272kg) of TNT. Immediately before being dropped, such charges were set to explode at the estimated depth of the enemy submarine. As ways were devised to project them, depth charges became heavier. For example, the British Mk10 of 1944 weighed 3000 lb (1360kg), and could reach a depth of 1500ft (457m).

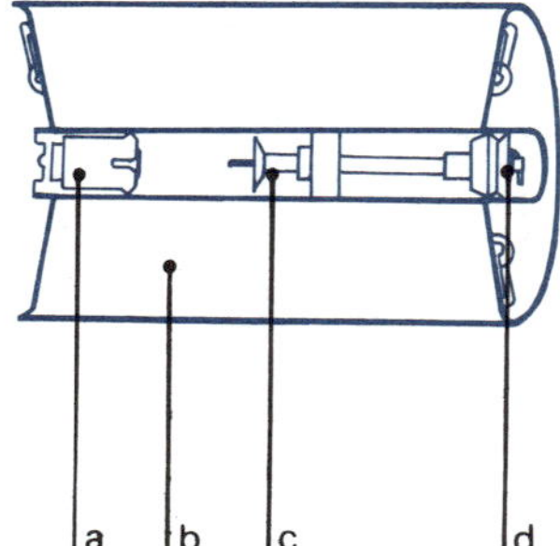

Parts of the MkVII

a Detonator
b Explosive charge
c Pistol
d Depth setting key

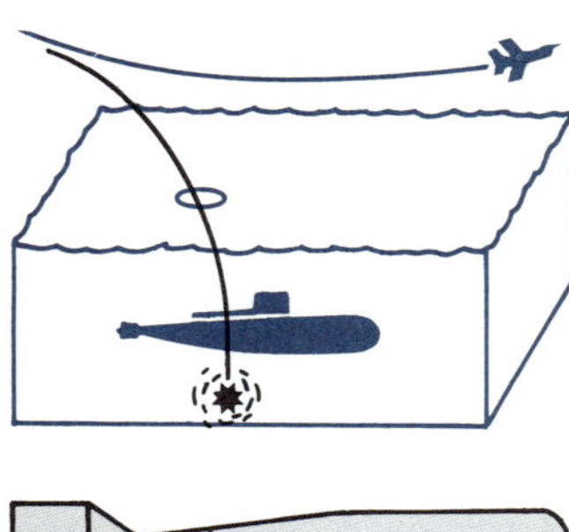

Aerial depth bombs (left) were developed in WW2. Modern atomic depth bombs such as the US "Lulu" (below left) and that carried by Subroc (see p.261) can afford to be relatively inaccurate as they have a high-radius kill capacity.

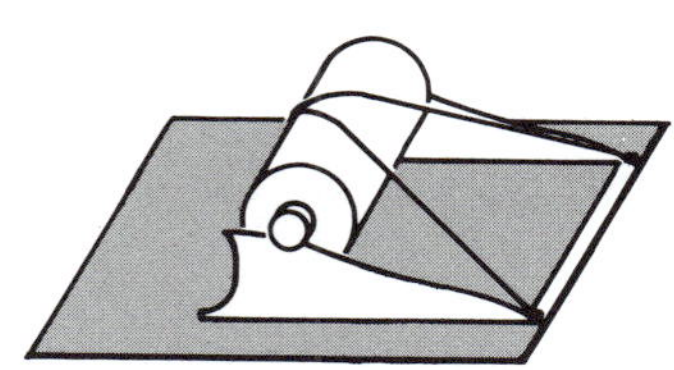

The original method (left) of delivering depth charges was simply to drop them over the side of a ship. They were rolled off chutes astern after the boat had passed over the last known position of the submarine. This was basically unsatisfactory, however, as it gave the submarine time to take evasive action.

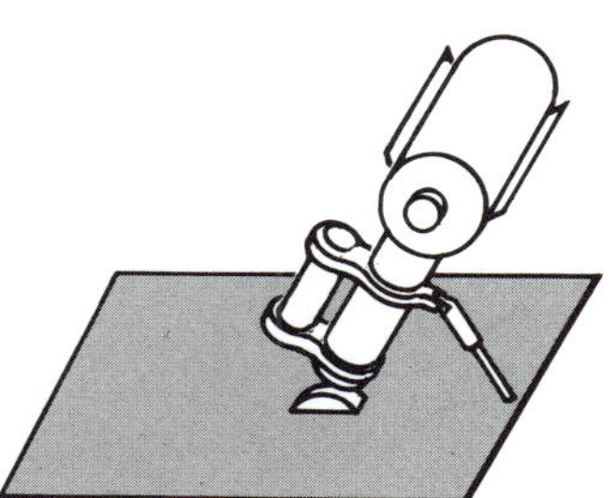

Depth-charge projectors (left) were usually fitted four to a boat, and enabled the attacking ship to cover a larger area. The British Thornycroft thrower was introduced in late 1917. The US depth-charge projector, or "K gun," which was basically a spigot mortar, had a range of up to 150yd (137m).

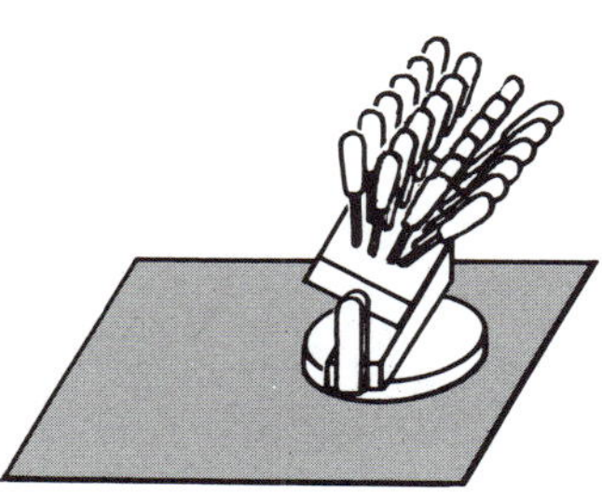

The Hedgehog (left) of 1941 was a British multi-spigot mortar that launched a salvo of 24 bombs, each with 31 lb (14kg) of HE, to a distance of 250yd (228m) ahead of the vessel carrying it. They landed in a circular pattern to increase the chance of a hit and exploded only on contact. Hedgehog allowed ships to attack submarines while still in sonar contact.

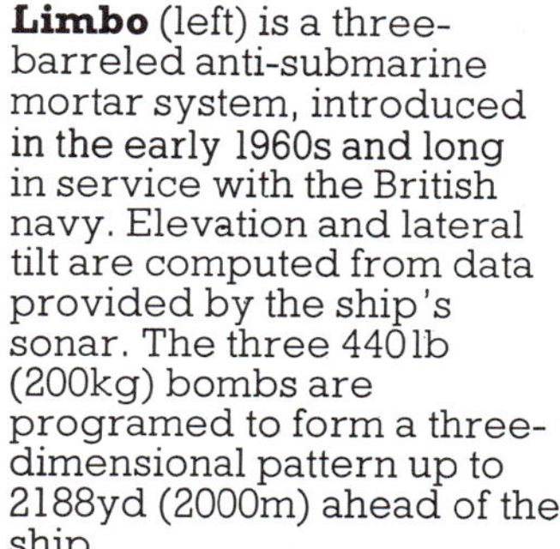

Limbo (left) is a three-barreled anti-submarine mortar system, introduced in the early 1960s and long in service with the British navy. Elevation and lateral tilt are computed from data provided by the ship's sonar. The three 440 lb (200kg) bombs are programed to form a three-dimensional pattern up to 2188yd (2000m) ahead of the ship.

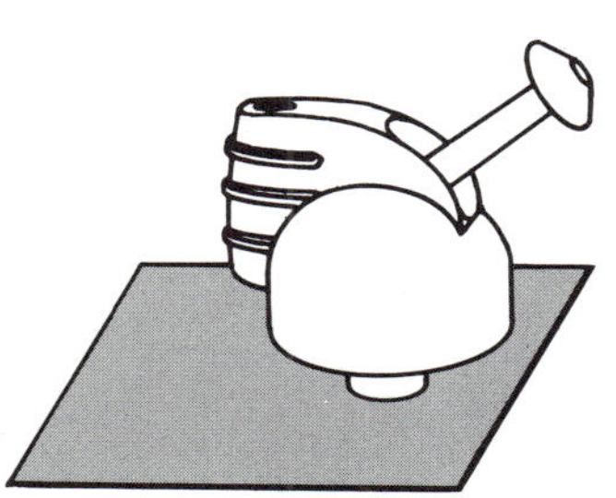
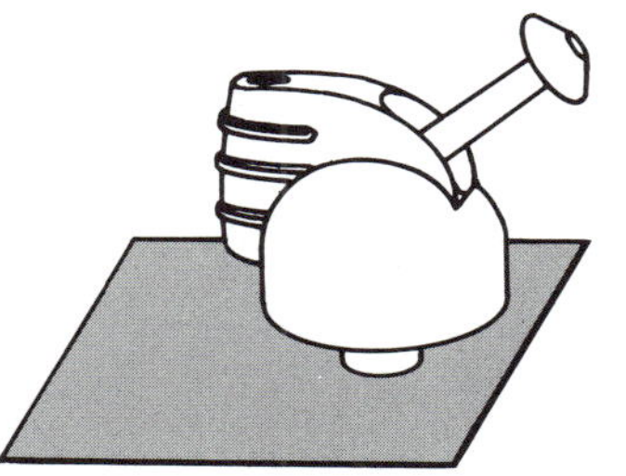

Weapon Alpha (left), first known as Weapon Able, was introduced by the US Navy in the mid 1950s, and was in service on Dealey and Courtney class escort ships until 1973. It fired a 12.75in (32.4cm), 500 lb (226kg) rocket-propelled depth charge a distance of about 1000yd (915m) from a Mk101 single-barrel launcher. It was designated RUR-4A.

Self-propelled missiles

Self-propelled missiles are those that carry with them their own motor—the means of imparting a forward velocity. The purpose of a military missile is to deliver a warhead as accurately as possible to an enemy some distance away.
On this page, by way of introduction, we explain the basis on which missiles are classified.

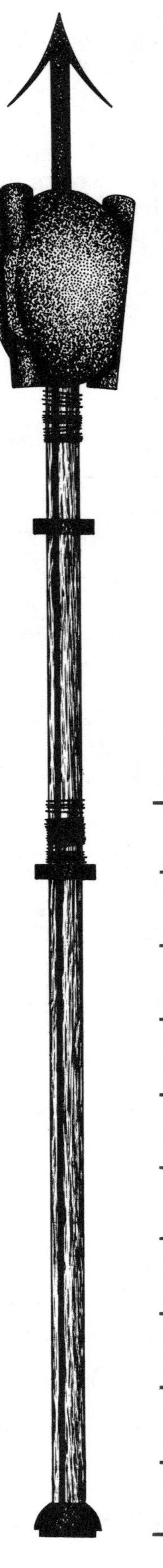

Rocket-spear (right) from 16th century Sweden, perhaps the oldest surviving self-propelled missile. It is thought to have been launched by being fired from a cannon, the four rocket motors near the point then igniting to prolong the spear's flight. Similar rocket-spears were used in 18th century India. (Kungliga Armémuseum, Stockholm.)

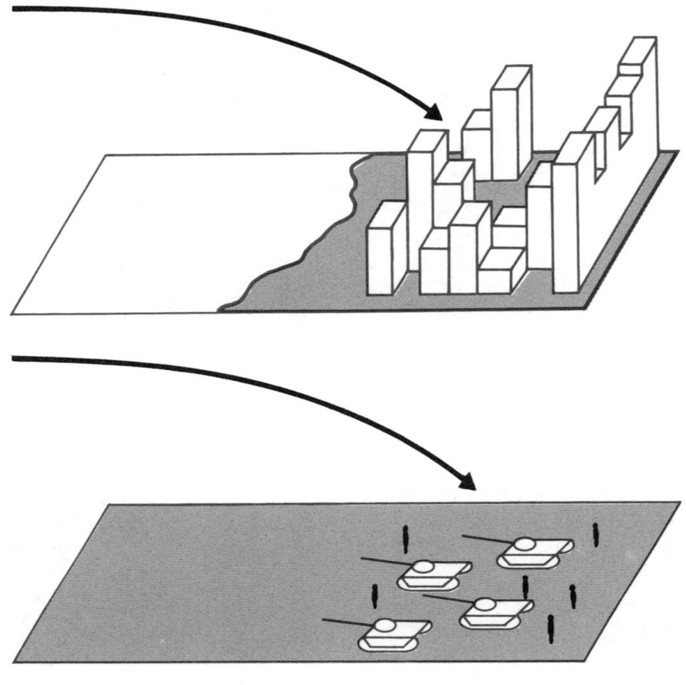

Strategic missiles (right) are designed to be used against targets such as enemy populations and centers of industry. They may be launched from the ground, on or under the sea, or from the air. (For specific examples see p.262.)

Tactical missiles (right) are designed for use within the context of a military battle, on land, at sea or in the air. They are more limited in their range and effect than strategic missiles. There are many specific sub-varieties, as explained below.

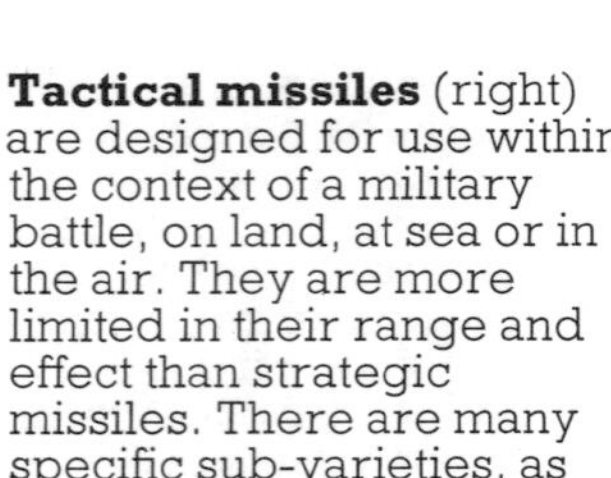

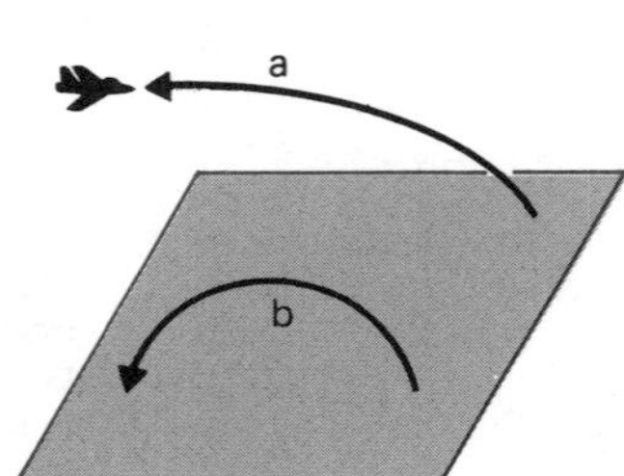

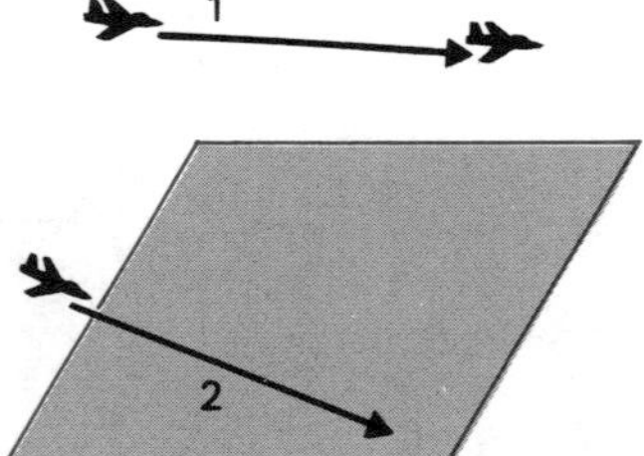

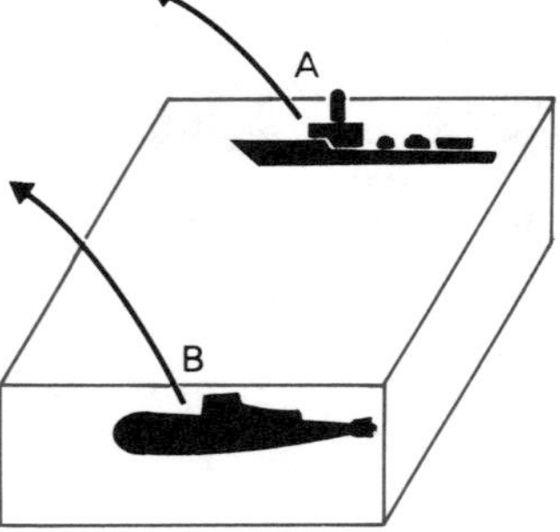

Ground-launched missiles (above) The two main kinds are ground-to-air (**a**), which are all tactical, and ground-to-surface (**b**), the surface being either land or sea. Category (**b**) has many sub-varieties, such as anti-tank missiles (see pp.254-5), general support or artillery rockets (see p.252) and tactical nuclear missiles (p.263).

Air-launched missiles (above) The main types are air-to-air (**1**) and air-to-surface (**2**); the surface may be either land or the sea. Tactical examples are shown on pp.258-9. There are also some strategic air-to-surface missiles, such as the Cruise missile (see p.262).

Sea-launched missiles (above) There are many varieties, ranging from the conventional torpedo (see p.242) to the Polaris strategic nuclear missile (see p.262). The primary division, however, is into ship- or surface-launched types (**A**) and submarine- or subsurface-launched types (**B**). Most tactical sea-launched missiles are shown on pp.260-1.

Methods of propulsion

All methods of missile propulsion are based on Newton's third law of motion—"to every action there is an equal and opposite reaction." Each method pushes water or air and/or hot combustion gases backward, producing a forward thrust from the consequent reaction. The three main kinds of missile propulsion—propeller, jet engine and rocket motor—are explained on this page.

a

b

Newton's third law of motion can be demonstrated with a toy balloon (left). The air inside a balloon exerts an equal pressure in all directions (**a**). When the neck of the balloon is released the air rushes out. This "action" of the air produces an equal and opposite "reaction," or thrust, that pushes the balloon in the opposite direction (**b**).

A rotating propeller, as on a torpedo (right), produces motion by pushing quantities of air or water backward (**1**), so creating a force of reaction that thrusts the propeller (and whatever may be attached to it) forward (**2**). A moving propeller pushes relatively large masses of air or water backward with a small increase in velocity.

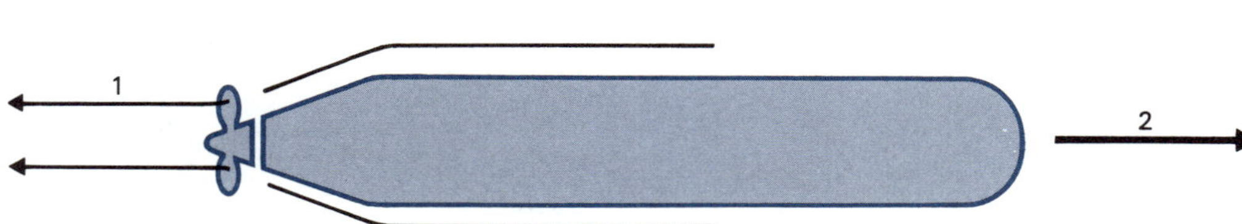

Jet and rocket engines (right) both work by jet propulsion, producing a forward thrust by the reaction to a backward stream of accelerated gases. A jet engine (**A**) accelerates the air it takes in, with a relatively large velocity increase. A rocket motor (**B**) produces gases by combustion and allows them to escape at speed through a back-facing vent.

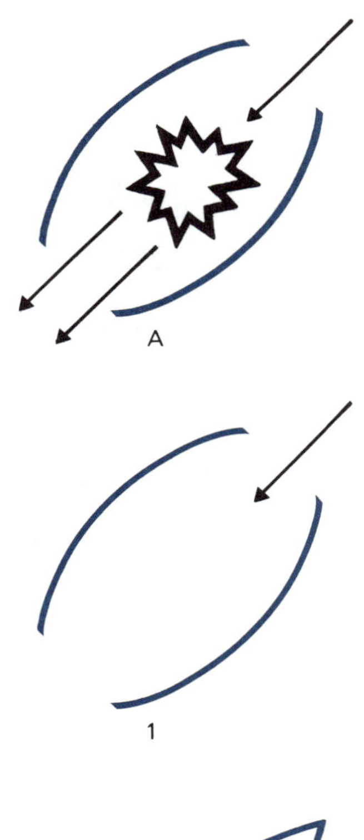

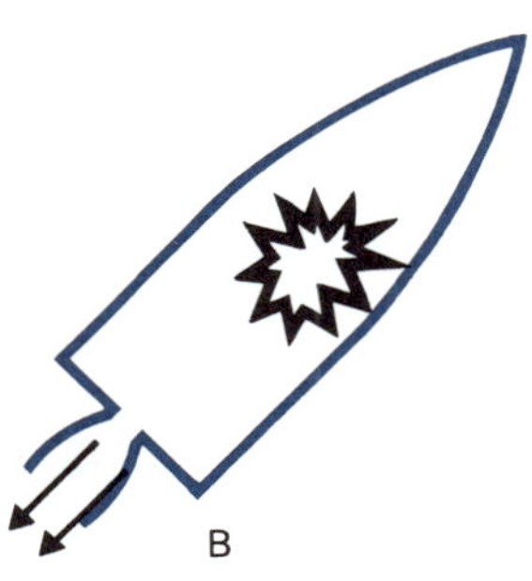

A jet engine (right) works by taking in air at the forward end (**1**). The velocity of the air is reduced and its pressure increased (**2**). Fuel is then injected and burned, and the hot, expanded air and combustion gases flow out at the rear with greatly increased velocity (**3**), thus creating the "action" on which the propulsion system is based.

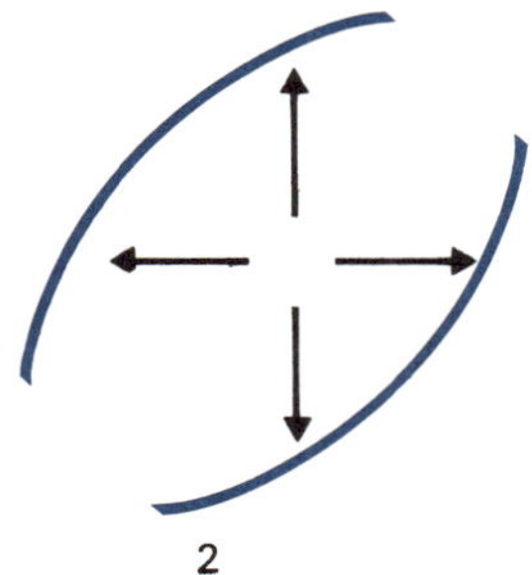

Rocket motors (right) burn their propellants in a combustion chamber (**a**), creating high pressure. The rush of gases through an opening (**b**) produces a forward thrust by reaction. The precise shape of this opening or nozzle is crucial.

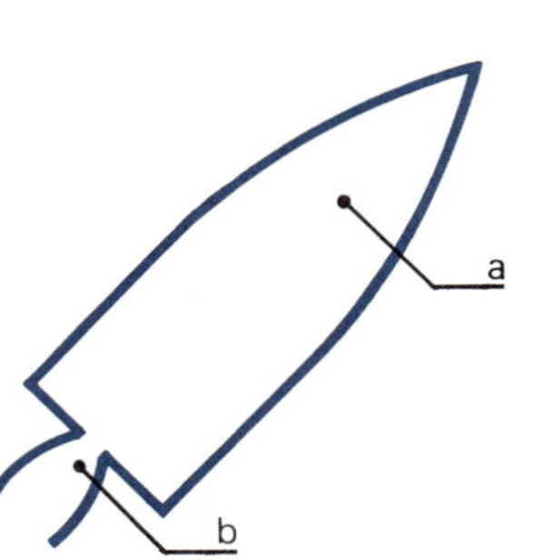

Rocket nozzle (right) The restricted part or throat (**A**) maintains the pressure in the combustion chamber. The cone-shaped expansion-chamber (**B**) reduces turbulence and produces a stream of efficiently directed gases. By providing a smooth, continual expansion and acceleration of the gases, their propulsive efficiency is maximized.

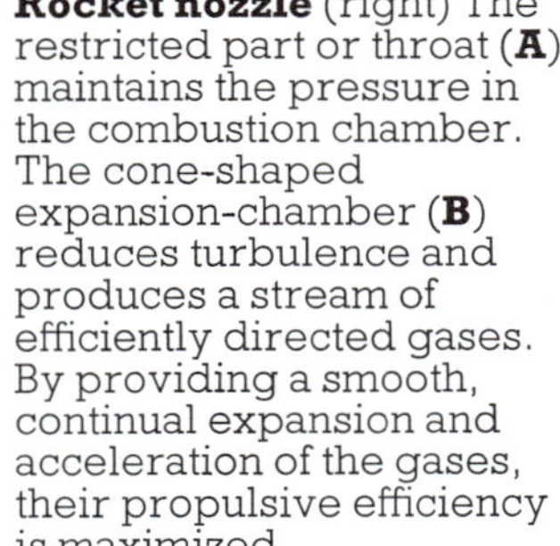

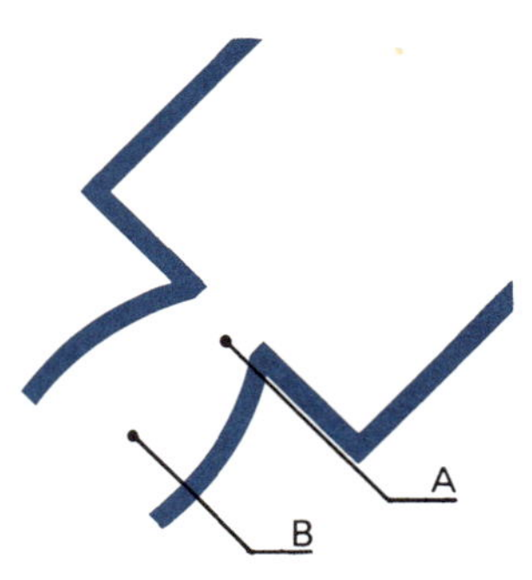

Propellers and torpedoes

The first self-propelled or "fish" torpedo was the British "Whitehead," invented in 1886. It was revolutionary, as it allowed small craft to attack capital ships. Since then it has been the main weapon of submarines and carrier-based aircraft.
Most torpedoes use an electric motor to power the propeller or screw by which they are moved through the water.

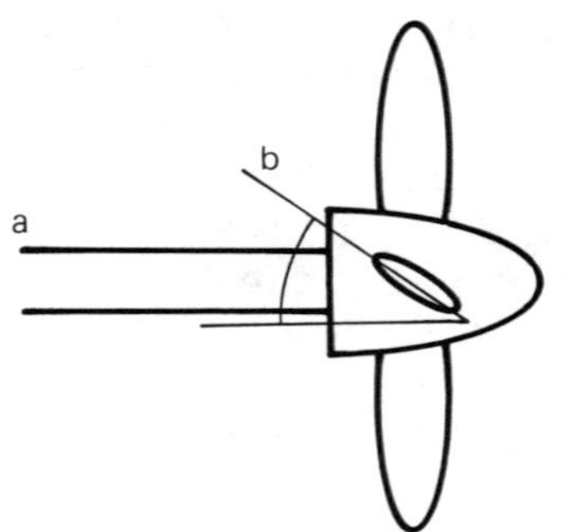

The propeller (left) consists of a number of angled blades attached to a rotating shaft (**a**). As the propeller rotates, the blades impart a momentum to a body of water proportional to their size and angle of incidence (**b**). This pushes the propeller forward as a reaction. Torpedoes usually have two contra-rotating propellers.

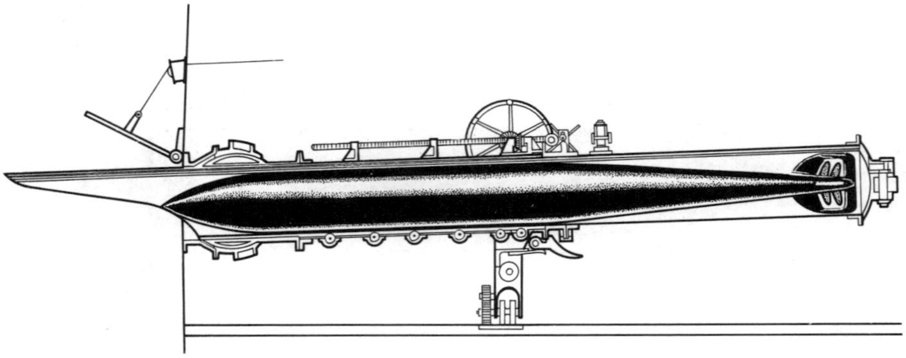

Whitehead torpedo (left) of c. 1890, shown inside its launching tube. The torpedo was loaded through a door at the rear of the tube, and the front of the tube emerged through a port in the side of the ship (as shown). Discharge of the torpedo from the tube was either by a blast of compressed air, or a small charge of cordite in the rear door.

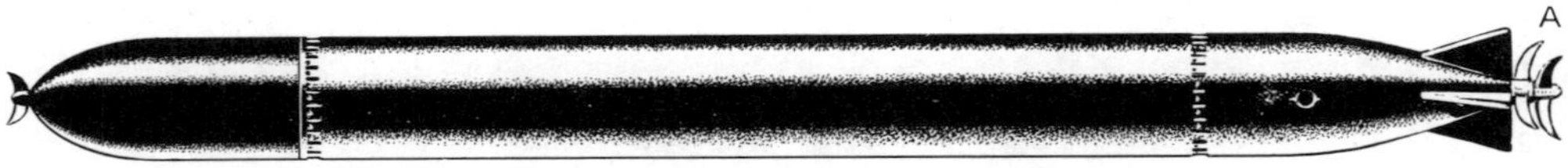

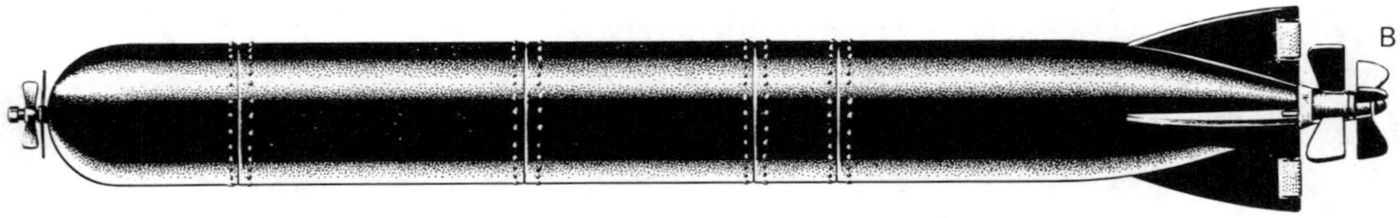

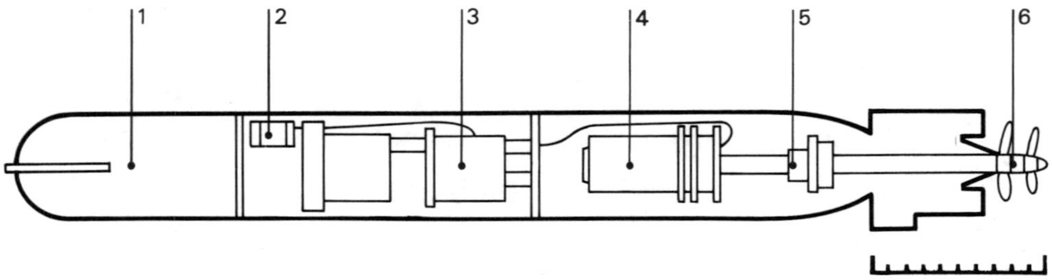

Torpedoes (left)
Data key
a Speed
b Total weight/charge weight
c Range

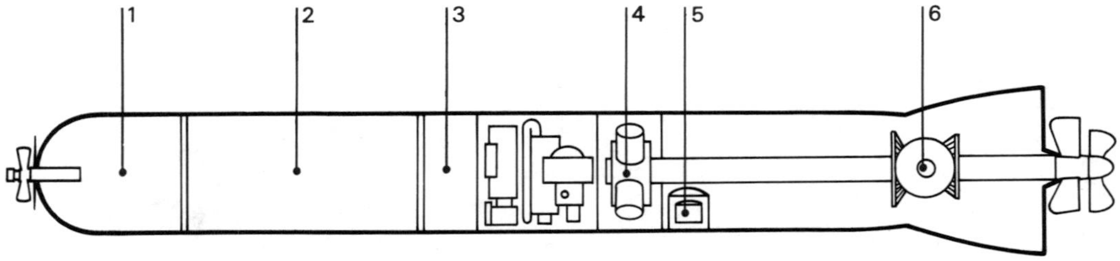

A German G7 of WW1.
Over 5000 of these were fired in WW1, of which at least 3000 missed their target.
a 36 knots
b 2491 lb/440 lb (1130kg/200kg)
c 6560yd (5996m)

B British Mk9 Mod of WW2
a 40 knots
b 2496 lb/1161 lb (1132kg/527kg)
c 15,000yd (13,710m) at 35 knots
Parts of the Mk9 :
1 Warhead
2 Compressed air chamber
3 Water chamber
4 4-cylinder hot-air driven radial engine
5 Gyroscope
6 Gearing

C US Mk44
Electrically powered ; other data not available. Also used by the UK, it is designed for launch from the air, from ships, or by the Asroc rocket system.
Parts of the Mk44
1 Warhead
2 Gyroscope
3 Battery
4 Motor
5 Gear
6 Propeller

Jet-engine propulsion

Three types of jet engine have been used in missiles. The pulse-jet, invented in France in 1910, was used by the Germans in WW2. The French ramjet (invented 1913) was developed after WW2 for use in long-range missiles. The turbojet, patented by Sir Frank Whittle in 1930, was first used to power a Heinkel He178 in 1939 and led to the development of the turbofan engine, as used in the US ALCM (see p.262).

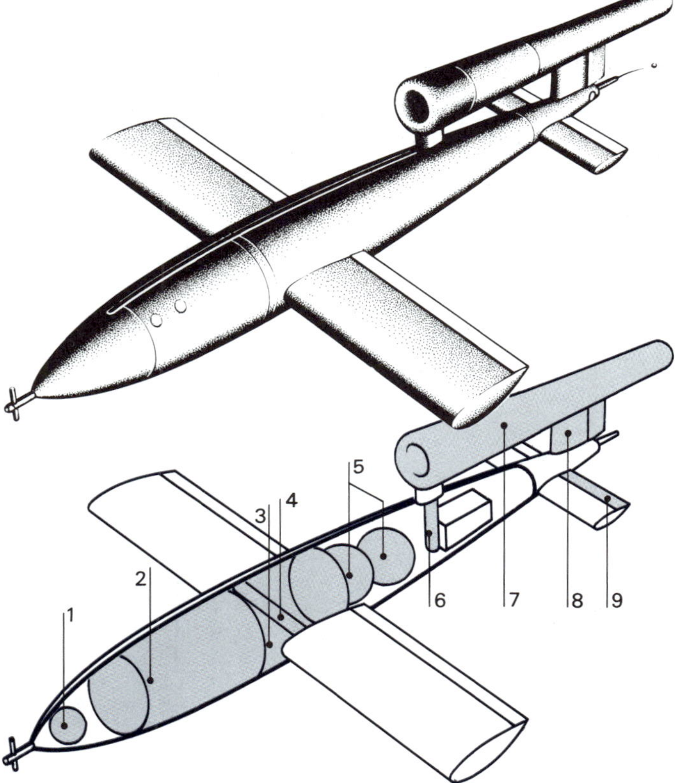

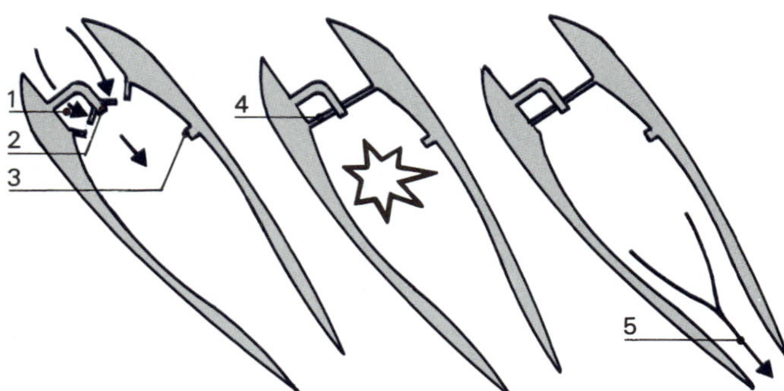

The pulse-jet (above) operates by a two-part cycle. To begin its operation there must be enough air pressure against the air intake valves to force them to open. This is achieved by catapult or rocket booster launch.
1 Air pressure opens valves.
2 Fuel is mixed with air as it enters combustion chamber.
3 Spark plug ignites fuel/air mixture.
4 Pressure of explosion closes valves.
5 Burning exhaust gases exit at high velocity to rear because of their high pressure. This causes the valves to re-open, air rushes in, and the process is repeated. After the first few cycles spark ignition is not needed as a residue of burning gases ignites the incoming mixture.

The German V1 (above) ("Vergeltungswaffe Eins") of WW2 was the first jet-powered guided missile. Propelled by a pulse-jet (the only operational use of this engine), its length was 27ft 3in (8.3m), its maximum speed 559mph (900km/h), and its range 150mi (240km) ; it flew at around 3000ft (900m). It was launched by catapult from a ramp, and the first (of over 8500) flew operationally against England on June 13, 1944.
1 Compass
2 HE warhead
3 Fuel tank
4 Main spar
5 Compressed air bottles
6 Fuel pump
7 Argus pulse-jet engine
8 Rudder
9 Elevator

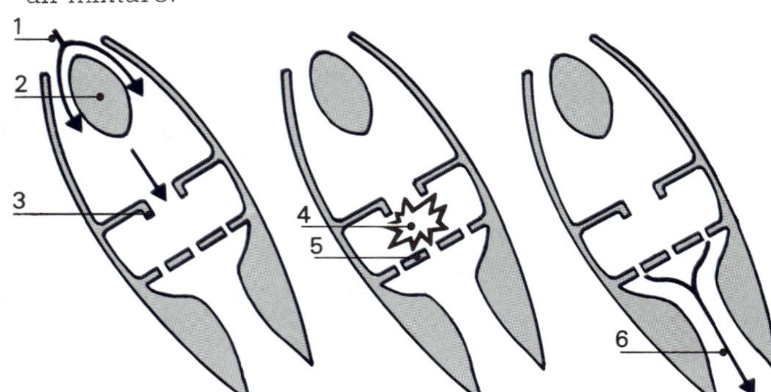

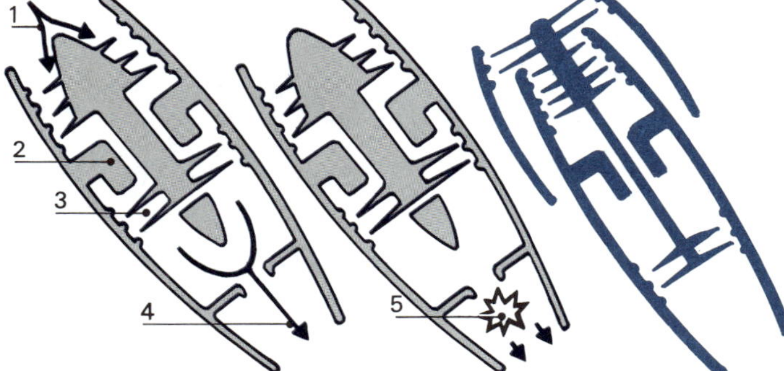

The ramjet (above) is the lightest and simplest jet engine. It is usually given the necessary high initial velocity by rocket boosters. It is used mainly in long-distance, high altitude missiles.
1 The forward velocity rams air into the air inlet.
2 Specially-shaped inserts or inner walls slow the air down and raise its pressure.
3 Fuel is injected and mixed with the air in the diffuser section.
4 The air/fuel mixture is ignited.
5 The flameholder prevents the flame from being blown out.
6 Exhaust gases rush out of the nozzle. The pressure of the entering air prevents exhaust gases from exiting forward. After initial ignition, combustion is continuous.

The turbojet (above) is the largest and most complicated jet engine.
1 The compressor draws in and pressurizes large amounts of air.
2 Fuel is injected and combusted.
3 The hot gases pass through the turbine wheels, and part of their energy is used to turn this, which drives the compressor.
4 The exhaust gases exit.
5 After-burners inject and combust more fuel to gain extra thrust.
The turbofan or fanjet (Far right) increases propulsive efficiency by directing air backward outside the engine casing (to increase the mass flow) by means of a fan before or after the compression chamber. A miniature of the front-fan type shown is used to power the US ALCM.

Solid fuel rocket propulsion

Solid fuels were used to power the earliest known rockets, and they still find wider use than liquid fuels. Here we illustrate a variety of 19th century war-rockets that used solid fuel, and go on to explain the ways in which solid fuels are applied in modern rocketry.

Rocket-propelled "fire-arrows," such as those held by the warrior (left), were fired by lighting the closed end of the container, and were developed and used by the Chinese from the 10th century. Rocket-launched explosive grenades existed by the 13th century. By 1250 the rocket had been introduced, mainly through the Arabs, to Europe.

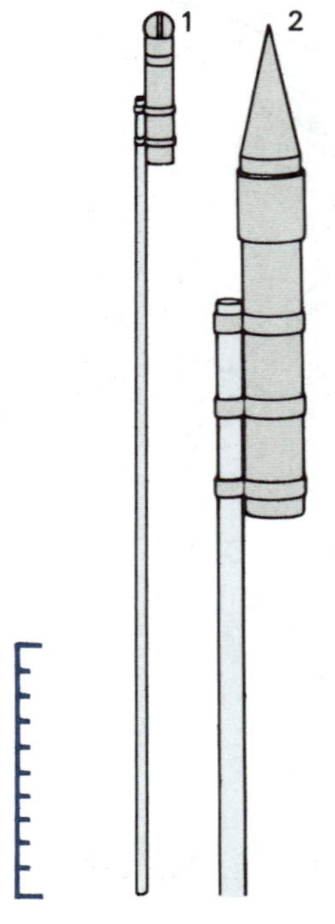

Congreve's rockets (above) were the first to be used by Western armies. They were made in ten sizes and with three main kinds of warhead. Shown are the complete 12-pounder size with shell warhead (**1**), and the head and motor of the 8in (203mm) "carcass" or bombardment type (**2**). The launching ramp for the larger versions is shown (below).

The Hale rocket (above), used, in several versions, in the American Civil War and by Britain. It had no stick, being stabilized instead by the spinning action of the propellant gas, acting on three vanes as it escaped at the rear. Shown in side (**A**) and rear (**B**) views, is the British 24-pounder model of the 1880s. The launcher is shown (below).

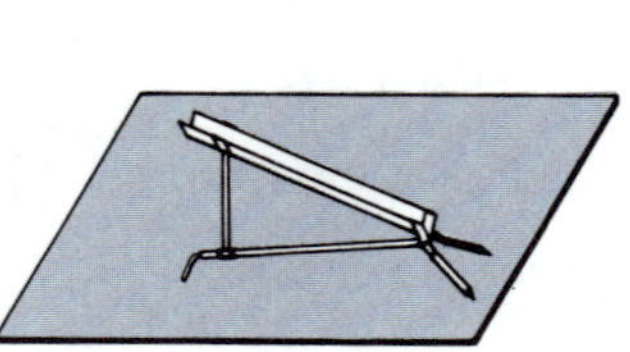

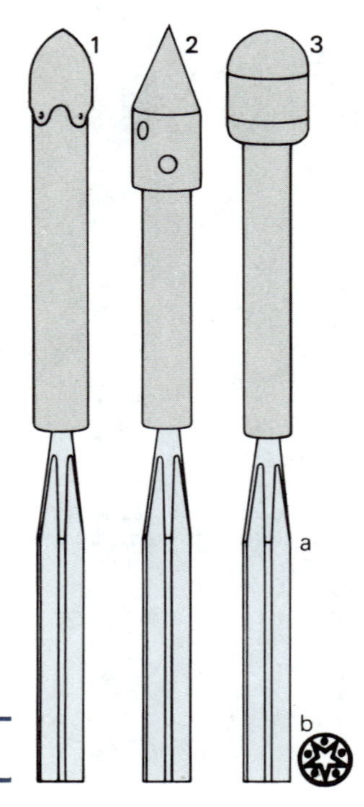

French artillery rockets of the 1870s (above) were fitted with three types of warhead: explosive (**1**), incendiary (**2**), or solid shot (**3**). They weighed 15.43lb (7kg). Stabilization was achieved by the grooved stick (**a**). The end view (**b**) shows the exhaust vents and the corresponding grooves in the stick. The launcher is shown (below).

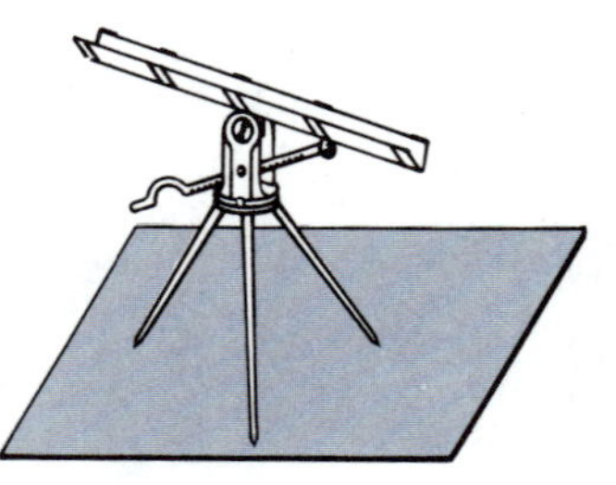

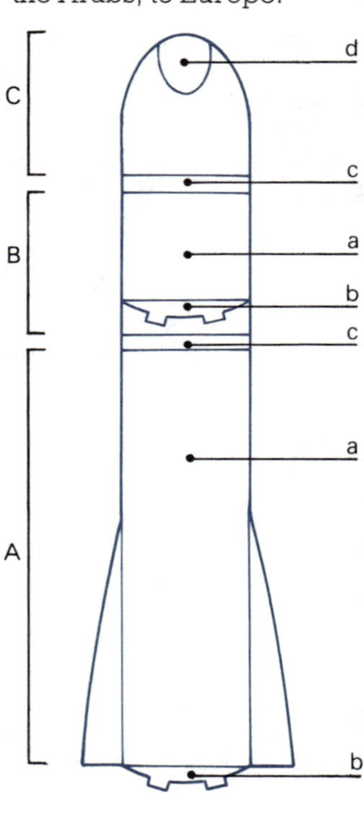

A basic two-stage solid-propellant ICBM (above) The first and second stages (**A** and **B**) of a two-stage rocket each contain a solid propellant charge (**a**), the exhaust nozzle system (**b**), and the thrust termination system (**c**), which shuts off the engine when the desired velocity has been reached. The re-entry body (**C**) contains the guidance and control systems that keep the missile on course, the auxiliary power supply, arming systems, safety systems, fuzes, and the warhead (**d**). Most contemporary re-entry bodies are termed re-entry vehicles, and are classed either as Multiple Independently-targeted Re-entry Vehicles (MIRVs), or Maneuverable Alternative target Re-entry Vehicles (MARVs) (see p.274).

Combinations (right) of solid fuel motors with other forms of propulsion.
1 Solid fuel boosters are sometimes fitted to ramjet and liquid-fueled missiles.
2 Integrated rocket/ramjet missiles exist, where the rocket motor (**a**) becomes, after burning out, the ramjet combustion chamber, with air-intakes (**b**). The ramjet fuel is at (**c**), and the warhead at (**d**).

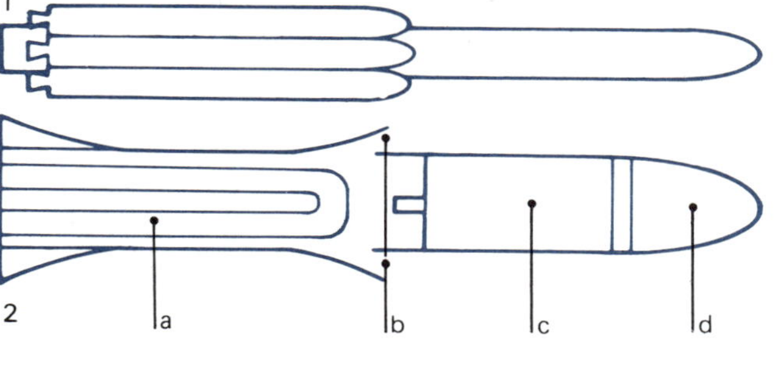

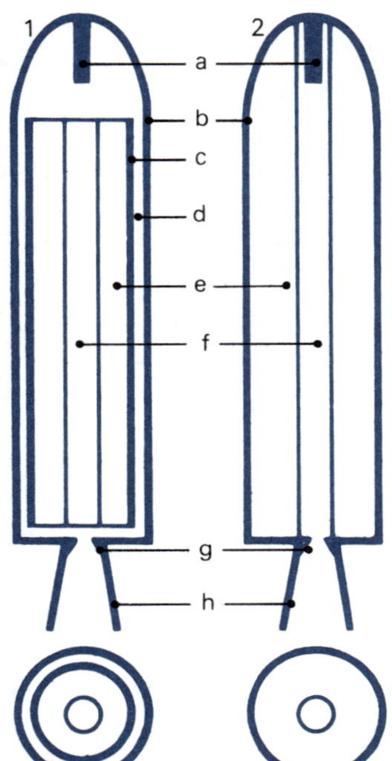

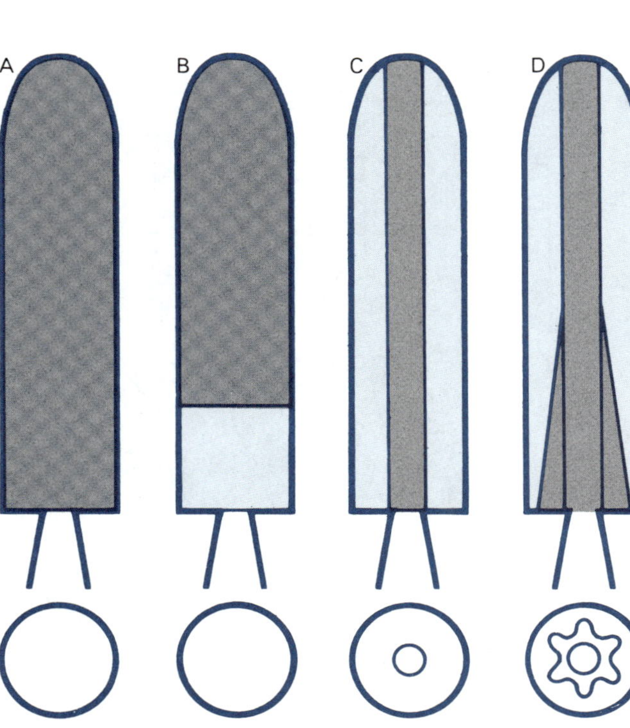

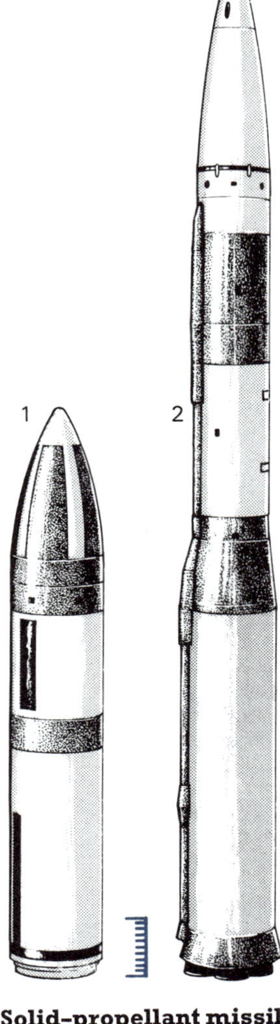

Rocket structure (above) Solid propellant rockets consist mainly of a solid propellant charge or "grain" contained within a case. The grain contains all the elements necessary for complete, smooth burning. It can either be contained within a separate case (**1**), or be bonded to the case—case-bonded (**2**)—which can reduce size and weight. The shape of the central conduit determines the surface area exposed to burning at any one time. Both those illustrated have a tubular grain type of configuration.
a Igniter
b Outer casing
c Insulation
d Inhibitor
e Charge
f Central conduit
g Throat insert
h Nozzle

Thrust levels and fuel configurations (above) The larger the surface area of the burning propellant, the greater is the motor's thrust. Thrust levels can therefore be controlled by the design of the charge shape. We show four examples.
A An end-burning grain burns only in one direction (like a cigarette) and gives a constant level of thrust.
B An end-burning configuration with two grains of different burning rates varies the thrust level, giving, for instance, initial high-level thrust followed by a lower-level thrust for sustained flight.
C Tubular-grain configuration produces a progressive thrust. As the period of burning continues the area of the burning grain and the resultant thrust progressively increase.
D This single-grain configuration will give an initial boost with the large star-shaped area and sustain the flight with the smaller burning area.

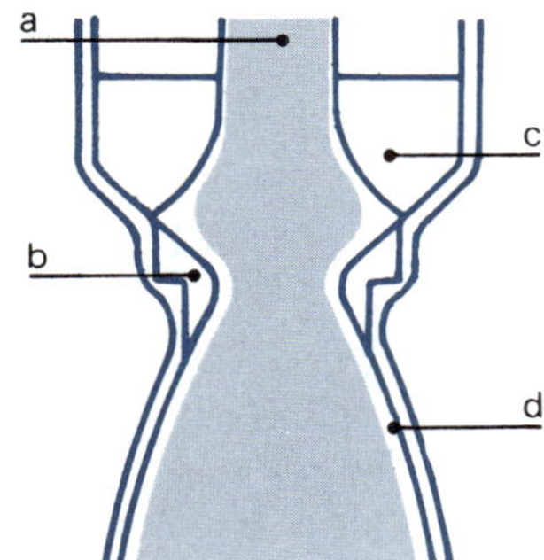

Solid-propellant missiles (above)
1 US Poseidon C3 two-stage submarine-launched ballistic missile. Targets 3230mi (5200km) away can be hit by fitting a Mk3 MIRV with ten 50KT warheads.
2 US Minuteman III three-stage intercontinental ballistic missile. Range over 8080mi (13,000km). It carries a Mk12 MIRV with three 170KT warheads.

Nozzle protection (left) To prevent the nozzle being damaged by the heat of the escaping exhaust gases (**a**), complex inserts of heat-resistant materials (**b**) are used. A ring of cool-burning propellant (**c**) inserted just above the nozzle provides a protective layer of cool gas (**d**) next to the nozzle.

Liquid fuel rocket propulsion

Liquid fuel rocketry was a theoretical possibility in 1903 through the work of the Russian pioneer Konstantin Tsiolkovsky. It became a practical reality during the inter-war years through the work of the American scientist Robert Goddard and others who experimented with fuel mixtures of liquid oxygen and gasoline. Liquid fuel mixtures are used now for the larger, military ballistic missiles.

Titan II (right), a US two-stage Inter-Continental Ballistic Missile (ICBM). Its motors burn nitrogen tetroxide and aerozine-50 storable liquid propellants. It can carry a 20 megaton (20MT) warhead 9300mi (14,966km), but is usually fitted with a five to ten megaton warhead plus electronic aids. 54 Titan II's are still operational.

Typical two-stage liquid propellant ICBM (right) The first and second stages (**A, B**) each have a rocket engine (**a**), fuel tank (**b**), oxidizer tank (**c**) and turbopump assemblies (**d**) that deliver propellants to the engines. There are also guidance and control systems (**e**), an auxiliary power supply (**f**), and the warhead (**g**), all parts of the re-entry body (**C**).

Tank arrangements (right) Various arrangements have been used, according to the way they affect the missile's center of gravity.
1 Tandem tanks with external piping
2 Tandem tanks with internal piping and common bulkhead
3 Concentric tanks
4 Multiple tanks for a group of engines

Fuel feed systems (right) There are two main kinds.
A Pressure feed systems have a high-pressure store of gas, such as nitrogen or helium. This flows into the propellant tanks and forces the propellants to flow out to the engines.
a Pressurizing gas tank
b Valve
c Liquid propellant tanks
d Valves
e Thrust chamber
B Turbopump feed systems pressurize the propellants with pumps driven by turbines, powered by the expansion of hot gases generated by the combustion of propellant.
i Liquid propellant tanks
ii Turbine
iii Propellant pumps
iv Gas generator
v Valves
vi Turbine exhaust
vii Thrust chamber

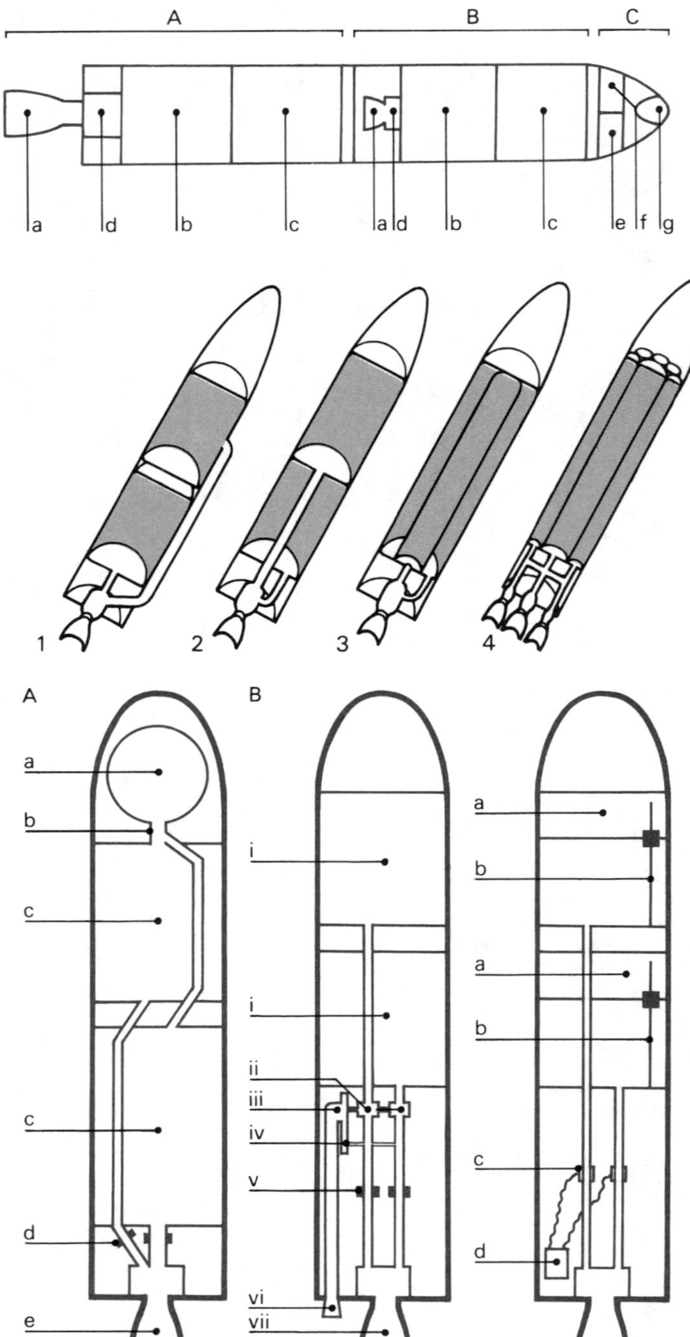

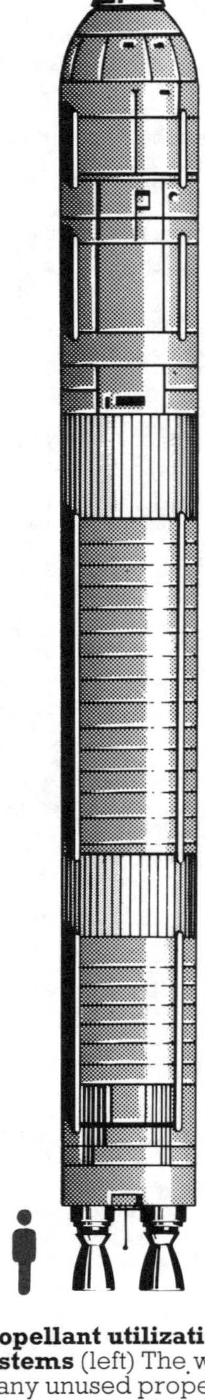

Propellant utilization systems (left) The weight of any unused propellant can seriously affect the accuracy and speed of a missile. For this reason, devices are fitted that adjust the flow-rate of propellants according to the amounts remaining.
a Propellant tanks
b Sensing devices
c Regulating valves
d Computer

Combustion and thrust (right) The diagram is a simplified representation of the combustion and thrust chambers of a bipropellant rocket, fuel and oxidizer being fed in through the pipes (**a**) and (**b**). We describe the process that follows.
1 In the combustion chamber the fuel and oxidizer are mixed and ignited. The temperature and static pressure of the gases are high, but their velocity is low.
2 At the "throat," the temperature is falling, static pressure is falling fast, but gas velocity builds up rapidly.
3 At the mouth of the expansion chamber static pressure is down to zero, the temperature is still falling, and gas velocity is at its maximum, to impart the desired thrust.

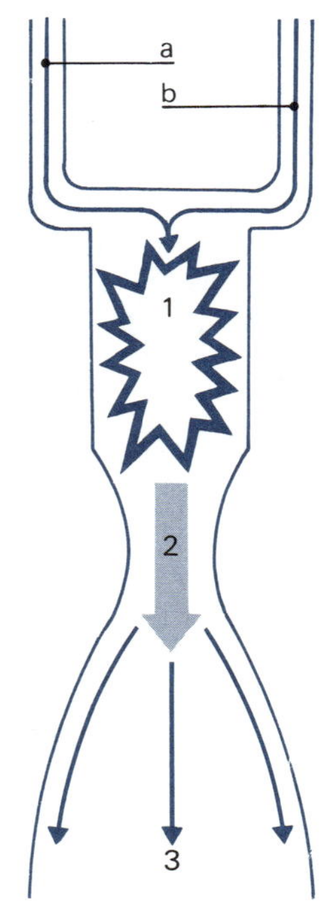

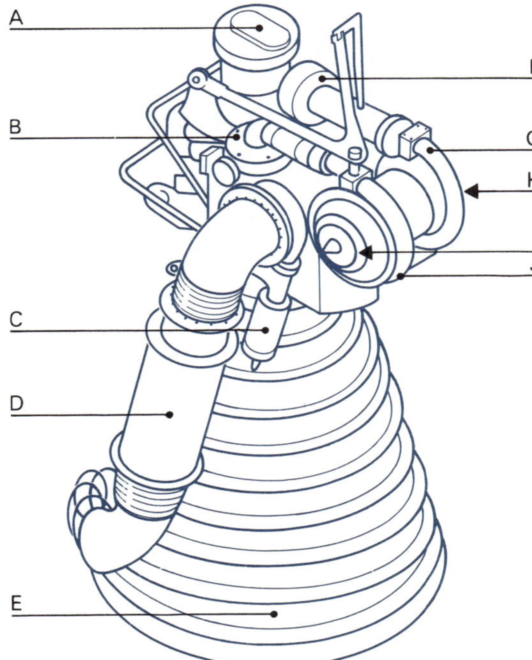

The US H-1 (above), a typical liquid-fueled rocket engine that burns kerosene and liquid oxygen. It has been used in several development projects since 1958, including the Saturn 1B and Skylab. Eight H-1 engines were used on the first stage of Saturn 1B, each generating a thrust of 73.65 long tons (74.84 tonnes).

A Gimbal
B Main fuel valve
C Turbine starter
D Heat exchanger
E Thrust chamber
F Main oxidizer valve
G Oxidizer pump
H Oxidizer inlet
I Fuel inlet
J Fuel pump

The coolant injection system (right) of cooling the thrust nozzle. In this method, below the propellant injector (**A**) there is a series of holes (**B**) for the injection of coolant liquid. This forms a protective lining (**C**) on the walls of the nozzle. A variation of this method injects more fuel at point (**B**), which has a similar effect.

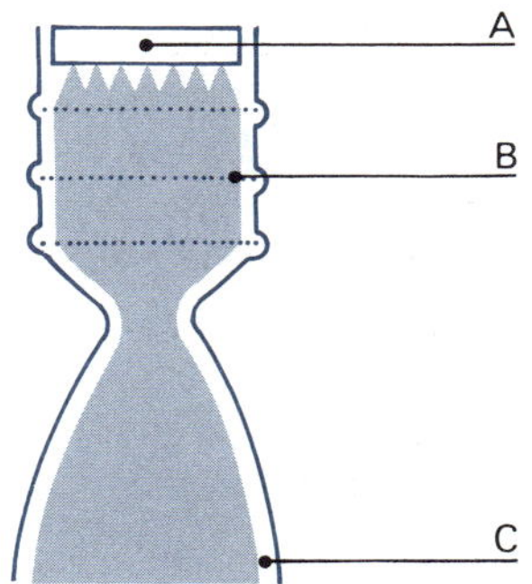

The regenerative cooling system (right) involves the circulation of one of the propellants through passages in the walls of the thrust chamber before it is injected for combustion. This method has the advantage that the heated propellant will then burn more efficiently. Typical temperatures in the various layers of a thrust nozzle with a regenerative cooling system are shown in the enlarged cross-section (lower right).
a Gases at center of nozzle, 2760°C.
b Outer gas film, 420°C.
c Inner wall, 200°C.
d Cooling fluid, 100°C.
e Outer wall, 65°C.

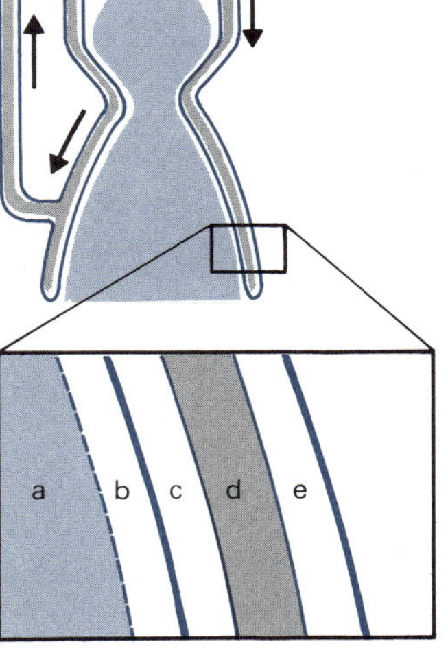

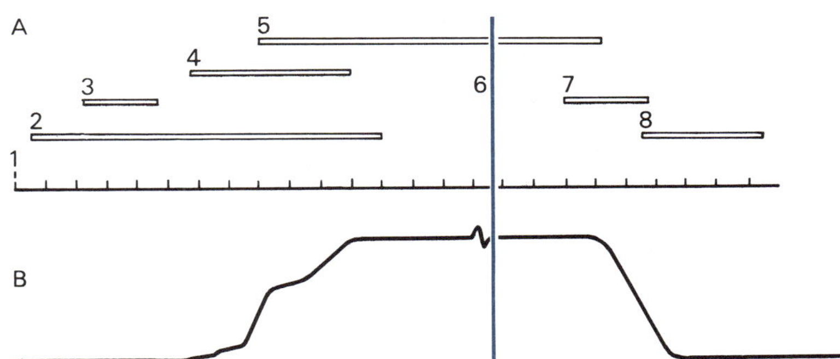

The sequence of events (above) in the ignition and shutdown of the H-1 engine is shown in the time-chart (**A**).
1 Electric ignition signal given.
2 Solid fuel gas generator operates.
3 Main liquid oxygen valve opens.
4 Main fuel valve opens.
5 Gas generator is now powered by the propellants.
6 Cutoff signal given.
7 Main liquid oxygen valve closes.
8 Main fuel valve closes.
The build-up of thrust to 188,000lb (85,275kg) and its decline after shutdown are shown to the same time-scale on the graph (**B**). The vertical line indicates the moment of shutdown. The time that the engine continues burning can of course be varied.

Launch methods

Here we introduce the methods that are commonly used for launching self-propelled missiles. In practice there are almost as many variations as there are makes of missile, the exact choice of method used being determined by considerations such as the guidance system to be used (if any), and the need for portability. More specific information will be found on subsequent pages.

Launching Congreve rockets (left) The rockets are being launched from the slope of an earth bank, to bombard a besieged town. Congreve also proposed to launch rockets from a variety of mobile ramps, and to let them slither across flat ground. (After Congreve's "The Details of The Rocket System," 1814.) See also p. 244.

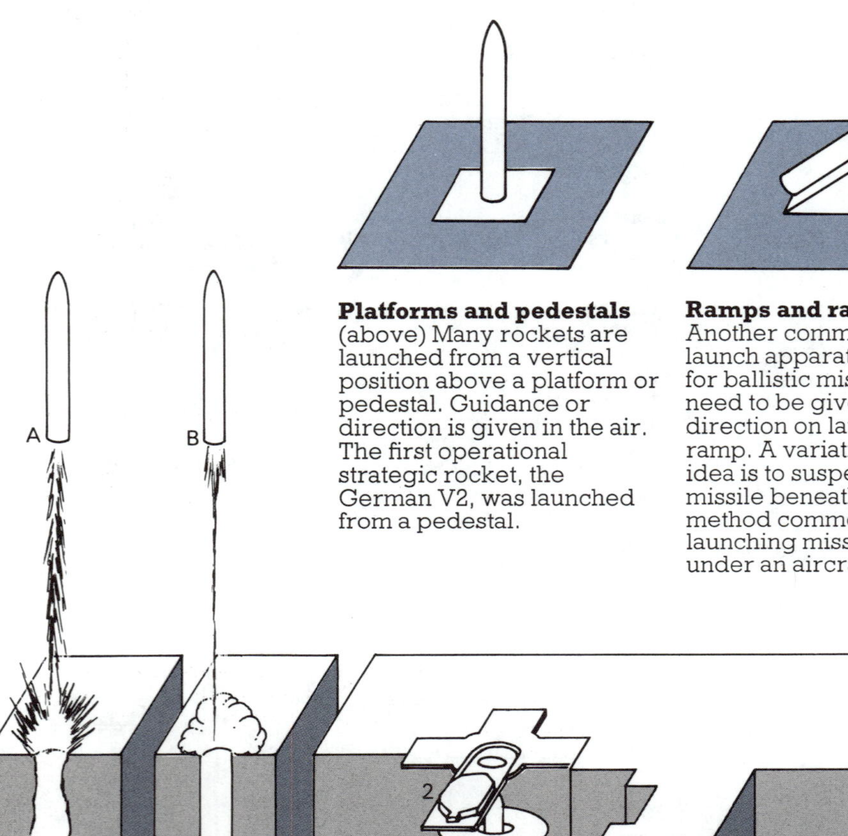

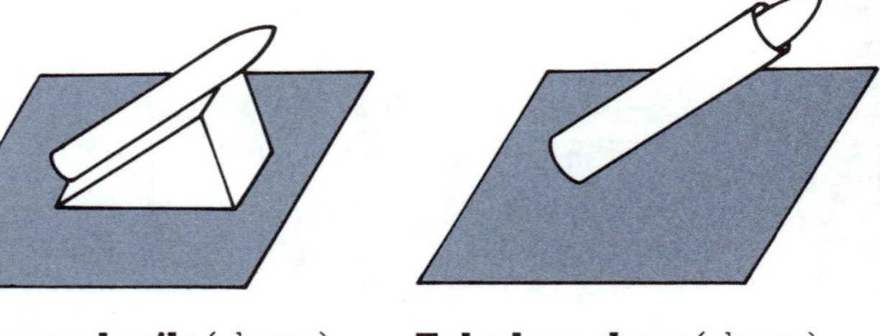

Platforms and pedestals (above) Many rockets are launched from a vertical position above a platform or pedestal. Guidance or direction is given in the air. The first operational strategic rocket, the German V2, was launched from a pedestal.

Ramps and rails (above) Another common type of launch apparatus, especially for ballistic missiles that need to be given an initial direction on launch, is a ramp. A variation of this idea is to suspend the missile beneath a rail — a method commonly used for launching missiles from under an aircraft's wing.

Tube launchers (above) These take two main forms. There is the permanent, immobile concrete silo, dug into the earth, and there is the portable, shoulder-held tube, such as the bazooka. Many tubular container/launchers are now in use with one-shot disposable anti-tank and anti-aircraft missile systems.

Missile silos are used to store, protect and launch many types of ICBM. Silo launch techniques can be divided into two main kinds.
A In a "hot launch" the main rocket booster is ignited in the silo, causing damage that must be repaired before reuse.
B In a "cold launch" the missile is ejected from the silo by gas generators before engine ignition.

US Minuteman III silo (above) The missile rests on a shock-absorbing cradle (**1**) and is covered by a large protective concrete slab (**2**) that opens 12sec before launch. The unmanned power facility is 15m away (**3**). Ten silos, placed at least 4.3mi (7km) apart, are controlled by a single launch control facility. Because of the inherent immobility of silos, and the consequent risk of their location and destruction by the enemy, silos are "hardened" to withstand all but a direct hit. The USA has 1000 silo-launched ICBMs deployed. The USSR's total is at least 1386. (IISS figures as of June 1988.)

Man-portable missile systems (above) now offer anti-tank and anti-aircraft protection to small and highly mobile units. They can be carried and launched by one or two men. The guidance and launch systems and the missile itself can all be carried in a light package, a part or all of which is usually disposable after use. (For examples, see p.254 and p.256.)

Missile subsystems

A modern self-propelled missile is composed of a number of subsystems, each contributing a particular function toward the correct working of the weapon. To explain the function of important subsystems, we take as an example a guided missile, as guided missiles contain the full range of complex subsystems, not all of which are necessarily present in other, simpler missiles.

Main subsystems (right) in a modern guided missile
1 Warhead or payload, which may contain its own complex subsystems.
2 Propulsion system, which may consist of up to three "stages."
3 Guidance systems, which monitor the missile's movements and actual position, and compare these with the desired position for a strike.
4 Control systems, which translate the signals from the guidance systems into movement.
5 Mission specific systems, for example, the command destruct system of an ICBM, through which its mission can be aborted.
6 Secondary power supply, providing power for subsystems 3, 4 and 5.
7 Airframe, the structure that contains the other subsystems.

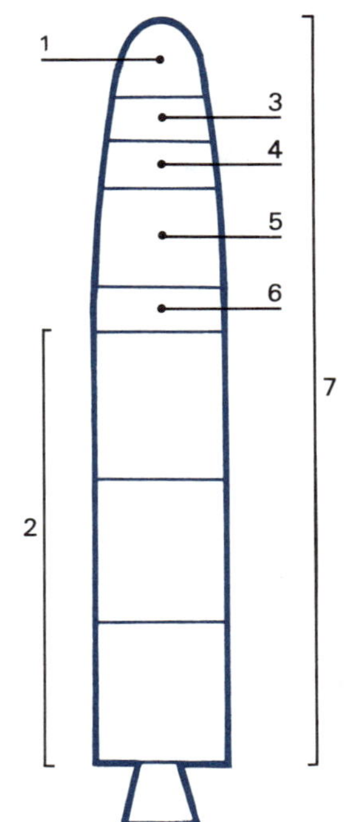

Three-stage propulsion (right) Rocket-propelled missiles may have three motors, used in sequence. The first "stage," at the rear of the missile, is designed for the task of lifting the missile clear of the ground (**1**) and propelling it through the dense lower air. When it has burned out it separates and falls away (**2**). The second stage motor then starts to burn. This may be adapted to flight and maneuver in the upper atmosphere. It too burns out and separates (**3**). The third stage motor then takes over. Its subsequent functioning will depend on whether the missile is of the guided or the ballistic type.

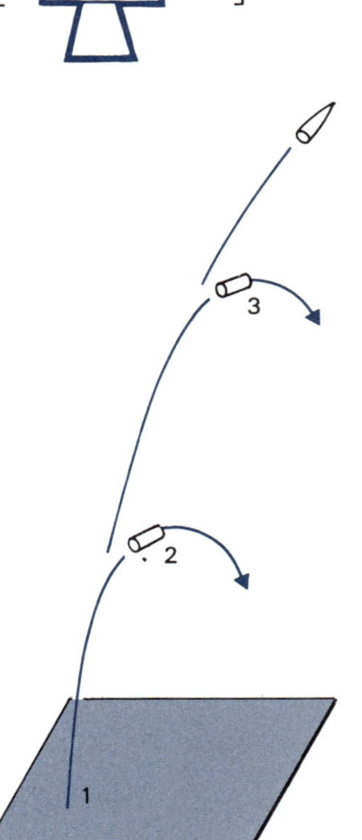

Guidance systems The flowchart (right) shows how the basic functions of a missile's guidance systems are interrelated.
A Determination of the missile's actual position.
B Knowledge of the desired position. (This may be preprogramed, or be deduced from (**A**).)
C Comparison of (**A**) and (**B**).
D Conveyance of commands to the control system.
E Reaction of the control system.
F Observation and measurment of the new position.

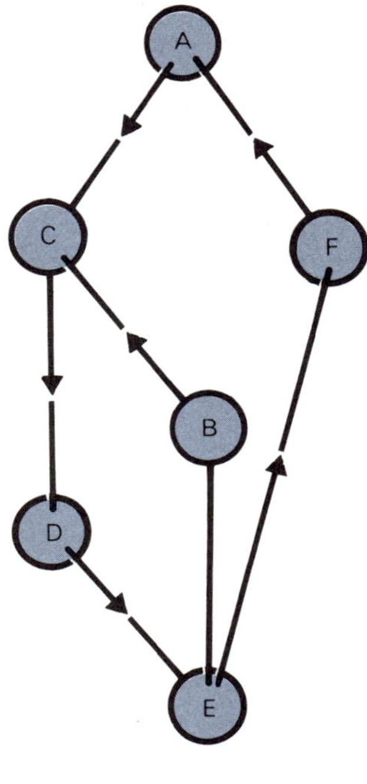

Attitude and its control (right) The attitude of a missile can be altered in several directions: roll (**a**), pitch (**b**), and yaw (**c**). Stability in flight is assisted by fixed fins (**d**), but some means is needed for making accurate alterations in attitude, and thus the course of the missile. Two main methods, described below, are used.

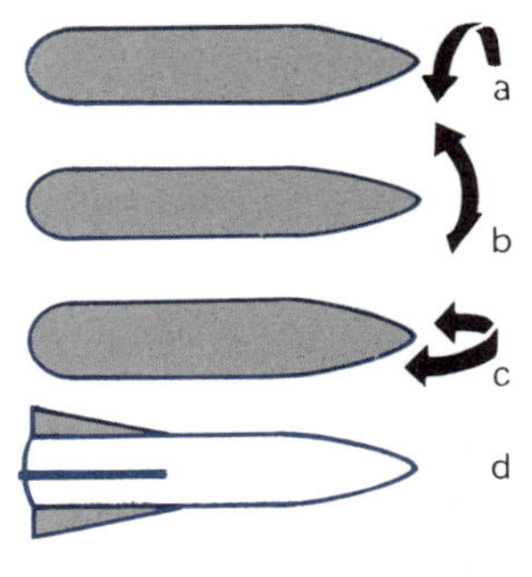

Control surfaces (right) Within the earth's atmosphere, the missile's attitude can be altered by control surfaces. These are adjustable vanes that are attached to the airframe, as part of the stabilizing fins (**A**), or behind them (**B**), or ahead of them (**C**).

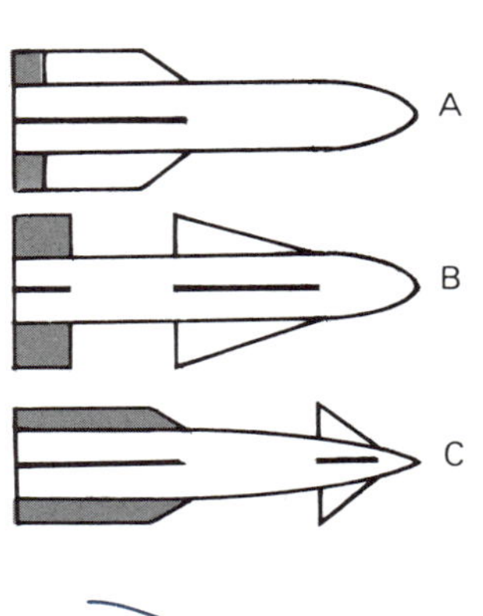

Thrust vector control (right) is used for missiles that travel outside the earth's atmosphere.
1 An entire liquid-fuel motor, or the nozzle of a solid-fuel motor, may be made to swivel on a gimbal.
2 Adjustable vanes may be fitted in the nozzle.
3 Fuel may be injected at the side of the nozzle, causing deflection of thrust by shock waves.

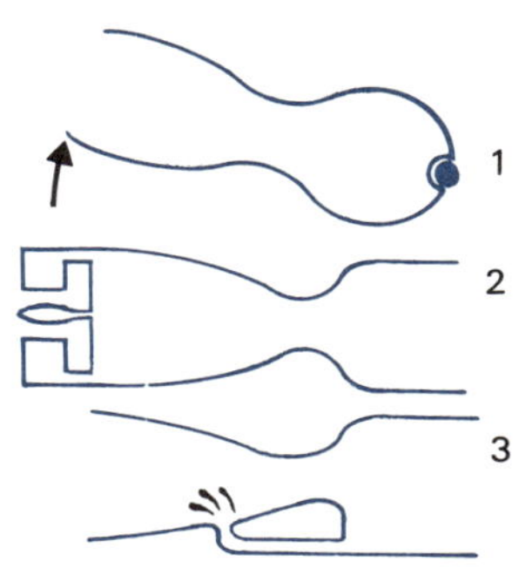

Guidance systems

There are three kinds of missile guidance system : inertial guidance, which may be aided by stellar reference ; command guidance ; and homing guidance, which may be active or passive. Inertial guidance systems, discussed on this page, are often used to keep ballistic missiles on course, but can be used only against stationary targets. Systems used with true guided missiles are shown on the opposite page.

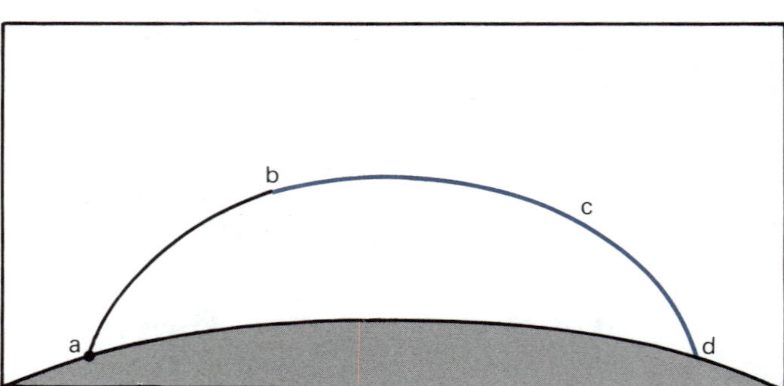

The trajectory (above) of an ICBM. The guidance and control of a ballistic missile is possible only during its period of powered flight, from the launch site (**a**) to the cutoff point (**b**). At this point, an ICBM will be above the earth's atmosphere but still under the influence of gravity. From point (**b**) it travels according to the laws of ballistics in a free-flight trajectory that is affected by many forces, all of which must be accurately calculated to achieve a hit. If the ICBM is fitted with a MIRV or a MARV its re-entry phase, from re-entering the earth's atmosphere at point (**c**) to the impact point (**d**), will also be controlled.

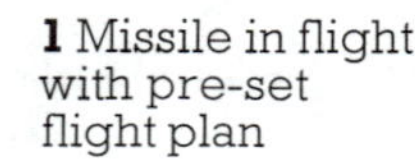

1 Missile in flight with pre-set flight plan

2 Accelerometer

3 Gyroscope

4 Programer

5 Computer

6 Control system

7 Flight control mechanisms

8 Adjustment of flight path

9 Follow-up unit

An inertial guidance system, as used in many ICBMs, is represented in the flow-chart (left). The system senses and compensates for any deviations from a flight plan fed into the missile before launch. In flight the accelerometers measure lateral, vertical and forward motion and velocity. The gyroscopes measure and control roll, pitch and yaw. The computer calculates the missile's position from this data and compares it with data on the desired position from the programer. An error signal is sent to the control system, and activates flight control mechanisms ; data is relayed back by the follow-up unit, so continually monitoring and adjusting the flight path.

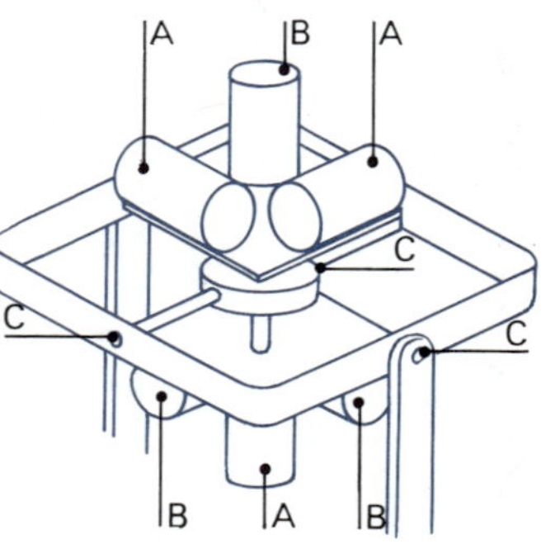

The inertial platform (left), the central part of the guidance unit, supports the accelerometers (**A**) and gyros (**B**). The accelerometer mountings must be kept horizontal to the force of gravity. The gyros keep the platform stable on its gimbaled supports (**C**) so that the accelerometers can function properly and provide the gyros with information.

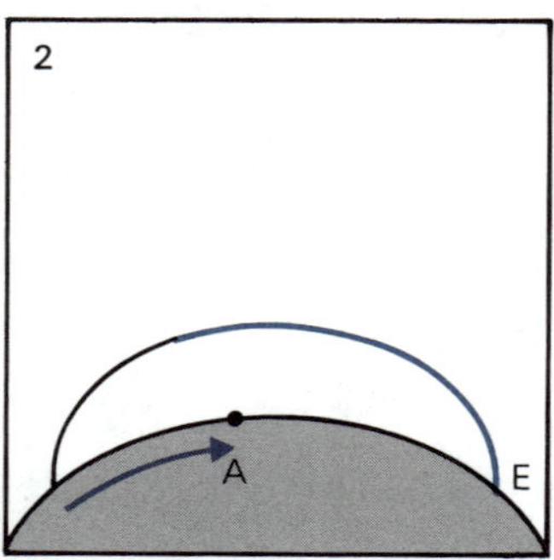

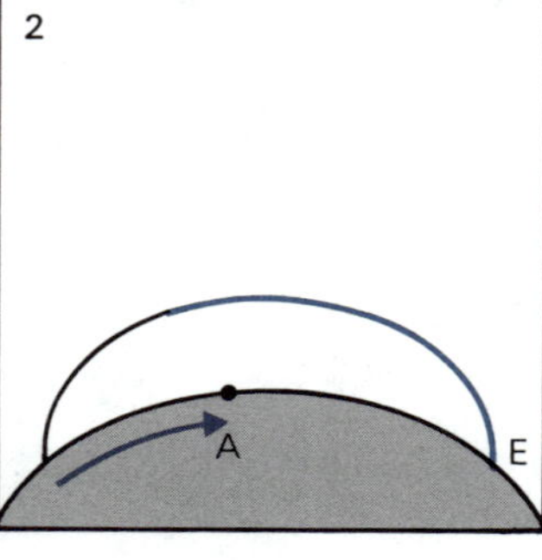

Two effects of the earth's rotation (above) on the accuracy of a ballistic missile. Both diagrams represent an ICBM traveling from west to east directly above the equator.
1 The missile is launched from point (**A**) on the earth's crust and travels under power until the motor cuts off at point (**B**). From this point the missile obeys the laws of ballistics. If the earth did not rotate, the missile would follow trajectory (**C**). However, the rotation of the earth imparts added impetus at launch, so extending the trajectory (**D**).
2 The second effect is that while the missile is in flight, the earth's surface has moved in the same direction, shortening the distance between (**A**) and the impact point (**E**).

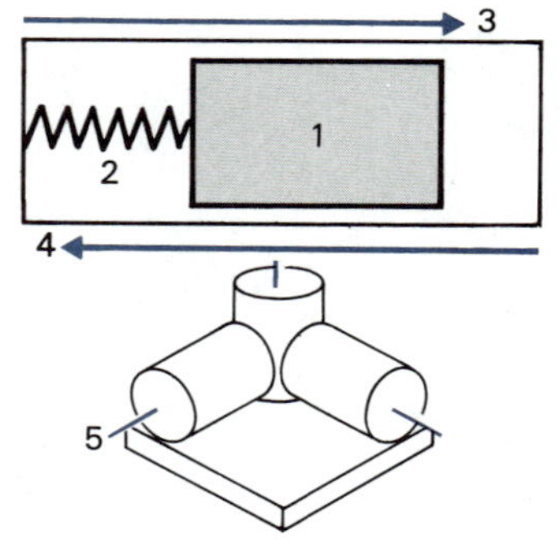

Accelerometers (left) consist basically of a known mass (**1**) subject to a specific constraint exerted by springs (**2**). Acceleration (**3**) along its axis exerts an equal, opposite force (**4**) that moves the mass. From the distance moved, acceleration, velocity and position are computed. Three accelerometers are arranged on mutually perpendicular axes (**5**).

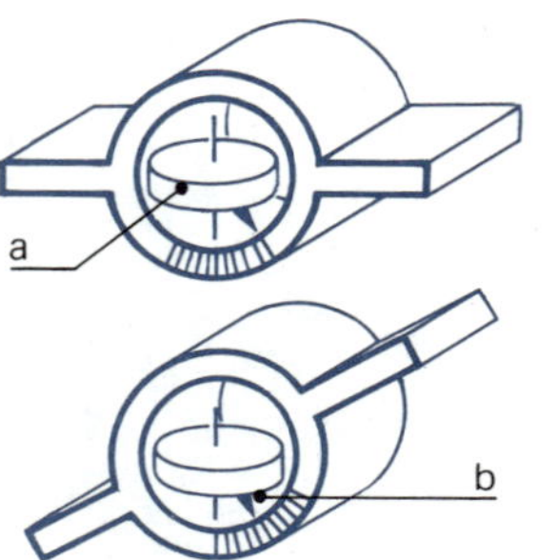

Gyroscopes (left) will remain stable in the plane of the spinning rotor (**a**). When the missile turns, the degree of the turn can be detected electronically from the angle between the gyro and frame, as indicated by the pointer (**b**). Yaw, pitch and roll are thus monitored. By pre-setting the gyro to a specific angle, controlled movements can be initiated when required.

Command guidance systems (right) In this case the missile contains no guidance equipment. It receives instructions to change course via a "command link" to external tracking equipment. Each system comprises a target tracker (which is often the "line-of-sight" of the operator), a missile tracker, a computer and a transmitter. The computer calculates the deviation of the missile's path from that indicated by the target tracker and sends corrective signals to the missile via the transmitter. Most command links are by wire (**A**) or radar (**B**). The missile is often tracked by the infrared radiations of flares in its tail. Beam-riding missiles fly within the cone of a radar beam, often "command-to-line-of-sight" (**C**).

1 Target tracker locks on target

2 Missile launched

3 Missile tracking system collects missile

4 Computer calculates deviation from path

5 Transmitter sends error signal

6 Receiver receives signal

7 Control mechanisms activated

8 Missile brought to path of interception

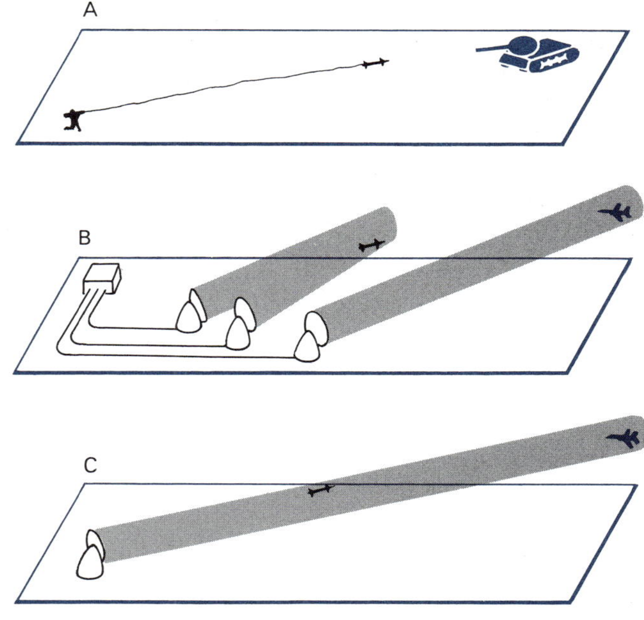

Homing systems The missile is sensitive to a form of electromagnetic radiation from the target, and can alter course accordingly to intercept the target.
Passive homing missiles (right) have a receiver that is sensitive to the heat generated by the target.

Semiactive (SA) homing missiles (right) have a receiver that picks up reflections of electromagnetic waves directed at the target by an external transmitter.
The external transmitter (**a**) may use either radar or laser radiations. The target (**b**) may be moving or stationary, surface or air. The missile may be air or surface launched.

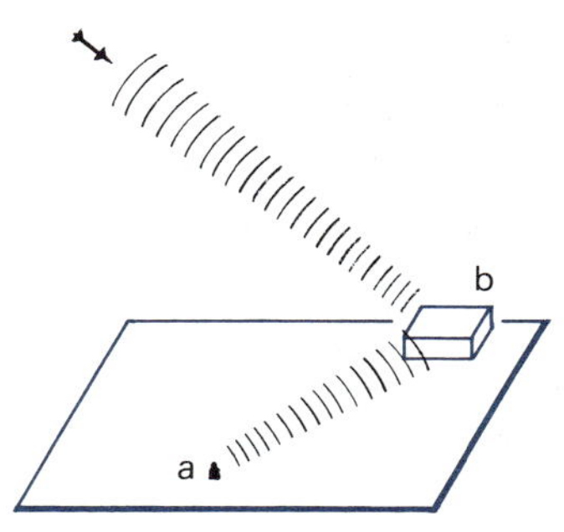

Active (A) homing systems are carried wholly in the missile. They home in on the reflected electromagnetic waves directed at the target by a transmitter contained in the missile itself (**a**). Their general form is shown (right). They are also known as "terminal guidance systems" when they are used in the final phase of a flight controlled by another, e.g. inertial, system. The US SLCM and ALCM (see p. 262) use Terrain Contour Matching (TERCOM) aided inertial guidance (**b**). After a preset point in the flight a downward-looking radio altimeter continually averages the elevations of successive areas 64ft (19.5m) square and compares them with stored terrain profiles, keeping the missile accurately on course.

1 Missile locked on target by launcher

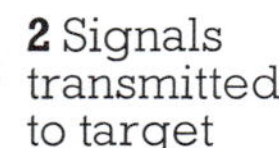

2 Signals transmitted to target

3 Reflected signals received from target

4 Computer calculates course

5 Control surfaces activated

6 Course to intercept target followed

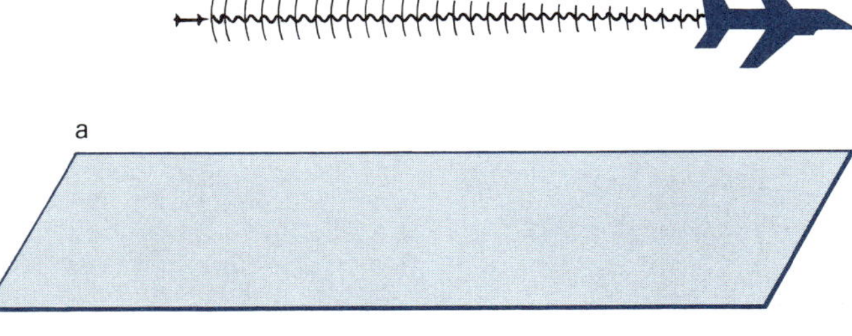

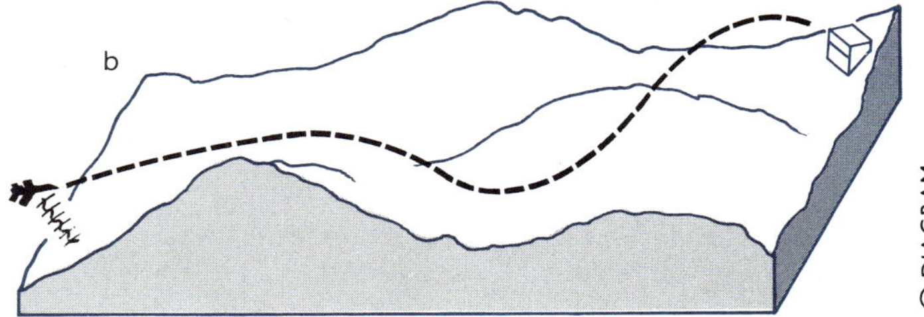

Rockets in World War 2

After going out of use in the later 19th century, the solid-propellant rocket made a comeback in WW2 in both artillery and anti-aircraft roles. Germany favored spin stabilization; the USSR, the USA and Britain favored fin stabilization as it was cheaper and easier to use although less accurate. By the end of the war, artillery bombardment and air-to-ground attack were the main roles for rockets.

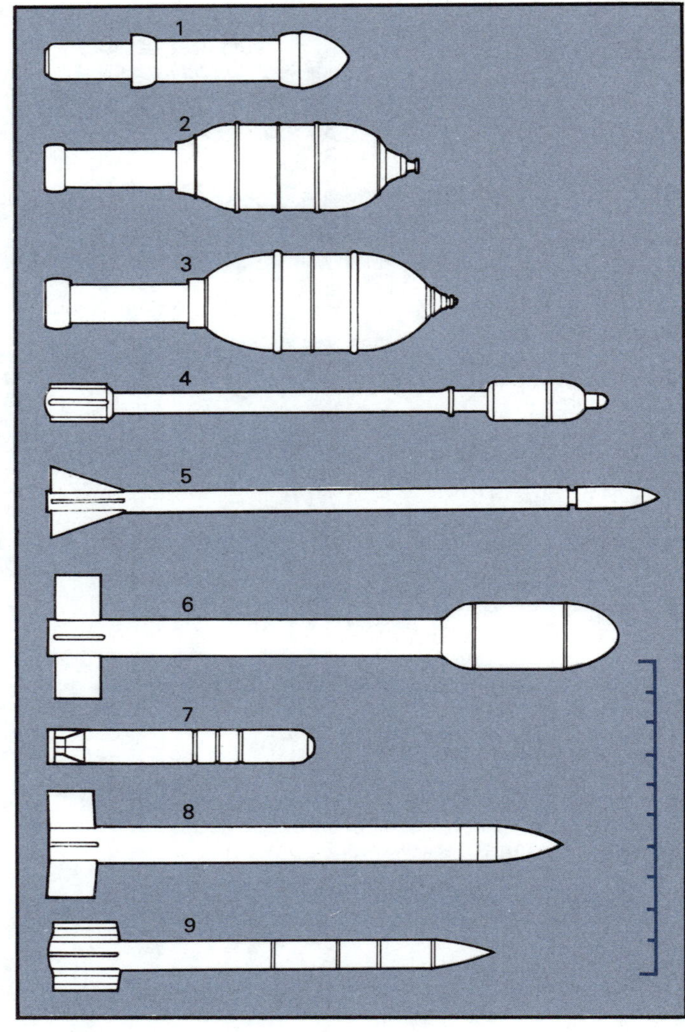

The first British rocket of WW2 was the 2in AA (Anti-Aircraft) rocket, closely followed by the favored 3in version. The first projector in mass use was the two-man No2 Mk1 (left), that fired two rockets. The No4 Mk1 and Mk2 fired nine rockets, and the No6 Mk1 fired 20. The 3in AA rocket had a ceiling of 22,200ft (6770m).

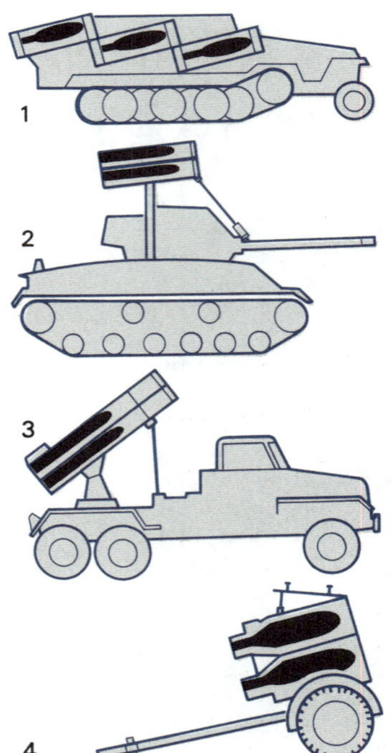

Rocket launcher/carriers (left) were developed for each kind of rocket to add the mobility desirable in all kinds of artillery.
1 The German *Schwerer Wurfrahmen 40* rocket frame converted the SdKfz 251 half-track into the SdKfz 251/1, capable of carrying and launching six rockets.
2 The T34 Calliope launcher for 60 US 4.5in rockets was fitted to the Sherman M4 tank.
3 Soviet rockets were launched from the famous *Katyusha* lorry-mounted launchers of various models.
4 The German *Nebelwerfer 41* was designed for the 28cm and 32cm rockets. Multiple rocket artillery systems are still used by many countries. The projected Italian/West German RS-80 system has a range of up to 37mi (60km).

WW2 rockets (above)
1 German 15cm HE rocket (warhead behind motor) Range 7723yd (7066m)
2 German 28cm HE rocket Range 2337yd (2138m)
3 German 32cm HE rocket Range 2217yd (2028m)
4 British "Land Mattress" Range 7900yd (7230m)
5 British 3in AA rocket Range (horizontal) 4070yd (3720m)
6 British RP-3 aircraft rocket for ground attack
7 US 4.5in HE M8 rocket Range 4600yd (4209m)
8 US High Velocity Aircraft Rocket (HVAR), 5in Accurate range 1000yd (914m)
9 Soviet 132mm rocket Range 9300yd (8500m)

Aircraft rockets were used in the later stages of WW2 for ground attack, usually being mounted on underwing rails (left).
Assault landing craft (below left) were often fitted with multiple rocket launchers to soften up shore defenses during a seaborne invasion.

The German A-4 (V2) and other experimental rockets of WW2 broke the developmental barrier between simple, unguided solid-propellant rockets, and missiles as we know them today. Apart from the then advanced A-4, many other experimental projects were under development by the end of the war, and served as the basis for post-war development.

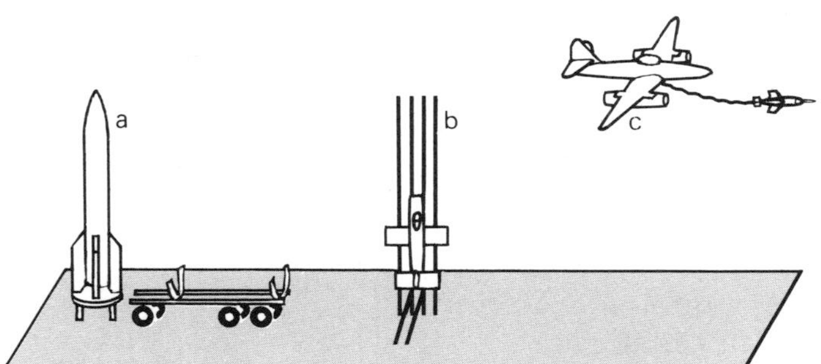

Launch techniques (left)
The A-4 (**a**) was vertically launched, originally from static sites, later from mobile platforms to escape allied air-raids. The Natter (**b**) was meant to be launched along guide rails into enemy bomber formations. The X-4 (**c**) was the first air-launched guided missile, and had wire guidance.

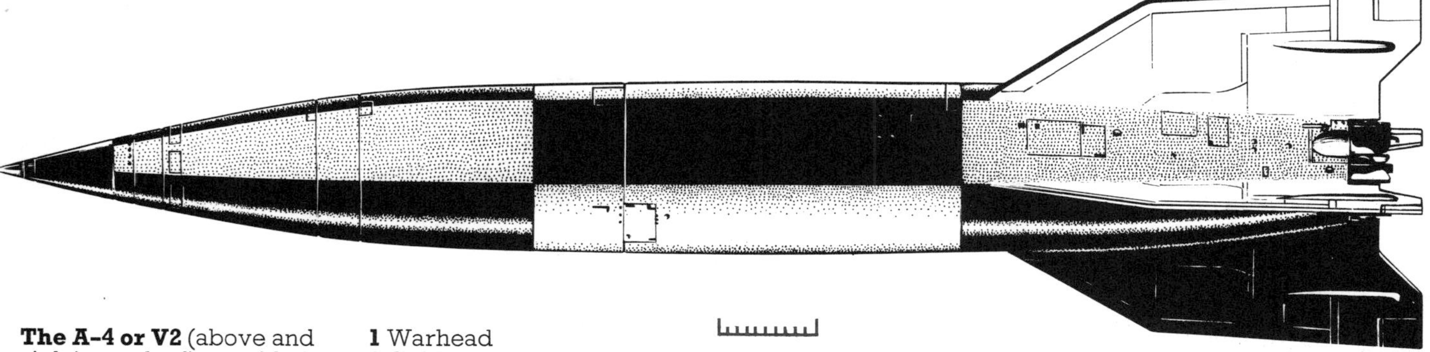

The A-4 or V2 (above and right) was the first guided ballistic missile to be used operationally. Between September 6 1944 and March 27 1945, over 4000 rockets were launched, mostly against London and Antwerp.
Launch weight 28,504 lb (12,930kg)
Warhead weight 2200 lb (998kg)

1 Warhead
2 Guidance and control
3 Alcohol tank
4 Liquid oxygen tank
5 Turbine and pump
6 Rocket engine
7 Control vanes

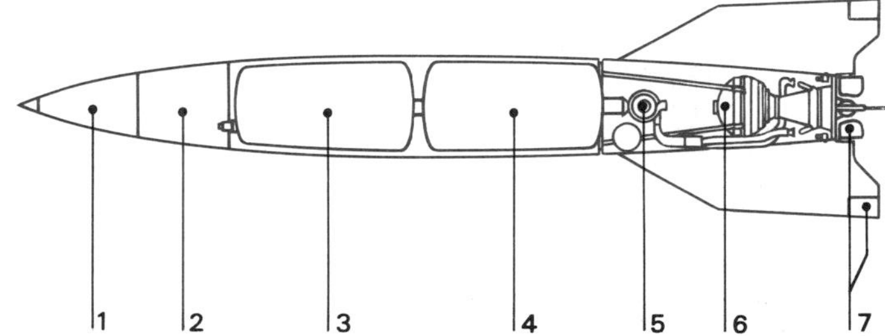

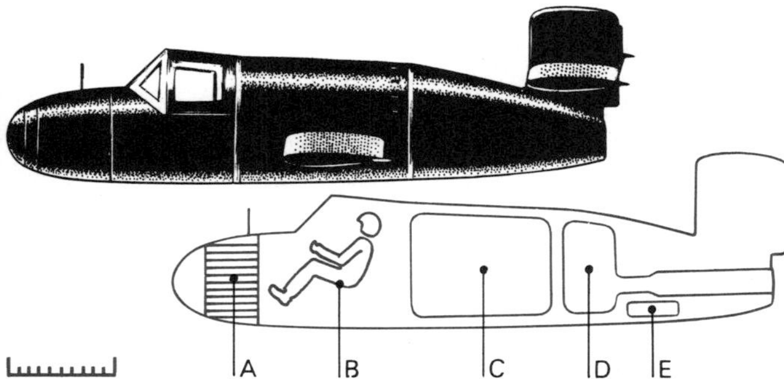

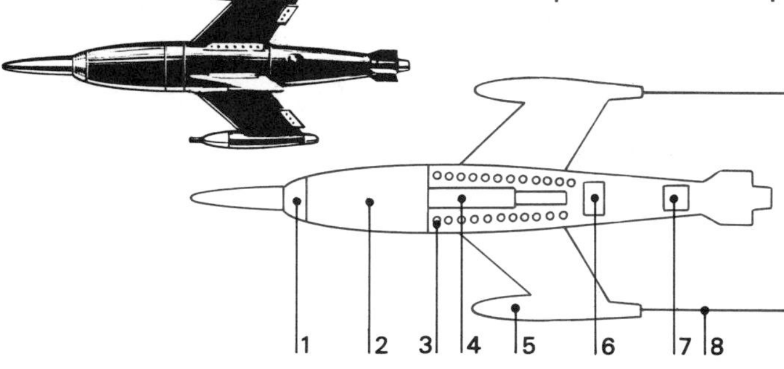

The Natter (above) was a rocket-propelled, piloted projectile launched by jettisonable solid-fuel motors and powered for up to 3 minutes by a liquid bipropellant rocket motor. It was launched in the direction of the target, and a bank of rockets in the nose was fired in salvo when in range — 100yd (91m). After this the pilot baled out and he and the Natter descended by parachute. It was never used operationally.
Max height 39,400ft (12,000m)
Max speed 620mph (998kph)
Radius of action at max height: 12.4mi(20km)
A Rocket tubes
B Pilot
C Fuel tanks
D Rocket motor
E Parachute

The Ruhrstahl A.G. X-4 (above) was a fin-stabilized liquid bipropellant, wire-guided, air-to-air missile. After release from the parent aircraft (FW 190 or Me 262) it could be guided over a range of 3.7mi (6km) — the length of the guidance wire. An automatic acoustic guidance system that would allow the pilot to take evasive action was under development.

Launch weight 132 lb (60kg)
Max speed 603.6mph (972kph)
Engine burn time 33 sec
1 Fuze housing (acoustic proximity and impact)
2 Warhead
3 Fuel tanks
4 Air bottles
5 Control wire housing
6 Gyro control unit
7 Battery box
8 Insulated control wire

Anti-tank missiles

Anti-tank defense is now a major role for self-propelled missiles. Most missiles of this type are solid fueled and carry HEAT warheads to penetrate armor (see p.199). Some are unguided. In Manual Command to Line-Of-Sight (MCLOS) systems the operator tracks both missile and target, and directs the missile's flight by a control lever. In Semi-Automatic (SACLOS) systems, tracking and flight corrections are automatic.

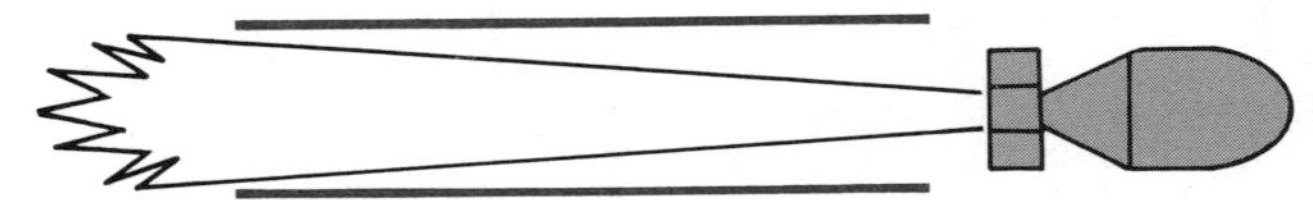

Anti-tank missiles are mostly tube-launched (above). In the early type of "point-and-fire" or bazooka systems, the tube is used to aim, ignite and launch the missile. These have now been largely replaced by guided systems in which the function of aiming is taken over by such devices as infrared tracking flares and wire-guidance.

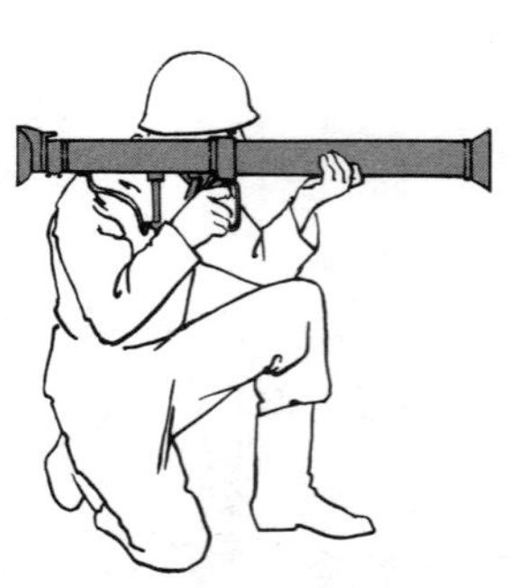

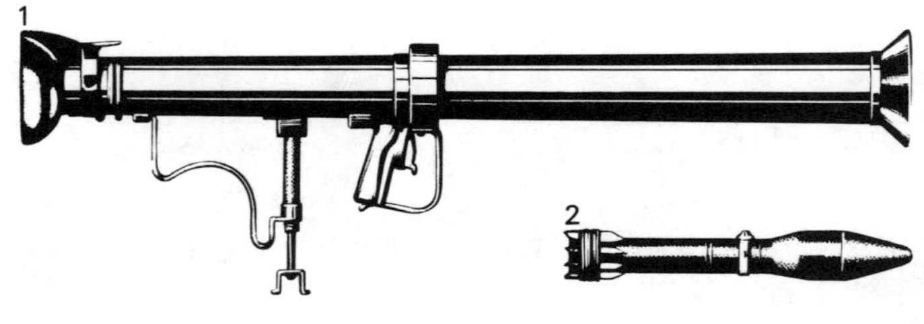

The US 3.5in M20 (left) or "Super Bazooka" rocket launcher replaced the 2.36in M9A1 Bazooka after WW2. It was a shoulder-fired, rear-loaded weapon. The tube (**1**) weighed only 12.1 lb (5.5kg) and was jointed at center for ease of carriage. The HEAT rocket (**2**) weighed 8.9 lb (4.04kg). Tactical range 120yd (110m). Extreme range 1130yd (1200m).

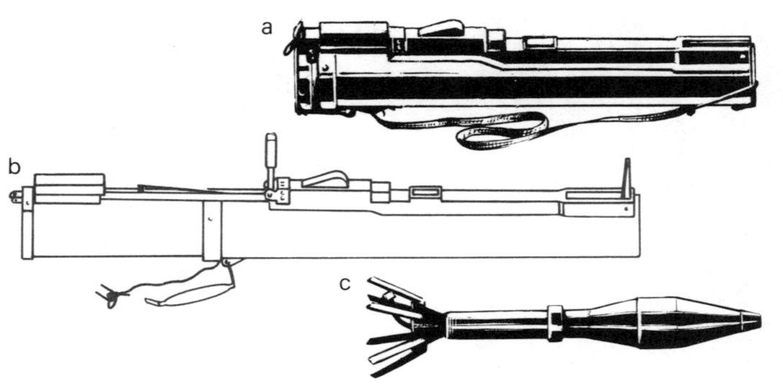

The US 66mm M72 A2 (left) is one of the latest adaptations of the bazooka. It is a one-man, single-shot throwaway weapon now used by several armies. The telescopic launcher-tube is shown closed (**a**) and open for firing (**b**). It weighs 3 lb (1.36kg), of which 2.2 lb (0.95kg) is the rocket (**c**), shown with fins deployed after launch.

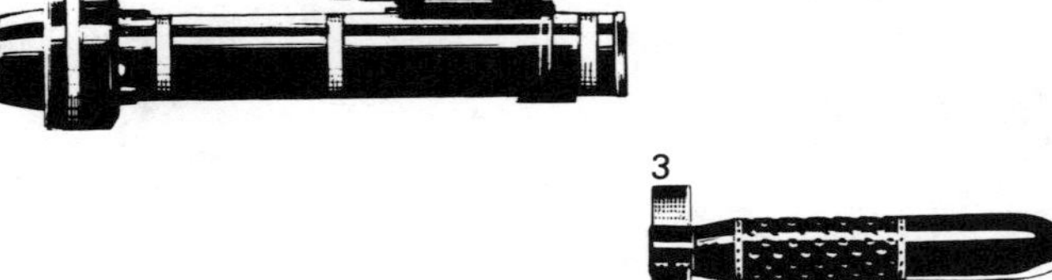

The US M47 Dragon (left) is a one-man, optically tracked, wire-guided system using command-to-line-of-sight guidance with infrared missile tracking. The carrier/launcher (**1**) is discarded after firing, but the tracker unit (**2**) is fitted to successive missiles. The fins on the missile (**3**) open out after launch. Total carrying weight 32 lb (14.6kg).

Vehicle-mounted and heavy AT missiles (right) complement the lighter infantry models.
1 Vehicle-mounted systems such as Snapper (AT-1), Harpon and Swingfire. With some vehicle-mounted systems the operator can be up to 100yd (100m) away to escape retaliatory fire (**1a**).
2 With ground-launched systems such as Cobra 2000 and Mamba, one controller can launch up to 18 missiles individually.
3 Heavy AT missiles, such as TOW and Sparviero, are launched from relatively long supported tubes (**a**) that can be easily mounted on jeeps (**b**), armored personnel carriers (**c**), and helicopters (**d**). Heavier missiles can penetrate thicker armor. The latest armors can be impenetrable to the lighter missiles.

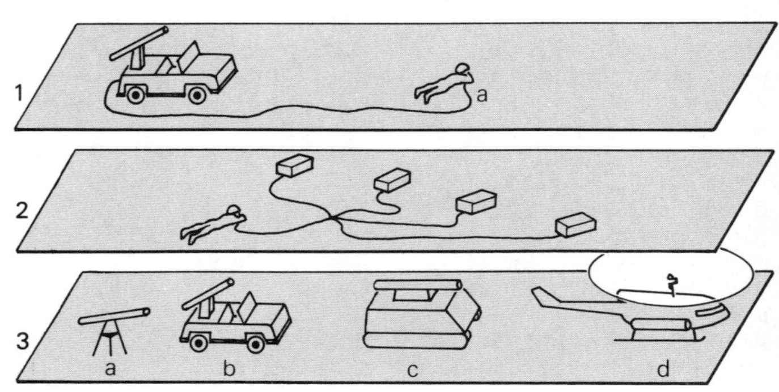

Anti-tank missiles (right)
1 Tow (USA)
a Two-stage solid
b 40 lb (18kg)
c 3280yd (3000m)
d Tube ; vehicle or ground
2 Harpon (France)
a Two-stage solid
b 67 lb (30kg)
c 3280yd (3000m)
d Guide rail ; vehicle
3 Mamba (W Germany)
a One-stage solid
b 24.7 lb (11.2kg)
c 2188yd (2000m)
d Ground jump ; one man
4 Cobra 2000 (W Germany)
a One-stage solid + booster
b 22.7 lb (10.3kg)
c 2188yd (2000m)
d Ground jump ; one man
5 Snapper (USSR)
a Solid
b 49 lb (22.25kg)
c 2950yd (2700m)
d Guide rail ; vehicle
6 Milan (France/ W Germany)
a Two-stage solid
b 14.66 lb (6.65kg)
c 2188yd (2000m)
d Tube ; one man
7 Swingfire (UK)
a Solid
b Not available
c 4376yd (4000m)
d Container ; vehicle (infantry possible)
8 Sagger (USSR)
a One-stage solid + booster
b 24.9 lb (11.3kg)
c 3280yd (3000m)
d Guide rail ; vehicle and single manpack
9 Sparviero (Italy)
a Three-stage solid – launcher, booster, sustainer
b 36.4 lb (16.5kg)
c 3280yd (3000m)
d Tripod ; infantry and vehicle
10 Hellfire (USA)
a Solid
b 94.79 lb (43kg)
c 5470yd (5000m)
d Helicopter ; air launch

Data key
a Propulsion system
b Missile weight
c Maximum range
d Launch and carriage method
Note: 1,2,6 and 9 use SACLOS systems ; 3,4,5,7 and 8 use MCLOS systems, and 10 has terminal laser guidance.

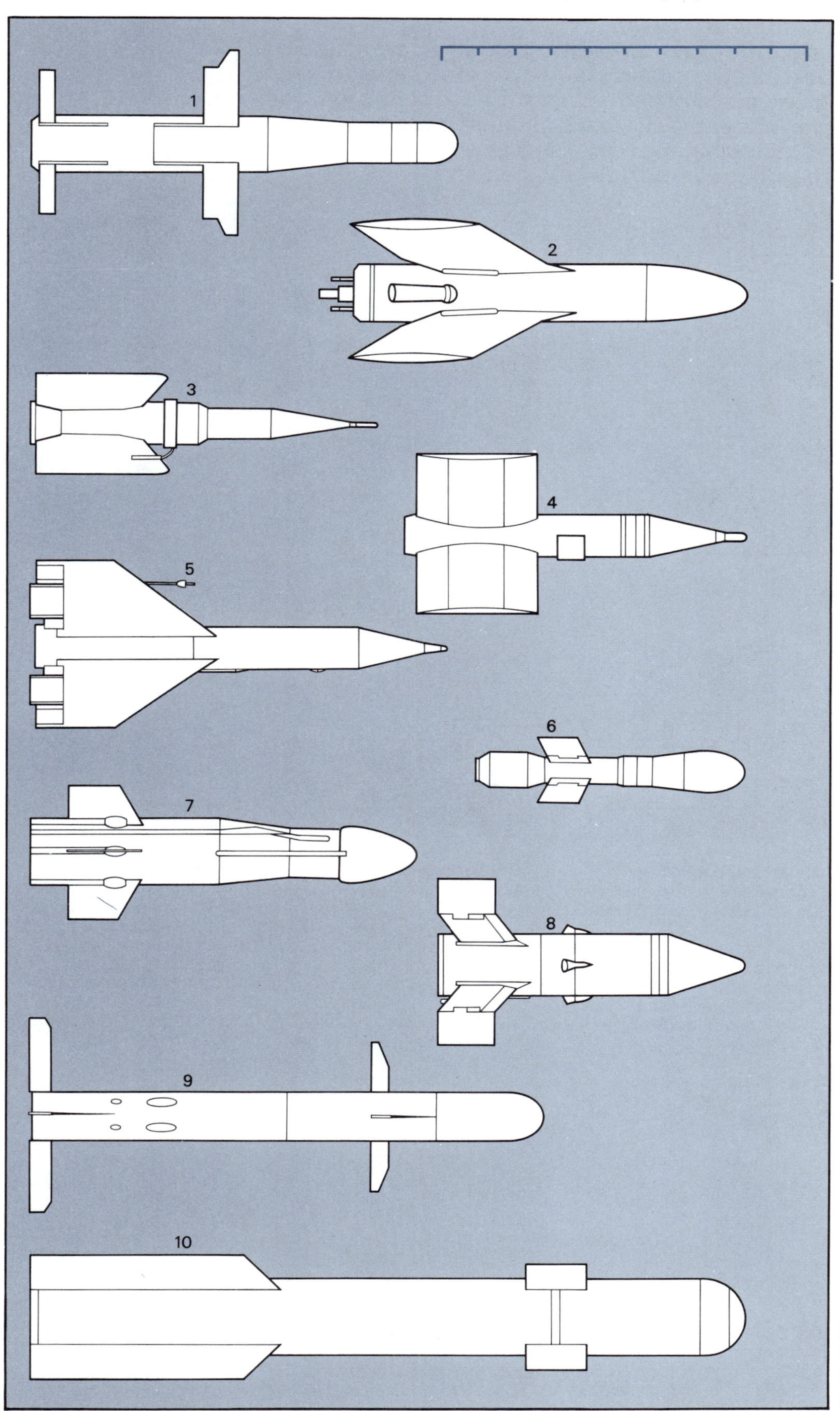

Air defense missiles

Air defense missiles offer protection to ground troops against attacking aircraft, and some can be used against other missiles. The three main varieties extend from large, permanently-sited missiles, through vehicle-transportable systems to single-missile, man-portable systems.

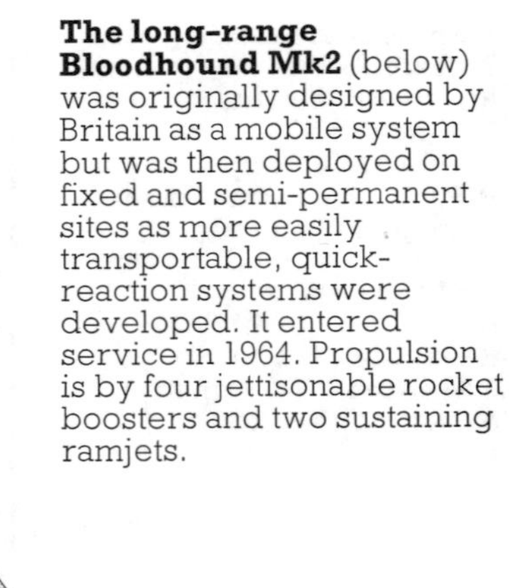

The long-range Bloodhound Mk2 (below) was originally designed by Britain as a mobile system but was then deployed on fixed and semi-permanent sites as more easily transportable, quick-reaction systems were developed. It entered service in 1964. Propulsion is by four jettisonable rocket boosters and two sustaining ramjets.

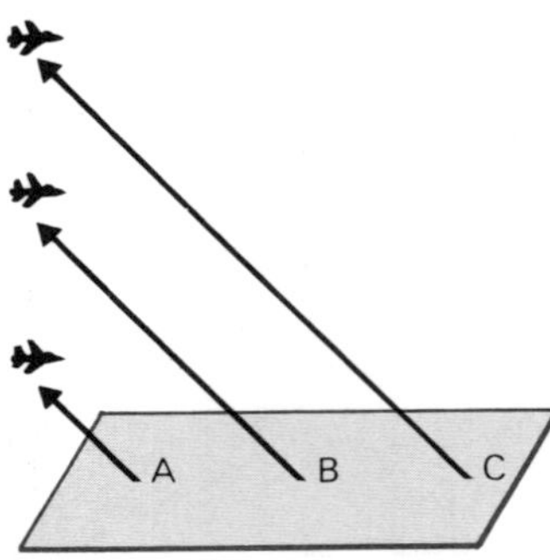

Air defense missiles (left) are designed to attack targets at different ranges. Generally, the shorter the range, the lighter and smaller the missiles. Approximate range categories are as follows.
A Short : to 6mi (10km)
B Medium : to 40mi (65km)
C Long : over 40mi (65km)
Long-range air defense missiles often use a ramjet after rocket boost.

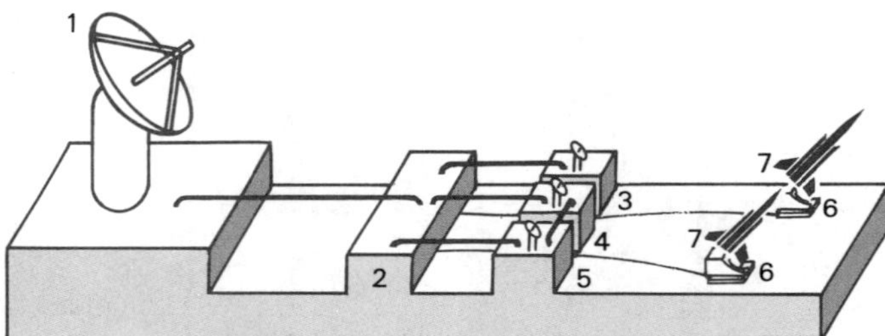

Air defense systems (above) are made up of seven basic units. In large systems they are often separate. In mobile systems, functions (**1**),(**3**) and (**4**) may be done by eye.
1 Acquisition radar
2 Control command post
3 Target tracking unit
4 Missile tracking unit
5 Command transmitter
6 Power units
7 Missiles

Vehicle-transportable systems (below) The medium-range US self-propelled Hawk system (**A**) carries three missiles and tows the tracking unit behind. The short-range European Roland (**B**) defends tanks and other forward units. The launcher tubes on either side of the turret are reloaded hydraulically from internal magazines after launch.

The Swedish RBS 70 (below) is an unusual short-range, man-portable system in that it uses a laser beam-riding guidance system. The stand enables the optical tracking system to be gyro-stabilized. Continual firing is possible with a two-man team.

One-man portable systems (below) such as Grail (SA-7), Blowpipe, Redeye and its replacement, Stinger, are usually short-range, shoulder-launched missiles used against low-level attacking aircraft by forward combat troops. The missiles' container/launchers are disposed of after launch, but launching units and tracking units are reusable.

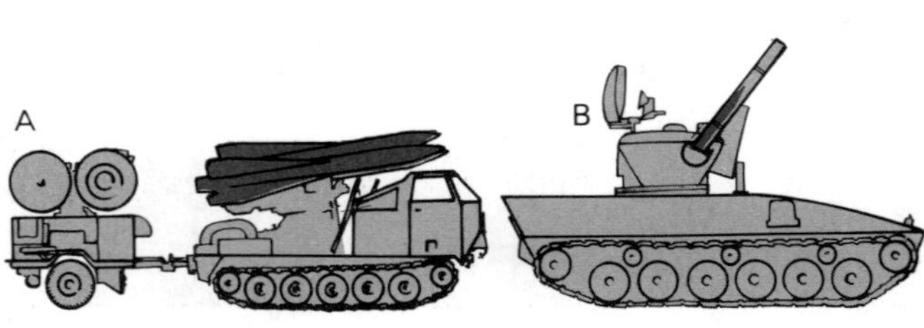

Air defense missiles (right)
Fixed/semipermanent
1 Gammon (SA-5) (USSR)
a 22,045 lb (10,000kg)
b About 155mi (250km)
c Command + A radar homing
2 Nike Hercules (USA)
a 9920 lb (4500kg)
b 87mi (140km) plus
c Command
3 Bloodhound Mk2 (UK)
b 50mi (80km) plus
c SA radar homing
Mobile systems
1 Ganef (SA-4) (USSR)
a 3968 lb (1800kg)
b About 47.5mi (70km)
c Command
2 Rapier (UK)
c Command to line-of-sight + radar tracking
3 Goa (SA-3, SA-N-4) (USSR)
b 18.5mi (30km)
c Beam-riding + SA radar homing
4 Gecko (SA-8) (USSR)
b 10mi (16km)
c Command
5 Gainful (SA-6) (USSR)
a 1212 lb (550kg)
b 37mi (60km)
c Command + SA radar homing
6 Crotale (France)
a 176.4 lb (80kg)
b 6.25mi (8.5km)
c Radio command
7 Hawk (USA)
a 265 lb (120kg)
b 22mi (35km)
c Radar
8 Patriot (USA)
c Command with Tracking Via Missile (TVM) homing
9 Roland (France/FDR)
a 1396 lb (63kg)
b 3.9mi (6.3km)
c Radio Command
Man-portable systems
1 Grail (SA-7) (USSR)
a 33 lb (15kg)
b 6.2mi (10km)
c Infrared homing
2 Blowpipe (UK)
a 28 lb (12.7kg)
c Radio command, optical tracking
3 RBS 70 (Sweden/ Switzerland)
a 44 lb (20kg)
b 3mi (5km)
c Laser beam rider
4 Stinger (USA)
a 30 lb (13.4kg)
c Passive infrared or ultraviolet homing

Data key
a Weight
b Range
c Guidance system
Note: missing information is not available.

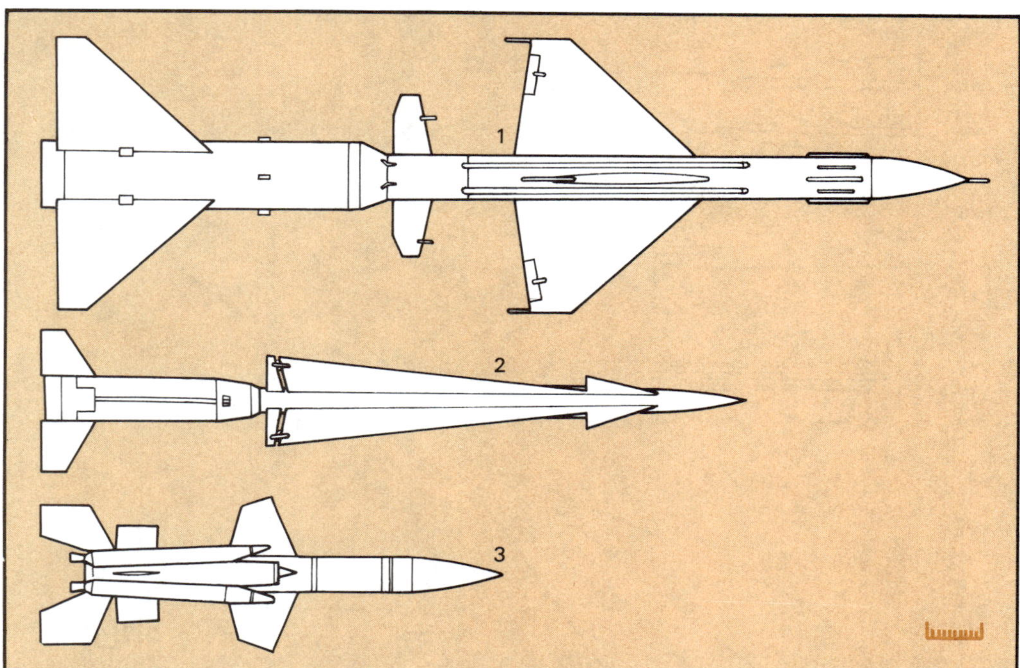

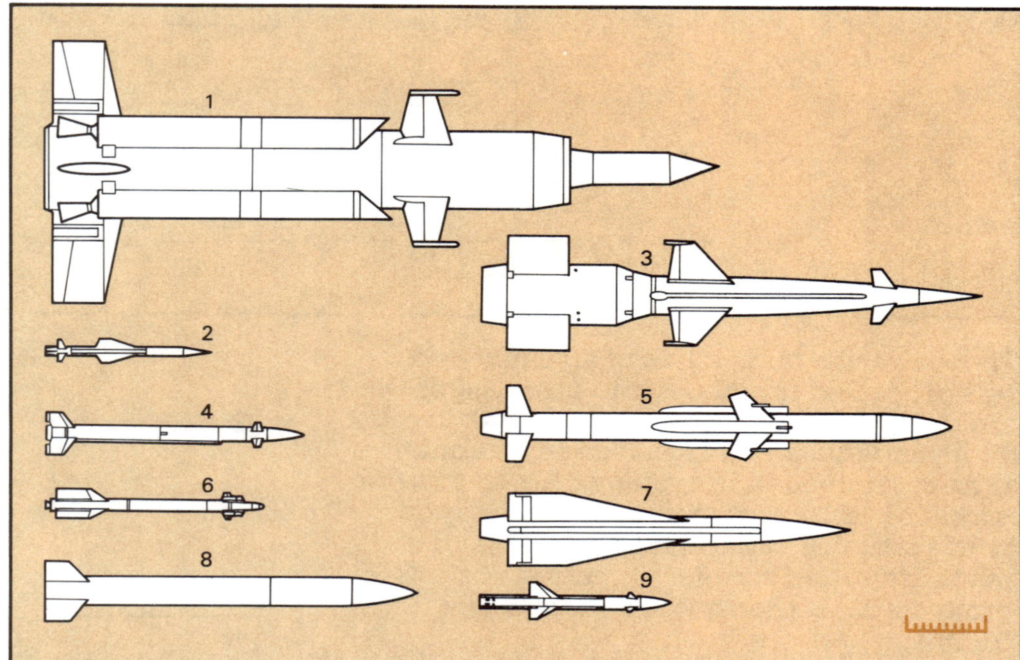

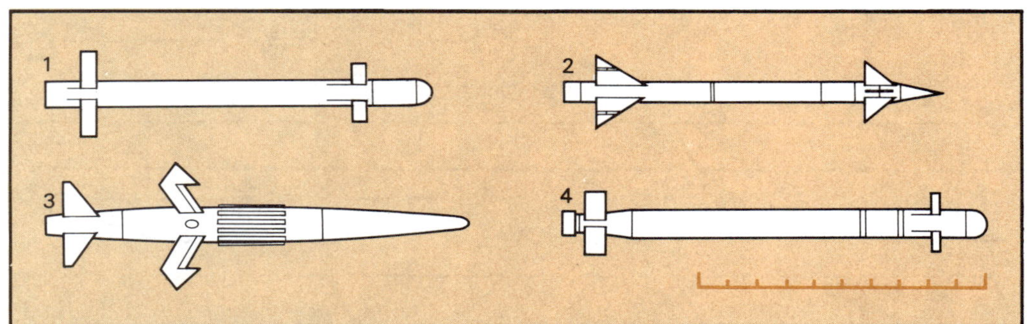

Air-launched tactical missiles

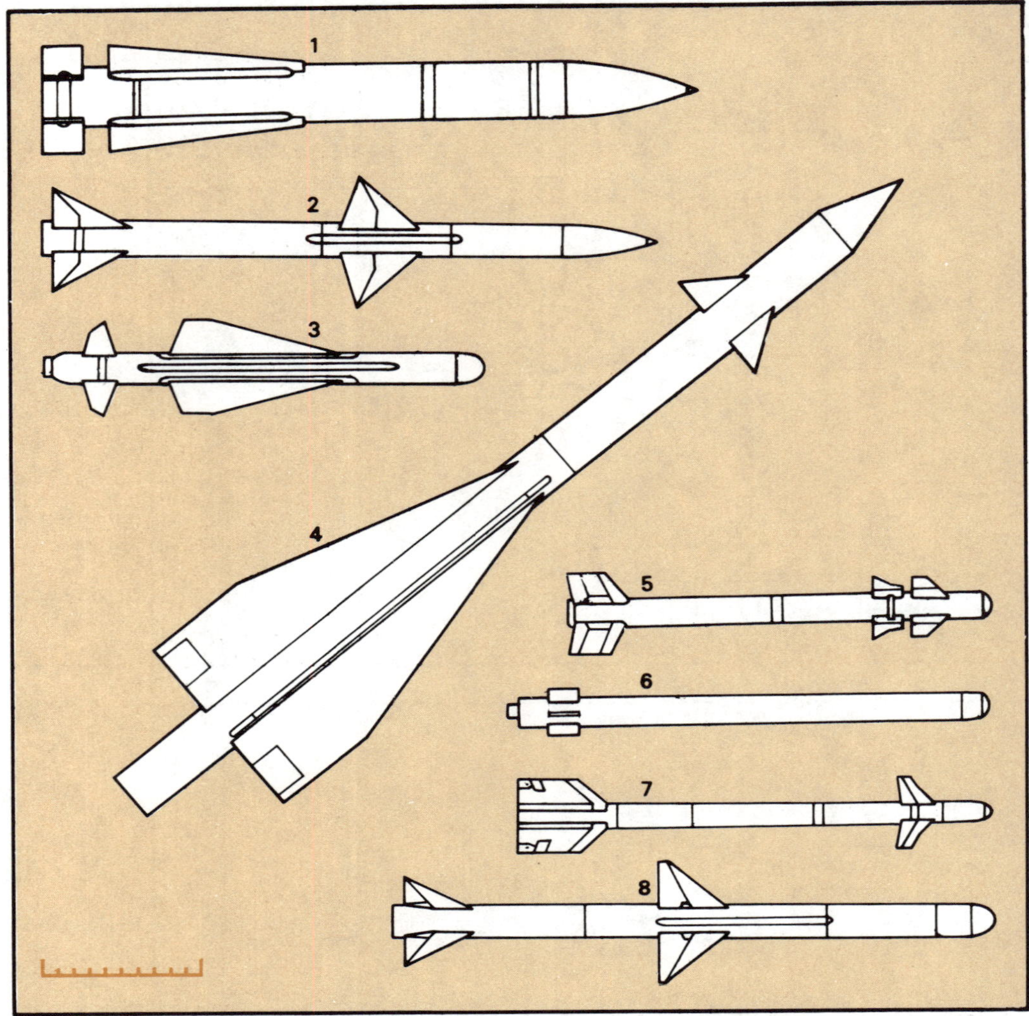

Air-to-air missiles (left)
1 Phoenix (AIM-54A) (USA)
a 838 lb (380kg)
b 100mi (160km)
c Radar (SA cruise, A terminal)
2 Aspide (Italy)
a 485 lb (220kg)
c SA radar
3 Saab 372 (Sweden)
a 242 lb (110kg)
c Infrared homing
4 Acrid (AA-6) (USSR)
a 176 lb (800kg)
b 31mi (6km)
c Infrared homing
5 Matra Magic R550 (France)
a 198.4 lb (90kg)
b 3.7mi (6 km)
c Infrared homing
6 SRAAM (UK)
b 5mi (8km)
c Infrared
7 Sidewinder (AIM-9L) (USA)
a 158.7 lb (72kg)
b 4.3mi (7km)
c Infrared
8 Brazo/Pave Arm (USA)
a 441 lb (200kg) ?
b 15.5mi (25km) ?
c Passive anti-radiation homing

Data key
a Weight
b Range
c Guidance system
Note: missing information is unavailable
A = active
SA = semi-active

There are two main kinds of air-launched self-propelled missile. Air-to-air missiles are designed to destroy other aircraft in flight, and thus need high maneuverability and accurate homing systems. Air-to-surface missiles include strategic nuclear weapons, cruise missiles, tactical missiles for land and sea targets, and simple, unguided rockets for ground attack. (For guided bombs, see p.238.)

Air-to-air "dogfight" missiles (left) need the following.
A High maneuverability, usually achieved by forward-mounted control surfaces or thrust vector control (as in the UK SRAAM missile).
B The ability to withstand the stress of tight turns.
C Guidance systems that enable the firer to take evasive action.

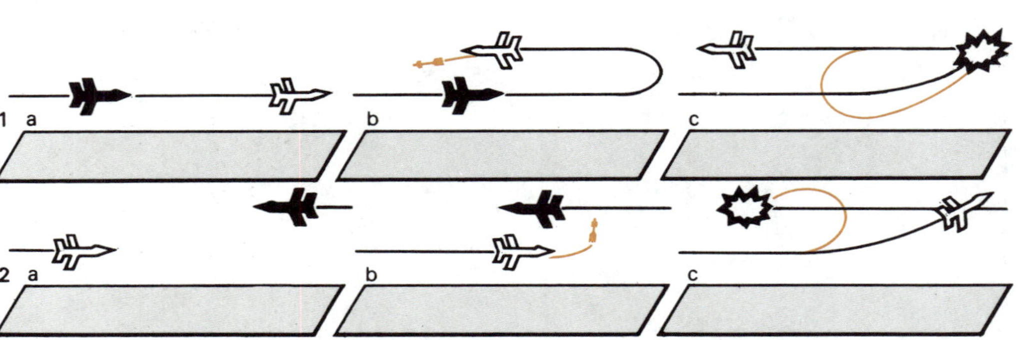

Two possible attack modes for an air-to-air missile (left). A "tail" attack is assumed to be preferable.
1 The white aircraft attempts to escape the black's tail attack.
2 Both aircraft attempt to achieve tail attack positions.
a Start positions
b The missile is fired
c Moment of impact

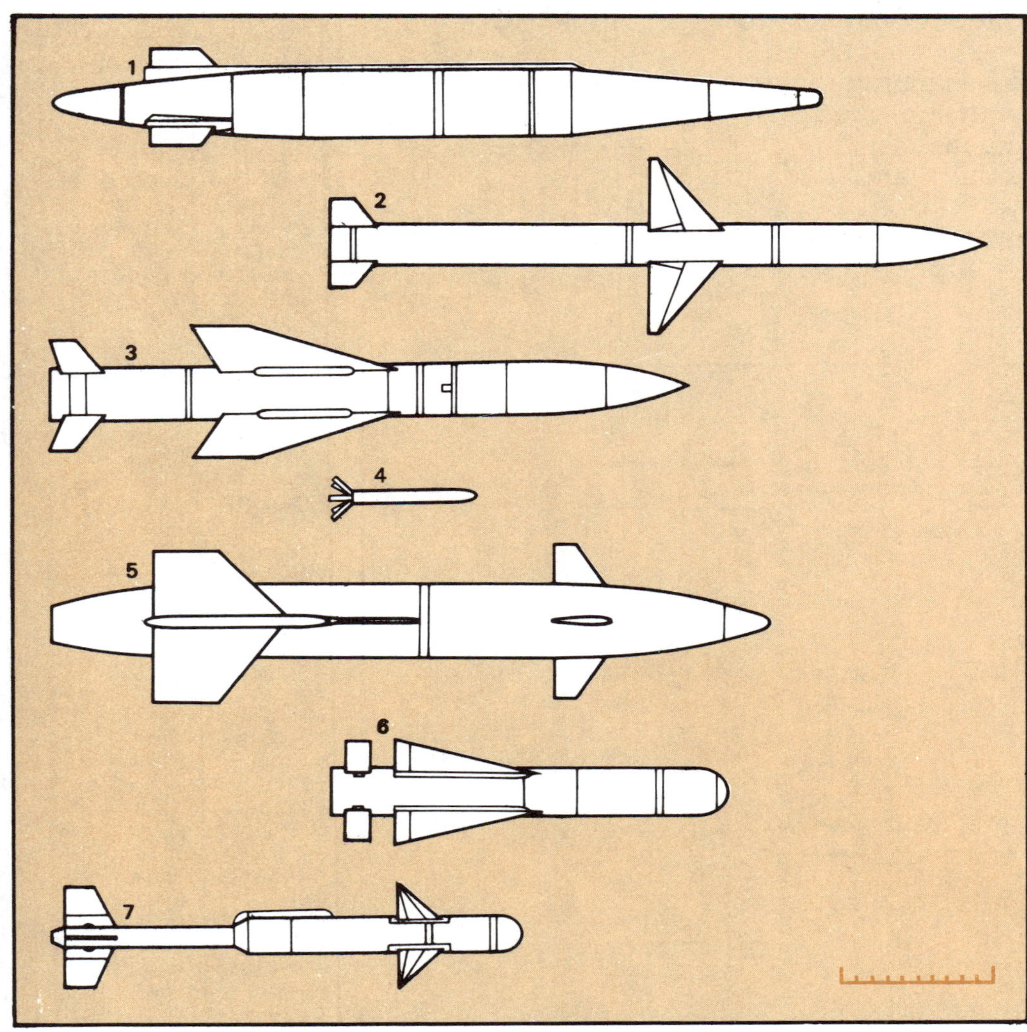

Air-to-surface missiles (left)

1 SRAM (Nuclear) (US)
a 2204 lb (1000kg)
b 100mi (160km)
c Programed inertial

2 HARM (US)
a 780.4 lb (354kg)
b 10mi (16km)
c Passive radiation homing

3 Kormoran (AS.34) (W Germany)
a 1323 lb (600kg)
b 23mi (37km)
c Inertial (cruise) A radar (terminal)

4 SNEB 68mm Aircraft Rocket (France and NATO)

5 RB O 4E (Sweden)
a 1323 lb (600kg)
b up to 20mi (32km)
c A radar

6 Maverick (AGM-65) (US)
a 460.7 lb (209kg)
b 30mi (48km)
c TV homing/laser/imaging infrared

7 Sea Skua (UK)
a 496 lb (210kg)
b over 9.3mi (15km)
c SA radar homing

Data key
a Weight
b Range
c Guidance system
A = active
SA = semi-active

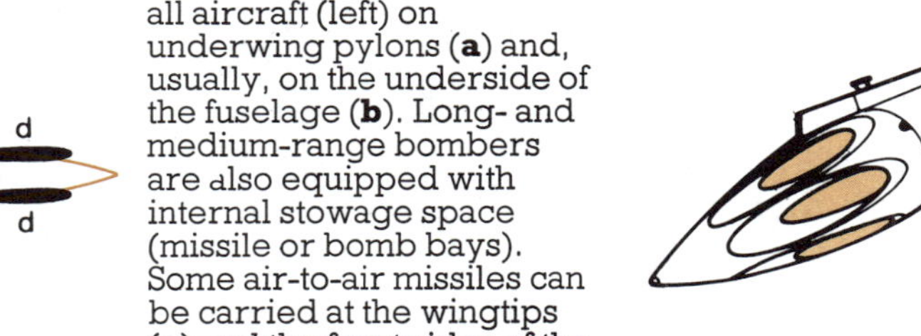

Missiles and other ordnance can be carried by all aircraft (left) on underwing pylons (**a**) and, usually, on the underside of the fuselage (**b**). Long- and medium-range bombers are also equipped with internal stowage space (missile or bomb bays). Some air-to-air missiles can be carried at the wingtips (**c**) and the front sides of the fuselage (**d**).

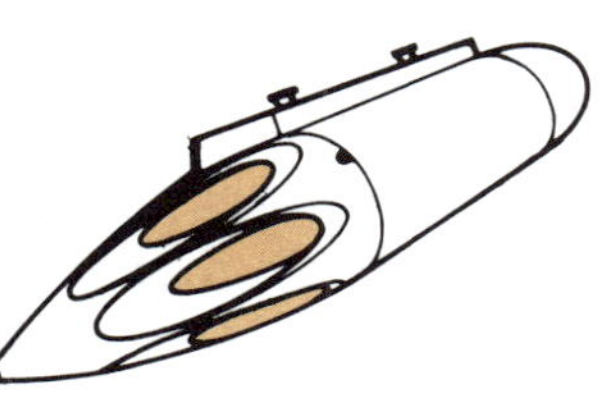

Unguided aircraft rockets (left), usually employed in an air-to-ground role, are now carried in specially designed underwing pods. Their fin stabilizers are folded for storage and open into position after launch. Pods can carry between 6 and 40 rockets at one time. Shown is the Swedish Bofors M70 pod, loaded with six ground-attack rockets.

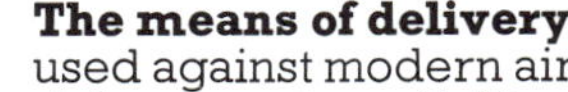

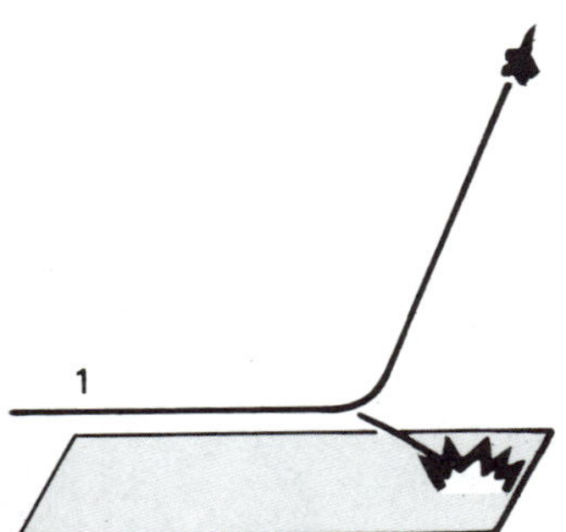

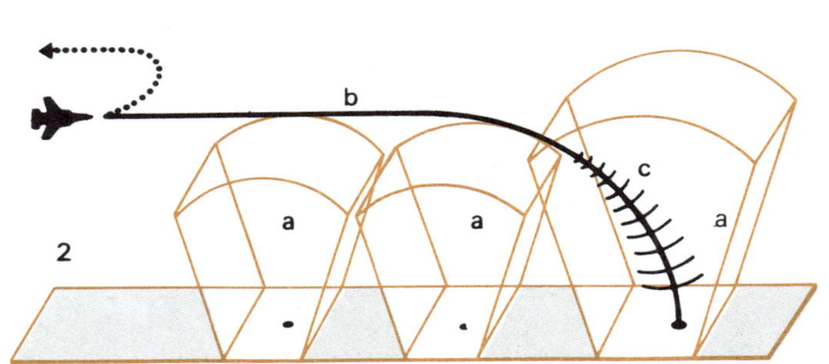

The means of delivery used against modern air-defense systems (left).
1 Low-level attacks attempt to fly under radar cover.
2 Stand-off missiles allow the delivery aircraft to remain above and beyond the defense systems (**a**). They use mid-course (**b**) and terminal (**c**) guidance systems. Missiles are designed specifically for each form of attack.

Sea-launched tactical missiles

The first naval self-propelled missiles were the solid-propellant rockets of the 18th and 19th centuries, but by the beginning of the 20th century these had been superseded by the torpedo. Nowadays, naval missile systems are as various as their land- and air-based counterparts.
Ground, air and naval systems are often interchangeable with only slight modifications.

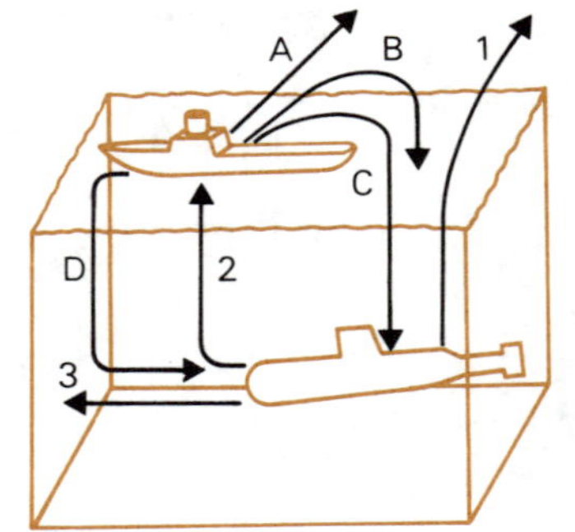

Types of naval missile (left) Some types of course can be included in other categories, such as air-defense missiles.
A Surface-to-air
B Surface-to-surface
C Surface-to-subsurface
D Torpedoes (see p. 242)
1 Submarine Launched Ballistic Missiles (SLBMs)
2 Anti-ship torpedoes
3 Anti-submarine torpedoes

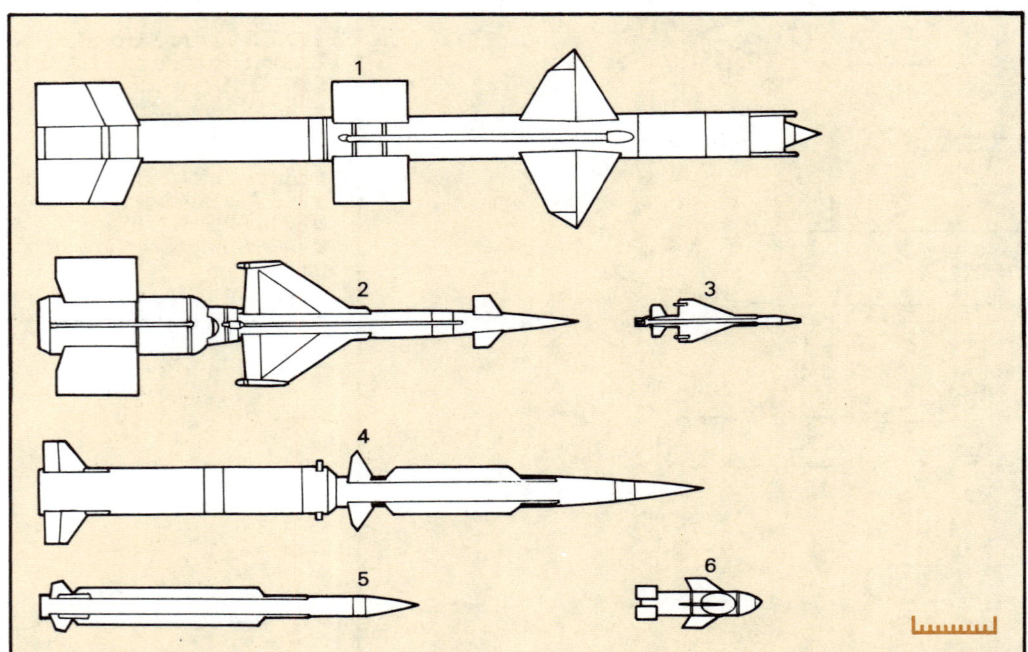

Surface-to-air missiles (left)
1 Talos (RIM-8) (USA)
a 7000 lb (3175kg)
b 75.4mi (120km)
c Beam riding + SA radar
2 Goa (SA-N-1) (USSR)
b 18.6mi (30km)
c Beam riding + SA radar
3 Seawolf (UK)
c Beam riding
4 Terrier (RIM-2) (USA)
a 3000 lb (1360kg)
b 21.7mi (35km)
c Beam riding + SA radar
5 Standard (SM-2 ER) (USA)
a 3000 lb (1360kg)
b 59.6mi (96km)
c Command + A radar
6 Seacat (UK)
a 150 lb (68kg)
b 2.2mi (3.5km)
c Radio command
Data key
a Weight
b Range
c Guidance system
Note: Missing information is unavailable

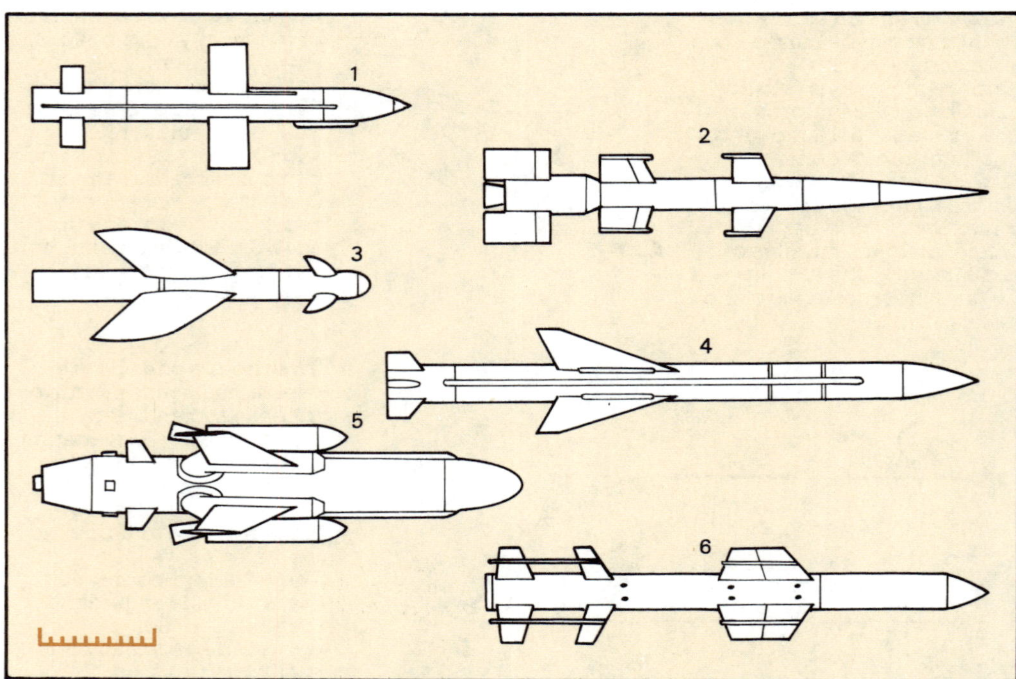

Surface-to-surface missiles (left)
1 Gabriel (Israel)
a 882 or 1102 lb (400 or 500kg)
b 13.6 or 25.5mi (22 or 41km)
c Inertial + terminal
2 Sea Killer Mk 2 (Italy)
a 661 lb (300kg)
b 12.4mi (20km)
c Beam riding/radio command
3 Penguin (Norway)
a 727 lb (330kg)
b 12.4mi (20km)
c Inertial + infrared
4 Exocet (MM40) (France)
a 1819 lb (825kg)
b 43.5mi (70km)
c Inertial + A radar
5 Otomat (Italy/France)
a 1697 lb (770kg)
b 124mi (200km)
c Inertial + A radar
6 Harpoon (RGM-84A) (USA)
a 1400 lb (635kg)
b 68.3mi (110km)
c Inertial + A radar

Surface-to-subsurface missiles (right)
Asroc carries a torpedo or nuclear depth charge; Ikara, a torpedo; Terne, a 110 lb (50kg) warhead; Subroc (submarine launched), a nuclear depth charge.
1 Subroc (UUM-44A) (USA)
a 4000 lb (1815kg)
b 35mi (56km)
c Inertial
2 Asroc (RUR-5A) (USA)
a 1010 lb (458kg)
b 6.2mi (10km)
c None in flight, acoustic torpedo in water.
3 Ikara (Australia/UK)
b Maximum sonar range
c Command + acoustic torpedo
4 Terne (Norway)
a 298 lb (135kg)
b 1.8mi (3km)
c None

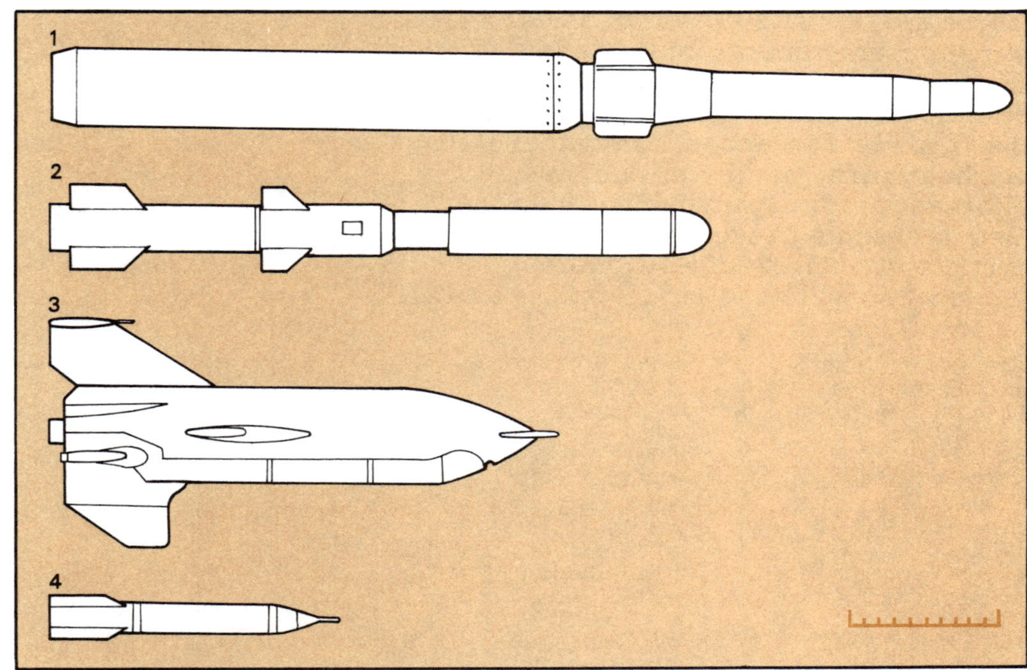

Asroc and Ikara (right)
Both of these are solid-fuel rockets used to deliver acoustic homing torpedoes.
A Asroc follows a ballistic trajectory with torpedo release at a pre-set point. It can also carry a nuclear depth charge.
B Ikara. Guidance and torpedo separation are via a command link through a computer that has data from the ship's sonar.

Subroc (right) is a submarine-launched, two-stage solid-fuel rocket carrying a nuclear depth charge for use against strategic missile submarines. After launch, the rocket motor ignites underwater, and the missile then surfaces to fly to the pre-set point at which the depth charge separates. The charge explodes at a pre-set depth.

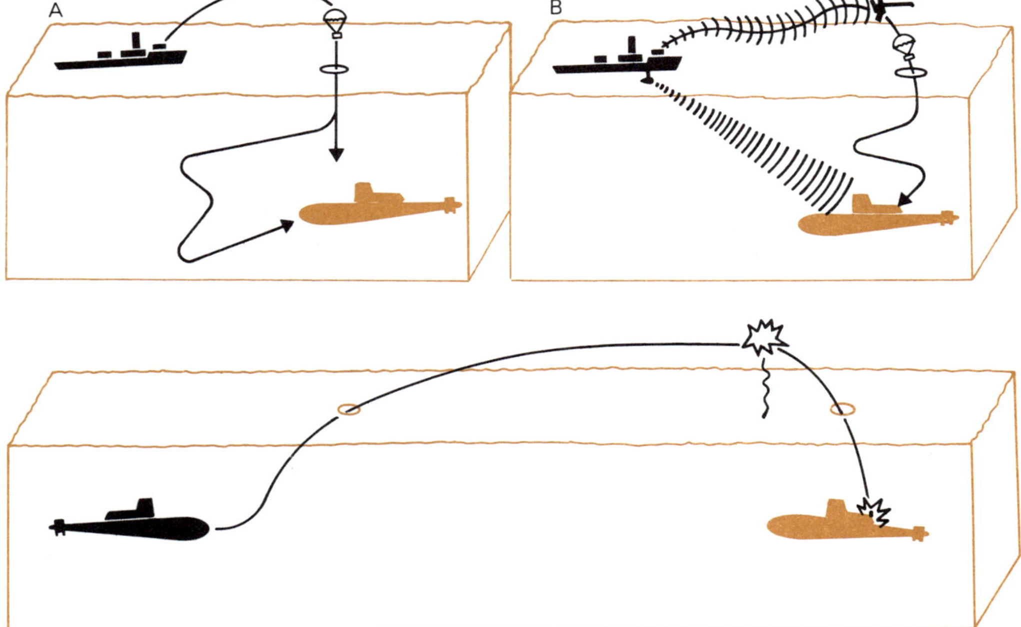

Guidance systems (right) have made torpedoes increasingly effective. Wire guidance (**1**), passive acoustic homing (**2**), and active acoustic homing (**3**) can be used. Torpedoes are also able to carry out "search," homing, and multiple re-attack procedures should the first attempt go astray.

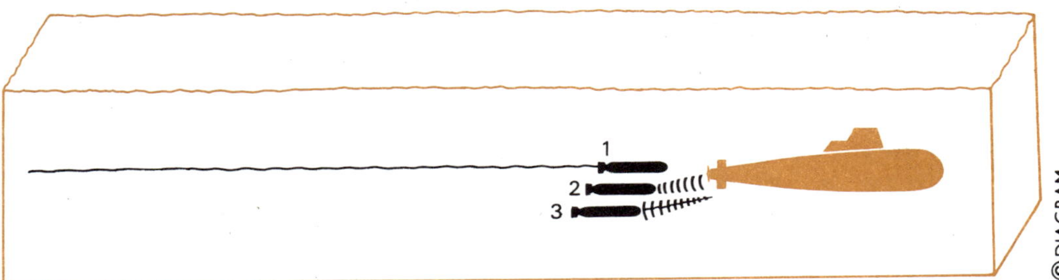

Strategic and tactical nuclear missiles

There are two categories of nuclear missile: strategic, and tactical (or battlefield support). Because of the danger of escalation to strategic nuclear warfare after the tactical use of nuclear weapons, conventional HE warheads are, or will be, available as alternatives for use on nuclear missiles. Details of some present and proposed systems are included here; more information will be found on pp.274 and 275.

Strategic ballistic nuclear missiles (right)
1 Sandal (SS-4) (USSR)
a IRBM
b 1 × 1MT
c 1242mi (2000km)
d 1959
2 Scarp (SS-9) (USSR)
a ICBM
b 1 × 18MT
c 7450mi (12,000km)
d 1969
3 SS-18 Mod. 2 (USSR)
a ICBM
b 8 × 1-2MT
c 7450mi (12,000km)
d 1977
4 SS-19 (USSR)
a ICBM
b 6 × 200KT
c 6210mi (10,000km)
d 1975
5 SS-17 (USSR)
a ICBM
b 4 × 200KT
c 6520mi (10,500km)
d 1975
Note: Nos 1 and 7 being eliminated under 1987 INF Treaty
6 SS-16 (USSR)
a ICBM
b 3 × 300KT ?
c 5900mi (9500km)
d 1977
7 SS-20 (USSR)
a IRBM
b 3 × 150KT
c 3540mi (5700km) **d** 1976
8 Minuteman III (USA)
a ICBM
b 3 × 350KT
c 8070mi (13,000km) **d** 1978
9 Trident C4 (USA)
a SLBM
b 8 × 100KT
c 4850mi (7800km) **d** 1980
10 MSBS M-20 (France)
a SLBM
b 1 × 1MT
c 1850mi (3000km) **d** 1976

Data key
a Type of missile
b Warhead
c Range
d Date of introduction
Note: the SS-20 is the top two stages of the SS16

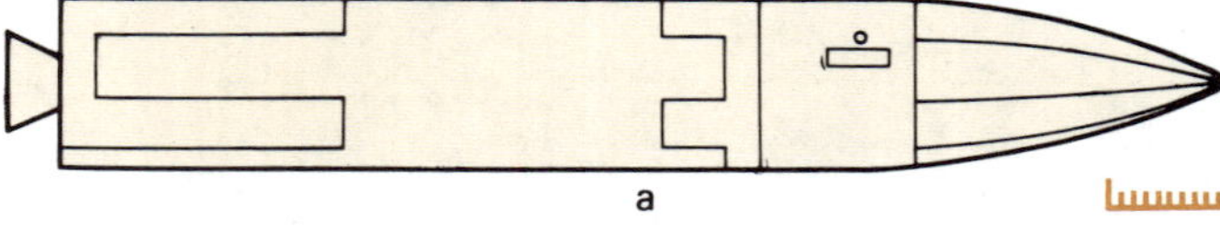

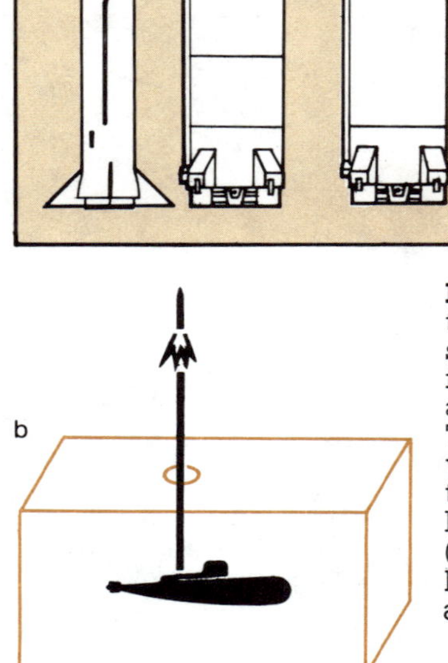

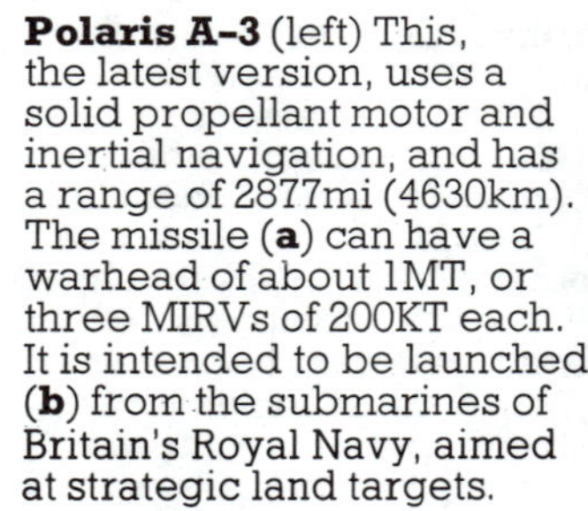

Polaris A-3 (left) This, the latest version, uses a solid propellant motor and inertial navigation, and has a range of 2877mi (4630km). The missile (**a**) can have a warhead of about 1MT, or three MIRVs of 200KT each. It is intended to be launched (**b**) from the submarines of Britain's Royal Navy, aimed at strategic land targets.

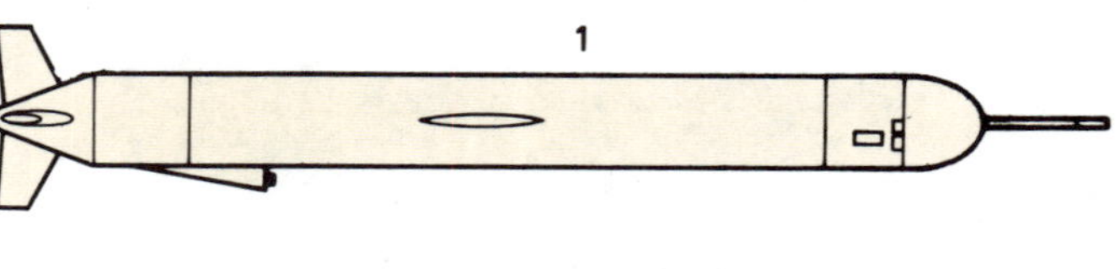

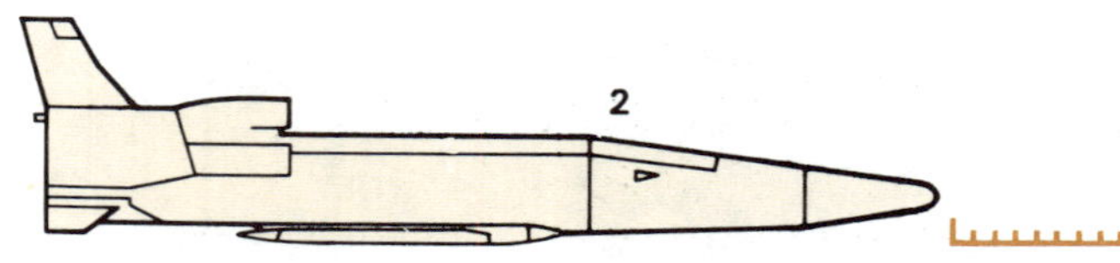

US Tomahawk and ALCM (left) Tomahawk (**1**) and the Air-Launched Cruise Missile (**2**) have the same basic subsystems, strategic and tactical roles, and can carry nuclear warheads. Tomahawk now arms 71 US Navy ships and submarines. ALCM (delivered 1981–86) equips up to 257 USAF bombers.

Propulsion: Turbofan
Guidance: TERCOM
Weight: 3200lb (1452kg)
Accuracy: within meters
Range: 1550mi (2500km)
Speed: max about 590mph (930kph); cruising 410mph (660kph) Warhead: W80 nuclear of up to 250KT

Pluton (right) This is the French army's current tactical nuclear ballistic missile (**a**), which has a range of about 75mi (120km) and has alternative 15KT and 25KT warheads. It is launched from an AMX-30 tank chassis (**b**) and is led to its battlefield target (**c**) by a simple inertial guidance system.

Lance (right) was first developed as a US tactical nuclear missile with simplified inertial navigation and a range of 75mi (120km). The missile (**a**) is launched from a self-propelled tracked chassis (**b**); one warhead development contains six or nine Terminally Guided Sub-Missiles (TGSMs) that are released to home in on individual targets (**c**).

Pershing (right) is the largest US tactical nuclear missile (warhead about 400KT). The Pershing II (**a**) is trailer-launched (**b**), and has a terminal guidance system; the "radar area correlation" compares images of the target seen by the missile (**c**) with images previously implanted from reconnaissance information. Its greater accuracy allows a smaller warhead.

Soviet tactical missiles (right)
1 FROG Series (Free Rocket Over Ground). FROGs 3, 4, 7 are in service. FROG 7 data:
Length: 29.7ft (9m)
Weight: 5952 lb (2700kg)
Range: 37.25mi (60km)
Warhead: HE or nuclear
Propulsion: 1-stage solid
Guidance: none
2 Scud series (SS-1)
Scud B is in service; C has been reported.
Length: 36.9ft (11.25m)
Weight: 13,888 lb (6300kg)
Range: 168mi (270km)
Scud C: 280mi (450km)
Warhead: HE or nuclear
Propulsion: storable liquid
Guidance: inertial
3 Scaleboard (SS-12)
Thought to be of similar length, guidance and propulsion to Scud, with a larger diameter, nuclear warhead perhaps of 1MT, and a range of 495mi (800km).

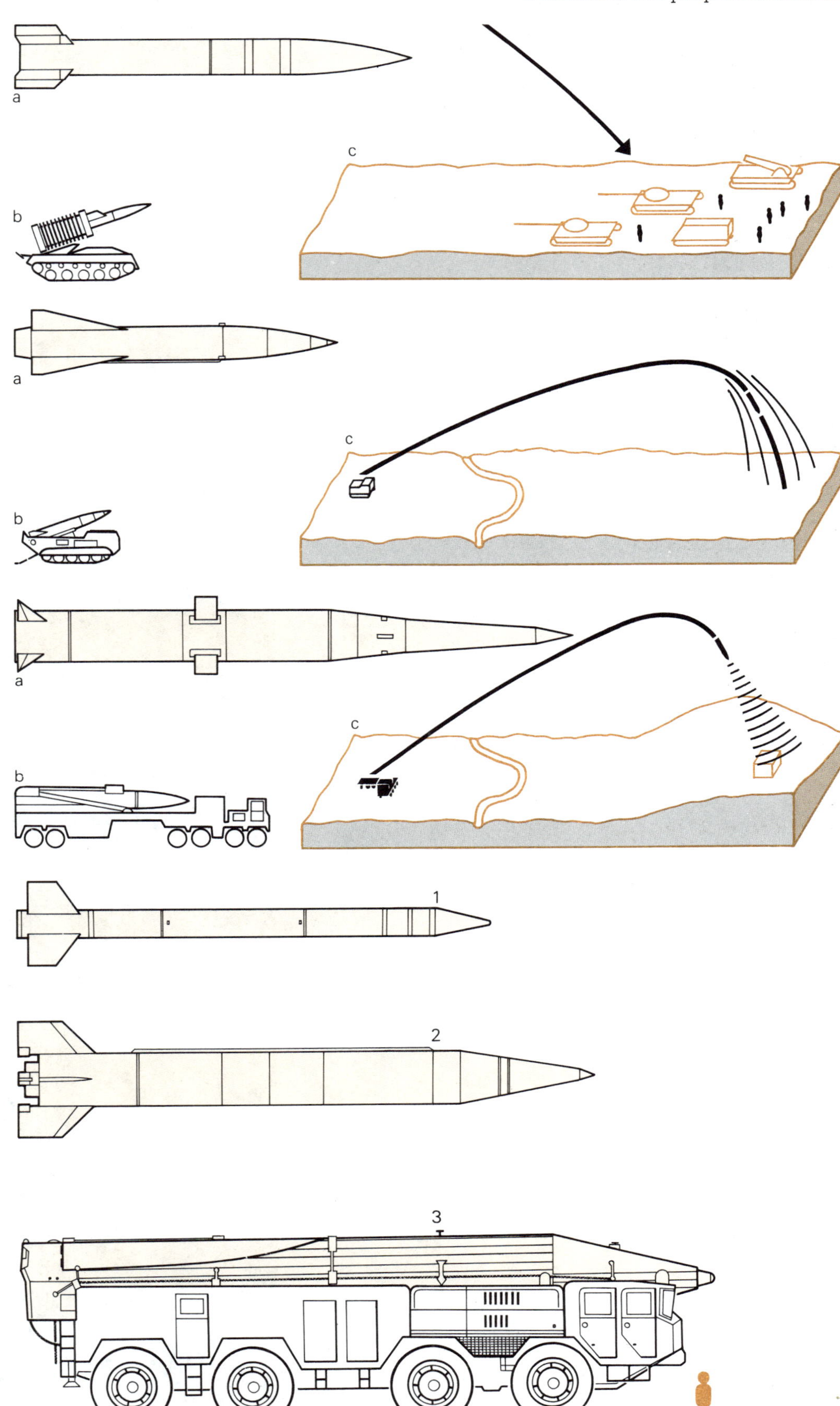

Chapter 7

CHEMICAL, NUCLEAR AND BIOLOGICAL WEAPONS

In this chapter we deal with certain major destructive agents that defy classification within our previous categories. They may be delivered by many of the weapon systems already shown, but their effects can be quite different. All of them have in common the vital characteristic that their effects can spread unpredictably, causing continued destruction.

Included in the chemical category is fire, long used as a weapon, but exploited as never before in the incendiary bombing of WW2. Then come the remaining chemical weapons, such as the poison gases of WW1. We also explain the physics, destructive effects and military uses of nuclear explosives. Lastly, the use of biological or "germ" warfare agents is discussed.

Soviet soldier (near right) photographed while on exercise, examining part of the "battlefield" for traces of chemical or radioactive agents, by means of a portable detector.

Nuclear test explosion (far right) at Maralinga, South Australia, in 1956. The pattern of smoke trails in the sky was formed by rockets, and was designed to act as a grid against which to measure the size of the fireball and mushroom cloud.

Incendiary weapons

Fire has been used as a weapon since time immemorial, but was for a long time limited in its effectiveness by the difficulty of delivering it. We survey the ways so far devised for using fire as a weapon, and list some common modern incendiary agents. Aerial bombing has become the main method for causing destruction by fire, and incendiary bombs are dealt with at greater length.

Ancient fire weapons (left) "Greek fire" was used as an incendiary agent by the Byzantine Greeks. Its basis was naphtha, mixed with various additives including quicklime. It is shown being fired through the "siphon." Fire pots, probably containing naphthon, were used in war throughout the second half of the first millennium BC and perhaps earlier.

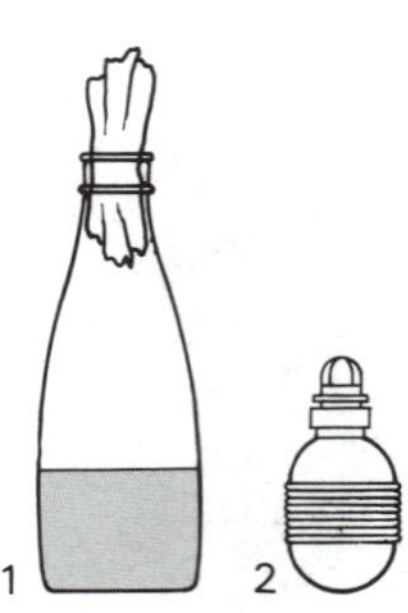

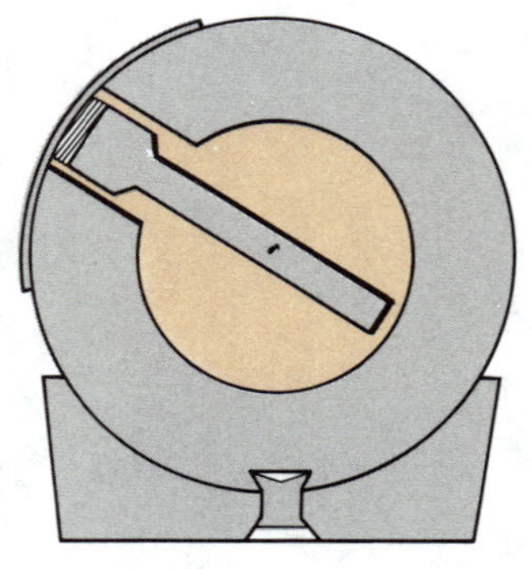

Hand-thrown fire weapons (above) "Molotov cocktails," consisting of bottles of petrol (**1**) with wicks to light at the neck, are a form of fire weapon often used by rioters. Regular armed forces have purpose-made incendiary grenades (**2**), most often containing white phosphorus which ignites on contact with the air.

Hand-held fire projectors (above) Flame-throwers, using a liquid agent that is squirted out in a jet and ignited, made their first appearance in WW1. Shown is a present-day US soldier wearing protective clothing while using a hand-held flame-thrower. Disposable, one-shot flame cartridges, and flame-throwers mounted on tanks, are also used.

Incendiary projectiles (above) Artillery has long been used to set fire to buildings and ships. The British "carcass" shell (above), to be fired from a 19th century smoothbore cannon, was an iron shell filled with a mixture of saltpeter, sulfur, rosin, sulfide of antimony, tallow, and turpentine. Incendiary shells and small arms bullets are in current use.

Incendiary bombs (above) Shown is a British 30lb (13.6kg) bomb of WW2. Although fire-bombs had been dropped from airships and fixed-wing aircraft in WW1, it was in WW2 that the bombing of cities with huge quantities of incendiaries became a major strategy.

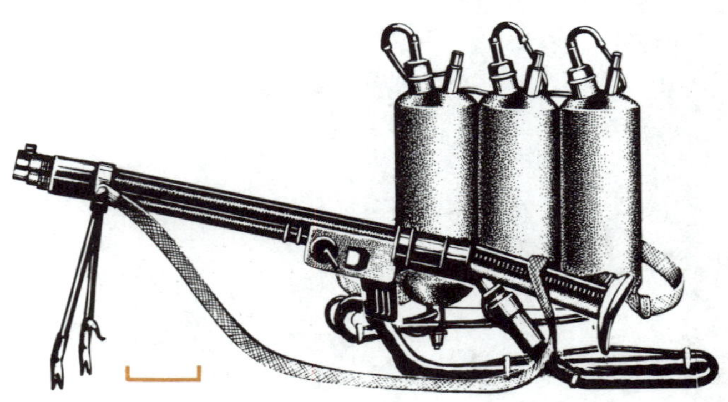

Flamethrower (above) This is the Soviet LPO-50. It has three 3.3 liter (0.87 US gal) tanks, each of which gives a two or three second burst of flame. Maximum range is 230ft (70m). Ignition is by battery.

The table (right) lists major military incendiary agents used in the 20th century. Some burn using oxygen from the atmosphere; others need the addition of an oxidizing agent. Some require a separate igniter. The metal magnesium has been used in incendiary bombs in the form of a thick casing which itself burns with intense heat.

Type	Examples
Igniters	**White phosphorus** (WP) Ignites spontaneously in air **Zirconium** **Depleted uranium** Both produce sparks of very high temperature
Metal agents	**Magnesium** **Aluminum**
Pyrotechnic mixtures (Agent plus oxidizer)	**Thermite** Powdered ferric oxide and powdered or granular aluminum **Thermate** Thermite plus pyrotechnic additives
Oil-based agents	**Napalm** **Napalm-B** 50% polystyrene thickener, 25% benzene, 25% gasoline

Aerial incendiary bombs (right) are of two main kinds.
A Intensive bombs These burn at extremely high temperatures at the point of impact, their main use being to set fire to buildings and equipment.
B "Scatter" type bombs These burst on impact, spreading burning fluid over a wide area, and can be used to attack personnel.

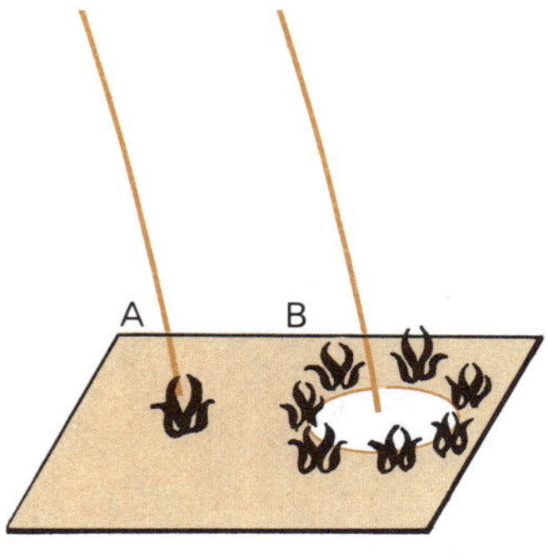

"Fire storm" effect (right) It was found during WW2 that if enough incendiaries were dropped on an area, such as a city, a "fire storm" could result. The heat at the center of the fire causes large masses of gas to rise, so sucking in air at ground level at gale force in an uncontrollable cycle of intensification.

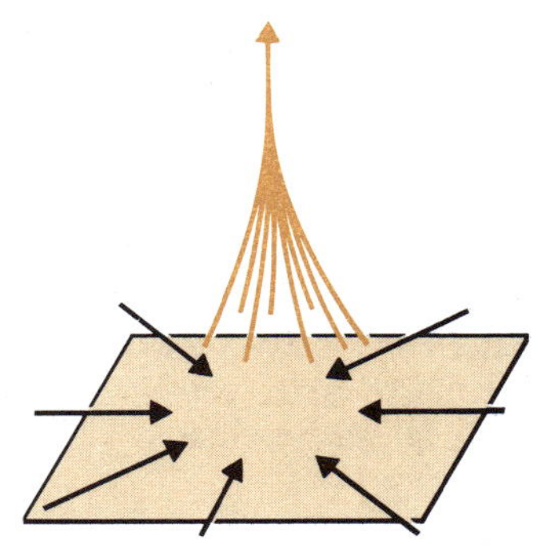

Early incendiary bomb (right) of a kind dropped from German Zeppelin airships over Britain in 1915. It is thought that the igniter was activated on release, setting fire to the thermite. This burned so intensely that the central metal funnel was molten on reaching the ground and helped spread the fire.

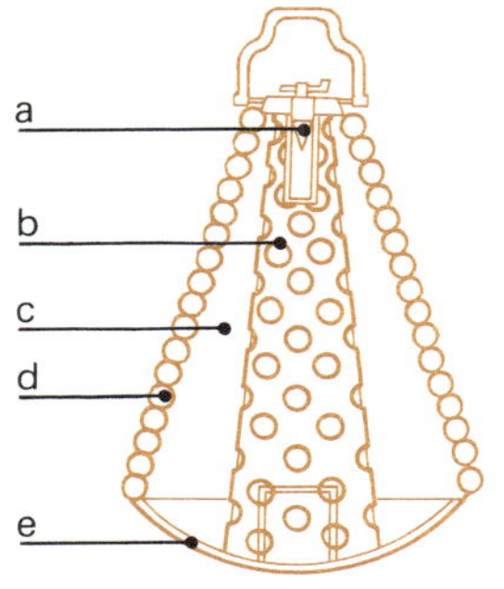

a Ignition device
b Perforated metal funnel containing thermite
c Resinous matter
d Rope binding
e Metal base

German B1 EZB (right), an intensive-type incendiary bomb of WW2. On impact, the detonator was thrown on to the striker, the resulting flash igniting the thermite filling. This in turn set fire to the magnesium casing around the perforations. The small explosive charge was to discourage firefighters. Weight 1kg (2.2lb).

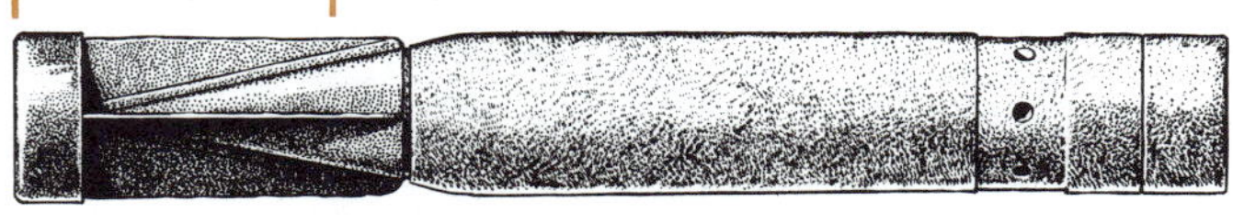
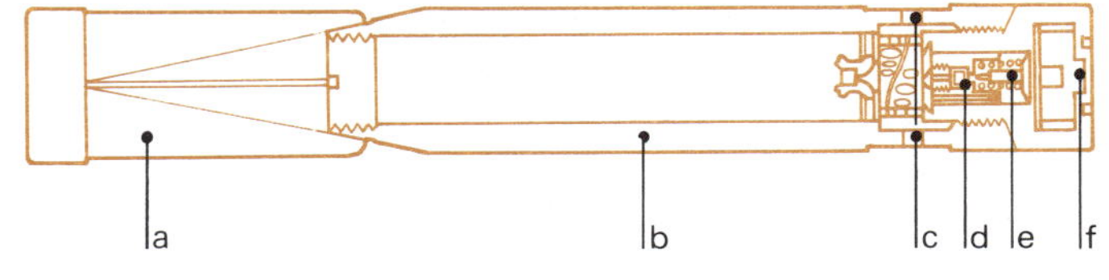

a Sheet steel tail fins
b Magnesium casing
c Perforations
d Detonator
e Striker
f Explosive charge

British 25lb incendiary bomb (right) of WW2. This was of an unusual kind. Its descent was retarded by a parachute. After hitting the ground the tail blew off and the seven fire-pots (of the intensive kind) were ejected rearward at intervals over a period of ten minutes. The charge of thermite in the nose then burned in situ for added effect.

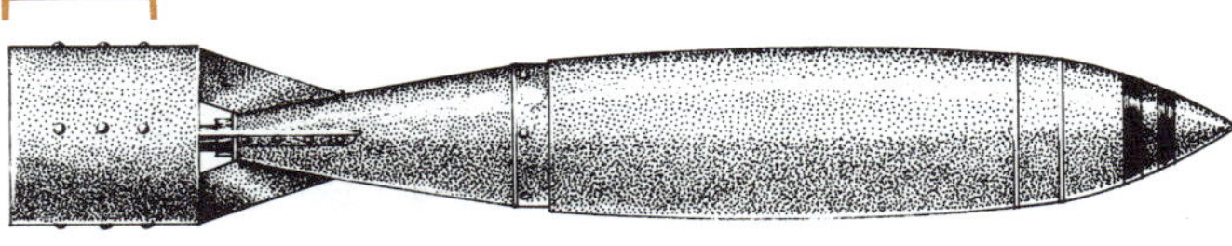
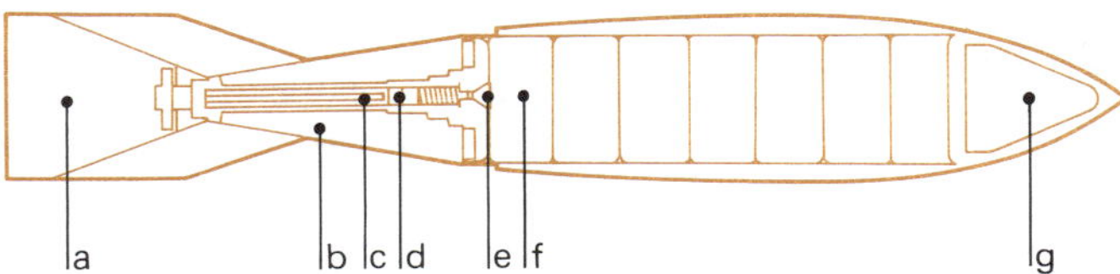

a Steel tail fins
b Steel tail cone
c Safety rod
d Striker pellet
e Blowing charge
f First fire-pot
g Thermite nose-filling

US Navy Mk78 Mod2 750lb Fire Bomb (right), one of several varieties of napalm bomb in US service in the 1960s and 1970s. This variety contained 110 US gallons (416 liters) of napalm. Napalm was invented in 1943 and derives its name from aluminum naphthenate and aluminum palmate, which were originally used to thicken petroleum into a gel. Napalm has now been superseded by Napalm-B, a liquid, not a gel, essentially consisting of polystyrene thickener, benzine and gasoline. It burns at about 1562°F (850°C) for two to three times as long as ordinary napalm, therefore causing more severe burning. Other second-generation napalms have extended burning times and increased adhesion.

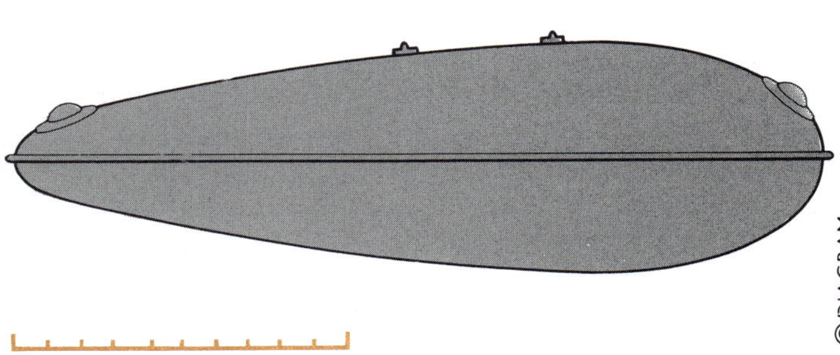

Chemical weapons

Although poisons have long been used against individual victims, organized chemical warfare may be said to date from April 22, 1915, when poison gas was first used on the Western Front. Non-lethal harassing agents were also used in WW1, and are now used for riot control. Despite treaties and wide condemnation, lethal nerve gases were used by Iraq from 1984.

Chemical agents The list (right) gives the general classification of Chemical Warfare (CW) agents. The table (below) gives more specific information on a selection of agents. The "LD50" level is the dose that will prove lethal for 50% of those affected. The effectiveness and persistence of CW agents depend on local conditions, particularly weather.

Lethal
Nerve agents
Blood agents
Choking agents
Toxin agents
Wounding or possibly lethal
Blister agents
Incapacitating
Harassing agents
Psychological agents
Indirect (on environment)
Defoliants

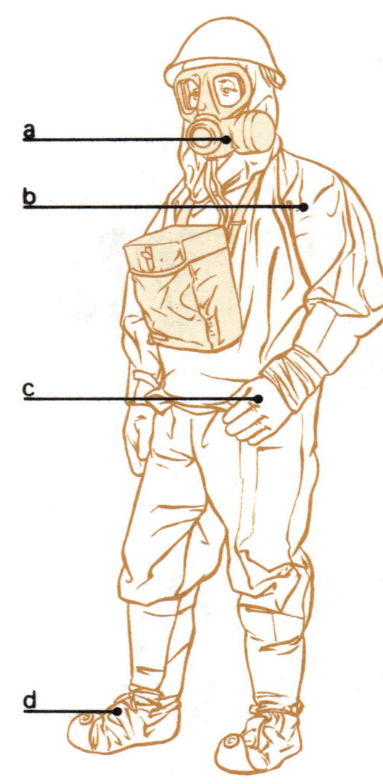

Chemical agents as weapons Chemical agents can enter the body and affect it in many ways, special clothing (left) being needed for protection. A respirator (**a**) is needed to protect the eyes and respiratory system. The British suit shown also protects the other entry routes—the skin and excretory exits—by completely enveloping them in impregnated paper (**b**), rubber gloves (**c**) and boot-covers (**d**). Nerve agents disrupt the nervous system. Blood agents prevent oxygen transfer to body tissues. Choking agents fill the lungs with body fluids. The term "toxin agents" covers a variety of general poisons. Blister agents attack exposed tissue, especially if wet. Indirect and anti-riot agents are explained opposite.

Type and name	Form	Smell	Parts of the body affected	Dosage (LD50)		
				Skin dose mg/man	Inhaled mg/min/m³	Digested mg/man
Nerve agents			Respiratory system, eyes, salivary and sweat glands, heart, digestive, excretory and central nervous systems; causes paralysis.			
Tabun "GA"	Liquid or vapor	Fruit		1000	400	40
Sarin "GB"	Liquid or vapor	Almost none		1700	100	10
VX	Liquid	?		15	36	5
Blister agents			Eyes and skin, lungs and other internal tissues; causes bronchopneumonia.			
Distilled mustard	Liquid or vapor	Garlic		4500	1500	50
Nitrogen mustard	Liquid or vapor	Fish or soap		4500	1500	50
Choking agents						
Phosgene	Colorless gas	New-mown hay	Respiratory organs; victims drown in their own mucus.		3200	
Incapacitating agents						
"CN"	Visible vapor	Apple blossom	Eyes and skin, respiratory system.		11,000	
"CS"	Visible vapor	Pepper	Nervous, respiratory and digestive systems.		61,000	
"BZ"	Vapor	?	Heart, central nervous system; causes hallucinations and manic behavior.		200,000	
Toxin agents						
Butolin "X," "A"	Powder or liquid	?	Body tissues, central nervous system; causes desiccation and paralysis.	0.00007 (via wound)	0.1	0.07
Saxitoxin "TZ"	Powder or liquid	?	Nervous system; causes paralysis.	0.05 (via wound)	5	0.5
Enterotoxin "B"	Powder or liquid	?	Digestive and excretory systems, body tissues, lungs.	Not known	200	500

Gas in WW1 (right) The table shows the quantities, in thousands of tons, of chemical warfare agents used in battle by the main belligerents in WW1. About 1.1% of fatal casualties in the war were caused by poison gas. (Data after "Chemicals in War," by A M Prentiss, New York, 1937.) In December 1987 the USSR admitted having 50,000 tons of chemical weapons.

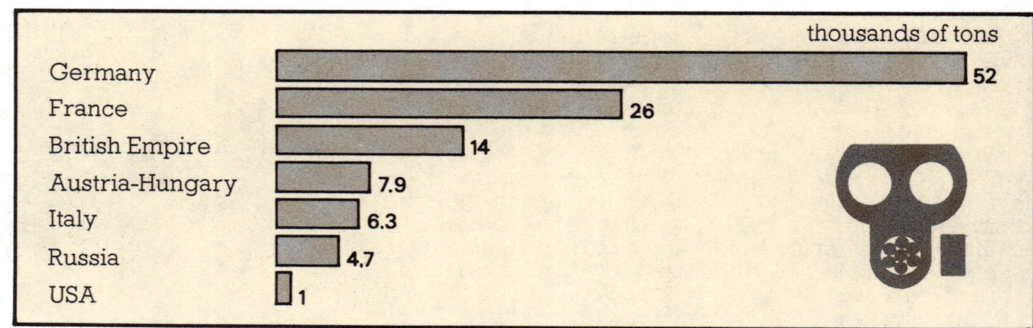

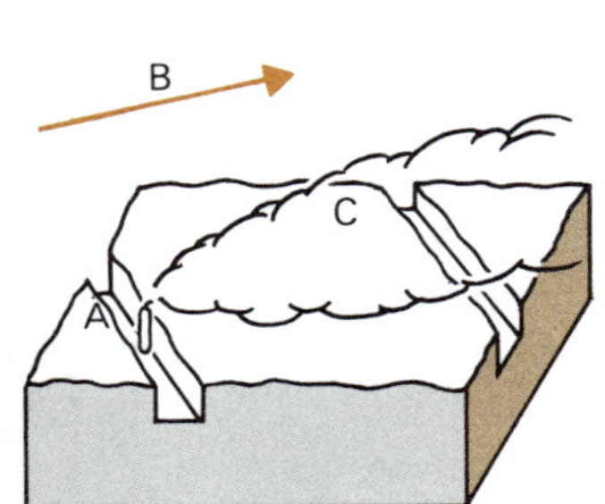

Gas clouds (above) Early gas attacks in WW1 were made in this way. Cylinders of gas (**A**) were hidden in the front line. If the wind (**B**) was blowing toward the enemy lines at the time of the attack, the taps of the cylinders were opened, and clouds of gas (**C**) drifted over to the enemy trenches. Friendly troops following up the attack needed gas masks.

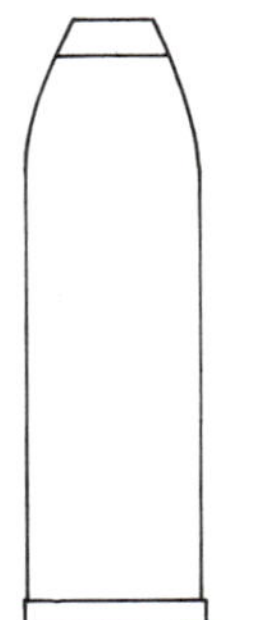

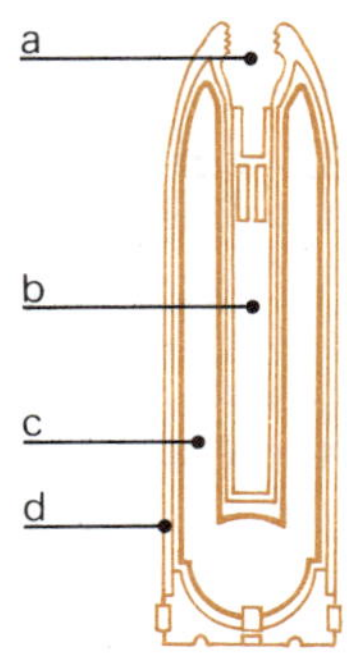

German gas shell (above) of WW1, for a *minenwerfer* or mortar. On impact with the ground, the fuze set off the bursting charge. This ruptured the outer casing and spread the liquified gas.
a Fuze pocket
b Bursting charge
c Liquified gas
d Casing

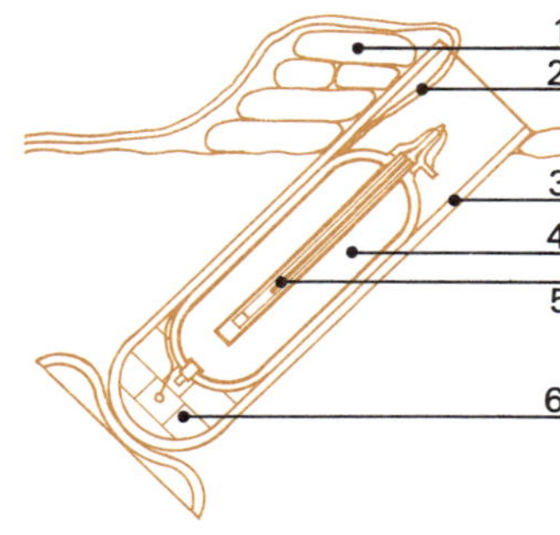

Livens projector (above), a British gas delivery system of WW1. A crude mortar which fired a cylinder of liquified gas, it was dug into the ground in rows of 25, to be fired in volleys.
1 Sandbags
2 Electrical leads
3 Barrel of thin metal
4 Cylinder of liquid gas
5 Exploder
6 Propellant charge

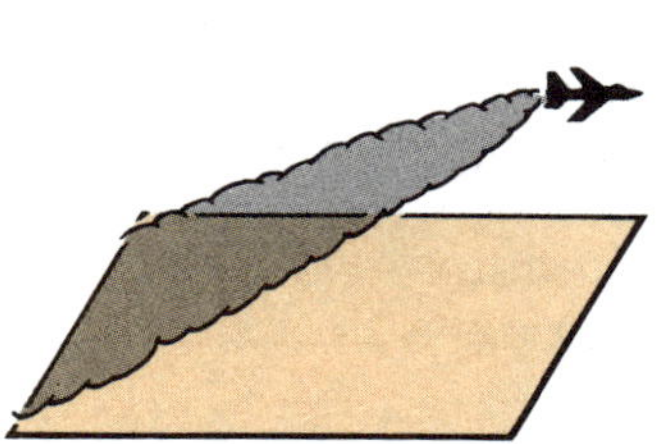

Indirect methods of chemical warfare are those aimed at the environment that supports the enemy. The ancient ploy of poisoning the wells of a besieged town or castle may be included here.
A recent application of the idea is defoliation, the killing of an enemy's crops or the jungle that hides him, by spraying from the air (above).

Incapacitating agents (right) are now commonly used in riot control. The theory is to inflict severe discomfort on the rioters, so that they are more concerned with finding relief than continuing the disturbance. They offer security forces an extra deterrent before recourse is had to weapons that may wound or kill. Anti-riot gas or smoke can be deployed in the form of aerosols (**A**), grenades (**B**), or cartridges (**C**) for riot guns and rifle-mounted grenade dischargers.
a French Type 63 FDM aerosol, emitting 30sec of CS gas.
b US ABC-M25A2 anti-riot grenade. Spreads CN1 gas on bursting.
c British L3A1 irritant cartridge for 1.5in (37mm) caliber riot guns and pistols.

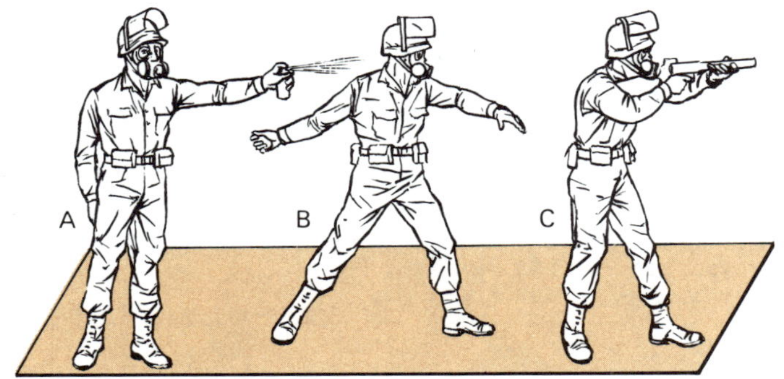

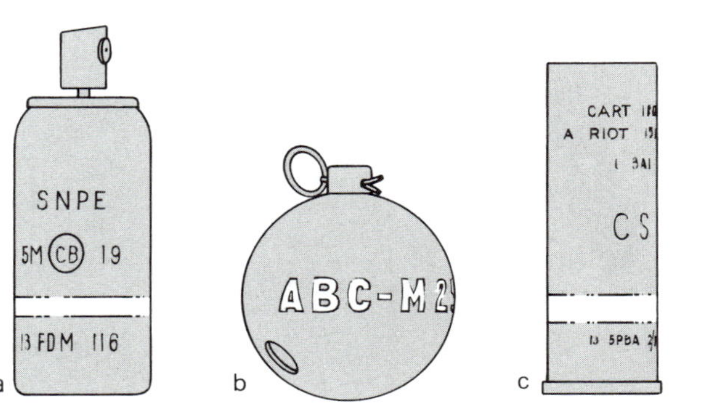

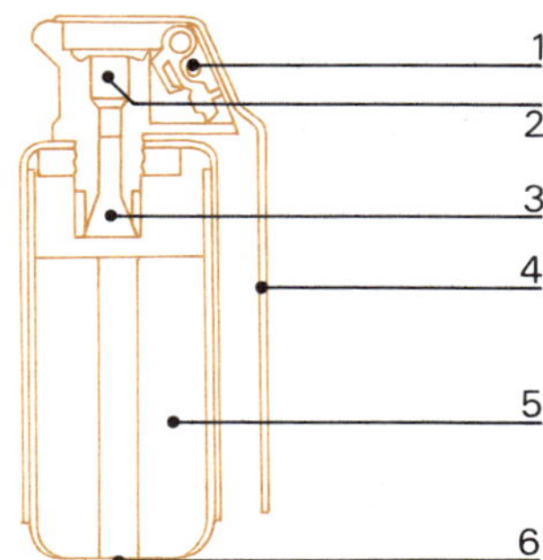

Typical chemical grenade (above) for discharging smoke or gas.
1 Safety pin
2 Detonator
3 Starter mixture
4 Safety lever
5 Pellets of agent set in pyrotechnic mixture
6 Emission hole

Anti-riot guns (right)
1 Smith and Wesson 210, a US riot gun able to fire various grenades up to 100yd (100m).
2 German P2A1 signal pistol converted to a launcher for gas grenades.
3 "Pistol, Pyrotechnic, 1½in, No4 Mk1/1," a British flare pistol sometimes used to project CS gas cartridges.

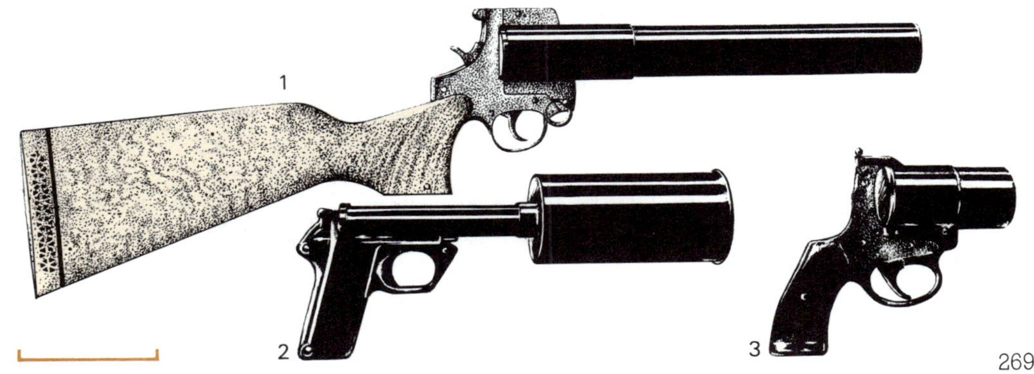

Nuclear explosive devices

All matter is composed of atoms. These have a center or nucleus, composed of protons and neutrons, around which electrons revolve in set orbits. When the structure of an atom is changed by releasing a neutron, energy is released. Nuclear weapons are based on this principle. Their power is measured in TNT equivalents : one kiloton equals a thousand tons (984 tonnes) of TNT, and one megaton equals one million tons (984,000 tonnes). On these two pages we explain the methods that may be used to create nuclear explosions, and also the phenomena that accompany them. On subsequent pages we deal with the form taken by nuclear weapons and their delivery systems, and explain their effects.

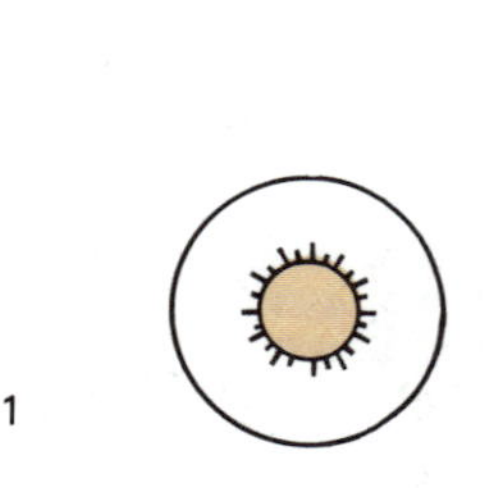

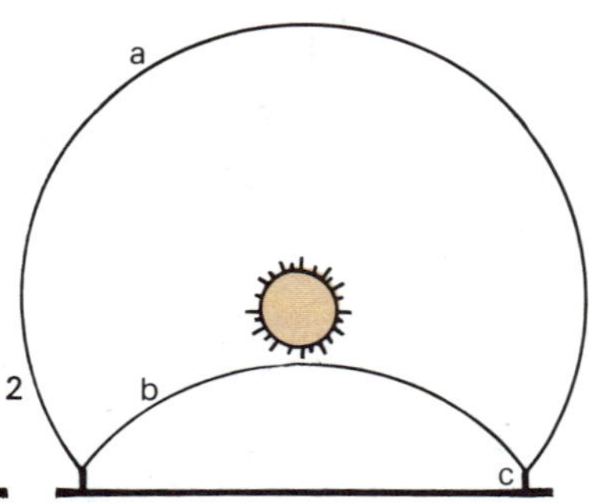

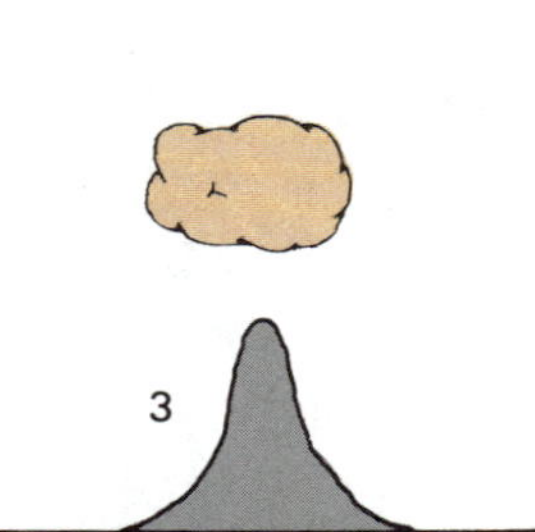

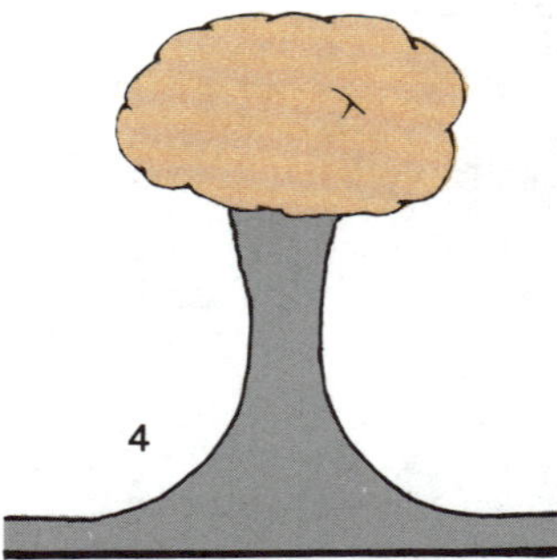

Sequence of phenomena in a nuclear explosion (above)
1 Immediately there is a blinding flash of bluish-white light and ultraviolet light. The surrounding air is heated to 18,000,000 °F (10,000,000 °C) and creates a fireball. The fireball generates radiant heat that travels at the speed of light.
2 The wave of heat is followed by the blast, in the form of a pressure wave (**a**) moving at 1150ft (350m) per second. Part of the wave is reflected up again by the ground (**b**). Where the reflected wave catches up with the original, the pressure is doubled and the "mach wave" (**c**) is formed.
3 The overpressure of the blast wave is followed by a negative pressure phase that draws winds of up to 620mph (1078km/h) into the destroyed area. This corresponds with the upward movement of the fireball and hot gases.
4 If the fireball has touched the ground, dirt and debris are sucked into the rising column of hot gases and smoke, and the familiar mushroom cloud is formed. The fireball will not necessarily touch the ground, as nuclear bombs are most effective when exploded in an "air-burst," from 2000 to 50,000ft (0.6 to 15.2km) above the ground.

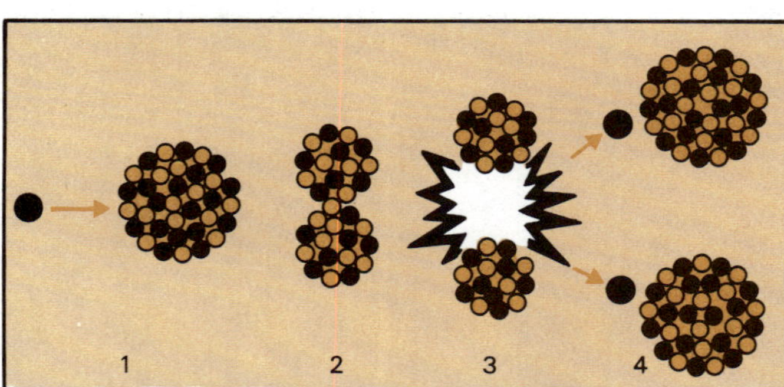

Fission atom bombs (above) depend upon the splitting or fission of uranium or plutonium atoms into two lighter atoms.
1 A free neutron from one atom collides with another uranium atom.
2 The collision causes the uranium atom to split into two smaller atoms.
3 This fission releases two spare neutrons and 32 picowatts (32 million millionths of a watt) of energy.
4 The two freed neutrons collide with two more atoms, which undergo the same reaction. In this way 1 lb (0.45kg) of U-235 can release over 36 million million watts of energy.

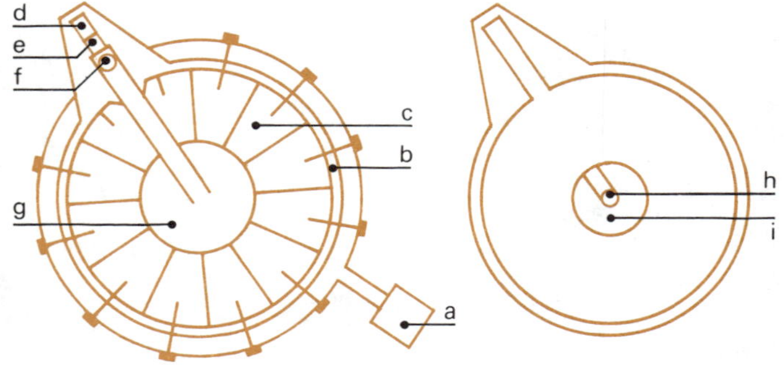

An atom or fission bomb mechanism (above) A subcritical mass of U-235 or plutonium is surrounded by high explosive in a tamper (neutron reflecting) casing. On detonation, the neutron source is shot into position in the U-235 or plutonium to initiate fission, and the high explosive detonates, so compressing the U-235 or plutonium into a supercritical mass that then undergoes rapid explosive fission.
a Detonating system
b Tamper casing
c High explosive wedges
d Explosive charge
e Tamper wedge
f Neutron source
g Subcritical mass
h Neutron source in position
i Compressed supercritical mass

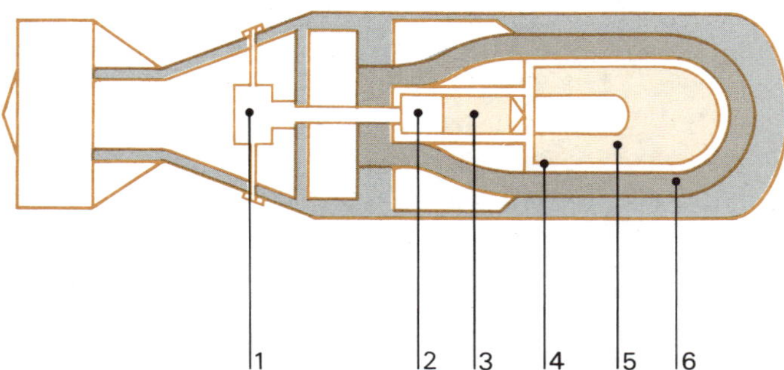

"Little Boy" (above) The 20KT U-235 bomb dropped on Hiroshima in WW2 was the simple "gun type" bomb. Before the reaction necessary for an explosion can take place, a certain amount of the radioactive material—Uranium 235—must be collected in a certain volume known as the "critical mass." A piece of U-235 slightly below critical mass is separated from a smaller piece. On detonation an explosive charge forces the smaller piece into the larger one, causing them to explode.
1 Air pressure detonator
2 Conventional explosive charge
3 Small piece of U-235
4 Neutron reflector
5 Large piece of U-235
6 Lead shield container

Weight of U-235	Volume of U-235	Equivalent weight/yield of TNT	Equivalent volume of TNT
1lb (0.45kg)	1in³ (16.38cm³)	9KT	210,000ft³ (5946m³)
11lb (4.98kg)	10in³ (163.8cm³)	90KT	2,100,000ft³ (59,465m³)
220lb (99.7kg)	200in³ (3277cm³)	1.8MT	42,000,000ft³ (1,189,314m³)
1100lb (498.9kg)	1000in³ (16,387cm³)	9MT	210,000,000ft³ (5,946,570m³)
2200lb (997.9kg)	2000in³ (32,774cm³)	18MT	420,000,000ft³ (11,893,140m³)

The table (above) compares the volumes of equivalent weights and yields of Uranium 235 and TNT, assuming 100% fission of the U-235. This great concentration of energy in a nuclear bomb means that one aircraft or missile can wreak as much destruction as thousands of bombers carrying conventional high explosives.

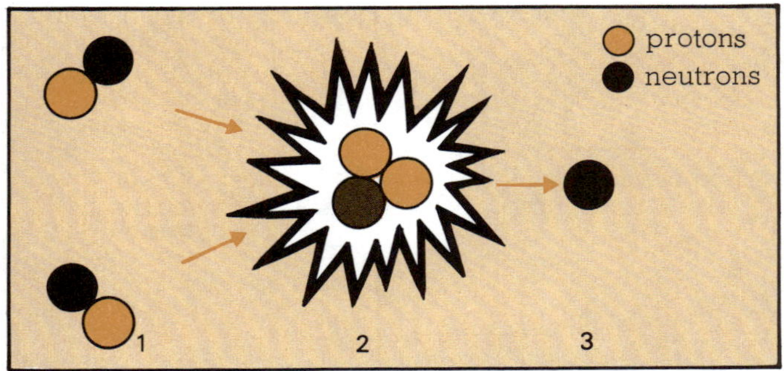

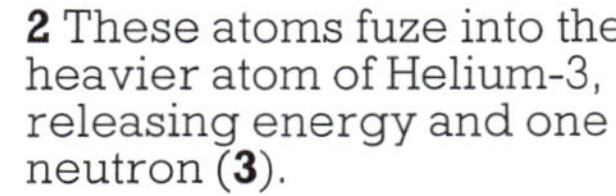

Fusion Unlike the atom bomb, which works by fission or the splitting of atoms, the "hydrogen" or "thermonuclear" bomb works by the fusion of atoms, made possible by the heat generated in a fission explosion.
Deuterium fusion (above)
1 In the heat of a fission explosion, two deuterium atoms collide.
2 These atoms fuze into the heavier atom of Helium-3, releasing energy and one neutron (**3**).

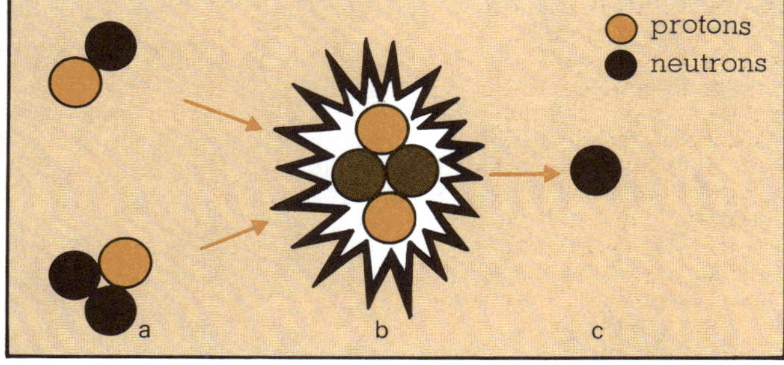

Deuterium/tritium fusion (above)
a A deuterium and a tritium atom collide.
b They fuze into a Helium-4 atom and release energy and one neutron (**c**).
Although the creation of Helium-3 and Helium-4 releases less energy than fission reactions, the atoms are much smaller and therefore thermonuclear fuels will give three to four times the energy of the same mass of fissile material and release up to six times as many neutrons. The materials are also relatively cheaper and more abundant than fissile material and are not subject to the dangers of "critical mass."

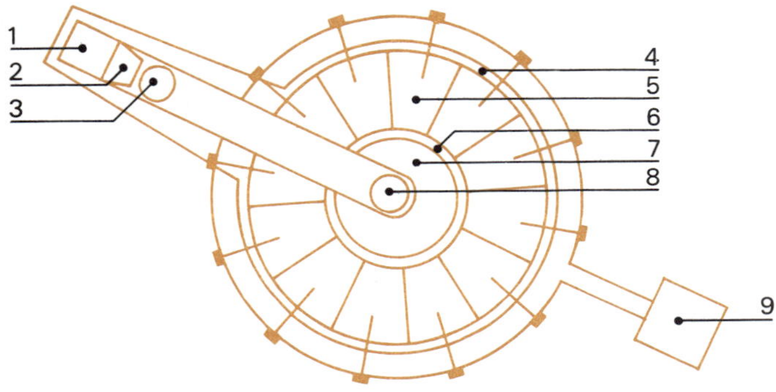

Thermonuclear warhead or H-bomb (left) A lithium deuteride core (containing lithium and deuterium) is surrounded by U-235 or plutonium, which in turn is surrounded by another relatively inert form of uranium—U-238. The fission reaction is set off as explained above. The heat generated causes the deuterium and tritium to undergo fusion, and the high-energy neutrons thus released cause the U-238 to undergo fission. This is known as a fission-fusion-fission bomb.
1 Explosive charge
2 Tamper wedge
3 Neutron source
4 Neutron reflecting tamper
5 High explosive
6 U-238
7 U-235 or plutonium
8 Deuterium tritium
9 Detonating system

Effects of nuclear explosions

The effects of a nuclear explosion fall into three categories: thermal (or heat) radiation, blast, and nuclear radiation. Thermal radiation vaporizes and burns whatever it meets. Blast creates pressure waves and high winds. Of the nuclear radiations, neutron and gamma (short wave electromagnetic emissions) radiations are the most dangerous, and can be lethal.

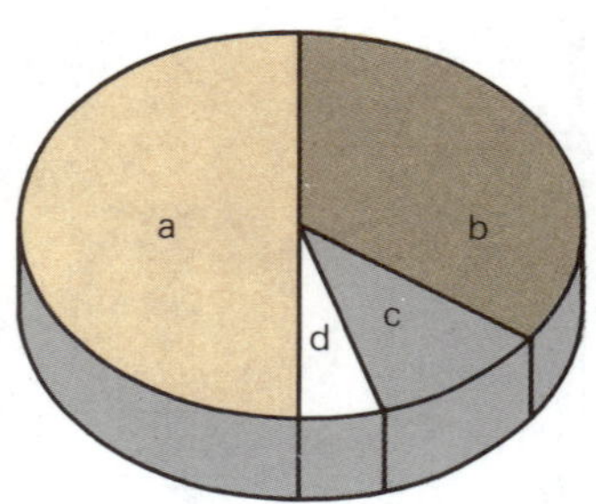

Energy distribution (left) An air burst initially releases 85% of its energy as thermal radiation, but a large amount of this is immediately transformed into the blast. The actual distribution is as follows.
a 50% blast
b 35% heat
c 10% residual radiation (remains in affected matter)
d 5% initial radiation

Thermal and blast effects of a 20KT bomb are superimposed (right) on a map of Washington DC, with mile and kilometer scales along the axes. The top segment of the diagram shows the zones over which particular heat effects are experienced, ranging in intensity from **A** to **G**; the characteristics of each zone are listed below the diagram. The lower segment of the diagram shows the lines representing specific blast overpressures and windspeeds, numbered from **1** to **9**; the zones between lines experience blast effects as listed. These heat and blast zones occur in the same ratios with nuclear bombs of different yields; the table (below) lists the distances from the explosion of the heat zones and blast overpressure lines for several bombs of higher yield.

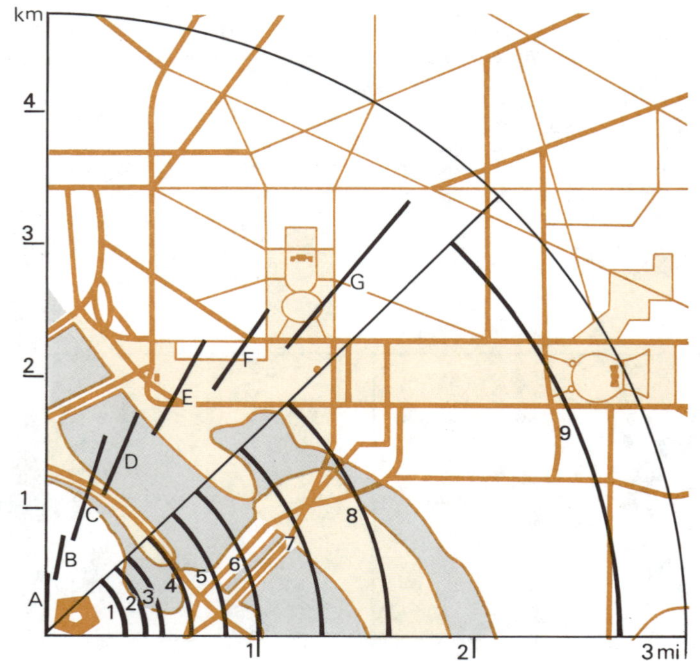

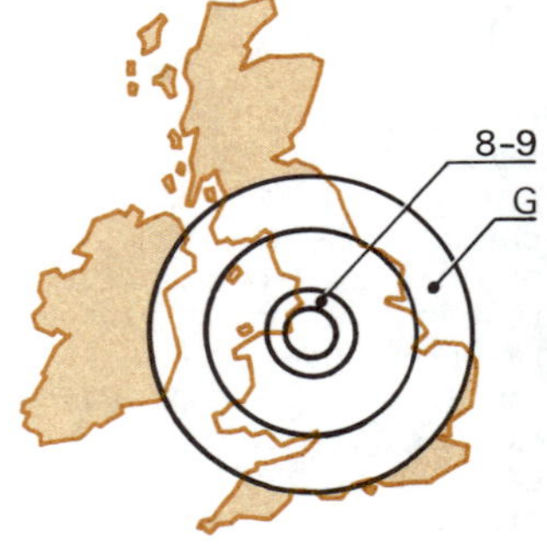

Extent of effects (above) of a large strategic nuclear bomb, superimposed on a map of the British Isles. The example taken is that of a 100MT airburst over Manchester. The bands shown on the diagram correspond to zone 8-9 and zone G as defined in the text (below).

Heat (thermal) effects in the zones indicated.
A Metals vaporize
B Metals melt
C Rubber and plastics ignite and melt
D Wood burns or chars
E Third degree burns (charring of skin)
F Second degree burns (blistering of skin)
G First degree burns (red and painful skin)

Blast effects on structures in the zones indicated.
0-1 Total destruction
1-2 Massive structures destroyed
2-3 Widescale destruction
3-4 Multistorey buildings damaged
4-5 Factories wrecked
5-6 Dwellings wrecked
6-7 Vehicles overturned
7-8 Brick houses damaged
8-9 Wooden buildings damaged

Blast overpressures The air pressures, in excess of atmospheric, and the windspeeds for the above effects at the zone lines are:
1 30psi/670mph
2 20psi/470mph
3 15psi/380mph
4 10psi/290mph
5 7psi/225mph
6 5psi/160mph
7 3psi/116mph
8 2psi/70mph
9 1psi/48mph

Yield	A	B	C	D	E	F	G
200KT	0-1.05mi (0-1.7km)	0.85-1.55mi (1.4-2.5km)	1.5-3.1mi (2.4-5km)	2.28-3.6mi (3.7-5.8km)	3.3-4.7mi (5.3-7.6km)	4.15-6.5mi (6.7-10.5km)	5.6-9.5mi (9-15.3km)
1MT	0-2.25mi (0-3.6km)	1.8-3.5mi (2.9-5.6km)	3.25-7.1mi (5.2-11.4km)	5.1-8mi (8.2-12.9km)	7.5-10.2mi (12-16.4km)	9.25-13.25mi (14.9-21.3km)	11.5-18.3mi (18.5-29.5km)
10MT	0-6.8mi (0-10.9km)	5.4-10.5mi (8.7-16.9km)	9.85-20.25mi (15.8-32.6km)	14.4-23.6mi (23.2-38km)	21.6-31.3mi (34.8-50.4km)	27.9-39.5mi (44.9-63.6km)	35.6-57.3mi (57.3-92.2km)

Yield	1	2	3	4	5	6	7	8	9
200KT	-0.85mi (-1.3km)	-1mi (-1.6km)	-1.1mi (-1.7km)	-1.4mi (-2.2km)	-1.8mi (-2.8km)	-2.2mi (-3.5km)	-2.8mi (-4.5km)	-3.4mi (-5.4km)	-5.9mi (-9.4km)
1MT	-1.4mi (-2.2km)	-1.8mi (-2.8km)	-2mi (-3.2km)	-2.5mi (-4km)	-3.1mi (-4.9km)	-3.8mi (-6.1km)	-4.8mi (-7.7km)	-5.9mi (-9.4km)	-10mi (-16km)
10MT	-3.1mi (-4.9km)	-3.8mi (-6.1km)	-4.3mi (-6.9km)	-5.4mi (-7.6km)	-6.8mi (-10.9km)	-8.2mi (-13.1km)	-10.3mi (-16.5km)	-12.8mi (-20.5km)	-21.7mi (-34.9km)

Radiation effects (right) The table shows the approximate effects of whole body gamma radiation, when acquired in an immediate exposure and also when the radiation is accumulated over one hour. Gamma radiation released during the first few seconds of the explosion can travel for several thousand yards, pass through soil, water, brick, lead and concrete, and disrupt the molecular structure of living tissue.

Whole body dose in RADS	Clinical effects	Incapacity in exposed persons	Mortality rate	Period of convalescence
0–25	Practically no effect			
100	Slight nausea and sickness; noticeable changes in the blood.	Up to 25%		7 days
200	Definite blood-cell damage; nausea, vomiting, diarrhea, hair loss, livid skin spots, fevers, hemorrhages, great fatigue; possible heart failure.	Up to 100%	About 25% in 30 to 60 days	Up to 40 days
400	Increased severity of the symptoms listed above; 50% fatalities among those exposed.	100%	Up to 50% in 30 to 60 days	Several weeks or months
600	Symptoms now very severe and quick to occur; death occurs more rapidly.	100%	Up to 75% in 20 to 35 days	Several months to years
800	Death likely; all the above symptoms plus rapid malfunction of circulatory and parts of nervous system.	100%	Up to 99% within days	Years
1000+	Very rapid onset of symptoms and death.	100%	100% within hours	

Approximate initial radiation yields (right) at set distances for bombs of different yields. Radiation is measured in Roentgens (r) and Milliroentgens (mr). Living tissue absorbs about 14% more radiation than air, on which the Roentgen is based, however, so the Roentgen Absorbed Dose (RAD) unit is used to measure tissue irradiation.

Weapon yield	Radiation at 1mi (1.6km)	Radiation at 2mi (3.2km)	Radiation at 3mi (4.8km)
10KT	90RAD	114mRAD	0.342mRAD
20KT	180RAD	228mRAD	0.684mRAD
50KT	500RAD	627mRAD	1.824mRAD
100KT	1140RAD	1.4RAD	4.2mRAD
200KT	2730RAD	3.4RAD	10.25mRAD
500KT	9120RAD	11.4RAD	34.2mRAD
1MT	19,150RAD	24RAD	71.8mRAD
10MT	456,000RAD	570RAD	1.7RAD

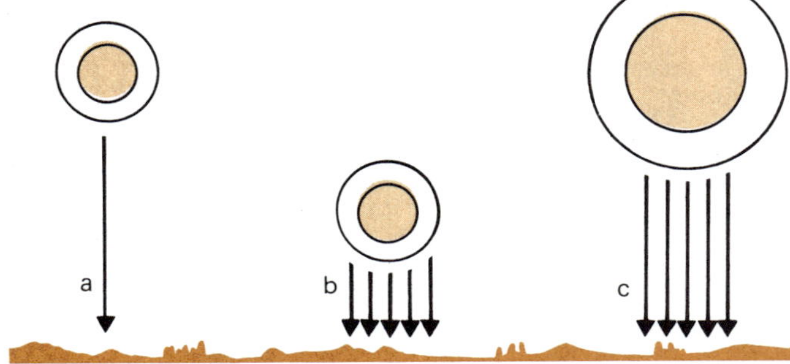

Optimum detonation height (above) The height at which a nuclear bomb is detonated is critical to its effects on the ground. If a 1MT bomb is detonated at 6000ft (**a**), its blast effect on the ground is only one-fifth that of a similar bomb detonated at 3000ft (**b**). The 1MT bomb at (**b**) has the same blast effect on the ground as a 10MT bomb detonated at 6000ft (**c**).

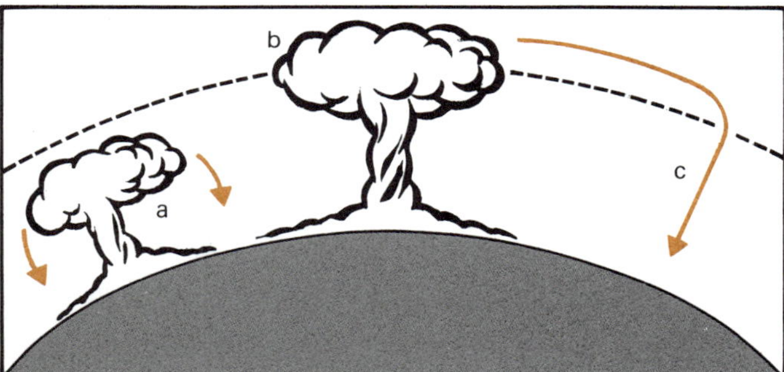

Local and global fallout (above) When the fireball caused by a nuclear explosion touches the ground, it sucks up matter that has been vaporized by its intense heat, so forming the mushroom cloud. This matter, together with the highly radioactive vaporized bomb parts, is heavily bombarded by the initial neutron radiation, and as it cools it falls back to earth as radioactive dust. With a small explosion, the mushroom cloud is within the troposphere boundary, and the fallout is relatively local to the explosion (**a**). When a large bomb is detonated and forms a cloud that reaches into the stratosphere (**b**), the particles are distributed by the upper air currents throughout the stratosphere, causing global fallout (**c**).

Applications of nuclear weapons

Here we explain the main ways in which nuclear weapons may be used — that is to say, the means used to deliver the warhead to the target, the precise type of warhead delivered, and the potential targets envisaged for a future war. We also list the nuclear weapons believed to be in current deployment. Further information on nuclear-tipped missiles is included in Chapter 6.

Since the 1950s, when nuclear weapons reached their present overshadowing prominence in world power-politics, there has been a general trend away from single warheads of huge power and toward multiple warheads of increasing accuracy. More than any other type of weapon, the success of nuclear arsenals is to be judged primarily in how well the threat they pose mediates against their use.

Delivery systems (right) Nuclear warheads can be delivered in three main ways: as a bomb dropped from an aircraft (**A**); as an artillery shell (**B**); or as the payload of a self-propelled missile (**C**), whether launched from land, sea or in the air.

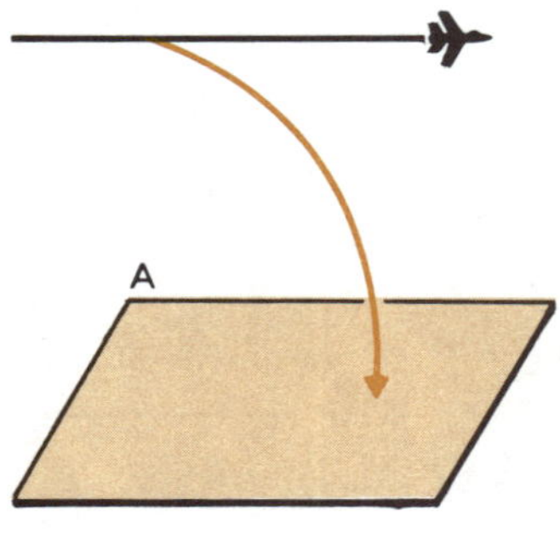

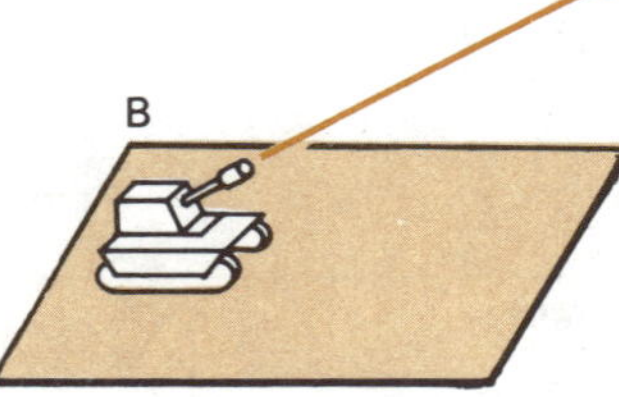

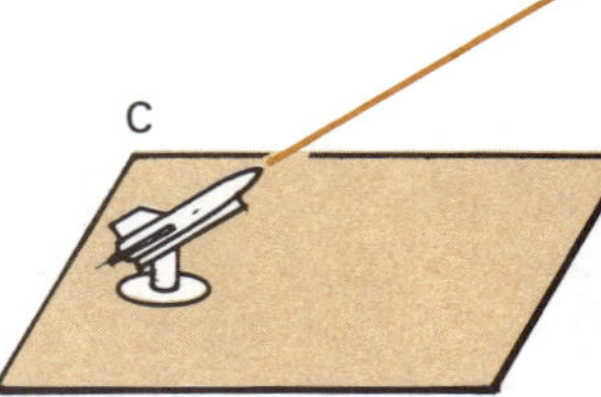

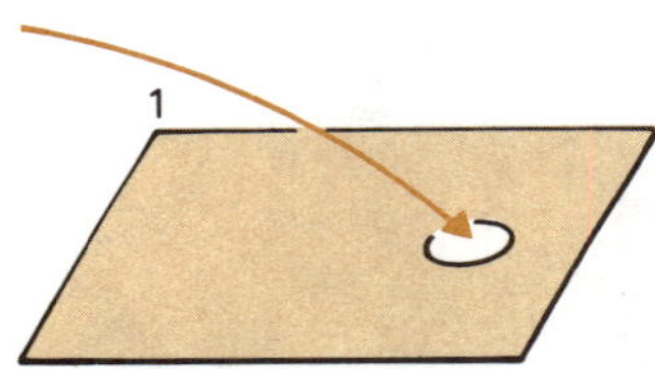

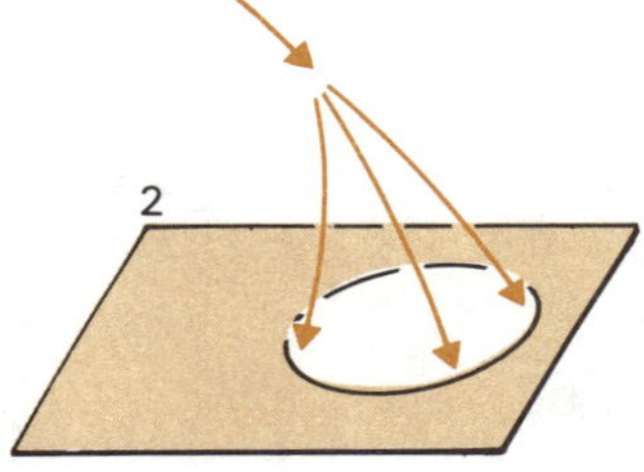

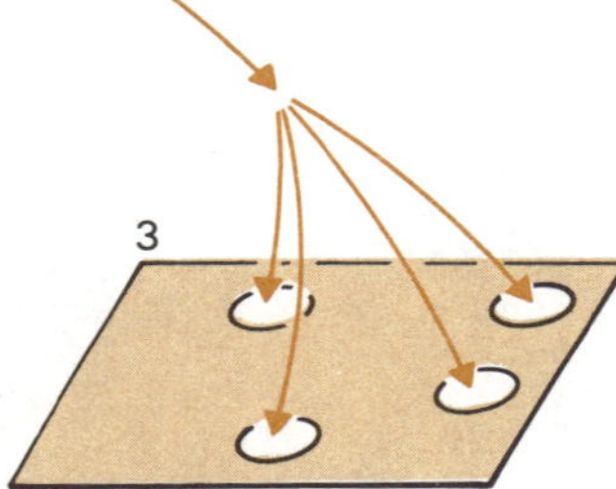

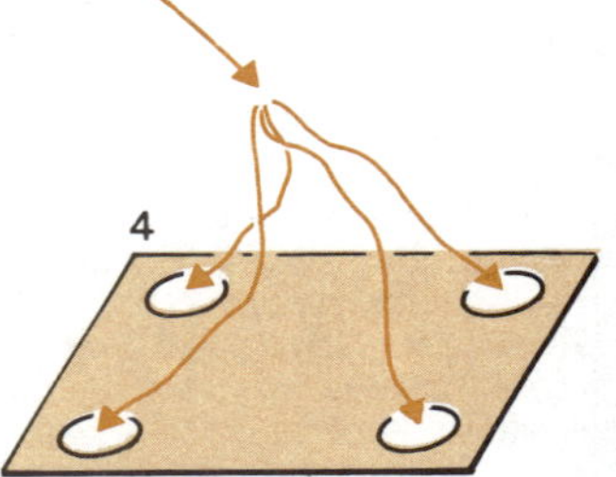

Types of nuclear warhead (above) The following classification of types applies principally to strategic self-propelled missiles.
1 Early nuclear missiles carried only one warhead. In the 1950s and 1960s, these warheads tended to be large—in the megaton range—but now the accent is on smaller warheads delivered more accurately.

2 Multiple Re-entry Vehicles (MRVs) are designed to deliver several warheads to one large target, in a saturation effect. This type was first deployed in 1970-71, but is already being replaced by the major powers with those of the MIRV and MARV types.

3 A Multiple Independently-targeted Re-entry Vehicle (MIRV) is a "bus" containing a number of warheads and usually some decoy devices to mislead enemy defenses. As the vehicle begins to descend, warheads and decoys are ejected toward separate targets which can be scores of kilometers apart.

4 A Maneuverable Alternative-target Re-entry Vehicle (MARV) differs from a MIRV in that each warhead has its own rocket and computer and can change course to a pre-selected alternative target if enemy Anti-Ballistic Missile (ABM) defenses are encountered. MIRVs and MARVs have multiplied the threat posed by each delivery missile.

Comparisons (right) of the current or potential arsenals of strategic nuclear weapons. (June 1988 data after IISS.)
Total of warheads
a USA 14,637
b USSR 11,694
c France 292
d China about 248
e Britain 192
f Israel up to 100 (est)
g India fissionable material to make 12–38 (est)
h Pakistan fissionable material to make 1–7 (est)

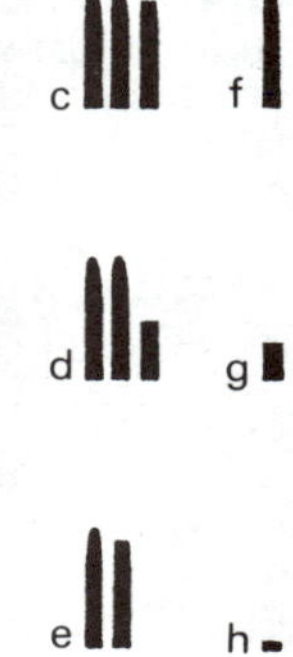

The table (right) attempts to list nuclear or potentially nuclear weapons in all categories. Data comes from *The Military Balance* and *Strategic Survey 1988–1989*, International Institute for Strategic Studies, London.

Abbreviations additional to list on p.234:
SRBM = Short Range Ballistic Missile (ie tactical)
LR = Long Range
MR = Medium Range
SP = Self-Propelled

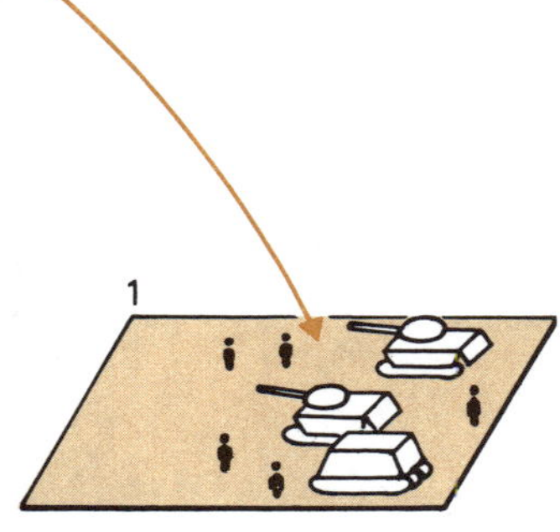

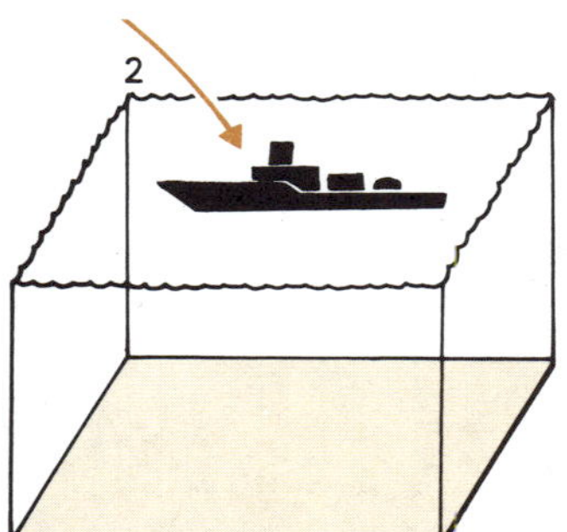

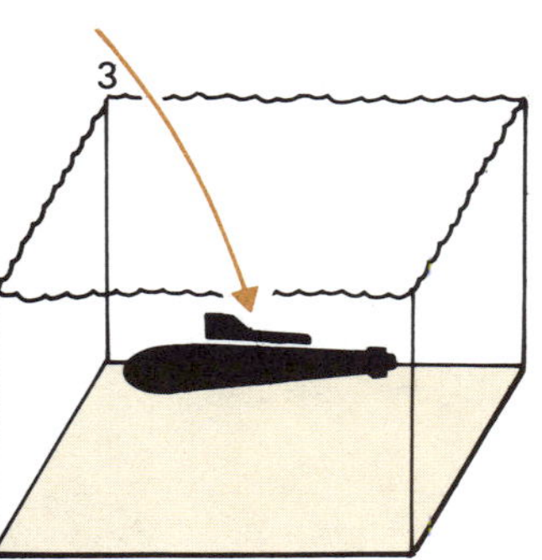

Range categories
Missiles: ICBM = over 4000mi (6400km)
IRBM = 1500-4000mi (2400-6400km)
MRBM = 500-1500mi (800-2400km)
SRBM = under 500mi (800km)
Aircraft: LR = over 6000mi (9650km)
MR = 3000-6000mi (4830-9650km)

Tactical roles for nuclear weapons (left)

1 Battlefield support
Tactical nuclear devices, in the shape of short-range missiles, artillery shells and even land mines and demolition charges, have important roles in the context of a land battle. Their most likely use is to destroy concentrations of enemy troops and armor.

2 Anti-ship weapons
Nuclear missiles can be used to increase the chance of sinking a specific ship, or to destroy a force of several ships. Missiles for this purpose are now deployed on many surface ships, in replacement of their former main armament of big conventional guns.

3 Nuclear depth charges
Another role for nuclear weapons has been found at sea. Conventional depth charges damage a submarine by setting up shock waves in the water that crush the vessel's hull. Nuclear depth charges produce more powerful shock waves, effective at greater distances, and reduce the need for accuracy.

4 Anti-aircraft missiles
Missiles with small nuclear warheads have also been devised specifically for shooting down aircraft. Some are of the surface-to-air kind, others are for air-to-air use, for one aircraft to use in shooting down another.

Countries with nuclear-capable weaponry

Missiles	
ICBM	US, USSR, China
ICBM (rail-based)	USSR, US (testing)
IRBM	France, China
MRBM	USSR, US, China, Israel, Iraq, Egypt, Argentina, Saudi Arabia, India
SRBM	NATO, Warsaw Pact, Israel, Iran, Iraq, Yemens, Saudi Arabia, Syria, India, Pakistan, Brazil, Argentina, Algeria, Cuba, Kuwait, Libya, Indonesia, S Africa (not confirmed), Koreas, Taiwan
SAM	Belgium, W Germany, Italy, Spain, Turkey (only 75 warheads left in service)
SLBM	US, USSR, Britain, France, China
SLCM	US, USSR
GLCM	US, USSR
ALCM	US, USSR
ASM	US, France, USSR
ABM	USSR
ASAT	USSR, US
ATBM	US, France & Italy (R&D), Israel (R&D), Japan (studying)
ASW	US, USSR
Aircraft	
LR bomber	US, USSR
MR bomber	US, USSR, China
Strike (carrier-based)	US, USSR, Britain, France, India, Spain, Argentina
Strike (land-based)	NATO, Warsaw Pact (exc Romania), most Third World countries
ASW	USSR, NATO
Atomic devices	
Bombs	US, USSR, Britain, France, China, Israel, India, Pakistan (for last 3 see foot of facing p. 274)
Depth charges	US, Britain, Netherlands, Spain, W Germany, Italy, USSR
Nuclear torpedoes	US, USSR (Britain and France research)
Sea mines	USSR, NATO
Land mines	NATO ones used to be in Turkey
Artillery	
SP	NATO (3 countries allow no nuclear warheads in their territory), Warsaw Pact (exc Poland and Romania)
Towed	NATO, Warsaw Pact (exc Poland and Czechoslovakia)
MRLS	US, Turkey

Note: Apart from Britain and France, all NATO and Warsaw Pact members would need US or Soviet permission to use nuclear weapons. Third World countries now possess many nuclear-capable launch systems, but for most of them reliable miniaturized nuclear warhead technology and accuracy is less easily acquired.

Anti-ballistic missile systems

Anti-Ballistic Missile or ABM systems use defensive, nuclear-tipped missiles to shoot down the enemy's attacking missiles. As such, they constitute a major factor in the nuclear competition between the superpowers. However, the SALT 1 agreement of 1972 between the USA and the USSR led to the dismantling of all ABM systems except one, defending Moscow. In March 1983 President Reagan announced the Strategic Defense Initiative or "Star Wars" program with the ultimate aim of making nuclear weapons harmless. He offered the Soviets the same shield, but President Gorbachev acknowledged a similar Russian scheme in 1987. Reduced funding and arms control makes SDI's future uncertain, but research and development continues.

Altitude of interception (right) ABM systems may be designed to intercept the attacking missiles above the earth's atmosphere (**1**). This method, known as exo-atmospheric interception, is preferable for several reasons, notably because the intruder need only be damaged, thus causing it to burn up on re-entry. Endo-atmospheric interception (**2**) may be used as a backup.

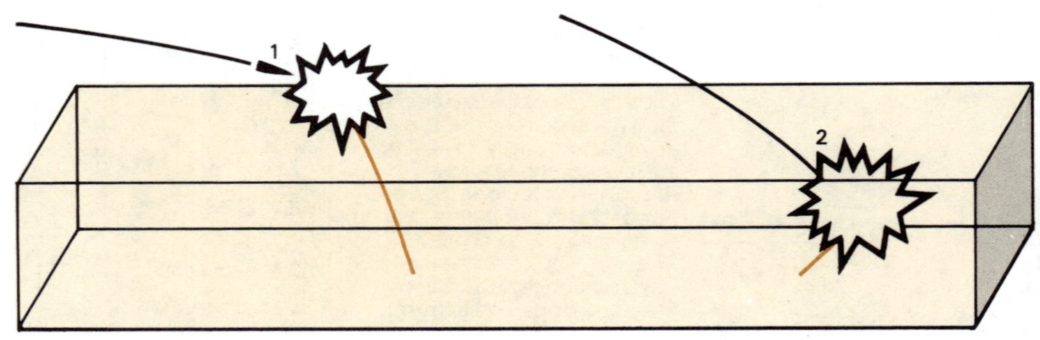

Galosh (right), as seen in a transportable container at a Red Square parade. This is the missile thought currently to be deployed on 16 launchers at the four remaining ABM sites around Moscow. It is believed to have a megaton-range warhead for interception above the atmosphere. Two improved ABMs, including a Galosh type, will fill the 100 launchers allowed.

Strategic defense (right) combines space and land-based ABM systems to detect and defeat in-coming nuclear missiles at every stage of their flight. Diagram based on an official US Army conceptual schema.

a ICBM launch
b Directed energy weapon fires during ICBM's boost rocket phase
c Neutral particle beam weapon attacks missile in midcourse
d Long wavelength infrared space probe tracks target
e Exoatmospheric ABM intercepts above earth's atmosphere
f Orbiting relay reflector focuses kinetic energy of ground-based weapon
g Airborne optical radar links
h Terminal imaging radar
i Last line of defense: Endo-atmospheric ABM intercepts
j ABM engages SLBM

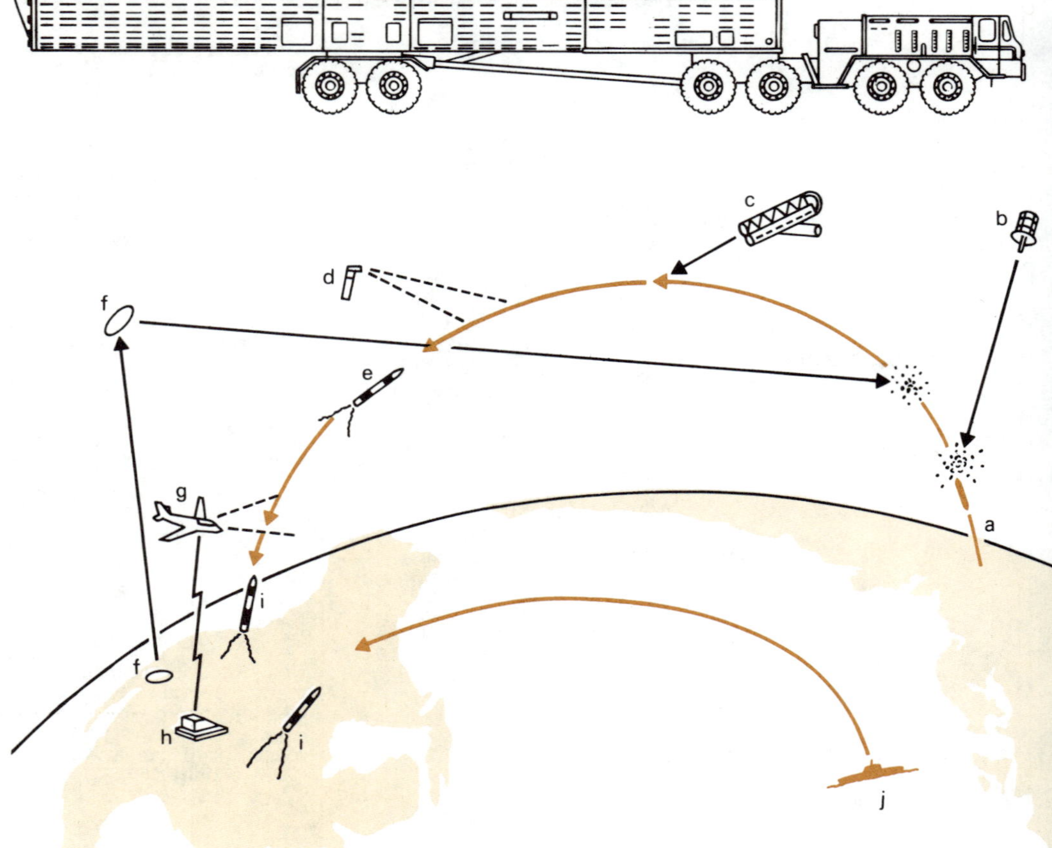

Biological weapons

Biological weapons seek to exploit man's natural susceptibility to disease, by deliberately spreading infection among the enemy. Despite attempts to limit the future use of such weapons by treaty or unilateral renunciation of "germ warfare," research continues in many countries. Here we explain possible means of dissemination, and list some likely diseases and relevant data.

Medieval germ warfare (below) The drawing, after a manuscript illustration, shows a dead horse about to be thrown into a besieged city to spread disease.

Delivery (right) of biological agents may be in aerosol form—that is to say, as finely divided particles of liquid or solid, distributed through a gas or air. The container may be a self-propelled missile (**a**) or a shell (**b**). Alternatively, "vectors" such as insects (**c**) or vermin (**d**) may be infected and released to spread the disease.

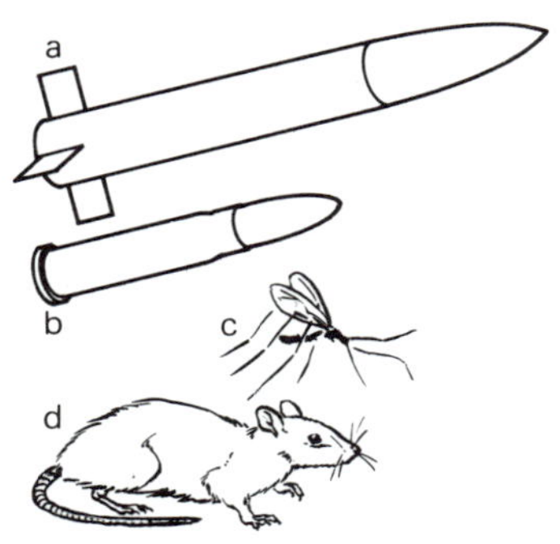

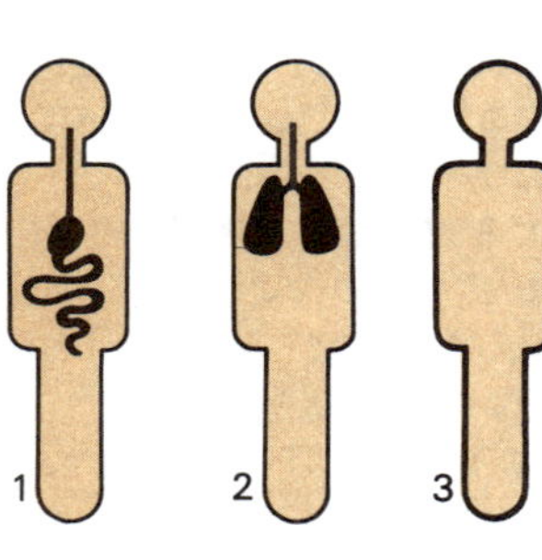

Main entry routes (left) into the human body for biological warfare agents.
1 Via the digestive system, in food or water.
2 Via the respiratory system, by inhaling micro-organisms in the air.
3 Through the skin, for example by insect bite. Of these routes, (2) is the most likely target for deliberate attack.

Types of agent (right) The headings in the table give the four main categories of possible biological warfare agent. Added under each is a list of specific diseases within that class.

Bacteria	Rickettsiae	Viruses	Fungi
Anthrax	African tick-borne fever	Encephalitis	Coccidioidomycosis
Brucellosis	Epidemic typhus	Influenza	Histoplasmosis
Cholera	Q-fever	Smallpox	Nocardiosis
Dysentery	Rocky Mountain spotted fever	West Nile fever	
Plague	Scrub typhus	Yellow fever	
Typhoid fever			

Table (right) giving data on a selection of likely biological warfare agents. The availability of vaccine for prevention does not imply 100% effectiveness.

Infectivity
- High
- Moderately high
- Low

Transmissibility
- High
- Moderate
- None

Antibiotic therapy
- None available
- Moderately effective
- Effective

Vaccination
- None
- Under development
- Available

Disease	Infectivity	Transmissibility	Incubation period (days)	Duration of illness (days)	Mortality	Antibiotic therapy	Vaccination
Encephalitis	High	None	5-15	7-60	1-80%	None available	Under development
Influenza	High	High	1-3	3-10	1%	None available	Available
Yellow fever	High	None	3-6	7-14	5-40%	None available	Available
Smallpox	High	High	7-16	12-24	5-60%	None available	Available
Epidemic typhus	High	None	6-15	14-60+	10-40%	Effective	Available
Anthrax	Moderately high	None	1-5	3-5	100%	Effective	Available
Brucellosis	High	None	7-21	14-60+	2-10%	Moderately effective	Under development
Cholera	Low	High	1-5	7-30+	5-75%	Moderately effective	Available
Pneumonic plague	High	High	2-5	1-2	100%	Moderately effective	Available
Typhoid fever	Moderately high	Moderate	7-21	14-60+	10%	Moderately effective	Available
Dysentery	High	High	1-3	3-21	2%	Effective	None

Chapter 8

THE THINKING BATTLEFIELD

Microelectronics have transformed modern weapon guidance systems, their sensors for detecting targets, and the fuzes for warheads to destroy them. Increasingly without direct human involvement, weapons are able to "think" for themselves once they have been fired, launched, or even just emplaced.
This new chapter attempts to chart key 1980s advances in weaponry that will affect the hardware carried well into the 21st century. It starts with the now rich arsenal available for internal security, from electrified nightsticks to armored riot control vehicles. The complete range of infantry weapons for the 1990s GI is detailed including Stinger-RMP and the M249 squad automatic. In artillery the highlights are the NATO Multiple Launch Rocket System (MLRS), binary chemical ammunition and self-propelled howitzer improvements. Anti-armor developments focus on "top attack" and fiber-optic missiles, and include ammunition becoming available to ordinary infantry mortars. Reactive armor and mechanized infantry combat vehicles form part of the defense half of the equation.
Aerospace coverage begins at battlefield level with the increasing refinement and development of anti-tank helicopters and remotely piloted vehicles. Higher in the sky the emphasis is on cluster bombs and runway denial systems with their growing range of submunitions. Armament for the new generation "stealth" technology aircraft is discussed. For space "Star Wars" developments, the reader should turn to p.276.
At sea the focus is on wire-guided torpedoes, sea skimming Exocet-type missiles and the revival of close-in weapon systems to defend valuable surface ships.
Few of these innovations constitute entirely new weapons, rather they represent quantum enhancements of existing technology or old ideas. It is increasingly difficult to classify weapons neatly by their purpose or arm of service, so versatile have they become. Similarly, sensors and guidance systems have become inseparable from the lethal part of the weapon.
High technology weapon costs have been a big inducement to the two superpower blocs to meet in meaningful arms control talks. Paradoxically, and in parallel, miniaturization and mass production have actually made some weapons simpler, cheaper and more accessible. Developing countries increasingly have arms industries of their own and since the mid-1980s the most threatening areas have been in chemical weapons ("the poor man's atomic bomb") and intermediate-range missile technology. Realistically, if bleakly, it is at this regional level and in countries' chronic internal strife down to the streets that the weapons of the future will actually be used. Elaborate, but treaty reduced and mutually-deterring, the strategic nuclear and lesser arsenals of NATO and the Warsaw Pact look like being an irrelevance in this kind of warfare.

Attack helicopters (right) are now very versatile weapons platforms. The US Army's AH-64 Apache (deployed since 1986) is a two-seater whose advanced sensors give it an all-weather, day and night capability (see pp. 290–291). They include a target acquisition designation sight and pilot night vision sensor, and a mast mounted sight. Armament includes the unusual underbelly Chain gun (see p. 290) and 8 TOW wire-guided or 16 Hellfire laser-guided anti-tank missiles. Alternatively, 4 2.75in (70mm) unguided 19-tube Hydra 70 rocket launchers can be carried with a choice of 8 warheads. Range 5mi (8km).

New technological directions

On these two pages we present a selection of recent and future weapons developments. Some take the form of improvements to an existing type of weapon that extend its usefulness. Others spring from general technological advances that have military applications. A few are entirely new destructive devices. Included also are devices that do not themselves kill, but are weapons in a more general sense.

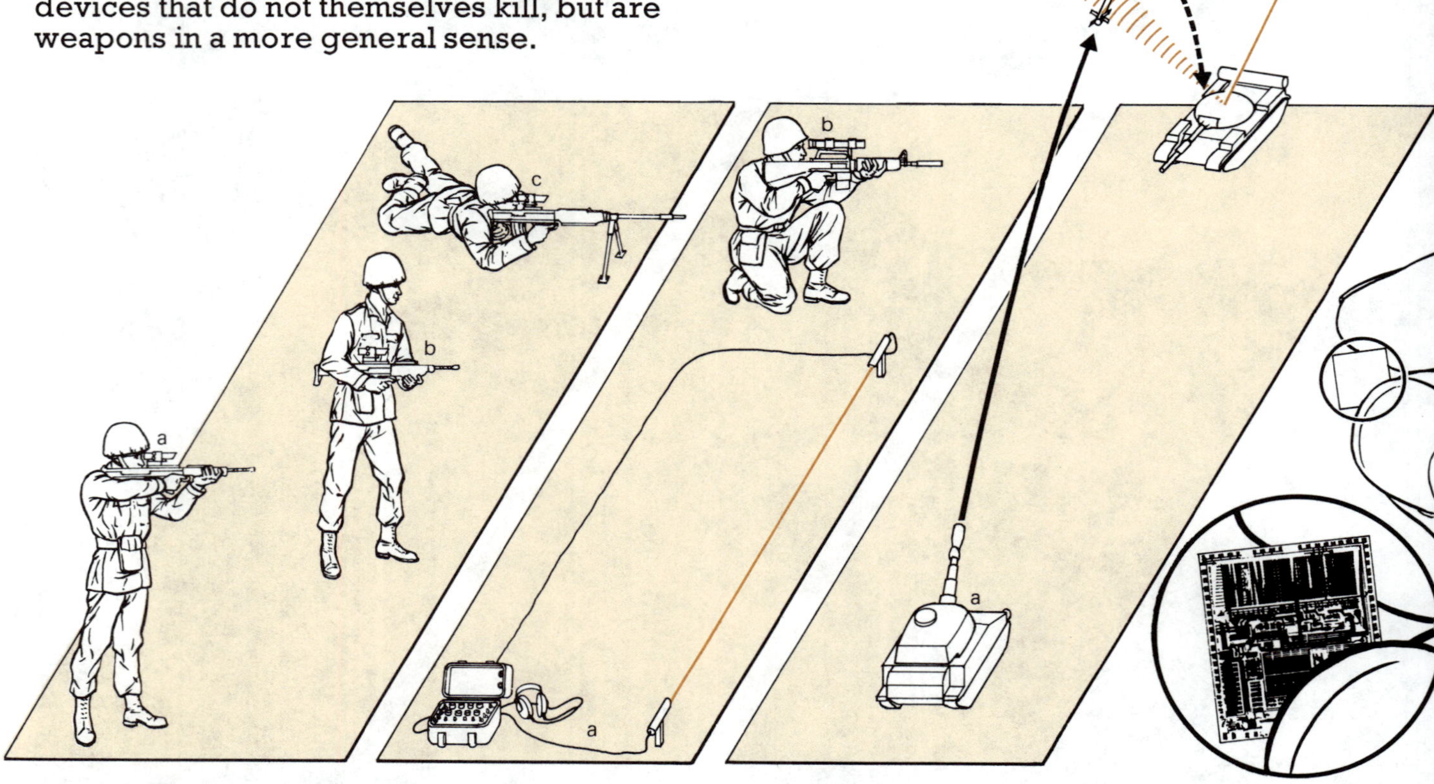

A better rifle (above) Even after 600 years of development, firearms are still being improved. The new service SA80 rifle for the British Army is easier for recruits and indifferent shooters to use accurately as a rifle (**a**), because of its low recoil and optical sights. It can be fired in bursts and is short and light enough to be used as a submachine gun (**b**). By exchanging a few components it can be adapted for use as a light machine gun (**c**). The cartridge for it is small and light, allowing more ammunition to be carried. The bullet flies on a flatter trajectory, so lessening the need for precise estimation of the range to the target. See p. 153 for its Individual Weapon foreunner and p. 284 for the bayonet.

Night surveillance aids (above) Future battles are likely to be fought at night, so much effort has been put into devising aids to night vision. Some take the form of intruder alarms (**a**) using, for example, an invisible beam or vibration-sensitive geophones, to warn of approaching enemy patrols. Another important device already in use is the passive night sight (**b**), that can intensify any ambient light (e.g. starlight) to permit one-color night vision. Such image intensifiers do not emit detectable rays, as did infrared sights, and thus are even harder for the enemy to detect. Image intensifiers can be used for general surveillance or as weapon sights.

Copperhead (above) is the name of a US Army project for developing a terminally guided anti-tank shell. This Cannon-Launched Guided Projectile (CLGP) is fired from a standard 155mm howitzer (**a**), and after leaving the barrel, fins fold out from the sides. As it approaches the target area (beyond the vision of the howitzer crew), an enemy tank is selected by a forward observer on the ground or one of several types of airborne surveillance craft (**b**). The observer illuminates the tank with a laser beam, so producing a "signature" on to which sensors in the projectile can direct it in the last few seconds of flight. Copperhead is thus a new departure, combining advantages of indirect artillery fire and guided missiles (see p. 286–287).

Silicon chip (above) The much-publicized silicon chip or microprocessor is certain to find many warlike applications. By making computers cheaper and smaller it will make them more readily available in quantity for existing roles, such as artillery target data processors. The miniaturization of computers will be especially advantageous in all airborne applications, such as missile guidance systems, and in satellites. The silicon chip is a classic instance of an improvement in general technology that has important military uses.

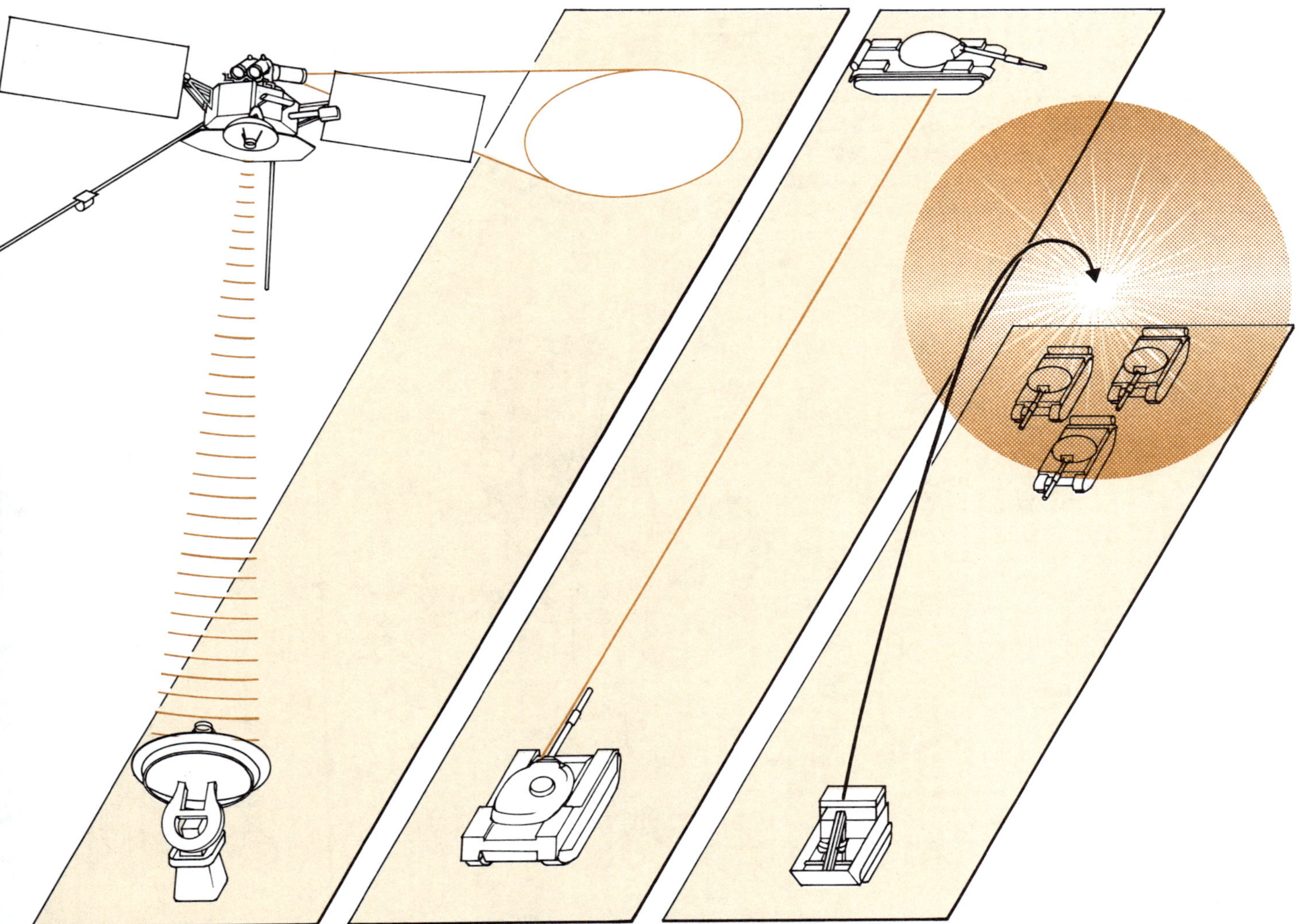

Satellite warfare
Military competition in space has already begun. Although the Outer Space Treaty of 1967 banned the positioning of weapons of mass destruction in space, satellites may still fill many military roles. The USA, USSR and China have launched military satellites of their own or for allies, and France followed in 1983. A satellite usually has one specific role, such as the early warning of missile attack, navigation and guidance, or communications. Remote sensing satellites for reconnaissance (above) can already detect individual foxholes on a battlefield. The USA and USSR have both been developing ASAT (anti-satellite) weapons to destroy hostile space vehicles.

Lasers are already in use as a part of various weapon systems, but not yet as the means of destruction itself. They can be used to mark targets onto which guided missiles can then home in. They are also coming into use as rangefinder/sighting systems for tanks (above). In this role they can replace ranging machine guns (explained on p.197). The advantage of a destructive agent that travels at the speed of light in straight lines with great accuracy is especially attractive for shooting down aircraft and missiles. However, the ranges attained in tests are said to be short. In space, high-energy lasers are being investigated for use in destroying enemy satellites.

Neutron "bombs" (above) or enhanced radiation warheads, are an entirely new category of nuclear weapon. The blast and heat effects from the explosion are minimal, but it emits a massive dose of enhanced neutron and gamma radiation that can penetrate thick armor plate or several feet of earth, and is highly destructive to living tissue. The US neutron warhead project, postponed in 1978, was for the production of warheads for the Lance tactical missile, and for 8in (203mm) and 155mm howitzer shells as a mass anti-armor weapon. These would be fired (above) to explode perhaps 650ft (200m) above the ground, disabling enemy tank crews within minutes, and leading to their deaths within days. Production resumed in 1981, but is limited to 925 shells.

Electronic warfare (EW) is a term that covers many activities, some of which are carried on in peacetime. It includes electronic reconnaissance, which covers activities such as listening in to radio traffic during maneuvers, to discover a potential enemy's organizational structure and level of efficiency. EW also includes Electronic Countermeasures (ECM). The increasing dependence of armies and their weapon systems on electronic aids such as radar prompts opponents to interfere with such systems through ECM. Communications may be jammed, or missile guidance hindered. These measures in turn prompt enemy Electronic Counter-Countermeasures (ECCM). EW is now closely related to satellite warfare.

Internal security weapons

Perhaps the largest expansion has been in the paramilitary field of anti-riot equipment and counter-terrorism. This weaponry confronts urban violence, both with firearms and without, and international terrorism, exemplified by the modern Czech-made plastic explosive Semtex used in such devices as letter bombs (of 1920s origin).

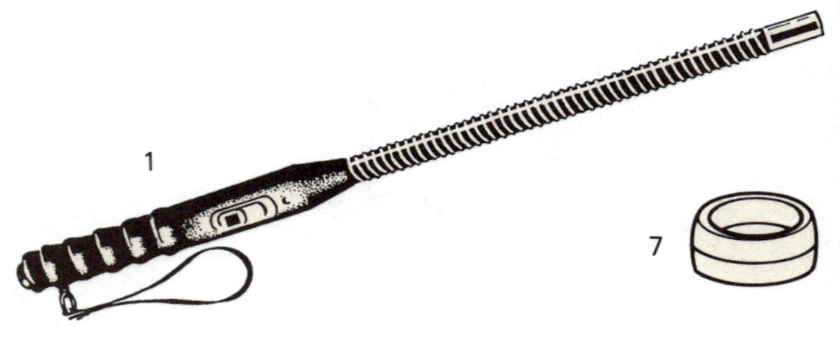

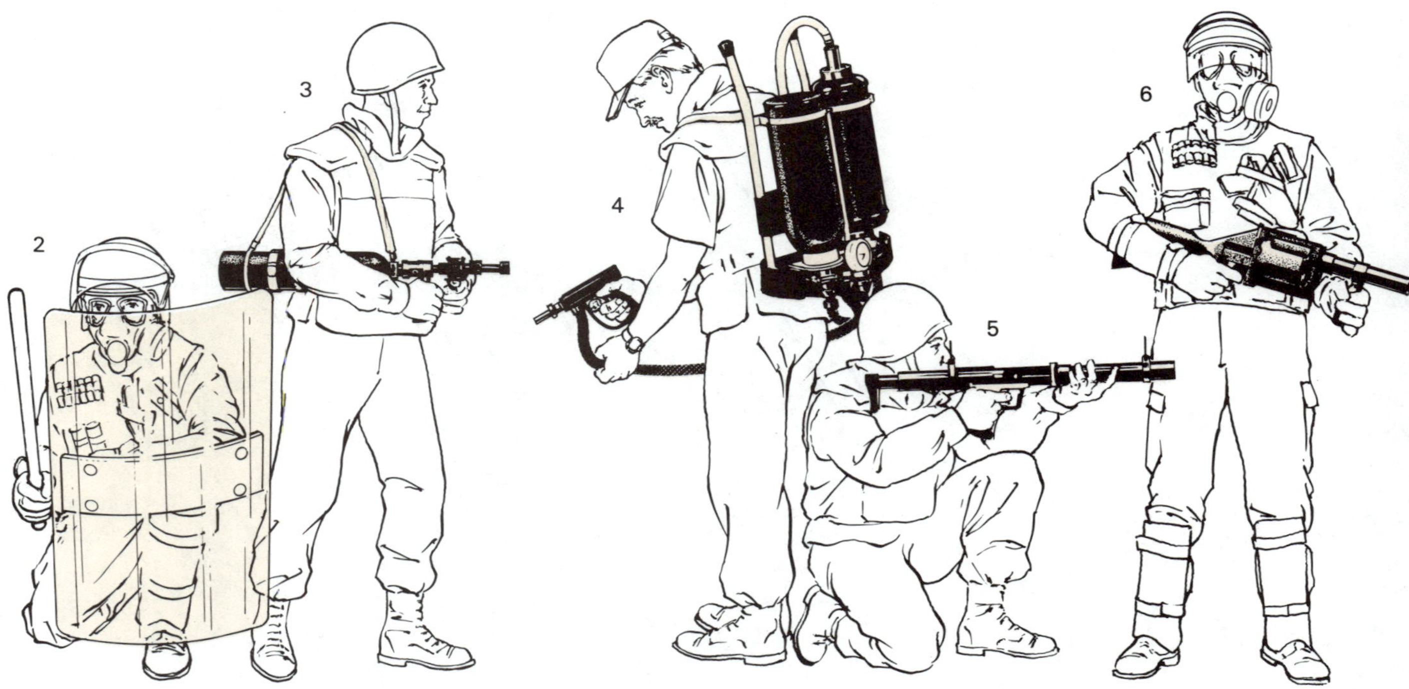

Personal weapons
1 Shockstick, SAS Developments SA121 adds a 6000-7000V local shock and crackling noise to the ordinary riot stick. Length 22¾in (57.8cm). Weight 12lb (0.54kg); sold to US police.
2 Riot policeman's snatch squad shield made of transparent polycarbonate. Dimensions 35.4in x 23.6in x 0.118in (90 x 60 x 3mm). Weight 4lb (1.8kg).
3 Projectojet CS fog projector (Israeli) to neutralize rioters 3yds each side of its 50ft (15m) range. Weight under 19.8lb (9kg).
4 Tear gas back pack dispenser (French Alsatex) Minimum range 32ft (10m). Weight 35-47lb (16-21.5kg) depending on whether gel, powder or liquid is loaded.
5 Anti-riot weapon (British Arwen Ace 37) fires five different types of ammunition accurately: AR1 kinetic energy baton round to "discourage" a rioter at 109yds (100m); AR2 multi-source irritant smoke round; AR3 frangible nose baton round with 2gm of CS powder; AR4 smoke screening round; AR5 barricade penetrating irritant round with CS powder to penetrate up to ½in (13mm). Caliber 37mm. Rate of fire 12rpm. Weight 4.6lb (2.1kg), lighter than its competitors; 500 sold to US police forces 1984-88.
6 Multi-shot riot gun (British Excalibur) carried by policeman in overalls, body armor and riot helmet with gas mask. Excalibur holds five 38mm rounds. Weight 8.8lb (4kg); 300 sold to Malaysia.
7 Soft/Sting rag ring airfoil grenade (US Edgewood Arsenal) for military police to fire from the standard M16 rifle. Soft rag contains CS powder.
8 Zigzag tear gas grenade (French Alsatex Gendarmerie model) designed with jacket and nozzle to be jerky when thrown and to bounce on the ground so rioters cannot throw it back.
9 Stun or flash bomb (French Alsatex model) gives one or more loud bangs and a bright flash for use against crowds or hostage-holding terrorists. First used on an hijacked airliner at Mogadishu, Somalia 1977 by German SAS-aided troops.
10 Baton rounds Better known as plastic or rubber bullets and first used in 1960s Hong Kong.
a British 1.5in plastic baton round to cause severe bruising at 65yds (60m).
b British 1.5in rubber baton round, similar but cheaper. Weight 6oz (170g), MV 328ft/sec (100/sec). Fired at too close range, 22yd (20m) or less these can be lethal projectiles.

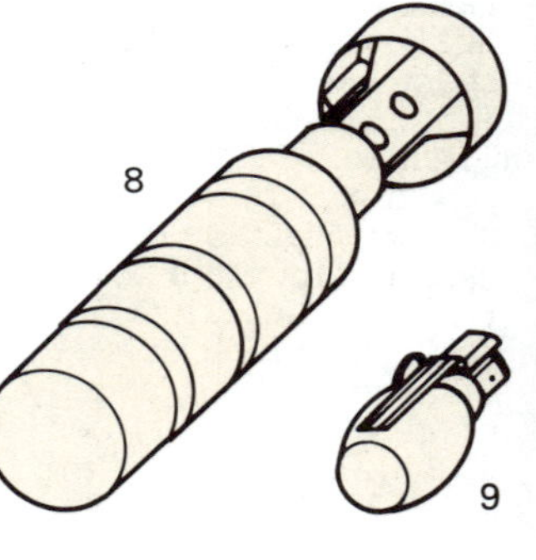

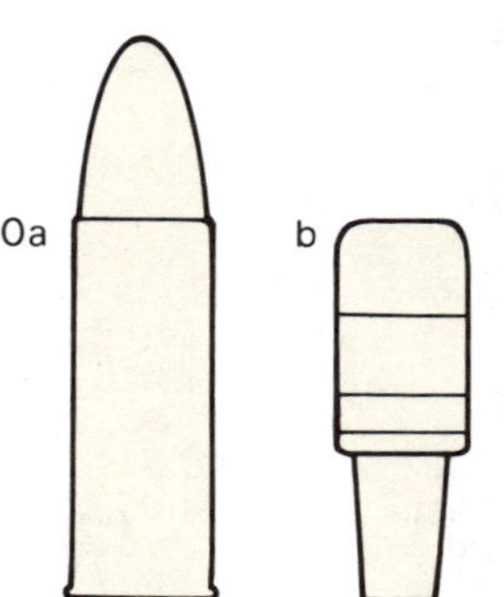

Internal security vehicles
These range from the simple patrol car to a fighting fortress like the AMAC. They can be fitted with bulldozer blades to push apart barricades and wire mesh screens as "people pushers" or police cover. Tear gas or smoke launchers can be fitted on if not part of the design.

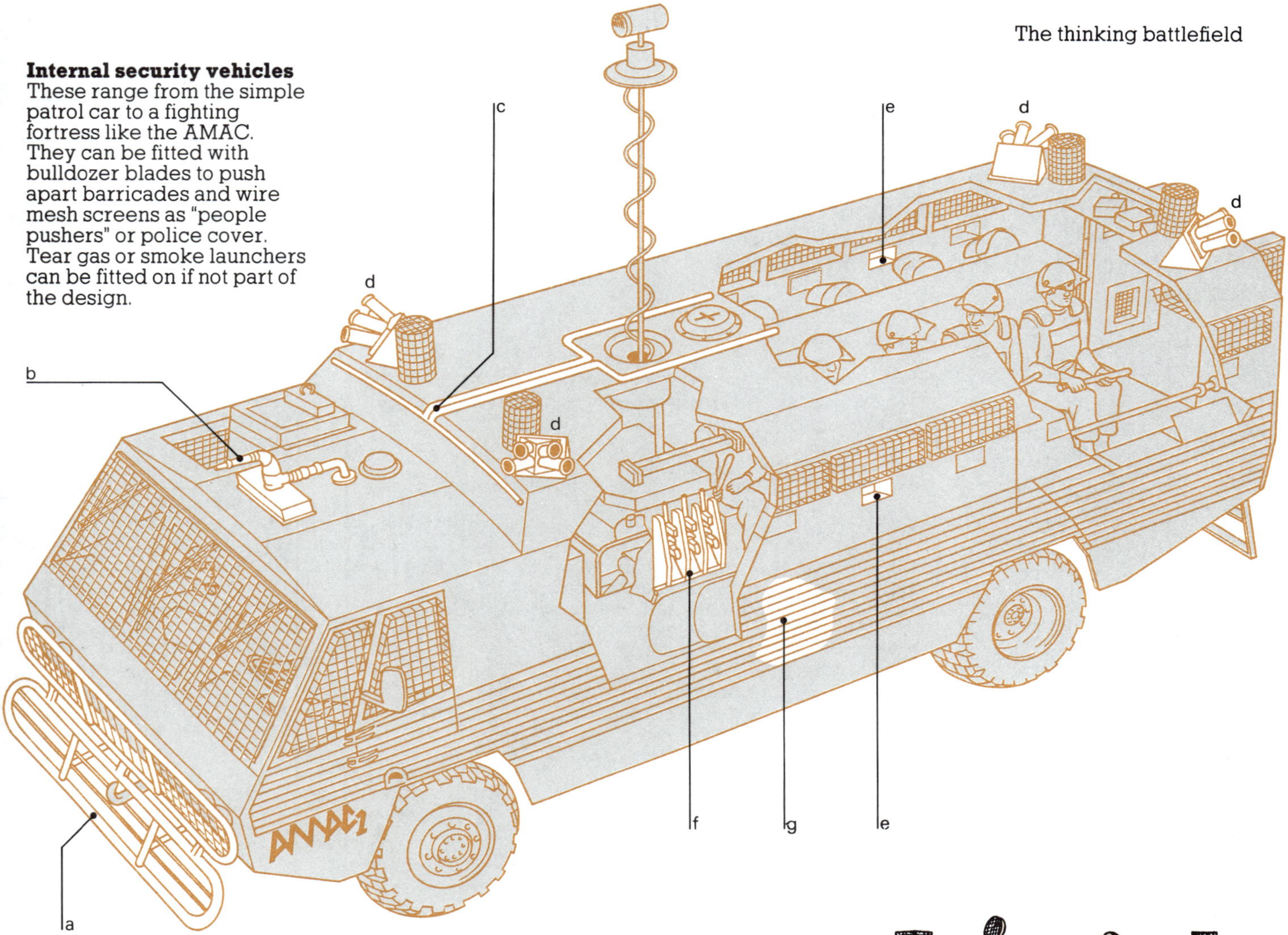

Armored mobile anti-riot control unit (AMAC) carries 12 security personnel at up to 55mph (88kph).
Pure water cannon (used since the 1960s) have the drawback of not enough water for sustained use, although by mixing CS or colored dye rioters can be further suppressed or marked for arrest. Sometimes a better use is dowsing burning barricades.
a Barricade remover
b Water cannon
c Water cascade pipes for keeping sides slippery
d 16 grenade launchers
e 18 weapon ports
f Weapon rack
g Electrically "live" bodywork to deter attackers

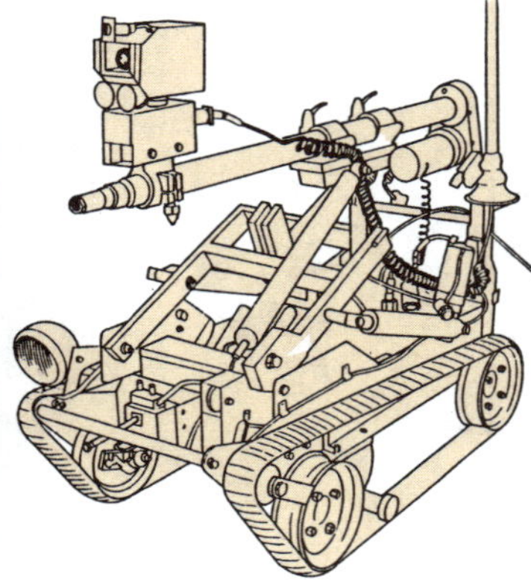

Remotely controlled bomb disposal vehicle (Morfax Wheelbarrow) in service since 1972 and first of many such tracked or wheeled robotic units for detonating terrorist explosive without exposing the human operator. Closed circuit TV camera examines suspect object while the operator controls it from up to 328yd (300m) away with cable or radio control. It can fire a shotgun charge to open a locked car door and/or disrupt a suspect bomb's circuitry. Endurance on electric batteries is about 2hrs. Such Explosive Ordnance Disposal (EOD) vehicles have helped the British Army dispose of 2767 tons of explosive in 40,000 bomb alerts and save an estimated $700 million of property damage in Northern Ireland (1969-89).

Hotspur Hussar Armored Land Rover (above) is a 6-wheel patrol vehicle able to carry 8 men. It has a barricade remover, spotlight and public address system.

Infantry weapons

No real revolution has occurred in infantry small arms. The trend towards greater lightness, accuracy and rates of fire has continued. Caseless ammunition being developed for next generation turn-of-the-century rifles may lead to a doubling (approximately) of the individual rifleman's magazine capacity and number of rounds carried.

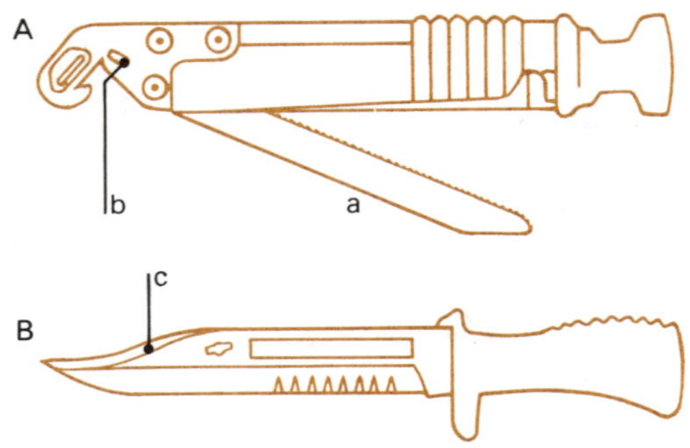

SA80 bayonet (above)
A Scabbard unit with hacksaw blade for wire-cutting (**a**). Bayonet blade fits onto lug (**b**).
B Knife bayonet with wire-cutting edge (**c**). Blade and handle are made of one casting. The British infantry SA80 bayonet, like most modern rifles' edged weapons, is more of a multi-purpose combat knife than the old-style thrusting bayonet.

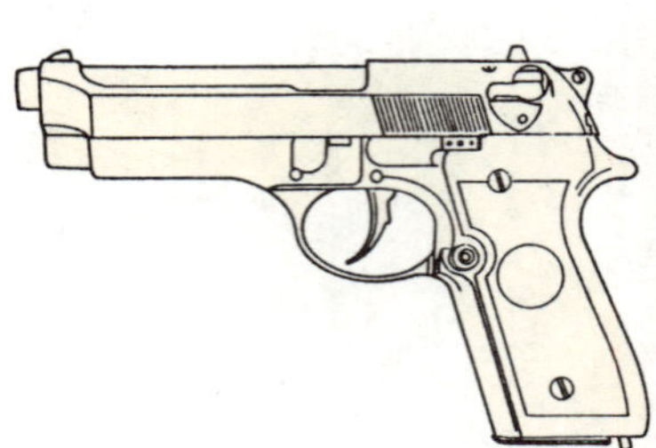

M9 Beretta 92 SB pistol (above) This weapon is replacing the veteran M1911A1.45 caliber pistol, arguably the longest serving side arm this century (see p. 147). M9 is lighter, safer and more lethal, firing standard NATO ammunition. Delivery of 315,930 pistols began in July 1986 for non-rifle carrying US personnel, aviators, military police, etc. 15-round magazine. Caliber 9mm.

Weapons of the 1990s US infantryman (up to company level)

- M9 multi-purpose bayonet
- 5.56mm M16A2 rifle (Advance Combat Rifle being designed for c2000)
- 7.62mm M24 Remington bolt-action sniper rifle (10x scope)
- 5.56mm M249 squad automatic weapon (see below)
- 40mm M203 grenade launcher (see p.154)
- 66mm M72A3 light anti-tank weapon (LAW) (see p.254 for A2); 84mm AT4 to replace.
- 40mm MK19-3 automatic grenade launcher (vehicle-mounted)
- 60mm M224 lightweight company mortar
- 81mm M252 improved medium mortar (armored and mechanized infantry)
- Stinger-RMP shoulder-fired, infrared homing anti-aircraft missile (see pp.256-257)
- Dragon M47 medium-range, wire-guided anti-tank missile with improved warhead (see p.254). Advanced Anti-Tank Weapon System – Medium under development

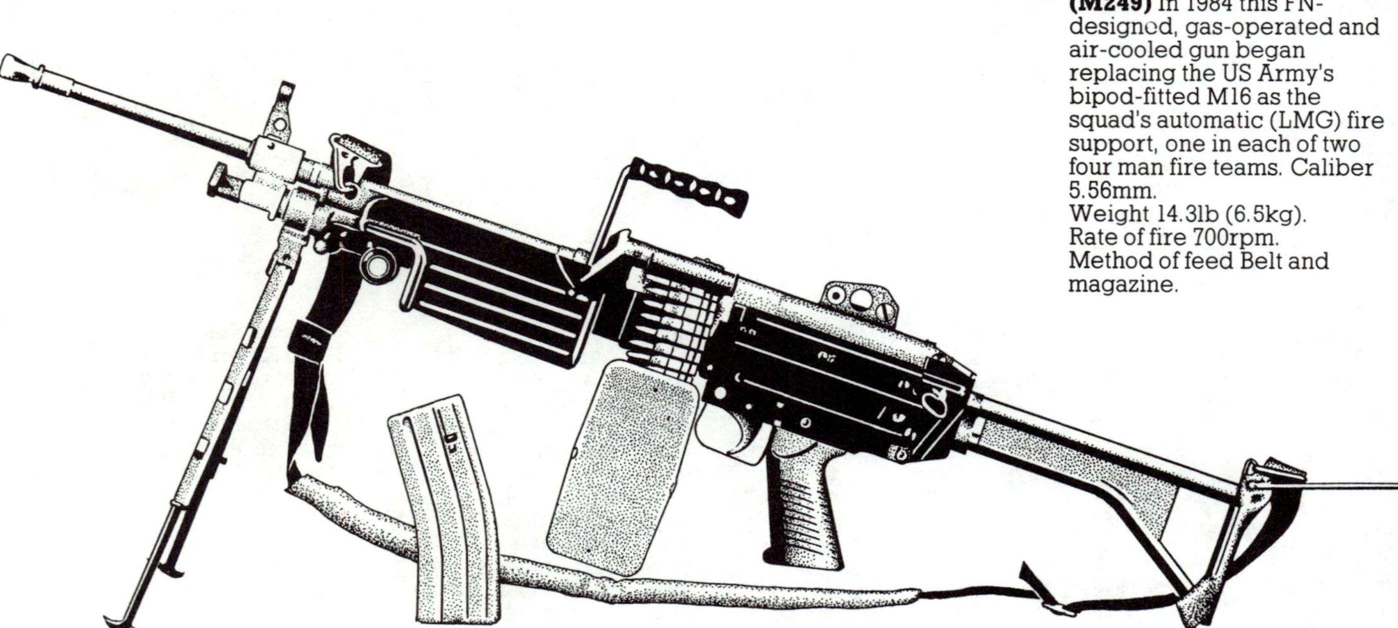

Squad automatic weapon (M249) In 1984 this FN-designed, gas-operated and air-cooled gun began replacing the US Army's bipod-fitted M16 as the squad's automatic (LMG) fire support, one in each of two four man fire teams. Caliber 5.56mm.
Weight 14.3lb (6.5kg).
Rate of fire 700rpm.
Method of feed Belt and magazine.

Caseless ammunition (right). This much-sought solution may increase infantry firepower. Caseless ammunition has a bullet fixed in a surround of explosive propellant (**a**). It has the advantage of weight saving, vital for the heavily loaded rifleman, as well as eliminating the need for a conventional cartridge (**b**) extraction system.
1 Primer
2 Propellant
3 Projectile
4 Booster mix (for propelling bullet into rifling before gas leakage can happen)
5 Brass cartridge case
6 Plastic end seal (ejected from muzzle)

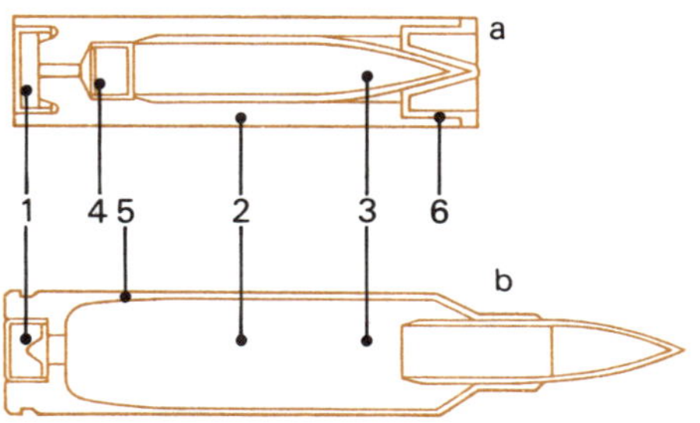

West German G11 rifle (far right) has a magazine feeding a caseless round into a rotating cylinder that aligns the round with the breech and fires. This small caliber Heckler & Koch design fires single shots or a 3-round burst from a 50-round magazine. The round can penetrate a NATO steel helmet at 656yd (600m). G11 is sole caseless contender for the NATO Advanced Combat Rifle design. Caliber 4.7mm

Ground sensors Although not themselves lethal weapons, hand emplaced or air delivered ground sensors, first widely used in 1970s Vietnam, form part of the layout for modern defenses with positioned weapons. They work on seismic, sound or metallic signals. The British Racal Classic system links up to 8 sensors with a monitor. The sensor uses a geophone or infrared detector and has signal-processing circuitry to classify the intruder and broadcast the result to the monitor which can display the information on an electronic screen or even print it out. Sensors may be buried, emplaced in cover or just camouflaged. The US Army Remotely Monitored Battlefield Sensor System (REMBASS) entered service in 1987.

Thermal Imaging While strictly not a weapon, thermal or heat imaging is the most sophisticated day and night vision equipment entering service and will change the character of warfare in the future. It detects and displays on a screen the minute differences in temperature between animate and inanimate objects. Hot engines in vehicles show clearly while men and equipment can be seen through conventional visual camouflage. Thermal imaging can also be used to find unconscious people in smoke-filled rooms or people trapped in rubble from collapsed buildings.

Protection & detection devices Razor barbed wire has existed for about 75 years (see p.223). By fitting a fiber-optic core to the wire a very effective perimeter security system is created. As an intruder struggles in the wire the fiber-optic core is broken and this sends a signal showing where on the perimeter an intrusion has taken place.

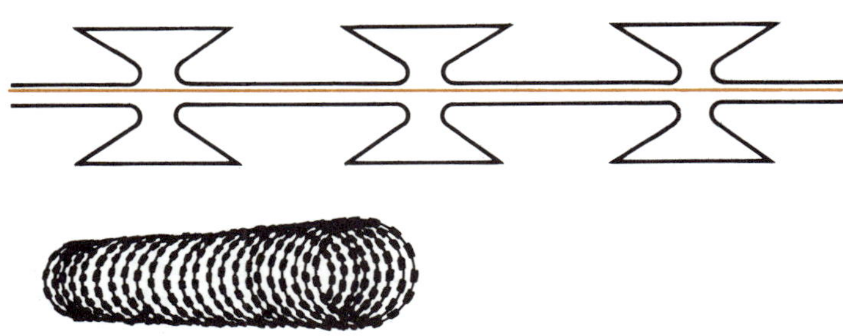

Artillery systems

Conventional artillery remains both towed and self-propelled, but the 1980s advent of terminally guided shells and binary chemical ammunition has vastly increased its hitting power and accuracy. Automated loading has reduced the size of human gun crews and better fire control means using less ammunition to destroy the target.

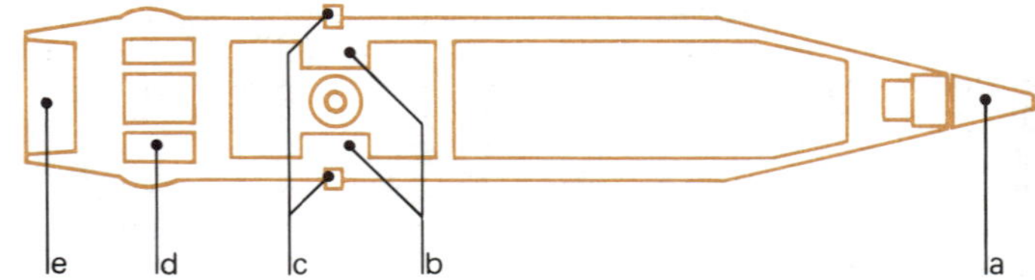

a Warhead fuze
b Fuel
c Venturi
d Guidance
e Tracer flare

Vickers AS90 155mm The new self-propelled howitzer ordered by the British Army in 1989 to replace its aging US-made M109A2/A3 (see p.187), a gun in NATO service since 1963. AS90 is not radically different, but has a crew of five not six plus room for improvements and longer barrels. Hydogas suspension allows higher cross-country speeds than conventional torsion bar systems, thus aiding swifter changes of firing position. Semi-automatic loading could be changed to a robotic system. The computer-based gunlaying system has optical and inertial navigation options.
Caliber 6.1in (155mm)
Range 27,012yd (24,700km) with standard ammunition
Max speed 33mph (53kmh)

Multiple Launch Rocket System MLRS is NATO's belated counter to the vast family of Soviet multiple rocket launchers developed since 1941 (see p.252). Delivered as M270 to the US Army since 1983 and to Turkey (1988); four nations have it on trial. MLRS fires 12 8.9in (22.7cm) unguided rockets from two self-contained six-round pods, either singly or in ripple fire lasting under a minute. The 13ft (4m) long rockets carry the M77 warhead with up to 644 submunitions for anti-personnel or anti-tank use. A terminal guidance warhead design was begun in 1985 and a binary chemical projectile has been developed. Computerized fire control makes MLRS far more lethal than the old-style area bombardment rockets.

Guided shells (left) Before firing, target details are fed to the shell thus programing it to follow the target. Venturi tubes on the shell allow course correction.
Copperhead, the first of its kind (see p.280), has been in US artillery service since 1980, its range is 10 miles (16km).

Binary chemical shell (right) This is a revolutionary step up from the ordinary gas shell basically unchanged since WW1 (see p.269). Instead of one lethal agent the 1980s binary shell has two harmless chemicals that only mix into nerve gas after the shell is fired.

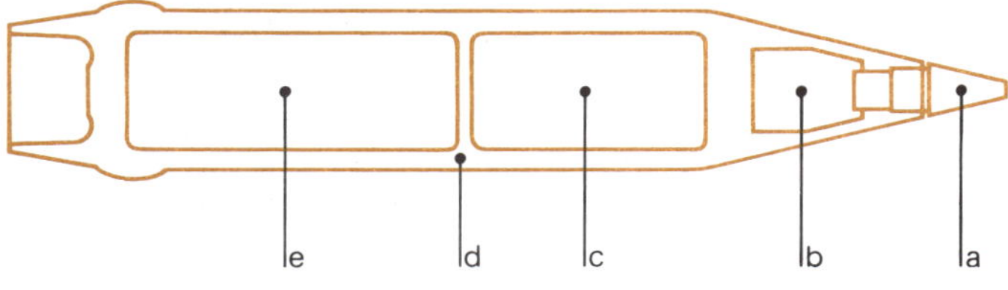

a Fuze
b Distributor
c Nose chemical reactant
d Separator
e Tail chemical reactant

Air Defence Anti-Tank System is the modern mobile missile concept of the old dual-purpose German 88mm AA and anti-tank gun (see p.195). Developed by Switzerland and the USA, this tracked, eight-launcher vehicle can engage both ground and aerial targets in what is fashionably known as AirLand Battle (US Army doctrine), the increasingly interlocked battlefield of the 1980s and beyond. One internationally designed vehicle with a common missile for two major fighting roles could mean fewer weapon systems at lower unit cost, a doubly desirable aim in an era of both superpower and European arms control and reductions. ADATS is laser-guided with TV, optic and infrared sensors.

Bradley fighting vehicle From being a battlefield "taxi" the armored personnel carrier has developed into the expensive mechanized infantry combat vehicle (MICV) with light direct-fire artillery in gun (cannon) and or missile form, plus enabling its infantry to fire small arms through ports from the moving vehicle. Bradley has a 1in (25mm) cannon in an automatically stabilized two-man turret; a coaxial 7.62mm MG; twin-tube TOW anti-tank missile launcher on the turret side (see pp.254-255); and 6 small arms firing ports covering the sides and rear. Delivery of over 10,000 Bradleys to the US Army began in 1983. The Soviet BMP with 73mm (2.8in) smoothbore cannon was the first MICV in 1967.

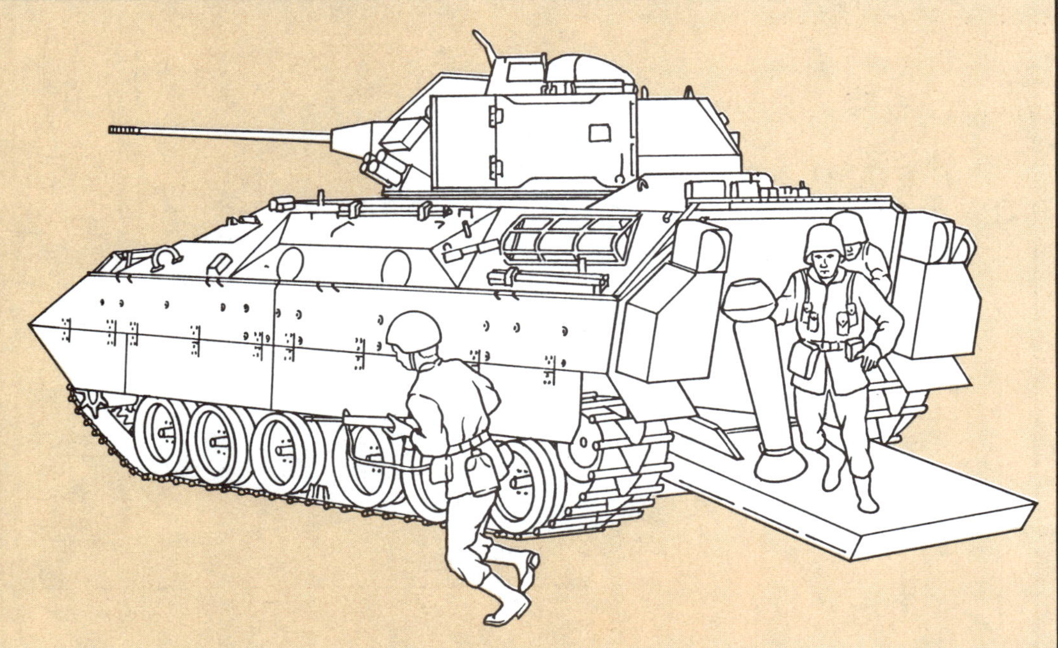

Anti-armor weapons

Top attack "fire and forget" missiles are beginning to make direct fire, line of sight weapons obsolete, but reactive armor has given combat vehicles an active form of protection to add to passive armor made of ever more advanced materials. Making mortars tank killers is probably the outstanding development.

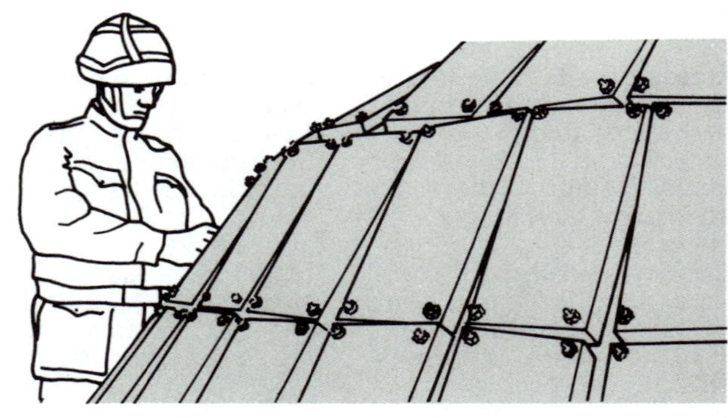

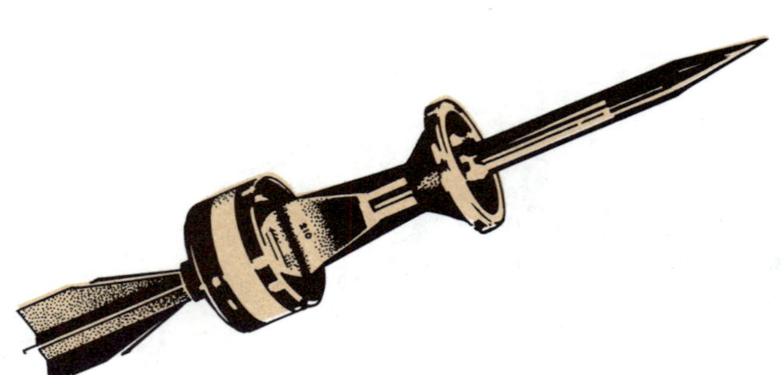

APFSDS or Armor-Piercing Fin Stabilized Discarding Sabot (left) takes the APDS concept (see p. 199) further. The solid shot is replaced by a super-hardened finned dart with a sharp and very hard point. The point will bite into angled armor and not glance off; some APFSDS have even penetrated despite glancing off tank gun barrels. Calibers 30mm-120mm.

Reactive armor (above) A secret technology first mentioned after 1982 when the Israelis captured a Syrian Soviet-made T62 tank in Lebanon's Bekaa valley. Reactive armor comes as boxlike slabs attached to an AFV's existing armor. A HEAT-shaped charge strike triggers a defensive reactive explosive that prevents penetration. Tandem anti-armor warheads are being tried to defeat it.

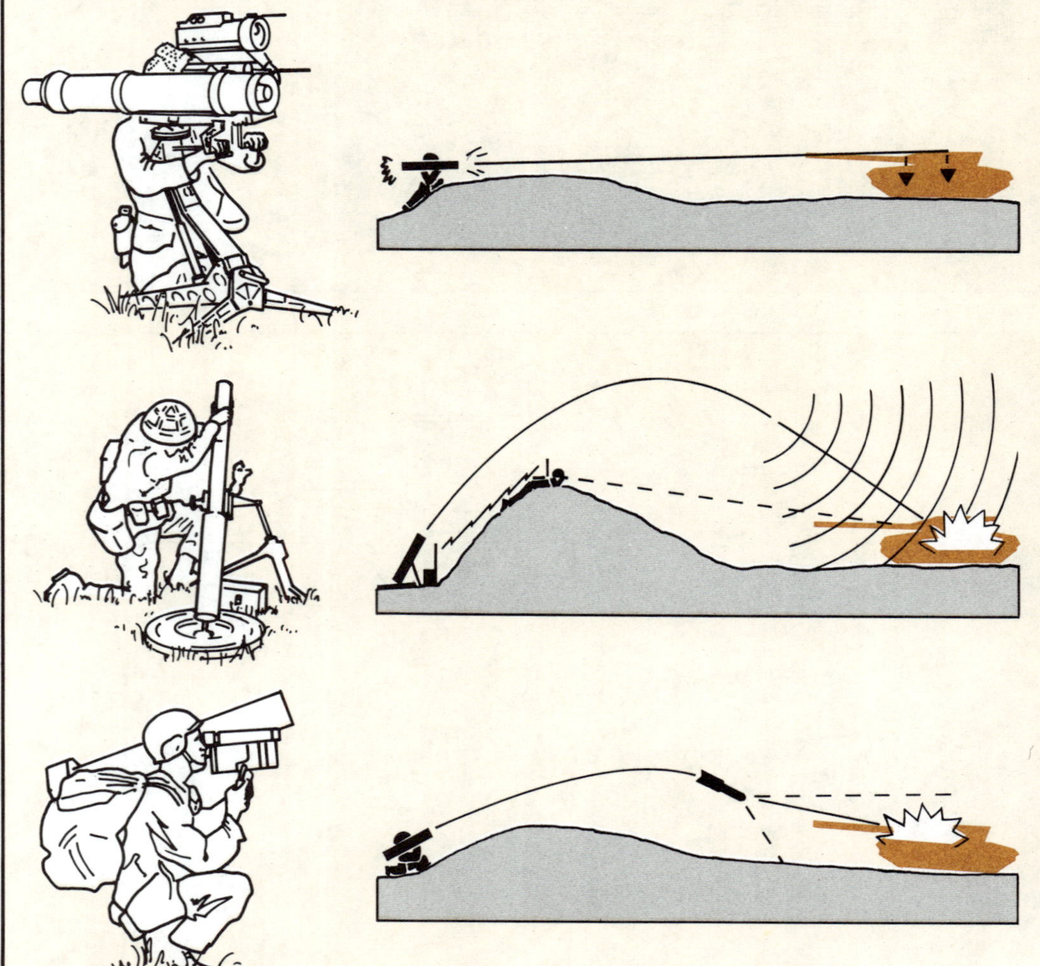

Top attack anti-tank missile does as the term suggests. It is wire-guided and the operator keeps the target in its sights as the missile moves into position above the target, then its onboard sensor triggers a downward-facing shaped charge which penetrates the driver's compartment, turret or engine. Sweden's Bofors

Guided anti-armor mortar ammunition is another form of top attack. Mortar fire controller observes enemy armor and sends its position to the mortar crew who fire a fin-stabilized bomb that homes on the target using millimetric radar in the nose to search a 328yd (300m) square area. The MERLIN system will give the British

Fiber-optic guided missile allows its operator to take cover after locating and engaging the target. A TV camera in the missile nose relays pictures (dashed lines) to the operator's sight allowing him to correct the flight path via the unjammable fiber-optic link.

Off-route mines (right) are getting near the non-human automated battlefield in which war is waged without troops. MINOS is a French Matra one-shot anti-tank weapon with a programed sensor head. It is installed to cover a minefield gap or a defile by firing at the targets it is instructed to engage. Two men with a truck could install such weapons along an entire defensive position days or weeks before an enemy advances into it.

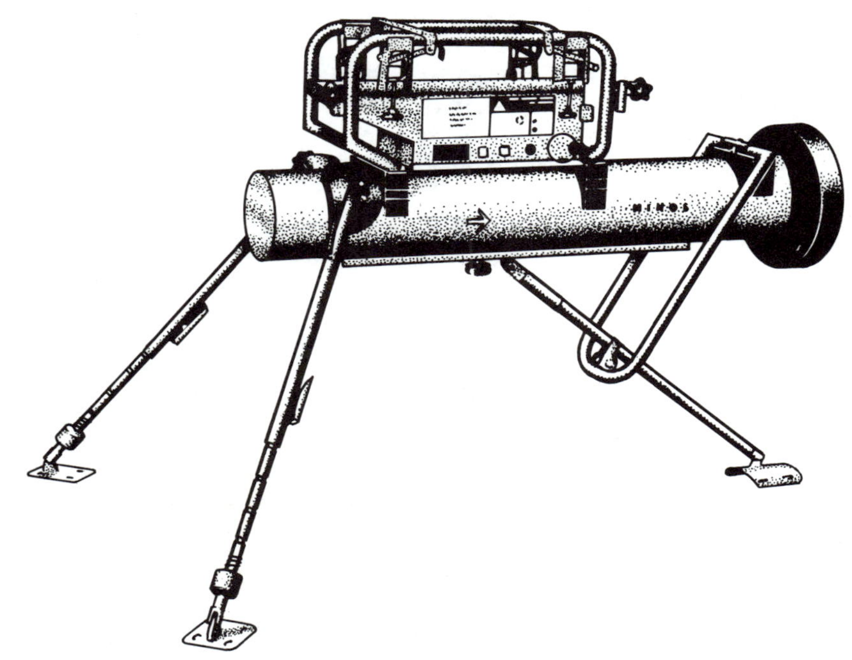

BILL system is an example of this method of attacking thinner top armor.

infantry 81mm mortar a revolutionary anti-armor capability from c1991 at ranges up to 4384yd (4000m), greater than conventional anti-tank missiles and much cheaper. Sweden's Strix system is for the 120mm mortar.

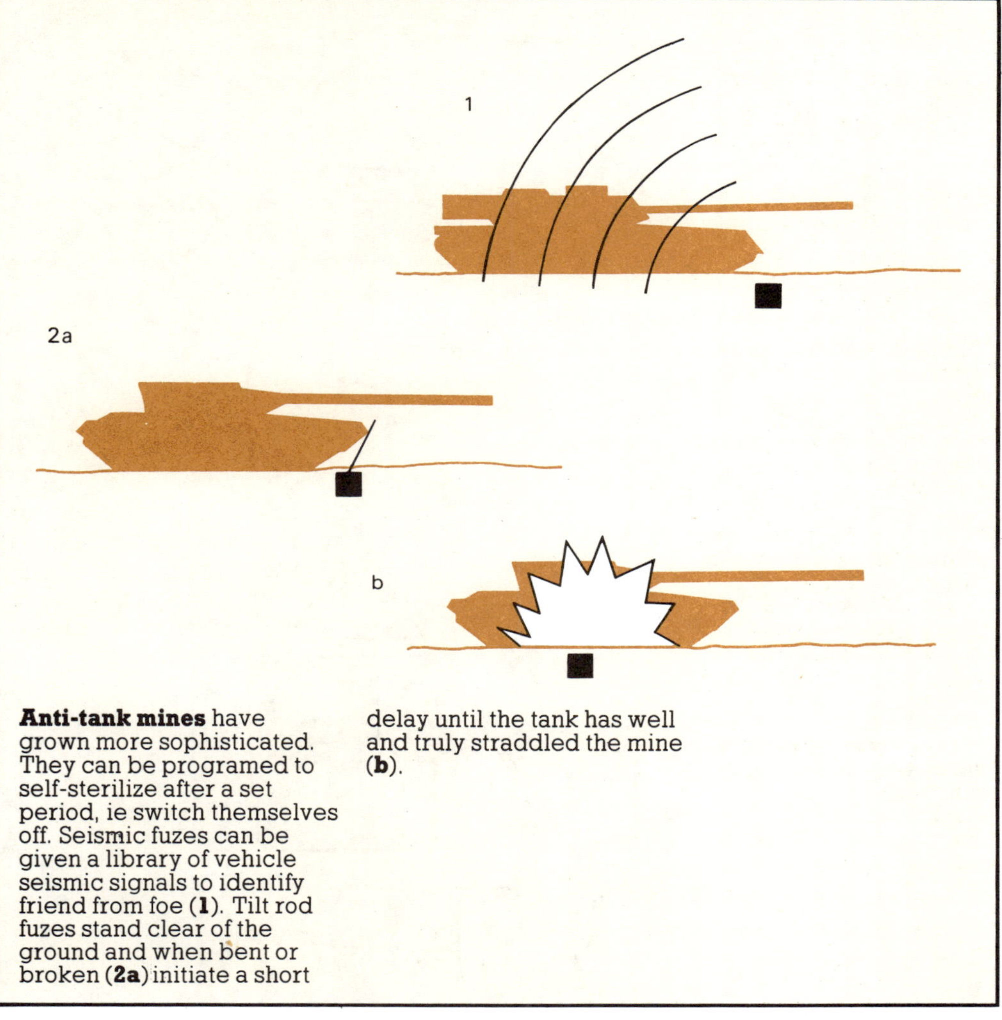

Anti-tank mines have grown more sophisticated. They can be programed to self-sterilize after a set period, ie switch themselves off. Seismic fuzes can be given a library of vehicle seismic signals to identify friend from foe (**1**). Tilt rod fuzes stand clear of the ground and when bent or broken (**2a**) initiate a short delay until the tank has well and truly straddled the mine (**b**).

Helicopter armament and RPVs

The technology of the tactical air battlefield centers on the role of helicopters, both assault and anti-tank varieties, and to a lesser extent remotely piloted vehicles or drones. Who should control these low-level weapons, army or air force? Different countries have different answers.

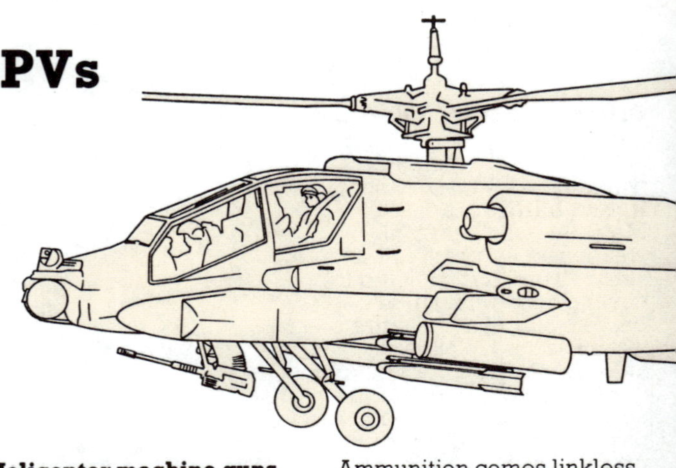

Helicopter machine guns (above) have developed advanced mounting and loading systems like the US 30mm M230 Chain gun for the Army's AH-64 Apache anti-tank helicopter deployed since 1986. The electric drive turret can turn 100° each way, 11° up to 60° down. The gun can be aimed by the AH-64's nose sensors or by either of the crew's helmet sighting systems. Ammunition comes linkless from a 1200-round box near the center of gravity. It feeds the gun along the starboard side and removes empty cases via the port side. A turret control box relays the gun 10 times a second after recoil. If there is a crash the gun comes up harmlessly between cockpits.

a

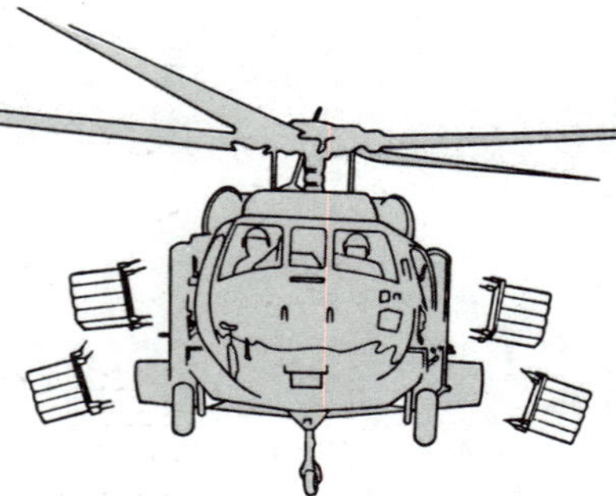

b

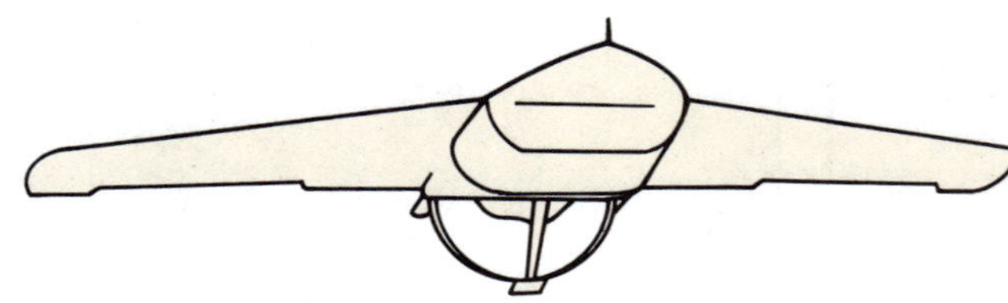

Air-launched landmine systems (above) are a growth area. From simple dropping (see p.230) and ramp delivery, the Italians have designed a suspended form of magazine dispenser (**a**) with up to 64 chutes holding 1536 anti-personnel scatter mines or 32 chutes dispensing 128 anti-tank mines, or a combination. The US Volcano system (**b**), proved in 1987, is a fixed tube dispenser in which 4 racks of 40 mine canisters each are ejected from a Black Hawk helicopter's sides. Up to 960 mines are randomly scattered into the target area.

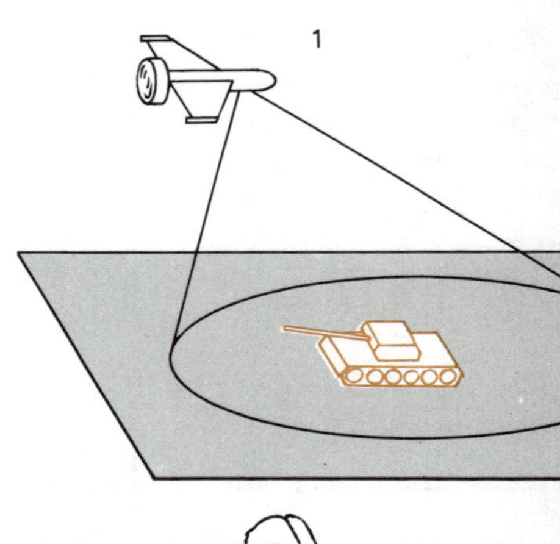

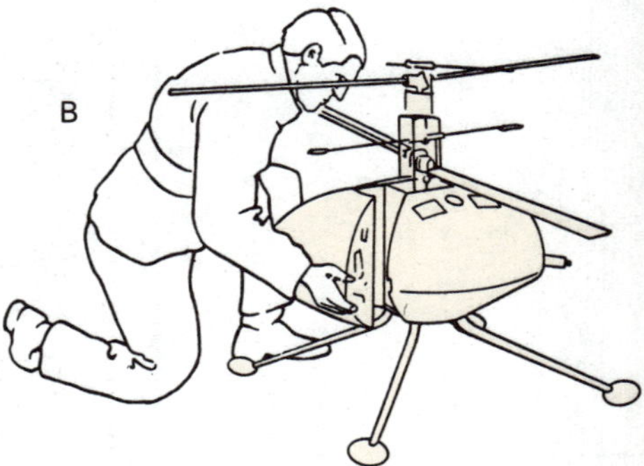

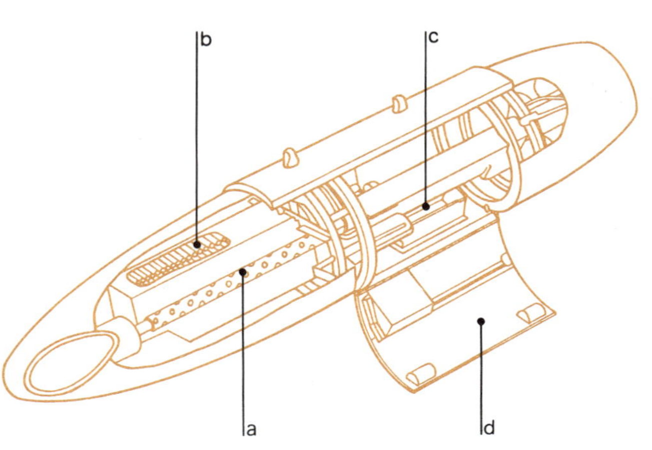

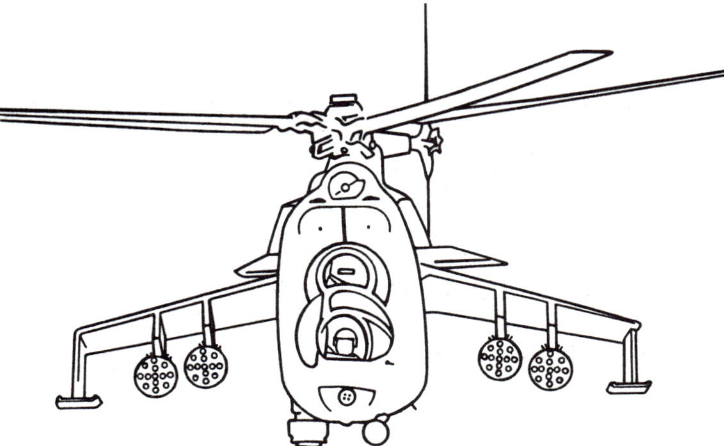

Gun pods (above) This type of weapon is fitted below aircraft or helicopters and has existed in many forms since the 1960s. Less accurate than internal guns, the pod is nevertheless a useful form of "bolt on" firepower. The example is a Swedish Uni-Pod 0127, the latest version has a rounds counter and inflight recocking.

a Caliber .50in (12.7mm) M3 Browning machine gun
b 200-round magazine
c Spent cases' ejection chute
d Spent links' ejection chute

Assault helicopters (above) like the famous Soviet Mi-24 "Hind", active in Afghanistan since 1979, carry unguided rocket pods (see p.259) on their stub wings and a multi-barrelled gun in a chin turret under the nose. Soviet rocket pods contain 32 57mm (2.24in) projectiles loaded from the rear, the single most numerous rocket type ever produced. Nine warheads are available including HE, fragmentation and chaff. The four-barrelled gun is of .50in (12.7mm) caliber and used by the nose weapons operator to suppress ground fire. The even more heavily-armed Mi-28 "Havoc" is expected from 1992.

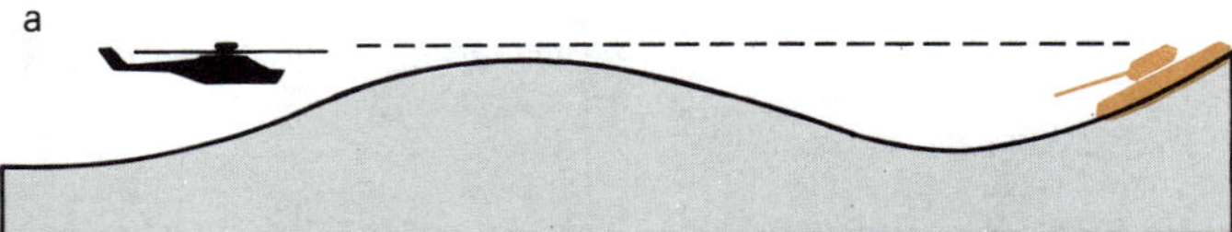

Anti-tank helicopters (above) can stand off a target after it has flown a groundhugging nap of the earth (NOE) approach and ambush it, out of range of its AA guns. Using its mast mounted sight, above the rotor blades, a modern anti-tank helicopter can see over cover (**a**) and having acquired the target, dip down behind again before launching missiles (**b**) at ranges up to about 4500yd (4114m) in all weathers, or even farther if a ground target designator assists. Although anti-tank helicopters saw action in Vietnam and the Middle East (1970s) and, less well documented, in the Iran-Iraq War (1980-88), they have yet to be used en masse in a modern armored battle. Despite this unproven status they have become a key system in the weapon counting of NATO and the Warsaw Pact.

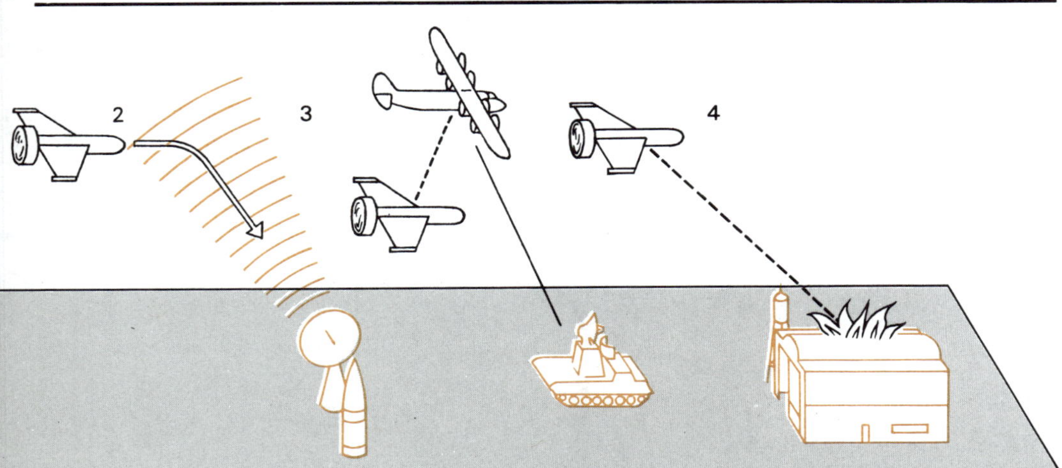

Remotely piloted vehicles (left) are an increasing part of the tactical air battlefield, either vehicle launched (**A**), or man launched like the British Sprite RPV helicopter (**B**). RPVs are small, low-cost unmanned, slow-flying machines developed since the 1950s from old gunnery target drones. They are used primarily for low-level target reconnaissance to assist artillery. Israel, which used them in the 1982 Lebanon invasion, has no fewer than six types under air force control. Clear Middle East skies lend themselves to good TV pictures.

RPV roles (above)
1 Reconnaissance with live TV pictures or bringing back film capsules. RPVs can also carry laser target designators.
2 Homing on hostile radar
3 Electronic warfare, causing hostile radar to switch on and reveal itself to electronic intelligence aircraft.
4 Direct or stand-off attack as a cheap flying bomb not using an expensive pilot.

Air missiles and cluster bombs

Air force weaponry's greatest advances during the 1980s have probably been in the ground attack role, whether in the extraordinary range of cluster submunitions for runway denial and anti-armor attack or in missiles for knocking out radar. Air defenses have responded with ingenuity to the challenge of stand-off attack.

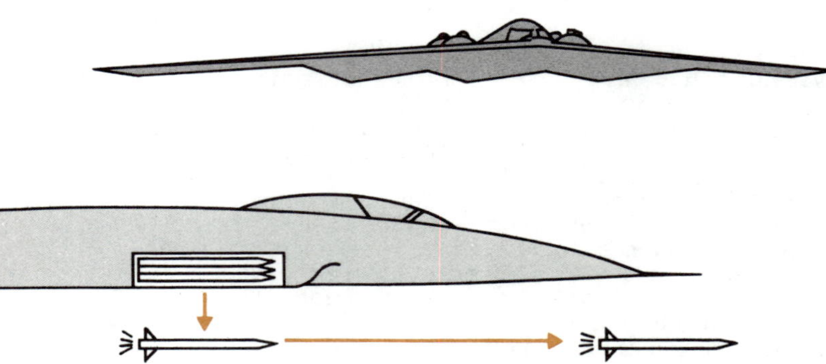

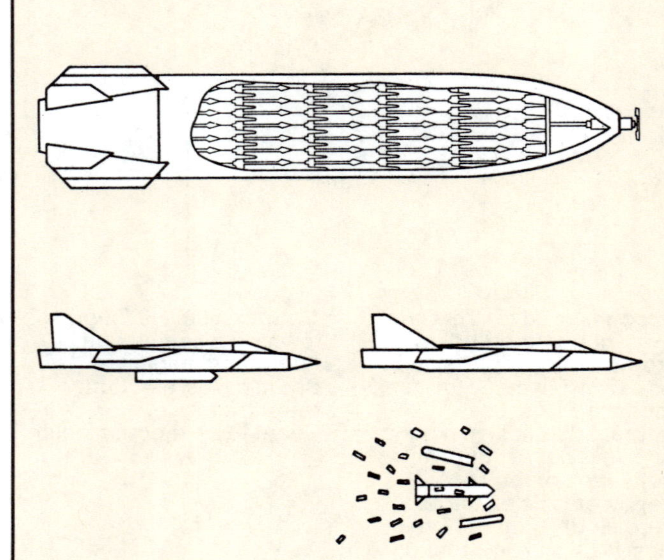

Stealth technology (top) is on the agenda for the 1990s. Ironically, precision guided weapons, often produced at gradually lower unit cost, have forced aircraft designers to turn to costly low-observable radar-baffling vehicles like the US B2 Stealth bomber, unveiled in 1988 ($500 million apiece at 1989 prices). No signs exist yet of novel weapons for it or the F117 Stealth fighter design.

Air-to-air missiles (above) of the future may be carried by fighters in internal drum launchers, not only giving more shots at the enemy but also not degrading aircraft performance. The missiles themselves will be smaller with only fold-out fins and rely on accurate homing rather than warhead size to kill the target.

Cluster bombs are shaped like ordinary bombs, but at a predetermined height shed their outer skin to release a mass of bomblets; the Chilean Cardoen CB-500 example (above top) contains 240. These can be anti-personnel fragmentation or shaped charge anti-vehicle bomblets. The forward motion of the releasing aircraft means that the spread of submunitions is a long oval, ideal against runways, road convoys or massed troops and vehicles. The Soviets pioneered such devices in the 1930s, but they have come into widespread use since the late 1960s.

Anti-radar missiles (right) are designed to beam ride down a radar beam from the search radar for an air defense system and destroy it, thus blinding the defenders. The radar on the ground can change frequencies, switch on and off and generally distract the missile. It can become a silent duel as to who will switch on or shoot first. Britain's Air Launched Anti-Radiation Missile (ALARM), selected 1983, is the most advanced and lightest of its kind. Its HE warhead has a precision laser proximity fuze. Unlike earlier anti-radar missiles, it can attack indirectly by (**a**) rocketing to 40,000ft (12,000m) and (**b**) deploying a parachute for loitering and scanning over targets. Once it has picked a target, the parachute is discarded (**c**) and the attack is a free fall trajectory.

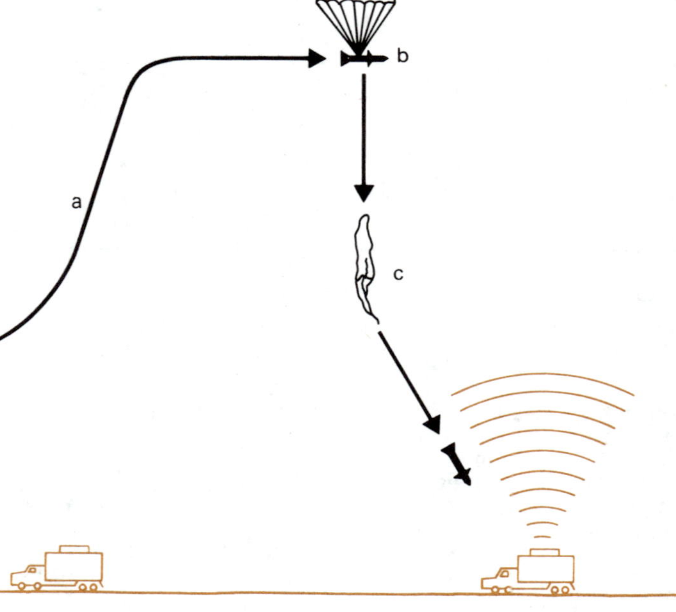

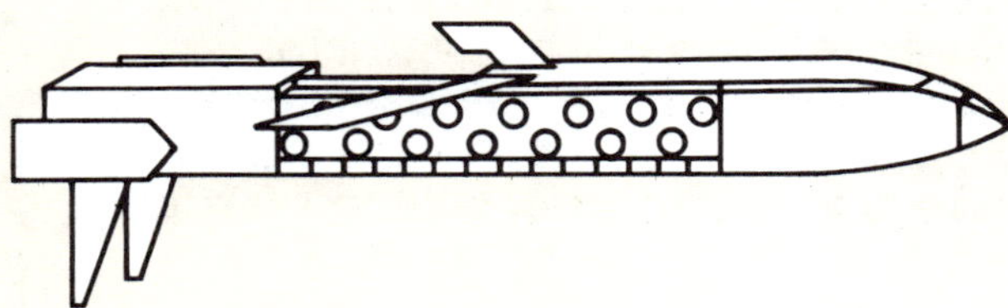

Cluster dispensers are a development since c1966 of the same area weapon principle in which the bomblets are dispensed sideways or rearwards from a container which either stays fixed to the aircraft or is released and parachute-braked. A weapon load typically covers an area of 65yd (60m) by 262yd (240m) or 3.5 acres. A drawback is that the launch aircraft must fly above 165ft (50m) at subsonic speeds over the target.

Container weapon systems are the latest extension of the cluster idea, eliminating the need for the aircraft to fly over the target. They are in fact subsonic small cruise missiles launched at long stand-off ranges and in the case of the Franco-German Apache system (1985 prototypes, destined to enter service 1992) strew their submunitions over an area 383yd (350m) by 1094yd (100m) or 86.5 acres.

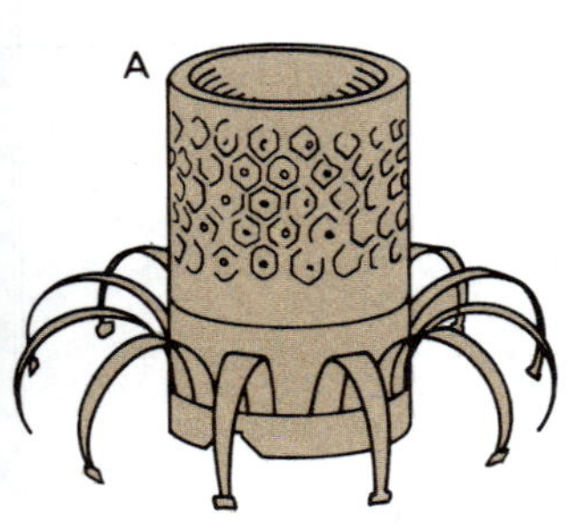

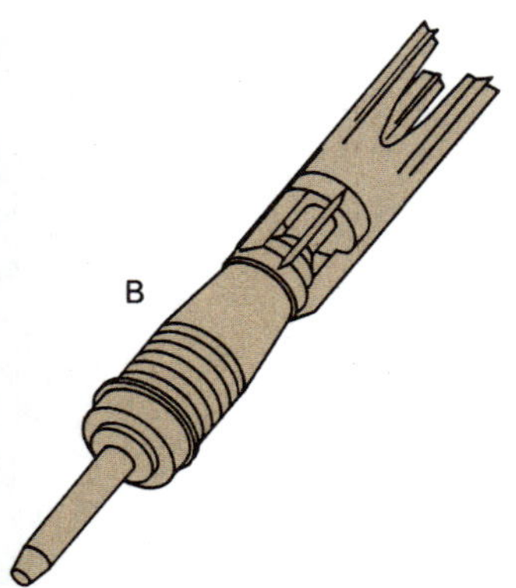

Bomblets (left) come in many shapes and sizes as cluster weapon submunitions. (**A**) HB. 876 area denial mine weighs 5.5lb (2.5kg) and comes to land on its sprung legs. It self-destructs after a preset period if not disturbed before. An RAF Tornado's JP. 233 dispenser can release 430 in one pass. (**B**) Armor-piercing bomblet (Chilean Cardoen, weighing 1.63lb/ 0.74kg and 14.2in/ 36cm long) with nose fuze probe to ensure maximum hollow-charge penetration (up to 6in/150mm). Runway cratering submunitions are similar but parachute retarded so that a piercing charge holes the surface concrete before, in latest versions, a main charge makes the crater. Anti-personnel bomblets work like hand-thrown grenades except they are larger and are dropped in hundreds.

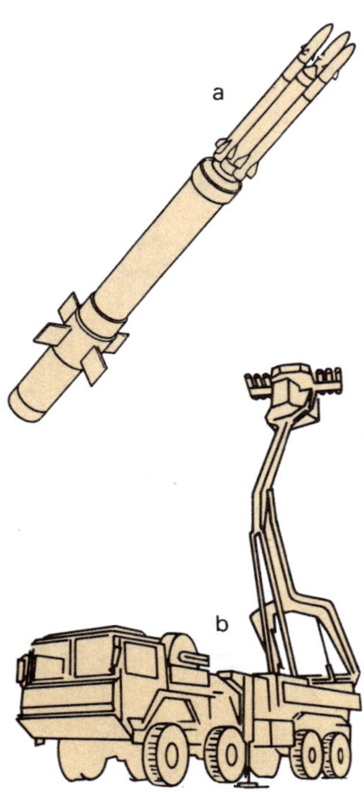

Air defense improvements (left) (**a**) Starstreak is Britain's revolutionary missile development that is designed to be fired at perhaps Mach 4.5 and in the terminal phase releases a formation of three laser-guided high-kinetic energy explosive darts. The system is intended for army (hand-held) and navy close air defense, but could be made into an air-to-air weapon as well. (**b**) Elevated mobile platforms allow tracking radars to be positioned behind cover or in deep woodland and missiles can be mounted alongside. Modern systems, like Sweden's RBS90 twin-launcher laser-riding missiles, can also be operated by remote control; the unmanned launcher is linked to command and tracking vehicles that are under cover a long distance off.

Maritime attack and defense

Sea skimming missiles have now proved themselves the deadliest non-nuclear naval weapon and prompted a return to close-in weapon systems to blast them from the wave tops before they hit valuable warships. Underwater, mines and torpedoes, the original guided missiles, have also attained a breathtaking ability to seek out their targets.

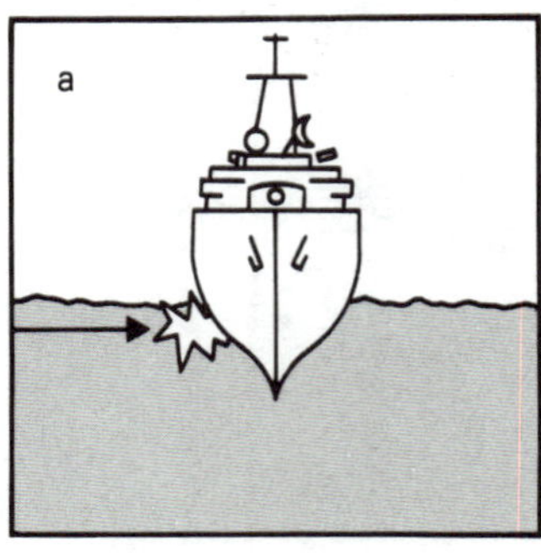

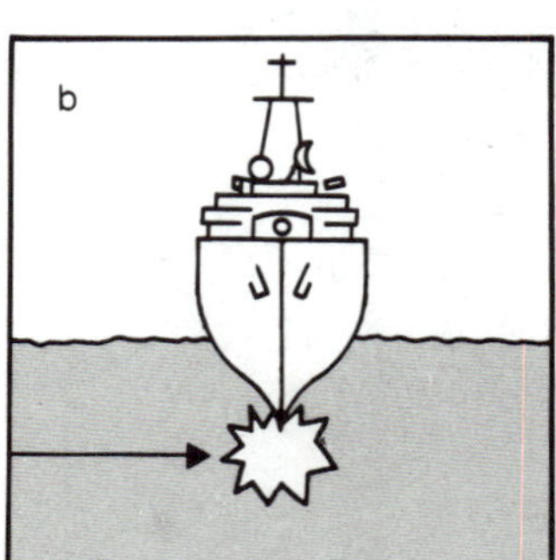

Wire-guided submarine torpedoes (right) have been in service since the late 1950s to improve on the accuracy of earlier electric-driven and acoustic torpedoes (see p.261). Wire guidance is proof against electronic countermeasures.
1 Submarine launches wire-guided torpedo.
2 Target changes course.
3 Wire guidance commands from submarine computer instruct torpedo to change course to hit target.
The British Royal Navy's Mk 24 Tigerfish wire-guided heavyweight torpedo uses self-contained acoustic homing. Its range may be 18.6 miles (30km). All torpedoes can have warhead fuzing (left) either to explode against a ship's hull (**a**) or delay detonation until beneath the keel (**b**) so breaking the vessel's back. Shaped-charge warheads are now widespread for piercing thick nuclear submarine hulls.

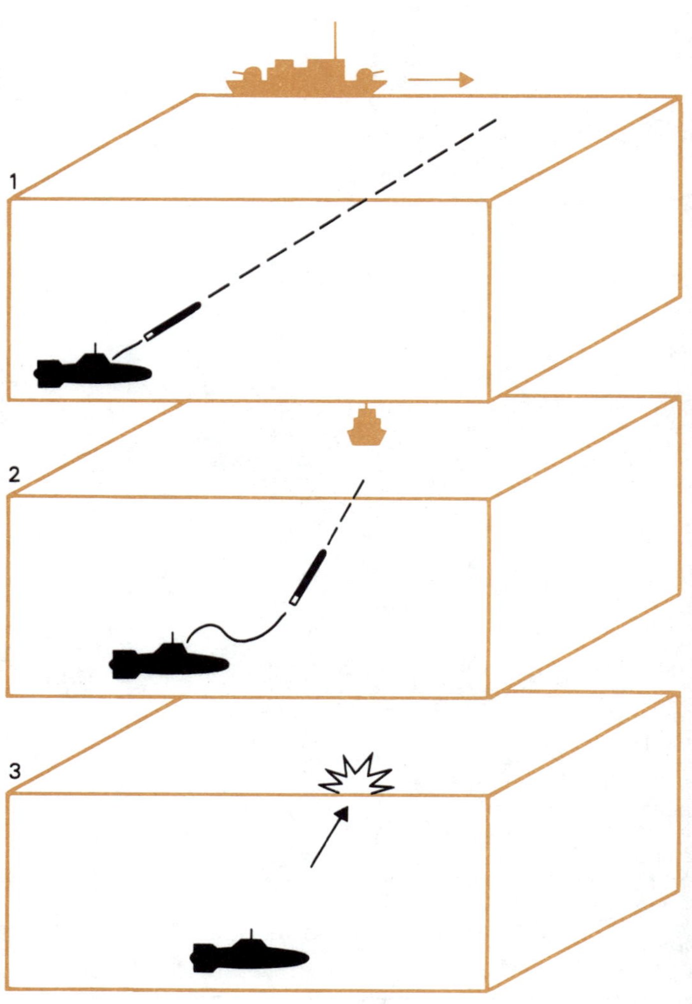

Anti-ship missiles have proliferated since the early 1970s. Best known of all is Exocet (see p.260) thanks to its record in the Falklands and Gulf Wars as an air-launched weapon (**A**), but it also arms fast attack craft (**B**) of 19 navies and has a coast defence variant (**C**) which damaged the British destroyer *Glamorgan* (June 12, 1982). France has also developed a submarine-launched version. ANS is a Franco-German Exocet replacement development of up to three times its range and speed.
The first ever major surface ship missile duel took place in the Gulf on April 18, 1988 when USS *Strauss* sank the Iranian frigate *Sahand*.

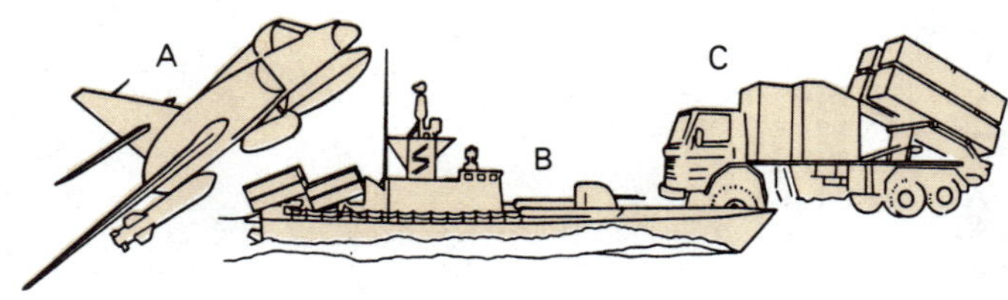

Exocet AM39 anti-ship missile (below)
a Tracking radar
b Radio altimeter
c Command guidance computer
d Explosive warhead 364lb (165kg)
e Sustainer rocket fuel
f Booster rocket fuel
g Steering mechanism
Length 15.3ft (4.69m)
Range 43.5 miles (70km)
h Narrow cross-section 31.4lin (0.8m).

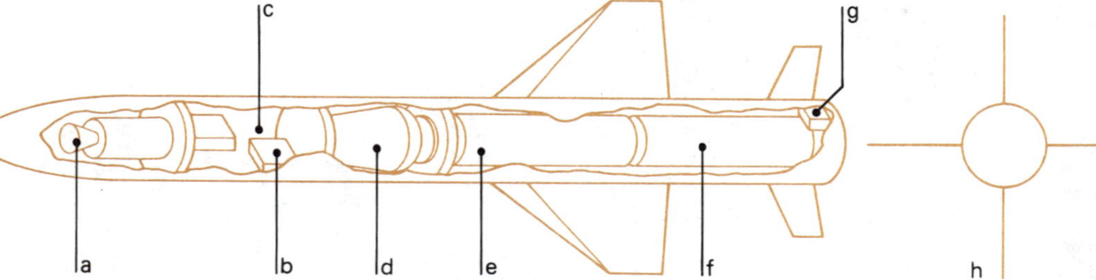

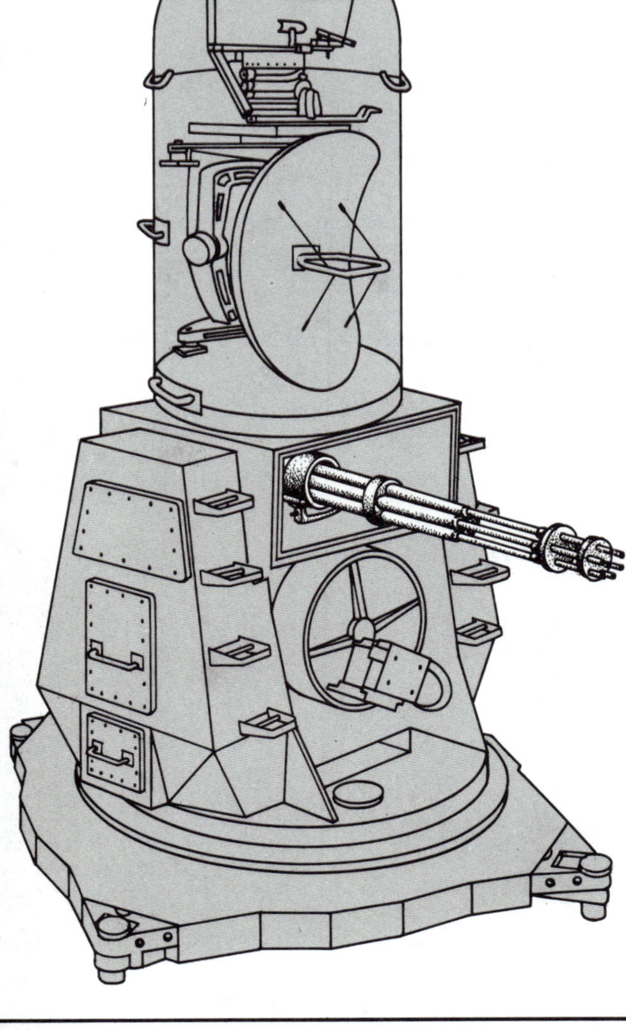

Close-in weapon systems (left and below) are a return to the naval multi-barrel pom-pom gun (see p. 205 and p. 218), a 1930s air defense concept (older still when applied against torpedo boats, see p. 192). The aim is to destroy the assailant by rapid close-range fire. The US M168 20mm Vulcan-Phalanx CIWS (left) is a late 1970s naval adaptation of a six-barrel 1953 air weapon design (see p. 193). Atop the gun housing is a radome containing tracking and fire control radars. The gun is automatically controlled (no crew) and fires up to 6600rpm of uranium-tipped ammunition up to 5000m. CIWS tracks the on-coming sea skimming missile with its own radar (**a**). Large-caliber CIWS (40mm and more) fire proximity-fuzed shells able to pick target reflections from those of the sea and destroy it with pre-fragmented tungsten shrapnel (**b**). Small-caliber CIWS like Phalanx rely on a "wall of steel" (**c**).

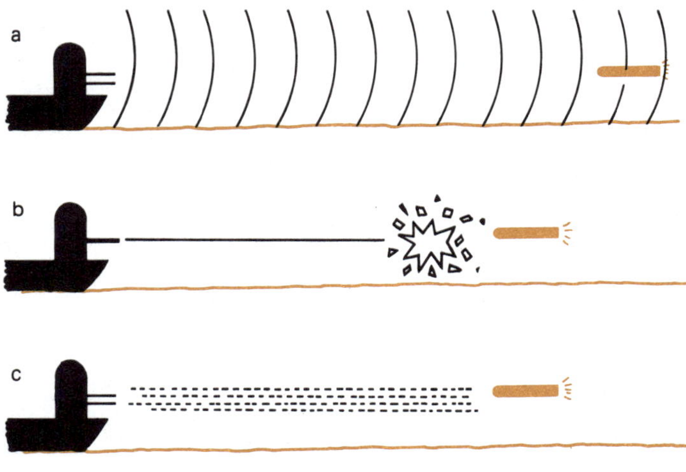

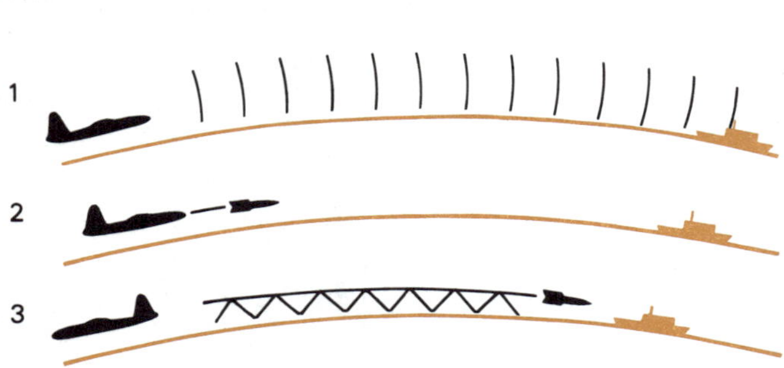

Sea skimming missiles (above) are air, ship or even land-based trailer launched over the horizon. (**1**) Launch vehicle "paints" target with its radar. (**2**) Missile is launched having received target details which it updates with its own onboard guidance. (**3**) As launch vehicle turns away, missile flies in wave reflections' radar-baffling "clutter". The missile's tracking radar homes in on the target and it strikes broadside on or topside, followed by detonation deep inside the hull. Even if the warhead fails to explode, as happened with the Falklands War hit on the British destroyer *Sheffield* (May 2, 1982), the still burning rocket sustainer can cause a lethal fire.

Modern sea mines (below) are increasingly versatile and "intelligent". Made in five warhead sizes (660lb/300kg size shown), Britain's Marconi Stonefish family has a tail electronics mount (**a**) and can be used at depths from 16ft (5m) to 656ft (200m). Laid life is over 700 days. It can be laid by helicopters, aircraft, surface ships or submarines. Sea mines today combine computer-programed magnetic, acoustic, and pressure actuation according to mission. Diameter does not often exceed 21in (533mm) since most mines must be launchable from submarine torpedo tubes. Non-metal materials like glass fiber, epoxy resin and plastics are used for lightness and strength, and to make mine countermeasures more difficult.

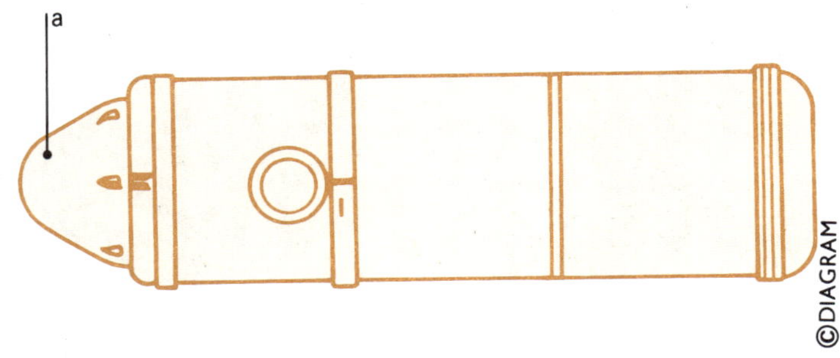

REGIONAL AND HISTORICAL INDEXES

The purpose of these regional and historical indexes is to provide further access to information in the main body of the book. Previously, our approach to the subject of weapons has been by function, bringing together similar objects regardless of period or culture. In the historical index, the European or broadly "Western" weapons that have been explained and illustrated in Chapters 1–7 are regrouped into historical periods. In the regional index, weapons from the rest of the world are regrouped by region. Thus, on one page, the reader can see a representative selection of weapons from, say, the islands of the Pacific, or that were in use in the American Civil War of 1861–65. The key under each heading in the index gives the page references for fuller information.

Regional index

Historical index

Using the visual index
If the reader wishes to know more about a weapon shown in silhouette in the index—for example the barbed spear under the heading "The Pacific" on the page opposite—then, by checking its number (6) in the key above it, the page numbers on which it and other spears from the region can be found are given in brackets. On referring to page 82 the barbed spear can be recognized from its shape. The caption relates that it comes from Hawaii and has links with Captain Cook the explorer. On looking over page 83, also listed in the index, another, shorter spear (or javelin) from the region will be found. The same procedure is used for the historical index, which begins on p. 302.

The lithograph (right) by the French artist Daumier is entitled "After you!" Although dating from the 1860s, the comment is ageless.

Australia and New Zealand

Covered here are the weapons of the Aborigines of Australia and the Maoris of New Zealand, to whom metals were unknown before the coming of Europeans. The Maoris are best known for their fine clubs of wood or stone, and the Aborigines for their boomerangs.
The figurine (right) depicts a tattooed Maori warrior with a club.

1 Clubs (15)
2 Adz (20)
3 Pick (20)
4 Dagger (27)
5 Wooden sword (35)
6 Throwing-clubs (78)
7 Boomerangs (79)
8 Spear (82)
9 Spear-thrower (83)

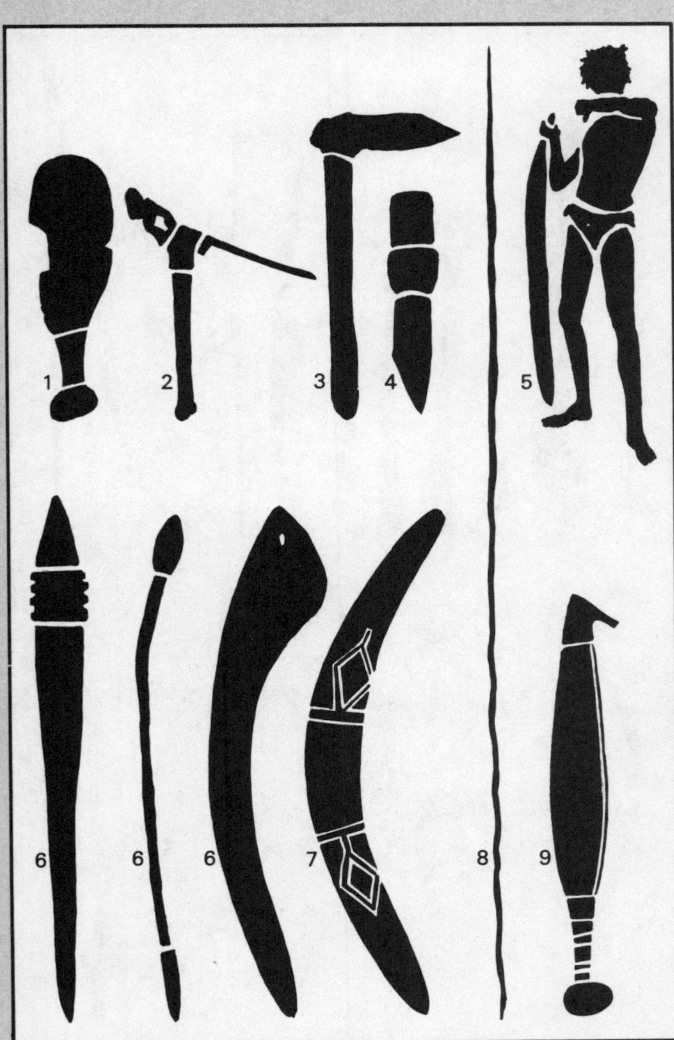

The Pacific

The weapons of Polynesia, Melanesia and Micronesia are included here. In the absence of metals, bone, teeth of animals and fish and suitable types of stone were used to provide sharp edges or points. The carved clubs of the region can be of the highest quality.
The figure (right) of a warrior was made in the Solomon Islands.

1 Clubs (15, 16)
2 Pick (20)
3 Proto-swords (35)
4 Sling (77)
5 Throwing-club (78)
6 Spears (82, 83)
(The numbers in brackets are page references for further information.)

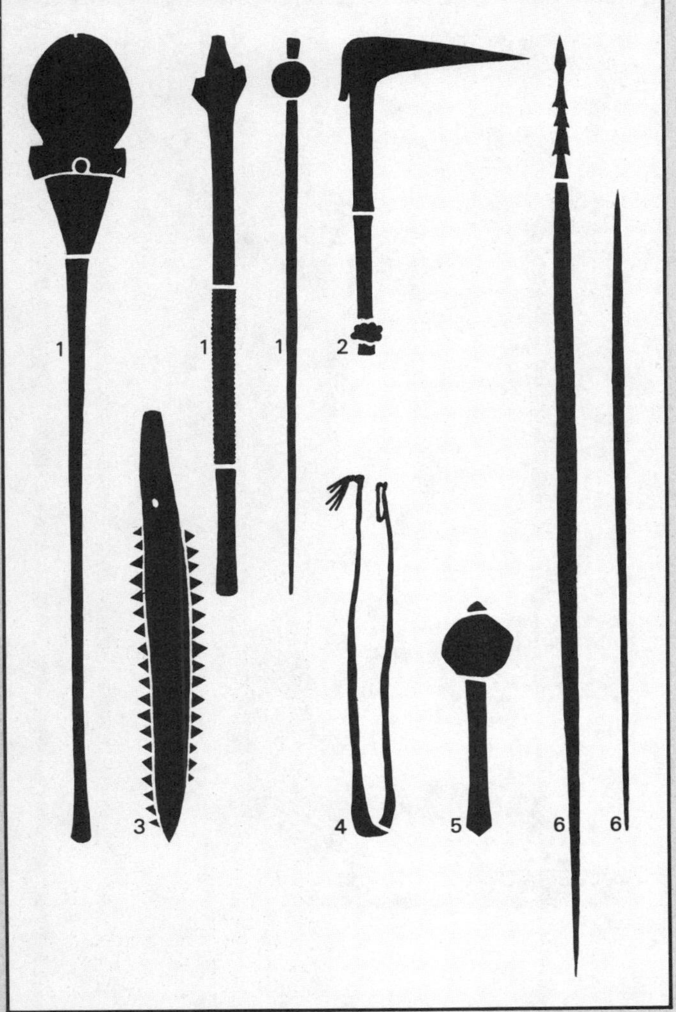

Southeast Asia

Included under this heading are weapons from the Malay Peninsula, Borneo, the Philippines, the Celebes and Java. Also indexed are some jungle traps that have been encountered in several 20th century campaigns in the region. **The statue** (right) is from Bali, and depicts the embodiment of martial ardor.

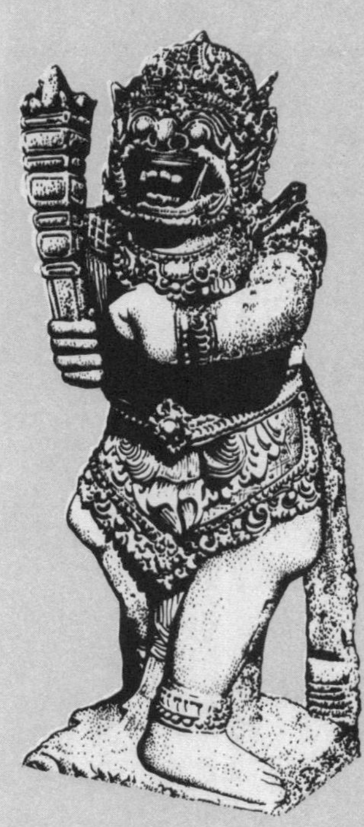

1 Axes (25)
2 *Kris* (30)
3 Swords (40)
4 Pole-arm (62)
5 Blowgun (106)
6 Swivel gun (173)
7 Traps (224, 225)
(The numbers in brackets are page references for further information.)

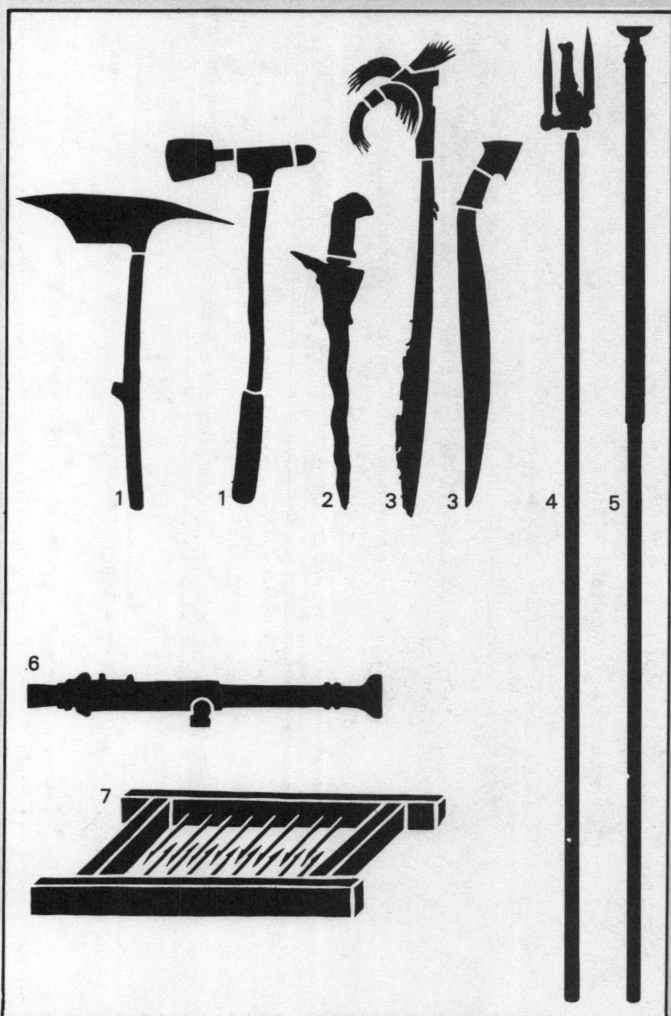

China, Burma and Assam

The selection of Chinese arms indexed here is by no means exhaustive. Much specialized research on the subject remains to be done, or is yet to be published in the West. More in comparison is known about the weapons of the peoples inhabiting northern Burma and Assam. **The figures** (above) are a detail from a tomb engraving from N China.

1 Mace (18)
2 Ax or *dao* (25)
3 Jade dagger (27)
4 Proto-sword or *dao* (35)
5 Swords (40)
6 Parrying weapon (73)
7 Chain/whip (73)
8 Naga spear (82)
9 Pellet bow (96)
10 Pellet crossbow (105)
11 Repeating crossbow (105)
12 "Fire arrows" (244)

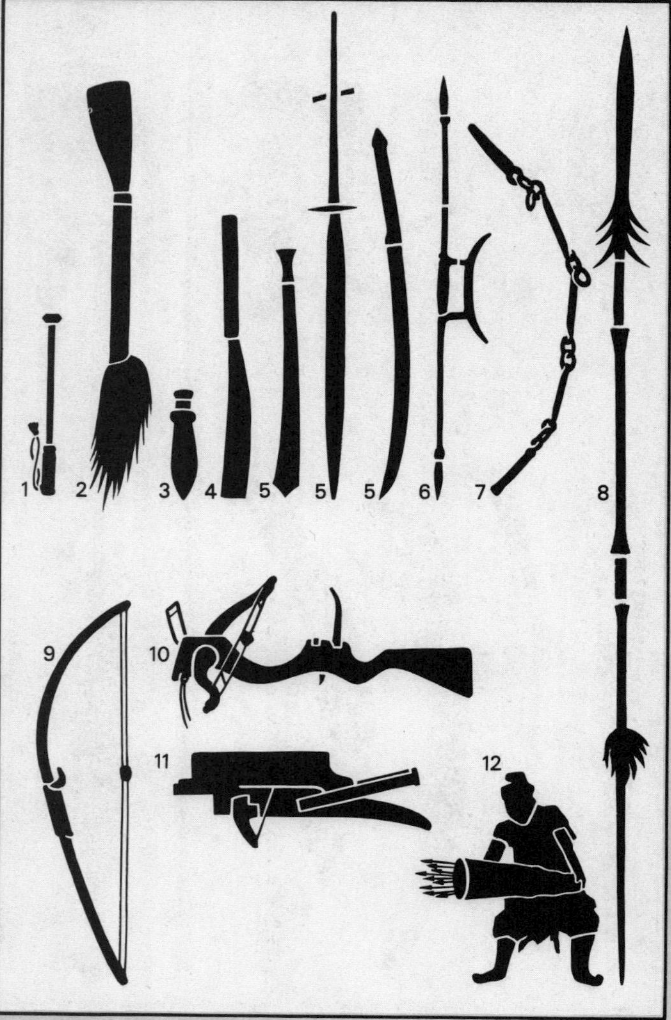

Old Japan

Almost as soon as trade with Japan began, the West appreciated the style and quality of Japanese art and artefacts. As a result there are many Japanese weapons in European and American collections. The swords especially are popular, and much has been published in European languages about the related terminology and lore. In addition to swords, we have included a selection of other traditional Japanese weapons.
The drawings (right) are by the artist Hokusai (1760-1849) and depict Samurai warriors engaged in weapon-training.

1 Club (16)
2 Flail (17)
3 Pick (20)
4 Dagger (28)
5 Swords (41-43)
6 Pole-arms (59, 62)
7 Hand weapons (73)
8 Javelin and dart (83)
9 Arrow case (95)
10 Bows (98)
11 Arrow and points (101)
12 Matchlock gun (117)
13 Matchlock pistol (122)

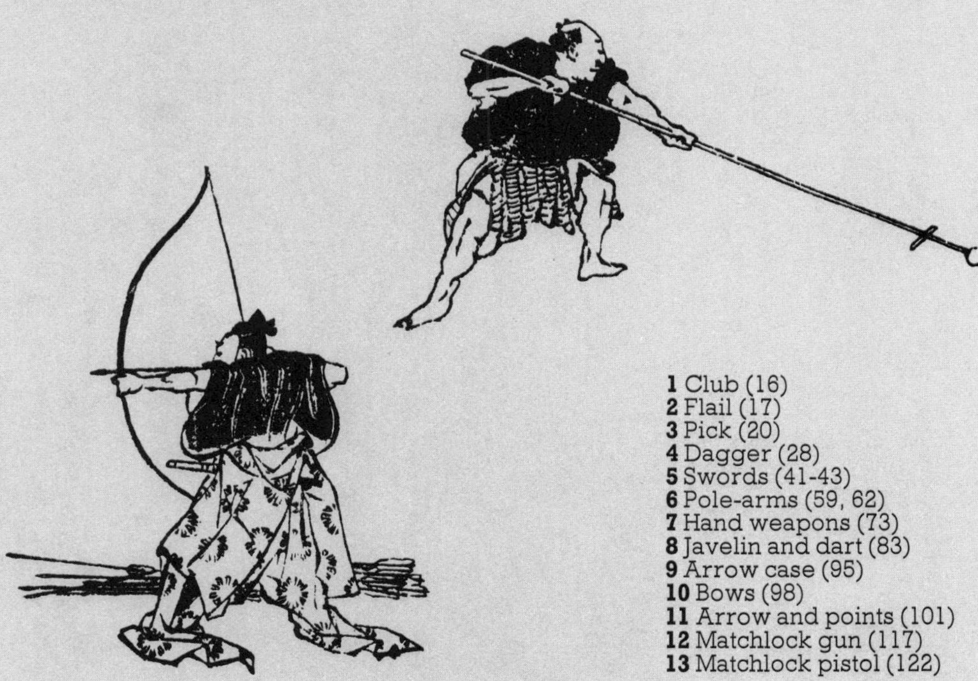

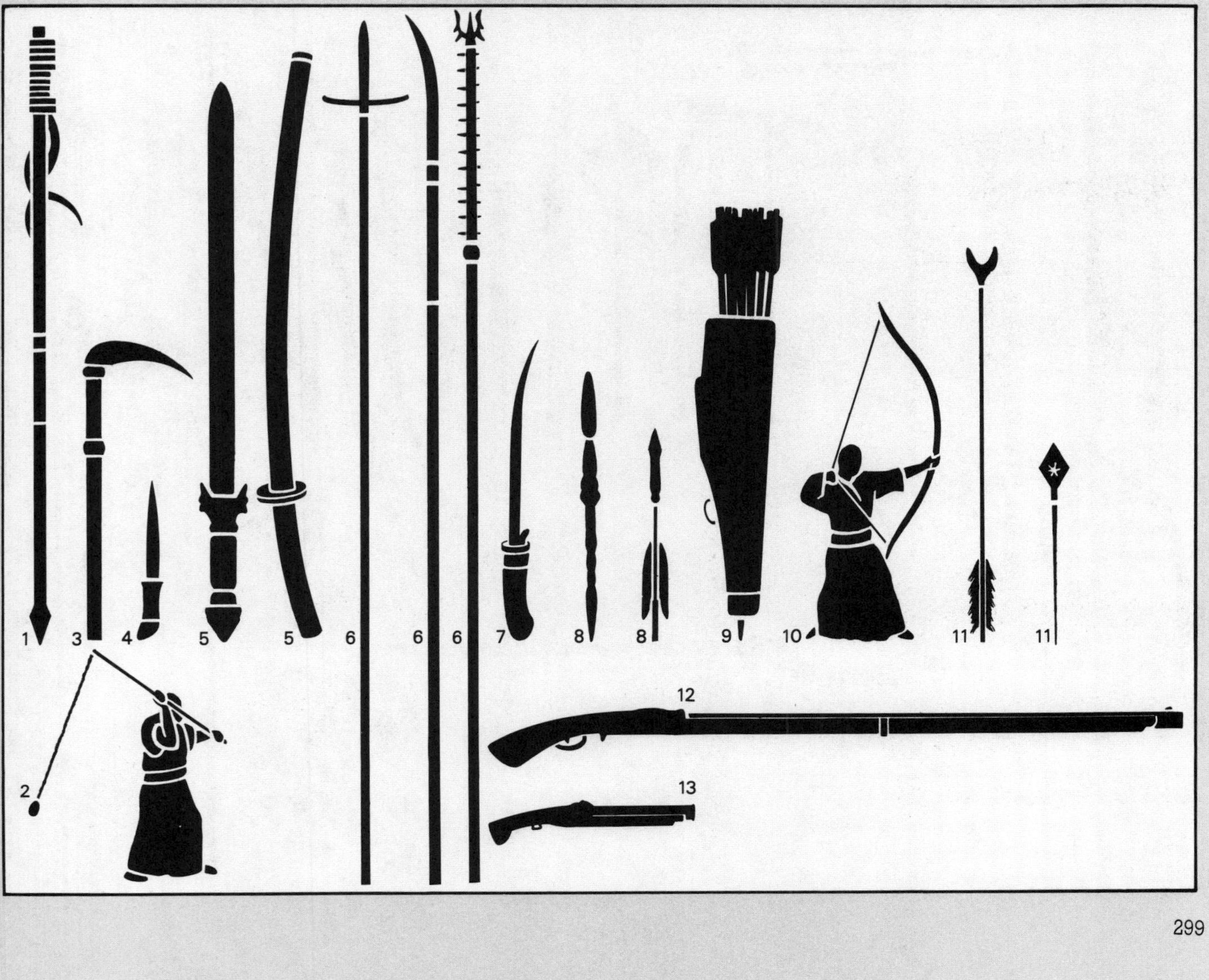

India and Persia

The extent of Persian influence in the form and decoration of Indian arms and armor is such that the weapons of the two regions are usually treated together. In addition to Indo-Persian weapons, a selection is included of those that originate with the other, older cultures of India.

The photograph (right) is of Rajput soldiers from Northern India, and was taken during the 1850s. They are armed with swords of the *tulwar* type, and a matchlock musket.

1 Club (16)
2 Flail (17)
3 Maces (18)
4 Pick (20)
5 War-hammer (21)
6 Axes (24, 25)
7 Daggers (28-30)
8 Swords (37-39)
9 Pole-arm (59)
10 Lance (63)
11 Hand weapons (72)
12 Quoits (81)
13 Spear (82)
14 Bows (99)
15 Arrow (101)
16 Matchlock guns (117)
17 Matchlock pistol (122)
18 Bronze mortar (169)

(The numbers in brackets are page references for further information.)

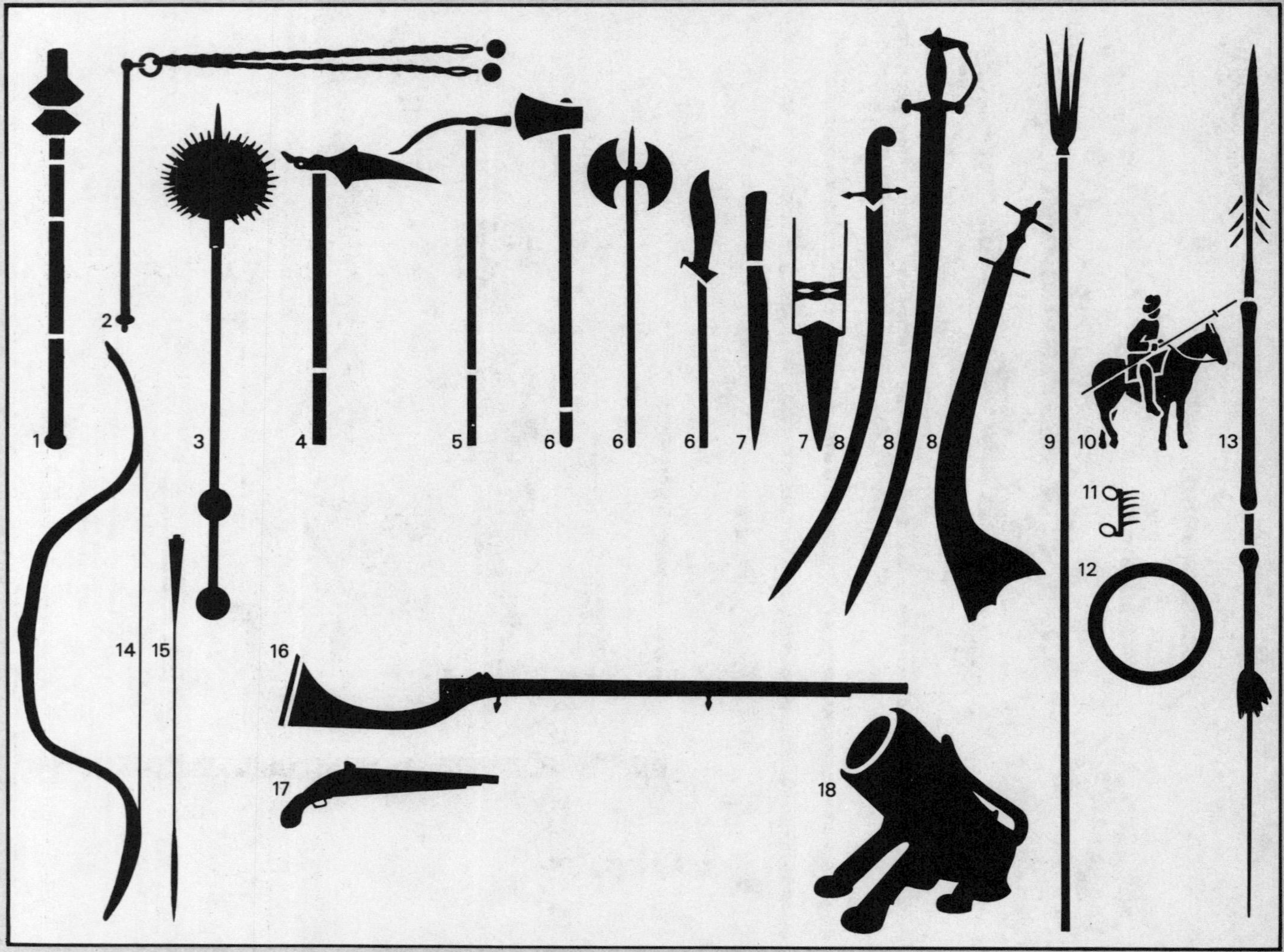

Africa

The limits of this section are geographical rather than cultural, and weapons of ethnic groups from North, South, East, West and Central Africa are represented. Ancient Egyptian weapons, however, will be found in the historical index under the title *Ancient Middle East*.
The illustration (right) is from a painting of a Zulu warrior.

1 Knobkerrie (15)
2 Axes (22, 24)
3 Daggers (28)
4 Swords (36)
5 Spear (58)
6 Throwing-club (78)
7 Throwing-knives (80, 81)
8 Spears (82)
9 Bows (96)
10 Crossbow (105)
11 Snaphance gun (118)

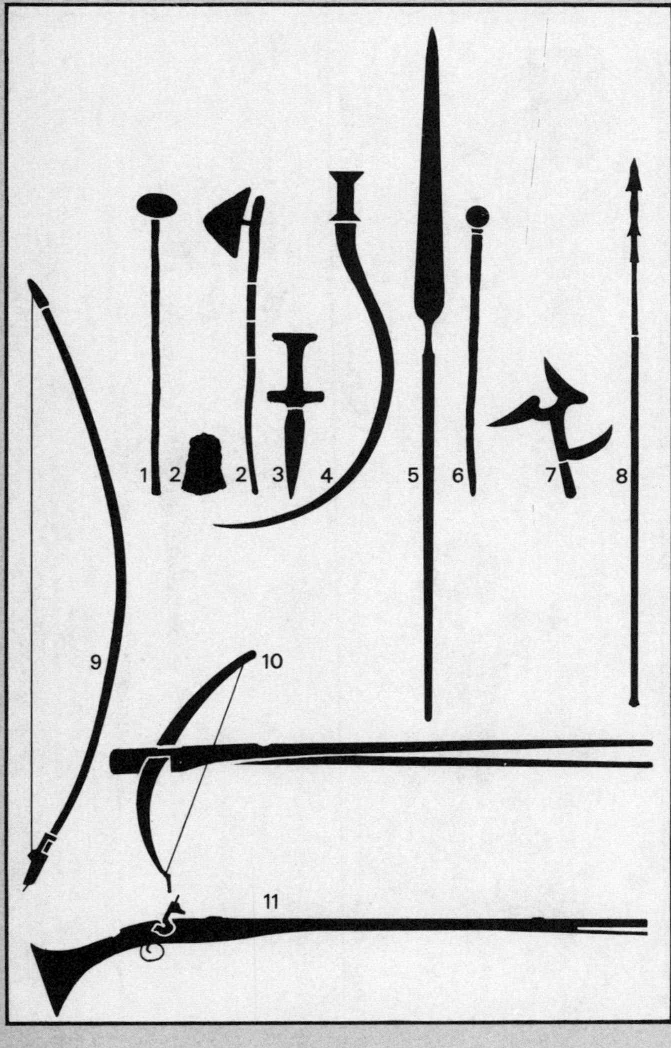

The Americas

In addition to weapons of the Indians of the USA and Canada, we include here those of the Eskimos of the far North, and a few from Central and South America.
The illustration (right) is after a drawing by a Mandan chief of a Cheyenne leader whom he had defeated in battle.

1 Clubs (15, 16)
2 Tomahawk (24)
3 Daggers (27, 28)
4 Tomahawk (80)
5 Quiver and bowcase (95)
6 Bow (97)
7 Arrow and points (101)
8 Blowgun (106)

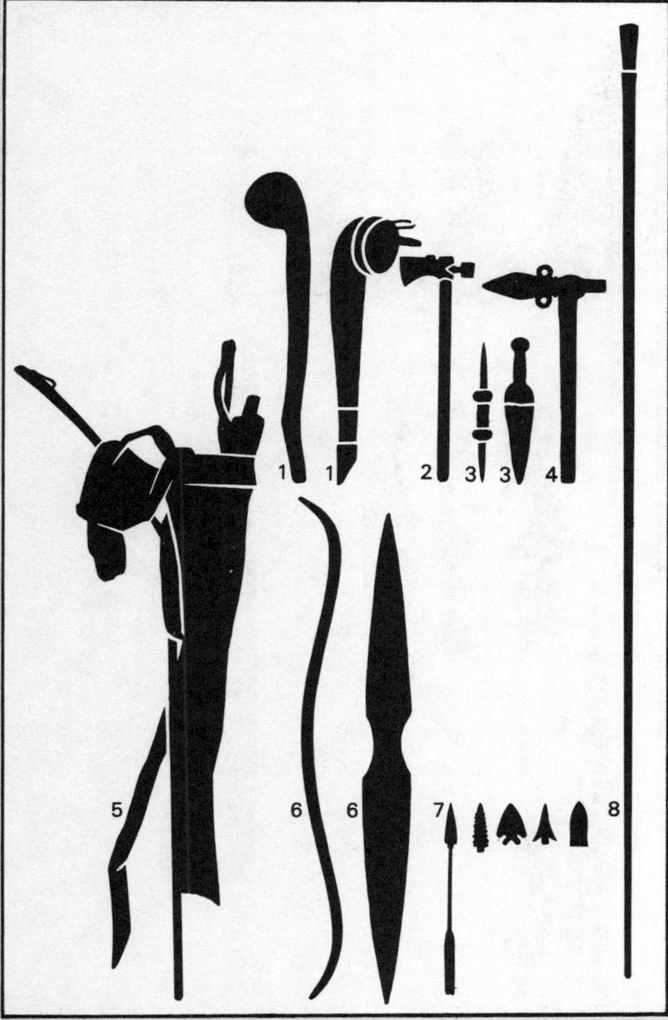

European Stone Age

The oldest European weapon included in this book is probably the wooden spearpoint shown on p.83, which is from the Clactonian culture of the early Palaeolithic period. Note that even after the discovery of metals, flint continued in use, especially for arrow points.
The cave painting (below) from Spain depicts a group of warriors.

1 Axes (22)
2 Daggers (27)
3 Spear points (83)
4 Bow (96)
5 Arrow points (101)

Ancient Middle East

Represented are the ancient cultures of Egypt, Luristan and Assyria, all of which used copper or bronze to make weapons.
The ivory handle (right) of a flint knife depicts men fighting with clubs and knives. It dates from c.3000BC, being from the Gerzean culture in Egypt. (Louvre, Paris.)

1 Mace-head (19)
2 Axes (22, 23)
3 Bronze sword (35)
4 Slings and bullets (77)
5 Throwing-stick (78)
6 Spearhead (83)
7 Bow (96)
8 Arrow points (101)

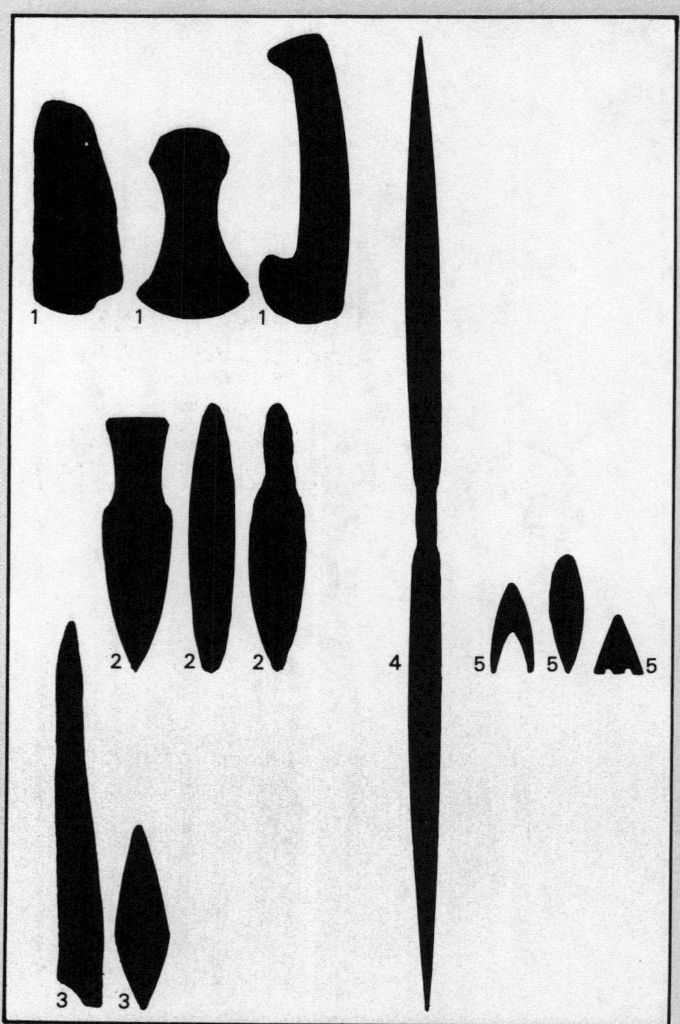

Ancient Greece and Rome

The selection of arms shown ranges from the bronze swords of the early Greek states to the iron weapons of Imperial Rome. It includes such missile-throwing weapons as slings, bows, and a variety of mechanical engines that were used as artillery. The Greeks, at various times, made extensive use of such mechanical artillery for defending cities. The Romans used them in besieging strongholds, and also sometimes on the open battlefield.

The marble relief (right) of about 500BC shows two Athenian warriors carrying shields and spears. (National Museum, Athens.)

Historical index

1 Dagger (31)
2 Swords (44, 45)
3 Spears (57)
4 *Amentum* (76)
5 Sling bullet (77)
6 Javelin (82)
7 Bowman (95)
8 Mounted crossbow (161)
9 *Onager* (162)
10 *Ballistae* (162)
11 Obstacles (222)
12 "Greek fire" (266)

(The numbers in brackets are page references for further information.)

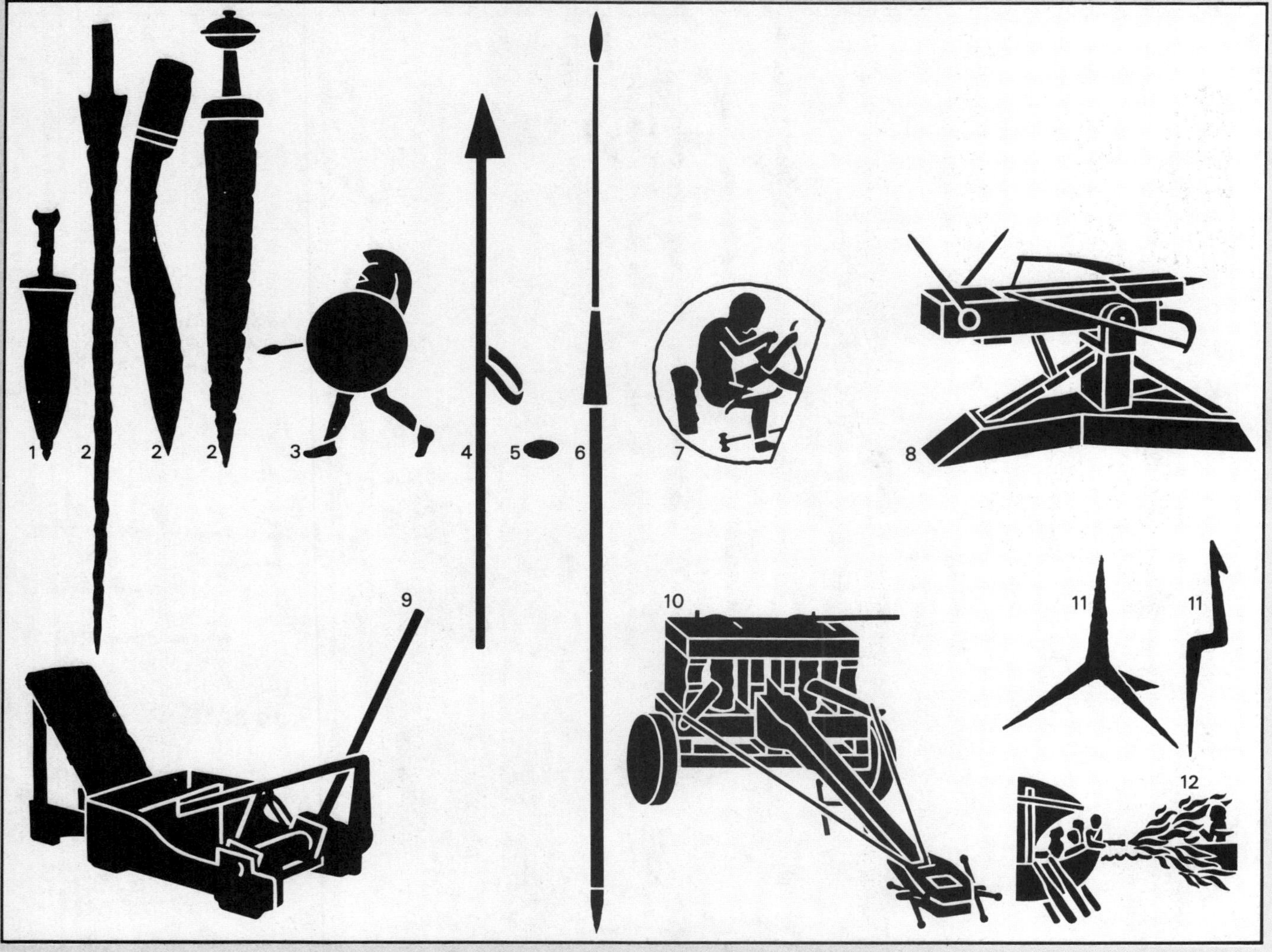

Medieval Europe

Notable developments in weaponry in medieval Europe were the rise of the crossbow and its competitor the longbow, and later the coming of gunpowder. These weapons were to have an important influence on tactics, armor and the use of other weapons, but did not immediately displace the basic arms in use with foot and horse soldiers. The former were armed predominantly with pole-arms of many kinds, and the latter with the sword, mace or lance. A dagger was commonly worn by men of all classes for show and as an implement and occasional weapon.

The detail (right) from the Bayeux Tapestry shows the Normans carrying arms down to their ships in preparation for the invasion of England in 1066.

1 Club (15)
2 Mace-head (16)
3 Flails (17)
4 Maces (similar) (18)
5 War-hammers (21)
6 Axes (24)
7 Daggers (31, 32)
8 Swords (46, 47)
9 Pole-arms (58-62)
10 Staff-sling (77)
11 Longbow (97)
12 Arrow points (101)
13 Crossbows (102-104)
14 Crossbow bolts (103)
15 Hand-cannon (109, 116)
16 Hand-cannon (127)
17 Spring engines (161)
18 Catapult (162)
19 Trebuchet (163)
20 ML cannon (166, 168)
21 BL cannon (178)
22 Obstacles (222)
23 Biological weapon (277)

16th century Europe

Historical index

The 16th century was more a period of refinement than of innovation in weaponry. Most medieval weapons continued in use—especially pole-arms, which became more extravagant and finely worked. Crude hand firearms gave way to arquebuses and then to matchlock muskets in the Spanish style. Wheellock ignition allowed horsemen to use a pistol one-handed. The crossbow and longbow declined in use. Muzzle-loading and some breech-loading cannon were used at sea and on land. A new kind of sword—the rapier—came into use as an item of dress.

The woodcut (right) is from a German book of 1529. Visible are hand-cannon, a mortar and ammunition as well as the cannon being loaded.

1 Maces (18)
2 War-hammers (21)
3 Ax (24)
4 Daggers (32)
5 Swords (48-50)
6 Pole-arms (58-62)
7 Lances (63)
8 Longbow (97)
9 Crossbows (103, 105)
10 Arquebuses (116)
11 Petronel (117)
12 Pistols (122, 123)
13 Double rifle (127)
14 Breech-loading gun (130)
15 BL pistol (132)
16 Grenade pistol (154)
17 Cannon (similar) (168)
18 Rocket-spear (240)

(The numbers in brackets are page references for further information.)

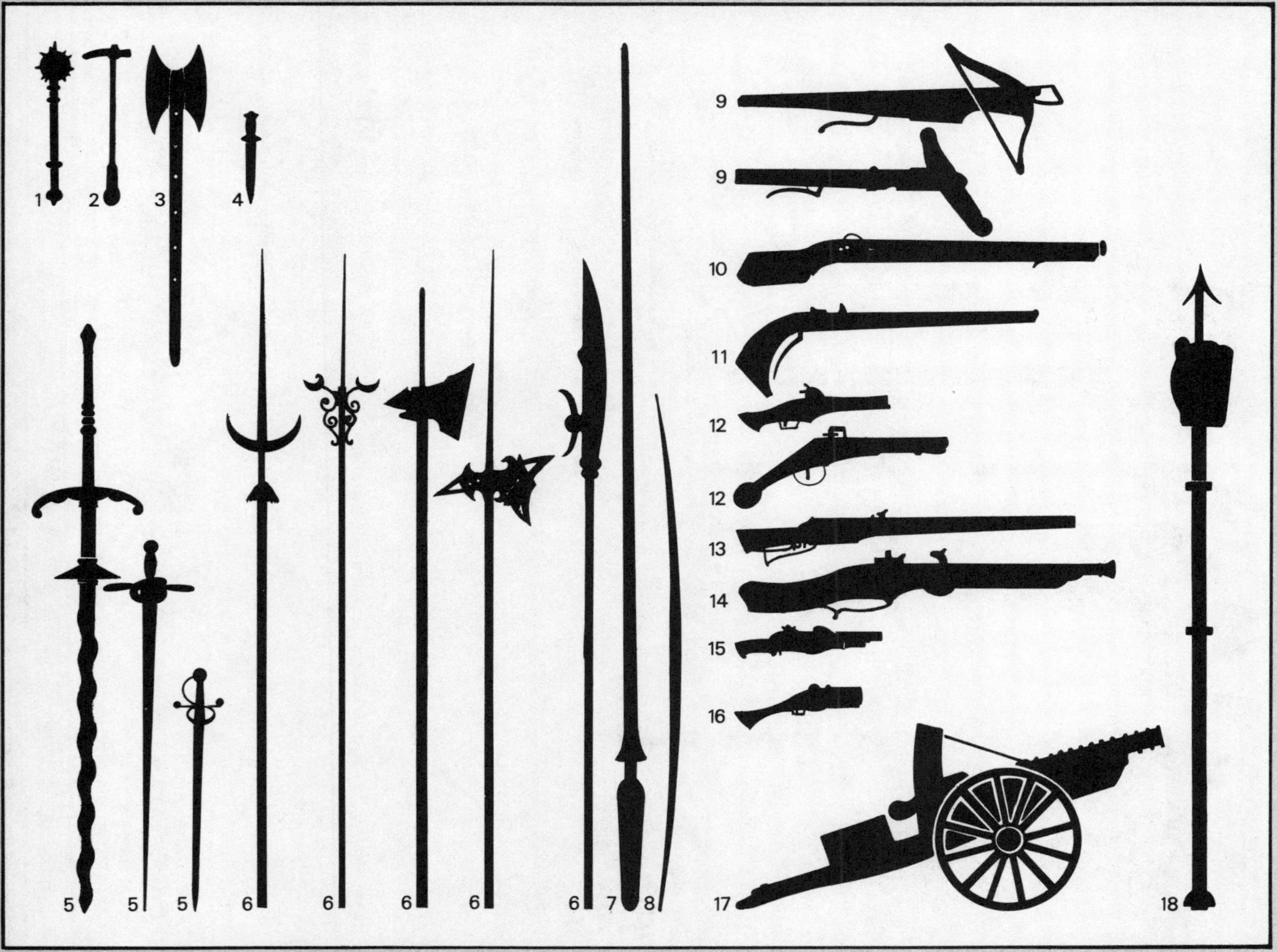

17th century Europe

17th century warfare was characterized by the use of musketeers and pikemen. The latter were to defend the former against attack by cavalry whilst loading, until later in the century simple bayonets allowed the musketeers to defend themselves. The cavalry used swords, and pistols or carbines. Perhaps the greatest innovation was flintlock ignition, which offered the convenience of the wheellock without the expense, so that it began to replace matchlock ignition on common soldiers' muskets as well. As for swords, rapiers and smallswords coexisted alongside broadswords.

The illustration (right) of musketeers and pikemen is from the French artist Jaques Callot's work on the Thirty Years' War, published in 1633.

1 Flail (17)
2 Dagger (32)
3 Dagger-bayonet (33)
4 Swords (49)
5 Rapiers (50)
6 Smallswords (51)
7 Pole-arms (58-62)
8 Bayonets (64, 66)
9 Longarms (117, 118)
10 Pistols (122, 123)
11 Double pistol (126)
12 Revolving rifle (128)
13 Revolving pistol (129)
14 Repeating rifle (136)
15 Falconet (169)
16 Naval cannon (173)
17 Volley gun (207)
(The numbers in brackets are page references for further information.)

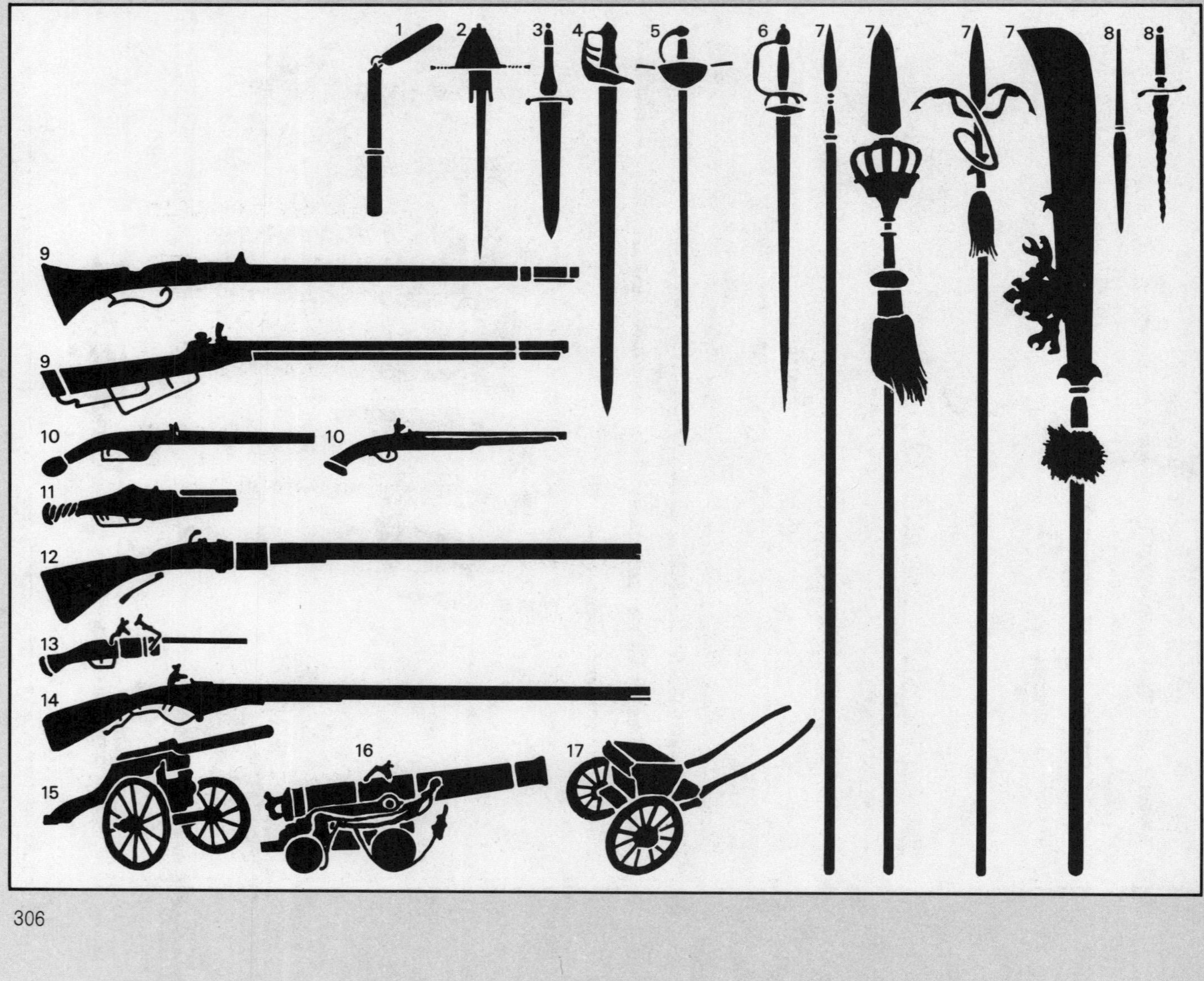

18th century Europe and America

Tactics in the 18th century became formalized into theories of drill movements culminating in the firing of disciplined volleys from the infantrymen's flintlock muskets. Infantry also carried short swords called hangers, and sometimes used hand grenades.
In the last quarter of the century, rifles saw increasing use for skirmishing, but did not replace smoothbore muskets. The cavalry still carried sabers, pistols or carbines.
A civilian might own a blunderbuss to defend his property, a pocket pistol to take on journeys, and from the 1770s, perhaps a pair of dueling pistols.
The illustrations (right) are from a drill manual of the time of the American Revolutionary War, in the 1770s.

Historical index

1 Dagger (33)
2 Smallswords (51)
3 Military swords (52)
4 Short sword (54)
5 Pole-arms (59-61)
6 Spring bayonet (67)
7 Socket bayonets (68, 69)
8 Tomahawks (80)
9 Grenade (84)
10 Blunderbuss (118)
11 Muskets (119)
12 Rifles (120)
13 Pistols (123, 124)
14 Double pistols (126)
15 Volley gun (127)
16 Turnoff pistol (132)
17 BL rifle (133)
18 Repeating rifle (136)
19 Grenade gun (154)
20 Grenade discharger (155)
21 Cannon barrel (169)
22 Cannon (170)
23 Depression carriage (172)
24 Naval cannon (173)
25 Puckle's gun (207)

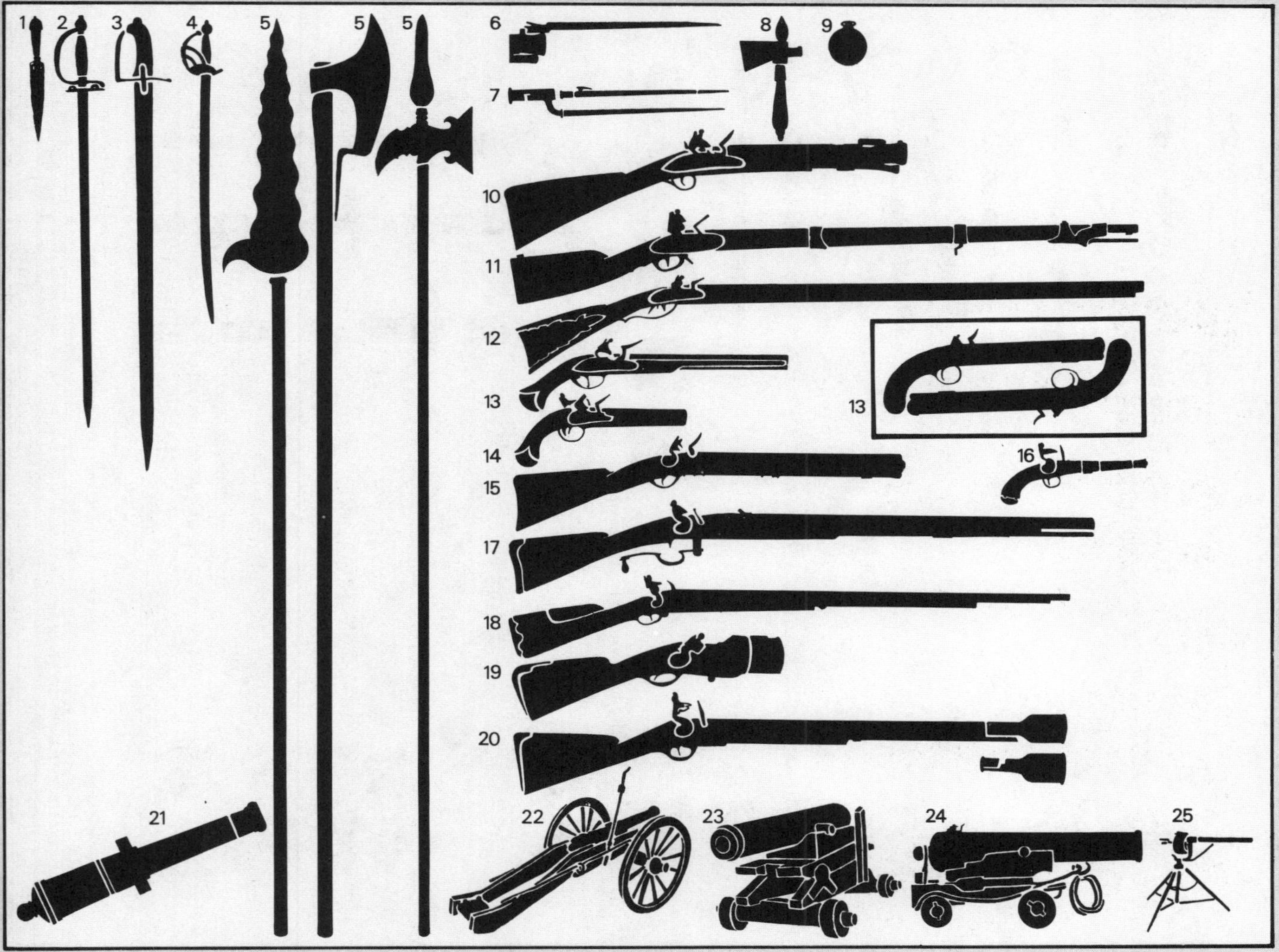

French Revolutionary Wars

The arms used in the major European wars that followed the French Revolution did not differ radically from those used earlier in the century. However, for the reader's convenience in tracing the exact style of weapons in use in the wars, this section of the index has been compiled.
The most notable innovation was the rocket, introduced by the British after seeing similar weapons used against them in India. Congreve's rockets continued in use until the mid-19th century.
The illustration (right) is from a French popular print of c.1816, and depicts French troops at the battle of Waterloo, June 18, 1815.

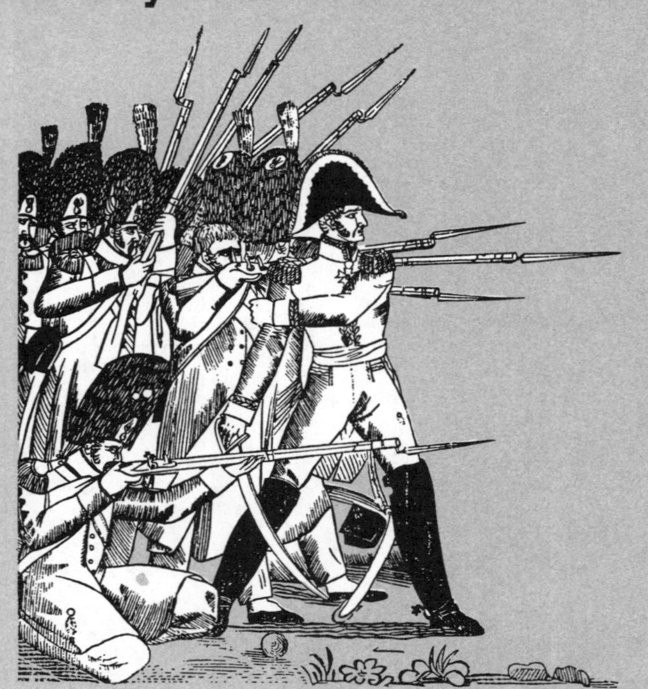

1 Dirk (33)
2 Saber (52)
3 Swords (53)
4 Cutlass (53)
5 Swords (55)
6 Spontoon (58)
7 Sword-bayonet (65)
8 Bayonets (68, 69)
9 Air-rifle (107)
10 Muskets (119)
11 Rifles (120)
12 Pistols (124, 125)
13 Cannon (170)
14 Garrison cannon (172)
15 Naval guns (173)
16 Congreve's rockets (244)
(The numbers in brackets are page references for further information.)

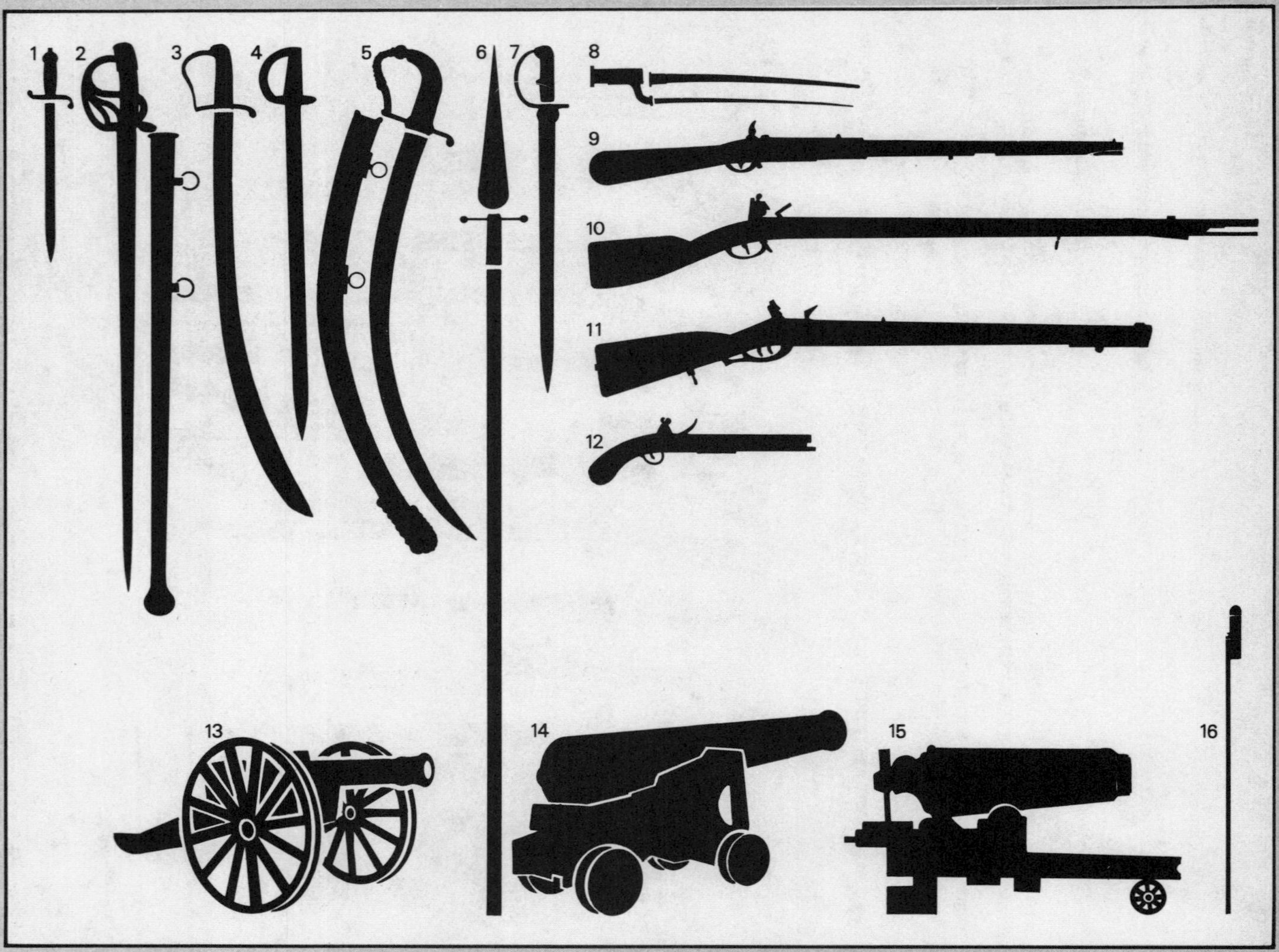

1816-60

Historical index

This period saw major improvements in small arms. Flintlock ignition was replaced for military use from c.1840 by the percussion system, which was more reliable, in wet weather especially, and required less skill from the soldier. Then, in the 1850s, Minié's bullet made smoothbore muskets obsolete, putting an accurate rifle in the hands of all infantrymen for the first time. Machinery and mass-production methods were coming into use by the end of the period, and general improvements in technology and industry were fast changing military armaments.

The engraving (right) shows British soldiers cleaning their arms and equipment at Gallipoli, en route for the Crimean War of 1854-56.

1 Saber (53)
2 Short swords (54)
3 Lance point (63)
4 Bayonets (68-70)
5 Air-cane (107)
6 Musket (119)
7 Rifles (120)
8 Minié rifles (121)
9 Pistols (124)
10 Pistol/carbine (125)
11 Double rifle (127)
12 Revolving rifle (128)
13 Revolvers (128)
14 Pepperbox revolvers (129)
15 Pistol (132)
16 BL carbine (133)
17 "Derringer" (135)
18 Repeating rifle (136)
19 BL revolver (142)
20 Cannon (171)
21 Congreve's rockets (244)

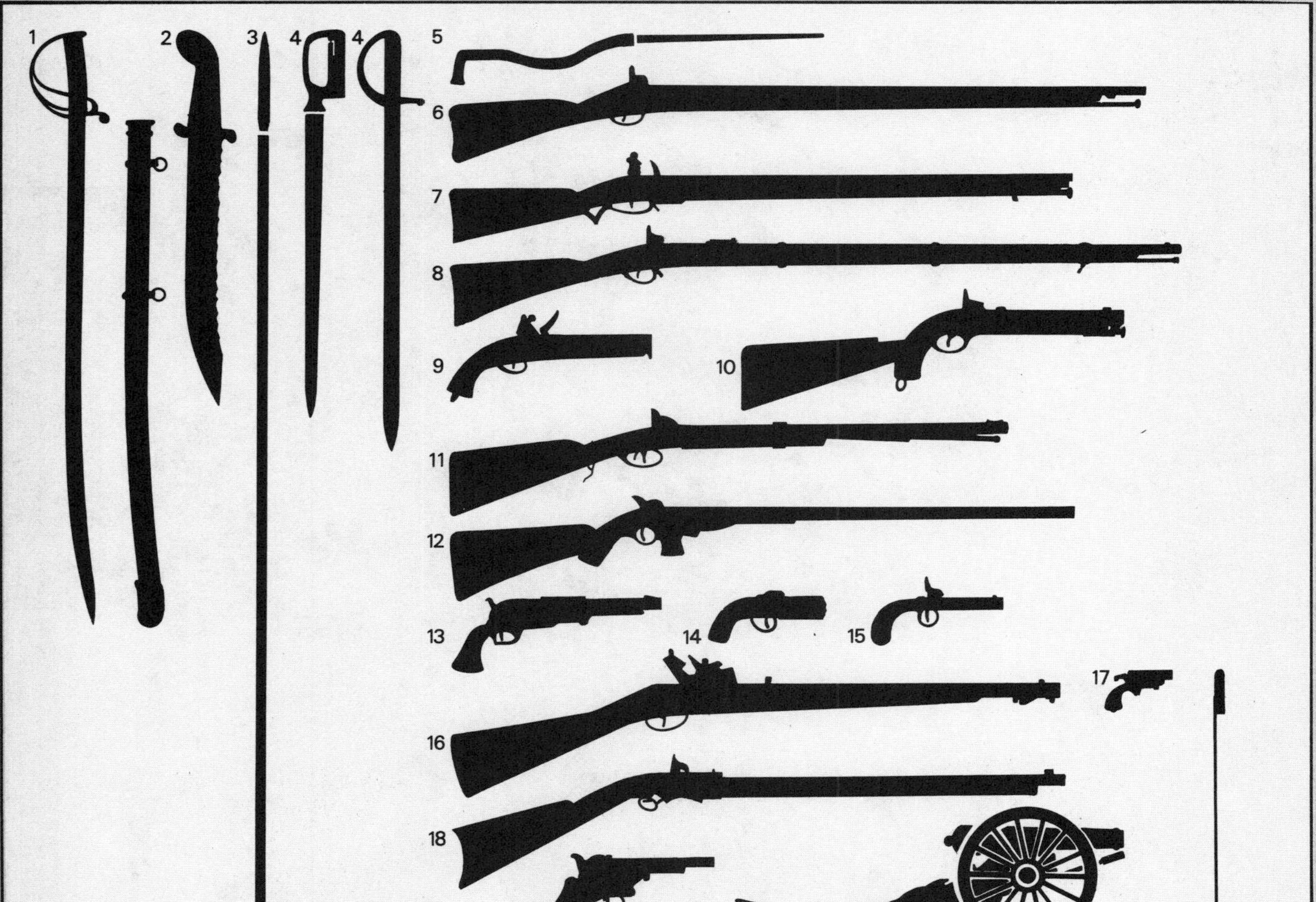

American Civil War

During the Civil War of 1861-65 many new weapons were seen in use on a large scale for the first time, and the armies and navies of the world took note. The list includes repeating rifles, hand-cranked machine guns, rifled and breech-loading artillery pieces, land and naval mines. The weapons that typify the War were, for infantry, the minié rifle with triangular-bladed socket-bayonet, for cavalry the front-loading revolver and breech-loading carbine, and for artillery the rifled field gun. As is true of most wars, though, many older arms that were technically obsolete were also pressed into service. Swords, knives and improvised weapons saw continued use.

The print (right) shows the manufacture of artillery shells.

1 Bowie knife (33)
2 Saber (53)
3 Bayonet (similar) (69)
4 Knuckle-duster (72)
5 Grenades (84, 86)
6 Musket (119)
7 Minié rifles (121)
8 Derringer pistol (125)
9 Revolving rifle (128)
10 Revolving pistol (128)
11 Revolving pistols (129)
12 BL carbine (133)
13 Multi-shot pistols (135)
14 BL repeaters (137)
15 BL revolvers (142)
16 Cannon (171)
17 Garrison cannon (172)
18 Naval swivel gun (173)
19 Smoothbore guns (174)
20 Rifled guns (175)
21 BL field gun (179)
22 Gatling gun (207)
23 Obstacles (222)
24 Land mine (230)
25 Naval mine (232)
26 Rocket (244)

1866-1913

This period began with muzzle-loading rifles and ended with bolt-action repeaters and fully-automatic machine guns of kinds that are still in use now. The most important single breakthrough was probably the metallic-cased cartridge that made possible the repeating rifle, the machine gun and the quick-firing field gun. At sea the iron warship was developed into the big-gun "dreadnoughts" that were the strategic weapons of the early 20th century. But these great ships could be sunk by the new self-propelled torpedoes, launched from the smallest of gunboats. **The illustration** (right) of British soldiers on service in India is from a periodical, "The Navy and Army Illustrated," of 1897.

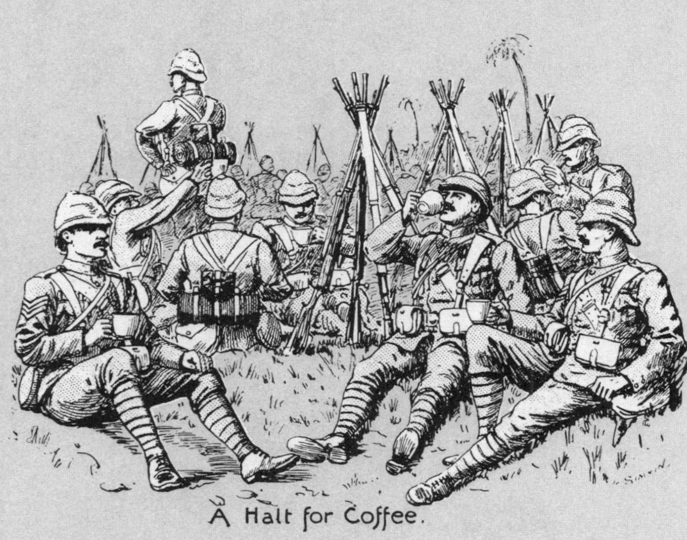

A Halt for Coffee.

Historical index

1 Knife-bayonet (33)
2 Swords (53, 55)
3 Lance (63)
4 Bayonets (65, 67-71)
5 Dagger/pistol (72)
6 Grenade (86)
7 Pistols (132)
8 Rifles (133)
9 Combat shotguns (134)
10 Multi-shot pistols (135)
11 Repeating rifles (137)
12 Bolt-action rifles (138-9)
13 Revolvers (142-144)
14 Semi-auto pistols (146-7)
15 Semi-auto rifle (150)
16 Field guns (182, 183)
17 Mountain gun (190)
18 Coastal guns (191)
19 Pom-pom (192)
20 Naval guns (202, 203)
21 Machine guns (206, 207)
22 Torpedo and tube (242)
23 Rockets (244)
(The numbers in brackets are page references for further information.)

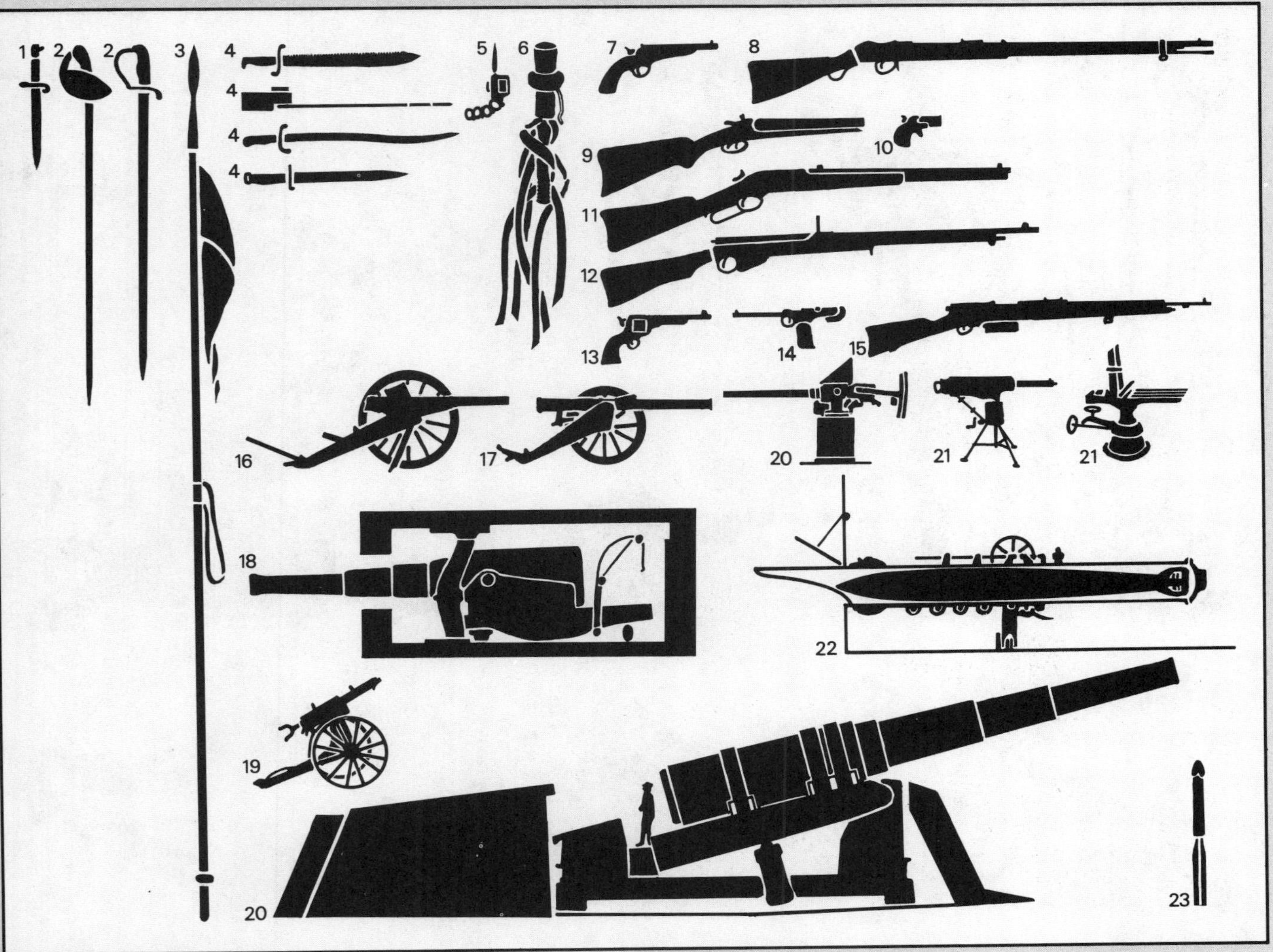

World War 1

World War 1 saw the first use in battle of submarines, tanks, aircraft, aerial bombs, flamethrowers and chemical warfare—in the form of poison gas. In response, depth charges, anti-tank rifles and anti-aircraft guns were developed. The defensive combination of machine guns and barbed wire led to trench warfare, and that in turn led to a revival of mortars and hand- and rifle-grenades. Bayonets, knives and clubs were used in trench raids. Artillery fire was used on a massive scale unthought of even at the war's outbreak. **Illustrations** (near right) from a British poster, listing achievements in war production. The German poster (far right) lists their gains in the offensive of March 1918.

(The numbers in brackets are page references for further information.)

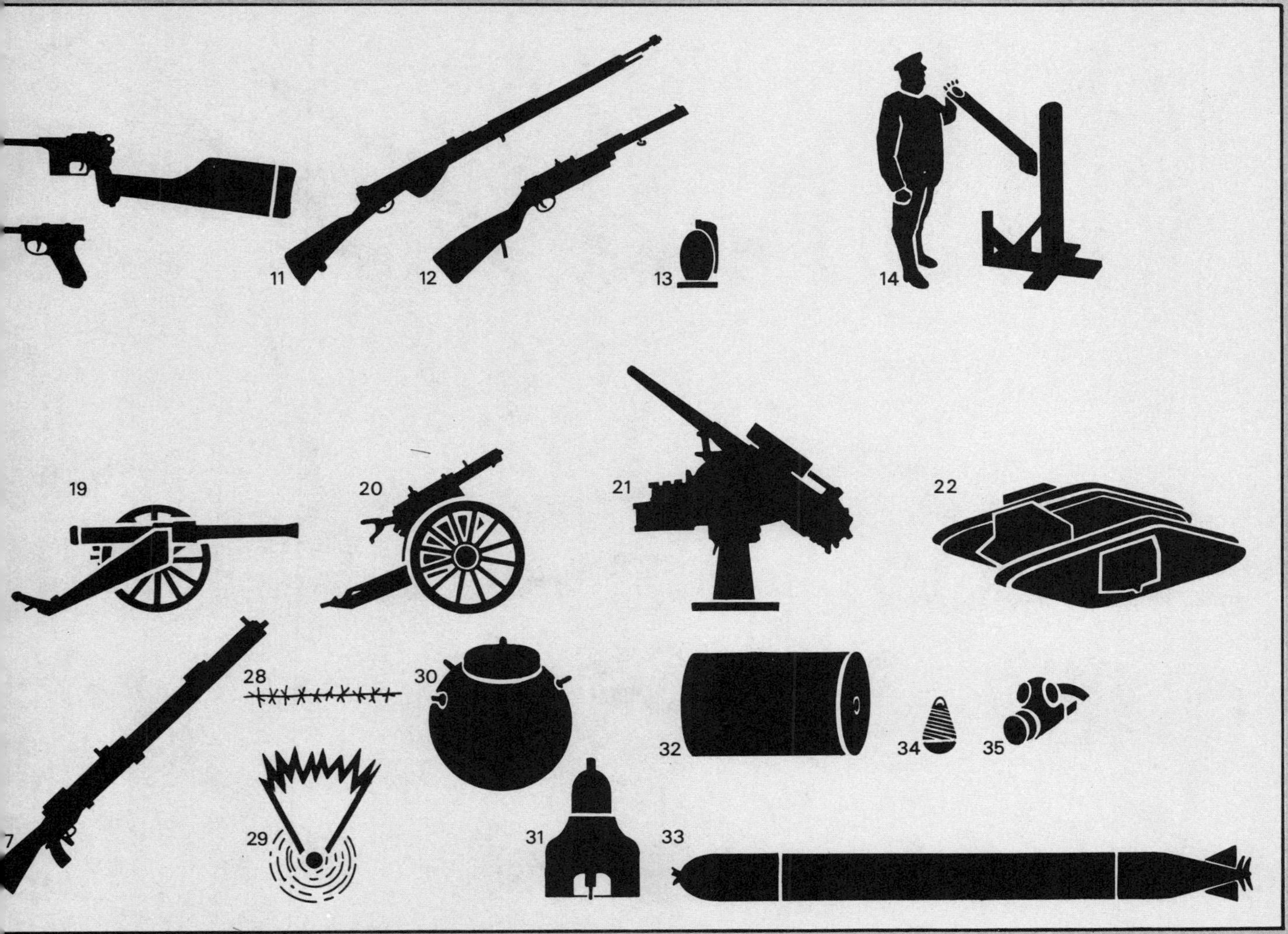

World War 2

As well as seeing wider use of most of the new weapons from WW1, in more highly developed form, the Second World War saw the first use of strategic missiles and the atomic bomb—weapons that still dominate world politics. In the air, it was the age of strategic bombing, and at sea too the use of aircraft began to render the big-gun battleships obsolete. On land, tanks now almost all had one main gun mounted in a rotating turret. More specialized kinds of machine gun were in use, and semi-automatic rifles were becoming common.

The painting (near right) by Lieutenant Ian Eadie depicts an amphibious landing on Sicily in 1943.

The emblems (far right) from US aircraft dramatize the role of the bomber.

"HELLSADROPPIN"

Jo-Jo's
SPECIAL
DELIVERY

Historical index

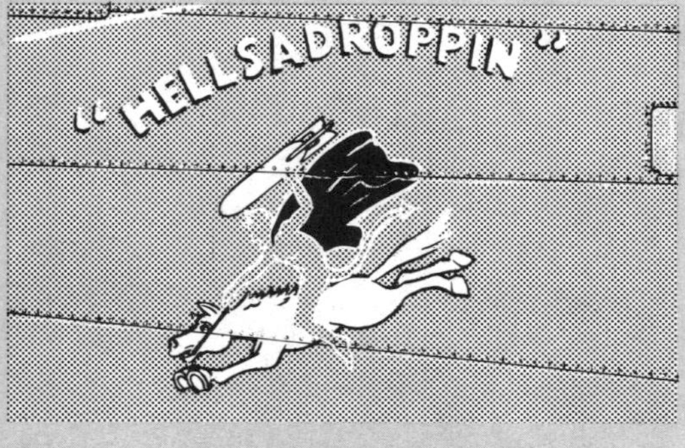

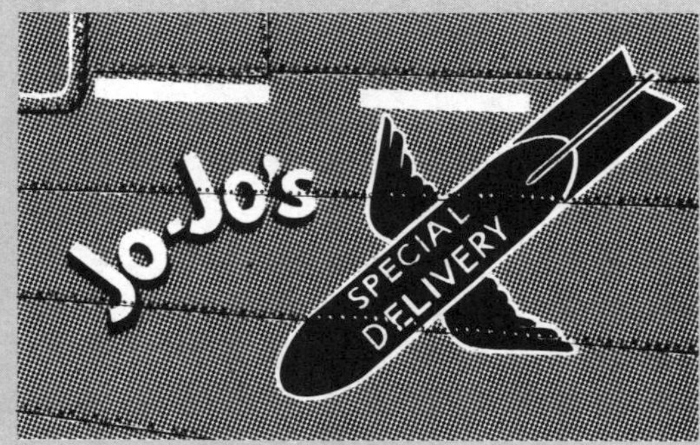

(The numbers in brackets are page references for further information.)

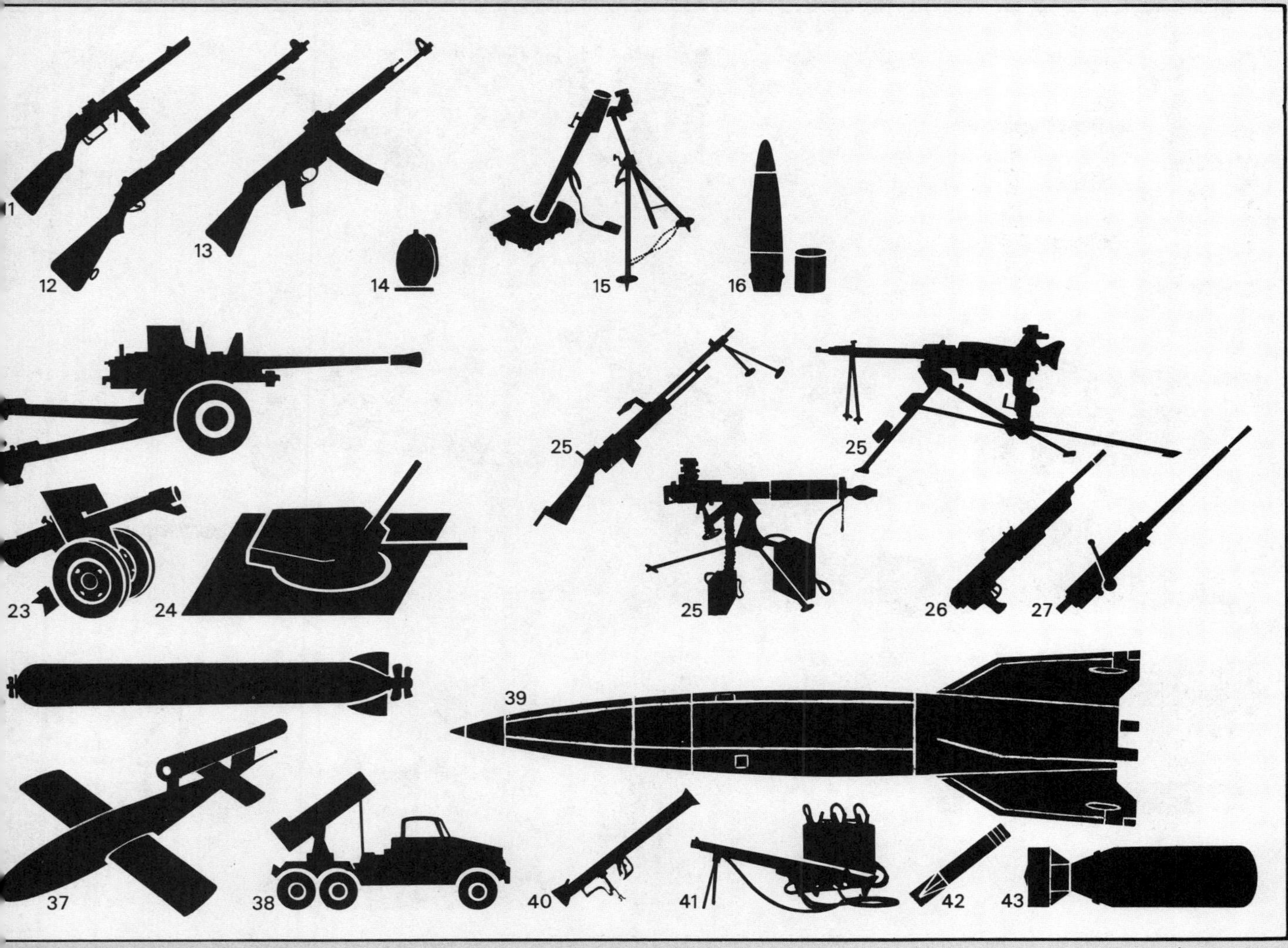

11
12
13
14
15
16
25
25
25
23
24
26
27
39
37
38
40
41
42
43

The modern world

Virtually all of the types of weapon ever devised by man are still in use, or are held ready for use, somewhere in the world today. The existence of multi-warhead nuclear missiles has not removed sticks and stones from the improvised arsenal of rioters. In other words, the choice of available weaponry goes on expanding, and what is obsolescent in the terms of regular armed forces may well find other users. For this reason, the weapons shown here range from the most sophisticated military hardware, through terrorist bombs and down to simple wooden truncheons.

The picture (near right) is from a North Vietnamese poster of the 1960s.

The poster (far right) was issued by the Committee for Nuclear Disarmament.

CountDown

14
15
16
17
18
19
20
28
30
32
34
36
38
29
31
33
35
37
50
52
51
53
54

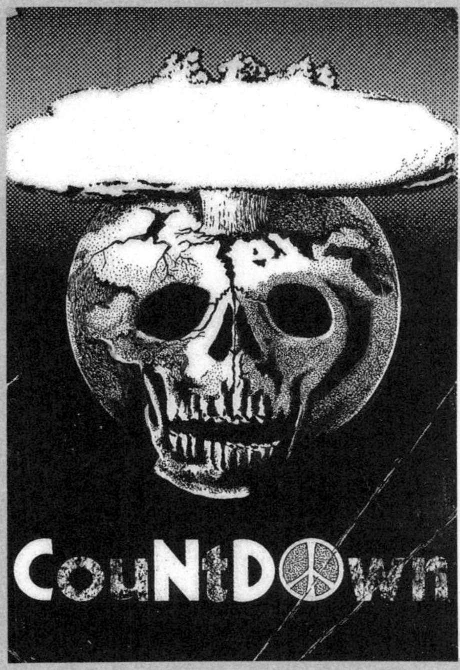

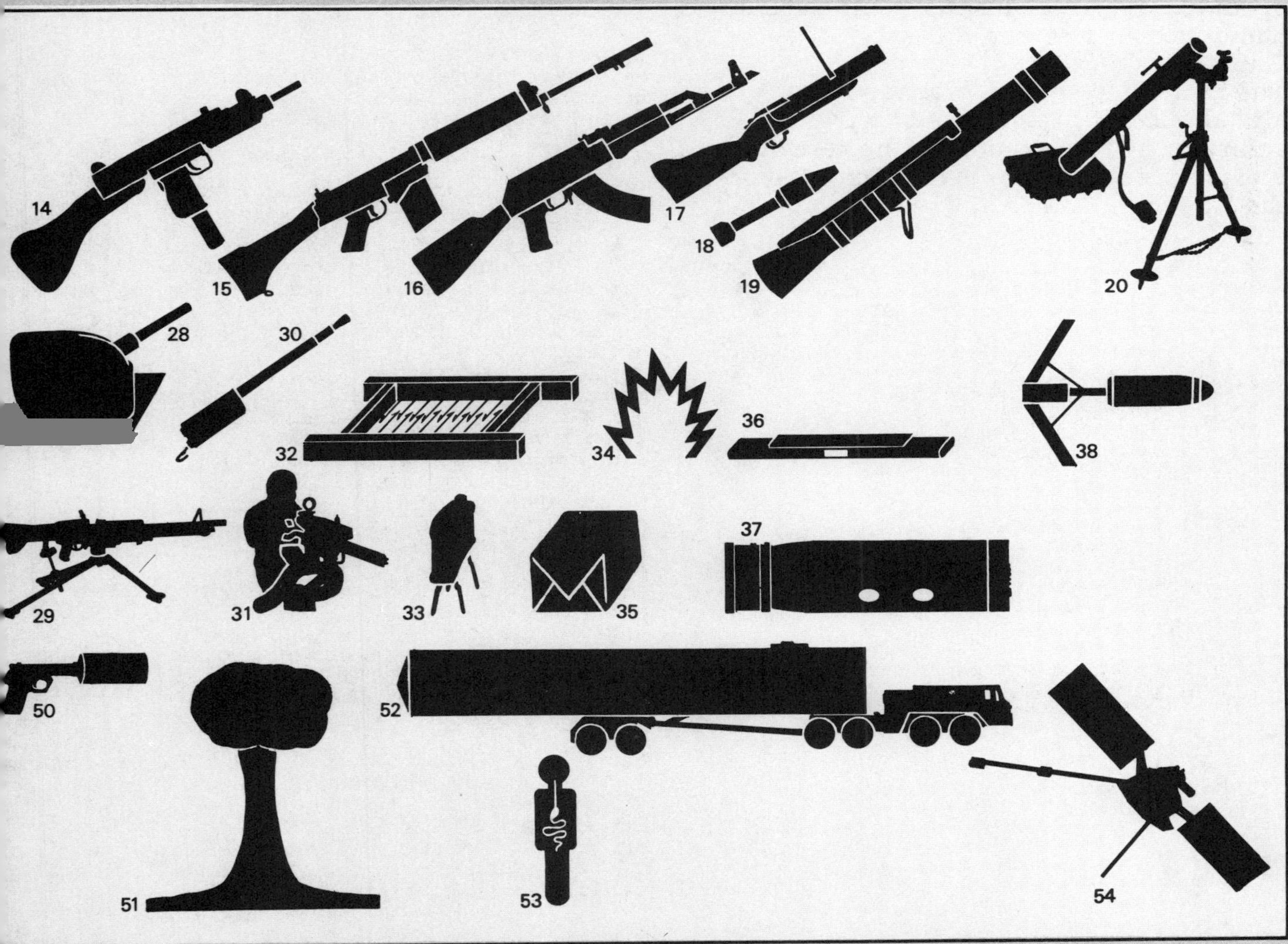

Famous names 1

The purpose of this section is to add to the information already given in the main body of the book. The emphasis here is on the designers, makers, scientists, arsenals, commercial companies and towns whose names are probably familiar even to many people previously quite unacquainted with the study of weaponry. Most will have heard, for example, of Springfield rifles or the Gatling gun. Here we explain that the former derive their name from the US arsenal in Springfield, Massachusetts, while the latter is named for its inventor, Richard Jordan Gatling.
The individual entries, arranged alphabetically, are followed by page references of illustrations of the relevant weapons, or of further textual information on the subject.

Adams, John and Robert
Brothers, both English gunsmiths, famous for a number of designs of revolver in the mid 19th century. (See pp.129, 142.)

ADEN
British aircraft cannon, developed in the late 1940s from a German WW2 gun, and still in use on some fighter aircraft. The name was made up from elements of its place of development, Armaments Development, ENfield. (See p.193.)

Allen, Ethan (1808-71)
Designer and manufacturer of sporting and self-defense firearms based in Massachusetts. Known chiefly for his distinctive pepperbox revolvers. (See p.129.)

Amakuni
The first Japanese swordsmith whose name is still known. He was active in Yamato province c.701AD.

Andrea Ferara
Properly Andrea dei Ferari. Italian swordsmith from Bellimo. His name was later used by many other makers, it being synonymous with high quality. (See p.49.)

Arisaka
A series of Japanese bolt-action rifles first produced in 1897. Named for Colonel Nariake Arisaka of the Tokyo Arsenal. (See p.141.)

Armalite rifle
The term "Armalite rifle" is now applied to a number of models of assault rifle that are derived from the AR10, first developed and marketed by Armalite Inc of California. Included is the AR15 (known in the US Forces as the M16 and M16A1 rifles) and the AR18. (See p.153.)

Armbrust
German word meaning "crossbow," adopted as the name for a new shoulder-held recoilless anti-tank gun. It represents a new application of the recoilless principle. (See p.157.)

Armstrong, William George (1810-1900)
1st Baron Armstrong. English inventor and engineer, particularly remembered for his successful design of breech-loading mechanism used on artillery pieces. (See pp.175,182,191.)

Austen
Name contrived for the Australian version of the British Sten submachine gun.

Baker, Ezekiel (d. 1836)
London gunsmith who produced sporting, self-defense and military arms. Best known as the designer of the first rifle to be used on a large scale by the British Army—the Baker rifle. (See p.120.)

BAT
Name contrived for a recent British series of Battalion Anti-Tank guns, including also the MOBAT, CONBAT and WOMBAT. (See p.201.)

Berdan, Colonel Hiram (d. 1893)
American soldier and inventor best known for his rifles, adopted by Spain and Russia, and for a design of cartridge primer still in use world-wide.

Beretta
Pietro Beretta SpA is an Italian armaments company, whose name is synonymous with its numerous designs of semi-automatic pistol.
Bergmann
Theodor Bergmann Waffenbau AG was a German arms manufacturing company. The name Bergmann is often used for the MP 18/1 submachine gun, which this company manufactured. (See p.148.)
BESA
British tank machine gun of WW2, a copy of the Czech ZB vz 53. (See p.218.)
Big Bertha
Popular name first applied to the 42cm howitzers used by the Germans and Austrians in 1914 (see p.188), and subsequently applied to other types of huge artillery piece in WW1 and WW2.
Bofors
Swedish armaments firm, known for its artillery developments, and especially for the series of light anti-aircraft guns (see pp.194,205) that have been used by most armies and navies of the world.
Bourgeoys, Marin les (c.1550-1634)
French painter and gunmaker, possibly the inventor c.1610 of the true flintlock.
Boutet, Nicolas-Noël (1761-1833)
French gunmaker famous for his highly decorated flintlocks, produced for the Royal, Revolutionary and Napoleonic régimes. (See pistol p.125.)
Bowie, Jim (1799–1836)
Adventurer from Kentucky, whose exploits popularized the large type of fighting knife that now bears his name (see p.33). Killed at the Alamo.
Boxer, Edward Mounier (1823-98)
British Artillery Officer and official at Woolwich Arsenal. Famous for three developments which bear his name : a shell fuze, the first successful metallic rifle cartridge, and a primer for it which is still in world-wide use. (See p.131.)
Braun, Wernher von (1912-77)
German engineer who featured prominently in all aspects of rocketry and space exploration, first in Germany and after WW2 in the USA where he became chief of the US Army ballistic weapon program.
Breda
Societa Anonima Ernesto Breda is an Italian company based in Brescia. They are mainly known for the Breda machine guns used by the Italian forces in WW2.
BREN
British light machine gun based on a Czechoslovakian design. The name is formed from BRno and ENfield, the two centers of its development. (See p.213.)
Brno
The town that has long been the center of the Czechoslovakian firearms industry.
Brown Bess
The unofficial name of a series of British smoothbore muskets of the 18th and early 19th centuries. The origin of the name is uncertain, and much disputed. (See p.119.)
Browning, John M. (1855-1926)
Major American designer of rifles, pistols and machine guns, most of which are still in use. Some of his products bear his name, while others were designed for the Winchester, Remington, Colt and FN concerns. (See pp.146, 208,209,211,214,215.)
Brunswick
The Brunswick two-grooved rifle was developed by George Lovell (qv) from a design by the Duke of Brunswick's field adjutant, a Captain Berners. It was used by the British and Indian armies from 1837 into the 1870s, and a version was also used by Russia. (See p.121.)
Carcano, M.
Italian government official involved in the development of the Mannlicher Carcano bolt-action rifle, introduced in 1891. (See p.141.)
Carl-Gustaf
Commercial name for a shoulder-held recoilless gun produced by the Forenade Fabriksverken company of Sweden. Currently in use with at least 11 armies. (See p.157.)
Carron Co
Scottish ironfounders who manufactured cannon, shot and shells in the 18th and 19th centuries. The carronade, a short naval cannon, was first made by them. (See p.173.)
Charleville
French town near the Belgian border which was a center of arms manufacture from the 17th century. The name is now commonly applied to the French Model 1763 military musket.
Chassepot, Antoine Alphonse (1833-1905)
Inventor of the M.1866 bolt-action rifle used by the French army in the Franco-Prussian War of 1870. (See p.133.) It is often compared with the Dreyse needle-gun which opposed it in that campaign.
Collier
The Collier revolver was a flintlock front-loading weapon made in at least two models. It was patented in 1818 by Elisha Haydon Collier of Boston, Massachusetts. (See p.129.)
Colt, Samuel (1814-62)
American designer of firearms and pioneer of modern mass-production, famous chiefly for his cheap, reliable revolvers. The company that he founded in 1836 still produces many of the old models, as well as the latest military hardwear. (See pp.128, 129,137,142,143,144,145, 147,214.)
Cominazzo
Celebrated family of Italian gun-barrel makers, active from the late 16th century in and near Brescia.
Congreve, Sir William (1772-1828)
British inventor of explosive rockets, a form of artillery used extensively in the 19th century. A range of different sized rockets bearing his name was used by the British, American and Indian armies. (See p.244.)
Cordite
A British propellant devised in 1891, still used extensively in small arm and artillery ammunition. It is formed from nitroglycerin, gun-cotton and mineral jelly, and resembles uncooked spaghetti in form and texture. (See p.112.)

Famous names 2

Creedmoor
A rifle-range on Long Island, New York, which gave its name to the sport of long-range rifle shooting in America, and hence to the rifles used.

Damascus
In the broadest sense, a damascus gun-barrel is one formed by winding a strip of metal spirally around a rod and welding the join by hammering it at white heat, a method once common in Europe, the Middle East and India. The link with the town of Damascus is tenuous.

De Bange
The De Bange system of sealing the breech of a breech-loading artillery piece was invented by a Frenchman of that name in the late 19th century. The general principle is still in use. (See p.178.)

Degtyarev, Vasily (1890-1959)
An eminent Soviet small arms designer. Three of his products are illustrated in this book. (See pp.213,214.)

Deringer, Henry (1786-1868)
An American gunsmith, famous for his small, single-shot muzzle-loading pocket pistols. His name, in various spellings, was later applied to many types of small pistol. (See pp.125,135.)

Dreadnought
The British battleship HMS *Dreadnought* was completed in 1906, and its modern design rendered all existing warships obsolete. Subsequently the term "dreadnought" came to be used for the general type of big-gun battleship used in WW1. (See pp.203-204.)

Dreyse, Johann Nikolaus von (1787-1867)
A Prussian gunsmith who once worked with Pauly (qv). He devised the Dreyse bolt-action needle-gun, with which the Prussians won many victories between 1841 and 1870. (See p.132.)

Dum Dum
A British arsenal near Calcutta which gave its name to a soft-nosed rifle bullet that was later forbidden by the Hague Convention of 1899. The term is now applied to any bullet designed to expand on impact—a form common in hunting but still banned in war.

Enfield
The Royal Small Arms Factory at Enfield in North London, founded in 1804, has given its name to several rifles, revolvers and a type of rifling. The British Pattern 1853 rifled musket (see p.121) is commonly called "the Enfield rifle." In the USA, the M17 rifle (see p.139) is often called the "Enfield." (See also Lee-Enfield.)

Essen
A German industrial town on the Ruhr and a center for arms manufacture. The main factory of the Krupps company (qv) was there.

Ferguson, Major Patrick (1744-80)
A British officer who fought in the American Revolution. For a time he led a unit armed with a breech-loading rifle which bore his name. (See p.133.)

FN
The initials of the Belgian arms manufacturers, Fabrique Nationale d'Armes de Guerre, one of the world's foremost arms producers. In England, the term "the FN rifle" is often applied to the L1 Self-Loading Rifle, of Belgian design. (See pp.151,217.)

Forsyth, Alexander John (1768-1843)
A Scottish Presbyterian minister who devised the first successful form of percussion ignition c.1805. This proved in time to be one of the most important steps in the history of firearms. (See p.111.)

Garand, John C. (1888–1974)
American designer of small arms, responsible for the M1 self-loading rifle used by the US Army in World War 2. Adopted in 1936, the rifle is commonly known as "The Garand." (See p.150.)

Gatling, Richard Jordan (1818-1903)
American-born inventor who, in 1862, patented the most successful early hand-cranked machine gun. (See pp.207, 209.)

Gerlich
The Gerlich principle, developed by a German engineer of that name, involved the use of a tapered bore in order to produce a high-velocity anti-tank gun. (See p.199.)

Girandoni, Bartolomeo (1744-99)
Inventor of a repeating air-rifle bearing his name, used by Austrian sharpshooters. The only air-rifle to have seen official use in war. (See p.107.)

Goddard, Robert H. (1882-1945)
The American pioneer of rocket engineering, born in Worcester, Massachusetts. (See p.246.)

Gras, Capitain Basile (1836-1904)
Designer of the French Model 1874 rifle, which bears his name. (See bayonet p.70.)

Greener, William (1844–69) and William Wellington (1864–1900)
English gunsmiths father and son. William the elder was a general inventor, a prolific writer, and one of the dominant characters in a vital period of firearms history. The son is known chiefly for his designs for breech-loading shotguns.

Gribeauval, Jean-Baptiste Vaquette de (1715-89)
French artillery officer responsible for a complete re-design of French artillery organization and equipment (the Gribeauval system). (See pp.165,171.)

Hall, John Hancock (1778-1841)
American inventor of one of the few successful flintlock breech-loaders, in limited use with the US Army from 1819. (See p.133.)

Henry, Benjamin Tyler (1821-98)
American designer remembered chiefly for the underlever repeating rifle which bore his name. It was a major step in the development of the famous Winchester rifle. (See p.137.)

Hispano-Suiza
Société Anonyme Suisse Hispano-Suiza, of Geneva, was for long one of the two leading producers of automatic cannon (see also Oerlikon). In 1972 the Oerlikon company gained a controlling interest in Hispano-Suiza. (See p.192.)

Hotchkiss, Benjamin Berkeley (1826-85)
An American responsible for the design and manufacture of many new developments in artillery and small arms, including a machine gun bearing his name. (See pp.212, 214.)
Jacob, Major General John (1812-58)
British Officer in the Indian Army who designed a number of rifles and bullets in the 1840s and 1850s. The Jacob rifle was eventually issued to two battalions of Indian infantry, and is now a prized collectors' item. (See p.127.)
Jäger (or Jaeger)
The German word for a hunter, and subsequently a military rifleman. The flintlock weapon of riflemen in the armies of German states in the late 18th century is called a Jäger rifle. (See p.120.)
Kalashnikov, Mikhail (b. 1920)
Kalashnikov, now a Hero of Socialist Labor and a winner of several Soviet prizes and a medal for gallantry in WW2, was the designer of the AK47 (Avtomat Kalashnikova of 1947), now probably the most numerous rifle in history. He also designed the PK (Pulemyot Kalashnikova) series of machine guns. (See pp.153,216.)
Kalthoff
A family of German gunsmiths who made repeating firearms in the 17th century. Their design is called by collectors the Kalthoff system. (See pp.111,136.)
Kentucky rifle
One name for the American Long or Pennsylvania rifle of the 18th and early 19th centuries. The most common of the three names, it nevertheless has the least basis in fact. (See p.120.)
Krag, Ole H. (1837-1912)
Norwegian firearms designer best known for his bolt-action rifle, the Krag-Jørgensen. (See p.138.)
Kromuskit
A design of breech for recoilless guns. The name was formed from those of the designers, Kroger and Musser. (See p.200.)
Krupp
German family concern of arms manufacturers, founded by Alfred Krupp in the 1840s, famous for their use of steel in armaments. Prominent in the arming of Germany in the two World Wars and still in production today.
Lahti
Finnish self-loading pistol named for its designer, Aimo Lahti.
Lancaster, Charles William (1820-78)
English gunsmith remembered for his oval-bored rifling system, and a successful early sporting breech-loader. His father also made high-quality sporting arms.
Lebel, Lt. Col. Nicolas (1838-91)
French designer remembered chiefly for the bolt-action rifle that bears his name (see p.139) ; it was the first military smallbore repeater using smokeless powder. His name is also applied to a revolver cartridge. (See p.144.)
Lee, James Paris (1831-1904)
Scottish-born firearms designer who worked chiefly in the USA and Canada. Famous for his invention of the box magazine and certain bolt-action designs. (See also Lee-Enfield and Lee-Metford.)
Lee-Enfield
A series of British military rifles produced from 1895-1957, based on the Lee bolt-action and Enfield rifling. (See pp.139,140.)
Lee-Metford
The first repeating rifle issued to the British Army, in 1888. It had a Lee bolt-action and Metford's rifling. (See pp.111, 138.) (See also Lee and Metford.)
Lefaucheux
19th century French gunmakers, father and son. Responsible for the pinfire cartridge (see pp.111,112,130), and a successful breech-loading shotgun and revolver (see p.142.)
LeMat
A revolver made in the USA, England and America in the 1850s and 1860s, named for its inventor J A F LeMat. (See p.129.)
Lewis, Isaac Newton (1858-1931)
American weapons designer, famous chiefly for his gas-operated machine gun. (See pp.212, 219.)
Liège
Belgian industrial city that has been one of the world's major centers of arms production, particularly of small arms.
Long Max
German long-range railroad-mounted guns of the latter part of World War 1. Named after Vice-Admiral Max Rogge, who was responsible for their deployment on land. The Paris Gun (see p.189) was based on Long Max.
Lorenzoni, Michele
17th century Florentine gunsmith, famous for his design of flintlock repeating firearms. (See p.136.)
Lovell, George (1785-1854)
English ordnance official responsible for many firearms designs used by the British Army from the 1830s to the 1850s.
Luger, George (1848-1922)
Austrian firearms designer, famous chiefly for his semi-automatic pistol (see p.147) used by the German, and many other, armies.
Maginot, André (1877-1932)
French politician, disabled as a soldier in WW1, who agitated for the building of a line of defense along France's border with Germany in the 1920s. The fortifications were built in the 1930s and were named the Maginot Line.
Manhattan Project
Name of the US War Department's plan to develop a superexplosive by using nuclear fission. Initiated in 1942, the project ultimately led to the dropping of two atomic bombs on Japan in 1945.
Mannlicher, Ferdinand Ritter von (1848–1904)
Prolific Austrian firearms designer, remembered chiefly for his bolt-action rifle. (See p. 139.)

Famous names 3

Manton, Joseph (1760-1835)
The most celebrated English gunsmith of his day, and the inventor of several improvements to sporting guns. His brother John was also a well-known gunsmith.

Martini-Henry
British Army rifle introduced in 1871 using Friedrich Von Martini's breech system and Alexander Henry's design of rifling. (See pp.131,133.)

Masamune (1264-1343AD)
One of the greatest Japanese swordsmiths, who worked in Sagami province. (See p.42.)

Maubeuge
French town near the Belgian border which was the site of the main French government arms factory from 1704 to 1830.

Mauser, Peter Paul (1838-1914)
German firearms designer, responsible for important designs of automatic pistols, self-loading rifles and also revolvers. He is best remembered for the series of bolt-action rifle designs, used world-wide. (See pp.138,139,141, 146.)

Maxim, Hiram Stevens (1840-1916)
American-born inventor who designed the first true modern machine-gun (see p.206). His revolutionary innovation was to use some of the cartridge's energy to work the gun's mechanism. (See also pp.165,192,209,212, 214,219.)

Metford, William Ellis (1824-99)
English inventor and firearms designer, responsible for several important discoveries and designs, chiefly related to rifling and accuracy. (See also Lee-Metford.)

Mills, Sir William (1856-1932)
British inventor of the "Mills bomb," a hand grenade introduced in 1915 and still in use with some armies. (See p.88.)

Minié, Claude-Etienne (1804-79)
French army officer who helped to perfect an expanding bullet which later bore his name. The design greatly improved the range and accuracy of muzzle-loading small arms, and affected military tactics. (See pp.111,121.)

Miquelet
A type of gun-lock popular in the Mediterranean area. The name originated in Spain, but the exact derivation is obscure. (See pp.115,118,123.)

Molotov (1890–1986)
Born Vyacheslav Mikhaylovich Skryabin, Molotov was Chairman and then Deputy Chairman of the Council of Ministers in the Soviet government in WW2. The term "Molotov cocktail" is often applied to improvised petrol bombs that use a glass bottle. (See p.266.)

Monitor
The name "monitor" came to be applied to shallow-draft armored gunboats generally, but it was originally the name of a specific vessel, the USS *Monitor*, which figured prominently in the American Civil War. (See p.174.)

Mosin-Nagant
A design of bolt-action rifle used by Russia from 1891, and still used in some countries. It was designed by Colonel Mosin, a Russian, and M. Nagant, a Belgian. (See p.140.)

Napoleon
The 12-pounder "Napoleon" cannon became famous in the American Civil War of 1861-65. Originally of French design, it was named for the Emperor Napoleon III. (See p.171.)

Nobel, Alfred Bernhard (1833-96)
Swedish chemist who developed several important explosives and propellants, including dynamite and nitrocellulose (see pp.111,112,165). He also instituted the celebrated Nobel prizes.

Nock, Henry (1741-1804)
English gun-manufacturer and innovator. He made ingenious multi-shot firearms, high quality sporting guns and also mass-produced military weapons and components. (See p.127.)

Nordenfelt, Thorsten (1842-1920)
Swedish entrepreneur, remembered for the manually operated machine gun, promoted by him, which bears his name. (See p.207.)

Oerlikon
Oerlikon-Bührte AG of Zürich are perhaps the world's best known producers of automatic cannon (see p.192). The term "Oerlikon gun" usually refers to the 20mm anti-aircraft cannon fitted to the ships of many countries in WW2.

Parabellum
The telegraphic name of the Deutsche Waffen- und Munitionsfabrik. It has also been applied to the Luger pistol, and a widely used 9mm cartridge. (See p.147.)

Parrot
The Parrot guns of the 1860s were distinguished by having a wrought iron band shrunk around the breech of their cast-iron barrel. The name derives from the inventor of this means of reinforcing the barrel. (See p.175.)

Pauly, Johannes Samuel (1766-c.1820)
Swiss-born inventor of a centerfire cartridge, patented in 1812. It had only a limited success, mostly for sporting guns, but was the forerunner of modern small-arms ammunition. (See pp.111,130.)

Pedersen
The Pedersen device was an adaptor which converted the American Springfield service rifle into a submachine gun, and was named for the inventor J D Pedersen. Although many were produced in 1918, none saw use in action.

Puckle, James (1667-1724)
British inventor and proponent of a quick-firing revolving gun, fired from a stand and sometimes regarded as an early machine gun. It was patented in 1718, but enjoyed little success. (See p.207.)

Purdey
Family of London gunsmiths, founded by James Purdey in the 19th century and still regarded as one of the world's foremost sporting-gun makers.

Radom
The departmental capital of the Kielce province in East Central Poland. In the field of weaponry, the name is best known from the term "Radom Mauser," referring to certain rifles of German design made there.

Rarden
The Rarden cannon is a modern British weapon fitted to a variety of armored fighting vehicles. Its name is derived from the initials of the research center where it was developed (RARDE) and of ENfield, where it is made. (See p.197.)

Remington
American firearms manufacturing concern, founded by Eliphalet Remington 1816. The name is now applied to many successful firearms designed by the company. (See pp.133,135,143.)

Ripoll
Town in Northeast Spain, famous for its distinctively styled firearms produced from the late 16th century until 1839 (see p.123). In that year the town was destroyed.

Ross, Sir Charles (1872-1942)
Designer of a series of straight-pull, bolt-action rifles that bear his name. They were used in World War 1 by the Canadian Army.

Saint-Etienne
Town in southeast France which has been a center of the French arms industry since the late 16th century.

Schmeisser, Hugo (d. 1945?)
German firearms designer, responsible for the MP18/1 or Bergmann submachine gun. His name is often applied to the MP38 and MP40 submachine guns (see p.148), although he did not design them, but merely took a part in the manufacture of the MP40.

Schmidt-Rubin
The name of a series of Swiss straight-pull bolt-action rifles, first produced in 1889 (see p.141). It is derived from the names of Major Rubin, director of a munitions factory at Thun who designed the bullet used, and a Colonel Schmidt who designed the rifle.

Schwarzlose, Andreas W. (1867–1936)
Austrian designer of firearms, remembered chiefly for his blowback-operated machine gun. (See pp.214,215.)

Sharps, Christian (1811-74)
American gunsmith, famous for the single-shot breech-loading rifle which bears his name. (See p.133.)

Shillelagh
Irish club, traditionally cut from a blackthorn tree (see p.14). The name has also been used for a US Army rocket system fitted to tanks in recent years.

Shrapnel, Henry (1761-1842)
Lieutenant, later Lieutenant-General. British Artillery officer who in 1784 invented an explosive shell containing many spherical bullets, designed to be burst over the heads of the enemy. His name has since been applied to several later developments of the idea. (See pp.165,167, 174,181.)

SIG
Schweizerische Industrie-Gesellschaft, of Neuhausen-am-Rheinfalls, Switzerland, are better known by their initials SIG. They have produced many successful designs of pistols, rifles and machine guns. (See p.216.)

Skoda
Major arms factory in Czechoslovakia that manufactured tanks and artillery throughout WW1 and WW2.

Smith & Wesson
Horace Smith (1808-93) and Daniel Wesson (1825-1906) were the founders in 1857 of a company which held a patent on the essence of the breech-loading revolver. They enjoyed a virtual monopoly until 1869, and the company is still world-famous for its revolvers. (See pp.142,143,145.)

Snaphance
A word of Dutch derivation, now applied to a certain type of gunlock (see pp.114,122) that was common in the 17th century. As with many old terms, its original usage was slightly different. Also spelled "snaphaunce."

Snider
A rifle, or more precisely, a breech mechanism designed by an American, Jacob Snider, in 1864. It was used by the British Army to convert muzzle-loading rifles to breech-loading. (See pp.131,133.)

Solingen
Town in northwest West Germany where the craft of swordmaking was established in the Middle Ages. Solingen blades were exported for setting up in many countries. (See pp.49,51.)

Spandau
A Western suburb of Berlin, once the site of an armaments factory. The name was applied by Allied Troops in World War 2 to the German MG34 and MG42 machine guns. (See pp.216,217.)

Spencer
The Spencer rifle was a successful repeater, patented in 1860 by an American, Christopher M Spencer. (See p.137.)

Springfield
A town in Massachusetts which, since 1777, has been the site of one of the most important US government arms factories. The name is also transferred to various models of rifle made there. (See pp.133,139.)

Sten
A British World War 2 emergency-issue submachine gun. The name was made up from the initials of the designers, a Mr Sheppard and a Mr Turpin, and of the Enfield small arms factory. (See p.148.)

Sterling
The current British Army submachine gun is sometimes called the Sterling, after the Sterling Armament Company which developed it.

Steyr
First mentioned in the 10th century, the town of Steyr was the center of Austria's medieval iron industry and is still an important manufacturer of iron and steel today. Outside Austria, the name is chiefly associated with Mannlicher rifles (see p.139) which were made there.

Stokes
The Stokes trench mortar of 1915, invented by Sir Wilfred Stokes KBE, was the forerunner of the most familiar form of modern mortar (see p.176). It consisted of a simple tube supported by a bipod.

Stoner
The "Stoner system" is a family of small arms that can be adapted to several roles by the exchange of a few parts (see pp.209,217). It is named for the designer, Eugene Stoner, who was also responsible for the Armalite rifle.

Famous names 4

Sun-tzu
Chinese author (c. 4th century BC) of perhaps the first treatise on warfare, entitled "The Art of War."

Thompson
The Thompson submachine gun was named for General John T. Thompson, the technical director of the Auto Ordnance Corporation, the company responsible for its development. (See p.149.)

Toledo
The famous steel and swords of Toledo (see p.49) in south central Spain are mentioned as early as the first century BC. Today the city still houses an important armaments factory.

Tower
The Tower of London was for centuries the main British arsenal. The word "Tower" thus appears on many firearms of the 18th and 19th centuries which were assembled there, and on cheap imitations of them.

Tranter
A 19th century English percussion revolver and its variants, designed by William Tranter, a major Birmingham gunsmith.

Tschinke
The name applied to a kind of light wheellock sporting rifle used in the 17th century. It derives from the town of Cieszyn in Poland, where the type developed.

Tsiolkovsky, Konstantin (1857-1935)
The Russian pioneer of the theory of modern rocketry. (See p.246.)

Tulle
A French town, the site of an arms industry since 1690.

Very
The Very pistol is not a true fighting weapon, being merely a device for launching a signal flare. Lt. Edward Very, a US Naval officer, invented the cartridge for it in 1877.

Vetterli
A bolt-action rifle used by Switzerland and Italy in the late 19th century. It was designed by Frederic Vetterli (1822-82), a Swiss. (See p.138.)

Vickers
British company involved in the manufacture of small arms and ships, their best known product being the Vickers machine gun (see pp.215,218), which was a modified Maxim design.

Viollet le Duc, Eugène-Emmanuel (1814-79)
French Gothic revival architect and restorer of buildings who studied and wrote about all aspects of medieval technology and architecture. In the field of weaponry he is best known for his studies into medieval siege engines. (See pp.161,163.)

Volcanic
"Volcanic" rifles and pistols were early magazine-fed repeaters made to Smith and Wesson's patents by the Volcanic Repeating Arms Company of Connecticut. The company eventually became the Winchester Repeating Arms Company, and their rifle was developed into the famous Winchester rifle. (See p.137.)

Wallis, Barnes (1887-1979)
British engineer and inventor, responsible for several revolutionary designs in aircraft. In weaponry he is best remembered for his "bouncing bomb," used to destroy German dams in 1943, and the "Tallboy" and "Grand Slam" earthquake bombs. (See pp.236,237.)

Walther
Carl Walther Waffenfabrik AG, German manufacturers of firearms, famous especially for the P38 and PPK semi-automatic pistols, which are often referred to as "Walthers." (See pp.146,149.)

Webley
British firearm manufacturing company founded by the brothers Philip and James Webley in the 1830s. The name now usually refers to a series of widely used revolvers, some of which are still in production. (See pp.143,144.)

Westley-Richards
English firearms manufacturers famous for their high quality sporting guns, and the W-R "Monkeytail" breech-loading system (see p.132). They are still in business in Birmingham, England.

Whitney, Eli (1763-1826)
American inventor and firearms contractor, remembered for his mass-production of interchangeable components, a design of revolver, and a machine used in the cotton industry.

Whitworth, Sir Joseph (1803-87)
An English engineer, famous for the standardization of measurements and gauges, and improvements in standards of accuracy. In the field of weapons, his hexagonal-bored rifle was famous for its accuracy but was not a military success. (See p.121.)

Wilkinson
British family of gunsmiths and sword-cutlers, active since the early 19th century. Wilkinson Sword Co. still makes swords and razor-blades in London.

Willie, Big and Little
"Little Willie" was the name given to an experimental tracked vehicle evaluated by the British in 1915-16. Its successors—MK1 tanks—were subsequently known as "Big Willies" and were the first tanks ever to see action. (See p.196.)

Winchester
The Winchester Repeating Arms Company was founded in Connecticut in 1866 by Oliver Winchester and is still active. The name is most commonly applied to their series of famous lever-action rifles. (See pp.131,137.)

Yasutsuna (c.806AD)
Japanese swordsmith from Hoki province who established the familiar classic shape of the Japanese sword.

Acknowledgements

The following companies kindly helped with the updated edition:

The AMAC Corporation
British Aerospace Dynamics Division, Stevenage, UK
Heckler & Koch Gmbh, Oberndorf, West Germany
Royal Ordnance Gun & Vehicles Division, Nottingham, UK
Vickers Shipbuilding & Engineering Ltd (VSEL Armaments), Barrow-in-Furness, UK

Our special thanks are due to the following individuals and institutions:

Nigel Arch, Esq., The Castle Museum, York
David Edge, Esq., The Wallace Collection, London
Lt. Col. Ulf G. Hjorth-Andersén, Kungliga Armémuseum, Stockholm
Professor Laurence Martin, The University of Newcastle-upon-Tyne
Jonathan and Diane Moore, Military Archive and Research Services
Helmut Nickel, Esq., The Metropolitan Museum of Art, New York
Lt. Cdr. W. F. Paterson, Society of Archer-Antiquaries

The Ashmolean Museum, Oxford
The British Museum, London
The Castle Museum, York
Compagnie Industrielle des Lasers, Marcoussis, France
Defence Research Information Centre, Orpington, UK
Department of the Air Force, USA
Department of Egyptology, University of London
Department of the Navy Historical Center, Washington DC
Department of War Studies, King's College, University of London
Germanisches Nationalmuseum, Nuremburg
Hallwylska Museet, Sweden
Imperial War Museum, London
International Institute for Strategic Studies, London
Koniklijk Nederlands Leger en Wapenmuseum, Delft, Netherlands
Kungliga Armémuseum, Stockholm
Kunsthistorisches Museum, Vienna
Landeszeughaus, Graz, Austria
Livrustkammaren, Stockholm
The Louvre, Paris
The Manchester Museum, Manchester, UK
The Metropolitan Museum of Art, New York
Ministry of Defence Library, London
Musée d'Armes, Liège, Belgium
Musée de l'Armée, Paris
Museo Civilta, Rome
Museo del Ejército, Madrid
Museo Nazionale di Castel S. Angelo, Rome
Museum of the American Indian, Heye Foundation, New York
The Museum of Mankind, London
Museum für Volkenkunde und Schweizerisches Museum für Volkskunde, Basel, Switzerland
National Maritime Museum, London
National Museum of Antiquities of Scotland, Edinburgh
Naval Ordnance Museum, Gosport, UK
Propellants, Explosives and Rocket Motor Establishment, Ministry of Defence, Waltham Abbey, UK
The Rotunda Museum of Artillery, London
Royal Air Force Museum, London
Schweizerisches Landesmuseum, Zurich
Scottish United Services Museum, Edinburgh
Skokloster Castle, Sweden
Statens Historiska Museum, Stockholm
Tøjhusmusset, Copenhagen
The Tower of London
US Army Ordnance Museum, Aberdeen, Maryland
US Embassy, London
US Marine Corps Historical Center, Washington DC
US National Park Service
The Victoria and Albert Museum, London
The Wallace Collection, London

Bibliography

General books on weapons
Jane's Weapon Systems (Jane's annual, 1969–)
Perkins, Ken *Weapons and Warfare: Conventional Weapons and Their Roles in Battle* (Brasseys, 1987)
Quick, John *Dictionary of Weapons and Military Terms* (McGraw-Hill, 1973)
Reid, William *The Lore of Arms* (Mitchell Beazley, 1976)
Stone, George Cameron *A Glossary of the Construction, Decoration and use of Arms and Armor in all countries and in all times* (Jack Brussel, 1934; reprinted 1961)
Edged weapons
Ashdown, C.H. *British and Foreign Arms and Armour* (T.C. & E.C. Jack, 1909)
Blair, Claude *European and American Arms c1100–1850* (Batsford, 1962)
Draeger, Donn F. *Weapons and Fighting Arts of the Indonesian Archipelago* (Charles E. Tuttle Company, 1972)
Fischer, Werner & Zirngibl, Manfred A. *African Weapons* (Prinz-Verlag, 1978)
Fuller, Richard & Gregory, Ron *Military Swords of Japan 1868–1945* (Arms and Armour Press, 1986)
Ginters, Waldemar *Das Schwert der Skythen und Sarmaten in Südrussland* (Verlag Van Walter De Gruyter & Co., Berlin 1928)
Mollo E. *Russian Military Swords 1801–1917*
Oakeshott, R. Ewart *The Sword in the Age of Chivalry* (Lutterworth Press, 1964)
Rawson, P.S. *The Indian Sword* (Herbert Jenkins, 1968)
Robinson, H. Russell *Japanese Arms & Armour* (Arms and Armour Press, 1969)
Robson, Brian *Swords of the British Army* (Arms and Armour Press, 1975)
Seitz, Heribert *Blankwaffen* 2 volumes (Klinkhardt & Biermann, 1965)
Stephens, Frederick J. *Fighting Knives* (Arms and Armour Press, 1980)
Wise, T. *European Edged Weapons* (Almark, 1974)
Bayonets
Stephens, F.J. *Bayonets* (Arms and Armour Press, 1968)
Stephens, F.J. *The Collector's Pictorial Book of Bayonets* (Arms and Armour Press/Hippocrene Books Inc., 1971)
Watts, John & White, Peter *The Bayonet Book* (published by the authors, 1975)
Wilkinson-Latham, R.J. *British Military Bayonets* (Hutchinson, 1967)
Bows
Bradbury, Jim *The Medieval Archer* (The Boydell Press, 1986)
Hardy, Robert *Longbow: A Social and Military History* (Patrick Stephen, 1976)
Heath, E.G. *The Grey Goose Wing* (Osprey Publications, 1971)
Payne-Gallwey, Sir Ralph, Bt. *The Crossbow* (The Holland Press, 1903; 1976)
Firearms
Barnes, Frank C. *Cartridges of the World* (Arms and Armour Press/ DBI, various eds.)
Blackmore, Howard L. *British Military Firearms 1650–1850* (Herbert Jenkins, 1961)
Caranta, Raymond *Les Armes de Votre Defense* (Balland, 1977)
Chapel, Charles Edward *The Gun Collector's Handbook of Values* (Coward, McCann & Geoghegan, 1972)
Greener, W.W. *The Gun and its Development* (1910; reprinted by Bonanza Books)
Gun Digest (annual and specialized publications, c1946–)
Guns & Ammo Annual (Petersen)
Held, Robert *The Age of Firearms* (Gun Digest, 1970)
Held, Robert (Ed.) *Arms and Armor Annual Volume 1* (Digest Books Inc., 1973)
Hobart, F.W.A. *Pictorial History of the Machine Gun* (Ian Allan, 1971)
Hoff, Arne *Feuerwaffen* 2 vols. (Klinkhardt & Biermann, 1969)
Hogg, Ian V. *Guns and how they work* (Marshall Cavendish, 1979)
Hogg, Ian V. *Revolvers 1870–1940* (Arms and Armour Press, 1986)
Hogg, Ian V. & Weeks, John *Military Small Arms of the 20th century* (Arms and Armour Press, 1973–)
Huon, Jean *Un Siecle D'Armament Mondial Tome 1 et 2* (Crepin-Leblond, 1976; 1977)
Jane's Infantry Weapons (Jane's annual, 1975–)
Nelson, T.B. *The World's Submachine-Guns* 2 vols. (Arms and Armour Press, 1981)
North, Alan & Hogg, Ian V. *The Book of Guns & Gunsmiths* (Chartwell Books Inc., 1977)
Peterson, H.L. *The Book of the Gun* (Hamlyn, 1962)
Peterson, H.L. (Ed.) *Encyclopaedia of Firearms* (The Connoisseur, 1964)
Pope, Dudley *Guns* (Spring Books, 1965)
Renette, Gastinne *Le Gastinne Renette des Armes de Poing* (Editions Garnier, 1978)
Reynolds, Major E.G.B. *The Lee-Enfield Rifle* (Herbert Jenkins, 1960)
Roads, C.H. *The British Soldier's Firearm 1850–1864* (Herbert Jenkins, 1964)
Skennerton, Ian *The British Service Lee; Lee-Metford and Lee-Enfield Rifles and Carbines 1880–1980* (Annual Armour Press, 1982)
Smith, W.H.B. *Small Arms of the World* (Stackpole Books/Arms and Armour Press, 1984–)
Smith, W.H.B. *Gas, Air and Spring Guns of the World* (Arms and Armour Press, 1978)
Swearengen, Thomas F. *The World's Fighting Shotguns* (T.B.N. Enterprises, 1978)
Swenson, G.W.P. *Pictorial History of the Rifle* (Ian Allan, 1971)
Tanner, Hans (Ed.) *Guns of the World* (Bonanza Books, 1972; 1977)
Thompson, Leroy and Smeets, René *Great Combat Handguns* (Blandford Press, 1987)
Walter, John D. *The Luger Book* (Arms and Armour Press, 1977)
Woodman, Harry *Early Aircraft Armament: The Aeroplane and the Gun up to 1918* (Arms and Armour Press, 1989)
Artillery
Ammunition for Aircraft Guns (US Depts of the Army and the Air Force, 1957)
Archer, Denis (Ed.) *Jane's Pocket Book 18: Towed Artillery* (Macdonald and Jane's, 1977)
Bellamy, Chris *Red God of War* (Soviet Artillery) (Brasseys, 1986)
Bethell, Col. H.A. *Modern Guns and Gunnery* (F.J. Cattermole, 1907)
Bidwell, Shelford *Artillery of the World* (Brasseys, various eds)
Hogg, Ian *German Artillery of WW2* (Arms and Armour Press, 1975)
Hogg, I.V. & Thurston, L.F. *British Artillery Weapons and Ammunition 1914–1918* (Ian Allan, 1972)
Hogg, Ian *The Illustrated Encyclopaedia of Artillery* (Stanley Paul, 1987)
Johnson, Curt *Artillery* (Octopus, 1975)
Kenyon, Capt. L.R. *Recent Development of Field Artillery Materiel on the Continent* (Royal Artillery Institution, 1903)
Marsden, E.W. *Greek and Roman Artillery* (Oxford, 1969 & 1971)
Miller, Col. H.W. *The Paris Gun (Harrap. 1930)*
Rogers, Col. H.C.B. *Artillery through the Ages* (Seeley Service, 1971)
Smith, R.E. *British Army Vehicles and Equipment* (Ian Allan, 1968)
Thouvenin, Capitaine L. *L'Artillerie Nouvelle* (Charles Lavauzelle et Cie, 1924)
Wilkinson-Latham, Robert *British Artillery on Land and Sea 1790–1820* (David & Charles, 1973)
World War 2 Fact Files (Macdonald and Jane's, 1975)

Naval weapons
Bacon, Admiral Sir Reginald H.S. (Ed.) *Britain's Glorious Navy* (Odhams, c1942)
Brassey's Naval & Shipping Annual (Wm Clowes & Sons)
Cooke, Commander A.P. *Naval Ordnance and Gunnery* (Wiley & Son, 1875)
Friedman, Norman *US Naval Weapons* (Naval Institute Press, 1983)
Friedman, Norman *Submarine Design and Development* (Naval Institute Press, 1984)
Hackman, W.D. *Seek and Strike: Sonar, Anti-Submarine Warfare and the Royal Navy 1914–1954* (HMSO, 1984)
Hodges, Peter and Friedman, Norman *Destroyer Weapons of World War 2* (Naval Institute Press, 1979)
Hogg, Ian & Batchelor, John *Naval Gun* (Blandford, 1978)
Lloyd, E.W. & Hadcock, A.G. *Artillery* (J. Griffin, 1893)
May, W.E. & Kennard, A.N. *Naval Swords and Firearms* (HMSO, 1962)
Missiles and nuclear weapons
Baker, David *The Rocket* (New Cavendish Books, 1978)
Chant, Christopher & Hogg, Ian *The Nuclear War File* (Ebury Press, 1983)
Gunston, Bill *Aircraft Armament* (Salamander, 1987)
Gutteridge, William (Ed.) *The Dangers of New Weapons Systems* (Macmillan, 1983)
Martin, Laurence *Arms and Strategy* (Weidenfeld and Nicolson, 1973)
The Military Balance 1979–1980 and 1988–1989 (The International Institute for Strategic Studies, 1979, 1988)
Parson, Nels A., Jr *Guided Missiles in War and Peace* (Harvard University Press, 1956)
Pretty, Ronald (Ed.) *Jane's Pocket Book 10: Missiles* (Macdonald and Jane's, 1978)
Jones, Rodney W. *Small Nuclear Forces* (Greenwood Press, 1984)
Sibley, C. Bruce *Surviving Doomsday* (Shaw & Sons, 1977)
SIPRI *Yearbook* (SIPRI, 1978–89)
Walmer, Max *An Illustrated Guide to Strategic Weapons* (Salamander, 1988)
Space weapons
Aspen Strategy Group *Anti-Satellite Weapons and US Military Space Policy* (University Press of America, 1986)
Graham, Daniel O. *The Non-Nuclear Defense of Cities* (Abt Books, 1983)
Hobbs, David *An Illustrated Guide to Space Warfare* (Salamander, 1986)
Payne, Keith *Strategic Defense: "Star Wars" in Perspective* (University Press of America, 1986)
Chemical weapons
Haber, L.F. *The Poisonous Cloud: Chemical Warfare in the First World War* (Clarendon Press, 1986)
Spiers, Edward *Chemical Warfare* (Macmillan Press, 1986 and 1988)
Spiers, Edward *Chemical Weaponry* (Macmillan Press, 1988)
Weaponry in specific periods
Bonds, Ray *Illustrated Directory of Modern Soviet Weapons* (Salamander, 1985)
Coggins, Jack *Arms and Equipment of the Civil War* (Doubleday, 1962)
Connolly, Peter *The Greek Armies* (Macdonald Educational, 1977)
Connolly, Peter *The Roman Army* (Macdonald Educational, 1975)
Gonen, Rivka *Weapons of the Ancient World* (Cassell, 1975)
Hackett, Sir John (Ed.) *Warfare in the Ancient World* (Sidgwick and Jackson, 1989)
Lord, Francis A. *Civil War Collector's Encyclopedia* (Castle Books, 1963; 1965)
Maringer, Johannes and Bandi, Hans–Georg *Art in the Ice Age* (George Allen and Unwin, 1953)
Petrie, Sir W.M. *Flinders Tools and Weapons* (The British School of Archaeology in Egypt, 1917/Aris & Phillips Ltd. with Joel L. Malter & Co., 1974)
Rosa, Joseph G. *Guns of the American West* (Arms and Armour Press, 1985)
Rosser-Owen, David *Vietnam Weapons Handbook* (Patrick Stephens, 1986)
US Army *United States Army Weapon Systems 1986*
Warry, John *Warfare in the Classical World* (Salamander, 1980)
Internal Security
Clapp, Wiley M. (Ed.) *Modern Law Enforcement Weapons and Tactics* (DBI, 1987)
Dewar, Michael *Weapons & Equipment of Counter-Terrorism* (Arms and Armour, 1987)
Limpkin, Clive *The Battle of Bogside* (Penguin Books, 1972)
McLean, Donald B. *The Plumber's Kitchen* (Normount Technical Publications)
Miscellaneous
Burland, Cottie *Men without Machines* (Aldus Books, 1965)
Congreve, Col. Sir William *The Details of the Rocket System* (London, 1814)
Egerton, Lord, of Tatton *A description of Indian and Oriental Armour illustrated from the collection formerly in the India Office* (W.H. Allen, 1896)
Hicks, Major James E. *French Military Weapons 1717–1938* (N, Flayderman & Co.)
Miles, Charles *Indian and Eskimo Artifacts of North America* (Bonanza Books, 1968)
Random, Michel *Les Arts Martiaux ou l'esprit des budô* (Fernand Nathan, 1977)
US Navy Department, Bureau of Ordnance *German Explosive Ordnance* Volume 1 (1946; reprinted by The Combat Bookshelf, 1969)
Weyer, Edward *Primitive Peoples Today* (Hamish Hamilton, 1959)
Museum catalogs and handbooks
British Museum *Handbook to the Ethnographical Collections* (1910)
British Museum *Flint Implements* (1968)
British Museum *Hunters and Gatherers* (1970)
British Museum *Man the Tool-maker* (1961)
City of Exeter Museums, Devon, England *Redmen of North America* (1974)
The Fuller collection of Firearms (US National Park Service)
Hallwyl House collection *Arms and Armour* Volume II (1962)
The Metropolitan Museum of Art, New York *Arms and Armor*
The Metropolitan Museum of Art, New York *The Art of Chivalry*
Royal Ontario Museum *Iroquoians of the Eastern Woodlands* (1970)
Tower of London *Crossbows* (1976)
Victoria & Albert Museum, London *Arms and Armour of Old Japan* (1951; 1963)
Victoria & Albert Museum, London *Swords and Daggers* (1963)
Wallace Collection European *Arms and Armour* Volume II (1962)
Wallace Collection *Oriental Arms and Armour* (1964)
Auction catalogs
Wallis & Wallis, Lewes, Sussex, England
Weller & Dufty Ltd, Birmingham, England

Index

H

I

J

N

O

P

Q

R

S

T

U

W

Z